POLITICAL DICTIONARY OF THE MIDDLE EAST IN THE TWENTIETH CENTURY

POLITICAL DICTIONARY OF THE MIDDLE EAST IN THE 20th CENTURY

Edited by:

Yaacov Shimoni and Evyatar Levine

Supplement Edited by:
Itamar Rabinovich and Haim Shaked

Quadrangle / The New York Times Book Company

First published in 1972

Revised paperback edition, 1974

Copyright © 1972, 1974 by G.A. The Jerusalem Publishing House Ltd., Jerusalem, Israel. All rights reserved, including the right to reproduce this book or portions thereof in any form. For information, address: Quadrangle/The New York Times Book Co., 10 East 53 Street, New York, New York 10022. Manufactured in the United States of America. Published simultaneously in Canada by Fitzhenry & Whiteside, Ltd., Toronto.

Library of Congress Catalog Card Number: 76-175628

International Standard Book Number: 0-8129-0482-6

Book design: Ofra Kamar

Text-Editor of the Supplement Rafi Grafman

Typeset by Keter Publishing House, Ltd., and
Peli Printing Works Ltd., Israel.

FOREWORD

The publishers and editors have produced this book in the belief that there is a need for a concise political compendium on the Middle East in the present and the recent past, a single volume in which the reader can find condensed information, alphabetically arranged, on countries and peoples, on national and political movements, parties and leaders, on ideas and ideologies, on disputes and wars, alliances and treaties. As far as can be ascertained, no such work in dictionary form exists in any language.

The entries were written by specialists, most of them professional Orientalists. Selecting the entries was not easy, and involved, of course, a measure of subjective judgment. The general criterion was what the intelligent reader could be expected to look for in a volume of his kind. Therefore certain important matters are not listed separately because they are not associated with some key word which the reader is likely to seek (although it is hoped that he will find them covered in entries on countries, movements, ideas).

The Dictionary is not in any sense a *Who's Who*. A limited number of entries, it is true, are devoted to leading personalities—kings, presidents and prime ministers, to the extent that they exerted significant historical or political influence, and other selected persons who have helped to shape the character and fate of the countries of the Middle East. These, however, are not official, formal biographies, but rather attempts to record and assess political character and influence.

An endeavour has been made to limit duplication by a system of extensive cross-references; but there has been no attempt to eliminate it entirely, the assumption being that the reader will want to find in any one entry all that he wishes to know on a particular subject, without having to jump constantly from one part of the Dictionary to another. The symbol ▷ has been used to indicate that a name or term has a separate entry (it may sometimes be found referring to an entry which for reasons of space had, in the event, to be deleted).

The years before World War I, in particular, are treated as an introductory period. By contrast, events of topical political importance are accorded more space than might perhaps be their due in the perspective of history (see, for example, the post-1967 government-guerilla confrontation in the entry Jordan).

Authors and editors alike have striven to present as accurate and objective a picture of the region as possible, in the full awareness that complete objectivity is an unattainable counsel of perfection. All of them are Israelis. One of the editors and several of the authors are members of the Israel foreign service. They obtained permission to write for the Dictionary, but do not, of course, speak on behalf of the Foreign Ministry or of the Government. Nor do other authors speak on behalf of the institutions with which they are connected.

Arabic, Hebrew, Turkish and Persian terms and names present complicated problems of spelling and transliteration. For Turkish names the standard Turkish usage has been followed (e.g. c for what, in English usage, would be transcribed as j; ç for English ch). For Arabic, Persian and Hebrew names, the transliteration is the one normally used in the international press, with some amendment towards a more correct transcription. For example, the guttural aspirate (Arabic: *'ayn*, Hebrew: *'ayin*) is always indicated by an inverted apostrophe ('), except where a name is commonly transliterated without it (e.g. Iraq, Aden). The non-guttural aspirate (Arabic: *alif*, Hebrew: *aleph*) is reproduced as an apostrophe (') only where it is needed to separate two vowels (*Ra'uf, Le'umi, Feda'i*). To simplify matters, diacritical marks have not been used: ض is d, ذ and ظ are z or dh. A certain freedom has been exercised — within the spirit of the Semitic languages — where vowels are concerned, and the generally accepted usage has been followed: Nasser (not Nasir); Hussein, Feisal, but Bahrain, Kuwait. A liberal attitude has also been adopted towards "wrong" but accepted transliterations: Ottoman, not 'Uthmani; Omar, not 'Umar. There is, therefore, no full consistency — which indeed, is unattainable where the same names are Gamal, Gumhuriyya in Egypt; Jamal, Jumhuriyya in Syria and Iraq; and Cemal, Cumhuriyet in Turkey.

With Arab names, the last has been taken as the family name and the entry appears accordingly: Nuri Sa'id under Sa'id, Nuri (except in the case of kings and princes, generally known by their first name: Hussein b. Talal under H; Feisal b. 'Abd-ul-'Aziz under F). The Arabic definite article, *al-*, is disregarded in the alphabetical listing; thus Jamal al-Husseini will be found under Husseini, al-, Jamal. The editors felt free, as far as the text was concerned, to use or drop the definite article at will, writing Badr or al-Badr, Husseini or al-Husseini. Names composed of 'Abd-ul- ("Servant of") and one of the epithets of God ('Abd-ul-Fattah, 'Abd-ul-Rahman) are regarded as one name and therefore appear under A (e.g. 'Awni 'Abd-ul-Hadi under 'Abd-ul-Hadi, 'Awni). An exception has been made for Gamal 'Abd-ul-Nasser, so well — though incorrectly — known as Nasser that he appears under that name.

An advisory committee of experts assisted the editors with its counsel, especially during the initial planning of the Dictionary, and thanks are due to its members — Professor Gabriel Baer of the Hebrew University of Jerusalem, Dr. Uriel Dann of the University of Tel Aviv, Dr. Alex Bein, Dr. A.P. Alsberg, Dr. Michael Heyman, Mr. Asher Goren, and Mr. Gabriel Cohen — as well as to the many others who gave generously of their advice. Thanks are also due to those who took part in the technical preparation of the volume — secretaries, typists, proof-readers, many of them faced with material of a dauntingly unfamiliar kind. For most of the authors, and for the two editors, English is a foreign language, and some of the entries had to be translated from Hebrew. The English text therefore required a considerable amount of styling, a task over which great patience was exercised by Pamela Fitton, Dennis Silk and Anthony Warshaw. The maps were prepared by Carta, Jerusalem, and photographs were kindly made available by Bar David, Israel Sun, David Harris, and Werner Braun.

Jerusalem, October 1971. THE EDITORS

INTRODUCTION TO THE SUPPLEMENT 1971–1974

The editors of the supplement, which brings up to date this *Political Dictionary of the Middle East,* have remained faithful as far as possible to the principles and conventions set out by the editors of the original edition. The updating was carried out in two ways: (a) by expanding original entries so as to cover the period of 1970–74; and (b) by adding new entries made essential by events and developments in the last four years. The Yom Kippur War in October 1973, and the political situation which ensued, naturally occupy an important position in this new edition, though not at the expense of other material entirely unrelated to the Arab-Israel conflict.

For the convenience of the reader, we have marked the entries which have been brought up to date with an asterisk(★), in both the Dictionary and the Appendix.

The editors wish to thank the staff of the Shiloah Centre for Middle East Research, of the Tel Aviv University, for their considerable assistance in the quickly-paced preparation of the present edition.

Jerusalem, May 1974 HAIM SHAKED, ITAMAR RABINOVICH

CONTRIBUTORS

A.K.	AARON S. KLEIMAN, Ph. D.	Sen. Lecturer, Dept. of Political Science, Tel Aviv Univ.
A.S.	ABRAHAM SETTON, B.A.	Orientalist, Jerusalem
A.Ly.	AHARON LAYISH, Ph.D.	Lecturer in the History of Muslim Countries, The Hebrew Univ., Jerusalem
Al.S.	ALBERT SOUD'I, B.A.	Orientalist
Am.S.	AMNON SELLA, Ph.D.	Lecturer in Inter.Relations, The Hebrew Univ., Jerusalem
A.G.	ASHER GOREN, M.A.	Assist. Dir., Res. Div., Min. for For. Affairs, Jerusalem
A.W.	ASHER WEILL	Man. Dir., Weidenfeld & Nicolson, Jerusalem
A.L.	AVIGDOR LEVI, Ph.D.	Lecturer, The Shiloah Centre for M.E. & African Studies, Tel Aviv Univ.
B.G.	BARUCH GILEAD, M.A.	Orientalist, Jerusalem
C.K.	CARL KEREN	Dir., Centre of Scientific & Technological Information, Tel Aviv
D.K.	DAVID KUSHNIR, Ph.D.	Lecturer, Dept. of the History of the Islamic Peoples, Haifa Univ.
D.M.	DAVID MENASHRY, M.A.	Research Worker, Shiloah Centre, Tel Aviv Univ.
D.T.	DAVID TOURGUEMAN, M.A.	Orientalist, Jerusalem
D.L.	DORITH LIFSHITZ	Research Worker, Shiloah Centre, Tel Aviv Univ.
E.B.	ELIEZER BE'ERI	Orientalist
E.A.	ELIYAHU AGRES, M.A.	Political Correspondent, "Davar" daily newspaper, Tel Aviv
E.L.	EVYATAR LEVINE	Jurist & Journalist
E.M.	EMANUEL MARX, Prof.	Dept. of Social Anthropology, Tel Aviv Univ.
E.Y.	EHUD YAARI, B.A.	Commentator on Arab Affairs, "Davar" daily newspaper, Tel Aviv
E.S	ESTHER SOUERI, B.A.	Research Worker, Shiloah Centre, Tel Aviv Univ.
G.B.	GABRIEL BAER, Prof.	Dir., Institute of Asian & African Studies, The Hebrew Univ., Jerusalem
G.H.	GIDEON HASID	Jurist
H.E.	HAGAI ERLICH, Ph.D.	Lecturer, Institute of Asian & African Studies, Tel Aviv Univ.
H.S.	HAIM SHAKED, Ph.D.	Dir. of Shiloah Centre & Sen. Lecturer in History of the M.E., Tel Aviv Univ.
H.Z.	HANNAH ZAMIR, B.A.	Research Worker, Shiloah Centre, Tel Aviv
H.H.	HAYYIM HERZOG, Ph.D.	Jurist, Military Commentator
H.C.	HAYYIM J. COHEN, Ph. D.	Sen. Lecturer, The Hebrew Univ., Jerusalem
H.L.-Y.	HAVA LAZARUS-YAFEH, Prof.	Dept. for Muslim Civilization, The Hebrew Univ., Jerusalem
I.M.	ISRAEL MEIR	Dept. for U.N. Political Affairs, Min. for For. Affairs, Jerusalem
It.R.	ITAMAR RABINOVICH, Ph. D.	Sen. Lecturer, Institute for M.E. & African Studies, Tel Aviv Univ.
I.G.	ITZHAK GROSSMAN	Speaker, The Jerusalem Municipality
I.R.	ITZHAK RAGER	Journalist

A

ABADAN. Town on an island of the same name in
the Shatt al-'Arab▷ River in the Iranian province of
Khuzistan▷. After an oil refinery was built there
(1912), it developed from a small village into a pros-
perous town with 270,000 inhabitants (1966 census).
The refinery became the largest in the world and covers an area of four square miles. It stood idle during the
Anglo-Iranian oil crisis (1951-3), but was subsequently further expanded, and about 20 million tons
of crude oil were processed there in 1969.   (B.G.)

'ABBAS HILMI, KHEDIVE (1874-1945). Ruler
of Egypt (Khedive), 1892-1914. He was considered
to be anti-British, and covertly in contact with
Britain's enemies. A kind of reconciliation between
him and the British occurred after Lord Gorst
succeeded Lord Cromer▷, in 1907, as British Agent
and Consul-General. 'A. H. was deposed in 1914,
when World War I broke out and a British protectorate was proclaimed. He was suspected of pro-Turkish
tendencies and anti-British machinations. He continued in the cultivation of contacts behind the
scenes, but did not return to play an active role in
Egyptian politics.   (S.L.)

'ABBUD, IBRAHIM, GEN. (b. 1900). Sudanese
officer and politician. Member of the Beja▷ tribe.
Educated at Gordon College and Military College,
Khartoum. Served in the (British) Sudan Defence
Force. During World War II, he participated, with
the Sudanese contingent in the British Army, in the
Libyan, Ethiopian and Eritrean campaigns. Deputy
Commander-in-Chief, Sudanese Army 1954; Commander-in-Chief 1956-64. In November 1957, 'A
staged a *coup d'état* and became President, Prime
Minister and Minister of Defence. He held supreme
power, suppressing several attempts to oust him.
In October 1964, his regime was toppled in a *coup
d'état* led by civilian politicians and supported by
some army officers. He spent two weeks as a figurehead President in the new regime and in Nov. 1964
retired from public life.   (B.G.)

'ABD-UL-'AZIZ b. 'ABD-UL-RAHMAN of
the House of Sa'ud—see Ibn Sa'ud▷.

'ABD-UL-GHAFFAR, HARDAN— see Tik-
riti▷, al-, Hardan 'Abd-ul-Ghaffar.

'ABD-UL-HADI, 'AWNI (1889-1970). Palestinian-Arab politician and lawyer, of a prominent
Nablus family. Active since 1910 in the Arab national

General Ibrahim 'Abbud

movement▷ in the Ottoman Empire, 'A. was a
member of the *al-Fatat* nationalist society and among
the organizers of the first Arab nationalist congress
(Paris, 1913). He was one of Amir Feisal's▷ secretaries
during his short-lived administration in Damascus,
1919-20 and accompanied him to the Paris Peace
Conference. He then served Amir 'Abdullah▷ in
Transjordan. 'A. returned to Palestine in 1924 and
became one of the chief spokesmen of the Palestinian-
Arab nationalist movement. In 1932, he founded
a Palestinian branch of the Pan-Arab *Istiqlal*▷
(Independence) party. Joining the Arab Higher
Committee in 1936, he was partially responsible
for the Arab rebellion of 1936-9, and spent 1937-41
in exile. In November 1945, 'A. joined a new Arab
Higher Committee, but in the internal disputes of
1946/7 he opposed the Husseini▷ leadership and was
not reappointed. In September 1948, he was appointed
Minister for Social Affairs in the abortive Egyptian-
sponsored "Government of all Palestine" in Gaza▷,
but resigned soon after, and settled in Jordan in 1949.
He served as Jordan's Minister (later Ambassador)
to Cairo, 1951-5, and was a Senator, 1955-8. In 1956
he briefly held the portfolios of Foreign Affairs and
Justice. In 1958 he was one of Jordan's representatives
on the Federal Council of the short-lived Jordan-Iraqi
Arab Federation▷. After 1958 he lived in Cairo and

served as chairman of the Arab League's▷ legal committee.   (B. G.-Y. P.)

'ABD-UL-HADI, IBRAHIM (b. 1901). Egyptian politican. One of the leaders of the *Sa'adist*▷ party. Minister of Foreign Affairs 1949, Chief of the Royal Cabinet 1947–8, Minister of Finance, 1946–7 and 1948–9, Prime Minister 1949. After the officers' coup of 1952 he was tried before a revolutionary court (accused, *i.a.*, of having, as head of the King's Cabinet, dragged the Egyptian Army into the 1948 Palestine War). In 1953 he was condemned to death and all his property was confiscated. The death sentence was commuted to life imprisonment. He was released in 1954 for reasons of health; his political rights, of which he was stripped in 1953, were restored to him in 1960.   (S.L.)

ABDÜLHAMID II (1842–1919). Thirty-fourth sultan of the Ottoman Empire. The son of Sultan Abdülmecid, A. succeeded to the throne in 1876, after his brother Murad V had been deposed on grounds of mental illness. The Empire was passing through a most difficult period. Having crushed revolts in the Balkans in 1875–6, it faced a Russian military intervention and lost the war in 1877–8. In the Treaty of Berlin (1878) it had to renounce most of its Balkan possessions as well as areas in north-eastern Anatolia. The remaining years of A.'s reign were relatively peaceful. Relations with Germany were fostered in order to counterbalance the economic penetration and political intervention of the other powers. Internal unrest among the non-Turkish nationalities also continued and an insurrection in Crete in 1896 led to a short war with Greece the following year. In order to secure the loyalty of his Muslim subjects, A. followed a strong Pan-Islamic▷ policy, emphasizing his title as Caliph, and initiating such projects as the Hijaz Railway▷ to serve the pilgrims to Mecca. He continued to modernize the state, especially in the fields of communications and education. Under the pressure of liberal reformists (led by Midhat Pasa) A. inaugurated the first Ottoman constitution in 1876; but early in 1878 he dissolved the newly established parliament and for the next 30 years ruled autocratically. In 1908 A. was forced by a military revolt, led by the Young Turks▷, to reactivate the constitution and convene a new parliament. In the following year, he was suspected of encouraging an attempted counter-coup and was deposed.   (D.K.)

'ABD-UL-ILAH b. 'ALI (1912–58). Regent 1939–53 and Crown Prince 1953–8 of Iraq. Born in Hijaz▷ to Sharif 'Ali▷, eldest son of Sharif Hussein▷, the future King of Hijaz. Moved to Baghdad with his father after Ibn Sa'ud's▷ conquest of Hijaz in 1925. He became Regent of Iraq on behalf of the infant King Feisal II▷, in 1939, after the death of his cousin and brother-in-law King Ghazi▷. When Feisal attained his majority in 1953, 'A. became the heir presumptive, retaining great influence over his nephew. 'A. remained strongly pro-British throughout his life. He fled Iraq in 1941 during the rule of Rashid 'Ali▷ and the officers of the "Golden Square" (who reputedly conspired against his life), and returned to Baghdad with the victorious British Army. From then on he collaborated closely with Nuri Sa'id▷. They were regarded by anti-Western Iraqis of all shades of opinion as the arch representatives of reaction and subservience to the foreigner. 'A. was believed to have intrigued for the throne of Syria in the 1950s. He was shot in Baghdad during the revolution of 14 July 1958 and his body was torn to pieces by the mob.
(U.D.)

'ABDULLAH b. HUSSEIN (1882–1951). Amir 1921–46, King 1946–48 of Transjordan, King of Jordan 1948–51. Born in Mecca, second son of Sharif Hussein▷ of Mecca, scion of the Prophet Muhammad's Hashemite clan of the Quraishi tribe.

In 1891 'A. accompanied his father to Istanbul, where Hussein lived under Ottoman supervision, and received his education there. He was active in Arab literary circles in Istanbul and associated with semi-secret Arab nationalist organizations there. After the revolution of the Young Turks▷ (1908), Hussein returned to Mecca as its Amir, again accompanied by 'A. In 1912 'A. became Deputy for Mecca in the Ottoman Parliament, and returned to Istanbul; later he was appointed Deputy-President of the House. In 1914 he returned to Mecca via Cairo, where he explored with the British Resident the possibility of receiving aid for a rebellion against the Ottomans, but received no positive answer. 'A. participated in the "Arab Revolt"▷ of June 1916, mounted by Hussein against the Ottomans after renewed contact with the British. In 1917, he became Foreign Minister and political adviser to his father, who had assumed the title of King of Hijaz. However, it was his brother Feisal▷, not 'A., who represented Hussein in the initial peace negotiations.

In Mar. 1920 a group of Iraqi nationalists, who met in Damascus, offered 'A. the crown of Iraq, but the British did not favour the proposal. At the same time Feisal was proclaimed King of Syria. When, in July 1920, the French (who had obtained a mandate▷ over Syria) expelled Feisal from Damascus, 'A. (no longer Foreign Minister) assembled troops in order to march through Transjordan to Damascus, to avenge his brother and restore Hashemite rule in

Syria. He arrived in Ma‘an in November 1920, and entered ‘Amman in March 1921. The British wished to avoid a clash between the French and the Hashemites. They felt themselves under an obligation toward the latter. The then Colonial Secretary, Winston Churchill, proposed to ‘A. that he settle in Transjordan. Britain pledged herself to recognize him as Amir (Prince) of the territory in exchange for his renunciation of plans to attack the French, and also of claims to the Iraqi Crown.

‘A. accepted the British proposals and became Amir of Transjordan in April 1921. In May 1923, Britain recognized Transjordan as an autonomous Amirate under ‘A., within the Palestine Mandate but with the Jewish National Home clause rendered inapplicable. ‘A. continued to cherish his vision of "Greater Syria"▷, i.e. a union of Transjordan, Palestine, Syria and Lebanon under his crown, and a "Fertile Crescent"▷ Federation of Greater Syria and Iraq. The British to some extent supported his aspiration, as did some elements in Syria, Iraq and Palestine. He was opposed violently by the French, the Syrian nationalists, the faction of the Mufti of Jerusalem, Amin al-Husseini▷, and other Arab rulers.

‘A. remained a loyal ally of the British during World War II; in 1941, he sent the Jordanian Army—the Arab Legion—to assist in quelling Rashid ‘Ali's▷ rebellion in Iraq, and was branded by his opponents in the Arab world as a British puppet. He also maintained good relations with the leaders of Jewish Palestine and favoured Jewish settlement in Transjordan—a plan that did not materialize, mainly because of British opposition. ‘A. was an autocrat and an arch-conservative, preferring the ancient ways of consultation with notables to modern democracy, which he considered unsuitable for Transjordan.

In May 1946, Britain granted Transjordan formal independence and ‘A. became king. In 1946-8, as the final Palestine crisis approached, he maintained contact with the Zionist leaders in an effort to reach an agreement. He was prepared to grant the Jews in Palestine autonomy—vaguely defined—within his greater kingdom, or even some degree of independence. But he could not resist Pan-Arab pressure, and his British mentors, too, seem to have advised him against seeking separate accommodation with Israel. Negotiations, that culminated in a secret last-minute visit of Golda Meir▷ to ‘A. (May 1948), failed. In May 1948, ‘A. was named Commander-in-Chief of the Arab armies which invaded Palestine; the title, however, was purely nominal and each of the invading armies followed its own plan and command. The Arab Legion took over most of Arab Palestine (except the Gaza Strip), almost without fighting. It seems to have avoided attacking Israel in the areas

allotted to her by the UN, a fact which corroborated charges of collusion between the King and the Israelis. Fighting took place mainly in Jerusalem and its vicinity (not allotted by the UN either to the Jewish or to the Arab State).

In Apr. 1949, while official Israel-Jordan armistice negotiations were being conducted in Rhodes, the most difficult points were settled in secret negotiations directly with King ‘A. The King maintained contact with Israel, and early in 1950 a non-aggression pact was negotiated; a final draft was actually ready for initialling in Feb.-Mar. However, before the pact was signed, ‘A. broke off the negotiations following strong opposition by the Arab states, who had got wind of the secret Jordan-Israel contacts and whose mounting pressure culminated in a threat to expel Jordan from the Arab League. The Arab states acquiesced, in return, in the annexation of Arab Palestine by Jordan, which they had violently opposed. This annexation was formalized in April 1950, and was the fulfilment of at least part of ‘A.'s dream of a greater, united kingdom. But it also undermined Jordan's stability and ‘A.'s position. The Palestinians he incorporated in his kingdom introduced modern, urban, nationalist politics; and many of them regarded the king as a collaborator with the British and the Jews. ‘A. was assassinated on 20 July 1951 by a Palestinian, while entering al-Aqsa Mosque in Jerusalem.   (B.G.-Y.S.)

‘ABD-UL-NASSER, GAMAL—see Nasser.

‘ABDUL, MUHAMMAD (1849-1905). Egyptian Muslim thinker, and the leader of Islamic modernism, which called for a renaissance of Islamic thought and reforms in Muslim society. Influenced by the Pan-Islamist ideas of Jamal-ul-Din al-Afghani. After the failure of the ‘Urabi revolt, ‘A. went into exile in the 1880s and published, together with al-Afghani, the Pan-Islamic journal *Al-‘Urwa al-Wuthqa* ("The Faithful Support") in Paris. ‘A. soon developed an independent line of thought; he advocated a renewal of Muslim values, which alone unite all the Muslims and establish their true identity, and their adaptation to modern life. He maintained this was Islam's only defence against Western criticism. He tried to prove that no contradiction existed between the tenets of Islam and those of the West.

In 1888 ‘A. was permitted to return to Egypt, appointed a judge, and was made a member of the Administrative Committee of al-Azhar▷ University in Cairo and of the Legislative Council. In 1899 he was appointed Grand Mufti of Egypt. His ideas caused an intellectual ferment and were intensely debated by supporters and opponents. Among his students was Qassem Amin, famous for his advocacy of equal rights for women in Muslim society ('A. also advocated the abolition of polygamy). 'A.'s doctrine was highly influential in the reawakening of Islam and consequently in the growth of Arab nationalism. (O.G.)

*ABU DHABI. The largest of the seven sheikhdoms or principalities of the Trucial Coast▷ (29,150 sq. about 90% of the total area of the seven). In 1967 the population was officially estimated at 30,000 but it is believed to have reached 50,000, possibly more. The fact that AD's borders are not delimited has led to several disputes with her neighbours. The most important of them involves the oasis of Buraimi▷. Most of AD's territory is not settled and is covered by sand or is saline. The capital, Abu Dhabi, with half of the sheikhdom's population, is situated on an island which was connected to the mainland by a sand causeway. It was a crowded medieval Arab city as recently as the 1960s. It has been modernized rapidly since oil was discovered there. Its main drawback is the absence of a deepwater port.

The Sheikhdom of AD has been under British protection since the 19th century (see Trucial Coast▷). The Protectorate is to lapse at the end of 1971 when AD plans to join a federation, the "Union of Arab Emirates". Her ruler, Sheikh Zeid ibn Sultan (who in 1966 overthrew, with British help, his brother who had been alleged to have been a tyrant and to stand in the way of progress and development) is temporary President of this federation which is in process of being established. Since 1966 AD has set up a small military force of her own. In 1939 the "Trucial Coast Development Company", a subsidiary of the Iraq Petroleum Company, was granted a concession for oil prospecting. A concession was granted for the offshore sea-bed in 1953 to the "AD Marine Areas Oil Co." (a British-French partnership). In 1958 this company discovered oil near the island of Das, and began production in 1962. The first-mentioned company discovered oil on land in 1962, and began producing in 1963. Since then concessions have been granted to other companies, American and Japanese. The land oilfields have been connected to the coast by a 67-mile-long pipeline. Oil production rose rapidly. It reached 29 million tons in 1969, 12 million from the sea-bed, AD's oil income reached nearly $200 million in 1968, and was estimated at $250 million in 1970 (a *per capita* income of around $5,000, the highest in the world). A five-year plan has been drafted to utilise this income for the development of agriculture, industry and public services. There are plans, also, for constructing a deepwater port. The Sheikh of AD donates part of his income for the development of the other Trucial sheikhdoms, and for general Arab political needs. (Y.K.)

ABU'L-HUDA, TAWFIQ (1895–1956). Jordanian politician. Born in Acre, Palestine. Served in the Ottoman Army and later with Amir Feisal's▷ short-lived administration in Damascus 1919–20. A. joined the Transjordanian civil service in 1922, and was director of the Agricultural Bank 1932–7; Prime Minister 1939–44; Foreign Minister 1945, 1947; again Prime Minister 1947–50. A. resigned in March 1950 because he opposed King 'Abdullah's▷ efforts to reach a separate peace agreement with Israel. He became President of the Senate in 1950. After King 'Abdullah's assassination in July 1951, A. served as Prime Minister 1951–3 and 1954–5. (B.G.)

ABU MUSSA. Small island in the Persian Gulf▷ involved in international disputes. In 1906, a flurry was caused by a concession for iron-oxide mining granted by the Sheikh of Sharja▷, one of the Trucial Coast▷ sheikhdoms, to German interests. British intervention compelled the Sheikh to cancel the concession, and a British landing party removed the Germans. More recently, Sharja's ownership of AM has been disputed by both Persia (Iran) and the Trucial Coast Sheikhdom of Umm al-Qaiwain▷. While the latter claim refers mainly to offshore oil rights, Iran claims territorial possession of AM and has given notice of her intention to take it by force as soon as British protection is removed from Sharja. (A similar Persian claim—and threat—refers to the neighbouring small Tumb Islands held by the Trucial Coast (Sheikhdom of Ras al-Khaima▷.) (Y.S.)

ADEN. Town and harbour at the western end of the south coast of Arabian peninsula. Chief town of South Yemen▷. Acquired in 1839 by Britain and developed as a coal depot and supply station for ships and as a base. A. was administered by the Bombay Government until 1932, and by the central Government of India 1932–7; it became a Crown Colony in 1937. In 1963 A. joined the short-lived Federation of South Arabia▷ as one of its memberstates; its Governor's title was changed to High Commissioner for A. and the A. Protectorates. In the 1950s and '60s A. served as the headquarters of the British ME Command. In 1967, when the Federation was transformed into the People's Republic of South Yemen, A. became part of the latter.

A. colony had an area of 75 sq. miles and occupied the two sides of a natural bay. On the eastern side, "Little A.", oil refineries are situated (built 1952–4 by the Anglo-Iranian Oil Co., with a capacity of

7.2m. tons per year), and near them there is a bunkering and oil port. The western side, A. proper, consists of A. harbour—a free port since 1850, which became one of the busiest ports in the world (in 1966, for example, 6,246 ships docked there). The western side also contains Khormaksar airfield and the town districts of Sheikh 'Uthman, Ma'alla, Mansura, Tawahi, Steamer Point and the Crater. Midway between A. and Little A., in the area of the Sheikhdom of 'Aqrabi, a new town was built; until 1967 it was called Al-Ittihad (Union), and after independence—Madinat al-Sha'b (People's Town); it became the capital of the Federation of South Arabia and subsequently of South Yemen.

As a result of A.'s economic development and the employment provided by the oil refineries, the port and British bases, tribesmen from the hinterland (i.e. the A. protectorates) and foreigners settled in A. Between 1951 and 1963 the population rose from 100,000 to 220,000, divided in 1963 as follows: Local Arabs and tribesmen from the protectorates —95,000; Yemenis—80,000; Indians and Pakistanis —20,000; Somalis—20,000; Europeans—5,000. There was also a Jewish community of about 1,000 who left the town in 1967 owing to anti-Jewish disturbances resulting from the Six Day War and the British evacuation (there had been earlier anti-Jewish pogroms, see Jews in the ME▷).

The Yemenis—the largest minority, estimated in 1965 at c. 100,000 out of a total population of 250,000 —were mostly unskilled labourers, retaining their tribal ties with Yemen; they were receptive to nationalist ideas and the traditional Yemeni claim that A. was an integral part of Yemen. Electoral rights were restricted to citizens, thus excluding the Yemenis and pushing them further into the arms of leftist, nationalist groups. (For political and constitutional developments see South Yemen▷ and South Arabia▷.)

The closure of the Suez Canal since the Six Day War and the evacuation of the British base and troops caused a grave economic crisis in A. The number of ships calling at the port was reduced to about 100 a month, the refineries worked at 30% of their capacity, and there was high unemployment.

In the hinterland of A. town, petty sultans and chieftains were brought, during the 19th and early 20th centuries, under British protection. For these A. protectorates, "Western" and "Eastern", see South Yemen▷ and South Arabia▷.   (Y.A.O.)

'ADHEM, AL-. Formerly British Air Force base, 15 miles south of Tobruk (Cyrenaica, Libya), retained by Great Britain, under the Anglo-Libyan defence treaty of 1953, in exchange for economic and military aid. Owing to nationalist and all-Arab (especially Egyptian) pressure, Libya requested the evacuation of British bases and troops in Libya, and in 1966 Britain evacuated those in Tripolitania. After the coup d'état of September 1969, the new Libyan regime demanded the evacuation of the remaining British bases in Cyrenaica: 'A., Tobruk and Benghazi. In December 1969 Britain agreed; the evacuation was completed in March 1970. The base was renamed in honour of President Nasser after his death in 1970.   (B.G.)

*'AFLAQ, MICHEL. Syrian politician and political thinker. Founder and ideologist of the Syrian Ba'th▷ party. Born in Damascus in 1910. A Greek Orthodox Christian. In the 1930s 'A. studied in Paris, and was close to the Communist Party. In the 1940s he founded, together with Salah-ul-Din al Bitar▷, the "Arab Renaissance Party" al-Ba'th) which in 1953 united with the "Arab Socialist Party" of Akram Hourani▷, to form the "Arab Socialist Renaissance Party". 'A. stood for Parliament in 1947, but was not elected. In 1949 he was appointed Minister of Education (in the government of Hashem al-Atassi▷, after Sami Hinnawi's▷ coup), but was again defeated when he stood for Parliament. Since then he has not filled any government posts, but has remained Secretary General of the Ba'th party. In the factional struggle that split the Ba'th party after it came to power through the March 1963 coup, he headed, with Bitar, the "civilian wing", which is considered more moderate. 'A. and his faction were ousted from Syria, together with the party they had founded, by the more extremist "Military Wing" in the February 1966 coup. They remained at the head of the "National (i.e. all-Arab) Command" of the party, seated in Beirut and Baghdad. Since 1966 there have virtually been two Ba'th parties, with 'A.'s faction ruling in Iraq. He himself lived in exile in Lebanon. In 1967 he emigrated to Brazil and abandoned all political activity, but in 1969 returned to Beirut and Baghdad in an effort to retain a position of Leadership. His book, "In the Ways of the Ba'th" (1959), is the accepted textbook of Ba'th party doctrine.   (A.L.–O.T.)

*AFRICA. Africa plays an important role in the policies of the ME, particularly the six African Arab states (Egypt, Sudan, Libya, Tunisia, Algeria, Morocco). Egypt and the other North African Muslim-Arab countries have for centuries radiated a strong influence on the African countries to the south: as the source of spreading Islam and a spiritual centre for its study; as an economic focus—the terminal of the caravan routes; as infiltrators and conquerors

(Sudan); and as merchants, including slave traders. The African Arab states consider the continent a natural arena for their activities, one of the circles in which their policy moves (in the words of Gamal 'Abd-ul-Nasser▷); newly independent African states for their part are influenced by the Arab states and look to them for guidance (although the memory of the slave traffic is still alive, and large colonies of Lebanese and Syrian traders in West Africa are unpopular).

The states of the ME are peripheral in both Asia and Africa. In Asia they are on the periphery of a continent with a cultural-national tradition and political experience superior to theirs, whereas in Africa there are only two non-Arab independent states—Ethiopia and Liberia, and from 1957 on also Ghana—and the weight and influence of the Arab countries is therefore considerable.

The Arab countries also participated actively in the organization of the struggle for African independence, and in the establishment of Pan-African state associations once African states began achieving independence, from 1960 onwards. Cairo became a very important centre for conferences and permanent secretariats—both of African states and (to an even greater extent) of popular movements and organizations. The latter refers mainly to underground and guerilla organizations and leaders-in-exile dedicated to the liberation of those countries still under colonial rule (of Portugal, South Africa or Rhodesia), and to political factions and movements which, not having won power in their countries, are fighting their own independent African governments (Congo, Cameroun, Chad, Ethiopia, etc.). Egypt also extends some technical aid to African countries, mainly in the field of Islamic education and religious personnel.

Among the numerous popular congresses in which Arab states were active, were the three Pan-African Peoples' Conferences (December 1958, Accra, Ghana; January 1960, Tunis; March 1961, Cairo). For the "Afro-Asian Peoples' Solidarity Organization", see Asia▷.) The association of independent African states commenced at a first conference in April 1958, in Accra, attended by only eight states, five of which were Arab: the June 1960 conference in Addis Ababa was attended by 11 states. However, once the process of African independence had gathered momentum, the liberated countries soon split into rival blocs. In January 1961 Ghana, Guinea, Mali, Egypt and Morocco established the revolutionary-leftist Casablanca▷ Bloc"; Algeria was an observer, joining in 1962 when she attained independence. Egypt's activity in the Bloc conformed to the general trend of her policy at the time—also sharply expressed in the Congo crisis, during which

Egypt actively supported the extremist-revolutionary forces (later-rebels); conservative-royalist Morocco did not really belong to this extremist group—she was experimenting with a foreign policy in sharp contrast to her character. In any case, the "Casablanca Bloc" was a complete failure; it attracted no further members from among the African states, nor did it develop as planned into the nucleus of an expanding African revolutionary bloc; and the alliance between its member-states deteriorated. By 1963 the Bloc was practically non-existent, and the brief Moroccan-Algerian war of October 1963 finally liquidated it. The more conservative African states formed a separate association—at the Monrovia Conference of May 1961, and the Lagos Conference of Jan. 1962—and started building a permanent organization; African states linked to the French Commonwealth also set up their own special organization. Of the Arab African states, Libya and Tunisia attended the Monrovia Conference; but they withdrew from further attempts at organization. The failure of the Casablanca Bloc paved the way for the establishment of an organization encompassing all African states with no ideological-political character other than an anti-colonial position and support for liberation movements. The "Organization of African Unity" (OAU) was established in May 1963 in Addis Ababa, Ethiopia, with the participation of all the independent states of Africa, including the six Arab ones; the latter still carry much weight in the organization, and its regular conference in 1964 was held in Cairo. The OAU maintains its permanent headquarters in Addis Ababa, and holds regular conferences and congresses.

Another ME state displaying an active interest in Africa is Israel. Israel has developed a network of technical co-operation—mainly instruction for trainees from developing countries and the despatch of technicians and experts to such countries—as well as technical-scientific aid for development projects, and a large part of these efforts was devoted to Africa. Many African states willingly accepted the aid offered, and ties of co-operation and sincere friendship developed between them and Israel. Israel maintains diplomatic missions in all non-Arab African states, with the exceptio of Mauritania and Somalia—both totally identified with the Arab states (and since 1967 also excluding Guinea, which severed relations with Israel in the wake of the Six Day War▷). Sharply anti-Israel resolutions are fairly often adopted at conferences of African states. Strangely enough, even countries professing sincere friendship towards Israel and actively co-operating with her, join in—or at least fail actively to oppose—resolutions denouncing Israel. This may be attributed in part to the tactics adopted by the Arab states, whereby they succeed in having such resolutions "passed by acclamation", without debate, at the last session; partly it is the result of the Arab states' threat to withdraw should their position not be endorsed; and in part it may result from a distinction consciously made between verbal political resolutions—considered as lip service and of little importance—and mutual assistance and co-operation in deed and real life which are the thing that counts.   (Y.S.)

AFRO-ASIAN. Conferences, organizations—see Africa▷, Asia▷.

AGRARIAN REFORM—see Land Reform▷.

AGUDATH ISRAEL. World Organization of Orthodox Jews. Founded in 1912 on the initiative of German leaders, together with eminent rabbis from Poland and Lithuania. It was bitterly opposed to Zionism because it believed that the nation should be governed only by the Lord's law, and that any attempt to achieve political independence in Palestine was heretical. Israel should wait for its redemption, which depended on the coming of the Messiah.

Nevertheless, a branch AI did advocate practical work in Palestine, and it became ascendant after the Second World War and the establishment of Israel. AI had boycotted the national institutions of the Jewish community in Palestine. Yet on the establishment of Israel it joined the government as part of the Religious Front, even though that Front included the *Mizrahi*▷ party (its principal rival for the support of the religious community). It has been in opposition since 1951, because its demand, that *Halakha* (traditional Jewish law) become the law of the State, was rejected. AI's educational institutions in Israel are independent of any official supervision but are subsidized by the State. It publishes a daily newspaper *Hamodi'a*, and is represented in the 7th *Knesset* (Parliament) (1969) by 4 members.
(E.A.)

AHAD HA'AM (Hebrew: One of the People) (1856–1927). Pseudonym of Asher Ginsberg. Believed that Zionism's main task was the revival of a cultural and spiritual centre in Palestine rather than the establishment of Herzl's▷ political entity (the doctrine of "Spiritual Zionism"). In 1891 he warned against neglecting the Arab question. Upon immigrating to Palestine, in 1922, he advocated a Jewish majority in Palestine as the only way to realize Zionism.   (S.H.)

AHDUTH HA'AVODAH (United Labour). a. A moderate leftist Zionist-Socialist party. Estab-

lished in 1919 by *Po'alei Zion*, individual members of *Hapo'el Hatzair* and non-partisan individuals in order to unify workers in Palestine. b. A radical leftist Zionist-Socialist party. Established in 1944 under the name *Tnu'ah le-Ahduth Ha'avodah* by dissidents from Mapai in opposition to the partition of Palestine which was assumed to be a consequence of the Biltmore Programme▷ and in order to throw more emphasis on Socialism (see Israel▷, Socialism▷, Zionism). c. A radical leftist Zionist-Socialist party, founded in 1954 by the merger of the *Tnu'ah le-Ahduth Ha'avodah* (see above) and *Po'alei Zion Smol* (see Zionism▷) under the name of *Ahduth Ha'avodah–Po'alei Zion*.   (E.L.)

AHMAD b. YAHYA (?–1962). Imam (religious head) of the Muslim Zeidi▷ sect of Yemen, and ruler of Yemen, 1948–62. Eldest son of Imam Yahya▷ He was chosen by the Imam to subdue rebellious tribes in the 1920s and '30s. In these campaigns A. won his spurs, acquiring a reputation for harshness and cruelty. He was chosen Imam in February 1948, following his father's murder. As Imam, A. continued the custom of taking hostages in order to assure the obedience of the insurgent tribes. At the same time he began to build a modern army and to subdue the ruling class of Zeidi notables (*Sada*—descendants of the *Khalifa* 'Ali). In August 1955 A. suppressed, with the help of his eldest son Muhammad al-Badr▷, a coup launched by two of his brothers, 'Abdullah and 'Abbas (both of whom were hanged), and by officers and *Sada*. In the remaining years of his reign he had to face many tribal revolts. He became ill, and delegated some of his authority to his son al-Badr and his brother Hassan b. Yahya. His death (19 September 1962) triggered the coup, or revolution, that toppled the monarchy.   (H.E.)

AHMADIYYA. Religious community derived from Islam, founded by Mirza Ghulam Ahmad (d. 1908) of Qadian, India, who claimed to be an incarnation of Krishna, Jesus (who died, according to him, in India) and Muhammad, and the Mahdi▷ of Islam. He expounded his doctrine in various publications, which show traces of Hindu influences, but reveal mainly Islamic mystical tendencies. Since the death of his first *Khalifa* (Arabic: successor), Hakim Nur-ul-Din, in 1914, his followers have been divided into two groups. The main faction, also called Qadiani, has its centre in Rabwah in Pakistan and branches all over the world, especially in India, Pakistan and West Africa; it engages in widespread missionary activities. This group believes that Mirza Ghulam Ahmad was also the "Seal of Prophets", *i.e.* the last prophet, a title usually accorded only to

Muhammad. The smaller faction, the "Lahoris", whose centre is in Lahore, Pakistan, are closer to orthodox Islam and regard the Founder as an innovating Islamic thinker rather than a Prophet. The Lahoris are also active in missionary work.

The Ahmadis claim to be the true community of Islam and denounce all other Muslims as unbelievers. They believe in the Qur'an—translated by one of the leaders of the smaller groups, Muhammad 'Ali (d. 1951), into English—and the basic tenets and commandments of Islam other than *Jihad*▷ (holy war). They prefer expansion through peaceful missionary activities and publish much material, including monthlies, etc., in which they expound their doctrines and explain their controversies with other religions, especially with Islam. Muslim religious leaders harshly denounce the A. movement and declare its adherents to be infidels, and sometimes also demand the confiscation of their estates (*e.g.* in Syria 1958). Estimates of the number of A. vary between 0.5 million and 2 million or more. (H.L.-.Y.)

*AHRAM, AL-. A daily Arab newspaper published in Cairo, Egypt. Founded in 1876 in Alexandria by the brothers Salim and Bishara Taqla, immigrants from Lebanon. In 1898 it was transferred to Cairo. Gradually it became the largest and most important Egyptian newspaper, with its own network of correspondents in foreign capitals, a rich variety of informative material and articles, and well developed printing techniques. Al-A. was political neutral, without party affiliation, yet loyal to the government of the day. After the officers' coup of 1952 the paper declined. But when Muhammad Hassanein Heykal▷ was appointed editor, in 1957, it recovered its leading position and won precedence over its principal competitor, *Al-Gumhuriyya* (established 1953 by the Free Officers). Heykal's weekly Friday editorial enhances the paper's prestige and circulation. At present, al-A.'s circulation is *c.* 250,000 copies. The paper was nationalized in 1960, together with all other Egyptian newspapers. During the last few years it has been regarded as the government's semi-official organ. (S.L.)

AID—see Foreign Aid▷.

'AJMAN. Smallest of the seven principalities of the Trucial Coast (Persian Gulf). Area—97 sq. miles, population *c.* 5,000, mostly nomadic though with some fishing also. The Sheikhdom of 'Ajman has been under British protection since the 19th century (see Trucial 'Oman▷). An oil exploration concession granted in 1962 to a small American company was not exploited, and expired in 1967. In 1970 a new concession was granted to the American Occidental Company. (Y.K.)

AL-. In Arabic names which begin with al- (the definite article), the 'al-' is not taken account of in the alphabetical order. E.g. look for Jamal al-Husseini under Husseini, al-, Jamal. In Arabic names constructed on the pattern 'Abd-ul-Rahman, 'Abd-ul-Qader, etc. (The Servant of God—with "God" replaced by one of God's epithets), the 'Abd-ul-epithet combination is considered as one name. E.g. look for 'Awni 'Abd-ul-Hadi under 'Abd-ul-Hadi, 'Awni. (Y. S.)

'ALA, HUSSEIN (1883–1964). Iranian diplomat and politician, Prime Minister 1951, 1955–7. Educated at London University. Ambassador to London 1934–6. Minister of the Court 1942–5 and 1951. Ambassador to Washington 1946–50. As Prime Minister, March-April 1951, 'A. tried to reach a compromise in the grave crisis between Iran and the British Oil Company. When fanatics threatened his life, he resigned and resumed office as Minister of the Court. After Gen. Zahedi's▷ resignation in April 1955 'A. once more became Prime Minister, serving until April 1957. He was again Minister of Court 1957–63 and served as a Senator 1963–4. (B.G.)

'ALAMI, MUSSA (b.1895). Palestinian-Arab politician and lawyer. Son of a prominent Jerusalem land-owning family. Educated at the American University of Beirut, 'A. joined the Legal Department of the Palestine Mandatory Government, attaining the senior position of Government Advocate. During the 1936–9 riots 'A. collaborated with the rebels under Hajj Amin al-Husseini▷. He was, however, considered to be a moderate, was not fully identified with any political party and had little political influence. In the mid-1930s—before, during and after the rebellion—he met Jewish leaders, headed by D. Ben-Gurion▷ and M. Sharett▷, in an abortive attempt to reach an agreement. In 1937, he was dismissed from the government and fled to Syria and Iraq, but returned to Palestine in 1941.

In the absence of an elected body of Palestinian Arabs, 'A. was appointed by the conveners of the Arab League▷ to represent the Arabs of Palestine at the preparatory meeting in Alexandria, October 1944, and at the foundation of the League, March 1945. In 1945, he was briefly a member of the Arab Higher Committee, but soon withdrew from such directly political leadership to establish two special projects: 1. in 1945 he founded Palestinian-Arab propaganda offices in Jerusalem, Beirut, London and Washington, staffed mostly by younger men; and

2. in 1944–5 he initiated a "Constructive Scheme" to buy and develop lands in Palestine to prevent their being sold to Jews and generally to develop the Arab village as the basis of the Palestinian-Arab national struggle. Both these enterprises were approved and supported by the Arab League.

After the 1948 Palestine War, 'A. founded near Jericho (in the Jordanian-occupied part of Palestine) an agricultural training farm for Palestinian-Arab youth, particularly orphans, supported by funds from abroad. In the 1950s, 'A. was reported to have been among the founders of the al-Ba'th▷ party in Jordan, then considered pro-Iraqi; but his political activity in Jordan was sporadic and he soon abandoned politics and devoted his time to his farm. His book "The Lesson of Palestine" ('Ibrat Filastin, 1949) was one of the first to analyse the underlying social reasons for the Arab defeat in Palestine. Since the Six Day War, 1967, 'A. has been living in London and 'Amman, and paying visits to Jerusalem and Jericho.
(B. G.-Y. S.)

*'ALAWIS, 'ALAWITES (or Nusseiris). Largest minority group in Syria. They live for the most part on the Syrian coast and in the Alexandretta▷ (Hatay▷) and Cilicia regions in Turkey, though small groups are found also in Lebanon. The 500–600,000 Syrian 'A. comprise 75% of the sect's total and 11.5% of the population of Syria. Most of them live in the mountain villages of the Lataqia district—known also as the 'Alawite region or the Mountains of the Nusseiris; they form two-thirds of the district's population, though they are a minority in its capital, Lataqia.

Little is known of the origin of the community. Some say that they are the remnants of an ancient Canaanite people which, surviving in the isolated mountainous region and retaining many ancient Syrian pagan customs, were influenced only slightly by Christianity and Islam. In the Middle Ages they adopted the Arabic language and the Islamic faith in the version of the Isma'iliyya▷ sect. They broke off from the Isma'iliyya and became a separate sect. The 'A.—part of whose beliefs are secret and known only to an esoteric circle of the initiated—believe in a holy trinity ('Ali, the Prophet Muhammad, and Salman al-Farisi, i.e. the Persian, one of the Companions of the Prophet).

Under Ottoman rule the 'A. enjoyed a certain measure of autonomy, but in the mid-nineteenth century the Ottomans began tightening their control. The 'A. were now tried in Sunni-Muslim courts. With the establishment of the French Mandate in Syria, 1920–2, the 'A. region was recognized as an autonomous territory or state within the framework of the Mandate, and ruled by a French governor. The French did much to advance the 'A. both economically and culturally. In 1936 the 'Alawite state was made a part of Syria, with partial autonomy. This special status did not survive the end of the Mandate and the departure of the French in 1944.

The percentage of 'A. in the army, particularly the officer corps, is much larger than in the population, since 1. under the Mandate the French encouraged the enlistment of members of the minorities as a means of curbing the nationalistic tendencies of the Arab-Sunni majority; 2 a military career was the only way for 'A. to achieve financial security and social advancement. Most 'A. officers come from villages, while most Sunni-Muslim officers come from urban families. Many 'A. joined the ruling Ba'th▷ party in Syria, which emphasizes nationalist-secular values rather than Islamic ties and traditions. As a result a relatively large number of 'A. are among Syria's military and political leaders (Jadid▷, Asad▷, Makhus, 'Umran—although the community as a whole is, from the economic and cultural point of view, the most backward in Syria.   (A.L.-O.T.)

ALEPPO (Halab). The second city in size and importance in Syria. Population c. 578,000 (1966). Situated in northern Syria at the feet of the Taurus Mountains on the banks of the small river Quweiq, A. is strategically and economically important as the crossroads between Syria, Iraq and Turkey, linking the Euphrates valley with the Mediterranean and southern Syria with Anatolia. As northern Syria's commercial and industrial centre (mainly textiles, cement and food products), A.'s economic activity exceeds that of Damascus. During the Ottoman period it served as the capital of a district (Vilayet). In 1921–4 it was the centre of a newly formed "State of A." (merged in 1924–5 with the "State of Damascus" to form Syria). As a centre of economic and political power, A. has been historically a competitor to Damascus. In the time of active parliamentary and political life, A. was the headquarters of the "People's Party" as opposed to the "National Party" centred in Damascus.
(A.L.-O.T.)

ALEXANDRETTA. A port and district (Sanjaq) at the head of the bay of A. in the Eastern Mediterranean. The district, whose area is about 1,814 sq. mi., was included in French-Mandated Syria, 1921–39, and was handed over to Turkey in 1939. Today it is known under its Turkish name Hatay. The city (in Turkish Iskenderun) has a population of about 30,000, and is an important Turkish port.

In the Franklin-Bouillon▷ Agreement of 1921 Turkey and France agreed on a border line which left A. within the area of the French Mandate in exchange for a French undertaking to allow it a special administrative régime with official status for the Turkish language. A. was included in the "State of Aleppo" in French-Mandated Syria. When the states of Damascus and Aleppo were merged into the "State of Syria" in 1924, a "special regime" was retained for A.

When the French-Syrian treaty was being negotiated in 1936, Turkey raised once again the A. question. She opposed the inclusion of the district in an independent Syria, claiming that she had surrendered it only to the French Mandatory regime. She demanded that the district be given the status of a separate state. Turkey claimed that Turks were the majority in the district, while the French and Syrians insisted that Turks were only 40% of the 220,000 inhabitants. The matter was raised at the League of Nations which decided in 1937 on a compromise according to which the district would form a separate entity with its own constitution, enjoying independence in internal affairs but connected to Syria in matters of currency, customs and foreign affairs. No military bases or fortifications were to be constructed in its territory; Arabic and Turkish would be the official languages; and Turkey would have special rights in the port of A.

This settlement caused unrest and the outbreak of violence between Turks and Arabs in the district. The powers were preoccupied with rising European tension, and Britain and France were interested in Turkish friendship. Turkey took full advantage of the circumstances and acted systematically and forcefully to gain control over the area, while France was a weak defender of Syrian interests. A Turkish army entered the district in 1938. Under Turkish pressure an electoral law was passed which gave the Turkish residents an absolute majority in the House of Representatives (22 out of 40). A Turk was chosen as President, and a Turk headed an all-Turkish government. The district was given an official Turkish name, "Republic of Hatay". Turkish laws, the Turkish currency and the Turkish postal service were introduced, and gradually ties between Hatay and Turkey were strengthened. In June 1939 France agreed to give up the district altogether and it was joined to Turkey.

The annexation of A. to Turkey caused an outcry in Syria against Turkey and France. Demonstrations were held demanding the return of the district to Syrian sovereignty, but to no avail. After gaining independence, Syria established diplomatic relations with Turkey which implied the acceptance of her borders, but officially she has never recognized Turkish sovereignty over the district. Every once in a while the demand is raised that A. be returned to Syria, and Syrian maps include the district within Syrian limits. The "A. question" is a permanent cause of tension in the relations between Turkey and Syria and other Arab states.   (A.L.-O.G.)

ALEXANDRIA (in Arabic *al-Iskanderiyya*. The second largest city in Egypt. It is Egypt's principal Mediterranean port.

A. was founded in 332 B.C. by Alexander the Great, and played an important role as a trade and cultural centre in the Hellenistic period. The city declined in importance after the third century A.D., and the Arab conquest in 641 completed this process. The revival of the city followed the conquest of Egypt by Napoleon and the rule of Muhammad 'Ali. The latter established a dockyard in A., and in 1819 dug the Mahmudiya canal which connected the city with the Nile. The rehabilitation of the city reached a climax during the rule of the Khedive Isma'il. During this period the population of the city rose to 200,000, of whom 50,000 were foreigners, and A. became an important Mediterranean port.

Its population today numbers about 2 million. A. is the seat of a Greek Orthodox and a Greek Catholic Patriarch (a reflection of the city's position in the Hellenistic world).

A. has had a University since 1942. The cosmopolitan character of the city did not survive under Nasser's▷ regime. Both Jews and foreigners left following the nationalization of their property after the Suez War▷ of 1956. A. is Egypt's main naval base—which is also, since the later 1950s, at the disposal of the Soviet navy.   (S. L.)

ALEXANDRIA PROTOCOL. In the autumn of 1944 a preparatory conference was held of the seven Arab states that had by then established their independence: Egypt, Transjordan, Iraq, Syria, Lebanon, Sa'udi Arabia and Yemen (with the participation of an appointed representative of the Palestine Arabs). The conference, held in Alexandria, discussed the establishment of a "Commonwealth of Arab States" (see Arab League▷). On 7 October 1944 five of the states signed a Protocol (the representatives of Sa'udi Arabia and Yemen were not empowered to sign without the endorsement of their kings). Its main points—chief of which was the conception of the League as independent and sovereign states rather than a federation —were later included in the League's Charter of March 1945. An appendix on Palestine stressed the right to independence of the Palestinian Arabs (along the lines of the British White Paper of 1939), and undertook to help them in their struggle. Another appendix confirmed the Lebanon's right to independence and her borders (as to why such a declaration was needed—see Lebanon▷).   (Y. S.)

*ALGERIA. A.—herself outside the scope of this Encyclopaedia—is deeply involved in ME affairs. Before she achieved independence (1962), support for her national struggle united and preoccupied Arab politicians and nationalists even in the eastern section of the Arab world, al-Mashriq, i.e. the ME. Her extremist nationalist leaders, who could not operate in France, established headquarters in Cairo, particularly after the outbreak of the armed revolt of the Algerian nationalists in Nov. 1954. The young leaders declared their revolt from Cairo and established the rebels' command there. The "Provisional Revolutionary Government of A." was set up in Cairo in Sept. 1958. The Arab governments were amongst the first to recognize this government, and Egypt had great influence over its political and military leaders. Since 1955, the Arab states had yearly raised the Algerian question in the General Assembly of the UN. They demanded independence for A. The Arab states, and in particular Egypt, granted the rebels financial assistance as well as military equipment. The recruitment of Arab volunteers, on the other hand, remained a propaganda idea only. The League Council invited the Algerian rebels in 1959 to send a representative as an observer to its meetings.

When A. gained independence (July 1962), she joined the left wing, 'progressive' camp amongst the Arab States. Muhammad Ben Bella, A.'s chief leader during her first three years of independence, was considered a "Nasserist". Nasser▷ was accused of interfering in the internal struggle within the Algerian leadership (in 1962) and assisting Ben Bella to defeat his adversaries; and Ben Bella always emphasized his close relationship with Nasser and his gratefulness to Egypt. Egyptian support was also given A. in her dispute with Morocco (1963); Morocco claimed that Egyptian arms, equipment and instructor-officers were being used against her. When Egypt, Syria and Iraq agreed, in Apr. 1963, to set up a new "United Arab Republic" on federal lines, A. was invited to join as well. Conflicting reports circulated about A.'s reaction to this invitation, but in any case the federation plan did not materialize. Around 1963 Ben Bella apparently began to draw away from Egypt: the new A. began to plan and act according to her own interests, her self-confidence increased, and Egyptian guidance became a burden from which she wished to free herself. On a number of issues A. took a more extreme position than Egypt, whilst on others her attitude was more Western, more sophisticated than that of the Eastern Arabs. It was then rumoured that Ben Bella was beginning to compete with Nasser for an all-Arab position of leadership. A state visit of Nasser to A. in May 1963 was not considered a success.

The Algerian coup d'état of June 1965 troubled relations with the Arab states for a certain period, as the Arab states, and in particular Egypt, had intervened in favour of the deposed Ben Bella, imprisoned without trial. However, the new Algerian leaders, Colonel Houari Boumedienne and his followers, withstood the pressure, and eventually the Arab leaders made up with the new regime. They did not interfere again when new purges were made. It was generally assumed that A. under Boumedienne would be less active in Arab affairs, and that Boumedienne would not compete for all-Arab leadership. But no drastic or fundamental change appears to have taken place in A.'s position.

A. has indirectly affected Israel's international situation since after the Algerian settlement France felt free to abandon her alliance with Israel and to restore her relations with the Arab states to a position of preference. A., like all the left-wing, revolutionary states in the Arab camp, has taken an extreme position on the Israel-Arab conflict. As the only Arab state ever to have conducted a successful guerilla war, she expressed her expert opinion that in this struggle too the Arabs could win only through a long people's guerilla war—which the Palestinians themselves must wage and in which the other Arab states, including A., could only assist (sometimes a note of impatient contempt for the Palestinian Arabs, Egypt and the whole Mashriq, and their lack of effectivity and courage, could be detected in these Algerian statements). A. sent a symbolic fighting force in June 1967 to participate in the Six Day War (estimates of its size run between 2,000 and 6,000) and left it on the Suez Canal front after the war. She refused to accept the Security Council resolutions—both that imposing a cease-fire, in June, and that drafting steps towards a just and lasting settlement, in November 1967—because she rejected in principle any settlement with the State of Israel. Her extreme attitude manifested itself in July 1968 when she held for over a month an El-Al plane highjacked to her territory as well as its Israeli passengers and crew. When President Nasser and King Hussein responded, in 1970, to an American initiative regarding a renewal of the cease-fire and indirect conversations with Israel through the Swedish ambassador Jarring, A. again reacted in extremist fashion: she opposed these steps, recalled her symbolic expeditionary force from Egypt, and refused to participate in high level inter-Arab consultations. A. also grants active assistance to the Palestinian-Arab feda'iyin▷ organizations, trains them and supplies them with arms. In their confrontation with the Jordan government and army, A. firmly—though not actively—supports the feda'iyin against King Hussein.   (Y.S.)

'ALI b. HUSSEIN (1880–1935). King of Hijaz, 1924–5. Eldest son of Hussein▷ b. 'Ali, the Hashemite Sharif of Mecca and King of Hijaz▷. Together with his brothers 'Abdullah▷ and Feisal▷ led the Hijazi Arab Revolt▷ against the Turks in 1916, though he played no major role. The Hashemites'▷ vague plans for a federation to be established after the Allied victory over the Turks apparently envisaged 'A. as ruler of Hijaz, and he remained with his father in Mecca while 'Abdullah and Feisal left for the Fertile Crescent countries. 'A. had little influence on his father's policies which, in 1924, culminated in a clash between Hashemite Hijaz, isolated and defenceless, and the Sa'udi▷ dynasty of Hajd▷. In October 1924, in order to save the throne for his dynasty, Hussein abdicated in favour of 'A. and left Hijaz as a refugee. Within ten days, however, Mecca was conquered by the Sa'udi Wahhabis▷; 'A. could not rule under Ibn Sa'ud's overlordship, and in December 1925 he renounced his throne and left Hijaz. Thus ended Hashemite rule in Hijaz and it became a part of Sa'udi Arabia. 'A. spent the rest of his days in Baghdad, at the court of his brother, King Feisal I. His daughter 'Aliya married Feisal's son King Ghazi▷ (King Feisal II▷ thus was his grandson). 'A.'s son Abd-ul-Ilah▷ served as regent of Iraq from 1939 to 1953, from the death of Ghazi until Feisal II reached his majority at the age of 18.   (Y.S.)

ALIGNMENT. An Israeli political bloc formed in 1969 in preparation for elections to the Seventh *Knesset* (Parliament). It comprised the "Israel Labour Party" and *Mapam*▷ but each of them maintained its own organizational and ideological independence. It brought about the dissolution of the previous alignment (1965) of *Mapai*▷ and *Ahduth-Ha'avodah Po'alei Zion*▷ which had been formed in preparation for elections to the Sixth *Knesset*, under the leadership of Levi Eshkol, to counter *Rafi*▷ (Ben-Gurion's "Israel Workers' List"), and had secured 45 seats against *Rafi's* ten.

The "Alignment's" policy was similar to that of the government ("Alignment" ministers constituted a majority of government ministers) in connection with the Arab-Israel conflict and the post-Six Day War crisis. It favoured direct peace negotiations and withdrawal from occupied territories to agreed, recognized and secure boundaries different from the pre-war boundaries which occasioned that war.

1. "Israel Labour Party" (affiliated to the Socialist International). Largest in Israel (some 300,000 members). Established in 1968 by the unification of *Mapai*, *Ahduth-Ha'avodah—Po'alei Zion* and *Rafi*. A moderate Socialist-Zionist party whose platform includes, among other aims, the concentration in Israel of most of the Jewish people, the strengthening of democracy and parliamentary regime, guarantee of euqal civil rights and personal liberties, the strengthening of the workers' society and economy and fulfillment of the principle of public ownership of natural means of production. In the 1971 convention 68% of the delegates were formerly *Mapai* members; 18% *Ahduth-Ha'avodah*, and 14% *Rafi*.

2. *Mapam* ("United Workers' Party"). A Marxist Socialist-Zionist party which believes in "pioneering Zionism and revolutionary socialism". Established in 1948 through the unification of *Ahduth-Ha'avodah —Po'alei Zion* and *Hashomer Hatza'ir* parties, the first breaking away in 1954. *Mapam* was Soviet-oriented in the beginning but its disillusionment with the USSR and the Communist world grew. As a result of the increasing Communist hostility towards Israel and Zionism since the Prague Trials, the arms deal between Egypt and Czechoslovakia, and the Six Day War, *Mapam* began stressing more the national part of its platform, while still believing in regional social revolution as a basis for understanding with Arabs. Many of *Mapam's* members and supporters come from *kibbutzim*▷, where the party's "ideological collectivity" is more zealously maintained.   (E.L.)

'ALI, RASHID—see Kilani▷, al-, Rashid 'Ali.

ALLENBY, EDMUND, Viscount (1861–1936). British officer and administrator. In June 1917, A. assumed command of the World War I British Expeditionary Force in Egypt. In October, he mounted an offensive against the Turkish forces in Palestine and entered Jerusalem on 9 December 1917. The offensive, which was temporarily halted, was resumed in autumn 1918, and Turkish resistance was broken at the Battle of Megiddo. Damascus, Beirut and Aleppo were taken in October 1918.

A. was put in charge of the provisional military administration of the occupied ex-Ottoman areas: Palestine and Transjordan, Syria and Lebanon. From October 1919 to 1925 he served as British High Commissioner in Egypt. He began his term of office by suppressing a nationalist uprising against the British in Egypt, but he was instrumental in promoting the partial *modus vivendi* resulting from the unilateral British declaration of Egypt's independence in February 1922. Towards the end of his term of office he faced a major Anglo-Egyptian crisis following the assassination of Sir Lee Stack▷, Commander-in-Chief of the Egyptian Army and Governor-General of Sudan (November 1924). He issued Egypt with a harsh, humiliating ultimatum, but was replaced before the crisis was resolved.   (Sh.H.-Y.S.)

*ALLON, YIG'AL (formerly Paicovitch) (b. 1918). Educated at Kadoorie Agricultural College and the Hebrew University of Jerusalem. In 1937 was co-founder of *Kibbutz* Ginnosar, of which he has been a member ever since. He served with the British Army in Syria and Lebanon, 1941–2, and was one of the founders of the *Palmah*▷—the commando arm of the *Hagana*—serving as its Commander-in-Chief, 1945–8.

During the Arab-Israel War, 1948, A. was the Commanding Officer of the Southern Front. In this capacity he secured the Negev, and expelled the invading Egyptian army. In 1950, A. retired from active service, as Major-General, and became Secretary-General of the *Ahduth Ha'avodah*▷ ("Labour Unity") party and a member of the Executive Committee of its *kibbutz* movement, *Hakibbutz Hame'uhad*. He has been a member of the *Knesset*, with a two-year interval for studies at St. Antony's College, Oxford, since 1955. A. was Minister of Labour 1961–8 and active in reuniting *Ahduth Ha'avodah* with *Mapai*▷ and *Rafi* to form the "Israel Labour Party"▷ in 1968. He became Deputy Prime Minister under Levi Eshkol▷ in 1968—and under Mrs. Golda Meir▷; in 1969 he also became Minister of Education.

A. has written several books about the *Palmah*, Israel's army and security problems. After the Six Day War, A. formulated the "Allon Plan" providing, in return for a peace treaty, for the return to Arab hands of Sinai (but with the right to occupy Sharm al-Sheikh and a connecting land bridge from Eilat) and most of the West Bank of the Jordan, with Israel keeping most of the Jordan River Valley as a security belt and strategic border (the Jordanian East Bank and the West Bank being connected by a narrow corridor).   (A.W.)

'AMER, 'ABD-UL-HAKIM (1919–1967). Egyptian officer and politician. Born into a wealthy family in Astal in the al-Minya province, son of the village headman. He graduated from the military academy in 1938, and took part in the 1948 Palestine War. 'A. was one of the ten founders of the "Free Officers' Committee" in 1949, and participated in the planning and execution of the July 1952 coup. In June 1953 he was promoted to general and appointed Commander-in-Chief of the Armed Forces. In 1954 he became also Minister of War. With the union of Syria and Egypt in 1958 he was promoted to the rank of field-marshal and served as Vice-President of the UAR as well as Minister of War in the central government. In 1960, when opposition to the UAR regime increased in Syria, 'A. was sent as a commissar to supervise all the affairs of the Syrian

region. After the dissolution of the UAR (1961) he continued to serve as Minister of War in Egypt. In 1962 he became one of the 12 members of the Presidential Council, but resigned as Minister of War. In 1964 he was appointed first Vice-President and Deputy Commander-in-Chief of the Armed Forces. On 10 June 1967, after the Egyptian debacle in the Six Day War▷, he resigned, or was dismissed, from his posts. In August 1967 he was arrested and charged with plotting a military takeover of the government; he committed suicide in prison.

Of all the members of the "Free Officers" junta, 'A. was the closest to Nasser▷. Their ties of friendship began at the military academy and continued through days of joint service in Sudan and during the Palestine War. Their views often differed. 'A. was more liberal and respected the traditional socio-religious values of Egypt, considering the new system which the Nasserist regime attempted to implant in Egypt as no more than a governmental necessity. His daily life showed no novel patterns: Relations between him and his subordinates remained paternalistic, and he often used his property and position to aid them and their relatives; his way of life, his private estates (estimated at 120,000 *feddan* or 124,560 acres), the drug deals he was involved in—did not match the image of the New Egyptian which Nasser strove to create. As a politician, 'A. tried to preserve the special status of the army in the administration, as well as his position within the army. This led to two crises between him and Nasser. In 1962, during the reorganization of the regime after the dissolution of the UAR, 'A. opposed the establishment of a presidential council, regarding it as the abrogation of the special status of the military in the state and of his own special ties with the army. The second crisis—the removal of 'A. and his followers from the army in the wake of the Six Day War—resulted in 'A.'s abortive plot, his arrest and suicide. 'A. also did not welcome the socialization of Egypt, accelerating since 1962. He discharged his duty as chairman of the "Committee for the Liquidation of Feudalism" (established in 1965) in as moderate a way as possible, and was criticized for this by the left. He also took issue with the single-party character of the regime. In 1962, and again during the 1967 crisis, he demanded the establishment of another party. However, 'A.'s non-conformist views became definite demands only at times of crisis; they were put forward in order to support his basic demand concerning the position of the army in the state, and to prevent the political "establishment" of the regime from emerging as a force counter-balancing the army. 'A. leaned toward the West, but did not openly condemn the movement towards the Soviet bloc and carried out

'Abd-ul-Hakim 'Amer

several important missions to Moscow (even being awarded the "Order of Lenin"); but he made things difficult for the Soviet instructors in the army, and removed from the army, or at least from delicate positions, officers returning from advanced training in Moscow. In 1965 'A. went to Paris, in an attempt to bring about closer ties with France. In internal discussions he apparently objected to Egypt's excessive rapprochement with the Soviet Union and estrangement from the West. (S.L.)

AMERICAN POLICIES, INTERESTS—see United States▷.

AMINI, Dr. 'ALI (b. 1905). Iranian politician, Prime Minister 1961–2. A member of one of Iran's largest land-owning families, related to the Qajar dynasty. Graduated from the Sorbonne, Paris. A. joined the Iranian civil service (Ministries of Justice, Finance and Customs) and became Director-General of the Ministry of Economy in 1939. He was Minister of Economy for some months in 1950. He was a supporter of Mossaddeq▷ and served in his government as Minister of Economy in 1951 but was dismissed in 1952 for opposing the Premier. A., appointed Finance Minister by Gen. Zahedi▷ in 1953, was Iran's chief negotiator in the talks which settled the oil dispute in 1954. Ambassador to Washington 1956–8. Prime Minister May 1961 to July 1962. In 1968 Premier Hoveida▷ accused A. of plotting against the government with foreign, *i.e.* American, support. He has played no further part in political life. (B.G.)

✶✶**AMMAN.** Capital of Jordan. 500–600,000 inhabitants (1970 estimate). Seat of the University of Jordan. Built on the site of the biblical Rabbat 'Ammon,

the Hellenistic Philadelphia. Its first settlers in modern times were Circassians▷, brought there by the Ottomans in the 19th century. Though 'A. became the capital of the newly established principality (later kingdom) of Transjordan in 1921, it remained a small town (population, 1948, *c.* 40,000). Its rapid expansion began after the Arab-Israel War of 1948 owing to the influx of Palestinian refugees, the development of the country and its separation from Palestine. (B.G.)

'AMMASH, SALEH MAHDI (b. 1924.). Iraqi officer and politician. From before 1958, one of the leading officers connected with the underground *Ba'th*▷ party. During the Qassem▷ regime, 1958–63, imprisoned several times. 'A. was one of the leaders of the coup which overthrew Qassem in February 1963, and served as Defence Minister in the *Ba'th* government established after the coup. After the fall of that government, in November 1963, he remained abroad, in virtual exile, until 1966. After the first Bakr▷ coup (17 July 1968), 'A. became Minister of the Interior, and after Bakr's second coup (30 July 1968) also Deputy Prime Minister. In April 1970 he was appointed Vice-President and gave up the Interior Ministry. 'A. is also a member of the Revolutionary Command Council. Despite his military background, he is first and foremost a politician, a member of the "moderate" sector of the *Ba'th* party, and the opponent of a rival faction headed by Hardan 'Abd-ul-Ghaffar al-Tikriti▷. He was often mentioned, in connection with factional disputes as a possible candidate for the presidency but lately his star declined. (U.D.)

✶**AMRI, AL-, HASSAN** (b. 1916). Lt.-Gen., Yemeni soldier and politician. Received his military education in Baghdad. Following the coup of September 1962, in which he played an active role, 'A. was appointed Minister of Transport, 1962, and of Communications, 1963, in 'Abdullah Sallal's▷ government. He became Vice-President in late 1963. 'A. displayed more independence than Sallal towards the Egyptians, then controlling Yemen through their military aid and expeditionary force, but took a hard line with the Royalists. In mid-1965, following military setbacks, the Egyptians, now on the defensive, made him Prime Minister. He held this post during Sallal's absence until late 1966. When Sallal was returned to power in September 1966, 'A. flew to Cairo and was detained there. In October 1967 he was released and, returning to San'a following the fall of Sallal, was appointed to the three-man Republican (*i.e.* Presidency) Council. He led the Republican forces which saved San'a in the siege of December 1967–February 1968. 'A. also served as Prime Minister 1967–9. He is considered the main leader of the non-tribal wing of the Zeidi▷–Republican regime.   (H.E.)

ANGLO-AMERICAN COMMITTEE—see Palestine▷, Committees and Commissions.

ANKARA. Capital of the Turkish Republic and, with a population of 905,660 in 1965 and 2 million in 1970, its second-largest city. A. is situated in the middle of the Anatolian plateau at an altitude of 2,880 ft. Known in ancient times as Angora, the town was during the Ottoman period an important station on the caravan route from Istanbul to the East. During the Turkish War of Independence A., still a small provincial town, became the centre of the nationalist struggle and was the venue of the first Grand National Assembly, 1920. It was proclaimed capital of the Republic on 13 October 1923, a decision motivated by its strategic position, its Turkish character and its record during the nationalist struggle. Henceforth A. underwent fast and extensive development and modernization, and was linked to the rest of the country by new railways, roads and air routes. A. is the seat of A. University (founded in 1946 through the unification of several colleges; the law faculty was founded in 1925), a "Technical University for the Middle East" (founded in 1959–60), and the Hacettepe University (1967–8).   (D. K.)

Kemal Ataturk boulevard in Ankara

ANSAR, AL- (Arabic: the assistants, the supporters). Originally the supporters of the Prophet Muhammad among the inhabitants of Medina (as distinct from those who came with him from Mecca, *al-Muhajirun*). Nowadays, the name of a religious-political movement in the Sudan, the sect of supporters of the *Mahdi* and his successors from 1880 onwards. For its religious-political character and history—see Sudan▷; *Mahdi*▷, *Mahdiyya*▷.

Al-A. is in addition the name of a Palestinian-Arab guerilla group established by the Communist parties in Jordan, Syria and Iraq. These parties (all of which are officially illegal) announced their intention to set up sabotage groups of their own early in 1970; the Palestinian interorganizational co-ordinating bodies have so far refused to accept them into their ranks. Few, if any, guerilla operations of al-A. are on record.   (Y.S.)

ANTI-SEMITISM. Arab spokesmen occasionally claim that Arabs cannot be anti-Semites, as they are themselves "Semites", but this is mere casuistry. Admittedly, the Arab countries and Islam were more moderate in their anti-Semitism than Christian Europe. The status of the Jews, however, was that of a "protected people" (*Ahl al-dhimma*) without full citizenship rights. Anti-Jewish feeling, at times fostered by Arab rulers and the Moslem religious establishment, occasionally expressed itself in persecution, pogroms, blood libels (Syria 1840; Jerusalem 1847; Dir el-Kamar, Lebanon 1847; the Yemen 1900, 1949), forced Islamization, and collective accusations against Jews of the murder of Muslims (see also Jews in the ME▷).

The political struggle in Palestine of Arab nationalism and Jewish nationalism (Zionism▷) obviously intensified anti-Jewish feeling. Hatred of the Jews on religious grounds was encouraged by Arab leaders, especially among the ignorant masses. There were pogroms during, or immediately following, religious ceremonies, or incited by preachers (Palestine 1920, 1929). Nazi propaganda during the 1930s, in which a number of Arab leaders participated, further encouraged anti-Semitism.

There has been a stronger injection of anti-Semitism into nationalist propaganda since the Arab states' defeat in the war of 1948 against Israel. There have even been attempts to start a *Jihad*▷ against Israel. The attempts of several Arab authors and intellectuals, to make a practical distinction between Israel and Zionism on the one hand and Jews on the other, have not succeeded. Internal propaganda in the Arab states, and their school curricula, have a strong anti-Semitic bias. It takes several forms:

poisonous publications, racial and religious incitement, distinctly Nazi-style caricatures depicting
the Jews (*per se* as nation and "race") as cruel, immoral,
cowardly and sly. "International Jewry" and "Jewish
capital" are depicted both as world-rulers and imperialist tools. The Arab propaganda machine even reprinted the libellous "Protocols of the Elders of
Zion"▷, which is about an alleged international
Jewish plot to take over the world, and distributed
this spurious document in Arabic and other languages
(President Nasser, for instance, referred to the
"Protocols" in at least one interview with a foreign
correspondent). It also reprinted and distributed
Hitler's "Mein Kampf". Nazi-German consultants
assisted the Arabs in the dissemination of anti-
Semitism.   (E.L.)

ANTONIUS, GEORGE (1892–1942). Palestinian-
Arab writer and politician, belonging to the Greek
Orthodox community. Born and educated in Egypt.
A. came to Palestine in 1921 and served in the Palestine
administration, 1921–30, in the Department of
Education. In 1930 he entered the employment of
C. R. Crane of the New York Institute of Current
World Affairs. He eloquently presented — both orally
and in his writings — the Arab case on Palestine and
Arab nationalism in general, especially in his contacts
with British personalities and the general public.
A. also appeared before the Peel▷ Commission
(1936–37) and participated in the London Round
Table Conference (1939) as an advisor. In 1938 he
published "The Arab Awakening", which, though
obviously pleading a cause, has become a classic
work on the Arab nationalist movement. A. maintained close ties with Hajj Amin al-Husseini▷
and his faction, though as a Christian he feared
Muslim extremism. He was sympathetic to the
idea of a Greater Syria of which Palestine would
form a part. He held several meetings with Zionist
leaders to explore the possibility of a Jewish-Arab
compromise, but no agreement was reached.

                                              (Sh. H.)

*'AQABA. Jordan's only port, at the head of the
Gulf of 'A. A small village during the Ottoman
period, 'A. became known in 1906 following the
"Aqaba Incident", which arose out of a dispute between Britain (acting for Egypt) and the Ottoman
Empire over the Sinai▷ Peninsula. The incident was
caused by a Turkish attempt to move troops into an
area considered by the British as Egyptian-Sinai territory. The Sultan had to submit to a British ultimatum and accept the inclusion of the whole Sinai Peninsula in Egypt. The 'A.-Rafah demarcation line later
became the border between Egypt and Mandatory

Palestine and, for most of its length, the armistice
line between Egypt and Israel, 1948–67. In 1917
'A. was occupied, with British assistance, by the army
of Sharif Hussein▷ of Mecca, the King of Hijaz, in
the course of his revolt against the Ottomans. Until
1925 its status was ambiguous, although it was administered by Hijaz. However, when Hijaz was
conquered by Ibn Sa'ud▷, Amir 'Abdullah▷ of
Transjordan, with British encouragement, claimed
'A. had been transferred to him by his father the
King of Hijaz, and annexed it (and also Ma'an, a
town inland). The Sa'udis acquiesced in that annexation, though they did not formally agree to it. In
1965, however, strips of land were exchanged by
agreement, Jordan gaining a length of coastline
near 'A; this agreement indicated full Sa'udi acceptance of the incorporation of 'A. and Ma'an
into Jordan. After the Arab-Israel War of 1948▷,
when Jordan could no longer use the ports of Palestine,
the port of 'A. was developed — partly with West
German and British aid. In 1960 it was linked to
'Amman by a modern highway. In 1968 the port
of 'A. handled 275 vessels and 850,000 tons of cargo.
During the years of border tension and Arab sabotage
incursions into Israel, Jordan ensured that Eilat▷,
opposite 'A. on the Israeli side, was not attacked from
the 'A. region, in order not to endanger 'A.   (B.G.)

ARAB, ARABS. The Arabic term *al-'Arab*
originally referred only to the nomads of the Arabian
desert. However, with the A.-Muslim conquests
of the seventh and eighth century and the spread and
gradual domination of the Arabic language the
term acquired a new meaning: all members of the
A. nation — *i.e.* in fact all those accepting Arabic as
their main language and not maintaining a separate,
distinct national character and consciousness. There
is no "official," generally accepted definition of the
A. nation today. One reasonable working rule is to
define as A. all those who speak Arabic as their main
and national tongue, consciously feel themselves
to be A., and have emotional ties to A. history and
its legacy. A. therefore form the majority in the
following countries: all the countries of the Arabian
peninsula and its northern rim (the Fertile Cres-
cent▷) with the exception of Israel and the Kurdish
regions of Iraq (all these countries are called *Mashriq*,
the East); and all the countries on the North African
coast, from Egypt to Morocco. In the "West"
(*Maghreb*, from Libya to Morocco) there are strong
non-A., Berber▷ elements, but the Arabic language
and A. consciousness dominate. The Sahara desert
is the southern border of the A.; Sudan considers
herself an A. country; but her southern part is
populated by African tribes, and African elements

have also penetrated into other parts of Sudan. All the A. countries have achieved full political independence (arrangements for British protection in the Persian Gulf▷ principalities are due to be terminated). Beyond the generally recognized realm of the A. countries, A. nationalists also claim Palestine, the Hatay▷-Alexandretta▷ district of Turkey, and the south-western portions of Iran (which they call "Arabistan"▷); some consider Mauritania▷, Eritrea▷ and Somalia to be A. or semi-A. countries.

This working definition of the term A. and the listing of the countries whose population is A. need not mean that the A. are one united nation. While some factors unite the A. as one nation (mainly language, literature, and national consciousness), other elements separating them may perhaps turn the A. in these various countries into separate nations (Egyptian, Syrian, Iraqi, Moroccan, etc.). Opinions differ as to whether the unifying or the dividing forces are stronger and which trend will prevail. See also Pan-Arabism▷, Arab Nationalism▷.
(Y.S.)

ARAB BOYCOTT. Economic boycott as a political weapon attracted the Arab leaders since the early days of their struggle against the Jews of Palestine. Local leaders campaigned for a B. against the Jews, their products and services back in the 1920s and the 1930s and tried to enforce it by violence. These efforts failed to stifle or slow down—on the contrary, in many instances accelerated and encouraged—the economic development of the Jewish community (*Yishuv*). Moreover, until the 1940s most of the Palestinian-Arab community continued using Jewish products and especially Jewish services (doctors, hospitals, lawyers, etc.) despite these efforts. In December 1945 the Arab League▷ Council proclaimed a complete economic B. against the Jews of Palestine. The Arab states, as opposed to the Arab community in Palestine, had the means to enforce their B. resolution; first laws to that effect were promulgated at the end of 1945 in various Arab states. This B. was automatically transferred, in 1948, from the Jews of Palestine to the State of Israel. Since the early 1950s it has been under the supervision of special B. offices of the Arab League.

The direct B. of Israeli goods and services is fully applied, and except for a few Israeli products that may reach Arab countries camouflaged under foreign labels, it severed all commercial, economic and transport relations between Israel and the Arab states. The damage done to Israel cannot be estimated in hard figures; the closing of all Arab markets, the severance of all ties between Israel and her neighbours, her natural trading area, undoubtedly

hurts Israel's economy to some extent. Yet, manifestly the AB failed to achieve its main aim: it did not prevent the economic development of Israel nor did it stifle it economically.

The main efforts of the AB officers are directed to non-Arab countries, in order to persuade them, their enterprises and companies, not to do business with Israel. Although many foreign commercial and industrial firms are angered by such an attempt to dictate to them the scope of their activities, no country has as yet forbidden or prevented that interference. The B. offices do not generally "ban" ordinary trade with Israel by foreign companies— albeit they request from every company full information about its ties with Israel, and if the opportunity arises, use pressure to prevent such trade. However, their main efforts are to persuade foreign firms not to invest in Israel, build plants, including assembly plants, maintain regional head agencies in Israel, permit Israeli products to carry their labels, or engage in any kind of cooperation that goes beyond regular trade. Companies and concerns that violate the instructions of the AB offices, are themselves threatened with B. This B. is applied ḥaphazardly and inconsistently. At times, a company insists on its continued co-operation with Israel—and remains unaffected; at times a company submits to the threat, and still its activities in the Arab countries are hampered; and there are in-between incidents— B. threats, and various arrangements to satisfy or evade them. In general, a company that stands firm in the face of a B. threat fares better than one that shows signs of surrender. There is no way to estimate the damage done to Israel: some foreign firms closed their plants, yielding to AB threats; others came in their place; still many others disregarded or resisted threats. Fear of the AB probably persuaded some firms not to extend their activities to Israel in the first place, and it may well be a partial or additional reason in other cases.

The AB is a partial factor in important transportation matters. Arab states do not allow any plane to land at their airports or even to overfly their territory, on its way to or from Israel (planes from Israel to the Far East, e.g., make a wide circle over the Mediterranean, Turkey and Iran). Ships, too, that called at Israel ports, are not permitted to dock in Arab ports (large cruise ships whose passengers are an important source of income are occasionally overlooked and exempted). Attempts to impose a complete B. on shipping and airlines that also serve Israel failed and were not pursued when they were met with firm opposition.

The AB includes at times international conventions and congresses—again, in a haphazard and inconsistent manner, since at the U.N. and many other international conventions Arab delegations participate in spite of the presence of Israeli representatives, yet in others they insist that Israeli delegates be barred as a price for Arab participation. Even important international bodies sometimes surrender, in one way or another, and bar Israeli participation in order to assure Arab participation. The B. offices also supervise the boycott of international artists, actors and their films, records, etc., if they are suspected of having too close ties with Israel; this B., too, is applied arbitrarily.   (Y.S.)

ARAB EXECUTIVE. Leading Palestinian-Arab political organization, 1920–1934, led by Mussa Kazem al-Husseini▷. See Palestine Arabs▷.   (Y.S.)

ARAB FEDERATION. Plans to combine all or several Arab states into a F. have mostly remained vague (see Pan-Arabism▷). The F. talked of was generally meant to include the Fertile Crescent▷ states (Iraq, Syria, Lebanon, Palestine, and Jordan) and occasionally the Arabian peninsula, but extended Egypt, Sudan, Libya, and the *Maghreb*. The Hashemite▷ princes, leaders of the Arab Revolt▷ of World War I, apparently intended to establish a federal kingdom in Arabia and the Fertile Crescent, though they never formulated clear-cut plans. When despite their efforts the area was divided into separate states (under European custody), the Hashemites and their followers continued to nurture the idea of a Hashemite-led F. such as the plan formulated by the Iraqi statesman Nuri Sa'id▷ in 1942 or the Greater Syria▷ scheme of King 'Abdullah▷ of Jordan. (Rival plans by a minor "Syrian Nationalist Party" led by Anton Sa'adeh▷, stressed Pan-Syrian, not Arab nationalism and, being Fascist-oriented, aspired to a unified, autocratic state rather than a F.) The Arab League▷, established in 1945 as an alliance of independent states, supported the status quo and opposed the formation of an AF. Though the Hashemite rulers of Iraq and especially Jordan continued to favour F., the opposing bloc (Egypt, Syria, Sa'udia) prevented the implementation of such ideas.

The formation of the Egyptian-Syrian United Arab Republic▷ (UAR) in 1958 — itself a complete union, not a F. — brought about the formation of two Fs.: a. The "Arab Union" (or F., *al-Ittihad al-'Arabi*) between Jordan and Iraq; formed as protection against the UAR and equipped with a fully federal constitution, it fell victim to the Iraqi officers' revolt of July 1958 and immediately dissolved into its two components. b. The "Union of Arab States" (*Ittihad al-Duwal al-'Arabiyya*), a F. of the UAR and

Yemen which was never implemented. In the 1950s and early '60s there was much talk of a Syrian-Iraqi F.; but it never came into being.

The leftist Pan-Arab Nasserist▷ and *Ba'th*▷ movements of the 1950s and '60s stand for complete, unitary-totalitarian union rather than F.; yet even among them federal or semi-federal plans have been formed. After the UAR was dissolved through Syria's secession (1961), Egypt, Syria and Iraq agreed in April 1963 to form a union that was federal in its structure and constitution, though not called a F.; but the agreement was never put into effect. Neither were decisions of 1964 and thereafter to progress gradually, through stages, towards an Egyptian-Iraqi union. Yemen (now a revolutionary republic) quickly joined that union, but since the Egyptian-Iraqi union was never formed, Yemen's membership remained purely symbolic.

Since 1969–70, a F. of Egypt, Libya and Sudan has been discussed; a decision to form it was announced in November 1970, and Syria announced her decision to join. The "Union (or F.) of Arab Republics" — without Sudan for the time being — was proclaimed on 17 April 1971 and endorsed by plebiscites in Egypt, Syria and Libya on 1 Sept. First constitutional principles were drafted — on loose confederal lines; but their implementation lies still in the future.

There have been several more limited, local-regional Fs. Libya▷, for example, upon attaining independence in 1951, established herself as a F. of Tripolitania▷, Cyrenaica▷, and Fezzan▷. This federal constitution was amended and power was somewhat centralized in 1962; the F. was abolished altogether, and Libya became a unitary state, after the revolution of 1969. In 1959, six small principalities of the Aden▷ Protectorate formed under British guidance, the "South Arabian F."▷ (so named since 1962, originally called "F. of Arab Emirates of the South"); by 1965, the F. included 16 principalities. In 1967, it was transformed into the Republic of South Yemen▷, which abolished her federal character and became a unitary state. The small principalities of the Persian Gulf▷, looking forward to complete independence in 1971 — the seven Trucial Coast▷ Sheikhdoms, Qatar▷, and Bahrain▷ — decided in 1968 to establish a F., to be called "Union of Arab Emirates". Though a temporary constitution has been worked out, there has been, by mid-1971, no real progress towards the implementation of the proposed F. In July-Aug. 1971 it was decided to establish it without Bahain and Qatar and without Ras al-Khaima, as well.   (Y.S.)

ARAB HIGHER COMMITTEE. The organization of the Palestinian-Arab political leadership in

1936, composed of the leaders of the six political parties then active and some non-party members, with Hajj Amin al-Husseini▷ as chairman. The AHC was outlawed on 1 October 1937 for its responsibility for the rebellion (the "disturbances") of 1936–7. It continued operating in exile—Beirut and Damascus —and leading the rebellion (which had by now become an instrument of terror within the Palestinian community itself) until it subsided in 1939. In 1945, a new AHC was formed in the absence of local agreement, through the good offices of Arab League▷ representatives. On the return of Jamal al-Husseini▷ from detention and exile, early in 1946, he expanded the committee and introduced his supporters. This angered the heads of rival factions and caused them to secede and form a rival "Arab Higher Front" in 1946. In the summer of 1946, the Arab League dissolved the two rival committees and appointed a new AHC; Hajj Amin al-Husseini was again its (absent) chairman; Jamal al-Husseini was vice-chairman and acting leader. The extremist Husseini faction dominated the committee. The AHC attempted to take control of the Palestinian-Arab war against partition and emerging Israel, 1947–8; but its attempt failed. The AHC maintained its formal existence after 1948. Its centre is in Beirut and it occasionally publishes declarations and pamphlets, but has little influence. See Palestine Arabs▷.   (Y.S.)

*ARAB-ISRAEL CONFLICT. Incipient Arab resistance to Jewish settlement in Palestine, and to the plans and policy it implied, can be discerned from the beginning of modern Zionist settlement at the end of the 19th century. There were many instances of good neighbourly relations; but sometimes peasants, shepherds and Bedouin feared that their rights of ownership, land tenancy or grazing would be adversely affected by the settlers. Bands of robbers and marauders also caused trouble for the new immigrants. The settlers were considered weak (Arabs sometimes derogatorily called them "Children of Death"), until they posted armed guards who formed the nucleus for organized self-defence. These clashes were, however, sporadic. They did not escalate into organized violence or a systematic struggle until after World War I. Settlement also aroused opposition on the part of politically-minded town notables. This opposition to some extent derived from the awakening Arab nationalist movement, but it also revealed itself as Muslim-Ottoman without specific emphasis on Arab nationalism. It usually took the form of protests to the Ottoman authorities and requests to prevent Jewish immigration and settlement. The authorities at times acceded to these requests. The first Arab newspapers, which began publication in Palestine at the time, also bitterly opposed Zionism and Jewish settlement.

During this period, contacts were established between the Zionist leadership (or local leaders of the Jewish *Yishuv*) and Arab leaders, in an effort to reach an understanding and find ways of co-operation, mainly in the framework of the Arab movement for the decentralization of the Ottoman Empire. Some of the contacts were made with Arab leaders outside of Palestine, e.g. in Beirut and in Egypt. These tentative contacts did not lead to full agreement.

FROM THE BALFOUR DECLARATION TO ISRAELI INDEPENDENCE. The Arab-Jewish confrontation entered a graver organized phase with the Balfour Declaration▷. Arab leaders now realized that the Jewish settlers had plans of great and far-reaching political significance, and that their plan was backed by the world powers. Furthermore, the very establishment of Palestine as a recognized and defined political unit was bound up with the programme to establish a Jewish National Home. The nationalist Pan-Arab leadership—King Hussein▷ of Hijaz and his sons, first and foremost Amir Feisal▷, who represented the Arab movement and its claims for sovereign independence (although they had received no formal mandate from the nationalist movement—the small urban nationalist societies in the Fertile Crescent, underground and hardly existing during the war) regarded the Jews of Palestine and the Zionist movement as a potential ally. They saw no contradiction between the Jewish enterprise in Palestine (whose borders had not yet been defined) or part of it, and the sovereign independence of the Arabs in the other parts of their homeland. They also hoped to obtain the assistance of influential world Jewry. Chaim Weizmann's▷ contacts with Feisal in Palestine and in Paris during the Peace Conference led in January 1919 to the Feisal-Weizmann Agreement▷, in which the Jewish and Arab national movement recognized each other's justice and provided for mutual support and full cooperation. The agreement had perhaps no legal validity, as Amir Feisal had added, in his own hand, that it would be valid only if all Arab national demands were satisfied—and the Arabs did not obtain full satisfaction at the time (though they have since attained the full independence they sought). It remains, however, a historical and moral fact that early Arab nationalism did not oppose a Jewish Palestine or regard it as an enemy. The agreement was open to conflicting interpretations on several points, but its essence is clear; it juxtaposed the Arab State and Palestine as two separate entities; it provided for co-operation between them and for reciprocal representation; and it expressed the support of the Arab nationalist movement for the Zionist enterprise.

The agreement was not implemented and left no real mark on future events, primarily because the Pan-Arab kingdom, in whose name Feisal spoke, was never established. The Zionist leadership continued their contacts with nationalist Pan-Arab leaders, such as the Syrian-Palestine office in Geneva and its counterpart in Cairo (Shakhib Arslan▷, Ihsan Jaberi▷, Habib Lutfallah, Riad al-Sulh▷) and others. But these were then politicals devoid of authority and power, and, moreover, extremist and anti-Zionist views began to dominate even among them. In contrast to Feisal and his advisers who had been prepared to allocate a place to a Jewish Palestine in their Pan-Arab vision, the local Palestinian-Arab leaders turned all their efforts against Zionism. If there were moderates among them, willing to compromise, they gave little or no public expression to their views; and they certainly did not attain influential or leading positions.

The political organization of the Palestinian Arabs is described in the entries Palestine▷ and Palestine Arabs▷. The struggle against Zionism—and the British Mandate, based on the Balfour Declaration and the obligation to assist in establishing a Jewish National Home—was, from the outset, the cornerstone of the programmes and platforms of all the organizations and parties. Their argument was clear and simple: the country belongs to the people living in it, whose majority is Arab; it is entitled to immediate independence as an Arab State; no Jewish immigration or settlement can take place without the consent of the country's owners (and this consent is refused); the British and the world powers had no right to promise a land that was not theirs, and their promise is null and void.

The Zionist counter-argument—that the Jewish people has a historical right to the land; that only in Palestine can it set up its homeland; that the rights of the Arab majority should be weighed not against the rights of the Jews already in the country but the whole Jewish people; that the development of the country would benefit both peoples; that the Jewish National Home was being created out of nothing, in deserts and uninhabited swamps; and that no Arab had been, or would be, expelled with the growth of the *Yishuv*—all these claims fell on deaf ears.

The organized political resistance which induced the Palestinian-Arabs to boycott all representative institutions proposed by the Mandatory Authorities and led to increasing clashes with the British was accompanied from the outset by violence. This violent struggle became continually more severe in tempo and scope: local outbreaks following incitement and demonstrations, on 4 Apr. 1920 and

1 May 1921; more prolonged and better-organized riots, including attacks on isolated Jewish settlements, in August 1929 (Muslim religious incitement, always an auxiliary means of inflaming the masses, played a more central role on this occasion, as a result of the conflict over the Western (Wailing) Wall and the claim that the Jews sought control of the Temple Mount, *al-Haram al-Sharif*); prolonged guerilla warfare, with the help of outside volunteers, and an incipient military organization, in 1936-9. This escalation of Arab resistance, strongly influenced by the rapid growth of Jewish settlement after 1933, in its turn induced the Zionists to greater efforts in immigration, economic growth and the organization of self-defence. The economic boycott declared by the Arabs as part of the 1936 disturbances moved the *Yishuv* to efforts to penetrate those economic branches then exclusively in Arab hands. The self-defence organization *Hagana*▷, which had until the 1930s been based mainly on the local defence of each settlement, gradually became a real military organization with a central command. There was bitter controversy among the Jewish leadership and public whether to continue the policy of restraint, *i.e.* static defence, or to take active, offensive reprisals against the centres of the guerilla gangs (in the course of which innocent people, women and children might also be hurt, which was repugnant to most). Offensive action against guerilla centres began in about 1937.

Throughout this period, the ideological content of the conflict did not change much. In the face of the increasing number, power and self-confidence of the Jews, no Arab thinker came forward with any idea or formula for a solution, beyond the demand for an immediate take-over by the majority, with the minority frozen in its status (if not expelled or liquidated)—an unrealistic formula, because no longer corresponded to the actual power situation. The Zionist leadership, in many contacts and discussions with Arab leaders, proposed the formula that had been the basis of the Feisal-Weizmann Agreement: a Jewish Palestine within a Pan-Arab or ME framework—federal or confederal, or in a close alliance. The assumption was that in an all-Arab framework, which would satisfy the Arabs' national demands and give them a feeling of strength and security, it would be easier to attain a Jewish-Arab agreement based on moderation and generosity. The formula was unacceptable to the Palestinian-Arab leaders. Another formula was suggested (in various versions) by unofficial Jewish leaders: a bi-national▷ state based on parity in all government institutions. The idea did not arouse much enthusiasm among the Zionists; but had there been an Arab leadership willing to accept it, many would undoubtedly have supported it within the Zionist camp, too (provided immigration and settlement could continue within its framework). However, no Arab leader accepted the bi-national idea. A proposal by Jewish personalities to base an agreement on a predetermined population percentage or an absolute number as a ceiling for Jewish population growth, was not acceptable to Jewish public opinion, particularly as the Arab notables contacted regarded a Jewish population of 35% or possibly 40% as the highest possible ceiling. No agreement was reached in any of these contacts, but talks between Zionist and Arab leaders continued in Palestine and in neighbouring countries, even during the disturbances. There were also close everyday contacts between the two peoples, mainly in the mixed cities, in the economic sphere, in mixed organizations (e.g. citrus growers, chambers of commerce), in government offices, etc. Most of these contacts ceased during the riots, from 1936, and were never resumed on their previous scale.

In 1937 the Peel Commission▷ proposed to partition the country and establish an independent Jewish State and an Arab State that would be united with Transjordan. The Commission assumed that both peoples were entitled to independence in Palestine, and that a compromise agreement on joint independence in a single state was unattainable. The Zionists were prepared to discuss partition; the Arabs totally rejected it. Amir 'Abdullah▷ of Transjordan was no doubt inclined to accept partition—the idea of uniting the Arab section of Palestine with his kingdom was not foreign to him—and his supporters in Palestine would have accepted it had it been decided and implemented vigorously and without delay. They were not prepared to fight for it openly, particularly as the Arabs of Palestine were then sinking into a blood-bath of internal terrorism. The Arabs' firm negative attitude brought them a great political victory: the partition plan was repealed and fresh consultations were held (in which the Arab leaders refused to sit at the same table and negotiate with the Zionists; this refusal turned the round-table conference into separate British consultations with the two sides). The White Paper▷ of 1939 was the result of these consultations. It virtually accepted the Arab' demands: independence (soon); giving the existing Arab majority full control, while the Jewish *Yishuv* was frozen; limited Jewish immigration for a short while, subsequently stopping altogether; land purchase limited.

In those years, the Arab states increasingly assumed the leadership of the Palestine struggle and the representation of the Palestinian Arabs. Important milestones in this process, apart from numerous conferences, declarations and political and diplomatic support were: a. in October 1936 the Arab kings (as yet without Egypt) intervened—at Britain's invitation after pre-arranged agreement with her—in the disturbances, asking the Palestinians to halt the strike and the armed struggle; b. late in 1938, Britain invited the Arab states to the 1939 London Conference (this time including Egypt—thus inducing her actively to enter both the Arab-Israel field and the all-Arab orbit). This obvious transfer of the leadership to the Arab states was not resisted by the Palestinian Arabs, as their most prominent leaders were in exile or imprisoned and the Palestinian-Arab public was left without strength after the blood-bath.

Jewish and Arab organization, positions and leadership in the period leading up to the decisive struggle in 1945-8 are described in the entries Palestine▷ and Palestine Arabs▷. The Jewish position was unequivocal: after the Biltmore Programme▷ of 1942, the Jews officially demanded independent statehood —if unavoidable, in part of the country. They made every effort to gain international support. After the UN recommended partition, November 1947, they realized that they would have to defend themselves and their new-born state against military attack. In the Arab camp, three conflicting attitudes were discernible: a. A few statesmen, led by King 'Abdullah▷, and Nuri Sa'id▷ of Iraq, realized that in view of international realities and Jewish strength, the grant of some kind of independence or autonomy to the Jews was inevitable and that the most the Arabs could achieve was to prevent total Jewish independence and secession by offering them partial autonomy in the framework of some form of Arab federation (both King 'Abdullah and Nuri Sa'id had different programmes for such a federation). Most Arab statesmen and the Palestinian-Arab leadership rejected these programmes, and their proponents did not continue arguing for them (although 'Abdullah tried to implement them on his own). b. The mainstream, the Arab states and the Arab League▷, in effect accepted the plan outlines in the 1939 White Paper: quick independence for Palestine, with an Arab majority and, therefore, an Arab character, with full civic rights (and possibly even a degree of cultural autonomy) for the Jews, but no further Jewish immigration (unless the Arabs agreed to it) and no further Jewish settlement. This was a clear, rigid and logical plan; but it lacked imagination and paid no heed to political realities. c. The Palestinian-Arab leadership was even more extreme; it wanted immediate independence (not by gradual progress in accordance with an agreed programme); and it was not prepared to commit itself to accept the existing Jewish *Yishuv* and to assure its minority and civic rights in the future Arab state.

For the 1947 UN resolution on Partition—see Palestine▷, and the war of 1948—see Arab-Israel War▷. Over and above the direct military defeat, the war was a grave political failure for the Arab states. The first five months, prior to the proclamation of the State of Israel and the invasion of the regular Arab armies, revealed that of the promised all-Arab assistance part was not supplied at all and whatever was supplied did not suffice; that despite committees and staffs and commands established there was no unified plan; and that there was no unity, no co-ordination and no mutual confidence among the Palestinian Arabs themselves, between them and their kinsmen in the Arab states and between the different Arab states. The Palestinian-Arab leadership deserted the battlefield when it left the country at the head of a stream of refugees. The failure of guerilla warfare and of the volunteers from the Arab countries forced the Arab states into a decision to invade Palestine with their regular armies—without adequate preparation and cancelling in a sudden move, an explicit decision not to do so. This *volte face* occurred only in the first week before the invasion. The military chiefs-of-staff advised and warned against the invasion, but the governments, primarily the government of Egypt, ignored their advice (later when trials were held for the sins of 1948, and the military proved that they had opposed the invasion, government leaders claimed that King Farouq▷ had forced his decision on them). The war ended with the Armistice Agreements of 1949 (see Arab-Israel War▷).

FROM 1948 TO THE SIX DAY WAR. The establishment of the State of Israel and the defeat of the Arab states in the 1948 War brought about a totally different situation. It was no longer a struggle for the fate and future of the country. That struggle had been decided (although the Arabs refused to accept the decision as final and the fight could break out again). The State of Israel had no claims on the Arab states, apart from requesting their agreement to end the war, their recognition of Israel and the establishment of a lasting peace. The Arab states have so far refused these demands. Arab leaders say sometimes—usually when addressing Western leaders rather than their own people—that they recognize the fact of Israel's existence (though not recognizing her diplomatically) and that their signature to the Armistice Agreements constitutes such recognition of the fact of Israel's existence. However, in the 23 years since 1948 no Arab government or leader (apart from a very few individuals with no power or influence) was pre-

pared openly and unreservedly to state their acceptance of Israel's existence and willingness to make peace with her. This Arab refusal to co-exist went with a rigid and uncompromising refusal of any direct negotiation with Israel.

Apart from the fact of Israel's existence, the 1948 War created a number of secondary problems. It was on just these issues that the Arab states thenceforth concentrated their diplomatic demands. a. While fighting a war of defence, Israel had expanded by *c.* 2,600 sq. miles, territory assigned to it in the UN resolution blueprint map, and she regarded the territory acquired as an integral part of the State. Israel argued that the UN map had been designed solely for implementation in conditions of peace and had not taken defence needs into account. As soon as the Arab armies invaded Palestine, it was no longer possible to preserve the details of the blueprint (such as, e.g., the intersection points—see map in Palestine▷). The independent Palestinian Arab State had not been created as planned, but its territories had been occupied by outside states which certainly had no claim to any Palestinian territory. Israel was also unwilling to abandon the Jews of Jerusalem; the UN had taken no steps towards the establishment of Jerusalem as a separate internationalized entity and had proven unable to defend its citizens and look after their needs. In any event, Israel argued, the Arab states that had rejected the UN resolution on partition and used the force of arms to prevent its implementation were not now entitled, either politically or morally, to claim appeal to that very resolution and clamour for the restoration of the details of the blueprint map. However, the Arab states now demanded the implementation of the 1947 Partition Plan and Israel's withdrawal from territories which, to Israel, had become an integral part of the State. This demand seemed to imply that the Arab states had accepted the fact of Israel's existence and would, after Israel's withdrawal make peace; but such a conclusion was never stated by the Arab states explicitly and binding On the contrary, when speaking to their own public the Arab leaders accompanied the claim for a withdrawal to the "borders of 1947" with incessant declarations that the State of Israel must be altogether liquidated.

b. A refugee▷ problem was created. There were initially 550–600,000 Palestinian-Arab refugees; over the years their number has grown to *c.* 1,300,000 (their number is disputed). This was a secondary problem, in the sense that it could have been solved in circumstances of peace and co-existence, *i.e.* with the solution of the main problem. It was, however, an important and real problem, and a tragic one. Hundreds of thousands of men and women were removed from creative and responsible life and made dependent on permanent relief. The Arab states demanded that the refugees be allowed to return to their homes, particularly as, they claimed, the refugees had not voluntarily fled but been expelled by Israel. UN institutions and large sectors of world public opinion also felt that the refugees were entitled freely to choose between returning to what had in the meantime become the State of Israel and receiving compensation. Israel declared its willingness to discuss the refugee problem in the framework of peace negotiations and as part of a peace settlement—or even outside of such comprehensive negotiations, in a sincere attempt to to find a separate constructive solution to the painful problem. But Israel was not prepared to accept the return of the refugees as an ultimatum, as a prerequisite for any arrangement, outside the framework of an overall solution. On the merits of the refugee question, Israel agreed to pay compensation for the immovable property left behind by the refugees (tentative estimates of the value of this property were made by a UN commission and Israel did not appeal against its findings). Israel also offered to absorb some of the refugees as a contribution towards solving the problem; in 1949 a figure of 100,000 was mentioned. This offer was rejected out of hand by the Arab states; so was the compensation offered (as accepting compensation would imply renouncing any further claims). However, Israel could not accept all the refugees within her borders; their absorption would have fundamentally altered her character as a Jewish State and, furthermore, would have implanted radically hostile elements, a populace that openly declared its unwillingness to live at peace in the State of Israel and to become its loyal citizens, and its fervent desire to destroy the State. It would also be better for future co-existence and Arab-Israel relations, so Israel held, not to create anew a substantial national minority that had been moved by history, albeit cruelly, in an unplanned exchange of population, to live among its own kith and kin.

These problems have been, since 1948, incessantly debated in the international arena, at the annual meetings of the UN General Assembly, in many international conferences, in the press and among world public opinion. In 1948, the UN appointed a mediator, the Swedish Count Bernadotte▷; but his proposals were unacceptable to the parties, and to the UN General Assembly as well. In September 1948, Bernadotte was assassinated in Jerusalem by members of a dissident, extremist group of the Jewish underground. The acting mediator who replaced him, Dr. Ralph Bunche▷, succeeded in initiating and completing negotiations on Armistice Agreements, and ceased his activities when they were signed. Late in 1948, the UN had also appointed a "Conciliation Commission" (PCC) composed of the representatives of the USA, France and Turkey. The PCC convened a conference in Lausanne (1949), but the Arab states refused to meet Israel, and the "conference" was no more than separate talks. It achieved nothing on the main issue: the parties agreed on a protocol, which provided for the 1947 UN blueprint map to be regarded as the starting-point for discussion. The Arabs interpreted the protocol as Israeli acceptance of the 1947 map, while Israel regarded it as only an opening for negotiations. The PCC formally still exists, but after the Lausanne Conference it has taken no bold steps and has achieved nothing. Nor has the annual debate in the UN General Assembly brought a solution closer. Every year, a similar resolution is passed on the refugee question. It usually reiterates a resolution of December 1948 that grants the right to choose between repatriation to Israel and compensation to those refugees "wishing to live at peace with their neighbours", or the version of 1950 that recommends "the reintegration of the refugees into the economic life of the Near East either by repatriation or resettlement". However, such resolutions were incapable of changing the situation or the positions of the parties. As to the problem of the borders, until 1967 the UN passed no resolution, and it hardly touched on the basic issue of peace and co-existence.

The Arab states conducted, throughout the period, hostile activities of various kinds against Israel. They declared a complete economic boycott of Israel, refusing to buy from or sell to Israel and refusing to grant Israeli aircraft and ships transit, docking and landing rights. Furthermore, they tried to compel other countries to comply with their boycott —if not concerning ordinary trade, then at least regarding investment in Israel, joint project assembly plants, etc.—and refused, in theory, to deal with any company that co-operated with Israel (in practice, enforcement of boycott decrees was arbitrary and haphazard and differed from case to case; it depended in no small measure on the courage and resistance shown by each company). There is no estimate in figures of the damage caused to Israel by the boycott. Israel overcame the obstacle, but there are probably enterprises in the world which refrained from co-operating with Israel out of fear of the boycott.

Egypt also closed the Suez Canal▷ to Israeli shipping and to any foreign ship en route to or from Israel. The Convention of Constantinople, 1888, obliged Egypt to keep the Canal open to ships of all countries, even in time of war (Art. 1); but Egypt cited article X permitting her to take measures for her defence even in contravention of certain articles of the Convention (although her right under this article specifically does not take precedence over the freedom of navigation, which remains the binding and leading principle of the Convention). In September 1951, the UN Security Council decided that the closure of the Canal by Egypt was unjustified and an unwarranted interference with the rights of free navigation, and called on Egypt to terminate these restrictions. Egypt did not heed the binding decision of the Security Council, and the Canal remained closed as before. Egypt imposed a similar blockade on the Straits of Tiran▷ and the entrance to the Gulf of 'Aqaba▷ (Eilat) after acquiring the islands of Tiran and Sanafir in the Straits from Sa'udi Arabia in 1950 (at that time promising the USA not to infringe the complete freedom of navigation in the Gulf). After a number of attempts by ships of different flags to reach Eilat despite the blockade, shipping to Eilat was, to all intents and purposes, paralysed until the blockade was lifted in the Sinai Campaign▷ of 1956.

Hostile acts of another kind, also strictly prohibited under the Armistice Agreements, were the incessant campaign of inimical propaganda and incitement against Israel conducted by all the Arab countries.

In the field, there were in the meantime many border clashes. Some of them were "ordinary" clashes of army patrols or exchanges of fire between army positions on the two sides of the border; most were incidents caused by deliberate infiltration and sabotage by the Arabs. Such sabotage acts became more fully organized and planned from the mid-1960s when guerilla (feda'iyin▷) organizations were fostered. In the preceding years they were more haphazard and had their ups and downs; but Arab acts of sabotage were carried out from the day Israel was established. A minority of them were acts of private initiative but most were organized by the Arab armies and their special and secret services or by Palestinian organizations. These incidents were dealt with by Mixed Armistice Commissions, each headed by a neutral officer of a force of truce observers established by the UN to supervise the Armistice lines (UNTSO). The Commissions considered many hundreds of mutual complaints. The observer-officer's vote usually decided the matter, as each side usually justified its own actions and voted against complaints by the other party. If the observer abstained, the complaint remained undecided. If a decision was made, it meant a censure of the party guilty of a breach of the armistice. The observers and the Mixed Commissions were powerless to remedy the situation or to prevent incidents. The

Commissions' regular work was sometimes interrupted by particularly serious incidents or disputes of principle. Israel boycotted the Israel-Jordan Commission from 1956 to 1959; it participated only in emergency sittings of the Israel-Syria Commission from 1952 to 1957, and boycotted them completely from 1957, as the Syrians insisted that the commission should also consider the demilitarized zones (see Arab-Israel War▷: Armistice Agreements), while in the view of Israel the Commission had no authority to discuss them. Israel regarded the Israel-Egypt Commission as abrogated from 1956.

These incessant acts of sabotage and infiltration were not prevented by the Arab states, as required by the Armistice Agreements. The Arab states in fact took no steps against them. On the contrary, they encouraged the saboteurs, organized and equipped them, supplied them with arms and funds, bases of operation and shelter. Israel for years had made unavailing complaints. The situation had not been remedied. She saw no alternative but to act herself against the saboteur bases and encampments beyond the borders. Major "reprisal" actions of this kind were taken from 1953 (among the best-known: Qibya— 14 Oct. 1953; Gaza—28 Feb. 1955; Sea of Galilee east shore—11 Dec. 1955; Qalqilya—10 Oct. 1956; Tawafiq—1 Feb. 1960; al-Nuqeib—16 Mar. 1962; Almagor—14 July 1966; al-Sumu'—13 Nov. 1966). The Arab states usually complained about reprisals to the Security Council, which generally censured Israel—usually without mentioning, let alone condemning, the chain of cause and effect, the incessant sabotage on Israel soil, that had preceded and caused Israeli action. (Of course, the reprisals were on a different scale from the acts of sabotage that caused them: each act of sabotage was relatively small, but their cumulative impact was to be weighed against Israeli counter-action.) Israel for her part submitted few complaints to the Security Council, because the USSR was almost certain to veto any decision unfavourable to the Arab states.

UN debates and the continuous political argument had little influence on the course of events in the region itself. That course was determined by the Arab states' effort to strangle Israel with a noose of military alliances and joint military commands of the states encircling Israel—states which strengthened their forces, 1955–6, mainly with Soviet arms, at an unprecedented rate—and through a tightened blockade of the Gulf of 'Aqaba, Israel's only outlet to the south and east. This threat of an immediate onslaught from the outside was accompanied by stepped-up attempts to undermine Israel's security and daily economic life by incessant sabotage inside. To these were added a noisy chorus of hate propaganda and predictions of approaching slaughter. It was this circle of immediate mortal danger that Israel felt compelled to break in October 1956—through the Sinai Campaign▷.

A future historian will determine the balance-sheet of the Sinai War. The sea-way to Eilat was open and secure, and the Egyptian border, particularly along the Gaza Strip▷, was quieter, less open to infiltration by saboteurs. The basic political confrontation, and the tactical claims of the sides had hardly changed. However, Arab suspicions that Israel had expansionist ambitions were probably reinforced. Arab national pride was hurt still more by this; further defeat and their desire for revenge strengthened. Arab spokesmen saw their claims that Israel was party to Western imperialism confirmed.

The basic constellation did not change in the decade between the temporary and partial arrangements made after the Sinai Campaign and the Six Day War▷. Three further factors were added:

a. The problems of the waters of the Jordan▷ River worsened, after coming close to a solution in the 1950s through the Johnston Plan▷. That plan was approved and agreed upon by the engineers and experts of both sides, but then rejected in principle by the Arab leaders for political reasons. When Israel prepared to implement her "National Water Carrier" scheme and pumping began from the Sea of Galilee▷, the issue became urgent and practical. As the Arab states could not, short of war, prevent Israel from implementing her share of the Johnston Plan, they devised a plan to divert the sources of the Jordan—the Baniyas▷ in Syria, and the Hasbani▷ in Lebanon—so that their waters would not reach Israel. The plan was approved at the First all-Arab Summit Conference in January 1964 (after Israel had announced the completion of the works in December 1963; the National Carrier began operating in spring 1964). Work on diverting the Baniyas and the Hasbani commenced early in 1965. However, as Israel made it clear that she would regard any diversion attempt as an act of hostility and take firm action against it, the Arab states debated at length the necessary military measures to protect the diversion works. As such protection was not fully assured—and Israel used several border incidents deliberately to strike at the diversion points in Syria— the diversion work did not proceed speedily or efficiently. In particular, Lebanon (neither military-minded nor extremist) clearly showed her lack of enthusiasm.

b. From the mid-1960s the guerillas again stepped up sabotage activities. They were now more organized, as guerilla action became the main sphere of operations, the *raison d'être* of new Palestinian-Arab

organizations, some of them, particularly *feda'iyin*▷ (commando) organizations, set up from the early 1960s on to revive a Palestinian-Arab national "entity" (see Palestine Arabs▷). Both the terrorist guerilla elements and the Palestinian-Arab political element had existed before, but their importance and the intensity of their activity now increased.

c. As clashes between Israel and the *feda'iyin* sharpened, regular Arab forces, particularly Syrian and Jordanian, were increasingly drawn into them. Terrorist incidents frequently developed into serious battles with regular forces, including the use of heavy arms. Israeli counter-actions also took on a more serious military character; from 1964 on, the air force was also used in such operations.

The Six Day War▷ is described in a separate entry. The War broke out following a chain of events similar, almost identical, to that of 1956: Arab military pacts clearly, even explicitly, directed against Israel; joint military commands of the various Arab armies, deliberately creating the impression that the strangling noose was closing on Israel; a growing concentration of forces on Israel's borders, primarily in the Sinai Peninsula; a growing intensity of threats of war, an ever-increasing incitement of the masses to a holy war of hate and revenge; the expulsion of the UN Emergency Force (UNEF▷); and the declaration of a renewed blockade of the Straits of Tiran leading into the Gulf of Eilat. The component elements were those of 1956. The course of events and the results were, necessarily, similar to those of 1956; on this occasion, though, no element of cooperation or coordination with imperialist powers entered the picture, as Israel stood alone.

1967 AND AFTER. Those who had hoped that the defeat in the Six Day War would bring the Arab states to a peace conference, and convince them they could not achieve a desirable solution through war, were mistaken. The latest defeat deepened the wounds, the bitter hurt to Arab pride and national honour. The old deep-rooted refusal to negotiate with Israel on peace terms became even more rigid now that Israel occupied Arab territories. Yet some changes seem to have taken place in the Arab position; attempts to summarize them are necessarily tentative, as events are too recent and it cannot be determined which of them are of a far-reaching and long-term nature or merely transient. a. The Arab leaders have realized that the violent war propaganda in which they indulged, calling to exterminate Israel, greatly damaged their position in world public opinion; furthermore, some of them realize that it also misled and deluded the Arab public at home and was, therefore, one of the causes of defeat. A change in propaganda methods was ordered—violent, emotional incitement was to be stopped, and world public opinion should be told that the Arabs had no intention of annihilating or expelling the residents of Israel and that their battle was only against the State, the establishment. b. The emphasis on the borders of the 1947 blueprint has been muted (although the demand has not altogether disappeared). A new, principal demand has replaced it, accepted by all the Arab states, despite their divisions over other essential political issues: the return of all the occupied territories, or, in the usual Arab political terminology, "The Liquidation of the Results of the Aggression of 1967".

As to the long-term fundamental aim, beyond the return of the lost territories, the Arab world is divided. The extremist camp — Syria, Iraq, Algeria, South Yemen and the Palestinian organizations (with Sa'udi Arabia and Kuwait usually joining the extremists in the Arab-Israel issue, while Sudan and Libya, otherwise extremist, generally accept Egypt's guidance) — takes a clear and simple position: it totally rejects the cease-fire imposed by the Security Council in 1967 and the November 1967 Security Council Resolution which calls for the establishment of a "just and lasting peace", based on "respect for and acknowledgement of the sovereignty, territorial integrity and political independence of every state in the area and their right to live in peace within secure and recognized boundaries" and on the withdrawal of Israeli armed forces from occupied territories. The Resolution also calls for freedom of navigation through "international waterways" in the area as well as for a "just settlement" of the refugee problem. The extremists could not accept this resolution, as it postulated the acceptance of Israel's existence and the establishment of peace with her.

The "moderates", led by Egypt under presidents Nasser▷ and Sadat▷, and Jordan under King Hussein▷, accepted the November 1967 Resolution — but with their own interpretation: Israeli withdrawal from all the occupied areas is a precondition for any settlement; the "secure and recognized" boundaries are the pre-1967 Armistice lines, with no need whatsoever to negotiate them; other matters, too, must be solved by the Security Council in accordance with UN resolutions, and need not be negotiated (the moderate leaders have implied, though they have not fully committed themselves, a willingness to assure the freedom of navigation in the Straits of Tiran, and possibly in the Suez Canal, to demilitarize the territories vacated by Israel, and to station international forces in them); the peace referred to in the Resolution means the termination of the state of war, but not necessarily a formal contractual peace

and certainly not normal relations. This state of "peace" is not intended by the Arab "moderates" to solve the Arab-Israel problem, the Palestine problem, but only to end the 1967 conflict and to "eliminate the results of the aggression of 1967", while the Palestinian issue, "the problem of 1948", would still remain open between Israel and the Palestinian Arabs as well as the whole Arab world. (It remained unclarified: would the "secure and recognized" boundaries and the state of non-belligerency apply only in the context of ending the 1967 conflict? Would they, therefore, be temporary, and would the guerillas continue their activities with aid, arms and money from the Arab states?) Even now the moderate Arab states have avoided a clear and unequivocal commitment to peaceful co-existence with Israel; their spokesmen have taken care to clarify that even President Sadat's desire for a "peace agreement" — voiced in February 1971 as the farthest reaching Arab statement in this direction ever made — did not mean a full, contractual peace treaty arrived at by peace negotiations.

Israel also accepted the Security Council Resolution — with her own interpretation. She saw a just and lasting peace as the main issue — peace rather than non-belligerency or a declaration on the termination of the state of war, a complete and contractual peace between the parties themselves (which could only be reached through direct negotiations). She therefore did not see the Resolution as a timetable which could be "implemented", but as a framework of, and starting-point for, negotiations to determine the details of peace, its provisions and guarantees, and, primarily, its "secure and recognized" boundaries. Israel has stated clearly that there can be no withdrawal except within the framework of a peace settlement and as part of it. Even then she has not committed herself to total withdrawal from all the occupied territories, insisting that total withdrawal was not requested by the Security Council, although the Arab states and the Soviet Bloc sought to interpret the Resolution in this way. Israel has refused to "draw maps" indicating from which territories and to which boundaries, she would withdraw; such maps could be drawn in negotiations with the Arab states and following agreement on the nature and character of the peace and security which would provide the framework for withdrawal (for some time even official government spokesmen, who repeatedly announced the acceptance of the Security Council Resolution, did not like to use the term "withdrawal", preferring "redeployment"; a section of the Israeli public was opposed to any withdrawal from the occupied areas and sought their annexation to the State of Israel). In the course of time,

Israeli leaders have indicated—as positions stated rather than conditions put forward as an ultimatum—acceptable boundary lines. No one even considered evacuating Jerusalem and redividing it; it was *de facto* incorporated in Israel as early as 1967, though Israel was willing to grant the world religions a special status and extensive rights to administer their holy places). It was generally assumed that the Golan Heights▷ should not be returned, and most people held this opinion on the Gaza Strip▷. All sought to maintain an Israeli presence at Sharm al-Sheikh▷, to guard the Straits of Tiran, and in a strip connecting it to Israeli territory (though that need not be annexed territory under Israel sovereignty). Opinions varied on Judea and Samaria, the "West Bank"▷. Even assuming that they would be demilitarized, with the immediate threat of armour and artillery removed from the vicinity of Israel's centres of population, many thought that it would be necessary for Israel to hold security outposts (with opinions divided on their siting and nature). In any case, the government, and the bulk of the public opinion would be prepared to, or even interested in, returning large parts of the occupied territories (some, even all of them) in exchange for real peace and security. No one, apart from isolated individuals on the fringes of public opinion, has even considered any withdrawal outside the framework of a peace settlement.

There is, therefore, still a large gap between the parties. Attempts to bridge it by the UN Special Representative, Dr. Gunnar Jarring▷, have so far failed. The Four Big Powers have also failed in their efforts to find a formula acceptable to them all. *Prima facie*, there is no great distance between their basic positions: they all speak of "peace" and of "Israeli withdrawal from occupied territories", with the USSR demanding, like the Arabs, total withdrawal, while the USA leaves room for adjustments of the pre-1967 lines. However, views differ on the nature of peace, the character of its security provisions and the image of future relations between Israel and the Arab states. Various plans and formulas, such as that of the US Secretary of State, (the Rogers Plan▷), were considered acceptable by some of the parties and powers, but agreement was only partial and superficial, and the differences soon reappeared. No "plan" acceptable to both the parties has yet been devised. Partial agreements—such as an agreement for the reopening of the Suez Canal and a partial Israeli withdrawal from the Canal and Sinai—have also been suggested (on their merits and/or as stepping stones towards broader agreements); none of them has so far come to fruition.

Meanwhile, guerilla operations of the *feda'iyin*, has continued; but acts of sabotage in Israel and the occupied areas have been surprisingly few and unsuccessful: Israel has succeeded in preventing sabotage on a larger scale, and the Arab residents of the occupied areas have not cooperated with the *feda'iyin*. Most guerilla operations were shellings from across the border, some acts of terrorism, and aircraft hijackings outside of the region. This guerilla war was a nuisance to Israel and gave much publicity to political propaganda abroad for the Palestinian-Arab cause, but it had no military value and no chance of defeating Israel (the more so as the *feda'iyin* were, since 1969–70, deeply involved in a war against the army and government of Jordan). Politically, all the *feda'iyin* groups were extremist—some more so, some less so (see Palestine-Arab guerilla organization▷)—and they totally rejected the idea of peace with Israel (even if she withdrew from all the occupied territories), the Security Council Resolution, the cease-fire and the Jarring mission. They also totally rejected the idea of the establishment of a Palestinian political entity in a partitioned Palestine, *i.e.* outside the borders of Israel—whether on the West Bank, to be separated from Jordan, or in Jordan, to become a Palestinian state. Their only aim was a Palestinian state in the whole of formerly Mandatory Palestine, *i.e.* including the territory of Israel, after her destruction. The *feda'iyin* groups succeeded in spreading in the outside world the slogan of a secular democratic state in the whole of Palestine, where Jews and Arabs would live as equal citizens. This slogan has no value as a realistic plan to solve the conflict, as no one in Israel could possibly take it seriously: no one could entrust the survival of the Jews of Israel to the generosity and peacefulness of the *feda'iyin*, and the Palestinian Arabs in general, engaged in a violent struggle with the country's Jews for more than two generations. Furthermore, the "new" *feda'iyin* slogan—which, in fact, is identical with the main line of Arab argument before 1948—ignores the existence of the Jewish people as a nation, over and above its members' physical survival, and Israel's right to independence and freedom. Instead of an attempt to throw the two peoples again together in one state, Israel prefers their peaceful co-existence in two neighbouring, separate independent states. The *feda'iyin* and other representatives of the Palestinian-Arabs have yet to agree to such co-existence.

The Arab-Israel conflict has not abated, nor have the beginnings of a solution been found, in the decades that have passed since 1948. On the contrary, it has grown worse. Israel still considers the only solution to be co-existence between the many Arab states (among which the Palestinian

Arabs will find their place) and the State of Israel. The Arab states do not believe in co-existing with the State of Israel as it is. Some of them, including the Palestinian *feda'iyin*, openly seek to destroy the State of Israel, though they no longer talk of annihilating its population. Others present demands which, if Israel were to accede to them, would change her character beyond recognition or would gradually lead to its destruction. All Arab bodies evade a binding definition of their recognition of Israel's existence. All the Arab states suspect Israel of having expansionist ambitions, while Israel declares it has none. Israel suspects the Arabs of aspirations to destroy her and is concerned for her security (seeing even territorial and border problems primarily in the light of security). In their internal anti-Israel indoctrination, Arab leaders diffused also anti-Semitic material of the worst kind (e.g. The Protocols of the Elders of Zion⊳, *Mein Kampf* and other Nazi hate-literature, "*Der Stürmer*"-type caricatures). This may be a propaganda ploy; it may be that the hatred of Israel has become so deep and total that hatred of the Jews—officially denied—has become an integral part of it. At all events poisonous anti-Israel indoctrination in the Arab countries is all-pervasive; it has penetrated the whole educational system, even school textbooks and first-grade primers. This indoctrination may even harm hopes for the future. For when the acute political conflict is some day solved, as it must be by a settlement based on some kind of compromise and concessions by both sides, peaceful coexistence will have to be established: the two hostile sister nations will have to live together.   (Y. S.)

ARAB-ISRAEL WAR OF 1948. The Resolution on the Partition of Palestine was adopted by the UN General Assembly on 29 Nov. 1947. It provided for the establishment of independent Jewish and Arab states and an international enclave comprising Jerusalem and its vicinity; all three were to constitute one economic unit. Although far from satisfying Zionist demands, the Resolution was welcomed by the Jews. It was rejected by the Arab Higher Committee and by the governments of the Arab states, who threatened to use violence to prevent its implementation.

PHASE I: 29 NOV. 1947 TO 31 MARCH 1948. Arab violence erupted the day after the adoption of the Resolution. A Jewish bus was fired upon near Lod (Lydda) airport, a general strike called by the Arab Higher Committee led to the burning and looting of the Jewish Commercial Centre near Jaffa Gate in Jerusalem. There were still about 100,000 British troops in the country, far superior to the fighting forces of either side. But, because of their opposition to partition, their general ME policy

and their forthcoming evacuation, the British were unwilling to crush the riots at the outset. They only intervened sporadically, and primarily to safeguard the security of British forces and installations. These interventions were often directed against the Jews. During this period the main Arab military activity consisted of sniping and throwing bombs at Jewish traffic along major routes, all of which passed through Arab villages and towns, and at isolated Jewish quarters in mixed towns and outlying settlements.

At first, the *Hagana*⊳, the underground military arm of the Jews, concentrated on defensive measures, limiting retaliation strictly to those directly guilty of assaults. The dissident *Irgun*, however, retaliated indiscriminately, e.g. by planting a bomb in a market place. (Later, in April, the *Irgun* attacked the Arab village of Deir Yassin near Jerusalem, killing about 250 villagers, including women and children. The attack—the only one of its kind by Jewish forces— was strongly denounced by the *Hagana* and the Jewish leadership, but, inflated by propaganda, created panic among the Arab population.) Between December 1947 and January 1948, the Arabs, with the help of volunteers from neighbouring Arab countries, made several attempts to capture outlying Jewish settlements (Kfar 'Etzion, Tirat Tzevi, Kfar Szold) but were repulsed by their Jewish defenders. Terrorist-type attacks, sometimes assisted by British deserters, were more successful, especially in Jerusalem. They included the dynamiting of the Jewish Agency building, the editorial offices of "The Palestine Post", and a number of houses on central Ben Yehuda Street.

In January 1948, an Arab volunteer force under Fawzi al-Qawuqji⊳ entered Palestine and took control of the Arab areas in the north; other volunteers, mainly from among the "Muslim Brotherhood"⊳ in Egypt, entered the Hebron-Bethlehem area in south. Qawuqji's force—the "Army of Deliverance"—was *c.* 2,000 strong in January and reached an estimated strength of 5–8,000 by April. It sent officers and small detachments to towns, such as Haifa and Jaffa, liable to Jewish conquest, and attacked Jewish settlements in the north (Tirat Tzevi, Mishmar Ha'emek, Ramat Yohanan); but it achieved no major success in these operations. It also attacked Jewish traffic along major routes, effectively isolating Jewish Jerusalem from the coastal plain, outlying settlements (including the 'Etzion bloc) from Jerusalem, the Negev from Tel Aviv, and Western Galilee from Haifa. These attacks almost achieved political success—late in March 1948 the USA proposed that Palestine become a UN Trusteeship rather than be partitioned into independent Jewish and Arab states, as had been decided.

Food convoy reaches besieged Jerusalem, 1948

PHASE II: 1 APRIL TO 14 MAY 1948. For political and military reasons the Jewish High Command decided to seize the initiative in order to gain effective control of the territories allotted to the Jewish State and to establish secure communications with Jewish settlements outside it. "Operation *Nahshon*" resulted in the reopening of the road to besieged Jewish Jerusalem, although only briefly. The *Hagana* captured the whole of Tiberias, where Jews had been besieged in the Old City (18 April); Haifa (22 April); the area connecting Tel Aviv with outlying quarters, and the Qatamon and Sheikh Jarrah Quarters in Jerusalem (this last had to be re-evacuated following a British ultimatum); Western Galilee; and all of Safad (there, too, the Jewish Quarter had been besieged). British intervention prevented a Jewish take-over of Jaffa (the town later surrendered, in May). Some Arab attacks, such as the one against a convoy to the University Hospital on Mount Scopus, caused heavy loss of life, but did not achieve any strategic advantage. Qawuqji's "Army of Deliverance" was virtually beaten during this phase. The creation of a continuous strip of territory under effective Jewish control caused the President of the USA to withdraw the Trusteeship plan, and made possible the proclamation of the State of Israel on 14 May 1948.

PHASE III: 15 MAY TO 10 JUNE 1948. On 15 May Tel Aviv was attacked by Egyptian planes. This signalled the beginning of the invasion by the regular armies of the Arab states. The Arab states had originally decided to aid the Palestinian Arabs with volunteers, money, arms and logistic support, and to draw up their regular armies on the borders—but not to use them for a full invasion. This decision had been reversed in the first half of May—against military advice. The decision to invade Palestine—in essence an Egyptian one—was reportedly imposed by King Farouq▷ on an unwilling government and army. Undoubtedly Egypt also wished to foil King 'Abdullah's▷ reported plans to annex Palestine (or, in rumoured agreement with the Jews, only her Arab part). The invading armies' original plan, never properly co-ordinated, envisaged the Egyptian forces moving north towards Tel Aviv, the Syrian, Lebanese and Iraqi forces converging on Haifa, and Transjordan's Arab Legion occupying the West Bank and Jerusalem.

The entry into battle of five regular armies against the war-weary *Hagana*, which as yet possessed no artillery, air force or armour, created a critical situation. The Egyptian Army moved along the coastal road, attacking nearby Jewish settlements, ultimately bypassing some (Nirim, Kfar Darom), and capturing others (Yad Mordekhai, Nitzanim). It was halted only 35 kilometres from Tel Aviv, by a hastily mobilized blocking force, assisted by the first fighter planes which had arrived the same day from Czechoslovakia.

The Arab Legion captured the 'Etzion bloc, Beit Ha'arava, and the Potash Works near the northern end of the Dead Sea; two other settlements north of Jerusalem were evacuated; and the Legion entered Jerusalem, where after bitter fighting it captured the isolated Jewish Quarter in the Old City, but failed, despite repeated attempts, to penetrate into the Jewish new city. *Hagana* was unable to dislodge the Legion from Latrun▷, which commanded the road to besieged Jerusalem. But an alternative route—the "Burma Road"—was built through which the city was saved from starvation or surrender for lack of arms and ammunition.

The Syrian Army occupied Massada and Sha'ar Hagolan, south of the Lake of Galilee, but was halted at the gates of Deganya, with home-made Molotov cocktails and sightless artillery pieces which had just arrived from France. Subsequently the Syrians turned north and established a bridgehead west of the Jordan at Mishmar Hayarden. The Lebanese Army captured Malkiya, but thereafter took little part in offensive operations.

By early June the Arab offensive had lost its momentum, and the confidently announced hopes

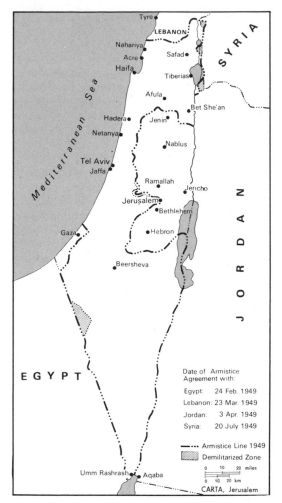

Map of Armistice Lines, 1949

in reducing the Syrian bridgehead near Mishmar Hayarden.

On the central front, "Operation *Dani*" brought about the capture of Ramla and Lod (including the vital airport) from the Arab Legion; the operation's second phase was designed to capture Latrun and Ramallah and to secure a wide corridor to Jerusalem, but there was no time to achieve this. In Jerusalem, an attempt to capture the Old City failed, and in spite of bitter fighting in various sectors the lines remained substantially unchanged.

In the south, the Egyptians again succeeded in closing the main road to the Negev and heavy fighting raged around *Kibbutz* Negba. An alternative route was used at night for Israeli north-south communications, while the intersecting east-west road to the Hebron mountains was used by Egyptian troops during the day. The initiative had passed to Israel, and it was probably as a result of an Arab request that the British representative on the Security Council proposed a truce of unlimited duration. This came into effect after 10 days' fighting, on 18 July.

PHASE V: 19 JULY TO 5 JANUARY 1949. The truce was uneasy. Efforts by Count Bernadotte▷, the UN mediator, to achieve a political solution were unsuccessful. Meanwhile, the nascent State of Israel was maintaining an army of over 100,000, close to one-sixth of her entire population. Clearly this situation could not continue indefinitely.

Following Egyptian attempts to isolate the Negev, aggravated by Bernadotte's plan to exclude the Negev from the Jewish State, Israel on 15 Oct. in a swift operation ("Yo'av"), succeeded in opening the road to the south, after bloody hand-to-hand fighting, capturing Beer Sheva on 21 Oct. The Egyptian forces in the Hebron mountains and on the southern outskirts of Jerusalem were now isolated from their bases. Simultaneously, "Operation *El Hahar*" (To the Mountain) succeeded in widening southward the precarious, narrow corridor to Jerusalem.

Meanwhile Arab irregulars, who had never accepted the truce, continued to harass Jewish settlements and forces in the north. Israel's counter-attack, "Operation *Hiram*" (29–31 Oct.), resulted in the capture of Upper Galilee in a pincer movement from Safad in the east and the coast in the west; some Lebanese territory adjacent to Upper Galilee was also occupied. "Operation *Horev*" (in Winter) was designed to expel the remaining Egyptian forces from Palestine. Israeli forces advanced southwards through the desert to the border village of 'Auja and into Sinai, capturing Abu 'Ageila and reaching the sea south of the Gaza Strip. Combined US-British pressure compelled Israel to withdraw from the Sinai Peninsu-

of a swift victory, backed by much expert world opinion, had evaporated. Jewish forces, though, had suffered heavily. Thus it was with relief that both sides accepted the Security Council resolution calling for a truce of 28 days, which came into effect on 10 June 1948.

PHASE IV: 10 JUNE TO 18 JULY 1948. When fighting resumed on 8 July, the situation had changed. Some heavy equipment, purchased before the proclamation of the State but imported only subsequently because of the British blockade, was incorporated into Israel's Defence Forces, which had been formed out of the *Hagana*. Larger formations had been created enabling several brigades to be used for one mission. Israel now took the initiative in the north; Operation *Dekel*" (Palm) resulted in the capture of Lower Galilee, including Nazareth, but "Operation *Brosh*" (Cypress) was only partially successful la, but her forces regrouped for attack east of the Gaza border. Now that Egyptian forces in the Gaza Strip were in danger of isolation, and the roads into Egypt were undefended, Egypt agreed, on 5 Jan. 1949, to negotiate an Armistice Agreement—called for by the Security Council on 16 Nov. A truce was reimposed on 7 Jan. (An Egyptian brigade remained besieged and cut off in a small pocket around Faluja; one of its staff officers was a young major named Gamal 'Abd-ul-Nasser▷.)

The War of 1948—Israel's War of Independence—caused very heavy Israeli casualties; over 6,000 dead, almost 1% of her population, including over 4,000 soldiers. Arab casualties were estimated at c. 2,000 dead for the invading regular armies, and an unknown number of Palestinian irregulars; but no reliable figures are available.

ARMISTICE. Negotiations with Egypt began on 13 Jan. 1949 in Rhodes, under the chairmanship of Dr. Ralph Bunche▷, the acting UN mediator. After six weeks of negotiations, and several crises over the evacuation of the besieged Egyptian brigade in Faluja, a "General Armistice Agreement" was signed on 24 Feb. 1949. Its preamble stated that negotiations had been undertaken in response to the Security Council's call and "in order to facilitate the transition . . . to permanent peace". This is followed by a non-aggression clause which forbids "resort to military force"; "no aggressive action shall be undertaken, planned or threatened against the people or armed forces of the other side"; "the right of each party to security and freedom from fear of attack shall be fully respected." The Agreement emphasizes that it does not prejudice the rights, claims and positions of either party in the ultimate settlement of the Palestine question; "the provisions of this Agreement are dictated exclusively by military considerations and are valid only for the period of the Armistice". Similarly, "the Armistice Demarcation Line is not to be construed . . . as a political or territorial boundary, and is delineated without prejudice to rights, claims". Warlike or hostile acts by irregular forces and their advance beyond the Armistice lines are prohibited; civilians are also barred from crossing the lines. The Israel-Egypt line was identical with the southern international boundary of Palestine, apart from the Gaza Strip, which was included in the territory under Egyptian control. The village of El-'Auja and its vicinity were demilitarized. A Mixed Armistice Commission was set up—to ensure the proper execution of the Agreement, and to deal with complaints presented by either side—under the chairmanship of an officer appointed by the UN, and with its seat in 'Auja.

The Armistice Agreement with Egypt served as a

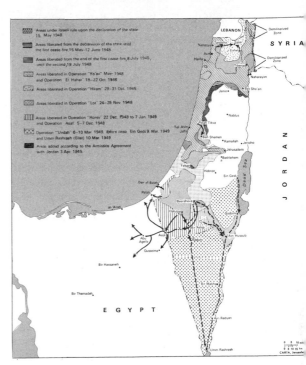

Map of the Arab-Israel War of 1948

model for similar agreements with Israel's other three neighbours. The agreement with Lebanon was signed on 23 March 1949 at the border point of Rosh Haniqra (Ras al-Naqura) and that with Transjordan on 3 April in Rhodes. The negotiations with Transjordan were complicated by the claims of both sides, concerning communications with and water supply to Jerusalem, the Hebrew University enclave on Mt. Scopus▷, the division of the southern Negev, the reactivation of railway lines, etc. Some of these issues were resolved in secret direct contacts with King 'Abdullah▷, which took place simultaneously with the "official" negotiations held in Rhodes; others, enumerated in Article VIII and agreed in principle, were to be arranged by a special committee. These included free access to the holy places of Old Jerusalem and to the Jewish cultural and humanitarian institutions on Mount Scopus (which were to resume normal functioning) as well as "free movement of traffic on vital roads". This clause was never implemented and the free access, free traffic and normal functioning envisaged were not established until 1967. Iraq, whose forces had participated in the War, had authorized the government of Jordan to negotiate "for the Iraqi forces" (which would be withdrawn) and the Armistice covered them.

The most complicated negotiations were those with Syria, whose forces were the only ones to hold, at the end of the War, territory allotted to the Jewish State under the UN Partition Resolution. The deadlock was resolved by a complicated and deliberately vague formula establishing demilitarized zones in these areas, which were to be evacuated by Syrian forces. Israel regarded these Demilitarized Zones as part of her sovereign territory, with limitations only on military forces and installations, as specified, while Syria considered them as areas in which Syria had special rights and which did not fully and finally belong to Israel; there were frequent clashes and a state of almost permanent crisis. The Armistice with Syria—with demarcation lines identical with the borders between Syria and Mandatory Palestine, except for the Demilitarized Zones—was finally signed on 20 July 1949.

The Armistice Agreement with Egypt was the first to break down owing to constant attacks against Israel by irregular forces with the active encouragement of the Egyptian authorities. Israel considered these attacks a complete invalidation of the Agreement and declared it null and void in 1956. The Agreements with Syria and Jordan, although more often broken than kept, remained officially in force until rendered ineffective by the Six Day War. However, since the 1950s Israel had stopped attending the Israel-Syrian Mixed Armistice Commission, as Syria insisted on discussing the Demilitarized Zones which were, Israel held, within the competence of the Commission's UN-appointed Chairman but not of the Commission itself and in which Syria had no standing. The Agreement with Lebanon, though more scrupulously observed, was also, in Israel's view, terminated in June 1967, when Lebanon declared war on Israel.   (N.L.-Y.S.)

*ARAB LEAGUE. The "League of Arab States" was established, in Mar. 1945, by the seven Arab states then independent or on the threshold of independence: Egypt, Iraq, Sa'udi Arabia, Yemen, Trans-jordan (later "Jordan"), Syria and Lebanon. The following states joined subsequently: Libya (1953), Sudan (1956), Tunisia and Morocco (1958), Kuwait (1961), Algeria (1962), South Yemen (1968). All 14 independent Arab states now belong to the L., and the principalities of the Persian Gulf are expected to join shortly. The Arabs of Palestine were represented (by a notable appointed by an all-Arab committee) at the conference which founded the L., and enjoy an ill-defined observer status, while at the same time constituting a kind of ward of the L. and the chief object of its activities.

While the AL is theoretically inspired by age-old visions of Arab Unity (see Pan-Arabism▷; Arab Federation▷), it is not a federal body and has no

power over its member states. During talks preparatory to its foundation (1942–4, partly initiated by the British) some Arab states—particularly Egypt, Sa'udi Arabia, Syria and Lebanon—who believed the only feasible association was that of sovereign states, rejected all federal or unionist schemes. The Charter of the L. states that member states are to be bound only by those resolutions of the L. Council for which they themselves had voted, *i.e.* that Council decisions would not be binding. Before agreeing to the L., Lebanon requested, and obtained, a solemn and specific recognition of her absolute independence and territorial integrity (as opposed to unspoken plans—by Syria—to annex her); this recognition formed an annex to the Protocol of Alexandria which prepared the L. Charter. Another special annex to the Protocol pledged L. support for the Arabs of Palestine in their struggle for independence.

The L.'s headquarters are in Cairo, and Egyptian influence on all L. activities has always been decisive. The Secretary-General has invariably been Egyptian: 'Abd-ul-Rahman 'Azzam▷ 1945–52, 'Abd-ul-Khaleq Hassouna▷ since 1952. Deputy secretaries-general and staff are recruited from all member states. The budget is raised according to a scale of fixed contributions by the member states; this scale is adjusted from time to time.

The AL had drafted and initiated many schemes for all-Arab co-operation, co-ordination or unification in the economic, cultural, technical and military fields. While a certain limited degree of co-ordination has been achieved, hardly any of the ambitious schemes for unification or joint ventures have materialized. A "Collective Security Pact", signed in 1950, was intended mainly to give more power to L. decisions, but it did not change the situation; a "Common Market" has been joined by only five of the member states and has anyway not progressed beyond a modest measure of trade co-operation. Joint shipping lines, tanker fleets, airlines, and a development fund have scarcely progressed beyond the blueprint stage.

The L.'s main functions have always been to present a common political front towards the outside world and to conduct information and propaganda work. It maintains propaganda offices in several world capitals. Its propaganda centred mainly on those problems and areas where Arab demands had not been fully satisfied—Syria and Lebanon in the 1940s; Morocco, Tunisia and Algeria in the 1950s; Aden, the Persian Gulf in the 1960s, and the Palestine problem and the Arab-Israel conflict, since its inception. The L. directs and supervises the economic boycott on those trading with Israel, and finances Palestinian-Arab organizations. The L. also decided upon and brought about the establishment of a Joint Military Command of the forces pitted against Israel (from 1964); but the Command did not in fact direct joint operations.

The L., while serving as a clearing-house and meeting ground for inter-Arab discussion, has not been able to prevent, arbitrate, or even significantly mitigate, the numerous inter-Arab conflicts; its own sessions have, in the course of these conflicts, been boycotted several times (by Tunisia 1958–61; by Iraq 1961–3; by Egypt 1962–3). It was always beset by internal conflicts—in the 1940s and 1950s an Egyptian-Syrian-Sa'udi bloc, guarding the inter-Arab *status quo*, against a Hashemite▷ Iraq-Jordan bloc with federalist-revisionist plans; in the 1960s a "progressive" socialist bloc (Egypt, Syria, Iraq, Algeria, South Yemen) against a "reactionary" or conservative group (Sa'udi Arabia, Jordan, Morocco). In the 1950s and again in 1966–7, a network of inter-Arab defence treaties, with Egypt at their centre, played an important role; none of them was concluded through the AL or within its framework.

During the 1960s the L., in the course of these antagonisms, lost most of its effectiveness, and inter-Arab politics, including efforts at co-ordination and co-operation, were conducted outside its framework. The L. had no say in the Yemen War (1962–7), which involved, apart from an internal-Yemini "civil war" with an Egyptian expeditionary force in the leading role, serious Egyptian bombardments of Sa'udi Arabia; nor did it mediate when Algerian and Moroccan troops fought each other (1963); the Pan-Arab attempts at settling the clashes between Palestinian-Arab guerillas and Jordan and Lebanon (1968–70) were not the result of AL efforts. In fact, the only inter-Arab clash in which the AL was directly involved in mediating and/or assisting the wronged side was the defence of Kuwait against Iraqi threats (1961). Complaints by Arab states against Egyptian subversive or aggressive activities (Sudan 1958; Tunisia 1958 onwards; Lebanon 1958; Jordan 1958 onwards; Iraq 1959; Syria 1962; Sa'udia, Morocco 1963) were useless. Major problems are discussed not by the L. Council but by special "summit" meetings of heads of states and governments, not convened through L. channels. Yet the L.'s existence has been maintained, and even its detractors do not seriously propose its abolition, because of its value as a common political front, a quasi-regional organization recognized as such, and an instrument of propaganda.
(Y.S.)

ARAB LEGION (*al-Jaish al-'Arabi*). Military formation established in Transjordan in 1920–1 by British administrators and officers; later became the army of the Kingdom of Jordan▷. (Y.S.)

*ARAB NATIONAL MOVEMENT, NATIONALISM. The term nationalism, in Arabic *Qawmiyya*, refers to the entire Arab nation as opposed to *Wataniyya*, patriotism connected with a specific Arab country. The geographic boundaries of AN are "from the (Persian) Gulf to the (Atlantic) Ocean" and embrace the Arabian peninsula, the Fertile Crescent, the Nile Valley and North Africa. It includes all of Palestine, the Turkish district of Alexandretta▷ (Hatay) (and some add the Adana and Mersin regions) and Khuzistan in Iran. Maps distributed by the Arab League often include Mauritania, Somalia, Chad, Niger, and Mali as well.

Who is an Arab? Most Arabs accept the definition that it is anyone of Arab origin or who is considered by other Arabs and by himself to be an Arab; some would add that he must be Arabic-speaking and follow an Arab way of life (see Arabs▷).

The emergence of AN was influenced by the penetration of Western civilization into the area and inspired by 19th century European liberation and romantic nationalism. It grew in opposition to the oppressive Ottoman regime and in reaction to Turkish nationalism, in Egypt against the British, in the *Maghreb* against the French. It is rooted in a cultural and literary renaissance in the Levant in the second half of the 19th century; among its leaders were two Christian Lebanese authors: Butros Bustani and Nazif Yaziji. It was influenced later by the modernist Islamic revival (Jamal-ul-Din al-Afghani, Muhammad 'Abdu▷, Rashid Rida)—without fully realizing that, although some areas do run parallel or overlap, there is an inherent conflict between supranational Pan-Islamism▷ and supra-religious Arab nationalism. Political conclusions were drawn by the ANM at the start of the 20th century (influenced in particular by the revolt of the Young Turks▷, in 1908) and the idea spread that the national (Arab) entity, rather than allegiance to the ruling dynasty or to Islam, ought to be the foundation of the state. As against the growing centralism of the new Turkish regime, the ANM pressed for decentralization. It made no clear statement as to whether it would be satisfied with such a decentralization within the Ottoman Empire or demand complete independence.

At the time the movement formed organizations such as the "Decentralization Party" (*Hizb al-La-Markaziyya*), the "Literary Club" (*Al Muntada Al-Adabi*), the "Pact Society" (*Al-'Ahd*), *Al-Qahtaniyya*, and the "Young Arab Society" (*al-Fatat*); the last three were clandestine. Members of these organizations later became the leaders of the Arab states. One of the leaders was 'Aziz 'Ali al-Masri▷; the thinkers included 'Abd-ul-Rahman al-Kawakibi and Najib 'Azuri. The total membership of all these organizations was about 100. They had little public or political influence, and no well-defined doctrine, only general ideas and emotions.

During World War I, Sharif Hussein▷ of Mecca, who with British aid had revolted against the Ottomans (1916), established contacts with the Arab nationalists of Syria and Iraq. After the war they became ministers and advisors to Hussein's sons, particularly Feisal▷, who attempted to establish an Arab state or a federation of Arab states. In 1919, these nationalists created the "Arab Independence Party" ("Al-Istiqlal▷ al-'Arabi"). Upon the creation, in the Fertile Crescent, of separate states under Western tutelage in place of one fully independent federated state, nationalist movements arose in each one of the Arab countries. They fought for independence from Britain and France, and in Palestine against Zionism also. These separate movements were linked by mutual sympathy. They supported one another, and they maintained a contact which was strengthened from 1936 onwards, particularly in the form of inter-Arab conferences on Palestine. However, with the exception of the Hashemite plan for a Fertile Crescent▷ or "Greater Syria"▷ Federation, whose implications were never thoroughly developed and the "Syria-Palestine" Representation in Europe which spoke in the 1920s for Pan-Arab nationalism, there were no all-Arab entities or organizations representing all-Arab nationalism. There were occasional nationalist demonstrations in the form of mass meetings, strikes and even insurrections. Efforts were made to elaborate a nationalist doctrine, but the ideology was largely emotional and ill-defined. It was purely political, and did not have a firm social foundation.

During World War II, the Axis Powers competed with Britain and her Western allies for the support of the Arab nationalists, who inclined generally towards Nazi and Fascist ideologies. The Arab League▷ (founded in 1945) was an alliance of independent states, not a movement towards all-Arab nationalism. Nevertheless, it provided a meeting-place and encouragement for all-Arab nationalists. After the war, the scope of AN widened: Egypt participated more actively in all-Arab affairs and even nationalists of the Maghreb▷ came into increasing contact with Eastern Arab Nationalists.

In the 1940s and '50s AN primarily appears in its pre-Socialist version. Among its principal thinkers were 'Abd-ul-Rahman 'Azzam▷, Sati' al-Husri and Constantine Zureiq.

The establishment of Israel and the Arab defeat in Palestine shocked Arab nationalists. New and radical forces emerged, which no longer restricted themselves to combating foreign rule and influence. They added a social dimension to AN. They aimed

at a nationalist-socialist revolution. The first of these forces was the Ba'th▷ party. Politically Nasserism▷ was even stronger. These two forces became the chief contenders for primacy in AN. Nasserism adapted the principal slogans of the Ba'th: Arab unity, freedom, socialism and revolution. The two doctrines shared other features: subversion of rival Arab regimes, whether feudal or revolutionary; and a totalitarian approach based on a one-party system and the imposition of their teachings and regime on the Arab world. The Ba'th and Nasserism clashed mainly over primacy in the Arab world. The Ba'th stressed collective leadership, Nasserism the charismatic leader. The Ba'th was doctrinaire, Nasser pragmatic. In contrast to the Ba'th, Nasser was often willing to co-operate with conservative Arab elements. The Nasserist ideology developed in the course of time from a few fundamental principles and endorsed post facto▷ moves already made by the Egyptian regime. The Ba'th advocated secularism, Nasserism paid lip service to Islam, and made use of it. The Ba'th works as a party and through cadres, Nasserism through the state bureaucracy, as it failed to establish any viable party apparatus. Nasserism's forte is the creation of slogans rather than an ideology; it has the better propaganda organization. Nasserism failed to establish an organized all-Arab movement outside of Egypt; pro-Nasser groups in Iraq and Syria clashed. The Ba'th on the other hand—with its two rival wings—is an all-Arab party. Pan-Arab unity is the first and sacred principle of the Ba'th yet the group did not succeed even in uniting its own two wings, which rule Iraq and Syria respectively. As both Nasser and the Ba'th regimes became increasingly dependent on the Soviet Union, their parties' ties with the Soviet Communist Party grew more intimate and the ideological influence of Soviet communism on Nasserism and the Ba'th increased.

A third Pan-Arab nationalist organization—the Arab Nationalist Movement (ANM) (Harakat al-Qawmiyin al-'Arab") emerged at the end of the 1940s under the leadership of George Habash▷. It originated at the American University in Beirut. At first it was mainly Pan-Arab nationalist, but in recent years it has moved very far to the left, and has established connections with China. It aims at the destruction of Israel; the disruption of the Arab regimes, particularly the conservative ones and, among those, principally Jordan and Lebanon; and the creation of revolutionary Arab unity. It inclines toward totalitarian notions and advocates terrorism. It is organized as an underground of fanatics, recruited primarily among educated young people and professionals, mainly in the countries of the Fertile Crescent and the Persian Gulf. The ruling party in South Yemen (NLF▷)

is linked with the ANM. From its inception, the ANM was interested in the Palestine questions; it is a sister organization of the "Popular Front for the Liberation of Palestine▷" (PFLP). The group owes no allegiance to any Arab regime. For years it received aid from Nasser, but recently it has been supported by the Iraqi Ba'th regime, despite the ANM-Ba'th rivalry. The group has split several times over the last year; Dr. Habash's faction remains the most important.

The aims of AN have changed with the passage of time. At first its aims were cultural revival, equal rights, decentralization and autonomy within the Ottoman Empire. Later they became independence, Arab unity, creation of a new Arab image, Arabization of all spheres of life, establishing Arab political, economic and military might, achieving a respected position in the world. Once independence had been achieved, the new emphasis was on nonalignment with the great powers, socio-economic change and the making of a modern nation.

The declared enemies and scapegoats of AN have been foreign rule and influence, imperialism and colonialism (the Western powers and in particular, of late, the USA), Zionism, feudalism, reaction, regionalism and particularism, "Shu'ubiyya" ▷ (non-Arab nationalism in Arab countries), opportunism, foreign agents and mercenaries. They are defined as the root of all evil in the Arab world. Salvation will ensue upon realization of AN's aims. These slogans mask the clashing interests of governments and pressure groups (the Hashemites, Nasser, for instance).

The religious factor has caused much trouble. In the Fertile Crescent, AN was created in opposition to the Muslim Ottoman Empire: in Egypt and the Maghreb it offset foreign, Christian rule. Some nationalists, in particular the Christians, hoped for a nationalism which would bridge religious differences and replaced religion as the touchstone of ME identity. They envisaged a secular nationalism. Some Christians continue playing important roles in AN (Aflaq▷, Habash). However, Islam and the Arab-Islamic past were keystones and sources of inspiration in nationalist thought. AN and Muslim solidarity and unity for many were identical. The Muslim masses were not capable of distinguishing between Islam and nationalism, and their nationalist awakening was essentially Islamic. However, as Arab Socialism grew stronger, the Muslim element in many educated nationalists weakened, and in many respects nationalism has replaced religion.

Social ferment and unrest among the masses has been one of the sources of AN. At first, the most active nationalists were well educated and from upper class families. They included officers and religious functionaries. The upper classes continued to occupy positions of leadership between the two World Wars, but educated, middle class people and professionals became increasingly prominent. AN is largely a movement of university and secondary school students. After the defeat by Israel (1948-9), army officers began to take over the nationalist leadership. Nationalism clashed with the traditional forms of social organization—the religious community, the clan, the tribe, minority groups—but under the cover of nationalism these groups often continued to function (e.g., Christian leaders; 'Alawites▷ in the Syrian Ba'th; the Druze Jumblat▷ in Lebanon).

AN's foundations are emotional and irrational. It inclines toward extremes and fanaticism; it instills proud dreams and is often the victim of its own overblown rhetoric. Yet it is frustrated by the gap between its aims and reality. AN dreams of power and demonstrations of strength. It is in fact rooted in weakness, in its sense of inferiority to the West, and jealousy of it. AN prefers dictatorship and totalitarianism to the rights and freedom of the individual. It contains an element of xenophobia and intolerance of minorities.

Despite common fundamental positions, AN has from the beginning developed in different and even conflicting directions. Separate nationalisms grew in Egypt, in the Ottoman Empire and in the Maghreb and these differences continued even when the separate streams seemed to merge into one movement. There is no universally accepted Arab nationalist doctrine. There are also different attitudes to methods of implementation. There is no general agreement on short-term aims. The principle of Arab unity and hatred for Israel provide the only base for agreement.

Despite this inherence, AN has been the decisive force in Arab public life and ideology since the end of World War II. It cannot bring about Arab unity but it is strong enough to prevent peace with Israel. AN has had its incissitudes. Yet there is no indication of the rise of non-nationalist, or anti-nationalist ideas among the Arabs, in spite of the increasing strength of the left.   (A.G.)

ARAB-PALESTINIAN SABOTAGE, TER-RORIST, GUERILLA ORGANIZATIONS, FEDA'IYUN, FEDA'IYIN—see Palestine-Arab Guerilla Organizations▷.

ARAB REVOLT or "The Revolt in the Desert". The name given to the uprising of Hussein ibn 'Ali▷, Sharif of Mecca, and his sons 'Ali▷, 'Abdullah▷ and Feisal▷, of the Hashemite▷ family, against the

Ottoman Empire during World War I (June 1916). The revolt was preceded by an exchange of letters between Hussein and Sir Henry McMahon, in which Britain promised support for Arab independence after the war (for details see McMahon-Hussein Correspondence▷). Britain financed the revolt with £200,000 per month, as well as supplying arms, provisions and direct artillery support. She also sent guerilla experts, among them the legendary (and controversial) T. E. Lawrence▷. Starting with an army of Hijazi Bedouin estimated at about 10,000, plus an additional 30–40,000 desert fighters semi-attached to it at times, the final strength of the army was an estimated 70,000 men. Several Arab (Syrian and Iraqi) officers of the Ottoman Army—both deserters and prisoners—also joined the revolt; but their number remained very small. The rebels conquered Mecca (with British artillery support) and 'Aqaba (with British naval support). Medina remained in Turkish hands, but was cut off and surrounded. The rebels' main operation was sabotaging the Hijaz Railway, the main Turkish supply route to Hijaz, 'Asir and Yemen. In 1917–8 the rebel army formed the right wing of Allenby's▷ armies advancing into Palestine, and Syria and was allowed to enter Damascus first and raise the Arab flag. The princes heading the revolt became the principal and recognized spokesmen for the Arab national cause at the peace conferences and in the settlement following the dismemberment of the Ottoman Empire. Though their connection to the Arab nationalists in the Fertile Crescent was at best only partial and remains altogether doubtful, the "Revolt in the Desert" is to this day seen as the "Golden Age of Arab Nationalism"▷. Several of its officers became spokesmen and leaders in the Arab states in the 1920s and '30s, and they continued to glorify the memory of the revolt (helped by the romantic and impressive writings of Lawrence).

(Y.S.)

*ARAB SOCIALISM—see Socialism▷.

*ARAB SOCIALIST UNION. Since 1962 the only legal political organization in Egypt, under the officers' regime set up following the 1952 coup d'état. It was preceded as the regime's single party by the "National Liberation Organization", 1953–8, and the "National Union", 1957–62. These previous efforts did not succeed in establishing a popular organization with real influence. The ASU, too, is part of the official establishment rather than an independent popular political organization. Its leadership is chosen by indirect vote, i.e. village and township committees send representatives to regional committees whose delegates form district committees

who in turn choose the national leadership. The latter—the top political leadership of Egypt—selects the candidates for election to the semi-parliamentary National Assembly of Egypt; it also proposes a candidate as President of the Republic. The Secretary-General of the organization was for a time 'Ali Sabri▷, but most of the time President Gamal 'Abd-ul-Nasser▷ himself was Secretary-General. From October 1970 to May 1971 'Abd-ul-Muhsin Abu-'l-Nur served as Secretary-General. In the crisis of May 1971 the ASU Executive Committee was the centre of opposition to President Sadat▷ and was purged. In July 1971 all ASU organs were reconstituted through new elections. (See, Egypt▷, Political History, Parties.)   (Y.S.)

*ARAB UNITY—see Pan-Arabism▷; Arab Federation▷.

ARABIA. The world's largest peninsula, 1.1m. sq. mi. with 13 million inhabitants (1967 estimate; no census has ever been taken, and there are conflicting estimates). Bounded by the Gulf of 'Aqaba (Eilat) and the Red Sea in the west, the Gulf of Aden and the Arabian Sea in the south, the Gulf of 'Oman and the Persian Gulf in the east. In the north, connected to Asia by the Syrian and Iraqi deserts. Mostly desert except for the south-west (Asir▷, Yemen▷) and the south-east (Dhofar▷, 'Oman▷) where there are summer rains. Seventy-five% of the peninsula is controlled by Sa'udi Arabia▷, but along the southern and eastern coasts other political entities are found: Yemen, South Yemen▷, Muscat-and-Oman▷, the Trucial Coast▷ sheikhdoms (principalities), Qatar▷ and Kuwait (map, see under Sa'udi Arabia).   (Y.K.)

ARABIC. The language of the Arabs▷. A Semitic tongue which originated in Arabia and spread through most of the ME and North Africa. There is a great difference between the written, literary language (in Arabic, Fusha—the pure, or Nahawi—the grammatical, tongue) and spoken A., divided into many dialects and differing from the written in grammar, composition and vocabulary. The dialects themselves are so different that Arabs from separate countries often cannot understand one another.

The written language, which retains the main qualities and structure of ancient A., is used in literature, newspapers, broadcasts, as well as in contacts between educated Arabs from different countries. But in everyday life, spoken A. in its local form is used. This dualism has caused much controversy among Arab nationalists. A minority favours abandoning the literary tongue and turning the various dialects into fully fledged, written languages. The majority claims that the *Fusha* is the only pure A. and cannot conceive the replacement of the language of the Koran and the classical literature with a jumble of inarticulate patois. Furthermore, if the dialects become written languages they will further divide the Arab nation, whereas classical A. by its very nature unites it. The advocates of *Fusha* have generally won out, but the debate continues as to the use of dialects in fiction, especially in plays and novels. Many plays are written in dialect, and novelists often put dialogues in dialect (in books otherwise written in classical A.).

Over the years, written A. has become a modern language with a large new vocabulary and constant changes in syntax and structure. It has been influenced by A. dialects and by various European languages (mainly English and French). The A. alphabet is still the ancient one, though a small minority has suggested latinizing it (as was done in Turkey). There are academies of A. in Cairo (the most prestigious), Damascus and Baghdad, but few changes proposed by the academies are accepted by the public.   (S.S.)

ARABISTAN ("Land of the Arabs"). Name used by some Arabs for the province of Khuzistan▷, in south-western Iran, to indicate that in their view the area is Arab and should be separated from Iran.
                                                          (B.G.)

ARABS OF PALESTINE—see Palestine Arabs▷.

✕**'ARAFAT, YASSER** (b. 1929). Palestinian-Arab guerilla leader and politician. Related to the al-Husseini▷ family, both on his father's and his mother's side (the Abu Sa'ud family). Educated in Egypt, A. graduated from Cairo University in 1956 as an engineer; he was chairman of the Palestine Students' Union in Gaza, 1951–7. 'A. served as a reserve officer in the Egyptian Army, 1957 and worked as an engineer in Kuwait, 1957–60. A leading figure in the *al-Fatah*▷ guerilla organization since 1958, he became its spokesman in Feburary 1968 and emerged as its chief leader. Since February 1969 he has been concurrently chairman of the Executive of the Palestine Liberation Organization▷ (PLO) and the main leader of its Central Committee, attempting to co-ordinate the activities of the various rival guerilla and sabotage groups. In September 1970, 'A. was appointed Commander-in-Chief of all Palestinian-Arab guerilla forces. In these capacities he has attended several all-Arab "summit" conferences, acting as chief spokesman for the Palestinian Arabs. While, as guerilla leader, he opposes any suggestion of a peaceful solution to the Arab-Israel conflict, he is considered to be under Egyptian influence and a "moderate", com-pared with the more extremist Habash▷ or Hawatmah and their "Popular Fronts"▷. Unlike his last-named rivals, who have leftist and Marxist leanings, he wishes to defer all discussion of internal ideological differences until such time as Israel is eliminated; this is considered a rightist position—and certainly 'A.'s background is both conservative and right-wing.   (E.Y.-Y.S.)

ARAS (Araxes). River flowing from south of Erzurum (Turkey) eastwards into the Caspian Sea and forming the natural boundary between Iran and the USSR. Length: 568 miles. Soviet-Iranian agreements of 1957 and 1963 provide for the joint development of the river for irrigation and power generation. Two dams, scheduled for completion in 1970, are still under construction: one in the USSR (Nakhjavan) and the other in Iran (Qaradiz); their water and power outputs are to be shared equally by the two countries.   (B.G.)

ARDAHAN. A small town and district centre in the province of Kars▷, in north-eastern Turkey, near the Soviet border. A. together with Kars had been ceded to Russia in 1878. It was recaptured by Turkey during World War I and formally returned to her in the Treaty of Brest Litovsk (1918). In 1945, the USSR re-claimed it (together with other demands) as the price for the renewal of the Soviet-Turkish Treaty of Friendship of 1925; this demand was rejected, and after Stalin's death, in 1953, the USSR renounced her claims.   (D.K.)

Yasser 'Arafat

'AREF, 'ABD-UL-RAHMAN (b. 1916). Iraqi officer and politician. President of Iraq, 1966–8. Brother of 'Abd-ul-Salam 'Aref▷. A member of the "Free Officers" group before the 1958 coup. He became involved in his brother's downfall in 1958–9. After the Feb. 1963 coup, his brother assumed the presidency, and 'A. received rapid promotion, serving 1963–6 as acting Chief of General Staff, although he had never passed through the Staff College. After 'Abd-ul-Salam's death in an air crash, in April 1966, the National Council of Revolutionary Command chose 'A. for the presidency as an inoffensive compromise candidate. During his service as President—and for some months in 1967 concurrently as Prime Minister—'A. tried to follow 'Abd-ul-Salam's line of independence with emphasis on nationalist pride and "prudent socialism" at home; but he lacked his brother's shrewdness and prestige and appeared to be a mediocre personality. On 17 July 1968, a coup headed by A. H. al-Bakr▷ and 'Abd-ul-Rahman al-Nayef ousted 'A. from office. He has since lived in exile.   (U.D.)

'AREF, 'ABD-UL-SALAM MUHAMMAD. (1920–66). Iraqi officer and politician. Son of a Sunni middle class family of Baghdad. Educated as a professional officer, 'A. served in the Arab-Israel War of 1948 with the Iraqi expeditionary force. About 1957, 'A. took the advice of 'Abd-ul-Karim Qassem▷, his friend and commanding officer, and joined the "Free Officers" Committee then conspiring to overthrow the monarchy. In the revolution of 14 July 1958, 'A. commanded the task force that took over Baghdad. Qassem appointed him Deputy Commander-in-Chief, Deputy Prime Minister and Minister of the Interior, but soon resented his advocacy of union with the UAR and his apparent eagerness to assume leadership of the revolution and state. In September 1958 'A. was dismissed from office; in November he was arrested and put on trial; and in February 1959 he was sentenced to death in Mahdawi's "People's Court" for attempting to assassinate Qassem. Qassem did not confirm the sentence, and in 1961 'A. was set free. He was one of the organizers of the 1963 coup that toppled Qassem and became President with nominal powers during the rule of the Ba'th▷ group. In November 1963, 'A. masterminded the bloodless overthrow of the Ba'th and henceforth he exercised real power. His policies were "nationalist", but not consistent. He maintained good relations with 'Abd-ul-Nasser▷. He signed an instrument of political union between Iraq and the UAR (May 1964), established an "Arab Socialist Union" modelled on Egypt's single-party system, July 1964, and decreed measures of far-reaching

'Abd-ul-Salam 'Aref

nationalization, July 1964. But the union did not materialize, as 'A. in effect insisted on Iraq's complete independence; the ASU did not come into being; and very few of the nationalization measures were put into practice. Though his closest colleagues and supporters were army officers, he appointed a trusted civilian, Dr. 'Abd-ul-Rahman al-Bazzaz▷, as Prime Minister in September 1965. 'A. did not succeed in solving the Kurdish problem, and despite several attempts at a settlement—including an agreement negotiated in June 1966 by Bazzaz, but not implemented—the war in the north dragged on, without the Iraqi forces gaining any advantage. An agreement with the Iraq Petroleum Co. signed in 1965 was not ratified because of leftist and nationalist pressure. 'A. was killed in an air crash on 13 Apr. 1966. Though no great statesman, he had developed a shrewd sense of political realities, and his prestige as a successful revolutionary had been considerable.   (U.D.)

ARLOSOROFF, Dr. CHAIM (1899–1933). Zionist Labour leader of the moderate Socialist *Hapo'el Hatza'ir* faction. Immigrated to Palestine in 1924 and was appointed head of the Jewish Agency's

Political Department in 1931. A. reached an agreement with the Amir 'Abdullah▷ and the Bedouin sheikhs about Jewish settlement in Transjordan, but met with determined opposition from the British authorities. In a confidential dispatch to Weizmann, A. expressed his doubts as to the possibility of ever attaining a Jewish majority in Palestine under the British Mandate. A. reached an agreement with the Nazi authorities of Germany enabling Jewish emigrants to transfer their capital to Palestine (*Haavarah*).

On 16 June 1933, A. was assassinated by unknown assailants. Two young Zionist-Revisionists▷ were charged with his murder; one was acquitted in the Lower Court, the other on appeal. The trial led to bitter dispute between the left and right wings of the Zionist movement. According to one theory A. was shot by Arab criminals.   (E.L.)

✳ARMED FORCES IN THE ME. The countries in the area may be divided into three categories: 1. those affiliated to Western alliances; 2. non-affiliated, but depending primarily on arms supplies from the West; 3. relying mainly on supplies from the Soviet Bloc. However, there are some countries receiving weapons from both sources (e.g. Iran) or still in the state of transition from reliance on one source to the other (e.g. Iraq, Libya, etc.). It is difficult to get accurate information, in particular about the third category. The figures given here are primarily based on data published in September 1970 by the Institute for Strategic Studies in London and reflect the situation as it existed in July 1970.

COUNTRIES AFFILIATED TO WESTERN ALLIANCES
a. The North Atlantic Treaty Organization (NATO): The only ME member of NATO is Turkey, which joined the Treaty in 1952. The Allied Forces Southern Europe (AF-SOUTH), with headquarters in Naples and commanded by an American admiral, are responsible for the defence of Italy, Greece and Turkey and for safeguarding communications in the Mediterranean and the Turkish territorial waters of the Black Sea. Turkey has assigned to it most of her armed forces (land, tactical air and certain naval forces). The United States Sixth Fleet is also earmarked for AFSOUTH, together with naval and maritime forces of Great Britain, Greece and Italy, and would become Strike Force South in the event of war. Maritime Air Force Mediterranean (MARAIRMED) was specially created to maintain aerial observation of the Soviet fleet in the Mediterranean and the Near East and is operating American, British and Italian patrol aircraft from bases in Greece, Turkey, Malta and Italy.

The total number of soldiers in the Turkish Armed Forces is 477,500, of which 390,000 serve in the army. In addition to 1 armoured division, equipped with American M-48 tanks, there are 4 armoured brigades with the same type of tanks and 1 armoured cavalry brigade. Out of 13 infantry divisions, 1 is mechanized. There are 3 additional mechanized infantry brigades and 2 parachute brigades. The Turkish Army is also equipped with American M-24 and M-41 light tanks, M-36 tank destroyers, M-8 armoured cars and armoured personnel carriers (APC) of the M-59 and M-113 types. The artillery has 105mm and 155mm self-propelled (SP) guns and 105mm, 155mm and 203mm. towed howitzers. There are also "Honest "Honest John" surface-to surface missiles. The anti--aircraft defence deploys 40mm, 75mm and 90mm anti-aircraft guns.

The total strength of the Turkish Navy is 37,000 seamen with 10 submarines, 10 destroyers and 46 smaller naval vessels and 25 (partly armed) support ships and auxiliaries. The United States has agreed to supply Turkey with at least 5 destroyers and 2 submarines in the near future.

The strength of the Turkish Air Force is 50,000 airmen with 310 combat aircraft, which include fighter bombers of the F-104G, F-5A and F-100C types, interceptor planes of the F-5A and F-86D/E/K types as well as all-weather interceptors (AWX) of the F-102A type. The reconnaissance squadrons are equipped with RF-84F and F-84Q aircraft. The transport squadrons include C-45, C-47, C-54 and C-130 aircraft. There are also 2 battalions (6 batteries) of Nike-Hercules surface-to-air missiles.

b. The Central Treaty Organization (CENTO): The members of this organization are Great Britain, Iran, Pakistan and Turkey (the last thus a member in both organizations, NATO and CENTO). The United States is associated with CENTO. The Treaty is designed to provide mutual cooperation for security and defence, but does not have an international command structure, nor forces allocated to it.

The total number of soldiers in the Iranian Armed Forces is 161,000, of which 135,000 serve in the army. There are 2 armoured divisions and 1 independent armoured brigade, 5 infantry divisions and 1 independent infantry brigade. The heavy equipment of these units includes American M-24, M-47 and M-60A1 tanks as well as M-8 and M-20 armoured cars. The army has American M-113 and Russian BTR-152 APCs, Russian 57mm and 85mm anti-aircraft guns, and American Hawk surface-to-air missiles (1 battalion). An aviation battalion is equipped with Huskie helicopters. An agreement with Italy for the supply of CH-47C Chinook helicopters was recently signed.

The total strength of the Iranian Navy is 9,000

seamen with 1 destroyer, 5 frigates (partly equipped with Seacat sea-to-air missiles) and 5 corvettes. There are also 34 smaller vessels (including 8 SRN-6 Hovercraft and 4 landing craft). The strength of the Iranian Air Force is 17,000 airmen with 175 combat aircraft, which include F-4D all-weather fighter-bombers with Sidewinder and Sparrow air-to-air missiles, F-5 tactical fighter bombers and F-86 all-weather interceptors. The tactical reconnaissance aircraft are of the RT-33 type and will be replaced partly by the RF-5 type. The transport squadrons include C-45, C-47, C-130E and Beaver aircraft. Helicopters are of the Huskie, Whirlwind and AB-205 types. Further helicopters of the AB-206A, Super-Frelon and UH-1D Iroquois will be supplied. For air defence Tigercat surface-to-air missiles are deployed. In May 1970 an agreement with Great Britain was signed for the supply of Rapier surface-to-air missiles.

COUNTRIES DEPENDING MAINLY ON SUPPLIES FROM THE WEST. ISRAEL: The total number of soldiers (men and women) in the Israel Defence Forces (IDF) is estimated at 75,000 regular cadre and conscripts, which can be raised to about 300,000 by mobilization of reservists (which is completed within 48-72 hours); 11,500 regulars and 50,000 conscripts (275,000 when fully mobilized) serve in the army. On active service are 2 infantry, 2 armoured, 1 mechanized and 1 paratroop brigade (some perhaps only in cadre form). In the reserves there are 26 brigades. For one-third of these armour is available. The armour includes 300 American M-48 Patton (with 105mm guns), 450 British Centurion, 200 Super Sherman (with 105 mm guns) and about 100 Russian T-54/55 tanks (the latter captured during the Six Day War). There are also some French AML-90 and AML-60 and American Staghound armoured cars. World War II American M-2 and M-3 half-tracks serve as APCs. The artillery has about 300 self-propelled pieces, including mortars and 155mm howitzers on Sherman chassis and 105mm howitzers on French AMX chassis. Additional SP howitzers will be supplied by the United States. The anti-aircraft defence deploys 20mm, 30mm and 40mm anti-aircraft guns. Anti-tank weapons include 106mm recoilless rifles, 90mm anti-tank guns, SS-10/11 and Cobra missiles.

The navy has 3,500 regulars and 1,000 conscripts (8,000 after full mobilization) with 4 submarines, 1 destroyer, 1 anti-aircraft frigate and 1 coastal escort, 12 Sa'ar type fast patrol boats with Gavriel sea-to-sea missiles, and 20 other vessels.

The strength of the Israeli Air Force (IAF) is 8,000 regular and 1,000 conscript airmen (17,000 after full mobilization) with 330 combat aircraft, which include French Vautour light bombers, American F-4E Phantom fighter-bomber interceptors, American A-4E Skyhawk fighter bombers, French Mirage IIIC fighter-bomber interceptors (some with R-530 missiles), French Mystère IVA fighter-bombers, French Ouragan fighter bombers, French Super Mystère interceptors, Fouga Magister jet trainers (to be used in ground-attack missions). The transport squadrons include Noratlas, Stratocruiser and C-47 aircraft. Helicopters are of the AB-205, Alouette, Super Frelon, CH-53 and H-34 types. There are 2 battalions of American Hawk surface-to-air missiles. Israel has ordered and paid for 50 Mirage V planes, but owing to the French embargo their delivery has been blocked. The delivery of further aircraft from the United States is under discussion.

JORDAN: The total number of soldiers in the armed forces is 60,250, of whom 58,000 serve in the army. There are 2 armoured brigades, 1 armoured Royal Guards battalion and 9 infantry brigades. The armour includes 160 American M-47 and M-48 Patton and 150 British Centurion tanks, as well as 130 British Saladin armoured cars and about 140 British Ferret scout cars. The APCs are 250 American M-113s and 100 British Saracens. The artillery includes 30 105mm and 155mm howitzers, a few 155mm and 203mm guns, as well as 3 regiments of World War II British 25-pounders. There is 1 anti-aircraft regiment, for which Tigercat surface-to-air missiles are on order. The navy operates only some patrol craft in the Gulf of 'Aqaba.

The total strength of the Jordanian Air Force is 2,000 airmen with 28 combat aircraft (American F-104A interceptors and British Hunter FGA6 and 9). There are also some C-47, Dove and Devon transport aircraft, as well as a few Alouette III and Whirlwind helicopters. The United States is due to deliver a further squadron of F 104A interceptors and Great Britain has agreed to supply 4 Hunter FGA-73 fighter bombers.

LEBANON: The total number of soldiers in the Lebanese Armed Forces is 16,250, of whom 15,000 serve in the army. There are 2 tank battalions, 1 motorized battalion and 9 infantry battalions. The armour includes 40 British Charioteer medium tanks, 40 French AMX-13 and American M-41 light tanks, various types of armoured cars and M-113 and M-59 APCs. The artillery includes 155mm. howitzers. The Lebanese Navy operates 5 small vessels of different types. The total strength of the air force is 1,000 airmen with 24 combat aircraft of the British Hunter fighter ground-attack and French Mirage IIIC interceptor (with R-530 air-to-air missiles) types. There are also about 6 transport aircraft and some Alouette II and III helicopters. France has agreed to supply a Crotale air-defence missile system. The Lebanese

Armed Forces are composed of volunteers (professionals) only. However, conscription for obligatory military service has been under discussion for some years and the first legislative steps have been taken.

SA'UDI ARABIA: The total number of soldiers in the armed forces (composed of volunteers) is 36,000, of which 30,000 serve in the army. There are 4 infantry brigades with 55 American M-47 medium tanks, 35 American M-41 and 30 French AMX-13 light tanks, about 200 French AML-90 and some American M-6 Staghound and M-8 Greyhound armoured cars, as well as some British Ferret scout cars. Anti-tank defence is provided by Vigilant missiles and anti-aircraft defence by 10 batteries of American Hawk surface-to-ground missiles. The navy operates 7 small vessels. Air-cushion vehicles for coastguard duties are on order from Great Britain. The total strength of the air force is 5,000 airmen with 75 combat aircraft of the F-86 fighter-bomber, BAC-167 Strikemaster ground-attack aircraft and Lightning interceptor types. There are 25 transport aircraft of the C-47, C-118, C-123 and C-130E types and about 30 helicopters of various types, as well as about 30 jet trainers. The air force deploys 37 Thunderbird surface-to-air missiles.

OTHER COUNTRIES: Great Britain has commitments in the area, as for instance to consult and co-operate in the defence of Cyprus and is responsible for the defence of Bahrain, Qatar and the Trucial States. The latter responsibility is to end, according to a British decision announced in 1968, by the end of 1971.

COUNTRIES MAINLY RELYING ON SUPPLIES FROM THE SOVIET BLOC. ALGERIA: (included here, though generally not covered in this Encyclopaedia): The total number of soldiers in the Algerian Armed Forces (drafted by limited conscription) is 57,000, of whom 53,000 serve in the army. There are 3 motorized infantry brigades, which include a certain amount of armour, 3 independent tank battalions, about 45 independent infantry battalions, 5 independent artillery battalions, 1 paratroop brigade and some companies of desert troops. The armour consists of 300 Russian T-34 and T-54 medium tanks, 350 Russian BTR-152 APCs and SU-100 SP assault guns. The artillery includes in addition to 85mm guns and 122-mm and 152mm howitzers, 140mm and 240mm rocket-launchers.

The total strength of the navy is 2,000 seamen operating Russian 9/Komar- and Osaclass missile patrol boats with short-range sea-to-sea missiles and 10 motor torpedo boats of the Soviet P-6 class.

The total strength of the Algerian Air Force is 2,000 airmen with 170 combat aircraft of the Russian MIG-15, MIG-17 and MIG-21 fighter and Il-28 light bomber types. There are 12 transport aircraft of the An-12 and Il-18 types, as well as 50 helicopters, mainly of the MI-4 type. There are also 30 trainer planes. France has agreed to supply 28 armed Fouga Magister jet trainers and 15 SA-330 Puma helicopters. One battalion of Russian SA-2 surface-to-air missiles is deployed.

There are 1,500 Soviet military personnel in the country, mainly in the capacity of instructors and advisers. Under the provisions of the Evian agreements of 1962 France still maintains about 400 Legionnaires and an air force detachment on Algerian soil.

IRAQ: The total number of soldiers in the armed forces is 94,000, of which 85,000 serve in the army. Since the Six Day War of June 1967, about 15,000 have been stationed in the Hashemite Kingdom of Jordan and c. 6,000 in Syria. There are 2 armoured divisions and 5 infantry divisions, equipped with 450 Russian T-54/55, 140 Russian T-34 and 55 British Centurion Mark 5 medium tanks. The armoured equipment also includes 40 American M-24 light tanks, 55 French AML-60 armoured cars, 20 British Ferret scout cars and Russian BTR-152 APCs. The artillery deploys Russian 120mm and 130mm guns.

The navy deploys about 25 small vessels.

The total strength of the Iraqi Air Force is 7,500 airmen, with 229 combat aircraft of the Russian Tu-16 medium bomber, Il-28 light bomber, Su-7 all-weather fighter-bomber types, the British Hunter Mark 9 ground-attack aircraft, the British T-52 Jet Provost light-strike aircraft types and the Russian MIG-21 interceptor, MIG-17 and Mig-19 fighter types. The transport aircraft are of the Russian An-2, An-12, An-24 and Il-14 types, and the British Heron and Bristol Freighter types. Helicopters include Russian Mi-1 and Mi-4 and British Wessex aircraft. Anti-aircraft defence is provided by Russian SA-2 surface-to-air missiles.

LIBYA: The total strength of the Libyan Armed Forces is 15,000 airmen, of whom 14,000 serve in the army. There are 2 armoured battalions, 5 infantry battalions, 2 artillery battalions and 1 anti-aircraft artillery battalion. The armour includes 6 British Centurion medium tanks, British Saladin armoured cars, British Ferret scout cars and British Saracen APCs. An order for 188 Chieftain heavy tanks from Britain is under discussion; in the meantime the delivery of an unknown quantity of Soviet armour and artillery was reported in July 1970. The artillery so far includes 105mm howitzers.

The navy operates one corvette and about 20 small vessels. One fast frigate is on order.

The total strength of the air force is 400 airmen

with 7 combat aircraft of the American F-5 interceptor type, 9 C-47 transports, 3 T-33 jet trainers and some helicopters. The United States agreed to supply 6 C-130 Hercules transports, and France will supply 50 Mirage V and 60 Mirage III interceptor aircraft.

SUDAN: The total strength of the Sudanese Armed Forces (composed of volunteers) is 27,450, of whom 26,500 serve in the army. There are 4 reinforced infantry brigades, 3 independent infantry battalions, 1 armoured regiment, 1 parachute regiment and 3 artillery regiments. The armour includes about 50 Russian T-55 medium tanks, 50 British Saladin and 45 American M-706 Commando armoured cars, and 60 British Ferret scout cars. The artillery includes about 90 pieces of 25 pounders and 105mm guns and howitzers, 20 120mm mortars, 40mm anti-aircraft guns of Western make and some Russian 85mm anti-aircraft guns.

The navy operates 6 small vessels.

The total strength of the air force is 450 airmen with 32 combat aircraft of which 16 are of the Russian MIG-21 interceptor fighter-bomber type and the others are British trainer and light-attack and counter-insurgency aircraft. There are also 11 transport planes: 6 of Western make and 5 Russian An-24s.

EGYPT (UAR): The total number of soldiers in the Egyptian Armed Forces is 288,000, of whom 250,000 serve in the army. The latter consists of 3 armoured divisions, 4 mechanized infantry divisions, 4 infantry divisions, 18 commando battalions, 2 parachute brigades and 15 artillery brigades. The Egyptian Army was compensated by the Soviet Union for its heavy material losses during the Six Day War of June 1967 and its armour again includes about 30 heavy tanks of the JS-III and T-10 types, 950 T-54/55, 250 T-34 medium tanks, 150 PT-76 amphibious tanks, in addition to about 10 British Centurion and 15 American Sherman medium tanks and 20 French light AMX-13 tanks still remaining. The APCs of the Egyptian Army include 900 BTR-40, BTR-50, OT-64 and BTR-152 vehicles. Artillery support is provided by about 150 SU-100 and JSU-152 SP assault and ZSU-57 SP anti-aircraft guns and by 1,500 122mm, 130mm and 152mm guns as well as by about 40 lorry-mounted rocket launchers. There are also about 50 short-range surface-to-surface missiles available.

The total strength of the Egyptian Navy is 14,000 seamen with 12 Russian submarines, 4 Russian and 1 British destroyers, and 86 other vessels of various types, among them 12 Osa class missile patrol boats and 7 of the Komar class, both with short-range sea-to-sea missiles and 18 landing craft.

The total strength of the air force is 20,000 airmen with 415 combat aircraft, which include Tu-16 medium bombers, Il-28 light bombers, MIG-21 interceptors, Su-7 fighter bombers, MIG-15 and MIG-17 fighter bombers. There are about 60 transport planes of the Il-14 and An-12 types and about 70 Mi-1, Mi-4 and Mi-8 helicopters, as well as 150 trainer aircraft, which can be partly armed.

The air defence is based on 37mm, 57mm, 85mm and 100mm anti-aircraft guns and by 250 SA-2 surface-to-air missiles, organized in batteries of 6 launchers each and geared to a radar system and MIG-21 interceptors. Since the increased Soviet involvement, commencing in the spring of 1970, it is assumed that about 100 MIG-21 interceptors are manned by Russian personnel. It is also believed that 22 SA-3 launching sites have been completed and that about the same number is under construction. All these SA-3 missile batteries are Soviet-operated. It is estimated that there were in 1970 about 10,000 Russian soldiers in Egypt, in the capacity of instructors and advisers as well as in operational functions. It is also assumed that the Soviet Union intends to supply a further 80 SA-3 launchers and 150 additional MIG-21 and 16 Su-7 fighter bombers.

Before the Six Day War there was a separate Missile Command, which was to operate Egyptian-made medium-range surface-to-surface missiles. It seems, however, that these missiles have not reached any operational capacity. The impression is that the whole programme has been abandoned and that the command may be disbanded, if this has not already been done.

SYRIA: The total strength of the Syrian Armed Forces is 86,750 soldiers, of whom 75,000 serve in the army. There are 4 armoured brigades, 4 mechanized brigades, 6 infantry brigades, 1 parachute battalion, 3 commando battalions and 7 artillery regiments. As with the Egyptian Army, the Syrian Army was also compensated by the Soviet Union for its material losses in the Six Day War and its armour again includes about 30 JS-III heavy tanks, 150 T-34 and 700 T-54/55 medium tanks, 100 Su-100 SP assault guns and 600 BTR-152 APCs. The artillery includes Russian 122mm, 130mm and 152mm guns; 40 SA-2 surface-to-air missiles are available for air defence.

The total strength of the Syrian Navy is 1,750 seamen with about 30 small naval vessels, among them 10 Komar class missile patrol boats with short-range sea-to-sea missiles.

The total strength of the air force is 10,000 airmen with 210 combat aircraft, which include MIG-15 and MIG-17 fighter bombers, Su-7 fighter bombers and MIG-21 interceptors. There are about 20 transport aircraft and the same number of Russian helicopters of different types.

It is assumed that there are about 1,000 Soviet military personnel in Syria in the capacity of instructors and advisers.

US AND SOVIET PRESENCE IN THE MIDDLE EAST. The USA has bilateral treaties with some of the countries in the area; the Soviet Union has none, though she supplies arms to a number of them. The USA has bases in Western Asia (e.g. Turkey); the Soviet Union has no such bases, but she has naval facilities on the southern shores of the Mediterranean (Algeria, Egypt, Syria) and east of Suez (Yemen, South Yemen, Somalia). Since the Six Day War of June 1967, the number of Soviet warships in the eastern basin of the Mediterranean has varied between 15 and 25. The Soviet Mediterranean Naval Squadron has included tank landing vessels and helicopter carriers and in addition to the warships a large number of auxiliaries.

MILITARY AGREEMENTS AMONG ARAB STATES. The Arab League, now comprising the 14 independent Arab states, established in 1950 (when it had only seven member states) and the Arab Collective Security Pact, with an Arab Defence Council. However, this was not an effective organization. A separate inter-Arab military agreement was concluded by Egypt, Syria and Sa'udi Arabia in 1955 (Jordan joined them in 1956, but both Jordan and Sa'udia seceded *de facto* in 1957). A Unified Arab Command was set up in 1964; its actual operation during and since the Six Day War of 1967 was limited, even doubtful, but officially it still exists. A defence agreement of November 1966 between Syria and Egypt provided for a Defence Council and a Joint Command, with the Egyptian Chief of General Staff as Joint Supreme Commander in the event of war. On 30 May 1967, on the eve of the Six Day War, a similar agreement was concluded between Jordan and Egypt. On 4 June the agreement was also joined by Iraq. It seems, however, that these agreements are no longer in effect. In 1968 a new "Eastern Command" (Iraq-Syria-Jordan) was set up within the framework of the Unified Arab Command and under Egyptian supervision; this was reinforced by Syro-Iraqi defence pacts of 1968 and 1969, but it was not effective and, according to reports in 1970, it was split up. Libya (under her new regime after the coup of 1969), Sudan and Egypt agreed in Dec. 1969 to co-ordinate military operations against Israel (in November 1970, this co-ordination extended into the proclamation of a federation).   (J. W.)

ARMENIA, ARMENIANS. A region of high plateaux and mountain chains south-east of the Black Sea. It is today divided among the USSR, Turkey and Iran. The Soviet Republic of A. has an area of 10,502 sq. mi., and a population of about 2m., 88% of whom are of Armenian nationality.

HISTORY. A succession of foreign rulers (Medes, Persians, Romans, Arabs and Turks) was interspersed with short periods of national independence. At the start of the 19th century, Russia seized substantial parts of A. from Turkey. Until World War I, there were about 2m. A. living in Turkey; like other Christian minorities in the Ottoman Empire, they were considered second-rate citizens. Owing to the intervention of the European powers, the Sultan in 1839 and 1856 granted equal rights to the A., as well as to all Christians within the Empire. But these edicts were never fully implemented. Following the uprisings of the Christians in the Balkans, which brought them independence, the Ottoman rulers decided to deal even more harshly with the A. in the Empire. When the latter tried to defend themselves, hundreds of thousands of them were massacred, 1894–6. The Young Turks▷, who came to power in 1908, did not solve the Armenian problem, as they favoured centralism and distrusted minorities. With the outbreak of World War I, matters came to a head, as the Turks accused the A. of disloyalty and collaboration with the Russians. During 1915–6 a systematic and ruthless massacre of civilians was carried out; this resulted in the death of more than 1m. A. and created many thousands of refugees. A short-lived Transcaucasian Federation (A., Georgia and Azerbaijan▷) was established during the Russian Revolution. In May 1918, the A. declared their country's independence, with Yerivan as their capital. The abortive Peace Treaty of Sèvres▷ between Turkey and the Allies (10 Aug. 1920) recognized an independent State of A. (A plan to impose a Mandate on A. was dropped when the USA declined to act as Mandatory Power.) At the end of 1920, however, free A. ceased to exist, as the Turks reconquered the former Turkish A. provinces, while the Russians took over the remaining part of A. After a national Armenian revolt, 1921, A. became a Soviet Republic. From 1922 to 1936 it formed part of a Transcaucasian Soviet Republic— with Georgia and Azerbaijan; it was re-established in 1936 when the Transcaucasian Republic was dissolved.

The Armenians' ethnic origin is unknown. Their tongue is Indo-European and their alphabet dates back, according to Armenian tradition, to 405 CE. Religion, which plays a major role in their national life, was in the past the main cohesive force among the A. and still serves to link the scattered worldwide community.

RELIGION. The Armenian Orthodox Church is Monophysite▷. It is incorrectly called the Armenian

Gregorian Church after St. Gregory the Illuminator, who converted the King and all his people in 303. The A., however, claim that Christianity was brought to A. earlier, by the Apostles Bartholomew and Thaddaeus.

The highest-ranking dignitaries of the Armenian Church bear the title Catholicos (of Etchmiadzin and of Cilicia), and Patriarch (of Constantinople and of Jerusalem). The seat of Etchmiadzin in Soviet A. is traditionally related to St. Gregory. When the Kingdom of New A. was established in Cilicia (Southern Anatolia), 1080–1375, the Catholicos moved from Etchmiadzin to Sis; but the seat of Etchmiadzin was subsequently re-established, and both seats persisted. When most of the A. were forced to leave Cilicia in 1920, following the re-occupation of this part of Anatolia by the Turks, the seat of Sis was transferred to Antelias in Lebanon. The Patriarchate of Constantinople dates from the 15th century, when the Sultan established the Armenian "Millet"▷, representing the Armenian nation throughout the Ottoman Empire. The Patriarchate of Jerusalem dates from 1311. For centuries there has been rivalry between the Catholicos of Etchmiadzin and that of Sis. The precedence of the seat of Etchmiadzin is now admitted for historical reasons, but there is a tendency in the dioceses of the Diaspora to turn towards the Catholicos of Sis in Antelias (Lebanon), because Etchmiadzin is situated in the USSR.

The Armenian-Catholic Church (see Uniate▷) is headed by a Patriarch, with his seat in Lebanon. There are also Armenian congregations within Protestant denominations.

There are about 4m. A. today—nearly 2.5m. in the USSR, more than .5m. in the ME, the remainder scattered throughout the world. Compact colonies are to be found in the ME (Cyprus, Turkey, Iran, Syria and Lebanon—with over 100,000 in each of the last three), where the A. have found it easier to maintain their traditional institutions and national consciousness. Over 200,000 A. live in the USA. In Lebanon and Iran, A. have representation in Parliament. A. in the ME have established their own political parties: Hantchak—at present with Communist leanings; Tashnak—pro-Western; and Ramkavar, with few adherents but economically influential and said to be close to the Hantchak.

After World War II, the Soviet government encouraged the A. of the Near East and the Diaspora to return to Soviet A. Some 200,000 came, but their situation seems to have discouraged further re-immigration.   (Sh.C.)

ARMISTICE AGREEMENTS (1949)—see Arab-Israel War, 1948▷.

*ARMY OFFICERS IN POLITICS. The ME has a tradition of interference of army commanders in government and politics, and of military rule; changes of governments and political systems have often been carried out by military means. In the later Middle Ages and up to the beginning of the 19th century the most persistent ruling class in many Arab and Muslim countries was a professional military elite—the Mamelukes (Mamluks)—and rulers and ruled alike became accustomed to the idea that the commander of the armed forces is also the head of the state.

Modernization and westernization, which characterize the public life of the ME in the last century, brought with them two different, even contradictory, trends: a strong movement towards constitutionalism, division of functions, and subordination of the army to a supreme civil authority; and, on the other hand, a strong emphasis on the military, "the cutting edge" of Western civilization and its most conspicuous instrument. In Ottoman Turkey in the 18th century, and in Egypt in the 19th, army officers became the first organized group of Muslim society which was systematically westernized. One of the results of this was the growth among army officers of a modern-nationalist mentality, a marked sense of their specific historical mission, and ostentatious political ambitions.

In those ME countries independent in the first decades of the 20th century—Iran and Ottoman Turkey—changes toward a modernization of regime, government and society were often made by military coups, or at least with army officers in controlling positions of initiative. This was the case in the Young Turks'▷ revolution of 1908, their recapture of power in 1913, Kemal Atatürk's▷ take-over in 1920-3 and Reza Pahlevi's▷ assumption of power in Iran in 1921. As Arab countries became independent, young army officers emerged there too, in dominant political positions. (The military revolt staged in 1881 in Egypt by Col. 'Arabi ('Urabi) served as a pretext for the country's occupation by the British in 1882, but had no major influence on the governance of Egypt thereafter.)

In the 1930s and '40s ambitious young men of the middle class often chose a military officer's career, regarding themselves as "intelligentsia in uniform". Many of them associated in clandestine oppositional officers' groups, the most successful of them being the Egyptian Free Officers Association of the early 1950s, which carried out the coup of 23 July 1952; it became afterwards the model for many other Arab officers' organizations and their activities. The military coup has become one of the outstanding features of the contemporary Arab political scene.

Iraq, the first modern Arab state to become formally independent (1932), was also the first to witness a military coup, that of Bakr Sidqi▷, in 1936. It was followed by a counter-coup, again of military officers, in 1937; and for five years, until the British military intervention in Iraq in 1941, Iraq was ruled *de facto* or behind the scenes by groups of army officers. This pattern repeated itself, with variations, during the 1950s and '60s in various Arab countries which became independent after World War II. Military coups became most frequent after the defeat of the Arab armies in the Arab-Israel War of 1948, first in Syria (March 1949 and thereafter on many occasions), then in Egypt (July 1952), later in Iraq (July 1958, February 1963, July 1968), Sudan (November 1958, May 1969), Yemen (September 1962), Algeria (June 1965) and Libya (September 1969). In many cases such military coups were followed by counter-coups and further military revolts. Military coups were also unsuccessfully attempted in Jordan (April 1957) and Lebanon (Dec. 1961) and several times in Syria, Iraq, Sudan, Libya.

The rebellious army officers generally describe themselves as revolutionaries. They promise to carry out fundamental social and economic reforms, to strengthen the armed forces of their respective countries and to fortify their independence, to liberate Palestine, and to return after a short transitional period to the barracks, handing over the government to democratically elected civilian leaders. These pledges have hardly ever been kept. In any event, in contrast to other areas in the world, the officers' coup in the ME appears in a leftist-progressive garb.

An exceptional case is Turkey. There, both the Young Turks of 1908 and, later, Kemal Atatürk, established a civilian-political government which administered the country—though in both cases the officers ruling retained ultimate power. The pattern was repeated in May 1960: a coup spearheaded and controlled by army officers was followed by popular elections initiated and supervised by the officers, leading to a civilian-political regime—with the implication that the officers reserve some right to intervene again should things go wrong (as they did, in Mar. 1971). In Persia, an officers' coup was used in 1953, by conservative and royalist leaders to oust the leftist revolutionary, Dr. Mossaddeq▷.

In no ME country outside Turkey has a dictatorship liquidated itself. In some cases, the officers received popular endorsement by plebiscite without opposition and sometimes even wide popular support, but insofar as the officer-politicians succeeded in establishing regimes of political and social stability, it was the stability of authoritarian totalitarianism, and mostly rather short lived. Army officers have shown themselves to be not less, but certainly not more, progressive and unselfish than other groups in modern Arab society. Their real advantage over others of the intelligentsia is their monopoly of institutionalized violence, the hierarchical organization of the army, and their readiness to take advantage of this power in internal controversies.

(E. B.-Y. S.)

ARSANJANI, DR. HASSAN (1922–69). Iranian lawyer and political leader. Born in Tehran. Founded the liberal *Azadi* (Freedom) party in 1945. When Azadi later merged with the communist *Tudeh*▷, A. seceded. In 1961, after many years in the service of the Ministry of Agriculture, A. was appointed Minister of Agriculture. He was the moving spirit of the Iranian Land Reform, but resigned in 1963. After serving as Ambassador to Rome, 1963–6, A. retired from politics and practised law. (B.G.)

ARSLAN. Clan of Lebanese Druze▷ notables, with the hereditary title of Amir (Prince). Until 1861 the feudal lords of the al-Gharb region east of Beirut, they headed one of Lebanon's two Druze factions (the rival faction being led by the Junblat▷ clan). During the French Mandate, the A. were opponents of the Mandatory regime; some of them even opposed separate status for Lebanon and took an active part in the general Pan-Arab nationalist movement (a contributing factor to this position was the Junblat clan's then staunch pro-French stand). During this period, the Emirs Shakib and 'Adel Arslan were particularly noted as active nationalist leaders. (Y.P.)

ARSLAN, 'ADEL (1882–1954). Syrian politician. Was a delegate to the Ottoman House of Representatives. Though a member of Arab-nationalist secret societies, he remained loyal to the Empire during World War I. After the War, he co-founded the Pan-Arab *Istiqlal*▷ party. Exiled from Syria-Lebanon during the French Mandate, he spent many years in Europe, Transjordan and Palestine, where he held various posts and engaged in political activity. A. returned to Syria in 1937. When the Allies occupied Syria in 1941 he fled to Turkey, because of his strong ties with the Axis. A. returned to Syria in 1945, but did not find his place in her parliamentary and political life. He served as Education Minister in 1946–7, and during the same period represented Syria in negotiations concerning the Palestine issue. He was Deputy Prime Minister and Foreign Minister under Husni Za'im▷ after Za'im's 1949 coup, and became Syrian Minister to Turkey, 1949–51.

(Y.S.)

ARSLAN, MAJID (b. 1904). Lebanese politician. First elected to Parliament in 1931 and a member of Lebanese cabinets since 1937, subsequent to the signing of the (unratified) Franco-Lebanese Treaty. A. was a staunch supporter of Bishara al-Khouri▷ and his doctrine and party (the "Constitutional Bloc") advocating closer relations with the Arab countries. A. was re-elected to Parliament in 1943. He was Defence Minister in the cabinet which was dissolved by the French, in November 1943. The members were arrested, but he escaped and organized the popular struggle against the French. He continued supporting Bishara al-Khouri and his Constitutional Bloc into the 1950s, when al-Khouri's decline began (his support stemmed also from the fact that Kamal Junblat▷ was a leading opponent of al-Khouri). A. was Defence Minister in many cabinets. He was elected to all parliaments in the 1960s (1960, 1964 and 1968) as a member for 'Aley in Mount Lebanon, heading a list of the Constitutional Bloc.   (Y.P.)

ARSLAN, SHAKIB (1869–1946). Syrian Pan-Arab politician and writer. A district governor under the Ottoman Empire, A. remained loyal to the Turks and joined the Arab Nationalists only after World War I. In the 1920s he was active in the "Syro-Palestinian Congress", which attempted to keep Pan-Arab activities alive, and was a member of its permanent delegation in Geneva. He edited the Pan-Arab weekly "The Arab Nation" (in French) and conducted negotiations with world statesmen (including fruitless contacts with Zionist leaders). He later became close to the Fascist movement and maintained strong ties with Italy and Nazi Germany. He also drew nearer to Pan-Islamic views and wrote a detailed biography of the modern Islamic thinker Muhammad Rashid Rida. He returned to Syria in 1937, but was not active in Syrian political affairs. During World War II he returned to Switzerland and called on the Arabs to collaborate with the Axis powers.   (Y.P.)

***ASAD, HAFEZ.** Syrian officer and politician. Prime Minister 1970–1, President 1971. Born in Lataqia, of 'Alawi▷ origin. Since the 1960s a member of the "national" (*i.e.* all-Arab) and Syrian High Command of the *Ba'th*▷ party. Appointed commander of the Syrian Air Force in 1963. Held the rank of Fariq (Lieutenant-General) since 1968. In the internal struggle for the leadership of Syria and the ruling *Ba'th* party, he belonged to the extreme left and the "military wing", which opposed the Bitar▷ and Amin Hafez▷ faction then in control. He led the *coup d'état* carried out by the military wing on 23 Feb. 1966. He became a leader of the regime following that coup, and served as Defence Minister. In the controversy within the ruling faction that followed the coup, A. was considered the leader of the "nationalist faction", opposed to Salah Jadid's▷ extreme left. A. opposed total identification with the Soviet Union and was critical of her position, rejected rigid ideological definitions, preferred a pragmatic approach to economic issues, and aimed at closer all-Arab co-operation and the resumption of the fight against Israel. A. gained control of the government in the spring of 1969 in a semi-coup, but compromised with his opponents. He again took control in Nov. 1970, and this time kept it, purging and dismissing his opponents and detaining their leaders. He became Prime Minister in Nov. 1970, and remained Minister of Defence. He was soon working for a *rapprochement* with Egypt and for Syria's more active participation in Arab affairs after a period of extremist isolation, and in Apr. 1971 he brought Syria into the projected "Federation of Arab Republics" (see Arab Federation▷). A. also reconstituted an (appointed) "People's Council". He was sole candidate for the presidency; in Mar. 1971 he was elected President.   (A.L.-O.T.)

ASIA. Various attempts were made following World War II to organize a bloc of the independent Asian states, often together with the African states. All-Asian conferences were held, for instance, at India's initiative, in 1947 and 1949. At times, such attempts were directed towards the creation of a "Third Bloc", neutral between the power blocs and "non-aligned" (see Neutralism▷). At the beginning of the 1950s, for example, Indian and other representatives attempted to organize the Asian delegations to the UN Assembly into a permanent policy-co-ordinating group; however, despite meetings held and views exchanged, no permanent group was formed. The Bandung▷ Conference, in April 1955, was primarily a festive demonstration, providing a stage for Asian leaders and an opportunity for a first get-together of all Afro-Asian countries (except those boycotted and not allowed to participate—see Bandung▷), but it did not lead to a permanent organization; nor was a much discussed "Second Bandung Conference" ever convened (the African states, on the other hand, established a permanent organization).

In contrast to the absence of a permanent Pan-Asian organization on a governmental level, semi-official groups were formed for specific spheres of activity (e.g., as an Organization of Asian Broadcasting Stations), and one-time conferences were held; the UN and its specialized agencies also set up regional organizations, committees and bureaux for the Asian states. However, membership in the former is in-consistent and at times haphazard, and certain Asian countries are sometimes deliberately boycotted while UN-sponsored Asian bodies do not include the ME. Though Asian sports events are held in various fields, attempts to hold "Asian Games" (e.g., Indonesia, 1962) have not yet established a permanent tradition.

On the other hand, a large number of Pan-Asian (or, mostly, Afro-Asian) popular organizations were founded, the most active being the "Afro-Asian Peoples' Solidarity Organization". Founded at a Cairo "Solidarity Conference" in 1957, it set up a permanent council and a secretariat in Cairo. Apart from special conferences and congresses (youth, writers, journalists, lawyers, economic experts, etc.), the organization held a number of multi-national plenary conferences (founding convention, Cairo 1957; Conakry, Guinea, Apr. 1960; Moshi, Tanzania, Feb. 1963; Accra, Ghana, May 1965; Tripoli, Libya, Nov. 1970). The organization was dominated by Arab and Communist activists and has virtually become a Communist cover or front organization; the Sino-Soviet conflict, however, has disrupted its work, and constant friction between pro-Chinese and pro-Soviet elements in its leadership and per-manent bodies have all but paralysed it.   (Y.S.)

✻'ASIR. A region on the Arabian coast of the Red Sea, between Yemen and Hijaz, consisting of a coastal plain ("Tihama") and a mountainous hinter-land. In 1910 the ruler of Sabya, the main district of 'A., al-Sayyid Muhammad al-Idrissi▷, of the Idrissi sect and dynasty, rebelled against the Ottoman Empire. He was defeated with the help of Sharif Hussein▷ of Mecca, but was saved by Italian aid. He rebelled again during World War I, in concert with British agents who promised him independence; agreements to this effect were signed in April 1915 and January 1917. When the British Army evacuated the Yemen coast in 1921, they allowed Sayyid Muhammad to occupy Hodeida▷. When Muham-mad died in 1923, a crisis over the succession weakened the little state into which Wahhabi▷ influence had begun to penetrate. Zeidi▷ tribesmen from Yemen conquered Hodeida in 1925. In 1926 the weakened Idrissi princes, quarreling among themselves, had to ask for Sa'udi patronage, and in 1933 'A. was formally annexed to Sa'udi Arabia. However, the Imam of Yemen disputed the annexation and claimed 'A. for his kingdom; the Italians encouraged him to carry out raids on 'A., now a Sa'udi possession, and in 1934 this led to war. Ibn Sa'ud▷ defeated the Yemeni Imam; the peace treaty of Ta'if allotted 'A.—both the Tihama and the inner region of Najran—

to Sa'udi Arabia. During the Yemen War, 1962–7, Egyptian planes occasionally bombed Najran, claim-ing that it was part of Yemen. The area served as an important supply base and refuge for the Yemeni Royalists.   (H.E.)

'ASKARI, AL-, JA'FAR (1885–1936). Iraqi officer and politician. Graduating from the Military Acade-my at Istanbul, 'A. served as an officer in the Ottoman Army. During World War I, he was sent to Cyrenaica (May 1915), to organize Sanussi▷ units for operations against the British in Egypt. Taken prisoner later in the same year, he was recruited in 1916 from the prison camp for Sharif Hussein's▷ army of the Arab "Revolt in the Desert". He became one of its leaders. 'A. was appointed Military Governor of Amman (1918) and, during Feisal's▷ regime in Syria (1919–20), Governor of Aleppo. After Feisal's withdrawal from Syria, he settled in Iraq. In 1921 'A. became Minister of Defence, and in this capacity organized the Iraqi Army. He was Prime Minister in 1923–4 and 1926–7, Iraqi Minister in London, 1928–33, and again Minister of Defence, 1935–6. 'A was strongly identified with the Hashemite dynasty and conservative-nationalist, pro-British governments. He was assassinated in Oct. 1936 by a group of army officers that overthrew the Yassin al-Hashemi government (the Bakr Sidqi▷ coup).   (B.G.)

✻ASNAJ, AL-, 'ABDULLAH (b. 1933). South Yemeni (Adeni) Labour leader and politician. Em-ployed 1951–62 by Aden Airways. Active in the Aden Trades Union Congress (ATUC), of which he be-came Secretary-General. In 1962 he formed and led the ATUC's political wing, the People's Socialist Par-ty. He joined the nationalist, anti-British revolution-aries and demanded the union of South Yemen with Yemen. Consequently he went into exile in the mid-1960s. In January 1966, he helped to found the Libera-tion Front (FLOSY▷) and became its Secretary-General. After the take-over of South Yemen (then "South Arabia"▷) by the rival NLF▷ in 1967, A. remained in exile. In Aug. 1971 he joined the (North) Yemen government as Foreign Minister.   (Y.A.O.)

'ASSALI, AL-, SABRI. Syrian politician. Born in Damascus in 1903. Active in the nationalist move-ment, 'A. took part in the Druze Revolt (1925–7). In the 1930s he joined the "National Bloc" but was also active in other, more extremist groups. He was several times elected to the Syrian parliament. In 1947, when the "National Bloc" disintegrated, 'A. was one of the founders of the "National Party" and became its Secretary-General and main leader.

From 1945 on he served as minister in several governments. 'A. became Prime Minister after the ousting of Shishakli▷ in February 1954. He served as head of four governments until the formation of the UAR▷ in 1958, when he was appointed one of the four deputies of the UAR president, 'Abd-ul-Nasser▷; he resigned that post after a few months and has since not been active in political life.

(A. L.-O. T.)

ASSYRIANS. Generally identified with the Nestorian Christians, or more precisely with those Nestorians living in the 19th century in the mountain region north of the Mesopotamian plain, between Lake Van in the west, and Lake Urmia in the east, which was later divided among Turkey, Iraq and Iran.

The Nestorian Church left the main body of Christianity after the Ecumenical Council of Ephesus in 431, which confirmed the Divine nature of Christ — a doctrine rejected by Nestorios, Patriarch of Constantinople, and his followers. The Nestorians' connection with the ancient A. has never been proved. The Eastern Syriac dialect, which was once their language, is today largely confined to their liturgy.

The A., a small minority among larger national and religious groups, lived in mountainous regions and had to struggle fiercely for survival. They were divided into several tribes. Their numbers dwindled because of losses inflicted by foes and defections to other creeds — mainly to the Catholic Church (Chaldeans▷, in Uniate▷), and to a lesser extent, to the Anglican and other Protestant churches.

At the beginning of World War I, most A. lived within the Ottoman Empire. Their situation, like that of other minorities, became critical as they were suspected of having connections with enemy countries. In October 1915, after repeated attacks by the Turks and their Kurdish neighbours, some 50–70,000 A. crossed the border to Iran under the leadership of their Catholicos-Patriarch and joined the Russian forces. When Russian forces occupied parts of Eastern Anatolia, the A. collaborated; they were exposed to Turkish retaliation when the Russians withdrew.

At the end of the war, the main group of Assyrians marched as an army to join the British Forces advancing into Iraq, and were followed by their families. A smaller group left for Russia, then in revolution. About 50,000 A. from Persia and Turkey were placed by the British in refugee camps in Iraq. Many of them succumbed to the hard conditions. The men were employed by the British Army as guards.

Vague plans, between the end of World War I and the emergence of Kemalist Turkey, to establish an independent Assyrian nation, embracing the various peoples whose liturgical language was Syriac

(A., Chaldeans and Syrian Orthodox), came to nothing. The A., who tried to return to their ancestral homes after the war, were very soon re-expelled by the Turks. They had to be content with a few areas in northern Iraq vacated by Turks and Kurds and not sufficiently large to maintain all of the A. Consequently many of them were practically refugees when, in 1932, the British Mandate in Iraq came to an end.

Under the independent Kingdom of Iraq, the A. met with considerable Iraqi animosity, as they were clamouring for far-reaching autonomy and had, moreover, been employed by the British as unpopular armed levies. Soon, bloody clashes broke out and in August 1933 hundreds of A. were killed. A large exodus followed. About 4,000 emigrated to America, 6,000 to Syria and some to the Lebanon. The French, with the support of the League of Nations, tried to settle some A. in Syria, but when that country became independent, the settlement project was discontinued. About 30,000 A. remained in Iraq; when in the 1950s the Kurdish rebellion was resumed, many of them moved southward to settle in Baghdad. Those A. who lived in the countryside in the north of Iran, also moved to the cities, mostly to Tehran, when life in the north became insecure.

There are more than 70,000 Nestorian A. in the ME today, 30–35,000 of whom are in Iraq, 20,000 in Iran and 15,000 in Syria. Some 20–30,000 live in the USSR and about 10,000 in the USA.

The Nestorian ecclesiastical hierarchy is headed by the Catholicos, who always bears the title "Mar Shim'oun" (Sham'oun = Peter). The office is hereditary, passing from uncle to nephew. Prior to 1933, the Catholicos' seat was in Mosul▷. but owing to the struggles which took place that year, Mar Eshai Shim'oun XXI was exiled to Cyprus. From there he emigrated to Medesto, California, and now has little contact with the ME. A Metropolitan and a Bishop reside in Iraq, and a Bishop in Iran. In 1968 a group critical of the permanent absence of the Catholicos elected the Metropolitan of Baghdad, Mar Thuma Darmo, as Catholicos. Mar Thuma died in 1969, but the movement which supported him still exists.

(Sh.C.)

ASWAN DAM. The first dam on the Nile▷ in Upper Egypt was constructed by British engineers (1898–1920) near the ancient town of A. It partially controlled the Nile floods and made possible the transfer of large tracts of land from basin-flooding to permanent irrigation. Its height was raised in 1907–12 and again in 1935. An electric power station and plant for chemical fertilizers (both opened in 1960) are among several recent development projects based upon this original dam. Egypt's most important development project is the construction of a new AD (the "High Dam"), five miles south of the original structure. One of the world's largest reservoirs, named Lake Nasser, is forming behind the High Dam and will cover 2,000 sq.mi. with 135–160,000m. cubic m of water. The new dam will enable the irrigation of an additional 1.3–2m. acres and the transformation of another *c.* 700,000 acres of partially irrigated land with one crop per year into a permanently irrigated multi-crop area. (This expansion of the irrigated area by 25–30% will not in itself provide a solution to Egypt's problem of overpopulation and limited agricultural lands.) AD is designed to generate about 2m.kw of electricity and thus to contribute significantly to Egypt's further industrialization. The capital invested in the project is variously estimated at $960–1,500m.

The High Dam was the subject of an international political crisis in 1956. Following the arms agreement between Egypt and the Soviet Bloc in 1955, the USA and the International Bank cancelled plans to extend financial aid for its construction. Egypt responded by nationalizing the Suez Canal, declaring that its profits would be used to support the project. This led to the Suez War of 1956. The USSR has advanced credits of 1,300m. rubles (*c.* $320m.) since 1958. Soviet experts, engineers and technicians participated in the design of the High Dam and its construction, using mainly Soviet equipment. Work began in 1960 and was completed in 1970. The reservoir began filling in 1967; power generation was started in 1968 and full capacity was reached in 1970. The dam was formally opened in January 1971. Lake Nasser will flood agricultural land and villages with a population of 100,000 (half of it in Sudan). The displaced villagers are being resettled and Egypt is paying compensation to Sudan. Sites of several ancient Egyptian monuments are being inundated by the new reservoir, including that of the famous temple of Abu Simbel. The temple has been lifted to a higher location, at tremendous cost, with the aid of contributions from many international organizations.

The High Dam and its storage-lake are liable to have negative side-effects, such as an increase in the incidence of Bilharzia in the region of the lake; the danger that, in the absence of the silt annually deposited by the Nile before the dam was erected, Egypt's coastline might recede, the sea seep in, and soil salinity near the coast increase; stronger erosion along the river is also feared (counter-measures are being planned). A sharp diminution of fish catches in the Mediterranean is already noticeable. It is too soon fully to evaluate the effects—both positive and negative—of the High Dam. (Y. S.)

The "High Dam" at Aswan under construction

ATASSI, AL-. A large Syrian land-owning family which provided many leaders of modern Syria. It is centred in Homs. When parliamentary government and political parties were permitted, members of the A. family were often in opposition to the main stream of the nationalist movement. In the 1940s and '50s they were among the founders and leaders of the "People's Party" (*Hizb al-Sha'b*).

The following were prominent members of the family: Hashem al-A. and Nur-ul-Din al-A., both Presidents of Syria—see entries below; Feisal al-A.— one of the leaders of the officers' coup which overthrew Adib Shishakli▷ in February 1954; Feidi al-A. and 'Adnan al-A.—both among the leaders of the "People's Party" and ministers in several governments during the 1950s; and Colonel Louai al-A.—Chief of Staff and President of the Revolutionary Council, Mar.–July 1963. (A. L.–O. T.)

ATASSI-, AL-, HASHEM (1874(?)–1960). Syrian politician. President of Syria 1936–9, 1950–1, 1954–5. Educated in Istanbul, A. served as district governor under the Ottoman regime. In 1920 he was chairman of the nationalist "Syrian Congress" and for a short time Prime Minister of King Feisal's▷ government in Damascus. During the French Mandate he was one of the leaders of the "National Bloc" which fought for Syrian independence. A. headed the delegation which signed the Franco-Syrian treaty of 1936 (which was not implemented) and became President of Syria, 1936-9. In autumn 1949, after Hinnawi's▷ coup, he became Prime Minister, and in Dec. 1949, following the coup of Adib Shishakli▷, President, but his actual powers were limited under Shishakli. After a long struggle between the politicians and the dictator, A. resigned in 1951 and worked towards the overthrow of Shishakli. Following Shishakli's fall, he returned to the presidency in 1954 and served until Sept. 1955, when he resigned.   (A. L.-O. T.)

*ATASSI, AL-, NUR-UL-DIN. Syrian politician (b. 1923? 1929? in Homs). President of Syria 1966-70. Doctor of Medicine (University of Damascus). Following the 1963 coup of officers close to the Ba'th▷ group, he was a member of the Revolutionary Council. In 1964 he became a member of the Presidential Council and Deputy Prime Minister. He was appointed President of Syria following the February 1966 coup of the extremist faction of the Ba'th officers. In October 1966 he was also made Secretary-General of both the "national" (i.e. all-Arab) and the "regional" (Syrian) commands of the Ba'th party (i.e. of the faction then ruling in Syria). From October 1968 he also served as Prime Minister. In the struggle between the factions of Hafez Asad▷ and Salah Jadid▷, A. was close to the latter, but tried to mediate between the rivals. In Asad's semi-coup of February-March 1969, A. retained his post, as part of a compromise settlement. But when Asad took full control of the government in November 1970, A. was dismissed from all his posts (President, Prime Minister and Secretary-General and was imprisoned.   (A.L.-O.T.)

ATATÜRK, MUSTAFA KEMAL (1881-1938). Founder and first President of the Turkish Republic. Born in Salonika. M.K. graduated from the Military Academy in Istanbul in 1905, and served in Syria, Macedonia and Tripolitania. After a brief spell as military attaché in Sofia, he distinguished himself in World War I in the Dardanelles▷, and on the Caucasian and Palestinian fronts. Initially, he had supported the Young Turks▷ and taken part in their conspiracies, but after the 1908 revolution he gradually became disenchanted with their policies. After the Armistice of Mudros, 1918, he was recalled from Syria to Istanbul and subsequently appointed Inspector of the Ninth Army in Erzurum. In May 1919 he began to organize in Anatolia nationalist resistance to Allied plans for the dismemberment of Turkey. He convened the two nationalist congresses of Erzu-

rum and Sivas, 1919, as well as the Grand National Assembly in Ankara, 1920. M.K. led the nationalists, in their struggle against both the Allies and the Ottoman Sultan's government, to final victory in the War of Independence and the proclamation of the Turkish Republic, 1923. He was elected the first President of the Republic and served in this office until his death in 1938. During this period A.— the surname he chose in 1935—was closely identified with the development of the Republic. Having achieved Turkey's independence, he embarked upon an ambitious programme of transforming the country into a modern, westernized, secular state (see Turkey▷, Political History). A. became a model for the leaders of many developing countries. His personality and ideas (Kemalism) still play a very important part in Turkish politics.   (D.K.)

Atatürk

ATRASH, AL-. Clan of traditional leaders of the Druzes▷ in the region of Jabal al-Druze (the Druze Mountain) in south-east Syria. According to one tradition the family is of Kurdish origin. It lived in the al-Jawf area in the Lebanon and moved to Jabal al-Druze in the 1860s. The heads of the clan were semifeudal *de facto* rulers; in addition, they were sometimes appointed governor. Thus, Salim-al-Atrash was appointed governor by the French in 1921.

Prominent in the last generation were: Sultan al-Atrash (born *c.* 1891); he was close to Amir Feisal▷

and later to his brother 'Abdullah▷, ruler of Trans-jordan, and supported the latter's "Greater Syria"▷ scheme; in 1925 he headed the Druze revolt (see Syria▷, Political History) as a result of which he spent ten years of exile in Transjordan. He returned to Syria in 1937 and since then has not been active in political affairs. He is still highly respected as a leader. Reports early in 1954, that he was about to be detained, caused an uprising which led to the fall of the dictator Shishakli▷.

His brother Zeid al-Atrash (born c. 1900) was also active in the 1925 revolt. Hassan al-Atrash (born 1908), who carries the title "Amir", was a Member of Parliament several times, a district governor (includ-ing the district of Jabal al-Druze, 1937–42), and a minister in several governments in independent Syria. He is no longer active since groups of left-wing offi-cers rose to power; but he has been suspected and put on trial several times for allegedly plotting to over-throw the regime—the last time in summer 1970 (he had been kidnapped in 1968 from his exile in Jordan).

Other well-known members of the family are Farid al-Atrash (born 1916), a popular singer and the composer of hit songs, and his sister Amal al-Atrash, known as Ismahan (1917–44), a singer and movie-star who was killed in Cairo in a mysterious accident (as she was involved in high society intrigues, there was suspicion of murder). It may be assumed that due to social and political changes in Syria the Atrash family has lost much of its status and influence.

(Y.S.)

*'AWADULLAH, ABU-BAKR (b. 1917).
Sudanese jurist and politician. Educated at Gordon College Law School, Khartoum. Held several posi-tions as judge. Elected to Sudan's first parliament, 1954, as a member of the National Unionist Party. Speaker 1954–7. Appointed judge of the Supreme Court, in 1957, he later became its President. Resigned in 1967 in protest against a ban imposed on the Com-munist Party by the government and endorsed by parliament in spite of the Supreme Court's ruling declaring the ban to be unconstitutional. After the coup of May 1969 he was appointed Prime Minister, Minister of Foreign Affairs and member of the Re-volutionary Council. Resigned the premiership in October 1969—reportedly after his pro-Communist views had brought him into conflict with Gen. Numeiri▷, the Head of the Revolutionary Coun-cil—and became Deputy President of the Revolu-tionary Council and Minister of Foreign Affairs and Justice. Since 1970 he has been Deputy Premier and Minister of Justice. In the pro-Communist coup attempt of July 1971 he remained loyal to Numeiri.

(B.G.)

AYYUBI, AL-, 'ALI JAWDAT (1886–1969).
Iraqi politician. Born in Mosul. A graduate of the Military College of Istanbul, A. served as an officer in the Ottoman Army. He deserted in 1916, and joined the forces of Sharif Hussein's▷ Arab rebellion. During Feisal's rule in Syria 1919–20 he was Governor of Aleppo. He returned to Iraq in 1921, and served as governor of several provinces. A. was Minister of the Interior 1923–4, of Finance 1930–3, Chief of the Royal Household and Private Secretary to King Feisal▷, 1933, Prime Minister 1934–5, Speaker of Parliament 1935, Iraqi Minister in London 1935–7 in Paris 1937–9, Foreign Minister 1939–40. During Rashid 'Ali al Kilani's▷ pro-German regime, 1941, A. left the country, to return after the restoration of the pro-British regime. He was Minister in Washing-ton 1944–8; Senator 1948–9, Foreign Minister 1948–9, Prime Minister 1949–50, Deputy Prime Minister 1953–4, Prime Minister 1957. After General Qas-sem's▷ coup of July 1958 he settled in Lebanon. Al-though A. was among the leaders of the right-wing nationalist *Al-Ikha* party which opposed the Anglo-Iraqi Treaty of 1930, he belonged to the group of conservative, pro-British politicians loyal to the Hashemite dynasty.

(B.G.)

AZERBAIJAN.
Province in north-western Iran, bordering on the Soviet Republic of A. along the Aras▷ River. Strategically situated between eastern Anatolia, Transcaucasia and Iran, A. has served throughout history as a crossroad and a battlefield. A.'s language is Azeri, a Turkish dialect. A. fills most of Iran's grain requirements. When Iran was divided into British and Russian zones of influence—1907, 1941—A. formed part of the Russian zone. In 1941 Soviet troops occupied A. for the duration of the war. In December 1945 the communist Tudeh▷ party, supported by the USSR, whose forces were still in occupation, created two independent republics in A.: A. and Kurdistan▷. These separatist regimes were crushed by the Iranian Army in December 1946, after the withdrawal of Soviet troops (see Iran▷ Political History). The nationalist anti-Western Pre-mier Dr. Mossaddeq▷ later received more support from A. than from any other province. In order to avert future separatist movements, A. was divided into two administrative provinces: East A. (popula-tion, 1966; c. 2.6m., capital: Tabriz) and West A. (population, 1966: c. 1m., capital: Rezaiyeh).

(B.G.)

AZHAR, AL-.
Famous centre for the teaching of Islam, founded in New Cairo in 970 by the Fatimid conquerors of Egypt as a mosque and centre of Shi'i-Isma'ili▷ preaching. Under the Sunni Ayyubids,

Al-Azhar University, Cairo

al-A. was transformed, in the twelfth century, into a Sunni orthodox centre. Since the 16th century al-A. has been regarded as the principal institution of Islamic religious teaching. From the 19th century onwards, several attempts were made—both from inside and outside al-A.—to reform its mediaeval methods of teaching. These attempts reached their peak with "Law 103", passed in 1961, which transformed al-A. into one of the five state universities of Egypt. In 1967/8 it had about 16,000 university-level students (about 3,000 of whom were foreign students), and 65,000 at primary- and secondary-level institutions affiliated to it; al-A. now includes various faculties of secular studies and admits women to its courses. However, its main function has remained that of religious teaching and preaching. Al-A. trains *Qadis*, *Muftis*, *Khatibs*, etc. (*i.e.* Islamic judges and preachers) for many Islamic countries—to a large part on its own or on Egyptian government scholarships—and sends out teachers; it issues legal religious decisions (*Fatwas*) in reply to questions from all over the world, arranges Muslim conferences, publishes and distributes Islamic publications (the best known of which is the monthly *Majallat al-Azhar*), and encourages Islamic missionary work in Africa and the Far East. The 'Ulama' of al-A. deal also with politics; nowadays they tend to co-operate with the government in spite of the latter's interference with the autonomy of the institution and its religious teaching. They issue *Fatwas* against Egypt's enemies (e.g. in 1959 against the communist rulers of Iraq), call for *Jihad*▷ (holy war) against Israel and publish anti-Semitic material, denounce the "Muslim Brotherhood"▷ and propound the doctrines of Islamic socialism.   (H. L.-Y.)

AZHARI, ISMA'IL (1900 or 1902–69). Sudanese politician. Educated at Gordon College, Khartoum; American University, Beirut. Official at the Department of Education of the Sudanese Government 1921–46. In 1938 he organized the "Graduates' General Congress"—the association of graduates of Gordon College and intermediate schools (most of them civil servants) that formed the nucleus of the nationalist movement in Sudan. He himself became secretary of the "GGC", In 1943, A. organized the first political party in Sudan, the *Ashiqa'* (Brothers). He and his group favoured union with Egypt, collaborating with the *Khatmiyya*▷ order. In 1952, various "Unionist" factions merged in the National Unionist Party and A. became its president. His party won the 1953 elections, during the transition period towards self-rule, and in January 1954, A. became his country's first Prime Minister, holding office till July 1956. Although in principle favouring union with Egypt, his government led Sudan, in 1955, to independence. In 1956, he lost his parliamentary majority and, until the fall of the parliamentary regime in 1958, became leader of the opposition. In 1961–2 he was detained by General 'Abbud's▷ military regime. A. played a part in the 1964 coup which restored civilian-political government. In 1965 he was elected a member, and later, permanent Chairman of the Presidential Council, a post he held till the coup of May 1969. After the coup he remained under house arrest until his death in August 1969.   (B. G.)

Isma'il al-Azhari

'AZM, AL-, KHALED (1900–1965). Syrian politician. Son of a wealthy family of Damascus notables which dominated the city in the 18th century. 'A. did not belong to the "National Bloc", the nationalist party which led Syria to independence and governed the country in the immediately ensuing period. He was an independent, and sometimes formed short-lived parliamentary parties. He was a minister in many governments and several times Prime Minister—in 1941–2 under the Vichy regime, 1948–9 (until the coup of Husni Za'im▷), 1949–50 and 1951. In 1955-7 he served as Minister of Defence, Finance and Deputy Prime Minister. Although a wealthy industrialist, he actively fostered close ties between Syria and the Soviet Union. Following the union of Syria and Egypt (1958) he ceased all political activity. After Syria's secession from the UAR (1961), 'A. became once more Prime Minister, in 1962–3; he was overthrown by the March 1963 coup of the Ba'th officers. He went into exile in Lebanon where he died.   (A.L.-O.T.)

'AZMA, YUSSUF. Syrian politician. Member of a Damascus family of notables. In 1920, 'A. was Minister of War in Amir Feisal's▷ government in Damascus. When, the French Army advanced on Damascus from Lebanon, following an ultimatum, he organized and commanded an Arab force of soldiers and volunteers which resisted the French at the Meithalun (Maisalun) Pass. The force was defeated and largely annihilated, and 'A. was killed in the battle. After his death he became a national hero and a symbol of the resistance against the French. Meithalun Day, 26 July, is a day of national mourning in Syria.

Other members of the 'Azma family were also active in the nationalist movement and held various governmental positions in Syria (e.g. Nabih al-'Azma —active in Pan-Arab nationalist organizations; 'Adel al-'Azma (died 1952)—Minister in 1948–9; Bashir al-'Azma—Prime Minister in 1962).   (A.L.-O.T.)

'AZOURI, NAJIB. Arab nationalist journalist and writer. A Lebanese of Greek-Catholic faith. At the beginning of the century, 'A. served in the Ottoman administration of the Jerusalem district. In 1904 he founded a "Livre de la Patrie Arabe" in Paris, which apparently received French support and published pamphlets calling for Arab independence and unity. In 1907–8 he also published a French monthly, "Indépendance Arabe". 'A. became well known after he published (in French) his book "The Awakening of the Arab Nation in Turkey and Asia" (Paris, 1905), in which he advocated independence for the Arabs in Asia (not including Egypt) and secession from the Ottoman Empire. He proposed establishing a Muslim spiritual caliphate in Mecca,

entrusted to the Hashemite sharifs. His willingness to break away from the Ottoman Empire and his conception of a caliphate modelled after the Christian-Catholic papacy may be explained by the fact that he was a Christian. He died in Cairo in 1916.   (Y.P.)

'AZZAM, 'ABD-UL-RAHMAN (b. 1893). Egyptian diplomat and politician. Studied medicine in London. From his youth active in the Arab nationalist movement. 'A. fought against the Italians in Libya before World War I. Member of the Egyptian parliament, 1924–36. One of the first protagonists of an active Pan-Arab policy for Egypt, he publicized the Pan-Arab idea from 1932 onward. 'A. served in the Egyptian diplomatic corps 1936–45, in Iraq, Sa-'udia, Turkey, Iran and Afghanistan. In 1939 'A. was Minister of Waqf (religious endowments) in the government of 'Ali Maher▷. In 1945, with the establishment of the Arab League▷, 'A. became its Secretary-General, until 1952. Since 1952 'A. has not been politically active.   (S. L.)

B

BAB AL-MANDEB (Arabic: Gate of Tears). Straits connecting the Red Sea and the Indian Ocean, of great strategic importance (as long as the Suez Canal is open and the Red Sea a main thoroughfare from the Mediterranean to the East). Perim Island▷ divides the Straits into an eastern channel—shallow and 2.2 mi. wide, and a western channel—deeper and 17.4 mi. wide. The Straits are bordered by South Yemen and Yemen on the Arabian side, and by Somali and Ethiopia on the African. They were controlled, since 1851, by Britain, through her possession of Perim. Gaining control of part of the eastern coast and Perim in 1967, the new People's Republic of South Yemen threatened to prevent the passage of Israel ships through the Straits. Palestinian-Arab guerillas shelled an Israel-bound oil tanker in June 1971.   (Y.A.O.)

BABISM—see Baha'is▷.

*BADR, AL-, MUHAMMAD (b. 1927). Imam of Yemen (head of the Zeidi▷ sect and ruler of the state) since 1962. Eldest son of Imam Ahmad▷ b. Yahya. Though not having much of a military reputation, Prince al-B. was the only member of the royal Hamid-ul-Din family who succeeded in organizing the northern tribes of Bakil and Hashid to save his father's throne during the rebellion of 1955. Thereafter he had greater power. He visited Russia (1956) and China (1958) as his father's representative, and

Muhammad al-Badr

BAGHDAD. Capital of Iraq, and of B. province. Founded by the 'Abbasid Khalif al-Mansur in 762 CE. Situated on the Tigris at its minimum distance from the Euphrates (22 mi.) Greater B. has a population of 1.95m. (1968), mostly Sunni and Shi'i Arabs, with considerable minorities of Kurds, various Christian sects, Shi'i Iranians, and c. 2,000 Jews. B. is Iraq's main communications centre, its rail and road hub (see B. Railway▷) and the site of its major international airport. Various colleges founded since the 1920s were incorporated in 1956 in the University of B. (U.D.)

BAGHDAD PACT. Unofficial name for the defence treaty ("Pact of Mutual Co-operation") concluded between Iraq and Turkey on 24 Feb. 1955. It was preceded by an agreement between Turkey and Pakistan, 2 Apr. 1954 and bilateral military aid agreements between the USA and Turkey (a member of NATO since 1951), Iraq, April 1954 and Pakistan, May 1954. Britain, Pakistan and Iran also joined the P. in 1955. It was the cornerstone of Western, particularly American plans for a ME Defence Treaty▷. Although overtures for such a defence arrangement were rebuffed by Egypt and other Arab states in 1951, negotiations were resumed in 1953–4; they now emphasized defence of the "Northern Tier"▷ (Turkey-Iran-Pakistan) with Iraq as the connecting link to the Arab countries. Although the USA provided the major support for this arrangement, participating in the various committees and providing most of the finance, she never formally joined the B.P. The treaty was denounced by Egypt as introducing great-power rivalries and the "cold war" into the ME, dividing the Arab world and threatening Egypt with encirclement. Egypt began the creation of a counter-alliance, and the division of Arab states into rival camps hardened. Apprehensions aroused by the P. played a major role in the gradual alienation of Egypt and her allies from

Aerial view of Baghdad, in the centre the al-Kadhimain Mosque

acted as Imam during his father's absence in 1959. In 1961 Imam Ahmad appointed B. Crown Prince and compelled the other princes to recognize him as the next Imam. On the death of his father, in September 1962, B. became Imam. Though considered a liberal, possibly even pro-Nasserist, he was overthrown a week later by an officers' revolt. For a few days B. was thought to have been killed, but in early October he appeared in the northern mountains and soon managed to rally various tribes, to lead them into war against the Republic proclaimed in San'a and to retain control over parts of Yemen (see Yemen▷, History). A sick man, Imam al-B. was forced to go for a cure to al-Ta'if in Sa'udi Arabia. In the critical period of November 1966–September 1968 he was out of Yemen. His power within the Royalist camp was reduced late in 1966, when an "Imamate Council" was formed under Prince Muhammad b. Hussein; however, al-B. resumed power early in 1969, following Prince Muhammad's failure to take San'a. The Royalist-Republican reconciliation of 1970 bypassed him, as it appeared to be based on the acceptance of a Republican regime and the permanent exclusion of the Hamid-ul-Din family; but al-B. has not renounced his claims and titles. He lives in exile in London. (H.E.)

the West, culminating in their *entente* with the Soviet Bloc in 1955–6. The P., therefore, failed in its major purpose: to erect a barrier against Soviet penetration. Iraq's anti-Western government, following the Qassem▷ revolution of July 1958, formally withdrew from the agreement in March 1959. The resultant rump alliance, renamed in 1959 Central Treaty Organization (CENTO▷), stressed economic and social co-operation and gradually lost much of its political and military significance.   (Y.S.)

BAGHDAD RAILWAY. A project for the extension of the Anatolian Railway to Baghdad and the Persian Gulf. Sultan Abdülhamid II granted its concession to the Deutsche Bank and the German-Anatolian Railway Company in 1899. The project formed part of the Ottoman government's policy of improving communications within its Empire. It was an object of rivalry between German, French and British companies. The newly formed Baghdad Railway Company, in which German interests predominated, was granted a final and definite concession in 1903. Britain, France and Russia, afraid of a strengthened Germany and fearing for their own interests, remained hostile to the project. Ultimately they reached agreements with Germany. Britain, the principal objector, stipulated in agreements concluded with the Ottoman Empire and Germany in 1911–14 that the lines should not extend beyond Basra to the Persian Gulf. The concession led to a great deal of diplomatic activity and several minor international crises over a period of 15 years. The construction of the line itself was hampered by technical and financial difficulties. By 1917 it had been completed from Istanbul to Nuseibin (on what later became the Turkish-Syrian frontier) and, in the south, from Baghdad to Samarra; the Nuseibin-Mosul-Samarra gap, c. 300 mi., was closed only in 1939–40, and the first train set out from Istanbul to Baghdad in July 1940.   (D.K.)

BAHA'IS. Baha'ism is an eclectic religion founded in Persia in 1862, by Mirza Hussein 'Ali, "Baha'ullah". It originally grew out of Babism, one of the sectarian deviations of Shi'ite Islam, whose founder, 'Ali Muhammad of Shiraz, "Bab-ul-Din" or "The Bab"—"The Gate" (or forerunner) of the Faith—foretold his mission in 1843. The principles of Baha'ism stress the "unity of all religions, world peace and universal education".

The B. faith and community were sometimes banned and persecuted in Persia and other Islamic countries. Their spiritual leadership is composed of a body of nine "Hands", called the Universal House of Justice. The main holy places are in Haifa (Tomb

The Baha'i Temple in Haifa

of the Bab) and in Bahji, near Acre (site of the Tomb of Baha'ullah). The B. throughout the world are reported to number approximately 2m. Few of them reside in the ME, where only Persia has a significant number. The B. are now banned in Morocco, Syria, Egypt and, since 1970, Iraq.   (Sh.C.)

BAHJAHJI—see Pachachi▷.

*BAHRAIN. Group of 33 islands in the Persian Gulf between the Qatar Peninsula and the Sa'udi Arabian coast (about 12 mi. from the largest island). Area: 230 sq. mi. The population is concentrated mainly on two islands: Bahrain and Muharraq, which are connected by a causeway. Of the population of 205,000 (1969 estimate), 90,000 are in the town of Manama, the capital, and 37,000 in the town of Muharraq.

B. Island was settled in ancient times, because of its springs and oases. In the mediaeval period, it was known for its pearls. After some decades of Portuguese rule, the islands were ruled intermittently by Persia (1602–1782), which claims sovereignty over them. Since 1783, they are ruled by an Arab sheikh from the house of al-Khalifa. As the result of several nineteenth-century treaties, especially the treaty of 1862, Britain took the islands under her protection, and established a naval and military presence (increased in 1966, prior to the liquidation in 1967 of the British base in Aden). The USA also maintains a small naval flotilla in the Persian Gulf, with headquarters at B. When Britain announced, in 1968, her decision to withdraw her forces and remove her protection from all the territories east of Suez by the end of 1971, Iran, claiming B. for herself, proposed a public opinion poll to be supervised by the Secretary-General of the UN. Such a poll took place in April 1970, and a decisive majority expressed its opinion in favour of independence (and not incorporation in Iran). Iran acquiesced, and independence was proclaimed in Aug. 1971. B. had planned to join a Federation of Arab Principalities (UAE; see Trucial 'Oman▷), but withdrew in 1971.

More self-government and free political organization have been demanded in B. since the 1930s. Attempts to establish elected councils were not entirely successful. In the 1950s and '60s such demands were renewed, and the ruling Sheikh established advisory bodies for education, health, etc. However, there are so far no representative government or elected councils.

The economy of B. is based mainly on oil. An American company discovered oil in 1932 and started production in 1933. It increased to 1.5m. tons by 1950, 3.8m. annually since 1968. B.'s oil refinery is the second largest in the Middle East; built in 1936, its production increased to 12m. tons by 1968. Most of the crude oil is brought from Sa'udi Arabia by two pipelines, 34 mi. long, 9 miles under sea). The B. Islands are an important commercial centre. Manama serves as free port for the entire Persian Gulf and has an international airport. A new port and dockyard were built in Mina Suleiman, not far from Manama. A plan to build an aluminium refinery is based on natural gas.   (Y.K.)

*BAKDASH, KHALED (b. 1912). Syrian politician. Leader of the Communist Party; called the Arab Communist Number One. Born in Damascus, member of a Kurdish notable family, studied law at the University of Damascus. Active since 1930 in the underground Communist Party, since 1936 its Secretary-General. During the French Mandate, he was sentenced to imprisonment. B. went as an exile to the USSR, and studied at the Communist International High School. He was a Member of Parliament 1954–8 and the first Communist member of any Arab parliament. Since his party was illegal, he campaigned as an independent. In 1957–8 B. opposed Syria's union with Egypt (considered by many as designed to counteract the growing Communist influence in Syria). On the establishment of that union (the UAR▷) in 1958, B. went into exile in Eastern Europe. He remained faithful to Moscow's fluctuating party-lines as exemplified for instance in the co-operation of Communist parties with non-Communist nationalist leaders. His articles and speeches were regarded as authoritative. He returned to Syria in 1966 and has since collaborated with the Ba'th regime, although the Communist Party is technically illegal in Syria. In 1968 he resigned as Party Secretary-General for reasons of health, but was later re-elected.   (A.L.-O.T.)

BAKHTIARIS. One of the great nomadic tribes of south Iran, between Shustar and Isfahan. The tribe numbers c. 350,000, most of whom have become sedentary, especially since the discovery of oil in the area. Ethnically the B. are thought to be akin to the Kurds; they speak the Luri dialect of Persian and are Shi'ite Muslims. The B. have often been influential in Iranian politics. They played a decisive part in the revolution which led to the granting of the Constitution in 1909. Their chiefs have frequently held prominent public office. Muhammad Reza Shah's▷ former wife, Soraya Isfandiari, is the daughter of a B. leader. In the past the B. tribes enjoyed a wide autonomy, and Iranian sovereignty was frequently only nominal. They were in close contact with the British, then dominating the Persian Gulf area, and the latter were often suspected of encouraging B. autonomist or even separatist tendencies. B. autonomy was, however, suppressed by Reza Shah in the 1920s.   (B.G.)

BAKR, AL-, AHMAD HASSAN (b. 1914). Iraqi Army officer and politician. One of the "Free Officers" who plotted the 1958 revolution, B. was among the first to quarrel with Qassem▷, the new ruler, and to be removed from the army, because he favoured union with the UAR. He was one of the main planners of Qassem's overthrow in February 1963 and served as Prime Minister in the 1963 Ba'th▷ government. After the dismissal of the Ba'th by President 'Aref▷, in November 1963, he continued to hold office for several additional weeks as Deputy Premier. He possibly never became a formal member of the Ba'th party, but was in sympathy with its right wing and in close contact with its civilian members. From 1965, if not earlier, his relations with the 'Aref brothers were strained. On 17 July 1968, he succeeded in toppling President 'Abd-ul-Rahman 'Aref▷, in co-operation with army officers, such as 'Abd-ul-Razzaq al-Nayef, who held operational key appointments. B. then became President of the Republic. On 30 July, Nayef and his group were in their turn ousted, and B. assumed the premiership and the supreme command of the armed forces, in addition to the presidency. He is also Chairman of the Revolutionary Command Council. B. has so far closely co-operated with the rightist, anti-Damascus, wing of the Ba'th party, headed in Iraq by Saleh Mahdi 'Ammash▷ and Sadam Hussein al-Tikriti, the Ba'th Secretary-General. But it is doubtful to what extent the party exercises real influence; it may simply provide an ideological façade. Though the political bases of B.'s regime is exceedingly narrow, he has scored a success by signing the Kurdish agreement of 11 March 1970 (which is not yet fully implemented).

The agreements' implementation and practical consequences are still in doubt.   (U.D.)

BALFOUR DECLARATION. A statement due mainly to Professor Chaim Weizmann's▷ efforts made on behalf of the British government by its Foreign Secretary, Arthur J. Balfour, on 2 Nov. 1917, in a letter conveyed to the Zionist Organization through Lord Rothschild. The statement was designed to ensure Palestine for Britain in the event of the collapse of the Ottoman Empire. The Suez Canal and the route to India would thereby be protected (though according to the Sykes-Picot▷ agreement of 1916, Palestine was to remain under international control): "His Majesty's Government view with favour the establishment in Palestine of a national home for the Jewish people, and will use their best endeavours to facilitate the achievement of this object, it being clearly understood that nothing shall be done which may prejudice the civil and religious rights of existing non-Jewish communities in Palestine, or the rights and political status enjoyed by Jews in any other country."

An alliance with the Zionist movement, suggested by Sir Herbert Samuel, was considered advantageous by British statesmen who hoped also that American Jews might influence the USA to enter the war, and Russian Jews prevail upon the Bolsheviks to remain in it, particularly as it was feared that the Germans might make a similar declaration.

The Declaration was made in spite of heavy opposition and was considered a great Zionist victory though it did not promise a Jewish state. Arab spokesmen condemned it on the ground that Britain was promising the Jews a land which had earlier been promised the Arabs (whether it had been promised remained controversial—see McMahon-Hussein Correspondence▷). The declaration was included in the text of the Mandate for Palestine of 24 July 1922. The Zionist leadership maintained that Britain failed to fulfil its obligations under the Declaration and the Mandate. The Mandate Commission of the League of Nations was also frequently critical of Britain's discharge of these obligations.   (Sh.H.)

BALKAN PACT. a. Treaty signed in Athens on 9 Feb. 1934, by Turkey, Greece, Rumania and Yugoslavia. The four states mutually guaranteed the security of their Balkan frontiers and agreed not to take action with or against any Balkan non-signatory without previous consultation. The treaty reflected the *rapprochement* among the Balkan states in the face of the growing menace of Fascism and Nazism.

b. Turkey, Greece and Yugoslavia signed another B.P. on 9 Aug. 1954, in Bled (Yugoslavia). This was a Treaty of Alliance, Political Co-operation and Mutual Assistance. It was an extension into a military defence pact of a Treaty of Friendship and Co-operation, which the three states had signed in Feb. 1953. Valid for 20 years, the BP stipulated that aggression against one or more of its signatories would be considered as aggression against all of them, and that in such a case all necessary assistance, including the use of force, would be given by the other parties. It created a permanent council composed of the foreign ministers and members of the cabinets of the parties, to convene twice a year. The P. was encouraged by the Western powers which saw it as an effective barrier against Soviet expansion southwards, and as a means of tying Yugoslavia to the West's defence alliance. Following the reduction of world tension, the Greco-Turkish rivalry over Cyprus, and the *rapprochement* between Yugoslavia and the USSR, the treaty lost its significance. Its provisions have, after some initial moves, not been implemented.   (D.K.)

BALKAN WARS. a. The first B.W. broke out in October 1912, when Montenegro, Greece, Serbia and Bulgaria (the B. League) attacked the Ottoman Empire in order to gain control of Macedonia. After suffering heavy reverses, the Turks ceded most of their European possessions, agreeing in the Peace Treaty of London, January 1913, to the Midye-Enez line in Thrace as the border, leaving as European Turkey only Istanbul and a narrow strip along the Straits.

b. The second B.W. broke out after the allies of the first failed to reach agreement on the division of the areas conquered. In June 1913, Bulgaria, coveting Salonika and other portions of Macedonia, attacked Serbia and Greece which were soon joined by Montenegro, Rumania and the Ottoman Empire. After Bulgarian losses, peace was made in Bucharest in August, leaving Greece and Serbia with the larger part of Macedonia. The Ottoman Empire, by a separate Treaty signed in Istanbul in September, regained most of Thrace, including Adrianople (Edirne).

The B.W. were instrumental in bringing both the Ottoman Empire and Bulgaria (bitter because of their defeat and loss of territories) on to the side of the Central Powers in World War I.   (D.K.)

BANDUNG CONFERENCE. In April 1955 the first conference of the independent states of Asia and Africa convened in Bandung, Indonesia. Its leading initiators were the prime ministers of India, Pakistan, Indonesia, Burma and Ceylon—Jawaharlal Nehru, Muhammad 'Ali, 'Ali Sastroamidjojo, U Nu, and Sir John Kotelawala. High-ranking delegations from

29 countries took part—23 from Asia and six from Africa (nine of them were Arab states— six from Asia, three from Africa). They included all the then independent Asian and African nations, except Israel and Korea who were not invited; Nationalist China (Taiwan-Formosa), which would not participate in a congress recognizing the People's Republic of China as representing China; the Asian states of the USSR, and Mongolia. Both South and North Vietnam participated. The sponsors of the BC, led by Nehru and U Nu, wished to invite Israel in order to assure the universality of the conference, but when the Arab representatives threatened to boycott it if Israel were invited, its initiators capitulated.

The BC began with the boycott of an independent Asian nation because of political pressure. Yet it was thought to mark a new era, the abolition of colonialism and the appearance of hitherto oppressed nations on the stage of history. The conference did not discuss disputed political issues; but it solemnly endorsed the "Five Principles" (*Panch Sila*) formulated by Nehru (in his joint statement with the Prime Minister of China, Chou En-lai, June 1954): 1. "Mutual respect for territorial integrity and sovereignty" of all states; 2. "non-aggression"; 3. "non-interference in the internal affairs" of another state; 4. "equality and mutual benefit"; 5. "peaceful co-existence". The trend of the BC, although the participating states had various political orientations and no binding decisions were taken, was towards non-identification and neutralism▷. The conference's resolution called for economic and cultural co-operation, and declared its support for the principles of human rights and self-determination, the abolition of colonialism, and world peace; it expressed support for the "Rights of the Arab People of Palestine" and called for the implementation of a UN resolution on Palestine and a peaceful solution; it also supported Yemen's position on Aden and the "Southern parts of Yemen known as the Protectorate" and urged the parties to arrive at a peaceful settlement of the dispute.

The People's Republic of China appeared for the first time, at the BC, in a major international assembly, and her Prime Minister, Chou En-lai, made many important contacts that assisted the creation of China's network of international relations. This was also the first appearance of Gamal 'Abd-ul-Nasser▷, Prime Minister (later President) of Egypt, among world leaders. Nasser's attendance at Bandung is often regarded as marking the beginning of a more activist Egyptian foreign policy.

Attempts to organize the family of Asian and African nations in a permanent body, or at least to convene more conferences of its leaders, have not succeeded. A second BC was planned, dates were set, but did not ensue. On the other hand, many non-governmental Afro-Asian organizations have been formed (see Asia▷, Africa▷).   (Y.S.)

BANIYAS. One of the main sources of the Jordan▷. The spring yields *c.* 120m. cubic metres (mcm) of water *p.a.*: in its course, the brook, sometimes called the Hermon Brook, carries *c.* 150 mcm. The spring issues from a cleft in a rock about 1.24 miles east of the border between Mandated Palestine and Syria, in the area administered since 1967 by Israel. In 1964–7 the Arab states planned to divert the sources of the Jordan from Israel (see Jordan▷ River). The B. would have been diverted southward, along the slope of the Golan hills to the Yarmuk River, and utilised in the Jordanian reservoir and development project. Work was actually begun; it was disturbed several times by military action, brought to a standstill and finally, in 1967, discontinued.   (Y.K.)

BANIYAS. Port city in north-west Syria between Lataqia (Al-Ladhiqiyya) and Tartus, serving since 1952 as the outlet of the oil pipeline from Kirkuk, in Iraq. An oil harbour was built by the Iraq Petroleum Company (IPC); in 1968, 29.5m. tons of oil were loaded.   (A.L.-O.T.)

The Baniyas waterfall

BANNA, AL-, HASSAN (1906–1949). Founder and leader of the "Muslim Brotherhood"▷ in Egypt. Born in Isma'iliyya to a pious Muslim family, he served as a teacher of Islam both in his birthplace and in Cairo. In April 1929 he founded the fanatic, conservative "Muslim Brotherhood" organization in Isma'iliyya. His simple doctrine and frugal way of life earned him sympathy and support. On 12 Feb. 1949 he was assassinated in revenge for the murder of Prime Minister Nuqrashi▷ by his "Muslim Brotherhood". The "Brotherhood" did not find another leader as powerful and able to unify them.   (O.G.)

BARAZI, AL-, DR. MUHSIN (executed 1949). Syrian politician. Member of a landowning family of Kurdish origin from Hama (of which Husni al-Barazi, Prime Minister of Syria in 1942, is also a member). B. served as minister in several cabinets in 1941–2 and 1947–8. Before Husni Za'im's▷ coup (March 1949) he was President Quwwatli's▷ personal assistant and speech-writer. In 1949 he served for a short time as Syrian Minister in Cairo. In June 1949, after Za'im was elected President, B. was appointed Prime Minister. At the time of Sami Hinnawi's▷ coup, August 1949, he was arrested, together with Za'im, tried by a military court, sentenced to death and executed. His cousin later killed Hinnawi in revenge.   (A.L.-O.T.)

***BAR-LEV LINE.** Unofficial name of system of Israeli fortresses erected at the Suez Canal between October 1968 and March 1969, as a means of defence in the Egyptian "war of attrition" launched in breach of the June 1967 cease-fire.   (E.L.)

***BARZANI** (or **BARZANI**). Originally a branch of the Sunni-Muslim Naqshabandi religious order, the B. assumed the characteristics of a secular Kurdish tribe about 100 years ago; their centre is the village of Barzan, about 50 miles north of Erbil in Iraq. The sheikhs were usually engaged in violent conflict with the authorities even in Ottoman times. Since 1915 the formal head of the community was Sheikh Ahmad B. (died 1969), a religious eccentric; in the 1930s and early '40s he was identified with the Kurdish rebel leaders, but managed to remain unattached during the political strife of the last 25 years.

Sheikh Ahmad's younger brother Mulla Mustafa B., born c. 1902, became the leader of the Kurdish national struggle in Iraq during the late 1930s. He has maintained this position throughout the vicissitudes of the Kurdish War which began in 1961. In 1946 Mulla Mustafa commanded the army of the Kurdish Mahabad▷ Republic in Iran. After its collapse he escaped with his followers to the USSR,

Mulla Mustafa Barazani (at centre) with bodyguards

where he stayed until permitted to return to Iraq after the 1958 revolution. He lived in Baghdad, which he was not allowed to leave, until late 1960 when he escaped to the Kurdish areas and resumed the rebellion. In the abortive agreement of 1966, and that of 1970, with the Iraq government he achieved—at least formally—many of his aims. Though his leadership is essentially of a traditional and tribal type, he formally heads the modernist-socialist "Kurdish Democratic Party". He was opposed by a rival wing, headed by Jalal Talabani; but after the Kurdish-Iraqi agreement of 1970 this opposing faction dissolved itself and accepted Mulla Mustafa's leadership.   (U.D.)

***BASES, FOREIGN MILITARY.** The right to maintain military forces and permanent MB in the countries of the ME was for many years an important policy aim of all the powers. It was to be attained either forcibly, through colonial or semi-colonial occupation (as usual till World War I), or by agreement of the host country (as preferred since World War I; see Imperialism▷). In the Ottoman Empire▷, till its fall in 1918, no power had such rights. The British maintained forces and MB in Egypt (since 1882), and in Cyprus (since 1878); the Italians in Libya (since 1912). The British had also a MB in Aden, and military privileges in the principalities of the Persian Gulf. In Iran, Russian and British forces sometimes operated as they saw fit without Iranian agreement; however, there were no permanent MB there.

The main FMB were developed between the two world wars. The Italians maintained their MB in Libya, the British theirs in Egypt (mainly in the Suez Canal Zone and Alexandria harbour), Cyprus, Aden and the Persian Gulf; they also obtained new privileges to keep forces and bases in Iraq, Palestine and

Transjordan. Britain's military presence received the approval of the host state in Iraq (treaty of 1930), Egypt (treaty of 1936), and in Transjordan (treaties of 1928, 1946, and 1948). The French maintained forces and MB, since 1920, in Syria and Lebanon. However, attempts to sanction this presence by agreements (in 1936) failed. The USA and Russia did not establish a military presence in the area.

During World War II Britain's military presence became stronger; France's was weakened by her defeat in 1940, but was re-established under British protection in 1941, through the occupation of Syria and Lebanon by British and Free French forces. Italy was expelled from Libya and in her place Britain and France established a temporary military presence. Russia sent forces to Iran (1941–6), and the US established a modest auxiliary military presence (transport, aviation, etc.) in Iran and the Persian Gulf area.

Since World War II most MB in the region have been abandoned. France was forced to withdraw her forces and bases from Syria and Lebanon in 1945–6. Britain removed her forces from Palestine in 1948, and from Jordan in 1957, without signing new agreements. Her MB in Egypt outside the Suez Canal⊳ Zone were turned over to Egypt in 1947; as to those in the Canal Zone, Britain agreed in 1954 to evacuate them while keeping technicians for their maintenance; their evacuation was completed by 1956 (the agreement to leave technicians was invalidated by Egypt in 1956–7 following the Suez crisis and the British invasion). Both British MB in Iraq—Habbaniya⊳ and Shu'eiba—were relinquished following the 1955 Anglo-Iraqi agreement providing for both countries' adherence to the Baghdad Pact⊳ (Iraq seceded from the Pact in 1959). The British base in Aden⊳ was abandoned in 1967, when independence was granted to South Yemen. Libya had agreed in 1953 to lease to Britain MB (mainly al-'Adhem⊳ and Tobruk⊳), but demanded in 1969 their liquidation; the bases were abandoned in 1970. In Cyprus British forces retained MB (Akrotiri and Dhekelia); according to agreements of 1959–60 they enjoy extra-territorial British sovereignty. Britain also maintains military privileges in the principalities of the Persian Gulf— Bahrain, Muscat-and-'Oman (especially Masira Island), and Trucial 'Oman (especially Sharja⊳); some of these are to be relinquished by the end of 1971, but some staging aviation and maritime rights may be maintained.

The USA obtained after World War II several MB in the region: a base leased by Libya under a 1954 agreement was developed into the major Wheelus Field⊳ air base; following Libya's demand in 1969 it was evacuated and handed over in 1970. In Dhahran⊳ in Sa'udi Arabia, the USA built an air base, completed in 1951; the lease agreement, signed in 1951, terminated in 1961 and the base was returned in 1962; however, the USA continues to enjoy certain aviation privileges. The USA also maintains several naval units in the Persian Gulf, with unofficial headquarters in Bahrain. The USA maintains forces in Turkey, and built MB there, in the framework of both bilateral agreements and of NATO. NATO's Eastern Mediterranean naval headquarters is in Izmir⊳. Most of the MB have been handed back to Turkey except that at Incirlik near Adana—for the most part an air base maintained by the USA on behalf of NATO. The USA maintains major naval contingents in the Mediterranean (the "Sixth Fleet"), but their base is in Southern Europe and not in the ME.

Since the end of the 1950s the Soviet Union maintains considerable naval units in the Mediterranean. The forces she maintains in Egypt and Syria are officially termed "advisors" and instructors. The ports and airfields of Egypt, Syria and Libya, among them Alexandria⊳, Port Sa'id and Mersa Matruh in Egypt and Lataqia⊳ in Syria, are at the disposal of the USSR (at Mersa Matruh, a major Soviet naval base is reported under construction); yet, officially, there is no mention of "MB". Further south, the port and airfields of Yemen, South Yemen and Sudan are also available to the USSR (reports of the construction of a Soviet base on Sokotra Island in the Indian Ocean off South Yemen are so far unconfirmed). As long as the Suez Canal remains closed the military importance of Red Sea ports is limited.   (Y. S.)

BASRA. Second largest city and main port of Iraq, capital of the province bearing its name. Situated on the Shatt al-'Arab⊳ 70 miles from the head of the Persian Gulf. Pop.: 420,000, 1968. An earlier B. was founded soon after the Muslim conquest and flourished in the middle ages. Modern B., built on its site, became important in the 18th century.   (U.D.)

*BA'TH, AL-. (Arabic: Renaissance). Pan-Arab socialist party. It originated in Syria, which has remained the area of its main activities and influence. The B.'s doctrine is radically Pan-Arab; it regards the "regional" parties of the various Arab countries as no more than branches of its "national" all-Arab structure; factional struggles within the party appear sometimes as a contest between the "national", i.e. all-Arab, and the "regional" command. The "national" command was seated, with the regional-Syrian one, in Damascus; but a deep rift occurred between the two in 1966, resulting in the transfer of "national" headquarters to Beirut and Baghdad. The slogan of the B. is "Unity, Freedom, Socialism—One Arab Nation, the Bearer of an Eternal Mission".

The B. was founded by two teachers from Damascus studying in Paris in the mid-1930s: Michel Aflaq▷, who became its chief ideologist, and Salah-ul-Din Bitar▷, later Prime Minister of Syria. The first congress of "The Arab Renaissance Party" (Hizb al-B. al-'Arabi), then a very small group of young men, was held in 1947; in 1949 party members stood—unsuccessfully—in the Syrian elections. In 1953 the party merged with Akram Hourani's▷ "Arab Socialist Party" (al-Hizb al-'Arabi al-Ishtiraki) to become "The Arab Socialist Renaissance Party" (Hizb al-B. al-'Arabi al-Ishtiraki). It played a part in the overthrow of Adib Shishakli's▷ dictatorship in February 1954. It won 15 seats in the 1954 elections, and in the following four years its influence in Syria increased steadily and spread also in Jordan, Lebanon and Iraq. Its attraction for young intellectuals and officers was largely due to its ideology. Unlike most Arab political parties, the B. has always had a well-formulated and systematically expounded political programme: its aims are socialist as well as Pan-Arab nationalist; its slogans are anti-capitalist, anti-imperialist and anti-Zionist; its propaganda towards the non-Arab world stresses the socialist component; its internal Arab propaganda emphasizes Pan-Arab nationalism. The B.'s political influence has been mainly due to its following among army officers; whenever it seized power it was through coups made by army officers.

In 1957, the Syrian B. was one of the main pressure groups pushing Syria towards a union with Egypt and the foundation of the United Arab Republic (UAR▷), 1 Feb. 1958. The B. expected to become the ruling party of the State and its ideological guide; but President Nasser▷ insisted on the dissolution of all parties other than his National Union, and of the B. in particular. His ideology of Arab Nationalism, in the later 1950s, and of Arab Socialism, in the 1960s, was influenced by B. doctrines, but he never admitted this debt and never wavered in his enmity to the B. as a political organization. During the period of the Union, the B. maintained some underground cells, but became almost extinct. Its leaders were gradually eliminated from their state positions of power and influence, and their growing opposition was one of the chief reasons for Syria's secession from the Union in September 1961. They were, however, bitterly disappointed with the new secessionist and anti-socialist regime. Caught in the contradiction between their Pan-Arab unionist doctrine and their secessionist role in 1961, they now advocated a rather looser reunion with Egypt on federal lines.

In March 1963, the B.—thereafter sometimes called (mainly by foreign observers) the Neo-B.—was the principal ideological partner in a new Syrian military coup. In Iraq, 'Abd-ul-Karim Qassem's▷ military regime had been overthrown a month earlier in a military coup led by 'Abd-ul-Salam 'Aref▷ and the Iraqi B. (whose militia imposed a reign of terror). In April 1963, the Syrian and Iraqi B. regimes worked out a new agreement with Egypt for a tripartite federal union. The federation plan remained abortive. In November 1963, the Iraqi B., weakened by bitter factional struggles, was eliminated from the Government, and Ba'thist-unionist Syria became more isolated in the Arab world than ever before.

In Syria the B. has been the ruling party since 1963, but rival factions struggled with, and carried out military coups against, each other. One faction, under the leadership of Gen. Amin al-Hafez▷ (politically and militarily) and Michel 'Aflaq (ideologically), controlled the "national", all-Arab leadership and ruled in Syria until February 1966. It was overthrown in a military coup by the faction based on the Syrian "regional" leadership, headed by Gen. Salah Jadid▷, and appearing more leftist-extremist. That faction soon split, with Jadid and Gen. Hafez Asad▷ heading rival groups engaged in a bitter power struggle; it was won—decisively in November 1970—by Asad. In fact the rival factions provided a doctrinal cloak for rival officers' juntas.

During the 1960s, and particularly after the coup of February 1966, the Syrian B. became increasingly radical: Marxist argumentation and terminology became widespread; Syria became the most openly pro-Soviet Arab state; her attitude towards Israel, both before and after the Six Day War was the most uncompromising and activist of all the Arab states—at any rate verbally and diplomatically. As the "national", Pan-Arab leadership had backed a losing faction in Damascus, the Syrian B. gradually became alienated from the national leadership, centred in Beirut, and "expelled" most of its leaders, including the party's founders 'Aflaq and Bitar. On the other hand, the Iraqi B. expelled its extremist, pro-Syrian faction and remained loyal to the "national" leadership. In July 1968, the Iraqi B. again assumed power—using a military coup and eliminating those coup leaders not subservient to B. party discipline.

The Damascus and Baghdad parties and governments have remained bitterly hostile. While both use the name of the B. party and doctrine, their organizations are completely separate. As Asad believes in closer coordination with Egypt and the other revolutionary Arab states his victory and the removal of Jadid's extreme left-wing group may result in a rapprochement with the Iraqi and all-Arab leadership. Neither of the rival B. factions has much influence outside Syria and Iraq—except for some links with the revolutionaries in power in Libya and South

Yemen, some cells in Lebanon and Jordan, and the Palestinian guerilla and sabotage formations established and maintained by Syria (*Al-Sa'iqa*) and Iraq ("Arab Liberation Front"). (E. B.-Y. S.)

BAYAR, (MAHMUT) CELÂL. Third President of the Turkish Republic 1950–60. Born 1884 in a village near Bursa, B. joined the Young Turks'▷ party and became the head of its Izmir branch. He took part in the resistance movement against the Greek invasion, 1919–22, and became a member of the first Grand National Assembly, 1920. A disciple of Atatürk▷, B. served as Minister of Economy 1932–7, and Prime Minister 1937–9. In 1945 he resigned from the Republican People's Party and in 1946 helped found the opposition Democratic Party. Following his party's victory in the 1950 elections B. was voted President of the Republic, a post which he held until the military revolution of 1960. B. was sentenced to death at the Yassiada trials, 1961; his sentence was commuted to life imprisonment, and he was finally released in 1964. His civic and political rights were restored in 1969. (D.K.)

Celâl Bayar

*BAZZAZ, AL-, DR. 'ABD-UL-RAHMAN (b. 1913). Iraqi lawyer, historian and politician. Sunni Muslim from Baghdad. Dean of Baghdad Law College 1955. A convinced nationalist, he was arrested in 1941 after the flight of Rashid 'Ali▷ for his anti-British and pro-German attitude, again in 1957 for his Nasserist sympathies, and in 1959 for suspected co-operation with Nasserist conspirators against Gen.

Qassem▷. After Qassem's fall, 1963, he became Ambassador to Cairo and London, and Secretary-General of OPEC (the Organization of Petroleum Exporting Countries). In September 1965 President 'Abd-ul-Salam 'Aref▷ appointed him Prime Minister. B. tried earnestly to restore civilian rule in Iraq, and in doing so fell out with the leading officers. He also initiated, in 1966, an agreement with the Kurdish rebels, in which he made far-reaching concessions to the Kurds▷; the agreement was not implemented, and the opposition it aroused contributed to B.'s fall, soon after. The new President, 'Abd-ul-Rahman 'Aref▷, was unable to give him his support, and B. was forced to resign in August 1966. When the Bakr▷ regime took over, after the coup of July 1968, B. was arrested for allegedly plotting treason with the Western Powers. No trial is known to have taken place. He was released late in 1970. (U.D.)

BEDOUIN. Arabic-speaking nomads raising camels, sheep and goats. The term B. (Arabic: *Badawi*, pl. *Badu*) denotes an inhabitant of the desert (Arabic: *Badiyah*). It is used chiefly by the settled population, from whose point of view any area which has no permanent settlement is a wilderness. The B. usually refer to themselves as "Arabs", *i.e.* tribesmen from the Arabian peninsula. All the B. tribes claim descent from the early Arab tribes. There are in the ME camel- and goat-raising tribes which are not Arabic-speaking, like the Qashqai▷ in Iran and the Tuareg in the Sahara; wandering Arabic-speaking tribes which do not raise camels and goats but rather cattle, like the Baqqara in Sudan, and the Ma'adan in Iraq; or groups of nomads who do not raise flocks, like the Sulluba, who are blacksmiths and hunters, and scattered all over the northern part of the Arabian desert. These tribes are not usually considered to be B. In the strict sense of the word B. are found primarily in the belt of arid land covering parts of the Arabian peninsula, the Fertile Crescent and North Africa.

A normal census cannot enumerate the B.; it is difficult therefore to establish their number. According to some estimates, there are about 7m. B. tribesmen in the ME. In the Arabian peninsula there are *c.* 4m. B., close to one-third of the population; in Iraq there are about 2m., which is over a quarter of the population (including groups which maintain a tribal form of organization, though no longer truly nomadic but partially or permanently settled); the half million B. in Libya form one-third of the population. In other countries of the ME, B. represent a smaller proportion. In Syria there are about 350,000 B., in Jordan *c.* 200,000, in Egypt *c.* 200,000 (including 60,000 in the Sinai Peninsula), and in Israel about 30,000.

The B. consider pastoralism their main occupation; it determines their nomadic way of life and influences their entire culture. Their tribal organization and mobility gives them a military advantage which in the past was very important, although today it has lost its value. Many B. also engage in farming, which has become a main source of income for a fair number of them. The balance between farming and pastoralism is determined to a great extent by conditions of soil, climate and political circumstances. Conditions for raising flocks are favourable where there is abundant land, the rains are sufficient but irregular and there is access to markets. Where political conditions are unsettled, the B. herds pasture on arable land. But governments prefer to establish farmers in such areas, and to transfer the B. to land that cannot be cultivated regularly. The B. are now in retreat under the pressure of farmers and settled cattle-breeders who encroach on their grazing areas. The battle of the desert and the sown continues, but the B. are losing ground steadily. Where B. combine farming and pastoralism, they keep their pasture and their farm-land distinct; they adapt their nomadic schedule to the ploughing and harvesting seasons and thereby prevent the destruction of tilled fields by the animals.

In order to defend themselves from outside enemies and make the best use of their land, the B. organize themselves into small groups of men related to each other through patrilineal descent. Tribes and tribal confederations—large territorial organizations sometimes comprising thousands of people—are made up of congeries of such groups. For example, the powerful Ruwala tribe in the Syrian desert numbers about 30,000 people whose tribal chief (sheikh) usually resides in Damascus. The fission and fusion of tribes, relocation and settlement, are constantly recurring processes, often extending over several generations.

The B. are dependent on settlements for the purchase of staples, such as flour, sugar, coffee, cloth and arms, as well as for the sale of animals and their products, such as wool and leather. Their diet consists mainly of cereals and milk and they eat meat very rarely. B. try to conserve their herds, since they are their main capital. Dairy products hold a secondary place in the diet of most B., especially in summer when milk production almost ceases. So even the tribes which penetrate deep into the desert retain contact with the settlements at certain points in their annual migrations. On the other hand, in recent generations the settlements are not dependent on the B. In the past the B. controlled some important overland routes of the ME and were the chief suppliers of beasts of burden. Modern means of transportation and new efficient weapons destroyed this economic branch. The dependence of the B. on the settlements, together with the settlements' independence of the B., has sometimes led the B. to conquer settled areas. They were not initially interested in permanent control of these settlements, but occupied them in response to seasonal and ecological pressures such as drought or locusts. In some cases, these settlements became the centres of short-lived B. states.

The Ottoman rulers mistrusted the B. since their large-scale political organization gave them a certain independence of the government. The Ottomans alternated between treating them as subsidised allies, or as enemies; they often incited tribes to fight one another. The states later established in the region no longer feared the B., but rather regarded them as an administrative nuisance and as a sector making a minimal economic contribution to the state. It is difficult to collect taxes from a wandering population or to recruit it for the army, and it is also difficult to provide it with amenities, such as schools and clinics. From the middle of the 19th century, there have been many attempts to settle the B. on the land. Yet the B. mode of life is adapted to the desert. Earlier attempts to change their way of life often caused economic hardship, and were bound to fail. Where the experiments involved good agricultural land, in parts of Iraq, for instance, the B. in some cases became serfs of the tribal chiefs, who became the legal owners of the land. In recent years there have been changes in the life of the B. due to the development that followed the discovery of oil in their areas. In Sa'udi Arabia, Kuwait, Libya, etc. the oil wells become nuclei of settlement. Permanent water supplies were installed near the wells and pumping stations. The B. settled nearby, some permanently; some became seasonal or permanent industrial labourers, though they continued to dwell in tents. It was generally a quick transition, unattended by problems. The tribal pattern sometimes is maintained even after the tribe has settled down in one place.

The importance of the B. as a political factor has decreased in recent generations. The states of the area have established order and security in the tribal areas and prevented the B. from controlling settled regions and from fighting and robbing one other. Camels and horses are no longer needed as beasts of burden or transportation, and the B. are no longer the exclusive suppliers of meat to the markets. Tribal organization has weakened since the B. began to take up various types of employment, often outside their territories. Only in Jordan do the B. still have a recognized, though indirect, influence on political life, since they are the backbone of the royal army.

(E.M.)

Menahem Begin

of Christians to Muslims and Druzes is 54 to 44 (2% are Jews and others).

B. is Lebanon's major administrative and financial centre, a hub of international traffic (port and international airport), and the focus of her trade and industry. B. became part of the State of Lebanon in 1920, when the French created "Greater Lebanon"; the area of autonomous Lebanon in the Ottoman period (1861–1914) had not included the city, which was then the capital of the Ottoman province *(Vilayet)* of B. (Y.P.)

BEJA. Hamitic-speaking tribes in Sudan, inhabiting the Red Sea hills and parts of the desert plateau sloping down to the Nile. They are camel-owning nomads, although there has been a certain amount of settlement. They have become Muslims and undergone varying degrees of Arabization. Estimated numbers: 600–700,000. (B.G.)

BENGHAZI. Second largest city of Libya and principal city of Cyrenaica. Pop.: *c.* 320,000 (unconfirmed 1970 estimates). During World War II B. changed hands five times due to the changing fortunes of the desert war fought by the British and Allied forces against the Italians and Germans. After the war it became the seat of the semi-independent regime of Amir Idris▷ and the Sanussis▷, and the capital of semi-independent Cyrenaica (under British protection), 1949–51. B. remained King Idris's favourite seat even after Libya's unification, and alternated as capital with Tripoli. Since the overthrow of Idris in 1969, and the establishment of a unitarian regime with a single centre in Tripoli, B. is no longer the capital. (B.G.)

*BEN-GURION (formerly Green), **DAVID.** Born in 1886 in Plonsk, Poland. Israeli statesman and first Prime Minister of Israel. He regarded Zionism▷ as a practical doctrine to be implemented through immigration to Palestine and conquest of the land by Hebrew labour.

He arrived in Palestine in 1906, spent several years as an agricultural worker, was active in the Socialist-Zionist *Po'ale Zion*▷ party. His approach to socialism was pragmatic, feeling the realization of Political Zionism had precedence over Marxist dialectics. Accordingly, at the party convention of 1907 he struggled successfully for the plank in its platform stating: "The party will strive for an independent state for the Jewish people in this country".

From 1910 he served as editor of the *Po'alei Zion's* organ, *Ahduth*, where he signed his first article with his new name Ben-Gurion, which had been the name of one of the last defenders of Jerusalem against the

*BEGIN, MENAHEM. Zionist underground leader and Israeli politician. Born 1913 in White Russia (later Poland). Head of Betar (the youth movement of the Zionist-Revisionists▷) in Poland, 1939. Played an active part in organizing illegal immigration to Palestine. Was arrested by the Soviet authorities in 1940 for Zionist activity and reached Palestine in 1942 with the Polish Army.

From 1943 until its dissolution in 1948, he headed *Irgun (T)zeva'i Le'umi*▷ (IZL), the militant underground organization which struggled for the establishment of a Jewish State by violent means.

In 1948 Begin founded the right-wing *Herut*▷ party, which he continues to lead, representing it in the *Knesset* (Parliament) since 1949. His policy is one of extreme nationalism with some religious emphasis and includes, in principle, the claim to a Jewish State "on both sides of the Jordan", opposition to socialist trends, and primacy of the State. B. sat on the opposition benches until 1967, the eve of the Six Day War▷, when he joined the Government as Minister without Portfolio. He resigned from the Government in August 1970, upon the withdrawal of *Gahal*▷ (the *Herut*-Liberal bloc) from the coalition, because the Government accepted Rogers'▷ Plan which entailed a withdrawal from territories occupied in June 1967 to "secure, recognized and agreed boundaries." (Sh. H.-E. L.)

BEIRUT. Capital of Lebanon and the major port city in the Levant. B.'s population exceeds half a million (in the absence of a census, there is no exact figure). Community distribution: Sunni Muslims *c.* 35%; Armenians (Gregorian-Orthodox and Catholic-Uniates together) 24%; Greek Orthodox 11%; Maronites 8%; Shi'ites (Mutawalis) 7.5%. The ratio

David Ben-Gurion

Jews. B-G. formulated the following policy at the beginning of World War II: "Fight the war as if there were no White Paper and the White Paper as if there were no war". He now looked to the United States for support. He was the *force de vivre* behind the 12 May 1942 "Biltmore"▷ Programme of the American Zionist Emergency Committee, on the establishment of a Jewish Commonwealth in Palestine. On the internal front, B-G. fought the "dissident" groups, who used terror against the British, and at the same time worked for the creation of a Jewish defence force.

On the establishment of the State in May 1948, B-G. became Prime Minister and Minister of Defence. He led the decisive struggle (the Arab-Israel War▷ of 1948) which accompanied the birth of the State. He built up the Israeli Defence Forces through a successful struggle with groups attempting to maintain separate organizations within the army. During his years in office he directed the absorption of large numbers of immigrants, the development of the wilderness, and the "ingathering of the exiles". He set up a uniform national education system. He took forceful positions on foreign policy and security, and called for self-realization and pioneering settlement, particularly in the Negev. In 1953 he left the government, "for a year or two", joined *Kibbutz* Sde Boker in the Negev, and transferred the premiership to Moshe Sharett. Pinhas Lavon▷ was appointed Minister of Defence. In February 1955, when Lavon resigned because of the "Lavon Affair"▷, B-G. returned to the government as Defence Minister, again becoming Prime Minister in July. He was the main architect of the Franco-Israel pact and against bitter opposition supported the establishment of relations with West Germany (which commenced with the Restitution Agreement▷). He was Prime Minister at the time of the Sinai Campaign▷ in October 1956 which was a reaction to armed infiltration and Egyptian threats following the Egyptian-Czech arms deal of 1955. In the years 1955–63 he initiated a number of secret, and unsuccessful, attempts at *rapprochement* with Arab leaders.

In June 1963 B-G. suddenly resigned from all his posts for "personal reasons". Levi Eshkol▷ became Prime Minister and Minister of Defence at his recommendation. But tension grew between the two men because of the "Lavon Affair". The "Affair" also provided the background for the struggle between the younger elements in Mapai, supported by B-G., and the veteran leadership. In June 1965, this struggle resulted in a split in Mapai. B-G. established the "Israel Workers List" *(Rafi)*, which won ten seats in the Sixth *Knesset* (Parliament). After the Six Day War, *Rafi* joined *Mapai* and *Ahduth Ha'avodah*,

Roman legions. After the revolution in Istanbul of the Young Turks (1908), he advocated (with Yitzhak Ben-Zvi▷) an Ottoman orientation for Palestinian Jewry. He hoped he would become a member of parliament and possibly even a Turkish minister. But Ben Zvi and B-G. were expelled from Turkey at the beginning of World War I. A year later, in New York, they established the *Hehalutz*▷ movement. On publication of the Balfour Declaration, in November 1917, B-G. wrote: ". . . a land is only acquired through the pains of work and creation, through the efforts of building and settling". A few months later he arrived in Palestine as a Jewish Legion▷ volunteer. His aim was the creation of an independent centre of Jewish strength in Palestine, which would become the bastion of Jewish settlement and the nucleus of the "state on the way". This nucleus was the General Federation of Labour in Palestine, the *Histadrut*▷, which was founded in 1920, with B-G. as its first Secretary-General. He was also active in the unification in 1930 of *Ahduth Ha'avodah*▷ and *Hapo'el Hatza'ir*▷ in *Mapai*▷. In 1935 he was elected chairman of the Zionist Executive and the Jewish Agency▷.

In 1937, together with Chaim Weizmann▷ and Moshe Shertok (Sharett▷), he supported the Peel Commission's plan for the establishment of a Jewish State in a small part of Palestine. After the plan was shelved, and the British clearly became pro-Arab, B-G. was one of the Jewish representatives at the St. James Arab-Jewish Round Table Conference held in London in February 1939. It was followed by the White Paper of 1939, which limited Jewish immigration to Palestine and land purchases there, and aimed at ensuring permanent minority status for the to form the "Israel Labour Party"; but B-G. held aloof. In the October 1969 elections he headed the "National List", which won only four seats in the *Knesset*. In June 1970, at the age of 84, B-G. retired from the *Knesset* and political life, and returned to Sde Boker.

Many regard David Ben-Gurion as the symbol of Israeli independence and the father of the country. His life in politics has not prevented him from enjoying a wide range of intellectual activities. He has published a large number of books and at present is working on his memoirs and a history of Israel.
(M. B.-Z.)

BEN YEHUDA, ELIEZER (1858–1922). Father of the revival of spoken Hebrew. Born in Lithuania, and settled in Palestine in 1881. Among the first to speak Hebrew in daily life and, though ridiculed and opposed, fought for its exclusive use as the language of Jewish national rebirth. He compiled a comprehensive historical Hebrew dictionary, coining many new terms to bring the language up to date. (Sh.H.)

BEN-ZVI, YITZHAK (ISAAC) (1884–1963). Zionist Labour leader, historian and ethnographer of Jewish communities in Palestine. Second President of Israel, 1952–63. Born in the Ukraine, where together with Boruchov▷ he founded the Zionist-Socialist *Po'alei Zion* party (1905). Settled in Palestine in 1907. One of the founders of *Hashomer*, the Jewish watchmen association, and of the first Hebrew socialist magazine in Palestine, *Ahduth*. At the beginning of World War I, he advocated a pro-Ottoman policy, but later, in the USA, together with David Ben-Gurion▷, he founded the *Hehalutz*▷ pioneer movement and organized the American Battalion for the Jewish Legion▷.

In 1920 he was among the founders of the *Histadrut* (Federation of Labour), and the Zionist-Socialist *Ahduth Ha'avodah*▷ (the later *Mapai*▷). He was a member of the Jewish National Council in Palestine (*Va'ad Leumi*▷), became its Chairman in 1931 and its President in 1944. A member of the *Knesset* (Parliament) for *Mapai*, until elected President. (Sh.H.)

BERBERS. Ancient pre-Arab inhabitants of Northwest Africa (the *Maghreb*). Their language belongs to the Hamite group and is related to ancient Egyptian. After the Arab-Muslim conquest, the B. accepted both Islam (though they retained many pre-Islamic customs), and, over a period of time, Arabic as their language. There is no reliable estimate of the number of B.: the majority of the *Maghreb* population are of full or part B. descent, but estimates vary as to the number and percentage of those still retaining

some B. distinctiveness, and the Berber language. One view is that they constitute 50% of the Algerian population and more than 50% of the Moroccan. There are B. also in Libya (estimates vary from 50 to 250,000). The distinctive character of the B. was preserved in the remote mountain areas rather than in the cities and villages of the lowlands. It tends to be conservative and separatist. No organization or political party explicitly represents B. interests or fosters B. nationality. Contemporary historical trends will probably encourage Arab nationalist hegemony, and the gradual disintegration of a Berber identity.
(Y.S.)

BERNADOTTE, COUNT FOLKE (1895–1948). A Swedish nobleman, President of the Swedish Red Cross, known for his efforts towards the end of World War II, to obtain the release of Scandinavians and others from German concentration camps. Appointed by the UN as Mediator for Palestine in May 1948, a few days after the end of the British Mandate, B. recommended the merger of the Arab part of Palestine with Jordan, the annexation of the Negev▷ to this Arab State, in exchange for Western Galilee (which was to remain in Israel's possession), and the repatriation of all Arab refugees who had fled from Palestine during the War of Independence (see refugees▷; Israel▷, history). The first version of B.'s plan provided also for Jerusalem▷ to be annexed to the Arab State; a second version recommended its internationalization. He suggested that Haifa be made an international port, and Lod (Lydda) an international airport. These proposals raised opposition from both Jews and Arabs. B. was assassinated on 17 Sept. 1948 in Jerusalem by members of a Jewish dissident group not under the national discipline of the Jewish leadership. The perpetrators of the murder were never found. Nevertheless, in 1950, Israel paid the UN $54,628 in compensation, following an advisory opinion of the International Court of Justice which established Israel's formal responsibility.

The second version of B.'s plan was published and discussed by the UN in September 1948; by its territorial suggestions, warmly supported by Britain, were rejected by the Political Committee of the UN General Assembly early in December 1948.
(Sh. H.-Y. S.)

BETHLEHEM—see Holy Places▷.

BEVIN, ERNEST (1881–1951). British Labour leader. Foreign Secretary 1945–51. As Palestine affairs had been transferred to the Foreign Office, B. was responsible for British policy there during the years of the decisive struggle preceding the termination of the British Mandate. Beginning with his policy statement of November 1945, B. scarcely altered British policy as laid down by the White Paper of 1939 (despite the Labour Party's promises in their election campaign); he barred the immigration of Jewish refugees from Europe and opposed the establishment of a Jewish State. Zionists therefore regarded him as a bitter adversary.

B. tried to involve the USA in the responsibility for a Palestine solution by sending an Anglo-American Investigation Committee to Europe and Palestine. He proposed keeping Palestine under British administration, perhaps under a UN Trusteeship, and in his statement of February 1947 he foresaw the possibility of dividing Palestine up into cantons. When his policy was rejected by both Jews and Arabs, B. handed the Palestine problem over to the UN (2 Apr. 1947). As the UN recommended partition, B. refused to allow the Palestine administration to co-operate actively in its preparation and implementation.

As Foreign Secretary, B. was also closely connected with the dispute over the evacuation of French and British troops from Syria and Lebanon (the B.-Bidault agreement of Dec. 1945); the crisis over the evacuation of Persia, 1945-6; and the abortive draft Treaty of Portsmouth▷ with Iraq, January 1948. Two abortive agreements of ME significance were (informally) named after B.: a. The B.-Sidqy▷ agreement of Oct. 1956 providing a formula to solve the dispute between Britain and Egypt over the presence of British troops in Egypt and the future governance of Sudan. (The agreement fell through when its two signatories publicly interpreted it in mutually contradictory terms—see Egypt▷, history). b. The B.-Sforza agreement of 1949, concluded with the Foreign Minister of Italy, providing for a ten-year trusteeship for Libya (this failed to obtain the required two-thirds majority at the UN—see Libya▷, History).   (Sh. H.-Y. S.)

BILTMORE PROGRAMME. Resolution adopted by an Extraordinary Zionist Conference, in May 1942 (named after the hotel in New York in which the conference was held), urging "that Palestine be established as a Jewish Commonwealth integrated in the structure of the new democratic world" after World War II. This was the first time that the Zionist Organization officially demanded a Jewish State in Palestine—henceforth its declared aim. As this demand was held necessarily to lead to the partition of Palestine, many Zionists opposed it.   (Sh.H.)

BI-NATIONALISM, BI-NATIONAL STATE IN PALESTINE. The establishment of a BNS

in Palestine was one of the solutions to the Jewish-Arab conflict proposed during Mandatory times. Submitting that both Jews and Arabs were in Palestine as of right, and that neither nation should dominate the other, and assuming that a solution to the conflict between the two nations could be found within an undivided Palestine, most plans for a BNS were based on the principle of parity in government irrespective of the numerical strength of either side, and the right of each nation to autonomy in its internal affairs. The BNS was envisaged as cantonal (consisting of several cantons—Jewish, Arab and mixed), federal, or unitary (based on communal rather than territorial autonomy for the two nations). BN was never the official policy of the Arabs, Zionists or British, though the idea was considered by the last two. Official Arab policy was unwilling to accept the Jews' right to free immigration and settlement in Palestine and insisted upon the establishment of an Arab State in which the Jews would enjoy—at most—minority rights. The Zionists, on the other hand appeared willing, in the early 1930s, to accept an eventual agreement based on political parity, but they were not prepared to forgo free immigration and the eventual establishment of a Jewish majority. The British were unwilling to impose a solution unpopular in both camps, and only their last proposals, in February 1947, contained some elements which might be termed BN. BN was mostly advocated by Jewish individuals and groups, such as *Brith Shalom; Hashomer Hatza'ir▷; Kedma Mizraha* (Hebrew: "Eastward", a group established in 1936 to prevent the deterioration of relations between Jews and Arabs; it advocated BN after 1937); the "League for Jewish-Arab *Rapprochement* and Co-operation" (established soon after the abortive London Round Table Conference of 1939, it united various groups advocating BN, published numerous pamphlets on Jewish-Arab relations and tried to arrange meetings with Arab groups); and *Ihud* (Hebrew: "Union", founded by Judah L. Magnes in 1942 after the Zionist organization had adopted the Biltmore Programme▷ for a Jewish State; its membership included the non-Marxist members of the "League" mentioned above). Various individual Englishmen also advocated a BN solution, but very few Arabs dared support it. Fawzi Darwish al-Husseini, one of the few Arabs openly to advocate BN, was murdered in 1946 by Arab nationalists.   (Sh. H.)

*BITAR, SALAH-UL-DIN. Syrian politician. Born in 1912 in Damascus. Studies at the universities of Damascus and Paris. In 1940 he founded, together with Michel 'Aflaq▷, the "Arab Renaissance

Salah-ul-Din Bitar

Party" (*al-Ba'th*▷) and became editor of its organ, *al-Ba'th*. In 1956–7 he was Foreign Minister, and worked for the union of Syria and Egypt. In 1958 he was Minister of State for Arab Affairs in the first UAR▷ government, and then Minister of National Guidance. He resigned at the end of 1959 when Nasser▷ began to curb the influence of the *Ba'th* leaders. After the *Ba'th* officers' coup of March 1963, B. headed five *Ba'th* governments. He was ousted in the coup on 23 Feb. 1966 staged by the "Military Wing" and the extremist faction of the *Ba'th*; B. was arrested but escaped to Lebanon where he has lived since in exile. He was expelled, together with 'Aflaq, from the *Ba'th* party (*i.e.* the faction ruling in Syria); he is not active in the rival faction of the party, controlled in exile by 'Aflaq and linked with the Iraqi regime.   (A.L.-O.T.)

BIZRI, 'AFIF. Syrian officer and politician. Born 1914 in Sidon, Lebanon to a family of Kurdish notables. In 1938 he joined the armed forces maintained by the French Mandate. In the early 1940s B. studied in Paris and became a leftist; whether he officially joined the Syrian Communist Party is not known; he did maintain close connections with the officers' cells of the *Ba'th*▷ group. B. attained the rank of colonel in 1955; in August 1957 he was appointed Chief-of-Staff of the Syrian Army and promoted to General. He was influential in bringing about the union of Syria with Egypt. Shortly after that union, because of pressure from Nasser▷,

he resigned his post as Chief-of-Staff of the UAR army in Syria. After the country seceded from the UAR (1961), he returned to Syria and the army and opposed Nasser's influence and the renewal of ties with Egypt. In 1965 B. was removed from the army by General Amin Hafez▷, but in 1967 he resumed political activity in Damascus.   (A.L.-O.T.)

BLACK SEA. Russia has been the strongest littoral country and in effective control of the B.S. waters ever since the Ottoman Empire lost control of it in the 18th century. Her fear of a warlike penetration of stronger maritime powers into the B.S. (as happened in the Crimean War, 1854–6) and her desire to ensure for herself free egress from the B.S. into the Mediterranean—*i.e.* that the Bosphorus and Dardanelles should be closed to foreign navies but open to the ingress and egress of Russian—were, for generations, a determinant of Russian policy and an important element of the "Eastern Question" (the great-power policy towards the Middle East and the Ottoman Empire). See Bosphorus▷, Dardanelles.   (Y.S.)

BLUDAN. Summer resort in southern Syria and a popular site for Arab conferences. The Pan-Arab non-governmental Conference of B. in 1937 was called by Arab political organizations to support Palestinian-Arab opposition to Zionism and Jewish settlement. In June 1946, the Arab League▷ convened its Council in B. Its partially secret decisions (the "Decisions of B.") concerned the mobilization of Arab military and political resources against the partition of Palestine. The Council rejected full military intervention by regular forces of the Arab states, assuming that a demonstration of force on the borders of Palestine, combined with financial and logistic support to the Palestinian-Arab irregulars and reinforced by "volunteers" from the Arab countries, would overcome Jewish resistance. With the subsequent defeat of these irregular forces, the decisions taken at B. were set aside in May 1948 and a full-scale military invasion was initiated (against the advice of the military staffs).   (Y.S.)

BORUCHOV, BER. (1881–1919). Propounded "scientific" synthesis of Zionism and Socialism. In his youth joined the Russian Social-Democratic movement, but later became one of the founders of the *Po'alei Zion* (see Zionism▷). Convinced that the liberation of the world proletariat would neither solve the Jewish problem nor eradicate anti-Semitism, he maintained that extra-territorialism was the cause of all anomalies in Jewish life. Therefore the Jews should concentrate in their own land (Palestine) to develop a working class there, which would establish

a strategic base for the class struggle. This working class would lead the liberation of the Jewish people.
(E.L.)

BOSPHORUS. Straits in north-western Turkey, connecting the Black Sea▷ to the Sea of Marmara (and ultimately, through the Dardanelles▷, to the Aegean and the Mediterranean). European Turkey forms the B.'s western shore with Istanbul▷ on its southern tip, and Asian Turkey (Asia Minor) its eastern shore. It is 16 miles long, and has an average width of one mile.

As the only outlet from the Black Sea, and a junction between Asia and Europe, the B. has always been of great commercial and strategic importance. The Ottomans took possession of the Straits in stages, culminating in the conquest of Istanbul in 1453. The B. first assumed strategic and economic significance (in modern times) in the 18th century, when Russia gained control of the northern shores of the Black Sea, which thereupon ceased to be a "Turkish lake". Russian foreign trade, and the defence of her southern frontier, became increasingly dependent on the Straits. Therefore Russia always attempted to gain direct control of the Straits or, if that were impractical, to establish rules that would ensure her own freedom of navigation but would minimize the entry into the Black Sea of fleets of non-riparian countries.

The question of the Straits was one of the major issues in the "Eastern Question", with Britain generally opposing any claims which might lead to Russian supremacy in the Straits. In the Treaty of Küçük Kaynarca, 1774, Russia acquired the right to send her merchant ships through the Straits, and this right was subsequently extended to other nations. Foreign warships were not permitted to pass through the Straits; but during the Napoleonic Wars Russia obtained the Sultan's special permission to send her navy through them, and for a time even his agreement to joint Russo-Turkish responsibility for their defence. In the Treaty of Hünkâr Iskelesi, 1833, Russia achieved a substantial gain when the Sultan agreed, as a price for Russia's support against Muhammad 'Ali of Egypt, to keep the Straits open to Russian warships and closed to those of other nations. After a diplomatic struggle between Russia and Britain, the latter succeeded in the Treaty of London, 1840, and the Straits Convention, 1841, in annulling Russia's preferential status.

The principle that the Straits should be closed to foreign warships prevailed until after World War I, although the Treaty of London, 1871, empowered the Sultan to grant the warships of friendly countries the right of free passage in certain cases. The admittance of two German battleships into the B., Aug. 1914, was

View over the Bosphorus to Scutari, with its Blue Mosque in the background

one of the chief reasons for Turkey's involvement in World War I. Attempts of the Allied fleets to force their way into the B. failed, and they occupied the Straits only after the armistice. Britain had departed from her long-established policy by consenting, in the secret Agreement on Constantinople, 1915, to the annexation of Istanbul and the Straits area to Russia, after victory; the Bolshevik Revolution rendered the agreement void.

The Treaty of Sèvres▷, 1920, left Istanbul to Turkey, but provided for control of the Straits by an international commission and their opening to merchant vessels and warships in both peace and war. The Treaty, never ratified due to the victorious nationalist struggle in Turkey, was replaced by that of Lausanne▷, 1923, which was much more favourable to Turkey and also made some concessions to Soviet Russia (which signed the Lausanne Straits Convention, though not the Treaty of Lausanne in its other parts; she never ratified the Convention). Unless Turkey were at war, merchant ships of all nations were guaranteed free passage; warships were allowed transit, but the size of the forces, which any one power might send through the Straits was limited to the size of "the most powerful fleet of the littoral powers of the Black Sea" (*i.e.* Russia). The Convention provided for the demilitarization of the Straits and an International Straits Commission to supervise navigation through them. The Lausanne arrangements remained in force until 1936, when Turkish pressure and the changing international situation led to the adoption of the Montreux▷ Convention, which abolished the international commission, permitted Turkey to fortify the Straits, and set new limitations for the passage of warships. In 1945 the USSR, dis-

satisfied with the new arrangements and angered by Turkey's neutrality during World War II, demanded to participate in the defence of the Straits and be given bases in their vicinity. Turkey, supported by the Western Powers, rejected this demand and it was dropped by the USSR in 1953, after Stalin's death.
(D. K.)

*BOURGUIBA, HABIB (b. 1903). Tunisian statesman; President of Tunisia since 1957. B. is the most important representative of modern Tunisian nationalism, and head of the political party embodying it (the "Neo Dustur" party, later "Socialist Dustur Party"). He led Tunisia to independence in 1956 and was Prime Minister until elected President in 1957. He is considered a moderate, Western and French in his culture and general approach, and pro-Western in policy, but his internal regime resembles a one-party, populist dictatorship. B.'s biography and career are outside the scope of this Encyclopaedia; only his involvement in ME affairs is discussed here.

B., like many leaders of nationalist movements in *Maghreb* countries, spent some time in exile in Cairo; but he differed from other leaders in being little influenced by the nationalism and socio-political conditions in the eastern Arab countries (the *Mashriq*) in general, and by Nasser's▷ doctrine in particular. From the time Tunisia joined the Arab League and began taking part in inter-Arab activity, there was personal hostility between B. and Nasser, and this was repeated at the general level of relations between Tunisia and Egypt and her allies. In spring 1958, on the eve of Tunisia's admission to the League, B. accused Egypt, and Nasser personally, of assisting

Habib Bourguiba addressing a meeting

conspirators in their plot to assassinate him and subvert Tunisia (the reference was to Saleh Ben-Yussef, B.'s leading opponent, who had found asylum in Egypt since 1956). In October-November 1958, B. repeated these accusations in speeches. In October 1958, the Tunisian representative walked out of the meeting of the Arab League council welcoming Tunisia's admission to the League; his parting speech repeated the above accusations, accused the League of being Egypt's tool, and expressed entire lack of confidence in Egypt. At the same time, Tunisia severed her diplomatic ties with Egypt. She returned to the League and renewed her ties with Egypt in 1961 after a number of attempts at mediation; however, relations remained cool.

B.'s non-conformist attitude toward the Arab-Israeli dispute caused much friction in Arab circles, and several crises. B. was not sympathetic towards Israel, but he did not indulge in Pan-Arab rhetoric and deplored the absolute refusal to negotiate with Israel or to consider peaceful co-existence—since that refusal was not based on the military power to solve the problem by war. B. was not always completely consistent, and sometimes wavered; but he usually held that: 1. There was no chance of a solution by force to the Israel-Arab dispute. It followed that the Arabs were deluding themselves, and were the victims of their own propaganda, in thinking in terms of revenge and a new war. 2. The Arabs should negotiate with Israel, in the clear understanding that negotiations could lead to recognition and peaceful co-existence. 3. In these negotiations the Arabs should persuade Israel to accept their conditions: Israel should withdraw behind the border of the 1947 partition plan, and allow all refugees back. Basically B.'s demands did not much differ from those of the other Arab leaders in their statements designed for external consumption (though at home they spoke in a different vein). But B. was the first brave enough publicly to draw the conclusion that if Israel were to accept the Arab demands, peace should follow. (No other Arab politician ever stated this conclusion clearly) and that a settlement could only be arrived at by negotiation. B. was the first to state his views openly to the Arab public at home. Sometimes, however, he would contradict himself. Despite his rejection of a solution by force, he would sometimes call on the Palestinian Arabs themselves for a more determined military effort, and for a people's war in Palestine which would receive the assistance of the Arab states.

B. often expressed his views on the Arab-Israel dispute. His frank non-conformity reached a peak during a tour of the ME in spring 1965 (when he also made an official visit to Egypt); during his trip he expounded his ideas to students, journalists, and political circles in Egypt, Jordan and Lebanon and formulated them into a plan. The solution he proposed caused a storm of protest and all the Arab states dissociated themselves from it. B. was called a traitor, and it was suggested he should be excommunicated. Egypt, Syria and Iraq recalled their ambassadors. He was informed that Tunisia's participation in Arab League sessions was undesirable. B. again deviated from the united Arab camp by his refusal to sever ties with West Germany. He was not alone in his refusal, Morocco and Libya also maintained their ties; but his refusal caused particular anger against the background of his heresy concerning Israel. In spring 1965, Tunisia did not attend the League council; in Sept. B. even absented himself from the all-Arab summit meeting (the third summit, in Casablanca, where a new Pan-Arab solidarity pact was signed. A poisonous propaganda war ensued between Tunisia and Egypt. B. again severed all relations with Egypt in October 1966 (those with Iraq had been severed previously).

The crisis of 1967 brought B. back to the fold: during the period of nationalist frenzy at the end of May, he declared his solidarity with Nasser, and called for war. In June 1967 he also resumed relations with Egypt. He himself did not attend the summit conference of Khartoum, in August, but he was represented by one of his chief ministers, and was a co-signatory therefore to the Khartoum decisions ("The Three No's"—no negotiation, no recognition, no peace—all of them flatly contradicting his views). B. continued expressing heretical views on the Arab-Israel dispute; but he did not provoke the same storm of protest. Relations between him and most Arab states remained cool and suspicious. (They did improve somewhat with neighbouring Algeria.) Tunisia's diplomatic representation in Egypt remained at below ambassadorial level until 1970. B. was sharply critical of Egypt's dictatorial behaviour in the Arab League. He attacked Egypt's evasion of responsibility for her defeat in 1967, and her refusal to draw the moral; in autumn 1968 Tunisia again absented herself for a considerable time from Arab League meetings. In 1968 she again severed relations with Syria. On the other hand, in 1970 B. sent his Prime Minister who played a major role as a mediator in the crisis between Jordan and the Palestinian guerillas. Despite these changes in B.'s inter-Arab policy the underlying pattern does not change: B. dissents, does not conform, gives public expression to his dissent. Until now, B.'s Tunisian colleagues have held the same views, or left their own views unexpressed. It has still to be seen whether his personal views will remain official Tunisian policy once B. himself no longer dominates the scene.

B. occupies a liberal position, also, in connection with Tunisian Jewry. Several times he has intervened personally to prevent progroms, or mob ugliness. One such intervention was in 1967.   (Y.S.)

BOYCOTT—see Arab Boycott▷.

*BRITAIN, BRITISH INTERESTS AND POLICIES IN THE ME. Great Britain first became involved in the ME in the 16th century, when London traders realized the commercial potential of the region. Thereafter, it was primarily a case of the flag following trade as the English mercantile system, European power struggles and British imperial dictates prompted the expansion of interests and control to the eastern periphery of the Mediterranean. The resultant commitments, reinforced by strategic considerations, came to be symbolized by the line of garrisons and naval bases starting at Gibraltar, under British control since 1704, and stretching to the Indian subcontinent and beyond.

Because, in this initial period, the lands of the Near and ME were politically subordinate to either the Ottoman Empire or the adjoining Persian Empire, British traders and statesmen sought to establish amicable relations with both Constantinople and Teheran. In 1553, Sultan Suleiman gave English merchants permission to trade within his realm on the same terms as were then enjoyed by the French and Venetians, and in 1578 the first British Ambassador presented his credentials to the Sublime Porte. Similarly, in 1566–8, Shah Tahmasp gave English merchants those privileges necessary to live and trade in Persia. Subsequent penetration of the ME thus came from the two directions of the Mediterranean and the Persian Gulf. The India Office developed a proprietary concern for Persia and the maritime corridors to India, while the Foreign Office, treating the Ottoman Empire as a sovereign entity, involved itself in Turkish affairs.

By the 19th century the Ottoman Empire had declined so appreciably that it became known as "the Sick Man of Europe" and posed before European diplomacy a sensitive "Eastern Question": what arrangements should replace the Ottoman Empire in the event of its demise? Great Britain was reluctant to see the Turkish domains, and especially Constantinople▷ and the Dardanelles▷, come under the control, direct or indirect, of either France or Russia. As a result, the survival, sovereignty and territorial integrity of the Turkish Empire endured as cardinal principles of British foreign policy. Attempts to promote legal, social and administrative reforms within the Empire proved unsuccessful, for Turkish leadership and society proved resistant to change.

Britain's commitment to Turkey often involved

her in the external and domestic affairs of the Empire. The Treaty of Paris, 1856, the Convention of London, 1871, and the Congress of Berlin, 1878, all attested to British diplomatic initiatives aimed at ensuring Turkish security, and British interests, by peaceful means. Yet on several occasions Great Britain used force: against France, 1798; in ending Muhammad 'Ali's defiance of the Sultan, 1839; and against Russian expansion during the Crimean War, 1854–6.

French and Russian designs on Turkish territory tested British resolve. They also heightened London's appreciation of the ME, and actually led to an extension of British control. Napoleon's abortive invasion of Egypt in 1798 alerted Great Britain to the vulnerability of her lines of communication to India as well as to Egypt's strategic importance for the entire region. The Sultan of 'Oman▷ and the sheikhs of Bahrain▷ and Kuwait▷ subjected their foreign relations to exclusive British control in 1891, 1892 and 1899 respectively; Britain acquired Malta in 1815 and Aden▷ in 1834. The Trucial Coast▷, which had been brought under "Trucial agreements" in 1820 and 1835, was "forevermore" pacified under a "Perpetual Maritime Truce" in 1853. Once the dream of a Suez Canal▷ became a reality in 1869 (inspired by a Frenchman, Ferdinand de Lesseps), British politicians realized its importance as the primary route between Europe and the Orient. At Disraeli's initiative, Britain acquired a major share in the Canal and obtained a voice in its management. This was reinforced by the British occupation of Egypt in 1882, transformed into a protectorate in December 1914. In 1878 Britain exploited renewed Russo-Turkish friction by annexing Cyprus▷.

In the decades before World War I the European Powers came to understand the importance of oil as a fuel both for industrial growth and the provision of a mobile war machine, and a scramble for oil concessions ensued. One of the first and most important concessions was granted to W.K. D'Arcy in 1901 by Persia; it was acquired in 1909 by the Anglo-Persian Oil Company, in which the British Government possessed from 1914 a controlling interest. British interests also competed for railway concessions, although few materialized, and endeavoured to frustrate rival powers' concessions, such as the German-controlled Baghdad Railway▷ project. River navigation was also an important British interest, especially on the Nile and Tigris-Euphrates systems.

In Iran, Britain exercised considerable influence, in constant competition with Imperial Russia. This imperial domination, and rivalry, culminated in an Anglo-Russian Treaty of 1907, dividing Iran into British and Russian zones of influence. (Germany appeared as a strong third competitor.)

The decision of the Turkish rulers to side with Germany in 1914 induced Great Britain to depart from precedent and consent to the eventual partition of the Ottoman Empire, with Russia taking possession of Constantinople and the Straits (Secret Agreement of April 1915). According to the Sykes-Picot Agreement▷ with France and Russia, 1916, Great Britain was to obtain possession of southern Mesopotamia with Baghdad, and Haifa and Acre in Palestine; central Iraq and the region that later became known as Transjordan were to become a British zone of influence; Britain was also to participate in an international administration of Palestine.

Estrangement from Constantinople induced Britain to deal directly with the Arabs. Great Britain hoped to protect its interests in the Arab world by negotiating with one Arab leader as spokesman for the Arabs as a whole. London considered Sharif Hussein▷ of Mecca to be the most appropriate spokesman (though Britain was, since 1915, in local treaty relations also with Ibn Sa'ud▷ of Najd▷, through the government of British India). In the Hussein-McMahon correspondence▷, 1915–6, Britain gave her qualified support for Arab independence, in return for which Hussein sponsored an Arab revolt against his Ottoman masters. The basic recognition of Arab nationalist claims was spelled out in Britain's pledge to support the independence of the Arabs in the large area bounded by Anatolia, the Red Sea and the Persian Gulf. Whereas Hussein and a future generation of Arab nationalists claimed the Mediterranean Sea as the accepted western border of their realm, the British felt they had excluded from this pledge the whole coastal belt of Syria, including Palestine. Similar considerations—staking out claims while satisfying friendly countries such as France and the USA; weakening the Central Powers; and attracting the support of uncommitted parties—led Britain, in November 1917, to issue the Balfour Declaration▷, which extended British support to world Jewry for establishing a national home in Palestine.

By 1920 Britain enjoyed an unprecedented primacy in the ME. No other great power offered a challenge. In the wake of the Bolshevik Revolution, Russia's new leaders had renounced traditional territorial claims; the Turkish nationalists under Mustafa Kemal▷ did not wish to restore the Turkish Empire; Germany was defeated; the USA did not want to play any part in the mandates and soon entered her isolationist period; France was weakened by the war effort and had to use force to assert her claim to Syria and Lebanon.

Local Arab nationalists were unwilling to accept British tutelage, and there were rebellions and unrest in Iraq (1920), Egypt (1919, 1921), and Palestine

(1920, 1921). The several conflicting wartime under-takings—to Hussein, to France and to the Zionist movement—aggravated the problem. Britain re-mained silent while France forcefully asserted her control over Syria and Lebanon in 1920. Gradually, however, national élites in Egypt and Iraq accepted the semi-independence granted them under British guidance. British authority was exercised in Egypt through a protectorate (*de jure* until 1922, *de facto* until 1936); in Palestine and Mesopotamia (Iraq) through mandates▷ confirmed by the League of Nations; and in Arabia and along the littoral of the Persian Gulf by direct treaty relationships with local sheikhs.

In an attempt to formulate a coherent, realistic policy to maintain the favourable *status quo*, respon-sibility for ME affairs was given to the Colonial Of-fice. Winston Churchill▷, then Colonial Secretary, summoned British authorities to a conference in Cairo in 1921, where several decisions were made which governed Anglo-Arab relations during the interwar period. The importance of the region for the British Empire was acknowledged; this, and the large invest-ments made over several decades, precluded any thought of withdrawal from the ME. However, Brit-ish interests and influence were to be ensured with minimal expenditure; the use of British troops could be avoided, it was hoped, by the efficient employment of air power, local Arab forces and monetary sub-sidies to various tribal leaders and rulers. Support was extended to Sharif Hussein in much of Arabia and to his sons Feisal▷ in Iraq and 'Abdullah▷ in Trans-jordan (created in 1921 and defined in 1922 in the League of Nations Mandate for Palestine). As for Pal-estine, British policy makers in London initially felt confident that the Jewish and Arab communities could eventually be brought to co-operate under Brit-ish rule; the Zionists considered British authorities in London to be well-intentioned, but most of the British administrators in Palestine antagonistic; with the passing of time, disillusionment replaced opti-mism and Britain tended to favour the Arabs, largely for political and strategic reasons. In the Arab coun-tries British interests were to be fostered by the creation of semi-independent states under indirect British supervision or guidance rather than direct con-trol; such high commissioners as Gen. Allenby▷ in Egypt, Sir Herbert Samuel▷ in Palestine and Sir Percy Cox▷ in Iraq reflected this spirit. The plan was to guide the Arab countries, gradually and peacefully, to full independence—while safeguarding British im-perial interests. The transition to independence, and the satisfaction of British interests after its achieve-ment, were to be laid down in treaties between Britain and the countries concerned.

In the period after 1921 British pre-eminence reached its peak. The discovery of rich petroleum sources, so important for European industrial growth, and the advantage of air bases in the region increased British appreciation of the ME. It slowly became ap-parent that around 70% of the world's petroleum reserves were located in an area centred on the Persian Gulf. This heightened the crucial nature of relations with Iran, Iraq, Kuwait and Sa'udi Arabia. It also led to friction between Britain and the USA, as the several oil companies vied with each other for access to, and concessions from, the oil-rich countries, and American companies felt themselves excluded by British imperial rule. By the mid-1920s, Britain had to admit American companies to areas of her con-cessions and interests, such as Iraq and later Kuwait and in the 1950s Iran.

Britain's relations with the countries under her tutelage were periodically aggravated when Arab nationalists renewed their struggle for more inde-pendence, to be codified in new treaties; where nec-essary Britain gradually made concessions. Thus the history of the Arab states diverged during the interwar period, since each became preoccupied in its own search for a *modus operandi* with Great Britain and obtained a different reaction.

In the two independent countries of Turkey and Iran—both Muslim and non-Arab—nationalists suc-ceeded in presenting Britain with a *fait accompli*. Mustafa Kemal and the Turkish nationalists tore up the peace treaty of Sèvres, imposed in 1920, and re-gained control of the whole of Anatolia and Con-stantinople and the Straits. Rather than engage in a protracted conflict, Britain made peace at Lausanne▷ in 1923. In 1926 a further treaty was concluded where-by Turkey agreed—after arbitration by the League of Nations—to relinquish her claims to Mosul▷ in favour of Iraq in exchange for the right to 10% of Iraq's oil production. The settlement included vague assurances that Iraq and Britain would safeguard the semi-autonomous privileges of the Kurdish minority in the disputed area; but Kurdish aspirations to auton-omy or independence were sacrificed. The improve-ment of Anglo-Turkish relations was symbolized by a courtesy visit paid to Istanbul by the British Medi-terranean fleet in 1929. Thereafter, Britain welcomed a strong and modernizing Turkey as a buffer against the USSR. Turkey did not interfere in Arab politics and, by 1936, shared Anglo-French concern at the growing threat of Germany and Italy in the Medi-terranean.

A comparable relationship evolved with Iran after Reza Shah seized power in 1921 and set out to en-force domestic reforms and to pursue an independent foreign policy. Relations were normalized by a treaty in 1928 which guaranteed the special status of the Anglo-Iranian Oil Company. However, Iran continued to suspect Britain of encouraging tribal unrest and separatism in southern Persia.

Britain clung tenaciously to her position in Egypt. In 1920 the Milner Commission recommended replacing the protectorate by a treaty of alliance under which Britain would defend Egypt, guide her foreign relations and control the Suez Canal. Unable to reach a bilateral agreement with either Sa'd Zaghlul▷ and his *Wafd*▷ nationalist party or the government, Britain in 1922 unilaterally proclaimed Egypt's independence with reservations. Britain retained full authority for the defence of Egypt and the imperial communications lines traversing the country, for the protection of foreign interests and for the governance of Sudan. Discontent continued, as did negotiations for a treaty; and only in 1936 did the two countries, anxious over the implications of the Italian invasion of Ethiopia, agree to a comprehensive treaty binding for 20 years. At first the treaty was warmly welcomed in Egypt but soon Britain's still-privileged position caused renewed resentment and agitation.

A similarly gradual emancipation took place in Iraq, where a treaty was concluded in 1922. Negotiations on renewed nationalist demands for greater independence culminated in the Anglo-Iraqi Treaty of 1930 which called for a 25 year alliance between the two countries. As a result, Iraq was admitted to the League of Nations in 1932 as a fully independent state and Britain's mandatory responsibility was terminated. Yet, Britain continued to exert considerable *de facto* influence through such leaders as King Feisal▷, until his death in 1933, and Nuri Sa'id▷. This reality bred resentment among younger Iraqi nationalists, finding expression in 1936 in a military coup led by Gen. Bakr Sidqi▷, and initially supported by the leftist-populist *Ahali* ("People's") group. In the late 1930s, officers' juntas were the *de facto* rulers, appointing and dismissing the governments. Most of the officers were extreme nationalists and bitterly anti-British.

Transjordan, created in 1921–2, provided the least troublesome relationship. The Amir 'Abdullah cooperated with Great Britain, upon whom he was dependent financially and militarily. Here, too, Britain gave the semblance rather than substance of independence through formal treaties; by the treaty of 1946, London recognized Transjordan as an independent state and 'Abdullah assumed the title of king. There were persistent rumours of British support for a planned Hashemite "Greater Syria"▷ or Fertile Crescent▷ Federation; the French, and anti-Hashemite Syrian and Lebanese politicians, certainly suspected such plans—as part of a secret British scheme

to oust France from the ME. In fact there was little British involvement in Syria and Lebanon during the interwar period, since British official policy studiously avoided interfering with France's position as mandatory power.

In Arabia, Britain acknowledged Ibn Sa'ud's primacy after 1925: aquiescing in his conquest of Hijaz and the ouster of Britain's Hashemite protégés, Hussein and his son 'Ali; a treaty with Ibn Sa'ud was signed in 1927. British influence endured in the Persian Gulf sheikhdoms. Efforts to gain influence in Yemen were not very successful.

On the eve of World War II, the greatest test of British preponderance in the ME occurred in Palestine. Periodic outbreaks of Arab violence (1920, 1921, 1929, 1936) illustrated the depth of animosity between the Arab and Jewish communities and Arab hostility towards the Mandate and the British. By 1937 British frustration was reflected in the Peel Commission's conclusion that the Mandate could not be implemented, and its recommendation to partition the country into separate Jewish and Arab states and a zone of direct British control; but the idea of partition—rejected by the Palestinian Arabs, accepted only with reservations by some, not all, Zionists, and viewed with scepticism in British government and public circles—was soon dropped by the British Government. An Arab rebellion was resumed. Separate conversations in early 1939 with Arab and Jewish representatives (the former including, at Britain's invitation, leaders of the governments of the Arab states) did not produce a compromise solution. In 1939 Britain imposed a White Paper severely restricting Jewish immigration and settlement and planning a future independent Palestine in which the Jews would be a perpetual minority with no further growth and no national autonomy; the Jews fiercely rejected this policy and turned against Britain.

That Britain had not gained the friendship of the Arabs was reflected in the sympathy which Italy and particularly Germany evoked in the region in the late 1930s. During World War II a group of Egyptian military officers and politicians were in contact with Italian and German officials; and Egypt's government only grudgingly granted Britain the co-operation and facilities agreed to in the Treaty of 1936. The former Mufti of Jerusalem and some of his supporters took refuge in Berlin; and so did pro-Nazi politicians from various Arab countries. In Iraq the pro-Axis government of Rashid 'Ali▷ made war on Britain in 1941, when Britain insisted on using the facilities and privileges provided for in the Treaty; pro-British leaders had to be reinstated by Britain through the supression of the Rashid 'Ali regime. In June 1941, British and Free French forces took Syria and Lebanon; Anglo-

French antagonism was concealed for a time, but soon reappeared—with Britain openly supporting the Syrian and Lebanese nationalists against the French. To secure Iran and deny her territory to the enemy, British and Russian troops occupied the country in August 1941, and divided it into two zones (Russia's Zone was much smaller than in 1907). 'Abdullah of Transjordan was loyal, and the Jews of Palestine, while fighting against Britain's White Paper policy, fully supported her war against Hitler though Britain was reluctant to form the 26,000 Palestinian-Jewish volunteers into a specifically Jewish Army, as they demanded (part of them was permitted to form a Jewish Brigade▷ in 1944).

The end of the war found Britain weakened and confronted by a new challenge from the USSR. In response, several means were used in seeking to maintain influence if not actual power in the region. Britain fostered the Arab League▷, 1945; joined the USA in insisting on a complete and speedy withdrawal of USSR troops from Iran, 1945–6; put pressure on France to withdraw from Syria and Lebanon by supporting the local nationalists, 1946; tried to retain a degree of influence on the Palestine conflict—jointly with France and the USA—by attempting to control arms supplies and offering a vague endorsement of existing frontiers, 1950; unsuccessfully promoted regional security organizations, such as the abortive MEDO▷, 1951, or the ill-fated Baghdad Pact▷, 1955; and even resorted to military force against Egypt during the Suez crisis of 1956.

Despite these efforts, Great Britain, attacked by forces both within and beyond the region, was unable to arrest the rapid decline of her position in the ME. From the 1940s onwards, Britain encouraged American involvement in the ME; she was overshadowed by the USA after 1950. In 1947 Britain, admitting failure in Palestine, relinquished her Mandate to the UN and, in May 1948, withdrew from Palestine. At the same time, she granted India independence, thus removing one of the major justifications for a strong British presence in the ME. A grave Anglo-Persian crisis, 1951–3, over the oil concession, ended with a compromise—but Britain no longer enjoyed special influence.

In 1954 Great Britain signed a new treaty with Egypt (now under a revolutionary government), in which she agreed to evacuate the Canal Zone bases and renounced any special privileges. Even this treaty was torn up by Egypt after the Suez War▷ of 1956, and any special treaty relationship ended. Sudan was granted self-determination in 1955 and assumed full independence without any special concessions for or treaty with Britain. In the following decade Britain's withdrawal from the ME accelerated.

Egypt's nationalization of the Suez Canal, and the abortive Anglo-French intervention in 1956 highlighted the impotence of the two former imperial powers, while the Egyptian arms deal with the communist bloc in 1955 indicated Soviet support for the Arabs. In 1956–7, Britain's special position in Jordan was ended by the dismissal of Brig. Glubb▷, the British commander of Jordan's Army, and other British officers, and the replacement of Britain's subsidy for the army by a Syrian-Sa'udi-Egyptian one. (However this subsidy was never implemented.) Britain again assumed a temporary role in July 1958, when her troops were asked by Jordan to ensure the latter's independence; but her privileged position in Jordan was not restored.

In Iraq, attempts to replace the Treaty of 1930 with a new one, were abortive. That Treaty was terminated, and new relations established, when both Britain and Iraq joined the Baghdad Pact▷, 1955. The Iraqi revolution of 1958 and the death of the last Hashemites ended Britain's privileges in Iraq (though Iraq seceded formally from the Baghdad Pact only in 1959, thus ending all special relations with Britain). Cyprus won her independence in 1960, after a painful period of strife and conflict with British forces. Kuwait followed in 1961—by peaceful means and in agreement with Britain; Kuwait immediately asked for British protection against Iraq. In 1967 British troops departed from the Crown Colony of Aden and the adjoining Protectorate under fierce attack by local nationalists. By 1970 Great Britain was completing this process of withdrawal from east and west of Suez by evacuating her bases in Libya. Those in the Persian Gulf were scheduled for liquidation in 1971. British protection for the petty rulers of the Gulf's Arabian coast was also due to end in 1971. Britain's new Conservative Government of 1970 was reconsidering the problem of a British presence and British protection in the Persian Gulf, but it appeared very doubtful if they could be restored.

Having profoundly influenced the politics, economics and social life of the ME during the last several hundred years, Great Britain has now yielded to the inhabitants of the region, and to the USA and USSR. British oil companies are no longer as powerful as they used to be—conditions and concessions have changed in favour of the owner-country; and Britain's share among the foreign companies has decreased from over 50% of production at the end of World War II to less than 30% in the 1960s. Britain's primary interest in unimpaired access to the sources of oil in the region still endures, as does a desire to retain a modest degree of influence in the region's capitals through normal diplomatic channels. Britain also remains a major supplier of arms, and

Martin Buber

attempts, sometimes, to use that position as a diplomatic lever. In 1969–70 she participated in Four-Power talks on the Arab-Israel dispute — but apparently as junior partner rather than as an equal to the two Super Powers.   (A.K.)

BRITH SHALOM (Hebrew: Covenant of Peace) — see Bi-national State in Palestine▷.

BUBER, PROF. MARTIN (1878–1965). Jewish philosopher and Zionist thinker, of German-Jewish origin. Together with Weizmann▷, he advocated 'practical' Zionism as opposed to Herzl's 'political' (see: Zionism▷). In 1940 he retired from organizational work but continued to partcipate in Zionist Congresses.

He advocated agreement and co-operation with the Arabs and saw Zionism as a bridge between East and West. He immigrated to Palestine in 1938 and once again entered active Zionist politics as a member of the *Ihud*▷ groups, advocating a bi-national▷ state. After the establishment of Israel he opposed Government policies on questions of Israel-Arab relations and the treatment of the Arab minority in Israel.
                                                        (Sh.H.)

BUNCHE, DR. RALPH (b. 1904). American UN official; Under-Secretary-General since 1954. Appointed Acting UN Mediator to Palestine after the assassination of Count Folke Bernadotte▷ in 1948.

Acted in this capacity from September 1948 until August 1949. Organized and chaired the Israel-Arab negotiations of 1949 at Rhodes (with Egypt and Jordan) and at border points (with Lebanon and Syria), which resulted in the armistice agreements between Israel and these four Arab states. He supervised various UN peace-keeping operations, including those on the Israel-Egyptian border ("UNEF"▷) and in Cyprus▷ ("UNFICYP"). In 1950 B. was awarded the Nobel Peace Prize.   (Sh.H.)

BURAIMI, AL-. Oasis in the Arab peninsula, on the border between Abu Dhabi and Muscat-and-'Oman. Area: 13,490 sq. miles. Pop.: *c.* 25,000 in eight villages, six of which belong to Abu Dhabi, two to Muscat-and-'Oman. In the late 1940s, when it became known there was a possibility of oil in B., a dispute over the oasis ensued between Britain (the power protecting Muscat-and-'Oman and Abu Dhabi) and Sa'udi Arabia. The latter claimed that B.'s inhabitants had been ruled by the Sa'udi Sultans of Najd in the 18th and 19th centuries; but in the Anglo-Sa'udi Treaty of Jedda (1927), in which the boundaries of Sa'udia were fixed, the status of B. is not defined. The opposing interests of the oil giants were apparent in the dispute. If the territory belonged to Abu Dhabi or Muscat-and-'Oman, the concession held by subsidiaries of the Iraq Petroleum Company would cover its oil; if it was Sa'udi territory, its oil would belong to (exclusively American) "Aramco". In 1952, following a period of claims and counter-claims, Sa'udi Arabia sent a military force to occupy B. Arbitration was agreed on in 1954 but was not carried to a successful conclusion. In 1955 B. was taken by military forces of Abu Dhabi and Muscat-and-'Oman, under British command. Sa'udi Arabia protested. She severed diplomatic relations with Britain in 1956, following the Suez War, and declared that they would not be resumed until the B. issue was settled. However, in Jan. 1963 relations were renewed, although the dispute was still unresolved. Sa'udia did not relinquish her claim to sovereignty over B.'s even when closer ties between her and the Gulf principalities (and Britain) developed at the end of the 1960s. As the withdrawal of British protection from the principalities was being prepared for the late 1971, Sa'udia was expected to press her claim. A compromise solution was being explored.   (Y.A.O.)

C

CAIRO (Arabic: *al-Qahira*). Also *Misr* (Egypt) or *Misr al-Qahira*. Capital of Egypt. Pop.: over five m. (1971). C.'s situation, 13 miles south of the apex of

Cairo railway station▷ (centre; 3,000 years old Ramses statue)

Cairo: Muhammad 'Ali Mosque and Old City Wall

Its newspapers (e.g. al-Ahram▷, in the past also al-Misri, al-Muqattam, etc.), its weeklies (Ahbar al-Yawam, Rose al-Yussuf, al-Mussawwar) and literary monthlies are read all over the Arab world. The rich and varied radio programmes of its broadcasting stations attract Arab listeners everywhere. C. possesses a large university (formerly Fu'ad I University, founded 1908, reorganized as a modern university 1925), the 'Ein Shams University (1950), a small American University (1953) and the al-Azhar▷ Islamic University (founded 969–70), famous throughout the Muslim world. C., with its shrines and pyramids, is an important tourist centre; its museums house fine collections, principally ancient Egyptian.

The Arab League▷ was founded in C. (March 1945); its headquarters and offices have remained there. Most League meetings take place in C. Other international organizations, particularly Afro-Asian, hold many congresses and meetings there. The second conference of the Organization for African Unity and the second summit conference of non-aligned states were held there (1964). The African and Asian People's Solidarity Organization (see Asia▷) was founded in C. in 1957 and has its headquarters there. C. provides refuge and headquarters for several revolutionary African underground organizations.

Among the political documents bearing C.'s name are: the C. Declaration of 1 Dec. 1943, in which Roosevelt▷, Churchill▷ and Chiang Kai-shek defined their war aims, mainly in relation to the Far East; the C. Agreement of 2–3 Nov. 1969, mediated by Egypt's rulers, which defined the relationship between the Lebanese Government and the Palestinian guerilla organizations, their operation, powers and conduct; and a similar C. Agreement with the guerilla organizations (27 Sept. 1970) imposed on King Hussein and the government of Jordan through all-Arab pressure.   (S. L.-Y. S.)

CALIPHATE (Arabic: Khilafa, Succession), **CALIPH** (Khalifa). The office of the head of the Muslim community, succeeding the Prophet Muhammad in his political and social functions (as distinct from his prophetic mission). After the Prophet's death in 632 the C. was first held by his friends the "Righteous" C.'s Abu Bakr, 'Umar (Omar), 'Uthman (Othman) and 'Ali, then by the Umayyad, 661–750, and 'Abbassid, 750–1258, dynasties. The office declined in importance with the emergence of rival C.'s, in the tenth century, the rise of military rulers, or sultans, in the C.'s court, and the general disintegration of the Muslim Empire. Various Muslim rulers later arbitrarily assumed the title of C. The Ottoman▷ rulers also assumed the C., but subordinated the office to that of Sultan. A change in Ottoman attitude first

the Nile Delta, is strategically important for it dominates the central approach axis to Upper Egypt. C. was preceded by Fostat, founded during the Arab conquest in 640 CE as an army camp and capital. C. itself was founded in 969 by the Fatimids, in between Fostat and a suburban settlement built by Ahmad Ibn Tulun in the ninth century. These cities were apparently unified and fortified during the reign of Salah-ul-Din (Saladin) in the 12th century. Saladin also added the citadel. The city reached the height of its prosperity in the fourteenth century. It scarcely expanded under Turkish rule. Its character changed under the Khedive Isma'il (1863–7), who tried to impose on it a Western image.

In the last two generations, C. has become the main centre of Arab literature and journalism, film-making, record production and, in general, of Arab culture.

became apparent in the Treaty of Küçük Kaynarca with Russia, 1774, stipulating that the Ottoman Sultan retain his spiritual authority as C. over the Muslim Tatars of the Crimea (which was granted independence). A similar provision was applied to Libya, when, in 1912, Turkey ceded her to Italy. The C. achieved great importance under Sultan Abdül-hamid▷ II, in line with his Pan-Islamic▷ policies, and was incorporated into the Ottoman constitution of 1876.

During World War I, the Ottoman Sultan used his office as C. to arouse sympathy for his cause among Muslims in the countries allied against him, e.g. India. Rumours of allied plans to dismember the Ottoman Empire and abolish the C. led to the formation of a *Khilafat* movement in India, from 1919 onwards, to protect the C. (Indian nationalists identified themselves with that movement). In spite of the Ottoman Sultan-C.'s great prestige, Mustafa Kemal (Atatürk▷) and the Turkish nationalists fought against the Sultan, 1920–3, (see Turkey▷, political history) and finally abolished the sultanate in November 1922, and the C. in March 1924, exiling the Ottoman dynasty.

The abolition of the C., in line with Kemal's policy of cutting Turkey's ties with her Ottoman-Islamic heritage, aroused puzzled, bitter hostility among the world's Muslims everywhere, particularly in India (where a movement for the defence of the C. gained Muslim and Hindu-nationalist support). Various Muslim rulers, e.g. Kings Hussein▷ of Hijaz, Ibn Sa'ud▷ of Arabia, Fu'ad▷ and Farouq▷ of Egypt, now began scheming to have themselves recognized as C. None of them gained much support. An Islamic Congress was convened in Cairo in 1926 to plan the renewal of the C., but, not being representative of all Muslims and failing to agree on a candidate, it dispersed with a call for future action. As no world-Muslim consensus was achieved henceforth either, and as secularism and nationalism spread, calls for the re-establishment of the C. have diminished and been largely disregarded.   (D.K.)

CANAANITES (Hebrew: *Kena'anim*). Group of "Young Hebrews" holding that in Israel a new Hebrew nation is growing, forming the nucleus of the larger Hebrew-C. nation which will embrace the various ethnic groups dwelling within its ancient "natural" borders. The C.'s ideas were finally shaped at the "United Hebrew Youth Committee" in 1944, and in the weekly journal *Aleph* (1948–53). The group remained very small, though with some influence on younger writers and poets. After the Six Day War (1967) the C. called for a federation of Israel, the Jabal Druze and Maronite Lebanon.   (Y.Shv.)

CAPITULATIONS. Foreigners living in the East were exempted from local jurisdiction by the C. The C. were set out in contractual chapters (Latin: *capitula*). (The word is not derived from *capitulare:* to capitulate.) The great mediaeval merchant powers Genoa, Pisa, Venice—were first granted the right to exercise jurisdiction over their nationals in the ME by the Crusader princes in the 11th and 12th centuries, and later also by the Byzantine emperors. With the consolidation of the new Ottoman▷ Empire the C. were renegotiated and treaties were made with Genoa 1453, Venice 1454, France 1535, and England 1583. Newly-formed Western states (USA, Belgium and Greece) were granted similar treaty rights as late as the 19th century. C. were also negotiated with countries from Morocco to Persia, south to Zanzibar and Madagascar and in the Far East (Siam, China and Japan).

The C. covered matters of personal status, penal jurisdiction, commerce, navigation, postal services, and educational, charitable and religious establishments. They included in most cases consular jurisdiction or Mixed Tribunals. For a long time the C., backed by foreign political power, gave foreigners a very necessary protection against the arbitrariness, corruption or xenophobia of local administrators and judges. Furthermore, as domestic law, through the Millet▷ system, granted non-Muslim communities the right to set up their own judiciary in matters of personal status, foreigners and minorities had a considerable degree of autonomy in religious matters, including the protection of Christian holy places, the running of charitable, educational and religious establishments (mainly by France for Roman Catholics, and Russia for the Orthodox). The C. encouraged development, as they implied an "open door" approach. They also stimulated education and research (archaeology).

Gradually, with the growth of strong nationalist movements (initiated by the Young Turks▷), the C. came to be resented as the result of illicit pressure by "imperialist" powers. This attitude was shared by the Soviet government which was the first voluntarily to renounce, 1921, its rights over the "weak". And yet, the disintegration of the C. originated in the West. As Western countries extended their own administrative responsibilities to the area covered by C. they abolished them—Rumania 1877; Bosnia-Herzegovina (Austria-Hungary) 1880; Serbia 1882; Tripolitania (Italy) 1913; Crete and certain Greek provinces 1914; Morocco (France) 1920; Palestine (including Transjordan) (Britain) 1922; Lebanon and Syria (France) 1922. The renunciation of capitulatory rights was also imposed in the Peace Treaties of 1919 on the Central Powers. Thus, the C. were generally terminated because other guarantees of protection were now available; where they were not, the C. were revived (as in the abortive Peace Treaty with Turkey, signed at Sèvres▷ in 1919). Otherwise, the C. were suspended under the mandates▷ or maintained under other contractual forms—mainly juridical reforms (Iran 1928; Iraq 1931; Egypt 1937).

Unilaterial acts to terminate the C. (such as that made by Turkey in 1914) were repudiated. But agreement was reached to conclude treaties for the abolition (Turkey, the Treaty of Lausanne▷, 1923) or phasing out (Egypt, 1937) of the then already modernized forms of C., i.e., the jurisdiction of Mixed Tribunals and/or Consular Courts. The Montreux▷ Convention with Egypt, 1937, provided for a transitional period of twelve years; thus in Egypt the remnants of the C. were abolished only in 1949. The mandates, too, served as a kind of gradual termination of the C. in the countries concerned.

The disappearance of C. left a void which it was difficult to fill. The process of protecting foreigners and minorities either came to a complete halt or was substantially slowed down and the protection of human rights in general remained underdeveloped. Moreover, formerly important minorities atrophied economically and were often forced to leave their countries of residence.   (J.L.)

CASABLANCA. Largest city of Morocco (itself outside the scope of this volume). An African summit conference, held in C. in 1961, drew up the C. Pact and formed the C. Bloc. The King of Morocco had called the Conference in particular to deal with the Congo problem. He had hoped the leaders of all the anti-Western African countries would attend. But only the Presidents of Egypt, Ghana, Guinea and Mali attended, with observers representing Libya, Ceylon, Algeria, the Palestinian Arabs and the Lumumba faction in the Congo. The Pact drawn up at the C. Conference, concerning the freedom and co-operation of African countries, had no influence on events in Africa or the development of an African political ideology. The C. Bloc did not rally the radical left; it remained limited to the five states whose leaders had met in C., with the addition of Algeria. This limited bloc rapidly disintegrated: a. when it became clear it had no influence or political importance; b. when the Congo problem was solved—or decreased in significance; c. after Morocco and Algeria had had serious armed border clashes in 1963 (Morocco charged that Egypt gave military aid to the enemy of her Moroccan ally). The enthusiasm of the conservative Moroccan monarchy for participation in a radical-revolutionary bloc had cooled. The C. Bloc virtually died in 1963.

An all-Arab summit conference was also held in C., in 1965. This conference signed a new all-Arab Solidarity Pact. It also affirmed previous decisions to frustrate Israel's Jordan River Project by diverting the sources of the Jordan in Syria and Lebanon.
                                                                         (Y.S.)

CASPIAN SEA. The world's largest inland salt lake, forming the border between Europe and Asia. Of its total shoreline of 4,000 mi., 3,350 mi. are in the USSR and 650 mi. in Iran. Principal ports in Iran: Bandar Shah and Pahlavi. The C.S.'s water level is falling. The sea is of economic importance to both the USSR and Iran, as a source of fish (caviar is taken from the C.S.'s sturgeon) and for transportation. From 1928 to 1952 a joint Iranian-Soviet concern fished along its southern shores. In 1953 Iran refused to renew the concession and a government company was formed to run the fishing and caviar industry.
                                                                         (B.G.)

CATHOLICS IN THE ME. There are about $1\frac{1}{2}$m. Catholics in the ME. They are mostly converts from the Eastern Christian communities, as a result of missionary activity by the Catholic Church, and the Uniates▷. About 20% belong to the Roman Catholic (Latin) Church proper (in Arabic, the term Roman Catholic—"Rum-Katholik"—denotes the Greek Catholic Church; what is in European languages termed Roman Catholic, is in Arabic "Latin"); c. 80%—to the Uniate churches. The Encyclical *Orientalium ecclesiarum dignitas*, promulgated in 1894, banned proselytizing among the followers of the Eastern communities by the Roman Catholic Church and entrusted their conversion to the Catholic Uniate churches.

The influence of the Latin Catholic community in the ME was strongly felt only in the time of the Crusades. The present members of the Latin Church are the descendants of the Crusaders, and of merchants from the Italian maritime cities, as well as former members of Eastern Christian communities who converted to Roman Catholicism. The community also includes some Roman Catholics from Western countries, who have settled in the ME. Many of the last left the region with the ending of the various mandatory administrations. The total number of Latin Catholics in the ME is approximately 330,000. In the territory under the ecclesiastical administration of the Latin Patriarch in Jerusalem there are 47,000 (24,000 in Israel, 20,000 in Jordan and 3,000 in Cyprus); Lebanon has 16,000; Syria 11,000; Iraq 5,000; Iran 12,000; Egypt 30,000; Kuwait 36,000 and Libya 28,000. A large number of Latin Catholics lived in Sudan (160,000 in 1960). Almost all of them belonged to the Negro tribes of the south and many left as refugees in the course of the rebellion and its suppression.

Administratively, the Latin Patriarchate of Jerusalem is responsible for Israel, Jordan and Cyprus. In the other countries of the ME, there are apostolic vicariates headed by apostolic administrators. Since 1938, Latin Catholics and their institutions in the ME have been under the jurisdiction of the Vatican Congregation for the Oriental Churches.

The oriental Catholic (Uniate) churches comprise the Maronites▷ (450,000), the Greek Catholics▷ (250,000), the Chaldeans▷ (190,000), the Coptic Catholics▷ (80,000), the Syrian Catholics▷ (60,000) and the Armenian Catholics▷ (50,000). Each of these six churches is headed by a patriarch.

In spite of the relatively small number of Catholics, their Church runs a great many educational and charitable institutions, mainly in Lebanon, Israel and Jordan—such as the University of St. Joseph in Beirut, various biblical institutions in Israel, and the seminaries for the Uniate churches maintained by Latin monastic orders. (Sh.C.)

CATROUX, GEORGES (1887–1969). French officer and diplomat. He served in Algeria (1900–2, 1936–9), Morocco (1907–10, 1928–31), Indo-China (1902–5, 1939–40), Syria and Lebanon (1931–5, 1941–3). When General de Gaulle▷ established the Free French movement, after the French collapse in June 1940, C. joined him. He was appointed de Gaulle's representative in the ME and took part in preparing the conquest of Syria and Lebanon (then held by Vichy French forces). On the day of the invasion (8 June 1941), C. revoked the French Mandate in Syria and Lebanon and declared both independent. A treaty to be signed later, he added, would ensure their independence and define their relations with France. C. proclaimed himself Free French "Délégué Général" in the Levant (Churchill▷ strongly advised against a reversion to the title "High Commissioner"). C. again proclaimed Syrian and Lebanese independence on 26 Nov. 1941. But what he and de Gaulle had in mind was a conditional and partial independence, with a privileged position for France—in the spirit of the Treaty of 1936 (see France▷, Lebanon▷, Syria▷). Disagreement over terms of the independence to be granted, and French delay in relinquishing control, led to a violent crisis between France and Syria and Lebanon (1943–5). C. was transferred in June 1943 to Algiers. The severity of his successor, Jean Helleu (see Lebanon▷), resulted in a crisis and C. was recalled to Beirut in November 1943 for a short time, to appease local sentiment. He was forced to reinstate the National Government dismissed by his predecessor, in other words to acknowledge

France's retreat from her position. C.'s many other posts and missions were not connected with the ME. He wrote several books, among them two memoirs of his work in the ME: *Dans la bataille de la Mediterranee* (1949) and *Deux missions au Moyen Orient* (1958). (J.B-A.)

CEMAL PASHA (1872–1922). Turkish military and political leader. Born in Istanbul. C. graduated from the War College. He joined the Young Turks▷, who opposed Sultan Abdülhamid's▷ regime, and became one of their leaders. After the Young Turks' revolution, 1908, he held various governorships. In 1913 he became Military Governor of Istanbul, and later Minister for Naval Affairs—forming, together with Enver▷ and Talât▷, a "Triumvirate" which ruled Turkey until 1918. As Military Governor of Syria and Commander of the Fourth Army, 1914–17, he suppressed suspected subversion by Arab nationalists and several trials ended with the execution of suspected rebels. He also tried or expelled Palestinian Jews suspected of disloyalty. After the Armistice of 1918 he fled to Berlin, then to Afghanistan and again to Europe. He was assassinated by an Armenian in Tiflis. (D.K.)

CENTO. Central Treaty Organization. Official name given in August 1959 to the 1955 Baghdad Pact▷, the defence alliance between Turkey, Iran, Pakistan and Britain; the USA associated itself with and supported the treaty. Its former name became inappropriate with Iraq's withdrawal in March 1959. The major political aims of the earlier Pact receded, particularly when Pakistan cultivated close relations with the USSR and China while assuming a neutralist posture. C. now concentrates on economic planning and co-ordination. Since 1964 Turkey, Iran and Pakistan have also maintained a "Regional Co-operation for Development" (RCD) which endeavours to co-ordinate economic planning and channel development projects. (Y.S.)

CHALDEANS. A branch of the Assyrian▷ (Nestorian) Church, which sought communion with Rome through the Uniate▷. They number about 200,000 and live mainly in Iraq and Iran with small communities in Lebanon, Syria, Turkey and Israel (Jerusalem). The movement for union with Rome began in the Middle Ages, but mass conversion took place only after World War I among the Assyrians who had left their original homes and settled in the larger towns of Iraq and Iran. As the largest Chaldean community was in Baghdad, the Patriarch, who bears the title of Patriarch of Babylon, moved his seat there from Mosul. (Sh.C.)

*CHAMOUN, CAMILLE (Sham'un, Kamil) (b. 1900). Lebanese politician. President of Lebanon, 1952–8. Maronite▷ Christian. In 1929 he was elected member of Parliament for Mount Lebanon. He was Minister of the Interior in 1938 and in 1943–4. In 1944 he was appointed Minister in London, and in 1946 headed the Lebanese delegation to the UN. C. belonged to the camp of Bishara al-Khouri▷ and the "Constitutional Bloc", who tried to impart an Arab character to Lebanon and integrate her in a Pan-Arab alignment. In 1947, he was appointed Minister of Finance in the government of al-Yafi▷, and later became Minister of the Interior in the government of Riyad al-Sulh▷. However, when Khouri was elected President for a second term in 1949, after the constitution had been suitably amended, and was accused of corruption and responsibility for a general decline in the standard of public administration, C. joined his opponents. In the summer of 1952, he carried out a kind of a quiet semi-coup which forced Khouri to resign. On 22 Sept., C. was elected President in his place. During his term of office, he pursued a policy of close relations with the Western Powers and of cautious neutrality towards the other Arab countries.

During the Syrian crisis in 1957–8, and after the union of Syria and Egypt, he was opposed to Lebanon's joining the Syrian-Egyptian camp. His pro-western policy, together with rumours that, like his predecessor, he proposed to secure a constitutional amendment to legalize his election for a second term, led in May 1958 to riots and a civil war. In July, C. requested and obtained the help of the US armed forces. As part of a compromise settlement, he withdrew his candidature for a further term of office. In September 1958, the Commander-in-Chief of the armed forces, Fu'ad Shihab▷, was elected in his place. C. then established a right-wing liberal, pro-Western opposition party: the "National Liberal Party". For a time, he withdrew from politics, but became active once again in the 1960s, when he established a "Tripartite Alliance" with Pierre Gemayel▷, leader of the "Phalanges"▷, and Raymond Edde▷, head of the "National Bloc". Parliamentary life in Lebanon often revolved around the conditions under which the representatives of this alliance were prepared to join the government or else the nature and intensity of their opposition. C. published his memoirs in 1949 and, in a revised edition, 1963.   (O.G.-Y.S.)

CHEHAB, CHEHABISTS—see Shihab▷, Fu'ad.

*CHINA. Until the 1950s, C. was not particularly interested in the ME, or active there. When the Arab states began to recognize Communist C. in 1956 (until then only Israel had recognized C., though diplomatic relations were not established), their diplomatic relations with "Nationalist" C. (Taiwan, Formosa) were severed. The same applied to Turkey and Iran in 1971. ME countries still maintaining relations with Taiwan are Cyprus, Lebanon, Jordan and Sa'udi Arabia.

Communist C. was interested in developing relations with the Arab states and securing their recognition. Her interest was evinced actively in 1955, when a Chinese delegation attended the Bandung▷ Conference and participated in efforts to establish an Asian Family of Nations. She made contacts with several Arab leaders, particularly Gamal 'Abd-ul-Nasser▷.

Since then the Chinese People's Republic has shown growing hostility toward Israel (whose recognition she had welcomed in January 1950 when Israel had been the only ME state to recognize her); she finally denounced Israel, in many statements and in her propaganda, as an aggressor and a tool of imperialism. C. even denied Israel's right to exist. When Egyptian and Syrian policies took on a more leftist complexion in 1955, many Arab states recognized Communist C.—Egypt, Syria and (Royalist!) Yemen 1956, Iraq, Sudan and Morocco 1958, Algeria 1962, Tunisia 1964, South Yemen 1967, Kuwait 1971. Turkey and Iran recognized Communist C. in Aug. 1971.

In 1963 the Prime Minister of C., Chou En-lai, paid official visits to Egypt, Sudan and the *Maghreb;* he again visited Egypt and Syria in 1965. Since C. had aided the Algerian rebels even before they achieved independence (while the USSR adopted a more cautious line), her relations with Algeria were cordial. Southern Yemen, which from the beginning of her independence had been ruled by a left-wing revolutionary regime, was also close to, and assisted by, C. This did not prevent C. from fostering relations with such arch-conservative regimes as pre-1962 Yemen and Kuwait, and extending aid to Yemen. Relations with Tunisia, on the other hand, marred by disagreements and an insulting exchange in 1967, were virtually frozen.

Chinese economic and technical aid generally comprised long-term and interest-free credits, mostly earmarked for specific projects; some 20% of the aid was in outright grants. According to Western estimates, 30–50% of Chinese aid that has been committed or agreed, is actually disbursed. Chinese experts are sometimes provided also. Among ME recipients of Chinese aid are Egypt (though in 1969–70 C. reportedly stopped aid because of her dissatisfaction with Egypt's policy), Syria, Iraq (?), Yemen, South Yemen, Sudan and Algeria.

C.'s wish to strengthen her relations with the Arab states and her willingness to extend aid (though not her ability to do so) increased with the intensification of the Sino-Soviet conflict and the struggle of C. and the USSR for ideological predominance and the support of the Communist world. Trade between C. and the ME is very restricted in contrast to the important place accorded the ME by C. in her foreign aid and her diplomacy. Both C. and the ME are trying to foster it.

C. is willing, like the Soviet Union, to establish links even with governments suppressing their local communists; at the same time she may support communists opposed to a friendly government. It is difficult to judge the exact amount of Chinese aid to various communist parties, though obviously such aid is given. C. also attempts to gain influence in various international organizations—e.g. various Afro-Asian groups such as the "Afro-Asian People's Solidarity Organization" (see Asia▷, Africa▷, Bandung▷), where there is a fierce clash among pro-Soviet and pro-Chinese elements in the leadership. Perhaps C. conceals and restricts her aid to groups fighting against friendly governments; she lends her unconcealed support to guerilla and other organizations who share common enemies with C. In this way C. aids the "Popular Front for the Liberation of the Occupied Arabian (*i.e.* Persian) Gulf", which wages, with the help of the rulers of Southern Yemen, a guerilla war against the Sultanate of Muscat-and-'Oman▷. In the same way, C. has assisted the left-wing nationalists in Algeria and South Yemen against their colonial rulers. C. also aids the Palestinian-Arab guerilla organizations—including Nayef Hawatmeh's "Popular Democratic Front" PDFLP and George Habash's▷ "Popular Front"▷ PFLP (both ideologically close to C.) and Yasser 'Arafat's▷ right-wing *Fatah*▷. Actual support—money, arms and equipment, instructors, know-how, training facilities in C.—is perhaps not large; its significance is mainly symbolic, political and propagandist.

(Y.S.)

CHRISTIANS IN THE ME. Christianity had its origin in Israel and from there spread rapidly to the neighbouring countries. Soon such cities as Antioch, Alexandria and Constantinople overshadowed Jerusalem as the main centres of the rising faith and the first seven Ecumenical Councils took place in ME cities. Schisms that split Christianity occurred at these assemblies of bishops. Political and national factors were often linked with the theological issues which led to the establishment of independent churches. The Islamic conquest caused a serious setback for Christianity in the ME, but most of the ancient churches of the first Christian centuries still survive in the region, (see Greek Orthodox▷, Maronites▷, Monophysites▷, Assyrians▷, Armenians▷, Copts▷, Uniates▷). The number of their followers has, however, been greatly reduced. Sizable Christian majorities exist only in Armenia and Cyprus, with about 2m. and ½m. Christian inhabitants respectively. The Lebanese Christian community, of over 1m., accounts for about half of the population and in large measure determines the character of the country. In all the other countries of the ME, the Christians are only small minorities—14% in Syria, less than 10% in most countries.

In the Ottoman▷ Empire, the Millet system▷ gave the Christian communities a large measure of autonomy, not only in religious life, but also in matters of personal status. This system, though adjusted to the conditions of modern life, still prevails today in certain countries of the ME (Lebanon, Israel, Jordan). In other countries, it has been partially or wholly abolished. Thus, Turkey adopted, after World War I, a secular system. Most Arab countries (Egypt, Sudan, Syria, Iraq), where Islam is the state religion, have tended to curtail the rights enjoyed by the Christian communities. Egypt for instance has abolished Christian religious courts and limited the activities of Christian educational and charitable institutions. Iraq has nationalized Christian educational institutions, and in Syria expropriation of Christian church property has severely affected Christian educational institutions. These restrictive measures derive only in part from religious intolerance. They are also due to the young national states' suspicion of Christian missionary institutions (which they consider to be a continuation of European colonialism or a concealed form of Western and American penetration) and largely to the generally totalitarian character of these states. In Sudan, the problem is that of the oppression of the Negro tribes of the southern provinces, among whom Christians number about 12%, 300–500,000, four-fifths of whom are Catholics. Many Christian missionaries were expelled, Christian schools were brought under government control, a day of rest on Sunday was abolished, etc.

A direct product of the uneasiness felt by the Christian minorities in the ME has been a progressive emigration to Western Europe and the Americas where large colonies of ex-ME Christians prosper.

(Sh.C.)

Christian Arabs, mainly from Lebanon, Syria and Palestine, played an important role in the Arab national movement, particularly in its early stages when it was a movement of enlightenment and literary revival rather than of political aspiration. As Muslims took over the leadership, and the dividing line between Arab nationalism and Islamic revival became blurred (see Arab Nationalism▷, Pan-Islam▷), and as Arab nationalism became a political force striving for statehood, Christians became somewhat less prominent. Some of them have, however, remained active figures.

Since Christians are a minority in most countries of the ME and in the ME as a whole, their attitude to Arab nationalism has tended to be ambivalent: some of them, concerned lest totalitarian nationalism (coupled sometimes with Islamic fanaticism, sometimes with Pan-Syrian expansionism) impair the remnants of Christian communal semi-autonomy, actively defend that semi-autonomy, dissociating themselves from Pan-Arab▷ nationalism, at least in its more extreme manifestations. In Lebanon even, the centre of Christian political awareness and activity, the idea of a "Christian National Home", with Lebanon as a home and refuge for all Christian Arabs, has been mooted. Other Christian-Arab leaders, however, have displayed an extremist Arab nationalism—some of them, perhaps, out of an age-old minority instinct to overstress conformity to the majority's ideals. There is a similar ambivalence in Christian-Arab attitudes to Israel: while many Arab Christians are no doubt more moderate in their hostility to Israel, particularly in Lebanon. They would not usually give public and straightforward expression to such moderation, and many of them even stress extreme anti-Israel attitudes. Many Christians are, of course, genuine Arab nationalists, striving to do away with the traditional communal distinctions and to merge them into a united, secular Arab nation.

(Y. S.)

CHURCHILL, SIR WINSTON LEONARD SPENCER (1874–1965). British statesman, Conservative Prime Minister 1940–5, 1951–5. C. made his main impact on ME affairs during his term as Colonial Secretary from February 1921 to October 1922. At a conference held in Cairo in March 1921, under his chairmanship, it was decided that Amir Feisal b. Hussein▷, who had been banished from Syria by the French, would become King of Iraq, while Amir 'Abdullah b. Hussein▷ would be given Transjordan, then part of the Palestine Mandate but soon to be excluded from the Jewish National Home. C. issued the White Paper▷ of 1922, the first major British policy statement on Palestine. Out of office, C. was considered sympathetic to the Zionist▷ cause; he favoured partition in 1937 and opposed the White Paper of 1939, restricting Jewish immigration and settlement. In 1944 he had approved the formation of the Jewish Brigade▷ Group, but the assassination of Lord Moyne by Jewish terrorists in Egypt, soon

afterwards, was viewed by him with great severity and he insisted on execution of the assassins.

As Prime Minister during five fateful war years and four post-war years, C. had a decisive influence on all major events in the ME. He participated in important war-time summit conferences in Teheran, November 1943 and Cairo, December 1943; at some of these meetings, and at a Cairo stop-over on his way back from the Yalta Conference, February 1945, he met top ME leaders. In the immediate post-war period C. advocated (in contrast to Roosevelt▷) a stronger Western stand against Soviet aspirations, including those in the ME. Stiffer Western resistance, which led to Soviet retreats over Turkey and the Straits▷, 1945, and in Persia, 1946, and an American commitment to the defence of Turkey and Greece in the Truman▷ Doctrine of 1947, were at least partially due to his influence. But in the war and post-war period, C. was not intimately connected with specifically ME events.   (Sh. H.–Y. S.)

CIRCASSIANS. One of the peoples of the Caucasus. Their region, formerly part of the Ottoman Empire,

Sir Winston Churchill

was transferred to Russia in 1829. After rebellions lasting until 1859, and the expansion of Russian control over additional regions in the Caucasus, many C., especially the Muslims, emigrated to the Ottoman Empire, which willingly accepted and settled them. Some of them reached Thrace, in European Turkey; others settled in the Asian and Arab parts of the Empire. The Muslim C., dispersed over Syria, Jordan and Palestine, were partially assimilated by the Arabs. They maintained their language for two or three generations, but in recent generations it has given way to Arabic. Yet the C. still maintain their distinctive character. There are 20–25,000 C. in Syria, about 10,000 in Iraq, 15–20,000 in Jordan, and several hundred in Israel. Some C. villages in the Golan▷ Heights in south-west Syria were abandoned in 1967, when Israel occupied the area. There are two C. villages in Israel (Kafr Kama and Rihaniya in Galilee), with several hundred inhabitants. In Jordan, many C. serve in the army (in the past also in the Frontier Force). Despite their small numbers, two seats are reserved for them in the Jordanian Parliament—unchanged since 1928, although the number of members of parliament has increased from 20 to 60. In the USSR, there is an autonomous region of the C., but their numbers are reported to be declining. There is no longer any connection between the C. in the ME and those in the USSR.

The migrating C. were joined, in the 19th century, by a small number of Chechens. In the course of time, the differences between these two related peoples disappeared, and the Chechens were assimilated by the C.   (Y.S.)

*CLERIDES, GLAFKOS (b. 1919). Cypriot lawyer and politician. Studied law in London. Served with the RAF during World War II. Shot down over Germany where he was imprisoned 1942–5. Practised law in Cyprus 1951–60, defending many EOKA▷ fighters arrested by the British. Head of the Greek-Cypriot group on the Constitutional Commission 1959–60. Minister of Justice 1959–60. President, House of Representatives, since August 1960. Considered as leader of the Right, in alliance with P. Georghadjis▷, he favours Cypriot independence (as against Enosis▷) and opposes Greek interference in Cypriot politics. In 1969 he founded the "United National Party", which obtained 15 seats, of the Greeks' 35, in the elections of 1970. C. is considered rightist and pro-West (as against President Makarios'▷ neutralism), and a rival—actual or potential—to Makarios; in domestic affairs he supports the government. Since 1968, he has conducted talks on behalf of the Greek Cypriots with Ra'uf Denktash▷ of the Turkish Cypriots in an effort to

find a solution to the island's communal problem. So far, the talks have yielded no agreement.   (B.G.)

COELE SYRIA (al-Biqa', Arabic: Valley). Wide valley between the mountains of the Lebanon and the Anti-Lebanon. Under the Ottoman Empire, most of C.S. was part of the province (Vilayet) of Damascus rather than of the autonomous district of Lebanon, since it has no decisive Christian-Maronite majority. According to the present administrative division, Shi'ite Muslims form about 31%; Sunni Muslims, 18.9%; Druzes, 3.5%; Christian communities, 46.4%. The annexation of C. to Greater Lebanon by the French, in 1920, together with the annexation of the Sunni-Muslim North and the Shi'ite Muslim South, destroyed Lebanon's homogenous communal structure. It became a multi-communal country, comprising many minorities. The annexation created severe problems, since the inhabitants had not been consulted. Most Muslims opposed it. With the acceptance of the "National Pact" of 1943 (see Lebanon▷, history) the dispute was settled, at least in principle, and the boundaries of Lebanon, including the three disputed districts which had been annexed, were accepted by all.   (Y.S.)

COLONIALISM. C. in the narrow sense of the term means the occupation of territory in foreign countries—mostly underdeveloped countries, and mostly overseas—by a world power (generally European and white) in direct ownership, sometimes accompanied by the permanent settlement of white settlers. Many colonies originated in the settlement of traders, planters, etc. In other cases conquest preceded settlement.

Direct colonialism, in the narrow sense of the term, occurred in the ME in only three instances. 1. Libya was conquered by Italy in 1911–2 and formally annexed, and Italian colonists were sent out and settled in an organized manner; 2. Aden was conquered by the British (operating out of India) in 1839 and ruled by the governors of Bombay Province, and later by the Government of British India; from 1937 onwards it was a Crown Colony; 3. Sudan was ruled by an Anglo-Egyptian Condominium from 1899 onwards. From the British point of view, this was not perhaps direct colonialism, as Britain did not view the Sudan as fully her territory; but the Egyptians advocated the "Unity of the Nile Valley" and claimed the Sudan as part of a single state united with Egypt under a single crown, denying the Sudanese the right to independence or self-determination.

Direct, fully-fledged colonialism has been eliminated in the ME. Libya was captured from the Italians during World War II and granted independence in 1951. Sudan became independent in 1956. Aden was admitted in 1963, as a semi-independent state, to the Federation of South Arabia, and became part of the People's Republic of South Yemen in 1967.

Colonialism in its broader sense can also mean the imposition of a European power's protection or indirect rule, or the attainment by political power or pressure of control and excessive influence in the economic field (oil-concessions, railways, shipping, canals, etc.). C. in this wider sense, whose exact limits cannot be defined, certainly prevailed in many places in the ME. Great Britain conquered Egypt in 1882, but recognized a symbolic Turkish sovereignty, always maintaining that the British occupation was "temporary". From 1914 to 1922, the British regime was defined as a "protectorate". The Ottoman Empire and the Persian monarchy remained independent; but the European powers exercised—in constant competition and bitter rivalry among themselves— a semi-colonial control over major sectors of the economy, including finance and taxation, obtained many concessions, supervised the arrangements affecting the Dardanelles and the Bosphorus, and intervened to secure partial autonomy for the Lebanese Christians (1861). Britain and Russia formally divided Persia into spheres of influence (1907). Britain imposed her protection on the principalities of the Persian Gulf—Muscat-and-'Oman, Qatar and the Trucial Coast in the course of the 19th century, Kuwait in 1899, the territory of Ibn Sa'ud early in the 20th century (although in that case no formal protectorate was ever established). Great Britain never annexed these principalities and claimed no sovereignty over them, yet her control of them followed an almost complete colonial pattern. Britain also imposed her protection on the south-Arabian desert sheikhdoms, from the border of Muscat and Dhofar, through Hadhramaut to Aden and its environs. These sheikhdoms became formal protectorates and colonial rule over them was almost direct.

In the places last mentioned the indirect, protectorate C. was eliminated only in the 1960s and '70s. The Aden Protectorate became a semi-independent federation in 1959, and an independent state (South Yemen) in 1967. Kuwait emerged from the British protectorate in 1961, and Britain was due to withdraw her protection and military forces from the rest of the Persian Gulf sheikhdoms in 1971. In the other areas of indirect C. this process had been completed long before. In Egypt, the British Protectorate was officially abolished in 1922, when Britain unilaterally recognized Egypt as an independent state; but Great Britain claimed certain special rights with regard to Egypt's defence, the maintenance of troops and bases

in Egypt, etc. This formula of a state in fact partially independent, granting a great power privileges and accepting its *de facto* protection, was to be formalized in a treaty. Such a treaty was signed, after years of negotiations, between Egypt and Britain, in 1936. It somewhat diminished British privileges and increased Egyptian independence; and officially it was a treaty between equals. Yet in fact it represented the continuation of a semi-colonial partial protectorate. The Treaty of 1936 was abolished with the signing of a new agreement in 1954, which was in turn abolished unilaterally by Egypt after the Suez War of 1956. Thus ended special treaty relations which had in fact constituted a partial protectorate and restricted Egypt's independence.

The mandatory system was a slightly more complete form of protectorate. When the victorious powers sought, in 1918–20, to settle the future of the Arab-Asian parts of the defeated and dismembered Ottoman Empire, they elaborated the mandate▷ as a compromise between the independence promised and imperialist plans for annexation and spheres of influence on which the powers had decided in secret treaties during the war. The mandatory power was charged to guide the mandated territory to independence. Britain was awarded the Mandate over Iraq and Palestine (at first including Transjordan), and Syria and Lebanon were entrusted to France. In practice, the type of regime which the powers established was very similar to a colonial one. Britain and France (and the Arab nationalists) strove to replace the Mandate with a treaty according a formally complete independence to the liberated state—and special privileges to the mandatory power. Britain signed such a treaty with Iraq in 1922, and again in an amended form in 1930. The latter treaty led to Iraqi independence and terminated the Mandate; it was replaced in 1955 by an agreement in the framework of the Baghdad Pact▷, which lapsed when Iraq seceded from the Pact in 1959. Britain signed treaties with Transjordan in 1928, 1946 and 1948. The first left Britain with a great deal of power, but each subsequent treaty accorded a greater degree of independence. The 1948 treaty was officially renounced in 1957, when Jordan agreed to accept from other Arab countries the aid needed to maintain her army and paid until then by Britain, and the King dismissed his British Commander-in-Chief, Sir John Glubb▷. France signed similar treaties with Syria and Lebanon in 1936, but did not ratify them. In 1941, Free France declared the Mandate terminated, and after a further struggle, 1943–5, the elimination of French domination and privileges was completed, without a further treaty. The Palestine Mandate ended in May 1948, with the establishment of the State of

Israel, and the occupation of the Arab areas by Egypt and Jordan. Thus, the indirect C. and semi-protectorate of the mandates ended in the 1940s and '50s.

Even in countries formally enjoying complete independence a kind of concealed semi-C. may obtain—e.g. through foreign control of vital sectors of the economy. Foreign influence in Turkey and Persia before World War I was regarded by many as a form of C. Since World War II the Western powers, particularly the USA, are often accused of "neo-C."—through control of markets, oil concessions, the manipulation of credit and the international banking system, etc. Iran's struggle against the Anglo-Iranian Oil Company, 1951–3, was described as anti-colonialist or anti-imperialist (the two terms have become virtually synonymous); the same holds for the Egyptian dispute over the nationalization of the Suez Canal, 1956. In effect, most nationalist struggles—political or economic—against Western powers are described as anti-colonialist. To what extent such a presentation of political claims is justified, and to what extent it is still possible to speak of C. or Neo-C. in the ME, is a matter of definitions and terminology, and of political opinion.   (Y.S.)

COMMON MARKET—see European Economic Community▷.

COMMUNICATIONS—see Transport▷.

*COMMUNISM, COMMUNIST PARTIES, IN THE ME. Communist activity—*i.e.* political activity defining its objectives and methods according to the Leninist or Stalinist interpretation of Marxism, and adopting the current ideological and political positions of the Soviet Union—began in the ME after World War I and the Bolshevik revolution. In 1920, an Armenian association entilted the "Spartacus League" was founded. In the same year, the Egyptian CP was founded in Alexandria; it was recognized in 1921 by the Third International (Comintern). These were small organizations, drawing most of their members from ethnic minorities and the intelligentsia. Far removed from the general public, they indulged in a great deal of internal ideological disputes, which led to schisms.

In Palestine, C. groups grew, from 1920 onwards, out of extreme left-wing elements in the Zionist-Socialist movement. These could no longer maintain the synthesis of Zionism with socialism, since C. had adopted an extreme anti-Zionist position, in both doctrine and practical politics. The conclusion they drew differed: some emigrated to the Soviet Union (where most of them died in the Stalinist purges of the 1930s). Others established the Palestine CP, which

supported anti-Zionist Arab nationalism, although most of its members for more than 20 years were Jews. The "Arabization" of the party, *e.g.* in the composition of its organs, was one of its main aims and slogans from 1924 onwards. The contradiction between Arab nationalist ideology and activity on the one hand, and a largely Jewish membership on the other, led to incessant disputes, changes in the party line, and factionalism.

In the Arab countries it was not until the 1930s that CPs with any continuity of activity and membership were founded; they were all illegal. The CP of Syria and Lebanon was established in 1930, that of Iraq in 1934 (in both cases, some sources give other foundation dates). They attempted—as a clandestine, underground movement—to penetrate the trade unions and to make contacts with the extreme anti-colonialist elements in the Arab nationalist movement. This led them to co-operate on occasion with elements connected with the Nazis such as the Mufti of Jerusalem in 1936, and Rashid 'Ali al-Kilani▷ in 1941.

In the 1940s, with the entry of the Soviet Union into the war on the Allied side and thanks to the impression created by Russia's victories, C. propaganda became respectable and important in the Arab world, and C. activists were able to emerge from the underground (although the parties were still officially proscribed). But the growth of their influence was arrested by two events: one was the elimination in 1946 of the separatist autonomous Republic of Azerbaijan▷ in northern Iran (which had been set up with Soviet help), and the other was Soviet support for the 1947 partition plan for Palestine (which the local CPs were obliged to support, albeit half-heartedly).

Soviet penetration of the ME, which commenced with the 1955 arms deal with Egypt and has grown apace ever since (see Russia▷), was accompanied only to a limited extent by a strengthening of the local CPs. The USSR forged links with the rulers, first and foremost Egypt, rather than with prisoners in jail. The Egyptian CP was in any case split into rival factions. Most of its activists were drawn from ethnic minorities whose standing and influence was impaired by the wave of nationalist fervour and the exodus of foreigners and minorities, and no C. leader of stature emerged. The schisms centered mainly around the attitude to be adopted towards the "bourgeois" national leadership, especially after 1952 when the latter became "progressive". The main faction of the party, the "Democratic Movement of National Liberation" (HDTW or MDLN) at first granted the new officers' regime its qualified support, whereas other factions opposed it. The regime did not reciprocate the sympathy of MDLN, especially after violent clashes with strikers in August 1952, and, from 1953 onwards, suppressed the CP.'s cells and arrested its leaders. There were further waves of arrests in 1955–6 and 1958. However, the increasingly close relations with the Soviet Union led to a softening in the attitude to the C.'s. Early in 1963, all the C.'s in jail were released, and many joined Nasser's administrative and propaganda establishment. At the beginning of 1965 the Egyptian CP decided to disband itself, and its members joined the regime's "Arab Socialist Union" on an individual basis.

The strongest and most active CP in the ME after World War II was that of Iraq. In the 1940s, it succeeded in extending its influence steadily, despite internal dissensions and brutal persecution on the part of the authorities. On several occasions, its leaders were captured and hanged, but new leaders always emerged in their place. The CP was one of the pillars of Qassem's▷ Republican regime, 1958–63. In 1959, when the regime's Nasserist opponents plotted to oust the C.'s from important positions they occupied in the army, the C.'s, most of them Kurds, helped to suppress a dangerous rebellion in the north. But the C.'s went too far in their demands; they claimed full partnership with Qassem, penetrated the regime's apparatus and set up strong cells in key positions. Qassem half-suppressed them, and from that time until his downfall, in 1963, he maintained a balance between the C.'s and the Nasserists. After Qassem's fall, the CP was once again persecuted, this time at the hands of the Nationalist-socialist Ba'th▷ party, and many of its members and supporters were arrested, tortured and killed. On the other hand, the Ba'thist regime, whose popular base was extremely narrow, was interested in forming a wider left-wing coalition, and endeavoured from time to time to attract C.'s—at least one or the other of the CP's rival factions—to join such a coalition as junior partners. Iraq's alliance with the USSR, which was becoming closer all the time, provided a further motive for some sort of partnership with the local C.'s. Conflicting attitudes towards the regime and the Ba'th party caused incessant splits of the CP into rival factions; so did differing views on the Kurdish problem. In 1969 it was reported that one of the three or four factions of the CP—the "Central Leadership" of 'Aziz al-Hajj—was cooperating with the Ba'th authorities, while the "Central Committee" faction of Zaki Kheiri and Baha-ul-Din Nuri was opposed to this. Since 1969, 'Aziz Sharif, who is regarded as a Communist, is a government minister.

The CP in Syria—which separated from that of Lebanon in 1943, with the dissolution of the Comintern and the attainment of independence by Syria and Lebanon—wielded a strong influence from the fall of Adib Shishakli▷ in 1954 until the union with Egypt in 1958. The fear of growing Communist influence was one of the motives which impelled the "Ba'th" officers and their allies in 1957 to negotiate the abortive union with Egypt. (The fear of growing Communist influence had not, however, impeded growing Soviet penetration and the ever-closer relations with the USSR.) In the mid-1960s the Syrian CP—still officially illegal—became in fact, if not in name, the partner of the Ba'thist military regime. Since the 1966 coup in which the extreme "military" wing of the Ba'th party seized power, at least one or two C. ministers have held office in the Syrian government. The veteran leader of the Syrian CP, Khaled Bakdash▷, is the outstanding C. personality in the Arab world. He spent many years in exile in Eastern Europe and returned to Syria in 1966

The CP in Lebanon, although illegal, conducts its activities quite openly, both in the trade unions (Mustafa al-'Aris) and in intellectual circles (Nicola Shawi). It has a nucleus of activists but has not achieved great political influence.

Sudanese C. had its beginnings in cells of Sudanese students in Cairo in the early 1940s. After World War II, a CP grew within the powerful Railway Workers Union in Khartoum and Atbara and was active in organizing strikes. In 1964, the C.'s were instrumental in the overthrow of Gen. 'Abbud's▷ military dictatorship. Their share in the government from 1964 to 1969 caused a bitter dispute which split the regime. Government and Parliament banned the CP late in 1965; the Supreme Court invalidated that act; but the regime refused to accept the verdict and annul the ban: these events shook the state and caused much unrest. At the same time, the C.'s succeeded in establishing strong front organizations— professionals, students, women, etc. They were a party to the military coup of May 1969 and remained partners of the Numeiri▷ regime that was established in its wake. It was not quite clear whether the four or five C. government ministers were card-carrying members of the CP, or belonged to dissident factions or crypto-C. front groups. The CP was split regarding its attitude to the regime; its Secretary-General, 'Abd-ul-Khaleq Mahjub, opposed collaboration with the regime, and the self-dissolution of the party; he was exiled to Egypt in 1970 and detained after his return. The government ousted some of its C. members in 1970 and the rest in 1971. After accusing the C. of complicity in an abortive coup, July 1971, it executed Mahjub and other CP leaders and brutally suppressed all communist groups and the trade unions.

In Palestine under the British Mandate, and in Israel, there have been repeated splits in the C. camp, most of them due to different attitudes to the Jewish-

Arab dispute and to the fate and future of the country. After its close co-operation with the Arab nationalists and rebels in the 1930s the CP, under Radwan al-Hilu ("Mussa"), had declined. Arab and Jewish sections were virtually separate. With the new respectability of the war years, stress was laid on trade unionist activities and front organizations; in Arab public life, the CP acted in the political sphere and among the intelligentsia through the "League for National Liberation", and in the field of trade-unionism through the "Arab Workers' Congress". These organizations were the only group among the Arabs which did not vigorously oppose the Partition Plan and the establishment of the State of Israel, or even supported them; they were thus the only Arab group in Israel whose leaders did not flee with the refugees, the only one still headed by its accepted leaders (Tawfiq Toubi, Emile Habibi, Emile Touma). In 1948, various C. factions united to form the "Israel CP". Israel is the only country in the ME in which the CP is legal, publishes its newspapers, and is represented in Parliament (the *Knesset*). In elections the C. have received between 2.8 and 4.5% of the votes, about half of them cast by Arab voters. Of the total Arab vote, the Communists received: in 1949 23%, in the 1950s 11–15%, in the early 1960s 22–23%, and in 1969 28–30%. A substantial proportion of these votes are cast not out of attachment to C. doctrines, but as a demonstration of dissent from Israel and her government, the C.'s being the only legal group in Israel opposed to the basic principles of the State. Under Israel's system of proportional representation, the C.'s usually obtain four of five (on one occasion 3, and on another—6) out of the 120 Knesset seats. The CP split again in 1965, mainly over the issue of loyalty to the State and the position on the Arab-Israel dispute. The "Israel CP" (*Maki*) views Israel's struggle as a just struggle waged in self-defence and, therefore, rejects the negative and hostile position of the Soviet Union. The "New C. List" (*Rakah*), on the other hand, aligns itself to a large extent with the Arab nationalist position, and totally with that of the Soviet Union. These differences of approach led to diametrically opposed attitudes of the two parties towards the Six Day War. Both parties lay claim to the title of the CP. Neither admits that the split parallels the division between Jews and Arabs. In point of fact, *Maki* consists entirely of Jews, while *Rakah* is overwhelmingly Arab.

In Jordan, the CP is illegal and lacks influence (although in the "West Bank"—annexed by Jordan in 1948–50 and held until 1967—there were left-wing currents of opinion). The leader of the CP, Fu'ad Nassar, has spent most of the last decades in prison, exile or hiding. In the elections of 1954 and '56, C.'s participated in lists submitted by a "National Front" and two or three of those elected from the "Front" lists were regarded as C.'s.

In Iran, the C. *Tudeh*▷ party was founded in 1941–2, when the northern part of the country was under Soviet occupation. It soon became a powerful force in the country, especially in the Autonomous Republic of Azerbaijan▷, which was set up in 1945–6, with Soviet support. But when Soviet forces evacuated Iran in 1946, the party was suppressed. In 1949 it was outlawed, and has existed ever since only underground.

In Turkey, the CP is illegal and—in contrast to the Arab countries—C.'s and their fellow-travellers are not permitted to operate in a semi-public manner (as "independents", or under the façade of some legal front organization). Little C. activity is reported in Turkey—although some would regard the Socialist Turkish Labour Party, vaguely leftist intellectuals and nationalist "New-Left" youth guerilla groups as C. There are also Turkish C.'s operating in exile (e.g. the well-known poet Nazim Hikmet, who died in 1963 in the Soviet Union).

Revolutionary Palestinian Arab organizations such as the "Popular Front for the Liberation of Palestine" (PFLP, see Palestine Arabs▷) cannot be regarded as true C.'s—although their leaders define themselves as Marxist-Leninist, are under strong Chinese-Maoist influence and no doubt have ties with C. cells.   (E.B.-Y.S.)

CONDOMINIUM. Term used for the joint Anglo-Egyptian rule of Sudan▷, from 1899 to 1955. The Anglo-Egyptian Agreement of January 1899 establishing joint rule is usually referred to as the C. Agreement, although it does not mention the term itself. Under the agreement both the British and Egyptian flags were flown in the Sudan; executive and legislative powers were concentrated in the hands of a Governor-General (in fact always a Briton) appointed by the Egyptian Khedive on the recommendation of the British government. Egyptian laws were not binding in the Sudan unless enforced by the Governor-General. Conditions for residing and trading in the Sudan were to be equal for the citizens of all European countries.

The Anglo-Egyptian C. was only symbolic, and Britain established a *de facto* colonial regime in Sudan. Its continuation, or abolition, its shape and Egypt's part in it, constituted for over three decades a principal bone of contention in Anglo-Egyptian negotiations and crises (see Egypt▷, Sudan▷). In October 1951, Egypt unilaterally abrogated the C. Agreement, and King Farouq▷ was proclaimed King of Sudan.

This act was not recognized by either Britain or large parts of Sudanese political opinion. Agreements of 1952–3, paved the way to self-determination, and Sudan's independence, in December 1955, terminated the C. (B.G.)

CONSTANTINOPLE. In the past an alternative name for Istanbul▷, especially current in Europe when Constantinople was still the capital of the Ottoman Empire (until 1920–3). Since the Kemalist revolution in Turkey, Istanbul has become the only acceptable name. On the city's geopolitical status, see Bosphorus▷. The "Convention of C." of 1888, between the Ottoman Empire and the Western powers, determined rules and obligations concerning freedom of passage through the Suez▷ Canal (see details there). (Y.S.)

CONSTANTINOPLE, CONVENTION OF— see Suez Canal▷.

COPTS. The Coptic Church is Monophysite▷. It has its centre in Egypt (Copt is a corruption of the word Egypt) and traces its foundation to the Evangelist Mark. Following the Arab conquest, many C. converted to Islam, thus greatly reducing the size of their community. Under Muslim rule (Arab and Ottoman), the C. were often discriminated against and persecuted. It was only at the beginning of the 19th century, under Muhammad 'Ali, that C. succeeded in acquiring a standard of wealth and education superior to that of the average Egyptian. A laymen's movement emerged among the C. which strove to administer the community's affairs. In 1883, a council was elected and given a constitution, empowering it to deal with matters of personal status, education and religious endowments. Coptic hopes that the British, who administered Egypt from 1882, would favour them as fellow Christians, were only partially fulfilled. Some C. were active in the Egyptian nationalist movement. C. have, however, complained of the self-identification of Egyptian nationalism with Islam, of their relegation to the status of second-class citizens and of discrimination in government employment and other positions. Only one C. has ever been Prime Minister of Egypt (Butros Ghali, assassinated in 1910, amid scenes of anti-Coptic mass agitation). One other C., Makram Obeid ('Ubaid) (1889–1961), attained a prominent position in the Egyptian national movement and high government office, mainly as Finance Minister; he also formed his own political party, the "Independent *Wafdist* Bloc" (*al-Kutla*), 1942–53.

The C. in Egypt number an estimated 2.5–3m. There are also small Coptic communities in Israel and

Coptic church, Nazareth

Jordan. The Church is headed by a Patriarch, whose seat is in Cairo. Because the clergy is, on the whole, poorly educated, Catholics have succeeded in establishing a Coptic Uniate Church (see Uniates▷, Catholics▷); Protestants have also been able to win Coptic converts. (Sh.C.-Y.S.)

COX, SIR PERCY ZACHARIAH (1864–1937). British colonial administrator. Army officer; political agent, Muscat 1899–1904; resident, Persian Gulf 1904–13; Foreign Secretary, Government of India 1913–14; Chief Political Officer to the British Expeditionary Forces in Mesopotamia (since 1917 "Civil Commissioner") 1914–18; Minister to Persia 1918–20; High Commissioner for Iraq 1920–4. C. was one of the last empire builders. A powerful personality and a brilliant administrator, his impact was particularly strong in Mesopotamia, where he laid the foundations for the modern State of Iraq. (U.D.)

COUPS D'ÉTAT—see Army Officers▷.

CROMER, LORD (previously Sir Evelyn Baring) (1841–1917). British colonial administrator. Scion of a family of bankers and civil servants. Trained as an officer, he held, after some years of service in the army, several posts in the Colonial Service. In 1877 he was appointed delegate to the Egyptian debt fund, and in 1879 British Inspector-General on the Anglo-French supervisory commission. A few months later he was transferred to India as financial advisor to the Viceroy. After the British conquest of Egypt (1882), in 1883 he was appointed "Agent and Consul-General" there (in fact, if not in name, governor of Egypt). He served in this capacity until 1907. He was made a baron in 1892, a viscount in 1898 and became the Earl of Cromer in 1901. In his 24 years of office in Egypt, he ruled the country in an autocratic manner. His outlook was a mixture of imperialistic concepts with liberal values; he believed in the British mission in Egypt and considered Islam a conservative factor. He adopted an independent policy which did not always accord with that of the government in London.

C.'s contribution to Egypt is in dispute. His critics point to the absence of drive and concern for development. His admirers point to his policy of economy and the restoration of the country's finances, in which C. himself saw his principal achievement. He alleviated the burden of taxation on the peasants and based the economy on agriculture, particularly cotton-growing, but retarded industrial development, restricted the social services and neglected the development of education (apart from those branches of education required to produce civil servants).

C. must be credited with the development of the administrative service, the regulation of the financial administration, the encouragement of irrigation projects, the expansion of the health services and the development of the railways. He scornfully dismissed Egyptian nationalism, which began to awaken during his incumbency. (S.L.)

*CYPRUS. Third largest island in the Mediterranean, and an independent republic since 1960, with an area of 3,572 sq. mi. Population: 627,500 (1968 estimate); Greek Orthodox Christians (ethnically Greek): 493,000 (79%); Turkish Muslims: 110,000 (18%); Armenians: 3,500; Maronite Christians: 3,000; others: 18,000.

Agriculture is the important economic activity in Cyprus. Most farmers own and occupy their land and belong to co-operatives. Principal crops: cereals, potatoes, carob, grape and citrus. Major industries: mining (mainly copper and iron pyrites), food processing and textiles. Most of the island's trade is with the Sterling Area and the European Common Market. Principal exports are foodstuffs and minerals. Principal imports are manufactured goods, machinery and fuel. Deficit in the balance of trade is met by the remittances of emigrants, the tourist industry and the expenditure from British and UN forces stationed on the island.

HISTORY. Cyprus was conquered by the Ottomans in 1571. In 1878 the British were permitted to occupy and administer the island in exchange for a pledge to support the Ottoman Empire against Russia. Formally, the island remained under Ottoman suzerainty until 5 November 1914, when it was unilaterally

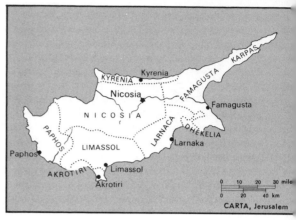

Map of Cyprus

annexed by Britain following Turkey's participation in World War I against Britain.

Britain offered to cede Cyprus to Greece in October 1915, on the condition that Athens enter the war to help Serbia (as she was obliged to do under the Greek-Serbian Treaty of 1913). Unwilling to relinquish its neutrality because of King Constantine's pro-German sentiments, the Greek government rejected the offer. Turkey gave retroactive recognition to Britain's annexation of the island in the Lausanne Treaty of 24 July 1923. Cyprus was declared a Crown Colony on 10 Mar. 1925. The British created an efficient judicial system and police force, and improved agriculture, education and other public services.

A movement advocating the island's union with Greece, Enosis▷, gradually became a strong factor in the political life of Cyprus. Severe violence occurred for the first time at Nicosia in 1931 when a crowd, led by a priest carrying a Greek flag, set fire to the Governor's residence. Similar anti-British demonstrations took place in other towns and villages. The British proclaimed a state of emergency, suspended the Legislative Council and banished a number of ecclesiastic and secular dignitaries from the island. Political life virtually came to a standstill.

Hostility between the British authorities and Greek Cypriots lessened after the Italian invasion of Greece in October 1940. As Britain and Greece became allies, Cypriots began volunteering for service with the British Army. In 1941 the British authorized the first political party in Cyprus, the AKEL (*Anorthotikon Komma Ergazomenou Laou*—Reform Party of the Working People), a cover for the Communist Party.

Municipal elections were held in 1943 and the British Colonial Secretary announced a plan of con-

Nicosia, aerial view

stitutional reforms on 23 Oct. 1946. It proposed participation of the Cypriot population in the administration of their internal affairs. These reforms were rejected by leaders of the Cypriot Church who declared that *Enosis* and only *Enosis* was the Cypriot goal. The Church organized a plebiscite, January 1950, on the future of the island. Of the 224,747 Greek residents who were considered eligible to vote, 215,108 favoured *Enosis*.

The movement for *Enosis* gathered momentum after the election of Makarios▷ as Archbishop, 1950. Under pressure from Makarios, Greece repeatedly raised the "Cyprus question" before the UN General Assembly (from 1954 to 1958). These overtures, however, failed to obtain an Assembly vote for Cypriot self-determination.

On 1 April 1955, EOKA▷ (a militant Greek Cypriot underground organization) began its armed struggle against the British. A state of emergency was declared on 27 Nov. 1955, imposing the death penalty for bearing arms and banning all political meetings. Negotiations between Makarios and the British Governor (from October 1955 to February 1956) reached an impasse. Makarios was deported to the Seychelles, March 1956, for alleged implication in the activities of EOKA. He was released in March 1957 and settled in Athens. During this interim Britain undertook a number of unsuccessful initiatives to find a solution to the Cypriot problem: the British-Greek-Turkish Conference in London, August–September 1955, Lord Radcliffe's constitutional reforms of 1956, and the Macmillan plan of 19 June 1958.

As the conflict between Britain and the Greek Cypriots dragged on, Turkish Cypriots and Turkey herself became involved. With the advent of inter-communal riots, Turkish Cypriots established their own underground organization. Until 1957 Turkey insisted there was no Cypriot problem, explaining

that the island belonged to Britain, and if Britain decided to relinquish the island, it must be returned to Turkey, its former owner. Turkish policy after 1957 was directed towards partition of Cyprus. This was difficult, however, because Turks and Greeks lived in mixed areas and no region possessed ethnic homogeneity.

As the Cyprus crisis began to jeopardize relations between Turkey and Greece, both members of NATO, the two countries began high-level talks. On 11 Feb. 1959, it was announced that the prime ministers and foreign ministers of both nations had met in Zurich and had reached a compromise solution. The final details of this agreement were completed in London when the ministers met with their British colleagues and with representatives of the Turkish and Greek Cypriot communities. Under the terms of the London agreement, the island was to become an independent republic under a Greek Cypriot president and a Turkish Cypriot vice-president, elected separately by their respective communities. Both *Enosis* and partition were rejected. Great Britain was to retain two military bases at Akrotiri and Dhekelia.

Elections for the presidency were held in December 1969. Archbishop Makarios was elected, with 144,501 votes, against 71,753 cast for John Clerides. (Opposition to Makarios came from those who continued advocating *Enosis*, those accusing him of "dictatorial methods", and the Communists.) Dr. F. Küçük▷ was elected unopposed to the vice-presidency. In July 1960 parliamentary elections took place. By an arrangement between Makarios and the Communists, 30 of the 35 seats allotted to Greek-Cypriots went to Makarios' supporters, and five to AKEL (the Communist Party); all 15 seats allotted to Turkish-Cypriots went unopposed to Dr. Kuçük's "Turkish National Party".

A constitution was drafted by a Joint Constitutional Commission composed of Turkish, Greek, Greek-Cypriot and Turkish-Cypriot representatives, and came into force on 16 Aug. 1960, the day Cyprus received its independence. The major provisions of the Constitution state:

1. Both the President and Vice-President were empowered to veto laws and decisions of the Cabinet and House of Representatives concerning foreign affairs, defence and security. 2. The Cabinet was to be composed of seven Greek and three Turkish ministers. 3. The House of Representatives was to consist of 35 Greeks and 15 Turks, elected by their respective communities, to serve for a term of five years. (No provision was made for the various other minorities, such as the Armenians and Maronites but, in fact, they were allocated seats in the House within the Greek quota.) Two communal chambers were given

jurisdiction over questions of religion, culture and education. 4. The civil service and police were to have a 70:30 Greek:Turkish ratio, while the army was to reflect a 60:40 ratio. 5. Separate Turkish municipalities were to be established in Nicosia, Larnaca, Famagusta, Limassol and Paphos. 6. Separate Greek and Turkish tribunals were to be established for each community, with mixed courts for cases involving both Greeks and Turks.

Three treaties were signed on 17 Aug. 1960, the day Cyprus gained its independence:

a. A TREATY OF ESTABLISHMENT between Britain, Greece, Turkey and Cyprus, defining the territory of the two bases remaining under British sovereignty.

b. A TREATY OF GUARANTEE between the same parties whereby Cyprus undertook to safeguard its independence and to refrain from political or economic union with any state, while the remaining signatories recognized and guaranteed the independence, territorial integrity and security of Cyprus.

c. A TREATY OF ALLIANCE for co-operation in mutual defence, between the Republic of Cyprus, Greece and Turkey, providing for a tripartite central command to be established in Cyprus with Greece and Turkey maintaining contingents of 950 and 650 soldiers respectively. (Unilaterally repealed by President Makarios on 4 Apr. 1964.)

Cyprus became a member of the UN on 20 September 1960 and a member of the Commonwealth on 14 March 1961. After independence serious problems arose between the two major ethnic communities regarding the interpretation and implementation of the new Constitution. The main points of friction concerned the structure of the army (the Greeks favoured integrated units while the Turks demanded separate ethnic units), the composition of the civil service, the jurisdiction of the House of Representatives in financial matters, and the question of separate ethnic municipalities. Negotiations between President Makarios and Vice-President Küçük yielded no results. The Archbishop proposed changes in the Constitution during November 1963: abrogation of the veto power held by both executives, cancellation of the requirement that both Greek and Turkish majorities in the House must approve financial legislation, and the establishment of single, fully integrated municipalities. Turkey rejected these proposals even before a reply was forthcoming from the Turkish Cypriots.

Tension mounted and violence between the two communities broke out in December 1963 and again in February 1964. Arms and armed "irregulars" abroad were brought into the island by both parties. General Grivas▷ (a Greek officer who commanded EOKA forces from 1955 to 1959) returned to the island and took command of the Greek forces.

The UN Security Council passed a resolution, 6 Mar. 1964, dispatching a "UN Peace-keeping Force" (UNFICYP) to the island. Authority for UNFICYP's presence on Cyprus, originally for a period of three months, has been extended repeatedly. A mediator, Dr. Galo Plaza of Ecuador, was appointed by the UN Secretary-General to study the crisis and submit recommendations. Dr. Plaza's report emphasized that the Cyprus problem could not be solved by restoration of the *status quo* prior to December 1963, and recommended that a new solution be reached consistent with the provisions of the UN Charter.

Tension increased again and Turkey declared its intention of invading Cyprus, June 1964, justifying this action under the terms of the Treaty of Guarantee. Invasion plans were called off because of international pressure, including a note from US President Johnson to Turkish Premier Inönu▷ stating that if Turkey were to attack, the USA would not assist Turkey in the event of Soviet intervention. The US Sixth Fleet was deployed between Turkey and Cyprus. But in August 1964, Turkish airplanes bombed Greek-Cypriot communities in northwest Cyprus in retaliation for Greek-Cypriot attacks on the Turkish village of Mansoura in northern Cyprus.

While the UN, NATO, Greece and Turkey were trying to effect a compromise between the two communities, President Makarios consolidated his own position. In March 1964 he appointed Greek ministers to replace the Turkish ministers who "failed to report for duty". On 17 June 1964 the House of Representatives passed a bill establishing a National Guard with six months compulsory service for all men between the ages of 18 and 59. In December 1964, legislation was passed creating unified municipalities and introducing income tax. In July 1965, a bill was passed which provided for unified elections on the basis of a common electoral roll. This abolished communal distinction between Greek and Turkish Cypriots.

In 1966–7 Greece and Turkey discussed proposals to merge Cyprus with Greece while establishing a Turkish base to protect the interests of the Turkish-Cypriots, but no agreement was reached.

In November 1967 there were clashes between the National Guard and Turkish units in the villages of Kophinou and Ayios Theodoros. The Turkish government threatened to invade the island. US President Johnson sent a personal representative, Cyrus Vance, to mediate between the parties. A settlement was reached, according to which Greek troops brought to Cyprus as volunteers were to withdraw, while Turkey agreed to cancel all plans for an invasion of Cyprus.

In December 1967 the Turkish community set up a "transitional administration" to govern the Turkish Cypriot areas" until such time as the provisions of the 1960 Constitution were fully implemented". Dr. Küçük headed the administration, Rauf Denktaş served as his deputy.

Presidential elections in February 1968 offered a choice between independence as advocated by President Makarios, and *Enosis* as advocated by Takis Evdokas. Makarios was re-elected by an overwhelming majority (221,000, against 8,500 for Evdokas). The Turkish community re-elected Küçük as Vice-President, without opposition.

In June 1968, following recommendations by the UN Secretary-General, talks between leaders of the Greek and Turkish communities were initiated, first in Beirut, then in Cyprus; they still continue, but have not yet yielded any results. The Greek Cypriots aim to restrict and diminish the special rights granted to the Turkish minority and to turn Cyprus into a unitary state. The Turkish Cypriots, on the other hand, want to achieve a separate administration which would act as a liaison between the Turkish population and the government.

Despite the law of July 1965, common elections were delayed by the tension between the two communities and the House of Representatives, attended only by its Greek members, annually extended its term of office (which expired in 1965). Elections were finally held in July 1970 — but for the two communities separately, despite the 1965 stipulation of joint elections. Of the 35 Greek seats, the United Party of Speaker G. Clerides▷ won 15 and the Communists nine, the rest being distributed among smaller parties and independents; T. Evdokas' list, advocating immediate *Enosis*, failed to obtain a single seat. The elections for the 15 Turkish seats, all won by the list of R. Denkas, were declared illegal by President Makarios.

In 1969–70 the "National Front", a terrorist group advocating *Enosis* and composed partly of ex-EOKA fighters, started a campaign of violence. It attacked, *inter alia*, British property. Government counter-measures included the introduction of administrative detention for up to three months. The Athens government also condemned the National Front. Acts of terrorism included an unsuccessful attempt on the life of President Makarios, 8 Mar. 1970, and the assassination, a few days later, of the ex-Minister of the Interior, P. Georghadjis▷ (himself allegedly involved in the attempt on the President's life).

The C. problem remains an unresolved international issue. Greece no longer encourages *Enosis*, but seems eager to find an agreed solution in direct co-operation with Turkey. Turkey strongly supports the Turkish Cypriots and regards herself as the guard-

ian of their rights to autonomy or even independence. Makarios and the government of C. continue rejecting any solution "imposed" by outside pressure or interference, including a bilateral agreement between Greece and Turkey. Internally, they reject both Turkish-Cypriot autonomy demands and Greek-extremist claims for immediate *Enosis*.

PRESS, RADIO AND TV. Greek-language publications include six morning and two evening newspapers, seventeen weeklies and fourteen monthlies. Turkish-language publications include two morning and one evening newspaper, and one weekly. There is an English-language daily newspaper. The Cyprus Broadcasting Corporation has radio and television programmes in Greek, Turkish, English and French. The Turkish Cypriots have their own radio station.

STATISTICS. Area: 3,572 sq. mi. Cultivable: 66%, cultivated: 16% (est. 1968). Population: 627,500 (1968). Birth rate: 24.4 per thousand (1968), natural increase: 1% *p.a.* Average life expectancy: 64 years for men, 68 for women. Infant mortality 26.7 per thousand (1965). GNP: $438.2m. (1968); (1970 est.: $540m.) National income *per capita*: $622 (1970 est.: $800). Exports: $95.9m., imports $203m. (1969). Budget: revenue $74.9m. (1970). Literacy: 82% (1968). Children at school 73% (Greeks only, 1965). Doctors: 1 per 1,300 (1968). Hospital beds: 1 per 1,930 (1966).   (B.G.)

CYRENAICA. Eastern part of Libya. Area of 350,000 sq. mi., with population of 450,000 (census 1964), mostly Bedouin. Principal town is Benghazi▷. The urban population includes many immigrants from the *Maghreb* (North-west Africa) and Tripolitania. C. is the centre of the Sanussi▷ Order. For its history, governance and politics, see Libya▷.   (Y.S.)

CZECHOSLOVAKIA. Apart from C.'s efforts to sell her industrial goods, and some credits granted Arab states to facilitate the export of C.'s machinery and know-how, her involvement in ME affairs has been threefold: a. In 1948, C. supplied arms to Israel, then engaged in her War of Independence, and allowed the transit of aircraft and arms from other sources. b. The Slansky trials of 1951–2 in which "World Zionism" was accused of crimes, espionage, subversion etc., inaugurated the Communist countries' new anti-Zionist, anti-Israel, and to a large extent anti-Jewish policy after a short initial period of support for the creation of Israel. c. Egypt's application for military aid and arms supplies from the Soviet Bloc, in 1955, was at first termed the "Czech arms deal". Though part of the first agreed consignment was C.-made or from C., the deal was no doubt principally made with the Soviet Union.   (Y.S.)

Damascus

D

DAMASCUS. Capital of Syria. Pop. 835,000 (1970). Situated in the north-west of the Ghuta bowl, a large oasis irrigated by the Barada and 'Awj rivers at the edge of the Syrian desert. D. is said to be the oldest continuously inhabited town in the world. It was the centre of the Omayyad Arab Empire (656–744). It was the capital of a province *(Vilayet)* in Ottoman times. At the beginning of the 20th century it became the centre of the Arab nationalist movement. In 1918 troops of the Arab Revolt▷, advancing on Allenby's▷ right flank, were permitted to occupy D. Amir Feisal▷ set up an Arab national government there and in 1920 was proclaimed King of Syria. The French, however, occupied D., and expelled Feisal. At the beginning of the French Mandate the city became the capital of a "State of D.". When this was merged in 1924 with the "State of Aleppo", D. became the capital of the "State of Syria". D. is a centre of industry, trade and culture, and has a university, but Aleppo surpasses it in economic activity. The two cities are historic rivals for the position of Syria's chief city. D. is linked by rail to the north of Syria as well as to Beirut port, and has a new international airport. (A. L.-O. T.)

DARDANELLES. Straits in north-west Turkey connecting the Aegean Sea and the Sea of Marmara, running north-east to south-west, between the Gallipoli▷ Peninsula in European Turkey in the north and Asia Minor in the south. The D. are 37 miles long, and have an average width of 2 miles. They have always been of commercial and strategic importance since they link the Mediterranean with Istanbul and, along with the Bosphorus▷, form the Black Sea's only outlet, Hence their control and the rules of navigation through them have played a major role in European diplomatic history. (See Bosphorus▷; for the D. in World War I, see Gallipoli▷). (D.K.)

DARFUR. The westernmost province of Sudan. Area: 191,505 sq.mi. Population: 1.5m. (1965) com-

posed of non-Arabs, especially the Negroid Fur (from whom the province takes its name), and largely nomadic Arab tribes. Capital: Al-Fasher. From the 17th century, the area was ruled by the Muslim al-Kayra dynasty. D. was conquered by Egypt in 1874, and subjected to the *Mahdi*'s▷ rule from 1883 to 1899. After the fall of the *Mahdist* regime, a descendant of the al-Kayra dynasty, 'Ali Dinar, established himself as a semi-independent sultan of D., under the suzerainty of the Sudanese government. When, in 1916, he rebelled against the British rulers of Sudan, the British conquered the province and incorporated it fully within Anglo-Egyptian Sudan. (B.G.)

DASHNAQ—see Tashnaq▷.

DAWALIBI, DR. MA'RUF (b. 1907). Syrian jurist and politician. Born in Aleppo, he studied at Aleppo, Damascus and Paris universities. He was a leader of the Syrian "People's Party", and elected to Parliament. He served as Minister for Economic Affairs, 1949–50 and President of Parliament, 1951. D. was Prime Minister for a single day (28 Nov. 1951) in the commotion of Shishakli's▷ second coup. D. was one of the first Arab politicians to propose a non-aggression pact with, and arms supplies from, the USSR. He was Minister of Defence following Shishakli's downfall in 1954 and tried to put an end to army intervention in Syria's political life. He opposed the *Ba'th* party and the union with Egypt and spent the period of the United Arab Republic▷ (1958–61) in self-imposed exile in Lebanon. He was again Prime Minister in 1961–2, following the dissolution of the UAR, until the military coup of March 1962. Lately he has been legal adviser to the Sa'udi Arabian government. (A.L.)

✻DAYAN, MOSHE (b. 1915). Israeli military and political leader, Minister of Defence since June 1967. Born in a co-operative village, D. was active in *Hagana*▷ (the underground Jewish self-defence force). During the 1936–9 Arab disturbances he fought in Orde Wingate's▷ special unit. In 1940 he was tried by the British for underground activity and sentenced to imprisonment. In 1941 he lost his left eye in an Allied operation against French (Vichy) forces in Lebanon. Later he was one of the first to join the *Palmah*▷ (the *Hagana*'s striking force). In the Arab-Israel War of 1948, he occupied command and staff posts in the Israel Defence Forces (IDF), was Jerusalem C.O. and represented Israel in the Armistice talks. As Chief of General Staff (1953–8), D. led the IDF to victory in the Sinai Campaign▷ (1956) and played a decisive role in the development of its tactics and fighting morale (including retaliatory raids on

Moshe Dayan (as Chief-of-Staff)

The hot, dry climate enables the production of salts by evaporation. A potash plant was built in 1934 at Kallia, at the northern end of the DS and a branch at Sodom, at the southern end in 1937. The Kallia plant was destroyed by Jordanian troops in the Arab-Israel War of 1948, and the southern plant remained cut off until the Beersheba-Sodom road was built (1953). The plant at Sodom has since been rehabilitated as a government company, "The DS Works Ltd.". It currently produces about 600,000 tons of potash *per annum*, as well as 100,000 tons of bromide and industrial salt. The Kingdom of Jordan plans to establish a potash plant on the eastern shore, but, due to financial problems, the plan has not yet materialized. (Y.K.)

DE GAULLE, GEN. CHARLES (1890–1970). French soldier and statesman. Founder of the Fifth Republic and its President, 1958–68, with wide powers under an amended constitution. In World War II, upon France's surrender in 1940, de G. established the Free French movement, whose forces continued the fight against Germany. In alliance with Britain and the USA, and despite sharp differences of opinion with Churchill▷ and Roosevelt▷, he led Free France to victory. Thereafter he served as Prime Minister, 1944–5. Out of office 1946–58, de G. was called to the presidency, to save a rebellious Algeria

saboteurs' bases). After his discharge (1958) D. studied at Jerusalem and Tel-Aviv universities. He represented the *Mapai*▷ labour party in the *Knesset* (Parliament) and in 1959 joined Ben-Gurion's▷ government as Minister of Agriculture. In 1966 he resigned over differences with Premier Eshkol▷ and joined Ben-Gurion in forming an opposition group (*Rafi*). Before the Six Day War, D. was appointed Minister of Defence by public demand. He is responsible for the post-Six Day War policy of "open bridges", which enables people and goods to move between the areas occupied by Israel and Jordan. He is pragmatic about the Arab-Israel conflict, and a moderate hard liner. In 1968 he reunited *Rafi* (without Ben-Gurion) with *Mapai*, which led to the formation of the Israel Labour Party▷. D. is very popular in Israel and a possible candidate for premiership. (E.L.)

DEAD SEA. The most saline body of water on earth, situated at the lowest point on earth, in the Jordan Depression, 1,302 ft. below sea-level. The DS is 48 m. long and its average width is 10.7 mi. Its surface is 405 sq.mi. and it contains about 150,000 million cubic metres. Salinity reaches 27%. The main chemicals are magnesium chloride (52%), sodium chloride (cooking salt, 30%), calcium chloride (12%), pottassium chloride (4.36%), magnesium bromide (1.46%). These are Israel's most important mineral resources. During the British Mandate, the border between Palestine and Transjordan passed along the median line of the DS. When Palestine was partitioned in 1948, the western half of the southern section, up to 'Ein Gedi, remained in the territory of Israel.

Charles de Gaulle

for France and to lead his country out of a period of instability and crisis. In direct contradiction to the policies and slogans that had brought him to power, he granted independence to Algeria (1962).

During the Algerian dispute de G. maintained his predecessors' policy of friendship and military assistance to Israel. However, after granting independence to Algeria (and the French colonies in Africa) he resumed France's traditional pro-Arab policy and turned against Israel, as part of his global policy of restoring France to her former position as one of the Great Powers. In May 1967, a few days before the outbreak of the Six Day War▷, de G. declared an embargo on arms to the ME (affecting mainly Israel) and refused to deliver to Israel 50 Mirage fighterplanes for which a contract had been signed. Military supplies to some Arab countries continued, officially justified by the claim that they were not directly involved in the Arab-Israel conflict. On the eve of the Six Day War, de G. also went back on France's undertaking in the Tripartite Declaration▷. He opposed any physical intervention to reopen the Tiran Straits▷ for unimpeded navigation. After the war, he insisted on total withdrawal by Israel from all the occupied Arab territories and denounced Israel's insistence that any withdrawal must be part of a peace treaty and accompanied by security guarantees. In his anti-Israel stance, de G. went so far as to accuse the Jews of being a domineering people throughout history—a remark interpreted by some as blatant anti-Semitism.

Through his anti-Israel policies, de G. succeeded in re-establishing some of France's prestige and standing in the Arab world. Some recent Franco-Arab transactions, such as the sale of a large number of Mirage planes to Libya (upheld even after Libya's decision, in 1970–1, to form a "Federation of Arab Republics" with Egypt and Syria, both directly involved in conflict with Israel) were successful. Others, such as the attempt to effect similar sales to Iraq or to obtain a concession in the North Rumeila oil fields in south Iraq, failed. With the termination, in 1971, of any special French-Algerian relationship, de G.'s Algeria policy also seems to have ended in failure. (E.L.)

DEIR YASSIN—see Arab-Israel War of 1948▷, *Irgun*▷ *(T)zeva'i Le'umi*.

*DEMIREL, SÜLEYMAN (b. 1924). Turkish statesman, Prime Minister 1965–71. Born in a village in the province of Isparta, D. studied civil engineering in Istanbul and the USA. He entered the Civil Service and became Director of the State Water Board. After the military revolution of 1960 he joined

the newly formed Justice Party (see Turkey▷, Political History), succeding Gen. R. Gümüspala as leader upon the latter's death. In 1965 D. became Deputy Premier in Suat Ürgüplü's coalition cabinet, and upon his party's 1965 election victory he became Prime Minister. Since his party was viewed as the successor to the Democratic Party, ousted by the 1960 revolution, D. took care not to antagonize the army, restrained the right wing of his party and followed a middle-of-the-road policy in both external and internal affairs. He also strongly maintained democratic order. However, social reforms were slow in coming and political pressures on the government degenerated into continuous disorders at the universities in particular and in the country in general. In March 1971 D. was forced to resign after an ultimatum presented by the chiefs of the armed forces. He was succeeded by a coalition government headed by Nihat Erim▷. (D.K.)

Süleyman Demirel (right)

DENKTAŞ (DENKTASH), RA'UF (b. 1924). Turkish-Cypriot lawyer and politician. Born in Paphos, educated at Lincoln's Inn, London. In legal practice in Cyprus 1947–9; Crown Counsellor and Acting Solicitor-General 1949–58. Chairman, Federation of Turkish Cypriot Associations 1959–60. Elected President of the Turkish Communal Chamber 1960. As a result of the inter-communal disturbances of December 1963, he was denied permission to return to Cyprus after a journey to London, and lived in Turkey 1964–8. D. returned clandestinely to Cyprus in 1967, was arrested and deported. Permitted to return in April 1968, he became Vice-President of the Turkish-Cypriot "Transitional Administration". Since 1968 he has conducted talks with the Greek-Cypriot leader G. Clerides▷ in an effort—unsuccessful so far—to reach agreement between the two communities. (B.G.)

DERVISH (DARWISH) ORDERS. Muslim mysticism, Sufism, wished to complement the stern, intellectual nature of orthodox Islam in its mechanical and external aspects, as stressed by the theologians and the juriconsults, with religious feeling and experience. Its aim was to come closer to God by gnosticism (*ma'rifa*), and to reach spiritual absorption (*fana*) in the divinity. The Sufis' indifference to the Muslim Law (*Shari'a*▷) brought them into conflict with the religious (and Islamic state) establishment. The great theologian Ghazzali (d. 1111) reconciled Sufism with orthodox Islam. Since then many theologians have taken part in Sufism, although there have always been tensions, and sometimes overt hostility, between the Sufis and the Islamic establishment.

The Sufi brotherhoods or orders (*tariqa*, plural *turuq*—literally "ways") have organized the Muslim masses, notably city artisans, since the 12th and 13th centuries. In theory, their organization was centralized: the head of the order (*sheikh al-sajada*), usually claiming family or spiritual descent from the founder of the order, had jurisdiction over the *khalifa*, the head of a local branch or sub-order; the latter led the adepts (*dervish*, in Persian, or *faqir*, in Arabic). In practice the branches have always been autonomous under the local leader. There were two kinds of Sufis: a. The "specialists", wanderers and beggars, reputedly able to perform miracles, and sometimes retreating to monasteries (*zawiya, taqiyya, khankah*). b. Laymen, usually from the lower classes. They used to parade in procession on their saint's or patron's (*wali*) anniversary (*mawlid*), wearing the colours of the order and carrying its flags and signs, and to visit the saint's tomb in order to invoke his blessing.

The central Sufi ceremony and practice is the *dhikr*, the ever-repeated uttering of God's name or some religious formula, until ecstasy is attained. Some orders, especially the *Rifa'iyya*, used to devour glass, walk on fire, play music, dance, take narcotics, play with serpents, etc. These practices, as well as the superstitious beliefs in saints living or past, were frowned upon by the religious and state authorities, but made the orders popular and were instrumental in converting non-Arab peoples, notably the Turks and the Berbers, to Islam.

The Turkish *Bektashi* order was a peculiar mixture of Sunni, Shi'i and Christian elements, thus appealing to both Balkan Christians and Anatolian peasants. This order had been associated with the Yenicheri (Janissaries) corps and was suppressed with them (1826). In the mid-19th century the order was revived. It supported the Young Turks'▷ revolution in 1908, and eventually accepted the measures of secularization promulgated by Kemal Atatürk▷. The second great

Turkish order is the *Mevleviyya*, named after the poet and mystic Mevlana Jelal-ul-Din Rumi (d. 1273), whose shrine in Konya still attracts many pilgrims. The Mevlevis were known in Europe as the Whirling D., because they danced in order to reach a state of ecstasy. The Mevlevis were an urban order and were looked upon favourably by the authorities.

Atatürk considered *all* orders to be reactionary and corrupt. In 1925 they were prohibited and their monasteries and mausoleums (*türbe*) were closed down. The Kurdish revolt in the same year was more nationalistic than religious, but it was supported by the *Nakshebendi* brotherhood. The orders seem to have survived to some extent, underground and outlawed. When the enforcement of secularization was relaxed in the late 1940s and under the Democratic Party (since 1950), a more favourable atmosphere was created for religion, both on the orthodox and popular levels. The mausoleums were reopened, and the DO, especially the *Mevleviyya, Bektashiyya* and *Nakshebendiyya* have since been tolerated and active. But D. processions are not permitted, and extreme orders remain outlawed. Thus, the north-African order of the *Tijaniyya* was suppressed and its leader Pilavoğlu imprisoned in 1952, for desecrating Atatürk's statues. The government also tries to stop the activities of the quasi-order Nur (*Nurju*).

Before the 20th century the orders were a most important social force in Egypt, and occasionally they expressed public opinion. The main indigenous orders are the *Ahmadiyya* or *Badawiyya*, named after Sidi Ahmad al-Badawi, whose *mawlid* in Tanta is still the most popular of the Egyptian feasts, although it has lost much of its commercial and social importance; and the *Brahimiyya*, named after Sidi Ibrahim of Dasuk. Also influential are the *Qadiriyya*, the *Rifa'iyya* and the *Shadhiliyya*, a north-African order. The *Qadiriyya*, which is considered to be the earliest order still in existence, is near to orthodoxy. Early in the 19th century Viceroy Muhammad 'Ali established state control over the orders, by creating a high council of the orders and nominating its head. Since then, government permission has had to be obtained before celebrating each *mawlid*. However, both the government and the religious establishment, whose stronghold is the al-Azhar▷ mosque-university, failed in their efforts to curb those practices of the Sufis that they considered offensive. Even nowadays, with the expansion of education, the changes of social values and the determination of the military regime to lead Egypt towards social progress and westernization, the *mawlids* are still popular and some of the customs considered objectionable are maintained. According to the present head of the Sufi in Egypt, there are now 60 orders in that country, most of them offshoots of the main ones previously mentioned. He presents contemporary Sufism as a respectable establishment, professes opposition to any religious innovation and loyalty to the government. Since 1958, he has published a journal to which even university professors have contributed. Yet membership of the orders seems to be declining. Most of the members come from the lower classes. With the exception of one new order, the *Hamidiyya-Shadhiliyya*, which is centralized and cohesive, the orders are loosely organized and multiple membership blurs the distinctions among them.

In the Arab countries of the Fertile Crescent the Sufi orders have never enjoyed influence or prestige comparable with their position in Egypt, Sudan and Turkey. The limited information on their present conditions there indicates that they are declining rapidly and may soon disappear from this area. Sufism may be a little more alive in Iraq. The tomb of 'Abd-ul-Qader al-Gilani (d. 1166) in Baghdad attracts many *Qadiri* pilgrims. The *Rifa'iyya*, also of Iraqi origin, the *Nakshebendiyya* and the *Bektashiyya* all have followers among the Arabs and Kurds of Iraq.

The *Sanussiyya*▷ in Libya and the *Mahdiyya*▷ in Sudan (and, similarly, the *Idrissis*▷ in north Africa and later in 'Asir▷) were founded in the 19th century. They originated from Sufi DO and adopted some of their methods and attitudes, such as a dislike of the theologians ('ulama') and of too much learning (*Mahdiyya*); the training of progagandists in monasteries (*Sanussiyya*); a central hierarchial organization (both movements); *dhikr* (*Sanussiyya*) and prayers peculiar to the order (both). But unlike the Sufis they were militant, fundamentalist and revivalist movements that aimed to restore the pure Islam of the Prophet and revolted against foreign (Turkish and European) domination and influence. They were firmly opposed to the superstitious innovations of the Sufis. At first, Muhammad Ahmad, the *Mahdi*, called his followers "Ds.", but later, to differentiate them from the Sufis, called them *al-Ansar*▷, after the Prophet's supporters in Medina. After the Anglo-Egyptian re-conquest of Sudan the rivalry between the *Mahdiyya* and its main competitor, the *Khatmiyya*▷ or *Mirghaniyya*▷ order, took a political form; the former supported the pro-British Umma party, while the latter favoured the pro-Egyptian *Ashiqqa'* party. Under the officers' regime, since 1969, both orders' power has declined; the *Mahdiyya* was suppressed in 1970. Some true Sufi orders are also active in Sudan. The most influential of these are the *Tijaniyya*, the *Sa'diyya* and the *Ahmadiyya*, all of which came from Egypt in the 19th century.

In the *Maghreb*, *i.e.* north-west Africa, especially in Morocco, the DO still have considerable though diminishing, influence. The most important orders are the *Shadhiliyya* and its sub-orders, the *Tijaniyya*, the *Madaniyya*, the '*Isawiyya* and the *Darqawa* (and in Libya—the quasi-order of the *Sanussiyya*).

Because of their lack of a positive ideology and their other-wordly and quietist attitude, many Muslims consider the DO to be irrelevant to the real problems of modern life. The DO are steadily declining but may continue to offer, in their *dhikrs*, a conservative atmosphere to those Muslims who cannot or will not participate in the new social and political activities of the contemporary ME.   (M.W.)

DHAHRAN. Town in eastern Sa'udi Arabia on the Dammam-Riyadh railroad, *c.* 6 mi. from the Persian Gulf shore. Headquarters of the Arabian American Oil Company ("Aramco"). Pop.: 12,500 (1967). A planned, modern city, the only one in the world with a central air-conditioning system, D. is inhabited chiefly by oil experts and officials. Towards the end of World War II a large American airbase was built near the town (completed only in March 1946, after the end of the war), to which Sa'udia granted her *ad hoc*, short-term approval, without formal treaty. A formal agreement was concluded only in June 1951 by an exchange of notes. This expired in 1961–2 and the base was evacuated and handed over in April 1962. However, the USA retained certain rights.
                                                              (Y.K.)

DHOFAR. Region on the south coast of the Arabian Peninsula, on the Arabian Sea. Since the 1870s D. constitutes the western part of the Sultanate of Muscat-and-'Oman▷, bordering on South Yemen's▷ Hadhramaut region. Est. pop.: *c.* 40,000, mostly nomadic tribesmen. The language spoken in D. is an ancient south-Semitic dialect. Since the mid-1960s an insurgent movement of left-wing revolutionary tendencies (the "Dhofar Liberation Front", later re-named the "Popular Front for the Liberation of the Occupied Arab Gulf") has fought the Muscat-'Omani regime. It enjoys South Yemen and Chinese support.
                                                              (Y.S.)

DODECANESE (Greek: The Twelve Islands). Group of islands in the southern Aegean, known also as Southern Sporades. The larger islands are Rodos (Rhodes), Karpatos, Kos, Kalymnos, Kasos, Syme, Leros, Patmos, Khalke, Lipsos and Astipalaia. There are another 40 small islands. The total area is 812 sq. miles and the population in 1961 was 122,000. The islands form a district of Greece with its capital at Rhodes. The economy is based on farming, but Rhodes (pop. 30,000) has become an international tourist centre.

The islands were part of the Ottoman Empire. In 1908 the Greek population revolted against the Turks. In 1912 the islands were seized by Italy as "security" for the evacuation of Libya by the Turks; but when the evacuation was completed, Italy refused to hand them over and held on to them throughout World War I. In 1920 their annexation by Italy was endorsed by the peace with Turkey (the abortive Treaty of Sèvres▷). The Italians had promised in 1919 to transfer the islands to Greece (with the exception of Rhodes, which they asked to retain for 15 years) and Greece never relinquished its claim to the D. Italy did not keep her promise but formally annexed the D. in 1924. The British occupied the islands towards the end of World War II and handed them over to Greece in 1947. (Y.K.)

DRUZE, DRUZES (also **DRUSES**). National-religious minority. Arabic-speaking. C. 350,000 in Syria, Lebanon and Israel. The Druze sect, an offshoot of the *Isma'iliyya*▷, developed in the 11th century around the figure of the Fatimid Caliph al-Hakim bi-Amr Illah, regarded by his followers as an incarnation of the divine spirit. They settled in Wadi al-Tim on the slopes of Hermon, and later in the southern parts of Mount Lebanon. There D. amirs (princes) exercised an autonomous feudal rule, even after formally submitting to Ottoman authority. Fakhr-ul-Din II (1585–1653), one of the emirs of the Ma'n dynasty, ruled over an area including most of Lebanon and parts of Syria and Palestine. His execution by the Turks marked the end of Ma'n power. In the 18th century the house of Shihab gained ascendancy over other feudal clans as lords of the region. Some of the Shihabs converted to Christianity. Under the Shihabi Bashir II (1786–1840) the power of the D. princes began to wane. At the same time tension arose between the D. and their Maronite Christian neighbours, especially in "mixed" areas where D. feudal clans lorded it over Maronite peasants. The Maronites (with French support) tried to achieve control, and the D. (with British encouragement) to regain their previous predominance. This inter-communal strife several times led to violent clashes, notably in 1840 and 1860. A D. massacre of Maronites in 1860 turned into generally anti-Christian outbreaks that spread as far as Damascus. The events of 1860 led to intervention by the powers, the dispatch of a French expeditionary force, and the creation of a semi-autonomous district (*Sanjaq*) of Mount Lebanon (see Lebanon▷, History).

Many D. emigrated to the Houran mountains in southern Syria, where some D. were living since the 18th century. This region now became the main D. centre, known as Jabal al-Druz, the D. Mountain.

Among the Jabal Druz leaders the al-Atrash▷ clan rose to prominence (Salim al-Atrash, regarded as the virtual ruler of the Mountain from 1914 onward, became governor in name as well in 1921, under the French). In Lebanon two chief clans disputed the leadership, Junbalat▷ (or Jumblat) and Arslan▷. In 1921 the Jabal Druz territory was granted autonomy under the French Mandate. Incipient friction intensified on the death of Salim al-Atrash in 1923, and as the D. families of notables were unable to agree on a local candidate, a French officer, Captain Carbillet, was appointed governor. His attempts to carry out administrative and economic reforms sparked off the 1925 uprising in the Mountain, which spread to the D. in the Mt. Hermon area (the "D. Rebellion") and soon turned into a national Syrian revolt. Heavy fighting took place before the French were able to put it down in 1927. The rebel leader, Sultan al-Atrash▷, escaped to Jordan, returning to the Jabal only ten years later.

In 1936 Jabal Druz became part of the Syrian republic, enjoying partial autonomy. In 1944, with the departure of the French, it lost this special status and became an ordinary Syrian province. The D. in Syria are today 160–180,000, 3% of Syria's total population—most of them in Jabal Druz, where they form 80% of the population. The D. participate in independent Syria's political and party life, but do not play too prominent a part. Traditional D. hostility to the rule of Damascus, coupled with their close ties with the British and the Hashemite▷ dynasty, has made D. leaders (of the al-Atrash clan and others) take a hand in some of the frequent Syrian coups—e.g. that by Col. Sami Hinnawi▷ (1949), the overthrow of Col. Adib Shishakli▷ (1954), the abortive pro-Iraqi and pro-Western coup of October 1956, and the attempted 1966 coup of Col. Hatoum▷.

In Lebanon c. 150,000 D.—6.3% of the total population—live mostly in Mt. Lebanon district and on the western slopes of Mt. Hermon, next to Hasbaya (a town which is also an important D. religious centre). They are represented in parliament, government and the civil service according to this percentage. By tradition—though this is not binding or permanent—the post of Defence Minister is usually held by a D.

In Israel, c. 33,000 Druzes constitute more than 1% of the population, or c. 8% of the non-Jewish inhabitants. They live mostly in 15 villages in Western Galilee and two on Mt. Carmel. Since the Six Day War they have been joined by another 8,000 in four villages on the Golan Heights▷. A long-standing friendship links Jews and D. in Israel. In Israel's War of Independence (1948) many D. fought by the side of the Jews to repel the Arab invasion. Since

1957, at the community's own request, young D. are subject to the same compulsory military service as Jewish citizens. In 1957 the D. were given the status of a distinct community with its own recognized communal-judicial institutions. Since 1970 D. affairs are no longer handled by the government departments in charge of matters concerning the Arab minority. One or two D. are regularly elected to Parliament (the *Knesset*).

The D. religion originated in the *Isma'iliyya*▷ (an extreme branch of Shi'i▷ Islam) but is considered by most as having seceded from Islam. It is a secret cult; its tenets are fully known only to the '*Uqqal* (those initiated into mysteries), who are the religious heads of the community (secular notables may also come from the ranks of the *Juhhal*, the uninitiated, or common people). The D. stress moral and social principles rather than ritual or ceremony. Their house of prayer is a small structure, the *khalwa*. The two great holy days observed are the Day of Pilgrimage (*Ziyara*) to the grave of Shu'aib (the legendary patriarch of the D., identified with Jethro) at Hittin, near Tiberias; and the Feast of the Sacrifice ('*Id al-Adha*), similar to that of the Muslims. In line with their isolationist tendency and in the wake of the persecutions they suffered, D. are permitted by their faith to keep their religious-communal identity secret (*Taqiyya*, secrecy, camouflage, was also practised among Shi'i Muslims).   (O.G.)

*DUBAI (also **DIBAI**). The most populous of the seven principalities on the Trucial Coast of the Persian Gulf, northeast of Abu Dhabi. Area: 1,175 sq. mi.; pop.: 65,000; 50,000 in the capital, D. The Sheikh of D. has been under British protection, in accordance with several 19th century treaties (see Trucial 'Oman▷), and D. was the residence of the British political officer responsible for the area. The capital comprises several settlements around a deep 9 mi. wide bay. Its excellent harbour serves all the principalities. Low custom duties turned D. into a virtually free port and a centre for smuggling between the Gulf and the countries of the Indian Ocean. Its trade income was used to convert it into a modern city even before oil was discovered. Concessions for oil exploration offshore and onshore were granted in the 1950s and 1960s to American, British and French groups, after previous concessions had expired or been returned. Oil was struck offshore in 1966 and production began in 1969. A large number of immigrants were attracted to D., so that the number of foreigners exceeds that of the local population. In the absence of any local resources apart from oil, D. must import all its needs.
                                                              (Y.K.)

DULLES, JOHN FOSTER (1888–1958). USA Secretary of State in President Eisenhower's Administration, from Jan. 1953 until his death. D. had the reputation of a cold war hard-liner and a pact-maker (as President Truman's special representative he had negotiated security treaties with Australia, New Zealand, the Philippines and Japan in 1950–1). He had little understanding for the neutralism▷ then gaining wide acceptance among Asian and ME nations and condemned it as an immoral evasion of a nation's duty to support justice. He toured the ME in May 1953, visiting Egypt, Israel, Jordan, Iraq, Syria, Lebanon, India, Pakistan and Turkey, with the intention of creating a ME Defence Treaty▷ or Organization. As a result of his findings, D. decided to base US policy in the region on the "Northern Tier"▷, *i.e.* a pact with Turkey and Iran to which Arab states should, if possible, be made to adhere. His efforts to persuade Egypt and other Arab states

to join were futile; the Baghdad Pact▷, as it emerged from his endeavours, with Iraq the only Arab state adhering, proved deeply divisive and pushed Egypt further into anti-Western policies. D. played a decisive personal role in US policies in the ME in 1956–7 (see Suez War▷, Sinai War▷, US Policies in the ME▷).   (Y.R.-Y.S.)

E

EASTERN COMMAND. A joint command of the Jordanian, Iraqi and Syrian forces was created in 1968. An Iraqi officer was named to head it and Iraq dispatched troops to Syria and Jordan (their numbers were variously estimated at 5–7,000 in Syria, 12–20,000 in Jordan). Formally the EC was part of the Supreme Arab Unified Command, established in 1964 (and never officially dissolved, although it failed to function, e.g., in the Six Day War, 1967) and headed by an Egyptian general. The EC was never operational; it had no real authority over Jordanian and Syrian forces, and had little success in getting them to co-operate. With the escalation of the conflict between Jordan and the Palestinian guerillas, supported by Syria and Iraq, the EC lost all effectiveness. It was dealt its deathblow when Syrian troops invaded Jordan in September 1970, attacked the Jordanian army and were defeated. The defence and foreign ministers of the states involved had decided already in summer 1970 to dissolve the EC so that the Jordanian Army should revert to the command of the King of Jordan, and the Syrian to the President of Syria (though the two armies should continue to aim at co-ordination and co-operation). Following the Hafez Asad▷ coup in Syria, November 1970, a revival of the EC was discussed (perhaps without Iraq). (Y.S.)

Abba Eban

*EBAN, ABBA (AUBREY). Israeli diplomat and politician. Born 1915 in South Africa and educated at Cambridge University. Israel Ambassador to the UN, 1948–59, and the USA 1950–9. Member of *Knesset* (Parliament) since 1959. Minister of Education and Culture, 1960–3. Deputy Prime Minister, 1963–6 and President of the Weizmann Institute of Science, Rehovot, 1958–66. Foreign Minister since 1966. E. is well-known for his scholarship and his oratory in several languages. Among his several books the best known is "My People—the Story of the Jews". He is generally considered as moderate in his attitude to the Arab-Israel dispute, and this has sometimes led him into conflict with other members of the government. (A.W.)

EDDE, EMILE (1886–1949). Lebanese lawyer and politician. President of Lebanon 1936–41. A Maronite Christian, French-educated and politically pro-French, E. served in the Mandatory administration and was Prime Minister 1929–30. He favoured close contact between the Lebanon, as a Christian state, and France as her protector. He opposed the notion that the Lebanon was part of the Arab world and should cultivate closer ties with it. He was consequently willing to reach an agreement with the Jews of Palestine and with Zionism. In 1934 he organized his supporters in the "National Bloc" party. In 1936 he was elected President, defeating Bishara al-Khouri▷. E. continued as Head of State even when the French suspended the Constitution, September 1939, and resigned only in April 1941. In November 1943 the French refused to acquiesce in the abrogation of those articles of the Constitution subjecting Lebanon to the French Mandate, declared their amendment null and void, suspended the Constitution, and imprisoned President Khouri and his government. E. agreed to be appointed Head of State by the French. However, British and American pressure compelled the French to retract and to reinstate the President, the Government and Parliament. E. was deposed. His political career ended in March 1944, when he was expelled by Parliament. He died in 1949.

His sons Pierre and Raymond continue to lead E.'s National Bloc. Raymond E. (b. 1913) was elected to Parliament in 1953 and 1957. He served for about a year as one of the four ministers of the compromise government set up after the Civil War in October 1958. In 1960 he was elected to Parliament in his home district Jubeil, together with five other members of his party. In 1964, however, he was defeated in the elections, and only two members of his party were elected. In 1965 he won a by-election. In 1968 he participated in the success of the right-wing Maronite bloc and was elected to Parliament with five members of his party. He was a minister in 1968–69 and held several portfolios. However, he is usually in opposition, particularly regarding the government's acquiescense in the activities of the Palestinian terrorists and its surrender to their demands.

Pierre E. (b. 1921) was elected to Parliament in 1951 and 1953. In 1953 he was Minister of Finance. In recent years he has devoted his time to running the family banking business and has taken little part in political life. He is active in economic affairs, but did not stand for Parliament. In 1968 he was once again Minister of Finance. (Y.P.)

EDEN, ANTHONY (EARL OF AVON) (b. 1897). British Conservative Prime Minister April 1955–January 1957. Foreign Secretary under Neville Chamberlain, from whose government he resigned in 1938 over the appeasement policy, and again under Churchill▷ 1940–5 and 1951–5. As Foreign Secretary, E. was instrumental in the formation of the Arab League▷, 1945. His speech of 29 May 1941, calling for a "greater degree of unity" among the Arab peoples, and promising British support, prompted Arab activity; it was followed by British efforts, first through Iraq and later through Egypt. E.'s main impact on the ME was felt in the bitter struggle with Egypt after she nationalized the Suez Canal in July 1956. This led finally to the mounting of a joint Anglo-French military operation and the occupation of the Suez Canal Zone (see Suez War▷). E. denied any foreknowledge of Israel's simultaneous attack on Sinai (see Sinai War▷). Under Russian, American and UN pressure, Britain and France were forced to withdraw. Severely attacked at home over his Suez policy, and owing to ill health, E. resigned the premiership in January 1957.   (Sh.H.)

EEC—see European Economic Community▷.

EGHBAL, DR. MANOUCHEHR (b. 1908, Meshed). Iranian physician and politician, Prime Minister 1957–60. Studied medicine in Paris and Montpellier. Professor of Medicine, Teheran University 1938–50. Minister of Public Health 1946–7, Posts 1947–8, Education 1948–9, Interior 1949–50. Governor-General of Azerbaijan Province 1950–1. Rector, Tabriz University 1951–3, Rector, Teheran University 1953–6. Minister of the Imperial Court 1956–7; Prime Minister April 1957, he resigned in September 1960 following allegations of irregularities in the general election. Permanent delegate to UNESCO 1960–3. Since 1963 President of the National Iranian Oil Company.   (B.G.)

*EGYPT. Independent republic at the north-eastern corner of Africa (her official name, 1958–71: "The United Arab Republic▷" (UAR) was changed in September 1971, to "The Egyptian Arab Republic"). Capital: Cairo. E.'s area is 386,000 sq. miles (incl. Sinai▷, which is about 29,160 sq. miles). The inhabited area is only some 13,510 sq. miles (approximately 3.5% of the total area), and lies in the Nile valley and its delta, and in a few oases, whilst the rest of the country is desert. Borders: In the north, the Mediterranean, 571 miles. To the east E. borders on Israel, in Sinai (since the Six Day War▷, on the Suez Canal, 99 miles in length); the rest of the eastern border is the Red Sea along 528 miles. In the south Egypt shares

with Sudan a desert border of 745 miles along the 22nd parallel, and in the west, with Libya (649 miles).

The population of E. numbers some 34 million (est. 1970). The vast majority speak Arabic; 90% are Sunni Muslims. The largest and most important minority are the Christian Copts▷, constituting about 8% of the population. Other minorities—Greeks, Italians, and Jews (about 2,000 Jews remain in E.)—have almost disappeared recently, mainly because of E.'s economic policy, based on large-scale nationalization. The Jewish minority have been subjected also to discrimination and persecution, especially after the Sinai Campaign▷ (1956), and to an even greater extent after the Six Day War (June 1967).

About 3.9 million of E.'s bread-winners engage in agriculture, about 1.1 million in industry and construction, and some 2.7 million in services (1969). C. 30% of the National Income is derived from agriculture, 23% from industry (1968–9; in 1952–3 industry constituted 16% of the National Income). In the last few years oil production has been developed (1.8 million tons in 1956; 12.5 million tons in 1968; 20 million tons in 1970). Because of the Six Day War, E. lost the oil produced in the Sinai Peninsula, estimated at the time at 5 million tons or 60% of E.'s output. The refineries at Suez were also damaged in the course of the "war of attrition" initiated by E. in 1969. E. also possesses various mineral resources; their exploitation is being actively developed.

Since 1953 (formally since 1956) E.'s regime has been a presidential republic. In the 19th century she was autonomous under the sovereignty of the Ottoman Empire, under a ruler titled since the 1870s "Viceroy" (*Khedive*). The present borders were fixed at the end of the 19th century. The border with Sudan

Map of Egypt

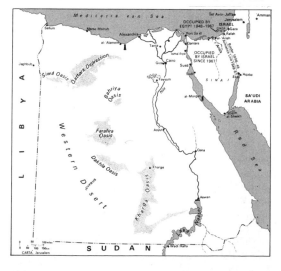

was determined in the Condominium▷ Agreement of 1899. The Sinai border was established in 1906 by British dictate to which the Ottoman Sultan was forced to yield, even though he did not renounce his claim to Sinai. The disputed western border was determined in an agreement with Italy in 1925. From 1882 E. was under a "temporary" British occupation, which became a protectorate, 1914–22. In 1922 E. received independence in a unilateral British declaration, endorsed and amended by an Anglo-Egyptian Treaty in 1936. E. became a member of the League of Nations in 1937 and is a founding member of the United Nations since 1945.

POLITICAL HISTORY. E. was under Ottoman rule, which was indirect and unstable, from the beginning of the 16th century. In 1798 she was occupied for two years by Napoleon—a conquest which symbolized the beginning of E.'s modern era. In 1805 an Albanian officer, Muhammad 'Ali, came to power. The dynasty he founded ruled until the deposition of King Farouq▷ (1952) and the abrogation of the monarchy in 1953. Muhammad 'Ali fought the Ottoman Empire, conquered Syria, reached Anatolia and endangered the very existence of the Empire. In 1840—with the intervention of the Powers and in exchange for his withdrawal to E.—the government of E. and the Sudan was formally conceded to Muhammad 'Ali and his successors. His successors continued to expand their independence. Isma'il Pasha managed to obtain from the Sultan, in 1867 and 1873, permission to make public laws of his own, enlarge his army, sign non-political arrangements with foreign states, and alter the order of succession in the ruling house; he took the title of Khedive—a Persian title meaning the monarch's deputy—which emphasized his semi-independent status as a ruler.

Muhammad 'Ali and his successors contributed to E.'s development: they fostered the beginning of industrialization, irrigation and transportation projects, cotton-growing and the construction of the Suez Canal▷. The concession to build and manage the Canal was granted in 1854 to a French engineer, Ferdinand de Lesseps. Work began in 1859, and in 1869 the Canal was opened. The plans for development and modernization, especially during the reign of Khedive Isma'il, placed E. under a heavy international debt. This debt, which reached £100m., served as a pretext for the intervention of the Powers. In 1876, Isma'il had to agree to the establishment of a British-French committee to supervise E.'s economy. Isma'il's unwillingness to cooperate with the Powers' representatives caused his deposition in 1879 and the appointment in his stead of his son, Tawfiq.

The increasing intervention of the Powers in E.'s affairs generated a ferment in the army. As early as 1879, before Isma'il's deposition, there were demonstrations by officers against the foreigners and against cuts in the military establishment. In 1882 the officers, led by Colonel Ahmad 'Arabi (correct: 'Urabi), forced the Khedive to appoint Sami al-Barudi, the Minister of War, as Prime Minister, and their leader, 'Arabi, as Minister of War. This government was not acceptable to the creditor states, especially Britain and France, because it tried to undermine the arrangements made by the Khedive to guarantee their financial interests. Britain occupied E. in 1882 and defeated 'Arabi and his army. The British conquest, though always defined as temporary, continued until 1922 (and, in fact, until 1947 or 1954). E.'s modern national movement, from the turn of the century, was therefore directed primarily against Britain (and not against the Ottoman Empire which held nominal sovereignty over E. until 1914).

On the eve of World War I, E. was, in international law, part of the Ottoman Empire, but actually ruled by the British. On 18 Dec. 1914, one month after war had been declared, Britain severed the formal link between E. and the Ottoman Empire and declared E. a British Protectorate. E. was promised that Britain would guide her toward self-rule and that the capitulations▷ would be abrogated at the end of the war. At the same time the British deposed the Khedive 'Abbas Hilmi▷ and replaced him with his uncle, Hussein Kamel, giving him the title of Sultan (he died in 1917 and was succeeded by his brother, Ahmad Fu'ad)▷.

The war intensified the Anglo-Egyptian antagonism. It emphasized the immense importance of E. to the British strategic alignment. The division of the Ottoman Empire after the war obliged Britain to find an arrangement that would guarantee her interests in E. but would not, on the other hand, completely ignore her promises to E. In E. the ever-increasing pressure of a war effort imposed on her inhabitants, soaring prices, martial law and censorship all caused growing resistance to the British and strengthened the nationalists who opposed both the Protectorate and the Egyptian Sultan. During the war a nationalist group formed, led by Sa'd Zaghlul▷, and demanded complete independence. This group differed from the other nationalist parties founded in 1907–8. Its leaders represented the nucleus of a new Egyptian (as opposed to Turkish-Circassian) élite: the landed gentry and commercial middle-class, with an economic interest in independence, and members of the free professions. This élite also managed to enlist active support in the villages—a new phenomenon in E.—as well as among the Coptic minority. The Zaghlul group demanded the right to represent E. in talks with Britain and disputed the right of the Egyptian Sultan (whose authority it wished to limit) and his government to conduct these negotiations. The claim of the nationalists to represent E.'s national demands in talks to be held in London was laid before the High Commissioner, Sir Reginald Wingate▷, on 11 Nov. 1918. Two days later the delegation, (Arabic: al-Wafd), constituted itself as a permanent body, the nucleus of the Wafd▷ party. At first the British government refused to recognize Zaghlul's group as the national leadership representing E. Demonstrations and strikes followed. The banishment of Zaghlul and his leading supporters (8 Mar. 1919) sparked off violent riots and the British backed down. Wingate was replaced by General Allenby▷. From the beginning, Allenby adopted a policy of conciliation. On 7 Apr., Zaghlul and his supporters were released and granted permission to travel to Paris to place the Egyptian demands before the Peace Conference. However, when the delegation arrived they learnt that the Peace Conference had recognized the British Protectorate in E. (May 1919).

In May 1919, the British government appointed the Secretary for the Colonies, Lord Milner▷, to investigate and suggest a regime that would grant to E. self-government under British guidance and safeguard British and foreign interests. Milner reached E. at the end of 1919. He was boycotted by the nationalists and public figures (except for palace and government circles), but later established contact with Zaghlul in Europe; Milner-Zaghlul talks were held in London in June 1920. Milner offered E. independence on condition that a treaty guaranteeing British interests be signed; but no agreement was reached as to the details of such a treaty. Milner presented his Report at the end of 1920; it was made public in February 1921. Now Zaghlul and the Egyptian government struggled as to who was to negotiate the proposed treaty with the British. Allenby tried to break the hold of Zaghlul and the nationalists and find a pro-British nationalist group that would accept independence on Britain's terms, but he failed. Zaghlul's exile to the Seychelles (December 1921) only intensified national ferment and caused renewed violence.

Seeing that an agreement on an Anglo-E. treaty was not feasible, the Lloyd George government decided to grant limited independence to E. unilaterally. On 28 Feb. 1922, Britain declared E.'s independence. Four matters were reserved to the British government until agreement could be reached upon them: a. security of British communications in E.; b. defence of E. against foreign aggression; c. protection of foreign interests and minorities; d.

administration of the Sudan. The Egyptians protested these restrictions, but in effect accepted the limited independence granted and began to establish the institutions of their state.

In March 1922, Sultan Fu'ad proclaimed himself King. A constitution was worked out by an appointed committee and promulgated in April 1923; and in Sept. 1923–Jan. 1924 a Parliament was elected (the Wafd won a sweeping majority). The 1923 constitution, the subject of a bitter struggle between the radical nationalists and the King and his conservative associates, was a conservative one. The King was to appoint and dismiss the Prime Minister, to dissolve parliament and postpone its sessions, to appoint the President of the Senate and one fifth of its members, and had the right to veto all laws. Despite this, the Wafd and the nationalists became the defenders of the constitution, in which they saw a guarantee against domination by the King, while the King viewed the constitution as restricting his rule. Conservative circles and court factions supported the King. Elections were initially indirect, but in 1924 the Wafd government provided for direct elections. The King and the conservatives again changed the Election Law in December 1925, introducing restrictions as regards property, taxes and level of education; in 1930 the government of Isma'il Sidqi▷ once again instituted indirect elections. In July 1928 the King dissolved parliament and postponed elections for three years; the Wafd succeeded in reversing this situation in 1929, and elections took place (again won by the Wafd). In 1930, parliament was again dissolved and Isma'il Sidqi annulled the 1923 constitution.

This instability in the internal political life of E., and the failure of the Wafd party to become a positive and decisive political force, prevented a parliamentary system taking root. They also were a major factor preventing Anglo-Egyptian agreement about a treaty. During these years a three-cornered struggle continued between the Wafd, the King and the British government. All three were keenly interested to replace the unilateral declaration of 1922 with a treaty between nominally equal, independent states. The four "reserved points" of February 1922 reflected, for Britain, vital interests which any treaty had to satisfy in some form. For the nationalists they represented restrictions on E.'s independence and a preference for foreign interests that no sovereign state could accept. The Royal Court found itself in the middle. On the one hand, Fu'ad knew that he owed his throne to the British, who were his chief support; on the other, the national struggle of the Wafd drove him to associate himself with the national resistance to the British.

Anglo-Egyptian negotiations on a treaty failed in

1924, 1927 and 1929–30—mainly over the problems of defence and the Sudan. E.—whether represented by the *Wafd* or by other governments—demanded the evacuation of British forces, the cancellation of restrictions on the strength of the Egyptian army and the transfer of its command from British to Egyptian hands. The British were unable to accept these demands and insisted on the presence of British forces in E. In regard to Sudan, the Egyptians feared British intentions to deprive them of their share in the joint administration as provided in the Condominium Agreement of 1899. This suspicion grew because of British pressure that Fu'ad should not be defined in the constitution as "King of E. and the Sudan", and the reprisals taken after the murder of Sir Lee Stack▷, 1924—the withdrawal of Egyptian troops from Sudan; the enactment of Sudan's budget without submission to E. for approval; the enlargement of irrigated areas in Sudan (implying the possibility of strangling E. by cutting off in Sudan the vital Nile flood-waters—an irritant removed by the Nile Waters Agreement, 1929, which guaranteed to E. an adequate share of the water supply).

The way out of the treaty impasse was found in 1936. Several factors made both Britain and E. ready for concessions. The conquest of Ethiopia by the Italians in 1935 threatened both British and Egyptian interests and both parties were interested in a quick agreement. The British, fearful of internal unrest fanned by the *Wafd*, now also supported the renewal of political-parliamentary activity and a restored balance between the King and the *Wafd*. They therefore supported the demand in 1935 to restore the 1923 constitution that had been abrogated in 1930. In 1936, elections took place and brought the *Wafd* to government. The delegation formed to negotiate with the British this time included the representatives of all the parties (excluding the "National Party" of Mustafa Kamel). King Fu'ad died at this time and was succeeded by his son, Farouq▷, a minor; a Regency Council was set up. These changes in the palace eased some of the tension between the Court and the nationalists.

The treaty between E. and Britain was signed on 26 Aug. 1936. A defence pact, valid for 20 years, allowed Britain to station a defined number of forces on the Suez Canal until such time as the Egyptian Army would be capable of defending it. In the event of war or threat of war Egypt was to furnish Britain with "all the facilities and assistance in her power, including the use of [her] ports, aerodromes and communications". Sudan would continue to be administered according to the Condominium Agreement. The protection of foreigners and minorities was recognized as the exclusive responsibility of the

Egyptian government. Britain was to support the abrogation of the capitulations▷ (which was agreed to in the international Montreux▷ Convention of May 1937). In May 1937, on Britain's recommendation, E. was admitted to the League of Nations▷.

The relaxation in Anglo-Egyptian relations that followed the 1936 agreement was disturbed by the outbreak of World War II. E. became vitally important to the British strategic set-up. This prevented Britain from adhering to all provisions of the treaty. The number of British soldiers in the Canal area still exceeded that stipulated in the treaty and, similarly, troops were not withdrawn from other parts of the country as stated in the treaty. During the war, E. served as a base for British forces in the ME and the number of troops stationed there increased further.

Many Egyptian politicians, including the King, displayed sympathy for the "Axis". E. refused to declare war on the "Axis" powers and instructed her troops on the western frontier not to engage "Axis" forces (that reached Mersa Matruh in 1940). This combination of the German-Italian military threat, and the anti-British and pro-German sentiments current in E., compelled Britain to intervene, during the war, more than ever in E.'s internal affairs. The Egyptian government was forced to dismiss the Chief-of-Staff, 'Aziz 'Ali al-Masri▷, who was (rightly) suspected of contacts with the enemy, and the Prime Minister, 'Ali Maher▷, who openly supported Italy. British intervention reached its peak on 4 Feb. 1942. In the face of the growing military threat of the "Axis" forces and the pro-German foreign policy of the King and his government, Britain compelled the King, by an ultimatum accompanied by a show of military force, to replace the cabinet with a *Wafdist* government more acceptable to the British.

The appointment of Mustafa Nahhas▷, the *Wafd* leader, as Prime Minister in February 1942, through British pressure, contributed toward the decline in the *Wafd*'s popularity. Nahhas, who had replaced Sa'd Zaghlul at the latter's death in 1927, did not enjoy Zaghlul's personal prestige. The Treaty of 1936 reduced the question of relations with Britain—which had been the central issue in the *Wafd* platform for several years—to secondary importance. The *Wafd* was unable to formulate a new programme that would answer E.'s new needs, especially the socio-economic ones. Indeed, the *Wafd* was dominated until the mid-1940s by individuals with vested economic interests. It was also weakened by internal rifts (dissident leaders had seceded and established a Liberal-Constitutional Party back in 1922; now the *Sa'adist* party split away in 1937, and the Copt Makram 'Ubaid—in 1942).

EGYPT

Attempts to improve relations between the Royal Court and the *Wafd* also failed. In 1936 the *Wafd* had pinned its hopes on the young King Farouq. However, Farouq was continuing his father's anti-*Wafd* policy. Relations between the *Wafd* and the Palace deteriorated when Farouq made use of appointments to the Senate, the budget, supervision of religious institutions, the appointment of army officers (after control of the military was handed over to the Egyptians under the 1936 treaty), as instruments against the *Wafd*. He relied for support on the anti-*Wafdist* parties, including the Fascist "Young Egypt" (*Misr al-Fatat*), founded in the mid-1930s.

In the late 1930s and especially during the 1940s, the influence of marginal extremist parties grew. On the right were the "Muslim Brotherhood" ▷ and *Misr al-Fatat*, and on the left the various factions of the Communist Party. These extra-parliamentary groups attracted youth, intellectuals and the middle-class. Their growth owed much to the decline of the secular-liberal system of values inculcated in E. by the British, and the increased influence of Fascist or religious anti-liberal doctrines. This change in ideological outlook, together with the continual conflict between the *Wafd* and the monarchy, the parties of the Court and extra-parliamentary groups, combined to cause the further decline of the constitutional regime. That regime, from its inception in 1923 until its collapse in 1952, did not display much stability. Only two houses of representatives completed their terms of office (1931–6, 1945–50), ten elections were held in those 29 years and there were 38 changes of government. Some of the causes of this instability are inherent in the 1923 constitution, which was vaguely phrased and granted the monarch much power. E.'s social conditions also contributed toward a number of negative phenomena of the parliamentary period, such as the rigging of elections, falsification and purchase of votes, etc.

During World War II, social and economic changes, the first signs of which had appeared since the beginning of the century, were accelerated and intensified, and contributed to the deterioration of the constitutional regime. Among these socio-economic trends were: a growing polarization in the distribution of capital and income and a decline in the standard of living. The population increased from 9.7m. in 1900 to about 22m. in 1952; but arable land, the source of subsistence of 75% of the population, was limited to *c.* 6m. *feddan* (acres), and industry did not develop fast enough to catch up with population growth. In 1952, 6% of landowners held 65% of all arable land. This situation created increasing socio-economic tension, and generated antagonism toward the constitutional

Egyptian pyramids

regime and its western ideological roots. The fact that the parties active within this regime devoted most of their energies to external-political problems (relations with Britain) and did virtually nothing to ease social and economic tension, further accentuated a tendency to side with extra-parliamentary forces, whose slogans expressed xenophobic nationalism and religious fanaticism, but who demanded social reform also. Things further deteriorated during the war, because of a decline in the urban standard of living, the increasing migration from country to town, and the creation of an unemployed or underemployed class which became a turbulent instrument in the hands of extra-parliamentary groups. This situation compelled the parliamentary parties to pay more attention to social and economic problems. On the eve of elections, they had to adopt slogans promising social reforms. Proposals for far-reaching socio-economic changes, such as land reform, were also discussed, Even within the *Wafd* party, controlled as it was by capitalists and landowners, a proposal was raised by leftist elements for agrarian reform and the limitation of ownership to a maximum of 500 *feddan* (acres); radical leftist circles demanded a limit of 50 *feddan*.

During the war E. became increasingly involved in an active regional Arab policy. Formerly, E. hardly took part in the Arab nationalist struggles outside its borders. She first became actively involved when she responded to a British invitation to attend the London Conference (1939) on the future of

Palestine. In 1942–3, the British renewed their active interest in the establishment of a Pan-Arab alliance, in the hope that such an alliance would provide support for Britain in the war, and induce in the Arab states, because of their feeling of increased power and self-confidence, a more moderate stance. The British realized that without E. such an alliance could not be built, and at their request (and also in order not to abandon this arena to King Farouq), Nahhas consented to head the consultations that were to bring about the foundation of the Arab League▷ (1944–5). E. became the major and decisive force in the League—the Secretary-General has been Egyptian since its foundation, and Cairo serves as its centre and headquarters. A growing involvement in Arab affairs dragged E. into the Palestine War (1948) — in breach of an explicit decision not to intervene in the war with regular forces and against the specific advice of the army commanders. Within the Arab League, E. opposed all plans for federation or a revision of the map of the Arab states and especially an expansion on the part of the Hashemite dynasty ruling Iraq and Jordan. Heading a bloc of states (Syria, Saʻudi Arabia, etc.), E. prevented this expansion (save for the occupation of the Arab part of Palestine by Jordan which she was unable to prevent) and saw to it that the Arab League should remain an association of sovereign states protecting the inter-Arab status quo. This policy line underwent a change only at the end of the 1950s when E. in turn tried to impose her rule on the other Arab states.

At the end of the world war, E. demanded the annulment of the 1936 Treaty. Her main demands were the evacuation of British forces, including those stationed on the Suez Canal, and "the Unity of the Nile Valley", in other words the unification of E. and the Sudan. Britain was prepared to discuss the expiry of the treaty before the twenty-year period agreed upon, on condition that the treaty be replaced by a defence pact that would satisfy Britain's strategic requirements in the Canal Zone. As for Sudan, the British advocated self-determination for the Sudanese, and an advance towards self-government in the meantime. In 1946, Ismaʻil Sidqi▷ reached an agreement with the British under which Britain was to withdraw her garrisons from Egypt within three years and a joint Anglo-Egyptian defence committee was to be established. With regard to Sudan, the two parties were to prepare her, "within the framework of the unity between E. and the Sudan under the joint Egyptian crown", for self-rule and self-determination. This formula was given conflicting interpretations by E. and Britain: to the British, "Egyptian-Sudanese unity" was no more than a token formula, mere lip service, whereas Sudan had been actually promised

self-determination; the Egyptians, in turn, claimed that the primary aim, that of Egyptian-Sudanese unity, had been conceded and achieved. The publication of these contradictory interpretations nullified the agreement. The question of Sudan was raised in 1947 in the UN Security Council by Prime Minister Nuqrashi▷, but the Council could arrive at no decision and E.'s argument against self-determination for Sudan failed to sway world public opinion. The impasse concerning relations with Britain, and the shift towards radicalization in E.'s internal political life during these years, resulted in 1951 in the unilateral abrogation by the *Wafd* government of the 1936 Treaty. Attempts to force the evacuation of British troops by a popular resistance movement caused prolonged and serious clashes in 1951–2.

Since the end of World War II, the radicalization of E.'s internal political life was accelerated. It resulted in a chain of political assassinations (Prime Minister Ahmad Maher▷ was murdered in 1945, Prime Minister Nuqrashi▷ in 1948; in 1949, Hassan al-Banna▷, the leader of the "Muslim Brotherhood"▷ held responsible for Nuqrashi's murder, was assassinated). The parties failed to neutralize the violence of the extra-parliamentary forces. Governments changed frequently (during the first half of 1952 six times). The debacle of the Egyptian Army in the Israel-Arab War (1948) and the shortcoming it bared in the military forces and the administration became a subject of dispute between the parties and the King, and increased political instability. This trend toward radicalism, which was to an extent supported by the King, revealed a political vacuum within the internal power system, which was to be filled by the "Free Officers" junta after their *coup d'état* on 23 July 1952.

The first steps of the "Free Officers" junta — headed by General Muhammad Nagib▷ and Colonel Gamal 'Abd-ul-Nasser — were concerned with safeguarding the revolution and the continuity of government. On the night of the coup itself the American ambassador was informed of the event and assured of the safety of foreigners in E. Thus the threat of foreign (*i.e.* British) intervention was averted. A civilian government was set up, led by the veteran anti-British politician, 'Ali Maher▷. King Farouq was deposed and exiled (26 July) and the crown transferred to his infant son, Ahmad Fu'ad. At first, the intentions and policy of the "Free Officers" were not clear. Some veteran *Wafdist* politicians thought the coup was intended to remove power from the monarch and restore it to the true representatives of the people, namely the *Wafd*. However, the intentions of the junta were soon evident. On 7 Sept., 'Ali Maher resigned, refusing to approve the agrarian reform bill as proposed by the "Free Officers". The same day a new government was formed with Nagib at its head, and the disputed land reform was immediately enacted. Land ownership was restricted to 200 *feddan* (acres) per person, with 100 *feddan* for other members of the family. The immediate significance of this law lay in the blow it dealt the class of land-owners who controlled the political and economic life of E. Another decree of the same day (8 Sept.) made the existence of political parties conditional on the approval of their leaders and programmes by the government. A decree of 31 July had ordered the parties to "purge themselves". These two laws indicated the political line chosen by the junta, namely an all-out attack on the old political system.

During October-December 1952, the parties, led by the *Wafd*, attempted to resist the officers and demanded the restoration of the constitution and a return to a parliamentary regime. The officers reacted with a propaganda campaign, the abrogation of the 1923 constitution (10 Dec. 1952), and the establishment of a court to judge ministers, members of parliament and civil servants who had "betrayed the trust of the people". Some of the men put on trial were sentenced to long prison terms and the loss of their political rights. All political parties were dissolved and their property confiscated (17 Jan. 1953); and a "Liberation Organization" was established (23. Jan. 1953) to fill the vacuum left by the disbandment of the parties. Pressure, however, for the renewal of the parliamentary system increased in 1953. This pressure was exerted by politicians, journalists and even by several members of the junta itself. The major struggle within the group was between Nasser and Nagib. It was partly a personal struggle for power: Nasser felt it was his right for his share in forming the "Free Officers" and directing the coup, while Nagib claimed it as a concomitant of his position as Chairman of the Revolutionary Council, Prime Minister and then President. But the struggle had also an ideological character. Nagib became, during 1953, the chief spokesman for those demanding the restoration of the constitutional regime and the return of the army to the barracks. Nagib was also rather more sympathetic to the "Muslim Brotherhood" ▷ (see below). The struggle became public with Nagib's resignation on 24 Feb. 1954 from his offices of President, Prime Minister and Chairman of the Revolutionary Council. This resignation aroused opposition among the public and the officers. Khaled Mohieddin (Muhyi-ul-Din), a member of the Revolutionary Council and a Marxist, supported Nagib against Nasser and, in a rapid military coup supported by officers of the Armoured Corps, restored Nagib

to his post as President (25 Feb. 1954). The temporary supremacy of Nagib over Nasser compelled the Revolutionary Council to proclaim, on 3 March, that elections for a constituent assembly would be held in July, and the military regime abrogated as of June. On 25 Mar. the Revolutionary Council announced that after elections political parties would be permitted and the Revolutionary Council dissolved.

Nagib's political victory was short-lived. Nasser and his supporters stirred up opposition within the military forces, decrying the threat to the revolution and calling for the abrogation of the measures taken. Transport workers struck, presenting identical demands. On 29 Mar., the Revolutionary Council deferred to 1956 the implementation of the March decrees. Evidently Nasser had emerged victorious from the political struggle against Nagib. In mid-April, Nagib was compelled to appoint Nasser Prime Minister; he himself remained President—without any real authority—and, in November, was stripped of this honorary position, too. In summer 1954 purges were carried out in regional and municipal councils, in the press, among politicians and in the army. More officers were brought into the government. This militarization of the government had begun in June 1953 with Nasser's appointment as Deputy Prime Minister; it was accelerated after the Nasser-Nagib clash, to consolidate Nasser's position. In April and August 1954, seven of the "Free Officers" became Ministers.

Parallel to the struggle between Nasser and Nagib, 1953-4, there was a contest between the new regime and the "Muslim Brotherhood". After the coup this was the only organization toward which the new regime did not adopt a negative attitude, and the "Muslim Brotherhood", for its part, welcomed the revolution. The new regime appeared willing to co-operate with them and even invited them to join the September 1952 government—an offer that fell through when two of their three nominees were rejected by the officers. The regime also agreed that the law on the dissolution of political parties should not apply to the "Brotherhood", as they were not a "party". Yet differences soon became apparent, since the "Brotherhood" wanted to be real partners in power and policy-making and demanded that the new regime adopt their principles and base itself on Islam—a demand which the officers rejected. A personal rivalry also sprang up between Nasser and Isma'il Hudeibi, the leader of the "Brotherhood". The conflict became more pronounced with the establishment of the "Liberation Organization" (January 1953), which put an end to the aspiration of the "Brotherhood" to become a popular civilian force on which the regime would rely. During 1953, the "Brotherhood" leadership was weakened by internal power struggles, encouraged by the regime. In January 1954, in the wake of student demonstrations which caused clashes between supporters of the "Brotherhood" and those of the regime, the government imprisoned the organization's leaders, disbanded it and outlawed its activities. Nagib's temporary supremacy (February-March 1954) brought with it the release of the "Brotherhood's" leaders and their support of Nagib against Nasser; with Nagib's fall, the rift grew.

In 1953-4, talks were resumed with Britain on the replacement of the 1936 Treaty by a new agreement, with the regime displaying a rational and moderate approach. On 12 Feb. 1953 agreement was reached on the question of Sudan—made possible by E.'s flexibility and a change in her position. It was agreed that the Sudan would prepare itself during a period of three years for self-determination and that the Condominium would be terminated. Talks begun in April 1953 on the evacuation of British troops from E. ended in October 1954 in an agreement that stipulated complete evacuation within 20 months. Britain was to return and use her bases in E. in case of an attack on one of the Arab League countries or Turkey, and British technicians were to continue maintaining the bases.

The agreement with Britain strengthened Nasser's position at the head of the Revolutionary Council and gave him the opportunity to remove Nagib and liquidate the opposition of the "Brotherhood". On 26 Oct. 1954, an attempt by the "Brotherhood" to assassinate Nasser was reported. A wave of purges followed which eliminated Nasser's last opponents. The "Brotherhood" leadership and some officers were arrested. Nagib himself was deposed on 14 Nov. 1954, as he was held implicated in the plot. By 1955, Nasser was consolidating his rule; his opponents in the Revolutionary Council, in the army and among the politicians and journalists, were fired, tried or detained. The leaders of the "Brotherhood" were condemned to death and some of them were hanged. (Yet the "Muslim Brotherhood" continued to exist underground, and was from time to time accused, during the 1950s and '60s, of plotting and treason, and purges, arrests and more trials followed.)

In 1953-4 during the struggle over the regime, Nasser published some of his political thoughts, later to be collected in his book "The Philosophy of the Revolution". He emphasized that the aim of the "Free Officers" was more than a mere change of government; they aimed at a revolution that would make E. free and strong. Towards this end action was necessary in three circles: the Arab, African and

Muslim, with E. at the centre of each of them. As to the form of government, at first the "Free Officers" had believed that, once they had defeated the corrupt regime, the people would follow them, take the power into its own hands, and carry out the hoped-for revolution. However, since this hope had not materialized, the leaders of the coup had to show the nation the way to political and economic freedom.

With Nasser firmly established in power and the problem of the treaty with Britain solved, the Nasserist regime began to conduct (for the first time in the history of an independent E.) an independent foreign policy. In 1955, Nasser attended the Bandung Conference▷. This was a turning point in Egyptian foreign policy both ideologically and practically. As a result of this conference, the Nasserist regime adopted "Positive Neutralism"▷ as a guiding line. Bandung was a mile-stone in E.'s separation from the West. Soon after the conference, and as a result of the contacts made at Bandung, E. recognized Communist China; an "Egyptian-Czech" (in fact Egyptian-Russian) arms deal, which first linked E. to the Soviet bloc, was revealed. Increased economic ties with the Soviet Union followed and massive Soviet aid including as its most significant item the construction of the High Dam at Aswan▷. E.'s requirements for arms since the adoption of an activist line towards Israel in 1955, and an activist inter-Arab policy, made for increasing dependence on the Soviet Union and Egyptian-Soviet military, economic and ultimately political co-operation, which reached their peak after the Six Day War of 1967 and were formalized in a Treaty of Alliance in May 1971. Increasing co-ordination with the Soviet camp resulted in E.'s recognition of North Vietnam, North Korea, the Vietcong, and, finally East Germany (1969) and the establishment of full diplomatic relations with them.

Tactical co-operation with the Soviet Union was, from 1966 on, on such a scale that it was in opposition to the declared Egyptian foreign policy doctrine of "Positive Neutralism". Those who formulated policy were quite aware of this disparity. In 1967, after the Six Day War, Muhammad Hassanein Heykal▷, the editor of al-Ahram▷, attempted to re-formulate a neutralistic Egyptian ideology and therefore advocated the re-establishment of some link with the USA. However, the escalation of the Israel-Arab conflict after the Six Day War, the full support given to E. by the USSR, and the total break with the USA compelled E. to abandon for the time being any thought of following a truly neutralist policy.

E.'s relations with the USA were complex and changing. During Nasser's years of entrenchment (1952-4) relations between the two countries were normal. However, after the Egyptian-Soviet arms deal of 1955, when the USSR began to replace the USA in supplying E. economic and military aid, the Nasserist regime adopted an anti-American policy that hardened over the years, despite the fact that the USA continued to provide much-needed economic aid. Several political steps taken by the USA in the ME were interpreted by the Egyptians as imperialistic plots against the independence of the ME countries and particularly against E.—thus, e.g., the Baghdad Pact▷ (1955); the suspension of Western aid for the High Dam at Aswan (1956); the Eisenhower▷ Doctrine (1957); US aid to royalist, "reactionary" countries such as Sa'udi Arabia; US aid to, and support for, Israel.

Relations with Britain and France arrived at a most serious impasse in 1956. In July, E. nationalized the Suez Canal, and after negotiations and a crisis that dragged on for several months, Britain and France invaded E. (the "Suez War"▷, October-November 1956), while Israel at the same time invaded Sinai (the "Sinai Campaign"▷). The invasion failed, as international, particularly US and Soviet, pressure compelled the three countries to call it off and withdraw. E. severed relations with Britain and France and confiscated the property of their citizens. Relations between E. and Britain were resumed only in 1959, and then at a lower level; only in 1961 were diplomatic relations restored to ambassadorial level. E. again broke off relations late in 1965 because of the Rhodesia crisis, and they were resumed only late in 1967. Relations with France were resumed in 1963. However, despite the resumption of diplomatic relations, neither Britain nor France was able to recover her former position of political influence in E. This was because of the bitterness felt towards them by many Egyptians; and also because they could offer E. only limited military or economic aid. Even de Gaulle's pro-Arab policy since 1965 (after France quit Algeria) did not restore France to a position of real influence because of France's limited strength. Diplomatic relations with West Germany were severed in 1965 in protest against German aid to, and recognition of, Israel.

Since 1955 E. adopted an activist line also in her Arab policies. She aimed at forging inter-Arab alliances under her leadership and protection—such as the 1955 military pact between E., Syria and Sa'udi Arabia, joined by Jordan and Yemen in 1956. E. continued to advocate Arab solidarity and the co-ordination of foreign policy, under her guidance, but not territorial union. The merger with Syria into the United Arab Republic▷, 1958, was contrary to E.'s Arab policy: in agreeing to it, E. was swept along by the tide of events (see UAR). In any

case, the union was dissolved three years later. E. also intervened in the affairs of other Arab states from the late 1950s in order to establish regimes or institute policies propitious to her. In this manner she intervened in Jordan in 1957, in Lebanon in 1958, and in Iraq in 1959. There is no Arab state that has not complained of Egyptian subversion and interference, that has not expelled Egyptian diplomats and military attaches, or broken off relations with E. The dissolution of the UAR in 1961 was a heavy blow to Egyptian prestige.

During 1962–3, there was a certain lull in Egyptian subversive activity in the Arab countries and hostile propaganda directed at them, except for E.'s military intervention in Yemen, in support of her revolutionary republican regime. At the same time E.'s Arab policy was revived. Instead of a "unified front" of the Arab regimes, each with its own character and orientation, against external pressures and dangers, a "unity of aims" was substituted. Unity was possible only through an identity of character and orientation of the respective regimes. E. was willing to co-operate with "progressive" regimes, but not with "reactionary" ones, which were bound to be toppled by revolution. All the same, at the end of 1963, E. tried to restrain Syria's over-energetic assault on Israel (regarding the Jordan waters dispute) and instituted all-Arab "summit" conferences—without distinction between "royalist-reactionary" and "progressive-revolutionary" regimes—in an effort to establish a unified all-Arab foreign policy. Within the framework of the summits, E. initiated the setting-up of the "Palestine Liberation Organization") (see Palestine▷ Arabs; and Palestine-Arab Guerilla Organizations▷). E. also directed attempts to divert the flow of the Jordan River, the establishment of the United Arab Command (which proved ineffective during the Six Day War), and the severance of relations with West Germany in 1965. However, since 1965–6, the summit policy was again abandoned and replaced by a confrontation of "progressive" and "reactionary" Arab states, between whom co-operation was impossible. On the eve of the Six Day War, E. worked again for Arab solidarity, and an acceptance of the differing character of regimes and states.

E.'s oscillating Arab policy thus necessitated numerous tactical changes. Since 1967, the Egyptian administration has cultivated close ties with leftist Arab regimes (especially post-1969 Libya and Sudan; relations with Syria and Iraq are very complicated; those with Syria have become much closer since 1970). At the same time E. has avoided a deterioration of relations with the conservative regimes, especially as several of those regimes extend enormous economic and financial aid to E. In the numerous crises that afflicted the Arab countries (particularly the imbroglio between Lebanon and Jordan and the Palestinian *feda'iyin*▷), E. appeared as a mediating force, even though her sympathy lay with the leftist and revolutionary forces. Since late 1970, new plans emerged for a federation (in reality, rather a confederation) between E., Libya and Syria; Sudan was expected to join later. The "Federation of Arab Republics" was proclaimed in April 1971—and endorsed by plebiscite on 1 Sept. 1971.

The radicalization that characterized Egyptian foreign policy, 1954–67, despite lip service to "Positive Neutralism", applied also to the Nasserist regime internally. It was the result, first and foremost, of Egypt's economic difficulties. Closer ties with the Soviet Union also had their effect. Over the first nine years, the revolutionary regime adopted a relatively moderate attitude to internal problems. After a three-year period of transition, in 1956, the military regime transformed itself into a civilian one. A new constitution defining the regime as "democratic-co-operative-socialist" was proclaimed and endorsed by plebiscite. But there were no far-reaching changes in a socialist direction, and the Nasserist regime was still groping for its ideological identity. On the other hand, in 1960, the regime nationalized and completely took over all newspapers. The turning point came with the nationalization laws of July 1961 and the publication of the "Charter for National Action" in May 1962, which laid the foundations for the concept of Nasserist "Arab Socialism" and initiated the "transitional stage of socialism". The sole legal political organization was called henceforth the "Arab Socialist Union" (ASU). Since 1962 the regime has been trying to keep a balance between liberal forces which have attempted to prevent further radical moves to the left and to apply the "National Charter" moderately, and the leftist forces which have tried to hasten E.'s transformation into a socialist state. These latter were greatly aided by E.'s closer ties with the Soviet Union. Since 1965, the ideological pressure exerted by the USSR (which at times resulted in cooler relations and even acrimony, e.g., in 1958—9) has borne fruit. Although the Communist Party is still outlawed (in 1965 it dissolved itself), Marxist ideas are voiced in the periodical *al-Tali'a* (founded in 1965), and the ASU maintains close ties with the Soviet Communist Party and is under strong Soviet influence. The 1971 Treaty with the USSR gives formal expression to E.'s admission to the Soviet camp.

The regime waited nine years until it decided on its ideological path. But in fact, it took radical steps internally from the very beginning. Inside two years, the regime liquidated the political forces of the pre-revolutionary era. It agreed to co-operate with some of their members, as individuals but not as leaders of parties, especially in the framework of the single popular organization it had set up, where their organizational and political experience was needed. Thus the regime made an attempt, at the beginning of the "Liberation Organization" (1953–8), to enlist the aid of the "Muslim Brotherhood". In the setting up of the "Arab Socialist Union" (1962) ex-communists were brought in. A new political élite arose, the nucleus of which was the "Free Officers" group, which was gradually joined by other officers and technocrats. This élite has monopolized the government since 1955.

Radicalization in the economic sphere matched that in the ideological. During its first nine years, the regime collaborated with capitalists and private enterprise. As investment in land was forbidden by the agrarian reform bill of 1952, it was hoped that capital would be invested in industry; these hopes did not materialize. After the Suez War a process of "Egyptianization" commenced, *i.e.*, the nationalization of the capital of foreigners and minorities. The principal stage of radicalization began with the nationalization laws of July 1961 and for the most part was completed in 1963. Through "Egyptianization" and nationalization, the state took upon itself economic development in general, and industrial development in particular. The traditional capitalists, still active in industry during the first years of the regime, did not establish basic industries which would have contributed a solution to the problem of over-population, regarded as the most desirable form of economic development. The regime decided therefore that the state had to take control of capital and direct it in the public interest according to a master-plan.

Alongside the nationalization of industrial, commercial and financial concerns, the July 1961 laws extended the scope of the agrarian reform of 1952, by restricting the maximal quota of land to 100 *feddan* (acres) per person. A third reform bill in 1969 reduced this further to 50 *feddan*.

In the mid-1960s the regime's financial difficulties increased, and it was torn by conflicting aims: radical leftist circles wanted further radicalization, more pressure on "national capitalists", so that rapid economic development could continue; while liberal circles wanted to restore economic health, even at the cost of freezing development and reforms. The Six Day War relegated this debate to the background. Now, most efforts are directed towards the search for ways and means of restoring the territories lost to Israel and adapting the national economy to the needs of the military build-up (since the end of the 1960s the military budget has risen until it reached 20% of the Gross National Product).

On 28 Sept. 1970, President 'Abd-ul-Nasser—a man regarded unanimously as the one, great leader of both Egypt and the larger Arab world—suddenly died. It appears that the succession was contested for on the one hand by a right-wing group with notions for liberalizing the economy and the regime, and of closer relations with the USA and the West— Zakariya Mohieddin▷ (Muhyi-ul-Din), 'Abd-ul-Latif Baghdadi, Muhammad Hassanein Heykal▷— and on the other by a leftist group headed by 'Ali Sabri▷. Several leaders and followers of Nasser, in particular Anwar Sadat▷, Sha'rawi Gum'a, Sami Sharaf, and especially the commanders of the army, held the balance between the two (with Soviet advisers keeping behind the scenes). Anwar Sadat, who had right-wing and nationalist tendencies, but was a kind of mediator and a member of the principal central faction of Nasser's followers, was elected President of the Republic and leader of the "Arab Socialist Union"; he appointed 'Ali Sabri and Hussein Shafe'i his vice-presidents and the technocrat diplomatist, Muhammad Fawzi, Prime Minister. Right-wingers remained outside the government (even Heykal, since spring 1970 Minister of Information and Guidance, in addition to his post as editor of al-Ahram, resigned his governmental position). The general trend was to demonstrate that, despite the mourning for Nasser and the sense of terrible loss, the administration's stability and the continuation of Nasser's policy were assured.

In May 1971, Sadat—regarded until then as no more than primus inter pares—took full power, emerging as E.'s leader. He announced the discovery of a plot for a coup and take-over by a group of leaders of the leftist faction (Vice-President 'Ali Sabri), the centrist faction of Nasser's close collaborators (Sha'rawi Gum'a, Sami Sharaf, Muhammad Fayeq), the top army leadership (Gen. Muhammad Fawzi), and the ASU leadership (Labib Shugeir, Dia-ul-Din Daoud, 'Abd-ul-Muhsin Abu'l-Nur). All those, and many others, were dismissed, and many were arrested. The government was re-formed by Mahmud Fawzi, new army leaders were appointed, and the ASU executive (considered the centre of the plotters' power) was dissolved. A certain liberalization, including a restriction of the powers of the secret police, was proclaimed. For the time being, Sadat had emerged victorious, in control of the state machinery. Even the Russians—who might well have been concerned, as some of those dismissed and arrested were generally considered to be "their men"— acquiesced and sent their President to sign a new pact with President Sadat.

ECONOMIC PROBLEMS. E.'s basic problem is the gap between the tremendous natural population increase and limited economic resources, accompanied by a rise in production that lags far behind the natural increase. During the 19th century, there was still a fast increase in agricultural production, due to the expansion of the cultivated area and the area under irrigation. However, this growth ceased at about the time of World War I. The cultivated area was enlarged, between that time and 1952, from 5,280,000 feddan (acres) to only 5,845,000 feddan. Nevertheless, following the expansion of the irrigation system (dams, water-storage, canals), the cultivated area increased during that period from 7.7 m. feddan to 9.3m. feddan (on 25% of the cultivated area cotton, the major export crop, was grown; on 50%—grain crops: wheat, barley, rice, sorghum, and millet). As against this meagre increase in production and cultivated land, the population doubled between 1900 and 1952 and continues to grow at a rapid pace. Since 1913, the average income per person has dropped.

Nor did industry flourish so as to match the population growth. In 1916, there were 15 industrial concerns in E., employing some 35,000 workers, most of them in sugar, food processing, textiles and building materials. World War II, which reduced imports, encouraged the development of local industries. Yet, those employed in industry were in 1952 only 10% of the labour force, whereas 60% were employed in agriculture; the share of industry in the National Product in 1952 was only 10%.

The economic policy of the officers' regime has been discussed above. What real economic change was achieved by it? A main achievement was the agrarian reform. The area sold by landowners, or appropriated from them, in accordance with the 1952 and 1961 laws, reached 1.2m. feddan, taken from approximately 7,000 owners. The majority of this land was distributed among 320,000 families. As a result of the reform, landowners with more than 200 feddan (who had, in 1950, owned 19.4% of all cultivated land) had disappeared, and owners of 5 feddan and less (some 94.3% of the owners) now held about 55% of all the land (as against 34% in 1950). However, 5.7% of the landowners still possessed some 45% of the land. Of the 4.5m. breadwinners engaged in agriculture, approximately 1.5 m. were landless in 1952. Even if the landless got land, the natural increase (2.5% 1947–60, 2.9% since) nullified the efforts to reduce their number, which has probably even increased.

A major development project was the High Dam at Aswan▷, the construction of which began in 1959 and was completed in 1969. The water stored behind the dam was to enlarge the cultivated area by 22% and increase agricultural production by 50% by 1980. In view of population growth and the decrease in the part played by agriculture in the National Product, opinions differ as to the influence of the High Dam upon the National Product. Other efforts at improving uncultivated land were also made. One major project in this sphere, the planned development of an entire area called "Liberation Province", failed; several other projects are in various stages of planning and implementation. Efforts were made to introduce modern agricultural methods and to combat pests.

The major change in the Egyptian economy was industrialization. Hopes that the owners of expropriated lands would invest the compensation they received in industry failed to materialize. But in 1957 the government laid down a plan for industrial development. In 1960, this plan was incorporated in the first Five-Year Plan. Industrialization was based on the nationalized concerns and foreign aid, including— from 1958—Soviet credits. The government devoted its energy chiefly to the development of basic and heavy industries, such as electricity, minerals, oil and oil products (on the oil industry in E.—see below, and Oil▷). The second Five-Year Plan was not carried out due to lack of finance. However, despite these difficulties, and certain plans that failed, the industrial production index went up (according to Egyptian data, often considered exaggerated) from 91 in 1951 to 100 in 1954, 124 in 1957, 142 in 1959. The average annual increase of industrial output was about 10%. The part of agriculture in the National Product went down from c. 40% in 1950 to 25% in 1969–70. At the same time, there was little change in the structure of employment: the number of industrial workers remained 11.12%, in other words, industry did not absorb the bulk of the population surplus. The regime hardly dealt with the problem of natural increase. It awoke to this problem during the 1960s, but there was no systematic attempt to deal with it and little success; the annual rate of increase from the mid-1960s has reached c. 3%.

E.'s development and economic advancement were also hindered by the enormous increase in her military expenditure due to the state of war with Israel. Until 1967, military expenditure was estimated at 8% of the GNP and up to 30% of the budget; in 1970, it was estimated at 20% and more of the GNP. The economy was also hit by the paralysis of the Suez Canal, the need to evacuate the Suez Canal Zone following the "war of attrition" against Israel, 1968–9, and the destruction of industry in the Zone.

GOVERNMENT AND POLITICS. The constitution of 1923 established a constitutional monarchy in E.

This regime and the parliamentary constitution were in force until the coup of 1952 (excluding the years 1931–5, during which the constitution was suspended). It provided for a two-chamber Parliament—a House of Representatives (general male franchise) and a Senate (partly elected and partly appointed). During the constitutional period, 1924–52, only two houses of representatives completed their terms of office according to the constitution (1931–6 and 1945–50), while all others were dissolved. Elections took place 10 times and there were 38 governments.

In December 1952, after the officers' coup, the constitution of 1923 was annulled, and in June 1953 the monarchy was abrogated and a republic proclaimed. After a transition period of military government, a provisional constitution was enacted in 1956; it was confirmed with minor alterations in the provisional constitutions of 1958 (UAR) and 1964. Its main provisions: The President of the Republic is elected by the National Assembly for a six-year term and endorsed by popular referendum. The President appoints the government which is responsible to him. A "National Assembly" with 350 members is the legislative authority. It is elected by universal franchise for a term of five years. Candidates are subject to the approval of the leadership of the regime's single popular organization (see below, Parties). In the first elections to the National Assembly, in 1957, 2,508 candidates presented themselves, of whom the "National Union" approved 1,318. The first National Assembly was dissolved with the establishment of the UAR, but the 300 Egyptian members of the UAR National Assembly were appointed from among its members (1960). From the break-up of the UAR in 1961 and until 1964 there was no "National Assembly". In 1964, a new Assembly was elected, which was replaced in new elections in 1969. This was dissolved in 1971. A new, permanent constitution was approved by plebiscite in Sept. 1971.

PARTIES. The first modern parties were established in E. in 1907–8. Only one of these, the "National Party" (al-Hizb al-Watani), established by Mustafa Kamel (d. 1908), continued to exist after World War I. It was extremist and anti-British; when the Wafd was established, in 1919–20, and took over the leadership of the national struggle, the National Party went into decline. It existed until the dissolution of all parties in 1953 as a small faction without influence.

The Wafd party—led by Sa'd Zaghlul▷, and after his death (1927) by Mustafa Nahhas▷—was modernistic, secular and nationalist; it was the sole party in E. to reach the rural population and establish a mass organization. The remaining parties of the constitutional period (1923–52) grew out of the Wafd, or were founded by former *Wafd* leaders (see *Wafd*▷). The Liberal-Constitutional Party was founded in 1922 by 'Adli Yakan and Muhammad Mahmud▷ and was considered to represent mainly the big land-owners. The Union Party, founded in 1925 by palace supporters, and the People's Party established in 1930 by Isma'il Sidqi▷, were founded for *ad hoc* purposes and did not last long. The *Sa'adist*▷ party (named after Sa'd Zaghlul) was founded in 1937 by Ahmed Maher▷, Mahmud Fahmi Nuqrashi▷ and Ibrahim 'Abd-ul-Hadi▷, who all seceded from the *Wafd;* the *Sa'adist* party claimed to be the true successors of Sa'd Zaghlul and the original *Wafd*, but they collaborated with the Court and the Liberals against the *Wafd*. The "Independent *Wafdist* Bloc" was established in 1942 by the Cop Makrem 'Ubaid, who left the *Wafd*; it remained a small faction.

Among extra-parliamentary parties were the "Muslim Brotherhood"▷, established by Hassan al-Banna▷ toward the end of the 1920s. The organization was banned in 1954, but continues to exist underground. "Young Egypt" under Ahmad Hussein operated during the 1930s as a Fascist party. The Communist Party▷ was founded in 1920, but split several times into numerous factions (see Communism▷). It has always been illegal. The officers' regime had its active members arrested since 1953–4 and again in 1955–6 and 1958. The *rapprochement* with the Soviet Union resulted in the release of all the communist detainees in 1963, and many party members joined the state machinery. In 1965, the Communist Party voluntarily dissolved itself.

All the parties were dissolved by the "Free Officers" regime in 1953. The revolutionary regime set up in 1953 the "Liberation Organization" as the sole political organization. In 1956, it was replaced by the "National Union". When E. began moving toward a socialist regime from 1961 on, the "National Union" was disbanded and was replaced, in 1962, by the "Arab Socialist Union"▷. These three organizations were defined as popular organizations and not as parties. Their activities were restricted and did not attract many followers. Two of the organizations failed; the "Arab Socialist Union" went through several reorganizations aimed at activating it as an effective instrument. In 1971 the ASU was purged and its executive organs dissolved, as President Sadat considered them the power centre of his adversaries plotting a take-over.

Since 1952, E. was actually ruled by a junta of officers, and although the body incorporating them is not a "party", it is worthy of a brief survey. The association of "Free Officers" was founded in 1949 — possibly influenced by the Syrian military coup of 1949; it was headed by a five-member committee,

which was shortly after expanded to 10 (Gamal 'Abd-ul-Nasser▷, Kamal-ul-Din Hussein, Hassan Ibrahim, Khaled Mohieddin (Muhyi-ul-Din)', 'Abd-ul-Mun'im Ra'uf, Gamal Salem, Salah Salem, 'Abd-ul-Hakim 'Amer▷, 'Abd-ul-Latif al-Baghdadi, and Anwer al-Sadat▷). In July 1952, four additional members joined the committee (among them were Zakariya Mohieddin▷ (Muhyi-ul-Din) and Hussein al-Shafe'i▷), and one member quit. These 13 officers, together with Muhammad Nagib▷, constituted, after the 1952 coup, the "Council of the Revolutionary Command". This nucleus was associated (according to Nasser's testimony) with 90 loyal officers and about 300 sympathisers. In 1950, 'Abd-ul-Nasser was elected President of the association. In January 1952 Nagib, the candidate of the "Free Officers" for the post of head of the Officers' Club, defeated the King's candidate. This victory aroused King Farouq to make an effort to regain control of, and influence in, the army. When Farouq appointed his brother-in-law, Isma'il Shirin, Minister of Defence (22 July), the "Free Officers" interpreted this as a threat to them and carried out their coup.

Of the 13 leaders of the "Free Officers", only two were left in government when Nasser died in 1970: Sadat and Shafe'i. In the first wave of purges, during 1953–5, left-wingers and supporters of Nagib were eliminated. Among them were Khaled Mohieddin and Gamal Salem; at the same time, Nagib was deposed. A second wave of purges, in 1963–4, removed Kamal-ul-Din Hussein and Baghdadi, mainly due to their opposition to the Yemen war. Hassan Ibrahim was dropped as Vice-President in 1966. Salah Salem died in 1962. In purges after the Six Day War, 1967, 'Amer (who later committed suicide) and Zakariya Mohieddin were dismissed and purges were also carried out amongst their supporters. Policy-making positions began to be filled by officers not connected with the central nucleus of the "Free Officers" junta. In spring 1971, Sadat removed many of Nasser's closest collaborators.

EDUCATION, CULTURE, PRESS. E. is the most important cultural centre of the Arab world. It has six universities, with a student body of some 150,000 students; four of them are situated in Cairo: the University of Cairo (est. 1908, modernized 1925), the 'Ain Shams University (1950), the *al-Ashar*▷ Islamic College (est. 970), and the American University; one is situated in Alexandria (1942) and one in Assiout (1957). E. is the centre of literature, art, production of books and records, theatre and the film industry for the entire Arab world. Her broadcasting stations are the largest and most powerful in the ME. Cairo Radio broadcasts in Arabic, English, French, Hebrew, German, Greek, Italian; the *Sawt al-'Arab* ("Voice of the Arabs") station, established in 1953, broadcasts in 20, mostly Asian, African and ME, languages. In 1967, there were in E. four million radio receivers and close on half a million television sets.

Until the nationalization of the press in 1960, E. had been the centre of Arab journalism, the home of a large, rich and free press—dailies, literary monthlies (*al-Kateb, al-Hilal, al-Thaqafa*) and political weeklies (*Akhbar al-Yawm, al-Ithnein, Rose al-Yusuf, al-Mussawwar*), which were read in all the Arab countries. Today, newspapers in Alexandria and Cairo appear in five languages: Arabic, English, French, Greek, Armenian. The most important Arabic dailies are *al-Ahram* (est. 1875), with a circulation of a quarter of a million, and *al-Akhbar* (est. 1952) with a similar circulation. *Al-Gumhuriyya* (est. 1953) is the daily organ of the ASU. Among the many literary and scientific periodicals and political weeklies, several of the well-known organs of past years still exist; but the entire press is now "directed".   (S.L.)

*EILAT. Southernmost town of Israel at the head of the Gulf of 'Aqaba (Eilat). Founded 1949. Pop: 13,200 (1969). Its port serves as Israel's only gate to East Africa, the Persian Gulf and the Far East. (Imports: 127,000 tons, excl. oil in bulk; exports : 281,000 tons—1969). E. is Israel's main oil harbour. One pipeline carries crude oil to the refineries in Haifa; another, with a diameter of 42 in. and a capacity of 60m. tons *p.a.*, carried oil to the terminal at Ashqelon (completed 1969). Main sources of income: copper mines at Timna, port activities and tourism (E. is a popular winter resort). Little industry. Egyptian complaints that the site of E. was occupied by Israel illegally, after the Armistice went into force, were rejected in 1950 by the Mixed Armistice Commission.
                                                                       (Y.K.)

The Gulf of Eilat

EISENHOWER DOCTRINE. US policy statement on the ME made by President E., on 5 Jan. 1957, requesting Congress to authorize military and economic assistance to countries of the area requesting such aid, and the use of the US Armed Forces to protect the independence and territorial integrity of any nation in the region "against overt armed aggression from any nation controlled by international Communism". Congressional authorization was given on 9 Mar. 1957.

The E.D. was invoked by Jordan in April 1957 when King Hussein▷ accused Communist-controlled forces of attempting to overthrow him; the USA sent the Sixth Fleet to the eastern Mediterranean and began giving economic aid to Jordan. Following Gen. Qassem's▷ *coup d'état* of July 1958 in Iraq, both Jordan and Lebanon invoked the E.D. and requested military aid. Britain sent paratroops into Jordan, and the USA sent 14,000 marines to Lebanon. The E.D. was linked to close US co-operation with the Central Treaty Organization (CENTO▷), following the signing of new bi-lateral agreements with Turkey, Iran and Pakistan in March 1959.
                                                                       (Sh.H.)

EMBARGO. An E. on arms and war material was several times imposed on the ME because of the Arab-Israel dispute. It is also an instrument in the Great Powers' struggle for influence in the ME, and the Powers have changed their attitude to it in accordance with circumstances.

When hostilities broke out in Palestine in 1947 the USA declared an E. On 5 Dec. 1947 she cancelled all arms export licences. Britain followed suit, but excluded from the prohibition arms which had been purchased under existing contracts. Zionist appeals for arms aid to defend Jewish independence, and for an E. on the Arab states intending to break the UN resolution, were of no avail.

On 29 May 1948 the UN Security Council placed an E. on all the countries involved in the conflict. Count Folke Bernadotte▷, the UN mediator, proposed that the entry of volunteers to the armed forces of the area should also be prohibited and Jewish immigration controlled. In accordance with this proposal, UN observers were placed in the ports and airports, but this control proved ineffective on both sides and was abandoned. Several countries were willing to break the general E. Czechoslovakia, for example, continued to supply arms and military equipment to Israel (in Sept. the US protested to Czechoslovakia about the use of aircraft belonging to American citizens and flown by them). After the armistice agreements were signed the Security Council lifted the restrictions, including the E., on 11 Aug.

1949 (with a call by the acting mediator, Dr. Ralph Bunche▷, to apply a "moral E." and abstain from supplying heavy arms). The USSR abstained on this decision, warning that the cancellation of the E. would encourage an arms race which would bring about the inferiority of the Israeli armed forces and renewed Arab aggression. Israel also preferred a continuation of the E.

The Tripartite Declaration▷ of May 1950 placed a *de facto* selective E. on the ME, as it stated that any request for arms would be reviewed in light of the needs of internal security, justified self-defence, and participation in the defence of the area as a whole. The USA, Britain and France set up a committee to co-ordinate arms supplies to the ME. Many requests by Israel and the Arab states were turned down. The selective E. on Israel by the three Western Powers continued even after the Soviet Union and Czechoslovakia began sending large quantities of arms to several Arab states, and the Tripartite Declaration had lost its meaning. It caused Israel difficulties in building up its armed forces and maintaining a military balance. During the 1950s Western countries used to request US approval before selling arms to Israel.

On the eve of the Six Day War▷ France placed a partial arms E. on countries involved, which in fact operated against Israel. Towards the end of 1968, after the Israeli raid on Beirut airport, the E. was widened. The French E. broke an existing contract between Israel and the French aircraft industry for the supply of Mirage war planes. Most of the states which supply Israel with arms place a partial E. on her. No equivalent limitation is known to exist in connection with the wide range of arms supplies by the Soviet Union and her allies to the Arab states. The E. and the breach of contracts have encouraged Israel to increase her own arms production.   (Z.S.)

✳**ENOSIS** (Greek: Union). The idea of union between Cyprus▷ and Greece, and the movement advocating this union. The Church and intelligentsia of the Greek Cypriots have cherished the idea of E. since Greece became independent, 1829. The movement gained momentum after World War II, and especially after Makarios▷ III became Archbishop, 1950. The development of events brought about the abandonment of E. in favour of independence. However, some Greek Cypriots still favour E.
                                                                  (B.G.)

ENVER PASHA (1881–1922). Turkish military and political leader. Born in Istanbul. E. graduated from the Military Academy and as a professional

officer played an active part in the events in Macedonia leading to the 1908 revolution of the "Young Turks". He served as military attaché in Berlin and returned to fight against the Italians in the Tripolitanian War, 1911. In January 1913 E. led a coup which brought down the Liberal Party then in power in Istanbul; together with Talât Pasha▷ and Cemal Pasha▷ he then formed a "triumvirate" that ruled Turkey until 1918. Having become a military hero by recapturing Edirne (Adrianople) from the Bulgarians in the second Balkan War▷, 1913, E. was promoted to the rank of General and appointed Minister of War. With strong Pan-Turkish▷ and pro-German inclinations, he was instrumental in bringing about Turkey's entry into World War I as an ally of Germany. During the war he led the Ottoman third army in a disastrous campaign on the Russian front. After the Armistice he was tried and sentenced to death; he fled to Berlin and then to Russia and Turkestan, where he intrigued against the new Kemalist Turkey and took part in a Muslim nationalist insurrection in the course of which he was killed.   (D.K.)

✳**EOKA** (Greek: Ethniki Organosis Kyprion Agoniston—National Organization of Cypriot Combatants). Militant Cypriot underground organization formed to achieve *Enosis*▷ (Cyprus' union) with Greece. Operated 1955–9 under the command of Col. Grivas▷. Its activities were directed against British personnel and installations as well as against Greek Cypriots suspected of collaboration with the British, and sometimes also against Turkish Cypriots. Stopped its operations after the conclusion of the Zurich and London agreements, 1959, and the achievement of independence, 1960.
                                                                  (B.G.)

ERETZ ISRAEL (Hebrew: Land of Israel). The usual and accepted Hebrew name of Palestine▷, roughly corresponding to Palestine within its Mandatory boundaries (including Transjordan). Under the British Mandate, the Jews of Palestine demanded that the government use "E.I." as the name of the country in all official publications in Hebrew (parallel to "Palestine" in English and *Filastin* in Arabic). The Government objected, and used *Paleshtina* in Hebrew. The dispute ended in a compromise: the official term became "Paleshtina (E.I.)"; the brackets enclosed the initials only. Palestinian Jews ridiculed the term and it never passed into popular usage.   (Y.S.)

✳**ERIM, NIHAT** (b. 1912). Turkish scholar and politician, Prime Minister, 1971. Born in Kandiar

(N.W. Anatolia), E. studied law in Istanbul and Paris, and was professor of law at Ankara University. He was elected deputy for the Republican People's Party in the National Assembly in 1945, was Minister of Public Works 1948, and Deputy Premier 1949. After the Democratic Party's rise to power in 1950, he returned to teaching and also worked for his party's newspaper, while continuing as member of the Assembly. He also served on international committees and participated in various conferences. In March 1971 E. was nominated Premier, after the Demirel▷ government was brought down by a military ultimatum. Resigning his party membership to become an Independent, he formed a coalition government largely composed of unaffiliated experts, and primarily committed to restoring order in the country and initiating social reforms. (D. K.)

✳**ERITREA.** Region in north-eastern Ethiopia▷, on the Red Sea. E. was an Italian colony from 1889, under British occupation from World War II until 1952, and federally united with Ethiopia from 1952, following a resolution of the UN General Assembly. The semi-autonomous federal regime was abrogated in 1962. An "E. Liberation Front", active since 1962, aims—through guerilla warfare and other violent means—at E.'s secession from Ethiopia and its independence. The main supporters of secession are E.'s Muslims—constituting 45–50% of her population of c. 1.6m. E. herself, apart for the role she plays in the policies of the Arab states, is outside the scope of this Encyclopaedia. Arabic is spoken to some extent as a second language in the coastal town. Many Eritrean Muslims consider themselves semi-Arab, and if she achieved independence E. would probably apply for membership in the Arab League. E.'s separatist-nationalist movement receives from the Arab states, especially the leftist-revolutionary ones, political support. They provide it also with money, equipment and bases for operations. The Liberation Front apparently maintains its main bases in Sudan, Egypt and Syria. This support damages the relations between Ethiopia and the Arab states, and in particular Egypt and Sudan. The E. Liberation Front maintains particularly close ties with the Palestinian-Arab guerilla organizations *(feda'iyin)*; its members train in *feda'iyin* camps, receive *feda'iyin* equipment and support and collaborate with them in operations (e.g. the hijacking of airplanes in Europe). (Y.S.)

ESHKOL, LEVY (1895–1969). Zionist Labour leader and Israeli statesman. Prime Minister 1963–9. Born in the Ukraine. E. immigrated to Palestine in 1913, where he worked in agriculture and as a

Levi Eshkol

watchman; was a co-founder of Deganiah Beth collective village *(kibbutz)*; volunteered for service in the Jewish Legion▷, 1918–20. He was active in the Labour Movement as promoter and director of several Trade Union *(Histadrut▷)* institutions and corporations. He also served on the Hagana▷ (Defence Organization) High Command, and as Secretary-General of the Tel-Aviv Workers' Council, 1944–8.

After the establishment of Israel, E. became Director-General of the Ministry of Defence, under David Ben-Gurion▷, and in this capacity founded and promoted Israel's arms industry. A member of the *Knesset* (Parliament) from 1951 until his death. He was Minister of Agriculture, 1951–2, and Minister of Finance, 1952–63, and exerted considerable influence on the growth of Israel's economy. He served simultaneously as Treasurer of the Jewish Agency▷, 1950–2 and Director of its Settlement Department, 1949–63, in which capacity he was responsible for the development of agricultural settlement in Israel and the absorption of many thousands of immigrants.

In 1963, E. succeeded D. Ben-Gurion as Prime Minister. Though Ben-Gurion had himself recommended him, he soon turned against E., accusing him of mishandling State business in general and the Lavon Affair▷ in particular. In the 1965 general elections, E.'s Labour Party *(Mapai)* beat the *Rafi* party, which had been established by dissident members of *Mapai* headed by Ben-Gurion and M. Dayan▷. From 1963 to '67, E. served also as Minister of Defence—a post he handed over, on the eve of the Six Day War, to Moshe Dayan, as a result of public demand. In 1967 his government was broadened into a "national unity" government, until 1970 when the *Gahal* bloc broke away.   (Y. R.)

ETHIOPIA. Kingdom, Empire in Northeast Africa; herself outside the scope of this Encyclopaedia, E. is involed in many ways in ME affairs. E. is the centre and home of the Ethiopian Church; her Church was for many years hierarchically and administratively dependent on the Coptic▷ Patriarchate in Egypt, and even now maintains close relations with the Coptic Church. Conservative E. must view with concern the activities of the revolutionary leftist Arab states—Egypt, Algeria, Sudan, Libya—on the African scene. Since the early 1960s, the Emperor of E. has played a leading part in all-African affairs, and his capital, Addis Abbaba, has become the permanent headquarters of the Organization for African Unity, OAU. There are specific points of friction between E. and several Arab states. Old border disputes between her and Sudan have not yet been fully settled and a mixed population on both sides of the border and wandering tribes exacerbate the problem. One of the two major sources of the Nile▷—the Blue Nile—rises in Lake Tana in E. Should the development of E.'s water works and diversions for hydro-electric plants or irrigation cause a decrease in the quantity of water Sudan receives, serious friction would arise, as Sudan's irrigation and agriculture are dependent on water from the Blue Nile. Sudan also accuses E. of encouraging the rebellion of Negro tribes in Southern Sudan, while E. on her part accuses Sudan of aiding a separatist guerilla movement in Eritrea▷. The other Arab states are also accused of supporting the "Front for the Liberation of Eritrea", at any rate politically and morally. Nevertheless E. maintains normal and close relations with Egypt and the other Arab states. She also fosters close ties with Israel and enjoys her technical aid and co-operation in various fields. This friendship with Israel is reinforced by the deeply rooted ancient tradition of the common origin of Israel and the kingdom of E. (the Kings of E. regard themselves as descendants of King Solomon, "The Lion of Judah" being one of their royal titles).   (Y.S.)

ETHIOPIAN CHURCH. Christianity was introduced into Ethiopia▷ in the fourth century. In the seventh century, Ethiopia was placed under the Monophysite▷ (Coptic▷) Patriarchate of Alexandria (later located in Cairo). In 1929 the Synod of the Coptic Church and the Emperor of Ethiopia reached an agreement whereby Ethiopian bishops were consecrated for the first time. An attempt to detach the Church of Ethiopia from the See of Alexandria

was made after 1935, during the Italian occupation. It was only in 1951, however, that the first Ethiopian *Abuna* (Patriarch) was consecrated by the Coptic Patriarch of Alexandria. In 1959, following an accord between the Coptic and the E. C., the latter, although canonically attached to the See of Alexandria, became administratively independent. Since then, the Ethiopian Patriarch is authorized to consecrate bishops for his country. The E.C. is the State Church of Ethiopia.

Ethiopian monks have lived in Jerusalem since very ancient times. The Ethiopians claim rights in the holy places, mainly in the Deir al-Sultan, a monastery situated on the roof of the Chapel of St. Helena, which is part of the Holy Sepulchre. These claims are disputed by the Coptic Church, which is actually in possession of the monastery. The dispute was discussed several times at governmental level, under the administration of both Jordan (1948–67) and Israel. A bishop was recently appointed to the Ethiopian convents in the Holy Land.   (Sh. C.)

EUPHRATES, RIVER (Turkish: *Firat*, Arabic: *Furat*). Together with the Tigris▷, the Karun▷, and their common outlet into the Persian Gulf, the Shatt al-'Arab▷, the E. forms the most important river system between the Nile and the Indus—one that created Mesopotamia almost as the Nile created Egypt.

The E. proper extends from the confluence of its two main sources, the Murat and the Kara-Su, near Keban in the east of central Anatolia (Turkey), to its junction with the Tigris at Qurna in southern Iraq, a course of about 1,250 mi. The Murat and the Kara-Su, both originating in the Armenian mountains, add 415 mi. and 275 mi. respectively. The E. crosses the Syrian frontier north of Jerablus, about 30 mi. after entering the plains. It crosses into Iraq below Abu Kamal after a run of 310 mi. through Syria. Still in Syria, the E. receives its last perennial tributary, the Khabur. From there the E. turns into a "tired" river, sluggishly winding through flat country, carrying ever-decreasing quantities of water, subject to changes of channel owing to abnormal floods or insufficiently effective damming. Large tracts of the middle and lower course lie amid lakes and marshes.

Among the major development projects on the E., designed in varying degrees for irrigation, flood prevention and power production, two in Iraq have been completed: the Hindiya Barrage on the Lower E., completed in 1913; and the Ramadi Barrage—diverting floodwaters into the Habbaniya Lake in the Abu Dibbis depression—completed in 1956. The Keban project in Turkey, and the Soviet-aided

Syrian Euphrates Dam project, are under construction. Both are major schemes. The Keban Dam is planned to create a lake 70 mi. long and storing *c*. 30,000m. cubic meters (mcm), and a power-generating capacity of over 600,000 kw, at a cost estimated at *c*. $350m. The Syrian dam is planned to create a lake 50 mi. long and storing, in its final stage 40,000 mcm—to irrigate over 1m. acres and creating a power-generating capacity of over 600,000 kw, at an estimated cost of $600m. Ideas for a similar major scheme on Iraqi soil have been long discussed, but have not crystallized into final plans. No Turkish-Syrian-Iraqi co-ordination or agreement on plans for the use of the E. has so far been reached.

The E. is of little importance as a trade route. Navigation is hampered by the shallow draft of the river most of the year. The Baghdad Railway▷, the rail link between the Persian Gulf and Europe, follows the Tigris for mainly political considerations which swayed its German and Turkish promoters at the beginning of this century. A new railway along the E. is being planned in Iraq and Syria.   (Y.S.)

*EUROPEAN ECONOMIC COMMUNITY, EEC, EUROPEAN COMMON MARKET.

Since the ECM was established in 1958, the volume of trade amongst its member states has grown beyond recognition. Yet trade with the ME still accounts for 5% of the foreign trade of the "Six".

In 1969, exports from ME countries to the CM totalled $5,154m., while the ME imported goods worth $2,620m. from the "Six". In 1957, on the eve of the establishment of the CM, the respective figures had been $845m. and $1,665m.

In 1969, 3.4% of the EEC's exports went to the ME, compared with 3.8% in 1957. EEC exports to the Arab countries declined from 2.1% in 1957, to 1.8% in 1969 (due to competition from Soviet bloc exports). In the same period, EEC exports to Israel dropped from 0.5% of the total to 0.4% (due to competition from British and American exports). EEC exports to Turkey and Iran remained 1.2% of the total throughout the period in question, thanks to an agreement signed with these two countries in 1963.

Whereas in 1957, 6.7% of CM imports came from the ME, in 1969 the figure was 6.9%, thanks to the rapid growth in oil imports. The ME countries, for their part, bought 22.5% of their imports in 1957 from the "Six", and over 25% by 1969. The Arab countries obtained 30% of their imports in 1957 from the CM, and 38% in 1969. The CM absorbed 40% of the exports of the ME in 1957, and 39% in 1969. For the Arab countries, the respective figures were 45% in 1957 and 41% in 1969; for Iran, Israel and Turkey, 25% in 1957 and 33% in 1969.

Already in 1959, first contacts were made between the governing bodies of the EEC and ME countries with a view to establishing Preferential Trade Agreements or Association Trade Agreements. Turkey, Iran and Israel were the first to seek such agreements and they were followed in 1970 by Egypt and Lebanon. (Egypt had originally claimed that the CM was a "neo-colonialist scheme" aimed at gaining control of the raw materials of the Arab countries and stifling their industrial development). By October 1970, agreements had been signed with Iran, Turkey and Israel.

a. An Association Trade Agreement with Turkey was signed in June 1963. The agreement is for a period of 12 years, and it can be expanded in scope, up to Turkey's admission to full membership of the EEC. Under the terms of the agreement, 37% of Turkish exports, including tobacco and dried fruit, enjoy reduced tariffs. Initially, Turkey was not required to grant the EEC reciprocal reductions. Turkey reduced by 60% her tariffs on industrial exports from the CM only in November 1969, when her economic development made it possible. In return, the CM reduced the duty on Turkish exports by 75%.

b. A preferential Trade Agreement with Iran was signed in September 1963. Duty on Persian carpets was reduced by 32%, and that on grapes was reduced from 8% to 1%. Duty on caviar was cut from 30% to 24%.

c. In May 1966, a three-year trade agreement was signed with Israel. Twenty-three Israeli products (including chemicals and clothing) enjoyed tariff reductions ranging from 10% to 40%. Duty on various fruits was reduced by approximately one-third. Quotas on imports of various industrial and agricultural products were abolished. In return, Israel was asked to grant concession to CM exports. In July 1967, Israel applied for associate membership of the EEC, but, out of political considerations, France vetoed the admission of Israel. In June 1970, a Preferential Trade Agreement was signed, under which Israel's industrial exports enjoy a tariff reduction of up to 55% and citrus, mango and avocado, a reduction of 40%. In return, Israel will gradually reduce tariffs on imports from the CM.

Meanwhile talks between the EEC and Egypt and Lebanon continue. Agreement has been held up by the search for a formula which would enable the two Arab states to continue their economic boycott of Israel without affecting European economic interests. Such a boycott would, in any case, contravene EEC regulations which ban discrimination by a member, associate member, or country in trade agreement with the EEC against a member or affiliate of the EEC.   (M.E.)

F

FAROUQ (1920–65). King of Egypt, 1936–52. Son of Fu'ad▷, Sultan and later King of Egypt; educated in England and Egypt. On the death of his father in May 1936, F. inherited the throne; as he was a minor, regents ruled for him until July 1937. F. continued the struggle between the royal dynasty and the *Wafd*▷ party and encouraged the rise of anti-*Wafd* parties—such as the already existing Liberal-Constitutional Party and the newly created *Sa'adist* party and also extra-parliamentary right-wing groups. During World War II F. was reported to share the pro-Italian and pro-German sentiments that permeated the administration, the army and public opinion, and were behind several cases of desertion and acts of treason. The British had to put pressure on him before he would honour Egypt's obligations to her and dismiss anti-British elements. In 1942, they forced him to dissolve his government and to appoint the *Wafd* leader Mustafa Nahhas▷ Prime Minister. F. removed the *Wafd* from rule in October 1944, as soon as the British no longer intervened actively in internal Egyptian affairs. The hasty decision of May 1948 to have the Egyptian army invade Palestine against army advice and in disregard of a previous decision not to involve the regular army, was imposed on government and army leaders, so they later claimed, by F. The 1948 defeat and revelations that followed of corruption in the Palace and the bureaucracy undermined F.'s position. His sybaritic life also was unpopular. In 1951 he proclaimed himself King of Egypt and Sudan, in a gesture of nationalist defiance of the British. (Ironically enough, a *Wafd* government made the decision). In July 1952, he was deposed in the officer's coup led by General Nagib▷ and Colonel Nasser▷. He was allowed to go to Italy. F. had three daughters, and a son Ahmed Fu'ad (b. 1952), from a second marriage—who was proclaimed King in 1952 (until the official termination of the monarchy in 1953). Throughout his life F. was known as a gambler and voluptuary and a frequenter of night-clubs. In July 1965, he died in exile in Rome. (O.G.)

FASCISM. No party or group in the ME openly and explicitly advocates F. However, its social doctrine on the corporate structure of the state, even more its nationalist character, its rejection of the order imposed by Great Power arrangements after World War I, its hostility towards the countries of the West, its hatred of Jews (particularly in F.'s German Nazi version), and its anti-democratic and anti-socialist

Ex-King Farouq (with daughter Fawziya)

nature—all these aroused in the 1930s and '40s much sympathy in the ME and especially among the Arabs, who were then fighting the British, the French and the Jews of Palestine. F. propaganda, originally broadcast from Italy (Bari) and then in increasing volume from Germany also, found attentive ears and exerted much influence. Many Arab nationalist leaders were among its leading spokesmen (Jajj Amin al-Husseini▷ and many of his associates among the Palestinian Arab leaders; Rashid 'Ali al-Kilani▷, Naji Shawkat, Yunis al-Bahri and other Iraqi leaders; Prince Mansur Daoud of the Egyptian royal family and other Egyptians; Fawzi al-Qawuqji▷ and other Syrians; etc.). This collaboration of Arab nationalist leaders with F. increased during World War II, when many hoped that the Axis Powers would win and take over the countries of the ME. Several highly-placed persons secretly collaborated; some even tried to cross the lines (e.g., 'Aziz 'Ali al-Masri▷ who was dismissed from his post of Chief-of-Staff of the Egyptian Army for his F. tendencies). The Rashid 'Ali al-Kilani▷ government of Iraq, in its war against Britain, in 1941, even requested German help, although unsuccessfully.

In the post-war world, few people expressed sympathy for F. But in the ME, in contrast to Europe, former association with F. did not constitute a black mark or an impediment to public office, and many leaders of the 1940s, '50s and '60s did not forget their past F. inclinations.

Among the groups of the 1930s and early '40s considered especially attached to F. were "Young Egypt" *(Misr al-Fatah)* led by Ahmad Hussein, and its "Green Shirts"; the "Syrian Nationalist Party" ▷ *(al-Hizb al-Suri al-Qawmi,* PPS) led by Anton Sa'adeh▷ in Lebanon and Syria, and the "Nationalist Action Group" *('Usbat al-'Amal al-Qawmi)* in Syria. Sympathy for F. and attitudes moulded by it were particularly common among younger army officers in Egypt and especially in Iraq, where in the late 1930s groups of officers such as the "Golden Square" ruled behind the scenes.

In pre-war Turkey, tendencies close to F. were found among pro-German and Pan-Turanian▷ groups. However, as Turkey was then ruled by a single party, pro-Fascist groups were unable to organize. In post-war Turkey, some consider the extreme Islamic right-wing close to F. Some of the younger army officers, especially Alpaslan Türkeş and his "National Movement" party (previously the "National Republic Peasant Party"), have been accused of F. (and issued angry denials). In Iran, as well, several groups have noticeable F. inclinations—mainly since World War II, as no free political organization was possible prior to it. In Iran, F. tendencies are sometimes reinforced by a special emphasis on the "Aryan" character of the Iranian culture and people. Among the groups which indulge in these ideas, were a "National-Socialist" Party in the 1950s and the "Pan-Iran" *(Mellat Iran)* party (Darius Foruhar, Muhsin Pezhekpour), with uniformed squads, and "Blood and Earth" as a slogan.

In Israel, too, extreme right-wing circles have sometimes been accused of a Fascist orientation, especially the Revisionist▷ and their *Irgun (T)zeva'i Le'umi*▷ (IZL) under the leadership of Menahem Begin▷. The "Israel Freedom Fighters" (LHY, Stern Group▷) attempted at the beginning of World War II to establish contact with the Axis Powers, in particular with Italy, to gain their support for the creation of an independent Jewish state. However, F.'s anti-Semitic character as finally manifested in German Nazism, with which no Jew could ever possibly sympathize, prevented any growth of real Fascist tendencies in Jewish Palestine and later Israel.

Since World War II no leaders or political parties have openly admitted to Fascist inclinations. The term F., on the other hand, is widely and loosely used as a derogatory synonym for right-wing nationalism and anti-socialism. In leftist circle the term F. has in effect become an insult to be levelled (like the epithet Imperialist) at political adversaries.   (Y.S.)

✥**FATAH** or **FATH.** Palestinian-Arab guerilla organization led by Yasser 'Arafat▷. (The name is the acronym of *Harakat Tahrir Filastin*, Palestine Liberation Movement, in reverse; it also means "conquest" in Arabic.) Founded in the late 1950s, F. is considered the strongest and most important guerilla group. See Palestine-Arab Guerilla Organizations▷.(Y.S.)

✥**FAWZI, MAHMUD** (b. 1900). Egyptian politician and diplomat. A native of Cairo, F. studied at the universities of Cairo, Rome and Columbia. A Doctor of Law (1929), he held many posts in the Egyptian Foreign Service: vice-consul in New York 1926–9; consul in Japan 1929–36; consul-general in Jerusalem 1941–4; counsellor at the Egyptian Embassy in Washington and Egypt's representative to the UN 1945–7. F. became Foreign Minister after the officers' coup, 1952, and kept that office until 1964 (1958–61 as Foreign Minister of the UAR▷); in 1964 he became Deputy Prime Minister for Foreign Affairs (in effect being relieved of his portfolio and removed from policy decision and execution), and in 1967 Special Presidential Adviser on Foreign Affairs. In October 1970, following Nasser's▷ death, F. was chosen Prime Minister, apparently to avoid a struggle between contending candidates and because, as a neutral, he was acceptable to the various factions. In terms of the Egyptian regime and its politics, F. is considered a liberal. He is thought of in the West as a skillful diplomat, with pro-Western inclinations.
(S. L.)

Dr. Mahmud Fawzi

FEDA'IYIN or **FEDA'IYUN** (Arabic: Suicide squads, commandos). A term based on mediaeval Islamic concepts, particularly on the Shi'ite-Isma'ilis and the *hashashiyin* (the "Assassins"). In the modern period the term F. designates commando and sabotage groups, guerillas and terrorists engaging also in political murder. The "Young Turks"▷ had their F.

groups. In Iran there is an extremist-terrorist group named Fedayan Islam▷. In recent years the term F. usually means Palestinian-Arab guerilla organizations▷.   (Y.S.)

FEDAYAN ISLAM (Persian-Arabic: "Those who sacrifice themselves for Islam"). A militant, fanatically right-wing, Iranian organization, founded in 1946 and inspired by the mediaeval Assassins' Order (see Isma'iliyya▷). In 1950–1, the FI co-operated with the right-wing religious leader Kashani▷ in a campaign against the Shah and in favour of oil nationalization. In March 1951, members of the FI assassinated Prime Minister Razmara▷ who had publicly opposed nationalization. Following the assassination Dr. Mossaddeq▷ became Prime Minister and oil was nationalized. In June 1951 relations between the FI and Kashani were broken off and Kashani formed his own terrorist organization. After the restoration of the Shah's power, brought about by Gen. Zahedi's▷ coup, 1953, the FI were forced to cease their activities. However, owing to their violent opposition to the social and economic reforms initiated by the Shah, members of the FI assassinated Prime Minister Hassan 'Ali Mansur▷ in 1965. Following this murder the authorities succeeded in liquidating the organization.   (B.G.)

FEDERALISM— See Arab Federation▷.

✳**FEDERATION OF ARAB REPUBLICS.** Federal (or rather confederal) alliance between Egypt, Syria and Libya proclaimed in April 1971 and approved by plebiscite on 1 Sept.—to be implemented gradually. Sudan—among the initiators of the plan— did not join but was expected to do so later. See Arab Federation▷, Egypt▷, Libya▷, Syria▷.   (Y.S.)

✳**FEISAL b. 'ABD-UL-'AZIZ** (of the House of Sa'ud) (b. 1905). King of Sa'udi Arabia since 1964. The second son of 'Abd-ul-'Aziz "Ibn Sa'ud"▷ (after the deaths of two elder brothers). In 1927 his father appointed him governor of the Hijaz▷ region, which had recently been conquered from King Hussein▷ and his son 'Ali▷, and entrusted him with its integration into the Sa'udi kingdom. In 1928 F. was made chairman of the Supreme Council of the 'Ulama', acting as the advisory State Council. He frequently represented Sa'udi Arabia in foreign matters and negotiations. Although Ibn Sa'ud's government was not organized along Western lines, F. was considered a kind of foreign minister. In 1953, after the death of Ibn Sa'ud and the succession of Sa'ud▷, F.'s older brother, F. was designated Crown Prince, Deputy Prime Minister and Foreign Minister, but sometimes

he was described as Prime Minister. A half-hidden fight for power between Sa'ud and F. flared up in 1958, when Sa'udia experienced a severe economic crisis and, at the same time, Nasser accused Sa'ud of attempting to have him assassinated. Sa'ud was forced to grant F. full powers in fiscal, internal and foreign affairs, and F. instituted administrative reforms and savings and attempted to eliminate corruption and waste. He managed to retrieve the economic situation and paid all state debts by 1962. The struggle with Sa'ud continued intermittently until 1964, with F. the virtual ruler. In 1964, Sa'ud demanded the restoration of his power, but F. refused. On 2 Nov. 1964, the 'Ulama' council deposed Sa'ud and proclaimed F. King.

King Feisal b. 'Abd-ul-'Aziz (with Queen of England), 1967

F. continued ruling as an absolute monarch but nevertheless introduced modernization and moderate reforms. He continued to act as his own Prime Minister. Despite objections from the tribes and the 'Ulama', he developed the educational system, communications, radio and television services. He relied on Western countries, particularly the USA, and equipped his army with Western arms. His relations with Nasser had their ups and downs: an attempt to reach agreement (including a settlement of the Yemen problem) in 1965; open animosity in 1966, when F. claimed the leadership of the Muslim world and attempted to forge an Islamic political bloc; suspicion and caution along with generous monetary aid, since June 1967.   (Y.A.O.)

FEISAL I. b. HUSSEIN (1885–1933). King of Iraq 1921–33. Born at Ta'if (Hijaz) as the third son of Sharif (later King) Hussein▷, F. grew up in Constantinople, where his father lived in exile; he returned to Hijaz in 1908, when Hussein was appointed Amir of Mecca. At the beginning of World War I he established ties with Arab nationalists in

Damascus. Upon the outbreak of the "Arab Revolt"▷ in Hijaz, 1916, he took command of the "Northern Army", which eventually entered Damascus, as part of General Allenby's▷ Allied Forces, on 1 Oct. 1918. F. assumed control of Syria, in the name of Arab nationalism and under the overall supervision of the Allies; he soon fell out with the French who wanted complete control of Syria. In March 1920 he was crowned King of Syria by an Arab-Syrian national congress, but was ousted by the French after armed clashes ("The battle of Meisalun" (Meithalun) 24 July 1920). Meanwhile, F. had presented his dynasty's claim to an independent Arab kingdom (or federation of kingdoms), and Arab nationalist claims in general, at the Paris Peace Conference. He had also signed a conditional agreement with the Zionist leadership on future co-operation between the Zionist movement and the future Arab State (see Feisal-Weizmann Agreement▷).

After F. was ousted from Syria, the goodwill of Churchill▷, on the advice of Lawrence▷ and the British "Arab Office" in Cairo, secured for him the projected Kingdom of Iraq, where he was enthroned after a "plebiscite" held in August 1921. From then until his death he remained on essentially good terms with the British, though he had to tread carefully to avoid alienating the nationalists, and he proved himself an astute politician. He promulgated a Constitution in 1925 (in force until 1958). The Anglo-Iraqi Treaty of 1930, and Iraq's consequent assumption of independence upon her admission to the League of Nations, in October 1932, were noteworthy successes his reign. Thereafter F. seems to have lost his grip, and his attempts in the summer of 1933 to restrain public fervour against the Assyrians▷ cost him much of his popularity. He died on 7 September 1933, and was succeeded by his only son, Ghazi▷.   (U.D.)

FEISAL II b. GHAZI (1935–58). King of Iraq 1939–58. Son of King Ghazi▷ and grandson of Feisal▷ I. On his father's death F., not yet four years old, became King. The Regency passed to his mother's brother (and his father's cousin) Prince 'Abd-ul-Ilah▷, who proved to be loyal and affectionate. During the Rashid 'Ali▷ crisis of 1941, F. and his mother were in the power of the nationalists but remained unharmed. F. was educated on English lines, partly in England (Harrow). In 1953 F. assumed his constitutional duties; in February 1958 he became head of the "Arab Federation"▷ of Iraq and Jordan (see Iraq▷, History). F. was not a forceful personality and had no appreciable effect on his country's policies, though he was not unpopular. His murder during the revolution of 14 July 1958 was probably planned

King Feisal II (left) and Crown Prince 'Abd-ul-Ilah, 1956 (with Queen of England)

so as to deprive adherents of the old order of a possible rallying point.   (U.D.)

FEISAL-WEIZMANN AGREEMENT. In his quest for an agreement with Arab leaders, Weizmann▷, then in Palestine at the head of the Zionist Commission, followed a British suggestion and met with Amir Feisal▷ b. Hussein, the leader of the Arab Revolt▷, on 4 June 1918, at the latter's encampment between 'Aqaba and Ma'an, and discussed future co-operation. A statement by Feisal describing Arab and Zionist nationalist aspirations as compatible was published in *The Times* on 12 Dec. 1918. During the Paris Peace Conference▷ further talks took place, and on 3 Jan. 1919 F. and W. signed a formal agreement. This provided for "the closest collaboration in the development of the Arab State and Palestine" (Preamble) and "the most cordial good will and understanding" between the two states (Art. I), whose boundaries would be established by agreement (Art. II). The Balfour Declaration▷ was specifically endorsed (Art. III), and it was agreed (Art. IV) that "all necessary measures shall be taken to encourage and stimulate immigration of Jews into Palestine on a large scale, and as quickly as possible to settle Jewish immigrants upon the land," while the Arab peasant and tenant farmers were to be duly "protected in their right, and shall be assisted in forwarding their economic development." F. added a hand-written note making the implementation of the agreement conditional on his demands concerning Arab independence being fulfilled. Proponents of Arab anti-Zionism, such as George Antonius▷, claimed that F. was influenced by T. E. Lawrence▷ and signed the agreement unaware of its implications. It was also claimed that F. had no authority to sign an agreement affecting the Palestine Arabs.

F. himself was somewhat ambiguous. In an interview with *Le Matin* (1 Mar. 1919) he declared that persecuted Jews were welcome to Palestine under a

Muslim or Christian government responsible to the League of Nations, but a desire to establish a Jewish state and claim sovereignty would lead to serious conflict. As the Zionists were disturbed by this statement, contradictory to the F.-W. A., the matter was clarified in an interview between F. and an American judge, Professor Felix Frankfurter, in the presence of Lawrence. A letter from F. to Frankfurter on 3 Mar. 1919 reassured the Zionists that "we are working together for a reformed and revived Near East, and our two movements complete one another ... There is room in Syria for us both." In 1929, asked about this letter, F. could not remember having written it. The F.-W. A. remained abortive.

(Sh. H.)

FERTILE CRESCENT. The countries on the northern edge of the Arabian peninsula: Iraq, Syria, Lebanon, Palestine (Israel and Jordan). Before the dismemberment of the Ottoman Empire▷ in 1918, it was administered by the Turks and divided into the provinces *(Vilayet)* of Basra, Baghdad, Mosul, Aleppo, Damascus and Beirut, the autonomous district of Lebanon, and the special district *(Sanjaq)* of Jerusalem. As protagonists of Arab independence during World War I, the Hashemite Sharif Hussein▷ of Mecca and his sons—'Ali▷, Feisal▷ and 'Abdullah▷—planned to establish a federation of independent Arab kingdoms in the FC under their rule. Their plan apparently envisaged one kingdom of Iraq and one of (Greater) Syria (including Lebanon and Palestine with Jordan), federated with Hijaz, their political centre and home, as a third kingdom. However, Great Power arrangements during and after the Paris Peace Conference, 1918–20, divided the FC into semi-independent states under separate mandates▷, with Britain administering Iraq and Palestine (including Transjordan) and France controlling Syria and Lebanon. For the next quarter-century, the region was under predominantly British influence accompanied by sharp Anglo-French rivalry. When the mandates were abolished and full independence won, these separate entities became firmly established. (Palestine was partitioned twice: when Transjordan was separated in 1922, and when Israel was established in 1948.) Nevertheless, the concept of a single political entity of the FC, completely united or at least federated, has persisted.

Various plans for a FC union have been suggested over the last half-century, sometimes openly but frequently through secret negotiations coupled with subversion. Most of these were put forth by the Hashemite▷ rulers and their associates. The Greater Syria▷ scheme, for example, was cultivated by 'Abdullah of Jordan; it provided for the union of Syria, Lebanon, Jordan and Palestine under his monarchy (with special autonomy for Jewish Palestine). Agitation for this scheme was particularly strong during the 1940s, on the eve of the establishment of the Arab League▷ and the partition of Palestine. Another plan sponsored in 1942–3 by Nuri Sa'id▷, the Iraqi leader, envisaged the union of Syria, Lebanon, Palestine and Transjordan (with semi-autonomy for Christian-Maronite Lebanon and Jewish Palestine) federated with Iraq. It was generally assumed that these various plans enjoyed British support, because of Britain's alliance with the Hashemites and the fact that several British statesmen proposed similar federations (e.g., Herbert Samuel▷ in 1920). The British secret services were also rumoured to be actively promoting these plans which France always suspected as British plots to put an end to French influence in the area. A union of the FC unlinked to the Hashemite dynasty but under the dominance of a republican Syria, was propagated by the Syrian Nationalist Party of Antoun Sa'adeh▷ (this clandestine organization later allied itself, beginning in the 1950s, with the Hashemites).

All these proposals were rejected by the Arab League and those Arab states insisting on maintaining their independence. They supported Pan-Arab co-operation on the basis of the *status quo* and their continued individual sovereignty. Proposals for the unity of the FC have, therefore, been dormant since the early 1950s. Egypt's transition, from a policy of *status quo* to revolutionary Pan-Arab unification in the later 1950s, has implicitly opened a new phase in the history of this concept. The union, for example, planned for Syria, Egypt and Iraq in 1963 would have partially brought about the unity of the FC and Jordan might well have been compelled to join (Israel was, of course, excluded). However, the creation of a "revolutionary", as opposed to a Hashemite, union in the FC was not successful, and such plans have also remained dormant since then, with efforts for closer co-operation between the existing states taking their place. Arab Federal plans have now moved outside the FC (see Arab Federation▷).

(Y. S.)

FEZZAN. The south-west area of Libya▷, a desert. Area: 220,000 sq. mi. Pop. 80,000 (1964 census). Principal settlement: Sabha. Following the liquidation of Italian rule in World War II, F. was under the provincial military administration of France 1943–51, while the rest of Libya was British-administered. For F.'s history, government and politics, see Libya▷.

(Y. S.)

FLOSY (Front for the Liberation of Occupied South Yemen, *Jabhat Tahrir Janub al-Yaman al-Muhtall*). Underground nationalist organization in Aden▷ and

South Arabia▷, founded in 1966 through a merger of several underground groups. Its aim was to liberate South Arabia from British rule and unite it with Yemen. Supported by Egypt, F. was at first considered the most extreme nationalist group; but in 1967 a more extremist group, the NLF▷, got the upper hand and eliminated F. Its leaders were suppressed or went into exile. See South Yemen▷, Political History.
(Y.S.)

*FOREIGN ECONOMIC AID. From the beginning of the century until 1945 foreign money came to the ME not as aid, but in the form of private investments or credit granted by financial institutions (governmental or private) to rulers or governments. Aid was given only in the form of imperial subsidies, generally to rulers—leading, explicitly or implicitly, to conditions of political protection or patronage. Of this type were the annual grants paid by Britain to the Persian Gulf▷ principalities, to Ibn Saʿud▷, Hussein▷ of Hijaz, and, later, to Transjordan▷ (for the maintenance of her army). The subsidies to Transjordan continued until 1956–7, and those to several Gulf principalities until 1971. After World War II foreign governments began offering aid to ME countries—grants or credits—without openly stated political conditions. The first to grant such aid

GOVERNMENTAL ECONOMIC AID* TO ME COUNTRIES
1945–69 (in millions of dollars)

| Countries receiving aid | Countries extending aid | | | | | General total |
| | OECD states | | Soviet Bloc | | Communist China | |
	Total	US share	Total	USSR share		
1. Non-Arab states						
Iran	829	736	758	520	—	1,587
Israel	1,916	945	—	—	—	1,916
Turkey	2,559	2,115	210	210	—	2,769
Total	5,304	3,796	968	730	—	6,272
2. Arab states						
Iraq	51	50	488	310	—	539
Jordan	657	587	—	—	—	657
Lebanon	89	88	—	—	—	89
Libya	283	203	—	—	—	283
Saʿudi Arabia	80	72	—	—	—	80
South Yemen (since 1968)	—	—	36	11	12	48
Sudan	133	94	70	22	—	203
Syria	50	50	423	233	16	489
Egypt	1,372	1,115	1,528	1,000	85	2,985
Yemen	46	45	101	88	56	203
Others**	155	—	—	—	—	155
Total	2,916	2,304	2,646	1,664	169	5,731
3. ME TOTAL	8,220	6,100	3,614	2,394	169	12,003

* Loans and grants from governments and state banks and institutions.

** Including the Persian Gulf principalities, Aden and the Federation of South Arabia (until 1967).

was the USA: following the enunciation of the Truman▷ Doctrine in 1947, she included Turkey and Greece (and actually Iran as well) among the receivers of "Marshall Plan" aid (earmarked for the rehabilitation of Europe) and "Point 4" aid (Jan. 1949). This aid was gradually expanded to include the other countries of the region; other Western countries and the Soviet bloc began granting aid in the mid-1950s.

In the years 1945–69 ME nations received more then $12,000m. in government economic aid, as grants or credit, of this more than $8,200m. from the West (OECD), $3,600m. from the Soviet Bloc and $170m. from Communist China (see table, p. 133). These figures are based on commitments and agreements which do not always tally with actual disbursements. This is so particularly in the case of the USSR and China where, according to some estimates, less than 50% of the committed aid is disbursed. The figures do not include military aid, which is usually kept confidential and concerning which no reliable figures are available.   (M.E.)

*FOUR-POWER TALKS. Talks on the ME held by the ambassadors to the UN of the "Big Four"— USA, USSR, Britain and France—during 1969–71. They commenced in April 1969 at France's initiative, after UN envoy Dr. Gunnar Jarring▷ had failed to bridge the gap between Arab and Israeli positions. The FP representatives attempted to arrive at an agreed interpretation of the Security Council resolution of November 1967, in order to pass it on to Dr. Jarring as a Security Council directive.

Israel opposed such an involvement of the FP in the ME conflict, objecting to any arrangement not negotiated and agreed upon by the governments concerned. The Arab states were more favourably disposed, hoping for pro-Arab decisions as the Soviet Union and France were known for their pro-Arab position, Britain was neutral, and only the USA was considered pro-Israel (with reservations and accepting several basic points in the Arab position). In over forty meetings held by the FP representatives, the USA recommended Israel's withdrawal from territories occupied by her (albeit possibly not from all, and with border adjustments), insisting on the principles of negotiation between the parties, secure and recognized borders for Israel, a contractual peace (to include cessation of all guerilla and terrorist warfare) and freedom of navigation. The USSR supported the Arab claim that Israel must evacuate *all* territories, her only recompense being a "cessation of belligerence" and not full peace based on agreement and a mutual contractual commitment.

In summer 1970, following a new American initiative for a cease-fire and the resumption of Dr. Jarring's mission (see Rogers Plan▷), the futile FP talks were suspended. They were resumed in October 1970 following Israel's withdrawal from the Jarring talks (the result of Egypt's violation of the standstill agreement along the Suez Canal). The talks were again suspended, January–February 1971. Meetings have since been held, but achieved no results.
(E. A.)

*FRANCE, FRENCH INTERESTS AND POLICIES IN THE ME. F.'s past and present interests in ME affairs are manifold as an ally and protector of the Catholic Church, F. takes a special interest in the Christian holy places and communities in the area; since her conquest of many Muslim lands, F. is conscious of being a "Muslim Power"; F.'s ME policies were often determined by Great Power aspirations and rivalries as well as consideration relating to the balance of power in Europe (which led to an early alignment with the Ottoman Empire, and to military expeditions such as the Napoleonic invasion of Egypt); prestige and strategic interests; trade and economic interests; and the dissemination of culture.

F. was deeply involved in the ME in the era of the Crusades, (1096–1291), assuming a leading part in eight of these. In 1535, François I signed a treaty of friendship with the Ottoman Sultan Suleiman I, which conferred upon France certain privileges or capitulations▷, including French jurisdiction over French merchants, and the virtual recognition of F. as the protector of Latin Christianity in the Empire. The capitulations were further extended in 1740, and by Napoleon in 1802.

In 1798 Napoleon invaded Egypt, to cut off Britain from her Indian possessions. He conquered all of Egypt, then under the rule of a Mameluk viceroy, and also advanced into Palestine and Syria. However, he failed to reduce Acre and was unable to proceed beyond Sidon on the Lebanese coast. In 1799 Napoleon returned to France, and by 1801 the French Army was forced to surrender to Britain. Though the expedition was spectacular, its main effects were in the cultural rather than the military domain. F. played an active role in the diplomatic and military manoeuvres of the Great Powers concerning the conflict between Muhammad 'Ali of Egypt and the Ottoman Sultan, in the 1830s, and in protecting the Ottoman Empire against Russia (the Crimean War, 1954–6).

F. granted her special protection to the Maronites▷ in Lebanon and intervened on their behalf in 1842–5 and again in 1860, when she exerted pressure upon the Sultan to establish Lebanon as an autonomous region, predominantly Christian; the Sultan had to concede this to F. and the other Western Powers supporting her. This led to a considerable extension of French political and cultural influence so that, upon the dismemberment of the Ottoman Empire after World War I, F. was able to stake a claim as the rightful trustee of the Levant. French interests had at the same time been active in the Ottoman Empire (railways, banking), Persia, and particularly Egypt. The Suez Canal▷ was devised and built by French engineers and largely with French capital. F., together with Britain, administered Egypt's foreign debts and was deeply involved in Egypt's whole economy. Even after the British occupation of Egypt (1882), which F. bitterly resented, French interests and influence in Egypt remained very strong.

F. claims to the Levant were put forward during World War I and recognized in the Sykes-Picot Agreement▷, under which F. was to obtain possession of the coastal strip of Syria-Lebanon and most of Cilicia in south-east Anatolia, as well as a sphere of influence to include the Syrian hinterland and the Mosul▷ province of Mesopotamia, and a share in an internationalized administration of Palestine. In November 1918 the French and British prime ministers, Clemenceau and Lloyd George, signed an agreement by which F. waived her claim to the Mosul area in favour of Britain, in return for a share in the oil resources of the area (and further compensation elsewhere, in Europe). F. also had to acquiesce in a British mandatory (rather than international) administration for Palestine. Her plans for annexing Cilicia were re-affirmed in the Peace Treaty of Sèvres▷ with Turkey (August 1920), but that treaty was torn up by the Turkish nationalists and the partition of Anatolia was abandoned.

In return for her concessions, F. was granted a mandate▷ over the whole of Syria and Lebanon, the distinction between direct administration in the coastlands and guidance-and-influence only in the Arab hinterland being dropped. In November 1919 French troops under General Gouraud took the place of British troops stationed along the Syrian coast. F. recognized Amir Feisal's▷ authority in the Syrian hinterland. However, when in the spring of 1920 Feisal accepted the Syrian crown, symbolizing complete independence, this was regarded by F. as a threat to her "rights" in Syria. General Gouraud's forces entered Damascus on 24 July 1920 and deposed Feisal, thus asserting French supremacy in Syria.

For the French Mandatory administration in Syria and Lebanon, and its struggle with the nationalists, see Syria▷, Lebanon▷. At first General Gouraud split Syria into four units: Greater Lebanon; the State of Damascus▷ (including the Jabal Druze▷ district); the State of Aleppo▷ (including the Alexandretta▷ district); and the Territory of Lataqia▷ ('Alawi▷ Territory). Jabal Druze was granted special status in 1922, and the Sanjaq of Alexandretta

gained autonomy in 1924; on 1 Jan. 1925 the states of Aleppo and Damascus were unified as the State of Syria.

F.'s endeavours to set up Western-type parliamentary institutions were more successful in Lebanon than in Syria. In treaties of September and November 1936 with Syria and Lebanon, the Léon Blum government granted independence within three years, in return for a military pact stipulating the presence of French forces and bases, a preferential status for F. and economic privileges, special provisions for French schools, etc. However, as a result of developments in F. such as the eclipse of the Socialist-led Popular Front and the preoccupation with the German and Italian danger, F. did not ratify the two agreements, reverting on the eve of World War II to unqualified colonial-type rule as Mandatory Power.

The danger of the approaching war also induced F. to surrender the district (Sanjaq) of Alexandretta▷, with its 40% Turkish minority, to Turkey. Turkish claims had been laid before the League of Nations which, in May 1937, had conferred upon the Sanjaq a special status: autonomy, with foreign relations entrusted to Syria, a monetary union with Syria, Turkish as an official language. However, Turkey continued to exert pressure and, in July 1938, F. was compelled to agree to the entry of Turkish forces into the Sanjaq. Elections, in September 1938, yielded a majority of 63% to the Turks and the administration became wholly Turkish. On 23 June 1939, F. consented to the annexation by Turkey of the Sanjaq of Alexandretta, known from then on as Hatay▷. At the same time, F. and Turkey signed a pact of non-aggression and mutual assistance.

In World War II, after the capitulation of F. in June 1940, French administrators and officers in Syria and Lebanon under General Dentz threw in their lot with the Vichy authorities. German and Italian troops were stationed in the Levant, under the guise of an Armistice Supervision Commission; Syria and Lebanon were expected to serve as the bridgehead of a fully fledged invasion of the ME, and on 8 June 1941, British and Free French forces went in. On the day of the invasion General Catroux▷ declared on behalf of "Free F." the end of the Mandate and the independence of Syria and Lebanon (future relations with F. to be determined by treaty). A British statement endorsed his proclamation, and General Catroux was appointed "Delegate General and Plenipotentiary of Free F. in the Levant" (rather than the traditional "High Commissioner") and instructed to negotiate treaties with Syria and Lebanon. On 28 Sept. and 26 Nov. 1941, Catroux again proclaimed the independence of Syria and Lebanon.

In February 1942, General Spears was nominated as the first British envoy to Syria and the Lebanon, and in 1944 the USSR and the USA recognized their independence. However, F. was not eager actually to transfer power to the local leaders; she insisted on the conclusion of a treaty conferring special privileges in the military, economic and cultural spheres—which the Syrian and Lebanese leaders, backed by the USA and particularly Britain, were no longer prepared to concede. French delays and evasiveness in the granting of full independence led to a series of severe clashes. One of the gravest occurred in November 1943, when the Lebanese government and Parliament formally abolished all articles of the Constitution limiting independence and granting F. special privileges. The French arrested the Lebanese leaders, including President Bishara al-Khouri▷ and Premier Riyad al-Sulh▷, but were compelled, mainly by a British ultimatum, to back down completely. Serious clashes again broke out in Syria early in 1945, as the French refused to withdraw their troops from the Levant. F. again had to retreat following a British ultimatum demanding that French forces cease fire and return to barracks. Early in 1946, the evacuation of French (and British) forces was discussed by the UN Security Council, and though no formal decision was adopted (owing to a Soviet veto), F. and Britain consented to withdraw their forces from Syria by 17 Apr. 1946, and from Lebanon by 31 Dec. 1946. This spelt the end of French predominance in the Levant.

The evacuation of French forces and the end of French rule over Syria and Lebanon left F. deeply embittered towards Britain, whom she saw as the chief cause of her dislodgement from the ME. Some French economic and cultural influence remained. In view of Lebanon's strongly Christian character—in no small measure due to F.—French efforts at maintaining strong cultural ties received considerable Lebanese support.

Although France voted in favour of the partition of Palestine on 29 Nov. 1947, her recognition of Israel was delayed in order to allay Arab sensitivities. France was elected in December 1948 to the UN Palestine Conciliation Commission▷ (PCC), with the USA and Turkey. Though F. had given generous assistance to survivors of the European holocaust, and had allowed the establishment of transit camps for Jews on their way to Israel, her ties with Israel continued to be marked by restraint. F. persisted in regarding herself as a Muslim power (i.a., in view of her African possessions).

The Algerian revolt proclaimed on 1 Nov. 1954 and soon actively supported by Egypt and most Arab countries, brought about a gradual change in F.'s attitude towards Israel. While still refraining from any demonstrative expression of friendship, F. became —after the Egyptian-Czech arms deal of 1955, and the Soviet-Syrian and Soviet-Egyptian ones following— Israel's main supplier of arms and military equipment. The nationalization of the Suez Canal▷ Company by Egypt, on 26 July 1956, led her to invade Egypt, in the Suez War▷, together with Britain (and in co-ordination with Israel's Sinai War▷). The Anglo-French Suez campaign failed to achieve its objective; in its wake, most Arab countries, headed by Egypt, broke off diplomatic relations with F.

F.'s relations with Israel now became even more intimate, in the military, economic and cultural spheres. F. was now firmly entrenched as Israel's main supplier of armaments, of which modern jet fighter planes were the most significant feature. Though closer, however, these relations were still discreet. F. gave no public expression to her sympathies and took, e.g., at the UN, a balanced position with a pro-Arab bias. De Gaulle's▷ return to power did not alter F.'s warm but discreet relations with Israel; when the President of F. welcomed Israel's Prime Minister Ben-Gurion▷ in 1961, he referred to his guest's country as "Israël, notre ami et notre allié" (Israel, our friend and ally).

The granting of independence to Algeria in 1962 paved the way for the resumption of normal relations between France and the Arab countries; the initiative came from the Arabs. The last Arab country to re-establish contact was Egypt in spring 1963. De Gaulle, rejecting all Arab pressure, proclaimed a doctrine of "parallelism" to guide F.'s dealings with both Israel and the Arab countries; this parallelism was accepted by the latter, and continued to guide French policy throughout the four years until the Six Day War.

The normalization of F.'s relations with the Arab countries, Algerian independence, and French interests in North Africa and particularly in Algeria, e.g. the oil resources of the Sahara, prepared the ground for increased political action by the Arab lobby in F. There was likewise a revival of F.'s traditional aspirations as a world factor and a Muslim power. Heading this trend was Maurice Couve de Murville, the French Foreign Minister, who had been ambassador in Cairo in 1952. Yet General de Gaulle carefully maintained the parallelism of F.'s relations with the Arabs and Israel, and on several occasions rejected Arab pressure to change course. In 1964, during the visit of Israeli Premier Levi Eshkol▷ to Paris, de Gaulle reiterated the phrase "Israel, our friend and ally". In 1965, F. supported Israel's plans for the "National Water Carrier" (based on diversion of the Jordan) against Arab attempts to divert the Jordan headwaters. De Gaulle was able to retain his honoured position both in the Arab countries and in Israel, and hoped that through the ME F. would be able to reassert her position as one of the Four Big Powers. In 1966, whilst on an official visit to the Soviet Union, de Gaulle, adopting Israel's point of view, advised the Soviet leaders to refrain from adding fuel to the flames in the ME.

The Six Day War▷ led to a change in France's position, as drastic as it was sudden. On 24 May 1967, Israel's Foreign Minister requested de Gaulle to use his influence with Nasser▷ and induce him to revoke the closure of the Straits of Tiran▷. De Gaulle advised Israel not to fire the first shot, fearing that this might touch off another world war. De Gaulle now suggested to the USA, Britain and the USSR that the Four Big Powers urgently consult on the ME crisis; the USA and Britain agreed, but the USSR objected. On 3 June, F. placed a total embargo on the supply of arms and military equipment to the ME. Since Israel was the chief buyer of such equipment from F., the embargo was aimed almost exclusively at her.

De Gaulle never forgave Israel for having "fired the first shot". Her protestations that the closing of the Straits of Tiran constituted a *casus belli* and was planned as the beginning of her destruction, left the French President unimpressed. During the extraordinary session of the UN in June–July 1967, France took up a distinctly pro-Arab position; she retained the embargo in full force; and at a press conference, in November 1967, de Gaulle was severely critical of Israel (using the notorious phrase "a chosen people with a domineering disposition", with its antisemitic undertone). This reversal in the French attitude was warmly praised by the Arab countries whereas relations with Israel steadily deteriorated.

The French arms embargo on Israel mainly affected 50 Mirage-V planes for which Israel had already paid. Following a retaliatory Israeli raid on Beirut airport on 28 Dec. 1968, de Gaulle—in view of F.'s special relations with Lebanon—placed a total embargo on arms supplies to Israel. F. took the initiative for talks on the ME by the UN Ambassadors of the Four Powers, beginning in April 1969.

It is too soon to conclude what considerations led to the *volte-face* in F.'s attitude and the abandonment of her policy of parallelism. No doubt de Gaulle's personal prestige (Israel had not listened to his advice . . .) carried considerable weight. At the same time the pro-Arab French lobby had certainly prepared the ground, providing a potent rationale for F.'s new political line.

De Gaulle's abdication and the accession of Georges Pompidou to the presidency in 1969 did not lead to a substantial change in French ME policy. Feelers put out at the end of 1969 with a view to reverting to a selective embargo were withdrawn when five gunboats, built for Israel but kept back by F. in accordance with the embargo, were taken out of Cherbourg harbour by Israel.

F. now considers the Mediterranean to be the most propitious arena for her political activity. She would favour an entente of Mediterranean countries, which would oust the two Super Powers from the region. French aspirations are now pursued in a rather less pretentious manner than under de Gaulle, and are mainly directed towards the countries of the *Maghreb*▷, into which F. would like to incorporate Libya as well. A large-scale arms deal with Libya (110 Mirages) announced at the beginning of 1970, exemplifies this line of thought. The French-Algerian crisis of spring 1971 terminating any "special relationship" between the two countries, has so far not led to a noticeable change in F.'s ME policies. As to the embargo, F. considers only the "front-line countries" (Israel, Egypt, Syria and Jordan) as subject to it; Lebanon is exempt in view of her particular character and also because she had not "joined the war". Other Arab countries, e.g. Iraq and Libya, are not included in the ban on the sale of arms and military equipment.

French economic interests in the ME fall mainly into two categories: oil, and trade relations and investment. As to oil, French companies operate in the following countries: a. Iraq. The Compagnie Française des Pétroles (CFP) has a share of 23.75% in the Iraq Petroleum Co. (IPC). ERAP, the French government company, won a concession for oil prospecting in an area of 4,150 sq. mi. (by 1971 already relinquished and returned in large part); b. Abu-Dhabi. CFP owns one-third of the Abu Dhabi Petroleum Co.; c. Dubai. CFP has a 25% interest in the Dubai Marine Areas (DUMA) Company; d. Muscat-and-'Oman. In the Petroleum Development ('Oman) Company, the CFP controls 10%; e. Iran CFP has a 6% share in the consortium (1954) producing most of Iran's oil; ERAP obtained new, separate concessions in the late 1960s; f. Libya. ERAP holds concessions in Libya.

French oil imports from the ME (including Iran) totalled 37.4m. tons in 1968 (out of total imports of 77.2m. tons) and 43.2m. out of 86.3m. total imports in 1969. About 90% of French oil requirements are covered by oil from Arab countries, including Algeria (27–30%) and Libya (13–17%). F. was endeavouring—even before the partial nationalization of Algerian oil led in spring 1971 to a grave French-Algerian crisis and to a virtual stop in oil imports from Algeria—to cut imports from Algeria and increase the supply from other Arab countries, so as to be less heavily dependent on Algerian fuel; the acute crisis was resolved in 1971.

As to trade, F. derives 10–12% of her imports from Arab countries (the percentage tending to decline), and ships to them 7–8% of her exports (see also European Economic Community▷).   (J. B.-A.)

FRANJIYEH, SULEIMAN (b. 1910). Lebanese politician. President of Lebanon since 1970. One of the leaders of a powerful Christian-Maronite clan in Zagharta, northern Lebanon, F. entered politics in 1960 only, when his brother Hamid F. (who had been a minister in many cabinets and a candidate for the presidency in 1952) retired. A Member of Parliament since 1960, F. held ministerial posts in cabinets headed by Sa'eb Salam▷, 1960–1, 'Abdullah Yafi▷, 1968, and Rashid Karameh▷, 1969–70. In August 1970 he was proposed for the presidency by a faction of the Centre, led by Salam, in opposition to the candidate (Elias Sarkis, Governor of the Central Bank) offered by ex-President Fu'ad Shihab's▷ bloc. F. gained the support of the Centre, a right-wing coalition led by the "Triple Alliance" of Camille Chamoun▷, Pierre Gemayel▷ and Raymond Edde▷ (who could not agree on a candidate of their own), and the left-wing faction led by Kamal Jumblat▷. He was elected President, on 17 Aug. 1970, by 50 votes to 49—the smallest majority ever in a Lebanese presidential election.   (Y. S.)

FRANKLIN-BOUILLON AGREEMENT. Agreement concluded in Ankara on 20 Oct. 1921 between France, represented by Henri F.-B. and Turkey, represented by Yusuf Kemal Bey (the Nationalist Government's Foreign Minister). The French had been defeated by Turkish forces in Cilicia, which France had planned to occupy in accordance with a secret agreement with her World War I allies. France now agreed to borders which left Cilicia in Turkish hands. The agreement, the first between an Allied Power and the Turkish Nationalist Government, gave rise to Anglo-French tension, as Britain wished to abide by Allied wartime and post-war arrangements and refused to recognize the Nationalist Government in Turkey.   (D. K.)

FU'AD (in full: Ahmad Fu'ad) (1868–1936). Sultan of Egypt 1917–22, King of Egypt 1922–36. The youngest son of the Khedive Isma'il (ruled 1863–79). In 1917 the British arranged for F. to succeed his brother Hussein Kamel as Sultan of Egypt (a title they introduced in 1914 when they made Egypt a protectorate) In 1922, following Britain's unilateral declaration of Egypt's independence, F. was proclaimed King (he claimed the title "King of Egypt *and Sudan*" and relinquished this claim only under intense British pressure).

During his reign the struggle continued for greater independence and a treaty with the British (the Treaty of 1936 was signed shortly after his death). The King did not play an active part in this struggle. He and his Court fought with the nationalist *Wafd*▷ party for the control of Egypt and about the extent of parliamentary freedom. F. preferred prime ministers from conservative circles close to him. He was keenly interested in the Egyptian educational system. The first Western-type Egyptian university was established at Cairo in 1925 and named after him. When F. died in 1936, his son Farouq▷ succeeded him.   (O. G.)

FUJAIRA. One of the seven Trucial Coast▷ principalities, on the east coast of the 'Oman Peninsula. Area: 763 sq. mi. Pop.: 4,000, mostly nomadic. F. was recognized only in 1952 as a separate sheikhdom under British protection. The Sheikh of F. signed in 1960 a treaty of federal co-operation with Sharja▷ (which had previously ruled F.). In 1966 oil exploration rights were granted to a German company.   (Y. K.)

G

GADDAFI—see Qaddhafi▷.

GAHAL. Israeli electoral bloc formed in 1965 by the *Herut* and "Liberal" parties in preparation for the elections to the Sixth *Knesset* (Parliament), with a view to providing an alternative to the leftist government. It was in opposition for two years but joined a National Unity Government on the eve of the outbreak of the Six Day War for a period of three years, after which it broke away (July 1970) in protest against government acceptance of the American peace initiative (see Rogers▷ Plan), interpreted by G. as consent to a new partition of, and a betrayal of Jewish historical rights to, Palestine and as jeopardizing security interests.

G.'s political platform is extremist. It advocates an activist approach to security problems and toward the Arab states leaning on Western support, and opposes Israel's relations with West Germany. In internal matters, G. advocates the elimination of the class struggle, the establishment of compulsory mediation in labour relations, limitations on government intervention in the economy, and the separation of labour unions from the ownership of workers' economy (see *Histadrut*▷). Two trends are in conflict within G., one toward complete unification of the two parties and the other for their continued separate existence.

In the first *Knesset*, the two parties, still not forming a bloc, together held 21 seats. In the present *Knesset* (elected 1969) the G. bloc holds 26 seats (as in the Sixth *Knesset*).

1. *Herut:* established in 1948 by veterans of the *Irgun (T)zeva'i Le'umi* ▷ (IZL), headed by Menahem Begin ▷, in the spirit of the "Zionist Revisionists" ▷ and Ze'ev Jabotinsky ▷, as a national party on the extreme right. Its influence in *Gahal* is decisive and most of its own platform became *Gahal's* (apart from *Herut's* assertion of Jewish rights to a greater Land of Israel on both sides of the Jordan, which it has not abandoned).

2. "Liberal Party": established in 1961 by the fusion of the "General Zionists" with the "Progressive Party" (the latter broke away with the establishment of *Gahal* and formed the "Independent Liberals"). The LP is a party of the centre, its members coming mostly from the middle and upper classes. It has conservative, anti-socialist ideas in internal affairs. In foreign and security matters, its approach is in general moderate though its third convention, held in July 1971, passed a resolution opposing the re-partition of *Eretz* (Land of) *Israel* (the former Palestine), *i.e.* the withdrawal of Israel from the West Bank ▷ and the Gaza Strip ▷ and their return to Jordan and Egypt respectively.   (E. L.)

GALILEE, SEA OF (also Lake Genezareth, Lake of Tiberias; Hebrew: *Yam Kinneret*). Situated in Israel. The world's lowest fresh water lake, 685 ft below sea level, derives its water from the River Jordan. Area: 99.8 sq. mi., maximum depth: 144 ft. The water volume is 4,236m. cubic metres (mcm), the average annual water supply—760 mcm, annual evaporation—270 mcm. The lake's shores serve as a winter resort (especially Tiberias, the only lakeside town), due to the hot climate and mineral springs.

Since 1964 the lake (in spite of its salinity: 280–300 mg/l, depending on the rainfall) has been used as the main source for Israel's "National Water Carrier", on which Israel's irrigation system is based; at present 320 mcm *p.a.* are pumped, and an increase is planned. The S. of G. is also a source of fish, and many inhabitants of Tiberias are professional fishermen.

Following the British occupation of Palestine and the French occupation of Syria in 1918, the British demanded the inclusion of all the shore lands in Palestine, so as to establish exclusive rights to all the waters of Jordan. The final boundary, agreed between the British and the French in December 1920 and March 1923, left within Palestine the entire S. of G. and a 328 ft wide strip of dry land, measured from the highwater mark of the lake, while

The Sea of Galilee

allotting the villages and their lands on the northeastern shore to Syria. Syrian fishermen were allowed to continue enjoying their traditional fishing rights.

After the creation of the State of Israel, the lake became a source of constant conflict with Syria. The Syrians occupied the 32.8 ft strip and the northeastern shore, claimed their fishing rights in the northeastern sector of the lake to be absolute and exclusive, and attempted to exclude Israeli fishermen by force. Armed clashes occurred frequently in this sector, sometimes involving artillery and aircraft. Further conflict often arose over cultivation rights in a Demilitarized Zone created in 1948 on the southeastern shore. A major air battle on 7 Apr. 1967, resulting in the loss of 6 Syrian planes, launched the crisis which led to the Six Day War ▷. Since the war, the area has remained peaceful under Israel's sole control.   (Y. K.-Y. S.)

GALLIPOLI. A peninsula projecting from the southern part of Turkish Thrace and bounding the Dardanelles ▷ on their northern side. Its major town bears the same name. During World War I, after allied warships had failed to force their way through the Dardanelles, allied (mainly British, Australian and French) forces landed on the G. peninsula in 1915, in an attempt to fight their way through to Istanbul. The expedition failed, and the peninsula was evacuated by early 1916. The failure of the G. campaign was instrumental in bringing Bulgaria into the war on the side of Germany and Turkey; it delayed the defeat of the Ottoman Empire and perpetuated the difficulties of sending supplies to Russia.   (D. K.)

GAZA. Arab town in southern Palestine, 2 mi. from the Mediterranean coast. Its population—mainly Muslim Arabs with a Christian minority—was 35–40,000 in 1948; it has since grown by the influx of thousands of refugees ▷ (see Gaza Strip ▷).

Known from ancient times as an important outpost on the *Via Maris* ("Way of the Sea") from Egypt to Syria, G. is mentioned in the Bible as one of the five Philistine cities and the place where Samson killed himself and the Philistines. In the Middle Ages there was a Jewish community in the town which declined towards the end of the 18th century. In 1882 Jews again settled in G., but left it after the disturbances of 1929. Under the British Mandate G. was a district capital and the largest exclusively Arab town in Palestine. Taken by Egyptian forces during the Arab-Israel War▷ of 1948, G. and the Gaza Strip▷ remained under Egyptian control under the Armistice Agreement. Here an attempt was made, in 1948, to establish a Palestinian-Arab government (see Palestine Arabs▷). On the Egyptian administration of G. and its occupation by Israel in 1956-7 and in 1967 see Gaza Strip▷. Since 1967 G. has been controlled by Israel. (O.G.)

*GAZA STRIP. The name given to the southern part of the coastal plain of Palestine which was occupied by the invading Egyptian forces in the Arab-Israel War of 1948▷ and administered by the Egyptians, until 1967 by authorization of the Israel-Egyptian Armistice Agreement of 1949. 25 mi. long and 4–9 mi. wide with a total area of c. 135 sq.mi. The population numbered 70,000 at the end of the British Mandate. In the course of the 1948 war it rose by more than 200,000 refugees▷. Housed mainly in camps, only a small number of them could find work in the GS; nevertheless they were not allowed to travel freely to Egypt (which did little to develop its economy), and many thousands remained unemployed, with only UNRWA▷ (the UN Relief and Works Agency) looking after their food, health, and education.

Egypt never formally annexed the GS, despite numerous appeals from the residents. She governed the GS through a Military Governor, under the Egyptian Minister of War. In 1958 an Executive Council was appointed by the governor and a Legislative Council (partly elected by indirect elections) nominated. (On the unsuccessful attempt to establish a Palestinian-Arab government in the GS, 1948—see Palestine Arabs▷.)

Prior to the Sinai-Suez War, the GS served as a base for guerilla-saboteurs (feda'iyin) for raids into Israel. These raids were one of the main factors leading to the Sinai Campaign▷, 1956, in the course of which the GS was conquered by Israel. When Israel was compelled to withdraw, early in 1957, a. UN Emergency Force (UNEF▷) was stationed in the GS. On the eve of the Six Day War terrorist attacks from the GS were renewed, and Egypt concentrated large forces in the GS and the Sinai Peninsula. On 5–6 June 1967 the GS was again taken by

Israel. Israel set up a military government, aided by a civilian administration which handles all economic-civilian affairs. Residents of the GS—whose number is now estimated at 350,000, of whom c. 260,000 are refugees from 1948 and their descendants—are permitted to work both in the West Bank▷ and in Israel, and 8–10,000 breadwinners usually do so (though the guerillas try to prevent them by terrorist methods).

Due to the large concentration of refugees and as a result of political and social frustrations accumulated over two decades, Gaza became a centre of sabotage and terrorist activity. This has lessened lately, i.a. because of economic development and a rising standard of living under the Israeli regime (see also Israel▷, Occupied Territories). (O.G.)

*GEMAYEL (JUMAYYIL), PIERRE (b. 1905). Lebanese politician. Maronite Christian. Leader of the Phalanges▷ Libanaises. A pharmacist, educated in Beirut and France. His political career is linked to the history of the Phalanges, which he founded in 1936. Designed to protect the Maronites▷, safeguard the Christian character of Lebanon and prevent the country's integration in a Pan-Arab scheme of things, this para-military organization in due course became more of a political party, making G. one of the leaders of the pro-Western Christian camp. During the civil war of 1958 he led the resistance to the pro-Nasser Muslim rebels. In September, when the dispute was being settled, he prevented, by threatening a coup, the formation of a government controlled by the rebels, and in October 1958 he was one of four members of the neutral caretaker government formed with the end of the crisis. A Member of Parliament since 1960, he held office in most Lebanese cabinets during the 1960s. As Minister for Public Works, he played a key role in President Fu'ad Shibab's▷ development scheme for under-privileged areas. G. introduced Lebanon's first national insurance legislation (1962) and was responsible for its implementation. The "Triple Alliance" established by G. with Camille Chamoun's▷ "National Liberal Party" and Raymond Edde's▷ "National Bloc", was in the 1960s the political mainstay of Lebanon's pro-Western Christians and the backbone of opposition to Nasserist tendencies. G. was also one of the principal figures to speak out openly against Palestinian guerilla-terrorists using Lebanon as a base for their raids and to oppose their growth as an independent 'establishment' within Lebanon (though he felt compelled to pay lip service to their activities as such). In 1970, standing for the presidency, G. withdrew in favour of a neutral candidate, Suleiman Franjiyeh▷, who was elected with his support. (Y.P.)

GENEZARETH—see Galilee, Sea of▷.

GEORGHADJIS, POLYCARPOS (1930–70). Cypriot politician. Joined EOKA▷ in 1955, and became one of its principal commanders. Minister of the Interior, 1960–68, and also acting Minister of Defence from 1964. Resigned in November 1968, after allegations that he was implicated in an unsuccessful attempt on the life of the Greek Prime Minister. He then became a rival to President Makarios▷, although the "United National Party" he formed in 1969 with G. Clerides▷ was supported by the President. Rumours attributed to him an unsuccessful attempt on the life of President Makarios on 8 Mar. 1970. He was himself murdered a few days later.   (B. G.)

✴GERMANY, GERMAN INTERESTS AND POLICIES IN THE ME. The G. Empire, founded in 1870, joined the Great-Power competition relatively late. Prussia had no interests outside Europe. Bismarck's united G. deliberately misled its neighbours, particularly France, encouraging them to engage in extra-European competition, with a view to diverting France from a *revanche* against continental G. Bismarck avoided acquiring colonies or spheres of influence in the ME or North Africa. He cultivated relations with Austria-Hungary, covered G.'s rear by a pact with Russia, in spite of their rivalry over the Balkans, and avoided any involvement in the "Eastern Question".

Bismarck's removal by Kaiser Wilhelm II brought about the collapse of this system of treaties. With G. launched on imperialist competition, the collision course was set, which led to the First World War. G. now preferred her Austrian alliance to agreement with Russia, and the Reich's interests in the Balkans and Turkey began to proliferate. In the 1890s German companies were building railroads in Anatolia, dreaming of a "Berlin-Baghdad axis" that would lead through Austria and Anatolia to the Persian Gulf, where oil prospecting had just started. Playing up the magnitude of G.'s role as a world power, the Kaiser clamoured for her "place under the sun" beyond European confines. Economic rivalry and an emotional and political contest with Britain for markets and investment opportunities all over the world, including the ME, were now added to G.'s friction with France and with Russia.

The turn of the century saw G., bolstered by a mighty navy, meddling wherever it could outside Europe. The Kaiser visited the ME in 1899, where he stressed G.'s friendship with the Muslim nations. Before his tour he had shown interest in Zionist efforts to obtain a Palestine charter from the Ottoman Porte; he had received a Zionist deputation led by Dr. Herzl▷ and accepted the view that support for the Zionist charter might win a foothold for G. in the Sultan's ME domains. Now, however, the Sultan explained his objections to autonomous Jewish settlement and persuaded the Kaiser that G. support for Herzl's project would be regarded as a departure from economic aid, and as a plot against the Ottoman Empire. Wilhelm, therefore, quickly abandoned the idea of taking the planned Jewish land company under his protection and described the Zionist delegation, which he received again in Jerusalem, as a kind of philanthropic body.

As Britain, France and Russia watched G.'s activities in Turkey, Morocco and other sensitive areas, coupled with the Kaiser's Near East travels, his intervention in the Boer War, and the growth of G. naval strength, they reached agreement on the division of spheres of influence in Africa and Asia (1904–07). The race which developed between their *Entente* and the Triple Alliance formed by Germany, Austria-Hungary and Italy later led to World War I▷. G. suffered two heavy diplomatic defeats over Morocco, first, when the preponderance of France's position in that country was recognized by most of the Powers (1906), and again when the French Protectorate over Morocco was confirmed (1911). The Balkan Wars of 1912–13 increased tension between G. (as Austria's ally) and Russia (as protectress of Serbia), and deepened G.'s influence on the defeated Ottoman army. The Young Turks▷ now in control of the Sultan's empire turned, by necessity as well as inclination, increasingly to G. for aid. At the outbreak of World War I▷ in 1914, G. gave first priority to the European theatre. Yet she did her best to strengthen Turkey with arms and experts. G. generals—von der Goltz, Liman von Sanders and Kress von Kressenstein—directed the Turkish defence effort from Mesopotamia (Kut al-Amara▷) to Gallipoli▷ and also helped to mount the Turkish offensive on the Suez Canal▷, which collapsed short of the waterway (1915). The blockade of the Dardanelles▷, imposed with G. help, cut off Russia from her allies, and hastened her withdrawal from the war in the wake of the Bolshevik Revolution. The contest for American public opinion (1917) that led England to issue the Balfour Declaration▷, induced G. to consider a similar proclamation on behalf of Zionism, but her hands were tied by her support of the Turkish Empire, and England got there first. In Palestine itself, throughout the war years, under Cemal▷ (Jamal) Pasha's ruthless rule, G. military advisers exercised a restraining influence which benefited the Jewish population.

Defeated in the war, rocked by upheavals during the Weimar period (1918–33), G. was no longer a power to compete in any extra-European arena, and the upsurge of Hitler's "Third Reich" (1933–45) made no difference to this at first. Nazi Germany's gradual involvement in the ME and North Africa began in the wake of its pact with Italy (1936) and its support of Mussolini's expansionist policies in Ethiopia and Cyrenaica. Aid to Franco's Spain and the pact with Japan likewise pointed towards increasing involvement. Palestine, as a haven for the Jews of the Reich and after the *anschluss* of Austria and the rape of Czechoslovakia, for the Jews of those countries as well, was of special interest to the Nazis, in view of their intention to expel these Jews and aggravate the Jewish problem till it became critical. They realized that they might be "helping" to build a Jewish homeland—and even permitted the transfer of capital under certain conditions. But they hoped that Jewish immigration to Palestine would add to Britain's difficulties in the ME. Nazi G. also supported the Palestine Arabs against the Jews and Britain, established secret contacts with their nationalist leaders, especially among the Husseini▷ faction, and enlisted their services as agents and spies. G. financial aid and propaganda support was extended to the Arab nationalist movement everywhere. The Nazis acquired many supporters and agents throughout the ME, including Egypt—particularly among intellectuals and young officers. From the end of 1938 onward, the official Nazi line favoured Jewish emigration to any place but Palestine: in practice they went on deporting Jews and pushing them towards Palestine.

In World War II▷, especially after Italy joined hostilities in 1940, Nazi G. became more directly involved in the ME—first in North Africa, where she had to step in militarily to help her Italian ally and, later, in the form of stepped-up support to Arab nationalists in Iraq, Egypt and Syria. In Iraq, the government of Rashid 'Ali al-Kilani▷, which was actually fighting Britain in 1941, appealed for G. military aid, but this failed to arrive in time. The G.-Italian Control Commission which had installed itself in Syria and Lebanon after the fall of France, establishing some air bases, tried to come to Rashid Ali's assistance, but the quick suppression of the Iraqi revolt and the 1941 conquest of the Levant countries by the British and Free French put an end to the immediate Italo-G. threat.

Meanwhile G. had been busily fanning the flames of anti-British sentiment throughout the Muslim and Arab world. The Nazis found active and loyal collaborators in such personages as Rashid 'Ali al-Kilani and the former Mufti of Jerusalem, Hajj Amin al-Husseini▷, both of whom spent most of the war years in Berlin, and many others. The Mufti not only recruited Muslims for the G. army, but also helped with the "Final Solution" of the Jewish problem, playing a direct role in Eichmann's extermination machinery. He also had a hand in espionage activities and some scattered G. parachute drops in the ME. In Egypt, willing agents and collaborators flocked to the G. side from the very start of the war—including a high proportion of army officers—from the Chief-of-Staff, 'Aziz 'Ali al-Masri▷ (dismissed for his connections with the Axis powers, and arrested while attempting to reach their lines) down to such junior officers as Anwar Sadat▷ (since 1970 President of Egypt). Pro-G. sentiment among Arab nationalists in North Africa and the ME—already strong under the influence of G.'s initial victories over the British and French—reached its peak with Rommel's 1942 advance to the gates of Egypt. Hitler's anti-Jewish doctrine was another attraction to some Arab minds (who lost sight of its implications for the Semitic-Arab "race"). The Jews of North Africa escaped the "Final Solution" because G. left Italy and Vichy France in political control. With Rommel's African defeat, the Gs. and Italians lost all their positions in Africa and the ME as well as all hope of Turkey joining the war on the side of the Axis—which G. had wished for and worked to achieve for years.

With G.'s defeat in 1945, and the rise, in 1949, of two separate, rival Gs. from the wreck of the Third Reich, there is no longer a single or unitary G. policy. At the start of the 1950s, West G., invoking the "traditional friendship" with the Muslims and the absence of a G. colonial past in the ME, and leaning on the considerable aid it was getting from the USA, began to cultivate large-scale economic interests in Egypt. The Cold War, the decline of French and British prestige throughout the Arab world, and the US desire to avoid direct involvement wherever possible, combined to lend point and value to this activity. West G. also gave Egypt considerable direct aid and credit guarantees. Similar assistance was extended to Jordan and Syria. Competing with West G. for recognition by the Arab states, West G. likewise offered increasing aid to any Arab country willing to ask for it. During this period, dozens, and sometimes hundreds, of G. experts, including known Nazis escaped from G., worked for Arab military industries, especially in Egypt, where they engaged in aircraft and rocket production, as well as intelligence and propaganda. West G. was unable to prevent their employment.

During the 1950s and '60s, West G. tried to square her ME interests with the special character, above and beyond ordinary policy considerations, accorded to her relations with the Jewish people and Israel.

Israel had put in a claim, forwarded to the two G. governments by the Allied Powers, for compensation and restitution for the G. crimes committed against the Jewish people. East G. has not responded to this day. West G. responded in 1950, both from a desire to improve the G. image in Western, particularly US, public opinion, and from a wish to atone to some extent for the horrors of the Holocaust, and also to strengthen within G. herself a democratic system of government based on law and justice. In 1952 a Restitution Agreement was signed, giving Israel c. $850 million in goods, mostly of G. manufacture. Another agreement signed simultaneously settled the personal claims of Jews (including Israeli citizens) for some, at least, of their despoiled properties and other damages suffered. The sum involved is about $8,000m. (of which $1,500m. go to Israeli residents), and is still being paid. With the signature of the agreements the West G. Chancellor, Konrad Adenauer, proposed the establishment of diplomatic relations with Israel. But the Israeli Premier, David Ben-Gurion▷, felt the time for such a far-reaching normalization had not yet arrived. When Israel was ready for that move, at the start of the 1960s, the Bonn government balked, fearing the Arab states might retaliate by extending recognition to the Pankow regime (and Bonn would have to cut relations with them—bound by its own "Hallstein doctrine" of 1955, to sever relations with any country, other than the Soviet Union, recognizing East G.). To compensate for withholding diplomatic recognition from Israel, Bonn was ready to continue with economic, and later military, aid. The volume of the assistance was expanded following a meeting between Ben-Gurion and Adenauer in New York (1960). At the same time G. went on cultivating her political and trade relations with the Arab countries, a tendency supported by a growing "lobby" of G. industrial and trade interests, as well as by some of the defence establishment out to forestall a possible Soviet penetration of Europe's "underbelly".

G.'s secretive policy towards Israel was upset when a new Chancellor, Ludwig Erhard, took over, and when, on the other hand, the Soviet Union and East G. launched an extraordinary effort to obtain Arab recognition for East G. While the Soviet Union exerted her political influence, East G. showered large-scale economic aid on Egypt, Syria, Iraq and Algeria. As a West G.-Israeli arms deal became known, the Arab states threatened a general rush of recognition for the Pankow government, and President Nasser▷ demonstratively invited the East-G. head of state, Walter Ulbricht, on an official visit to Egypt (1965). In an attempt to induce Nasser to call off the visit, Erhard cancelled the arms deal; but as Nasser did not yield, West G. announced her readiness to establish diplomatic relations with Israel and to substitute economic aid for arms. Erhard and Premier Levi Eshkol▷ exchanged messages, and relations were established the same year (1965). Israel has since received economic aid at the rate of c. DM 140m. a year.

The Arab states retaliated by severing their relations with West G. in 1965—all but Morocco, Tunisia and Libya. By the end of the decade most of them—excluding Jordan, Lebanon, Libya, Sa'udia, Tunisia, Morocco and Yemen—had recognized East G. Only Jordan (1967) and Republican Yemen (1969) had resumed official relations with West G. In the meantime the West-G. government under Chancellor Willi Brandt (since 1969) has virtually abandoned the "Hallstein doctrine" and is ready to maintain diplomatic relations with countries that also recognize East G. Bonn is, in fact, endeavouring to persuade the Arabs to resume normal relations with G., though not at Israel's expense.   (S.A.)

*GEZIRA (Jazira, Arabic: island or peninsula). The part of Sudan situated between the Blue and White Niles as they converge. Principal cotton-growing and development area of Sudan. Two British plantation syndicates received concessions to develop and exploit large areas—reaching 400,000 acres in the 1930s—in the G., through tenants obliged and guided to use modern methods of intensive irrigation and cotton production. Work started in 1925, after the completion of the Sennar Dam on the Blue Nile enabled irrigation to be carried out. In 1950 the concessions expired and the enterprise was taken over by the government. A new barrage on the Blue Nile at Ruseiris (first stage completed in 1966) made it possible to enlarge the area cultivated in G. to over 2m. acres.   (B.G.)

GHAZI b. FEISAL (1912–39). King of Iraq 1933–9. Born in Hijaz, the only son of Sharif (later King) Feisal▷, third son of Sharif (later King) Hussein▷. G. became heir-apparent when his father was installed as King of Iraq in 1921. Educated in Baghdad, with a brief, and unhappy spell in England (Harrow). He mounted the throne in September 1933, upon his father's death. G. married his cousin 'Aliya, daughter of Ali b. Hussein▷. G. was popular for his Arab nationalism and his reputed hate of the British, but carried little political weight. He had no influence on the officer cliques which succeeded one another as the real rulers of Iraq after 1936. G. was killed on 4 Apr. 1939 in a car crash. His son Feisal II▷ succeeded him to the throne.   (U.D.)

GILAN. A province in north-west Iran, near the Caspian Sea. Pop: c. 1.5m. (1966). Main town: Resht. G.'s economy is based on fishing, the cultivation and processing of tea, rice, maize, wheat and fruit. There are also holiday resorts on the Caspian coast. A Persian dialect, Gilaki, is spoken. A separatist rebellion, supported by the USSR, resulted in a short-lived "Persian Socialist Soviet Republic" of G. in 1920. It was crushed by Reza Khan (later Reza Shah▷) in 1921.   (B. G.)

GLUBB (PASHA), SIR JOHN BAGOT (b. 1897). British army officer. Served during World War I in France and Iraq. In the Iraqi civil service, 1926–30. Transferred to the Arab Legion, i.e. the Transjordanian Army, in 1930, G. became its Second-in-Command and, from 1938 until 1956, its Commander-in-Chief, attaining the rank of Lieutenant-General. Although he served under contract (not seconded from the British Army), the nationalists regarded him as a symbol of British imperialist domination of Jordan, and blamed him for the defeat of the Arab Legion in the 1948 Palestine War (especially the loss of Lydda and Ramla) and the Legion's failure to capture West Jerusalem. As the tide of nationalism in Jordan rose, King Hussein▷ dismissed G. in March 1956, and he retired to Britain. His published works include "The Story of the Arab Legion", 1948; "A Soldier with the Arabs" (his memoirs), 1957, as well as books about Arab history and the Arab-Israel conflict ("Peace in the Holy Land", 1971). G. expresses strongly pro-Arab views, especially on the Arab-Israel issue.   (B.G.)

GÖKALP, ZIYA (1875(?)–1924). Turkish poet and writer, the theorist of Turkish nationalism. Born in Diyarbekir (Eastern Anatolia). G. made contact with the Young Turks▷ at an early stage, and after the Revolution of 1908 he was elected to the council of the "Committee of Union and Progress" in Salonika. There, and later in Istanbul where he became Professor of Sociology at the University, G. wrote his main nationalist essays and became the spiritual leader of the Young Turks. After the Proclamation of the Republic, 1923, he was elected to the National Assembly. Prior to the dissolution of the Ottoman Empire, G. favoured the preservation of the supranational state, but called for the revival and promotion of Turkish national culture, the acceptance of European scientific and technical knowledge, and the relegation of Islam to an ethical and personal religion. For some time an advocate of Pan-Turkism▷, later his thoughts grew closer to those of Atatürk▷. His social and cultural ideas paved the way for many reforms during the Republican period.   (D. K.)

∗GOLAN, GOLAN HEIGHTS. Part of the provinces of Quneitra and Fiq in Syria, since the Six Day War▷ of 1967 occupied by Israel. Area 714 sq. mi. Pop. pre-1967: 40,000; since 1967: 5–6000 (1971), mainly Druzes▷ (most Muslims having moved to Syria in 1967). The G. is a volcanic plateau at the southern foot of Mount Hermon. It was one of Syria's economically most backward regions. After the Arab-Israel War of 1948 the GH were turned by the Syrians into a military fortress. Commanding the Lake of Galilee, the Hula area and the fertile northern Jordan Valley, they were often used for artillery shelling of Israeli settlements and traffic, the Hula Drainage Project and Israel's water works (the "National Water Carrier"). In the Six Day War, the GH were taken by Israeli forces after intense fighting. Under Israel's military administration, a number of military-agricultural settlements have been set up.   (Y. K.)

∗GOLDMANN, DR. NAHUM. Zionist politician. Born 1894 in Poland. President of the World Zionist Organization 1956–69. Chairman (since 1936) and President (since 1953) of the World Jewish Congress▷. Publisher of the Encyclopaedia Judaica in Berlin 1923–33. Jewish Agency▷ representative with the League of Nations in Geneva 1934–40. Member of the Executive of the World Zionist Organization and the Jewish Agency since 1934. Played a major role in the Restitution Agreement with West Germany▷. Though he does not live permanently in Israel and is a controversial figure there, G. has lately expressed considerable criticism of Israel's leaders and policies, advocating the neutralization of Israel and greater flexibility towards the Soviet Union and the Arabs. In 1969 the Israel government refused to endorse his proposal to meet President Nasser▷ (it has remained in doubt whether Nasser was really prepared to meet him).
                    (A. W.)

GORDON, AHARON DAVID (1856–1922). Spiritual leader and philosopher of Socialist Zionism, and in particular of the Hapo'el Hatza'ir party. Born in Russia, G. came to Palestine in 1909. He put stress on "self-perfection", and worked as a farm-labourer, later joining Kibbutz Degania. He idealized physical work, especially farming, co-operation and mutual aid, as the base of Jewish national renaissance and a major means for improving the individual. At the centre stands man, who reveals himself in the community. The perfect community would be "collective man", "the nation of man". He infused his nationalism with a cosmic sense by merging the nature spirit of the homeland with the spirit of the nation. Barriers between man and the external world were to be removed. (E. A.)

GREATER SYRIA (*Suriya al-Kubra*). From October 1918 until July 1920 Damascus was under semi-independent Arab rule, headed by the Amir Feisal▷ b. Hussein. After Feisal was ousted by the French, his brother 'Abdullah▷ attempted to march on Syria from Hijaz▷ and to reconquer it. The British, who wished to avoid trouble with the French, suggested to 'Abdullah that he stop in Transjordan, where they would set him up as Amir. 'Abdullah agreed, but continued to dream of the renewal of Hashemite▷ rule in a GS. As long as the French remained, his plans had little hope of realization; and though the French suspected that the GS notion and similar plans were the result of British plots to eject them from the area, official British support was always partial and reserved.

During World War II▷, when it was becoming clear the French would not return to the area, 'Abdullah made public overtures to the Syrians concerning GS. He received negative replies from many leading people. They claimed that while his country was still under a British Mandate, Syria was on the way to independence. However, when in Mar. 1946 a new treaty with Britain granted independence to Jordan (which became a kingdom), 'Abdullah thought the major obstacle to the realization of his plans had been removed. At the opening session of Parliament in Nov. 1946, he declared his intention to work towards the union of "the natural GS". He proposed uniting Syria, Lebanon and Palestine with his country under his crown. To the Jews of Palestine he proposed an autonomous status in this united country.

'Abdullah's plan had very few avowed supporters. Among them were a faction of Aleppo politicians from the "People's Party" and a small group of Damascene politicians (Hassan al-Hakim and Munir al-'Ajlani, and others who secretly supported the scheme). The GS plan was attacked from all sides. Lebanon categorically refused to become part of a Muslim state. The ruling "National Bloc" faction in independent Syria refused to turn their country into a district of a country whose capital would be in 'Amman; the memory of Feisal's rule in Damascus was dearer and more glorious to the Hashemites than to the political élite of Damascus. The Sa'udis opposed any plan which might strengthen the Hashemites, their past enemies, who most probably had not given up the idea of reconquering Hijaz. The Egyptians also opposed a plan which might strengthen the Hashemite bloc in the Arab world. Even Arab nationalist extremists, advocating an immediate Arab unity, opposed 'Abdullah's plan, for they despised 'Abdullah since 1941, when he assisted the repression of the revolt of Rashid 'Ali al-Kilani▷ in Iraq. The Hashemites of Iraq and the politicians around them nursed plans of a federation under their own leadership and gave 'Abdullah little support. The Arab League▷ strongly opposed GS. Even Britain, 'Abdullah's ally and main support, was not enthusiastic, since she feared both the reaction of the French and the hostility of the other Arab nations, particularly Egypt. The murder of 'Abdullah in 1951 terminated his plan.

Others who advocated GS, e.g. the "Syrian Nationalist Party"▷, envisaged a non-Hashemite GS. although certain connections were made in the 1940s and '50s. This faction was in any case without power or influence. The GS plan has not been resurrected.   (Y. P.)

GREEK CATHOLICS. Former Greek Orthodox Christians (also called Melkites—from *Melk*, Emperor, in Syrian) mainly of the patriarchates of Antioch, Jerusalem and Alexandria, who sought communion with Rome through the Uniate▷. They follow the Byzantine rite and their liturgical language is Arabic. In the ME, they number about 270,000: 120,000 in Lebanon, 70,000 in Syria, 30,000 in Egypt, 25,000 in Israel, 15,000 in Jordan, and a few thousand in other ME countries. There is also a large diaspora in the two Americas. The Church is headed by the "Patriarch of Antioch and the whole ME, Alexandria and Jerusalem", whose seat is in Damascus. The present incumbent, Patriarch Maximos V Hakim, was formerly Archbishop in Israel.

A tendency to leave the Greek Orthodox and join the Catholic Church began in Syria in the 17th century. Among its causes were the proximity of the Catholic Maronites▷ in Lebanon, and French intervention in favour of the Christian subjects of the Sultan. In 1725, the Holy See appointed the first Greek Catholic Patriarch (Serephim Tannas, who took the name of Cyril VI), but owing to persecution by the official, Ottoman-backed Greek Orthodox Church, he was forced to leave. It was only in 1837 that the Patriarch (Maximos III Masloum) was officially recognized as head of an independent Greek Catholic Millet▷ and took up residence in Damascus. In 1882, a Greek Catholic Seminary was opened by the White Fathers at St. Anne's Church in Jerusalem, which thereafter produced most of the educated priests of the Greek Catholic Church. (Following the reunification of Jerusalem in 1967 it was transferred to Harissa, in Lebanon.)

(Sh. C.)

GREEK ORTHODOX. The origin of the Greek Orthodox of the ME can be traced back to the official Church of the early Christian Hellenistic and Byzantine period—also known as *Melkite*, from *Melk* (Syrian word for Emperor), in contrast with those churches embracing the schismatic doctrines of the Nestorians▷ and the Monophysites▷. (The term *Melkite* is, however, mainly used for the Greek Catholic▷ Church).

Since ancient times, the G.O. Church in the ME has comprised four autocephalous entities: the patriarchates of Constantinople, Alexandria, Antioch and Jerusalem. The Patriarch of Constantinople, who is considered *primus inter pares*, was accorded a special status under the Ottoman Empire. He was considered not only the spiritual leader of Orthodoxy, but, at least during the early centuries of Ottoman rule, as the head of all the Christian inhabitants of the realm, other than the Armenians▷.

Until the end of the 19th century, the senior clergy of the four patriarchates were priests of Greek origin, even though the majority of the faithful in the patriarchates of Antioch, Jerusalem and to a lesser degree Alexandria, were Arabs. Since 1899, the hierarchy of the Patriarchate of Antioch, with its centre in Damascus, has been composed exclusively of Syrian and Lebanese Arab clergy. That Patriarchate now numbers about 450,000 G.O. faithful, all of whom are Arabic-speaking. During the past hundred years, it has lost many adherents to the Greek Catholic Church as a result of Catholic missionary activities. In 1969–70 a crisis threatened to split the Patriarchate into Lebanese and Syrian sections.

The Patriarchate of Constantinople, whose members are of Greek origin, was greatly reduced by the exchange of population between Greece and Turkey in 1920–23. The G.O. population of Turkey is now 30,000, concentrated mainly in Istanbul. A split is threatened by a separatist movement which advocates an independent Turkish Orthodox Church.

In the Patriarchate of Jerusalem, the Greek character of the senior hierarchy has been maintained, although the Arab community, supported by the lower clergy, has been struggling to abolish or at least reduce it. There are 60,000 faithful, mostly Arabs, in Israel and Jordan.

Following the restrictive measures of the Egyptian government towards foreigners many Orthodox of Greek origin emigrated, thus reducing the Patriarchate of Alexandria to about 25,000.

In contrast to the decline of Orthodoxy in the four patriarchates, the autocephalous Church of Cyprus▷, with its 450,000 adherents, prospers under Archbishop Makarios▷, who is also the Head of the State. (Sh. C.)

GREEKS IN THE ME. G. have been migrating to other Mediterranean countries since the dawn of history. At present the most important G. concentrations in the ME are in Cyprus, Egypt and Turkey.

Modern Greek migration to Egypt took place during the 19th century. The G. in Egypt earned their livelihood mainly from commerce, industry, banking, craftsmanship and clerical jobs, and contributed to the development of their host country. Before World War II they numbered about 120–150,000, mainly in Alexandria—also the seat of a G. Orthodox Patriarchate—and Cairo. They retained their G. nationality and language, and kept close ties with Greece. G. foreign policy—e.g. on the Arab-Israel conflict—has been strongly influenced by the existence of the G. colony in Egypt. After the *coup d'état* of July 1952 the G. community in Egypt declined, owing to the economic and social policy of the new regime. Though not officially directed against minorities, the take-over of foreign enterprises, beginning in 1956–7, and the expropriation of most of the private sector of the urban economy, since 1961, undermined the economic basis of the G. community. Its members started to emigrate to Greece and elsewhere, and by 1970 the community had shrunk to about 15,000.

After the Ottoman conquest of Asia Minor and Constantinople, in the 14th–15th century, the G. population stayed and enjoyed considerable religious freedom. G. were prominent in administration and economic life. In 1908 the new regime of the Young Turks▷ embarked on a policy of Turkification, which caused the G. community to decline. The First Balkan War▷, 1912–13, in which Greece and Turkey were on opposing sides, added suspicion of and hostility towards the local G., as did Greece's entry into World War I on the Allied side in 1917. On the eve of World War I▷ the G. in the Ottoman Empire numbered about 3m. (*c.* 2m. in Asia Minor and *c.* 1 m. in Constantinople and Eastern Thrace); large parts of the Western coastlands of Asia Minor were

Greek-Orthodox Patriarch Benediktus I (with T. Kollek, Mayor of Jerusalem, left)

dominated by them (such as the town and port of Smyrna or Izmir▷). G. attempts to conquer and annex Asia Minor and the G.-Turkish War of 1919–22, compelled many G. to leave Turkey. This exodus culminated after the defeat of the G. Army in the autumn of 1922. The victorious Turks destroyed many G. towns, such as Izmir. During the Peace Conference of Lausanne▷, Greece and Turkey reached an agreement, in January 1923, under which all G. still living in Turkey, except those resident in Istanbul (Constantinople) prior to 1918, were to be repatriated to Greece; Turks living in Greece, except in Western Thrace, were also compelled to leave. (The seat of the Oecumenical Greek Orthodox Patriarchate was to remain in Constantinople.) The exchange of populations, inasmuch as it had not *de facto* taken place before the agreement, was carried out between 1923 and 1926, and continued on a smaller scale until 1936. About 1.26m. G. left Turkey, while Turkey received 400,000 Turks from Greece.

The situation of the G. who remained in Turkey, mainly in Istanbul, deteriorated in the 1950s owing to the tension between Greece and Turkey caused by the Cyprus▷ problem. In September 1955, anti-G. riots erupted in Istanbul, and property belonging to G. (and other minorities) was damaged and plundered. A new G. exodus from Turkey started, and today the G. population is estimated at about 35,000 compared with 85,000 in 1955.

For the G. in Cyprus—see Cyprus▷.

There are small G. communities in other ME countries, e.g. Libya (*c.* 800) and Sudan (*c.* 300).
(B. G.-Y. S.)

defeated the Greeks and by the middle of September they had been driven out of Anatolia.

By the Treaty of Lausanne▷, Greece gave up all claims to T. territory, and in a special agreement the two countries arranged to exchange populations (excluding the Greeks in Istanbul and the Turks of Western Thrace). The exchange affected, together with war-time refugees, *c.* 1.3m. Greeks and 400,000 Turks. When it was completed, G.-T. relations improved, and the two countries signed a Treaty of Friendship, 1930; they both joined alliances such as the Balkan Pacts▷, 1934 and 1954, and NATO▷, 1951–2. But the Cyprus question has caused a renewed deterioration in G.-T. relations in recent years (see Turkey▷, Political history; Cyprus▷).   (D. K.)

General George Grivas (left)

GREEK-TURKISH RELATIONS.

Relations between the Ottoman Empire▷ and Greece, its first Balkan province to gain independence, 1829, remained cool during the 19th and the early 20th centuries, and, in 1897, erupted into war over Crete. Greece's dreams of re-establishing her rule over Constantinople▷ and Western Anatolia played a significant role in her entry into World War I▷, in June 1917, against the Central Powers and the Ottoman Empire. After the war, in May 1919, G. forces landed in Izmir▷—with the blessing of the Western Powers. This invasion stiffened T. nationalist resistance to allied plans for the dismemberment of Turkey. Full-scale war between Greece and the T. nationalists broke out in 1920, after the terms of the Treaty of Sèvres▷ became known and Greece was assigned the task of breaking nationalist power in Anatolia. In summer 1920, Greece launched an offensive in Thrace and Anatolia, but the Turks were able, after serious reverses, to check its advance on the Sakarya River in September. A T. counter-offensive, in Aug. 1922,

*GRIVAS, GEORGE, LT.-GEN.** (b. 1898). Cypriot-born Greek officer. Career officer in the Greek Army. Retired in 1945 with the rank of colonel. Invited to Cyprus in 1951 by Archbishop Makarios▷ to organize a "Pan-Cyprian National Youth Organisation". Returned to Greece but arrived in Cyprus clandestinely in 1954 to head EOKA▷, the underground nationalist organization, under the assumed name of Dighenis (a legendary mediaeval Greek hero). Left Cyprus, March 1959, after the signature of the Zurich and London agreements. Promoted to Lieutenant-General by special law of the Greek Parliament. After unsuccessfully attempting to enter political life in Greece, he returned to Cyprus in 1964 and commanded the Greek forces stationed there as well as the Cypriot National Guard. Recalled to Greece in November 1967. Being a staunch supporter of *Enosis*▷, union with Greece, his relations with President Makarios have deteriorated since the latter abandoned *Enosis* in favour of independence.
(B. G.)

GUERILLA ORGANIZATIONS—See Palestine Arab Guerilla Organizations▷.

GÜRSEL, CEMAL (1895–1966). Fourth President of the Turkish Republic 1960–6. Born in Erzurum. Educated as a professional officer, G. fought in Gallipoli▷ and Palestine during World War I. Appointed Commander of the Land Forces in 1957, he resigned in May 1960 in protest against the conduct of the Democratic Party government. After the army coup that same month he was chosen by the rebel officers to head the Committee of National Unity and to serve as President, Prime Minister and Minister of Defence. He successfully led the country to a return to parliamentary rule, ridding the Committee of its more radical officers. In Oct. 1961, he was elected President of the Republic and held office until incapacitated by a stroke in Mar. 1966.   (D.K.)

General Cemal Gürsel

H

*HABASH, DR. GEORGE (b. 1925). Palestinian political and guerilla leader. Born in Lod (Lydda). Greek-Orthodox Christian. Graduate in medicine of the American University of Beirut. Resident in 'Amman, Jordan, since the early 1950s, H. was one

Dr. George Habash (with female guerilla)

of the founders of the Arab Nationalist Movement▷ (ANM, Arabic: *Harakat al-Qawmiyin al-'Arab*), an extreme nationalist, Pan-Arab group, in opposition to the established Arab states and their governments, and of increasingly leftist-Maoist tendencies. In December 1969, he became the leader of the Popular Front for the Liberation of Palestine▷ (PFLP—an extremist guerilla and sabotage group that grew out of the ANM and remained connected with it). His PFLP is a bitter rival to the leaders in the mainstream of Palestinian political and guerilla activity, such as 'Arafat▷, and co-operates only partially and reluctantly in their joint roof organization.

For doctrinal and factional reasons, H. was also involved in a violent clash with the leftist-revolutionary *Ba'th*▷ government of Syria; he bitterly opposed Egypt's President Nasser, who had been his first sponsor. For some time he seems to have drawn support mainly from Iraq. In 1970 his PFLP became known for its daring and brutal hijacking of foreign planes, the passengers of which were held as hostages. H. and the PFLP are also held responsible for triggering the bloody clashes between guerillas and government troops that erupted in Jordan in the summer of 1970.   (E.Y.-Y.S.)

HABBANIYA. Town in Iraq in the province of Ramadi, on the Euphrates, west of Baghdad. From 1938 to 1955, H. was the main British air base in Iraq. It was under siege by the Iraqi Army in April 1941, during Rashid 'Ali's▷ last government, but held out. After 1955, it remained at Britain's disposal, under the Baghdad Pact▷, until 1959, when Iraq, under Qassem, repudiated the Pact. The last British personnel were evacuated in May 1959. (For Lake H. see Euphrates▷.)   (U.D.)

*HADHRAMAUT. A region in the southern part of the Arabian peninsula named after Wadi H., a stream that flows southeastward along 248 mi. into the Indian Ocean and serves as agricultural centre and main trade route for the entire region. H. includes four principalities: Wahidi in the west, Qu'aiti and Kathiri in the centre and Mahrah in the east, all in the formerly British "Eastern Protectorate" of Aden▷. H.'s main city is Mukalla, on the coast of the Indian Ocean.

In the 1930s Ibn Sa'ud laid claim to H. or parts of it, and the British endeavoured to strengthen their hold. Between 1936 and 1939, they signed truce and protectorate treaties with over 1,300 tribal chiefs and put an end to inter-tribal warfare (Harold Ingrams, who directed these operations, wrote several books about the area). In 1940, the British formed from amongst the H. tribesmen a military force of about 1,000–1,500 men, the Hadrami Bedouin Legion, mainly for policing the area.

When the Federation of South Arabia▷ was formed, Wahidi was the only eastern protectorate principality to join it (1962). In Sep.-Oct. 1967, all the H. principalities were taken over by the NLF▷, and integrated into the People's Republic of Southern Yemen▷; the princes were deposed. H. was divided among several districts in order to erase the identities of the separate principalities.

There was a small number of Jews in H., of whom very little is known. With the emigration of the Jews of Yemen to Israel, the H. Jewish community seems to have been liquidated, but possibly isolated groups still exist. (Y.A.O.)

*HAFEZ, AMIN. Syrian officer and politician. Born in Damascus in 1911. Veteran member of the Ba'th▷ party. After the Ba'th coup of 8 Mar. 1963, H. was recalled from his post of military attaché in Argentina to become Deputy Prime Minister and Minister of the Interior in the Bitar▷ cabinet. Rose to prominence in the factional struggle within the Ba'th, and over the period 1963–5 was appointed Head of the Revolutionary Council, Military Governor, Commander-in-Chief and Defence Minister, Prime Minister (twice) and President. At first, H. held extremist views but gradually tended to the moderate "civilian" faction of 'Aflaq▷ and Bitar. In the coup of 23 Feb. 1966 H. was deposed by the extremist "military faction" of Jadid▷, wounded and imprisoned. After the Six Day War▷, H. was released and went to Lebanon. Since then he has been active, in exile, in the former "national" leadership of the Ba'th, i.e. the 'Aflaq-Bitar faction, connected with the Iraqi regime and opposed to the present regime in Syria. (A.L.-O.T.)

HAGANA (Hebrew: Defence). Jewish underground organization established in 1920—upon a resolution passed at the *Ahduth Ha'avodah* ("Labour Unity") party convention—"to defend Jewish life, property and honour". Its establishment followed Arab riots (particularly in the Jewish quarter of Jerusalem) and the British failure to defend the Jews there, which was compounded by severe measures taken against the Jewish Legion (see World War I▷), intervening under its commander, Vladimir Jabotinsky.

Organized Jewish self-defence began early in the 20th century with the founding of *Hashomer* ("The Watchman") to defend settlers against hostile Arabs, whose hope of plunder was later reinforced by awakening Arab nationalism.

The H. was closely linked with the *Histadrut*▷. In 1931 seceding members of the H. founded a rival body, later known as the *Irgun (T)zeva'i Le'umi*▷ (IZL, "National Military Organization"). The two organizations merged in 1937, under the authority of the Jewish national institutions. However, Zionist-Revisionist▷ members of IZL maintained their separate organization (from which the Stern Group▷ —"Fighters for the Freedom of Israel"—seceded). During the Arab riots of the 1930s, the H. and the IZL disagreed on methods of defence. The H. followed a policy of restraint and opposed retaliation against the bases of Arab guerilla bands, in order to avoid harming innocent people and to safeguard prospects of agreement with the Arabs; the IZL advocated retaliation. There was later a similar disagreement when the H. argued that the Jews of Palestine could not defeat the British Empire by force of arms, which the IZL advocated. In addition, the H. strongly opposed individual acts of terrorism carried out by the IZL and the Stern Group

Each Jewish settlement was responsible for its own defence under the general supervision of the H. High Command. However, after the massacre of the Jews of Hebron in 1929, its organization was more centralized. It organized smuggling and storing of arms; later, it manufactured weapons. During the 1936–39 disturbances, the emphasis was on defence of settlements. Members of the H. joined the super-numerary Jewish police set up by the government. Gradually, a more active policy was adopted, and Arab guerillas were attacked in their own bases ("Field Units", 1937; "Special Night Squads" under Wingate▷, 1938).

In World War II H. members, acting on its orders, joined the British Army. Meanwhile the *Palmah*▷— permanently mobilized commando units—was formed and assisted in operations against Vichy-French Syria and Lebanon. Several H. members parachuted behind enemy lines in Europe, on various operations and also to help the Jews in Occupied Europe. At the end of the war, H. members serving in the British Army in Europe smuggled Jews to the coast. From there the *Palmah* transported them to Palestine, running the gauntlet of the British blockade of Jewish immigrants (see Palestine▷; White Papers▷). In 1946–8, when the struggle in Palestine intensified, the H., despite repressive British measures, became more active in the armed resistance (mainly smuggling in Jews and related activities), sometimes in co-operation with the IZL and the Stern Group. This struggle was one of the factors that led to the establishment of Israel in 1948.

By the end of 1947, the H. comprised the following units:—a. a permanent cadre of about 400 men; b. about 2,000 supernumerary police; c. three *Palmah* battalions (11 armed companies, four reserve companies, air and naval and special reconnaissance units) of about 3,000 men; d. about 10,000 men in the infantry (*Hish*) between the ages of 18 and 25, who underwent intensive week-end training; e. reserve units of guards (*Him*) comprising men aged over 25; f. youth brigades (*Gadna'*) whose members, aged 15–18, had undergone pre-military training. The H. formed the nucleus of the armed forces which fought during the initial stages of the Arab-Israel War▷ of 1948 and from it envolved the Israeli Defence Forces. It was dissolved in 1948 upon the establishment of independent Israel. (E.L.)

HAIFA. Main port of Israel, handling 71.8% of all imports and 36.7% of all exports (1969 excl. oil in bulk). Pop: 217,000 (1970), including 7,000 Arabs; 100,000 more live in the suburbs of the conurbation.

General view of Haifa

Dag Hammarskjöld (with Golda Meir)

Industrial centre (oil refinery, cement, chemicals, glass, iron foundries, textiles). H. started growing only at the beginning of the 20th century with the construction of the narrow gauge railway to the Hauran and Damascus (1905) and particularly the normal gauge one along the coastal plain and to the Suez Canal (completed at the end of World War I; linked northwards to Beirut in 1941). H.'s rapid development began in the 1920s and '30s, with Jewish settlement and the opening (1932) of the modern port. H. is the terminus of an oil pipeline from Iraq (1934), blocked and dismantled by Iraq in 1948.

During the Arab-Israel War of 1948 agreement to avoid a civil war in the town was reached between Jewish and Arab leaders; but the Arab signatories failed to obtain the approval of their high command, then in Cairo and Damascus, and returned instead with a recommendation (complied with) to evacuate. (Y.K.)

HAMMARSKJÖLD, DAG (1905–61). Swedish economist and administrator. Secretary-General of the UN▷ from 1953 until his accidental death in the Congo in September 1961. In the ME, he was particularly involved in the establishment of the UN Emergency Force (UNEF) designed to replace British, French and Israeli forces occupying Egyptian territory after the Suez War▷ and the Sinai Campaign▷ of 1956. The arrangements H. made for UNEF did not contain clear-cut provisions as to who would be competent to demand or order its withdrawal. A memorandum drafted by H. limited Egypt's freedom in this respect; but it was intended for the files and does not seem to have acquired official status or committed Egypt. (Sh.H.-Y.S.)

HANTCHAK. A political party which evolved between the world wars among the Armenians▷ dispersed in ME countries, particularly in Lebanon and Syria. Its political ideology changes. Lately it is considered leftist and pro-Communist—as opposed to the rival *Tashnaq*▷ party. Its main concern is the welfare of the Armenian community.   (Y. S.)

HAPO'EL HAMIZRAHI—see National Religious Party▷.

HASA, AL-. The eastern region of Sa'udi Arabia, along the Persian Gulf. Area: 41,167m. Pop.: about 300,000—among them a substantial minority (about 12% of Isma'ili▷ Shi'ites▷. Al-H. is known for its many oases, among them the great oasis at Hofuf, which was the centre for the export of dates. Agricultural development projects have been introduced in the oases. Since World War II H. has become Sa'udi Arabia's centre of oil production. Along the coast modern oil cities have sprung up—Dhahran (administrative centre of the "Aramco" oil company), Ras Tanura (refineries and oil port), Dammam (oil port and railhead to Riyadh).   (Y.K.)

HASBANI (Hebrew name: *Senir*). The northern source of the Jordan▷ River; originates in springs near the Lebanese town of Hasbaya about 12 mi. north of the Israeli border. The springs produce about 120m. cubic metres of water a year, and the rains add flash floods to about the same amount. The Arab plan of 1964–7 for the diversion of the Jordan sources called for the diversion of the H. waters, partly through a tunnel to the Litani▷ River in Lebanon and partly in an open canal eastward to the Baniyas▷ (thence, together with Baniyas waters, towards the Yarmuk▷). See Jordan▷.   (Y.K.)

HASHEM, IBRAHIM (c. 1884–1958). Jordanian politician. Born in Nablus, Palestine, graduate of the Istanbul Law School, 1906. Held several positions in the Ottoman civil service (Attorney-General in Beirut, Damascus and Jaffa, President, Court of Appeal, Damascus). In 1919–20, H. was active in the Arab nationalist movement under Amir Feisal▷ in Damascus. After Feisal's expulsion, H. returned to Palestine and engaged in private law practice. In 1922 he was called by Amir 'Abdullah▷ to Transjordan, and was appointed Minister of Justice, a position he filled until Nov. 1933, when he became Chief Minister, he resigned in Sept. 1938, because of friction with the British Resident, Colonel Cox. In May 1945, he was re-appointed Chief Minister, and went with 'Abdullah to Britain in 1946 to negotiate fuller independence for Transjordan. When the country became independent in May 1946, his title changed to that of Prime Minister. H. resigned in Feb. 1947, after the conclusion of the Jordan-Turkey

Pact of Friendship, apparently because he disagreed with that Pact's implied support of Turkey's possession of Hatay▷ (the formerly Syrian district of Alexandretta▷). He headed caretaker governments from Dec. 1955 to Jan. 1956 (after the resignation of the Majali▷ cabinet over the issue of Jordan's adherence to the Baghdad Pact▷), and again from July to Oct. 1956 (to prepare for general elections).

Considered a staunch pro-Hashemite▷ and supporter of the West, H. was again appointed Prime Minister in Apr. 1957, after King Hussein▷ dismissed the leftist Premier Suleiman Nabulsi▷ and purged the army of pro-Egyptian elements. In May 1958 he was nominated Deputy Premier of the Iraqi-Jordanian Arab Federation▷. He was assassinated on 14 July 1958, in Baghdad, during the *coup d'état* which toppled the Hashemite regime in Iraq.   (B.G.)

HASHEMI, AL-, TAHA (1888–1961). Iraqi officer and politician, brother of Yassin Hashemi▷. Born in Baghdad. Educated at the Istanbul Staff College, H. served as an officer in the Ottoman Army, 1809–18. He participated in the Arab nationalist societies, but did not desert, during World War I, to Sharif Hussein's▷ Arab rebel forces. During Amir Feisal's▷ rule in Syria (1919–20), he was Director of Defence. After Feisal's fall, H. went to Iraq and joined the army there, retiring in 1926 with the rank of Colonel. After service in various civilian posts, he returned to the army, in 1929, became Chief of General Staff, 1929–1936, promoted to Lt.-General in 1936. During Bakr Sidqi's▷ *coup d'état* (Oct. 1936) he was in Turkey, where he remained until after the restoration of the old regime in 1937. In Nov. 1937, H. was co-founder and president of the "Society for the Defence of Palestine" in Baghdad. He also began intriguing with the group of pro-German officers that later became known as the "Golden Square". Under the governments they installed, he was Minister of Defence and the Interior, 1938–40, Minister of Defence 1940–1. As Prime Minister, Feb.-Apr. 1941, he prepared the way for Rashid 'Ali's▷ return to power by a semi-coup (May 1941). When the British toppled Rashid 'Ali's regime and restored the Hashemite King and Regent, H. fled to Turkey where he stayed till 1946. In autumn 1947 he was mentioned as Commander-in-Chief of the Arab forces preparing to invade Palestine, but the project was dropped (probably because he was not *persona grata* with the regime in Iraq); he served, however, in 1948, as military adviser to the all-Arab Committee co-ordinating the Palestine struggle. In 1951–3 H. was active in attempts to form a right-wing opposition National Front. He was Vice-Chairman of the Development Board, 1953–8. After the July 1958 coup his appointment was not renewed and he stayed out of public life. H. published several books on geography and military subjects. (B.G.)

HASHEMI, AL-, YASSIN (1884–1937). Iraqi politician. H. was active in the clandestine Arab nationalist societies, 1911–3, but during World War I he remained loyal to the Ottoman Army, in which he served as a Colonel. After Iraq became independent, he played an active part in her political life, serving as Minister of Finance several times and as Prime Minister in 1924. He was one of the leaders of the right-wing nationalist party of National Brotherhood (*Hizb al-Ikha' al-Watani*, active 1931–5), which opposed the Anglo-Iraqi Treaty of 1930. In 1935–6 he again became Premier. His government was overthrown by a group of army officers under Bakr Sidqi▷ and he was banished to Damascus, where he died in 1937. (B.G.)

*HASHEMITES, HASHEMITE DYNASTY, HOUSE OF HASHEM. According to Muslim tradition, Banu Hashem are the family, or clan, of the Qureish tribe from whom the Prophet Muhammad is descended. In the 20th century, the name H. has come to refer to the family of the Sharifs of Mecca, from whom came the kings of Hijaz, Iraq and Jordan. The H. are descendants of the ancient H. of H. and the Prophet Muhammad, through his daughter Fatima and his son-in-law 'Ali and their son al-Hassan. In the H. family, the honorary title, "Sharif of Mecca", has been handed down from father to son.

The Sharif Hussein▷ b. 'Ali (1852–1931) was appointed Amir of Mecca in 1908; in 1916, after an exchange of messages with Sir Henry McMahon▷, the British High Commissioner in Egypt, he proclaimed the Arab Revolt▷, and declared himself King of Hijaz▷. In 1924, he took steps to declare himself Caliph▷, but was compelled to resign the same year, in order to save his throne for his dynasty (he died in exile). His son 'Ali (1879–1935) succeeded to his throne, but after less than a year he was driven out by King Ibn Sa'ud▷ ('Ali died in exile, in Baghdad). His two brothers, the second and third sons of Hussein, founded dynasties. Feisal▷ (1885–1933), Hussein's third son, reigned for a short time in Damascus, 1919–20, and was driven out by the French; in 1921 he was proclaimed King of Iraq by the British and reigned there until his death. His son, Ghazi▷ (1912–39), succeeded him. Killed in an accident, after six years of rule, he left a young son, Feisal II▷ (1935–58), whose uncle 'Abd-ul-Ilah▷ b. 'Ali (1921–58) acted as regent. When Feisal was crowned in 1953, 'Abd-ul-Ilah became crown prince. With their assassination in

the July 1958 coup in Baghdad, the Baghdad branch of the H. house came to an end.

The second son of Hussein b. 'Ali, 'Abdullah▷ (1882–1951), was made Amir of Transjordan, which was established by the British for him in 1921; in 1946 he took the title of King. In 1948, he changed the name of Transjordan to "The Hashemite Kingdom of Jordan" and annexed the Arab part of Palestine (the "West Bank"). He was assassinated in Jerusalem in 1951, at the entrance to the al-Aqsa Mosque. His son, Talal▷ (b. 1909), succeeded him, but was deposed in 1952, when found to be mentally ill; he has been in an Istanbul hospital ever since. Talal's son Hussein▷ (b. 1935) has reigned in Jordan since 1953. The crown prince is his younger brother Hassan (b. 1948) rather than his brother Muhammad (b. 1945). (Hussein's own sons are apparently not considered heirs to the throne, because they are sons of an Englishwoman, although she has become a Muslim.)

The leadership of the H. dynasty stood at the cradle of Arab independence in the Fertile Crescent▷, after World War I▷. When their plans to found a single kingdom, or a federation of kingdoms, failed, they found themselves in power in two countries in the region: Iraq and Jordan. The idea of reviving the original scheme and establishing a H. Federation, in other words, to bring Syria under their domination, continued to animate some of them. 'Abdullah was the chief protagonist of this idea (see Arab Federation▷, Greater Syria▷, Fertile Crescent▷); there was always some doubt about the degree of support the Iraqi branch of the H. dynasty afforded the scheme—and similar doubts as to British support. Another aim of the H. was to return and rule in Hijaz; this idea, although sometimes broached, never had serious prospects, and it was finally shelved in the late 1940s and the '50s, when a H.-Sa'udi *rapprochement* took place. The expansionist plans of the H. played a prominent part in inter-Arab policies and always met strong opposition from Egypt, Sa'udia and Syria. After 'Abdullah was assassinated in 1951, and H. rule over Iraq ended with the last of the Baghdad dynasty murdered in the 1958 revolution, these plans were abandoned.

The H. family has many branches and, until 1958. many of its members held state positions in Iraq (e.g. the Sharif Sharaf who was appointed regent instead of 'Abd-ul-Ilah in 1941 by the rebels under Rashid 'Ali al-Kilani▷). Many still hold positions in Jordan, especially in the army (e.g., the Sharif Hussein b. Nasser, who was Prime Minister in 1963–4 and 1967, and the Sharif Nasser b. Jamil Commander-in-Chief in 1969–70 whose dismissal was demanded and obtained by the Palestinian guerillas). Only the

THE HASHEMITE DYNASTY

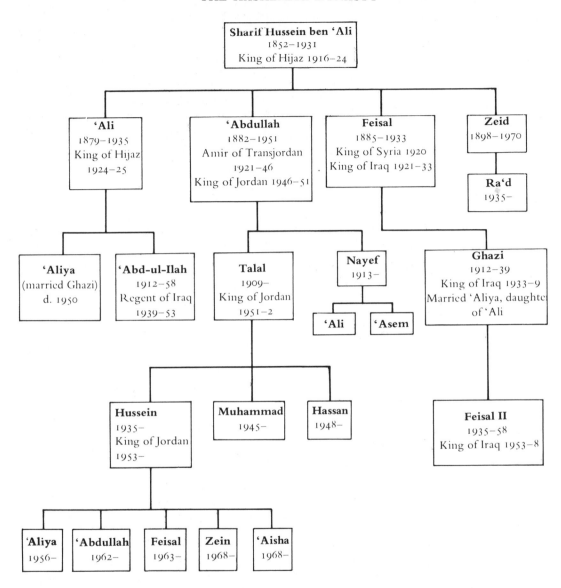

most prominent members of the main branch are mentioned here and in the table above.   (Y.S.)

HASSUNA, 'ABD-UL-KHALEQ. Born in Cairo, 1898. Egyptian politician. Son of a leading Muslim religious scholar, H. studied law at Cairo and Cambridge Universities. Worked for the Egyptian Foreign Ministry and rose to the position of Ambassador and Under-Secretary of State. In 1942, he was appointed Governor of Alexandria. In 1949, he became Minister for Social Affairs, and, in 1952, served as Minister of Education in the 'Ali Maher▷ government, and then as Foreign Minister in the two administrations of Nagib al-Hilali▷. After the July 1952 revolution, he was elected Secretary-General of the Arab League▷—a position he still holds.   (S. L.)

HATAY. Province in southern Turkey on the Syrian border, previously known as the Sanjak of Alexandretta▷, formerly part of French-mandated Syria. It was incorporated into Turkey in 1939, after a protracted crisis (see Alexandretta▷). Its new name recalls the Hittites, whom present-day Turks count among their ancestors. The province has a population of over 1m. and includes the city of Antakya (the ancient Antioch), the capital, and the important port of Iskenderun (Alexandretta).

(D.K.)

HATUM, SALIM (d. 1967). Syrian-Druze army officer. H. was commander of the Syrian commando units with the rank first of major, then colonel. He was in charge of military operations in the coup of 23 Feb. 1966 that brought to power the "military wing" and extremist faction of the Ba'th▷ party, headed by Salah Jadid▷. On 8 Sept. 1966, he attempted a counter-coup with the aid of the deposed "National Leadership" of the Ba'th, and apparently also with the help of the Jordanian government. On its failure, he escaped to Jordan with his supporters. During the Six Day War▷, 1967, he returned suddenly to Syria, to put himself, as he said, at the service of the army. However, the regime maintained he had returned to overthrow it. He was arrested, sentenced to death by a military court and executed in June 1967.

(A.L.-O.T.)

HEBREW LANGUAGE. A Semitic tongue, the official language of the State of Israel. The revival of the H. language is an unprecedented social-linguistic phenomenon. Within a few decades H. changed from a language of literature, prayer and religious study, into a living language. In the Middle Ages, and particularly in Muslim Spain, a rich H. literature flourished; it served also as means of communication between Jews of different countries. Christians also learned H., to study and debate the sources of the Jewish religion in their original tongue. In the 18th and 19th centuries Jews began making more use of H. as a literary language; several H. periodicals were founded (e.g. Hame'assef, Vienna, as early as 1783), as part of the Jewish Enlightenment.

The disillusionment with European rationalism and its Jewish counterpart—the Haskalah (Enlightenment) movement—together with the revival of European nationalism, brought about the emergence of a Jewish national movement. This was a reaction to previous trends towards the assimilation of Jews among the nations, inspired by a belief in European liberalism. Peretz Smolenskin (1842–1885) declared that the Jews are a nation with its own spiritual attributes—the H. language and the messianic idea. Herzl▷, the founder of the Zionist movement, did not consider H. important, but felt that the strongest of the tongues brought by the new immigrants to the "Jewish State"—in his opinion, German—would become its language. Nevertheless, the revival of H. was fostered by Zionism▷ which had come to realize that the H. language was an inseparable element of national unity and identity.

The revival of H. as the main spoken language of the Jewish population of Palestine was brought about largely by Eliezer Ben Yehuda▷, who immigrated to Palestine in 1881 and waged a stubborn public battle to achieve this goal. Opposed to him were most of the major spokesmen of the earlier Jewish settlement; the Turkish authorities also harassed Ben Yehuda. In 1905, the Hapo'el Hatza'ir ("Young Worker") party, founded the same year, declared its support for a Jewish spiritual revival based on H. as both a spoken and literary language. The "language dispute", marked the victory of H. over German. It began when Ezra, a German-Jewish philanthropic organization decided (1913) to establish an Institute of Technology and a secondary school in Haifa, and declared that due to the poverty of H., the natural sciences would be taught in German. As a result, the majority of the students went on strike and the teachers resigned. The "Teachers' Central Committee" (founded 1903) opened a seminary for H. teachers. In the meantime World War I broke out. When the Institute reopened at its conclusion, H. was its only language of instruction. This victory together with the growth of a H.-speaking generation in Palestine, the establishment of local Jewish institutions, and the upsurge of Jewish nationalism following the Balfour Declaration▷ assured the role of H. in the educational system of Palestine and it began to penetrate the administrative sector as well. Finally it was proclaimed—along with Arabic and English (which under the British Military Government had been the only official languages)—an official language (1923), despite the opposition of the local Arab leaders.

Between the two world wars the Zionist movement and the Mizrahi▷ religious party set up a wide network of H. schools in Eastern Europe (the Tarbut and Tahkemoni networks), as well as teachers' colleges. H. literature flourished both in Palestine and Eastern Europe. In post-revolutionary Russia religious instruction was forbidden and, under this guise, the teaching of H. as well (in 1919). From 1920 the Yevsekzia (The Jewish section of the Communist Party) banned the publication of H. books (though Yiddish was encouraged) and the study of H., at the penalty of imprisonment and exile. This was part of the Communists' struggle against Zionism.

World War II brought a bitter end to Eastern European Jewry and its Jewish and H. cultural achievements. In the Western world a movement, begun in the late 1950s, and intensified since the Six Day War, tends towards identification of world Jewry with Israel, Jewish nationalism and the H. language. Several European and American universities have opened departments in H. studies.

With the founding of the State of Israel, H. became the language of the country. In 1953 a H. Language Academy was established (replacing a "H. Language Committee") to modernize and enrich the language. The immigration of one and a quarter million Jews since the establishment of Israel in 1948 has posed a serious threat to her lingual unity and necessitated the creation of methods for the rapid teaching of H. and the cultural absorption of the immigrants. Intensive study centres (*Ulpanim*) were set up (the first in 1950 by Nahum Levine, 1901–59).

In Israeli H. there are no dialects, though there are some differences in pronunciation among the immigrants from various areas. Israeli H. uses the *Sefardic* pronunciation, *i.e.* that of the Jews of Spain (rather than Eastern Europe).

SCRIPT AND SPELLING. The "Assyrian" script used by H. since the 4th or 5th century BC. is still used today. H. spelling—print and daily writing do not usually indicate vowels—causes difficulty both in writing and reading. Demands for the latinization of the alphabet have been made, but supporters of this idea have always been a minority. Others have suggested the addition of letters or symbols to indicate vowels. To simplify reading, the Academy has abolished the use of several grammatical rules, sometimes contravening biblical spelling and the rules of classical grammar.   (E. L.)

HEHALUTZ (Hebrew: The Pioneer). Zionist youth organization in the Diaspora (organized during World War I after earlier beginnings). Prepared its members for manual labour and settlement in Palestine, and the revival of Hebrew culture. Its world organization was set up in 1921 closely connected with the *Histadrut*▷ (General Federation of Jewish Labour). Membership 100,000 in 1939. The holocaust of World War II virtually annihilated H.
                                    (E. L.)

HELOU, CHARLES (b. 1912). Lebanese politician, President of Lebanon 1964–70. Son of a middle class family of the Christian-Maronite▷ community, native of Beirut. Graduated in law, during the period of the French Mandate was a lawyer and journalist. In 1936, he took part in the establishment of the Phalanges▷ Lebanaises, but later left that organization and joined Bishara al-Khouri's▷ "Constitutional Bloc". In 1949, he was Minister of Justice in the government of Riyad al-Sulh▷. In 1951, he was elected to Parliament in Beirut, on a list supporting President Bishara al-Khouri. During President Chamoun's▷ first years in power, he participated in the government as Minister of Justice and Health (1954–5), but in 1957 joined his opponents. Together with his colleague Henri Far'oun, he headed the "Third

Force" of Christians, mostly supporters of Bishara al-Khouri, who opposed Chamoun and his efforts to be elected President for another term, but stood aside and were neutral when the opposition adopted violent methods. This neutral stand, and his retirement from active politics (in 1960 he did not stand for Parliament), aided his election as President in 1964 as a neutral—and rather colourless—compromise candidate. As President, H. continued the policy of his predecessor, General Fu'ad Shihab▷, in Lebanon's foreign relations (with a slight shift towards neutrality in inter-Arab affairs and less identification with the Nasserist bloc), in the field of administrative reforms and concerning development. In 1964, he assigned the task of cleaning up the administration to a non-parliamentary government headed by Rashid Karameh▷ (himself a Member of Parliament, but unable to overcome factional disputes). During his presidency, the strong personality of Fu'ad Shihab continued to cast its shadow over Lebanese politics, with the army and the intelligence services under his strong influence.   (Y.P.)

HERUT—see Gahal▷.

HERZL, DR. (THEODOR) BINYAMIN ZEEV (1860–1904). Visionary of the Jewish State, father of political Zionism▷ and founder of the World Zionist Organization (1897). Born in Budapest of a semi-assimilated family, he moved at the age of 18 to Vienna, where he studied law. Realizing that he could never become a judge because he was Jewish, Herzl turned to journalism and literature. He published hundreds of feuilletons, and many plays.

The Dreyfus Affair, which he observed as Paris correspondent (from 1891) of "Neue Freie Presse", impressed on him the power of French anti-Semitism and led to his absorption in the Jewish problem. He concluded that the only solution was the exodus of the Jews from their Diaspora and their ingathering in a sovereign state. He first thought of Argentina (where Baron Hirsch had attempted to settle Jews) but later decided on Palestine (but see also Uganda Project▷).

His book, "The Jewish State" (1896), set out his ideas and evoked a powerful response among Jews. He organized the First Zionist Congress in Basle (1897), to recruit support for his plan. There the World Zionist Organization was founded, Herzl was appointed President (a post he held till his death), and the aims of Zionism▷ were defined. (About Herzl's activities, see Zionism▷).   (E.A.)

*HEYKAL, MUHAMMAD HASSANEIN (b. 1924). Egyptian journalist. H. began his career as

correspondent of the weekly *Rose al-Yussuf*, joined *Akhbar al-Yawm* in 1945 and became famous as war correspondent in the Israel-Arab War of 1948. His acquaintance with 'Abd-ul-Nasser▷ began there, in the battle of Faluja. He also reported the Korean War. He was appointed editor of the weekly *Akher Sa'a* in 1954, and editor of the semi-official Egyptian daily *al-Ahram*▷ in 1957. His weekly article is considered to reflect the opinions of the Egyptian regime. H. was thought to be President Nasser's closest adviser and confidant; he accompanied him on many of his foreign journeys. In the Egyptian factional struggle, H. is thought to tend to the West and to belong to the (relatively) liberal right-wing faction. H. was appointed Minister of Information in 1970. On the death of Nasser, he resigned this post, but retained his position as editor of *al-Ahram*.
(O.G.)

HEYKAL, MUHAMMAD HUSSEIN (1888–1956). Egyptian writer, journalist and politician. Son of a wealthy landowning family in Lower Egypt. He studied law in Cairo and France, where he obtained his doctorate. On his return to Cairo, he devoted himself to politics and writing. He was one of the founders of the "Liberal Constitutional Party", 1922, and edited its organ *al-Siyassa*. In 1937, he joined the government as Minister without Portfolio; later he was Minister of Education until 1942 and again in 1944. On the death of the party leader, Muhammad Mahmud▷, in 1941, he took his place. He was President of the Senate 1944–9. H. is considered as one of the creators of the modern Egyptian novel, mainly because of his story "Zeinab", published during World War I, which portrays Egyptian village life. He wrote many books and articles about Egypt.
(O.G.)

HIGH COMMISSIONER. Formerly a title of colonial governors, generally in territories not under direct colonial rule (those were ruled by a governor), but under protection, indirect rule or international trusteeship such as a mandate▷. In the ME the title of HC was used as follows: a. The chief British representative in Egypt was called HC from 1914, when Egypt became a protectorate, until 1936 (the British HC and, from 1936, the British Ambassador, in Egypt also held for some time the title HC for the Sudan, though he fulfilled no function in that country). b. In all mandated areas the chief of administration held the title HC—British in Palestine with Transjordan and in Iraq, French in Syria and Lebanon (see lists appended to entries Palestine▷ and Syria▷). c. The Governor of Aden became a HC from 1963 (when Aden ceased to be a colony

and joined the Federation of South Arabia) until 1967.—The title HC is also used instead of ambassador in the mutual diplomatic representation of member states of the British Commonwealth (in the ME —only Cyprus).
(Y.S.)

HIJAZ. Western region of Arabia, in present-day Sa'udi Arabia. Capital: Mecca▷. Area: 1,134 sq. mi. Pop.: 1.3m. (1967 est.), half of whom are settled. H. is 745 mi. long and consists of a narrow plain (*Tihama*) along the Red Sea coast, and 186 mi. wide granite and basalt plateau. The northern section, along the eastern shore of the Gulf of 'Aqaba▷, is formed by the mountains of Midian. In the 1920s and '30s, the Sa'udi rulers half-heartedly demanded the whole area as far as 'Aqaba, but eventually agreed to the incorporation of 'Aqaba in Jordan. In 1965 Sa'udia ceded to Jordan—in exchange for some territory inland—a narrow strip of coast several miles long (15–19 sq.mi.) in order to extend the hinterland of 'Aqaba.

The H. coast is barren and access is blocked by coral reefs, except for a few small harbours, such as Yanbu' and Jidda▷, which has become Sa'udia's chief port. Most of the inhabitants of the inland plateau are Bedouin. Several depressions contain large oases (Tabuk, Taima, 'Ula and, most important, Medina▷). A historic trade route follows the line of these depressions: the "Spice Route", or "Frankincense Road", which leads from the South Arabian coast through Yemen, Mecca and Medina to 'Amman and Damascus. This road was the main pilgrimage route to Mecca and Medina and along it the Turks built the H. Railway▷, which reached Medina in 1908 but was not completed as far as Mecca. In World War I▷ the railway was sabotaged and not repaired after the war. In the 1960s an asphalt road was built linking Jidda, Mecca and Medina.

The local rulers have always enjoyed special prestige due to the location of the holy cities of Islam, Mecca and Medina, in H. In the days of the Ottoman Empire, the Turks tried to maintain effective rule at least in these cities, the roads to them and the coast. The local amir, the Sharif of Mecca, had limited authority (except during periods of weakness and decline of the Empire). In the interior, effective authority was in the hands of the tribal chiefs. In 1916, the "Arab Revolt"▷ broke out, led by the Sharif Hussein▷ of the Hashemite▷ dynasty and supported by the British. In 1916–17, Hussein declared himself "King of H.". However, in 1918–19, he came up against the growing power of the Sa'ud▷ dynasty in Najd▷; Hussein was the weaker party in the conflict, since he rejected a protective alliance with Britain and remained without friend or support. In 1924, he even attempted to declare himself Caliph▷ of all Muslims. Ibn Sa'ud▷ then declared war on him and captured Mecca in 1924. Hussein abdicated in favour of his son 'Ali▷ and went into exile; but, in 1925, Ibn Sa'ud drove out 'Ali and annexed H. to his kingdom. In 1926, he was proclaimed King of H. and Najd; in 1932, his kingdom was renamed "Sa'udi Arabian Kingdom". Since then H. has been a region of Sa'udia. Mecca is Sa'udia's second capital, Ta'if her summer capital and the port of Jidda her diplomatic capital. With the discovery of oil deposits in the eastern parts of the Arabian peninsula, the economic centre of Sa'udia has moved over to the east coast.   (Y.K.)

*HIJAZ RAILWAY. 807 mi.-long railway connecting Damascus in Syria to Medina in Hijaz. Built in 1900-08 at the initiative of Sultan Abdülhamid▷, who hoped by this means to consolidate his central rule in the Ottoman Empire and to prevent rebellion in the Arabian peninsula. To keep the railway out of naval range, it was not built along the coast but in the interior.

The official purpose of the HR was to transport pilgrims to Mecca▷ and about a third of its cost (£3m.) were contributions from the Muslim world. After the Young Turks'▷ revolution (1908), the HR was not completed as far as Mecca and Jidda▷, as planned. However, a branch line was built to the Mediterranean, linking Der'a' in Southern Syria to Haifa. During World War I▷, the guerillas of the Arab Revolt▷ sabotaged the HR and destroyed many parts of it. To this day, it has not been repaired and only sections of it, in Syria and Jordan, are used. Since the early 1950s, Sa'udia, Jordan and Syria have drafted joint programmes to repair it and resume operation. International tenders have been issued and contracts signed, but, due to political and financial difficulties, repair work has not progressed.
                                                                (Y.A.O.)

HILALI, NAGIB (1891–1958). Egyptian politician and lawyer. Minister of Education and Commerce 1935-6. He joined the *Wafd*▷ in 1937 and was Minister of Education 1942-5. H. was expelled from the *Wafd* at the end of 1951. Since he was no longer identified with any party but considered neutral, he was appointed Prime Minister in 1952 at a time of grave crisis, both in Anglo-Egyptian relations and internal. He again formed a cabinet (for one day only) on 22 June 1952, the day preceding the Officers' coup. After the coup, H. was imprisoned for a while, and in 1954 was deprived of all political rights.   (S.L.)

HINNAWI, SAMI (1898–1950). Syrian army officer. Born in Idlib near Aleppo, of Kurdish ancestry. H.

served in the Ottoman Army, then in the "Special Forces" formed by the French, and in the Syrian army, rising to the rank of colonel. On 14 Aug. 1949 he engineered a military coup against Husni Za'im▷, executed both Za'im and his Prime Minister Muhsin Barazi▷ and appointed himself President of the "Revolutionary Council" and Army Chief-of-Staff. He allowed political activity and held elections. He was close to the "People's Party" (*Hizb al-Sha'b*) and encouraged its association with the administration. He initiated closer ties with the Hashemite▷ kingdoms, Jordan and especially Iraq, and was suspected of planning a union between Syria and Iraq. H. was deposed by Adib Shishakli▷ on 19 Dec. 1949; he was arrested, then released, and allowed to leave for Beirut. There he was murdered in 1950 in vengeance for Barazi.   (A.L.-O.T.)

HISTADRUT. General Federation of Labour in Israel. Established in 1920 (an earlier attempt had been made in 1905) as a Federation of Jewish Labour. In 1969 it opened its doors to full membership for Arab workers (see below). In 1970 the H. had a membership of *c.* 1m. workers (*c.* 4,500 in 1920) — 75% of Israel's labour force, 95% of salaried workers.

The aims of the H., as formulated in its revised statutes of 1927, are to organize and unite all workers who live by their own work "without exploiting the labour of others"; to defend their national, economic and social interests; to raise their standard of living and foster co-operation and mutual aid; and to develop a labour society in Israel, with individual freedom in matters of conscience and religion. The H., through The General Co-operative Association of Labour in Israel (*Hevrat Ha'ovdim*), which is identical with the H., though legally separate, acts also as Israel's second biggest employer (the biggest being the government) in industry, agriculture, commerce, public transportation and public services. Consequently the H. is responsible for 65% of Israel's agricultural product; 40% of her building activities (350,000 live in H.'s housing projects); and 25% of her industrial product; the Workers' Bank is the third biggest bank in Israel, and the H. owns one of the largest insurance companies in Israel. Most bus companies are run by H. co-operatives, and the H. is a partner in Israel's shipping and air lines.

Membership of the H. is personal and non-political. But the formation of the H.'s governing bodies and those of its constituent unions is usually organized on political party lines, *i.e.* political party lists — including non-socialist and anti-socialist parties like the Independent Liberals and *Herut*▷ — compete in internal elections. In practice, the H. has been continuously led by the various Social-Democratic

Labour parties, particularly *Mapai*▷ (since 1968: Israel Labour Party).

The H. negotiates working conditions, wages and labour contracts through the affiliated trade unions; country-wide annual labour agreements are usually signed by the employers' association and the H. (centrally). The H. also assists in the absorption of new immigrants; fosters increased labour productivity, work safety and hygiene; develops co-operative associations for credit, production (see above) and consumption (the H. co-operatives are responsible for 35% of Israel's private consumption); cares for working women; provides, under mutual aid schemes, assistance to the elderly and needy and the dependents of the deceased. It provides adult and youth education (workers' university, vocational schools, evening classes, choirs, dancing groups, youth centres, Israel's largest youth movement—which also provides trade-union services for working youth), encourages sports activities (its sport club *Hapo'el*, the largest in Israel, has 600 branches with 70,000 members); publishes a daily newspaper, *Davar*, and maintains the country's largest publishing house. The H. provides 70% of the population with medical care through its Sick Fund (*Kupat Holim*), and owns a large number of hospitals and over 1,000 clinics, employing a great many medical personnel.

The H. maintains strong links with foreign labour organizations. It was a member of the Amsterdam International and the World Federation of Trade Unions (until the end of World War II). In 1950, it joined the International Confederation of Free Trade Unions. It represents Israel's workers in the International Labour Organization. It maintains an Afro-Asian Institute for Labour Studies and Co-operation, which, since 1960, has trained over 1,000 students from 57 developing countries.

For 40 years, the H. held that Arab and Jewish workers should be organized in autonomous national units federated in a joint roof organization. It founded and maintained an Arab Trade Union of its own; but owing to the nationalist struggle over Palestine this union was never very strong. Arab workers objected to separate unions, particularly after the establishment of Israel; gradually they obtained membership of various H. institutions, and finally—full, direct and equal membership of the H. itself. The number of Arab members was about 50,000 in 1969—*c.* 150,000 with their families, *i.e.* about one half of Israel's Arab population.

Some of Israel's foremost leaders were active in H. affairs and members of its Executive (Meir▷, Eshkol▷, Sharett▷). David Ben-Gurion▷ and Pinhas Lavon▷ are among its past Secretaries-General.
(E.L.)

HISTADRUT HA'OVDIM HALE'UMIT (National Workers' Organization)—see Zionist-Revisionists▷.

HODEIDA—see Hudeida▷.

HOLY PLACES. JEWISH. All the Land of Israel is holy for Jews, but the Temple Mount in Jerusalem is especially sacred. The Western (or Wailing) Wall▷ which borders the Temple Mount, is today the only part of that site at which Jews worship. The Wall is the last remnant of the Second Temple, and according to Jewish tradition the Divine Immanence (*Shekhinah*) still abides there even though the Temple was destroyed in 70 CE. Orthodox Jews do not visit the Temple Mount area itself. Under Muslim rule, access to the Wall by Jews was severely curtailed owing to Muslim veneration of their own religious sites on the Mount. Under the British Mandate, the authorities tried to settle the conflicting claims and rights to the Wall on the basis of the *status quo*. But there was much dispute over the Wall—culminating in serious disturbances in 1929 (see Palestine▷). When the Old City of Jerusalem was occupied, in 1948, by Jordan, a Jordan-Israel agreement provided for free passage for Jews to the Wall. However this agreement was not honoured by Jordan, and Israelis were barred from access between 1948 and 1967. (Since June 1967, all HP, under Israeli rule, are freely accessible to all.)

There are other sites, mainly tombs of patriarchs, matriarchs and sages, which are objects of veneration and the goal of devout pilgrimages, mostly

Inside al-Aqsa Mosque

Birthplace of Jesus, inside the Church of the Nativity, Bethlehem

The Cave of Makhpelah

during the major festivals. These, however, do not really merit the name of "HP", and if such terminology is employed it is the result of the influence of other religions. Such so-called "HP" include the cemetery on the Mount of Olives; the Tomb of the Patriarchs (Cave of Makhpelah) in Hebron▷; the Tomb of Rachel on the outskirts of Bethlehem; the Tomb of Shim'on Bar-Yohai in Meron; the alleged Tomb of King David on Mount Zion▷; the tombs of Rabbi Me'ir Ba'al Haness and of Maimonides in Tiberias; the Synagogue of Rabbi Yitzhaq Luria (the "Holy Ari") in Safed, and many others of lesser importance.

CHRISTIAN. The Christian HPs are sites associated with events related in the Christian Scriptures. Churches were generally built at these sacred spots to mark the locality and make it a centre of worship. There are about 100 Christian HPs in Israel belonging to the Catholic, Orthodox and Monophysite churches. (The Protestants do not single out specific sites for veneration.)

The most important sanctuaries in Jerusalem▷ are the Church of the Holy Sepulchre at the traditional site of the Crucifixion and the Tomb of Jesus; the Via Dolorosa, with its Stations; the Cenacle (the Room of the Last Supper); the Mount of Olives, with the Tomb of Mary, the Garden of Gethsemane and the Church of the Ascension. In Bethlehem, the most important HPs are the Church of the Nativity and the nearby Shepherds' Field. In Nazareth, the most important sanctuaries are the Catholic Basilica of the Annunciation and the Church of St. Gabriel, which the Orthodox believe to be the site of the Annunciation. HP in the Galilee include the Church of Cana, the place of the first miracle, and Mount Tabor, the site of the Transfiguration. The Lake of Galilee is venerated for its association with many miracles performed by Jesus. Many churches and chapels near its shores mark scriptural episodes such as the Sermon on the Mount and the multiplication of loaves and fishes. The River Jordan, the traditional site of the baptism of Jesus, is considered as especially holy.

In many HP there are both Catholic and Orthodox churches. Several very important sanctuaries are jointly owned by several donominations and are the objects of conflicting claims. Typical examples are the Church of the Holy Sepulchre, the Church of the Nativity, the Tomb of Mary and the site of the Ascension. The ownership of and worship at such sites are regulated by the rules of the *status quo*, which were defined by a Firman of the Ottoman Sultan in 1852.

MUSLIM. The holiest city of Islam is Mecca, the birthplace of the Prophet Muhammad, and the site of the Mosque of the Ka'ba, the venerated black stone. One of the five central precepts of Islam is to make a pilgrimage to Mecca (*Hajj*) at least once in one's lifetime. The most venerated city after Mecca is Medina (*al-Madina*), where the Prophet took refuge and where, according to Muslim tradition, his tomb stands. Third in order of holiness is Jerusalem. There, on the Temple Mount area, called by Muslims *al-Haram al-Sharif*, the Noble Sanctuary, stand the mosques of *al-Aqsa* (the Farthest One) and the Dome of the Rock (also called the Mosque of 'Omar). According to Muslim tradition, Muhammad ascended to heaven from this place, while his horse, al-Buraq, remained tied at the Western Wall. By choosing the site of the Temple as one of its HP Islam emphasized its ties with Judaism and with Christianity.

The Tomb of the Patriarchs in Hebron, mentioned above as sacred to Jews, is also deeply venerated by Muslims—particularly that of Abraham ("God's Friend", *Khalil Allah*, in Muslim tradition). A mosque, *Haram al-Khalil*, built in the 7th century on earlier, ancient foundations, enshrines the burial cave.

To the Shi'ite▷ branch of Islam, the mosque built above the grave of Hussein, grandson of Muhammad, in Karbala in Iraq, near where he fell in battle, is also a HP and the site of pilgrimages. Another HP is the Iraqi town of al-Najaf—according to Shi'ite tradition, the site of the tomb of 'Ali, Muhammad's son-in-law and the fourth caliph. Two additional towns in Iraq, al-Kazimain and Samarra, containing the tombs of later heads *(Imam)* of the Shi'a, are places of pilgrimage and important centres of Shi'ite learning, as also are Mashhad and Qum in Iran.

Muslim masses in most ME countries also venerate a large number of tombs of saints, holy men, prophets, etc., many of them legendary—some connected with biblical names and traditions. Islam has never formally sanctioned this veneration of tombs, but neither has it ever denounced or banned it.

The Druze▷ sect venerates the tomb of Shu'aib, the legendary ancestor of the community (identified with Jethro the Midianite, Moses' father-in-law). The tomb is situated at Hittin in Israel. Another Druze H.P. is the tomb of Sheikh 'Abdullah al-Tanukhi at 'Abaya in Lebanon. For other H.P. see also Baha'is and Samaritans. (Sh.C.)

HOPE-SIMPSON, SIR JOHN. British administrator sent to Palestine in 1930 to investigate development and land problems and the absorptive capacity of the country. In his report, he concluded that the country could not absorb many more immigrants. See Palestine, Commissions▷. (Y.S.)

HOURANI, AL-, AKRAM. Syrian lawyer, journalist and politician. Born 1914 in Homs. He participated in Rashid 'Ali al-Kilani's▷ seizure of power in Iraq in 1941 and in the war with Israel in 1948. He campaigned for agrarian reform, won support of the farmers in the Homs district and was elected to Parliament in 1943, 1947, 1949 and 1954. He took part in the three military coups of 1949. In 1950, he founded the "Arab Socialist Party". When this party united in 1953 with the "Arab Renaissance Party" (al-Ba'th▷) of 'Aflak▷ and Bitar▷ to form the "Arab Socialist Ba'th Party", H. became one of the leaders of the united party. He was Minister of Defence under Adib Shishakli▷ in 1950, but fell out with him and escaped to Lebanon. After Shishakli's downfall in 1954, he became President of Parliament. After the union with Egypt and the formation of the UAR▷ (1958), he became Vice-President and Minister of Justice of the united republic, but resigned at the end of 1959, having become an outspoken opponent of Nasser▷. After the UAR was disbanded (1961), he left the *Ba'th* party because he opposed its ideas of renewed co-operation with Egypt. During the

coup of the *Ba'th* officers, 8 Mar. 1963, he was arrested and, when freed, went into exile to Lebanon. He attracted a group of Arab socialists who opposed the existing regime in Syria and in 1968 again formed (in exile) an "Arab Socialist Democratic Party", advocating the liquidation of the military regime in Syria and the establishment of parliamentary government with a free economy and social reforms. (A.L.-O.T.)

*HOVEYDA, AMIR 'ABBAS.** Iranian politician. Born in Teheran, 1919. Educated at Brussels University, (Political Sciences and Economics), Ph. D. (History), Paris University. Served in the Ministry for Foreign Affairs, 1945–58. Member of the Board of Directors of the National Iranian Oil Company 1958–64. In 1963 H. joined the *Iran Novin* (New Iran) party, established the same year, and became a member of its executive committee and its Deputy Secretary-General. Minister of Finance 1964–5; Prime Minister since 1965. (B.G.)

*HUDEIDA** (often spelled Hodeida). The main port of Yemen. Pop: *c.* 50,000 most of whom are Shafe-'is▷. In 1921 the British, who were evacuating the area, allowed the ruler of neighbouring Sabya (Asir▷) to occupy H., as a reward for his assistance during World War I. Yemeni tribesmen, taking advantage of 'Asir's growing weakness, reoccupied H. for Yemen in 1925. H. port (opened 1961) was developed with Soviet aid and new roads were built to San'a▷ and Ta'izz▷ with Chinese and Soviet assistance, respectively. H. was the main Egyptian supply base in the Yemen war of 1962–7, but owing to its non-militant Shafe'i population and its remoteness from the mountainous Zeidi▷ tribesmen it remained calm. After the Egyptian withdrawal in late 1967, it became a centre of Shafe'i opposition to the new Zeidi-Republican regime in San'a. (H.E.)

HULA. Valley and lake, adjoined by swamps, in northern Israel, at the confluence of the headwaters of the Jordan. The lake and swamps were drained (1950–8) and the valley turned into one of the most fertile regions of Israel, with 20 villages and 14,000 inhabitants producing mainly cotton, sugarbeet, fodder and apples, with fishponds also covering large parts. Drainage work was disturbed by frequent Syrian shelling, from the commanding positions of the Golan Heights▷. Syria also complained in 1951 and 1957 to the UN Security Council that the drainage gave Israel military advantages contrary to the 1949 Armistice Agreements▷, particularly in the demilitarized zone; but after a brief suspension of work the complaints were not upheld. However,

The Hula nature-reserve, after the draining of the swamps

an Israeli plan to divert the Jordan▷ waters from a point in the demilitarized zone near the H., was changed, to avoid long debates, in 1953, and the diversion was made from the Sea of Galilee▷ instead.   (Y.K.)

HUSSEIN b. 'ALI, SHARIF, KING (1852 [or '53 or '54]–1931). Sharif of Mecca, King of Hijaz (1916–24). Hashemite▷ descendant of the Prophet Muhammad. He was kept for years in exile in Istanbul by Sultan Abdülhamid▷. After the revolution of the Young Turks▷ (1908, he was allowed to return to Hijaz▷ and was appointed Amir of Mecca. H. opposed the continuation of the Hijaz Railway▷ into Hijaz itself. There was rivalry between him and Ibn Sa'ud▷ in Najd▷, as well as between him and the house of Rashid, rulers of the Shammar tribes in Ha'il.

In 1914 he contacted the British High Commissioner in Cairo to enquire about British help in the event of his revolting against the Turks. These contacts were renewed in July 1915, when the British became more interested in the notion of a revolt. Apart from help for the revolt itself, H. demanded independence for "Arabia". The British accepted, but had reservations concerning his territorial demands (see McMahon-Hussein▷ Correspondence). Without reaching a clear and signed agreement, H. and his sons 'Ali▷, 'Abdullah▷ and Feisal▷ started the Arab Revolt▷ (see also World War I▷). H. wanted to proclaim himself "King of the Arab Lands", but the British and their allies objected to that; as a compromise he was proclaimed and recognized, in Oct. 1916, King of Hijaz.

At the end of World War I H. sent his son Feisal to represent him at the Paris Peace Conference▷.

Since he did not receive complete satisfaction, and in protest against the Sykes-Picot Agreement▷ and the setting up of mandates▷ instead of complete independence, H. refused to endorse the peace treaties. He likewise rejected in 1920–1 British proposals for an Anglo-Hijazi treaty, including British aid and guarantees against outside attack, since he refused to recognize, in return, the arrangements made in Iraq, Syria and Palestine. (As to Zionism▷, H. at first identified himself with Feisal's friendly attitude and his readiness to reach an agreement—see Feisal-Weizmann Agreement▷—but later changed his mind.) H. also refused to send delegates to a British-initiated convention in Kuwait, 1923, to settle border problems in the Arabian peninsula.

In armed clashes between his tribesmen and those of the Sa'udi▷ Najd tribes in 1919–20, he suffered defeat, but was saved from a total debacle by British intervention with Ibn Sa'ud▷. After the Turkish National Assembly abolished the Caliphate▷ in Mar. 1924, H. proclaimed himself Caliph that same month. H. had not obtained the agreement of any Islamic leaders and his step was unrealistic in relation to his strength and position. It caused anger and consternation, especially among Ibn Sa'ud's *Wahhabis*▷. In September 1924, the *Wahhabis* mounted an offiensive which H. could not withstand. After Ta'if was captured by the Sa'udis, H. abdicated in favour of his oldest son 'Ali▷, hoping thus to save the kingdom of Hijaz for his family. But in Oct. Mecca was captured by Ibn Sa'ud. H. escaped to 'Aqaba▷ ('Ali was overthrown by the end of 1925 and escaped). In July 1925, H. was taken by a British naval vessel to Cyprus. He lived in exile there or with his son 'Abdullah in Transjordan. He died in 'Amman in 1931 and was buried in Jerusalem.
(Y.A.O.)

✻HUSSEIN b. TALAL (b. 1935). King of Jordan. Born in 'Amman. Educated at Victoria College (Alexandria), Harrow and Sandhurst Military Academy (Britain). Succeeded his father Talal▷ in 1953. Crowned in May 1953. Married, in 1955, Princess Dina (member of another, distantly related, branch of the Hashemite family), but divorced her in 1957. Remarried in 1961, Antoinette Gardiner, daughter of a British Army officer. She converted to Islam and assumed the name Muna al-Hussein. Under pressure from nationalistic circles, Hussein decided in 1965 to name as Crown Prince his brother Hassan and not his son by his formerly British wife.

Having ascended the throne at a very young age, H. became increasingly independent. He had to make important concessions to nationalist groups, e.g. an amendment to the constitution enabling parliament to dismiss the government by a simple majority, 1954; the withdrawal of a decision to adhere to the Baghdad Pact▷, 1955 and the dismissal of General Glubb▷, the British Commander of the Arab Legion, 1956. When the leftist-nationalist National Socialist Party won the elections of October 1956, the king had to appoint its leader, Suleiman Nabulsi▷, as Prime Minister. The same month he approved Jordan's adherence to the Egyptian-Syrian Defence Pact and Joint Command and, early in 1957, the abrogation of the Anglo-Jordanian Treaty and the replacement of British aid by Egyptian, Syrian and Sa'udi subsidies. However H. dismissed Nabulsi in 1957, when the leftist trend reached its climax in Nabulsi's cabinet's decision to establish diplomatic relations with the USSR, and Egyptian-supported subversion led to an officers' plot against him which he succeeded in averting by an act of personal courage. In February 1958 H. became Deputy-Head of the "Arab Federation"▷ of Iraq and Jordan (established in reaction to the Syro-Egyptian merger); but the Federation collapsed in July 1958, as a result of the *coup d'état* in Iraq. Jordan's isolation, and the fear of UAR intervention already prepared for by subversion, impelled H., in July 1958, to ask Britain to send troops to protect Jordan; they stayed until October 1958. H. succeeded in preserving his throne in spite of numerous plots, sponsored by Egypt or Syria, to overthrow his regime. His relations with

King Hussein

Egypt have been subject to incessant fluctuation; Egyptian information media, and President Nasser himself, alternately called him traitor and imperialist stooge with whom "progressives" could not co-operate, and noble king of an Arab sister country.

In May 1967, H. signed a defence treaty with Egypt, placing his army under Egyptian command. He entered the Six Day War▷—as described in his memoirs—after personally deciding to disregard Israel's warning and promise not to attack him. Jordan's defeat and the loss of the West Bank were a heavy blow to his position and prestige. Moreover, his position was continuously undermined by the Palestinian-Arab guerilla organizations which he permitted, step-by-step, to establish in Jordan a state within a state. For several years, King H. endeavoured to preserve his throne by co-operating with the guerilla organizations and making concessions to them, while trying to prevent large-scale operations against Israel from Jordanian territory which would entail Israeli reprisals. His senior army officers were pressing him to take stronger action to impose control over the guerillas. His attempts to keep the guerillas under control and to maintain Jordan's law and sovereignty within her territory brought him into ever-increasing conflict with the guerillas, despite his concessions. Incessant clashes, terminating in repeated cease-fires, erupted into fully-fledged civil war in September 1970. The king and the army emerged victorious—at a heavy price in casualties and an irreparable loss of popularity ("H. the Butcher", "Nero b. Talal")—but another compromise was forced on him by Pan-Arab intervention. However, in renewed clashes, in spring and summer 1971, H. seems to have subdued the guerillas and re-established his full control.   (B.G.-Y.S.)

HUSSEIN-McMAHON CORRESPONDENCE—see McMahon-Hussein Correspondence▷.

HUSSEINI, AL-. Prominent Arab family in Jerusalem. Claims descent from the Prophet Muhammad and therefore the standing of a *Sharifian* family. A member of the H. family was Mufti in Jerusalem in the 17th century and one was *Naqib al-Ashraf* ("Chief of the Descendants of the Prophet") of Jerusalem. In the middle of the 19th century, Mustafa al-H. was appointed Mufti of Jerusalem. He was succeeded by his son Taher, Taher by his son Kamel, Kamel by his stepbrother, Muhammad Amin al-H.▷. The family meanwhile advanced socially and accumulated large amounts of land, mainly in the villages north-west of Ramallah. Its members held many administrative posts, including on several occasions the post of Mayor of Jerusalem (Salim al-H. in the 1870s, his son Hussein Salim al-H. 1909–18, and his younger son Mussa Kazim al-H.▷. 1918–20). Sa'id al-H. was elected in 1908 and again in 1914 as one of the three delegates of the Jerusalem district to the Ottoman Parliament. Some prominent members during the 20th century will be found in the following entries.

During the 1920s, '30s and '40s, the name al-H. denoted not only an influential family, but a political camp or party. In view of the dominant influence of Hajj Amin al-H. and the Supreme Muslim Council▷ which he headed, their supporters were called *Majlisiyin*—"Council Men"; the opposing camp was called *al-Mu'aridin*—"The Opposition". But many called the *Majlisiyin* "Husseinis"; their opponents were called Nashashibis▷ after the prominent family at their head. When the "Arab Palestine Party" was established in 1935, and became the political instrument of the *Majlisiyin*, it was often called "The Husseinis".   (Y.P.)

HUSSEINI, AL-, JAMAL (b. 1892 or 1894). Palestinian-Arab politician. Son of Muhammad Saleh al-H. (a member of the City Council of Jerusalem) and of the sister of Mussa Kazim al-H.▷. Educated at the Anglican School in Jerusalem and the American University of Beirut, H. started studying medicine, but was interrupted by the outbreak of World War I▷. After the war, he served in the British Military Government as an official in the Health Department, as "local adviser" to the Military Governor of Nablus and as assistant to the Governor of Ramla. His political activities began in 1921, when he was appointed Secretary to the Arab Executive▷, in part because of his command of English. He held this post and was the moving spirit of the Committee until 1934 when it ceased activities. In 1928–30, H. served as Secretary to the Supreme Muslim Council▷. With the disintegration of the Arab Executive Committee, he organized the political framework of the H.▷ faction— the "Palestine Arab Party"—and was one of its representatives on the Arab Higher Committee▷ established in Apr. 1936. When that Committee was dissolved, in October 1937, H. absconded; but in 1939, he was permitted to head the Palestinian-Arab delegation to the London Round Table Conference. In 1940–1, he was active among Palestinian exiles in Iraq and supported the revolt of Rashid 'Ali-Kilani▷. In 1941, he escaped from Iraq, but was caught by the British in Teheran and exiled to Rhodesia. Freed in 1945, he was allowed to return to Palestine in 1946. He soon established a new Arab Higher Committee, but his factionalism impelled his opponents to form a rival committee. In June 1946,

the Arab League▷ intervened, disbanding both committees and forming a new one, appointing H. as its Vice-President (the presidency was reserved for Hajj Amin al-H.▷ then in exile). H. now reorganized his party and its paramilitary youth organization *al-Futuwwa*. He presented the Arab case before the 1946–7 Committees of Enquiry. Under his leadership and the influence of Hajj Amin al-H., the Arab Higher Committee rejected the Partition Plan and called upon the Palestinian Arabs to prevent its implementation by force. During the 1948 War he was in Cairo, Damascus and Beirut. Following the Arab defeat in that war, he was active in the Arab Higher Committee that continued to operate in Beirut. He later joined the service of the Sa'udi Arabian government and retired from political activity.

                                    (Y.P.)

❋HUSSEINI, AL-, HAJJ (MUHAMMAD) AMIN (b. 1893, or 1895 or 1897). Palestinian-Arab politician and religious leader. H. studied *i.a.* for one year at the Jewish "Alliance" school in Jerusalem. Before World War I▷, he studied about a year under Sheikh Muhammad Rashid Rida at al-Azhar▷ in Cairo, without graduating, and at the Turkish School of Administration in Istanbul. He served in the Ottoman Army during the war. During the British occupation, he was recruiting officer for Feisal's▷ army, and later an official in the British Military Government. He was president of *al-Nadi al-'Arabi* (the "Arab Club") in Jerusalem, the organization of the supporters of all-Syrian unity. He headed anti-Jewish demonstrations on 4 Apr. 1920, and was sentenced by a British military court to 15 years in prison for his part in inciting to riot. He absconded, but in September 1920 was pardoned by the High Commissioner. In March 1921, the Mufti of Jerusalem, Kamel al-H., H.'s stepbrother, died. H. offered his candidacy but lost the first stage of the election. The H. family and its supporters now exerted great pressure on the High Commissioner to appoint H., although he was not among the three elected candidates from whom the High Commissioner was to appoint the Mufti. One of those elected withdrew in his favour, and the High Commissioner appointed him Mufti; H. had promised to exercise his prestige and that of his family to assure quiet in Jerusalem. The High Commissioner also obviously wished to keep a balance between the rival clans: the position of Mufti had been previously held by the H. family, and the position of Mayor of Jerusalem had just been taken from them and given to the head of the opposition, the Nashashibi▷ family.

In January 1922, H. was also elected President of the Supreme Muslim Council▷ formed by the

Mandatory Government. The Council became his, and his family's, tool. He used it to fight his opponents among the Palestinians (the Nashashibis), the Zionists, and the National Home policy of the Mandate▷. He fostered the Muslim character of Jerusalem and the position of its two great mosques and injected a religious character into the struggle against Zionism. This was the background of his agitation concerning Jewish rights at the Wailing Wall▷ that resulted in the disturbances of August 1929. After these riots H. became the most important leader of the Palestinian Arabs. From that time he aimed at political leadership, and began to undermine the position of Mussa Kazim al-H.▷ (although he left the leadership of his political faction in the hands of Jamal al-H.▷). The death of Mussa Kazim, 1934, gave him his chance, and in April 1936, when an Arab Higher Committee▷ was formed, he was elected its President. As such, he was the chief organizer of the 1936 riots, and of the rebellion and the internal Arab terror in 1937.

In October 1937, he was dismissed by the government from his position as President of the Supreme Muslim Council, which was disbanded; the Arab Higher Committee was outlawed. H. escaped to Syria and then to Iraq where he was close to Rashid 'Ali al-Kilani▷ and the pro-Nazi army officers. After the collapse of Rashid 'Ali's revolt, H. escaped to Italy and Nazi Germany. There he worked as a propagandist, mobilizing Muslim public opinion throughout the world and recruiting Muslim volunteers from Bosnia and Yugoslavia, for the Nazi war effort.

After the war, H. escaped arrest and returned to Egypt (he was not allowed to return to Palestine). From there, he conducted the Palestinian struggle against Partition, while the presidency of the Arab Higher Committee was reserved for him. Although the Arab states financed and equipped the struggle, H. demanded for himself supreme leadership. This created tension between him and the Arab leaders. After the defeat, in 1948, he tried unsuccessfully to form an "All-Palestine Government" in Gaza. He moved to Lebanon and tried to revive the activities of the Arab Higher Committee. The Hashemite▷ regime in Jordan was one of his targets; King 'Abdullah▷ was assassinated, 1951, by his supporters. His influence then declined. The Arab Higher Committee was relegated to publishing a monthly. H.'s decline was accompanied by that of his family, as a result of its political failure and steps taken by the Hashemite administration.   (Y.P.)

HUSSEINI, AL-, MUSSA KAZIM (1850–1934).
Son of Salim al-H., Mayor of Jerusalem. Educated at the Istanbul School of Administration, H. joined the Ottoman administration and was promoted from *Qaimaqam* (Sub-District Governor)—Gaza, Safad, ('Akkar (Lebanon), and 'Ajiloun (Transjordan)—to *Mutasarref* (District Governor) of several districts in Anatolia, Transjordan, and the Arabian peninsula. He retired on the eve of World War I▷.

In March 1918 H. was appointed Mayor of Jerusalem by the British, following the death of the mayor, his brother Hussein. He was appointed on condition that he stay out of politics. H. did not honour this condition, and in March 1920 greeted Arab demonstrators who demanded that Feisal▷ be recognized as king of a United Syria, including Palestine; in April he welcomed Nebi Mussa celebrants involved in anti-Jewish riots. For this he was dismissed from his position by Ronald Storrs, the Military Governor of Jerusalem. MKH became a top leader of the Palestinian Arabs' national movement when he was elected in December 1920, at the third Palestinian Congress, as President of the Arab Executive▷—a position he held until his death in 1934. He headed, in the 1920s and '30s, every Palestinian delegation that went to London to persuade the British government to abandon its policy based on the Balfour Declaration▷. In 1929, he withdrew his previous opposition to all British suggestions for the establishment of home rule institutions, and agreed, together with Ragheb al-Nashashibi▷, to the appointment of a Legislative Council; but the riots of August 1929 prevented its implementation.

One of his sons, 'Abd-ul-Qader, was in the early 1930s among the organizers of a "Congress of Educated Muslims", which fought against alleged discrimination in government service. In 1936–9 and in 1948, 'Abd-ul-Qader was a commander of guerilla gangs in the Jerusalem area, one of the few members of a prominent family who actually joined such guerillas. He was killed in the battle for the Qastal Hill in April 1948.   (Y.P.)

I

IBADIS, IBADIYYA. An unorthodox Islamic sect which developed from the Khawarij (or Kharijiyin, Kharijites) sect during the seventh century. The Khawarij rebelled against evolving Islamic laws of governance and succession, both in their Sunni and Shi'i versions (the latter allowed positions of leadership in the state or community only to the descendants of 'Ali). Their Ibadi heirs gradually became a separate sect. The I. form the majority of the population of 'Oman-and-Muscat, and their doctrine is the state religion. Small groups of I. also exist in Tripoli, Libya, Tunisia and Algeria (as well as in countries reached by emigrants from ʻOman, such as Tanzania). (Y.S.)

IBN SAʻUD. The name by which King ʻAbd-ul-ʻAziz ibn ʻAbd-ul-Rahman ibn Feisal Aal Saʻud (1880–1953) was known. His ancestors had ruled Najd▷. They had sponsored the puritan-conservative Wahhabi▷ school of Sunni Islam. In the 19th century the Saʻudi dynasty had been rivalled in its Najdi domain by the Rashidi dynasty of Haʼil; in 1891 they were forced to flee, and IS grew up in exile in Kuwait. In 1901 he recaptured the city of Riyadh and re-established the rule of his dynasty in Najd. In 1913 he conquered the al-Hassa▷ region on the Persian Gulf. The rule of IS and the independence of Najd were recognized by Britain in an agreement concluded by the government of British India in 1915; he was also paid a monthly subsidy of £5,000. The British encouraged IS in his fight against the pro-Turkish Rashidis, but were content with his benevolent neutrality in World War I. IS soon clashed with another of Britain's clients, the Hashemite Sharif Hussein▷ of Mecca, King of Hijaz▷. In 1918–19, IS was victorious in battle, but under British pressure did not follow up this victory. Instead, he defeated his rival Ibn Rashid (1919–21), incorporating his territory into his own domain and, from 1921, called himself Sultan of Najd and its Dependencies. Raids on Iraq and Transjordan were stopped in 1922 by treaties concluded under British auspices and establishing agreed frontiers; IS also undertook to refrain from attacking Kuwait▷ and Hijaz. However, hostilities between IS and the Hashemites in Mecca broke out again in 1924. Mecca was taken in 1924, Jidda and the rest of Hijaz by the end of 1925. Only the threat of British intervention prevented an attack on Transjordan.

In Jan. 1926, IS was proclaimed "King of Hijaz, Najd and its Dependencies." By 1931 most of the major European countries, including the USSR, had recognized him. In the Treaty of Jidda, 1927, Britain recognized his complete independence (instead of the veiled protectorate of the Treaty of 1915). In 1932, IS renamed his kingdom Saʻudi Arabia. During the 1920s, IS had brought the region of ʻAsir▷, south of Hijaz, under his control, and in 1933 he annexed it. This brought tension with Yemen to a climax and war broke out in 1934. IS won, but left the Imam of Yemen independent. In 1936, IS was one of the mediators bringing about the end of the Arab general strike in Palestine. He was one of the first to recognize Italy's annexation of Ethiopia, and received Italian arms, aeroplanes and training facilities in

King Ibn Saʻud

return. In World War II, IS was suspected of pro-Axis leanings, but remained neutral. When the USA entered the war and President Roosevelt▷ was induced by American oil interests to grant IS military and development aid, IS declared in 1945 his support for the Allies. By then he was considered, in particular, the ally of the USA (and her oil interests—as against British oil interests). Attempts by the Zionists to obtain IS's help towards a settlement with the Palestine Arabs failed; he took an extreme anti-Zionist stand and used his influence, e.g. in his meeting with Roosevelt in 1945 and later in correspondence with Roosevelt and Truman, to promote the Palestinian-Arab cause. However, his financial and military aid to the Palestinian war effort in 1947–8 was small.

In the Arab League, he was allied with Egypt against Hashemite plans for a revision of the Arab map, the inclusion of Syria in a Hashemite-ruled federal union, etc. However, in the early 1950s a Saʻudi-Hashemite reconciliation was gradually effected.

IS ruled his kingdom as an autocrat, consulting the tribal sheikhs and his advisers in the traditional manner, but reserving decisions to himself. He permitted no modern political representative government, and kept the unruly tribal chiefs—whom he had to suppress in the late 1920s by armed force—under strict control, by paying them subsidies, keeping their sons at his Court and marrying their daughters to his sons. He enforced Wahhabi Islam in its strictest forms, though little was later heard of his initial efforts to establish a nucleus of armed Wahhabi "Brethren" (*Ikhwan*) in colonies in which these Bedouin were to settle on the land. He permitted little economic or social modernization, except for the development of the oil industry by the American Aramco company (through which he became, from the early 1950s, immensely rich). Despite the rule of strict Islamic law, corruption and excessive luxury became common among the dynasty and the ruling class during his later years. IS was said to have over 40 sons.   (Sh.H.-Y.S.)

IDRIS, KING—see Sanussi, Muh. Idris▷.

IDRISSI (house, dynasty, sect). The Is, a dynasty of North African origin, gained political power and religious influence in the region of 'Asir▷ (between Yemen and Hijaz) in the mid-19th century under Ahmed al-I. Claiming descent from the Khalifa 'Ali, the Is. founded a Muslim school or order (*Tariqa*), similar to Dervish orders▷ but traditional and fundamentalist in content, and influenced by the Wahhabis▷. Their state gained brief independence at the beginning of the 20th century, but was annexed to Sa'udi Arabia in 1933 (see 'Asir▷), and the dynasty lost its position.   (H.E.-Y.S.)

IHUD (Hebrew: Union)—see Bi-national State▷.

IMAM. In Sunni Islam▷, the I. is the head of a mosque, a leader in prayer, and often also a preacher (in the larger mosques there is a preacher—*Khatib*, or, in special cases, *Wa'iz*).

In Shi'i Islam▷, the I. is the head of the Muslim community (*Umma*) and, in theory the ruler of the country. He must be a descendant of the Prophet Muhammad, his daughter Fatima and his son-in-law 'Ali. Shi'i Islam gradually came to attribute to the I. mysterious and superhuman qualities. According to its main stream—the *Ithna-'Ashariyya* ("Twelvers") or Imamites—the twelfth I. disappeared in the 9th century and has been in hiding since, with no I. being revealed; at the end of time he will return as the *Mahdi*▷ (The "Guided One") and redeemer, and institute a reign of justice. According to the *Isma'iliyya*▷ sect, the seventh I. in the 8th century was the last legitimate one, and has been hidden since. However, another branch of the same sect believes in a living I., the "Aga Khan". The *Zeidiyya*▷ stream in Yemen also recognizes an unbroken line of legitimate, revealed, living Is. The Zeidi I. is elected as head of the community and the ruler of Yemen (though at times there are several claimants).

Some esoteric schools of Sunni Islam which have, though orthodox, absorbed certain elements of Shi'ism and Muslim mysticism (Sufism)—e.g. the *Mahdiyya*▷ movement in Sudan—also call the head of their order I.   (Y.S.)

IMPERIALISM. The expansion of a great power (or "Empire") through conquest of foreign countries and/or their economic or military exploitation. Though there is no generally accepted definition of modern I., it is commonly regarded as an expansionism chiefly motivated by the economic needs of the advanced European states, at first by a search for raw materials, then for markets for their industrial produce, and, finally, as a field for profitable investment. According to Lenin's definition, this is the highest and final stage of capitalism. A number of nineteenth century philosophers and statesmen, particularly Englishmen, defended I., the expansion of the British Empire and the subjugation of foreign nations. They justified it as of advantage to backward peoples, and regarded it as a moral obligation, or "the white man's burden" ("mission civilisatrice"). In the course of time, the epithet I. became a kind of insult. No state would admit to being imperialistic. American and European oil magnates would not consider the development of the natural resources of foreign counries under concessions as I., nor the great banks their credits to developing countries. Neither would the Soviet Union view the expansion of her rule to Eastern Europe, or her penetration of the ME as I. In the absence of a scientific, factual definition, it becomes a question of terminology and of political opinion whether or not a political or economic act, state policy or even a state itself, are to be termed Imperialistic.

For the under-developed countries, in particular those overseas, I. is almost synonomous with colonialism▷, in daily if not scientific usage. Britain, France and Italy were the powers which acted on straightforward colonialist and imperialist principles in the ME, and tried to divide the region between them particularly during World War I▷ (see Sykes-Picot▷). Their direct and indirect rule is described in greater detail under colonialism▷. Germany's colonial and imperialistic ambitions led to her increasing penetration, in the period immediately preceding World War I, of key positions in the economy of the Ottoman (and to a lesser extent the Persian) Empire. However, her defeat in the war prevented her from realizing her ambitions. In the same way, Nazi Germany's much more embracing ambitions were checked by her defeat in World War II▷.

Tsarist Russia▷ had pronounced imperialistic aims, particularly in connection with the Bosphorus▷ Straits and the regions of Northern Persia and Eastern Anatolia. She acquired decisive influence in Northern Persia through the Anglo-Russian treaty of 1907, which divided Persia into spheres of influence. Through secret agreements in 1915–16, Russia obtained British and French acquiêscene in her claims concerning Turkey and the Straits. However, Bolshevik Russia, following the October 1917

Revolution, abandoned these claims and denounced the imperialist agreements. In time, however, the Soviet Union herself began to nurse many of Tsarist Russia's strategic and political aims, which she reformulated in agreements and diplomatic negotiations with Nazi Germany (1939–40) and in her demands on Turkey and Persia (1945–6) (see Russia▷). The ties connecting the Soviet Union and several Arab states, her increased military, political and economic influence in Egypt, Syria, Iraq, Algeria, Libya, Yemen, and Southern Yemen, and her naval presence in the Mediterranean, can be regarded as fulfilling the traditional aims of Russian I.

Britain, France and Italy still preserve many of their interests in the ME, even though they no longer predominate. Their opponents term these interests, particularly their oil holdings, imperialist. The foreign power with the greatest influence, and the most commanding position (except for the Soviet Union), is the USA. The USA never maintained a direct or indirect colonial rule in the region. Her influence prior to World War II was particularly centred in the oil economy. Since the war, she has assumed the task of defending the area against the USSR, entered into treaties with Turkey, Iran, Sa'udi Arabia and Libya, attempted to set up a regional defence treaty (MEDO▷, Baghdad Pact▷) and built military bases in Turkey, Libya and Sa'udi Arabia. She has given extensive economic aid to Turkey, Iran and other ME countries. The USA has assisted (without formal treaties) the economies and defence of Israel, Jordan and Lebanon. Her adversaries call this I., the USA and her allies—defence of democracy and the freedom of small nations.

Military bases▷ are often regarded as a clear indication of I. Yet some at least were set up at the request of the host country, as with the American bases in Turkey. Such distinctions between various kinds of bases again depend upon political opinion. The only remaining full-scale Western military bases in the ME are in Turkey (NATO▷ and US). There is some Western military or semi-military presence in bases disguised as staging and refuelling stations for aircraft—e.g. Dhahran▷ in Sa'udi Arabia (US air base), Bahrain▷ (US naval; British), Sharja▷ (al-Shariqa; British), and Massira (an island near the southern coast of Muscat-and-'Oman▷, British). Several of these small naval and air installations will be evacuated and liquidated in 1971. The main Western bases in the Arab states were abandoned one by one: Syria and Lebanon (1945); Egypt (1954–6); Jordan (1957); Iraq (1955, 1959); Aden (1967); and Libya (1970). The Soviet Navy and Air Force have many supply points in friendly Arab states: the ports of Alexandria▷, Port Sa'id▷, and Mersa-

Matruh in Egypt, the port of Lataqia▷ in Syria, ports in Iraq, Libya, Sudan, Yemen, and Southern Yemen, and many airfields in these states. These friendly supply points have not been officially designated "bases". The question as to when a friendly port becomes a base once again depends upon one's political views and semantics.   (Y.S.)

⋇**INDIA.** On her path to independence, nationalist I. developed close relations with the ME. The Indian nationalists, as leaders in a country with a large and influential Muslim minority, took care to show sympathy with Islamic problems and solidarity with the Muslims of the ME. Thus, during World War I, when the Ottoman Sultan-and-Caliph called for the help of the Muslim world and for a *Jihad*▷, he found a sympathetic response in I. She did not really join in a holy war, but many—mainly Muslims, but also non-Muslims—were sympathetic to the Turkish cause (also because of anti-British feeling). After the war, the Indian nationalists were no less keen in demonstrating solidarity with the ME Muslims. From 1919, a *Khilafat* movement operated in I. to defend the Ottoman Caliphate▷ against alleged Western schemes to abolish it; the Indian National Congress joined this Muslim movement *en masse*. (The movement expired quietly in 1924, when the caliphate was abolished, not by imperialist Western plots, but by the Turkish nationalists.)

The Indian nationalists also developed close relations with the Arab nationalist movements, particularly the Egyptians since the 1920s. On the other hand, the Indian nationalists, with the exception of a

Nehru meeting Nasser, Cairo 1960

few individuals, displayed no sympathy for Zionism, the national movement of the Jewish people; they fully supported the Arab view on Palestine and even put pressure on the British in this respect. An Indian judge served on the 1947 UN Palestine Commission; he opposed the partition programme supported by the majority. I. spoke and voted against the November 1947 Resolution on the Partition of Palestine (Indian opposition to any partition proposal was at least in part motivated by the trauma of the partition of I. herself, which the nationalists had resisted for long, but finally had to accept).

Independent I. (from 1947 onwards) continued the same policy as the pre-independence nationalist movement and developed close and friendly relations with the Arab states, particularly Egypt. This co-operation was intensified after the Egyptian Revolution of 1952, with the Indians regarding the new Egyptian leadership as men of their own kind—progressive, secular, socialist, and neutralist. Nehru and Nasser▷ and their colleagues formulated the concept of neutralism▷ and "non-alignment"; and a personal friendship developed between the two. Indo-Egyptian co-operation went as far as a joint programme to develop jet aircraft (the programme failed and was abandoned) and nuclear research.

Relations with Israel, on the other hand, reflected the attitude of the Indian leaders to Zionism. I. recognized Israel *de jure* and without qualifications in Sept. 1950, but refused to establish normal diplomatic relations. She permitted the opening of an Israel Consulate in Bombay, but not an Embassy in New Dehli. I. has consistently spoken against Israel at international conferences and refrained from co-operation in trade, cultural exchanges, etc., even though public opinion and the press are quite sympathetic to Israel and often protest against the government's policy. The government sought at all cost to avoid giving offence to the Arab states whose friendship it assiduously solicited; it feared the anger of Indian Muslims, on whose votes the ruling party depended; and it wished to deny to Pakistan propaganda advantages in the Muslim world, such as branding I. a "friend of Israel". It also took care not to endanger I.'s position in Kashmir by friendship with Israel, on account both of local Muslim opinion and the need of Arab support in the international arena. I.'s relations with Turkey and Iran were correct but cool because of those countries' close links with the West and with Pakistan.

The Arabs did not respond with generosity to I.'s hope that, in exchange for her friendship, they would support her against Pakistan in general, and in the Kashmir dispute in particular. The more conservative states, Sa'udi Arabia, Jordan and, until

1958, Iraq, felt closer to Pakistan and supported her, discreetly or openly, in the Kashmir dispute. The revolutionary and "progressive" states, with friendly Egypt at the head, professed friendship and sympathy for I.; but even they did not fully identify themselves with I. against Muslim Pakistan. They were, at most, neutral in the Kashmir dispute and often spoke of Kashmiri rights of self-determination—a formula close to Pakistan's position and opposed by I. Nasser and the other Arab leaders showed no more than sympathetic neutrality in the frontier dispute between I. and China which turned into open warfare in 1962. Nasser even tried unsuccessfully to mediate between I. and China, together with other neutralist countries. I. sustained the greatest injury to her prestige at the hands of the Arab states in 1969, when she was rebuffed by them on seeking to take part at the Muslim "summit" following the fire at the al-Aqsa Mosque in Jerusalem: I., as representing a large Muslim community, was eager to demonstrate her solidarity with the Arab states and Islam; but her high-level delegation was not even admitted to the conference.

The Indian public (where, notwithstanding official government policies, there is much anti-Muslim sentiment) is no doubt offended and disappointed over the policies of the Arab states which do not return I.'s friendship in kind. However, Indian official policy remains one of fostering friendship and close bonds with the Arab states in general, and Egypt and the other left-wing "progressive" regimes, in particular.   (Y.S.)

*INDUSTRIALIZATION. Industrialization began in the ME after World War I▷. It received a boost after World War II▷, due to exploitation of the soil resources and the attainment of independence by the countries of the region. Between the two World Wars, the process was reflected mainly in the change from outdated, traditional handicraft industries to relatively modern small-scale industries. After World War II, medium and heavy industry developed, often at an advanced technological level. The progress of I. was reflected in the growth of the industrial labour force and in the percentage of the gross national product accounted for by industry. At the turn of the century, about 750,000 persons worked in industry—mostly in handicrafts—in the ME; by the 1950s, the total had risen to 1—1.5m.; by 1968 the industrial labour force totalled some 2.5m.

Industry (excluding oil) has accounted since the 1950s for 2%–8% of the GNP in Iran, Sa'udi Arabia, Libya, Iraq and Sudan; 11%–13% in Syria, Lebanon and Jordan; 13%–25% in Kuwait, Turkey, Egypt, and Israel.   (M.E.)

Ismet İnönü

*İNÖNÜ, ISMET (b. 1884). Turkish statesman. Second President of the Republic 1938–50. Prime Minister 1923–4, 1925–37, 1961–5, Born in Izmir, İ. graduated from the Military Academy of Pangalti in 1906 and served in various military assignments, including that of Commander of Ottoman forces in Yemen, 1910–13. During World War I he was Commander of the Second Army and fought on the Russian, and later the Syrian and Palestinian fronts. In 1920 he was elected to the Grand National Assembly. In 1921 he was appointed Chief-of-Staff and Commander of the Western front, winning the two battles of İnönü (from which he took his family name). He became Foreign Minister in 1922 and successfully led the Turkish delegation at the Lausanne▷ Peace Conference.

On the proclamation of the Republic, 1923, he became Prime Minister, a post which he held, except for a brief interval in 1924–5, until 1937. Upon Atatürk's▷ death in 1938, I. was elected President of the Republic and leader of the Republican People's Party. He carried on Atatürk's policies and kept Turkey out of World War II. After the War he permitted the growth of a multi-party system, and in 1950 he was replaced by Celäl Bayar▷, the leader of the Democratic Party. He led the fight against the Democratic regime in the 1950s, and although he did not take part in the 1960 revolution, he exercised strong influence on its leaders. I. and his party emerged from the elections of 1961 as the strongest party but without an overall majority, and until 1965 he led three successive coalition governments. In 1965 the Justice Party won the election and İ. again became leader of the opposition. In 1971 he gave his blessing—reluctantly and with reservations—to the ultimatum of the military chiefs that toppled the Demirel▷ government and to his party's participation in a new coalition. İ.'s Republican Peoples' Party has adopted, since about 1964, under his leadership, a left-of-centre ideology (with

a right-wing faction seceding) with an increasingly socialist slant.   (D.K.)

IRAN (or Persia). Independent kingdom between the Caspian Sea and the Persian Gulf, comprising most of the plateau of Iran. Pop. (1970 estimate): 28m., most of them Shi'ite▷ Muslims, speaking Persian, an Indo-European language. In Azerbaijan▷ a Turkish dialect is spoken. Sunni-Muslim minorities include c. 1m. Kurds▷, 300,000 Turkmens (Turcomans) and 40,000 Baluchis. An Arabic-speaking minority, in Khuzistan▷, numbers c. 300,000, mostly Shi'ite but including some Sunnites. The main non-Muslim minorities are c. 200,000 Armenians▷ (of the Gregorian denomination); 65,000 Jews; 30,000 Zoroastrians▷; 25,000 Assyrians▷ (Nestorian Christians), and c. 60,000 Baha'is▷.

The first four groups are recognized as religious minorities and entitled to representation in Parliament (2 Armenians, 1 each for the other three); but the Baha'is are not recognized and are officially considered as Muslims.

I. is bordered in the north by the Caspian Sea and the USSR, in the east by Afghanistan and Pakistan, in the south by the Persian Gulf and the Gulf of 'Oman, and in the west by Iraq and Turkey. The area is 628,000 sq. mi. of which about 50% is considered cultivable, but only about 5% is actually under cultivation.

The population is about 25% urban and about 75% rural and nomadic. Most of it is engaged in agriculture and fishing, producing livestock as well as wheat, barley, rice, tobacco, dates, cotton and sugar. Industrial enterprises include textile, cement, carpets and vehicle assembly plants.

I.'s major industry is the production of oil (see Oil▷). A concession was granted in 1901 to the Australian W. K. D'Arcy; oil in commercial quantities was discovered in 1908, and in 1909 the Anglo-Persian Oil Company was formed (changed in 1935 to "Anglo-Iranian Oil Company" and in 1954 to "British Petroleum"). After a long series of disputes with the Anglo-Iranian Company, Iran nationalized the oil industry in 1951, but was unable to operate it on her own. In Oct. 1954 it was agreed to replace the concessionaire by an international Consortium consisting of British Petroleum (40%), American companies (40%), Royal Dutch Shell (14%) and a French Company (6%). The Consortium's concession is valid until 1979. Ownership of oil deposits outside the Consortium's area is vested with the National Iranian Oil Company, an Iranian state enterprise, which now handles about 10% of Iranian oil either independently or through foreign companies as contractors.

I. is now the largest oil producer in the ME, having overtaken Kuwait and Sa'udi Arabia. The closure of the Suez Canal in 1967 and the temporary stoppage of production in some Arab countries contributed to this development. Crude oil production in I. amounted to 141.5m. tons in 1968, 168m. tons in 1969. Government revenue reached $1,000m. in 1969.

Adverse geographical conditions have greatly restricted communications in I. Road construction is difficult, but continues. Important railways, linking north-to-south the Caspian Sea, Teheran and the Persian Gulf and branching out also to the west and east have been constructed. Recently Persian Gulf ports, especially Bushire, are being developed—partly to lessen I.'s dependence on the port of Khorramshahr on the disputed Shatt al-'Arab▷ River, whose entrance is under Iraqi control. CENTO▷ has planned and developed roads into Turkey and Pakistan. The large distances within the country—1400 mi. from north-west to south-east—have encouraged the development of domestic air traffic. I. was a founder-member of both the League of Nations and the UN.

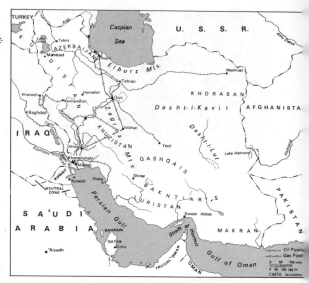

Map of Iran

POLITICAL HISTORY. I. declined during the reign of the Qajar dynasty, 1797–1925, owing to disunity, misrule and growing foreign interference. Since the 19th century Britain and Russia have been competing for influence in I. The interplay of conflicting British and Russian interests dominated not only the country's foreign policies but also, to a great extent, the shape of internal affairs. To cover his deficits, the King (Persian Shah) of I. used to sell concessions to foreigners and contract foreign loans and mortages. This policy paralysed the country's economic growth and caused discontent among the people.

During the reign of Muzaffar-ul-Din Shah, who ascended the throne in 1896, popular discontent led to the formation of a constitutional movement among intellectuals influenced by Western liberal doctrines and religious elements headed by a Pan-Islamic preacher, Jamal-ul-Din al-Afghani (these elements opposed the Shah's policy of granting concessions to foreigners and curtailing the power of the clergy), as well as the merchant class frustrated because of foreign commercial deals. Britain favoured the constitutional movement because it aimed, *inter alia*, at freeing the country from its involvement with Russia. A bloodless revolution took place in July 1906 in Teheran. Some 10,000 people flocked to the grounds of the British Legation where they could not be arrested and voiced their demands for a constitutional monarchy. At the same time, the entire clergy left the capital to show their solidarity. On 5 Aug., the Shah gave in. He issued an order con-

vening a National Assembly and promising reforms, a modernized Court of Justice, an amnesty, etc. The constitution was drawn up the same year. It provided for an Assembly (*Majlis*) of 120 members elected by seven groups or classes representing only a fraction of the population: members of the Qajar dynasty, princes, nobles, religious leaders, landowners, merchants and the guilds. *Majlis* ratification was required, as the constitutionalists had advocated, for the Shah's transactions regarding concessions, foreign loans, public property and national revenues.

In 1907, Britain and Russia concluded an agreement—part of their new *entente*—to divide I. into zones of influence: the south-east was recognized as a British sphere, the whole north as a Russian sphere, and the rest of the country was to be neutral.

Muzaffar-ul-Din Shah died in 1907. His successor, Muhammad 'Ali Shah, made several attempts to overthrow the constitution and restore an absolute monarchy. A counter-revolution led by the Shah and his Persian Cossack Brigade (created on a Russian pattern with Russian officers), took place in 1908. In June 1908 the Cossacks shelled the *Majlis* building and the Shah declared the dissolution of Parliament. To aid the Shah, the Russians occupied I.'s northern provinces. However, the Nationalists resisted the Shah's forces and an army including a considerable number of Bakhtiari▷ tribesmen marched on Teheran and defeated the Cossack Brigade in July 1909. Muhammad 'Ali Shah fled to Russia and the second *Majlis*, inaugurated in Nov. 1909, crowned the Shah's 11-year-old son Ahmad. Two years later

Muhammad Shah tried to return and seize the throne, but he failed and left the country never to return.

The Constitutionalists failed to achieve unity among themselves and to give the country a strong central government. To improve financial management, it was decided to engage an American expert, Morgan Shuster. He arrived in May 1911 and under his guidance some progress was made in the reorganization of the country's financial system. However, reactionary elements, strongly backed and encouraged by Russia, opposed his work and presence in I. In 1911 Russia presented I. with an ultimatum demanding his dismissal. The ultimatum was rejected by the *Majlis* but accepted by the cabinet. Shuster left Iran in Jan. 1912 and wrote his classic "The Strangling of Persia." Russian influence was now quite dominant.

On the outbreak of World War I, Ahmad Shah declared I.'s strict neutrality. But he was not able to carry out the policies he desired as he lacked an army strong enough to guard the country's frontiers. A Turkish invasion of Azerbaijan in 1914 was soon followed by a Russian invasion of all the northern provinces. In the south, the British Major Percy Sykes recruited the "South Persia Rifles" to protect the Persian Gulf and British oil interests. This formation rapidly gained control over all the southern section of I. German agents were active in stirring up the tribes in the vicinity of Shiraz and trying to win them over to the German cause. In fact, some circles in I. believed that siding with Germany could provide a way out of the Anglo-Russian game of interests, and an impending pro-German revolt was rumoured.

After the war, I. faced social and economic chaos. The government's bid to participate in the Versailles peace talks was rejected. Instead Britain offered I., in 1919, a treaty which would have helped her solve some of her most urgent problems but would have put her under pronounced British influence. The treaty was accepted by the Shah and the government, but the *Majlis* refused to ratify it.

On 20 Feb. 1921, Zia-ul-Din Tabatabai▷, a journalist and politician, seized power with the help of the Persian Cossack Brigade—now without its Russian officers and commanded instead by a Persian officer, Reza Khan▷. Zia ul-Din formed a new Cabinet and Reza Khan was appointed Minister of War and Commander-in-Chief of the Army. However, the two coup leaders clashed and Zia-ul-Din was forced to resign; he left I. and was given refuge by the British in Palestine. Reza Khan remained Minister of War in several successive cabinets, seeking to build up an army and an internal security force strong enough to exert control through-

out the country. He succeeded in this task and was able to suppress a number of political and tribal revolts. In October 1923 Reza Khan became Prime Minister. A few months later Ahmed Shah, the last ruler of the Qajar dynasty, left I. In 1925 a special Constituent Assembly chose Reza Khan as Shah of I. The new Shah chose the name of Pahlavi▷ for the dynasty established by him.

The reign of Reza Shah was an era of reforms. His main purpose was to modernize the country, make it self-sufficient and free it from dependence on foreign aid. He reorganized the army, equipped it with modern weapons and improved its training. With its help, he was able to defeat a separatist Soviet-supported rebellion in the northern province of Gilan▷ (1921) and several other plots and uprisings, and in the mid-1920s subdued the separatist great tribes of the south. In 1929, '30 and '31, the Shah had to deal with strikes in Abadan, Tabriz and Isfahan. In 1930 there was an uprising of Kurdish peasants in Khorassan. He also suppressed Communist activities.

To modernize I. the Shah had to destroy a deeply rooted social order. Though he was inspired, at least in part, by Kemalist Turkey's example, he modernized gradually without breaking with traditions. He curtailed the power and wealth of the clergy; the *Shari'a* (religious law) was replaced by civil and criminal codes based on French law; the whole judiciary system was Westernized and a hierarchy of courts of justice was established on the Western model; civil marriage and divorce registers were set up; the position of women was improved; the wearing of the veil was banned; religious schools were replaced by state schools. Elementary and secondary schools were improved and expanded, adult education courses initiated to combat illiteracy, physical education and scouting were introduced in all schools, the level of technical education improved. In 1935 the University of Teheran was founded.

The keynote to the Shah's economic policy was state control. Thanks to the secularization of the judiciary system, the capitulations (foreign privileges and extra-territorial rights) could be legally abolished. On the other hand, the merchant class lost its freedom of enterprise and was drawn into the governmental system of monopolies and trade control. Priority was given to industrialization and to the development of national resources. Many factories were built (textiles, sugar refining, cement, etc.). Efforts were made to devise an efficient method of collecting taxes (rather than imposing new ones). One of the most spectacular achievements of Reza Shah was the construction of the north-south Trans-Iranian Railroad. The expenses of this costly enterprise were covered by revenues derived from the tea and sugar monopolies.

In World War II I. declared her neutrality. But Reza Shah allowed Germany to use I. as a base for subversive activities in the Middle East. To prevent the expansion of German influence and to open a secure supply line to the USSR, Britain and the Soviet Union invaded Iran in Aug. 1941. Reza Shah capitulated after two days' struggle. He abdicated in favour of his son, Muhammad Reza▷, and was exiled to South Africa. Soviet troops occupied the north of the country, while the British occupied the south, joined, in 1942, by American troops. They developed ports and constructed roads through which millions of tons of war material were sent to Russia.

In Jan. 1942 a Treaty of Alliance was concluded between I., Britain and the USSR. The two powers undertook to respect I.'s territorial integrity, sovereignty and political independence, while I. granted the Allies the use of all her means of communications. Allied forces were to be withdrawn from I. not later than six months after the cessation of hostilities between the Allies and the Axis.

The Russians kept their zone of occupation under firm control, denying the Iranian authorities freedom of movement. Furthermore, they pressed Teheran to grant them oil concessions; in Apr. 1946, the Iranian government agreed to establish a joint Russian-Iranian oil company but this decision was later shelved by the *Majlis*. The Russians encouraged separatist movements in North Iran. In Dec. 1945, they engineered the creation of two puppet governments: an "Azerbaijan▷ Republic" with headquarters in Tabriz, and a (much smaller) "Kurdish Republic" with headquarters in Mahabad▷. The Russian army prevented Iranian troops from entering Azerbaijan to crush the rebellion. Even after the evacuation of Russian troops from I. in May 1946, Russia pressed Teheran not to send troops to Azerbaijan. Only in Dec. 1946 were Iranian forces able to recapture the northern separatist provinces.

Iranian complaints to the UN Security Council had preceded these developments. In Jan. 1946, I. denounced Soviet interference in her internal affairs, and in March she complained bitterly that the USSR had not withdrawn her troops from I., as she was committed to do. (British and American troops were evacuated by Mar.) These complaints, supported and encouraged by the Western Powers, and the ensuing discussion at the Security Council were the first open post-war East-West clash, the first signs of the impending Cold War. Russia was compelled to withdraw her troops by May. (I.'s unwilling agreement to the joint oil company was a

kind of return concession extracted by the Russians).

During the period of occupation many Communist detainees had been released as a result of a general amnesty to political prisoners, and a Communist party called *Tudeh*▷ ("The Masses") had been established, especially in the Russian-occupied north. In 1943–4 *Tudeh* participated in the parliamentary elections and won 8 seats. In Aug. 1946 Premier Qavam al-Saltaneh▷ took three *Tudeh* men into his cabinet. They were, however soon ousted, and the government began suppressing the party; in Feb. 1949, it was outlawed.

While unrest and discontent at misgovernment grew, the oil issue increasingly dominated the Iranian political scene. Dr. Muhammad Mossaddeq▷ established a faction called the "National Front", composed mainly of urban intellectuals, and started a campaign for the nationalization of I.'s oil. Under his influence, the Oil Commission of the *Majlis* rejected in summer 1950 a revised oil agreement with the A.I.O.C. which granted more favourable conditions than the original agreement. Mossaddeq's views were opposed by the Premier, General 'Ali Razmara, who stated that I. was not yet able to run the complicated oil industry by herself. In March 1951 Razmara was assassinated by a member of a terroristic ultra-religious group, *Fedayan Islam*▷, and a few days later the *Majlis* passed a bill nationalizing the oil installations. In April Dr. Mossaddeq, whose popularity had risen tremendously, became Prime Minister. The A.I.O.C. and the British government brought the dispute before the International Court and the Security Council, but with no result. American mediation efforts also remained unsuccessful. By Oct. 1951 A.I.O.C. technical staff left Abadan, the refinery ceased to work and Iranian oil exports came to a standstill. Relations with Britain were severed in Oct. 1952.

Mossaddeq's "National Front" was composed of several groups with different ideologies, both socialist and right-wing, with anti-British sentiment and the will to reduce the Shah's power as the common denominator. Besides his Front, Mossaddeq was supported by different groups with opposed inclinations, such as the fanatical religious circles headed by Ayatullah Kashani▷, the *Tudeh* party, proscribed in 1949 but allowed by Mossaddeq to operate again, and the merchants of Teheran's Bazaar. These groups shared the Front's hatred of the British and anti-Shah attitude. Mossaddeq held that the Shah should reign, not rule, and strove to curtail his power. In Feb. 1953 the Shah publicly announced his intention of leaving the country. He was persuaded to stay by a large pro-royalist demonstration (allegedly organized by Kashani who feared that the abdication of the Shah would strengthen Mossaddeq's position beyond control).

As no oil was being sold, the economic situation deteriorated alarmingly and the country faced bankruptcy. As the impasse dragged on friction between Mossaddeq and his supporters increased, and in July 1953 there were resignations from the *Majlis* in protest against Mossaddeq's policy. In order to forestall a vote of non-confidence, the Prime Minister held a "referendum" and claimed that its results authorized him to dissolve the *Majlis*. The Shah now dismissed Mossaddeq and appointed Gen. Fazlollah Zahedi▷ as Prime Minister (16 Aug. 1953). But Mossaddeq refused to obey the decree; and as Zahedi, after an unsuccessful attempt to arrest Mossaddeq, disappeared, the Shah left I. However, the army had remained loyal to the Shah, despite Mossaddeq's efforts to win it over. Zahedi and the army now rapidly took control of the capital, arrested Mossaddeq and enabled the Shah to return (19 Aug. 1953).

Gen. Zahedi's government resumed diplomatic relations with Britain, and started negotiations to solve the oil problem. In Sept. 1954 it was agreed to replace the A.I.O.C. by a Consortium of several oil companies including a large share for US companies (see above).

The Shah now proceeded to consolidate his position. All political parties and groups were disbanded, and till 1957 no political parties were allowed. The army and other security services were purged of disloyal elements. Gradually the Shah's position changed from that of a symbolic Head of State to that of a chief executive on the US pattern. In the early 1960s the Shah initiated a land reform programme, which he had already unsuccessfully tried to commence in 1950-1 by distributing crown lands. He had then urged the landowners in vain to follow the royal example and distribute some of their lands. A bill providing for a mild form of land distribution was approved by the *Majlis*, where an influential group of landowners prevailed, in so mutilated a form that hardly any land was earmarked for distribution. The oil crisis had then shelved the land reform for several years. In 1960 the *Majlis* once again obstructed land reform plans, but this time the Shah, assisted by an energetic Minister of Agriculture, Dr. Hassan Arsanjani, persisted.

In Jan. 1963, between the dissolution of one *Majlis* and the elections to the new one, the Shah submitted his plan for social and economic reforms, called the "White Revolution," to a referendum. With an overwhelming majority of 98% the electorate approved Land Reform, i.e. the requisition of large estates and their distribution to the peasants working

them; the nationalization of forests; the sale of shares in government factories to provide funds for the land reform programme; a scheme for a workers' share in the profits of state factories; the amendment of the electoral law and the granting of the franchise to women; and the formation of a "Literacy Corps," *i.e.* conscripted army officer cadets to be trained as teachers and to serve in villages.

Following the referendum, steps were taken to break up the large estates and transfer ownership to peasants. It is estimated that at present about three million rural families own the land they cultivate.

Opposition to the Shah's reforms came from the landowners and also from the religious-conservative circles. The latter initiated in June 1963 a series of riots in Teheran, Tabriz, Isfahan and Meshhed. At least 100 persons were killed and some 200 injured. A land reform official was also killed in the province of Fars, and security forces clashed with rebel tribal elements. Hundreds were arrested, including some *mullahs* (religious leaders). The Shah declared that there had been a deliberate plot to overthrow the regime, while the Chief of Security claimed there were "strong indications" that President Nasser was behind the disturbances. However, reforms were carried out according to plan. In the elections of Sept. 1963 women participated for the first time.

In 1965 there were more outbreaks of violent opposition to the reforms. In Jan., Prime Minister Hasan Ali Mansur▷ was assassinated by a member of the fanatic *Fedayan Islam* (he was succeeded by the Finance Minister A. A. Hoveida▷). In April, an unsuccessful attempt was made on the Shah's life, apparently by a secessionist pro-Peking *Tudeh* faction. However, the implementation of the "White Revolution" made headway. In 1966-7, six more points were added to the original programme: the formation of a Health Corps, a Development Corps, and local village courts and arbitration councils, to shorten and simplify legal procedures; the nationalization of water resources; a building programme to provide better housing; and administrative and educational reforms, to create a more efficient civil service.

In the elections of Aug. 1967 the reform programme was the main issue Boycotted by extreme-right and extreme-left circles, the elections were won by Premier Hoveyda's *Iran Novin* ("New Iran") party.

In Oct. 1967 the solemn coronation of the Shah took place, to emphasize the stability of his regime. Since then there has been calm in the internal scene in Iran and accelerated economic progress at a 7% rate of annual growth—despite sporadic small-scale unrest and leftist agitation.

In 1968 for the first time a woman, Mrs. F. Parsa, was included in the cabinet as Minister of Education.

RECENT FOREIGN POLICY. In the early 1960s a new phase began in Iranian foreign policy. Political stability, the continued growth of economic development projects, social reforms—all these gave the regime a feeling of self-confidence. I. began to appear as an independent factor of increasing importance in the region, and to demonstrate her independence of the Big Powers. I.'s basic orientation remains pro-West and she maintains special ties with the USA. A bi-lateral defence treaty signed with the USA in 1959 is still in force. I. is a member of CENTO▷ (previously the Baghdad Pact▷), and an American military training mission operates in I. Yet, since the mid-1960s, I. has shown her independence of the West in general, and the USA in particular. The Shah would like to refute the charge that he was reinstated during his struggle with Dr. Mossaddeq by the Americans and keeps his position through their support, and that he signed the 1954 oil agreement with the consortium under American pressure.

I. has strengthened her defensive power by acquiring modern arms. In particular, she ensured the protection of the vulnerable oil installations, especially the oil refineries in Abadan▷ and the oil port on the island of Kharg. In 1964–5, the government obtained *Majlis* approval of two defence loans of $200m. each, the first one explicity from the USA. The second loan was to strengthen I. in view of approaching changes in the Persian Gulf, and was earmarked in particular for the construction of ports, naval bases, anti-aircraft defences and the purchase of naval craft. It was decided to end US economic aid at the end of 1967, as I., because of her economic development, no longer needed it. American aid, 1950–67, half of it military, reached *c.* $700m.

Since the early 1960s, great changes have taken place in I.-Soviet relations. In Dec. 1962, I. informed the Soviet Union that as an act of good will and to foster friendly relations, she would not permit the stationing of foreign missile bases on her territory. At the same time Premier Bulganin publicly dissociated himself from past Soviet activities against I. The USSR had apparently abandoned her hope that hostile propaganda and subversion would bring leftist forces to power in I., and decided to co-operate with the existing regime. Since late 1963, there have been exchanges of high-level visits and missions with the Soviet Union and other Soviet Bloc countries (the Shah visited the USSR in 1956, 1965 and 1968). Trade and economic ties were increased and there is an impressive Soviet and Eastern European economic presence in I. Under an important agreement of Jan. 1966 the Soviet Union is to erect a steel

mill near Isfahan (to produce, at first, 600,000 tons a year and later double that amount). A $230m. Soviet loan for the plant will be repaid in natural gas to be transported through a 42-inch pipeline from the oil fields near Ahwaz in the south to the Russian border west of the Caspian Sea. The $550 m. pipeline will be constructed in its southern section by I. (by Western companies and with partial Western credits) and in its northern section by the USSR. Natural gas exports will also cover I.'s other debts to the USSR—for a machine-tool plant being constructed near Arak and various projects agreed upon in Dec. 1963 (e.g. power station on the river Aras▷ and the construction of 33 grain silos, of which eleven have already been completed). Under further agreements more factories were to be constructed by the USSR in return for natural gas, agricultural produce and manufactured goods (June 1968), while I. was to purchase from the USSR arms and military equipment for $110m. (Feb. 1967). This deal caused some tension in relations with the USA, and criticism in the American press met with an angry reaction in the Persian. In Apr. 1967, I. also granted the USSR concessions for oil exploration. Similar agreements were signed with other Soviet Bloc countries, e.g. for the construction of a tractor factory in Tabriz by Rumania. On the other hand, I.'s economic relations with East Germany were frozen in 1969 due to her anti-I. position in the I.-Iraq dispute (I. maintains diplomatic relations with West Germany).

Relations with the Soviet Bloc have remained ambivalent. Every once in a while there is sharp reaction in the Iranian press to Persian-language Communist radio propaganda from the USSR and East Germany. The I. Foreign Ministry in Aug. 1968 deplored the Soviet invasion of Czechoslovakia, but the Shah was the first non-Communist Head of State to visit the USSR after the invasion, and Soviet naval units paid a friendly call at the port of Bandar-'Abbas in Feb. 1969.

In Aug. 1971, I. recognized Communist China and established official relations with her.

Relations with Britain were influenced by passing tension over the Persian Gulf▷, and Britain's plan for a federation of the Gulf principalities, including Bahrain▷. The renunciation of I.'s claim to Bahrain, in 1970, ended this dispute (see below). I. has acquiesced in the termination of Britain's presence in the Gulf in 1971, *i.e.* the removal of her protection from the principalities, and opposed the plan of the Conservatives to review this decision. There is occasional tension in relations with both Britain and the USA due to frequent Iranian demands that the oil consortium should raise its output. A new agreement over oil prices and taxes ended a grave crisis, in Feb. 1971.

I.'s relations with Turkey and Pakistan were tightened when all three joined the "Baghdad Pact" (1955), later CENTO. But this politcal and military treaty has never been very effective, Pakistan's membership is only symbolic and partly suspended, and I. no longer attaches real importance to it. At a conference of the three heads of state, in Istanbul, in July 1964, an Organization for Regional Co-opera-tion and Developmet (RCD) was set up parallel with CENTO but without Anglo-American partici-pation. I. and Turkey are also planning a $1,100m. oil pipeline from Ahwaz in southern I. to Iskenderun on the Mediterranean, to free I. from dependence on the passage of her oil through Arab territory or the Suez Canal. The 42-inch pipeline will be 1,055 mi. long, and 60m. tons of oil will flow through it annually.

Despite this co-operation with Turkey and Pakis-tan, neither gave I. the political and moral support which she had hoped for in the disputes with the Arab states on the questions of Khuzistan▷, Bahrain, Shatt al-'Arab▷, and the Kurds▷ in Iraq. On the other hand, I. supported Turkey in the question of Cyprus, and Pakistan in that of Kashmir. I. views Pakistan as the country closest to her, rather than Turkey.

I.'s relations with Egypt deteriorated in the 1950s and were completely severed 1960–70. The dispute began with the "Baghdad Pact". President 'Abd-ul-Nasser▷ saw the Shah as a tool in Western imperialist hands, and his royalist regime—precisely because of its stability and successful development, its reforms and improved relations with the Soviet Bloc—as an antithesis to the Egyptian revolutionary regime. An open conflict broke out in July 1960, and relations were broken off, following the Shah's declaration that I. recognizes Israel de facto and carries on normal trade and economic relations with her. Since then, Egypt has supported Arab claims to the Iranian province of Khuzistan ("Arabistan"). I. considered Egyptian intervention in the Yemen war as Egyptian expansionism in the direction of the Persian Gulf (which the Arabs call the "Arab Gulf") and a threat to herself. Every opposition movement in I. has since then enjoyed the support of the Egyptian propaganda machine. There were bitter mutual attacks through all communications media, with I.'s ties with Israel playing a major role in Egyptian propaganda. Various Arab heads of state attempted to mediate between I. and Egypt. Since 1968, I. has softened her position, i.a. due to Egypt's defeat in the Six Day War which has made her appear less dangerous. I. is also interested in an understanding with Egypt over the Persian Gulf on the eve of the British evacuation. The constant tension between I. and Iraq and the wish to isolate Iraq have strengthened this desire. Efforts at concilia-tion wcre made at the Muslim summit conferences of Rabat (Sept. 1969) and Jidda (Mar. 1970). In June 1970, senior representatives were unofficially exchanged and later in the year full diplomatic rela-tions were resumed.

I. did not have close ties with Sa'udi Arabia. The contrast between Wahhabi▷ rule in Sa'udi and Shi'i Islam in I. (which the Wahhabis consider a heresy), and between Sa'udi theocracy and secular reforms in I., led to estrangement and mutual suspicion. In addition, there was competition between the two as oil-producing countries (Sa'udi Arabia—and Iraq and Kuwait also—had taken advantage of I.'s oil nationalization crisis in 1951–3 to boost their own production, and I. resented that, too). Relations began to improve in 1963. Egypt's dispatch of troops to Yemen created a community of interest between I. and Sa'udi Arabia. They both fear Egyptian (and Iraqi) ambition in the Persian Gulf and the Arab peninsula. As conservative monarchical regimes with a pro-Western orientation, they are also both ap-prehensive of leftist and Nasserist elements in the Persian Gulf principalities. King Feisal's▷ visit to Teheran in Dec. 1965 signalized this rapprochement, and led to an agreement on the delimitation of submarine oil rights in the Persian Gulf (finally signed in Oct. 1968). In Nov. 1968, the Shah paid a royal visit to Sa'udi Arabia. The question of Bahrain occasioned a temporary crisis only.

Relations with Kuwait▷ have been close. I. was the first country to recognize her independence and supported her against Iraqi threats, 1961. Rela-tions have deteriorated since Arab nationalism grew stronger in Kuwait and she became, at the instigation of Egypt and the Arab League▷, a centre of anti-Iranian propaganda. Tension also arose over the status of I. residents in Kuwait (60–80,000), as well as the delimitations of submarine oil rights in the Persian Gulf. It appears, however, that mutual interests oblige I. and Kuwait to reach compromise settlements, for both are anxious to prevent instability and the rise of revolutionary forces in the Gulf region.

In the Persian Gulf▷, I. aims to achieve political and cultural influence, and a strategic hinterland for her defence. She fears Egyptian penetration and an Iraqi presence in support of radical Arab nationalist movements which could endanger the stability of the regimes in the larger principalities, and in Sa'udi Arabia, once the British leave at the end of 1971.

The Bahrain▷ question has been a bone of conten-tion for many years. Since 1927, when the British-Hijazi Treaty of Jidda recognized British claims over Bahrain, I. has been demanding the return to her of the islands. She complained to the League of Nations in the 1930s over the oil concession granted to American companies by the Sheikh of Bahrain. In 1957, I. proclaimed the Gulf islands, including Bahrain, a province under her control, but the claim has remained dormant. When Britain announced in Jan. 1968 her intention to evacuate her Persian Gulf bases by the end of 1971, to terminate her protectorate over the principalities, and to set up a federation of independent amirates, I. announced that she would not recognize that federation if it were to include Bahrain. However, after the Shah's visits to Kuwait and Sa'udi Arabia in Nov. 1968, he agreed, in Jan. 1969, to a referendum or public opinion poll in Bahrain to be carried out by a representative of the UN Secretary-General. A UN representative arrived in Bahrain in March 1970, and reported that her inhabitants preferred independence. On 11 May 1970, the Security Council approved these findings, and I. accepted them. I.'s claim to Abu Mussa▷ and the Tumb Islands create a dispute with the Trucial▷ sheikhdoms.

Tension grew between I. and Iraq after the establishment of a republican regime in Iraq, in 1958. It concerned the Shatt-al-'Arab▷ border, the continental shelf in the Persian Gulf, oil rights in the areas of Naft-i-Shah and Naft Khaneh, grazing rights of nomadic tribes, the Kurdish problem, the status of the Shi'ites in Iraq, the treatment of the I. minority (of several hundred thousand) in Iraq, and I. pilgrims to the Holy Places in Iraq. Iraq accused I. of turning a blind eye to aid from her territory to the Kurdish rebels, and of affording them even direct assistance. I. rejected these charges; but she had actually provided limited support to the Kurds in Iraq. I. would prefer Iraq as an entity composed of three groups: Sunni Arabs, Kurds and Shi'ites (both Arabic- and Persian-speaking), rather than as an Arab State. At the Shatt-al-'Arab, I. maintained that the border should be the thalweg or median line of the river. The issue led to a series of crises (1961, 1965, 1969), accompanied by military confrontations; in 1969 I. repudiated the 1937 agreement—imposed on her, she claimed, by Britain—which had left the whole river in Iraqi hands except for one short section. In order to reduce her dependence on shipping in the Shatt-al-'Arab and to counter Iraqi infiltration in the Persian Gulf, I. recently laid a pipeline from Abadan to Mashur on the Persian Gulf, and is constructing a large port at Bandar 'Abbas.

Relations with Syria are also tense. Following a declaration by the Syrian Prime Minister in Oct. 1965 that Khuzistan is Arab, the ambassadors of both countries were recalled, though diplomatic relations were not broken off.

Relations with Lebanon, which had always been friendly, were marred in Jan. 1966. In a speech in Beirut, a Kuwaiti minister said that Teheran had become "a centre of Zionist activities". The Iranian Ambassador in Beirut reacted sharply and the ambassadors of both states were recalled. Towards the end of 1966, the two countries patched up the quarrel for a short time. A new breach occurred when Lebanon gave asylum to General Teymour Bakhtiar▷, former head of the security services in I. I. broke off relations and applied economic sanctions.

I. has been relatively active in attempts to organize an association of Islamic states. These began after visits by King Hussein of Jordan in Sept. 1965 and King Feisal of Sa'udi Arabia in Dec. 1965; they continued during 1966, but yielded no results. I. supported the establishment of a permanent secretariat of the Islamic states, as decided on by the Muslim Foreign Ministers Conference at Jidda (in Mar. 1970).

I. accorded *de facto* recognition to Israel in 1950 and sent a diplomatic representative. In 1951, he was recalled because of pressure by religious groups and to gain the support of the Arab states in the struggle over oil nationalization (though, officially for financial reasons). Since then, relations have developed in many directions, including trade and economic ties, Israeli technical assistance in the development of I., but I. has stopped short of full official diplomatic relations. In the Arab-Israel conflict, I. politically supports the moderate Arab (Egyptian-Jordanian) position, particularly since 1967. The Shah and government have, however, repeatedly reconfirmed the recognition of Israel in press interviews, resisting all pressure to withdraw it.

CONSTITUTION AND POLITICS. I. is a constitutional monarchy. The executive power is vested in the Shah. The Shah appoints the Prime Minister who must be approved by the *Majlis* (Parliament). An amendment to the constitution promulgated in 1949 empowered the Shah to dissolve the *Majlis* provided that new elections are ordered to take place soon afterwards. The legislative power is vested in the *Majlis*—elected for a period of four years—and the Senate, of whose 60 members 30 are appointed by the Shah and 30 are elected (15 in Teheran and 15 in the rest of the country).

Political parties are a recent phenomenon in I. Till the late 1950s the only modern political party was *Tudeh* (Communist) proscribed 1949. At the initiative of the Shah, and to provide for a two-party system, two parties were founded in 1957–8: the *Mardom* ("People's") party and the *Melliyun* ("National") party—the former as an opposition. They do not seem to have taken root. The *Iran Novin*

("New I.") party was founded in 1963. In the mid-1960s a faction of the extreme right-wing "Pan-Iran Party," which once formed part of Mossaddeq's "National Front," was allowed to renew its activities.

PRESS, RADIO, T.V. Teheran is the centre of the Iranian press. There are about 25 dailies and 60 periodicals. The most important dailies are the after-noon newspapers *Ettel'at* and *Kayhan*, and the morning paper *Ayandegan*—all of which belong to private publishers. There are also some newspapers in English, French and German.

There are radio stations in Teheran and in 12 provincial centers broadcasting in Persian, Arabic, German, English, French, Russian, Turkish, Armenian, Assyrian, Urdu, Kurdish and Baluchi. There are T.V. stations in Teheran and Abadan.

STATISTICS. Area: 628,000 sq. mi.—c. 50% of the total area is considered cultivable; 5% is under culti-vation. Pop.: c. 28m. (1970 est.). Birthrate: 5%. Natural increase: 2.8%. Life expectancy: 40 years. Infant mortality: 20 per thousand. GNP: $9,000m. (1969). National income p.a.:: $303, (1969). Exports (1969, excluding oil): $245m. Imports: $1,300m. (1969). Budget: balanced at 400,000m. Rials ($52,632) (1970–1). Literacy: adult population (10+): c. 35%. Children (6–14) schooled: 90% (urban), 43% (rural). Doctors: 1 p. 2,5000 (1970). Hospital beds: 1 p. 940 (1968), 76 Rials = US $1.

(B. G.-D. T.)

IRAQ. Independent Republic. Pop: 8,261,527 (1965 census); it was estimated to approach 10m. in 1970. The mother tongue of about 80% of the people is Arabic. About 25% of the population are Arab Sunni Muslims inhabiting the upper Euphrates region from the Syrian border to the west of Baghdad, and the upper Tigris region between Samarra and Mosul. They are traditionally the politically dominant ele-ment of the country. About 50% of the population are Arabic-speaking Shi'is inhabiting the south and the centre up to the vicinity of Baghdad. They are by I. standards backward and parochial. The Kurds▷, Sunni Muslims by religion, make up 18–20% of the population. They live in the mountains of the north and north-east, with considerable com-munities in all the large cities of I.; they have, as a rule, preserved their native tongue—Indo-Aryan, of the Iranian group—and their group loyalty is to their tribe (except for the detribalized Kurdish city dweller) and beyond that to their Kurdish nation. Smaller minorities are Turcomans (Sunnis speaking a Turkish dialect), about 100,000 of whom live in Kirkuk and along the border between Arabs and Kurds; Yazidis▷, numbering about 40,000, are congregated mainly in Jabal Sinjar west of Mosul;

Sabaeans▷, of whom there are about 20,000, live along the lower Tigris; and Jews, of whom at most 3,000 are left, all inhabit Baghdad. There is an unknown number of Persians—partly along the eastern border and mainly in the cities holy to Shi'i Islam and in Baghdad. Christians total at most 4% of the population; the overwhelming majority of them belong to Eastern churches, or their Uniate Catholic off-shoots. An estimated breakdown is: Orthodox rites: Nestorians, 25,000; Syrian Jacobites, 30,000; Armenians, 20,000; Greek Orthodox, 2,000. Uniates: Chaldeans, 200,000; Syrian Catholics, 80,000; Armenian Catholics, 3,000; Greek Catholics, 1,000. There are also a few thousand Latins and Protestants.

In all these groups loyalty to the community ex-ceeds identification with the state, which is still not common except, perhaps, among Arab Sunnis. These last are also the carriers of Arab nationalism in I. Arab nomads (Bedouin) are estimated to form 5% of the population; but if semi-nomads at an advanced stage of settlement are taken into account the per-centage is far higher.

The area of I., including half of the Neutral Zone with Sa'udi Arabia, is 169,683 sq. mi.—exclusive of territorial waters in the Persian Gulf which are claimed by I. The borders are: with Kuwait, 99 mi.; Sa'udi Arabia, 345.5 mi.; Jordan, 56.7 mi.; Syria, 233 mi.; Turkey, 118 mi.; Iran, 507.5 mi.

I. is a predominantly agricultural country of immense antiquity, drawing its water from the Tigris and Euphrates, and in particular from their yearly floods. Since the security and the centralistic regime necessary for the rational harnessing of the twin rivers have often been absent for centuries, swamps and salt wastes have come to cover large areas of formerly fertile land. However, over the last 60 years much land has been reclaimed through a number of spectacular damming and irrigation projects and modern methods of soil preservation. The main produce is subsistence crops; barley, wheat, rice and lentils. A vital cash crop is dates—I. is the largest exporter in the world. Tobacco and fruit are of importance in the north, and cotton in the centre.

The main wealth of I. is its oil produced in com-mercial quantities since 1934 (for the terms and history of the concessions—see Oil▷). In 1970 the output was 77m. tons, from which the government received $495m. in royalties. The oil-producing concession-aires are so far only the I. Petroleum Company and its subsidiaries—the Mosul Oil Company and the Basra Oil Company—except for marginal quantities pro-duced by the Khanaqin Oil Company, nationalized in 1958. The importance of oil for the national economy cannot be overestimated; on it depend not merely whatever development is carried out, but also the day-to-day administration of the state. Mining and industry are of little importance as yet. Of about 2m. earners an estimated 1.6m. live on agriculture, and about 160,000 are in government service (including the armed forces). There is considerable unemployment, both in the cities and on the land.

The country suffers from two main social problems—that of rapid urbanization unaccompanied by industrialization on any comparable scale, and the presence of an uprooted, under-employed and disgruntled intelligentsia, flooding the liberal professions and unskilled in coping with the material challenges of I. society. The Agrarian Reform Act of 1958 (see below) has been the basis for much useful work, and for the distribution of land among, so far, some 57,000 peasants; but it has not solved the basic problems of rural poverty, backwardness and exploitation, and its administration has been slack for some years.

GOVERNMENT. According to the Provisional Constitution of 16 July 1970 I. is a "Sovereign People's Democratic Republic". The supreme body in the state is the Revolutionary Command Council of (maximal) 12 members who are recruited from among the Regional (i.e., Iraqi) Command of the Ba'th▷ party. The chairman of the RCC is also President of the Republic and Supreme Commander of the Armed Forces. The present incumbent is Lt.-General Ahmad Hassan al-Bakr▷, in power since the coup of 17 July 1968 (see below). The cabinet is appointed by the President and accountable to him. A National Assembly with legislative powers is envisaged by the Provisional Constitution, but no steps have been taken so far to implement that article, and no legislative or consultative body exists.

The press is government-controlled by law, and of a low standard compared with that of Egypt and Lebanon. On the other hand, higher education has developed rapidly in the last decade, with Baghdad University (1967–8—20,000 students) in the lead.

I. is divided into 15 provinces. The 15th, Dohuk, was carved out of the Kurdish districts of Mosul province early in 1970, in anticipation of a settlement with the Kurdish national movement (see below).

I. has existed as a political entity since 1920–1. She achieved independence in 1932 upon joining the League of Nations. She is a founding member of the United Nations Organization.

POLITICAL HISTORY. At the beginning of the century, what is today I., the ancient Mesopotamia, was loosely covered by the three Ottoman provinces (Vilayet) of Mosul, Baghdad and Basra. Though "Turkish Arabia" (Mesopotamia) was backward even by Ottoman standards, modernization had started

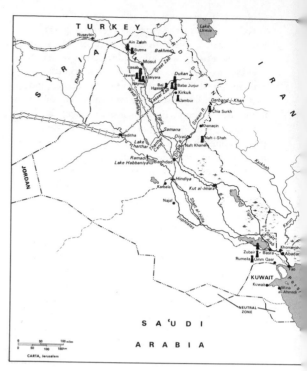

Map of Iraq

by then in the shape of improved provincial and municipal administration (brought about by the governorship in Baghdad of Midhat Pasha, 1869–72), a rudimentary school system on the Western pattern (the Baghdad Law School, founded 1908), the extension to the region of international rivalries, and in particular communications projects (outstanding among which was the German-inspired Baghdad Railway scheme), and the appropriation of oil rights among British, German and Dutch interests.

Remarkable at a different level were stirrings of Arab nationalism, not easily distinguishable from a striving for greater local independence, which centred, after the Young Turks' revolution, about a group of Sunni-I. officers in the Ottoman Army, and in Basra about the Shi'i *naqib* Sayyid Talib ibn al-Sayyid Rajab. It is certain, however, that these movements, for all their symptomatic significance, touched only a very small part even of the urban population.

Within a week of the declaration of World War I the British invaded Mesopotamia. The invasion was mounted from India, owing to the importance attributed to southern Mesopotamia as part of the western approaches to that subcontinent. Originally intended to exclude the Ottomans and their German allies from the head of the Persian Gulf, and to safeguard the oil installations of south-west Persia,

British strategic aims steadily expanded. Despite a heavy setback (surrender of the Sixth Division under Maj-Gen. Townshend at Kut, Apr. 1916), by Mar. 1917 a powerful army carried its offensive beyond Baghdad, and reached the outskirts of Mosul at the time of the armistice. At the same time an efficient civil administration was built up under the forceful direction of Sir Percy Z. Cox▷ and his assistant and deputy, Lt.-Col. (later Sir) Arnold T. Wilson▷.

At the time of their entry into Baghdad, and later immediately after the armistice, declarations by the victorious army and the Allies in general gave grounds for the expectation that I. would be granted independence through the mechanism of self-determination. However, Wilson, by then Acting Civil Commissioner of Mesopotamia, with the Government of India behind him, believed in the imperial necessity of direct British rule, strong and lasting, and was firmly convinced that I.'s native population was not capable of full self-government. Discontent grew throughout the country, uniting for the moment the Shi'i *mujtahidin*, resentful of Christian domination, with the Sunni intelligentsia, disappointed in their hope for speedy independence according to the Arab-nationalist interpretation of the McMahon-Hussein correspondence; the tribal sheikhs, too, were traditionally a disturbing element hostile to settled authority, though by and large Wilson and his collaborators had managed to establish better relations with them than with other élite groups. In June 1920, a major insurrection broke out in the middle Euphrates and spread quickly over large parts of the country, shaking for some time the hold of the army of occupation. Though hardly a "Great Revolution" this movement clinched the argument in London for a radical departure towards self-government. Wilson left, and with Cox's return as "High Commissioner" I. was reconstituted as a nominally independent country, "guided" by Britain under a Mandate▷ conferred by the League of Nations (San Remo▷, 1920, finalized in 1922). Feisal b. al-Hussein▷, recently expelled by the French from Syria, was appointed King of I. as a result of British pressure, and after a dubious plebiscite, July-Aug. 1921. This arrangement—a Mandate under the League of Nations and "a sovereign state, independent and free" (the Organic Law of 1925, following an Anglo-I. Treaty, 1922) on the other hand—was resented by the I. élite and marred the political atmosphere till the termination of the Mandate. However, there were hardly any violent disturbances there during this period, except in the north (see below). Administration developed on sound lines, guided by British "advisers"; a national army came into being.

Educational progress, starved of funds, and economic progress were comparatively slow. But the newly organized I. Petroleum Company struck oil in large quantities near Kirkuk in 1927. Nationalist pressures in I.; optimism generated by public security; the good will created by Britain's success in retaining the Mosul area for I. against Turkish aspirations (1925–6); the philosophy of the Labour government in office in Britain since 1929; and, last but not least, the general political atmosphere during the heyday of the League of Nations, combined to bring about the Anglo-I. Treaty of 1930 which provided for the termination of the Mandate upon I.'s admission to the League. Important privileges, strategic, economic and diplomatic were reserved for Britain. On Britain's strong recommendation, I. was admitted to the League and thus became independent on 3 Oct. 1932.

The political history of I. during the following nine years was not a happy one. With British prestige and responsibility removed from the domestic scene, the politicians were unable to rule the country for long. Within a year of the granting of independence the long-standing quarrel between the Baghdad authorities and the Assyrian▷ (Nestorian) community, displaced during World War I from their homes to the north of the later I. frontier, and under special British protection under the Mandate, came to a head and resulted in the slaughter of hundreds of Assyrian men, women and children at the hands of the I. Army. Nevertheless, the disturbances throughout the Shi'i south and centre, always smouldering and often breaking out into uprisings, encouraged or bloodily suppressed by the rival factions in Baghdad, assumed a far greater political importance. King Feisal died in September 1933; there are signs that the situation had previously been growing beyond his control. His son and successor Ghazi▷, was young, rash and unstable. Though not unpopular, he had no real influence in the face of the growing political power of army officers. By the end of 1936 the situation was ripe for the first of the many military coups which have since shaken I. Gen. Bakr Sidqi▷, at first supported by a group of leftist intellectuals (the *al-Ahali* group), was himself overthrown, and assassinated, in 1937; but he set a pattern of military dictatorship, thinly veiled by civilian governments with the Organic Law nominally preserved, which lasted till 1941. King Ghazi's death, Apr. 1939, and the succession by his infant son Feisal II▷ under the regency of his pro-British uncle 'Abd-ul-Ilah▷ did not change this situation. In the spring of 1941 the then ruling group of colonels, the "Golden Square", slithered into a war with Britain—caused, essentially, by their resentment of Britain's privileged position, and expressed in their refusal to let Britain make full use of I.'s territory and communications for the war effort. This "Rashid 'Ali movement" (named after Prime Minister Rashid 'Ali al-Kilani⊳—who was little more than a hesitant figurehead) represented critical time of World War I. A brief campaign from the overbearing patron power. To Britain it came as a dangerous threat from the rear at a most critical time of World War I. A brief campaign in May ended with the rout of the I. Army, and the flight abroad of the "Golden Square", Rashid 'Ali and the Mufti of Jerusalem who had backed and inspired the movement. After May 1941 I. was secured to the Allied side by the co-operation of the Regent and an establishment of senior politicians among whom Nuri al-Sa'id⊳ predominated. Economically the pre-war years saw the inauguration of the Kirkuk-Haifa and Kirkuk-Tripoli (Lebanon) pipelines, 1935, opening the marketing of I. oil on a commercial scale. The exploitation of oil from the Mosul and Basra areas was envisaged and prepared for.

Throughout the period from 1941 to 1958 official I. showed an interest in various schemes for a Fertile Crescent⊳ Federation, the real motive of which was to obtain predominance in the Syrian area. These schemes were pursued intermittently, unenthusiastically and ineptly. Their net result was to bring to the surface Egypt's latent mistrust of I. and to cause disunity in the Arab League⊳ and resentment among the great majority of the Syrian public.

The post-war period till the revolution of 1958 falls into two main periods, with Nuri Sa'id's return to power in the autumn of 1954 as a dividing line. The first lacks a common denominator. Times of political liberalism alternated with strict police rule, comparative quiet with violent disturbances. A new draft treaty with Britain, signed at Portsmouth in January 1948, was abandoned after fierce demonstrations brought the country to the verge of chaos. Steadily rising oil royalties—especially since the half-and-half profit-sharing principle was adopted in 1952—produced a surplus for major development purposes that was, on the whole, sensibly invested; at the same time the absence of import and distribution policies, unbridled speculation and an overall lack of social awareness on the part of the authorities more than once brought the masses close to famine. An appreciable part of the I. Army—about one division—took part in the Palestine War of 1948. It returned home in the spring of 1949 without victory and added its share to the general malaise.

In Sept. 1954 Nuri Sa'id was recalled to head the government, after the freest elections I. was ever to know had returned a sizable opposition to parliament.

Nuri in practice prohibited all party activity and remained for the coming four years the ruler of I., whether in office or out of it. He determined the country's policy, which meant externally close collaboration with the West, and domestically a police state, though in retrospect Nuri's rule may look less repressive than it did then. Economic development plans inaugurated in the early 1950s were pursued with vigour, but little thought was given to social progress or the alleviation of immediate misery. The army, though well cared for and considered a bastion of the existing order, was kept strictly away from politics. Each of these factors tended to make the regime unpopular with the politically articulate forces of the kingdom—whether Arab nationalists, liberals, communists, traditionalists or army officers.

Discontent was focussed after 1955 on the Baghdad Pact⊳, joining I. with Turkey, Iran, Pakistan and Britain in a defence treaty backed and sponsored by the USA. Britain and I.'s common membership had also provided the basis for a new Anglo-I. Treaty, Apr. 1955, which abolished most of Britain's remaining privileges. The Baghdad Pact was disliked equally as an alliance with "colonialist" Britain, as a threat to the USSR, newly revealed as a friend of the Arab world, and as a separatist move harmful to Arab unity and hostile, at least by implication, to Egypt's leader 'Abd-ul-Nasser⊳, embodiment and hero of that ideal. Nuri's ambiguous stand during the 1956 Suez crisis enhanced Egyptian and nationalist antagonism. A federation with Jordan was hastily set up in Feb. 1958 as a counter move to the establishment of the UAR⊳, but it remained unpopular and unconvincing; its implementation was cut short by the fall of the Monarchy, in July 1958. The coup was not engineered by Nasser; he does not appear to have been informed in advance. But his hostility to the regime was a powerful stimulant as well as an advance justification.

The Kurdish north remained largely unassimilated to the I. state throughout its existence. From the earliest days of British rule the British occupation authorities had promised administrative decentralization and cultural self-expression, so as to induce the Kurdish tribes to accept any form of subjection to Baghdad. Throughout the 1920s Kurdish resistance centred about the eccentric personality of Sheikh Mahmud Barzenchi of Suleimani, for a short time ruler of a south Kurdish "kingdom". By the early 1930s the heads of the Barzani⊳ tribe, Sheikh Ahmad and his younger brother Mulla Mustafa, succeeded to this role. Their struggle to keep the influence of the central government out of the Kurdish homeland met with reverses and, although suspended by occasional truces, was basically unrelenting. The

I. Army garrisoned towns and patrolled a few main routes; whenever a new outbreak of fighting developed the air force strafed and bombed Kurdish villages, causing heavy losses and sometime driving whole tribes across the frontiers to Turkey and Iran. There was no pacification. In 1945–6 Mulla Mustafa took part in the establishment of a Kurdish republic at Mahbad▷, on the Iranian side of the border (liquidated at the end of 1946). After 1947 he and thousands of his followers found refuge in the USSR. The United Democratic Party of Kurdistan, with Mulla Mustafa as its nominal President, represented Kurdish nationalism among the urban Kurds; it remained strictly illegal.

The Revolution of 14 July 1958, was prepared by a conspiratorial group of "Free Officers" who had come together over the previous four or five years. While determined in their hostility to the Monarchy, they were as divided as the civilian opposition in their attitudes as to the remedies and policies to be applied. On the burning question of the day—that of Arab unity i.e. union with Nasser's UAR, they did not reach agreement beyond affirming general principles of Arab solidarity. As a body the "Free Officers" expected the future regime to be guided by an officers' council to be elected from among themselves. Co-operation with civilian enemies of the regime was rudimentary, and certainly touched upon no operational matters. Brig. 'Abd-ul-Karim Qassem▷, a Baghdad-born Sunni of lower middle class origin, was elected chairman of the executive commitee. Qassem in turn appointed as his assistant Col. 'Abd-ul-Salam 'Aref▷, his friend and erstwhile subordinate.

The occasion for the revolution arrived, when the government decided to send to Jordan via Baghdad the brigade in which 'Aref served as batallion commander, at the height of the Lebanese crisis. The take-over was effected with speed and reasonable efficiency, though a more determined stand by the main leaders of the Monarchy—King Feisal II, Crown Prince (former Regent) 'Abd-ul-Ilah, and Nuri Sa'id—might have changed the outcome. 'Aref commanded the units which occupied the capital and in the process killed the King and the Crown Prince at their residence; Nuri was killed by the mob the following day while trying to escape abroad.

Qassem, in his first broadcasts, announced a "Popular Republic" with himself as Commander-in-Chief, Prime Minister and acting Minister of Defence, laying the groundwork for a military dictatorship. 'Aref became his deputy. No officers' council was established then or later, and the majority of "Free Officers" thus had a major grievance against Qassem from the first. The presidency of the Repub-

lic was vested in a "Sovereignty Council" of three respected but powerless individuals. The cabinet, on the other hand, also appointed by Qassem, included leading personalities representing all the shades of opposition to the defunct regime—a near-communist, liberal socialists, Arab nationalists of various hues and nationalist Kurds (though not members of the UDPK).

The revolution was received throughout I. with enthusiasm. The UAR and its Arab allies, as well as the Communist Bloc, recognized the new regime with alacrity. The West followed within less than a month; its acceptance was made easier by soothing statements from Qassem which included promises not to touch existing oil concessions. I. even refrained for the time being from leaving the Baghdad Pact, though its membership was henceforth a mere formality (it was formally abrogated in Mar. 1959). The atmosphere of general rejoicing and harmony did not last. Nasserists and adherents of the Ba'th▷ group soon discovered that Qassem was determined to guard I.'s full independence vis-à-vis Nasser and Pan-Arab unity, and they started undermining his position, with Qassem's deputy, 'Aref, as leader. For his part, Qassem was thrown into alliance with the communists who, taught by the Syrian example, bitterly opposed I. falling under Nasser's domination. An atmosphere of intrigue and violence speedily spread. 'Aref was stripped of his home offices in Sept. 1958 and forced into exile as Ambassador at Bonn. When he returned from Europe against Qassem's order (never having arrived at Bonn), he was charged with an attempt to assassinate Qassem. In February 1959, he was sentenced to death in a "People's Court" presided over by Qassem's cousin Mahdawi, but reprieved.

As communist influence and self-assurance grew, various nationalist bodies took to carefully laid conspiracies. Worth mentioning are those of a group about Rashid 'Ali in Dec. 1958, a rising of anti-communist officers, chiefly at Mosul, in Mar. 1959, and a Ba'thist attempt on Qassem's life in Oct. 1959. All these conspiracies were foiled and repressed—the Mosul rising with heavy bloodshed—with communist help. By the spring of 1959 all Arab-nationalist activity was virtually paralyzed, and a communist take-over appeared possible. However, Qassem outmanoeuvred the communists by threatening them with suppression by the army after a communist-led massacre at Kirkuk in July 1959, and at the same time promising legalization of political parties from the beginning of 1960. The communists shied away from an open contest with Qassem in the belief that half a year's restraint would bring them easy victory through their superior élan and organization. From then on their fortunes waned; the authorities increasingly harassed them and street terror started to turn against them. In January 1960 Qassem issued a decree legalizing political parties but it was hedged with safeguards enabling the regime legally to interfere with their activities whenever it so chose. The communists in particular were cheated of their expectations when Qassem licensed a dissident communist with virtually no following as chairman of a legal "I. Communist Party"; the communists, though very bitter, acquiesced. The licensed parties quickly withered away under the unfriendliness and obstruction of the regime. In the process Qassem made enemies of the liberal-socialist National Democratic Party, hitherto generally friendly to him, which put great hopes on constitutional devolution. By 1961 the cabinet had lost practically all its political members, who had been replaced by technicians or mere protégés of Qassem. Measures of social reform taken immediately after the revolution (the most important being the Agrarian Reform Law of September 1958) came to a stop as the political atmosphere darkened.

There was no internal political activity during the last two years of the Qassem period. These years are noteworthy for the Kurdish rising, Qassem's claim to Kuwait and his quarrel with the oil companies. A full-scale rising broke out in the Kurdish north in Sept. 1961, with Mulla Mustafa Barzani as acknowledged leader and the Barzani tribe as nucleus of an incipient national army. This came at the end of 18 months of deteriorating relations between the Kurds and the regime, when the former had finally despaired of receiving anything approaching autonomy from Qassem, while Qassem saw the Kurds as treacherous malcontents ignoring his readiness to grant them "equality". Barzani quickly established dominion over most of the open mountainous country of the north, while the I. Army held the towns, most of the larger villages and, intermittently the main lines of communication. The Kurds held their own, though they suffered heavily from blockade and air bombardments.

The Kuwait crisis broke out when Qassem publicly claimed the principality as a former district of Basra province, after Britain had granted it independence in June 1961. Qassem's move met with fervent opposition from all other Arab countries, even to the extent of despatching an all-Arab force to Kuwait; and since Qassem made no move to enforce his claim, a stalemate ensued which brought him much ridicule at home and abroad. His successors recognized Kuwait's independence, in 1963.

Qassem's dispute with the oil companies, the IPC and its subsidiaries, broke out in 1960 over the demand for new contracts assuring I. of greatly increased benefits. It led, in Dec. 1961, to "Law No. 80" which limited the companies' concession to about one percent of their former area (areas actually producing were not affected). The companies protested but production was not interfered with.

On 8–9 Feb. 1963, Qassem fell before a conspiracy joined by the clandestine Ba'th group and sympathizers from among army officers. For nine months civilian leaders of the Ba'th tried to rule I., with 'Abd-ul-Salem 'Aref nominal President of the Republic. They failed, through their own administrative inexperience and mutual jealousy, the failure of negotiations with the Kurds and new defeats in the north, the hostility of Nasser who did not forget the role the Ba'th had played in the breakaway of Syria from the UAR, the antagonism aroused by the unbridled violence of the Ba'thist militia, and the jealousy of the military. On 18 Nov. 1963 the officers around 'Aref brushed the Ba'th government aside, forcibly broke up the militia, and established themselves as the rulers of I. The new regime lasted till the coup of 17 July 1968. 'Aref died in an air crash in Apr. 1966, and was followed, as President, by his elder brother, Gen. 'Abd-ul-Rahman 'Aref▷.

The period was one of restlessness and little was achieved. For some months in 1965–6 an attempt was made to reintroduce a semblance of civilian government with Dr. 'Abd-ul-Rahman al-Bazzaz▷ as Prime Minister. Bazzaz too was forced out of office by the jealousy of the military. A settlement with the Kurds which he had negotiated was tacitly abandoned and the Kurdish rebellion flared up again. A planned federation with Syria and Egypt, solemnly proclaimed in Apr. 1963, came to nought; an I.-Egyptian "Union" agreement of 1964 was never implemented, except for some partial and tentative measures. Far-reaching nationalization decrees were published but not carried out. An "Arab Socialist Union" on the UAR pattern was founded, as a single party, but never became firmly established. An end to the constitutional "transition period", a term for the resumption of some form of representative government, was fixed, and put off. An agreement with the oil companies was initialled, but remained unratified in view of nationalist and "progressive" attacks. I.'s part in the Six Day War was limited. She built up a strong force in the north of Jordan, withdrawn only in 1971. The Nasserist Brig. 'Aref 'Abd-ul-Razzaq staged two coups which failed. Finally in the wake of two successive coups in the second half of July 1968, Gen. Ahmad Hasan al-Bakr▷ came to power at the head of a group claiming to represent the Ba'th, or rather its right wing. The new regime led an undistinguished existence, without much honour either on the domestic or the Arab scene. It gained prominence through the savage persecution of its enemies, whether real or proclaimed. The simmering quarrel with Iran over the status of the Shatt al-'Arab▷, and border problems further north, flared up afresh in 1969. Relations with the rival *Ba'th* clique in Damascus were openly bad.

In Mar. 1970 the regime scored a prestige victory when Bakr was able to announce the signing of another agreement with the Kurds, entailing concessions to the latter which went beyond those conceded in the past. While it did not grant the Kurds complete autonomy or a part in the administration of oil revenues, as they had demanded, a far-reaching local semi-autonomy and a larger part in the governance of I. were accorded them. I. was proclaimed (not for the first time) to consist of two nations, Arab and Kurdish—and Barzani and his colleagues declared themselves satisfied. In spite of Kurdish complaints concerning the efficacy and speed of the agreement's implementation, it is too early to judge.

STATISTICS: Area: 169,683 sq. mi. Area cultivated: *c.* 23.160 sq. mi. Pop.: *c.* 9m. (1970). Birth rate: 55 p. 1000 (estimated). Natural increase: *c.* 3% *p.a.* Infant mortality: 300 p. 1000 (estimated). GNP: ID 737m. ($2063.3m.) (1967). National Income *p.c.*: *c.* ID 90 ($252) (1967). Exports: ID 27.5m. ($77m.) (including re-exports, excluding crude oil) (1968). Imports: ID 144.1m. ($403.48m) (1968). Budget (actual): Revenue ID 158.6m. ($444.08m.); expenditure ID 192.4m. ($538.72m.) (1966/7). Doctors p. 1000: 0.2 (1967). Hospital beds p. 1000: 2 (1968). Literacy: 17% above age 5 (1967). I. Dinar 1 = $2.80 = £1.17.   (U.D.)

IRGUN (T)ZEVA'I LE'UMI (IZL), *Etzel.* Hebrew: National Military Organization). Armed Jewish underground movement, founded 1937 by Zionist-Revisionists▷ seceding from *Hagana*▷, the Jewish illegal self-defence organization. IZL, more militant, opposed *Hagana's* mainly defensive character, particularly its reluctance to retaliate against Arab attacks. (The dissidents were reviving a similar split that had occurred in 1931; most of the dissidents of 1931 had rejoined *Hagana* in 1936; others joined the IZL about a year later.)

After the publication of the White Paper▷ of 1939, IZL began directing its activities against the British Administration in Palestine, but agreed to call a truce upon the outbreak of World War II. Then a further split took place. The more extreme wing, led by Avraham Stern, seceded from IZL to form *Lohamei Herut Yisrael* ("Fighters for the Freedom of Israel," LHY), which initially sought contact with the Axis Powers in order to obtain from them a firm pledge of Jewish independence in Palestine. LHY also

advocated terrorist attacks on individuals (see Stern Group▷).

In Jan. 1944, IZL resumed its activities. When the post-war British Labour Government failed to diverge from the policy laid down in the White Paper of 1939, *Hagana*, IZL and LHY cooperated for some time in sabotaging British installations and activities. However, this co-operation soon came to an end because the two latter refused to submit to the discipline of the elected Zionist and Palestine-Jewish institutions when these decided to discontinue acts of sabotage and, as before, rejected acts of individual terror. In July 1946, IZL blew up the offices of the British Army command and the Palestine Government Secretariat in the King David Hotel, Jerusalem. In 1946, IZL had 5,000 members, hundreds of whom were arrested and exiled to Africa; a few were executed and became symbols of heroism.

Upon the UN decision to partition Palestine (29 Nov. 1947), when Arab irregulars started an armed insurrection IZL continued to act independently of *Hagana* (apart from occasional co-ordination). IZL was responsible for an attack on the Arab village of Deir Yassin near Jerusalem, in which about 250 inhabitants were killed; *Hagana* strongly denounced the attack, but the news, spread and magnified by Arab propaganda, caused panic among the Arabs.

After the proclamation of the State of Israel (14 May 1948), IZL refused to surrender unconditionally all its newly-arrived cargoes to the nascent Israel army (formed mainly out of *Hagana*); in June IZL's arms ship "Altalena" was blown up by Israeli artillery off Tel-Aviv. In Sept. 1948, IZL was disbanded by order of the Provisional Government of Israel and its members were incorporated in the army.

Until May 1941, IZL was headed by David Raziel (killed in Iraq on a mission for the British), then by Ya'akov Meridor, and after Dec. 1943 by Menahem Begin▷. Besides its military activities, IZL brought many illegal immigrants into Palestine before World War II. There were periods of partial co-operation with *Hagana*—in 1945–6 against the British, and in 1947–8 against guerillas. But IZL's doctrine and activities were constantly opposed by the official Zionist and Jewish-Palestinian authorities as undermining national unity and discipline. (Sh.H.-E.L.)

✳**IRYANI, AL-, SAYYID 'ABD-UL-RAHMAN** (b. 1905). Yemeni politician. Member of a family of Zeidi▷ "Sada" (descendants of the Khalifa 'Ali). After receiving a traiditional Islamic education, he became a religious judge (*Qadi*). Disappointed with Imam Ahmad's▷ regime, I. exiled himself to Aden and Cairo, where, together with Ahmad Muhammad Nu'man, he established a "Free Yemeni" movement. After the coup of 26 Sept. 1962 he joined the Republic and was appointed Minister of Justice, 1962–3, and of Local Administration, 1964. As a Zeidi leader and a *Qadi*, I. was able to exercise substantial influence on the Zeidi tribes. He became a member of the Presidency Council during Sallal's▷ absence, Apr. 1965–Sept. 1966, and was responsible for convening the pro-Republican Tribal Conference of Khamir, May 1965. The resolutions adopted there reflected I.'s conservative and anti-Egyptian policy. He was detained in Cairo, Sept. 1966–Oct. 1967. Following the fall of Sallal, 5 Nov. 1967 and the establishment of a new, more conservative republican regime, I. was appointed Head of the new Republican (*i.e.* Presidency) Council. Through this high office, and his close relations with the paramount Sheikh of the Hashid tribal confederation, 'Abdullah al-Ahmar, I. became one of the strongest leaders of the new Zeidi-Republican regime in San'a.   (H.E.)

ISLAM, MUSLIMS. The Islamic faith, which swept the ME in the seventh century and the centuries following, remains the ruling faith of most of its countries to-day. The majority of the population of the ME adheres to it; it shaped social patterns and deep-rooted modes of thought, and even determined the constitutions of several ME countries. M. constitute the overwhelming majority of the population in all countries of the region, with the exception of Israel (where they number about 12%), Cyprus (about 20%), and Lebanon (almost 50%—counting Druzes as M.). Considerable non-M. minorities are to be found in M.-majority Sudan (25–30%) and Syria (30%—if Druzes▷ and 'Alawites▷ are considered non-M., 15% if they are considered M.).

There are two main divisions in I.: Sunnites▷, who follow the *Sunna*, the traditional practice of Muhammad as set forth in the *Hadith* ("Traditions"), and Shi'ites▷ (the *Shi'a*, the "faction" that held that only descendants of the Prophet Muhammad and his son-in-law 'Ali could legitimately head the Islamic community). The Sunnites form the majority of M. in all ME countries with the exception of Iran (Persia), Iraq, Yemen, Bahrain, and Muscat-and-'Oman. Within Sunni I., there are four major schools (*Madhhab* pl.: *Madhahib*): a. *Hanafi*—widespread in Turkey, Syria and Iraq and among urban Palestinian M., and predominant in official Islamic institutions in countries formerly of the Ottoman Empire; b. *Shafe'i*▷—widespread in Lower Egypt, among rural Palestinians, the Kurds, in Hijaz and 'Asir, Yemen and Southern Yemen; c. *Maliki*—widespread in Upper Egypt, Sudan, Bahrain, Kuwait, Libya; d. *Hanbali* —in Sa'udi Arabia, where it gave birth to the Wahhabi movement of conservative and puritanical

reform, which took root among the tribes of Najd and, thanks to the conquests of the Sa'udi▷ dynasty, dominated other parts of the Arabian peninsula as well. To a greater or lesser extent, the Wahhabi school influenced other reforming or revivalist movements and schools, e.g. the Idrissis▷ in 'Asir, the *Mahdiyya*▷ and *Mirghaniyya*▷ in Sudan, the Sanussis▷ in Libya. These schools, though orthodox and opposed to Islamic mysticism (Sufism) and the Dervish▷ orders which sprouted from it, were influenced by their methods of organization and set up orders of their own.

The principal trend of Shi'i I.—the *Imamiyya* or *Ithna-'Ashariyya* (the "Twelvers") (see *Shi'a*▷)— dominates Iran, where it is the official State religion. In Iraq, too, most M. are Shi'ites, and in Bahrain about half the population. Imami Shi'ites are a minority in the rest of the ME. Zeidi▷ Shi'ites hold sway in the Yemen, where they form some 55% of the population. A trend on the fringe of Shi'ite I.—considered by many as outside I.—is the *Isma-'iliyya*▷. Members of this sect are a small minority in some ME countries. Two sects which grew out of the *Isma'iliyya*, or were greatly influenced by it, are the Druzes▷ (in Syria, Lebanon and Israel) and the 'Alawites▷ or Nusseiris (in Syria and in Turkey's Hatay▷-Alexandretta▷ district); these two sects are considered by most M. as outside the pale of I. A dissident sect which seceded from both Sunni and Shi'i I. is the *Ibadiyya*▷, which developed out of the Kharijite school in the seventh century; it forms the majority, and is the State religion, in Muscat-and-'Oman; some Ibadis live also in Tripolitania and Algeria.

I. is the State religion in all ME countries except for Turkey, Lebanon, Israel and Cyprus which have no State religion. The link between I. and the State was particularly strong in Sa'udi Arabia (whose growth and conquests are linked to the spread of Wahhabism), in Yemen, (where the king, as *Imam*▷, was simultaneously head of Zeidi-Shi'i I.), and in Libya (whose king was also head of the Sanussi order). However, even in more modern states, based on Western-type administrations and constitutions, I. is recognized in the constitution—either formally as the State religion (Egypt, 1923; Iraq, 1925; Jordan, 1928 and 1952; Libya, 1951), or by the stipulation that the Head of State must be a M. (Syria, 1930). The coups of the 1950s and '60s and the revolutionary-socialist, leftist character of the regimes established in their wake, effected no basic change in this context. I. figures as the State religion in Egypt's 1956 and 1964 constitutions, in the provisional constitutions of revolutionary Iraq (1958 and 1970), in Syria's constitutions of 1950 (as before, the President must be a M. and, in addition, Islamic Law is to constitute the principal source for legislation) and 1964. Libya's revolutionary regime did not follow this pattern and its provisional legislative principles, published in Dec. 1969, say nothing about I. Independent Sudan has not completed the drafting of a constitution, and the post-1969 revolutionary regime has not published any constitutional principles. Those laid down by Southern Yemen concern administrative details but not basic principles. Yet the status of I. as a central pillar of State and society has evidently not been affected even in the revolutionary regimes aiming at State socialism.

For the position and nature of Islamic Law *(Shari'a)* and the Islamic establishment, and changes wrought in them in the present century—see *Shari'a*▷. (Y.S.)

ISMA'ILIYYA, ISMA'ILIS. A group that grew out of Shi'i Islam. Recognizes as seventh Imam Isma'il (d. 755?), the son of the sixth Imam, Ja'far al-Sadiq, and derives its name from him. Its main doctrines are based on esoteric interpretations of the Qur'an and on adaptations from Neoplatonic teachings. It embraced sects that propagated radical social and political ideas as well as religious-philosophical ideologies, such as the Qarmathians *(al-Qaramita)* of eastern Arabia and the Fatimids (tenth-twelfth centuries) who founded an independent state and dynasty in North Africa, conquered Egypt and built Cairo▷ as the capital of their empire and the mosque-university of al-Azhar▷ as a citadel of the faith and its propagation. The I. Fatimids also ruled Syria, Sicily, the Red Sea coast of Africa, the Yemen and the holy cities of Mecca and Medina.

After the conquest of Cairo by Salah-ul-Din, 1171, the I. soon disappeared from the *Maghreb* and Egypt. However, it survived through two rival branches—the *Musta'lis* or Western I. and the *Nizaris* or Eastern I.—in Syria, Persia and the Yemen. The Druze▷ movement was an earlier schism from the I.

The *Musta'lis* believe in a hidden Imam and their apparent religious leader is called the chief *da'i*. He resided in the Yemen until early in the 17th century, when the *Musta'li* centre was moved to Gujarat in India, which has been his residence ever since. Today the Musta'lis are known as *Bohras* or *Bohoras*, or *Tayyibis*. Most of them are merchants, converts or descendants of converts from Hinduism, and some are descendants of refugees from Yemen, Arabia and Egypt. Outside India, *Bohra* communities exist mainly in Burma, Tanzania, Kenya and Somali. The *Bohras* lack efficient leadership and are divided amongst themselves; many see their future in assimilation to other Muslim communities. In general they

are reluctant to share their religious literature with non-*Bohras* and most of it exists only in manuscript.

The *Nizaris* gained control of a number of fortresses in Syria and Persia, and passed into history as the Assassins. Following the destruction of their strongholds by the Mongols in the 13th century, their movement was crippled. Surviving only underground and within certain Sufi (mystic) orders, it gradually lost its violent character. In the 19th century, the Shah of Persia conferred on the 45th Imam of the *Nizaris* the title of Agha Khan, and gave him his daughter in marriage. The first Agha Khan, however, was later forced to flee Persia and joined his followers in India, 1840. The British government granted him the hereditary title of "His Highness", but firmly discouraged his ambitions to sit upon the throne of Persia or obtain a territory to rule in India. The title of the Agha Khan has been perpetuated by his descendants. The Agha Khan claims descent from the Fatimid Caliphs of Cairo and the Caliph 'Ali b. abi Talib. He is also considered to be the earthly incarnation of the Divinity, and his word is law among the I. Today the Agha Khan's followers in India are called *Khojas*. In Persia they are called *Muridan-i-Agha Khan* and in Syria, I. The 'Alawis▷ (Nusseiris), the largest sect in Syria to derive from the *Shi'a*▷, grew at least partly out of the I. Significant *Khoja* communities are to be found in Kenya, Tanzania and in South Africa. Most of them are merchants, shopkeepers and entrepreneurs. They foster community-consciousness, practise mutual help and maintain elaborate welfare, health and educational institutions under the supervision of the Agha Khan. Though the *Khojas* claim to be adherents of Islam, they follow some religious-legal doctrines which derive from Hindu law and custom. Their number is estimated at 15-20m. (of whom about 100,000 are in the ME—in Syria, Yemen, and the al-Hasa province of Sa'udi Arabia. (Y.E.)

***ISRAEL.** Independent republic at the eastern end of the Mediterranean Sea. Established on 14 May, 1948, through the partition of Mandatory Palestine. I. is the realization of a two-thousand-year-old Jewish dream. She generally grants every Jew the automatic right to immigrate and become a citizen. Citizenship may be granted, in certain circumstances, even to Jews still in their countries of origin. I. has no State religion. Capital: Jerusalem▷. (Pop.: 291,700 in 1970). Economic and cultural centre: Tel-Aviv▷. (Pop.: 384,000 in 1970).

AREA. According to the Armistice▷ Agreements of 1949-67: 7,993 sq. mi. (the area of the occupied territories▷ under the 1967 cease-fire is 26,476 sq. mi.) Physical structure: I. is divided lengthwise into three sections (from west to east): the coastal plain; the mountain region (maximal height—1,208 m. (3,682 ft.) Mt. Meron in Galilee); the Jordan valley, along the Jordan River▷. The Negev▷ desert lies south of the Hills of Judea and extends as far as the Gulf of 'Aqaba▷ (Eilat▷).

BORDERS. In the north: the international border with Syria▷ and Lebanon▷. In the east: the international border with Syria; with Jordan▷: the international border, after that—the 1949 cease-fire line, and in the southern part—again the old international border. In the south: the international border with Egypt▷. The western border is the Mediterranean Sea and, in the southern part, the Gaza Strip▷, which was under Egyptian military rule, 1949–67. The cease-fire lines since the 1967 Six Day War▷ are shorter than the 1949–67 borders:

	1949–67	since 1967
with Lebanon	50.9 mi.	63 mi.
with Syria	47.8	50
with Jordan	376	298
with Egypt	167.7	112
Total	642.4	523
Maritime borders	157	620

LANGUAGES. I.'s principal language is Hebrew, and among the non-Jewish communities Arabic, which is also in official use and may be used in Parliament. English is widely used and is the principal foreign language taught in school.

POPULATION. 3,001,400—2,561,400 Jews and 440,000 non-Jews (including 75,000 in East Jerusalem) (1970). On 31 Dec. 1970 non-Jews constituted 14.65% distributed as follows:

Community	Number (1000)	% among non-Jews	% of total pop.
Muslims	328.6	74.7	10.9
Christians	75.5	17.2	2.5
Druzes and others	35.9	8.2	1.2

The number of Jews living in Palestine over the last 2,000 years varied from a few thousand to 200,000, depending on the attitude of the governing power. There were some 24,000 prior to the beginning of Zionist immigration in 1882, and 650,000 in 1948, when I. was established. After the Arab-I. war of 1948, there were 150,000 non-Jews, out of c. 700,000 before the war, i.e. c. 550,000 Arabs abandoned Israeli territory during the 1948 war (see Refugees▷,

and Palestine Arabs▷). From 9.77% in 1948 the non-Jewish population grew to 14.65% in 1970, despite the large-scale Jewish immigration. This was due to: a. 31,000 additional Arabs under the 1949 cease-fire agreement with Jordan; b. the return of c. 40,000 refugees, under the family re-union scheme; c. the addition of 68,000 inhabitants of East Jerusalem; d. natural increase: 39 per 1,000 (15.9 among Jews).

Between 1948 and 1970 over 1.25m. Jews immigrated to I., including over ½m. Jews from the Arab countries in the ME and North Africa. On 1 Jan. 1970, 55% of the Jewish population was foreign-born.

JEWISH POPULATION OF ISRAEL BY COUNTRIES OF ORIGIN

Continent of birth	Nov. 1948 (1,000)	%	End 1970 (1,000)	%
Israel	253.7	35.4	1,182.8	46.2
Asia	57.8	8.1	317.2	12.4
Africa	12.2	1.7	357.4	14.0
Europe and America	393.0	54.8	704.1	27.4

Of the Jewish population (1970) 89.3% is urban (among non-Jews: 42.8%). The vast majority of Muslims (83.1%) and Druzes▷ (90.8%) live in villages. Most Christians (61.3%) live in towns.

THE MINORITIES IN I. Of the non-Jews 74.7% are Muslim Arabs. Most Christians are Arabs; their main denominations are: 23,000 Greek Catholics, 21,000 Greek Orthodox and 15,000 Roman Catholics. The Druzes number c. 34,000. There are also several hundred Circassians▷, Baha'is▷ and Samaritans▷.

The minorities live in homogeneous settlements, in mixed settlements with Jewish majorities (e.g. Jerusalem, Tel-Aviv, Haifa) and in mixed Muslim-Christian settlements (e.g. Nazareth and Shafa 'Amr or Shefar'am). On 1 Jan. 1971 most of the minorities were concentrated in the Jerusalem area (76,585) and in Galilee (202,671). There were 26,281 Bedouin in the Negev▷ (approximately half I.'s entire area). Most of the Christian population is concentrated in East Jerusalem (an estimated 15,000) and in Nazareth and Shefar'am (32,000). The Druzes are concentrated in Galilee and on Mount Carmel, near Haifa.

The minorities have autonomy in culture and religion. However, I. was obliged for security reasons to limit the freedom of movement in certain border areas under military government. Military government was abolished on 1 Dec. 1966, after earlier relaxations since 1957; some of its emergency powers were transferred to the civilian authorities.

Members of the minority groups enjoy all civil liberties and personal freedoms. There are seven Arab representatives in the present *Knesset*

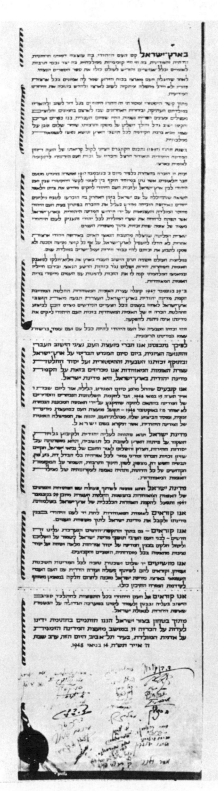

Israel Declaration of Independence Scroll

(Parliament), and one of its vice-chairmen is an Arab. Several Arab judges have been appointed. One Arab was made a Vice-Minister in May 1971. Arabs vote in general elections. Of the non-Jewish electorate 85% voted in the elections of 1969 (a proportion higher than among the Jews). Of them 28–30% voted for the "New Communist List" (*Rakah*), which adheres to Moscow's extreme anti-Israel line; 37.3% voted for specifically Arab or Druze lists, connected with Jewish parties, and 18.5% voted for general, Jewish parties. Attempts to establish nationalist Arab parties failed in 1950, 1958, 1959 and 1961. The application of such a group, *al-Ard*, to put up candidates in the elections of 1965 was rejected, the Supreme Court ruling that the State is not obliged to permit activities of a political body whose aim is to destroy it.

The Arabs of I. have come to accept I.'s existence. During the Six Day War▷ the Arab minority refrained from hostile activity (although subsequent closer contacts with the Arabs of the occupied territories has caused a certain revival of Arab nationalism). Israel has refrained from testing the loyalty of the Arab minority, her assumption being that there is a sense of affiliation between the Israeli Arabs and the neighbouring Arab nations.

I. has established an Arabic-language school network. In 1969–70 there were in Arab elementary schools 2,524 teachers and 113,087 pupils (with some more Arab pupils in Hebrew schools). Arabs sometimes avoid sending their children — especially girls — to school; yet gradually the Law of Compulsory Education is being fully applied. The percentage of girls among Arab elementary school pupils was in 1948–9 18.6%; in 1969–70 it had grown to 43.9%. In 1969–70 there were about 470 Arab educational institutions, 35 of which were secondary and vocational (one in 1948–9). Although only 1.5% of the population aged 14+ had completed more than 13 years of education (12.4% among the Jewish population, 4.3% among the Jewish population of Asian and African origin), 27.5% had received from five to eight years of education (31.7% among the Jews). In 1969–70 549 Arab students studied at Hebrew universities (Hebrew is taught in Arab schools as the first foreign language).

The Arab minority is politically conscious and active; intellectuals tend to be strongly nationalist, presumably because of their limited possibilities in the social and political hierarchy. Opinions are freely expressed in two Arabic daily newspapers (both published in Jerusalem) and eight weeklies and monthlies (in addition to four in the West Bank; three more are planned, also in the West Bank). There are also three Arabic-language publishing-houses (one of them owned by the *Histadrut*▷).

The Knesset in session

numbers among the non-Jews were 10.6 and 10.2.

The legal status of Arab women has been made equal to that of men; polygamy and divorce against the wife's will are forbidden; she is her children's guardian and has equal rights to inherit and to be party to legal proceedings. She is entitled without reservations to all benefits under social legislation. She has the right to vote and be elected. Her effective equality is being held back by the patriarchal structure of Arab society and conservative Muslim traditions; but these traditional structures are crumbling. The extended Muslim and Druze patriarchal family—the *hamula*—is in drastic decline. The Bedouin are abandoning their traditional nomadic life, and their tribal structure, under the leadership of the Sheikh, is being undermined.

The Druzes—whose identification as a community was initially religious, as a sect—have an almost national consciousness and, though speaking Arabic, regard themselves only partially as Arabs. They fully regard themselves as Israelis. Compulsory military service is applied to the Druze community at its own request. For reasons of security, and out of consideration for their national feelings, conscription has not been imposed on Israeli Arabs—though they may volunteer for the security forces (mainly Bedouin and Christians do).

All religious communities in I. have complete freedom of worship. The Muslim community maintains 90 state-supported mosques, and some 200 Muslim clergy and *Qadis* (judges in Muslim law-courts), whose independent status is guaranteed by law. The Christians hold services in 200 churches (half of them in Jerusalem), officiated over by 2,500 priests.

There are also almost 1,000 monks and nuns in I. Despite the Arab-I. conflict, regular communication is permitted between Christian communities and their spiritual leaders resident in Lebanon and Jordan. Religious communities own property and administer it freely—whether in the form of endowments and trusts (see *Waqf*▷) or through full ownership by monasteries and churches. Every community has its own law-courts dealing with questions of personal status—mainly marriages, divorces, conversions and probate. Sometimes, their authority is parallel to the civil courts (see below).

THE ESTABLISHMENT OF THE STATE, CONSTITUTION AND GOVERNMENT. I. was founded following a resolution of the UN General Assembly, on 29 Nov. 1947, recommending the termination of the British Mandate for Palestine, the partition of Palestine and the establishment of two independent states, one Arab and one Jewish, and the internationalization of Jerusalem as a separate body, the three units to con-

Between 1962 and 1967 the government invested $24m. in developing the Arab economy (including industry); between 1968 and 1973 $33m. more will be devoted to this purpose. Five banks, one of them an Arab bank, operate in the minority towns and villages. Out of 98 Arab villages, 34—including all the large ones—had by 1970 been connected to the electricity grid (none before the establishment of I.). By 1970 almost all Arab villages received a regular supply of running water (none did before 1948). Due, *i.a.*, to the modernization of agriculture, the area under cultivation in the non-Jewish economy grew from 85,000 acres in 1948–9 to 217,000 in 1968–9. Access roads lead to most Arab villages. Construction of dwellings among non-Jews rose from 200,000 sq. m (2,150,000 sq. ft.) in 1961 to 300,000 sq. m (3,230,000 sq. ft.) in 1969. The average income of an Arab urban family (Nazareth) was IL6,500 per year, while the oriental Jewish family's was IL6,300. In 1964, 5.4% of the non-Jews owned electric refrigerators and 24.5% gas cookers, while in 1970 the corresponding numbers were 26.8% and 62.6%.

Of the rural Arab bread-winners 50–65% work as wage-labourers (in Jewish agricultural settlements, building and services)—their wages usually commensurate with those of the Jewish worker and are based on the latter's standard of living. The non-Jewish average labour-force in 1969 was 91,000, of whom 4,100 were unemployed.

Arabs fully insured medically through the *Histadrut*▷ Sick Fund numbered 130,000. Infant mortality was 39.4 per thousand in 1970 (180 per thousand in 1948; 19 among Jews, 83 in Egypt, 22 in the USA). In 1969 8.2 per 1,000 Jewish men and 8.5 Jewish women could expect to reach the age of 75; the corresponding

stitute an economic union. The British refused to admit a UN committee (sent to plan elections, the establishment of governments and constitutions and the transfer of power to the two states). Accordingly, on 4 May 1948, the Executives of the *Va'ad Le'umi*▷ (Jewish National Council) and the Jewish Agency▷ constituted themselves as the "National Council"; it comprised 37 members (including 11 representatives of political groups not represented on either of the two constituent bodies: Zionist Revisionists▷, *Agudath Israel*▷, the Communists and the *Sephardim*). The Council elected 13 of its members to serve as a provisional government.

On 14 May 1948, the head of the National Council, David Ben-Gurion▷, read the Proclamation of Independence; the Council became the "Provisional State Council" which sat until the "Constituent Assembly" elected in 1949 convened and declared itself the First *Knesset* (Parliament) of I. (14. Feb. 1949). The Constituent Assembly defined in general terms the status and tasks of President, Government and Parliament. On 16 Feb. 1949, Professor Chaim Weizmann▷ was elected first President of the State. The number of *Knesset* members was fixed at 120, corresponding to the "Great *Knesset*" of the First Return to Zion (6th century BC). During the Arab-Israel War of 1948, when Jerusalem was cut off, the Council met in Tel-Aviv. On 11 Dec. 1949, the *Knesset* decided to transfer its seat to Jerusalem, the capital of I. *Knesset* proceedings are in Hebrew, translated simultaneously into Arabic; Arab members may address the House in Arabic.

A manifesto published together with the Proclamation of Independence, determined the separation of powers and rescinded the White Paper▷ of 1939, which had limited Jewish immigration and the right of Jews to purchase land. Existing laws remained in force subject to changes deriving from the establishment of the State. Thus, the legal system is based on remnants of Ottoman law (gradually being abolished), English Common Law and Equity, Mandatory decrees and *Knesset* legislation. The influence of English law is declining, as current legislation and local court decisions gradually replace it.

The First *Knesset*, realizing that the State was still in formation, and to avoid disputes about its character (e.g. secular versus religious), decided on 13 June, 1950 not to enact a constitution but only fundamental laws which eventually, taken together, would serve as a constitution. Four fundamental laws were enacted, three of which determine the separation of legislature and executive. The separation and independence of the judiciary, existing in fact before, were formally enacted in 1953. The *Knesset* is sovereign to pass whatever laws it pleases. However, it regarded itself bound by a Supreme Court ruling, in 1969, which invalidated a specific law for "contradicting the spirit of democracy", and thus established the Supreme Court as entitled to supervise legislation in certain circumstances. *Knesset* members enjoy parliamentary immunity—as the sovereign legislator, the *Knesset* sanctions the government by a vote of confidence and supervises its activities; it elects the President. Its term of office is four years, but the *Knesset* may decide on earlier elections. Government operations are controlled also through a discussion of the report of State Comptroller (appointed by the President on the recommendation of the *Knesset* Committee).

Every citizen over 18 may vote, and every citizen over 21 may stand for election. The *Knesset* is elected in general, national, direct, secret, proportional elections based on equal suffrage. Voters (average turnout: 80%) choose between lists of candidates presented by political parties (or 750 backers). Each list is entitled to *Knesset* seats according to its proportion of the national vote—provided it obtained at least 1% of all votes. For many years there has been a struggle, headed by David Ben-Gurion, for constituency elections on the majority system. However, despite considerable public support, only in 1969 did the I. Labour Party resolve to replace the proportional system by a compound system, under which some members will be elected in constituencies and some proportionally on national lists, as at present. A bill providing for direct elections of mayors constitutes a step in this direction.

Because of proportional representation, no party has ever obtained a majority in the *Knesset* (although the labour parties together have always formed a majority); consequently all governments have been coalitions—always dominated by *Mapai*▷ (since 1968: "Israel Labour Party"). In the Nov. 1969 elections the "Alignment"▷ ("I. Labour Party" and *Mapam*) obtained a majority, but preferred a coalition government of national unity. The cabinet collectively, and each of its ministers individually, are responsible to the *Knesset*. The Supreme Court as High Court of Justice is empowered to supervise administrative activities of the government.

The President is elected by the Knesset for a five-year term; his major function is representative and symbolic and his power very restricted.

The complete independence of the courts is guaranteed by law. Judges are generally appointed for life. Following Byzantine, Islamic, Ottoman and British usage, religious courts (Jewish, Muslim, Christian and Druze) have jurisdiction—sometimes corresponding to the civil courts—in matters of personal status (marriage, separation, divorce, custody of children, maintenance and alimony, probate of wills, conversions, etc.) and charitable trusts (see *Waqf*). Military courts established in accordance with the Geneva Convention function in the territories occupied by Israel since the Six Day War▷, according to local criminal law and complementary military law (see Israel, Occupied Territories▷).

The powers of the *Knesset*, the cabinet and the President, are laid down in fundamental laws (1958); those of the courts and the status of judges in regular laws. A fundamental law (1960) determined that land owned by, or in the possession, of the State, or by the Jewish National Fund, may not generally be sold in perpetuity but may only be given on lease. The Law of Return grants every Jew the right to immigrate to I. and generally become a citizen automatically.

A distinction may be made between citizenship (Israeli), ethnic 'nation' (Jewish, Arab) and religious community (Jewish, Muslim, Christian). As to Jews, the general Jewish view is that their nationhood and their religion are identical. Some, however, criticize this historical identity and claim the right to belong to the Jewish nation without belonging to the Jewish religion. The problem is still unsolved. The Supreme Court has ruled that the Jewish nationality of an individual may be determined by his own declaration. The *Knesset* reacted with a law stating that an individual's Jewishness, as well as conversions, must be determined by religious law. The *Knesset* ruling regarding conversions does not correspond with a previous judgement of the Supreme Court, where a Jew who had been converted and became a Catholic monk was refused—contrary to Jewish religious law—recognition as a Jew. At present, one is considered a Jew by nation only if one is of the Jewish religion; and anyone who according to Jewish religious law is a Jew, automatically belongs to the Jewish nation. This formulation has been bitterly criticized.

The supreme authority of the Jewish community is the Chief Rabbinate (not recognized by *Agudath Israel*▷ and *Neturei Karta*▷), which supervises 500 local religious councils and 400 rabbis. It follows the orthodox trend and does not recognize the legal acts of progressive religious currents.

I.'s security is based on her army (I. Defence Army: *Tzahal*, usually *Zahal*, established 26 May 1948). In addition to the usual branches, the IDA includes *Nahal* ("Pioneering and Fighting Youth") units, service in which includes the establishment of outpost settlements along the borders (about 20 along the cease-fire lines of 1967), doing agricultural work and military duty at the same time. Regulars form the nucleus of the army, but its main strength lies in the reserves, which include most of the adult population and can be mobilized immediately, to-

gether with civilian vehicles and heavy equipment. I.'s military industry manufactures most of her light arms and much of the heavier ones. Foreign experts report that I. manufactures at least two kinds of missile ("Jericho" and "Gabriel"; I. has admitted only to the latter) and will soon start production of fighter planes and tanks. Men are drafted for three years (ages 18 to 26) and women for twenty months. Men serve in the reserves until age 55 and unmarried women as well as married ones without children, until 38. Orthodox women are exempted if they so desire. Youth between 14 and 18 receive pre-military training in the *Gadna*' (youth brigades).

I.'s small size, together with strategic and tactical reasons, dictate a military doctrine (also applied against guerillas and infiltrators) of rapid breakthrough into enemy territory and the concentration of heavy fire-power. It follows that the armoured corps and air force are I.'s main military strength. The IDA fosters the skill of each individual soldier and a spirit of volunteering effort (hence an extremely high casualty rate among officers). The army also plays an important educational role in integrating young men from different backgrounds into one nation and completing the elementary (sometimes also secondary and higher) education of those who lack it.

The army has ensured the continuance of normal life in the occupied territories since the Six Day War. Their inhabitants govern themselves, and maintain controlled contact with the neighbouring Arab states (the "open bridges" policy).

POLITICAL HISTORY AND FOREIGN RELATIONS. The violence with which the Arab states and the Palestinian Arabs resisted the establishment of Israel had its roots in a long conflict (see Arab-Israel Conflict▷). Immediately after the UN resolution of 29 Nov. 1946, guerila fighting broke out inside the country (local Arab guerillas being assisted by an 'Army of Deliverance' of Arab volunteers from abroad); an invasion by the regular armies of seven Arab states followed on 15 May 1948 (see Arab-Israel War▷, 1948). On the same day, engaged in her struggle for survival, I. was recognized by the USA, and two days later also by the USSR (within a year, 55 states had extended their recognition).

Hostilities ceased on 7 Jan. 1949, and Armistice agreements were signed shortly afterwards between I. and Egypt, Syria, Jordan and Lebanon. Previous attempts by the UN mediator, Count Folke Bernadotte▷, to work out compromise proposals had failed. At the end of 1948 the UN set up a "Conciliation Commission" (USA, France and Turkey), but it achieved nothing. In 1948 and 1949 the UN Assembly reiterated its recommendation that Jerusalem be an international *corpus separatum*, but it did nothing to implement either this or the economic union of Jerusalem, I. and the abortive Arab State (whose territory had been occupied by Jordan and Egypt). The UN did not return to the original partition map: it never laid down that the Armistice lines should be final borders but it accepted them as a *fait accompli*. However, it resolved that Arab refugees▷ from the war should have the right to choose between returning (to what had meanwhile become I.) and receiving compensation (first resolution: Dec. 1948). I. was ready to compensate the refugees for their property left in I., and to admit a limited and agreed number of them, but considered it impossible to absorb hundreds of thousands of potential enemies. She maintained that the bulk of the refugees should be absorbed by the Arab states; this would have constituted a population exchange, as I. had absorbed a similar number of Jewish immigrants from the Arab countries. (Since the 1967 Six Day War I. has made efforts to assist in the integration of those Arab refugees under her rule—by providing work, housing, electricity, water and a network of roads. Post-1967 I. would probably be prepared to absorb many of them within the framework of a settlement.)

Another major problem is the Arab states' rejection of peaceful co-existence with I. The Arab states presented numerous demands, but they have never accompanied them by recognizing, in return, I.'s right to exist. Their attitude has prevented any solution, and resulted in an endless series of acts of sabotage and terrorism on their part, of retaliation on I.'s, and finally of war. War preparations against I. and threats to destroy her led to I.'s surprise actions in 1956 and 1967 (see: Sinai Campaign▷ and Six Day War▷). At Khartoum, Aug.-Sept. 1967, and at Damascus, Aug. 1971 (at the proclamation of the proposed federation of Egypt, Syria and Libya), the Arab leaders reiterated their refusal to recognize, negotiate or make peace with I.

Nevertheless, Egypt and Jordan were engaged in indirect negotiations with I. through Jarring▷, the emissary of the UN Secretary-General, and accepted the Rogers Plan▷. In 1971 Egypt declared her readiness to sign a peace agreement if I. would retreat to her pre-Six Day War borders and respect "the rights of the Palestine people"; I. could not accept the pre-1967 lines, that had twice led to war, as the frontiers of future peace; she also regarded Egypt's second condition as implying I.'s destruction, for Arab "rights", by Arab definition, include the establishment of a Palestinian state to replace I.

Other major problems in I.'s first decades were the tremendous efforts needed to absorb a million and a quarter immigrants from all over the world (including about half a million refugees from Muslim countries in the ME and North Africa); the process of nation-building and development; relations between secular and orthodox Jews; and relations with Germany.

The religious parties, occasionally supported by *Herut*▷ (later *Gahal*▷), insisted that I. be governed by Jewish religious laws. They based their stand on a *status quo* agreement with Prime Minister David Ben-Gurion▷. Their struggle had begun with the very establishment of the State. They had questioned the secular phrasing of the Proclamation of Independence. Later they fought successfully for the exemption of religious girls from military service; for imposing religious law in matters of personal status; for a free choice between religious and general state education (in addition to an independent ultra-religious network recognized by the State and administered by *Agudath Israel*▷). Religious leaders claimed that emissaries of the Jewish Agency and the government forced secular education upon immigrant children. The crisis led in 1951 to new elections. The Second *Knesset* very much resembled the first: *Mapai*▷ and the religious bloc lost one seat each, *Mapam*▷ lost four, the right-wing gained six. But when the right-wing remained in opposition, hopes for an alternative to the Labour-dominated government were dashed. (The right was still in opposition even in the Fifth *Knesset* when it formed a bloc of 34—though it sometimes participated in the government coalition.) The government formed by the Second *Knesset* was again led by *Mapai*▷ and Ben-Gurion.

Meanwhile, the absorption of masses of immigrants (many of them unemployed and in camps), the founding of new settlements (350 since the establishment of the State), and the development of means of production created economic pressures and a grave national problem. A policy of austerity failed. I.'s enormous security needs, surpassing all her other problems, undermined her economy. "Selective immigration" resulted and the resort to loans, contributions and grants (through the United Jewish Appeal, the US administration and government bonds).

I.'s economic difficulties were one of the reasons for the conclusion of the "Restitution Agreement"▷ with West Germany▷ (1952), by which the latter undertook to aid the rehabilitation in I. of the Jewish victims of the holocaust with a sum of $770m. Many Israelis, led by the nationalist *Herut*▷ party and its leader, Menahem Begin▷, opposed this agreement in violent demonstrations, which led to a grave internal crisis. Another aspect of Germany-I. relations —a libel action brought by a war-time Hungarian-

Jewish leader against the charge of having co-operated with the Nazis and, rejected, as the charge was held to be true (his appeal was eventually allowed in part)—caused the government to resign. A new government was formed without the right-wing "General Zionists" (see below, Parties and Zionism▷).

In the elections to the Third *Knesset*, (July 1955), *Mapai* gained 40 seats (a loss of 5) and the "General Zionists" 13 (loss of 7), but *Mapai* again headed the coalition government. Ben-Gurion again became Premier, after having withdrawn in 1953 and returned in Jan. 1955 as Minister of Defence in Moshe Sharett's▷ government.

Ben-Gurion returned against the background of a sharp increase in acts of terrorism by Arab infiltrators, both from the Jordanian-controlled West Bank and from the Gaza Strip, under Egyptian control, accompanied by belligerent declarations of Arab leaders. In 1954 Egypt blockaded Eilat▷ and the Gulf of 'Aqaba. The Syrians attempted to prevent by force of arms the Hula▷ Development Project. I.'s counter-action, mainly retaliatory raids on bases of hostile action, increased in proportion to the attacks (1955: raids on Gaza, Khan Yunis, Kuntila, Nitzana, Syrian posts on the eastern shore of the Sea of Galilee). The Gulf of Eilat and the Suez Canal remained closed to I. shipping (a test boat, the *Bat Galim*, was seized at the Canal). When the Egyptians signed an agreement with Czechoslovakia on the supply of large quantities of arms (1955), and a joint military command of Egypt, Syria and Jordan was set up (1956), I. invaded the Sinai Peninsula and the Gaza Strip in Oct. 1956 to liquidate hostile bases there and re-open the Gulf of Eilat. This was done in co-ordination with England and France who invaded Egypt a few days later, when Israeli forces had almost reached the Suez Canal. (see Arab-I. Conflict▷; Sinai Campaign▷; Suez War▷). Under combined American-Soviet pressure I. was soon forced to withdraw, while a UN Emergency Force▷ was formed to guarantee free navigation.

American pressure led to tension in I.-US relations. Relations with the USSR had become very strained, as the USSR had turned against Israel, linking her ME policy with the Arab countries. The Soviet Bloc had denounced Zionism as an imperialistic, international Jewish plot (the Prague trials). The USSR again intensified the repression of her Jewish minority. These changes in Soviet policy led to a split in *Mapam*▷; its leftist faction, led by Dr. M. Sneh▷, seceded and joined the I. Communist Party (*Maki*).

After the Sinai Campaign the immediate threat to I.'s security was eased. With the UNEF in the Gaza Strip and the Sinai Peninsula, I.'s major struggle was now against Syria (Battle of Tawafiq, 1960,

Nuqeib 1962) and terrorists from Jordan. I. developed the port of Eilat and strengthened her commercial ties with Africa and the Far East. New waves of immigrants arrived—pennyless Jewish Egyptian refugees and Jews from Poland and Hungary (refugees of the Hungarian Revolt of 1956). Construction and development continued. Most transit camps for immigrants were eliminated. The drainage of the Hula swamps was completed. An oil pipeline was laid from Eilat to Haifa, and the first stage of the Yarkon-Negev pipeline for irrigating semi-desert land in the south. Mass immigration created problems of integration. In summer 1959 fights broke out against alleged "ethnic" or communal discrimination and a number of ethnically-based lists participated—unsuccessfully—in the elections to the Fourth *Knesset*. At the same time there was a government crisis over the sale of arms to the German Army.

Mapai gained seven seats in the Fourth *Knesset*, bringing the total up to 47, *Herut* obtained 17 seats, the "General Zionists" fell to 8, *Ahduth Ha'avodah*▷ to 7 and *Maki* to 3. The Fourth *Knesset* was dissolved in 1961—in a crisis caused by the conclusion of a Ministerial Committee that it was not Pinhas Lavon, the Minister of Defence in Sharett's government, who had ordered sabotage activities against American institutions in Egypt in July 1954 (see Lavon Affair▷).

The new government devalued the currency and liberalized trade, to ease financial problems caused by the continued absorption of immigrants, and to create an appropriate background for negotiations with the European Common Market.

The revival of the Lavon Affair▷ by Ben-Gurion in December 1964 led eventually to the secession of several of his supporters from *Mapai* and the establishment of *Rafi* ("Israeli Workers' List"), under his leadership. In the 1965 elections the principal struggle lay between *Rafi* and an alignment▷ of *Mapai* and *Ahduth Ha'avodah* led by L. Eshkol▷. *Rafi* obtained ten seats in the *Knesset* but the "Alignment" retained its full strength of 45. A new government was formed by Eshkol; it held office until the Oct. 1969 elections, though Eshkol himself died in Feb. 1969 and was replaced by Golda Meir▷.

In Oct. 1963 Eshkol removed some of the restrictions on the freedom of movement in border areas which, for security reasons, had been under military rule since 1948; in Dec. 1966 military government was abolished altogether. Its powers were conferred upon the civilian authorities to be used only in emergency cases.

During this period I.-US relations grew closer. During Premier Eshkol's visit to the US, President Johnson declared the USA's support for the territorial integrity of all ME states and opposition to all aggression and use or threat of force. A joint US-I. project for desalinating water was announced. On the other hand, I.'s relations with the USSR progressively deteriorated. I.'s close relations with France grew cooler, after the Algerian problem had been resolved. The call by the I. Foreign Minister, Abba Eban, for the application of the 'Tashkent spirit' to the I.-Arab conflict went unanswered.

Meanwhile, I.'s relations with the Arab countries grew still more strained. There were two acute problems—the freedom of navigation in the Suez Canal and, mainly, Arab objection to I.'s "National Water Carrier" project, designed to pump 320m. cubic metres of Jordan River⊳ water *p.a.* from the Sea of Galilee⊳ to the Negev⊳. In Jan. 1964 the Arab leaders decided to set up in Cairo a joint command and to prevent the implementation of I.'s Jordan scheme by diverting the source of the river to Syria, Lebanon and the Kingdom of Jordan. I. warned the Arab leaders that she would view such action with the utmost gravity. The National Water Carrier went into operation in summer 1964.

At the same time there was an increase in planned military attacks from over the Syrian border and Syrian-trained guerilla and sabotage attacks through Jordan. In 1966 the Syrian Prime Minister proclaimed his government's support for the activities of *al-Fatah*⊳. In Nov. 1966 I. made a large-scale retaliatory strike against a Syrian guerilla base in the Jordanian village of Samu'. Tension rose and clashes increased. In an air battle over the Sea of Galilee, in Apr. 1967, six Syrian "MIG" planes were shot down. From this point on events rapidly deteriorated, culminating in the Six Day War⊳, which was precipitated by active Soviet interference.

The Security Council's resolution of 22 Nov. 1967 demanded I.'s withdrawal to secure and recognized borders in the framework of a lasting peace agreement. Since the Arab states were not prepared to conduct peace negotiations no progress was made, not even through the good offices of the UN Secretary-General's emissary, the Swedish diplomat, Dr. Gunnar Jarring⊳. This political deadlock was accompanied by a vast increase in border clashes, particularly along the Suez Canal—the cease-fire line with Egypt—where Soviet installations were reinforced to an unprecedented degree and Russian officers were brought in to conduct operations. Terrorist activities continued, including attacks on I. institutions abroad and the hijacking of passenger planes (see Arab-I. Conflict⊳). From 11 June 1967 to Sept. 1970 Israeli casualties amounted to 700 killed and over 2,000 wounded.

I. stood firm in the territories she had occupied—prepared to withdraw from them only in the context of a secure peace and to agreed borders. Daily life in the occupied territories continued; all attempts to establish a network of underground terrorist cells failed; thousands of workers found employment in Israel; and the bridges across the Jordan to the Arab countries remained open for goods and people—an unprecedented step in occupied territory.

From May 1967 until July 1970, when I. decided to accept the American Rogers⊳ peace initiative, a Government of National Unity held office, under the leadership of Golda Meir (14 ministers from the "Alignment", 6 from *Gahal*, 3 from the "National Religious Party" and one "Independent Liberal"). Its principle tasks were the struggle to achieve peace with the Arab countries, or at least prevent war; defence against guerilla terror and Egypt's "war of attrition" (1969–70); and the effort to solve the country's economic problems intensified by defence needs. Additional taxes were imposed, and I. now takes first place in the world in the tax/GNP ratio. When the Government accepted the American Rogers peace initiative, the six *Gahal* ministers resigned and the National Unity Government broke up. The new Meir Government has an ample majority in the *Knesset*.

Egypt's violation of the new cease-fire agreement by advancing Soviet ground-to-air missiles to the Canal Zone impelled I. to announce that she would not participate in the Jarring⊳ talks until the previous situation had been restored; but she withdrew this policy later to show good will. She also agreed (1971) to discuss the re-opening of the Suez Canal through a separate interim agreement that would not contradict her policy of no retreat without an agreed and secure peace. I.'s attitude towards the terrorist organizations remains that the responsibility for their actions rests on the countries from which they operate.

I.'s foreign policy was initially that of preserving non-alignment and a balance between the two major powers. I. had to bear in mind the existence of large Jewish minorities in both the Soviet Bloc (2–3m. in the USSR) and the West (almost 6m. in the USA alone); she remembered the USSR's support in the UN for her creation and independence, and hoped that Russia's gates would be opened for Jews to emigrate. While the USA had in 1948 imposed an embargo on arms shipments to the ME, the Communist Bloc had assisted I. in her hour of need through a Czechoslovakia-I. arms agreement and by training Israeli teams.

I.'s balanced stand was initially well received by both the USA and the USSR. Both recognized I. shortly after the Proclamation of Independence. I. was one of the first countries to recognize the Chinese People's Republic (1950), although no diplomatic relations were established. However, the USSR reverted rapidly to its former, aggressive anti-Zionism, and was unwilling to allow active contact between Russian Jews and I. She also sought closer relations with the Arabs. This, and I.'s increased dependence on assistance from the US government and Jewry, led I. to abandon non-alignment in favour of closer relations with the West and the USA. Increasingly strained relations between a leftist-revolutionary Egypt and the West formed the background to this *rapprochement*.

Since 1955 the USSR had adopted an aggressively negative policy towards Israel, eventually severing diplomatic relations in 1967 and actively supporting the Arabs in their war against I. China's attitude to I. is even more extremist. After 1967 Rumania was the only country of the Soviet Bloc which continued to maintain diplomatic, even friendly, relations with I. Yugoslavia, which was initially friendly towards I., preferred to foster relations with Egypt, within the framework of the non-aligned nations, and displayed considerable hostility towards Israel.

After the mid-1950s I. had particularly friendly relations with France▷ (whose policy was influenced decisively by the Algerian war). In view of the US embargo on arms to the ME France, being engaged in the suppression of the Algerian revolt, became I.'s major arms supplier, counter-balancing Czech arms supplies to Egypt. This close link led to political and military co-operation in the Suez-Sinai Campaign▷, in 1956. France severed the link—a betrayal in the eyes of I.—in 1967, adopting a pro-Arab stand since.

I. has maintained since 1965 diplomatic relations with West Germany, despite the memory of the Holocaust and the annihilation of the Jews of Europe by the Nazis. Full relations were preceded by a wide-ranging network of ties based on the 1952 Restitution Agreement▷, by which Germany paid the Israeli government $770m. over a period of thirteen years (1952–65)); Germany has also been paying individual victims of the Nazi regime compensation for personal persecution and loss of property (about $1,500m. so far). The Restitution Agreement and I.'s consent to establish relations with Germany aroused violent dissension in I. But the money assisted I. in developing the economy and in absorbing and rehabilitating immigrants. After the termination of the agreement Germany assisted I. with development credit, and economic and political relations between the two countries remained close. Germany has also helped I. in her efforts to achieve a preferential agreement with the European Common Market (signed in 1970 after several interim agreements).

I. has been a member of the UN (the 59th) since 11 May 1949. She offered co-operation and technical (not financial) assistance in the fields of economic, social and scientific development to the developing countries of Africa, Asia and Latin America (over the years some 3,000 Israeli experts have served in 80 countries and *c.* 14,000 trainees from these countries have been trained in I.); Israeli companies have planned or implemented development schemes. Israeli military advisors have operated in five countries (Ethiopia, Uganda, Congo-Kinshasa, Nepal and Singapore). I.'s annual investment in assistance amounts to $1£30–35m. I. maintains diplomatic representations in all the African countries apart from the Arab African states, Mauritania and Somali, which usually identify with the Arab states, and Guinea, which severed relations with Israel in 1967—after the Six Day War. Anti-I. resolutions are often passed at conferences of African and Asian states—among them some who maintain friendly relations with, I. ; they often claim that such resolutions constitute political lip service only. In 1971, the Organization for African Unity nominated ten African heads of state to help work out a solution for the ME conflict; a sub-committee of four presidents was to visit Israel and Egypt for consultations. India represents a particular problem for I. Although she has recognized I. fully, *de jure*, and I. maintains a consulate there, India does not wish to establish full diplomatic relations and usually identifies herself with the claims of the Arab states. I.'s relations with the Far East are generally in the process of quiet development, with Israeli technical aid and growing economic ties as an important element—and some countries' fear of the Arab boycott▷ as a brake or an irritant.

This boycott constitutes an additional foreign policy problem for I., since the declared aim of all the Arab countries participating in it is to prevent the supply of goods to I. by any country in the world, thus imposing economic isolation on I. I. has managed to rise to this challenge, occasionally arousing public opinion in the countries concerned, and has thus limited the damaging results of the Arab boycott.

POLITICAL PARTIES. When the State of I. was founded in 1948, the parties which had been active within the framework of the Zionist Organization and the Jewish Community of Palestine continued to operate. There was considerable fragmentation among the parties. 21 lists participated in the elections to the First *Knesset* (Jan. 1949), and 12 obtained the minimum vote needed (1%). But with the passage of time there was a tendency towards the unification of political groups into blocs. In the First *Knesset* the 120 seats were split among three lists of the left (*Mapai*▷—46; *Mapam*▷—19; the Communist Party, *Maki*—4), five of the centre and right (*Herut*▷—14; "General Zionists" —7; "Progressive Party"—5; *Sephardi* List"—4;

"Stern Group"▷—1) and one religious bloc: 18 ("United Religious Front", comprising the *Mizrahi*▷, *Hapo'el Hamizrahi*▷, *Agudath Israel*▷ and *Po'alei Agudath Israel* parties). A Yemenite and a women's list had 1 each. In the Seventh *Knesset* (1969) the seats were distributed as follows: The "Alignment"▷ ("Labour Party" and *Mapam*)—56; *Gahal*▷ (*Herut–*"Liberals")—26; "National Religious Party"▷—12; *Agudath Israel*▷—4; *Po'alei Agudath Israel*—2; "Independent Liberals"—4; "State List"—4; Arab lists linked with the "Alignment"—4; "New Communist List"—3; *Ha'olam Hazeh-Koah Hadash* —2; "The Free Centre"—2; *Maki*—1.

The largest political party in I. is the "I. Labour Party"▷, which was established in 1968 through the merger of *Mapai*▷ ("The Eretz-Israel Labour Party"), *Ahduth Ha'avodah*▷ and *Rafi* ("Israel Workers' List") (see also Zionism▷, Palestine▷). *Rafi* had been created in 1965 by members seceding from *Mapai*, led by David Ben-Gurion▷, a main motive being Ben-Gurion's demand to renew the investigation into the Lavon Affair▷. In the elections to the Sixth *Knesset* in 1965 *Rafi* obtained ten seats while the "Alignment"▷ (an alliance of *Mapai* and *Ahduth Ha-'avodah*) obtained 45 seats, 36 of them going to *Mapai*.

To its left is *Mapam*▷, which was established in 1948 through the merger of the *Ahduth Ha'avodah-Po'alei Zion*▷ movement with *Hashomer Hatza'ir* (see Palestine▷; Zionism▷). In 1969 an "Alignment"▷ of the "Labour Party" and *Mapam* was set up.

In 1958 a leftist group, under the leadership of Dr. Moshe Sneh▷, broke away when *Mapam* was unable to accept the group's demand to identify with the USSR over the question of the "Doctors' Trials" and the "Prague Trials". Later Dr. Sneh's "Left Front" united with *Maki* ("The Israel Communist Party". See below).

In 1954 the *Ahduth Ha'avodah-Po'alei Zion*▷ party broke away from *Mapam* because of differences of opinion over the question of joining the government, methods of operation in the *Histadrut*▷, the admission of Arab members to the party and various other issues.

Two communist parties exist in Israel since 1965: a. "I. Communist Party" (*Maki*), mostly Jewish—in recent years stresses its solidarity with the Jewish nation and the Zionist movement, and opposes Moscow's anti-I. line; b. "New Communist List" (*Rakah*), mostly Arab—adheres to Moscow's line and is in effect an Arab nationalist party. It regards the Six Day War as an aggressive, imperialistic war. (See also Communism▷.)

After the establishment of the "Alignment" a few hundred dissenters broke away from *Mapam* and, together with several *Maki* activists who opposed their

party's support for the government in the Arab-Israel conflict, established the "Israeli New Left▷" (*Siah*). Another group which broke away from *Mapam* is "The Zionist-Socialist Leftist Association", which also advocates a more moderate line on the Arab-Israel conflict but regards the Six Day War as a war of aggression, supporting the USSR's attitude to the ME problem. Another group—*Matzpen*▷—accepts the view of New Left circles that the State of I. is an imperialistic-colonialist creation and does not support her continued existence as a sovereign Jewish State. *Matzpen* supports those Arabs advocating a democratic, socialist Palestinian State and justifies even Arab terrorist and guerilla methods.

The centre and right section within Israel established the *Herut*▷-Liberal Bloc (*Gahal*▷) in 1965 as an alternative to the government of the left. (For the background see also Zionism▷, Zionist Revisionists▷.) *Gahal* remained in opposition for two years. On the eve of the outbreak of the Six Day War *Gahal* joined the National Unity Government, resigning in 1970 over the Rogers Plan▷. The "National Religious Party"▷ (*Mafdal*) represents the linking of two religious Zionist parties: *Mizrahi* and *Hapo'el Hamizrahi*. It has participated in government coalitions since the establishment of the State. It was mainly through its influence that the laws governing personal status of Jews in I. have been based on Jewish religious law.

The *Ha'olam Hazeh-Koah Hadash* movement was established in 1965 by Uri Avneri, the editor of the weekly *Ha'olam Hazeh* ("This World"), as a protest movement against the slander and libel bill. Avneri was elected to the Sixth *Knesset*, 1965, and obtained two seats in the Seventh *Knesset*, 1969. He advocates I.'s assimilation into the region, the recognition of the "Palestine Entity"▷ and withdrawal from all the occupied territories in return for peace. His movement does not recognize Zionism and the connection between I. and the Jewish nation. It carried on the tradition of the "Canaanites"▷ and advocates a separation between state and religion.

The Six Day War gave birth to the "Land of Israel Movement", which contains active members from several parties and opposes the return of territories occupied during the war. The "Movement for Peace and Security" was established by a group of intellectuals in opposition to the "Land of Israel Movement".

ECONOMY. A large part of the nation's resources are state- or public-owned; 73.2% of the land is owned by the government, 17.1%—by the Jewish National Fund, and less than 10% is private. The generation and supply of electricity is concentrated in the hands of a government-controlled company. All mines, quarries and other natural resources (*i.e.*, potash and bromine of the Dead Sea, oil) are state property and can be exploited only under licence. Water is national property; most of it is pumped and distributed by a licensed public company. Railways are state-owned; much of public road transport is handled by co-operatives affiliated to the *Histadrut*▷ (General Federation of Labour). This concentration of the principal means of production in the hands of the government derives from the Zionist-Socialist outlook of most of I.'s inhabitants, from her historical growth as a developing state with nearly no capitalistic free competition, and also from the needs of her security situation. Yet, the government encourages private enterprise by special concessions and incentives. From 1965 to 1969 total foreign private investment amounted to over $400m. In 1969, the balance of government investment was 1£3,803.3m. in loans and 1£1,188.2m. in shares (in addition to expenditure of 1£1,154.3m., the nature of which, *i.e.* loans or shares, has not been determined yet, and investment of 1£707.1m. in assets in creation).

The absorption and integration of vast numbers of new immigrants (over 1.25m. since 1948) and the mobilization of all the national resources for defence have presented I. with immense economic difficulties. The extent of investment in the absorption and integration of immigrants is reflected by government investment in building (principally for new immigrants): 1£1,510.9m. in 1969 alone, plus 1£693.3m. for electricity and water. Security requirements amount to nearly 1£6,000m. devoted either directly or indirectly to defence—almost 50% of the national budget (1£11,234.8m. in 1970–1) and 30% of the gross national product (the highest percentage in the world).

It was necessary to impose extremely high taxes in order to cover this vast expenditure. In 1970 I. took first place in the percentage of taxes of the gross national product (more than 40%). Still, I. was unable to solve her immense economic problems without grants, aid and credits from governments, international banks and world Jewry (mainly through the United Jewish Appeal).

GRANTS AND CONTRIBUTIONS (IN US DOLLARS)

1. The United Jewish Appeal (1949–69): 2,130m. (of which 1,700m. was from the USA).

2. Personal reparations from Germany (1952–70): 1,475m.

3. Reparations from Germany to the Israeli government (1952–65): 770m.

4. Grants from the US government, food surpluses, other products and technical aid (ended in 1961): 320m.

Total: 4,695m. dollars.

GOVERNMENT DEBTS (1969)

1. Internal debt: 1£6,075m. (1£400m. in 1956).

2. External debt (repayable in 1£): 1£798m. (1£56m. in 1956).

3. External debt (repayable in foreign currency): $4,927m. ($628m. in 1956).

I.'s labour-force—approximately one million in 1970 (of which an average of 4.5% were unemployed) —was distributed as follows: industry 26.8%, agriculture 8.9%; services 43%. In 1969 I.'s gross national product (at current market prices) was 1£15,861m. The annual growth of the gross national product 1969 to 1970 was 6.8%; the average was 10–12% *p.a.* (with the exception of 1966 and 1967)—one of the highest in the world. Average (annual) income *p.c.* reached 1£4,512 in 1969 (1£1,578 in 1959).

The net national product in industry and mines was 1£4,205m. in 1970 (1£184.3m. in 1952); in agriculture it was 1£956m. (1£275m. in 1952). The growth in agriculture is also due to the completion of the National Water Carrier which carries 320m. cubic metres *p.a.* from the Sea of Galilee to the Negev.

Since I. has no basic raw materials (apart from chemicals, copper and some oil), or sources of energy, her industry is largely based on imported raw materials. The following are I.'s main industries: diamond cutting and polishing, food and drink, chemicals and phosphates, oil refining, textiles and clothing, tobacco, arms and armaments industry and the aircraft industry (servicing and repairs, as well as plane manufacture). Lately the development of science-based industries, such as the electronics industry, has been fostered. Similarly, industries based on know-how and local raw materials, such as petro-chemical and chemical industries, are being encouraged. Most Israeli industry is concentrated in private hands, only 20–25% being in the public or *Histadrut* sector. I. encourages both foreign and local private capital investment in industry by providing grants, loans on easy terms and tax concessions or exemptions.

Despite the continual increase in exports, they still fall well below imports, and the adverse balance of payments is on the rise. In 1970 the net export of goods and services was $775.6m., while the net import of goods was $1,451.2m. (In 1949 exports were $29m. and imports $253m.; in 1958: $142m. and $430m.) I.'s main exports were diamonds, citrus fruits, machinery, plastic goods, edible oils, medicines, cement, books and cult articles, arms, ammunition and military equipment, and airport service. In 1970, out of total exports of goods, amounting to $775.6m., 26.2% was exported to the Common Market countries; 53.1% to Europe as a whole, 21.2% to the USA and Canada and 20.4% to Asia and Africa. Of imports, 30.7% came from the Common Market,

59.6% from Europe as a whole, 23.6% from the USA and Canada and 7.3% from Asia and Africa. Israel signed in 1969 a preferential trade agreement with the European Common Market (see European Economic Community▷). One of I.'s most important sources of foreign currency—$102m. in 1969—is tourism (over 436,900 tourists in 1970, 117,662 in 1960). I.'s electricity consumption in 1970 was 5,697m. Kwh. (Production in 1948 was 246m. Kwh.)

COMMUNICATIONS AND TRANSPORT. Communications and transport are particularly important to I. because of her security needs and geopolitical situation. I.'s merchant fleet numbered in the beginning of 1970 109 vessels with a gross tonnage of 1.25m. ton. The national airline El-Al, with eleven passenger planes, including one "Jumbo" Jet, flies to four continents (in 1969 it carried 45.6% of all air passengers to and from I.). Fifteen foreign airlines regularly serve I.'s international airport, Lod. I.'s three major ports are Haifa (40% of outgoing freight, 70% of incoming), Ashdod (50% and 25% respectively) and Eilat (10% and 5% respectively—not including oil). Internal transport is mainly motorized road transport. The bus companies are co-operatives. There are several truck and car assembly plants. There are 5,600 mi. (9,000 km.) of asphalted roads. The number of vehicles is c. 260,000, including 4,000 buses and trucks. The state-owned railway—476 mi. (765 km.)—is used mainly for the transport of goods, and operated through diesel engines.

SCIENCE AND NUCLEAR RESEARCH. I.'s sole sources of energy are electricity and fuel (oil and gas). Fuel produced in I. supplies only a small percentage of her needs. Electricity is produced by a public-governmental company in several thermal power stations and transmitted by a high voltage grid. I. has no commercially useable natural deposits; in the Negev there are phosphate deposits with a low uranium content. Nuclear research began even before the establishment of the State, and I.'s scientists have received further training abroad. During the late 1950s and early '60s, I. co-operated with France in nuclear research. I.'s nuclear research—in physics, organic chemistry, chemical engineering, metals' research, biology and medicine—is concentrated in three main centres: the Weizmann Institute, Nahal Sorek (five reactors), and Dimona (a 24 megawatt reactor operating on the basis of natural uranium and heavy-water). I.'s nuclear research is extensive and advanced and I. is considered capable of producing an atomic bomb. A non-nuclear naval missile, "Gavriel", is being produced. I. has declared that she will not be the first to introduce atomic weapons into the ME and that her research is directed towards peaceful purposes only.

There are dozens of research institutes in the various branches of science, and c. 40 public scientific libraries, containing over four million volumes, two million of them concentrated in the National and University Library in Jerusalem.

EDUCATION. The Law of Compulsory Free Education (1949) applies to all children between the ages of five and 14 (and to youth aged 14–17 who have not completed their elementary education). Two more years have been recently added, but this law is not yet fully implemented.

The national elementary education system maintains general and religious schools (parents being free to choose between them). There are also private schools recognized by the Ministry of Education. In the past schools were divided into three streams—workers', general and religious—but these distinctions were abolished in 1953. Secondary education is neither compulsory nor free; however, public grants regulate the payment according to the parents' financial means and the pupil's abilities.

There were in 1970–71 807,500 pupils in I., 116,700 of them Arab. Almost 100% of the Jewish children of compulsory education age attend schools, but only approximately 85% of Arab children because of the deep-rooted opposition to the schooling of girls (92.1% of boys attend, only 76% of girls). The language of tuition in Jewish schools is Hebrew and in Arab schools Arabic. Arabic is taught in the Jewish schools and Hebrew in the Arab ones. The principal foreign language is English from the fifth grade). Many Arab children attend Hebrew elementary and secondary schools. About 9,000 students in 1969–70 attended the 56 Hebrew teachers' training colleges, 370—Arab ones. There is an extensive network of vocational and agricultural schools, and special schools for retarded children. Higher education is provided for 43,000 students (1971)—16,350 at the Hebrew University of Jerusalem (established in 1925), 11,500 at Tel Aviv University (1956), 7,500 at the Technion in Haifa (1912) and the rest at Bar-Ilan University (religious, Ramat Gan, 1953), the universities of Haifa (1964) and Beer-Sheva (1965) and the Weizmann Institute of Science (research). Thousands more study at eleven other higher institutions (all these figures include also students from abroad) and in religious seminaries. The government supports the institutions of higher learning by providing more than 50% of their budgets, but does not interfere in their administration or academic freedom. Special institutes (ulpanim) teach Hebrew to new immigrants; the number of their pupils averages c. 35,000.

PRESS, RADIO AND TELEVISION. The multiplicity of political fragmentation in I. has created a lively and active press. The press is free. Censorship is imposed on military and security matters only, generally with the press's agreement and by means of a committee of its own editors; there is no political censorship. There are 26 morning newspapers and two afternoon papers, seventeen of them in Hebrew, two in Arabic, and nine in other languages (including English, French, Polish, Hungarian, Rumanian and Yiddish). Overall circulation is 600,000 per day, c. 20 per 100 population. About 400 journals are published, 50 of them weeklies and 150 fortnightlies; 260 are in Hebrew and the rest in eleven other languages. Various newspapers are identified, whether officially or not, with political parties. The most important daily papers are: *Ha'aretz* (independent); *Ma'ariv* (independent); *Yedi'ot Aharonot* (independent); *Davar* (owned by the *Histadrut*▷, and in effect supporting the Labour Party); *'Al Hamishmar* (*Mapam*); "Jerusalem Post" (English independent); *al-Anba'* (Arabic, close to the government coalition parties); *al-Quds* (Arabic, independent). One daily newspaper, *Omer*, is intended for new immigrants and is written in easy, vowelled Hebrew (owned by the *Histadrut*).

Radio and television are government-owned, but managed by the National Broadcasting Authority—an autonomous body whose administration comprises representatives of the government and public (it occasionally clashes with the government).

WELFARE, HEALTH AND PUBLIC SERVICES. I. is a welfare state. The National Insurance Act of 1954 guarantees the support of dependents, the aged, the disabled (including medical care), and families with many children. It also assures the provision of maternity benefits. The National Insurance Institution pays the wages of reservists serving in the army (up to I£1,500 per month).

The Ministry of Welfare cares for the needy, underprivileged youth and children, the chronically sick and the mentally defective. It also deals with community development. It runs work-shops for pre-vocational training, centres for delinquent youth and centres for deaf children. Public welfare bodies, financed by voluntary contributions, are also supported by the government (*Malben*, "Joint", *Wizo*, *Ort*, The *Histadrut*'s Working Women's Council, Hadassah, School for the Blind, etc.). First aid is provided on a voluntary basis by *Magen David Adom* (Red Shield of David).

The government deals with public health through government hospitals and clinics, and by supporting public health associations, the largest of which is the Histadrut Sick Fund, which provides medical care for 72% of the population.

STATISTICS. Area: 7,993 sq. mi.; cultivated area; (1970): 1,630 sq. mi. (20.5%). Population (1971): 3,001,400. Birth rate (1969): 2.62%; natural increase

(1969): 1.92%. Life expectancy (1969): Jews: males 69.5, females 73.3; non-Jews: males 68.6, females 71.2. Infant mortality (1969): 23.5 per thousand births. Gross National Product (1969): I£15,861m. (at current prices). National income *p.c.* (1969): I£5,067 ($1,206). Exports (goods and services, 1969): $1,386m.; imports: $2,605m. Budget (1970–1): I£11,234.8m. Population over 14 never schooled (1968): Jews: 10.4%; non-Jews: 42.8%. Children (6–14) at school (1967–8): Jews: 98%; non-Jews: 84.4%. Doctors (1969): 1 per 422 population (c. 2.3 per 1,000). Hospital beds (1969): 7.9 per 1,000 population. Rate of exchange: I£4.20 = $1.-.   (E.L.)

ISRAEL LABOUR PARTY—see Alignment▷.

✻ISRAEL, OCCUPIED TERRITORIES. The territories occupied by Israel during the Six Day War▷ (June 1967) include the Golan Heights▷ (Syria), the West Bank▷ (Kingdom of Jordan), the Gaza Strip▷ (Egypt) and the Sinai Peninsula▷ (Egypt). They extend over 27,000 sq. mi., 3.5 times the size of Israel itself. Their population is approximately one million (1 Jan. 1971)—610,000 in the West Bank; 372,000 in the Gaza Strip and northern Sinai; 40,000 in central and south Sinai; and 7,000 in the Golan Heights. This number included (Sept. 1967) camps housing 194,000 Arab refugees▷ from the Arab-Israel War of 1948—45,000 in the West Bank and 149,000 in the Gaza Strip (according to the Israeli definition of refugees: "A family whose head was born in the area in which Israel was established"; according to UNRWA's▷ admittedly unreliable figures, the camps population was 269,500, while the total number of refugees in the OT was 510,000). Some 200–250,000 of the inhabitants of the OT had fled to Jordan during the Six Day War: 18,595 of them were permitted to return.

The OT are administered by a military government responsible for the maintainance of public services and order, in accordance with international law. Most public services are run by local municipalities and councils set up under the Jordanian regime. Civil courts and judges also conform to Jordanian law.

Israel adopted, despite the state of war, an "open bridges" policy, which allows the passage of goods and people between the OT and the Arab countries through Jordan. She assists the OT's economy through guidance and budgetary support or long-term loans, and provides employment (35–40,000 breadwinners are employed inside Israel). She has also permitted tens of thousands of citizens of the Arab states to visit both the OT and Israel. Israel tries to minimize her presence in the T. so as not to antagonize the Arabs or disturb their sentiment. She has cut down military movement and restricted the activities of Israeli officials. The latter number less than 5% in the T. Those few soldiers and policemen who have molested local residents have been severely punished.

The inhabitants of the West Bank generally do not co-operate with guerilla-terrorist organizations. There is more subversion in the Gaza Strip, due to the overcrowding and frustration of the refugee camps. There has been a decrease in the number of acts of terrorism there in 1970 (455–30% less than in 1969). Terrorists often attack Israelis in places where Arab civilians gather; this results in large numbers of Arab casualties, including women and children. The ratio of Arab to Israeli casualties caused by terrorists in the Gaza Strip was 3.5:1 in 1970. The number of terrorists killed in the OT by the Israeli security forces was 1,901 by 31 Mar. 1971.

Under Jordanian Defence Regulations in force, houses in which arms and sabotage materials had been found, or in which terrorists found shelter or operated, were blown up (716 by the end of 1970). Administrative detention is also applied. Military courts, established in accordance with the Geneva Convention, have passed no death sentence despite their power to do so. By Mar. 1971 they had tried 27,601 cases; 600 were acquitted, approximately 20,000 fined. Only 466 were sentenced to imprisonment of more than ten years. (These figures include non-resident guerilla-terrorists who had infiltrated into the OT). People in jail in the OT numbered (31 Mar. 1971) 3,674, including 478 administrative detainees (whose release or continued detention are periodically reviewed by a public committee).

The Arab states proposed that a UN committee investigate alleged infringements of human rights in the OT. Israel agreed on condition that the committee would also investigate infringements of the human rights of Jews in the Arab states. As this condition was rejected, Israel refused to co-operate with the committee appointed by the UN General Assembly in 1969 and consisting of representatives of Ceylon, Somalia and Yugoslavia—all three hostile to Israel and maintaining no official relations with her. Being unable to carry out its task within the OT, the committee heard evidence—often mere hearsay—in places outside the OT; parts of these hearings, with grave charges against Israel, were published by the Committee. Red Cross reports, on the other hand, based on its continuous close observation of the OT, usually confirm the humane conduct of Israel's occupation. As the OT are open to tourists and visitors, many thousands have been able to form their own impression of daily life under Israeli administration.

On the future of the OT and their bearing on the Arab-Israeli conflict—see Arab-Israeli Conflict▷; Palestine Arabs◁.   (E. L.)

ISRAEL WAR OF INDEPENDENCE—see Arab-Israel War of 1948▷.

ISTANBUL (Constantinople). City in north-western Turkey, on the Bosphorus Strait and the northern shores of the Marmara Sea. Pop.: 1,743,000 (1965), nearly 3m. (1970), Turkey's largest city. The city served as the capital of the Ottoman Empire since 1453, when the Turks captured it from the Byzantines. With the establishment of the Turkish Republic in Oct. 1923 the capital was moved to Ankara▷, but I. has retained its economic and cultural importance. It is an industrial, commercial and communications centre, and its port and airport are the largest in Turkey. It also has most of Turkey's publishing houses and newspapers, two state universities and many other institutes of learning and culture. The city also retains its former cosmopolitan flavour, with its Greek, Armenian and Jewish communities.

                                                                               (D. K.)

ISTIQLAL (Arabic: Independence). I. appears in the names of many Arab nationalist parties, societies and organizations (though *Tahrir*, "Liberation", has become more popular in recent years). Arab nationalist circles, who had founded some societies before, established an I. party immediately after World War I. This I. party was in contact with Amir Feisal▷ during his brief reign in Damascus, and close to plans for an Arab Federation▷. As these plans proved abortive, and separate, semi-independent, Arab states were set up in the Fertile Crescent▷, the I. remained a loose group rather than an organized party. It continued to foster Pan-Arab▷ views. In 1932, 'Awni 'Abd-ul-Hadi▷, an I. veteran, founded an I. party in Palestine, but this, too, was not really active as a permanent organization. The name I. was also appropriated by parties not con-

Galata Bridge, Istanbul

nected with the original group, e.g. Muhammad Mahdi Kubbeh's I. party in Iraq (comprising nationalist rightist elements after World War II) or the I. party in Morocco (outside the range of this Encyclopaedia). The name was also made use of by some short-lived factions in Lebanon, such as 'Abdul-Hamid Karameh's I. party in 1945.   (Y. S.)

*ITALY, INTERESTS AND POLICIES IN THE ME.

Italian interests in the ME go back to the Middle Ages, when Italian cities traded in the Eastern Mediterranean. Large colonies, churches, monasteries, schools, hospitals, and missions existed in many ME cities.

In modern times, I.'s active involvement in the ME began with the Italian-Turkish War of 1911–12, which broke out as a result of Italian complaints of Turkey's treatment of her interests in Tripolitania▷ and Cyrenaica▷, and Turkish suspicions of Italian designs. I. emerged from the war in possession of Libya▷ and the Dodecanese▷ Islands. When I. joined the *Entente* in World War I, she pursued further expansionist interests in the direction of Asia Minor. In the Treaty of London, Apr. 1915, Britain, France, and Russia agreed that I. should obtain the south-western part of Anatolia upon the defeat and dismemberment of the Ottoman Empire. The agreement of St. Jean de Maurienne, Apr. 1917, was even more specific, harmonizing the promises to I. with the Sykes-Picot▷ Agreement (and the French aspirations to south-east Anatolia incorporated in it) and assigned to I. the districts of Izmir▷ and Anatolia and the whole of south-west Anatolia. Italy assured the Zionist leaders in May 1917 of her support for the Balfour Declaration▷ and Zionist aspirations.

Under the terms of the secret inter-Allied agreement accompanying the abortive Peace Treaty of Sèvres▷ with Turkey, August 1920, I. was to be accorded south-west Anatolia as her sphere of influence (but Izmir was given to Greece). However, as the Treaty with Turkey was abrogated the accompanying agreement remained inoperative and I. lost her share of the spoils (except for the Dodecanese).

Fascist I. began in the early 1930s to take a more active interest in the ME. At first she continued to support Zionism; in 1934, Mussolini suggested to Weizmann the cantonization of Palestine as a solution. But Mussolini soon began wooing the Arabs of Palestine and the ME. I. subsidized Arab nationalists, such as Hajj Amin al-Husseini▷, the Mufti of Jerusalem, and Radio Bari broadcast anti-British propaganda directed to the Arabs. I. became more deeply involved through her conquest of Ethiopia in 1935–6, which made her a Red Sea power. She

began supplying Ibn Sa'ud▷ with arms on favourable terms and trained his pilots, in return for his early recognition of her annexation of Ethiopia. She also renewed in 1937 a treaty of friendship with the Imam of Yemen which she had concluded in 1926, and her influence in the Yemen increased. In the 1930s, I. also attempted to woo the government of Iraq by offering arms on credit and free training for Iraqi air-force officers. An Anglo-I. agreement of April 1938 only temporarily halted Italian anti-British propaganda broadcasts. It also contained assurances that neither power would acquire a "privileged position of a political character" in Sa'udi Arabia and the Yemen. For I.'s colonial rule of Libya and Libyan resistance, see Libya▷.

When I. entered World War II, on 10 June 1940, the ME became a threatre of war, with Egypt as an immediate target for Italian attack from Libya. I.'s offensives—repelled and resumed, in a see-saw sequence, with German troops playing an ever-increasing role—brought her deep into Egyptian territory, but were finally halted in 1942 at al-'Alamein▷. By 1942–3, I.'s North African empire was lost (see World War II▷). She had entered the war with obvious ambitions in the ME, particularly in Egypt and the Sudan, which were recognized by the Germans (Hitler had stated, in June 1940, to Mussolini and his Foreign Minister Ciano that "the Mediterranean and the Adriatic had from ancient times belonged to the historical sphere of influence of the Apennine peninsula"). Though she needed Germany's military help, she was not pleased with German intervention in Eastern Mediterranean affairs.

After the fall of France, 1940, an Italian Commission was sent out to Lebanon and Syria (then under Vichy control), to supervise the fulfilment of the armistice agreement. The Commission seems to have taken no interest in Arab nationalist demands, but its presence was seen as a grave threat to the Allies and as preparing the ground for a German-Italian invasion of the ME.

Throughout the war, I. and Germany negotiated with Hajj Amin al-Husseini▷ and Rashid 'Ali al-Kilani▷ (both in Germany since 1941) for an Axis declaration in favour of Arab independence and Pan-Arabism. I. had supported Rashid 'Ali when he became Prime Minister of Iraq, 1941, but had been unable to come to his rescue when he made war on Britain and was defeated. Mussolini supported a declaration in favour of Arab independence in Iraq, Syria, Lebanon, Palestine and Transjordan, but was not eager to extend similar support to the idea of Arab unity or Arab independence in Egypt and Sudan—two countries on which he had designs.

Husseini had discussed with Mussolini, in May 1942, the formation of an Arab Legion, and Arab units were actually formed by both Germany and I. However, the pro-Axis Arabs preferred Germany to I., because of I.'s colonial record in Libya and her military defeat in the western desert in February 1941.

Mussolini's overthrow in July 1943 and I.'s capitulation in Sept. 1943 removed her from the ME arena. Since World War II, I.'s activities in the ME have been purely economic, in particular through her vigorous national oil company, ENI▷, which began operating in the 1950s in several ME countries. Her attempts to retain possession of at least part of her Libyan empire—in the form of a trusteeship over Tripolitania—continued throughout the peace negotiations, but finally failed in 1949 (see Libya▷, and see Bevin▷ for the abortive Bevin-Sforza Agreement). The number of her colonists in Libya, many of whom had been withdrawn during the war, continued to decrease; in 1970 their departure was further accelerated by the confiscation of their properties by the new, revolutionary-nationalist regime, the total remaining having fallen to around 15,000. Whatever actual interest I. retained in Libya, was now mainly economic.   (Sh.H-Y.S.)

IZL — see Irgun (T)zeva'i Le'umi▷.

IZMIR (SMYRNA). Third largest city of Turkey, situated on the Aegean coast; pop.: 412,000 (1965), 1.4m. (1970). I. is Turkey's second port, a major commercial centre, the venue of an annual international fair, and the seat of the Aegean University. I. had a large Greek population until after World War I. In 1919 invading Greek forces occupied the town. Under the abortive Treaty of Sèvres▷, 1920, the area was to be under Greek administration for five years, after which a local parliament or a plebiscite would determine whether it should be incorporated into Greece. I. and its surroundings were, however, reconquered by the Turkish nationalists in September 1922. The Peace Treaty of Lausanne▷, 1923, did not revive the Sèvres proposal, thus confirming Turkey's right to retain I. The remaining Greek population left the town during the overall exchange of populations between Greece and Turkey (see Greek-Turkish Relations▷).   (D.K.)

J

JABAL 'AMEL. The southern part of Lebanon, south of the Litani▷ River. With a mainly Shi'ite▷

population (see Mutawalis▷), JA has been part of Lebanon since 1920. See Lebanon▷, Political History.   (Y.S.)

JABAL DRUZE. The "Mountain of the Druzes" in south-eastern Syria. See Druzes▷, and Syria▷, Political History.

JABERI, AL-. Wealthy family of Syrian notables in Aleppo, some of whom became leaders in the Arab and Syrian nationalist movement. Most prominent were Ihsan al-J. and Sa'dullah al-J.

JABERI, AL-, IHSAN. Active in the Pan-Arab▷ movement during the 1920s when he headed the Geneva office of the "Syro-Palestinian Congress" and engaged in political negotiations with diverse groups, including the Zionist leadership. These attempts to work out a Jewish-Arab agreement (persuant to the Feisal-Weizmann Agreement▷) were fruitless.

JABERI, AL-, SA'DULLAH (1892–1947). An active Syrian nationalist since his youth, and one of the leaders of the "National Bloc" at the time of the French Mandate, S. was arrested on numerous occasions by the French. He served in several Syrian governments of the "National Bloc", 1936–9, and was twice Prime Minister when the "Bloc" returned to power, in 1943–4 and 1945–6. In 1944–5 he was President of the National Assembly.   (A.L.-O.T.)

JABOTINSKY, ZEEV (VLADIMIR) (1880–1940). Zionist leader, ideologist and writer. Born and educated in Russia. During World War I, together with Joseph Trumpeldor▷ and Pinhas Rutenberg, he persuaded the British to form two (out of four) Jewish volunteer units in Egypt (1915) and England (1915–17) (see Jewish Legion▷). In 1920 J. was sentenced by the British to 15 years' imprisonment for organizing the defence of the Jewish Quarter of Jerusalem, but his sentence was quashed afterwards due to public pressure.

J. was elected to the Zionist Executive in 1921, but resigned in 1923 in protest against the White Paper▷ of 1922 which tore Transjordan from Palestine and its acceptance by the Zionist Organization to which he had earlier agreed. He formed the World Union of Zionist Revisionists▷, in 1925, in opposition to "official" Zionism, and a youth movement, *Betar* (*Brith Trumpeldor*). In 1929 he left Palestine for the Zionist Congress in Zurich and the British authorities refused to grant him re-entry. In 1935, mainly because of the refusal of the Zionist Congress to declare a Jewish State as its immediate aim, he led the Revisionists in their secession from the Zionist Organization and the establishment of their own "New Zionist Organization" of which he was elected President. The latter reunited with the Zionist Organization in 1946. J. advocated increased Jewish immigration to Palestine, militant opposition to the Mandatory authorities and an immediate struggle for a Jewish State, in both Palestine and Transjordan, and opposed vigorously plans for the partition of Palestine. J. was the spiritual leader of the dissident military underground organization, *Irgun (T)zeva'i Le'umi*▷ (IZL). He died in the USA in 1940 and was reinterred in 1964 on Mount Herzl in Jerusalem. His philosophy has remained the ideological basis of the *Herut*▷ party in Israel.   (A.W.-E.L.)

JABR, SALEH (1896–1957). Iraqi jurist and politician. Shi'ite Muslim. Born in al-Nasseriyya (al-Muntafiq Province). Graduate of Baghdad Law School. Judge 1926–30. Member of Parliament since 1930. Minister of Education 1933–4. Governor of Karbala 1935–6. Minister of Justice 1936–7. Director General of Customs and Excise 1937–8. Minister of Education 1938–40, Social Affairs, 1940. Governor of Basra 1940–1, Acting Minister of Foreign Affairs 1941–2 and 1943, Minister of Finance 1942–3. Prime Minister (the first Shi'ite to reach this position) from Mar. 1947 to Jan. 1948. Considered a moderate and pro-British, of Nuri Sa'id's▷ school (though not of his faction), J. negotiated with Britain the Portsmouth Treaty▷ of Jan. 1948 that was designed to replace the Anglo-Iraqi Treaty of 1930. However, after violent demonstrations, he had to resign and the Treaty was scrapped by his successor. He rejoined the government, as Minister of the Interior, in 1950. In 1951 he established a short-lived conservative "People's Socialist Party", but did not return to high office.   (B.G.)

JACOBITES. Synonymous with Syrian Orthodox Monophysite▷ Christians. The name derives from Jacob Baradeus, who lived in the 6th century and reorganized the Syrian Orthodox Church in spite of the oppression of the Monophysites by the Byzantine authorities. The Church's liturgy is very close to that of the primitive Church of Jerusalem and its language is ancient Syriac-Aramaic. Today there are about 100,000 J. in the ME—60,000 in Syria, and the remainder in Lebanon, Iraq, Turkey and Israel (and *c.* $\frac{1}{2}$ m. J. in India). Their religious head, the Patriarch, always bears the title Mar Ignatios; at present he has his seat in Damascus. The Church is divided into eleven dioceses. The seat of the Archbishop of Jerusalem is the ancient convent of St. Mark. The J. have certain privileges in the Church of the Holy Sepulchre and in the Church of the Nativity in Bethlehem.   (Sh.C.)

＊JADID, SALAH. Syrian officer and politician of 'Alawi▷ origin. Born 1929 at Lataqia. Deputy Secretary of the *Ba'th*▷ party (1966–70) and leader of its military faction. Politically active since the *Ba'thist* officers' coup of 8 Mar. 1963, which he helped to engineer. He was appointed Army Chief-of-Staff before the year was out, after a sharp intra-party struggle. Member (since 1964) of Syria's Presidential Council and the *Ba'th* party's "national" (all-Arab) and "regional" (Syrian) leadership councils, J. headed the extremist military wing of the party against the more moderate line of the "civilian" wing led by Michel 'Aflaq▷, Salah-ul-Din Bitar▷ and Amin al-Hafez▷. Hafez, then Head of State, dismissed him in Sept. 1965 as Chief-of-Staff; but within six months J., leading another coup (23 Feb. 1966), deposed the "national" *Ba'th* leadership and brought to power extremists of the "regional" leadership and the military wing. They have ruled Syria since, with J. filling no formal government post but wielding power as Deputy Secretary of the *Ba'th* party (1966–70).

The ruling group was split by constant factional rivalries. J. led the "progressives", standing for a swift and radical re-organization of Syria's regime and economy along Marxist lines and close co-operation with the Soviet Union (as against the "nationalist" wing of Hafez Asad▷). J., now a major-general, played a prominent part in organizing Syrian-Palestinian guerilla groups to fight Israel. His power, and that of his faction, began to decline in Oct. 1968, and in 1969 the struggle between him and Asad grew more intense. A semi-coup staged by Asad in Feb. 1969 was successful, but Asad agreed—apparently under Soviet and Egyptian pressure—to a compromise settlement, with J. remaining Deputy Party Secretary and in effective control of the al-Sa'iqa▷ guerilla organization. However, in Nov. 1970, Asad seized the helm and kept it. J. was dismissed and imprisoned.   (A.L.)

JAFFA. One of the oldest ports on the coast of Israel, dating back to the third millennium BC. The town started to grow with the opening of the Suez Canal▷, and became in the early 20th century the centre of modern economic activity in Palestine. Later it was overtaken by its former suburb of Tel-Aviv▷ (founded in 1909) and by the modern deep-water ports of Haifa▷ (1932); it remained the town with the largest Arab population in Palestine (*c.* 65,000, 1944).

The Partition Plan of the UN Special Committee (UNSCOP), 1947, allotted J. to the Jewish State. This was changed in the plan adopted by the UN General Assembly on 29 Nov. 1947, which envisaged J. as an enclave belonging to the Arab State. The

View of Jaffa

Arab attacks of 1947–8 made such an enclave untenable, and as soon as British rule was terminated, in May 1948, J. surrendered to Jewish forces. Most of its population had fled during the preceding fighting. Arabs in J. numbered 8,000 in 1969. In 1950 J. was joined to the municipality of Tel-Aviv, since called Tel-Aviv-J.   (Y.K.)

JAGHBUB. Oasis in Cyrenaica▷ (Libya) near the Egyptian frontier. In 1856 it was made the centre of the Sanussi▷ order, because of its strategic position between Cyrenaica, Tripolitania, Egypt and Sudan, on the main pilgrim route from North Africa to Mecca, and its remoteness from the administrative centre. After the Italians conquered Libya (1911–12) J.'s status became a matter of dispute between the Italians and the British, then ruling Egypt. After Egypt achieved independence in 1922, Italy entered into new negotiations with Cairo, and by an agreement of 2 Dec. 1925 J. was awarded to Libya, in return for concessions elsewhere. J., then still held by the Sanussis rebelling against Italian rule, was conquered by the Italians a year later.   (B.G.)

✻ **JAPAN.** J. was not particularly active in the ME until World War II. After the war, its growing need for ME oil and the wish to invest capital and export goods and know-how prompted her to action in the ME. Japanese oil companies acquired their first concession in the ME in 1958 on the sea-bed off the Neutral Zone▷ between Kuwait▷ and Sa'udi Arabia▷, and began production in 1961. These and other Japanese companies acquired in the late 1960s further concessions in the Persian Gulf, particularly the Trucial Coast▷. A consortium of Japanese companies also obtained, in 1969–70, a concession in Egyptian waters, in the Gulf of Suez. By the end of the 1960s oil produced in the ME by Japanese

companies covered 10–15% of J.'s growing oil imports, and the companies hoped to expand their activities and increase the percentage. Most of J.'s oil imports were, however, still covered by straight purchase—mainly in Iran and the Persian Gulf. The ME, including both Japanese production and purchase, provided nearly 90% of J.'s oil needs, the Arab countries—c. 50%.

Japanese companies also sought to participate in development projects, particularly the construction of power stations, harbours and dockyards, petrochemical industries, assembly plants for Japanese products, roads, railways (for example, a Japanese company successfully tendered to build the Hijaz Railway▷, but the contract was subsequently cancelled). An expansion of Japanese activities and interests is to be expected. Politically, J. maintains normal relations with all the countries of the region.   (Y.S.)

✻**JARRING, Dr. GUNNAR** (b. 1907). Swedish scholar and diplomat. Having served during World War II and in the early 1950s in Turkey, Iran, Iraq and Pakistan, J. was Swedish Permanent Representative to the UN 1956–8. As President of the Security Council during that tenure, he tried briefly, and unsuccessfully, to assist a settlement of the Kashmir problem (1957). Following the Six Day War▷, J., now Sweden's Ambassador to Moscow, was chosen by the Secretary-General of the UN in Nov. 1967 in accordance with a Security Council resolution, as special envoy to the ME, to "promote agreement and assist efforts to achieve a peaceful and accepted settlement" to the Arab-Israel conflict▷. As the Arab states refused to meet and talk to Israel, J. was obliged to commute between Jerusalem and

Dr. Gunnar Jarring

the Arab capitals. His talks were suspended in spring 1969, without results, when the representatives of the Four Powers began to discuss the ME issue. In Aug. 1970 the J. talks were resumed, after an American initiative had resulted in a renewal of the cease-fire and a standstill in the military situation (see Rogers▷). Israel walked out again when it became clear that Egypt had, with Soviet assistance, violated the standstill agreement. In Dec. 1970 the resumption of the J. talks was agreed. Exchanges of views and memoranda, early in 1971—including certain proposals submitted by J. himself—led to no progress, and the J. mission was, in spring and summer 1971, in semi-suspension.   (Sh. H.-Y. S.)

JAZIRA, AL-. (Arabic: island or peninsula). Region between the Euphrates and Tigris rivers, in north-west Iraq and north-east Syria. Syria's J. is today divided into three administrative districts: Hasake, Deir al-Zor and Raqqa. The J. is a semi-desert area where the average rainfall is less than 12.7 in. a year. Until the early 20th century, it was the desolate range of the nomadic Shammar tribes. When France obtained the mandate for Syria (1920, formally: 1922), she set up an administration for the J. region, granting the Bedouin limited autonomy. The region was merged in 1924 in the "State of Syria". French rule restrained the Bedouin tribes, and, with the development of modern communications and new farming methods, the J. attracted many settlers and quickly became Syria's main area of agricultural development. In the 1930s, the French encouraged separatist and autonomist tendencies in the J., but Syrian nationalism halted that trend.

During World War II▷, with the Allies exerting themselves to encourage food production in the ME, more virgin land was developed in al-J., and this hastened the settlement of more Bedouin and other migrants (see below). During that period, a special agency was established for grain cultivation. The cultivated area of the J. grew from 50,000 acres in 1942 to almost 1.25m. acres in the 1950s, and hundreds of new villages sprang up. Until recent years, the development of al-J. was undertaken mainly by private entrepreneurs, owners of tractors and farming machines, through the extensive cultivation of wide areas and partial irrigation, chiefly by pumping from the Euphrates. The further development of al-J. is one of the most important Syrian projects. Its acceleration and extension depend on the completion of the Euphrates▷ Dam now being built at Tabqa and designed to irrigate an area of 1.5-1.75m. acres. In 1957, oil was struck in the J.; production in 1968 was 950,000 tons. That year, a 403 mi. long oil pipeline was laid from the J.

wells to a refinery built at Homs and to the oil port of Tartus▷.

Al-J. has the largest concentration of ethnic minorities in Syria, for whom it became an asylum over the last few generations. The Sunni▷ Muslims (who are the majority in Syria) are a minority in the J. The most important groups are Kurds▷, who fled from Turkey during the 1920s and '30s; Armenians▷, who preceded them, fleeing from Turkey in World War I▷; Assyrians▷, who left Iraq after the massacre inflicted on them in 1933; and Syrian Orthodox Jacobites▷, a Monophysite Christian community. Afraid of the growth of separatist national ambitions among the minorities, the Damascus government resorts to sharp suppressive measures, especially against the Kurds, who form the largest group in the area (c. 300,000 out of al-J.'s total population of 700,000).   (A. L.-O. T.)

*JERUSALEM. Capital of Israel (Pop.: 291,700, in 1970). Holy city of the three major religions (according to a list compiled by the UN there are fifteen places sacred to Christians, five to Muslims and ten to Jews—see Holy Places▷). During the British Mandate (1922–48) J. served as Palestine's capital. From 1950 it has been the seat of the Israeli President, the *Knesset* (Parliament) and Government (and also the centre of the Zionist Movement). The Old City and the eastern part of J. were occupied in 1948, during the Arab-Israel War▷, by the Kingdom of Jordan, except for Mount Scopus▷, which became an Israeli enclave. Since the Six Day War (7 June 1967), Israel holds the whole city and its environs.

J., built on the Judean Hills, approximately 2,600 ft. above sea-level, is first mentioned in Egyptian sources of the 17th and 18th centuries BC and was Jewish from King David's time (1037–969 BC) until the destruction of the Second Temple by the Romans (70 CE). During the Second Jewish revolt, led by Bar-Kokhba (in 135), Jerusalem became Jewish once more; after the suppression of the revolt, it was re-named by the Romans *Aelia Capitolina* and Jewish settlement was forbidden. The Persians (614–29) allowed Jewish re-settlement. From the time of Muslim conquest (638) there have always been in J. both a large Muslim, Arabic-speaking community and a Jewish community. J. was briefly under Christian rule 1099–1187 and 1229–44 when Jews were not allowed to settle in J.

The history of new (West) J. begins in 1860 with the building of Jewish quarters outside the walls of the Old City. Jewish settlement within East J., on the other hand, was forcibly interrupted on 28 May 1948, when the Jewish Quarter (1,700 inhabitants) surrendered to the Jordanian Arab Legion.

POPULATION OF JERUSALEM 1860–1948

Year	Total	Jews	% of Jews
1860	12,000	6,000	50
1892	42,000	26,000	61.9
1922	63,000	34,000	53.9
1942	140,000	86,000	61.42
1948	165,000	100,000	60.6

The UN resolution of 29 Nov. 1947, providing for the partition of Mandatory Palestine and the establishment of a Jewish and an Arab State, recommended that J. should be under an international regime, which would be separate from the two states and under the supervision of the UN Trusteeship Council. Nevertheless, the UN did nothing to defend the city and its inhabitants, or to secure their physical needs. Nor were steps taken towards the elaboration of a "detailed Statute", as resolved, or for an administration.

The plan for internationalizing J. presented by Count Folke Bernadotte, the UN mediator, was rejected both by the Arabs and the Jews and was not approved by the UN. However, the General Assembly re-affirmed on 11 Dec. 1948, that J. should be "under effective UN control". The "Palestine Conciliation Commission" (PCC▷) just appointed was instructed to prepare a "detailed proposal for a permanent international regime" for J., while the Security Council was to ensure the demilitarization of Jerusalem (but in fact did nothing). In Dec. 1949, the Assembly "restated its intention" to establish an "international regime" in J., which would provide adequate protection for the holy places, and charged the Trusteeship Council with preparing the "Statute of J.". Jordan stated during the debate in the Assembly that she would not discuss any plan to internationalize Jerusalem.

The Jews had accepted the 1947 Assembly Resolution but the Arabs had rejected it claiming that it denied the Palestinians' (i.e. Arabs') right to self-determination. Rejecting the Jews' right to self-determination, the Arabs embarked on war. West J. was shelled by "Qawuqji's▷ Army of Deliverance". Several Arab areas were conquered by the Israelis, but the Old City and East J. fell to Jordan on 28 May 1948. On 1 Dec. 1948 Jordan established her administration there, and on 24 Apr. 1950 she officially annexed—despite the bitter opposition of all the other Arab states (see Jordan▷, Palestine Arabs▷)—most of the West Bank▷, including the eastern part of J. Jordan again emphasized her objection to the

Jerusalem, General view with Temple Mount

The new building of the Knesset.

internationalization of J. Israel too withdrew her agreement, claiming that the Arab invasion restored to the Jews their historic right to J., and that she would guarantee the safety of the holy places.

In its report published in June 1950, the Trusteeship Council again proposed that J. be a *corpus separatum* under international administration. The USSR withdrew her support for internationalization in view of the opposition of both its Arab and its Jewish inhabitants. In January 1952 the General Assembly passed a resolution placing on the governments concerned the responsibility for reaching agreement about all disputed points, in accordance with previous UN resolutions. This resolution, which practically recognized the *status quo*, was the last one on this subject to be passed by the UN until 1967.

The Israel-Jordan Armistice Agreement of 3 Apr. 1949 crystallized the complete partition of J. already existing *de facto*. The agreement provided for a joint committee to ensure free access to the holy places, to the Jewish cultural institutions on Mount Scopus and to the Jewish cemetery on the Mount of Olives. (It also placed a limit on the amount of arms allowed into Jerusalem.) This joint committee never met and the Jordanians ignored their commitment to allow Jews access to the holy places. The Jewish cemetery on the Mount of Olives was desecrated. Access to Mount Scopus was granted a limited number of Israeli policemen only.

On 23 Jan. 1950 the *Knesset* declared J. to be Israel's capital. Only 17 out of 57 diplomatic missions accredited to Israel were resident in J.

On 29 June 1967, following its occupation, Israel applied to East J. the Israeli "law, jurisdiction and administration". (Bethlehem's request to come under the same jurisdiction was rejected.) This decree did not automatically make the residents of East J. Israeli citizens, but it entitled them to travel freely in Israel or abroad, and to participate fully in Israel's economic life. Later legislation (Aug. 1968) cancelled the status of 'enemy aliens' with regard to the residents of East J. In 1971 the Ministry of Justice announced its intention to draft a bill which, when passed, will entitle East J. residents to compensation for their real estate located in Israel and abandoned by them during the Arab-Israel War of 1948. This step aroused, especially in Jordan, protests against the so-called transformation of J. into a Jewish city. East J. residents have the right to vote in the elections to the municipality of united Jerusalem; and in the 1969 elections thousands did. Opinion in the Israel Supreme Court was divided as to whether the application of Israeli law amounted to annexation.

With the applications of Israeli law to East J. and its environs (43.5 sq. mi.), some 68,000 inhabitants—(57,000 Muslims and 11,000 Christians)—were added to Israel. The new total population of united J. was 266,000, c. 200,000 of them Jews.

The *de facto* annexation of East J. to Israel aroused opposition both among the Arab states and in the UN. The UN General Assembly resolved on 4 and 14 July 1967 that the steps taken by Israel to alter J.'s status were invalid and called on her immediately to cease all such action. (It is not clear whether the Assembly referred to the status determined by its resolution of 29 Nov. 1947 or to the Jordanian regime which preceded the Six Day War.) In two sharply-worded resolutions the Security Council called on

Israel, on 21 May 1968 and 3 July 1969, to cancel all steps taken to annex J.

After the Six Day War, some Arab leaders indicated that the Arabs would now be ready to accept the internationalization of J. Most Arab spokesmen, however, demanded that East J. be returned to Jordan.

Since the unification of J. Israel has maintained the security of the holy places, freedom of access and worship for all, and the rights of the various religious communities to their holy places. The government forbade Jews to pray on the Temple Mount, which is holy to the Muslims and the site of two venerated mosques and protected by their own guards. It was these guards who failed to prevent a mentally disturbed person from entering the al-Aqsa Mosque and setting fire to it, in Sept. 1969.

In order to facilitate worship at the Wailing (Western) Wall▷, the Jews' most sacred place, houses close to the Wall were demolished and their occupants transferred to other houses and compensated. The Jewish Quarter in the Old City has been rehabilitated, and the aim is to resettle it. Apartment houses have been built in the northern part of East J., and there are plans also for building to the south. The buildings of the Hebrew University and the Medical Centre on Mount Scopus have been repaired and new student accommodation has been provided.

According to plans, J.'s population should rise by 100,000 within a few years.   (E. L.)

JEWISH AGENCY FOR PALESTINE. Article 4 of the Mandate▷ for Palestine provided for the establishment of "an appropriate JA" which would be recognized as a public body to advise and co-operate with the administration of Palestine "in such matters as may affect the establishment of the Jewish National Home and the interests of the Jewish population" and to "assist and participate in the development of the country". "The Zionist Organization, insofar as its organization and constitution are appropriate in the opinion of the Mandatory Government, shall be recognized as such an agency..." Until 1929 the Zionist Organization fulfilled the tasks of the JA. In 1929, after prolonged discussions, the JA was formally established with the intention of absorbing both non-Zionists and Zionists from different political groups. Its basic aims were: a. the facilitation of Jewish immigration to Palestine; b. the advancement of the Hebrew language and Hebrew culture; c. the purchase of land in Palestine for the Jewish people, through the Jewish National Fund▷; d. the development of agriculture and settlement on the basis of the principle of Jewish labour; e. fulfilment of Jewish religious needs in Palestine

without infringing on individual freedom of conscience. It was determined that, unless otherwise decided, the President of the Zionist Organization would also be President of the JA.

Prior to World War II the JA and the Zionist Organization were separate bodies, though the JA represented the Zionist Organization vis-à-vis the British government, the Palestine government, the League of Nations and the various committees dealing with Palestine affairs. During World War II, the distinction between the two bodies disappeared.

After the establishment of Israel, the Government of Israel took over many of the JA's activities. Except for those tasks which the Government is by law obliged to fulfil, the JA, from its Jerusalem headquarters, provides all services in the fields of immigration and the absorption of immigrants in Israel, including social welfare services, education, youth care and training, agricultural settlement, housing. Yet, since the establishment of Israel, and despite an expenditure of over $4,500m. from Oct. 1948 until Mar. 1970, the JA has lost much of its former importance.

Since 1971 the JA is composed in equal parts of representatives of the Jewish communities in the Diaspora and the World Zionist Organization. By the same agreement the JA is established as the representative of World Jewry.   (E. L.)

JEWISH BRIGADE IN WORLD WAR II. Palestine Jews volunteered for service in the British Army, particularly the East Kent Regiment (the Buffs), three companies of which became the Palestine Regiment. Others served with sappers and commando units and fought in Ethiopia, on the Western Front and in Greece, and some served in the British Air Force and the Navy. Palestinian volunteers numbered some 26,000 Jews (out of a population of about 450,000) and 9,000 Arabs (out of about 1m.).

The JB was formed in Sept. 1944 under Brig. Ernest Frank Benjamin, an English Jew, after heavy Jewish pressure and years of British objection on economic and political grounds. The JB numbered about 5,000 men, with its own flag and emblem, and saw service in Egypt, the North Italian front, and north-west Europe. Men of the JB did much to aid Jewish survivors of the Holocaust, and helped to smuggle them to Palestine.

The JB was disbanded in the summer of 1946. Many of the future leaders of the Israel Defence Forces received their military education in its ranks.
(Sh. H.)

JEWISH LEGION. Jewish battalions in World War I consisted of the 38th (recruited in England

Soldiers of the Jewish Brigade

1915–17), 39th (organized in America, 1917–18, by D. Ben-Gurion▷ and Y. Ben-Zvi▷) and 40th (mainly from Palestine, 1918) Battalions of the Royal Fusiliers, and the Zion Mule Corps (initiated and organized by Jabotinsky▷ and Trumpeldor▷ in Egypt in 1915 and led by the latter who was one of its captains). They totalled around 6,400 men and were collectively called JL.

The JL was formed as a result of the Zionists' conviction that they should support Great Britain and her allies in order to accelerate the establishment of a Jewish National Home in Palestine. The JL's formation had been preceded by lengthy discussion, some Zionist leaders advocating neutrality as the right policy for the movement.

The JL was disbanded in May 1921 (because of the participation of JL soldiers in the defence of the Jewish quarter of Jerusalem against Arab rioters and in the smuggling of arms for Jewish self-defence). Many members of the JL were later active in the formation of the *Hagana*▷.   (Sh.H.-E.L.)

JEWISH NATIONAL FUND. Land and development fund of the Zionist Organization, founded in Dec. 1901. The lands it purchased in Palestine became by statute the inalienable property of the Jewish people. They are leased for settlement, mostly to co-operatives (*kibbutz*▷, *moshav*), for 49 years. The lease, which may be extended, is conditional upon the land being cultivated by the lessee himself (not by hired labour). Upon his death his successors may carry on the lease under the same conditions.

Land purchases began in 1904 and continued throughout the British Mandate. Restrictions were imposed by the British Administration in 1940, following the White Paper▷ of 1939, which banned further purchases in most of Palestine. When the State of Israel was established the JNF held about 250,000 acres of land; after 1948, it acquired an additional 600,000 acres—mostly abandoned property (the purchase price being held by the Custodian of Abandoned Property towards the payment of compensation in a future settlement of the Arab

refugee problem). The JNF has also prepared land for agricultural settlement and industry, drained swamps and worked in hill reclamation and afforestation. It is financed by contributions from world Jewry.   (Sh.H.-E.L.)

JEWISH STATE. A book by Theodor Herzl. See Zionism▷.

JEWS IN THE ME. Jews form the majority of the population in Israel (*c.* 2.6m. in 1970). This reflects, in part, the drastic change which has taken place in the distribution of Jewish populations in the rest of the ME during the past 50 years. The total number of J. in the ME (other than Palestine), was 425,000 in 1917, 485,000 in 1947, but only 118,000 in 1968.

JEWS IN THE ME - ESTIMATES FOR 1917–68
(THOUSANDS)

Country	1917	1947	1968
Iraq	85	125	2.5
Egypt	60	66	2
Yemen and Aden	45	54	0.5
Syria	32	19	3
Lebanon	3	6	3
Libya	25	35	—
Total, Arab countries	250	305	11
Turkey	100	80	37
Iran	75	100	70
Total in the region (outside Israel)	425	485	118

In the first period (1917–47) approximately 17,000 J. left the Yemen for Palestine; many others emigrated from Syria and Turkey, mainly to Palestine. A small number emigrated from Iraq, Egypt, Iran and Libya. However from 1948 to 1968 they departed from the Arab states *en masse*, leaving very few J. behind. Only in the non-Arab countries—Turkey and Iran—do Jewish communities of any size exist today.

This mass emigration was partially motivated by religious sentiment for the Holy Land, while the younger generation was also attracted by Zionist movements (established in all countries of the ME, except Yemen, from 1930 onwards) advocating the rebirth of the Jewish State. However, religious or Zionist aspirations were not responsible for the mass migration of any Jewish community to Palestine. The principal cause of this movement to Palestine, and later Israel, was the deterioration of a local

Front view of the Cairo synagogue

community's social and political security in Arab society. A few migrated for religious or Zionist reasons; the majority did so only when their personal safety was endangered. In addition, Islamic law and custom only accepts non-Muslims as protected subjects, if they pay a specified poll-tax *(Jizya)*. This mediaeval statute remained in force for the J. of Yemen▷ as recently as this century. J. were segregated and humiliated, and Jewish orphans forcibly converted to Islam. These regulations applied even during the "liberal" reign of Imam Yahya▷ (1905–48). Yemenite Jews, therefore, emigrated whenever the opportunity presented itself. Between 1919 and 1948 about one-third left Yemen for Palestine and the remaining 45,000 followed in 1949–50 (mainly via an airlift from Aden supported by the State of Israel). These immigrants included all the J. of Hadhramaut▷, South Arabia, who, though subject to less segregation than their brethren in Yemen, were in an equally bad economic position. The 4,000 J. of Aden lived peacefully until Dec. 1947 when several were killed, hundreds injured and much of their property destroyed, during a pogrom. Many immigrated to Israel. The immigration begun in that year was virtually completed after further anti-Jewish outbreaks in 1958 and 1967. Pogroms in Dec. 1947 also prompted the few hundred J. of Bahrain▷ to leave. Similar conditions resulted in the emigration of some 35,000 from Libya▷. This ancient community escaped extreme persecution under the Italian occupation, 1911–42, although the fascist regime discriminated against them after 1936. Large numbers left Libya only when many J. were killed in two pogroms, Nov. 1945 and June 1948. Some 6,000 still remained in 1952. This remnant also departed gradually and its last members emigrated after renewed anti-Jewish outbreaks in June 1967.

Acts of violence and discrimination against the Jewish populations in Iraq▷, Syria▷ and Egypt▷ were increasingly aggravated by government dis-

crimination from the 1930s onwards. Individual J. were attacked by nationalist-oriented Arab youth, and large-scale pogroms were organized in Baghdad, June 1941, Aleppo, Dec. 1947 and Cairo, June 1948. Beginning with the Arab-Israel War, May 1948, the Arab governments participated actively in the oppression of their Jewish subjects, although formally denying that their military intervention in Palestine or the ban on Zionist organizations reflected an anti-Jewish policy. Hundreds of J. in Iraq, Syria and Egypt were sent to concentration camps or otherwise detained in May and June 1948; many were sentenced to several years of imprisonment on charges of Zionism or Communism, or both. In view of such measures, many fled these countries. The Iraqi government permitted their emigration in Mar. 1950 and within a year almost the entire community had disappeared (settling mainly in Israel). Most Syrian J. emigrated illegally during the same period, crossing the border into Lebanon. Approximately 6,000 remained in Iraq, 5,000 in Syria, and 40,000 in Egypt in 1952. The Suez crisis of 1956 resulted in a further deterioration of the status of Egyptian J. Thousands were expelled from the country, with little or no preliminary notice, and the community was reduced to 15,000. Hundreds were again placed under arrest or in concentration camps, including the rabbis of Cairo and Alexandria, during the Six Day War▷. Later, many of those detained were released and left Egypt; others, however, still remained in concentration camps. The status of J. remaining in Iraq after 1951 deteriorated when 'Abd-ul-Salam 'Aref▷ seized power, 1963. Many were detained and their business assets frozen. After show trials in 1968–9, several J. and Arabs were executed as "Zionist and Western spies". The situation of J. in Iraq is one of continued distress. After 1948 J. in Syria were not permitted to emigrate. Nevertheless, most of the community managed to escape. Those who remain are subjected to economic discrimination; the majority have been dismissed from their jobs and their assets frozen.

In Lebanon▷ the J. were never mistreated by the government either before or after 1948. In periods of tension, May and July 1948, June 1967, the Lebanese government posted guards in the Jewish quarter of Beirut and no J. were harmed. Given equal civil rights and a free economy, few left the country while many Syrian J. found a safe haven there. However, a considerable number left after the Lebanese crisis of 1958 and more followed after the Six Day War. Emigrants were permitted, in contrast to Egyptian and Iraqi practice, to take their possessions with them. They emigrated to Israel, the USA, Latin America and Europe.

Until 1906 the J. of Iran▷ were, like those in Yemen, subjects without citizenship and required to pay the *Jizya*. They were guaranteed equal rights by the new Iranian constitution of 1906, but their status did not improve until the coronation of Reza Shah▷ in 1925. Thereafter, they were admitted to state schools, the army and the civil service. The Shi'ite Muslim leadership also became less fanatic and their anti-Jewish sentiments less acute. With improved educational and economic status after 1925, the more successful members of the Jewish community have remained in Iran and only the indigent immigrated to Israel. Among the immigrants were most of the "Maranno" J. of Mashhad (Meshed). Their ancestors were compelled to convert to Islam in 1839, but remained crypto-J. at home, leading a double life, each with a Muslim name and a Jewish one, conducting double ceremonies (marriage, etc.), a Muslim one and a Jewish one, and trying secretly to observe Jewish dietary laws. Since the 1880s many started to leave Mashhad for Palestine, later Israel, where they live as J. The few Marannos living in Mashhad today are still outwardly Muslims, and known as "*Islam-i-Jedid*" (New Muslims).

J. in the coastal towns of Turkey▷ suffered under the Greek occupation of 1918–22; many fled to the interior and Istanbul, or emigrated from the country. The Lausanne▷ Peace Treaty, July 1923, obliged Turkey to continue granting non-Muslims autonomous jurisdiction in matters of family law and personal status (see Millet System▷).

However, the government of the Turkish Republic subsequently compelled the J. and other minorities to relinquish these privileges, 1925–6. Despite their Turkish citizenship, they were the object of discrimination, and anti-Jewish outbreaks in Thrace (European Turkey) compelled many to emigrate in 1934. In 1942 the minorities of Turkey claimed that a revised property-tax (of 1%) was applied in a discriminatory way imposing on them a disproportionate burden. In fact, many J. were impoverished, leaving Turkey immediately thereafter. Although some 28,000 immigrated to Israel, 1948–51, many still live in Turkey where they enjoy full rights of citizenship with religious and economic freedom.   (H. C.)

JIDDA. Chief port of Sa'udi Arabia, on the Red Sea, 43 mi. from Mecca▷, and main reception centre for Mecca pilgrims arriving by ship and plane. Pop: 148,000 (1967). J. virtually serves as Sa'udi Arabia's administrative capital and is the seat of the Diplomatic Corps. Handling most of the country's imports, J. is developing a growing industry, and there has been much building and modernization in the city.

In the Treaty of J., May 1927, Britain recognized the independence of Ibn Sa'ud's▷ kingdom (then called Kingdom of Hijaz▷, Najd▷ and Dependent Territories), while Ibn Sa'ud undertook to respect the British Persian Gulf protectorates. The Treaty also established normal relations between the two countries.

The J. Agreement of Aug. 1965 represented an attempt by President 'Abd-ul-Nasser▷ and King Feisal▷ to put an end to the Yemen war and to reach agreement on that country's regime (see Yemen▷).   (Y.K.-Y.S.)

JIHAD (Arabic: holy war, literally "great effort"). Muslims are obliged to fight non-Muslims until the latter accept either the religion of Islam, or the status of protected subjects (*Dhimmi, Ahl ul-Dhimma*), the latter choice being open only to the "People of the Book", *i.e.* to Jews, Christians and Sabaans-Mandaeans▷. This fight, J., is one of the fundamental tenets of Islam. The world is divided into *Dar-ul-Islam*, the "House of Islam"—comprising countries in which Muslims and their religion prevail, and *Dar ul-Harb*, the "House of War"—countries to be fought and conquered. Some traditions mention a third realm, *Dar ul-Sulh*, the "House of Truce"—countries paying tribute to the Muslims. According to one view, since the concept of J. was born in the particular circumstances of the Arabian peninsula during the 7th century, when the founders of Islam fought for control of their homeland and centre, it is an injunction applying to those historic circumstances alone. Orthodox Islamic tradition, however, holds that J. is obligatory in all generations and circumstances.

Since the 8th century, when the wave of Islamic conquests stopped and the borders of Islam were stabilized, theologians have differed on the question of how to fulfil the duty of J. in circumstances under which continued wars of conquest are no longer possible. Does J. imply *constant* warfare? Must all Muslims engage in it, or could a number of chosen fighters fulfil the injunction on behalf of the community? In the absence of a caliph▷, with no recognized head of the faithful, who proclaims J.? Who proclaims it for Shi'i▷ Muslims whose recognized leader, the Imam▷, remains hidden until the Day of Judgement?

In principle, any war by a Muslim country against a non-Muslim one may qualify as J., but Muslim tradition requires J. be proclaimed officially. Many Muslim rulers did so but their pronouncements did not commit Muslims in other countries. In modern times, too, Muslim countries engaging in war have tried to obtain the support and sympathy of

Muslims everywhere by proclaiming J. The Ottoman Sultan and Caliph did so upon Turkey's entry into World War I▷ in 1914. His call aroused pro-Turkish feelings among the Muslims of the world (e.g. in India), but brought him no active military help, nor did it stop Muslim rulers and peoples from rising against him—thus failing as a resort to J. Muslim fighters have more than once, without formally proclaiming J., conferred that name on their operations and called themselves *mujahidin*, holy warriors; so did, for instance, the Algerian rebels, 1954–62. On the other hand, Muslim governments have had recourse to the term J. for various purposes and efforts; e.g. in Tunisia, the 'Ulama', the Muslim sages, permitted the easing of the Ramadhan fast because the country was waging an "economic J.", a holy war for its existence.

In the Arab-Israel conflict, Arab leaders also tried to reinforce their strength by declaring J. The sages of al-Azhar▷, the foremost Islamic University, proclaimed it from Cairo in 1948, and the pronouncement was frequently repeated by 'Ulama' and Muftis, in speeches and sermons or in religious rulings (*Fatwa*). On the eve of the Six Day War▷ in 1967, the J. slogan helped to rouse the Arab masses to fever pitch. The definition of the war with Israel as J. also led the Palestinian guerilla organizations to apply for formal recognition as *mujahidin*, holy warriors, so that contributions to their funds would qualify as a religious duty or even as part of the charity payments (*Zakat*) obligatory for Muslims. While there is no all-Islamic authority whose decree would commit all Muslims, some Muftis did issue the requesting ruling. Some Arab governments, such as Libya, with the blessing of their 'Ulama', established J. funds, and the Sa'udi Arabian government has been collecting a "J. tax" in aid for the guerillas. 'Ulama' congresses continue to call for J. or to define as J. the struggle against Israel, and particularly the operations of the guerillas; the latter mostly avoid calling themselves *mujahidin* and prefer the term *feda'iyin*▷— "those who sacrifice themselves", but this term is also taken from the traditional Islamic dictionary and connected with J. Some 'Ulama' have ruled that the holy war waged by the Arab armies and guerillas does not discharge the J. obligation of the entire community, and that every single individual has to wage this war personally.

While the J. slogan encouraged many Muslims in non-Arab countries to lend their support to the Arab cause in the conflict with Israel, it has not carried them to the point of active warfare. Among the Arabs themselves, the call for J. is always sure to cause great enthusiasm, but, in the long run, it does not seem to mobilize fresh resources.   (Y.S.)

JOHNSTON, ERIC (1896–1963). American businessman, sent by President Eisenhower in 1953 to draft, and obtain agreement on, a unified or co-ordinated regional water development plan for the exploitation of the Jordan River▷ for the benefit of the riparian countries (Lebanon, Syria, Jordan and Israel). After protracted negotiations, he presented in 1955 a plan for the distribution of the Jordan waters approved by the technical experts from the nations concerned (and, in Israel's case, by the political authorities as well). The "J. Plan" foundered eventually on the refusal of the Arab leaders to concur in any scheme having Israel for a party or beneficiary. Israel and the Kingdom of Jordan proceeded to implement their own water development projects independently, though in a manner consistent with the abortive "J. Plan." (See Jordan River▷.)   (Y.S.)

*JORDAN, KINGDOM OF (official name: The Hashemite Kingdom of J.); formerly (1921–48) Transjordan. A kingdom bordered in the north by Syria, in the north-east by Iraq, in the east and south by Sa'udi Arabia and in the west by Israel. Capital: 'Amman. J.'s pre-June 1967 area was 37,000 sq. mi.—including the Arab part of Palestine (the West Bank▷ of the J. River) which she had occupied in 1948, and which has an area of *c.* 2,165 sq. mi. In the Six Day War▷ of 1967 J. lost the West Bank and reverted to her pre-1948 (Transjordanian) area of *c.* 35,000 sq. mi.

J. has existed as a state since 1921 (then "Transjordan")—see below. She became independent in 1946. She was a founding member of the Arab League▷ in 1945 and was admitted to UN membership in 1955.

The borders of Transjordan were largely defined in 1921–3, and some parts of the desert borders with Sa'udi Arabia in 1925. The same year 'Aqaba and Ma'an, also claimed by Hijaz, were annexed. (The matter, left vague and open as long as the Hashemite King Hussein ruled Hijaz, became important when Hijaz was conquered by Ibn Sa'ud). Sa'udi Arabia acquiesced (in the Anglo-Sa'udi Treaty of Jidda, 1927), and formally consented in 1965—when an exchange of territory also took place and J. acquired a coastal strip south of 'Aqaba in return for an inland area of equal size. In 1948, Jordan occupied—and in 1950 formally annexed—the Arab parts of Palestine (except for the Gaza Strip); in June 1967, she lost the areas annexed in 1948–50.

The population on both banks of the J. River was estimated in 1967 at *c.* 2 m. about equally divided between the East and West banks. Most of J.'s inhabitants were Sunni Muslim Arabs. There were about 150,000 Christian Arabs. About 200,000 were

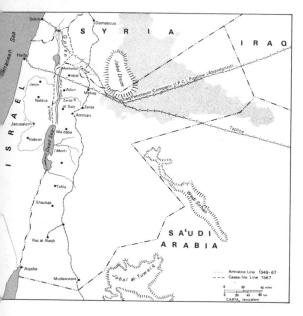

Map of Jordan

Bedouin (nomads, semi-nomads and settled dwellers) and 15–20,000 Circassians▷ and Chechens (Muslims of Caucasian origin), all of whom lived on the East Bank. About 60,000 Jordanian citizens live abroad, mainly in Kuwait and Sa'udi Arabia. Owing to natural increase, the influx of 1948 refugees, continuous migration from the West Bank, 1948–67, and the influx of new refugees in 1967, the population of the East Bank only, that had been *c.* 450,000 in 1948, was estimated to have grown to 1.5–1.8m. in 1969–70.

ECONOMY. The pre-1967 population on both sides of the J. River was 42% urban, 53% rural and 5% nomadic; 54% were engaged in agriculture; 27% in administration, police and the army; 8% in industry; 6% in the building trades; and 5% in commerce and services.

J.'s economy is handicapped by lack of capital, minerals, water, skilled manpower, and a market for developing industries. J. is, therefore, heavily dependent on foreign aid.

Until the annexation of the West Bank in 1948–50, J.'s economy was based mainly on primitive agriculture and stock-breeding. The annexation of the West Bank (with a population disturbed by the Arab-Israel war of 1948 and augmented by refugees) and the influx of Palestinian refugees to the East Bank changed the general character of the population: it grew three times and came to include townsmen with a higher standard of living. J. was obliged to develop her resources, in order to absorb the

additional population. For political reasons the government encouraged mainly the development of the East Bank.

Only 10% of the total area is under cultivation (on the East Bank—the former Transjordan—5%). Wheat, barley, vegetables, grapes and olives are the main products. To increase the area under cultivation, the government initiated a scheme which uses the waters of the Yarmuk▷ River for the irrigation of the J. Valley area (*Al-Ghor*).

An oil pipeline (Aramco's "Tapline" from Dhahran, Sa'udi Arabia, to Sidon, Lebanon) traverses J., in return for which royalties are paid to the government. J.'s own mineral wealth is small. No oil worth developing commerically has been found. Valuable deposits of potash and bromine in the Dead Sea have not yet been exploited owing to lack of capital. However, rich beds of phosphates at Rusaifa, a few miles north-east of 'Amman, are being exploited and constitute J.'s chief export. Industry is limited to the manufacture of soap, matches and cigarettes, and food processing. In 1966 a cement factory was established.

Poor communications are a major obstacle to economic development. The only railway is the single-track narrow-gauge Hijaz line, the southern parts of which are out of order. (Its joint repair and reconstruction by Syria, Jordan and Sa'udi Arabia has been planned for years, but has been delayed, mainly for political reasons.) 'Aqaba is the country's only port, linked to 'Amman by a 200 mile-long road, opened in 1960. J. also uses the port of Beirut, but this involves passing through Syrian territory—a passage which is often disturbed by political tension. Consequently J. has endeavoured to improve the port of 'Aqaba so as not to be dependent on Beirut.

Before the Six Day War tourism was an important contributor to J.'s economy. In 1966 the number of tourists, visiting mainly Old Jerusalem and Bethlehem, was about 600,000, giving the country an income of about JD 21m. ($58.8m.). Though Transjordan also has sites of interest to tourists, such as Petra and Jarash, the number of visitors has considerably declined.

Until 1956 J.'s public finances were heavily subsidized by Britain. J. is a member of the sterling area, and the Jordanian Dinar (subdivided into 1,000 fils) was at par with the £ sterling till the latter's devaluation in Nov. 1967 (the present rate of exchange is JD 1 = £1.16½). Up to the abrogation of the Anglo-Jordanian Treaty in 1957, budgetary deficits were covered by Britain, who also paid the cost of J.'s Army (the "Arab Legion"). Between 1946 and 1956 the United Kingdom gave J. an estimated £80m. in the form of subventions and grants-in-aid. Since

1957, J. has also received US economic aid; Britain continues to assist J., but on a modest scale. At the Arab summit meeting in Khartoum, Aug. 1967, Kuwait, Libya and Sa'udi Arabia undertook to pay J. an annual subsidy of £40m. ($112m.) "until the effects of the aggression are eliminated". Additional aid from Abu Dhabi and Sa'udi Arabia, amounting to £5.8m. and £15m. respectively was also promised.

POLITICAL HISTORY. What is now J. was created by Britain in 1921 as the Amirate of Transjordan, and 'Abdullah b. Hussein▷, of the Hashemite dynasty, was installed as amir. Transjordan was under the Palestine Mandate, but after 1922 excluded from the clause concerning the Jewish National Home. By installing 'Abdullah, Britain accommodated a loyal ally, prevented him from making trouble with the French (who had just expelled his brother Feisal▷ from Damascus) and fulfilled the British war-time pledge to his father Hussein▷ recognizing this area as Arab and independent (under British tutelage).

Initially, Transjordan had about 300,000 inhabitants, half of whom were nomads or semi-nomads. Most of the population was Arab Muslim, with about 25,000 Christians and 10,000 Circassians. The amirate was totally dependent on British economic aid, as most of its area was desert and it lacked economic resources. Assisted by a small number of British advisers, at the head of which was a Resident, representing the High Commissioner in Jerusalem, Amir 'Abdullah ruled his country in autocratic and patriarchal fashion. The British helped 'Abdullah create a military force, which started as a desert police unit and later developed into the best Arab army—the Arab Legion, commanded till 1956 by a British officer (F. G. Peake Pasha, 1921–39; J. B. Glubb▷ Pasha 1939–56).

In Feb. 1928 Transjordan signed a treaty with Britain which gave her rather more independence, but financial and foreign affairs continued to be handled by the British Resident. A constitution of Apr. 1928 provided for a Legislative Council, in part indirectly elected. In 1934 Transjordan was authorized to establish consular ties with her neighbours: Egypt, Syria and Iraq. In 1939 the powers of the British Resident were reduced, a Cabinet of departmental heads, responsible to the ruler, was formed, and an elected Legislative Assembly of 20 members established. During World War II, 'Abdullah remained loyal to his British allies.

In Mar. 1946 a new Anglo-Transjordanian treaty granted J. formal independence, while providing for a political and military alliance and for British aid. Britain was authorized to maintain troops and bases in Transjordan. This treaty was modified in Mar.

1948; the new treaty stressed Transjordan's independence and the equal status of the two contracting parties. 'Abdullah assumed the title of "King" in 1946, and from 1948–9 the country was officially referred to as "The Hashemite Kingdom of J.".

'Abdullah cherished ambitions to create and rule a "Greater Syria"▷, i.e. a union of J., Palestine, Syria and Lebanon. This was to be followed by the unification of the Fertile Crescent, i.e. the inclusion of Iraq in the kingdom on her federation with "Greater Syria". The British—or at least some British agencies—supported 'Abdullah's aspirations as long as the French remained masters of the Levant states (reportedly to oust the French). 'Abdullah also received some support from the pro-Hashemite establishment in Iraq and from some elements in Syria and Palestine. He was opposed by the French, the rulers of Egypt and Sa'udi Arabia, most Syrian and many Palestinian nationalists (these last were led by the Mufti of Jerusalem, Hajj Amin al-Husseini▷).

'Abdullah felt that the first step towards the implementation of his scheme should be taken in Palestine. He maintained close contacts with prominent Palestinian families, such as Nashashibi▷ of Jerusalem, Touqan▷ of Nablus and Ja'bari of Hebron. He also endeavoured to reach an agreement with the Jews in Palestine. In 1930 he had agreed to, and even encouraged, Jewish settlement in Transjordan; but the plan had to be shelved because of local opposition (and British obstructionism); in 1933 a law forbidding the sale of lands to foreigners was enacted. Prior to the Arab-Israel War of 1948 'Abdullah sought a peaceful solution with the Jewish leaders—he was reported to favour Jewish autonomy or even independence in part of Palestine, hopefully under his crown. When he felt compelled to join the war, he avoided attacking the areas earmarked for the Jewish State, and the fighting centred on Jerusalem (designated as an international enclave).

The 1948 War enabled 'Abdullah to start implementing his aspirations. His army took over Arab Palestine, except for the Gaza Strip (and the Iraqi Expeditionary Force handed over to him the areas it had occupied, as Baghdad refused to sign an Armistice Agreement with Israel). In Dec. 1948, a conference of Palestinian notables in Jericho—preceded and followed by similar gatherings—implored 'Abdullah to save Palestine by becoming her King. An Armistice Agreement between Israel and Transjordan, signed in Apr. 1949, confirmed Transjordan's de facto occupation of Arab Palestine. In Mar. 1949 the military government in the occupied Palestinian areas was replaced by a civil administration. In May Palestinian ministers were included for the first time in the Jordanian Cabinet, and in June 1949, the country's name was changed to

"The Hashemite Kingdom of J." (thus emphasizing that it was no longer confined to the "other" side of the River) and officially gazetted. In Apr. 1950 the Palestinians participated for the first time in parliamentary elections, and later the same month the new Parliament decreed the formal annexation of the West Bank. Only Britain and Pakistan formally recognized the annexation (but most countries accepted it *de facto*). The Arab League was vehemently opposed to the annexation and threatened to expel J.; in particular, Egypt, Syria and Sa'udi Arabia objected to any territorial aggrandizement of the Hashemite dynasty. A compromise formula was devised by the Prime Minister of Iraq: the West Bank would be held temporarily by J. in trust, until its restoration to its owners would be possible. In fact a "deal" was made: the League accepted the annexation of the West Bank, under this face-saving formula—in return for 'Abdullah's renunciation of his plan to sign a separate non-aggression treaty with Israel (of which a draft had been negotiated in Feb. 1950).

The annexation of the West Bank, and the influx of Palestinian refugees to the East Bank, modified considerably J.'s ethnic and social features: the population increased nearly three times (from *c.* 450,000 to *c.* 1.2m.; of the new population, about 400,000 were Palestinians living in the West Bank, 200,000 were refugees who had joined them there, and 100,000 were refugees in Transjordan). Most of the new inhabitants were town and village dwellers with a higher standard of living. The population of the East Bank had as a whole been loyal to 'Abdullah, although pockets of opposition existed, mainly among the tribes of the north, connected by blood to their brethren in Syria, and in the towns of al-Salt and Irbid. This opposition was considerably reinforced by the Palestinians, many of whom supported 'Abdullah's foe, Hajj Amin-al-Husseini. The Palestinians, who occupied half the seats in Parliament, soon made their presence felt. They demanded that the monarch's powers be curtailed, that the Cabinet be made responsible to Parliament and that political life in J. become democratic. Opposition to the King increased as rumours of his secret negotiations with Israel spread.

On 20 July 1951, King 'Abdullah was assassinated by a Palestinian, while entering al-Aqsa Mosque in Jerusalem. (Among those tried and executed for the murder was a prominent member of the Husseini clan.) 'Abdullah's eldest son Talal▷ succeeded to the throne (his younger son Nayef having failed to usurp it). Talal gave in to the opposition's demands and in Jan. 1952 he approved a change in the constitution which made the Cabinet responsible to Parliament. (A majority of two-thirds was required to dismiss the Cabinet; this was amended in 1954 to a simple majority.) The King also pursued a different foreign policy from his father. He strove for a *rapprochement* with Egypt and Syria and joined the Arab Collective Security Pact of 1950. But in Aug. 1952 Talal was found to be mentally ill; Parliament declared him unfit to rule and deposed him. His son Hussein▷ was crowned (after regents had briefly ruled for him until he reached the age of 18) in May 1953.

J.'s third King had to continue facing an opposition eager to shake off her financial (and political) dependence on Britain, and to improve ties with Egypt and Syria. The refugees from Palestine to whom J. gave full citizenship—the only Arab country to do so—aggravated the political unrest. Foreign policy difficulties increased as the cold war between the world powers grew in intensity. One such problem was a result of J.'s desire to join the Baghdad Pact▷, concluded in Feb. 1955 between Turkey and Iraq as the nucleus of a US-inspired defence treaty. When, in Dec. 1955, the Chief of the British Imperial General Staff visited 'Amman, it was rumoured that he had persuaded the government to join the Baghdad Pact. Violent demonstrations, in all major cities, against Jordanian participation forced the resignation of the Cabinet, headed by Hazza' al-Majali▷, who was known to support the Pact. The new government announced that J. would not join the Pact. Another setback to the West was the dismissal, in Mar. 1956, of the British commander of the Arab Legion, Lt.-Gen. Glubb, who was regarded by the nationalists, despite the many services he had rendered to the Arab cause, as the symbol of British imperialist domination.

In Oct. 1956 leftist nationalist parties won the parliamentary elections for the first time, and the leader of the "National Socialist Party", Suleiman al-Nabulsi▷, became Prime Minister. At his initiative, J. joined, the same month, the military alliance of Egypt, Syria and Sa'udi Arabia, and the Egyptian-Syrian Joint Military Command. However, J. did not take part in the Israeli-Egyptian Sinai War▷ of Oct.-Nov. 1956, although she allowed Sa'udi, Iraqi and Syrian troops to take up positions on her territory (they were withdrawn when the crisis had passed). In Jan. 1957 an agreement was signed among Egypt, Syria and Sa'udi Arabia, providing for an annual subsidy of £12.5m. to J. over the next ten years (Egypt and Sa'udi Arabia were to give £5m. each, Syria £2.5m.) to cover J.'s defence expenditure and thus enable her to abrogate her treaty with Britain. The Anglo-Jordanian Treaty of 1948 was indeed annulled in Mar. 1957 and all

British troops were evacuated by July. In Apr. 1957 the government decided to establish diplomatic relations with the USSR, following a parliamentary recommendation, and to accept Soviet aid.

In Apr. 1957 King Hussein attempted to halt this increasingly rapid movement towards the left. He announced the discovery of a Syrian-Egyptian plot against him and dismissed the leftist Cabinet. This led to riots and demonstrations, and all political parties were suppressed. A plot of army officers supported by Egypt was averted when the King himself appeared in the Zarqa Camp and persuaded the officers to support him. The Chief-of-Staff, Gen. 'Ali Abu Nuwar, was dismissed and fled the country. Purges in the army and the civil service followed. The USA emphasized its support of the King by sending units of the Sixth Fleet to the eastern Mediterranean, in line with the Eisenhower Doctrine ▷. The USA also from now on supplied economic and military aid.

The King's swing to the right naturally worsened relations with Egypt and Syria. The two countries did not pay the subsidy agreed in the Cairo Treaty of Jan. 1957 (only Sa'udi Arabia paid one instalment of $5m.), launched a violent campaign of defamation against J. and encouraged subversion within J. The merger of Syria and Egypt, on 1 Feb. 1958, into the United Arab Republic caused grave concern in 'Amman and paved the way for an Iraqi-Jordanian Federation established on 14 Feb. 1958 and called the "Arab Union" or "Arab Federation"▷. King Feisal II▷ of Iraq became the Head of the Union and King Hussein his deputy. A federal parliament with equal representation for both countries was formed and a federal government was set up to handle foreign affairs, defence and monetary policy. Each country continued to preserve its parliament, cabinet and civil service.

The "Arab Union" came to an end after the Iraqi coup d'état of 14 July 1958 which toppled the Hashemite regime (and killed several top Jordanian leaders; as well as those of Iraq). King Hussein now proclaimed himself Head of the Union and prepared to invade Iraq, but soon abandoned his plans, as there was apparently no support for them in Iraq. The UAR was actively inciting subversion within J. and had closed its air-space and roads to Jordanian traffic, and Hussein expected immediate UAR-Iraqi hostilities against J. (possibly co-ordinated with a coup). He, therefore, asked Britain to send troops to protect his Kingdom, and a contingent of British paratroopers from Cyprus arrived in Jordan in July 1958 (via Israeli air-space). J. also severed diplomatic relations with the UAR and lodged a complaint against her to the UN Security Council (for sending heavily armed infiltrators across the borders). US proposals to replace British troops in J. (and American troops in Lebanon) with a UN force were vetoed by the USSR and the issue was transferred to a special session of the UN General Assembly. In Aug. the Assembly adopted a compromise resolution, drafted by the Arab states, noting that these states had agreed, in the Arab League Pact, to respect each other's sovereign independence, welcoming their renewed assurances to observe that commitment, and requesting arrangements to be made that would "facilitate the early withdrawal of the foreign troops". British troops were withdrawn by October.

As it became clear that the new regime in Iraq was no satellite of the UAR, relations between 'Amman and Baghdad improved and diplomatic ties, severed after the Iraqi coup of 1958, were renewed in Dec. 1960, despite the blood-feud the coup had caused. Relations with Sa'udi Arabia also improved. King Hussein cast aside the old enmity between the Hashemite dynasty and the House of Sa'ud which had driven his great-grandfather Hussein from Hijaz; the Sa'udi ruler now realized that his conservative monarchy was also threatened by Egypt and abandoned his alliance with her. J.'s diplomatic relations with the UAR were renewed in Aug. 1959, but the latter continued to support subversion—culminating in the assassination of Prime Minister Hazza al-Majali▷ in Aug. 1960. Relations were again severed in Sept. 1961 when Egypt denounced J.'s recognition of Syria (which had just seceded from the UAR) and accused her of conspiring with the secessionists.

Relations with Egypt were restored in Jan. 1964, during the first Arab summit conference held in Cairo. At the Conference J. agreed to co-operate with other Arab states to prevent Israel from diverting the waters of the J. River, and also to recognize the Republican regime in Yemen. J. did not sound enthusiastic about these decisions at a second summit. She was even less happy about the creation of a "Palestinian entity", a Palestine Liberation Organization▷ (PLO) with a military force— decided at a second summit conference in Alexandria in Sept. 1964. Any recognition of a Palestinian national entity was likely to cast doubts on J.'s annexation of Arab Palestine. J. also rejected proposals to station Arab troops on her territory to protect her from Israel. J. recognized the PLO only reluctantly and allowed it to open an office in Jerusalem. But relations were tense, and in July 1966 the Government closed down the PLO office, claiming that its Secretary-General was indulging in pro-Communist activities.

The intensification of Arab guerilla activities against Israel from Jordanian territory, brought about Israeli retaliation in Nov. 1966 when Israeli troops attacked the village of Samu' in the Hebron district. King Hussein was accused of neglecting the defence of his people—mainly by the Syrians and the PLO who called on the Jordanians to revolt against the King. Egyptian broadcasts also described the King and his government as "imperialist stooges" with whom no co-operation was possible.

As tension rose between Israel and the Arab states in spring 1967, as President Nasser spoke confidently of his forthcoming victory, and as war seemed inevitable, King Hussein flew to Cairo and signed a defence agreement with Egypt, 30 May 1967, placing his troops under Egyptian command. When the Six Day War▷ broke out, on 5 June 1967, the Israeli government advised King Hussein via the UN to stay out of the war and assured him that Israel would not attack. J. King Hussein ignored this advice, and shelled Israeli Jerusalem and other Israeli areas. In the war that followed J. lost the West Bank. A new influx of refugees, estimated at 200–250,000 people, crossed the J. River eastwards. They formed an additional burden on J.'s economy already hard hit by the loss of the West Bank. However, Israel's "open bridges" policy enabled commercial exchanges and continuous personal contact between Transjordan and the West Bank to be made. Jordanian authorities also maintained ties with the West Bank leadership and even continued to pay salaries to many former civil servants.

After the war, King Hussein campaigned vigorously to gain international sympathy for his country's cause. He visited several countries, including—in Oct. 1967—the USSR (with whom diplomatic ties had been established in 1963). Closer economic relations with the Soviet bloc were initiated; however the King turned down Soviet proposals for military assistance. J. takes part in the conferences of "neutralist" countries, but she maintains her ties with the West, especially the USA, and receives economic aid and arms supplies. J.-US relations are sometimes tense (e.g. the cancellation, in Apr. 1970, of a scheduled visit of a US Assistant Secretary of State, after anti-American demonstrations, and the expulsion of the US Ambassador in 'Amman). But such incidents have been handled with restraint and have not caused major crises. When a real crisis occurs, it is to the West that J. looks for help.

Within the Arab world Hussein continued to strengthen relations with Egypt. In Mar. 1969 J. joined the "Eastern Command" initiated by Egypt to co-ordinate military activities against Israel to lessen Israeli pressure on the Egyptian front. It included troops from Iraq, Syria and J. under an Iraqi

general (under overall Egyptian command). The Eastern Command was not successful and was disbanded in 1970. J. also participated in the meetings of those Arab countries bordering Israel, and, therefore, directly involved in fighting against her.

With J.'s agreement, Iraqi, Sa'udi Arabian—and sometimes Syrian—troops were stationed on her territory with the declared aim of helping to defend her against Israel, but probably also with a view to looking after their own interests (which might include seizing parts of J. if the regime collapsed). There was also a large Pakistani training mission in J. Iraqi and Syrian troops were evacuated in 1970–71.

J.'s main political problem, which affects the very root of her existence, is the relationship between the authorities and the Palestinian guerilla organizations▷ (feda'iyin▷). The feda'iyin—permitted since 1967 to grow into large organizations, lavishly financed and heavily equipped—gradually assumed control of the refugee camps and gained widespread support among Jordanian youth. In their relations with the regime four phases can be distinguished:

1. JUNE 1967 TO NOVEMBER 1968. The guerillas established themselves securely in J. and even moved their headquarters to 'Amman. They took effective control of wide areas along the border and increased their operations against Israel, especially the shelling of Israeli villages from Jordanian territory. This brought about Israeli retaliations, notably an attack, in Mar. 1968, on Karame, a village which served as an advance base for the guerillas. The creation of a "State within the State" not subject to Jordanian law and control created mounting tension. In Nov. 1968 serious clashes occurred between the Jordanian Army and the guerillas and a civil war seemed imminent. However, the King wished to avoid a full-scale confrontation, and agreement was eventually reached: the guerilla organizations were permitted to issue their own identity cards; they undertook not to recruit deserters from the Arab Legion or men liable for conscription; J. would not hold up the passage of arms destined for the guerillas; targets in Israel would not be shelled by the guerillas from Jordanian Army positions; guerillas would strike at targets in Israel only from positions situated at least 6 mi. inside Israel or the Israel-occupied areas; they would operate in co-ordination with the Jordanian forces; no operations against Israel would be mounted from 'Aqaba.

2. NOVEMBER 1968 TO FEBRUARY 1970. The Nov. 1968 agreement, vague on many crucial points, was never fully implemented. Several severe clashes took place. The guerillas wanted both freedom of action and cover by the Jordanian Army for all their operations against Israel. The King was reluctant

to give the guerilla leaders all the credit for fighting Israel. During this period the problem of the future of the West Bank and the status of the Palestinians and the refugees within J. became more acute. The King announced several times his readiness to grant the Palestinians self-determination after the defeat of Israel, and kept emphasizing the need for all Arab forces to co-operate. Yet, the struggle for the control of J. continued with the *feda'iyin* wielding increasing influence—and the King vacillating between his hard-line army supporters and pro-guerilla elements. There were repeated government reshuffles (invariably interpreted as either pro- or anti-guerilla).

3. FEBRUARY TO AUGUST 1970. In Feb. 1970, after an attempt to impose stricter regulations, fresh clashes, and a retreat by the King, a new agreement was reached, confirming the agreement of Nov. 1968, but putting more emphasis on the equality of the two parties. Yet the army Commander-in-Chief, Nasser b. Jamil, a hard-liner and the King's uncle, was taking active measures to control and restrict the guerilla organizations; the army also resented the guerillas' impertinent behaviour which hurt their prestige. Tension between army and *feda'iyin* mounted, and early in June very serious clashes erupted, causing many hundreds of casualties. The army bombarded refugee camps near 'Amman held by the guerillas and attacked the guerilla centre in the capital; the *feda'iyin* gained control of several districts in 'Amman, including hotels in which foreign guests were held as hostages. Several Arab states, especially Egypt, Iraq and Libya endeavoured to mediate, and the King again backed down. On 10 June an agreement to cease hostilities was reached, but it was implemented only after the King yielded to the guerillas' demand to dismiss Nasser b. Jamil (the King himself becoming C.-in-C. of the Army) and Zeid b. Shaker, the Commander of the armoured division. The agreement provided, *inter alia*, for an exchange of prisoners; the creation of several mixed commissions—one to devise measures to prevent future clashes, one to inquire into the causes of the riots, and one to supervise the implementation of this and previous agreements. An unofficial summit conference in Tripoli (Libya) in June, set up a committee composed of representatives of Egypt, Libya, Algeria and Sudan to tackle disputes between J. and the guerilla organizations "in a manner that both the sovereignty of J. and *feda'iyin* action be preserved". By agreeing to the creation of this committee, King Hussein in fact accepted a sort of inter-Arab guardianship, while the guerilla organizations obtained a status equal to that of the King, Government and Army of J.

The King's letter of appointment to Prime Minister 'Abd-ul-Mun'im al-Rifa'i▷ who formed a new government in June 1970, stressed the freedom of action for the guerillas and asked the new cabinet to work for "national unity". Obviously the King wanted to improve relations between his government and the *feda'iyin*—especially with the moderates such as Yasser 'Arafat▷ and his *al-Fatah*▷. The growing importance of the Palestinians in Jordanian public life was reflected in the composition of the new Government: of the 17 ministers, nine were Palestinians. Several ministers from both banks were sympathetic towards the guerilla organizations. Furthermore, the King abolished conscription, thus enabling Jordanian youths to join the guerilla organizations if they so wished.

The events of June 1970 seriously undermined the King's position and the army's prestige. The majority of the guerilla organizations had not, so far, attempted to overthrow the regime but had, while striving for greater freedom of action, gladly left the responsibility of administration to the Jordanian authorities. This attitude changed in summer 1970.

Relations between the King and his government and the Palestinian guerillas created a virtually permanent state of crisis. In a new agreement, 10 July 1970, the King had to make further concessions. The guerillas renounced any military presence in the cities, except for some guard units for their leaders and offices, and undertook to refrain from military exercises in inhabited areas, to restrict the movements of their vehicles, to identify themselves at army checkpoints, and to respect the civil law of J. The government undertook to abolish its emergency measures (*i.e.* to withdraw the army from the towns), to support the propaganda activities of the guerillas, to allow them freedom of action, and (by implication) not to use the "special units" of the army against them. Mixed Commissions were to supervise the implementation of the agreement.

4. AUGUST TO SEPTEMBER 1970, AND AFTER. King Hussein's agreement, in August, along with President Nasser▷, to the American peace plan and the renewal of the Jarring▷ talks further strained his relations with the guerillas, who vehemently opposed any such initiative. On the other hand, Hussein felt more confident, as he now counted on President Nasser's backing. Moreover, the King was pressed for anti-guerilla action by senior army officers, who felt humiliated by the concessions made to the guerillas. Hussein reappointed General Zeid b. Shaker to a senior army post, and went to Cairo for talks with Nasser, 20–23 Aug. A few days later, clashes began between the guerillas and the Jordanian Army, mainly in the 'Amman area. Anarchy soon

prevailed in J., and the government lost control over large areas, especially in the north. On 6 Sept. the guerillas brought to an airstrip near Zarqa two hijacked foreign airplanes, and a third plane a few days later, and prevented the army from approaching the planes or rescuing their passengers. On 16 Sept. the King proclaimed martial law. Premier Rifa'i resigned and a Military Government was appointed, with Brig. Muhammad Daoud, a Palestinian, as Prime Minister, to crush the guerillas' independent military-political establishment. A vigorous army offensive against guerilla concentrations—many of them in towns, especially 'Amman, and refugee camps—hit civilians in large numbers (casualties were variously estimated at anything between 700 and 20,000 killed). The guerillas now called openly for the overthrow of the King and the regime.

Deep shock engulfed all the Arab countries. King Hussein was denounced as a butcher and a "Nero". Kuwait and Libya suspended financial aid to Jordan, Libya severed diplomatic relations, Tunisia recalled her envoy. Iraq and Syria promised aid to the *feda'iyin* and threatened intervention. On 19 Sept., Syrian armoured units, disguised as forces of the "Palestine Liberation Army", invaded J. and occupied a strip in northern J., including the town of Irbid. They retreated four days later—whether defeated by Jordanian troops, or because of Soviet and Arab pressure or the fear of American or Israeli intervention, is a matter of conjecture. The Iraqi expeditionary force in J. did not intervene. The USSR, for her part, warned the USA against intervention (planned or at least considered, as had been reported). Egypt, despite the King's confident expectation of her backing, recommended a compromise, so as to end the fratricidal bloodshed and prevent foreign intervention. But the leftist-revolutionary Arab states refused to attend an unofficial summit conference convened in Cairo. President Nasser succeeded in imposing a compromise. A four-member delegation, headed by Sudan's President Numeiri▷, came to 'Amman to mediate for a cease-fire; on 26 Sept. Brig. Daoud resigned, and the King appointed another Palestinian, Ahmad Touqan▷, as Prime Minister.

An agreement to end the dispute was signed in Cairo, on 27 Sept., by J., Egypt, Libya, Sa'udi Arabia, Sudan, Yemen, Kuwait, Lebanon, and Yasser 'Arafat on behalf of the guerillas. This created a "Supreme Arab Committee" under the Prime Minister of Tunisia, to supervise and enforce the normalization of relations between the Jordanian authorities and the guerillas; both the army and the guerillas were to withdraw from 'Amman, government administration was to be restored everywhere, including the guerilla-held Irbid area in the north; commando operations against Israel were to continue with J.'s full support, while the guerillas were to respect J.'s sovereignty and operate "within the law, except where necessary for commando action". The Arab co-signatories of the agreement undertook to intervene against whichever side broke it. The agreement was a fragile compromise, imposed under the threat of outside intervention. In fact, King Hussein seemed to have emerged much stronger; in Oct. 1970, he changed his government (Wasfi Tall▷—Prime Minister). In spring 1971 he reimposed his control by constant pressure and immediate reaction to provocations or attacks of the guerillas. The crisis was not solved, but the King had the upper hand; after further operations in summer 1971, he proclaimed that the problem was finally solved.

CONSTITUTION AND POLITICS. According to the Constitution of 1952, the official religion of J. is Islam, and her official language Arabic. The Legislative power is vested with the National Assembly and the King. The National Assembly consists of a House of Representatives elected—one-half from the East Bank and one-half from the West Bank—in a secret ballot of men only, for a four-year term of office; and a Senate appointed by the monarch. The government is responsible to the House of right-wing group, similar to the Muslim Brotherhood, the "Liberation Party" (*Hiz al-Tahrir*), was promised, but has yet to be granted.

Parliament's increasing powers encouraged the formation of political parties—including Suleiman Nabulsi's▷ "National Socialist Party" mentioned above, and a Jordanian Branch of the *Ba'th*▷ party, led by 'Abdullah al-Rimawi, which in the early 1950s stood for Union with Iraq and later became Nasserist; the party was proscribed. An extremist right-wing group, similar to the Muslim Brotherhood, the "Liberation Party" (*Hiz al-Tahrir*), was accused of several plots and attempted coups and outlawed; its leaders were imprisoned. However, apart from these marginal left- and right-wing opposition groups, political parties have not struck roots.

PRESS, RADIO, T.V. Transjordan's press was not highly developed before 1948. The oldest paper, *al-Urdunn* ("The Jordan") was founded in 1919. In 1948, with the occupation of the Palestinian West Bank, several lively Palestinian papers were transferred to East Jerusalem—including *Filastin*, founded in Jaffa in 1911, and *al-Difa'* ("Defence"), founded in 1934 in Jaffa. In Mar. 1967 the licences of all dailies and weeklies were revoked and stringent conditions were attached to the issue of new licences. Six dailies had to close down—including *Filastin* and *al-Difa'*. The latter re-established itself in 'Amman later in 1967, and a new paper appeared—*al-Dustour* ("The Constitution"). In both papers the State's holdings amounted to 25%. *Al-Difa'* had its licence revoked in 1971. A new, Government-sponsored, paper, *Al-Ra'i*, appears since 1971.

The Hashemite Jordan Broadcasting Service transmits from 'Amman in Arabic, English and Spanish, Television—in Arabic and English.

STATISTICS: Area: 35,000 sq. mi.★ (1921–48, and post-June 1967); 37,000 sq. mi.★★ (1948–67). Area cultivated: *c.* 5%★; 10%★★. Pop.: *c.* 2m.★★ (1967 estimate); 1.5–1.8m.★ (1969 estimate). Birth-rate: 4.6%★★. Natural increase: 3%★★. Life expectancy: 52 years★★. Infant mortality: 30 per 1,000★★. GNP: $520m.★★ (1966); $500m.★ (1969). National income *p.c.*: $252★★ (1966); $240★ (1968–1969). Exports: JD 8.8m.★★ ($24.6m.) (1966); JD14m.★ ($39.2m.) (1968). Imports: JD67m.★★ ($187.6m.) (1966); JD 67m.★ ($187.6m.) (1968). Budget: revenue: JD50m.★★ ($140m.) (1966), expenditure: JD52m.★★ ($145.6m.) (1966); revenue: JD84m.★★ ($235.2m.) (1970), expenditure: JD88m.★★ ($246.4m.) (1970). Literacy: 35%★. Children at school (age 6–14): 57%★★ (1965). Doctors: 1 per 4,700 persons★★ (1965). Hospital beds: 1 per 570 persons★★ (1964). *Note*: 1JD = US$2.80.   (B.G.)

★ East Bank only.
★★ Both banks of J.

JORDAN RIVER (DEVELOPMENT SCHEMES).

Most development projects for the JR are based on Walter C. Lowdermilk's 1942 plan to channel the J. waters *via* the mountainous central region of Palestine to the coastal plain and the Negev. The original plan suggested concentrating all the tributary sources of the JR at the northern end of the Hula▷ valley and channelling their waters through force of gravity to the Beit-Netofa Valley, which would serve as the main reservoir, and thence through a pipeline to the coastal plain. An alternative project, the Cotton Plan, which was ultimately accepted, was based on utilizing the Sea of Galilee▷ (Lake Tiberias) as the principal reservoir and point of diversion into the "National Water Carrier." The Carrier was opened in 1964. Water is pumped from the Lake up the hills into open channels which take it to the Beit Netofa Valley where a small auxiliary reservoir has been constructed. From there, a 108-inch pipe leads to Rosh Ha'ayin, the point of origin of the Yarkon-Negev Works. Because of the salinity of the Sea of Galilee, the water is mixed with sweeter water from regional projects.

In the early 1950s, the Kingdom of Jordan also began planning the "Ghor Scheme" to utilize the waters of the Yarmuk▷—the JR's main eastern tributary—for irrigating the eastern side of the J. Valley (the "Ghor"). A main canal starting from the Yarmuk runs along the eastern edge of the J. Valley, supplying the water for irrigating the valley.

Since the USA was asked to help in financing both projects and regarded their separate implementation as likely to cause a clash (Syria and Lebanon also had claims), several attempts were made to produce a unified or co-ordinated plan for utilizing the waters of the J. and its tributaries. In 1953, President Eisenhower sent a special envoy, Eric Johnston▷, to prepare a plan approved by the riparian countries and ensuring a fair and agreed allocation of the J. waters. After lengthy negotiations with the Arab states and Israel (separately, since the Arab countries refused to hold direct talks with Israel), an agreed plan was drafted in 1955. The waters of the J. and the Yarmuk were to be allocated approximately as follows: Kingdom of Jordan— 46.7%; Israel—38.5%; Syria—11.7% Lebanon— 3.1%. The agreement included the commitment by the country upstream (Syria and Lebanon as regards Israel; Israel as regards the al-Bouteiha valley in Syria, north of Lake Tiberias, and the Kingdom of Jordan south of Naharayim; Jordan as regards Israel concerning part of the Yarmuk waters) not to interfere with the flow of the agreed quantities of water to the downstream country. Experts from the four countries (as well as Egyptian experts brought into the talks by Johnston) reached agreement on that distribution as well as inspection procedures, technological details, etc. (Only the problem of water storage was not completely solved.) However, the agreement was never signed, as the Arab states refused to sign any accord to which Israel would be a party or a beneficiary.

Israel and Jordan thereupon began implementing their separate projects on the tacit understanding that the quotas of the Johnston Plan would be followed. Israel's National Water Carrier carries, since 1964, *c.* 320 million cubic metres yearly to the coastal plain. As the Arab states failed in their endeavours to prevent Israel from implementing her scheme, they decided in 1964–5 to deny to Israel the sources of the J. (the Baniyas▷ and the Hasbani▷). The plan was to divert the Hasbani partly westwards into the Litani▷ in Lebanon and partly eastwards into the Baniyas in Syria, which would itself be diverted southwards into the Yarmuk. The waters of the Yarmuk and the Baniyas were to be stored in a large reservoir formed by the Mukheiba Dam, which was begun in 1966. Diversion work was started in 1965. Israel warned that she would regard any attempt to divert the sources of the J. as a matter

The Jordan River

of utmost gravity, and in the course of retaliatory operations against raids from Syria, diversion works were hit several times (see Arab-Israel Conflict▷). The Six Day War▷, in which Israel occupied the area of the Syrian diversion works, put an end to these plans. Construction of the Mukheiba Dam also stopped and the Jordanian Ghor Project continued to operate (if not disturbed by guerilla raids or border clashes) without storage of Yarmuk waters, on the smaller scale of its initial stage.   (Y. K.-Y. S.)

JUDAEA—see West Bank▷.

***JUMAYYIL,** Pierre—see Gemayel▷, Pierre.

***JUMBLAT (or JUNBALAT).** Prominent Druze▷ family in Lebanon, one of the two clans struggling, for generations, for the leadership of the country's Druze community (the other, rival, clan: Arslan▷). The J. clan descends from a Kurdish chieftain from Aleppo, who migrated to Lebanon, gained control of the al-Shuf region in the central Mount Lebanon and found his home with the Druzes there. The family acquired large tracts of land as semi-feudal lords. During the French Mandate, the family, headed by Nazira J., was a loyal ally of the French.

JUMBLAT (JUNBALAT), KAMAL (b. 1917). Lebanese politician. Son of Nazira J. and present head of the family. Studied sociology and law at Beirut and the Sorbonne. J. was in his youth a supporter of Emile Edde's▷ pro-French "National Bloc", but after Edde's "treachery" in 1943, he gave his support to Bishara al-Khouri▷. However, soon after becoming Minister of Economic Affairs in 1947,

he turned against President Khouri. In 1949, he founded the "Progressive Socialist Party" (*al-Hizb al-Ishtiraki al-Taqaddumi*) which advocated farreaching social reform and claimed to be above communal interests. To show how serious he was about reform, J. distributed some of his land among al-Shuf farmers. His party turned increasingly radical and began to support Nasser's▷ policies and his Arab socialism, while continuing to rely for its own support mainly on the Druze▷ population in the J. family fief, al-Shuf. In 1952, J. joined forces with Camille Chamoun▷ to bring about the resignation of President al-Khouri, but in 1958 he was Chamoun's open enemy and among the leaders of the insurrection which caused the civil war. Elected to every parliament since 1947, he failed in 1957 (partly because of changes in the al-Shuf constituency delimitation), but regained his seat in 1964 (when Chamoun's rival list suffered a resounding defeat) and again in 1968. Having held several cabinet posts since 1958, he became Minister of the Interior at the end of 1969. In this capacity, he voiced enthusiastic support of the Palestinian *feda'iyin*▷ and their guerilla war against Israel, including free movement for terrorists through Lebanon (though apparently trying to restrain and control them). This attitude brought him into conflict with the heads of the army and the secret services (and with ex-President Fu'ad Shihab▷, who backed them). J. is the author of several books on Lebanese political problems ("The Truth of the Lebanese Revolution", "In the Current of Lebanese Politics") and of translations from the French. For some years, he taught history of economic thought at Beirut University.

(Y. P.)

K

KARA'ITES (from the Hebrew *Qara:* to read, study the Scriptures). Jewish sect, based on individual righteousness, asceticism, social justice and the belief in national redemption, which was formed by 'Anan Ben-David in Persia in the 8th century against the background of messianic hopes encouraged by the Muslim conquest of Persia (640) and the collapse of the Umayyad dynasty (750). The K. recognize only the written Scriptures and reject the oral, Talmudic tradition and hence the authority of the Rabbinate. The movement flourished between the 10th and 12th centuries, spreading to Palestine, from there to Egypt and Syria, and into Europe by way of Spain and Byzantium. Most East European K. were killed by the Nazis in the World War II Holocaust. Some 1,500 K. immigrated from Egypt to Israel after 1948 and, though they are not recognized as Jewish by Israeli Orthodox Jews, nevertheless the majority of non-religious Jews, the government and the Jewish Agency treat them as Jews. In 1971 a plan was submitted to the *Knesset* (Parliament) to allow them their own religious tribunal. The total number of K. in the world is unknown.   (E.L.)

*KARAMEH, RASHID** (b. 1921). Lebanese politician. Scion of a Sunni-Muslim family of notables from Tripoli. Members of the family held in the past for a long time the office of Mufti of Tripoli. RK's father, 'Abd-ul-Hamid K., also served as Mufti, was the religious and political leader of the Muslims of Tripoli, and headed their representatives in parliament. In 1945, he replaced Riyad al-Sulh▷ as Prime Minister for several months. RK, who had received a legal education in Cairo, was elected to parliament on the death of his father, (Abd-ul-Hamid), in 1951, and rapidly inherited his place among the Sunni Muslims in Tripoli, and in all Lebanon. He continued his father's policy of opposition to the regime of Bishara al-Khouri▷ and was one of the opposition leaders who brought about his downfall, 1952. When Camille Chamoun▷ became President, he wanted to appoint K. Prime Minister, but Parliament, largely composed of supporters of Bishara al-Khouri, denied him its confidence. In 1955, he became Prime Minister, but he soon fell out with President Chamoun: the latter tended towards the West and its allies within the Arab world, whilst K. was one of the foremost spokesmen

Rashid Karameh

of the pro-Nasserist▷ school in Lebanon. This rift deepened until, in 1958, K. became one of the leaders of the fight against the Chamoun regime. After the civil war, with the end of Chamoun's presidency and the election of General Fu'ad Shihab▷ as President in the summer of 1958, K. formed a "Government of National Salvation" of four members intended to heal the breaches in the national structure (his first attempt to form a government of conciliation resulted in a crisis and almost a renewal of the civil war, because he favoured the Nasserist rebels and afforded them an exaggerated preference). Since 1959, K. and the Sunni-Muslim leaders of Beirut (Sa'eb Salam▷, 'Abdullah al-Yafi)▷ have alternated as Prime Minister. K. held the post during the Six Day War▷; reportedly he instructed the army to enter the war, but its commander, General Emile Bustani, a Maronite▷, refused to involve Lebanon in this venture. Palestinian guerilla operations from Lebanese territory after 1967 involved K. in a crisis. Some of his supporters in Tripoli clamoured for stronger support to the *feda'iyin*▷, while K. tried to co-ordinate and control their operation, so as not to upset the delicate balance existing in Lebanon. In 1970 the new President, Suleiman Franjiyeh▷, chose Sa'eb Salam rather than K. for Prime Minister, in order to preserve the old balance between Tripoli and Beirut, and perhaps also on the assumption that a leader from Beirut would be better able to restrain the guerillas.   (Y.P.)

KARS. Town in north-eastern Turkey. Pop.: 41,000 (1965). Centre of a province of the same name (pop.: 606,000), adjacent to the USSR. Controlling the road from Anatolia to the Caucasus, K., a fortified town, has always been of stragic importance. It was allotted to Russia in 1878 by the Treaty of Berlin following the Russian-Ottoman War of 1877–8. During World War I, Turkey captured the region, and in the Treaty of Brest Litovsk, 1918, the Bolsheviks formally returned it to her; this was confirmed in 1921 in a Turco-Soviet Treaty of Friendship. In 1945 the Russians again claimed K., along with other demands, as the price for the renewal of the Soviet-Turkish Treaty of 1925. The demand was rejected, and the USSR formally renounced its claim, in 1953, after Stalin's death.   (D.K.)

KATZNELSON, BERL (1887–1944). One of the leaders and spiritual guides of Socialist Zionism in Palestine. Born in White Russia, he studied at the *heder* and with private tutors. Came to Palestine in 1909, worked as a labourer, and became friendly with A. D. Gordon▷ and Y. H. Brenner. K. founded the Federation of Agricultural Workers and was active in the *Po'alei Zion* party. In World War I he volunteered for the Jewish Legion, and there, together with David Ben-Gurion▷ and Yitzhak Ben-Zvi▷, was active toward the unification of the workers of Palestine. In 1919 K. was one of the founders of *Ahduth-Ha'avodah* party (which unified *Po'alei Zion* and independents); in 1920, of the "General Federation of Labour" (*Histadrut*) in 1930, of the "Palestine Workers' Party" (*Mapai*), which unified *Ahduth Ha'avodah* and *Hapo'el Hatzair*. He founded the *Histadrut* daily *Davar* (1925) and its publishing house '*Am 'Oved*. His central aim was the achievement of unity of the Jewish workers of Palestine. He initiated various workers' economic projects, and during his last years he concentrated on educational and cultural activities.   (E. A.)

KEMAL, MUSTAFA—See Atatürk▷, Mustafa Kemal.

KEREN HAYESOD (Hebrew: Foundation Fund). Founded at the World Zionist Conference in London in 1920 with the object of enlisting funds from the Jewish people to finance immigration to and settlement in Palestine as a central instrument for the development of the country. Since 1939, it is known as the "United Israel (abroad—Jewish) Appeal".

The KH is the largest voluntary fund-raising organization in the world, and has raised $1,620,000,000, 92% of it in 54 countries since the establishment of Israel (1948). The money was invested in hundreds of agricultural settlements, in shipping, industry, education and (until 1948) in defence. KH finances the "Jewish Agency" in the spheres of immigration, absorption, settlement and culture. Dr. Israel Goldstein was chairman, 1961–71.
                (E.A.)

KHALIDI, AL-. Prominent family of Jerusalem notables. It claims descent from Khalid b. al-Walid, the great 7th century Muslim general. During the Ottoman period, the family was noted for its religious learning, and many of its members held key posts in the Muslim religious establishment. Outstanding members: Yussuf Dia' al-Kh.—member of the first Ottoman parliament, 1876, and its Vice-President. Ruhi al-Kh.—Ottoman consul in Bordeaux, elected in 1908 and 1912 as one of the three Jerusalem members of the Ottoman parliament. Al-Hajj Ragheb al-Kh. (b. 1866)—*Shari'a*▷ Qadi Magistrate and District Judge, and founder of the Khalidiyya library in Jerusalem. Sheikh Khalil al-Kh. —a well-known Muslim sage, President of the Jerusalem *Shari'a* Appeals Court 1921–35. Mustafa al-Kh.—Beirut Chief of Police during the Ottoman period, Judge of the Jerusalem High Court 1920–37,

appointed Mayor of Jerusalem 1937–44 in place of his relative, Dr. Hussein al-Kh. (see below) who was exiled from the country. Ahmad Samih al-Kh. (1896–1951) was a well-known writer and educationalist, Principal of the Jerusalem Arab College. His son, Professor Walid al-Kh., worked in 1945 for the Palestinian-Arab propaganda office and is now a Lecturer in History at the American University of Beirut, one of the heads of the Institute for Palestine Research and author of several books and political essays. In recent years, the status of the family has declined; its members have dispersed, and Jerusalem is no longer their main centre.

KHALIDI, AL-, DR. HUSSEIN FAKHRI (1894–1962). Palestinian-Arab politician and physician, graduate of the American University of Beirut, 1915. He served in the Palestine Government Health Department. Breaking with his family tradition, Kh. joined the Husseini▷ faction in 1934 in their opposition to Ragheb Nashashibi, the Mayor of Jerusalem. The Nashashibis were defeated, and he was elected Mayor of Jerusalem (with the help of Jewish votes). A year later, he established a "Reform Party". Though that party was not really active, he became in 1936 its representative on the Arab Higher Committee▷. On the dissolution of this body, in 1937, he was dismissed from the mayoralty and exiled to the Seychelles. Kh. was released in 1938 and settled in Beirut; he returned to Palestine in 1943. In 1945, Kh. was a member of the revived Arab Higher Committee, but resigned in 1946 because of the factional intrigues of Jamal al-Husseini▷ and joined a rival committee established by the opposition. On the dissolution of both committees by the Arab League▷, he was appointed to a new High Committee formed by the League. After the Arab defeat of 1948 and the annexation of the West Bank▷ by Jordan, he briefly joined the abortive Palestine Government formed in Gaza, but soon returned to Jerusalem; in 1953–4, he was Foreign Minister, acting chief *Qadi* (Head of the *Shari'a* judicial system) and Minister of Social Affairs in the Government of Jordan. In 1955–6, he served as Minister of Health and Social Affairs and then Foreign Minister. Appointed Prime Minister during the crisis of April 1957, he held this post for only nine days. Afterwards he retired from public life.   (Y.P.)

KHALIL, 'ABDULLAH (1892 (1888?)–1970). Sudanese soldier and politician. Prime Minister 1956–8. Served in the Egyptian Army 1910–24, and the Sudanese Defence Forces, 1925–44, the first Sudanese to attain the rank of Brigadier. In 1945 he founded the *Umma* party, advocating independence for Sudan (as against union with Egypt), and served as its

Secretary-General 1945–7. When a Legislative Assembly was created in 1948, he became its leader. Later the same year he was appointed to the Governor General's Executive Council, serving as Minister of Agriculture, until 1953. In 1956 he joined Azhari's▷ coalition government as Minister of Defence, and in July he became Prime Minister, leading a coalition government dominated by his *Umma* party, retaining the defence portfolio. He held the premiership until the military coup of 1958 when he retired. In 1960–2 he was under house arrest, suspected of subversive activities against the regime.   (B. G.)

KHANAQIN. Town in eastern Iraq, in the province of Diyala, on the Baghdad-Kermanshah road, close to the Iranian frontier. Pop.: 24,000 (1968). K. lies in an oil-bearing area ceded by Persia to Turkey in 1913. According to an agreement concluded at that time between Turkey and Great Britain, exploitation rights remained with the Anglo-Persian Oil Company which set up a subsidiary, the K. Oil Company, in 1926. The KOC produced oil in small quantities and also built a refinery at Alwand near K. (362,000 long tons of finished products, 1968). The KOC was partially nationalized in 1951, continuing operations as contractor on behalf of the government. This relationship was terminated by agreement and nationalization completed in 1958.   (U.D.)

KHARTOUM (Arabic: elephant trunk). Capital of Sudan. Pop.: 170,000 (1965.) Founded in 1823 by the Egyptians, then masters of Sudan, on the junction of the White Nile and the Blue Nile. Forms one urban conglomeration together with North Kh. (Pop.: 80,000) and Omdurman (180,000). Cultural and press centre of Sudan. Seat of a university, founded 1951, as well as a branch of Cairo University. A river port and an important transportation junction. Kh.s fall to the *Mahdi*▷, in 1885, Gordon's death, and Kh.'s reconquest, in 1898, greatly stirred the imagination of the West. In Sept. 1967 Kh. was host to a "Summit Conference" of Arab heads of state which resolved not to recognize Israel, not to negotiate with her and not to make peace with her (the "Decisions of Kh.").   (B.G.)

KHATMIYYA, AL-. A fundamentalist Islamic order in Sudan, opposed to Islamic mysticism (Sufism, see Dervish Orders▷). Rival and opponent of the *Mahdiyya*▷ order. Also named *al-Mirghaniyya*▷ after its founder and leaders.   (Y. S.)

KHAZ'AL SHEIKH (?–1934). Semi-independent Arab tribal chief who controlled Muhammarah (Khorramshahr▷) and the left (eastern) bank of the

Shatt al-'Arab▷ in the Iranian province of Khuzistan▷. After the discovery of oil in the region, 1908, he concluded an agreement with Britain: in return for his promise to maintain security and not to disturb oil prospecting and extraction, the British undertook to protect him against external attack and pay him an annual subsidy. However, when, in 1924–25, Reza Shah▷, in his efforts to curtail the power of local chieftains, sent troops to Khuzistan, Britain did not come to K.'s help. K. submitted but was arrested and brought to Teheran, where he was detained till his death.   (B.G.)

KHORRAMSHAHR (Arabic: Muhammarah). Town and port in the Province of Khuzistan▷, in south-west Iran, on the north-eastern bank of the Shatt al-'Arab▷. Pop.: 90,000 (1966). During the 19th century Khuzistan had an Arabic-speaking majority, and the Teheran government was unable to exercise effective control there. Real power was concentrated in the hands of the Sheikh of Muhammarah, and Arab feudal chieftain. After the discovery of rich oil deposits in Khuzistan early in the 19th century Sheikh Khaz'al▷ of Muhammarrah concluded agreements with the British Oil Company, 1909, and government, 1910, by which he undertook not to interfere with the oil drilling operations, in return for a measure of British protection and an annual subsidy. In 1924–5 Reza Shah▷ crushed the rebellious Sheikh's autonomy and incorporated Khuzistan fully into Iran's administration. The town's name was Persianized, and it was developed into a major port. However, the development of Iran's ports on the Persian Gulf, prompted by her dispute with Iraq over navigation on the Shatt al-'Arab, operated to the detriment of K.   (B.G.)

KHOURI, AL-, BISHARA (1892–1964). Lebanese politician, Maronite▷-Christian. President of Lebanon 1943–52. Lawyer educated in Beirut and Paris. During World War I, he escaped to Egypt, later returned to Lebanon and served in the French mandatory administration. In 1927–8, he first served as Prime Minister of Lebanon. After the constitution was abrogated in 1932, he formed the "Constitutional Bloc" party that fought for the restoration of the constitution and was considered firmly anti-French. His rival was the pro-French Emile Edde▷. In 1936, he lost to Edde the election to the presidency; but in Sept. 1943, with the intensification of the struggle for independence and just before its attainment, Kh. was elected President of the Republic. His election was due, in no small measure, to the alliance he made with Riyad al-Sulh▷, leader of the Sunni Muslims, and the unwritten agreement he reached with the

Muslim leaders. This "National Covenant" of 1943 bound Muslims and Christians to uphold Lebanon's independence within her existing borders; Lebanon would not be aligned with France on the one hand, nor unite with any Arab state on the other; Lebanon would foster her Arab character; public service positions would be allocated among the various communities according to a fixed key (see Lebanon▷, Constitution), whereby, e.g. the President would be a Maronite Christian, the Prime Minister a Sunni Muslim and the Speaker a Shi'i▷ Muslim, and the ratio of Christians to Muslims and Druzes▷ in parliament would always be 6:5.

In 1948–9, Kh. sponsored a change in the constitution that enabled him to be elected in 1949 for a second term. This unconstitutional act raised a public storm. It was preceded by irregularities in the elections of 1947; Kh. was also accused of corruption and considered responsible for the deterioration of public administration. In Sept. 1952, a semi-coup was staged by a group of his opponents led by Camille Chamoun▷; Kh. was forced to resign, and his public career was terminated. His brother Salim and later his son Khalil (b. 1923) succeeded to the leadership of his "Constitutional Bloc" but the "Bloc" did not regain its leading position.   (Y.P.)

KHOURI, AL-, FARES (1877–1962). Syrian politician, Protestant Christian. One of the few Christians who rose to first-rank leadership in nationalist Syria, and the only one who served as Prime Minister. Before World War I▷. Kh. represented Damascus in the Ottoman parliament. He was a member of King Feisal's▷ Damascus government in 1920. He participated in the Syrian-"Druze" rebellion (1925–7), was arrested and exiled to Lebanon. In the 1930s Kh. was one of the leaders of the Syrian "National Bloc", and, when it came to power, became President of Parliament (1936–9). He served as Foreign and Finance Minister in 1939. He resumed the presidency of parliament in 1943, when the "Bloc" was returned to power, and again in 1945–9. In between he served as Prime Minister 1944–5. After the "National Bloc" broke up, he became from 1947 one of the leaders of the "National Party". After the fall of Adib Shishakli▷, he served as Prime Minister, 1954–5.   (A.L.-O.T.)

KHUZISTAN. Province in south-west Iran, the country's main oil-bearing area. Capital: Ahwaz. Pop.: 1.7m. (1966). At the turn of the 19th century most of K.'s inhabitants were Arabic-speaking nomadic tribesmen. The area assumed a new importance when rich oil deposits were discovered at the beginning of the 20th century. The government

in Teheran was weak and *de facto* control of the province was in the hands of the Arab Sheikh Khaz'al▷ of Muhammarrah (Khorramshahr)▷. In 1910 Britain signed an agreement with the Sheikh. In return for his promise to maintain internal security and not to interfere with oil extraction, Britain guaranteed to protect him against external attacks and to pay him an annual subsidy. When Reza Shah▷ came to power, he put an end to the semi-independent rule of the Sheikh of Muhammarrah, 1924–5. During Reza Shah's reign, Arab nationalism in K. (called by the Arabs "Arabistan", *i.e.* land of the Arabs) posed no very serious problem. However, in 1946, at the height of the Qashqai▷ rebellion in the neighbouring province of Fars▷, several Arab chieftains called for K.'s incorporation into Iraq. After the coups in Egypt, 1952, and Iraq, 1958, an Arab irredentist movement, encouraged by Cairo and especially Baghdad, began to grow. In 1965 Iran recalled her ambassador from Damascus, after the Syrian Prime Minister described "Arabistan" as one of the lost Arab territories that had to be recovered. In recent years the Teheran government has been endeavouring to develop K. and to strengthen its Iranian character.   (B.G.)

KIBBUTZ (or **KVUTZA**). Collective agricultural settlement in Israel (occasionally including some industry), based upon equal sharing in both production and consumption. The K. was the product of the difficult living conditions in Palestine at the beginning of this century, competition with cheap Arab labour, and the Socialist-Zionist background of the Jewish immigrants.

The first attempt to establish a collective was at Sejera in 1908; this was a collective of wage-earning workers. The first k. settlement was established at Umm-Juni (later known as Deganya), on the shores of the Sea of Galilee, in 1909. Among the initiators of the idea were Joseph Trumpeldor▷, Zvi Shatz and members of Deganya A. D. Gordon▷ and Joseph Bussel. Dr. Arthur Ruppin, then director of the Palestine Office (see Zionism▷), fostered and aided the first *kibbutzim*.

The basic principles of the K. are: collective organization of production, administration and services; collective ownership of all means of production and consumption; shared responsibility for the satisfaction of all the members' needs; common education of all the children. The K. is based on the principle: "From each according to his abilities, to each according to his needs." The K. movement expanded as a result of immigration to Palestine after World War I. It split into four movements, two unofficially affiliated with the *Mapai*▷ and *Ahduth*

Ha'avodah▷ parties (now the Labour Party▷), one with *Mapam*▷ and one with the religious *Hapo'el Hamizrahi*▷. The number of *kibbutzim* today is 240 with a population of *c.* 100,000, (about 5,600 belonging to religious *kibbutzim*). The average population of a K. is about 600.

Kibbutzim constitute only 3.5% of the general population, but they constitute a pioneering élite. They were among the first to organize Jewish illegal immigration to Palestine, and made a major contribution to the *Hagana*▷ and *Palmah*▷. Those in the Negev▷ and south, in the Jordan Valley and Galilee, stopped the Arab invasion during the Arab-Israel War of 1948▷. Today K. youth constitute 25% of the volunteers to the select army units. K. members hold important posts in the *Histadrut*▷ leadership (a K. member is its present Secretary General), and in the workers' parties. Four government ministers are K. members.

The growing industrial sector in the *kibbutzim* (10% of Israel's industrial total output) led to a manpower shortage, and social problems resulted from the necessity to employ hired labour.

Ideological differences between the various movements have become less marked, and the movements co-operate within the framework of the "Union of K. Movements". The process of unification of Israel's labour parties may well lead to a union of K. movements.   (E.L.)

KILANI (also KAILANI, GAILANI), RASHID 'ALI

(1882–1965). Iraqi lawyer and political leader. Born in Baghdad, a scion of its leading Sunni-Muslim family. First joined the government in 1925, as Minister of the Interior. Co-founder of the nationalist *al-Ikha'* (Brotherhood) party which rejected the Anglo-Iraqi Treaty of 1930; Prime Minister for the first time in 1933. Minister of the Interior, 1935–6. K. regarded World War II as an opportunity to emancipate Iraq from British influence, though he was cautious and hesitant as to the means. The ex-Mufti of Jerusalem, Hajj Amin al-Husseini▷, then in Baghdad, and the four colonels who were the *de facto* rulers of Iraq ("The Golden Square"), rabidly anti-British and admirers of Germany, projected him into the premiership in 1940 and again, in a virtual coup, in Apr. 1941. In the crisis that followed— military operations against Britain, a call for German help, the dismissal of the pro-British Regent and the purge of his supporters (see Iraq▷, History)—K. was little more than a puppet. He fled with those who had placed him in power when defeated by the British at the end of May, and proceeded to Germany, where he became a leading Arab collaborator and propagandist for the Nazi war effort. After the war,

he lived as an exile in Sa'udi Arabia and Egypt, until Sept. 1959. He then returned to Baghdad in the hope that Gen. Qassem's▷ new regime would effect a union with Egypt. Disappointed, and scared of social reform, he gave his name to a futile plot against Qassem. He was sentenced to death, but pardoned. He played no further part in politics.   (U.D.)

KILLEARN, LORD

(formerly Sir Miles Lampson) (1880–1964). British administrator and diplomat. Joined the Foreign Service in 1903 and held a number of diplomatic appointments in the Far East. He was appointed High Commissioner▷ in Egypt in Sept. 1934. When that office was abolished under the terms of the Anglo-Egyptian Treaty of 1936, he became British Ambassador to Cairo, a post which he held until 1946. In 1936, he headed the British delegation to the talks which led to the conclusion of the treaty. During the ten years of his ambassadorial tenure, he enjoyed wide influence in Egyptian political affairs, including internal matters. On 4 Feb. 1942, with the help of British tanks and troops, he compelled King Farouq▷ to dismiss the Hussein Sirri government (supported by the King) and to appoint as Prime Minister Mustafa Nahhas▷, leader of the *Wafd*▷ party, who, K. believed, would support the British war effort more efficiently and willingly. This act, and Lord K., became—in the eyes of Egyptian nationalists—symbols of British imperialist interference.   (O.G.)

KING-CRANE COMMISSION.

A commission headed by the Americans Henry C. King and Charles R. Crane, sent in 1919 to Palestine and Syria to investigate the wishes of the population on the future of the two countries. It was originally intended that a commission including experts from additional Allied countries should be sent, but the British and French delegates never set out. K. and C. reported general opposition to Zionism and to the imposition of a French Mandate▷ in Syria. They recommended that a "Greater Syria"▷, including Lebanon and Palestine, be established. They reported that, if it were at necessary to establish a mandate, the inhabitants would prefer an American or—failing that—a British one. The K.-C. Report was never acted upon.   (Y.S.)

KIRKUK.

Fourth largest city of Iraq and centre of its foremost oil-bearing area, capital of a province. 150 miles north of Baghdad near the foothills of the mountains of Kurdistan. Pop.: 176,000 (1965); majority of Kurds, with considerable minorities of Turcomans and Arab Sunni Muslims. K. has a record of bloody communal riots (the last of which occurred in July 1959).   (U.D.)

KITCHENER

KITCHENER, HORATIO HERBERT, EARL
(1850–1916). British Field-Marshal and administrator.
Commissioned Second Lieutenant 1871. Conducted
some surveys in Cyprus and in Palestine. Attached to
the Egyptian Army 1883. From 1896 onwards he
directed operations against the *Mahdi's*▷ Army and
won the decisive battle of Omdurman in 1898.
Governor-General of Sudan Jan. 1899. Transferred
to South Africa in Dec. 1899. British "Agent and
Consul-General" (*i.e., de facto* Governor) in Egypt
1911–14. Secretary of War in the 1914 British Cabinet.
Died in 1916 when a submarine taking him to Russia
for a visit was sunk. (B.G.)

KÖPRÜLÜ, MEHMET FUAT (1890–1966).
Turkish scholar and politician. Born in Istanbul. K.
became a scholar of world renown in Turkish
literature and history, teaching at Istanbul and Ankara
universities and other institutes of higher learning.
He served for many years as a deputy in the National
Assembly for the Republican Peoples' Party, but
resigned from the party in 1945, with Bayar▷ and
Menderes▷, and was one of the founders of the
Democratic Party in 1946. When it won the elections
in 1950 and gained office, he became Foreign Minister.
In 1956 he resigned, and in 1958 left the party in
protest against its undemocratic conduct. (D.K.)

Fuat Köprülü (being arrested)

Dr. Fadil Küçük

*KÜÇÜK, FAZIL, DR. (b. 1906). Turkish-Cypriot
politician. Born in Nicosia, K. studied medicine at
Istanbul, Lausanne and Paris. Returned to Cyprus
in 1938 and began practising medicine. K. took a
keen interest in the problems of the Turkish community in Cyprus. He was editor of a Turkish-
language daily, *"Halkin Sesi"* 1941–60, leader
of the Cyprus Turkish National Union Party 1943,
chairman of the Evkaf High Council (administering
Muslim endowments), 1956–60. K. was elected
Vice-President of Cyprus in Dec. 1959. After the
inter-communal clashes of Dec. 1963, he ceased in
fact to fulfil vice-presidential functions, though he
did not resign. In Dec. 1967 he created the "Transitional Administration of the Turkish Community"
and became its President. (B.G.)

KUFRA. An oasis in southern Cyrenaica (Libya).
In 1895, the headquarters of the Sanussi▷ order were
transferred from Jaghbub▷ to K., because of its
strategic position at the intersection of caravan
highways. Anxious to be protected from the French,
advancing from the south, the Sanussis agreed in
1910 to receive a Turkish Governor and to fly the
Turkish flag in K. The Italian rulers of Libya conquered K. in 1931 and thereby put an end to Sanussi
resistance. (B.G.)

KURDISTAN—see Kurds▷.

*KURDS. The K. are one of the oldest nations on
earth: they have inhabited Kurdistan at least since
2000 BC when Sumerian sources mention the Kuti
as living in present-day Kurdistan, and from then
on the historical record is unbroken. Kurdistan,
the domicile of a population predominantly Kurdish
in speech and consciousness, is bounded by the Aras

river in Iran and Turkey in the north, the Kara-Su and upper Euphrates in Turkey in the west; the border between mountain country and undulating plains and the Mosul-Kirkuk-Khanaqin line, in Iraq, to the south; and the Hamadan-Lake Rezaiyeh-Maku line, in Iran, to the east. However, these are not precise borders; many non-K. live within this area, and many K. outside it. There are large and long-established Kurdish communities in several cities outside Kurdistan, the most important being in Baghdad, Basra, Damascus and Aleppo. All these are Sunni Muslims. Lastly, some Shi'i tribal groups, chiefly the Lurs (Faylis) and Bakhtiaris▷ in Iran, are occasionally considered as K., mainly by Kurdish nationalists. The non-Muslim Yazidis▷ of Jabal Sinjar are best treated as non-K., even though they speak Kurdish.

Kurdistan thus falls mainly within the political frontiers of Turkey, Iraq and Iran, with much smaller adjacent areas in north-east Syria and Soviet Trans-caucasia; its area is approximately 135,100 sq. mi. There are about 8m. K. in Kurdistan, 3m. of whom live in Turkey, rather less than 3m. in Iran, 2m. in Iraq; 300,000 live in Syria and 100,000 in the USSR. Nearly another million live in the above-mentioned cities outside Kurdistan. Kurdish sources tend to give larger figures: 20m. or more.

The K. speak an Indo-European tongue, closely akin to Persian. It is split into a number of very different dialects, none of which has been adopted nationally; it remains undecided whether Kurdish should be written in Latin or Arabic script.

The Kurdish homeland is largely mountainous, with few easy passes and few wide valleys suitable for agriculture. Thus the K. have remained essentially a nation of rough pasture shepherds living in tribal communities, to whom they owe their first loyalties. They are not easily amenable to outside influence. Owing to their tribal structure and language problems, modern nationalism appeared late among the K., and therefore the post-World War I map of the area was drawn to their disadvantage. It is thus difficult to deal with "Kurdish nationalism" as a single subject. One should rather distinguish between the Kurdish situation in Turkey, Iran and Iraq, and consider separately the efforts of Kurdish intellectuals outside Kurdistan, and largely outside the ME.

Until the middle of the 19th century Kurdistan was divided into a number of principalities ruled by local dynasties, which loosely united numerous tribes, under the nominal suzerainty of Sultan or Shah. These principalities broke up, but the tribes remained largely unaffected by central authority. However, towards the end of the century there grew up in Constantinople, and later in Europe, a Kurdish intelli-gentsia which began working for national survival, first culturally, and soon after politically. Tradi-tionally leading families, like the Badr Khan and Baban, who had recently been deposed as rulers, formed the nucleus of this national intelligentsia. From these circles sprang the first Kurdish political societies and later parties. They had some effect in Europe, but little or none in Kurdistan. Thus the most significant success of early Kurdish nationalism, the provision for Kurdish autonomy, with an option for later independence, made by the abortive peace treaty of Sèvres▷ between the Allies and Turkey (1920), was eliminated in the Treaty of Lausanne▷ three years later (owing to Turkish opposition), without any Kurdish participation in the negotiations.

Kurdish political societies and "parties" springing up among exiles in the 1920s remained unrepresented in, and unrepresentative of, the homeland. The first nationalist society akin to a modern political party was Khoibun ("Independence"), founded c. 1927 in Beirut; from its initiation, its most influencial leader has been Kamuran 'Aali Bedir-Khan, a member of an old princely house. Khoibun remained essentially an organization of exiles, mostly in Europe, but played a part in fostering the rising in eastern Turkey in 1930 (see below). It was non-socialist and pro-Western. Khoibun dwindled away, when nation-alist organizations began to grow in Kurdistan itself—such as the right-wing Heva ("Hope") party and the Marxist Rizgary ("Salvation") in Iraq, and the left-wing Komala ("Committee", or more correctly Komala i-Zhian i-Kurdistan—"Committee of Kurdish resurrection"), in Iran. In late 1945 the Komala reconstituted itself in Mahabad as the Kurdish Democratic Party, which soon absorbed Rizgary, and later Heva. With the steady, though slow, advance of urbanization, de-tribalization and formal education along the fringes of Kurdistan, the KDP has come to provide the link between the sophisticated diaspora and the incipient nationalist consciousness of the tribes. The KDP remains the focus of Kurdish nationalism at the organizational as well as the ideological level. Branches are known to exist, or to have existed, in Iraq, Iran and Syria. Significantly, the links among them are weak. The organ of the KDP in Iraq between 1956 and 1966 was Kha-bat ("The Struggle"), and since then Ta'akhi ("Brother-hood"). Both occasionally appeared legally, but more often they were clandestine.

Kurdish nationalism is weakest, at least to outward observation, in Turkey. The K. there were respon-sible for at least three major rebellions against Ankara's centralist policy—in 1925, 1930 and 1937; all three were harshly suppressed. There is no trace of ad-ministrative autonomy. Tribal authority has been destroyed. Kurdish culture has no recognized status in Turkey; the very name "Kurds" has been replaced by "Mountain Turks". However, recently the authorities appear to have become liberal to the extent of not interfering with the daily life of the Kurdish rural population. But all matters under the jurisdiction of the state, including education, are conducted exclusively in Turkish, in accordance with the concept of one united Turkey.

Relations between the government and the K. in Iran have usually been better than those elsewhere. A situation has evolved in which traditional Kurdish society is left undisturbed, and the cultural activities of the younger generation are not interfered with, on the understanding that the K. remain politically loyal. The exception to this *modus vivendi*, the rebellious attempt, in 1946, to establish a separate, independent Kurdish Republic in Mahabad▷, was due to the then abnormal situation in north-west Iran.

In Iraq, Kurdish tribal society was exposed to contact with a central government relatively unused to authority and, being Arab, held in traditionally low esteem by the K. Moreover, under the British Mandate, 1922–32, the K. received a number of half-promises and witnessed a number of half-measures, which made their subordination to an independent government in Baghdad extremely difficult from the start. From 1932 onwards the Kurdish north was seldom at rest. The struggle, entirely tribal at first, became increasingly "national" as the detribalized intelligentsia in the towns, including Baghdad and other cities outside the Kurdish area, became more deeply involved. This synthesis found its expression in the assumption of the presidency of the Iraqi KDP by Mulla Mustafa Barzani▷.

Since autumn 1961 the unrest assumed the character of war, in which the bulk of the Iraqi Army was engaged against the Kurdish nationalists—without decisive success. The Iraqi government set up irregular units from among Kurdish tribes hostile to the Barzanis, named the "Jsah" and, later, the Salah-ul-din cavalry; the impact of these bodies on the struggle was slight. Politically, the central authorities were assisted since about 1966 by a former chief lieutenant of Mulla Mustafa, Jalal Talabani, who set up a rival "Kurdish Democratic Party" in Baghdad. However, after the agreement of Mar. 1970 Talabani seems to have ceased to play an independent role.

Kurdish national aims can be summarized as full autonomy within Iraq. After a number of arrangements and agreements which were never implemented, a "peace treaty" was signed on 11 Mar. 1970, between the Iraqi government of Gen. Bakr and representatives of Mulla Mustafa. The treaty recognized the K. as one of the nations of Iraq and

conceded many Kurdish demands, including the right to keep their armed forces virtually intact. It is too early to judge the longterm significance of this agreement and the degree to which it is being implemented.   (U.D.)

KURIA MURIA. Group of five islands in the Arabian Sea, 40 miles south of Muscat-and-'Oman. Area: 25 sq. mi., pop.: *c.* 80. The islands were ceded to Britain in 1854 by the Sultan of Muscat-and-'Oman. A cable station was later built. Though legislation by the British Governor in Aden and the protectorates applied to KM, the islands were administered by the British Political Resident in the Persian Gulf. When Britain granted independence to South Arabia (South Yemen), in Nov. 1967, she announced that the KM islands would be handed back to Muscat-and-'Oman. South Yemen claimed them—though their distance from the South Yemen border is about 200 mi.—and appointed a governor to symbolize their take-over. However, the islands were transferred to Muscat-and-'Oman without incident.   (Y.A.O.)

*KUWAIT. A principality at the north-western extremity of the Persian Gulf▷; area: 6,081 sq. mi., all desert, with a few oases. The area of K. encircles the Bay of K., the only deep-water bay in the Persian Gulf, which afforded K. an important role as a gateway to the Arabian peninsula and Iraq. It was because of K.'s strategic importance that Germany planned, at the end of the nineteenth century, to extend the planned Baghdad Railway▷ as far as the Bay of K. Britain saw in this plan a threat to her sea route to India and this was one of the reasons for placing K. under a British protectorate, in 1899. According to the protectorate agreement Britain conducted K.'s foreign affairs and in effect supervised also law and administration. The agreement remained valid until 1961. K. then received full independence, under the rule of a sheikh, or amir, of the House of Sabah▷, which has governed K. since 1756.

Until World War II, K. had a population of 75,000, mostly Bedouin, who lived at a minimal level of subsistence, and a few fishermen, pearl divers and boat builders. The discovery of oil made K. rich, with the highest *per capita* income in the world (until Abu Dhabi▷ took its place recently). An oil concession was granted in 1934 to a partnership of the Anglo-Iranian Oil Company and the American Gulf Company. Oil was discovered on the eve of World War II, but its production was postponed until after the war. Today, K. ranks among the biggest producers in the world (for several years it held the first place in the ME; today Iran, Sa'udi Arabia and Libya surpass it). Production in 1970 reached 138m. tons; oil produced in the Neutral Zone▷ between K. and Sa'udi Arabia totalled 27m. tons in 1970, of which *c*. 60% was offshore. Income from oil royalties is estimated at $800–900m. *p.a.* The oil industry brought in its wake the development of K. as a wealthy city with all modern services.

The labour market in the oil industry, building and the developing city has attracted immigrant workers, particularly from the Arab countries (including 70,000 Palestinians). In 1965, K.'s population was 468,000, of whom a minority were Kuwaitis and some 250,000 foreign. The 1970 census showed a population of 733,000, of whom 387,000 were foreign and 346,000 Kuwaiti. The population enjoys all the advantages of a developed welfare state: education (including a university) and medical and telephone services are free; electricity (the 1968 production capacity was 390 megawatts) is supplied at the lowest price in the world. Approximately one half of the population of K. live in the city of K., a planned city which ranks amongst the most modern in the world. It is linked through an extensive network of roads to the inhabited areas of the country and has a large international airfield.

K.'s economy is based upon oil. All the oil installations are concentrated in the town of Ahmadi, and its port—Mina al-Ahmadi—is the largest oil port in the world. South of Ahmadi a second oil port has been constructed—Mina 'Abdullah. There are oil refineries in both towns with a combined production of 23m. tons. An extensive petrochemical industry has been established (although it cannot yet exploit the vast quantities of natural gas generated by the oil industry). Other K. industries produce for the local market, mainly food, clothing and footwear. Water is K.'s biggest problem: she has no water sources of her own. Large quantities of water are transported from Iraq in container vessels, but most of the supply comes from giant desalination plants. In 1964, an agreement was signed between K. and Iraq for the supply of 1,500m. cubic metres (mcm) of water each year from the Shatt al-'Arab▷ River; it has yet to be decided if the transportation is to be *via* pipeline or canal.

K. became economically and politically viable with the development of her oil resources and the resulting enormous income and economic boom. Britain had no objections when, from the late 1950s onward, K. demanded more independence. In 1960–1, the government of the sheikh-amir took over administrative departments that had previously been in British hands (Justice, Finance, etc.); in Apr. 1961 a special Kuwaiti currency was established (the Dinar—replacing the Indian Rupee which had until

then been K.'s legal tender); and in June 1961 the abrogation of the British protectorate and the complete independence of K. were proclaimed. Iraq thereupon presented a claim to sovereignty over K. (a claim made in the past as well, but dormant while K. was under British protection), and her declarations implied a threat of occupation by force. The Amir of K. immediatedly requested Britain to return her military forces, and also lodged a complaint with the UN Security Council (Iraq lodged a counter-complaint: in her view, the British presence suppressed K.'s independence and threatened Iraq, whereas Iraq itself had no intention of using force). The Security Council found itself deadlocked, when the draft resolution recognizing K.'s independence was vetoed by the USSR, and an Egyptian appeal for the withdrawal of British troops did not secure a majority. In July 1961, the Arab League accepted K. as a member —in the face of Iraqi protests (whereupon Iraq boycotted the League until 1963)—and established a Pan-Arab force (actually mostly Jordanian and Sa'udi) to defend K. With the recognition of the Arab world and its symbolic defence thus demonstrated, the Amir of K. asked the British troops to leave; they were withdrawn in Oct. Iraq withdrew her claim and recognized K.'s independence in the autumn of 1963 after the downfall of General Qassem▷; at the same time she received a grant of $84m. from K. In 1963, the Soviet veto was also withdrawn and K. was accepted as a member of the United Nations.

Rich K., whose reserve funds and investments have played an important role in the financial markets of London, Beirut and Switzerland, has used her wealth also to aid the Arab states. A "K. Fund for Arab Economic Development" was set up in 1962 with a capital later reaching $560m., to aid development plans in Arab countries with credits; the K. government also used its reserve funds for direct aid in large sums. Since 1967, K. pays an annual subsidy of $154m. to Egypt and Jordan. K. separately also pays large sums (not made public) directly to the Palestinian *feda'iyin*▷. Although K.'s regime is conservative, in her inter-Arab policy she adopts a radical line, generally endeavouring to co-ordinate her positions with Egypt's, but sometimes even more extreme; in 1970, for example, K. announced the suspension of her aid to Jordan and her monarch, out of solidarity with the Palestinian guerillas. It is a matter of opinion to what extent this is a policy of "re-insurance" and a diversion of *feda'iyin* revolutionary energy towards a front far from K.

The government of K. has remained conservative. In 1961, elections took place for the first time (only

Aerial view of the city of K.

men voting) for a Constituent Assembly, which passed in 1962 a constitution providing for a constitutional monarchy, with a single-house parliament elected by male suffrage. The first National Assembly was elected in 1963 and new elections duly held in 1967 and 1971. Nasserist▷ left-wing forces or supporters of the Ba'th▷ gained only a few seats. Only K. citizens voted, not immigrant workers (many of whom hold extremist and leftist views and constitute a source of turbulence encouraged by Iraq).

Executive powers have remained almost exclusively in the hands of the ruling dynasty, the al-Sabah family. There is a dynastic dispute between rival branches — the Jaber al-Sabah branch, which held the amirate in 1915–16 and 1921–50, and the Salem al-Sabah branch, which ruled 1916–21 and since 1950 ('Abdullah Salem al-Sabah 1950–65, and his brother Sabah Sahem al-Sabah since 1965). This internal dispute has not had grave repercussions. (Y.K.-Y.S.)

KUZBARI, DR. MA'MOUN. Syrian jurist and politician. Born in Damascus in 1914, he studied at the universities of Beirut and Lyons and was a professor of law at the University of Damascus. K. served as a government official in various juridical capacities 1948–53. During the military government of Adib Shishakli▷, K. was President of Parliament (1953–4) and also headed the "Arab Liberation Movement" founded by Shishakli. After Shishakli's deposition in Feb. 1954, K. declared himself acting President, but was forced to resign within two days. He served as a minister in several governments 1955–8, until the merger of Syria with Egypt and the establishment of the United Arab Republic▷. After Syria seceded from the UAR, in Sept. 1961, through a coup headed by one of his relatives, Colonel Heidar al-K., K. became Prime Minister. He was deposed in a military coup on 28 Mar. 1962. He retired from politics after the Ba'th▷ take-over in 1963. (A.L.-O.T.)

L

*LAND OF ISRAEL MOVEMENT. Group established in 1967 in Israel by members of various parties. It opposes withdrawal from the territories occupied by Israel in the Six Day War (see Israel▷). (E.L.)

LAND REFORM. For various economic, social and political reasons the ownership of land in the ME tended during the 19th century and the first half of the 20th century to be concentrated in the hands of a small number of large landowners. By the middle of this century, the distribution of landed property in some of the main Arab countries was as follows:

| Country | Year | % of total registered area in hands of | | |
		small scale owners	medium scale owners	large scale owners
Iraq	1951	15.7	17.2	67.1
Syria	1952	13.0	38.0	49.0
Egypt	1950	35.3	30.5	34.2
Transjordan	1950	36.3	49.5	14.2

(For purposes of comparison, a small landowner is taken to be one who owns less than 100 dunams (about 25 acres; one metric dunam is 1,000 sq. metres) in Syria and Transjordan, less than 100 Iraqi dunams (250 metric dunams, about 62.5 acres) in Iraq, or less than five *feddan* (about five acres) in Egypt. Large scale owners are taken to be those who own over 1,000 dunams, 1,000 Iraqi dunams, or 50 *feddan* (250 acres, 625 acres, 50 acres), respectively.

Generally large landowners lived in the city while their property was tilled by *fellahin* who were themselves landless. As a result, the land was often neglected by both parties. Since the *fellah* enjoyed only a small part of the fruits of his labour, he made no effort to introduce improvements. Moreover, the "monopoly" of large landowners and their power enabled them to maintain rents at a high level or even to raise them from time to time, while keeping farm wages low. The resulting low incomes were barely sufficient for the basic needs of most *fellahin* of the Arab countries. Thus two-thirds of the population subsisted at a very low standard of living. Economically this state of affairs diminished the domestic market for the emergence of local industry, while socially it was responsible for a high incidence of disease, ignorance and an inferior level of culture. On the other hand, because of the high rents, the greater security of landed property (as compared with other possessions) and the social and political status of landowners, capitalists preferred to invest their money in land rather than in industry. Finally, the concentration of great economic resources in the hands of a small number of large landowners gave them great political power. In many cases this was the reason why progressive social and economic legislation and development projects were delayed or completely frustrated. By the middle of the 20th century this situation brought about much tension and unrest in the countryside, but the ruling groups and parties were unyielding in their objection to any reform in the agrarian system. Land reform in the Arab countries had to wait until the old regimes were overthrown by military revolts. (The situation was different in Iran, where the Shah introduced, and forced through, certain measures of reform, see Iran▷.)

It was in Egypt, after the revolution of July 1952, that the first comprehensive land reform law in the ME was enacted. The main clauses of the Egyptian Law of Agrarian Reform of 8 Sept. 1952, may be summarized as follows: a. The maximum extent of landed property was limited to 200 *feddan* per head of family plus a further (temporary) allowance of no more than 100 *feddan* for children. (One *feddan* = 1.038 acre.) b. The excess area was to be confiscated within five years, compensation to amount to ten times the value of the rent, payable in government bonds at 3% interest, redeemable within 30 years. c. Expropriated land was to be distributed within five years, among *fellahin*, in plots of two to five *feddan*. The recipient was to repay the government, within 30 years, for the compensation it had paid, plus annual interest of 3%, as well as 15% of the cost to cover expenses. d. Those benefiting by this distribution, together with the other owners of land whose property did not exceed five *feddan* would set up co-operative societies— under government supervision—to supply credit, marketing facilities, seeds and equipment, and to improve cultivation and social services. e. It was forbidden to split agricultural land into units smaller than five *feddan* through inheritance or by any other means. f. It was forbidden to lease agricultural land to anyone who did not himself till that land. Rent must not exceed seven times the original tax or half the crop after deduction of expenses. The lease was to be for a duration of at least three years, and by written contract. g. Wages of agricultural labourers would be reviewed each year by a special committee. Agricultural labourers were allowed to set up unions for the protection of their rights.

Since 1952 this law has been amended several times, but its basic tenets are still in force. Among the major additions and changes are the laws which formed part of the socialist legislation of 1961. By these laws the maximum limit of land ownership was reduced (to 50 *feddan* per individual, 100 *feddan* per family), as were payments due on land distributed, while interest due from beneficiaries has since been waived altogether.

When Syria merged with Egypt to establish the UAR, a law was passed, Sept. 1958, providing for the implementation of an agrarian reform along lines similar to those of Egypt. Since the separation of Syria from the UAR frequent changes have been introduced into this law. A similar law was enacted, also in September 1958, in Iraq, after the military coup of that year. Syrian and Egyptian legislation also affected *Waqf*▷ (endowment) lands: it abolished family *waqf* and ordered the transfer of charitable *waqf* from private administration to the state and, in Egypt, if the property were agricultural land, to the Land Reform Committee for distribution.

Expropriation of land proceeded more or less according to law, although the process was slower in Syria and Iraq than in Egypt because of deficient land registration and stronger opposition of former landowners. Nevertheless, the economic aim, namely to divert capital from land acquisition to industrial investment, has not been achieved in any of the three countries, all of which had recourse to large-scale nationalization of industrial enterprises. Distribution, too, made faster progress in Egypt than in the other two countries. The change in the distribution of landed property in Egypt brought about by the different stages of land reform is reflected in the following official figures;

Owners of	% of land held	
	1952	1964
less than 5 *feddan*	35.4	54.7
5–10 *feddan*	8.8	10.1
10–50 *feddan*	21.6	21.9
50–100 *feddan*	7.2	6.4
100–200 *feddan*	7.3	6.9
more than 200 *feddan*	18.7	—

However, because of the tremendous increase in population land reform was unable to prevent even the relative growth of the class of landless peasants in Egypt. While the average annual increase in the number of landowners remained, even after 1952, 1.2%, the average annual increase of the population, including of course the rural population, rose to 2.5

to 3% in the 1950s and 1960s. The prospects that land reform will solve at least the problem of widespread landlessness are, despite greater difficulties in implementation, much better in Syria and Iraq than in Egypt.

Since many of the expropriated large estates were leased in small units before 1952, the reform did not involve, in most cases, a reduction in the size of the unit of operation. Therefore, on the whole, redistribution did not lead to a fall in crop yields. Some Egyptian sources claim that the average yield per acre even increased.

It is difficult to evaluate the effect of other measures provided for by land reform legislation, in addition to redistribution of land, in Syria and Iraq. As to Egypt, there can be no doubt that the income of the peasants who benefited from land distribution has risen considerably. However, the co-operatives have failed to bring about the social advancement of the *fellah*. Moreover, beneficiaries spent their additional income on consumption and on arranging early marriages and only negligible sums were invested in the farms. Tenants achieved greater security and in some places rents went down, although most landowners (even official bodies) evaded the legal rent limit. (The prohibition of splitting agricultural land into small units has been ignored.)

Agricultural labourers were the most deprived of all. Many were dismissed when the estates were distributed among small peasants and the reform law provisions for a minimum wage in agriculture failed utterly. Finally, the organization of agricultural labourers in trade unions has made no significant progress.   (G.B.)

*LATAQIA (*al-Ladhiqiyya*). Chief seaport of Syria and capital of L. district. Pop.: *c.* 90,000 (1967), mainly Sunni▷ Muslims (in contrast to two-thirds of the district's population, who are 'Alawites▷). During the French Mandate, L. was capital of an 'Alawite Autonomous Region. Development of the port began with Syrian independence; the government wanted to ensure its independence of Lebanese ports. Work began in 1953 and was completed in 1959. In 1967, the port handled 1,526 vessels which unloaded 1,294,000 tons and loaded 331,000 tons.
                                                   (A.L.-O.T.)

LATIN. In Arabic, Christians of the Roman-Catholic rite are called L. (whereas the term *Rum-Katholik*—Arabic: Roman Catholic—usually designates the Greek Catholics▷—see Catholics▷). (Y.S.)

LAUSANNE, TREATY OF. a. Peace T. signed on 24 July 1923—after eight months of negotiations —between Turkey and her World War I enemies: Britain, France, Italy, Japan, Greece, Yugoslavia and Rumania. The T. replaced the T. of Sèvres▷ signed in 1920 by the Ottoman government and invalidated after the Turkish nationalists' successful military struggle against the dismemberment of their homeland and the restriction of its sovereignty. In the T. Turkey renounced all claims over the non-Turkish provinces of the former Ottoman Empire, but her full sovereignty in Anatolia was reconfirmed. The clauses in the T. of Sèvres concerning Greek administration in Izmir, Armenian independence in Eastern Anatolia and Kurdish autonomy were dropped. Turkey undertook to safeguard minority rights and arranged, in a separate agreement with Greece, a Greek-Turkish▷ exchange of populations. Turkey retained control of Eastern Thrace and of the Aegean Islands of Imbros and Tenedos. The capitulations▷ were abolished, and so were the Ottoman Public Debt Administration and pre-war foreign concessions and contracts.

A new Convention of the Straits, in the formulation of which the USSR also played a part (though she did not sign it), was added to the T.; it stipulated freedom of navigation for all merchant vessels and warships with certain limitations in the event of Turkey being at war, and with restrictions on the forces of non-riparian states allowed into the Black Sea▷ (see Bosphorus▷). Although the Straits were under full Turkish sovereignty, Turkey agreed to their demilitarization and supervision by an international Straits Commission. The rival claims of Turkey and Britain (acting in the name of Iraq) to the Province of Mosul▷ were not resolved in L. but left for future negotiations and arbitration (completed in 1926 in favour of Iraq). The T. represented a great victory for the Turkish nationalists nearly all of whose demands were met, and allowed Turkey to devote the subsequent years to internal reform and modernization.

b. In another, less famous T. of L., signed in Oct. 1912 between the Ottoman Empire and Italy after the war that followed the Italian invasion of Tripolitania▷ (Libya▷), the Empire agreed to withdraw its forces and in fact renounced its possession of Libya (though it never did so *de jure*). The Ottoman Sultan was, however, to be represented in Tripoli in his capacity of *Khalifa* (Caliph) of all Muslims.

c. L. was also the meeting place, Apr. to Sept. 1949, of the UN Palestine Conciliation Commission▷ with delegations from Israel and the Arab states, for discussions that proved abortive. A protocol of 12 May 1949 signed by the delegations and establishing a basis for discussions, is sometimes referred to as the Protocol of L.   (D.K.-Y.S.)

LAVON AFFAIR. Pinhas Lavon was a government minister for four years (1951–5) and twice Secretary-General of the *Histadrut*▷ (1948–51, 1956–61). As a result of the LA he was dismissed from his posts, withdrew from *Mapai*▷ and disappeared from Israeli public life.

Eleven Egyptian Jews were arrested in Egypt in 1954 on suspicion of having placed—on behalf of the Israel secret service—bombs in cinemas, the post-office and the US Information Service premises in Cairo and Alexandria, in order to impair relations between Egypt and the West (at the time of the Anglo-Egyptian negotiations for British withdrawal from Suez). An Egyptian military court sentenced two of them to death and six others to long prison terms. Two other accused, Israeli espionage-officers according to the prosecution, were tried *in absentia*.

The Prime Minister, Moshe Sharett▷, had not known about the operation. L., the Minister of Defence, also pleaded ignorance, whilst the head of Intelligence, Col. B. Givli, claimed that he had acted upon L.'s oral order. The Chief-of-Staff, Moshe Dayan▷, also held the Minister of Defence responsible. The Prime Minister appointed an investigation commission. The commission was unable to decide whether Givli had received the order from L., who thereupon resigned. Sharett appointed David Ben-Gurion▷, at that time in retirement at Sdeh Boker, in his place.

At the end of 1960 L. appealed to Ben-Gurion for rehabilitation on the basis of new evidence which proved, in his opinion, that the higher echelons of the Ministry of Defence had conspired to remove him from his post. Ben-Gurion rejected this appeal, but a committee of seven ministers determined, and the government endorsed, that L. had not given the order to Givli and had not known of the operation in Egypt; Ben-Gurion thereupon resigned, claiming that the government was not competent to act as judge, and new elections to the *Knesset* were called (1961). The *Mapai*▷ central committee dismissed L. from his post as Secretary-General of the *Histadrut*▷, in order to facilitate Ben-Gurion's return as Prime Minister after the elections.

Nearly two years later, in 1963, Ben-Gurion resigned. He demanded in 1964 that the Prime Minister, Levi Eshkol▷, set up a board of inquiry to determine whether the "committee of seven" had acted correctly. Eshkol refused. A struggle in the *Mapai* convention of 1965 ended with 60% support for Eshkol and 40% for Ben-Gurion. The dissident elements seceded and established the "Israel Workers' List" (*Rafi*), which gained 10 seats in the *Knesset* (1965). *Rafi*, without Ben-Gurion, re-united with *Mapai* (together with *Ahduth-Ha'avodah*▷), to form the "Israel Labour Party" in 1968. In the 1969 elections Ben-Gurion's "State List" secured four seats.

(E. A.)

LAWRENCE, THOMAS EDWARD (1888–1935), "Lawrence of Arabia". British archaeologist, officer and ME expert. Attached in 1917 to the Hijaz Expeditionary Force assisting the Arab revolt. On Gen. Allenby's▷ staff from 1918. Played a leading role in Sharif Hussein's▷ Arab revolt against the Turks, as described in his book "Seven Pillars of Wisdom" (privately printed 1926, published 1935); the book and L.'s true part in the revolt have remained controversial. He participated in raids on the Damascus-Medina Railway and the conquest of communication centres. L. entered Damascus with the Arab forces in Oct. 1918.

He was a member of the British Delegation at the Peace Conference in 1919 and acted as adviser to Amir Feisal▷; he was intermediary in the Feisal-Weizmann▷ agreement.

He sometimes felt the Arabs had been let down in the post-World War I settlement, but several times stated that, in his view, Britain had honourably fulfilled her commitments to the Arabs.

He supported the Balfour Declaration▷ and was not opposed to Zionism▷. L. was Adviser on Arab Affairs in the ME Division of the Colonial Office, 1921–2. He later joined the RAF under an assumed name.

(Sh.H.)

T. E. Lawrence

LEAGUE OF NATIONS. Set up in 1919–20 as a permanent international organization "to promote international co-operation and to achieve international peace and security". The Covenant of the L. of N. provided, *i.a.*, for arbitration in disputes between member states. The USA never joined the L.; several powers belonged to it only for part of the inter-war years. Four ME countries belonged to the L.: Persia was a founder-member; Turkey joined only in July 1932, though she had participated in the L. Council negotiations, 1924–6, over the status of the Mosul▷ area; Iraq was admitted upon gaining independence in Oct. 1932 (and the following year was very severely censored by the L. for failing to prevent the massacre of her Assyrian▷ minority); Egypt joined the L. in May 1937 following the Anglo-Egyptian treaty of Aug. 1936. The 15-member L. Council always included at least one of the Muslim member states (the four ME states and Afghanistan).

ME issues dealt with by the L. included aid to refugees from Turkey in the early 1920s; the Mosul question mentioned above (the district was awarded to Iraq); the concession of the Anglo-Persian Oil Company, 1932; the Turco-Persian border dispute of 1934; and the Franco-Turkish dispute over Alexandretta▷. As a part of the ME came under the new mandates' system—a post-World War I compromise between the distribution of imperial zones of interest and the independence promised and claimed—Palestine (including Transjordan), Syria and Lebanon, and Iraq were regularly discussed by the Permanent Mandates Commission (see mandates▷). The L. of N. lost much of its prestige and influence in the 1930s; it was formally dissolved in 1946 after the establishment of the United Nations Organization.   (Sh.H.)

✵**LEBANON.** Republic on the eastern coast of the Mediterranean ("the Levant"), with an estimated population of 2.3 m. (1968). Arabic is the predominant language. None of its various religious communities constitutes a majority, although all Christian groups together are said to form 53% of the population: Maronites▷: 29%; Greek Orthodox▷: 10%; Greek Catholic▷: 6.3%; Armenian Orthodox ("Gregorians"): 5.1%; Armenian Catholics: 1.1%; Protestants▷, Syrian Orthodox▷ and others: 2.2%; all Christian communities: 53.7; Sunni▷ Muslims: 20.8%; Shi'i▷ Muslims ('Mutawalis'▷): 18.2%; Druzes▷: 6.3%; all Muslim and Druze communities: 45.3%. These figures are based upon the official census of 1932 and it is possible, as many Muslims claim, that a Christian majority no longer exists; for political reasons, however, no census has been taken since 1932 and the data quoted are still recognized for constitutional purposes.

The Maronites are concentrated in the Mount L. districts; Sunni Muslims in the Tripoli district of the north, in the southern coastal area and the capital city of Beirut▷; Shi'i Muslims in the south ("Jabal 'Amel") and in Coele Syria▷ ("al-Biqa'", the plain lying between the L. and Anti-L. mountain ranges); Druzes are concentrated in Mount L. and the south-eastern districts of Hasbaya and Rashaya; the Greek Orthodox reside mainly in the north. Between 1.5 and 2m. Lebanese emigrants reside abroad mainly in the Americas, and some 150–200,000 still retain their Lebanese citizenship.

Bordered on the north and east by Syria and on the south by Israel, the largely mountainous area of L. totals 4,015 sq. mi. of which less than half is considered cultivable. About 55–60% of this arable land is under cultivation. The economy is more modernized than in most ME countries and supports a higher national income.

The population is 57% urban, 43% rural and semi-urban; 35–40% engage in agriculture, 20–25% in industry, transport and construction. Of the national income (about $400 *p.c.*) less than 15% derives from agriculture. Although fruit is exported, staple foods must be imported. Tourism, shipping, banking and finance (with unrestricted gold and currency transactions) play an important role. Beirut is a major world centre for the gold trade and banking. More than 50% of the national income stems from trade, finance and services.

The nature of its economy forces L. to maintain a system of free enterprise and to eschew controls and state planning. A customs and currency union with Syria, inherited from the period of French rule, was dissolved in the 1950s soon after full independence was attained, as Syria favoured a protectionist and controlled economy. Some sections of the infrastructure that had previously been leased to concessionaires were nationalized—e.g. the railways and the port of Beirut; otherwise, L. has avoided any nationalization of the economy. Even river development for irrigation and power, reserved for state initiatives, has not been very enthusiastically managed. The Orontes▷ River, flowing north into Syria, is still untapped, and a project for the development of the Litani▷ River had made only slow progress since its inception in the early 1950s.

L. is a communications and transport centre. Its railways, however, are underdeveloped; a narrow gauge line runs to Damascus (opened in 1895), sections of the standard-gauge Aleppo-Rayak line (built 1903–14) cross the country and a coastal line (1941) joins the pre-World War I Tripoli-Homs-

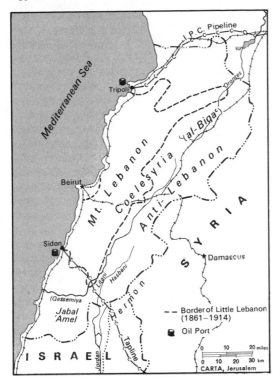

Map of Lebanon

Aleppo railway (its southern connection to Haifa and Egypt was cut in 1948). Beirut is a major port, facilitating the transport of goods by road to Syria, Jordan, Iraq and the Persian Gulf. Beirut also has a large international airport and L.'s "Middle East Airlines" (largely owned by private shareholders) is the largest in the ME. Oil pipelines from Iraq and Sa'udi Arabia (the "Tapline"▷) terminate at the Mediterranean in Tripoli and near Sidon respectively; both are privately owned and pay royalties to the government of L. (See Oil▷).

POLITICAL HISTORY. What is now L. was part of the Ottoman Empire▷ until the end of World War I. Parts of it formed the semi-autonomous district (*Sanjaq*) of Mount L. under a Christian (but non-Lebanese) Governor with a degree of Great Power supervision. This arrangement was imposed on the Empire by the Great Powers in 1860–61 after anti-Christian riots. Maronite Christians formed nearly 60% of the population in this district; the Christian communities as a whole amounted to 80%; Druzes were more than 11%, while Sunni and Shi'i Muslims represented less than 10%. The rest of what is now L. formed part of the Ottoman provinces (*Vilayet*) of Beirut and Damascus.

At the outbreak of World War I, the Ottomans abrogated the special semi-autonomous status of Mount L. Beirut had been, since the eve of the war, one of the centres for Arab and Syrian-Lebanese societies, some clandestine, striving for independence, autonomy or at least a decentralization of the Ottoman Empire (see Arab Nationalism▷). Some of these societies also advocated a wider autonomy for L., possibly with an enlarged territory (the distinction between Pan-Arabism▷ and a specifically Lebanese nationalism being then quite vague). Several Lebanese Arab leaders were in contact with the Western Powers, particularly France. Thirty-three Arab notables, including several Lebanese, were tried and executed by the Turks in 1915–16 as rebels. However, they were tried solely on the basis of suspicion and their previous contacts with French diplomats, and in fact there was no nationalist insurrection in L. throughout the war. The country was occupied in 1918 by Allied Forces under Gen. Allenby▷ and placed under a temporary Allied (*de facto* French) military administration. Attempts to establish a nationalist Arab government, as had been done in Damascus under British supervision, were foiled.

In accordance with the decisions of the Paris Peace Conference▷, and after a protracted Anglo-French dispute, L. and Syria were placed under a French Mandate▷ on behalf of the League of Nations▷ in July 1922. On 31 Aug. 1920, long before the Mandate was formally confirmed, a French decree created "Greater L." by annexing the overwhelmingly Muslim districts of Tripoli▷ in the north, Coele Syria▷, in the east, "Jabal 'Amel" and the Tyrus and Sidon coastlands in the south, and the city of Beirut, to the predominantly Christian district of Mount L. This created an economically viable political entity with a major city and port, but it destroyed L.'s homogeneity and predominantly Maronite-Christian character. Lebanese society consisted thereafter of many communities, each a minority with almost half of the population composed of non-Christian groups divided among themselves.

The populations of the annexed districts were not consulted before the annexation and most of the Muslim inhabitants opposed and resented it. Some of them advocated the absorption of all L. into Syria (as did many Syrian nationalists), while other favoured at least the incorporation of those newly annexed Muslim districts into Syria. Not all Muslims thought like this, nor was every Christian the protagonist of an independent Greater L. In general, however, the Christian communities, particularly the Maronites, supported the new state and developed a separate Lebanese, as opposed to Syrian or Arab, nationalism. This fundamental dichotomy found little open expression in the political parties which were mainly formed by coalitions of pressure groups and networks of prominent semi-feudal families and their retainers. Nevertheless, this very real and profound ideological division ultimately determined L.'s fate.

The struggle against foreign tutelage and the Mandate, although fundamentally similar in all ME countries, could not be waged with the same extreme intensity in L. because of its unique conditions. France had created L.'s enlarged boundaries and French support guaranteed its existence. Protagonists of Greater L.'s independence were often regarded as pro-French, while the radical anti-French Arab nationalists had less regard for L.'s independence and integrity.

At first, France ruled with an appointed administrative commission. A Representative Council, indirectly elected by the various communities, was established in 1922. This Council participated in the drafting of L.'s constitution, enacted by French decree in 1926. This constitution, with several amendments, remains the basic law of the land. Its provisions include—as a "transitory measure"—an equitable communal representation in parliament, government and public administration (see below). Since implementation of the constitution was made "subject to the rights and obligations of the Mandatory Power", France retained *de facto* authority.

The new constitution did not work successfully and was therefore suspended in 1932 by the French High Commissioner; the President ruled thereafter without parliamentary sanction. A struggle to restore constitutional government ensued. The faction which most consistently fought for restoration, and refused to co-operate with the government, was consolidated in 1934 as the "Constitutional Bloc" under Bishara al-Khouri▷. Its chief rival, the "National Bloc," led by Emile Edde▷, also advocated a speedy return to constitutional government but was prepared in the meantime to co-operate with France. Authority to elect the President was restored to parliament in 1936. Edde defeated Khouri for the presidency, and the constitution was fully restored in 1937.

The struggle for constitutional government had temporarily overshadowed the issue of complete independence with a treaty-between-equals replacing French tutelage. After protracted negotiations, such a treaty was signed (parallel with a Franco-Syrian pact) in Nov. 1936. L. was to become fully independent *de jure*. Under the treaty of alliance that replaced French tutelage, France agreed to defend L. in return for military bases and the right to station French troops on Lebanese soil. Signed by the Popular Front Government of Léon Blum, the treaty was not ratified by its successors and never took effect.

While French rule remained colonial, and L.'s independence was postponed, the draft-treaty had a far-reaching impact on the political situation. It was evident that its signature meant affixing the seal of final international recognition to the country's independence and territorial integrity, not only *vis-à-vis* France but Syria also. Indeed, the parallel Franco-Syrian draft-treaty included Syria's implicit but clear recognition of L.'s independence. Those elements in L. (mostly Muslim) still objecting to L.'s separation from Syria, or at least to the inclusion of the "new" Muslim districts within its borders, now resumed their agitation. Their opponents defended L.'s independence. Although the resulting tension was over a basically political problem, it had distinct communal (Muslim-Christian) undertones. Young Maronite activists founded a para-military organization for the defence of their community, the Phalanges▷ *(al-Kata'eb)* led by Pierre Gemayel▷ (Jumayyil). Other communities established similar groups (e.g., the Muslim Najjada▷). The proliferation of para-military formations was also encouraged by the growing influence of Fascist Italy and Nazi Germany. A clearly Fascist, Pan-Syrian organization, the Syrian Nationalist Party▷ *(Parti Populaire Syrien* — PPS), was founded by Antoun Sa'adeh▷ and outlawed in 1936.

Partial self-government in L. was further restricted with the approach of World War II. Parliament was dissolved and the constitution suspended in 1939; President Edde resigned in 1941. French administrators and officers in L. remained loyal to the Vichy government after the fall of France in 1940. Under the armistice concluded with France, a German and Italian base was gradually built in L. and Syria and full-scale German-Italian penetration into the ME seemed imminent, particularly since German assistance had also been requested by the pro-German revolutionary regime in Iraq. British and Free-French forces invaded and occupied Syria and L. during a brief campaign in June 1941.

Gen. Catroux▷ now proclaimed, in the name of Free France, the termination of the Mandate and the independence of L. and Syria; British statements concurred. Nevertheless, French pronouncements and an official exchange of Anglo-French notes clearly indicated that France intended to retain a predominant position in L. and Syria. Lebanese nationalists found this unacceptable. The elections of 1943 brought the Constitutional Bloc to power with Maronite Bishara al-Khouri▷ as President and the Muslim Riyad al-Sulh▷ as Prime Minister. In Oct. 1943, the new Government and Parliament enacted the abolition of all articles of the constitution restricting L.'s independence. After their warnings had gone unheeded, the French arrested the President and members of his government, declared the measures taken unlawful, and appointed Emile Edde▷ President. Some Ministers, however, escaped to organize demonstrations and resistance. Invoking the needs of security and the war effort, the British Commander of the ME supported the nationalists and, under the threat of armed intervention, demanded the restoration of parliamentary rule and the legitimate government. France had to yield, the national government was reinstated, and Edde was discredited. The final end to French domination came in 1945-6, when France evacuated her military forces and transferred locally recruited troops to L. to become the nucleus of her national army—after a struggle mainly conducted by Syria, and following a complaint to the UN Security Council. L. was now completely independent.

The crisis of 1943 had led to an unwritten "National Pact" between Christian (mainly Maronite) and Muslim leaders—principally Khouri and Sulh—on the political future and character of L. In substance, the Muslims accepted the country's separate independence and territorial integrity within its post-1920 frontiers, while the Christians abandoned their dependence upon French protection and accepted independent L.'s integration into the Arab family of nations. This agreement also formed the basis for the country's association, at first hesitant and reserved, with the Arab League▷. Lebanese apprehensions compelled the Arab states to append to the Protocol of Alexandria▷ (which laid the foundation for the League) an appendix solemnly recognizing L.'s independence. When the League proved to favour co-operation between separate, sovereign states, rather than a policy of Pan-Arab unification, L. became an active member and ardent supporter.

In her nation-building and internal politics, L. was less successful. The unity of 1943 was born of crisis and proved unstable. Permanent and responsible parties did not develop. Governments rose and fell in quick succession, and accusations of nepotism and corruption were frequent. The elections of 1947, returning the Constitutional Bloc of Khouri and Sulh to power, were denounced as rigged. Louder protests were heard when an acquiescent parliament amended the constitution in 1948 to permit the re-election of President Khouri for a second term. A right-wing coup by the Syrian Nationalist Party (PPS) was reported to have been attempted and suppressed in 1949; Antoun Sa'adeh was summarily tried and executed (Premier Sulh was assassinated, in revenge, in 1951). A bloodless coup compelled President Khouri to resign in 1952 and Camille Chamoun▷ (Sham'un) was elected President.

L.'s gravest crisis occurred in 1958. The traditional Christian-Arab antagonism now focused upon L.'s inter-Arab orientation. The left and many Muslims favoured integration with an Egyptian-led Nasserist revolutionary union or bloc. Most Christians, and the Chamoun regime, opposed such an integration, insisting on L.'s separate independence, and favoured a rightist, pro-Western policy and neutrality in inter-Arab affairs. An opposition "National Front" came together in 1957 under the predominantly Muslim leadership of Sa'eb Salam▷, 'Abdullah al-Yafi▷, Rashid Karameh▷ and Kamal Jumblat▷. Officially, the aim of the Front was to prevent a constitutional amendment permitting President Chamoun's election for a second term. The real, fundamental issue was the question of L.'s inter-Arab integration. Violence flared up in 1957, turning into a general rebellion in May 1958. The government and its supporters insisted that the rebellion was a Nasserist attempt to seize power, organized and supported chiefly by Syria (then the "Northern Region" of the UAR▷). Maintaining that the crisis was purely domestic, the rebels consistently denied these accusations. The Lebanese government submitted a complaint to the UN Security Council in May 1958, charging the UAR with interference in its internal affairs. In June the Security Council dispatched an international military observers' group ("UNOGIL") to L. They failed to detect the infiltration or presence of foreign forces or arms (giving rise to grave doubts as to the value and effectiveness of such UN missions).

A leftist revolution in Iraq, July 1958, aggravated the crisis. Concluding that L.'s independence was being threatened, President Chamoun appealed to the USA for assistance. President Eisenhower▷ agreed that "indirect aggression from without" threatened L. and dispatched US troops to the country. US proposals to replace her troops (and the British contingents sent to Jordan during the crisis) with UN forces were vetoed by the USSR. In view of this deadlock, the issue was transferred to a special session of the UN General Assembly. An Arab draft resolution was adopted by the Assembly in August, noting that the Arab states were committed to respect their separate independence, welcoming their renewed undertaking to "observe" that commitment, and requesting arrangements to be made that would "adequately help in upholding the principles of the Charter . . . and facilitate the early withdrawal of the foreign troops." US troops were evacuated in October; their bloodless intervention—controversial as to its merits and effects—had demonstrated the West's willingness to protect its allies against revolutionary subversion and coups engineered from without.

The struggle within L. was conducted with restraint and never became a full-fledged civil war. The Lebanese Army, under the command of Gen. Fu'ad Shihab▷ (a Maronite Christian), did not intervene, thus avoiding a final confrontation that might have prevented future reconciliation and destroyed the army's apolitical and non-communal character. President Chamoun let it be known that he did not intend to run for a second term. At the end of his term, Gen. Shihab was elected President. Under his strongly paternalistic administration, the Nasserist rebels of 1958 were appeased and returned to play a leading role in the government; their leaders (Karameh, Yafi, Salam) headed virtually all governments after 1958, while Chamoun and his associates went into temporary political eclipse. An approximate balance later was achieved in parliament between the Nasserist, Pan-Arab left and a "Triple Alliance" (under Chamoun, Pierre Gemayel and Raymond Edde) of right-wing moderate Christians who placed L. before Pan-Arabism. When Shihab declined Parliament's offer to amend the constitution and re-elect him for a second term in 1964, this balance was preserved and politically neutral Charles Helou▷ became President.

However, the atmosphere of crisis and uncertainty with regard to L.'s future, implanted by the events of 1958, did not disappear entirely. Some Christian leaders returned to the concept of a smaller, more homogeneous Christian L. that would relinquish the non-Christian districts and thus reduce the exposure of L.'s internal affairs to Pan-Arab tensions. The country was also affected by the Arab-Israel crisis mounting in the early 1960s. Arab plans to prevent Israel's use of the Jordan River▷ included the diversion of its Lebanese tributaries into the Litani River. Such schemes called for a military protection which L. could not provide, and as she did not choose to invite Arab forces into Lebanese territory, the country was not eager to implement those plans. While formally participating in the Arab-Israel War of June 1967, L. escaped defeat by refraining from military action and thus avoiding countermeasures from Israel.

The political equilibrium was critically endangered again in 1968–9. Palestinian-Arab guerilla groups (feda'iyin▷), based in L. or infiltrating across the Syrian border, stepped up their sabotage operations against Israel. Israel could not acquiesce in the operations conducted from Lebanese soil and retaliated. The guerillas also demanded a freedom of action tantamount to a state-within-a-state. The "Triple Alliance" of the right opposed feda'iyin presence in, or operations from, L. (although their objections were not always openly expressed), while

the Nasserist left encouraged them. President Helou and the army favoured the right-wing position and objected to commando operations from Lebanese soil. Several compromise formulas (such as commando operations controlled by the Lebanese Army, use of Lebanese territory for transit only, etc.) were suggested and rejected. Following a grave crisis late in 1968, aggravated by an Israeli raid on Beirut's International Airport, a new crisis in Apr. 1969 left the country with only a caretaker government for seven months, with the ever-present threat of an army take-over or a non-parliamentary presidential government. (Gen. Fu'ad Shihab was often mentioned both as the potential author of a coup and as a candidate for the presidency in 1970.) Nov. 1969 saw an easing of the crisis, with an agreement reached between the Lebanese Army and government and the feda'iyin organizations, in which President Nasser mediated. The agreement (published later) contained a modus operandi for the commando groups, prescribing their bases and location (in the south-eastern corner only), limiting their sabotage operations against Israel, and imposing some army control. It was a brittle, unstable agreement that laid L. open to future crises apt to grow out of misunderstandings between the feda'iyin and the government, and out of Israel's counter-measures against operations conducted from Lebanese territory. L.'s south-eastern corner, in particular, remained virtually outside government control.

In the summer of 1970 a new President was elected. Shihab refused to present his candidacy on realizing that he was not guaranteed a decisive majority; the right-wing factions, the "Tripartite Alliance", opposed a candidate sponsored by Shihab, and Jumblat and his leftist faction also refused to support such a candidate. A neutral, Suleiman Franjiyeh▷, was elected and entered office in Sept. 1970. Sa'eb Salam became Prime Minister.

CONSTITUTION, GOVERNMENT AND POLITICS. L. is a republic. The President is elected by Parliament for six years. The Prime Minister and his government require the confidence of a parliamentary majority. The unicameral Parliament is elected by a general adult franchise (women were enfranchised in 1953) for a four-year term. Representation is based on a predetermined communal proportion for each multi-member constituency. The President is enjoined by the constitution (as a "temporary" measure) to assure equitable communal representation in Parliament, government and the civil service and administration. Since 1943 the number of deputies is by custom always a multiple of eleven with a ratio of six Christians to five non-Christians. By a similar firmly established custom, the President is always a

Maronite Christian and the Prime Minister a Sunni Muslim; the Speaker of Parliament is usually a Shi'i Muslim, and the Minister of Defence often a Druze.

Political parties are generally loose coalitions of factions and pressure groups. Each party presents lists for the various constituencies containing members of the various communities. Thus, no party is entirely or officially identified as Christian or Muslim. In elections, doctrines or ideology are of little importance.

L.'s press is highly developed. A plethora of dailies, weeklies and monthlies appear in Beirut, most of them with a small circulation. Since the nationalization of Egyptian newspapers in 1960, Beirut remains the principal source of free, uncontrolled political information in (and about) the Arab countries. Some of Beirut's newspapers are propaganda organs of, and probably financed by, foreign countries, international movements, and political factions. There are several foreign-language publications—e.g., "L'Orient", "Le Jour" (merged in 1971), "Daily Star". Among the more important Arabic-language daily newspapers are: al-Hayat and al-Nahar (pro-Western, right-wing), al-Anwar and Al-Ahrar (left). Several weeklies are mouthpieces of leftist, Marxist, Maoist factions and guerilla groups.

Beirut is an important educational and intellectual centre with the University of Lebanon (founded in 1951) and Arab University (1960), a Catholic University (St. Joseph, established in 1875) and an American University (founded in 1866 as the Syrian Protestant College, a university since 1920). The American University in particular attracted students from all Arab countries and became an important educational centre of the modern nationalist Arab élite.

STATISTICS. Area: 4,015 sq. mi. Cultivated: 600,000 acres (23% of the total area, 57% of the arable). Pop.: c. 2.3m. (estimate, 1968). Birth-rate: 3.2%. Natural increase: 2.7–2.8%. GNP: c. $1,000m. National income p.c.—c. $400. Imports: c. $640m. p.a., exports, $118m. p.a. Budget: c. $200m. Literacy: adult pop. (15+) c. 50%. Children (6–14) schooled: 70%. Doctors: 1:1,300 (0.77 per 1,000). Hospital beds: 6.5 per 1,000.   (Y.S.)

LEVANT. "Lands of the Rising (Sun)". Originally designated the entire East, as seen from southern Europe, but particularly the eastern coast of the Mediterranean from Greece to Egypt. It gradually changed in concept to include only the coastlands of Asia Minor, Syria-Lebanon and Palestine. Recent usage limits the Levant to Syria and Lebanon.   (Y.S.)

LIBERAL PARTY IN ISRAEL—see Gahal▷.

✳ **LIBYA.** Republic on the southern shores of the Mediterranean. Pop.: 1.8m. (estimate 1970). Ethnically, Libyans are a mixture of Arabs and Berbers▷; their language is Arabic, and the Berber element can no longer be distinguished. About 97.5% are Muslims. Minorities include 15–20,000 Italians (after the departure of many Italian colonists following World War II and, again, in 1969–70), 2,500 Maltese, 800 Greeks, 300 Jews (after the departure of most of the ancient Jewish community which numbered c. 30,000 in the 1940s).

L., with an area of 680,000 sq. mi., is bordered on the north by the Mediterranean, in the east by Egypt and Sudan, in the south and south-west by Chad and Niger, in the west by Algeria and in the north-west by Tunisia.

The main economic resource of the country is oil, in production since 1959 60. But over 75% of the population is still engaged in agriculture and animal husbandry. Peanuts, olive oil, citrus fruits and almonds are exported. Fishing yields tuna, sardines and sponges. Apart from oil production no industry has yet been developed.

L. has existed as an entity since 1934, when the country was formed out of the provinces of Tripolitania▷, Cyrenaica▷ and Fezzan▷, then under Italian rule. L. has been independent since 24 Dec. 1951, and a member of the UN since Dec. 1955.

POLITICAL HISTORY. L. was conquered by the Ottomans in the middle of the 16th century. The area had some degree of autonomy between 1711 and 1835. In 1711 a Ttipolitanian notable, Ahmad Qaramanli, defeated the Pasha sent from Istanbul and secured recognition for himself as Pasha by Sultan Ahmed III. His descendants, the Qaramanli dynasty, continued their rule under nominal Ottoman suzerainty and engaged in piracy in the Mediterranean. Concerted action by the European powers brought an end to their exploits and caused the ruin of the last of the Qaramanlis, Yusuf. In 1835 the Ottomans reoccupied the territory to counter expanding French influence in North Africa.

In the mid-19th century, there emerged a movement of religious reform, the Sanussi▷ order, which spread among the local tribes especially those in Cyrenaica and in the desert hinterland where neither the Qaramanlis nor the Ottomans had ever been able to exert effective control. The Sanussi movement gave the nomads of Cyrenaica, Fezzan and southern Tripolitania the rudiments of a social structure and a sense of national unity which grew into a political and military force.

In the late 19th century, when colonialism was at its zenith, Italy began to covet L., aspiring to acquire "her share" of North Africa, where other powers,

Map of Libya

operations. The Ottomans prevailed upon Ahmad al-Sharif to attack Egypt so as to ease British pressure on them. The Sanussis first overcame the small British garrison at al-Sallum and advanced as far as Sidi al-Barrani, but a British counter-offensive forced them to retreat in 1916. Ahmad al-Sharif then left the country aboard a German submarine for Istanbul, relinquishing political and military control in Cyrenaica to his cousin and rival, Sayyid Idris al-Sanussi▷, who had all along opposed any action against the British and had in fact co-operated with them, taking up residence in Egypt.

Early in 1917, negotiations took place at Ikrima between Britain, Italy and Sayyid Idris, who was recognized as "The Grand Sanussi". Britain and the Sanussi leader agreed on mutual co-operation. Negotiations with Italy were more difficult, as the Italians could not agree to Libyan or Cyrenaican-Sanussi independence, but they eventually led to a precarious agreement on a cessation of hostilities.

After World War I the Socialist Government of Italy, wishing to pursue a more liberal colonial policy in line with the ideas of President Wilson of the USA, took certain steps towards granting civil and political rights to the people of Cyrenaica and Tripolitania. Separate statutes for the two provinces provided for a parliament and a government council for each province and local councils. In a new accord, signed at al-Rajma in Oct. 1920, Idris al-Sanussi was recognized by Italy as "Amir" (Prince) at the head of a self-governing Sanussi regime in the interior of Cyrenaica, comprising the oases of Jaghbub▷, 'Ajila, Jalu and Kufra▷, with the right to use Ajdabiya as the seat of his administration, which was to be subsidized by Italy. The Amir, for his part, was to ensure the disbandment and suppression of any armed Sanussi formations. This obligation the Amir was unable to fulfil, and so, a year later, the Bu Maryam accord provided that, until the establishment of full Italian control, Sanussi formations still existing would be maintained jointly by Sanussis and Italians in "mixed camps".

In view of the favourable terms obtained by Idris al-Sanussi at al-Rajma, the Tripolitanians—who had established a semi-independent regime of their own before the Italians had been able to exert full control over them—decided to make him their leader and invested him formally with the Amirate of Tripolitania on 28 July 1922. When the Italians took steps to prevent this extension of Sanussi self-government to Tripolitania, Idris al-Sanussi broke with them and reopened a bitter conflict. Yet he was not strong enough to fight. He left the country for Egypt in Dec. 1922; his exile was to last more than 20 years.

especially France, were increasingly expanding their influence. By a series of separate agreements signed with Austria 1887, Britain 1890, France 1900 and Russia 1909, Italy secured the backing of the five major European powers for the conquest of the Turkish provinces of Tripoli and Cyrenaica. In Sept. 1911 Italy declared war on Turkey and Italian troops landed at Tripoli. They encountered unexpected resistance on the part of local tribesmen and Sanussis, who fought together with the Turks under the command of a number of able Turkish officers, such as Enver▷ Pasha and Mustafa Kemal (later known as Atatürk▷). However, owing to growing difficulties on other fronts, the Ottomans were compelled to make peace with Italy in Oct. 1912, relinquishing their sovereignty over L. in the Treaty of Lausanne.

Libyan tribesmen, however, continued a guerilla war against the Italians, inflicting heavy losses on several occasions. In Apr. 1915 after defeating an Italian force at Qasr bu Hadi, in the desert of Sirte, the Sanussis under Safi-ul-Din tried to unite the whole of Tripolitania under the Sanussi flag; but he was thwarted by the traditional feud between the Sanussi nomads of Cyrenaica and the interior and the Tripolitanian urban and coastal nationalists headed by Ramadan al-Suweihili. Safi-ul-Din was defeated by Ramadan in 1916 and thereafter resistance against the Italians, mainly in Cyrenaica, was led by the Sanussi chief, Sayyid Ahmad al-Sharif, aided by a number of Ottoman troops who had remained in the country despite the treaty of 1912.

After Italy's entry into World War I in 1915, Sanussi resistance became a part of the general war

After 1922 Fascist Italy hardened her policy towards L., being determined to subjugate the rebellious tribes and gain complete control of the country. In 1923 the Italians declared null and void all previous Italo-Sanussi accords, seized the "mixed camps" in a surprise action, and attacked the rebels. This second phase of the Libyan guerilla war was to last nine years. It was led by a Sanussi follower, 'Omar al-Mukhtar▷ and based on small, mobile bands usually made up of members of the same tribe. Gradually, the Italians grew familiar with local guerilla tactics and took the Sanussi strongholds one after another; Jaghbub fell in 1926, Kufra—the last —in 1931. The Sanussi rebel leader, Sheikh Rida (Idris' brother) surrendered in 1928. The Italians barred the rebels' arms supply routes by running a barbed wire barrier along the Egyptian frontier. 'Omar al-Mukhtar, continuing a desperate fight, was wounded and captured in Sept. 1931. Tried and publicly hanged the same month, his name became a symbol of L.'s fight for freedom. With al-Mukhtar's death, resistance broke down almost completely. In 1934 Italy nominally united Cyrenaica and Tripolitania (comprising also Fezzan) and named the combined area L.

The colonization of the territory by Italian settlers started in 1920, but was severely hindered by unrest and the guerilla war. In 1933 settlement was given a new impetus by the Italian administration, and agencies were created to help and finance it. By 1940 the number of Italian settlers had reached c. 90,000 in Tripolitania and 60,000 in Cyrenaica. In the process of colonization, the Italians extended the cultivated areas. They also enlarged cities, set up public buildings and established a network of roads. But they did little to raise the standard of living and the cultural level of the local population.

When Italy entered World War II, Sayyid Idris al-Sanussi, in his Cairo exile, endeavoured, at Britain's suggestion, to recruit a Sanussi force which would help the Allied forces to liberate L. A meeting of Cyrenaican and Tripolitanian leaders, in Aug. 1940, endorsed his plans—despite the opposition of a number of Tripolitanian leaders. Idris al-Sanussi was also asked to negotiate L.'s future independence with Britain. The Sanussi force raised consisted of five battalions and took part in the campaign in the Western Desert. In return, the British Foreign Secretary, Anthony Eden, expressed in Jan. 1942 his government's appreciation of the Sanussi force's co-operation and pledged that "the Sanussis in Cyrenaica will in no circumstances again fall under Italian domination". Britain, the disappointed Libyans were told, could not commit herself any further before the end of the war.

Oil drilling rig in Libya

During the war, L. became a battlefield, on which Rommel's Afrika Korps and the Eighth Army fought for control of the Western Desert. After changing hands three times, Cyrenaica was taken by the Allied forces in Nov. 1942, and Tripoli in Jan. 1943, Fezzan falling to the Free French forces advancing from Chad. By Feb. 1943 the last of the Axis forces had left Libyan territory, and the Italian rule of L. was at an end.

After the war disagreement between the Powers delayed a settlement of L.'s future and from 1943 to 1951 the country was ruled by a Provisional Military Administration, British in Cyrenaica and Tripoli, French in Fezzan. The question of L.'s future was linked with the fate of the other Italian colonies in Africa and formed part of the long-drawn peace negotiations with Italy. It was agreed that L. should be brought under a temporary UN trusteeship, but there were conflicting views as to its form and the identity of the trustee country or countries. Finally, in the Italian peace treaty of 1947, the disposal of the Italian colonies was deferred for a year; should no agreement be reached by the end of that time, the matter would be referred to the UN General Assembly. No agreement was reached, and the issue was discussed at the UN General Assembly in Apr. 1949.

In the meantime, Britain and Italy had agreed in the so-called Bevin-Sforza Plan to place L. under three UN trusteeships for ten years; Tripolitania was to go to Italy, Cyrenaica to Britain and Fezzan to France. After ten years, L. would be granted independence upon a recommendation by the General Assembly. The plan caused sharp protests and disturbances in L. It was adopted in the UN Political Committee, in May 1949, but in the General Assembly it fell short, by one vote, of the required two-thirds majority, and was thus rejected. Instead, on 21 Nov. 1949, the Assembly ruled, by 48 votes against 1, with 9 abstentions, that "L., comprising Cyrenaica, Tripolitania and Fezzan" should become independent by 1 Jan. 1952 at the latest. A UN Commissioner was to advise and assist in the establishment of an independent government and the formulation of a constitution, in co-operation with an Advisory Council comprising one representative from each of the three provinces of L., one from her minorities and one each from Egypt, France, Italy, Pakistan, Britain and the USA.

In Dec. 1949 Adrian Pelt of the Netherlands was appointed Commissioner. With the assistance of the Advisory Council, he set up a 21-member committee to prepare the establishment of a Constituent Assembly. The Assembly convened in Nov. 1950. The main difficulty in the drafting of a constitution lay in the rivalries between the three provinces, and Cyrenaica's and Fezzan's insistence on status and representation equal to that of Tripolitania, despite the great difference of population and area. Cyrenaica had been declared independent on 31 May 1949 by Idris al-Sanussi, with himself as Amir, with British support and for the time being under the supervision of the British military administration. Elections for a Cyrenaican Parliament were held in June 1950. Provisional representative assemblies for Tripolitania and Fezzan had also been established in 1950. Provincial Executive Councils were set up in 1950 and a provisional government of L. in Mar. 1951. The constitutional problem was solved by the establishment of L. as a federation, giving wide internal autonomy to each of her three component parts. The constitution was adopted in Oct. 1951, the throne of L. was offered to Amir Idris al-Sanussi, and on 24 Dec. 1951 L. was declared independent under King Idris.

Friction between Tripolitania and Cyrenaica bedevilled L.'s internal affairs. From the start, Tripolitania had strongly favoured a unitarian state, whereas Cyrenaica and Fezzan advocated federalism. Prior to the first elections, Feb. 1952, an (opposition) National Congress of Tripolitania campaigned against the federal constitution. The elections were won by moderate pro-government candidates, except in the city of Tripoli, where riots occurred. These were suppressed, the National Congress leader, Bashir Sa'dawi (holder of a Sa'udi passport), was expelled and the National Congress ceased to exist. Rivalries between Tripolitania and Cyrenaica frequently turned into conflicts between provincial and federal authorities; but the king and his government were in firm control. Subsequent elections were held without major trouble.

Nationalist elements, mainly in Tripolitania, disagreed with the king's conservative regime and his pro-Western policy; and with the rising tide of anti-Western nationalism in the ME and North Africa their influence grew. In 1963, as a result of their pressure, the king abolished the federation and a new unitary

constitution was adopted by parliament. The traditional division of L. into her three provinces was replaced by ten administrative districts. L.'s sudden economic boom, following the exploitation of her oil resources since 1960, made the country independent of Western financial assistance and strengthened the nationalists. They were also increasingly under Nasserist influence and favoured L.'s integration in an Egyptian-led Arab alliance based on socialism within and neutralism in external relations.

King Idris, 1951–69, followed a pro-Western foreign policy. Treaties signed with Britain, July 1953, and the USA, Sept. 1954, allowed these countries to maintain military bases and forces in L., in exchange for military and economic aid (then still badly needed). An agreement with France, Aug. 1955, gave her forces communication facilities in the south-western desert areas. Close ties were also maintained with Turkey and Greece. Within the Arab League▷— which she joined in Mar. 1953—L. supported the conservative bloc, despite insistent demands by the urban intelligentsia for a pro-Egyptian and neutralist policy. Nasserist Egypt, for her part, encouraged subversive activities in L., and Egyptian diplomats and military attachés were on several occasions expelled. However, after Egypt's defeat in the 1967 Six Day War, conservative Lybia supported Egypt (and Jordan) by extensive annual subsidies.

Under the combined internal and external pressure for the liquidation of foreign bases, the government felt compelled publicly to favour their early evacuation, but it took few practical steps. In Feb. 1964, for instance, President Nasser publicly called for the liquidation of the American and British bases in L.; a day later, the Libyan government declared that the military agreements with the USA and the UK would not be renewed upon their expiry (i.e. in 1971). The USA and Britain agreed to this, in principle, in 1964. In June 1967, the government officially requested Britain and the USA to liquidate their bases "as soon as possible". The evacuation of some bases and posts was agreed. However the matter was only taken up with determination under the post-1969 revolutionary regime.

In the African arena, L. was a founding member of the Organization for African Unity, May 1963, and according to its resolutions she closed her air and sea ports to Portuguese and South African aircraft and ships. Talks took place with Tunisia, Algeria and Morocco, aiming at closer economic co-operation among the Maghreb states.

On 1 Sept. 1969, a bloodless military coup d'état took place. A Revolutionary Command Council proclaimed a "Libyan Arab Republic" that would strive for a revolutionary, socialist and progressive L.

and fight against imperialism. The constitution was abolished, the king deposed, and the government dismissed. All nationalist prisoners were released. There was no resistance, either by the police, thought to be loyal to the king, or the tribes of the interior, traditionally linked to the Sanussi dynasty. The king (visiting Turkey at the time) made a feeble attempt to ask for British help (rejected by Britain) but gave up without further resistance and renounced his throne.

The Revolutionary Command Council formed a government under Dr. Mahmud S. al-Maghrebi. The strong man of the new regime was Col. Mu'ammar al-Qaddhafi▷, aged 28; he was made Commander-in-Chief of the Armed Forces and later emerged as Chairman of the twelve-member Revolutionary Command Council, the supreme body of the new republic. In Jan. 1970, he became Prime Minister as well. His chief aide was 'Abd-ul-Salam Jallud. Internal strife within the junta was suppressed. In Dec. 1969, a conspiracy of the ministers of Defence and the Interior to overthrow the regime was foiled. The two officers were tried and sentenced to prison for life (and in a re-trial, on popular demand, to death).

The new regime declared that it would not nationalize the oil concessions but would honour contracts with the oil companies "as long as they honour the rights of the people". Most companies soon submitted to pressure to increase tax and royalty payments to the government and follow strict government instructions as to production and development, etc. In Nov. 1969 foreign banks were nationalized (i.e. it was decreed that 51% of capital and full control must be in Libyan hands). The takeover by the state of heavy industry and mining was proclaimed in Apr. 1970. The use of foreign languages in public places was banned; so was the employment of foreigners, except in the case of experts and by special dispensation. The properties of Italian settlers and Jews was confiscated in July 1970, and most of the remaining Italians started leaving. At the same time, the new regime was interested in foreign investment (in fields chosen by the regime). In spring 1971, L. obtained, after tough negotiations, new, still more favourable terms from the foreign oil companies (see Oil in the ME▷).

L.'s new regime turned towards the "revolutionary" Arab states. Of these, Egypt's influence seemed the strongest, and an intensive tri-lateral co-operation between L., Egypt and Sudan began to develop, culminating in plans for a tri-partite union. A "Federation of Arab Republics"▷ to consist of L., Egypt and Sudan, was pre-announced in Nov. 1970, and proclaimed—with Syria replacing Sudan as the third member—in Apr. 1971 (see Arab Federation▷).

By way of contrast, ties with Algeria and the Maghreb appeared to weaken; in 1970, L. ceased to participate in Maghrebi meetings and commissions on economic co-operation. (Within the ruling junta, there seems to have been some opposition to this veering towards the "Egyptian line", and a preference for a more "nationalist" balancing of various external influences.) L., under the new regime, gave very active aid to Palestinian-Arab guerilla organizations—in the form of finance and political and moral support (to the extent that in Sept. 1970 she severed relations with Jordan in protest against King Hussein's measures against the guerillas). Qaddhafi also sought to play a large part in Pan-Arab affairs.

In Dec. 1969, agreements were reached with Britain and the USA on the evacuation of all their military bases. Evacuation was completed by Britain (al 'Adhem▷ and Tobruk▷ bases) in Mar. 1970, and by the USA (Wheelus▷ Field base) in June. A much publicized deal with Britain for the purchase of missile defence systems was cancelled. France, on the other hand, agreed in January 1970 to supply 110 military aircraft (mostly Mirages). The USSR also agreed to supply military equipment. L. retained several conservative-Islamic features, but belonged politically and emotionally to the leftist-revolutionary camp; yet she professed neutralism and endeavoured to keep channels open to the West too—not least for the sake of the oil sales on which her economy is entirely dependent. In autumn 1970 negotiations with Britain on the question of arms purchases were also resumed.

PRESS, RADIO, TV. Owing to the high percentage of illiteracy, the Libyan press is poor and its circulation is small. During the regime of King Idris the government subsidized the press and, in return, received its support. After the coup of Sept. 1969, the new regime closed down all existing newspapers and started publishing its own daily, al-Thawra (The Revolution). Gradually other newspapers began to appear, such as a daily, al-Haqiqa (The Truth), and several weeklies. The Libyan Broadcasting Service broadcasts from Tripoli and Benghazi; a National Television Service was inaugurated in Dec. 1968.

STATISTICS: Area: 680,000 sq. mi. Area cultivated: 2% Pop.: 1.8m. (estimate, 1970). Birth-rate: 2.5% (1964). Natural increase: 1.5%. GNP: L£665.9m. ($1864.5m.) (1967). National income p.c.: $800 (1967). Exports L£670m. (oil included) ($1,876m.) (1968). Imports: L£230m. ($644m.) (1968). Budget: balances at L£426m. ($1192.8m.) (1969–70). Literacy: 27% (1966). Children (6–15) schooled: 46% (1965). Doctors: 1 per 3,160 persons (1966). Hospital beds: 1 per 310 persons (1965) L£1 = US$2.80.
(B.G.)

LITANI. Major river of Lebanon. It rises near Baal-bek and flows for most of its 105.5 mi. course from north to south through the Biqa' (Coele Syria▷), the valley separating the mountains of Lebanon and Anti-Lebanon. In its upper reaches, the L. is used for irrigation of large expanses in the Baalbek and Zahle districts. Near Merj 'Ayun, it makes a sharp western turn and continues through a deep gorge until it enters the Mediterranean, north of Tyre. This stretch is called al-Qassemiyya. Since the 1950s the utilization of the river for irrigation and elec-tricity by means of dams and tunnels is planned; but work on the initial stages commenced only in the 1960s and so far no stage of the scheme has been completed.

In course of Anglo-French negotiation over the Palestine-Lebanon border 1918–23, the British pro-posed, with Zionist support, the inclusion of the L. within Palestine, for Jewish settlement and develop-ment schemes to utilise its waters; but the frontiers fixed left the L. to Lebanon. Israeli planners continued to think of making use of its waters through a mutually advantageous agreement. In the light of the Arab-Israeli dispute there is, however, little early prospect of such an Israeli-Lebanese agreement. (For the repercussions of the Jordan River problem on the L. see Jordan River▷).   (Y.K.-Y.S.)

LLOYD GEORGE-CLEMENCEAU AGREE-MENT. An A. between French Premier Georges Clemenceau and British Prime Minister David Lloyd George, signed on 30 Nov. 1918. It modified the Sykes-Picot A.▷ on the division of the Turkish Empire. (Following its repudiation by the Bol-sheviks, the latter A. was no longer considered as fully binding.) According to the LG-CA the oil-rich Mosul▷ district was to be within the British rather than the French sphere of influence, and Palestine, with enlarged boundaries, was to be controlled by Britain and not by an international body. In return, France was to be given a share in the revenues from oil discovered in Mosul and to have full control of (as opposed to indirect influence in) the A Zone of the Sykes-Picot A. In addition, Britain made concessions to France in Europe.   (Sh.H.)

LOWDERMILK PLAN. Irrigation development plan for Palestine published by Dr. Walter C. Lowdermilk (b. 1888) of the US Bureau of Agri-culture in his book "Palestine—Land of Promise", 1944. A Jordan Valley Authority was to use the waters of the upper Jordan▷ to irrigate the Jordan Valley, the plains of Jezreel (Esdraelon) and Beit She'an and some parts of Galilee. The plan also in-volved diverting sea water from the Mediterranean to the Dead Sea for the generation of hydroelectric power. The LP served as a basis for later Jordan diversion projects, such as the Johnston▷ Plan and the scheme implemented by Israel (the "National Water Carrier").   (Sh.H.)

M

*MAGHREB, AL- (Arabic: "West"). The Arabic-speaking North African countries—Morocco, Al-geria and Tunisia—together (and also the Arabic name of Morocco alone); some include in the term M. also Libya, or at least Tripolitania, her western part. After achieving independence (Libya, 1951; Morocco and Tunisia, 1956; Algeria, 1962), the countries of the M. have become quite influential in all-Arab affairs, though they are reluctant to intervene overmuch in issues of the ME (*Mashreq*: "East", as opposed to M.); the exception is Libya which has become very active in inter-Arab affairs following her 1969 revolution. There are marked differences—ethnic, in dialect and in customs—be-tween the Arabs of the M. and those of the ME. Berbers▷ form a large proportion of the population of the M.

Attempts have been made, since they achieved independence, to unify the M. states, or at least to achieve close co-operation in economics, develop-ment and other spheres. Complete union does not seem feasible; even close co-operation and some measure of economic integration have not yet been achieved, due to political problems, differences of regime, mutual distrust and conflicting interests. Permanent committees have been formed to foster inter-M. co-operation, and occasionally ministerial conferences deal with it. Libya, which used to take part in these meetings, has ceased to since 1970. (Y.S.)

MAGNES, JUDAH LEON (1877–1948). Ameri-can Rabbi and Jewish leader. Immigrated to Palestine in 1922 and became President of the Hebrew Uni-versity in 1925. M. advocated bi-nationalism▷ as a solution to the Palestine problem within a ME federa-tion, in opposition to official Zionist policy, and with no success with the Arabs. In 1942 he organized the *Ihud* Association to forward his idea.   (Sh.H.)

MAHABAD, REPUBLIC OF. Autonomous Kurdish republic, established in 1946. The Soviet penetration of north-west Iran during the latter part of World War II gave encouragement to Kurd-ish nationalist aspirations there. They found expres-sion in the Komala Party which was reconstituted towards the end of 1945 as the Kurdish Democratic

Party. The collapse of Iranian central authority enabled the Kurdish nationalist leader Qazi Muhammad to proclaim (with Soviet encouragement) an autonomous Kurdish republic on 22 Jan. 1946. M. (also called Sauj Bulaq) became the capital of the state, which controlled a narrow strip of territory east of the Turkish and Iraqi frontier, from the Soviet border to the northern approaches of Saqqiz. The government of M. was in the hands of Kurdish intellectuals and town merchants; its armed forces were made up of tribesmen, chiefly Barzanis▷ from Iraq led by Mulla Mustafa. Despite its Soviet connection the regime was basically conservative. After futile negotiations with Teheran the Republic of M. collapsed when the USSR abandoned the separatist government they had established in Iranian Azerbaijan▷ and began withdrawing their troops from northern Iran; Iranian troops entered M. on 17 Dec. 1946 without resistance. Qazi Muhammad was court-martialled and hanged; Mulla Mustafa and the Barzanis escaped over the Soviet frontier.   (U.D.)

*MAHDI, MAHDIYYA. The M. (Arabic: the Guided One) is in Islamic theology a divine leader chosen by God at the end of time to fill the earth with justice and equity (and sanctioned to overthrow the existing regime). In 1881, in Sudan, Muhammad Ahmad ibn 'Abdullah (c. 1840–85) claimed to be the Imam (the head of the Muslim community), chosen to restore the community established by Muhammad, and the long awaited M. His followers established a religious order, the Mahdiyya—also called al-Ansar▷ (Arabic: the Helpers; the original Ansar were the "Helpers" of the Prophet Muhammad in Medina). The M. movement, encouraged by the discontent of the population with Egyptian rule and economic dislocation (partially caused by the suppression of the slave trade), was also supported by entire tribal groups, such as the Ja'aliyin, Danaqla and Baqqara tribes.

The M. called for a holy war against the infidels, including Muslims who did not acknowledge his mission. His fanatical followers, whom Europeans incorrectly called "Dervishes" (a term usually applied to members of the mystic Sufi orders, strongly opposed to the M. movement), defeated the Egyptian troops sent against them and conquered the provinces of Kordofan, Darfur and Bahr al-Ghazzal. The British advised the Egyptians to evacuate these territories and sent Gen. Gordon, former Governor-General of Sudan, to organize the evacuation. But the M. besieged Gordon in Khartoum, and took the town in Jan. 1885, killing Gordon, and established his rule over Khartoum and most of Sudan. The M. died in 1885 and was succeeded by 'Abdullah Ibn

Muhammad, the Khalifa (successor). The order lost much of its vigour and failed to establish a well-ordered state. In 1896, the British sent an Anglo-Egyptian force commanded by Gen. Kitchener▷ and reconquered Sudan, 1896–8. The Khalifa was killed in battle. Continuing resistance was quelled at the beginning of the 20th century.

The Mahdiyya gradually changed from a fanatic-military revolutionary force into an ordinary sect or order which, in time, gained great political influence. It later became generally pro-British, anti-Egyptian and was in favour of Sudanese independence (as opposed to union with Egypt). Its main rival was the fundamentalist Khatmiyya▷ or Mirghaniyya▷ order. The Mahdiyya is strongest in central and western Sudan. It claims 2–3m. adherents. In the 1950s and 1960s it was a focus of opposition to the military-revolutionary regimes controlling Sudan. In Mar. 1970 the order was accused of bringing about a rebellion which was suppressed; its last Imam, al-Hadi al-M., was killed, and no successor was proclaimed.

The Mahdiyya order (al-Ansar) was led by Sir 'Abd-ul-Rahman al-M. (1885–1959), the posthumous son of the M. (al-M. gradually became a kind of family name). During World War I he helped the British to combat the Pan-Islamic propaganda of the Ottomans. He gradually took a pro-British line and was knighted in 1926. In the 1940s he became the patron of the Umma party, which campaigned for Sudanese independence (as opposed to union with Egypt). Efforts to elect him as President for life, of an independent Sudan, did not succeed.

Sir 'Abd-ul-Rahman's son, Siddiq al-M. (1911–61), succeeded him in 1959 as head of the order (and patron of the Umma party). Under him the Mahdiyya became the spearhead of resistance to Gen. 'Abbud's▷ military rule.

Siddiq was succeeded as leader of the order, in 1961, by his brother al-Hadi al-M. (1915–70). He caused a schism in the Umma party, 1966, by patronizing its conservative right wing. He was a strong candidate for the presidency but his ambitions were thwarted by the coup of May 1969. After the coup he retired to the Nile island of Aba. He was considered to be a leader of the opposition to the new regime, and in Mar. 1970 was accused of fomenting a rebellion. When the rebellion was crushed, the Imam al-Hadi was killed, reportedly while trying to escape to Ethiopia.

Sadeq al-M., the son of Siddiq and nephew of the Imam al-Hadi (b. 1935, educated at Oxford), became —while holding no official position in the order— the leader of the progressive-modernizing faction of the Umma party and Prime Minister July 1966–May

1967. Under arrest since the coup of May 1969, al-M. was expelled, in Apr. 1970, in the wake of the *Mahdiyya* rebellion, to Egypt.   (B.G.-Y.S.)

MAHER, Dr. AHMAD (1886–1945). Egyptian politician, prominent in the *Wafd*▷. In 1937, M. was expelled from the party by Mustafa Nahhas▷ because of differences over relations with the King and, together with Mahmud Fahmi Nuqrashi▷, formed the *Sa'adist*▷ party (named after Sa'd Zaghlul▷), which claimed to represent the true traditions and ideology of Zaghlul and the *Wafd*. Eventually, this party collaborated with the court against the *Wafd*. M. was Prime Minister and Minister of Interior 1944–5. He was assassinated in Feb. 1945, when Prime Minister, on the day he declared war on Germany, and in reprisal for this declaration.   (S.L.)

MAHER, 'ALI (1883–1960). Egyptian politician. Born in Cairo, A graduate of the Law School and a wealthy landowner, M. became a member of the *Wafd*▷ in 1919, but soon joined the conservative royalist camp. A Member of Parliament from 1924, he served as chairman of its constitutional committee. M. was many times a minister (Education 1925–6; Finance 1928–9; Justice 1930–2) and Head of the Royal Cabinet 1935 and 1937. On the death of King Fu'ad▷ in 1936, he was a member of the Regency Council, until King Farouq▷ came of age in 1937. M. was Prime Minister and Minister of Foreign Affairs in 1936 and 1939–40. He was forced to resign in 1940, because—within Egypt's neutrality and beyond it—he displayed marked pro-Axis sympathies. He became again Prime Minister and Minister of Foreign Affairs and War in January 1952, following riots against the British, foreigners and minorities ("Black Saturday"). Following the July 1952 Revolution, the "Free Officers" asked him to form a government; but he resigned in Sept. in opposition to the agrarian reform and the revolutionary tendencies of the officers.   (S.L.)

＊**MAHJOUB, MUHAMMAD AHMAD** (b. 1908). Sudanese lawyer and politician. Educated at the Engineers' and Architects' School, Gordon College, Khartoum, and Khartoum Law School. In 1947 he was among the founders of the *Umma* party, advocating independence for Sudan (as opposed to union with Egypt). Member of the Legislative Assembly 1948–53; and of Parliament from 1954. Minister of Foreign Affairs 1956–8. During the military regime of Gen. 'Abbud▷, 1958–64, he practised as a lawyer. After its fall, he was again Minister of Foreign Affairs 1964–5. Prime Minister 1965 and 1967–9, leading a coalition with the National Unionist

Party. After a split in his own *Umma* party, he led the conservative faction loyal to the head of the *Mahdiyya*▷ sect, the Imam Hadi *al-Mahdi*▷. The May 1969 coup removed him from politics.   (B.G.)

MAJALI, AL- HAZZA' (1916–60). Jordanian politician. Born in Karak. Education: Damascus University (Law). Practised law until 1947, when he was appointed Chief of Protocol to the Royal Palace. Later served as Mayor of 'Amman and Minister of Justice and of Agriculture (1950–1). Pro-Western in his politics and a king's man, M. supported Jordan's proposed adherence to the Baghdad Pact▷; he was appointed Prime Minister in Dec. 1955 to finalize Jordan's entry into the Pact, but resigned five days later following riots and demonstrations against such participation. He served as Chairman of Jordan's Development Board until 1958, when he was appointed a Minister of the Royal Court. In May 1959, M. again became Prime Minister. Early in 1960 he denounced Egyptian agents for plotting against the regime and the life of its leaders, and predicted an attempt on his own life. He was assassinated in Aug. 1960.

Other prominent sons of the same Majali clan include 'Abd-ul-Wahhab al-Majali: several times minister (Interior, 1965; Finance, 1967; Defence, 1970); and Field-Marshal Habes al-Majali (born 1913); one of the top leaders of the Jordanian Army, Chief of General Staff 1957–65, Commander-in-Chief 1965–7, Minister of Defence 1967–8, Commander-in-Chief and Military Governor 1970 (during the strife between the Jordanian Government and Army and the Palestinian-Arab guerilla organizations.   (B.G.-Y.S.)

＊**MAKARIOS, ARCHBISHOP (MICHAEL CHRISTODOULOU MOUSKOS)** (b. 1913). President of Cyprus and head of the autocephalous Greek-Orthodox Church. Born in Ani Panayia (western Cyprus). He entered Kukko Monastery at the age of 13, became a novice and trained for the priesthood. He enrolled in Athens University in 1938, reading theology and law. On being ordained a priest, in 1946, he took the name of M. (Greek: Blessed). He was awarded a scholarship for postgraduate studies at the University of Boston, Mass., by the World Council of Churches. Elected Bishop of Kition, he returned to Cyprus in 1948 to become head of one of the island's four sees. M. became actively involved in the struggle for *Enosis*▷ (union with Greece). He was elected Archbishop and enthroned in Oct. 1950, as Makarios III. Between 1951 and 1954, M. visited Greece, the USA, Egypt, Syria and Lebanon, and attended the Bandung Con-

Archbishop Makarios

ference▷ in 1955, to enlist support for *Enosis*. The British exiled M. to the Seychelles, in March 1956, for alleged implication in EOKA▷ terrorist activities. He was released in 1957 on condition that he not return to Cyprus; he settled in Athens. M. returned to Cyprus after signature of the Zurich and London agreements in Mar. 1959 (see Cyprus▷). He was elected President in Dec. 1959, and took office on 16 Aug. 1960, when Cyprus became independent. M. was relected in 1968, for a second term.   (B.G.)

* MAKKAWI, 'ABD-UL-QAWWI (b. 1918). South Yemeni (Adeni) politician. Born to an Aden middle-class family and qualified as a lawyer, M. worked as a company manager in Eritrea and Aden. On election to the Aden Legislative Council, M., who had nationalist sympathies, became leader of the Opposition. In Mar. 1965 Britain attempted to appease the nationalists and appointed M. Chief Minister; but in Sept. he was dismissed because of his nationalist and pro-revolutionary views (the Government and Legislative Council were dissolved and the constitution suspended), and went into exile. When, in Jan. 1966, the insurgents formed a united Liberation Front (FLOSY▷), he joined it and became the head of its Political Bureau. After the take-over of South Yemen by the rival NLF▷, in 1967, M. remained in exile, with the intention of continuing the fight against the NLF regime.
    (Y.A.O.)

MANDAENS (also Sabaeans or Sabians). A small community in Lower Iraq, variously estima- ted at 5–30,000. For the most part they live in towns and are artisans, mainly silversmiths. Their religion contains Christian and Muslim elements and borrowings from other faiths. The M. speak Arabic but use an ancient Chaldean-Aramaic language in their religious rites. Ritual immersion in a river is an important part of their religion, and they are sometimes termed "Christians of John the Baptist".
    (Y.S.)

MANDATES. After World War I the victorious Allies devised a new system for the ex-German colonies and the Asian areas severed from the Otto- man Empire. The system was a compromise between the principle of self-determination for all nations— generally accepted and proclaimed, in particular, by US President Wilson▷—and secret war-time agree- ments among the Allies to divide the areas into imperial zones of influence. Article 22 of the Covenant of the League of Nations▷ speaks of "peoples not yet able to stand by themselves", whose "well being and development . . . form a sacred trust of civiliza- tion"; "tutelage of such peoples should be entrusted to advanced nations . . . as Mandatories on behalf of the League."

Three types of M. were created: The "A" M. included Palestine and Transjordan, Mesopotamia (Iraq), and Syria (and Lebanon), which were con- sidered civilized but not yet ready for independence. The Mandatories were to give administrative advice and assistance and—in the case of Iraq and Syria—to "facilitate the progressive development" of these territories "as independent states"; constitutions were to be drawn up within three years. The "B" and "C" M. comprised the overseas possessions of Germany in Africa and Oceania; as their populations were considered less advanced, the Mandatories were given more sweeping powers. However, in all cases the Mandatories had to submit annual reports to the Permanent M. Commission of the League of Nations (see below).

The distribution of the M. was decided at the San Remo Conference▷ of the principal Allies, Apr. 1920, and finalized (except for Iraq) by the League of Nations Council on 24 July 1922. The M. for Palestine, conferred upon Great Britain, recognized the "historical connection of the Jewish people with Palestine" and obliged the Mandatory to assist in the establishment of a Jewish National Home. In Sep. 1922 the League of Nations Council approved the exclusion of Transjordan from the last-named provision. While the terms of the Palestine M. did not include a clause concerning independence and a constitution, the Mandatory was made "re- sponsible for the development of self-governing institutions, and also for safe-guarding the civil and religious rights of all the inhabitants of Palestine, irrespective of race and religion". Attempts to set up a Legislative Council, following the White Paper of 1922 and of 1930, failed. The Peel▷ Commission Report of 1937 declared the Palestine M. to be unworkable because of the Jewish-Arab conflict, but Britain continued as Mandatory. In spring 1947, she handed the Palestine problem over to the UN, thus implying that she was unable to continue administering the M. or to find any other satisfactory solution to the problem. Following a UN resolution, 29 Nov. 1947, to partition the country into a Jewish and an Arab State, and an international enclave of Jerusalem, the M. lapsed and the British Administration was liquidated (though not handed over to the successor states) on 14 May 1948. The M. over Transjordan was terminated in Mar. 1946, when Britain recognized Transjordan's independence and signed a treaty of alliance with her. The UN gave full recognition to Transjordan's independence, by admitting her to the UN, only in Dec. 1955.

Iraq was to have become an "A" M.; but Britain, as Mandatory, agreed—after a two-year struggle with the Iraqis, who opposed any form of M.—to set out the main terms of the Mandatory relationship in the form of a Treaty with Iraq, Oct. 1922, rather than an instrument conferred by the League upon the Mandatory. A constitution came into force in 1925. A new Anglo-Iraqi Treaty of June 1930 granted Iraq full independence; in Oct. 1932 she was admitted to the League of Nations and the M. was terminated. Iraq became a founder member of the UN in 1945.

The M. for Syria and Lebanon was granted to France. In May 1926 Lebanon became a republic with a formal constitution. The Mandatory Power now acted in an advisory rather than an executive capacity, but retained control of defence and foreign affairs and the right to veto any law liable to affect the "rights and obligations of the Mandatory Power". In Syria internal disturbances delayed constitutional developments. A constitution was drawn up in 1930; as in the case of Lebanon, its implementation was subject to the "obligations contracted by France in respect of Syria". In 1936 France signed treaties with Syria and Lebanon granting both countries independence and terminating the M., but never ratified them. When, in June 1941, Syria and Lebanon were occupied by the British and Free French forces ousting Vichy France, the Free French leaders proclaimed the independence of these territories and the termination of the M. France tried, however, to retain control of the area and to obtain a preferential treaty. The constitutional clauses subjecting Syria and Lebanon's independence to France's Mandatory obligations were removed by Lebanon in Nov. 1943

(causing a grave Franco-Lebanese crisis), and by Syria in Jan. 1944. French and British troops were withdrawn in 1945–6. Syria and Lebanon became founder members of the UN in 1945.

THE PERMANENT M. COMMISSION was constituted in Feb. 1921 as an auxiliary political agency of the League of Nations. It studied the annual reports of the governments of the mandated territories and advised the League Council whether or not the conditions of each M. were being strictly observed. It also accepted representations from inhabitants of the various territories and summoned governors and other high officials for questioning. Five ME territories came under the supervision of the Commission: Lebanon and Syria (French "A" M.), and Iraq and Palestine-and-Transjordan (British "A" M.).

The Commission was often critical of the Palestine Mandatory administration. In 1930 it sent out a commission to investigate Jewish and Arab claims concerning the Wailing Wall▷. In 1937 it expressed preference for the cantonization of the country rather than its partition in accordance with the Peel Report. It also declared the White Paper of 1939 to be opposed to the spirit of the M.

In 1930–1, the Commission was asked its opinion on Britain's recommendation to terminate the Iraq M. It had grave misgivings over the fate of the minorities, particularly the Kurds▷ and Assyrians▷ (who had also petitioned the Commission), in an independent Iraq. The Commission advised the League Council to make its approval of the termination of the M. conditional upon formal guarantees for the minorities, to be written into Iraq's constitution. This was implemented; but the Assyrians were suppressed soon after, and the Kurds kept complaining and rebelling.

In the UN the M. Commission has been replaced, with modified functions, by the Trusteeship Council.
(Sh.H.-Y.S.)

MAPAI (Initials of Hebrew: *Mifleget Po'alei Eretz Israel*, Palestine, later Israel, Workers' Party). Established in 1930 by a merger of *Ahduth-Ha'avodah*▷ and *Hapo'el Hatza'ir*. Largest party in Palestine and since 1948, Israel. Moderate Zionist-Socialist.

M. aimed at "the revival of the Jewish people in Palestine as a working and free nation rooted in all branches of agriculture and industry and developing its own Hebrew culture". It is part of the world working class in its struggle against social servitude and discrimination. It advocates public ownership of the means of production, equality and freedom.

M. was affiliated to the Socialist International. It always had the decisive majority in the *Histadrut*▷ (General Federation of Labour.) It also politically dominated the Zionist institutions and the representative organs of the Jewish community in Palestine. In 1932 it became part of a world-wide association of Zionist-Socialist parties, *Po'alei Zion*.

In 1944 a dissident faction broke away from M. and re-established *Ahduth Ha'avodah*, as a reaction to the Biltmore Programme▷ and M.'s implied consent to the partition of Palestine. However, M.'s leading position was hardly affected. After 1948, M.'s leaders headed the Government of Israel (David Ben-Gurion▷, Moshe Sharett▷, Levi Eshkol▷, Golda Meir▷). In 1965 M. formed an "Alignment"▷ with *Ahduth Ha'avodah* to counter Ben-Gurion's *Rafi* ("Workers of Israel List") which had seceded because of the Lavon Affair▷. In Jan. 1968, M. merged with *Ahduth Ha'avodah* and *Rafi* to form the Israel Labour Party▷.   (E. L.)

MAPAM (United Workers' Party)—see Alignment▷; see also Zionism▷, Socialism▷.

MARDAM, JAMIL (1888–1960). Syrian politician. Born in Damascus. One of the founders of the Arab nationalist association *al-Fatat* (Paris, 1911) organizer and secretary of the first Arab Congress in Paris in 1913. (See Arab National Movement▷.) M. was a member of the Syrian-Arab delegation to the 1919 Paris Peace Conference▷. He took part in the Syrian "Druze" revolt (1925–7). In the late 1920s and early 1930s, M. was one of the founders and leaders of the "National Bloc" in Syria, but he supported co-operation with France and therefore did not belong to its inner circle. M. took part in the negotiations which brought about the Syrian-French treaty of 1936 (which remained unratified). He was Prime Minister in Syria's first national government 1936–9 and served again as Prime Minister after Syria became independent, 1946–8. With the disintegration of the "National Bloc", M. was among the founders of the "National Party", but was not politically active after 1948–9.   (A.L.-O.T.)

MARONITES. An Eastern Christian Church in communion with Rome, with its centre in Lebanon. There are about ½ m. M. in Lebanon and smaller communities in Syria, Israel, Cyprus and Egypt. A large Diaspora has also grown up in the Americas.

According to M. tradition, the Church was founded in the fifth century by a monk called Maron, who lived in the Orontes River Valley. A large monastery was founded on the spot, which became the spiritual centre of the M. It seems that during the seventh century the M. adhered to Monothelism, which emphasized the "one will" of Christ. Emperor Heraclius of Byzantium tried to use this doctrine to reconcile the Orthodox and the Monophysitic▷

churches; but his efforts failed and the Monothelites turned into a schismatic community of their own. The M. sought contact with the Catholic Church during the Crusades but formal union with Rome was established only in the early part of the 18th century (see Uniate▷). The M. Church, headed by a Patriarch, retained a certain autonomy and its own liturgy, the Antiochene rite, the liturgical tongue of which is Syriac (Aramaic).

At the beginning of the 19th century, the M., until then concentrated in the northern part of Lebanon, moved southwards into a region mostly inhabited by Druzes. M.-Druze clashes, culminating in 1860 in massacres of the Christians, brought about the intervention of the European Powers and the establishment, in 1861, of an autonomous district of Mount Lebanon, which had an absolute majority of M. (see Lebanon▷)

In "Greater Lebanon", created by France in 1920, the M. became a minority (about 29%); but they remained the largest single community. The M. were the chief defenders of independent Greater Lebanon, with a specific multi-communal and Christian character, and opposed full integration into a Pan-Arab union. By firmly established custom, the President of the State is always a M., as is the Commander-in-Chief of the Army. The "Phalanges"▷, founded in the 1930s as a para-military organization (today a political party) is composed mainly of M. and defends the interests of the community (see Lebanon▷).   (Sh.C.-Y.S.)

MASRI, AL-, 'AZIZ 'ALI (1878–1965). Egyptian officer and politician. Born in Cairo into an Arab-Circassian merchant family, M. studied at the Military Academy in Istanbul and from 1901 served in the Ottoman Army. He was one of the first members of the Young Turks'▷ "Committee for Unity and Progress". After their revolution (1908), he expected the Ottoman Empire to grant the Arabs independence, or autonomy, and hoped for the establishment of a joint Turkish-Arab kingdom. When this hope did not materialize, M. began, in 1909, Arab nationalist activities. He was co-founder of the clandestine *al-Qahtaniyya* association and one of the initiators of *al-'Ahd* (1913), a secret society of Arab officers in the Ottoman Army. He was arrested and sentenced to death, but thanks to public pressure was released and permitted to leave for Egypt. Despite the rift between him and the Turks, he refused to join the British against them during World War I. Only after the McMahon-Hussein▷ correspondence, which envisaged Arab independence, did he join the Arab Revolt▷ (1916) as Chief-of-Staff of the Sharif's army; but he resigned the same year.

M. was anti-British and pro-German. As early as 1916 he had attempted to bring German influence to bear on the Turks in favour of autonomy for the Arabs within the Ottoman Empire. He remained loyal to this pro-German orientation after the war. In 1939, he was appointed (by the pro-German Prime Minister Ali Maher▷) Chief-of-Staff of the Egyptian Army. He was suspected of collaboration with the Germans and dismissed under British pressure, in 1940. He thereupon deserted and tried to reach the Axis forces in the Western Desert, but was caught and tried, together with other officers. M. had a certain influence on the "Free Officers", later the instigators of the 1952 coup, as he symbolized the Egyptian nationalist officer fighting the British rule; he maintained contacts with Anwar Sadat▷ as early as the 1940s. In 1953, he was appointed Ambassador to the USSR by the new regime, a post he filled for only one year, retiring in 1954.   (S.L.)

MATZPEN (Hebrew: Compass). A small Israeli political group (less than a hundred) which believes a socialist revolution in the whole ME and the abolition of "imperialistic-colonialistic" Israel as a separate state will solve the Arab-Israel conflict.   (E. L.)

***MAURITANIA.** Situated in north-west Africa, M. does not really come within the scope of this Encyclopaedia; but she is involved in ME affairs. M. considers herself virtually an Arab country. Though most of her tribes do not speak Arabic, to a certain extent it serves as an auxiliary language. There has been talk of M. joining the Arab League▷, but she has still to apply for membership. However, M. is a faithful supporter of the Arab states in all international issues, such as the Arab-Israel conflict. M. also takes part in international Pan-Islamic▷ activities. On the other hand, the establishment of M. as an independent state caused much controversy, since Morocco claimed M. as part of her territory and denounced her creation as an imperialist conspiracy. Not a single Arab state supported Morocco. However, the Arab states were not eager to foster close relations with M. while the dispute was unresolved. Eventually, Morocco had to accept the existence of M. and, in 1970, she recognized her and formal relations were established.   (Y.S.)

McMAHON-HUSSEIN CORRESPONDENCE. Ten letters exchanged between 14 July 1915 and 30 Mar. 1916 by Sharif Hussein▷ of Mecca and Sir Henry M. (1862–1949), the British High Commissioner in Egypt, 1914–16.

The correspondence discussed the terms under which Sharif H. would ally himself with the British

and revolt against Turkish rule. H. asked Britain to recognize the independence of the Arab countries and to support the re-establishment of an Arab caliphate▷. Britain accepted these principles, but could not agree with H.'s definition of the area claimed for Arab independence—all of the Arabian peninsula (except Aden) and the whole Fertile Crescent▷, including parts of southern Anatolia. In his second note, 24 Oct. 1915, M. excluded certain areas: "The districts of Mersin and Alexandretta and portions of Syria lying to the west of the districts of Damascus, Homs, Hama and Aleppo, cannot be said to be purely Arab, and must on that account be excepted from the proposed delimitation." The interpretation of this sentence later gave rise to a long argument between Britain and the Arabs as to whether Palestine was part of the excluded area (as she was west of the Province of Damascus, which covered all of Transjordan, but not geographically west of the general area of the above four towns). Britain always argued that she had never intended to include Palestine in the area of Arab independence—as confirmed by M. himself in a letter to the Colonial Office, 12 Mar. 1922. However, several British spokesmen admitted that it was unclear whether Palestine had been excluded from the area. So did the Government, when publishing the correspondence in 1939 (". . . the language in which this exclusion was expressed was not so specific and unmistakable as it was thought to be at the time.") The Arabs claimed that Palestine was included in the area promised to them and that both the Sykes-Picot Agreement▷ and the Balfour Declaration▷ contradicted M.'s promises to H. and revealed Britain's bad faith. M. also claimed a special position for Britain in the provinces of Baghdad and Basra, and H. implicitly accepted this claim. As to the coastal lands of western Syria, H. did not accept their being granted to France, but indicated that he would claim them after the war.

No complete agreement was reached in the M.-H.C. and it does not constitute a formal treaty. But an Arab-British Alliance was established, and the revolt started on the assumption that Britain would generally support Arab independence. The Sykes-Picot Agreement and the post-war settlement were regarded by Arab leaders—far beyond the question of Palestine and specific territorial claims—as a betrayal because they substituted zones of imperial influence, or even direct imperial control, for the full independence promised.   (Sh.H.)

MECCA. Capital of the Hijaz▷, now part of Sa'udi Arabia▷. Pop.: 159,000 (est.). Holiest city of Islam, the birthplace of the Prophet Muhammad. Due

The Ka'ba Stone, Mecca

to its ancient sanctity as the site of the well Zamzam and the Black Stone of the Ka'ba, and as a juncture of important trade routes, M. served from earliest times as a commercial centre. M. is the goal of the annual Muslim pilgrimage, the *Hajj*, with some 300,000 pilgrims participating from abroad. Today most of the pilgrims arrive at Jidda▷ by plane or ship. The control of M. is a source of great prestige for Arab rulers; the Hashemite▷ Sharif of M., Hussein b. 'Ali▷, proclaimed here the Arab Revolt of 1916 against the Turks and declared himself king of Hijaz; in 1923–4 he took the title of Caliph▷. The capture of M. by Iban Sa'ud▷ in 1924 terminated the rule of the Hashemite dynasty in M. and the Hijaz, and through this victory Ibn Sa'ud gained great prestige and became the guardian of the holy places for all Islam.   (Y.K.)

MEDINA (AL-MADINA). Holy City in Hijaz▷, now Sa'udi Arabia▷. In ancient times, M. was an important trading centre, known as Yathrib. The Prophet Muhammad fled there from Mecca in 623 (the *Hijra*). He and his successors, the Caliphs Abu Bakr and Omar ('Umar), are buried there. For

Medina

the Islamic world, M. is second only to Mecca as holy city and a place of pilgrimage. Until World War I M. was the final station on the Hijaz Railway▷, but the railway was not repaired after its destruction during the war. M. is connected now to Mecca by an asphalted road and to other parts of Sa'udi Arabia by airways. Pop.: 72,000 (est. 1967).   (Y.K.)

MEDITERRANEAN SEA. Six ME countries border on the MS: Turkey, Syria, Lebanon, Israel, Egypt and Libya; a seventh, Cyprus, is a M. island. The MS has a central position in the economy, communications, and political and strategic alignments of these countries, and the entire ME. Throughout history, until the advent of aviation, the MS was the main approach-route to the whole ME, and through it to India and the Far East. Until 1869, the route to the Far East was by ship to Egypt and the Levant, from there by land to the Red Sea or the Persian Gulf, then again by ship. With the opening of the Suez Canal▷, a direct shipping route was created from the MS to the Red Sea and the Indian Ocean.

The control of this route, and of the whole MS (including the coasts of southern and south-eastern Europe), was a primary task of British and French strategic policy and an important issue for every European country with Great Power ambitions. Italy's ambition to control the MS led to her expansionist policies. The M. is particularly important to Russia: a. as a base for attack by potential enemies on her southern parts; b. as an outlet from the Black Sea and southern Russia to the world's oceans. The importance of the M. to Russia is enhanced by the fact that her northern ports are ice-bound in winter.

During World War II, there was a fierce struggle for control of the M. between Britain and Italy-and-Germany. Since the war, the fleets of the West—co-operating since 1949 in the framework of NATO▷ (one ME country, Turkey, is a member)—has controlled it. Since the 1950s, the USA has maintained a strong presence there through the Sixth Fleet. However, since the 1960s the USSR has also established her presence in the M. The strength of the two rival fleets varies, but some experts lately consider the Soviet presence stronger than the American.

The M. plays a vital role in the transport of ME oil to Europe: most Iraqi oil and a large proportion of Sa'udi Arabian oil is transported by pipeline to Lebanese and Syrian ports; Israel, too, has laid a pipeline from Eilat, on the Red Sea, to the M.; Egypt is planning a similar pipeline from Suez to the M. Egypt, and particularly Libya (as well as Algeria, outside the scope of this Encyclopaedia), enjoy a great advantage through the reduced costs of transporting oil from their territory to Europe. Until 1967, the Suez Canal was also used to transfer large quantities of oil from the ME (the Persian Gulf▷ region) to the MS and Europe.   (Y.S.)

MEDO—see ME Defence Organization, Treaty▷.

✻**MEIR** (formerly **MEYERSON**), **GOLDA** (b. 1898). Zionist-Socialist leader, Prime Minister of Israel since 1969. Born in Russia and educated in the USA (as a teacher), M. immigrated to Palestine in 1921 and went to live in a *kibbutz*▷ (1921–4). Active in the General Federation of Labour (*Histadrut*▷), she became Secretary of its Council for Women Workers in 1928, a member of the Executive Committee in 1934, and the Head of its Political Department in 1936. M. played an active role in the Palestinian Workers' Party (*Mapai*▷) and the Palestinian Jews' political struggle for immigration, self-defence and independence (see Palestine▷, Zionism▷). In 1946, when Moshe Sharett▷ was arrested by the British, M. replaced him as Head of the Political Department of the Jewish Agency▷. She met secretly with King 'Abdullah▷ of Transjordan in an effort to reach agreement with him. In May 1948 she was appointed Israel's first Minister to Moscow.

A Member of the *Knesset* (Parliament) since its establishment in 1949, M. was Minister of Labour,

Golda Meir

1949–56, and Foreign Minister 1956–66. She initiated Israel's policy of active co-operation with the newly independent countries of Africa.

In 1965, M. was appointed Secretary-General of *Mapai*. In this capacity, she succeeded in reuniting *Mapai* with the breakaway factions of *Ahdut Haavoda*▷ and *Rafi* in the Israel Labour Party▷ (1968). On the death of Levi Eshkol▷ she became Prime Minister, on 17 Mar. 1969, forming a coalition government of national unity; in July 1970, the *Gahal*▷ bloc left the government because of the latter's acceptance of US Secretary of State Rogers'▷ proposal. M.'s views on the Arab-Israel conflict are those of a moderate hard-liner.   (I.R.)

MENDERES, ADNAN (1899–1961). Turkish statesman, Prime Minister 1950–60. Born in Aydin. M., a landowner, studied law at Ankara University. He was elected to the National Assembly for the Republican People's Party. In 1945 he resigned from the party, together with Bayar▷, Köprülü▷ and Koraltan, demanding a policy of far-reaching liberalization. In 1946 this group formed the Democratic Party, and upon its 1950 election victory, M. became Prime Minister. During the ten years of his premiership he greatly strengthened Turkey's Western alignment by sending a Turkish brigade to Korea, 1950, joining Nato, 1951–2, and fostering economic, technical and military co-operation with the USA. He also embarked upon an ambitious programme of economic development, and adopted a permissive attitude towards religion (as opposed to Kemalist secularism) policies which earned him the trust of Turkey's peasant majority. He was, however, rejected by the intellectuals, and later the army, because of his allegedly irresponsible economic policy, his repression of the Opposition, and his deviation from Kemalist principles. He was ousted by an army coup in May 1960. M. was tried with other leaders of the Democratic Party and the government on Yassiada Island on charges of contravening the constitution, and corruption; he was sentenced to death and hanged.   (D.K.)

MIDDLE EAST. The area east of Europe and the Mediterranean, and south of Russia and Central Asia. The term has come into use mainly since World War II ("ME Forces"; "ME Command"; "ME Supply Centre"). Previously, the term Near East was more usual—meaning primarily the western parts of the ME, *i.e.* Anatolia and the eastern coast of the Mediterranean (the "Levant"▷), sometimes including Greece and the Balkans (not now covered by the term ME), and sometimes the whole Ottoman Empire▷. Some try to distinguish between such a

Near East and the ME—which would then mean mainly Iraq, Iran and the Persian Gulf area; but such a distinction is not usual. No precise definition of the term ME has ever been generally accepted. Turkey, Israel, the Arab countries of Asia, Egypt and Iran are included by all; Cyprus, Sudan and Libya by many (including this Encyclopaedia); Afghanistan, even Pakistan to the east, and Ethiopia and Somalia to the south, by some (not this Encyclopaedia). Because of the ambiguity of the term and its European orientation, some prefer "Western Asia"—thus Indian official usage; but this would exclude Egypt and the rest of north-east Africa.

Racially, most of the peoples of the ME belong to mixed Mediterranean sub-groups of the white, Caucasian or Europiform race, except for southern Sudan, which is populated by Negroes; negroid admixtures are decreasingly noticeable northwards, in Sudan, Egypt and the Levant. (Other attempts at racial classification speak of Armenoid and "orientalid" elements.) Small groups in northern Sudan and southern Egypt belong to Erythriot groups (Nubians▷; Beja▷).

Ethnically and linguistically, most of the ME countries are Arab (Semitic by language), though some pre-Arab and non-Arab minorities▷ survive in the Arab areas. The north-eastern and eastern parts are Iranian (Persian), linguistically Aryan or Indo-European; Kurds▷ and Armenians▷ are nations of their own, while their languages belong to the Iranian family. The north and northwest are Turkish, Cyprus—part Greek, part Turkish. Israel is the home of the Jewish nation, whose language is Hebrew. Nilotic and Hamitic languages survive among the tribes of Sudan.

Religiously, most of the inhabitants of the ME practise Islam▷ in its various forms. Most ME countries have considerable Christian▷ communities of various denominations; they form the majority in Cyprus and about half the population in Lebanon. In Israel the majority is Jewish. Various non-Islamic communities, other than Jewish or Christian, or heterodox groups on the fringes of Islam, add to the ME's diversity and pluralism (see minorities▷).

The whole ME was united in one political framework only once in history—in the Persian empire of the sixth to fourth centuries BC and in the reign of Alexander the Great which briefly followed it; even then the Arabian peninsula and southern Egypt and Sudan were not included. The Arab-Islamic Empire of the seventh and eigth centuries CE embraced most of the ME but left out Anatolia; it soon broke up. The Ottoman▷ Empire, 16th century to 1918, ruled large parts of the ME, but never included Iran.

No modern political movement aimed at establishing the ME as such as an entity—the Pan-Islamic▷ one aspired to a much larger area (and had no clearly defined political aims); the Pan-Arab▷ one, anyway not politically effective, addressed itself to the ME's Arab parts only; as has the Arab League▷, since 1945. The great powers of the West, particularly the USA and Britain, often toyed with the idea of establishing a ME Pact; but their plans affected only parts of the region, and in any case never came to fruition (see ME Defence Treaty▷; Baghdad Pact▷). The UN and its specialized agencies, such as the WHO (World Health Organization), also sometimes planned or attempted to establish regional institutions for the ME. These attempts were, however, blunted by the refusal of the Arab states to co-operate in a regional entity with Israel; Turkey always preferred to be aligned with Europe rather than the ME.   (Y.S.)

MIDDLE EAST DEFENCE ORGANIZATION, TREATY. With the emergence of the Arab states into full independence after World War II, and the withdrawal of the Western powers from military bases and positions of privilege, Western policy planners suggested a multilateral defence pact, or command, for the ME states. Such a defence arrangement, linked to and guided by the West, was clearly directed against military and political penetration into the region by the USSR, and efforts were accelerated with the intensification of the Cold War. It was also hoped that such a multilateral treaty would solve bilateral problems that had proven insoluble (e.g. the future of British military bases and privileges in Egypt and Iraq).

Britain and the USA were the most active in the search for such a MEDO, while France and Turkey associated themselves with their efforts. In Oct. 1951 Britain, the USA, France and Turkey presented Egypt with a plan for a MEDO, also known as the Supreme Allied Command for the ME (SACME), and invited Egypt to join as an original signatory. Other states in the region were kept informed, on the understanding they could later enter the arrangement. Egypt rejected the concept outright both in its original form and as amended in Nov. 1951. Other ME states were not receptive and negotiations were suspended. With the American Secretary of State, John Foster Dulles▷, as the prime mover, overtures were renewed in 1955 (see Northern Tier▷) and led to the conclusion of the Baghdad Pact▷, which included only one Arab state, Iraq. Iraq's withdrawal from this pact in 1959 underscored its failure as a MEDT. The Pact had greatly antagonized Egypt and her allies and, far from creating a concerted MEDO, had split the ME and generated much anti-Western feeling. It also failed completely to prevent the political and military penetration of the ME by the USSR. The Arab League▷, confining itself to the Arab states in the region and not the entire ME, has always given special attention to the military and strategic aspects of its charter. In 1950 the League established an "Arab Collective Security Pact" (Treaty of Joint Defence and Economic Co-operation); but it did not develop into an effective Defence Treaty.   (Y. S.)

MIDFA'I, AL-JAMIL (1890–1958). Iraqi politician. Born in Mosul. Graduate of the Istanbul Engineering School. M. served in the Ottoman Army during the Balkan wars (1912–13) and in World War I. A member of Arab-nationalist societies, he deserted in 1916 and joined Sharif Hussein's▷ Arab Revolt▷. In 1918–19 he acted as military adviser to Feisal▷, then ruling in Damascus. Returning to Iraq in 1920, M. participated in anti-British riots, and had to flee to Transjordan, where he remained until 1923. After his return to Iraq, he served as governor of several provinces. M. belonged to the Hashemite-loyal, pro-British camp headed by Nuri Sa'id▷ (though not to the latter's faction). He thus became one of the group of politicians among whom ministerial office and the premiership usually rotated. He was Minister of the Interior 1930–3, Prime Minister 1933–4, 1935, 1937–8, 1941. During Rashid Ali's▷ coup, he fled with the Regent and Nuri Sa'id to Transjordan and Palestine, returning after the restoration of the regime. In 1944–5 M. was President of the Senate, in 1948 Minister of the Interior. He again became Prime Minister in 1953, and was President of the Senate, 1955–8.   (B.G.)

*MILITARY, FOREIGN BASES—see Bases, Foreign Military▷.

MILITARY COUPS, JUNTAS—see Army Officers in Politics▷.

MILITARY FORCES—see Armed Forces▷.

MILLET, MILLET SYSTEM. The Turkish term "M.", derived from the Arabic *Milla*, meant any one of the religious communities within the Ottoman Empire. The MS was the organization of the non-Muslim population into religious communities. It established their rights and obligations under their ecclesiastical leaders. Following Islamic and ME practice, the Ottomans granted the Christian and Jewish religious communities wide autonomy in matters of personal status, community affairs, legal

procedure and education, and gave their heads jurisdiction over their members. These leaders were responsible for the maintenance of order within their communities, and the payment of the *jizya*, the poll tax, and other taxes required of non-Muslims. Until the 19th century there were three M.s: the Greek Orthodox▷, the Armenian▷ Gregorian, and the Jewish. Subsequently, separate M. status was given to various other denominations and sects, so that by 1914 the number of Ms. had risen to 14. The MS by its very nature helped preserve religious divisions, and as those sometimes coincided with ethnic divisions (e.g. the Armenians or in the Balkans), it promoted the rise of nationalism among the non-Muslims of the Empire, and also encouraged foreign intervention on their behalf. Consequently, in the 19th century the Ottoman government sought, for the sake of the independence and integrity of the Empire, to undermine the system. One method was introduction of M. "constitutions" in the 1860s, seeking to increase lay participation in the affairs of the community. Owing to foreign pressure, and the M.s' insistence on self-preservation, the MS was maintained until after the final dissolution of the Empire, when the new Turkish constitution established the principle of national unity and equality. The rights of minorities featured, however, as a major issue in the Lausanne▷ Peace Conference (1923) and the Western Powers secured an undertaking by the Turkish government to uphold some of the traditional religious, judicial and educational rights of the non-Muslims, which were to be guaranteed by the League of Nations. These rights were voluntarily renounced by the Jewish, Armenian and Greek communities in 1925–6 following the steps taken by the Turkish government to secularize the state.
(D.K.)

MILNER, ALFRED, LORD (VISCOUNT) (1854–1925). British administrator and politician. Served in various imperial posts, including Egypt (1889–92). As Secretary for the Colonies, he headed a mission to Egypt in 1920 to examine the cause of the crisis of 1919 and suggest a solution. He negotiated with representatives of the Egyptian government and—in Europe—of the nationalists led by Sa'd Zaghlul▷. His recommendations were presented late in 1920 and made public in Feb. 1921 ("The M. Report"); they provided a basis for British policy for many years. M. recommended the replacement of the British Protectorate by a treaty between an independent Egypt and Britain, by which Britain would guarantee Egypt's defence and would, in exchange, be granted a special status and rights, especially that of maintaining an army and bases in Egypt.

The British government was also to have the authority to protect foreigners and minorities and their interests; Egyptian foreign policy would be co-ordinated with that of Britain. M.'s recommendations were rejected by both the Egyptian government and Zaghlul and the nationalists; but they constituted the basis of Britain's unilateral declaration of Egypt's independence in Feb. 1922.   (S. L.)

MINORITIES. In the ME, for many centuries, the primary social framework of loyalty and allegiance was the communal-religious group. In the present century, this has been largely replaced by nationalism; but communal-religious entities, quasi-national in many cases, still play a very important role. Since all the ME nations are racially mixed, "race" cannot constitute a mark of identity—except in Sudan, which is divided between negroes and Arab Muslim non-negroes. Because of the mixture of nations, national-ethnic classifications cannot be fixed objectively, but depend largely on subjective national group-consciousness and primarily on linguistic identities. "M" may be classified as all those groups that differ from the majority of the nation or state in their ethnic-linguistic or religious character.

The majority is ethnic-linguistically Turkish and religiously Sunni Muslim in Turkey; Iranian (Persian) and Shi'i Muslim in Iran; Greek and Christian (Greek Orthodox) in Cyprus; linguistically Hebrew and ethnically and religiously Jewish in Israel (in the case of the Jews, the ethnic and religious aspects coincide, *i.e.* the Jewish nation and the Jewish religious group are identical). In the Arab countries, the ruling majorities are linguistically Arab and religiously Sunni Muslim—with the exception of Lebanon, where no single community constitutes a majority and all Christian groups together form about one half. The Sunni Muslim predominance is also qualified in the following countries. In Iraq, the majority is Arab Shi'i Muslim; yet the ruling group is the Sunni Muslim minority, while the (majority) Shi'ites display many of the characteristics of a minority. Yemen is almost equally divided between Arab Sunni Muslims of the *Shafe'i*▷ school and Shi'i Muslims of the Zeidi▷ branch, with a slight majority for the latter; in the days of the Kingdom the Zeidis were the ruling group, while the situation in the Republic, since 1962, is not yet clear. In Muscat-and-Oman the majority and ruling community is Arab and Ibadi▷ Muslim, while in Sa'udi Arabia and Qatar the ruling majority is Arab Sunni Muslim but of the Wahhabi school. Islam is the state religion in Iran and all Arab countries except Lebanon; the revolutionary leftist or socialist orientation of some Arab governments has resulted in little change in that

respect. (See Islam▷ for some qualifications). There is no state religion in Turkey—which numbers secularism, "laicism", among the basic principles of her political philosophy—or in Israel.

The M. of the region can be classified schematically into those differing from the ruling majority both ethnically and religiously, those differing ethnically only, and those differing only in their religion. In this Encyclopaedia, each group is treated separately under its own heading and that of its country of domicile; a schematic list follows:

DIFFERING BOTH ETHNIC-LINGUISTICALLY AND RELI-GIOUSLY. Armenians in Turkey, Iran, the Fertile Crescent countries and Egypt; Greeks in Turkey and Egypt; Turks in Cyprus, and those Turks and Tur-comans in Iran who are Sunni Muslims; Negro-Africans in southern Sudan; Arabs and Druzes in Israel; Italians in Libya; Kurds (Sunni Muslims) in Iran; Kurdish-speaking Yazidis and Shabak in Iraq; Persians in Iraq (if Shi'i Islam is considered a minority religion there); a few non-Muslim Indians in South Arabia and the Persian Gulf area; Jews outside Israel who, though speaking the language of their country of domicile, undoubtedly form a distinct ethnic entity. Border-line cases consist of a few ancient communities, mostly Christian, whose distinctive tongue has gradually fallen out of use and survives only partially, or as a liturgic cult language: Nestorian Assyrians and Syrian Jacobites in Iraq and Syria, Maronites in Lebanon, and Sabaeans-Mandaeans in Iraq—all with Syriac-Aramaic as their ancient tongue —and Egypt's Copts, preserving remnants of ancient Egyptian.

DIFFERING RELIGIOUSLY ONLY. The Christian com-munities of the ME (the degree to which they still regard themselves as separate, quasi-national entities or else as part of the majority nation, varies—with the strongest consciousness of "national" distinction in the border-line groups mentioned above and the greatest solidarity with majority nationalism in the Greek Orthodox and Greek Catholic communities); Shi'i Muslims in those countries in which Sunni Islam is the official or majority school (for the special cases of Iraq and Yemen see above); the heretic com-munities on the fringes of Islam—*Isma'iliyya*, Druzes and 'Alawites in Syria and Lebanon; Zoroastrians in Iran.

DIFFERING ETHNIC-LINGUISTICALLY ONLY. Kurds in Iraq, Turkey and Syria; Turks and Turcomans in Iraq, Syria and Iran; Azerbaijanis and Qashqai tribes (speaking Turkish dialects) in Iran; Arabs in south-western Iran ("Arabistan") and the south-eastern border regions of Turkey, including the Alexandretta (Hatay) District; Baluchis in Iran; Muslim Indians and Pakistanis in southern Arabia and the Persian Gulf.

Minorities make up a considerable part of the population, and therefore pose a political problem, actual or potential, in the following ME countries: Lebanon—a country composed of minorities only; Cyprus (Turks—20%); Iran (linguistically non-Persian—25–30%); pre-June 1967 Israel (Arabs and Druzes—14–15%; if the areas occupied in 1967 are included, Arabs and Druzes would constitute 36–38%); Iraq (Arab Shi'i Muslims—53–55%; Arab Sunni Muslims—20–21%; Sunni-Muslim Kurds—13–15%); Syria (non-Arab in language—17–18%, non-Muslims and non-Sunni Muslims—31–32%); Yemen (Sunnites and Zeidi Shi'ites—c. 50% each); Bahrain (Sunnites and Shi'ites—50%each); Sudan (non-Arab non-Muslims—25–30%, constituting almost the total population of the three southern provinces).

All minorities wish to enjoy equal rights and yet preserve their distinctive character, whether ethnic-linguistic or religious-communal. In the past (under foreign rule) some of them were given a degree of local autonomy—such as the Syrian Druzes▷ and 'Alawites▷ under the French Mandate (when the French were accused of using Druze and 'Alawite separatism against Syrian aspirations towards unity and freedom).

Some struggled for a greater measure of autonomy, and failed—as in the case of the Assyrians▷ in Iraq. Armenian efforts to establish, after decades of persecution and dispersion, and independent Armenia in Eastern Anatolia failed, 1917–21. Azerbaijan in Iran had in the 1940s an autonomous regime under Soviet protection, but since its liquidation, 1946, there have been no reports of any autonomist movement there. The Kurds▷, particularly in Iraq, rebelled for may decades—and it is too early to judge whether the agreement reported in Mar. 1970 will be satisfactorily implemented and solve their problem.

Some minorities no doubt hope that their distinctive character will be preserved under the rule of the national majority-state—a hope that is unlikely to be realized in the long run, in view of modern nationalism's centralistic, totalitarian, equalizing tendencies. Few minority groups pursue an active and continuous struggle for national independence or autonomy

Country	Differing ethnically and religiously	Differing religiously only	Differing ethnically only
Turkey	Armenians, Greeks, Jews	Turkish Christians	Kurds, Arabs
Iran	Armenians, Jews, Kurds, Arabs (if Sunni), Turcomans (if Sunni)	Persian Christians, Zoroastrians	Shi'i-Muslims Turcomans, Azerbaijanis, Qashqai, Baluchis (if Shi'i) Arabs (if Shi'i)
Cyprus	Turks	non-Greek–Orthodox Christians	
Israel	Arabs (Muslim and Christian), Druzes		
Iraq	Armenians, Jews, Iranian[1] Sabaeans[2], Yazidis, Shabak Assyrians[2]	Shi'i Arabs[1], Assyrians[2] and other Christian Sabaeans[2]	Kurds[1], Turks, Tucomans[1]
Syria	Armenians, Jews	Assyrians[2] and other Christians, Isma'iliyya, 'Alawites, Druzes	Kurds
Egypt	Armenians, Greeks, Jews	Copts[2] and other Christians	
Arabia and Persian Gulf	non-Muslim Indians	Shi'i Muslims	Muslim Indians, Pakistanis, Somalis
Sudan	Negroes, southern tribes	Arab Christians	Remnants of ancient peoples (Beja, Nubians, Nuba)
Libya	Jews, Italians		Berbers

[1] Iraq is treated here as if Arab Sunni Muslims were the majority, as they are the dominant group, though in fact Arab Shi'i Muslims are the majority.

[2] Ancient linquistic-ethnic distinctions surviving as remnants and partially only; these—and some others, too—are borderline cases. Lebanon is not included in this table, as all its communities are minorities.

—and fewer still can have any real hope of achieving such an aim. A few possible exceptions are the Turks in Cyprus, the Kurds—particularly in Iraq, and the African tribes of southern Sudan.   (Y. S.)

MIRGHANI, MIRGHANIYYA. An Islamic religious order in Sudan, named after its founder, Muhammad 'Uthman al-Mirghani (1793–1853). Called also *Khatmiyya*. A rival to the *Mahdiyya*▷ order—though both stand for a revival and purification of orthodox Islam. Unlike the *Mahdiyya*, which advocated the overthrow of the existing regimes, the M. recommended co-operating with them. Leadership of the order has been held exclusively by the descendants of the founder. The leaders during this century were al-Sayyid 'Ali al-M. (1870–1968), and his son 'Uthman.

The M.-*Khatmiyya* order usually supported the pro-Egyptian party (*Al-Ashiqqa*'), from 1952 the "National Unionist Party"; from 1956 they backed the "People's Democratic Party", and since 1967, the "Democratic Union Party" issuing from the merger of the two latter groups. The order was considered more friendly than the rival *Mahdiyya* towards the revolutionary regime which came to power in the coup of May 1969.   (B. G.)

MISSION, MISSIONARY. M., *i.e.*, propagation of the faith among unbelievers, has always been regarded by the Christian Church as one of its main tasks. M. activity in the ME by both Catholics and Protestants has been directed mainly at proselytizing members among the Eastern Christian churches, no less than among Muslims and Jews. M. work among Muslims and Jews has met with very little success.

Catholic religious orders have been engaged in M. activity in the ME since the Crusades. In the 17th century the establishment of a special Vatican Congregation for the Propagation of the Faith helped to increase the efficiency of Catholic proselytizing. In the 19th century, the increasing weakness of the Ottoman Empire gave M. work greater opportunities for development; Catholic monastic orders and congregations established hundreds of educational and charitable institutions all over the ME.

Protestant and Anglican Ms. also began proselytizing during this period. The first missionaries of the American Board of Commissioners for Foreign Ms. landed on the shores of Syria in 1819, the Presbyterians to work in Syria and Lebanon, and the Congregationalists in Armenia. German and Swiss Lutherans became active mainly in Palestine and Lebanon. The Anglican Church worked in Palestine, Iran, Egypt, Sudan and Libya, *via* two agencies: the Society for Promoting Christianity among the Jews and the Church Missionary Society. Later on, Ms. were established in the ME by such denominations as the Baptists, Pentecostals and Mormons.

As a result of this activity, the membership in local Protestant and Anglican Churches—practically non-existent before—grew to 250–300,000. In 1927, the Near East Christian Council was founded, as a meeting ground for the Evangelical M. Societies. In 1958 the Council underwent a structural change, becoming a regional component of the World Council of Churches.

Prominent M.-established educational institutions are the University of St. Joseph of Beirut, founded in 1875 by the Jesuits; the Coptic Catholic Seminary of Ma'adi in Egypt, also founded by the Jesuits; a Syro-Chaldean Seminary of Mosul, founded by the Dominicans; the Greek Catholic Seminary of St. Anne, established by the White Fathers in Jerusalem (transferred to Lebanon in 1967). The most important educational institutions established by Protestant Ms. are the American universities of Beirut (1866, university since 1920) and Cairo (1919), and Robert College, Istanbul (1865). The Protestant-established institutions of the YMCA also became important social-educational centres.

The various religious orders and congregations have also founded numerous hospitals and clinics, which greatly contributed to the development of public health in the region.

Islamic M. activity was directed only outside the area of the ME (e.g. Africa); Islamic institutions in the ME, such as the al-Azhar▷ University in Cairo, served as its centre. Judaism does not engage in M. activity.   (Sh. C.)

MIZRAHI—see National Religious Party▷.

MOHIEDDIN (MUHYI-UL-DIN), ZAKARIYA. Egyptian army officer and politician. Born 1918 in a village in Dakhaliyya region, he graduated from the Officers' Academy in 1938 (together with 'Abd-ul-Nasser▷). He was close to the "Free Officers" and joined them on the eve of their coup of July 1952. M. held important posts in the Revolutionary Government. He was Minister of the Interior 1953–62, one of the heads of the Secret Service, and responsible for internal security. From 1961 he was also Vice-President. M. was Prime Minister in 1965–6, and again Vice-President in 1966–7. When Nasser resigned on 9 June 1967, after the Six Day War▷, he appointed M. President in his place, but both resignation and appointment were withdrawn following mass demonstrations. In 1968, M. was removed from the government.

M. is close to, and popular with, US and West European financial and government circles and on occasion acted as Nasser's go-between with them. On the eve of the Six Day War, he was about to leave for the USA to discuss the crisis with President Johnson; the war foiled this plan. M. has tried to moderate the regime's socialism. Confronted by Egypt's increasing financial difficulties in the 1960s, he recommended a slow-down of the pace of development, the shelving of grandiose industrial schemes, the consolidation of industries already established and the further development of agriculture. On the strength of these views M. was appointed Prime Minister in 1965, but he had to resign in 1966, after supporting recommendations of the International Monetary Fund that Egypt should cut her budgets so as to improve her financial position.

On the death of Nasser in Sept. 1970, M. was considered a possible candidate for the presidency. His candidacy enjoyed the support of the right-wing and the West. According to unconfirmed reports he struggled to win power, but failed. In the crisis of May 1971, he reportedly lent his support to President Sadat▷; but he himself has not been reinstated in any official position. (S.L.)

MONOPHYSITES. The M. doctrine is adhered to by the Orthodox churches of the Ethiopians▷, the Armenians▷, the Copts▷, and the Syrian Jacobites▷. There are approximately 20m. M.: 12m. Ethiopians, 4m. Armenians, 3m. Copts and 700,000 Jacobites.

The M. churches originated from a schism at the Council of Chalcedon, 451, concerning the nature of Christ. M. doctrine maintains that there is only one (*monos*) nature (*physis*)—divine—in the person of the Incarnate Christ, while the Orthodox believe that Christ has a double nature, divine and human. The rift was as much political as theological, rooted in the traditional hostility of the provinces of Egypt and Syria to Byzantium. Many unsuccessful attempts were made to reconcile the M. to Orthodoxy. In later centuries, parts of the four M. churches seceded to form parallel churches in union with Rome (see Uniate▷). (Sh.C.)

MONTREUX CONVENTION. a. Agreement concerning the Straits of the Bosphorus▷ and the Dardanelles▷ signed on 20 July 1936 by Britain, France, the USSR, Bulgaria, Greece, Rumania, Yugoslavia, Australia, Japan and Turkey. The MC, still in force, replaced the one appended to the Treaty of Lausanne▷. The MC—signed as a result of Turkish pressure and the rising threat of Fascism in Europe, which brought the Western powers closer to Turkey

and the USSR—abolished the International Straits Commission and gave Turkey the right to remilitarize the Straits. Merchant vessels were allowed free passage, but Turkey reserved the right to ban passage of enemy ships when at war. Warships of non-riparian powers were allowed to pass through the Straits to the Black Sea in times of peace, provided that their aggregate tonnage did not exceed 30,000 tons and that they did not stay longer than 21 days. In time of wars in which Turkey was not involved, passage was to be granted to non-belligerents only. But if Turkey became a belligerent or considered herself threatened with war, the passage of foreign warships was left to her discretion (see Bosphorus▷).

b. Another MC was concluded on 8 May 1937 between Egypt and the twelve powers that had enjoyed the special privileges of the capitulations▷ (particularly extra-territorial jurisdiction over their citizens, which led to extensive economic advantages). In return for an Egyptian undertaking that laws applied to foreigners would be consistent with the principles of modern legislation and would not discriminate against foreigners or foreign companies, the capitulations were abolished. During a twelve-year transition period, mixed courts were to adjudicate cases of "mixed interest" and criminal cases affecting foreigners, while consular courts were to continue handling matters of personal status affecting their own nationals. These mixed courts functioned satisfactorily; their powers were assumed by Egypt's national courts when the transitional period ended in June 1949. (D.K.-Y.S.)

***MOROCCO.** M. (in Arabic: *al-Maghreb*) is herself not within the scope of this Encyclopaedia. Her part in ME affairs was initially passive: the Arab states supported the struggle of M.'s nationalists for the liquidation of the French Protectorate and full independence. A number of Moroccan nationalist leaders spent years of exile in Arab countries, especially in Cairo, and established there the centres of their movements and organizations. The Arab states raised the problem of M. in the UN General Assembly in 1951–2, despite France's vehement protest. The debate held and the resolutions adopted had no real, immediate influence, but they helped pave the way toward France's withdrawal and M.'s full independence in 1956.

In 1958, M. joined the Arab League▷. M.'s relations with the Arab countries were not always good. The problem of Mauritania▷ caused difficulties; the Arab countries had for a time reservations as to the separate independence granted to Mauritania, but they did not fully accept M.'s claim to all of Mauritania as part of M. (Tunisia even supported

Mauritanian independence, and in 1960 M. severed relations with her and only restored them in 1964.) A serious border dispute erupted between M. and Algeria in 1963 and led to serious military encounters; it exacerbated the problem: no Arab state identified itself with M. while Egypt secretely supported Algeria and even sent her, so M. claimed, military aid. Consequently, M. broke off relations with Egypt (renewed at the beginning of 1964); she also refused to raise the dispute for discussion, let alone arbitration, in the Arab League, a body which, M. claimed, was controlled by Egypt and therefore biased in Algeria's favour (the problem was discussed instead in the Organization for African Unity, which took steps towards conciliation and a gradual lessening of the tension).

The M.-Algeria crisis, and other international developments, sobered M. and made her wary of the radical-leftist camp in the Arab world and Africa. Formerly she had adopted a radical foreign policy, in strange contradiction to the very conservative character of her internal regime and social patterns. M. had been propelled towards this "leftist" position a. by her support of the Algerian rebels, 1954–62; b. by the problem of Mauritania; and c. by her involvement in the Congo crisis. In 1961, the conservative M. monarch was the host and one of the initiators of the Casablanca Conference▷ of the radical left-wing states in Africa, and M. became a member of the bloc established there (M.-Egypt-Ghana-Guinea-Mali-Algeria). After the failure of the Casablanca bloc, and following M.'s disappointment over, and isolation in, her dispute with Algeria, she abandoned her radical-leftist external policy. However, she did not adopt an overt pro-Western stand. While M. maintained good relations with the USA (American bases were evacuated and officially handed over to M. in the early 1960s, but a certain degree of co-operation was maintained, her official policy was neutralist and she took part in international neutralist conferences (see Neutralism▷). In inter-Arab affairs, too, M. usually takes a neutral line, though her own character and regime tended to bring her closer to the conservative camp (Jordan, Sa'udi Arabia, Lebanon).

M. supports the unification of the *Maghreb*▷ and the gradual establishment of joint institutions and co-ordinating bodies, especially in the economic sphere, but does not promote this trend with much zeal or extremism. As to Israel, M. follows the hostile line common to the Arab states but her stand is not extreme. M. sympathizes with Pan-Islamic▷ activities; after the fire at the al-Aqsa Mosque in Jerusalem (Aug. 1969), M. convened an Islamic summit conference in her capital, Rabat.   (Y. S.)

MORRISON-GRADY PLAN. Proposals for solving the Palestine question, drafted in 1946 by Herbert M., a British politician and member of the Labour Government, and Henry P. G., an American diplomat, and special representative of President Truman. The proposals were based on the recommendations of the Anglo-American Committee of Enquiry and included the partition of Palestine into semi-independent Jewish and Arab cantons under British Mandatory rule. Since the MGP was vague about Jewish immigration and the solution of the Jewish refugee problem in Europe, it was not accepted by the Jews; the Arab leadership also rejected it. See Palestine▷.   (Y.S.)

MOSLEM—see Muslim▷.

MOSSADDEQ, DR. MUHAMMAD (1881–1967). Iranian lawyer and politician. Prime Minister 1951–3. Educated at the École des Sciences Politiques, Paris, and Neuchâtel University, Switzerland. Member of the *Majlis* (Parliament) 1915–17, 1926–8, 1944–53. Governor-General of Fars 1920–1; Minister of Justice Jan.-Oct. 1921; Governor-General of Azerbaijan 1922–3; Foreign Minister June-Oct. 1924. Owing to his strained relations with Reza Shah▷, M. retired from political life in the 1920s. He was under arrest in the late 1930s and was later restricted, until Reza Shah's abdication in 1941, to his country estate. He then resumed political activities and was elected to the *Majlis* in 1944. That same year he introduced a bill barring any minister from negotiating the grant of oil concessions to foreign parties without the approval of the *Majlis*. In 1950, M. was elected chairman of the oil commission of the *Majlis*, in which capacity he was a very strong advocate of oil nationalization. He created a "National Front" which was joined, after he assumed the premiership, by many factions and formed a majority in the *Majlis*. M. became Prime Minister in Apr. 1951, after the assassination of his predecessor, Gen. Razmara▷, and amid great tension, holding office until Aug. 1953. He nationalized the Anglo-Iranian Oil Company's installations—causing a grave political crisis and bringing Iran to the brink of bankruptcy. M. also clashed severely with the Shah. He was dismissed after a military coup in Aug. 1953, was tried and sentenced to three years' imprisonment. After his release, he retired to his country estate.
                                                        (B. G.)

MOSUL. Third largest city of Iraq and capital of the province of that name. M. is situated on the Tigris opposite ancient Nineveh; centre of an important oil-bearing area and of transit trade with

Turkey and northern Syria. Pop.: 343,000 (1968); majority Arab Sunni Muslims, with considerable minorities of Sunni-Muslim Kurds and various Christian sects.

M. and its area were intended by the Sykes-Picot▷ Agreement of 1916 to become part of a French zone of influence. However, in Dec. 1918 Premier Clemenceau acceded to Prime Minister Lloyd George's request to transfer the area to the British zone, in exchange for British concessions on the Rhine and a share for France in the reorganized Turkish Petroleum Company. Turkey, however, refused to forgo her claim to M., arguing that the population was preponderantly "Muslim-Ottoman" (*i.e.*, non-Arab) and that it had not been in British hands when the armistice of Mudros▷ was signed on 30 Oct. 1918. The dispute had not been solved when the peace treaty of Lausanne▷ was signed between the Allies and Turkey, in 1923. It was handed to the League of Nations▷ for arbitration which decided, in 1925–6, in favour of Iraq (then under a British Mandate). Iraq had to agree to an extention of British tutelage. Turkey was given, as compensation, a 10% share for 25 years, in Iraq's oil revenue.   (U.D.)

MOUNT SCOPUS. A ridge (828 m., 2,717 ft.), north-east of Jerusalem, connecting to the south with the Mount of Olives. The site of the Hebrew University (inaugurated in 1925), including the National Library and the Hadassah Hospital. In the Arab-Israel War of 1948▷ it was often attacked. A convoy carrying physicians, nurses, and academic staff was ambushed on 13 Apr. 1948, and 68 people were killed. Yet MS held out, separated from the rest of Jewish Jerusalem. The Israel-Jordan Armistice Agreement of Rhodes (1949) provided for MS to remain in Israeli hands as a demilitarized zone, and its academic and medical institutions to operate. A small garrison of Israeli police was supposed to be changed every fortnight, crossing through Jordanian-held territory, under UN supervision. However, the Jordanians permitted neither the hospital nor the cultural institutions to function, and refused to set up the agreed joint special committee to work out detailed arrangements. There was much friction and the Israeli police post on MS was often attacked. The change of garrisons was also a frequent cause of trouble; as was the passage through MS of the Arab villagers of 'Isawiya, included in the demilitarized zone. In the Six Day War▷, MS was occupied by Israeli forces and incorporated in the reunited municipality of Jerusalem (to which Israel Law was applied). In 1968 reconstruction of the University campus began, and since 1969–70 its use for lectures, etc. has been resumed.   (Y.K.-E.L.-Y.S.)

MUDROS. Principal port of the Island of Lemnos, in the north-eastern Aegean, where, on 30 Oct. 1918, World War I hostilities between the Ottoman Empire and the Allied powers were terminated by an Armistice. Its terms included opening the Straits of the Bosphorus▷ and Dardanelles▷ to the Allies and the occupation of their forts; the demobilization of the Ottoman Army except for troops required to defend the borders and preserve order; and the right granted to the Allies "to occupy any strategic points" in any situation threatening their security. The Allies used these terms as a pretext to occupy Istanbul and parts of Anatolia later the same year (after the Armistice).   (D.K.)

MUFTI. Muslim religious official who issues rulings (*Fatwa*), in general in response to questions. In most Islamic countries the M. is government-appointed. A M. has a highly respected status and great spiritual and social influence, but plays no executive or political role. An exception to this was the M. of Jerusalem, Hajj Amin al-Husseini▷ (appointed 1921, dismissed 1937), who exploited his position to consolidate his political leadership (see Palestine Arabs▷).   (Y.S.)

MUHAMMAD REZA SHAH (b. 1919 in Teheran). King or Emperor (Shah) of Iran. Educated in Switzerland and at Teheran Military Academy. Ascended the throne in Sept. 1941, upon the abdication of his father, Reza Shah▷. Unlike the latter, whose refusal to co-operate with the Allies resulted in Britain and the USSR occupying Iran, 1941, MR permitted the Allies to use Iranian territory as a supply route to the USSR. MR was divorced twice (from Princess Fawzia, the sister of King Farouq▷, of Egypt, and Soraya Esfandiari, neither of whom produced a male heir), and in 1959 he married Farah Diba, who, in 1960, bore him a son, Crown Prince Reza. In 1950–1 MR began the distribution to farmers of over 2,000 villages of the Crown estates; but he had to shelve his plans for agrarian reform, owing to the opposition of the landowners ("the thousand families"). The Shah left Iran in Aug. 1953 after Premier Mossaddeq▷, refused to obey an order dismissing him, but returned a few days later after Mossaddeq was ousted by Gen. Zahedi▷. MR has since been able to consolidate his position. From 1959 he enforced a far-reaching land reform, which was further extended in 1962. In 1963 he put his social and economic reforms (known as "the White Revolution") to a plebiscite and won an overwhelming majority. Politically, he keeps tight control of the government and—with the aid of a large conservative majority—parliament and exerts a strong personal influence.

Internationally, MR has strengthened Iran's ties with the West. In 1946 he appealed to the UN and the West for help in getting the Soviet occupation forces out of Iran. In 1955 he brought Iran into the Baghdad Pact▷ (later CENTO▷). However, since the mid-1960s the Shah, while maintaining his pro-Western orientation, has followed a more balanced policy between East and West and led Iran to a spectacular *rapprochement* with the USSR. He is the author of two books: "Mission For My Country" and "The White Revolution". (B.G.)

MUHYI-UL-DIN, ZAKARIYA—see Mohieddin▷, Zakariya.

MUKHTAR, AL-, 'UMAR (OMAR) (*c.* 1862–1931). A leader of the Libyan resistance against the Italians. Born in Cyrenaica▷ and educated in Sanussi▷ *Zawiyyas* (lodges). M. took part in the war against the Italians in 1911–12 and in resistance activities afterwards. In 1922, he followed Sayyid Idris al-Sanussi▷ into exile in Cairo, but returned to Cyrenaica in 1923 and spent the next eight years leading a guerilla war against the Italians. He was captured in Sept. 1931 and hanged in public. He became a symbol of Libya's struggle for independence, and was commemorated by the 'OM Society, established by young Libyans after World War II to struggle for independence. (B.G.)

MUSCAT (MASQAT)-AND-'OMAN (since 1970 officially called 'Oman). Sultanate at the southeastern tip of the Arab peninsula, on the coast of the Gulf of 'O. and the Arabian Sea. The country comprises three regions: a. Ras ul-Jabal (or Ru'us al-Jabal), the tip of the 'O. peninsula which blocks the entrance to the Persian Gulf▷ at the Strait of Hormuz; this part is separated from the rest of M.-and-'O. by the principalities of Trucial 'O.▷; b. 'O. herself; c. Dhofar▷ in the south-west, bordering on South Yemen in the west. The borders are undemarcated especially in the inland region, the Rub' al-Khali (Empty Quarter) Desert.

The area (without Dhofar) is estimated at 82,000 sq. mi. and the population at 750–900,000. The population is concentrated along the coast of the Gulf of 'O.; some 40,000 inhabit the Dhofar region—mostly Bedouin tribes; and some agricultural settlements are scattered on the slopes of Jabal Akhdar, a mountainous range which rises to a height of 9,938 ft. and receives summer rains. Most of the inhabitants belong to the Islamic Ibadi▷ sect, and *Ibadiyya* Islam is the state religion. The *lingua franca* is Arabic, but the Dhofari dialect—South-Semitic—is sometimes defined as non-Arabic. Tribal and political

differences between the inhabitants of the coast—fishermen, traders, boat-builders and pearl-divers—and the agricultural mountain-dwellers and nomadic tribes, led to civil war in the 1950s (see below).

M.-and-'O. also ruled the tiny peninsula of Gwadar (270 sq. mi.) on the Pakistan coast across the Gulf of 'O. but in 1958 sold it to Pakistan. She also holds the Kuria Muria Islands and the island of Masira, where the British constructed an airfield. The sultans of M.-and-'O. in the past also controlled areas in Eastern Africa, especially the island of Zanzibar; the latter was separated from M.-and-'O. in 1856 under a branch of the ruling family. Dhofar was annexed in 1877, but it was to witness many insurrections.

M.-and-'O. was the first country in the Persian Gulf area to sign a protectorate treaty with Britain—in 1798; the first British governor settled in M. in 1800. The treaty was amended several times, but Britons (mostly by contract rather than seconded from the British government) have headed the army and directed much government activity. Since the 1950s, Britain has presented M.-and-'O. as an independent state. It is not clear whether, at the end of 1971, the British protectorate will end entirely, as with the Persian Gulf principalities, but M.-and-'O.'s independence will undoubtedly be reaffirmed. M.-and-'O. (officially now 'O.) has applied for membership in the UN and the Arab League▷.

M.-and-O.'s economy was extremely backward until 1968. Marine activity diminished because it could not compete with modern economic conditions. There were no roads, there was not even an airfield. Urban development was minimal. The capital, M., has a population of only 6,000, and the largest town, the near-by port of Matrah, only 14,000. Sultan Sa'id ben Taimur deliberately obstructed all progress. His harsh policy also prevented the development of elementary health and educational services.

Oil concessions were granted in 1937. and passed through several hands. In 1964, "Shell" discovered oil in commercial quantities, but the development of transport facilities took several years, as the oil fields lie inland across the mountain range. In 1967, a pipeline was completed to an oil port constructed at Sa'ih al-Malih, north-west of the town of M. Production reached 2.8m. ton in 1967, and 16.5m. ton in 1970. Accelerated modern development of 'O. is now to be expected.

Since the late 1960s, both British advisers and the British government (sharply criticized for its semi-colonial protectorate in M.-and-'O.) began to press for reform and modernization. When Sultan Sa'id ben Taimur continued to resist, they encouraged a *coup d'état* by his son, Qabus, in July 1970. The new Sultan, who had been held under house arrest in the palace for many years, promised modernization, a reformed administration and the beginnings of representative institutions. He appointed his uncle, who had been exiled for his modernizing tendencies and opposition to the Sultan, as Prime Minister. 'O. has no intention of joining the planned Federation of the Trucial and Persian Gulf Principalities. 'O. applied in 1971 for admission to the UN and the Arab League. Both requests are kept pending.

'O. has been disturbed for years by two separate rebellions. Among the inland tribes of 'O. an Imam▷ arose, head of the Ibadi sect, and claiming not only spiritual and religious authority (which the Sultan is willing to concede), but autonomy or even political independence for 'O. proper (as apart from the other parts of M.-and-'O.) under his leadership. The demand is based on an agreement signed in 1920 in Sib; the Sultan does not recognize its validity and claims that, even if valid, it grants only limited local autonomy. The Imam Ghaleb b. 'Ali, who holds this position since 1953, attempted to achieve independence through armed revolt and was supported by several tribes. He was defeated by the Sultan's army in 1955 and 1957, with the help of British forces. The Imam (who lives in exile, usually in Egypt or Iraq) claims that his guerilla forces continue the fight; this is denied by the Sultan and his government.

Since the Imam's rebellion was opposed by an establishment aided and guided by the British, the Arab states supported the Imam and presented his revolt as a national and anti-colonial struggle (Sa'udi Arabia does not advance this leftist-revolutionary argument, but she joined the political campaign against the Sultan and the British and aided the Imam for geopolitical reasons and interests of her own). Since the late 1950s, the Arab states have tried to involve the United Nations in the problem, with the support of the anti-colonialist Afro-Asian forces. The UN even sent a Swedish diplomat to investigate the problem (1963) and also set up a sub-committee (1964-5). No conclusion was reached on the Imam's claims, the counter-claims of the Sultan, and the guerilla war the Sultan was denying. The sub-committee found, though, that the problem was "international" and invited the UN De-colonization Committee to examine it. The latter and, in its wake, the General Assembly every year since 1965 have appealed to Britain to withdraw her forces from M.-and-'O. and grant her full independence. Britain and the sultanate deny the right of the UN to interfere a. in the matter of the uprising, which is an internal problem, and b. in the relations between independent 'O. and Britain, as long as neither of the two has asked for UN intervention.

Another revolt erupted in Dhofar, in 1966. A "Front for the Liberation of Dhofar" was set up there, which later changed its name to "Popular Front for the Liberation of the Occupied Arab Gulf". The "Front" aims apparently at the overthrow of the government not only in M.-and-'O. (and perhaps the secession of a revolutionary Dhofar), but in all the principalities of the Persian Gulf. It attempted to assassinate the Sultan in Apr. 1966, and clashes and raids are reported from time to time; but the "Front" has so far not succeeded in initiating large-scale revolutionary action, or making its impact on events in the Gulf region. It is, however, associated with leftist Iraq, with Nasserist▷ and *Ba'thist*▷ circles, and with the Palestinian-Arab guerilla organizations, and receives aid and training from South Yemen▷ (behind which stands Communist China). There are reports of another "Liberation Front" in the 'O. area. The conservative elements in the Gulf region (Iran, Sa'udi Arabia) are becoming increasingly concerned, and seem willing to work together against the threat from the left. The new, modernistic regime of Sultan Qabus b. Sa'id is also denounced both by the Imam and the "Liberation Front".   (Y.K.-Y.S.)

✶MUSLIM BROTHERHOOD. An ultra-conservative religious and political association founded in Egypt in 1929 by Hassan al-Banna▷, "Supreme Guide"—a title taken from the vocabulary of the Dervish orders and the Muslim mystics (Sufis), along with many of the Brotherhood's organizational and missionary techniques. The aim of the association is to impose the laws of Islam upon the social, political and constitutional life of the Muslim nations. Its conception of Islam is basically fundamentalist, though it also displays certain conservative reformist tendencies. The MB's Pan-Islamic▷ aspirations are mixed with Pan-Arabism▷ and strong xenophobic and anti-Jewish sentiments.

The MB's strength in the 1940s was variously estimated at anything between 100,000 and 1m. members. It also maintained a para-military youth organization. It has generally taken a position of extreme opposition to all Egyptian governments and political parties. On the single occasion that Hassan al-Banna stood for election to the Egyptian parliament, in 1945, he was defeated.

The MB's power and influence was extra-parliamentary and manifested through demonstrations and agitation in the streets. It was held responsible for the wave of political assassinations that engulfed Egypt in 1945-8. The association recruited volunteers in 1948 to join the Arab irregulars fighting the Jews in Palestine; they saw action in southern Palestine.

The MB was banned in Egypt in Dec. 1948 by Prime Minister M. F. Nuqrashi▷. In retaliation, Nuqrashi was assassinated. Measures against the MB were tightened and al-Banna was himself murdered in Feb. 1949. The movement then went underground. It was permitted to resume activity in Egypt during the spring of 1951 on condition that it would not engage in political activity nor maintain any military organization, limiting its functions to spiritual, social and cultural matters.

Under the leadership of Sheikh Hassan Isma'il al-Hudeibi (the new "Supreme Guide"), the movement failed to regain its previous strength and influence. When the new revolutionary regime of the "Free Officers" banned all political parties in 1953, the MB insisted that it was not a political party, and was therefore exempt from the decree. It was divided on the issue of whether to support the new regime. The regime, however, suspected the MB of subversion and banned it in Jan. 1954. The struggle for power in 1954 between Gen. Nagib▷ and Col. Nasser▷ was fostered, in part, by Nagib's attempt to soften the regime's attitude towards the MB which reportedly supported Nagib. When Nasser won, further measures were taken to suppress the association. An attempt to assassinate Nasser (Oct. 1954) was ascribed to the MB. The government took stronger action and thousands were arrested. Hudeibi and six other top leaders were sentenced to death, after a show trial, in Dec. 1954; six were executed, while Hudeibi's sentence was commuted to life-imprisonment.

But the MB—now reportedly without a "Supreme Guide" and under "collective leadership"—was apparently not completely broken. The regime has continued to denounce its plots and hold it responsible for various political difficulties. In the 1960s thousands were again arrested and new trials held. (Hudeibi, released in 1966, was rearrested and sentenced to a prison term; he died the same year in prison.) Student unrest in the latter part of 1968 was also ascribed to the MB.

Attempts to create branches of the MB in other Arab countries were only partially successful. Beginning in 1945, religio-political clubs bearing its name were established in Palestine and some Arab states. Many were short-lived and those surviving (e.g., in Jordan—also under the name "Liberation Party") attained little influence. Their association with the Egyptian movement was also rather loose. Apart from Egypt, the only country where the MB exerted some political influence was Syria (appearing under various names: Islamic Front, Islamic Liberation Party, etc.).   (Y.S.)

MUSLIM COUNCIL, SUPREME. Council charged with the administration of Muslim community affairs in Palestine during the British Mandatory regime. It was formed in 1922 by decree of the Mandatory Government (through indirect elections by a restricted group of electors in accordance with the pre-war Ottoman Election Law). Hajj Amin al-Husseini▷, the Mufti of Jerusalem, was elected president. The SMC soon became a tool in the hands of its chairman and was exploited for the political purposes of his extremist faction. This caused the Palestine Arabs to split into two political factions—"Council-Supporters" (al-Majlisiyin), headed by the Husseini family, vs. "The Opposition" (al-Mu'aridin) headed by the Nashashibi▷ family. The SMC was dissolved and its members dismissed by the Mandatory administration on 1 Oct. 1937, after they were accused of involvement in the nationalist Arab rebellion in 1936-7. From then on and until the end of the Mandate in 1948, the SMC ceased to be a political body and its members were government appointees or officials.   (Y.S.)

MUSLIMS—see Islam▷.

MUTAWALIS (Arabic, plural: *Matawila*, singular: *Mutawali*), (Shi'i Muslims of the *Ithna-'Ashariyya Shi'a*▷, in Lebanon are called M. They are concentrated in southern Lebanon (the Jabal 'Amel▷ region and the towns of Tyre and to a lesser extent Sidon) and also in the northern part of al-Biqa' (Coele Syria▷), the Baalbek region. The areas inhabited by the M. were not part of the semi-autonomous *Sanjak* of Lebanon during the Ottoman period, but were added to it on 1 Sept. 1920, when the French established "Greater Lebanon". At first, the M. were not sympathetic toward the French Mandate or to their incorporation in Lebanon. However, in 1926 they changed their stand, after the administration recognized them as a separate religious community (a recognition denied them by the Ottoman Sunni▷-Muslim administration).

Most M. are farmers and villagers. The traditional ME social structure has in their region been better preserved than in any other part of Lebanon. Land is mostly owned by large landowners who wield economic and political control over their dependants. The clan and extended family continue as units of social organization.

The M. are the third largest community in Lebanon, constituting 18.2% of her population, according to the 1932 census. The office of President of Parliament is traditionally given to a member of the M. community. In southern Lebanon, the M. constitute 58% of the population, and in the Biqa' province—31% (in the Baalbek district of that province—67.5%, in the Harmal district—60.2%).

(Y. P.)

N

NABLUS. Town in Samaria, Palestine, in the part occupied in 1948 by Jordan and called the West Bank▷. Pop.: 44,000 (1967) (together with refugee camps and suburbs: 65,000). Administered by Israel since the Six Day War. The heir of biblical Shekhem, N. (the name is a corruption of Greek Neapolis) lies in a narrow valley between Mount Ebal in the north and Mount Gerizim (the holy place of the Samaritans▷) in the south. Situated in the midst of the main olive-growing area of Palestine, it has developed some small industry: olive oil, soap, matches, conserves, carpentry. During the British Mandate it was a centre of Arab nationalism; under the Hashemite Kingdom of Jordan, of Palestinian unrest and opposition.   (Y.K.)

✻**NABULSI, AL-, SULEIMAN** (b. 1910). Jordanian politician. Born in al-Salt. Educated at the American University of Beirut. Employed by the Agricultural Bank of Transjordan, he later served as its Director until 1946. N. was Minister of Finance and Economy 1946–7 and 1950–1, and Ambassador to London 1953–4. N. was one of the founders of the "National Socialist Party", 1954, and became its main leader — while it grew into a leftist, pro-Egyptian, anti-West, and anti-Hashemite force. The NSP won the elections of 1956, and N. became Prime Minister and Foreign Minister, Oct. 1956–Apr. 1957. He was dismissed by King Hussein▷ after his government had led Jordan into an alliance with Egypt and Syria, terminated the Anglo-Jordanian Treaty, and decided to establish diplomatic relations with the USSR (an act then still considered a bold move to the left). N. has not held office since. Nor has he been a Member of Parliament, but instead he heads an extra-parliamentary leftist, pro-Egyptian opposition. He supports the Palestinian-Arab guerilla organizations and advocates an extremist attitude towards Israel.   (B.G.)

✻**NAGIB, MUHAMMAD, GENERAL** (b. 1901). Egyptian army officer and politician. President of Egypt 1953–4. Born in Khartoum (Sudan), the son of an Egyptian army officer N. graduated from Cairo University (law) and the military academy, 1921. He joined the regular army and was promoted colonel 1948, general 1950. He was wounded as a brigade commander in the Arab-Israel War of 1948. He became commander of the frontier force and,

in 1951, of the army. In military circles, N. was admired for his integrity. He demanded army reforms and the elimination of corruption.

Though not a member of the "Free Officers" group, N. was in contact with them through his operations officer, 'Abd-ul-Hakim 'Amer▷. He was their candidate in 1952 for the presidency of the "Officers Club". His election contributed to tension between the officers and the King and his supporters. According to the later official version, N. did not take an active part in the July 1952 coup, but was asked by the young revolutionaries formally to represent them as a sort of figurehead, while Nasser▷ was the leader. (N. himself claims that he joined the "Free Officers" in 1949 and was their real leader in 1952.) After the coup, N. was appointed Commander-in-Chief of the Armed Forces. When the civilian government formed after the coup resigned in Sept. 1952, N. was appointed Prime Minister and Minister of War. On the proclamation of the Republic in June 1953, N. was nominated President and Prime Minister but released from his military posts. In Feb. 1954, N. resigned all his posts; he returned as President later in Feb. 1954 and as Prime Minister in Mar. In Apr. 1954, N. was relieved of the premiership, and retained only the presidency. In Nov. he was dismissed from this honorary post, too, and placed under house arrest.

The erosion of N.'s position, from June 1953 until his final dismissal, and the vicissitudes of Feb.-Apr. 1954, were due to a rupture between him and Gamal 'Abd-ul-Nasser. N. felt that the high office he held should carry real authority and a decisive share in formulating policies. Nasser, however, regarded him only as a figurehead. There were also fundamental differences of opinion. N. thought, contrary to Nasser, that the army should return to barracks, and parliamentary rule be restored, a view supported by right-wing circles (such as the "Muslim Brotherhood"▷), the *Wafd*▷, and the left. These differences of opinion came to a head in Feb. 1954 when it was decided, without N.'s knowledge, to ban the activities of the "Muslim Brotherhood". N. resigned in protest, but Khaled Mohieddin (member of the "Free Officers" Council and a left-winger) forced his return to power after a show of strength by several army units. However, at the end of Mar. Nasser engineered counter-demonstrations of workers and army units and won the upper hand; his views won out and he deposed N. (in two stages, as described above). N.'s followers in the army and his civilian supporters were removed, or their activities curtailed. His dismissal from the post of President came some days after the campaign against the "Muslim Brotherhood" had begun (they were accused of an attempt on Nasser's life, and it was hinted that N. was involved in their plot).

In 1955, N. published his memoirs, "Egypt's Destiny". N. is thought of as a father-figure and a moderate, and many ascribe the moderate and reasonable appearance of the officers' regime in its first two-three years to his views and influence. (S.L.)

NAHHAS, MUSTAFA (1879–1965). Egyptian politician. A leader of the nationalists and one of the founders of the *Wafd*▷ party, N. was elected head of the party on the death of Sa'd Zaghlul▷, in 1927. In 1928 and 1930 he was, for short periods, Prime Minister. In May 1936, his party won the elections and N. formed a new *Wafd* government. In Aug. of the same year, he headed the delegation which negotiated and signed the Anglo-Egyptian Treaty giving Egypt nominal full independence in exchange for a defence pact and certain privileges for Britain (see Egypt▷, political history). In 1937, King Farouq▷ dismissed N. and the *Wafd* went into opposition. In Feb. 1942, the British forced the King to restore N. to power, because they thought that only a *Wafd* government would be capable of full co-operation with them in the war effort. In 1943–4, N. initiated and chaired the discussions towards the establishment of the Arab League▷; he headed the preparatory conference in Alexandria, Oct. 1944. The day after the conference, he was dismissed by Farouq (the British had by then ceased to intervene in Egypt's internal affairs).

The *Wafd* party won the Jan. 1950 elections and N., once again, formed a government. In Oct. 1951, he abrogated the treaty with Britain and proclaimed the incorporation of Sudan under the Egyptian crown. He also rejected a Western invitation that Egypt co-sponsor a ME Defence Pact. He started a violent popular struggle to eject the British troops from Egypt, and, in Jan. 1952, in the serious crisis which followed, his government fell. His regime had also been accused of corruption.

During the purges after the "Free Officers'" coup in 1952, N. did not face trial, but the *Wafd* party was compelled to dismiss him from its leadership; his wife was tried for corruption. In 1954, he was deprived of his civil and political rights; they were restored to him in 1960, but he did not return to political life. (O.G.)

NAJD. Central region of Sa'udi Arabia, about half Sa'udia's area (400,000 sq. mi.). Pop.: *c.* 2m. (estimate), more than half of them Bedouin. N. is a region of desert plateaus and vast expanses of sand; here the Bedouin way of life has reached its full development, and the strongest Bedouin tribes have

been centred. Some permanent settlements are located in oases which follow a line of topographical depressions with subterranean water: Riyadh▷ (the capital of Sa'udi Arabia), Laila, Shaqra, 'Anaiza, Buraida and Ha'il. Caravans used to pass through N. from the coast of the Persian Gulf and Iraq to Mecca▷ and Medina▷ and the Red Sea coast; today, a road and railway link Riyadh to the oil centres on the Persian Gulf, a road—to Mecca and Jidda on the Red Sea.

N. was a region of dispute between the great tribes, especially the House of Rashid▷ of the Shammar tribe, whose stronghold was in Ha'il, and the House of Sa'ud▷ of the 'Anaza tribe, centred in Riyadh. The Rashids gained the upper hand in the 1880s and '90s but in 1902 'Abd-ul-'Aziz Ibn Sa'ud▷ succeeded in restoring his rule in Riyadh and subduing the rival tribes; he conquered the strongholds of the Rashidis in 1921 and ended their rule. In 1922, Ibn Sa'ud proclaimed himself "Sultan of N., al-Hasa, Qatif and Jubail and their dependencies"; in 1926, after the conquest of Hijaz▷, he took the title "King of Hijaz, N. and Dependencies", and in 1932 changed the name of his kingdom to "The Sa'udi Arabian Kingdom". (Y.K.)

NAJJADA, AL- (from an Arabic root indicating both help and bravery). Name of several paramilitary organizations or adult scout movements. The best known: a. A paramilitary organization founded in Lebanon in the 1930s, mainly as a reaction to the foundation of the Phalanges▷ *(al-Kata'eb)*. These organizations were not openly and explicitly communal; but just as the Phalanges were intended to protect the Christian community, especially the Maronites▷, and the Christian character of Lebanon, so the N. was founded for the protection of Lebanon's Muslims against Christian domination. The founder-leader of the organization was Muhyi-ul-Din al-Nassuli; during the 1950s and '60s its outstanding leader was 'Adnan al-Hakim. The N. now appears as a political organization or party; al-Hakim was elected several times to parliament. In the 1958 civil war, the N. constituted the main military force of the pro-Nasserist▷ rebels.

b. A paramilitary organization of the same name was founded by Palestinian Arabs in 1946, led by Muhammad Nimr al-Hawari; the N. was not under the control of the extremist "Husseini"▷ faction—which, therefore, established a rival military organization of its own named *al-Futuwwa*. Neither organization played an important military role in the 1947–8 War. (Y.S.)

NASHASHIBI. Palestinian-Arab family in Jerusalem, which became prominent during the last half century of Ottoman rule. At the beginning of the 20th century, 'Othman al-N. stood out as head of the family; he amassed great wealth and was elected a member of the Ottoman Parliament in 1912. After his death, his relative Ragheb al-N. was elected to the Turkish Parliament in 1914. He became head of the family and one of the chief leaders of the Palestinian Arabs (see below).

Other notable members of the last generation: Fakhri al-N., a political organizer and the family's "strong-man", one of the organizers of the "Defence Party", 1934, and also of trade unions. He organized guerilla bands during the disturbances of 1936; when the bands embarked, from 1937 onwards, mainly upon internal terror, he organized counter-bands, the so-called "Peace Gangs". He was assassinated in Baghdad in 1941.—Anwar N., a lawyer, was active in the Palestinian-Arab propaganda offices, 1945. He was a member of the Jordanian government, as Minister of Justice, Development, Public Works in 1956 and 1959-60. He was Jordanian Ambassador to Japan and Taiwan 1966-9 and to India, from 1969. —'Azmi N. was a government official under the Mandate and afterwards head of the Jordanian Jerusalem (Ramallah) Broadcasting Service, 1949; Minister of Transport 1955; Jordanian Ambassador in Japan and Taiwan 1958-9.—Muhammad Is'af N. was a well-known author.—Nasser-ul-Din N. is a journalist of note, living mostly in Egypt.

In the 1920s and '30s and, to a lesser and decreasing extent, in the 1940s, the name N., besides being that of a large and prominent family, symbolized the political group which the family headed: the group in opposition (Mu'aridin) to the Supreme Muslim Council▷ and its Husseini▷ nationalist leadership. The official policy of the N.s, who founded the "Defence Party" in 1934, was not very different from the official nationalist programmes of the other parties. However, in practice they were ready to co-operate with the British Mandatory regime, maintained close relations with Amir 'Abdullah▷, and were more moderate with regard to the Jews. In 1936, the N.s joined in organizing the "disturbances" in their early stage, but when these became terrorist in character and the guerilla bands launched a campaign of internal terror directed at the N.s, the opposition, they organized counter-bands, "Peace Gangs" (see above, Fakhri N.)

During the 1940s, the N. family and their political faction declined in influence and power and many of their members took public and political positions conflicting with the family tradition. In any case, the leading role of prominent families has diminished. The family and its political history are reflected in the life of Ragheb N.▷, below.   (Y.P.)

NASHASHIBI, AL-, RAGHEB (1875, or 1881,–1951). Palestinian-Arab politician. An engineer by profession and a graduate of Ottoman universities, N. was Jerusalem district engineer at the time of the Turks and, from 1914, represented Jerusalem in the Ottoman Parliament. He was a Turkish army officer in World War I. After the British occupation, he initiated the "Literary Club" (al-Muntada al-Adabi) in opposition to the "Arab Club" (al-Nadi al-'Arabi) dominated by the Husseini▷ family. Both clubs regarded Palestine as the southern part of Syria and envisaged her political future in the framework of a Greater Syria. When Mussa Kazem al-Husseini▷ was dismissed as Mayor of Jerusalem, N. was appointed to this post (1920–34). He co-operated with the British authorities and advised the Arabs to participate in self-government bodies which the British proposed and which the nationalist Arabs rejected. In Nov. 1923, his adherents formed the "National Party" (al-Hizb al-Watani) which displayed extremist slogans and to all appearances differed little from the Husseini nationalist faction. The party did not last long.

N. strongly opposed the Supreme Muslim Council▷ dominated by the rival Husseini family and its extremist faction, and succeeded in recruiting many Arab mayors as associates in his struggle. He won the Jerusalem municipal elections of 1927, and his supporters triumphed in all the towns, except for Gaza. But in 1934 N. was defeated in the Jerusalem elections. That same year, he organized the "National Defence Party". As head of this party, he became a member of the Arab Higher Committee▷ formed in 1936. He supported the general strike and the first stage of the 1936 "disturbances" but in 1937, when they deteriorated into internal terror, he resigned from the Arab Higher Committee and turned against the Husseinis. The conflict between the two factions in the years 1937–9 led to a blood bath, to Husseini-inspired terror and to counter-terror on the part of the N. militants.

In 1937, N. was inclined to accept the Partition proposals, but did not dare to say so publicly. He supported King 'Abdullah▷ and was one of his confidants. He was considered a moderate on the Arab-Jewish problem, though he gave no public expression to his dissent and moderation. During the 1940s, N. displayed no active independent policy and let many of his followers be won over by the Husseinis. In 1948, N. actively supported the Jordanian annexation of the West Bank▷ and was appointed as its first governor. In 1950, N. was Jordanian Minister of Agriculture and later of Transport. In Jan. 1951, he became Minister in charge of al-Haram-al-Sharif and Guardian of the Holy Places. He died the same year.   (Y. P.)

NASSER (full name: **'ABD-UL-NASSER, GAMAL**) (1918–1970). Egyptian officer and statesman. President of Egypt 1956–70. Born in Bani Mor, Assyut district, he completed his secondary studies in Cairo in 1936. After some law studies, he was admitted in 1937 to the military academy and graduated in 1938. In 1939 he was posted to Sudan, and in 1941 he was appointed instructor at the military academy. In 1948, after advanced training at the staff college, N. was sent with the invading forces to Palestine, commanding a battalion. He took part in battles in the Negba area and was besieged with his battalion in the Faluja pocket. He returned to Egypt only after the armistice agreement was signed in 1949. In 1951 he was promoted colonel and appointed lecturer in the military college.

Gamal 'Abd-ul-Nasser

During those years he was a participant in the "Free Officers" group, which prepared a military *coup d'état* against King Farouq's▷ regime, and carried it out on 22 July 1952. According to some, N. was the leader of the junta even then and Muhammad Nagib▷ was admitted to the plotters' group only at the last stage and headed it as a symbolic figurehead only. Within the junta now in power a confrontation between Nagib and N. soon began, partly on a personal basis, but mainly concerning the regime and the character of the government. Nagib wished rapidly to revert to a parliamentary system and permit the re-establishment of parties, etc. N. opposed these steps. In Jan. 1953 all political parties were banned and N. established the only legal political organization—"The National Liberation Organization"—and was appointed its Secretary-General. In May 1953 he was appointed Deputy Secretary-General of the Revolutionary Council, and in June, Deputy Prime Minister and Minister of the Interior.

In Feb. 1954 the struggle between N. and Nagib came to a head. N. became Prime Minister and tried to remove Nagib from the leadership; Nagib returned and N. was deposed; demonstrations and counter-demonstrations took place. The struggle ended in Apr. N. became Prime Minister and Nagib was relegated to a presidency stripped of all real power; in Nov. he was dismissed from this post too.

N. now took action against remnants of the traditional parties, as nuclei of potential opposition, and especially against the "Muslim Brotherhood"▷. In Oct. 1954 an attempt to assassinate N. was ascribed to the "Brotherhood", and they were severely suppressed and subjected to show trials. At the same time N.'s government turned to initiating the first reforms (an agrarian reform law had been enacted in 1952) with the distribution of agricultural land amongst landless families. In 1954 various development plans were begun in both industry and agriculture.

From about 1955–6 N. began to disseminate the ideas of "Arab Socialism".

In Jan. 1956 a new constitution was proclaimed, and in a June referendum N. was elected President for a six-year term. In Feb. 1958, with the proclamation of the Egyptian-Syrian union, he was elected president of the United Arab Republic▷. After the dissolution of the UAR (29 Sept. 1961) and the failure of attempts to establish a popular organization (since 1957 the "National Union" had replaced the "Liberation Organization"), N. convened in 1962 a congress of "popular forces", founded a new ruling party, which he called the "Arab Socialist Union", and formulated a "National Charter" as the basic doctrine (henceforth socialist) of both the party and the nation. A new "National Council", elected in Mar. 1964, ratified the nation's new constitution. In Mar. 1956 N. was elected President of Egypt for a second term of six years. In his internal policy N. tried to strike a balance between different trends and factions—animated by rivalries both personal and ideological—and political trends (see Egypt▷, Parties) and kept the decisive power in his own hands.

Besides the emphasis N. placed upon social reform and economic development (his major prestige-project was the "High Dam" at Aswan▷), and upon the doctrine of "Arab Socialism", he paid much attention to the enhancement of Egypt's inter-Arab and international status. His first appearance on the inter-Arab scene was an act of moderation: agreements conceding Sudan the right of self-determination (1952 and 1953)—a concession which all Egypt's former rulers had opposed. In his book "The Philosophy of the Revolution" (1954), N. described Egypt's position at the centre of three circles, Arab, Islamic and African. Even before the union with Syria in 1958 he endeavoured to extend Egypt's predominant influence over the Arab states — at first mainly through his struggle against the Baghdad Pact▷ (1955) which he denounced as an imperialistic conspiracy. Although Egypt already wielded decisive influence as the centre of the Arab League▷, she signed separate agreements and pacts with Sa'udi Arabia and Syria in Mar. 1956; with Sa'udi Arabia and Yemen in Apr. 1956; with Syria and with Jordan in Oct. 1956. It was not N. but the Syrians who initiated the union with Syria in 1958; but once he agreed to it he enforced Egyptian control over Syria. And in Nov. 1959 he signed a new agreement with Sudan regarding the division of the Nile's waters.

Syria's secession and the dissolution of the UAR in 1961 were a major blow to N.'s prestige and inter-Arab position. Then in Oct. 1962 he became involved, for a period of more than five years, in the military intervention in Yemen, which brought Egypt neither honour nor power, and disturbed the relations between it and Sa'udi Arabia in particular. Through-out those years Egypt was conducting subversive activities in various Arab countries; Iraq, Syria, Jordan, Lebanon, Algeria, Libya, Tunisia, Morocco — all complained and accused her of supporting plots and hatching conspiracies — and more than once N. was charged with personal responsibility, even for plots to assassinate Arab leaders. Similar activities were directed towards countries not yet independent (Aden and South Arabia, the Persian Gulf princi-palities, African countries).

This subversive activity levelled off since 1964, and Arab "summit conferences" were held, which restored much of N.'s prestige. In 1966–7, N. again bitterly took issue with those Arab leaders opposing his line; but in the frenzy of enthusiasm on the eve of the Six Day War▷ in 1967, they all joined his banner (for the defeat and N.'s resignation — see below). After the Six Day War N. adopted a moderate and conciliatory attitude toward the Arab states (Sa'udi Arabia, his old rival, and Kuwait paid vital subsidies to Egypt). He also made great efforts to strengthen Egypt's ties with Sudan and Libya (which resulted, after his death, in the proclamation of a federation between Egypt, Libya and Syria). He also acted as mediator in the crises in relations between the Palestinian guerillas and their host states Lebanon and Jordan. His last all-Arab meeting, on 27 Sept. 1970, one day before his death, yielded the "Cairo Agreement" designed to resolve the dispute between the guerillas and Jordan.

N.'s foreign policy began with the successful completion, in 1954, of negotiations with Britain on the total withdrawal of British troops and the abolition of the Treaty of 1936 and the special privileges it had accorded to Britain (a success partly based upon the agreement concerning Sudan which had preceded it). However, N.'s moderation, that had made Anglo-Egyptian agreement possible, did not last long. In 1954–5 he began to incline towards the "Third World" and became one of the leaders of the neutralist bloc; on the other hand, he drew closer to the Soviet Union and became in-creasingly dependent upon her.

The following are milestones in N.'s international appearances: in Feb. 1955 he met for the first time with Tito and Nehru; in April 1955 he visited India and participated, in Indonesia, in the Bandung▷ Conference of Asian leaders, emerging, for the first time, as a well-known international figure. In 1955 the arms deal with Czechoslovakia was con-cluded, marking the budding alliance with the Soviet Bloc. In July 1956, in the wake of N.'s disappointment at the West's refusal to aid in the Aswan▷ project, the Suez Canal▷ was nationalized; from the crisis that erupted — see Suez War▷ — N. emerged triumphant, as the leader of a new, developing nation, which imperialism had failed to enslave. In December 1957 an Afro-Asian solidarity conference was held in Cairo. In April and July 1958 N. paid his first visits to the Soviet Union. In 1961 he participated in the founding conference of the Casablanca▷ Bloc, and later in a neutralist summit conference in Belgrade. In May 1963 he took part in a summit conference of the Organization for African Unity in Addis Ababa, and, in July 1964, in its second conference in Cairo. In October 1964 the second conference of the non-aligned nations was held in Cairo, with N. participating.

There was a decline in his attendance at inter-national gatherings after 1964. On the other hand, he continued to participate as their moving spirit in the inter-Arab gatherings already mentioned, and to receive in Cairo an endless flow of Arab statesmen. Egypt's political and military ties with the USSR grew increasingly close, after 1967, and N. visited the USSR several times, mostly for "medical purposes" (1968, 1969, 1970), but undoubtedly also for political.

In his attitude toward the Arab-Israel conflict▷ N. has been regarded by some observers as moderate and aspiring to peaceful solution. In his speeches, too, he often referred to a peaceful solution, although never to real peace and co-existence with Israel. Despite this element of moderation, he spoke on innumerable occasions of the need to solve the Pales-tinian problem by military means, and in speeches meant for internal consumption generally emphasized this approach. His first direct contact with the Palestinian problem was as an officer of the Egyptian army invading Israel in May 1948. During his first years in office he did not stress the Palestinian problem as a major and central issue for Egypt. He began doing so from the mid-1950s (he stated that the Israeli reprisal raid against Gaza in Feb. 1955 was an important turning point). N. encouraged and tirelessly expressed the refusal of the Arab states to recognize Israel, negotiate or make peace with her. In his prosecution of the Arab struggle against Israel, N. ordered an economic boycott, the closure of the Suez Canal▷ to Israeli shipping and the blockade of the Tiran Straits▷, the encouragement, organization and financing of infiltration and sabotage in Israel—including sabotage against civilian targets (acts that served as a major cause of the Sinai Campaign▷ in 1956), and the suppression of the Jews of Egypt. The whole cycle was repeated in 1967. N. encouraged terrorist warfare, made inflammatory speeches, signed military pacts for the encirclement of Israel and, finally, blockaded the Tiran Straits. To crown it all, he demanded the withdrawal of the UN forces (UNEF▷) from Sinai and concentrated huge forces on the borders. The steps he took brought about the Six Day War▷. N. was *the* leader, who himself made all important political decisions. His personal responsibility for the steps taken cannot be doubted. His own speeches provide the record of responsibility. Many observers claimed after the Six Day War that N. had not wanted war but only a political victory (deterring Israel from reprisal raids against Syria; the blockade of the Tiran Straits). Maybe in the early stages of the crisis that was all he had wanted. Even then he should have known, as an experienced statesman, that the blockade of the Tiran Straits would constitute a *casus belli* for Israel. In any case, during May and the first days of June, Nasser was no doubt swept along in the excitement of his own speeches and by the frenzy of the masses that he had fanned himself. Certain of victory, he had decided to go to war.

The defeat in the June War was the low point in N.'s political career; on 9 June 1967 he resigned, publicly taking responsibility for the debacle. Some think that his resignation was a calculated performance, designed to provide a public demand for his return. The stormy demonstrations which "forced" N. to withdraw his resignation, turned even this day of defeat into a personal victory. N. had become the leader of his people to the extent that the masses were easily convinced that without him the state could not exist; leading officers, led by his close friend 'Abd-ul-Hakim 'Amer▷, who did not think so and tried to oust him and overthrow the regime, were removed.

N. persisted in his ambivalent stand on the conflict with Israel even after the 1967 War. He first "accepted" the cease-fire and then the Security Council resolution of 22 Nov. 1967. He thereby became the leader of the "doves" (in contrast to hawkish Algeria, Syria, Iraq and the Palestinian guerillas). On the other hand he completely ignored that part of the Security Council resolution calling for peace, and the fact that Israeli withdrawal was envisaged only in a context of a peace agreement. In numerous speeches he stated that he would not be satisfied with the "abolition of the results of the 1967 aggression" (*i.e.* Israel's withdrawal from the areas she had occupied), but that after the restoration of what was lost in 1967 the struggle would continue against Israel's very existence. It was he who formulated the "Three Nos" of Khartoum (No peace, no negotiations, no recognition of Israel). In a speech on 23 Nov. 1967 he said: "What was taken by force, will be returned by force". In speeches made in 1968 and 1969 he blueprinted the stages of the war: a war of defence; a preventive war of attrition and deterrence, of "active defence" (which had, he claimed, begun in spring 1969); and a war of liberation. In July 1970 N. accepted the American initiative which intended to reactivate the Jarring▷ talks and stressed that these talks were aimed at real and lasting peace. Yet he still spoke of a military solution, and he quickly violated the stand-still at the Suez Canal, which had been one of the conditions of the American initiative. As to N.'s long-term intentions *vis-a-vis* Israel, opinions differed; but most observers agreed that he did not sincerely aspire to peaceful coexistence with her. The final balance sheet of N.'s achievements as against his failures is for history to draw up. It will have to balance development schemes, reforms (begun but left uncompleted), a new pride instilled in the Egyptian people, on the one hand, against the creation of a police state, and the suppression of freedom of speech, of newspapers and organizations, on the other. It will have to account for the huge sums spent on the army instead of on development, industrialization, hospitals and schools, and for the military adventures and defeats in which Egypt was bogged down. Such contrasts will have to be noted as Egypt's hegemony in the Arab world and her attempts to undermine the regimes of sister state; the Arab-Israel conflict which he intensified and left unresolved. The liberation of Egypt from British rule will be counterpointed against her dependence on, and perhaps even enslavement to, the Soviet Union. Yet one thing is clear, No Egyptian-Arab figure in recent generations has made such a mark on the history of Egypt and the Arabs as Gamal 'Abd-ul-Nasser.   (Y.R.-Y.S.)

NASSERISM. The political and social attitude of Arabs in many countries who regard Gamal 'Abd-ul-Nasser▷ as the leader of all Arabs, and republican Egypt as the prototype of a nation progressing towards national freedom and social justice. N. is neither a well-defined ideology nor an organized movement; it is a general political-emotional outlook, which takes its inspiration from the personality, actions and utterances of the late Egyptian president. It was for some years the most popular force in the Arab world. It developed against the background of disillusionment with other ideologies and the poor performance of previous Arab leaders.

N. grew and flourished in the second half of the 1950s, when Nasser espoused an actively Pan-Arab nationalism, took a fierce stand against the West, nationalized the Suez Canal, triumphantly prevailed upon the USA and the USSR jointly to coerce Israel, Britain and France to withdraw from Egypt after the war of 1956, and, with the Egyptian-Syrian Union, 1958–61, was at the peak of his power and prestige. In the next decade, 1958–67, N. had become a sort of self-sustaining force, skilfully exploited for Egypt's interests by a first-rate propaganda machine. In spite of failures as in Syria in 1961 or the involvement in the Yemen War, 1962–7, Nasser's self-confidence became ever more secure, particularly as the weakness of his Arab rivals and the irresolution of his Western adversaries became increasingly evident. Even after the Arab defeat in the Six Day War▷ of 1967, which was to a great extent Nasser's responsibility and which led to his swift resignation, as speedily withdrawn, Arab public opinion and popular feeling seemed to remain loyal to his leadership as the only foundation on which to rebuild the nation's life in a deep political and emotional crisis. Yet there was some erosion of the spell of Nasser and N. Disillusionment became gradually stronger, and when, in the summer of 1970, Nasser accepted the American initiative towards a peaceful solution of the conflict with Israel, only part of Arab public opinion followed his lead.

N. had, since about 1961–2, acquired a more doctrinal appearance. To its nationalism, anti-Western neutralism and reformism, socialism was now added. However it is a populist-totalitarian version of state socialism, remote from Western social democracy. It would be difficult to define precisely the doctrinal difference between N. and the ideology of the Ba'th▷ group, though N. and Ba'thism were the chief rivals wooing the Arab left; the main differences seemed to concern power. N. was much more pragmatic, less doctrinaire.

N. had, even at its peak, no organized, unified instruments outside Egypt—no party, youth or militant organization openly describing itself as Nasserist. Small groups of Nasserists in Syria and Iraq, locked in combat with Ba'th factions, were split and powerless, and gradually diminished from the mid-1960s onwards, as the Ba'thists consolidated their power. However, the underground leftist-nationalist Pan-Arab *Harakat al-Qawmiyyin al-'Arab* (Arab Nationalist Movement▷) that grew in the mid-1950s, mainly among students and intellectuals, was to a large extent a concentration of younger Nasserist elements. Intimately linked with the Palestinian-Arab guerilla groups, and especially the "Popular Front for the Liberation of Palestine" (George Habash▷ was in the forefront of both), the ANM was in the later 1960s growing more and more extremist, and moving into the orbit of Maoist-Castroist ideas, so that by 1970 it could no longer be described as Nasserist. Though N. had remained a powerful general attitude, none of the Arab states outside Egypt was fully committed to its leadership, and no political group or organization expressed, and fought for, its tenets. (See also Socialism▷ and Arab Nationalism▷.)   (E.B.–Y.S.)

*NATIONAL LIBERATION FRONT FOR OCCUPIED SOUTH YEMEN (NLF). Nationalist underground organization in Aden▷ and South Arabia▷ (later South Yemen▷). Founded in 1963 under the leadership of Qahtan al-Sha'bi▷ and considered the strongest group in the nationalist rebellion which broke out in Oct. 1963 and continued intermittently until the achievement of independence in 1967. In 1966 the NLF joined a roof-organization, FLOSY▷, but seceded the same year. In a violent struggle between the two groups the NLF won out. In 1967 it gained control of the South Arabian principalities one after the other, until the British had to transfer authority to them (and not to the princes or to FLOSY). The NLF formed the ruling group, single party and government of the new People's Republic of South Yemen. Although at first sometimes supported by Egypt, the NLF was always associated with the extremist Arab Nationalist Movement▷ (*Harakat al-Qawmiyyin al-'Arab*) and influenced by Leninist-Maoist ideas. From 1967 it veered further to the left, amidst internal struggles and purges. Sha'bi was removed in 1969 and the leadership transferred to Muhammad 'Ali Haitham as Prime Minister and 'Abd-ul-Fattah Isma'il as Party Secretary. See South Yemen▷, Political history.
                                        (Y.S.)

NATIONAL RELIGIOUS PARTY (Hebrew initials: *Mafdal*). Established in 1955 by a merger of two religious Zionist parties: *Mizrahi* and *Hapo'el Hamizrahi*. *Mizrahi* was founded in 1902 in Vilna (then Lithuania) and in 1918 in Palestine, as "The Zionist NR Organization dedicated to Building the Land according to the Written and Oral Law". Its aim was to restore religious values and to establish obedience to the commandments in all walks of life. It initiated the establishment of the Chief Rabbinate for Israel which is still the highest authority on Jewish religious matters, including all those pertaining to personal status. *Hapo'el Hamizrahi* was founded in 1922 in Palestine as a labour union of religious workers with progressive social views, regarding labour as a value *per se* and as a means toward the implementation of national purposes. The party co-operates with the *Histadrut*▷ (General Federation of Labour) while maintaining its own labour union.

The NRP regards the *Torah* as Israel's fundamental constitution and aims to establish "a society based on its spiritual social-legal foundations", and legislation based on the "Laws of the *Torah*". In the Seventh *Knesset* (Parliament), 1969, the NRP won 12 out of 120 seats. The NRP has always participated in Israel's government coalition. It has often been in a position to tip the coalition scales, and has therefore obtained agreement to maintain the *status quo* on religious matters (Sabbath observance, exemption of religious girls from military service, personal status of Jews governed by religious law). The NRP believes in Jewish historical rights to the whole of Palestine and in Jewish settlement on the West Bank▷. Many of its members, possibly the majority, oppose the demand that Israel withdraw from the territories occupied in the Six Day War▷.   (E.L.)

*NATO—see North Atlantic Treaty Organization▷.

NEGEV (Hebrew: drylands, south). The southern half of Israel, stretching from the Mediterranean coast to the head of the Gulf of 'Aqaba▷ (Eilat▷). The climate is arid and hot.

The first eleven Jewish settlements in the N. were erected in 1946—in the space of one night because of anticipated opposition from the British Mandatory administration. About 70 more have been founded since 1948 with the aid of the National Water Carrier (see Israel; Jordan River; Water in the ME▷). The area of the erosion cirques in the south and east and the lowlands between them contain the main mineral resources of Israel: phosphates (production: 1 m. tons, 1967), natural gas, gypsum, glass sand and fireclay. The Dead Sea▷, 3,300 ft. below, contains large quantities of potassium (production: 1 m. tons, 1970–71), bromide and salt. The sandstone at Timna, in the southern N., contains copper ore, which is exploited and concentrated into copper cement (export: over 10,000 tons, 1969–70). The central part of the N. is completely barren, with no scope for agricultural settlement.

The eastern boundary of the N. is the depression of the Arava (Hebrew: steppe), stretching from the southern end of the Dead Sea to the Gulf of 'Aqaba (Eilat), a distance of 109 mi. Along its centre runs the boundary between Israel and Jordan. A small number of agricultural settlements has been set up since the late 1950s.

Because of its aridity the N. was unoccupied by permanent settlement throughout history, except for short periods between the 3rd century BCE and the 7th century CE, by the Nabbataeans. Up to 1946 only Bedouin (nomads and semi-nomads) roamed through the northern N.; they used also to sow some barley. Most of these Bedouin (about 27,000 in 1970) have adapted to a semi-settled way of life.

The main urban centre is Beersheba (pop.: 75,000, 1970)—a Bedouin townlet and market place with 4,000 inhabitants until 1947. Dimona (pop.: 22,000, 1970) founded in 1955, has textile industries and an atomic reactor nearby. Arad (a few thousand inhabitants), founded in 1961, will be based chiefly on a large chemical combine and on tourism.

From a geo-political point of view, the Arab states regard the N. as the land connection between Egypt and Jordan and the rest of the Arab ME. For Israel, it is an important source of raw materials, a potential area for agricultural settlement, and a vital link in her foreign trade, especially with the Persian Gulf, Africa, and the Far East; and it gives her a vital strategic and tactical depth.

In May 1948, Egypt invaded the N. in the course of her invasion of Palestine; but she was pushed back and Israeli control over the N. (allotted to Israel under the UN Partition plan of 1947) was established. Egypt's complaint in 1949/50 to the Mixed Armistice Commission, that Israel's possession of Eilat and the southern N. was illegal, was rejected. British plans,

Agave field in the Negev

in 1946–8, had not envisaged the N. as part of the future Jewish State. Britain seems to have advised the ruler of Jordan—secretly—that he should occupy the N. and that Britain would support him. The UN mediator, Count Bernadotte▷, also recommended that the N. be given to Jordan. Ideas and schemes for the renunciation of the southern N. by Israel, so that Egypt and Jordan could have a common border, continued to be mentioned or rumoured. They found, however, no response in Israel and were, in fact, wholly unrealistic. (Y.K.-E.L.)

NESTORIANS—see Assyrians▷.

NETUREI KARTA (Aramaic: Guardians of the City). A small group (centered in Jerusalem and in Brooklyn, New York) of extremely anti-Zionist ultra-orthodox Jews, who oppose the State of Israel and refuse to recognize its laws and to obey its authorities, their doctrine being that only God can bring about the redemption of the Jewish people, and therefore any human effort is heretical. Thus NK denounce also Zionist religious leaders, bodies or parties (Mizrahi▷, Agudat Israel▷, the Chief Rabbinate of Israel).

Regarding the Arab-Israel War of 1948 as a "godless" battle, NK appealed to the British Mandatory Government to remain in Palestine. They also attempted to contact the Arabs, to surrender to their rule. NK isolate themselves completely from the general community; they maintain their own law-court, boycott all local and national elections, and refuse to pay taxes to the Israeli government; their sons and daughters refuse military service, taking advantage of the general exemption granted to religious scholars. The Israeli government tolerates their activities—except when they disturb the public peace (e.g. by attempting forcibly to prevent Sabbath traffic). (M.S.)

NEUTRAL ZONE. In the course of negotiations over the northern frontiers of Najd▷ (later Sa'udi Arabia▷), there were large areas on the borders of Iraq and Kuwait the ownership of which remained in dispute. All the border areas were in effect the domain of nomadic Bedouin tribes, who ignored political boundaries and a centralized governmental control. A frontier agreement was signed in Dec. 1922 at a meeting in 'Uqair between Sultan (later King) Ibn Sa'ud▷ and the British High Commissioner for Iraq, Sir Percy Cox▷. The agreement included the setting up of two zones of "neutral and common ground", one on the Najd-Iraq frontier, the other on that of Najd and Kuwait. In the latter, oil was later discovered and exploitation

rights were given separately by Sa'udi Arabia and Kuwait to different companies; however, since no frontiers were delineated, the companies on both sides were compelled to co-operate. In 1964–5, Sa'udi Arabia and Kuwait agreed in principle to divide the NZ between them and negotiations over agreed demarcation of the frontier were concluded in 1969–70. (Y.S.)

NEUTRALISM. Neutrality in time of war is an accepted and well-based concept of international law. Several ME states have retained their neutrality in time of war—sometimes in practice as well as in theory (e.g., Turkey during World War II), and sometimes in theory only (while in practice one of the belligerents enjoyed the right to use bases and lines of communication—e.g., Egypt and Iraq during World War II). N. in time of peace, as distinct from neutrality in time of war, and embodying a doctrinal principle, was born after World War II. Several statesmen claimed to have fathered it. But the man who really gave the notion currency was Jawaharlal Nehru of India.

In general small states prefer not to get involved in the struggle of power blocs (especially when that struggle is waged between two blocs, each with its ideological character—capitalism vs. communism). Nehru added two dimensions to this assumption: first, he attributed moral value to the doctrine of N., asserting that it was not only politically useful, but morally good; secondly, he argued that N. is a particularly appropriate stance for the newly independent states of Asia and Africa. From this stem two features associated with N.: a. a critical attitude to those Afro-Asian states which supported, and were supported by, a power bloc and did not consider N. a sacred principle; b. an extreme anti-colonialism which became—sometimes only by implication—anti-Western. Thus, N. has not maintained an equal distance from the two power blocs: it has generally dissociated itself from the American-Western bloc more readily than from the Soviet.

Some prefer the term "non-alignment" to N. There are conflicting versions as to the coining of this concept, too; it has been attributed to Moshe Sharett. Attempts have been made at fine distinctions between the two terms, but they are generally considered synonymous.

The doctrine of N., or non-alignment, was quickly adopted from the 1950s on by leaders of many Asian and African countries. The President of Egypt, Gamal 'Abd-ul-Nasser▷, gave it currency in the ME, naming his version Positive N., i.e., an active N. not content with negative neutrality in relation to the powers but following paths and doctrines of its own.

N. became the official doctrine of the leftist revolutionary regimes in the Arab world: Egypt,
Syria, Algeria, Libya, Iraq, Sudan, Yemen and South
Yemen. The tendency of these regimes to move
closer to the Soviet bloc, their *de facto* alliance with
the USSR, has not prevented their verbal adherence
to N. and non-alignment.

There is no objective, generally accepted definition
of either the doctrine of N. or the identity and nature
of states adhering to it. Several countries have taken
part in conferences of non-aligned states despite the
fact that they are in formal treaty relations with one
of the Great Powers, have granted them military
facilities, or actually belong to a power bloc. Indeed,
the inviting and accreditation of such countries has
been vigorously debated at the conferences. Non-
aligned conferences—mostly taking the form of
"summit meetings" and usually preceded by consultations at the level of foreign ministers—were held
in Belgrade, Sept. 1961 (25 states participating);
Cairo, Oct. 1964 (46 participants, 11 observers);
Belgrade, July 1969 (preliminary conference, 44
participants, 7 observers); and Lusaka, Zambia,
Sept. 1970 (52 participants, 8 observers). The number
of countries invited was 60–70.

N. determines general principles only; it is for each
country to interpret them in the light of its own
historical and political circumstances, its understanding and interests. In their voting at the General
Assembly of the UN, various states of the "non-
aligned" bloc have often taken different or opposed
positions—e.g. in connection with Korea, the Congo,
Cameroon (this notwithstanding the fact that in
"colonial" issues, such as the last two, the bloc has a
common anti-Western point of departure). There
are neutralist countries which, in their scrupulous
N., do not maintain diplomatic relations with either
North or South Korea, North or South Vietnam;
others maintain relations with South Korea, South
Vietnam and West Germany (but not with their
communist counterparts); some neutralists (e.g.,
Egypt, Syria, Iraq, Sudan, South Yemen) maintain
relations with the communist halves of those divided
countries; and there are other variations and half-way
houses.

In reality, then, there is no unified bloc of neutralist
countries, and each country adopts its own posture.
In fact, within the neutralist camp there is a leftist
pro-Soviet bloc (Egypt, Iraq, Algeria, Syria, South
Yemen, Tanzania, Guinea, Zambia, Ceylon—some
of them even gravitating toward China); another
group (including India) which maintains a more intermediate position; and other neutralist countries which
tend to support the West. At congresses, the leftist-
extremists often succeed in imposing their views and
shaping the resolutions adopted. This applies, in
particular, to the imposition of pro-Arab views,
concerning the Arab-Israel conflict, on non-aligned
conferences, although many of the participating
countries maintain friendly relations with Israel.

No neutralist country takes a favourable view of
non-alignment or N. when its own interests are
concerned. India, for example, one of the leading
proponents of N., does not pardon even friendly
nations who adopt a neutralist position with regard
to her dispute with China or the problem of Kashmir.
In matters vital to her, she requires alignment with
her position.

In the world of practical politics, N. therefore does
not unite its supporters in a particular, common
posture. Nevertheless, it is a doctrine attracting and
keeping together some 60–70 countries. Even the
super-Powers, both of whom at its inception rejected
N. outright, since the second half of the 1950s have
tolerated it and shown themselves ready to render
economic, and sometimes even military, aid to
countries not aligned with them but professing,
at least in theory, a strict N. There are neutralist
states which, through careful manoeuvering, have
succeeded in obtaining simultaneous assistance from
both super-Powers.   (Y.S.)

＊NEW LEFT (Israel). Political movement founded in
1969 by dissenters from *Mapam* opposing the
"Alignment"▷, and dissenters from the Israel Communist Party opposing its support of the government's policy after the Six Day War (see Israel▷,
Parties).   (E.L.)

NILE. River in Africa—the longest in the world
(*c.* 4,160 mi.). Its two main sources, the White N.
and the Blue N., join and form the N. north of
Khartoum. The White N. rises in equatorial East
Africa. It flows from Lake Victoria, from a height of
3,937 ft., forming a series of rapids, through Lake
Kyoga and Lake Albert to the savannah plains of
Sudan. In the flat region, the waters spread and form
large swamp areas, the *Sudd*, where half the water
evaporates. The White N. supplies a major part of
the N. waters during the eight months when the
river is low. The Blue N. rises in the Ethiopian
plateaus at a height of 14,764 ft., and passes through
Lake Tana. Plentiful rainfall in this region
causes flooding from June to Oct. After the confluence of the White and Blue Ns., the N. encounters
one more important tributary from the east—the
Atbara. The average annual flow on the Sudan-Egypt
frontier reaches nearly 85,000 m. cubic metres (mcm),
25,000 mcm coming from the White N., 50,000 mcm
from the Blue N., and 10,000 mcm from the Atbara.

View of Cairo (the round building: Television Head-quarters)

After receiving the Atbara, the N. enters the desert and makes its way through a narrow valley. Rock barriers form five cataracts along this valley; near the northernmost one, the Aswan Dam▷ was built. North of Cairo, the river branches out into a large delta, formed by silt deposits, and then flows into the Mediterranean.

The period of high waters is vitally important for Sudan, and even more so for Egypt, whose agriculture and sustenance depend on irrigating her lands with the N. waters. Since the quantities of water available during the dry season are not sufficient, both countries have built a system of dams to control and store the water; this permitted, from the beginning of the twentieth century, a transition from basin irrigation by flooding during the high water season to irrigation throughout the year, and, as a result, the harvesting of two or three crops. The greatest and most complex dam is the High Dam of Aswan (completed 1970–1), which is intended to store 130,000 mcm of water. Other important works are the Delta Barrage (completed 1891) and the barrages of Asyut (1901), Isna (1908), Nag' Hamadi (1930), and the first Aswan Dam (1902)—all in Egypt, as well as the dams at Jabal Awliya on the White N. (1937) and at Sennar (1926) and Russairis (1966) on the Blue N.—in Sudan.

The division of the N. waters between Egypt and Sudan was one of the causes of the Anglo-Egyptian dispute. In 1920, Egypt objected to the allocation of water from the N. for the development and irrigation of the Gezira▷ region in the Sudan, for fear of loss of water and competition of Sudanese cotton. In 1925, Egypt also rejected the recommendations of a commission for the distribution of the N. waters during the various seasons, taking into account the interests of Egypt and Sudan. Despite Egyptian objections, the British implemented the recommendations of the committee. In May 1929, with the formation of the Muhammad Mahmud government, Egypt and Britain (for Sudan) signed an agreement on the use of the N. waters which approved additional quantities of water for Sudan in exchange for granting Egypt priority rights and the privilege to inspect Sudanese irrigation works. According to the 1929 agreement, Sudan received 4,000 mcm and Egypt 48,000 mcm.

The importance attached by Egypt to the control of the N. sources was one of the reasons for her demand for the "Unity of the Nile Valley" (*i.e.* the annexation of Sudan by Egypt) as part of her struggle with Britain. By ensuring her rule over Sudan, Egypt intended to prevent any injury to her lifeline. Only in Feb. 1953, following the Officers' Coup and during the rule of Muhammad Nagib▷, did Egypt officially renounce her demand for the "Unity of the Nile Valley" in its direct form, but she continued to strive for decisive influence in Sudan.

A re-distribution of the N. waters between Egypt and Sudan became necessary in the 1950s, as arrangements had to be determined in connection with the construction of the Aswan High Dam, but principally because Sudan was pressing for a more equitable share than that of 1929. Negotiations were held from Sept. 1954 to Nov. 1959, when a new agreement was signed for the allocation of water after the completion of the Aswan High Dam and for co-operation in exploiting the N. waters. Sudan's share was considerably increased, to 18,000 mcm, while 55,000 mcm were allocated to Egypt. The agreement assumed that new works would enable the use of larger quantities of water. Should the al-Sudd swamps be drained and developed, and evaporation (estimated at 18,000 mcm *p.a.*) prevented, Egypt and Sudan will share the extra water equally. (O.G.)

NILI. Jewish espionage organization, formed in Palestine 1915–17, in protest against Turkish mal-treatment of Palestinian Jews and in the hope that helping the British would oblige them to hand Palestine over to the Jews after victory. N. did not succeed in mustering widespread Jewish support. It remained controversial, and sometimes persecuted by the organized majority, especially because of the

fear of Turkish reprisals. Most of its leaders were captured and imprisoned or executed by the Turks. It broke up in May 1919 upon the accidental death of its last leader, the agronomist Aharon Aaronsohn.
(Sh.H.-E.L.)

*NLF—see National Liberation Front▷.

*NOMADS—see Bedouin▷.

NON-ALIGNMENT—see Neutralism▷.

*NORTH ATLANTIC TREATY ORGANIZA-TION, NATO. Established with the signing of the North Atlantic Treaty on 4 Apr. 1949 by ten European countries, the USA and Canada; later West Germany, Greece and Turkey also joined. NATO is involved in ME affairs a. in that it views the Mediterranean▷ as part of the area to be defended since it formally entrusted NATO under the treaty with the defence of most of its northern shores; NATO'S Naval Command for South Eastern Europe is at Izmir▷ in Turkey; b. in consequence of Turkey's membership (agreed upon in 1951, and effectuated in 1952); c. the undisturbed supply of ME oil to Europe and the European defence establishment is of vital interest to NATO.   (Y.S.)

*NORTHERN TIER. Term used by American policy-planners, headed by US Secretary of State John Foster Dulles▷, referring to Turkey and Iran, since these countries represented the northern-most strip of the ME, bordering on the Soviet Union. When Dulles and his aides despaired of creating an all-inclusive ME defence pact (in 1950-1, see ME Defence Treaty▷), mainly due to Egyptian opposition, they decided that at least on the NT, on the Soviet border, a defence wall should be set up to protect the ME from attack from the north; those countries interested might join the NT pact. It was this line of thought that led to the "Baghdad Pact"▷, 1955, based on the NT concept (Turkey, Iran and Pakistan). Iraq was the only Arab state which joined the Pact, and then only up to 1958-9.   (E.A.)

NUBA. Negroid tribes in western Sudan, mainly in Kordofan. Most of them are pagans, but there is a Muslim minority. Those of northern Kordofan are completely Arabicized, though maintaining their own tribal customs. Some N. groups in the south of Kordofan have taken the names of the Arab tribes they once served as slaves. The diversity of the N. languages has caused Arabic to become a *lingua franca* among them. They are believed to number about 600,000.   (B.G.)

NUBIA. The area between Upper Egypt and Sudan, from the Red Sea to the Libyan desert. Consists mainly of almost rainless, sandy desert and arid steppes and plateau bisected by the Nile. Divided politically between Egypt and Sudan. The Nubians (also called Barabira or Danaqila) form the major part of the population between Khartoum and Upper Egypt. They are descendants of an ancient people, with a strong admixture of Egyptian, Negro and Arab elements. They are Muslims. Their livelihood is derived mainly from agriculture. Many of them migrated to urban centres in Sudan and Egypt, where they are employed mostly as cooks, servants or watchmen. Beside their own African language, most of them also speak Arabic. Nubians are estimated to number 300–350,000. Most of those displaced by the Aswan▷ High Dam, and resettled, are Nubians.   (B.G.)

NUCLEAR ENERGY IN THE ME. Four research reactors are operating in the region. In Israel there is a 5MW(T) pool reactor using enriched uranium at the Soreq N. Research Center and a 26 MW(T) natural uranium reactor at the Negev N. Research Center. Egypt and Iraq each has a 2 MW(T) tank-type reactor. The Egyptian reactor at Inshass went critical in 1961 and the Iraqi one, near Baghdad, in 1968.

Plans for large-scale dual-purpose (power/desalination) reactors have been studied in Israel and Egypt at various times since 1967; none has been implemented as yet because of the high cost of the desalinated water expected with existing technology. Iraq, Israel and Egypt have active research and development programmes concerning reactors. In Israel reactor research is carried out both in the establishments mentioned of the Atomic Energy Commission and in the institutes of higher learning. In Iraq and Egypt such research is almost entirely the responsibility of the Atomic Energy Centres, although university staff play a large role, particularly in Egypt. Israel, Egypt, Iraq and Lebanon use disotope and radiation techniques extensively in agricultural and medical applications and Israel and Egypt also in industrial applications. Some of the isotopes used, especially very short-lived ones, are produced locally.

At present fissionable material is imported by all countries. Prospecting for workable ore deposits is proceeding in Iraq, Israel and Egypt. Traces of uranium have been found in phosphate deposits, and Egypt has investigated the use of its thorium deposits.

N. training in Iraq is provided by Baghdad University in cooperation with the AEC. In Israel nearly all the institutions of higher learning have nuclear programmes on their curricula. In Lebanon, courses are given at the American University of Beirut. In Egypt the Atomic Energy Establishment and the universities train N. specialists, and a radio-isotope training center for the Arab countries is operated at Inshass. There is no significant N. research or development activity in Turkey and Iran.

None of the countries mentioned is known to have developed N. weapons, and all have declared at various times that the use of N. energy for peaceful purposes is the only object of their research. Foreign observers have sometimes credited Egypt and Israel with having an option to produce fissionable material should they desire to do so.

All countries of the ME, members of the UN, are also members of the International Atomic Energy Agency whose headquarters are in Vienna.

(C.K.)

*NU'MAN, AHMAD MUHAMMAD (b. 1910). Yemeni politician, Sunni-Shafe'i▷. Educated at the Islamic University of al-Azhar, Cairo, graduated 1941). As one of the few Yemeni intellectuals with a modern education, N. was able to wield considerable influence at the Imam's court where he demanded more liberalization and modernization. N., disappointed by the failure of a revolt in 1955, went into exile in Cairo and Aden, where he established a movement of "Free Yemenis". N. praised Prince al-Badr's▷ promises of liberalization and blessed him when he became Imam, 1962. He did not give the officers' rebellion of Sept. 1962 his whole-hearted support, preferring to serve the new Republic in its first two years abroad as representative to the Arab League. In 1964 he was appointed Deputy-Chairman of the Executive Council. When the Egyptians had to adopt a defensive posture in Yemen and more moderate policies were introduced, he was appointed Prime Minister, Apr. 1965. N., though a Shafe'i, exercised a substantial influence on the Zeidi tribes. He was among the chief organizers of a pro-Republican tribal conference at Khamir in May 1965. Soon afterwards he resigned as Premier but continued to play an important role on the Republican (i.e. Presidential) Council, June 1965 — Sept, 1966. Together with 'Amri▷ and 'Iryani▷, he was detained in Cairo from Sep. 1966 to Oct. 1967. On his release, N. did not return to San'a though he was offered his place on the Republican Council, but went to Beirut and continued calling for a Republican-Royalist reconciliation in Yemen. After such a reconciliation was achieved, in 1970, following the political and military decline of the Royalists, N. was appointed a member of the Republican Council. He was not reappointed in Apr. 1971, but was Prime Minister May to Aug. 1971. (H.E.)

*NUMEIRI, MUHAMMAD JA'FAR (b. 1930). Sudanese officer and politician. Educated at the Military College, Khartoum, and in military studies in the USA, 1966, N. was given various assignments in the Sudanese Army and attained the rank of Brigadier-General. He led the leftist-military coup of May 1969 and became head of the National Revolutionary Council, the supreme state organ. Prime Minister since Oct. 1969, he groped for a middle-of-the-road course, balanced between the army (his mainstay), conservative groups (some of which he suppressed) and the Communists (whose orthodox main faction he tried to suppress, while letting other factions participate in his government). Since 1969–70 he began to participate in inter-Arab affairs as an active Pan-Arab leader. N. was overthrown in July 1971 in a coup headed by leftist officers whom he had purged in 1970; but a counter-coup returned him to power three days later and he savagely suppressed his communist foes. N. was elected President in a plebiscite in Sept. 1971. (B.G.)

NUQRASHI, MAHMUD FAHMI (1888–1948). Egyptian politician, Prime Minister 1946–8. Engineer by profession. A leader of the *Wafd* party, N. seceded from the *Wafd* in 1937 and, together with Ahmed Maher▷, formed the *Sa'adist*▷ party. N. was Minister of Transport 1936–7, Minister of Interior 1940, Foreign Minister 1944–5, Prime Minister 1945–6 and 1946–8. In 1947, while Prime Minister, N. took the Anglo-Egyptian dispute over Sudan to the UN Security Council, but his arguments failed to convince the Council and the discussion was inconclusive. During his tenure of office, Egypt went to war with nascent Israel in 1948. In the course of his struggle with the *Wafd*, he uncovered and denounced cases of corruption that had occurred under *Wafd* rule. When the "Muslim Brotherhood"▷ stepped up in 1948 a campaign of violence, N. outlawed the organization and ordered its disbandment. N. was assassinated by one of its members in revenge. (S.L.)

NUSSEIRIS, NOSSAIRIS — see 'Alawis▷.

O

*OIL IN THE ME. In the past half-century, the ME has become a vital source of crude oil. Oil production has caused a basic transformation of the area: barren tracts of desert have become hives of industrial and commercial activity and centres of communication. Obscure little sheikhdoms have grown immensely rich overnight.

The existence of oil deposits in this region has been known for thousands of years, but modern oil prospecting began only late in the 19th century. The first important well was discovered in 1908, east of Abadan▷ in Persia, by William Knox D'Arcy, an Englishman who had in 1901 obtained a 60-year concession. In 1914, the British government acquired the largest share in the company operating the Persian concession—the Anglo-Persian (later Anglo-Iranian) Oil Co., founded in 1909, the present British Petroleum Company—mainly, to make the Royal Navy independent of Dutch and American firms which then controlled oil production and marketing.

Fears of an American oil crisis (rooted in the misapprehension that USA oil resources, which then accounted for 80% of total world production, would soon be exhausted) impelled the large oil companies urgently to procure concessions in the ME. The American oil companies, backed by the State Department, objected to Franco-British arrangements after World War I which excluded American interests from participation in Iraqi oil developments. In 1925, after protracted negotiations (finalized in 1928), US companies—Standard Oil of New Jersey and Socony Vacuum—were admitted to participation in the Turkish Petroleum Co., the concessionaire in Iraq; the Anglo-Persian Oil Co. relinquished half its holdings to the American group, thus giving the latter a 23.75% share. In return for its admission, the US group had to agree, as had the other partners in the TPC, not to seek separate concessions in the Asian territories of the defunct Ottoman Empire (except Kuwait, and the Khanaqin district of Iraq)—the "Red Line Agreement" of 1928. (This was unilaterally broken by the American partners to the company—since 1929 called the Iraq Petroleum Co. (IPC)—in 1946, when they joined an American group that sought, and obtained, concessions in Sa'udi Arabia.)

The power contest soon led to the partition of the region between the large oil companies of the West. In Iran (Persia) the concessionaire was British; American groups operated in Bahrain and Sa'udi Arabia; Iraq had an international company, IPC (US-British-French-Dutch); Kuwait's oil was prospected for by a joint American-British group; and in Qatar and other Persian Gulf sheikhdoms, subsidiaries of the IPC took out concessions.

Oil was soon struck—1927 in Iraq, 1932 in Bahrain, 1938 in Sa'udi Arabia and Kuwait, 1940 in Qatar. Exploitation, however, proceeded at a slower pace. The European powers, on the eve of World War II, needed at home the steel and heavy equipment necessary for oil production; during the war it was easier

and safer to transport oil to Europe from the American continent than to risk drawing it from the ME. Thus, as late as 1938 Britain still drew 57% of her oil requirements from the western hemisphere, 18% from Persia, and no more than 4% from the rest of the ME. Aggregate ME oil production stood at 320,000 barrels per day (16m. tons *p.a.*)—about 6% of total world output.

The great forward thrust came after World War II, and particularly after 1948 when Europe's reconstruction, with US (Marshall Plan) aid, created a tremendous increase in the demand for petroleum and its by-products. Controlling all the hitherto discovered oil deposits in the ME, the seven largest oil companies—ESSO (Standard Oil of New Jersey), Gulf, Mobil, Standard Oil of California, Texas Oil, BP (British Petroleum), Shell—had succeeded from the 1920s to the mid 1950s, while competing for concessions and markets, in maintaining a steady flow of oil at stable prices. Now, under the pressure of the producing countries, a new system of payment was gradually adopted (by more or less concerted action of the several companies): fixed royalties per barrel were replaced by a profit-sharing arrangement between the companies and the producing countries, generally on an equal basis. The first to conclude such a 50:50 agreement was an American company, Aramco, which thus broke informal intercompany agreements. The new arrangements had no adverse effect on the companies' profits, since the American ones in particular now remitted to the local governments the taxes hitherto paid to the American Treasury. Their control of the markets, in keen competition between the companies themselves, prevented producing countries from engaging in independent marketing.

This pattern came to an end in 1957 through the actions of ENI, the national oil company of Italy. ENI's dynamic manager, Enrico Mattei, had failed in his efforts to obtain from the leading oil companies a share in their concessions, and was looking for new prospects. He offered Persia a joint enterprise assuring the Persian Treasury 75% of the profits (50% as partner plus half ENI's 50% as government). Profit-sharing agreements of this order have since become usual, some new contracts increasing the producing country's share to as much as 82%. ENI itself entered into a similar partnership with Egypt (its Sinai oilfields, captured by Israel in the Six Day War, yielded 4.5m. tons annually).

In the wake of ENI other smaller companies joined the race. The producing countries liked the new system of partnership in the production process itself, which put an end to the semi-colonial character of the older-type concessions. The relinquishment and return of parts of older concession areas, nationalization acts and the development of novel methods of offshore submarine drilling opened the field to many new companies, while the domination of the big companies declined. By 1965 the latter accounted for 75% of world oil production outside North America and the Soviet Bloc, as against 90% in 1952; their share in refining decreased from 72% to 60%. As a result of increased international competition, and also enlarged Soviet exports to non-Communist markets, the price of oil dropped. Accordingly the profits of the big concerns fell from 19% of their net assets to 11–12%. In 1967 the total income of the "Big Seven" amounted to $4,040m. (the five US companies earning $3,320m., of which $1,370m. outside the USA).

In recent years there has been mounting pressure for increases in oil prices (mainly the "posted price" which serves as the basis for the calculation of taxes and royalties), and changes in favour of the producing country in taxes and other payments, as well as continuous increases in production. After a protracted crisis, a five-year agreement was signed in Teheran in Feb. 1971 between 23 Western oil companies, among them the "Big Seven", and six oil-producing countries in the Persian Gulf. The posted price of oil was raised by $0 35 a barrel, with additional increases of 5 cent *p.a.* in the coming years, and also a 2.5% *p.a.* compensation for world inflation; the tax on profits was raised to 55%. The average income of the Gulf states from a barrel of oil was to rise from $0.98 to $1.30 now, to almost $1.50 by 1975. The agreement was to increase the six Gulf states' oil income in 1971 by $1,200m. with further annual increases. Over the five years of the agreement, the six countries will receive a total increment of $10,000m.; and while their annual income in recent years was *c.* $4,400m., by 1975 it will reach $7,500m.

In Apr. 1971 the Government of Libya and the Western oil companies reached a similar five-year agreement, raising the posted price from $2.55 to $3.45 a barrel, with an annual increase of 7%, plus 2.5% to compensate for the reduced value of money. Libya's oil revenue was to rise from $1,300–$1,600m. in 1970 to $2,000–$2,200m. In June, a similar agreement with Iraq and Sa'udi Arabia applied a similar posted price increase to oil shipped to Mediterranean ports through the IPC pipeline and the "Tapline" (the two countries' Persian Gulf oil is covered by the Teheran agreement). A French-Algerian oil crisis—triggered in part by these disputes and agreements in the Persian Gulf, Libya and the Mediterranean pipeline-ports—is itself outside the scope of this Encyclopaedia.

The producing countries of the ME and North

Africa derived from oil about $4,000m. in 1967, and far more than $5,000m. in 1970. Foreign currency assets of the most important oil-producing ME countries increased between 1958 and 1967 by more than 150%, as compared with a total international growth of less than 25%. Some 70% of the world's known oil reserves are in the ME and North Africa. The share in world oil production of the ME without North Africa rose from 3.3% in 1930 to 16.7% in 1950, 30.5% in 1970 (nearly 40% if North Africa is included).

Five out of the eight largest oil-producing countries in the world are in the ME, viz. Iran, Sa'udi Arabia, Libya, Kuwait, and Iraq; a further four countries are large-scale producers. Production costs in the ME, including payments to the local governments, were, until 1971, the lowest in the world, at about one-third of parallel outlay in the USA. World oil consumption is expected to rise by 100% within the next 10–12 years, and the role of the ME and North Africa in the supply of oil to the West is bound to grow at an even faster rate (unless Alaskan oil should flow into the world market in large quantities or other hitherto untapped sources be discovered). Both Western Europe and Japan depend heavily on the ME and North Africa for oil, their chief source of energy. In 1969 the ME and North Africa supplied 473 out of 580m. tons imported by Western Europe and 151 out of 170m. tons imported by Japan.

"Mediterranean" oil (Libyan, Algerian, and that transported by pipeline from Iraq and Sa'udi Arabia to Mediterranean ports) supplied 40% of Western Europe's oil consumption in 1970, while oil brought by tankers from the Persian Gulf supplied about 33%.

THE OIL-PRODUCING COUNTRIES. A country-by-country survey of the rise of the oil industry in the ME follows:

IRAN: The main Persian oilfields are concentrated in southern Iran, not far from the Persian Gulf. The discovery of the Masjid-i-Suleiman field in 1908 marked the beginning of the ME oil industry. The Anglo-Iranian Oil Co., formed in 1909 to operate the concession granted in 1901 to W. K. D'Arcy, was the only concessionaire. By World War II, Persian oil production had reached a stable level of *c.* 10m. tons *p.a.* During and after the war, demand increased and production rose to 25m. tons in 1948, 32m. tons in 1950. Iran was then the ME's largest producer.

In 1951 a grave crisis broke out between the government and the company—mainly about conditions of payment, royalties, dividends (see also Iran▷, political history). A similar conflict in 1932 had caused the abrogation of the concession by the government; after the matter had been raised with the League of Nations, a new concession was negotiated (1933) — valid until 1993 — increasing royalty payments and reducing the concession area. Now, however, Iran's demands were not satisfied by the company's offers; an agreement of May 1949 was rejected by the Iranian parliament (*Majlis*). In Mar. 1951 the *Majlis* decreed the nationalization of the oil industry and the company's installations; the leader of the extremist advocates of nationalization, Dr. Muhammad Mossaddeq▷, became Prime Minister. In Apr., the Abadan▷ refinery was closed; the company's property was seized, British experts departed, and production stopped. The company warned off all buyers of oil offered for sale by the newly established National Iranian Oil Company. The International Court ruled, in June 1952, that it had jurisdiction only in disputes between governments, not between a government and a private company. American mediation efforts failed. The dispute, with its almost complete interruption of oil production and sales, hurt both Britain and Iran, but particularly the latter; oil revenues had been one-third of the country's GNP, 65% of its foreign currency income.

The dispute was resolved only after the fall of Mossaddeq, in Aug. 1953. In Aug. 1954, a "Consortium" of companies reached a new agreement; British Petroleum (the former Anglo-Iranian) sold 60% of its holdings and retained only 40% in the new Consortium; 40% were now held by five American companies (in 1955, they gave up 1% each, and nine smaller US companies also joined), 14% by Royal Dutch Shell, and 6% by the French Petroleum Co. (Compagnie Française des Pétroles) Large-scale production was resumed late in 1954. The Consortium's contract provided for a fast increase in production — to reach in 1957 30m. tons (actually 36.2m.), with 13m. tons refined at Abadan. By 1970 production reached over 190m. tons — mostly from the area operated by the Consortium — whereas the Abadan refineries processed over 21m. tons. Persian oil deposits during 1968 constituted about 10% of proven world oil reserves. The Iranian government receives from the Consortium royalties to the tune of 12.5% on aggregate oil production, as well as an income tax of 50% on profits. Its oil revenues reached $1,225m. in 1970; over $1,675m. were expected for 1971 — after the Feb. 1971 agreement described.

Since all the oilfields were located inland an impressive network of pipelines to the shores and the Abadan refineries was laid. Until recent years the export of crude oil was carried out through Bandar Mashur near Abadan. However, limited anchorage and shallow waters restricted loading and thus curbed the expansion of production. A more suitable terminal was developed at the island of Kharg, 25 miles from the coast. Pipelines were laid from the oilfields; the loading facilities, initially designed to handle 100,000 ton tankers, are being expanded to serve tankers with a loading capacity of up to 250,000 tons. The old Bandar Mashur terminal, serving tankers with a loading capacity of 40,000 tons, now exports only the products of the Abadan refinery. A major pipeline from the south Persian oilfields to Iskenderun, on Turkey's Mediterranean coast, is under discussion.

Oil prospecting has also continued in other regions of Iran and offshore in the Persian Gulf, vigorously encouraged by the government (the Oil Act of 1957). Agreements for joint prospecting — offshore, and outside the area of the Consortium — were signed with several foreign concerns, among them Italian, American and German firms. The terms negotiated secured for the Iranian partner, the National Iranian Oil Company (NIOC), a 50% share in whatever oil was struck; income tax raised the Persian share in the profits to 75%. Oil was struck in four of these joint ventures: by IPAC (NIOC-Pan American); SIRIP (NIOC-ENI); LAPCO (NIOC, Atlantic, Union, Murphy, Sun); and IMINOCO (NIOC, Phillips, ENI and the Indian government).

Natural gas is also produced in southern Iran in large quantities. A huge pipeline to the Soviet Union, running through the entire length of Iran, is under construction. It will also provide gas for home consumption.

A refinery was set up in 1912 on the island of Abadan, then a desolate spot, but close to the oilfields and to the Persian Gulf. By 1951, the refinery had reached a processing capacity of 25m. tons *p.a.* When nationalized in 1951, the Abadan refinery came to a virtual standstill. Operations were resumed under the 1954 agreement, but did not revert to the former level of production. By 1968, a production rate of 21m. tons *p.a.* was attained. Refineries of smaller size, or for preliminary processing, operate at Kermanshah, Elburz and Masjid-i-Suleiman. A new refinery in Teheran with a capacity of 4.25m. tons *p.a.* was opened by NIOC in 1968.

IRAQ: Iraq is, with 76m. tons (1970), the fourth largest oil-producing country in the ME. Keen competition for the acquisition of oil concessions in the part of the Ottoman Empire that is now Iraq began in the early 20th century. Before the outbreak of World War I, a preliminary concession was obtained by a group of British, Dutch, German and French companies. After the war, the French took over the German interests; American companies joined in 1925–8. An international group — later

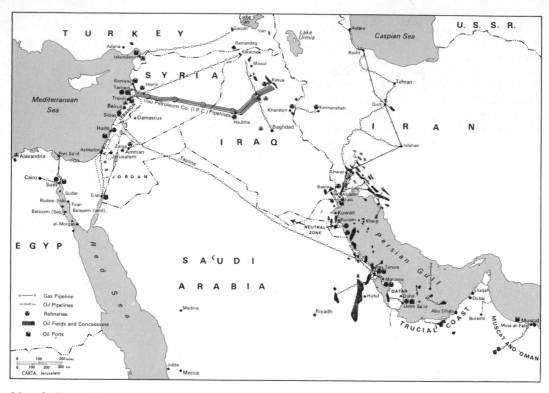

Map of oil resources in the ME

named Iraq Petroleum Company, IPC—renegotiated the concession (1925). In the IPC, the Armenian
oil magnate C. S. Gulbenkian held 5%; the rest
was equally divided between BP (AIOC), Shell,
Compagnie Française des Pétroles and a US group
comprising Standard Oil of New Jersey and Mobil,
each of the four groups holding 23.75%.

Drilling began in 1927 and the same year oil
was struck and the Kirkuk oilfield discovered—
still the largest oil-producing site in Iraq. Production
reached 4m. tons in the later 1930s and began to rise
steeply after 1951: 18m. in 1952, 33 in 1955, 47 in
1960, 76 in 1970. As Kirkuk is far away from the sea,
pipelines (12", 4–4.5m. tons capacity) were laid in
1934 to the Mediterranean, at Haifa▷ (Palestine)
and Tripoli▷ (Lebanon)—a distance of some 510 mi.
A new 16" pipeline to Tripoli was laid after World
War II. In 1948 the flow of oil to Haifa, now in Israel,
was cut off, and work on a new 16" pipeline abandoned. The two lines leading to Tripoli now have a
capacity of 10m. tons *p.a.* In 1950–2 a new 30/32" pipeline was laid from Kirkuk to Baniyas▷ in Syria,
and in 1961 a new 30/32" Kirkuk-Tripoli line was
completed. By 1965 all these pipelines conveyed
40m. tons *p.a.*, 64% of Iraq's oil output; by 1970
a capacity of over 50m. tons was reported.

The IPC's original concession covered almost
all of Iraq. During the late 1950s, the government
sought to regain from the IPC areas where the
company had not actively prospected, also demanding
a larger share of the profits. Negotiations yielded no
agreement and, in Dec. 1961, General Qassem's▷
revolutionary government issued a degree limiting
the concession held by the IPC and its two subsidiaries—the Mosul PC and the Basrah PC—to
736 sq. mi., 0.44% of its original area. The possibility of doubling the concession area under certain
conditions was left open and the IPC hoped to
regain in particular the promising North Rumeila
field; these hopes have remained unfulfilled. In August
1967, all the territories formerly held by the IPC
were transferred to the National Oil Company of
Iraq. This government company plans some projects
to be undertaken on its own, with Soviet Bloc aid,
while it will operate in other cases in partnership
with several foreign firms, including, *e.g.*, the French
government-owned ERAP.

Even before the Kirkuk oilfield was discovered,
oil had been struck near the Persian border. This
field was connected with an adjacent oil-bearing
area in Persia, and was operated at a low production
rate by a subsidiary of the Anglo-Iranian Oil Co.

(see Khanaqin▷). In the 1950s, oil was also struck near the Syrian and Turkish borders.

All the early discoveries of oil in Iraq were made in the northern part of the country, which even now accounts for two-thirds of the national output. Prospecting in the southern regions was begun after World War II. In 1951, oil was struck at Zubeir, and late in 1954 at the Rumeila field near the border of Kuwait. The southern fields are connected by pipelines with terminals at Fao, Umm Qasr and Khor al-'Amayeh on the Persian Gulf. In 1968 the southern fields yielded 16.2m. tons.

Only small quantities of the crude oil are refined locally, the bulk being exported. The capacity of the principal refinery, near Baghdad, is 2.5m. tons. Five more refining plants are much smaller. Before the Palestine War of 1948, part of Iraq's oil was processed at the refinery in Haifa.

SA'UDI ARABIA: The discovery of oil at Bahrain in 1932 stimulated prospecting in the Arabian peninsula, and in 1933 an extensive concession was granted by the Sa'udi government to an American company (later to be joined by others and to develop into Aramco—composed of Standard of California, Texas, Standard of New Jersey (30% each) and Mobil (10%). In 1936 oil was struck at Dammam on the Persian Gulf. Production started in 1938 but picked up speed only after the war. By 1946, production reached a level of 8m. tons p.a. More fields were discovered in a large area, constituting in fact one vast oilfield. Offshore production, providing over 20% of output, began in 1957 (marking the first oil extraction from under the sea-bed of the Persian Gulf). Sa'udi Arabia's total production reached 40m. tons in 1952, 141.1m. tons in 1968, 175m. in 1970. Sa'udi Arabia is now the second largest oil producing country in the ME, and disposes of considerable untapped resources. Her proved subterranean reserves are the largest in the world, exceeding those of the entire American continent. Her own needs are small and she exports the bulk of her production.

Most Sa'udi wells are near the Persian Gulf and most of her exports pass through the Ras Tanura terminal; but 20% of the output is carried to the Mediterranean by pipeline. Known as the "Tapline", it carries crude oil through Jordan and Syria (crossing also the Golan Heights▷, occupied since 1967 by Israel) to Sidon in the Lebanon. The line, completed in 1950 at a cost of £80m., is over 1,000 mi. long and has a diameter of 30/31''; its initial capacity of 15m. tons p.a. was increased to 22–25m. tons by 1958. (In May 1970 the "Tapline" was damaged by Palestinian-Arab saboteurs in Syria, and its repair was permitted only in Jan. 1971.)

A large refinery at Ras Tanura has been functioning since 1940. Its capacity has been increased several times and now stands at 19–20m. tons p.a. Since 1961, it has also produced concentrated hydrocarbon gas for export. Large quantities of Sa'udi Arabian oil are conveyed by submarine pipeline to the nearby island of Bahrain and refined there.

KUWAIT: The sheikhdom of Kuwait, a desert region with a population of 730,000, is now the third largest oil producer in the ME. A concession was granted to a British-American (Anglo-Iranian/Gulf) partnership in 1934, and oil was discovered in 1938. Commercial exploitation began only after World War II, and by 1970 the output was 138m. tons. Kuwait's main field—the Burgan field—is said to possess the largest untapped resources in the world. One of the largest export terminals in the world was built at Mina al-Ahmadi, permitting the loading of several tankers at once, including vessels of 300,000 tons and more. A small refinery was built nearby (1949), with an initial output of about 1m. tons p.a., increased in 1958 to 8.5m. and in 1963 to 12m. tons. A second refinery with a capacity of more than 5m. tons is located at Mina 'Abdullah, mainly for the preliminary processing of crude oil from the nearby Neutral Zone▷ (see below). The government-owned KNPC operated a third, 4.7m. ton refinery at Shu'aiba (1968).

THE NEUTRAL ZONE: On the borders of Kuwait and Sa'udi Arabia, in areas where no agreed demarcation was achieved, a Neutral Zone was established in which both countries possess equal rights. American companies acquired concessions in the Zone in 1948–9—American Independent for the Kuwaiti half, Pacific Western (Getty) for the Sa'udi half. The two companies operated jointly. Drilling began in 1949 and oil was struck in 1953 at Wafra. Pipelines to Mina 'Abdullah in Kuwait were laid immediately.

Oil was also found offshore. Concessions for prospecting under the sea-bed were granted to a Japanese company that discovered the Khafji field in 1960 and in Apr. 1961 began exporting to Japan. Khafji together with the Safania field off the Sa'udi shore is considered the world's largest submarine oilfield.

Oil output in the Neutral Zone was 21.1m. tons in 1968 (usually included in the production figures of Sa'udi Arabia and Kuwait). A refinery at Mina Sa'ud with a capacity of 2.5m. tons (opened 1968) deals in preliminary refinery only, similar to that of Mina 'Abdullah in Kuwait, which also serves the Neutral Zone.

QATAR: Qatar's oil resources are much smaller than those of nearby Sa'udi Arabia. The only oilfield of the sheikhdom, Dukhan, was discovered in 1939 and went into production ten years later. The

Oil wells, South Iran

concessionaire is a subsidiary of the Iraq Petroleum Company. During the past years output has been maintained at a steady rate of 8–9m. tons *p.a.*

Oil was discovered off the shores of Qatar by Shell in 1961, and commercial exploitation began in 1964. An offshore terminal has been constructed at Halul Island. Output is about 7.5m. tons *p.a.*, raising Qatar's total production to 16.2m. tons (1968).

BAHRAIN: The discovery of petroleum at Bahrain in 1932 by the American concessionaire (Standard of California and Texas) gave the initial impetus to the vast oil development in the Arabian peninsula and the Persian Gulf. At Bahrain itself, oil is found in modest quantities only. Present oil output is about 3.8m. tons *p.a.* A refinery plant was initially set up (1936) to process the island's own oil. After World War II, however, it was enlarged to refine also oil produced in the nearby Sa'udi Arabian fields. These now supply two-thirds of the 10m. tons *p.a.* processed at the refinery. Offshore concessions were recently granted to additional American companies.

TRUCIAL COAST (TRUCIAL 'OMAN): Intensive oil prospecting was conducted after World War II throughout the entire region of the Persian Gulf, including the seven British-protected sheikhdoms of the Trucial Coast. So far oil has been struck in the largest of these sheikhdoms, Abu Dhabi, and in nearby Dubai. Offshore and inland prospecting continues in the remaining sheikhdoms as well.

ABU DHABI's oil resources, offshore and inland, are considerable. The first oilfield to be exploited on a commercial scale (1962) was discovered by the Anglo-French Abu Dhabi Marine Areas Co. some 60 mi. from the coast, 20 mi. east of Das Island, where a large oil terminal has been built, handling tankers of up to 200,000 tons. Output has reached 6m. tons (1968). A second field operated by the same com-

pany since 1967 produces some 10m. tons *p.a.*

In 1960 an inland oilfield was discovered at Murban by a subsidiary of the IPC. A terminal capable of serving large tankers was built at Jabal Dana, with an annual capacity of 12m. tons. Exports started in 1963. Abu Dhabi's total oil production stood at 24m. tons in 1968, 33m. tons in 1970.

DUBAI: Inland and offshore concessions were granted in 1963 — after previous licences had been relinquished—to two international groups. Oil was struck offshore, and production, at an initial rate of 1m. tons, started in 1969.

'OMAN: In Musca-and-'Oman oil in commercial quantities was struck in 1964, by an international group of companies, in the Fahud area, 156 mi. inland. A terminal was built on the Gulf coast, capable of serving 150,000 ton tankers, and pipelines were laid. Exports began in mid-1967 at an initial rate of 6–7m. tons *p.a.* Production in 1970 was 16m. tons. Another group of companies is prospecting offshore.

EGYPT: Oil prospecting in Egypt began in 1885 on the shores of the Gulf of Suez. The first well was located in 1909, but output was poor and the field was closed down in 1927. Other wells were at Hurghada (1913) and Ras Gharib (1937). Output was increased during World War II and production reached 1m. tons *p.a.* A new oil-bearing area was discovered in 1946 in Sinai, on the eastern bank of the Gulf of Suez, at Ras Sudr and other places. By 1949, Egypt's oil output had grown to over 2m. tons *p.a.* and this level was maintained for several years. In 1957, production increased with the development of new wells east and west of the Gulf of Suez. By 1965 it had reached a rate of 6.5m. tons *p.a.* Egypt's main oil resources, in the submarine al-Morgan field in the Gulf of Suez, were discovered in 1965. Since 1966, oil has been struck—by American companies (Phillips, AMOCO)—in the Western Desert; some of these wells are considered of major importance.

Egypt's oil production reached 8.3m. tons in 1967. She lost about one half, deriving from the inland and offshore fields of Sinai, to Israel in the Six Day War. Yet, despite the loss, Egypt's output has risen to nearly 20m. in 1970—most of it from the al-Morgan offshore area and from the new al-'Alamein field in the Western Desert. Natural gas deposits have recently been located in the Nile Delta.

British and American companies played an important part in the development of the Egyptian oil industry. In recent years the Egyptian government decided to take a more active part in oil prospecting. Accordingly a national authority was set up with an overall responsibility for oil prospecting and refining.

For several years the Egyptians operated oilfields requisitioned from British and other foreign interests following the Suez crisis of 1956. The requisition orders were revoked in 1959, but in 1964 the Egyptian government nationalized the oilfields in question. Since then the national oil authority, the Egyptian General Petroleum Corporation, has been in charge of oil prospecting throughout Egypt, advised by Soviet experts and mostly in partnership with American and Italian interests. Japanese companies have also recently acquired prospecting interests.

The Suez Canal constituted until 1967 the world's main artery of oil transport. Before the Six Day War, c. 167m. tons of oil passed through the canal annually into the Mediterranean. Since the war it has been closed. As the new giant tankers would anyhow be unable to traverse the canal, even if reopened, Egypt decided to lay, with the aid of foreign capital, a 205 mi. pipeline with a planned capacity of 60–80m. tons p.a. Work has not yet begun.

Until 1967, three refineries, two at Suez and one at Alexandria, produced c. 8.5m. tons p.a. The two Suez refineries were destroyed during the post-1967 Egypt-Israel artillery clashes; they were to be rebuilt in the vicinity of Cairo.

LIBYA: Libya has in recent years rapidly become a major oil producer, with an output of over 160m. tons in 1970. The first concessions were granted in 1955, and wartime minefields had to be cleared before ground exploration could be carried out. Oil was first found towards the end of 1957 in the Fezzan area, about 50 mi. south-east of Algeria's Edjelch field. Subsequent finds have been numerous, and a dozen important oilfields are now in operation, representing between them a total of some 800 producing wells.

Commercial production started in 1961, reached 55m. tons in 1965, 160m. in 1970. Libya's proximity to Europe facilitated transportation and stimulated production. The closure of the Suez Canal since 1967 has further accentuated her advantageous position.

The largest producing field is Zelten, discovered in 1959, about 200 mi. from Benghazi and within 100 mi. of the coast. An extensive pipeline system links Zelten with the terminal at Marsa al-Brega; it may be extended to include future fields. The most remote of the larger Libyan fields is Sarir field in Cyrenaica, some 250 mi. south of Tobruk. A 34" 320 mi. pipeline (1967) carries oil to Tobruk. Other pipeline systems terminate at Ras Lanuf, al-Sidr and Zuweitina.

Concessions have been parcelled out to a large number of companies—about 40 now, including some of the giants (ESSO, Shell, Mobil, BP). US companies are responsible for about 90 per cent of present production. Libya has also established a national oil company—Lipetco—which has concluded exploration contracts with several foreign oil companies. Libya's oil revenue, starting in 1961 with $3m., passed the $1,000m. mark in 1968–9. The post-1969 revolutionary regime obtained substantial increases in Sept. 1970, after hard pressure on the companies and a protracted dispute; after the Apr. 1971 agreement, over $2,200m. are expected for 1971. Natural gas is also produced in large quantities; a large liquefaction plant, completed by ESSO in 1970, was kept closed for many months by the payments dispute, but began operating in 1971.

(Libya's neighbour, Algeria—outside the scope of this Encyclopaedia—is another major oil producer. Oil discoveries there preceded Libya's by a few years.)

ISRAEL: Oil output in Israel has remained low in spite of extensive oil prospecting carried out over several years by government as well as private firms. Production began in 1955 when the Lapidot Company struck oil at the Heletz field. During 1965, output at this site reached a peak of 200,000 tons; it has steadily declined since, and in 1969 only 100,000 tons were produced. Natural gas is produced in the 'Arad region by the Naphta Company since 1961 (equivalent of 133,000 tons of oil in 1969). Pipes carry the gas to the Dead Sea Works and other industrial enterprises in the Negev.

Following the opening of the passage to Eilat in 1956–7 (with the Suez Canal closed to Israel by the Egyptian blockade) a 16" pipeline was laid from Eilat to Haifa; its capacity was increased several times and is now 6m. tons p.a. In 1967 70 a 42" 22m. ton Eilat-to-Ashkelon pipeline was laid; its capacity could be increased to 60m. tons. Whereas the Eilat-Haifa line was designed to cover Israel's local needs, the larger pipeline is meant to serve as a land bridge between the Mediterranean and the Red Sea, shortening the route between the ME oil producers and the European consumers (made considerably longer since the closure of the Suez Canal). Once the Suez Canal is reopened, giant tankers that cannot use it may serve the Eilat-Ashkelon land bridge, thus lowering the cost of ME oil to Europe. A third pipeline carries oil products from the Haifa refineries to Tel Aviv and Ashkelon.

Refineries were built at Haifa by the British Petroleum Company and began in 1939 refining Iraqi oil conveyed through the 4m. ton Kirkuk-Haifa pipeline. In World War II they played an important part in the Allied war effort. In Apr. 1948 the flow of oil from Kirkuk was stopped by Iraq and the refineries were closed down. Work was resumed in 1950, at government request, to cover the country's fuel requirements (then c. 1m. tons p.a.; by 1969 over 5m. tons). In 1958 the refinery was acquired by the Israeli government. It was overhauled and enlarged, raising output to 6m. To the refining plants were added devices for the production of high-grade petrol, the removal of sulphur from diesel oil and a plant for the production of basic lubricants. A second, 3.5m. ton, refinery is planned at Ashdod, near the terminal of the Eilat-Ashkelon pipeline.

SYRIA: While long deriving benefits from ME oil production as transit territory for all the pipelines leading from Iraq and Sa'udi Arabia to the Mediterranean, Syria has only lately entered the field as a producer. The first oil deposits in commercial quantities were discovered in 1956 at Karachuk in the north-east, near the Iraqi border. In 1959, oil was discovered at Suweidiya in eastern Syria, also near the Iraqi border. Production totalled 1m. tons in 1968, 4.5m. in 1970. A 400 mi. pipeline was laid (1968) from Karachuk to the Tartus terminal on the Mediterranean coast, with a branch line to the Homs refinery (whose capacity was recently increased to 2.7m. tons p.a., now processing local oil). The Syrian oil industry was nationalized in 1965.

TURKEY: Turkey is peripheral to the main oil-producing area of the Persian Gulf. It had been supposed for centuries that oil was to be found, and the first concession for prospecting was granted as early as 1887. Yet commercial quantities of oil were discovered only in 1940, in the Ramandag area, by a state oil company. Production began in 1949, but yielded only small quantities.

Prospecting is also undertaken in other parts of south-eastern Turkey, in Thrace and lately also on the Anatolian inland plateau. Since 1954, private companies have also prospected, in central and south-eastern Turkey, with several successful drillings in 1960 and 1961. The largest field, north of Batman, yielded 600,000 tons in 1968. Turkey's total oil production in 1970 was 3.5m. tons, of which 1.2m. was produced by TPAO, her state company, 1.8m. by Shell, and 0.5m. by Mobil.

Turkey has a 3m. ton refinery at Mersin and two smaller plants at Izmit and Batman, the latter being state-owned. Total refining capacity is 5m. tons p.a. An expansion of the existing refineries and a new 3m. ton refinery at Izmir are planned. So is a 35 mi. pipeline from Batman to Dörtyol on the Bay of Iskenderun.

Hopes of discovering oil resources are also entertained by countries which have hitherto found none. Extensive drilling is being undertaken at present throughout the ME, especially in the Persian Gulf

area, onshore and offshore. Lebanon and Jordan, where no oil has been found, are connected with the oil industry, and benefit from its royalties, as transit territories for the pipelines connecting Iraq and Sa'udi Arabia with the Mediterranean. Some of the non-producing countries derive considerable profits from refining operations. A striking example is Aden, whose refinery (1954) now has an annual capacity of 7m. tons. Lebanon has two refineries with a total output of 2.5m. tons p.a., and Jordan refines 350,000 tons in a small plant.

MARKETING. Of the oil produced in the ME, 90% is exported. The large-scale supply of distant markets has posed some difficult transport problems. The nearest sea outlet to the ME's largest oilfields, excepting the Kirkuk wells in Iraq, is the Persian Gulf. The Suez Canal was a vital link; about half the ME's oil output—167m. tons in 1966—was until 1967 exported through the Suez Canal, the bulk (c. 80%) to Britain and the Common Market countries.

The pipelines connecting Iraq and Sa'udi Arabia with the Mediterranean convey 60–70m. tons p.a. Egypt's Suez-Alexandria pipeline and Israel's Eilat-Ashkelon pipeline at its final capacity may each equal that amount. Persia plans a pipeline from her oil-producing areas to the Bay of Iskenderun in Turkey; a similar project is being considered in Iraq.

OIL IN THE ME'S ECONOMY. The development of the ME oil industry has led to far-reaching economic and social changes in the producing countries and the entire area. Revenue derived from royalties and other payments help finance the budgets of the producing countries and to a lesser extent of neighbouring lands. The oil companies set up social services for the local population such as their own governments were then still unable to provide. They established schools, which they later transferred to the care of the governments, supported secondary schools and universities and provided vocational and technical instruction to train skilled personnel for the oil industry. They built modern housing for their workers, set up medical services, including hospitals and clinics, and introduced preventive medicine which led to a decline in the incidence of diseases. They constructed roads and assisted local authorities in the installation of street lighting and drainage systems.

In several countries the oil companies continue to provide such services. However, as the revenues of the producing countries rose they were able to take over these functions. The aggregate payment in royalties and other forms made by the oil companies to Kuwait, Sa'udi Arabia, Iran, Libya, Iraq, and Abu-Dhabi now totals about $4,600m. p.a. and is expected to reach c. $10,000m. by 1975.

TABLE 1. CRUDE OIL PRODUCTION (millions of tons p.a.)

	1935	1940	1945	1950	1955	1960	1965	1969	1970
Abu Dhabi	—	—	—	—	—	—	13.6	28.9	33.4
Algeria	—	—	—	—	0.06	8.6	26.5	44.5	46.4
Bahrain	—	1.05	—	1.51	1.5	2.3	2.9	3.8	3.8
Dubai	—	—	—	—	—	—	—	0.5	4.2
Egypt*	0.3	0.9	1.3	2.2	1.7	3.1	6.5	14.0	19.0
Iran	7.9	9.1	17.9	33.2	16.4	52.6	94.8	168.1	191.7
Iraq	3.9	2.8	5.0	7.0	34.9	47.6	64.4	74.9	76.4
Israel	—	—	—	—	—	0.1	0.2	0.1	0.1
Kuwait	—	—	—	17.2	55.2	81.9	109.0	129.5	137.3
Neutral Zone	—	—	—	—	1.2	7.3	19.1	23.3	26.3
Libya	—	—	—	—	—	—	58.7	149.8	159.6
Morocco	—	—	—	—	—	—	—	0.1	0.04
'Oman	—	—	—	—	—	—	—	16.4	16.4
Qatar	—	—	—	1.7	5.7	8.2	11.0	17.0	17.0
Sa'udi Arabia	—	6.9	3.0	27.3	48.9	62.1	100.8	148.6	175.7
Sinai	—	—	—	—	—	—	—	2.5	4.4
Syria	—	—	—	—	—	—	—	3.5	4.5
Tunisia	—	—	—	—	—	0.2	0.2	3.4	4.1
Turkey	—	—	—	0.1	0.2	0.4	1.5	3.6	3.6

* Data up to 1965 include Sinai wells; 1969 and 1970 data do not.

TABLE 2. CRUDE OIL PRODUCTION (daily average in thousand barrels)

	1935	1940	1945	1950	1955	1960	1965	1969	1970
Abu Dhabi	—	—		—	—	—	282	601	683
Algeria	—	—	—	—	1	183	552	1,017	980
Bahrain	—	19	—	30	30	45	57	76	76
Dubai	—	—	—	—	—	—	—	10	84
Egypt*	5	18	26	45	35	62	123	240	361
Iran	157	181	358	664	329	1,068	1,908	3,314	3,871
Iraq	78	56	100	140	697	972	1,313	1,518	1,560
Israel	—	—	—	—	—	3	4	2	2
Kuwait	—	—	—	344	1,104	1,692	2,360	2,575	2,732
Neutral Zone	—	—	—	—	24	136	361	481	503
Libya	—	—	—	—	—	—	1,219	3,110	3,320
Morocco	—	—	—	—	—	—	—	2	n.d.
'Oman	—	—	—	—	—	—	—	328	323
Qatar	—	—	—	34	115	175	233	356	359
Sa'udi Arabia	—	14	58	547	977	1,314	2,206	2,993	3,548
Sinai	—	—	—	—	—	—	—	50	90
Syria	—	—	—	—	—	—	—	63	90
Tunisia	—	—	—	—	—	3	4	70	87
Turkey	—	—	—	—	3	7	30	64	71

* Data up to 1965 include Sinai wells; 1969 and 1970 data do not.

TABLE 3. REVENUES FROM OIL (in million US$)

	1935	1940	1945	1950	1955	1960	1965	1969	1970
Abu Dhabi	—	—	—	—	—	—	34	191	220
Iran	9	16	22	45	90	285	522	938	1,225
Iraq	3	7	10	15	207	266	375	483	495
Kuwait	—	—	—	14	282	465	671	812	840
Libya	—	—	—	—	—	—	371	1,132	1,300
Qatar	—	—	0.5	1	29	54	84	120	125
Sa'udi Arabia	—	1	5	112	270	335	655	1,008	1,300

Lebanon, Syria and Jordan receive considerable royalties on the transit of oil through their territories. Egypt, too, profited a great deal, until 1967, from the transit of oil through the Suez Canal. Several Arab countries benefit from the financial aid granted or loaned by their oil-producing neighbours for development projects. Moreover, Egypt and Jordan have received, since 1967, considerable permanent subsidies from their oil-rich sister countries, Sa'udi Arabia, Kuwait and Libya (though Jordan's subsidies from the two latter are often suspended for political reasons). The Palestinian Arab guerilla and sabotage organizations are also largely financed by the oil-rich Arab regions, particularly Libya, Kuwait and the Persian Gulf sheikhdoms.

What about the future? Estimates of oil reserves are rising at an unprecedented rate. In 1968 some 60% of all the known world resources were in the ME. Assessments fluctuate, but as the ME still remains largely unexplored, prospecting in this region may reasonably be expected to yield further large quantities of oil. Taking into account the large-scale production and vast reserves of the ME, coupled with the expected rise in world consumption, the affluence of the area seems assured. It may also be assumed that the international oil companies will continue to develop the ME oil industry, even though they may have to transfer a rising share of their profits to the producing countries themselves. (M.C.)

OIL IN ME POLICIES. The search for oil and the rush for concessions have been, since the end of the nineteenth century, an important, sometimes a principal, factor in the penetration and growing intervention of the powers in the ME. It was, in many cases, oil interests that pushed their governments into the struggle for concessions, influence, hegemony. And after concessions were granted and oil began to be produced in large quantities, it became an economic, political and strategic necessity to protect the installations and vast investments and to ensure the regular supply of oil. Relations between the oil companies and the oil-producing countries (their governments, and their nationalist movements) were an important factor in the relations between the imperial powers and those countries. This was true even for countries under the West's dominating influence (e.g. Iraq in the 1920s, Bahrain, Kuwait), let alone for more fully independent countries.

After the termination of Western imperial or semi-colonial rule in the ME, oil interests continued to play an important part in the powers' policies in the region. Concession conditions became more and more favourable to the producing country at the expense of the oil companies' share and the powers were no longer able to intervene, as in the past, in the relations between producing country and company. However, the Western Powers remained most interested in the free and undisturbed flow of ME oil—especially to Europe. True, it transpired that in times of crisis the West could manage without ME oil and obtain its vital fuel from other sources (as, for instance, in 1967); but Europe still depended on ME oil in normal times (see figures above). The Western powers' interest in defending their investments also remains important, and the major oil companies still retain a considerable influence on the West's foreign policy (generally in the direction of pro-Arab pressure).

As to the Soviet Bloc's part in ME oil affairs, opinions differ. Till now, the Soviet Bloc countries had no direct interest in, or need for, ME oil. In times of conflict, they might attempt to deny ME oil to the West; otherwise, they were content to aid the countries of the region with political support in their struggle with Western oil interests, and technical and financial aid in their efforts to develop an independent national oil industry. However, Soviet Bloc countries began appearing as buyers (e.g., the USSR—of natural gas from Iran; Rumania and others—of Iranian oil). Some experts believe that in the 1980s the Soviet Bloc will need large quantities of ME oil. Should this turn out to be true, it will have far-reaching political implications.

(Y.S.)

MAJOR OIL COMPANIES. Dozens of oil companies, large and small, operate in the ME. Especially after World War II, many small companies entered the field (in Libya, Iran, the Persian Gulf, and Egypt), and we cannot survey them all here. The major oil companies are frequently mentioned above, in the survey by countries; see also fuller details on each company in Table 4, below. The following survey of major companies refers only to companies specially linked to, or mainly active in, the ME.

1. ENTE NAZIONALE IDROCARBURI (ENI): The "Italian Government Hydrocarbon Company" was established in 1953 at the initiative of Enrico Mattei, who was its manager and the moving spirit of Italian oil policy until his death in 1962. ENI's efforts to acquire sources of oil in the ME brought it into open rivalry with US and British companies with a traditional hold on the region's oil production.

Mattei urged the creation of a direct link between oil-producing and -consuming countries, by-passing the "international" companies. He pioneered the so-called ENI-type concessions, i.e. the 75:25 formula, on the pattern of ENI's 1957 agreement with Iran, based on the equal partnership of the foreign company and the national oil company of the producing country. Following the death of Mattei, there has been some rapprochement between ENI and the British and American oil companies.

ENI's principal assets in the ME and North Africa (through its subsidiary AGIP), are oil concessions in Iran, Sa'udi Arabia, Qatar, Egypt, Libya, and Tunisia, in conjunction with local and foreign companies. In 1969, the total crude oil production of the ENI group of companies was 8.1m. tons, of which 6.6m. tons were from Tunisia, Iran and Qatar. ENI's oil assets in Sinai are under Israeli control since 1967.

2. BRITISH PETROLEUM COMPANY (BP): One of the world's biggest oil companies, BP originated and operated for a long time mainly in Iran. It was called, until 1935, the "Anglo-Persian Oil Company" and later the "Anglo-Iranian Oil Company". It was formed by a British syndicate in 1909, immediately after the discovery of oil in Persia, and was at first owned by the Anglo-Australian financier William Knox D'Arcy, who obtained the original oil concession from the Persian government in 1901, and following financial difficulties sold in 1905 most of his concessions to the "Burmah Oil Company". After oil was discovered in Persia, and in view of the British Admiralty's plan to change the fuel of the Royal Navy from coal to oil, the company's capital was increased and the British government, at the initiative of Winston Churchill, acquired more than half its shares. About a quarter of the shares remained in the hands of the "Burmah Oil Company"

and the remainder in those of private investors. This ownership structure remained virtually unchanged until 1967, when the government's share dropped to 49%, following an increase in the company's capital.

BP still remains at the head of ME oil producers, though it lost its position as sole oil concessionnaire in Persia through the nationalization of 1951, and its share in the international consortium set up in 1954 to run the Persian oil industry is 40%. For details of BP's other principal oil assets in the ME see Table 4. BP has lately tended to intensify exploration and production in other parts of the world, because of the political dangers inherent in the concentration of its production assets in the ME.

3. IRAQ PETROLEUM COMPANY, (IPC): British-registered company producing oil in Iraq. It originated in a syndicate of "African and Eastern Concessions", formed in 1911 as an Anglo-German concern to obtain a concession and produce oil in Mesopotamia, then under Turkish rule. In 1812, the company's name was altered to "Turkish Petroleum Company". It was renamed IPC in 1929. An agreement of Mar. 1914 allocated 50% of the shares to the "Anglo-Persian Oil Company" (later "British Petroleum"), 25% to "Shell" and 25% to the "Deutsche Bank"; benefit rights to 5% (without voting rights) were allocated from the share of the first two partners to the Armenian C. S. Gulbenkian who was one of the founders of the company. Though the Turkish government had granted the concession, World War I postponed its activities.

After the war, the "Deutsche Bank" shares were handed over to France under the 1918 Lloyd George-Clemenceau agreement and the 1920 San Remo oil accord. US pressure secured, after some time, the participation of American oil companies (organized for this purpose in the "Near East Development Corporation Group") at the expense of the "Anglo-Persian Company's" share. The Group Agreement, signed after prolonged negotiations in July 1928, divided the ownership as follows:—23.75% "Anglo-Persian", 23.75% "Anglo-Dutch Shell", 23.75% "French Petroleum Company", 23.75% NEDC (initially made up of seven companies, later owned in equal partnership by "Standard New Jersey" and "Mobil"), 5% Gulbenkian. This agreement incorporated the "Red Line" condition, under which all participants undertook not to operate separately in the search for oil or its production in any of the territories of the former Ottoman Empire (marked in red on the map appended to the agreement), but only to do this jointly. This condition was annulled following much litigation after World War II and this enabled participation of American companies in Aramco.

TABLE 4. MAJOR ME OIL PRODUCERS: (a) OWNERSHIP OF OPERATING

Country	Operating Company	Ownership British Petr. Co.		Royal Dutch Shell Group		Standard Oil Co. (New Jersey)		Mobil Oil Corp.	
		(a)	(b)	(a)	(b)	(a)	(b)	(a)	(b)
Iran	I. Oil Explor. & Producing Co.	40.0	59.0	14.0	21.5	7.0	9.4	7.0	10.5
Iraq	IPC Mosul PC, Basrah PC	23.7	17.7	23.7	17.7	11.9	8.8	11.9	8.8
S. Arabia	Aramco					30.0	44.6	10.0	14.9
Kuwait	K. Oil Co.	50.0	53.4						
Qatar	QPCE	23.7	2.2	23.7	2.2	11.9	1.1	11.9	1.1
	Shell Q.			80.0	6.2				
Abu-Dhabi	ADPC	23.7	4.1	23.7	4.1	11.9	2.0	11.9	2.0
	AD Marine Areas	66.7	6.8						
'Oman	Petr. Development (O.)			85.0	14.0				
Bahrain	BP								
	ME Total (without North Africa)		143.2		65.7		65.9		37.3
	Libya		8.7		12.9		32.2		8.4
	World Total		162.1		195.6		249.3		80.0

★ Production figures do not necessarily correspond to ownership percentages because individual companies may, within certain limits, "under-lift" or "over-lift" their production shares according to inter-company arrangements. Figures may not total because of rounding.

The concession treaty with Iraq, signed in 1925 and amended in 1931, granted the company oil rights for 75 years in the region east of the Tigris. After some time, IPC shareholders (under the name of "Mosul Petroleum") acquired similar concessions in the area west of the Tigris and north of latitude 33° (1941), and also in the remaining areas of Iraq south of latitude 33° (under the name "Basrah Petroleum Co.", 1938). For IPC production and pipelines—see above, under Iraq. See there also for "Law No. 80" of 1961 confiscating 99.53% of the concession area of the IPC and its subsidiaries. The company denies the validity of the law, but the Iraq government is applying it in effect.

Outside Iraq, the IPC company acquired many concessions in ME countries (in the former Ottoman Empire territories, in accordance with the "Red Line" condition) by means of a roof company, "Petroleum Concessions Limited"; but they have not yielded any oil and were abandoned, except for the Qatar PC and the Abu-Dhabi PC.

4. COMPAGNIE FRANÇAISE DES PÉTROLES (CFP): The "French Oil Company", founded in 1924 by French banks and foreign oil companies then operating in France, mainly to exploit the oil assets promised to France following World War I. Thus, CFP acquired all the French oil concessions in Iraq (see above, IPC). Under the San Remo oil agreement, the government holds 35% shares and has 40% voting rights. Most of the French company's production is in the ME (see Table 4), and the remainder is mainly in Algeria. The company markets its products under the commercial name "Total".

5. ARABIAN AMERICAN OIL COMPANY (Aramco):

COMPANIES (%) (b) 1969 PRODUCTION (IN MILLION METRIC TONS)*

Standard Oil Co. of California		Texaco		Gulf Oil Corp.		Cie. Française des Pétroles		Others		Total	
(a)	(b)	(a)	(b)	(a)	(b)	(a)	(b)	(a)	(b)	(a)	(b)
7.0	9.0	7.0	8.9	7.0	8.3	6.0	11.3	5.0	16.7	100.0	154.7
						23.7	17.7	5.0	3.7	100.0	74.5
30.0	44.6	30.0	44.6							100.0	148.8
				50.0	76.1					100.0	129.5
						23.7	2.2	5.0	0.5	100.0	9.5
								20.0	1.5	100.0	7.7
						23.7	4.1	5.0	0.8	100.0	17.1
						33.3	4.9			100.0	11.7
						10.0	1.6	5.0	0.8	100.0	16.4
50.0	1.9	50.0	1.9							100.0	3.8
	55.5		55.4		84.4		41.8		24.0		573.7
	9.1		9.1								80.4
	113.9		146.2		142.4		52.6				1,142.1

Source of production figures: Petroleum Times, 3 July 1970.

A joint subsidiary of four large American oil companies holding an oil concession in Saʻudi Arabia. The original concession, which covered all the Al-Hassa▷ region in eastern Saʻudi Arabia, was acquired for 60 years in 1933, by the "Standard Oil Company of California". To operate it, the latter formed "Casoc" ("Arabian Standard Oil of California"). "Texas Oil" joined in 1936, and "Casoc" became an equal partnership of the California and Texas companies—similar to the partnership formed a year earlier to operate another California-held concession in Bahrain▷ ("Bahrain Petroleum Company"). At the end of World War II, "Standard Oil of New Jersey" and "Mobil Oil" ("Socony") joined the concession after they had freed themselves of the limitations of the "Red Line" agreement (see above, IPC); the company was renamed "Aramco", in which the California, Texas and New Jersey companies held 30% each, and "Mobil" 10%. "Aramco" was the first company in 1950 to agree to pay half of its profits to the government (instead of the customary royalty per ton or barrel). In addition to producing oil, "Aramco" operates refineries in Ras Tanura, which refined 19.5m. tons of crude oil in 1969. "Aramco" has in Saʻudi Arabia 10,865 employees, of whom 83% are Saʻudis and 9% Americans. It is the most important economic enterprise in Saʻudia. For the development of "Aramco's" production see above.

6. TRANS-ARABIAN PIPELINE COMPANY (TAPLINE): An American company of the same structure as "Aramco", operates the oil pipeline from Saʻudi Arabia to Sidon in Lebanon—see above under Saʻudi Arabia.   (S.Y.)

OKYAR, ALI FETHI (1880–1943). Turkish politician, Premier 1923, 1924–5. Born in Pirlepe. O. graduated from the Military Academy and served in various military posts, but left the army in 1913 to become a parliamentary deputy and, in 1917, Minister of the Interior. A close friend of Mustafa Kemal▷. He was a deputy in the first Grand National Assembly, 1920, and served again as Minister of the Interior, replacing Ra'uf Orbay▷ as Premier in Aug. 1923, and Ismet Inönü▷ in Nov. 1924. After a few years as Ambassador to France, he formed, in 1930, a liberal opposition party (Free Republican Party), but dissolved it shortly after. O. served as Ambassador to Britain 1934–9 and Minister of Justice 1939–41.
(D. K.)

'OMAN. A peninsula protruding northwards from the south-eastern part of the Arabian peninsula into the Persian Gulf▷ and the Gulf of 'O. and separating the two. The name 'O. is also applied to the whole south-east of the Arabian peninsula, the Sultanate of Muscat-and-'O.; but there are various definitions of 'O., and some restrict it to the hilly inner region, the area controlled by the rebel Iman of 'O. (see Muscat-and-'O.▷) The 'O. Peninsula contains the seven principalities of the Trucial Coast▷, or Trucial 'O. Its tip, Ras al-Jabal or Ru'us al-Jabal, belongs to the Sultanate of Muscat-and-'O. from which it is separated by the principalities. In 1970 the official name of the Sultanate of Muscat-and-'O. was changed to the Sultanate of 'O.
(Y. S.)

*ORBAY, HÜSEYIN RA'UF (1881–1964). Turkish politician, Prime Minister 1922–3. Born in Istanbul, O. studied in the Naval College, served in the Ottoman Navy and on diplomatic missions, and became Minister for Naval Affairs in 1918. A deputy in the first Grand National Assembly from 1920. He first co-operated with Atatürk▷ during the nationalists' struggle in Anatolia, and in 1922–3 served briefly as Premier. His conservatism led him, however, to break away. In 1924 O. was among the founders of the short-lived opposition "Progressive Republican Party", and in 1926 he took part in a plot on Atatürk's life. He fled and lived abroad for ten years, but returned to serve as Ambassador to London 1942–4.
(D. K.)

ORONTES (in Arabic — al-'Assi). River starting in al-Biqa' ("The Valley") or Coele Syria▷, in Lebanon, and flowing northwards through Syria, passing through the towns of Homs and Hama, and into the Mediterranean near Antakia (Antioch) in Turkey. It is 310.5 mi. long and the largest river in western Syria. The utilization of its waters for irrigation is an important Syrian development project. The O. creates the extensive al-Ghab swamps, north-east of Hama; 55,000 acres were drained by 1961 and reclaimed for agricultural purposes and the project is to be expanded. No agreement with Lebanon over the distribution and utilization of the waters of the O. has so far been reached.
(A. L.-O. T.)

ORTHODOX — see Greek Orthodox▷.

OTTOMANS, OTTOMAN EMPIRE. The OE arose from a small Turkish principality founded in the second half of the 13th century in north-western Anatolia, on the Byzantine border. Originally a vassal of the Seljuks, Osman I asserted his independence around 1300 (traditionally 1299) and gave his name to a dynasty which ruled for over 600 years. The O. rulers, originally known as Emir or Bey, soon acquired the traditional Islamic titles of Sultan and Khalifa (Caliph), though this last was not, until modern times, of great importance to them. After continued expansion the O. ruled, under Süleyman the Magnificent (1520–66), an Empire stretching from Hungary to Yemen and the Abyssinian coast, and from the Moroccan border to the Persian Gulf. After Süleyman, Ottoman advance was halted by the beginnings of disintegration in its army and administration, and by powerful enemies in the East (Persia) and West (the Habsburg Empire); various territorial gains, though, were still made occasionally.

However, the OE's real decline began after the failure of the siege of Vienna, 1683, and in the Treaty of Karlowitz, 1699, it lost control over a large part of the Balkans. The OE suffered further defeats during the 18th century mainly at the hands of Austria and Russia, while the rise of powerful autonomous local rulers and chiefs limited the Sultan's authority even within his own domains. By the first decades of the 19th century the fate of the Empire (the "Sick Man on the Bosphorus") had become a major European concern (the "Eastern Question"); British opposition to Russian designs to advance southwards was largely

Map of the Ottoman Empire

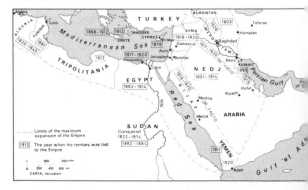

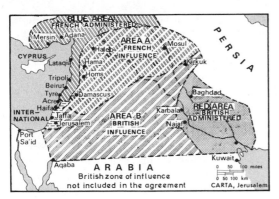

Partition of the Ottoman Empire as planned by the Sykes-Picot Agreement

responsible for the Empire's survival. The Great Powers' efforts to acquire territorial gains, extend their capitulatory rights (see capitulations▷) and obtain economic concessions, was now complicated by the emergence of nationalist movements, aiming at self-rule and independence for the OE's various ethnic communities. The OE reacted by introducing —often under Great Power pressure—a series of administrative legal, military and educational reforms (the *Tanzimat*) and by adopting a policy of Ottomanism, designed to induce loyalty to the dynasty and the state among the various ethnic and religious communities. The O., who implemented these reforms inefficiently (and too late to arrest the process of disintegration), were unable to stand up against nationalist insurrections and Great Power encroachments; during the 19th and early 20th centuries the O. lost all their Balkan and African provinces, and at the outset of World War I they were left with only Anatolia, part of Thrace and the Arab provinces in Asia. The entry of the OE into World War I on the side of the Central Powers hastened its final dissolution, and by the time of the Armistice of Mudros▷ it had also lost its Arab provinces. As the O. government was discredited by failure and defeat, and by its acceptance of the Allied peace terms (Treaty of Sèvres▷, 1920), the Turkish nationalists under Kemal Atatürk▷ were able, in Nov. 1922 and March 1924, to abolish the O. sultanate and caliphate. The dynasty was permanently exiled from Turkey. (D.K.)

P

PACHACHI (also Bahjahji), **AL-, HAMDI** (died 1948). Iraqi conservative, right-wing nationalist politician, son of a family of big landowners. Minister of Social Welfare 1941–4. P. was Prime Minister,

1944–6, but had to resign when the Regent wanted to liberalize political life in Iraq. After the nationalist riots in protest against the Draft Treaty of Portsmouth▷, Jan. 1948, he served as Foreign Minister in Muhammad al-Sadr's right-wing cabinet from Jan. 1948 until his death in Mar. 1948.   (B.G.)

PACHACHI (also Bahjahji), **AL-, MUZAHIM.** Iraqi politician and diplomat, b. 1891. Prime Minister 1948–9. Graduate of the Istanbul Law School. Active in the pre-World War I Arab nationalist movement, he founded a newspaper, *Al-Nahda* ("The Revival"), 1912, and a "National Scientific Club", 1913; both were closed down by the Ottomans when war broke out. In 1924, P. was a member of the committee drafting the Iraqi constitution. The same year he was appointed Minister for Communications and Public Works, a post he held until 1925. Member of Parliament 1925–7; Representative of Iraq in London 1927–8. P. opposed the Anglo-Iraqi Treaty of 1930, as not satisfactory to nationalist demands, but moderated his opposition when appointed, in 1931, Minister of Economics. Minister of the Interior 1931–3. Representative to the League of Nations, Geneva 1933–5. Minister to Italy 1935–9, France 1939–42; during the occupation of France he stayed in Switzerland 1942–5. After his return to Iraq, P. showed active concern with the Palestine problem: appeared before the Anglo-American committee in 1946, member of the committee for the Defence of Palestine 1946–7. He served as Prime Minister and Minister for Foreign Affairs from June 1948 to Jan. 1949. His cabinet rejected the truce imposed on Palestine by the UN Security Council and recognized the Palestinian "Gaza Government" (see Palestine Arabs▷ and Gaza Strip▷). Briefly Deputy Prime Minister and Minister for Foreign Affairs, Dec. 1949 to Feb. 1950, in Mar. 1950 he led the opposition to the law allowing the Jews of Iraq to leave the country. In 1951, after failing to establish a pro-Egyptian party, P. left Iraq and spent most of his time abroad. He returned after the 1958 coup, but was not politically active.   (B.G.)

*PAHLAVI. The dynasty ruling Iran. Founded in 1925 by Col. Reza Khan (later Reza Shah▷), when he ousted the Qajar dynasty and made himself King. The name P., chosen by Reza Shah as his family name, was originally the name of the Persian language, spoken during the Parthian dynasty (*c.* 250 BC to 150 CE). The present Shah, Muhammad Reza▷, is the second monarch of the P. dynasty.   (B.G.)

*PAKISTAN. P.'s involvement in ME affairs is anchored primarily in her Islamic character. As a

Muslim nation, P. is interested in forging close ties with the Muslim countries of the ME. She has always declared her solidarity with the Arab states in their struggle against Israel, refuses to have any relations whatsoever with the latter, and participates in all Arab activities against Israel in the international arena. P. has aided Jordan and Sa'udi Arabia with military instruction, mainly in their air forces, and has lent them pilots. There were also reports—never confirmed—of Pakistani volunteers or mercenaries joining in military and guerilla activities against Israel.

P. refrains from adopting a stand in inter-Arab disputes. It is apparent, however, that her leaders are more in sympathy with the conservative pro-Western regimes, such as Jordan and Sa'udi Arabia, then with the revolutionary leftist ones. This sympathy is also consistent with P.'s close ties with Iran. P. has also taken Pan-Islamic▷ initiatives and organized all-Islamic conferences and organizations, and this, too, drew her closer to Sa'udi Arabia and the conservatives. P.'s eagerness for Pan-Islamic activities—chiefly conducted by political leaders and groups and not necessarily by the government has considerably lessened in recent years.

P. is tied to the ME, beyond her Islamic links, by a formal alliance. In Apr. 1954, she signed a treaty of friendship with Turkey (and a mutual defence treaty with the USA). From this followed her adhesion in Sept. 1955 to the Baghdad Pact▷, comprising P., Turkey, Iran, Iraq, and Britain, with American support. The decline of this Pact and the disillusionment of its members occurred at a time when P. was adopting a more neutralist policy and seeking to foster ties of friendship with the Soviet Union and Communist China. She has since been anxious to play down the political and military implications of the Baghdad Pact. P. continues, nevertheless, to participate, with Turkey and Iran, in a "Regional Cooperation for Development" (since 1964). Her relations with Turkey and, in particular, with Iran have remained close.

In exchange for her friendship, P. expects the ME nations to support her in her conflict with India in general, and in the Kashmir issue in particular. Such support is forthcoming from Iran, Turkey and the conservative Arab states to a greater extent than from the leftist Arab states. The latter foster their friendship with India and seek her support; but even they do not fully support India on the Kashmir question, but subscribe to a vague formula of self-determination for the people of Kashmir, that is in effect close to P.'s official position.   (Y. S.)

PALESTINE (Arabic: *Filastin*, Hebrew: *Eretz-Israel*). Country on the eastern shores of the Medi-

terranean, between Lebanon and Syria in the north and the Sinai desert and the Gulf of 'Aqaba in the south. Some regard the desert as P.'s eastern border, thus including Transjordan within her boundaries, while others consider the River Jordan as her eastern frontier. In ancient times most of P. belonged to the Kingdoms of Judah and Israel; later, most of it was known as "Judaea", but in 135 CE, following an unsuccessful rebellion of the Jews, the Roman rulers renamed the province *Syria Palaestina*, in order to obliterate its Jewish national character.

From 1516 to 1917–18, P. formed part of the Ottoman Turkish Empire. She did not, however, constitute a political or administrative unit. Northern P. belonged to the Province Normal *(Vilayet)* of Beirut, southern P. to the Special District *(Samaq)* of Jerusalem, and Transjordan to the *Vilayet* of Damascus.

As a political unit in modern times, P. was created in 1917–22, as a British Mandate, including Transjordan▷ (in 1922 Transjordan was excluded from the Mandate provisions concerning the Jewish National Home). In May 1948, when Israel was created in one part of P., while the Arabs declined to form an independent state in their part and permitted her occupation by Jordan and Egypt, P. ceased to be a political unit. Various P. Arab groups are endeavouring to re-create an Arab P. State or at least a vaguely defined "P. Entity" (see below).

The area of P., 1922–48, excluding Transjordan, was 10,800 sq. mi. Its population was in 1922 about 750,000: 590,000 Muslims, 5,000 Druzes, 71,000 Christians, most of whom were Arabs, and 84,000 Jews. In 1946, the last official estimates of the Mandatory Government indicated a population of about 1,912,000 (1,143,000 Muslims, 10,000 Druzes, 145,000 Christians, 608,000 Jews).

POLITICAL HISTORY. There have always been some Jews in P.; Jews have immigrated to P. throughout the twenty centuries of their dispersion. However, since the 1880s, Jewish immigration was inspired by the idea of Zionism▷. Unlike previous Jewish immigration, which was mainly for religious purposes, these immigrants came with the intention of turning the country into a Jewish homeland, thus staking the Jewish nation's political claims. At first there were sporadic, small-scale armed clashes with Arab villagers, while the Arab urban intelligentsia articulated its opposition by petitioning the Ottoman authorities to ban Jewish immigration and settlement (which were, indeed, only semi-legalized and sometimes formally banned).

At the same time, Arab nationalism▷ made its first, tentative steps, directed in part against Jewish settlement and in part towards independence from Ottoman rule. These stirrings of nationalism were in part Muslim rather than Arab in character and most Arabs remained loyal to the Muslim Ottoman Empire; their aims—whether separation from the Empire and complete independence or a greater degree of local autonomy within the Empire—were not spelled out precisely. Neither was their aim specifically Palestinian; the movement was part of Arab nationalism in the Fertile Crescent▷. In the first two decades of the 20th century, P. Arabs founded some societies, and a few of them belonged to Arab nationalist societies of a more general character (see Arab nationalism▷). Most P. Arab leaders took no part in these activities and remained loyal to the Ottoman rulers. Arabic newspapers were also launched in P., e.g. *Al-Karmel*, 1908; *Filastin*, 1911 (both by Christian Arabs).

Contacts between Zionist and Arab nationalist leaders—both Palestinian and non-Palestinian—were frequent, and attempts were made to reach agreement; but they remained inconclusive, and hostility to Jewish settlement and aspirations gradually became dominant.

During World War I—in which Turkey was allied with Germany—the Ottoman authorities, suspicious of rebellious movements and contacts with the Allied Powers, suppressed both Arab nationalists and the Jews of P. Several suspected Arab and Jewish leaders were arrested, and some were executed. Many Jewish leaders were expelled and deported (while others served in the Turkish Army). In 1916–17 British forces under General Allenby▷ advanced northwards from Egypt; in Dec. 1917 they conquered Jerusalem. British military rule was replaced by a civil administration on 1 July 1920, following the decision of the San Remo Conference▷ (Apr. 1920) to confer the Mandate▷ for P. upon Britain, and Sir Herbert Samuel became the first British High Commissioner for P.

The Mandate for P.—confirmed by the League of Nations in 1922—held the Mandatory "responsible for putting into effect" the British Balfour Declaration▷ of 2 Nov. 1917 "in favour of the establishment of a National Home for the Jewish people", without prejudice to "the civil and religious rights of existing non-Jewish communities".

The local Arabs claimed that Britain had promised independence to P. (southern Syria, as they put it) in the McMahon-Hussein Correspondence▷ of 1915–16, as part of the all-Arab State of Federation. They vehemently rejected the Balfour Declaration as invalid, alleging that Britain had had no right to promise the country to a third party. Nevertheless, in Jan. 1919, Prof. Chaim Weizmann▷, the President of the Zionist Organization, signed a formal agreement with Amir Feisal▷, Sharif Hussein's▷ son

New immigrants on the deck of Hagana ship "Jewish State", 1947

(the man representing Arab nationalism and the planned Arab Federation), providing for close co-operation between the Arab and the Jewish nationalist movements, the "Arab State" on the one hand and "P" on the other; the Zionists were to give aid to and advice on the economic development of the Arab State, and Feisal agreed that large-scale Jewish immigration and settlement in P. be encouraged. The agreement was never implemented; Feisal stipulated that it would be void if Arab independence plans were not satisfied; Feisal lost his Damascus throne in 1920, and the Arab Federation, in whose name he had signed, did not come into being. Zionist contacts with Syrian, Pan-Arab Federalists continued in the early 1920s; but the extreme nationalism of the local Arab leaders came to determine the Arab attitude to Zionism and the Jews of P.

Local Arab hostility against the Jews broke out in demonstrations early in 1920, and in violent disturbances on 4 Apr. 1920, at the Muslim festival of Nebi Musa. A second bloody riot, followed by a massacre of Jews in Jaffa, occurred in early May 1921, as a result of the Jewish celebration of May Day. The British Administration appointed a local commission of inquiry, the Haycraft Commission, to report on the cause of the riots. A Jewish self-defence organization, *Hagana*▷, was formed in 1921 out of local defence groups.

The first British White Paper on P., was subsequently issued on 3 June 1922. It proposed to provide a measure of self-government by establishing a legislative council. It denied Arab allegations that the British intended to turn P. over to the Jews, stressing that they merely intended to establish such a Home *in* P. It limited Jewish immigration to P., and proposed establishing a quota determined by the economic absorptive capacity of the country.

At the same time Transjordan▷, in which the Hashemite Prince 'Abdullah▷, another son of Sharif

Hussein▷, had been installed by the British, in 1921, as "Amir", was excluded from the Mandate's provisions concerning the establishment of a Jewish National Home (while remaining, officially, under the British Mandate); the League of Nations had, on Britain's request, authorized this *de facto* partition of P. The Zionists protested. They also interpreted the White Paper as an attempt to appease the Arabs but reluctantly accepted it; however it was rejected by the Arabs as it did not put a stop to the development of the Jewish National Home. The Legislative Council, rejected by the Arabs, was not established, and in the absence of any representative institution the administration, headed by a High Commissioner, remained of the colonial type. There followed seven years of relative peace in P. This period saw the development of local Jewish and Arab communal organization.

BRITISH HIGH COMMISSIONERS FOR PALESTINE

Sir Herbert Samuel▷	1920–5
F.M. Lord Plumer	1925–8
Sir John Chancellor	1928–31
Maj. Gen. Sir Arthur Wauchope	1931–7
Sir Harold MacMichael	1937–44
F.M. Lord Gort	1944–5
Sir Alan Cunningham	1945–8

The Jews elected a "Representative Assembly", *Assefat Hanivharim*, in Oct. 1920; this Assembly nominated a "National Council", *Va'ad Le'umi*▷, as a sort of cabinet for Jewish communal affairs, recognized as such in 1926 by the Mandatory Government. (The Jewish Agency▷, identical until 1929 with the Zionist Organization, was recognized by the Mandate as a World-Jewish body to advise and co-operate with the government on matters concerning the National Home and the development of the country.)

Jewish political parties existed mainly within the Zionist movement (see Zionism▷)—though there were some specifically Palestinian-Jewish groups, such as *Hapo'el Hatza'ir* ("The Young Worker"), a non-Marxist socialist pioneer group, formed 1905, and *Ahdut Ha'avoda*▷ ("Labour Unity"), a socialist party founded in 1919 and embracing the Zionist-socialist *Po'alei Zion* party. A Jewish federation of labour, the *Histadrut*▷, later to become quite powerful, was set up in 1920. Two groups remained outside the Jewish communal organization: *Agudat Israel*▷, an ultra-orthodox organization, opposing Zionism as an improper interference with Providence, and the communists (outlawed by the Mandatory Government), opposing Zionism as a nationalist movement.

P. Arab leaders, participating also in the Syrian-Arab congresses of 1919–20 as representatives of "Southern Syria", created local national committees. In 1920, the Third Arab Congress set up a permanent Arab Executive, with Mussa Kazem al-Husseini▷ as Chairman. The Executive would not co-operate with the British Administration and refused to have any dealings with the Jews. In 1921–2 the British Administration set up a Supreme Muslim Council▷ to manage Muslim religious affairs; Hajj Amin al-Husseini▷, nominated in 1920 as Mufti of Jerusalem, was elected President of the Council (both appointments were interpreted as government encouragement to the nationalist extremists). Husseini gradually turned the Muslim Council into a forceful political weapon.

The Jewish population doubled between 1922 and 1929, mainly through immigration. There was an economic crisis in P. in 1926–7 and Arab nationalists hoped that the Zionist endeavour would collapse from within (in 1927 there had been a net Jewish emigration from P. of 2,350). However, the economic situation improved and in 1929 the Zionist movement was strengthened by the creation of the Jewish Agency▷, which included non-Zionists.

In 1928 tension developed over the *status quo* at the Wailing Wall▷, the Jewish holy place below the Temple Mount, on which the mosques of al-'Aqsa and 'Omar are situated. Rumours that the Jews were about to take over the area of the holy mosques resulted (1929) in a massacre of Jews in the old Jewish centres of Hebron and Safed, and the British forces were inadequate to prevent the violence. A Commission, headed by Sir Walter Shaw▷, blamed the outbreak on the Arabs, but emphasized their fear of, and opposition to, the continuing development of the Jewish National Home. In 1930 Sir John Hope Simpson found the economic prospects for further Jewish settlement and immigration very limited and recommended their restriction.

A British White Paper of 1930 re-emphasized the safe-guarding of Arab rights, urged the restriction of Jewish immigration and land purchases, and proposed once again setting up a Legislative Council as a step towards self-government. But, owing to strong Zionist protest, the British Prime Minister, Ramsay MacDonald, denied in a public letter to Weizmann the interpretation of the White Paper as intending to water down the Balfour Declaration and the Mandate and reaffirmed Britain's obligation to the Jewish people. Futile discussions about the formation of a legislative council continued until 1936. The Arabs demanded a council with an Arab majority and real powers, through which they could undermine the Jewish National Home. The Jews demanded numerical parity, to prevent Arab obstructionism. The government, which had planned to have official representatives on the Council as the real decision-makers, was unable to come up with a proposal acceptable to all parties.

In Oct. 1933 the Arabs launched a new campaign of violence; this time it was directed against the British, but also protested against continuing Jewish immigration and land purchase. The following year, Mussa Kazem Husseini▷ died, and the Arab Executive virtually ceased to exist. The Executive—and the Muslim Council—had been torn by factional struggles between the supporters of the nationalist leadership led by the Husseini▷ clan, and an opposition led by the Nashashibi▷ clan. By 1935, these factions had coalesced into Arab political parties, which differed from one another in personalities rather than in political programmes—all of them advocated the maintenance of the Arab character of P., resistance to the establishment of the Jewish National Home and the improvement of the social, economic and political conditions of the Arabs in P. The "P. Arab Party" was dominated by Hajj Amin al-Husseini, and formally headed by his cousin, Jamal al-Husseini▷. The "National Defence Party", headed by Ragheb Nashashibi▷ (Mayor of Jerusalem, 1920–34) formed the main opposition. It was believed to be more moderate and was in contact with Amir 'Abdullah▷ of Transjordan. Smaller groups included the Istiqlal▷ (Independence) party, advocating the creation of an Arab Federation and considered extremist, with 'Awni 'Abd-ul-Hadi▷ as its main leader; a "Reform Party" led by Dr. Hussein Khalidi▷ (Mayor of Jerusalem after 1934); a Youth Congress headed by Ya'qoub Ghussein; and a "Nationalist Bloc" based in Nablus and headed by 'Abd-ul-Latif Salah. There were also some Arab communists who co-operated with the Jewish communists, but, being extremely anti-Zionist, gradually adopted an Arab nationalist policy.

There was a considerable increase in Jewish immigration between 1933 and 1935, caused mainly by the rise of National Socialism in Germany and Polish anti-Semitism (1933; 30,327; 1934: 42,359; 1935; 61,854). The immigrants included a large proportion of highly skilled professionals and "capitalists" (according to the Immigration Ordinance of 1933 the immigration of capitalists of independent means was not limited, while a "labour schedule" for pioneers and workers was fixed annually by the government on the basis of the estimated economic absorption capacity; the entry of students, persons of religious occupation and dependants of local inhabitants was permitted provided that their maintenance was assured).

For the first time there was a real possibility of a Jewish majority in Palestine within the foreseeable future.

Attempts to reach agreement with the Arab leadership, made by both the official Jewish-Zionist leaders and by dissenters, such as the advocates of a Binational▷ P., consistently failed. Arab apprehensions concerning the rapid growth in the Jewish population, and nationalist unrest in Syria, Lebanon and Egypt, coupled with the moves towards independence planned in those countries, were the main cause for Arab unrest in P.

A general strike was proclaimed in Apr. 1936, and an Arab Higher Committee, composed of ten leaders of the various factions, was set up. The strike was accompanied by continuous violence against the Jews, communications and the security forces. In Aug., local Arab guerilla bands were reinforced by a

The Peel Commission partition plan, 1937

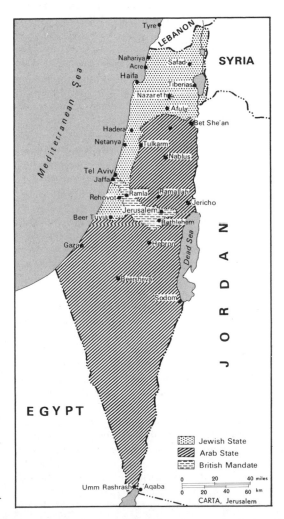

Jewish State
Arab State
British Mandate

0   20   40 miles
0   20   40   60 km
CARTA, Jerusalem

volunteer army from Syria, Lebanon and Transjordan under Fawzi al-Qawuqji▷. The *Hagana*▷, still restricting itself to passive defence, was split by the founders of the *Irgun (T)zeva'i Le'umi*▷ (IZL) for not adopting more active tactics. Yet, Arab violence proved a failure. The strike also caused severe damage to the P. Arab economy. The insurrection was ended in Oct. 1936 upon a pre-arranged joint appeal by the rulers of Transjordan, Iraq, Sa'udi Arabia and Yemen. (Egypt was not then considered as part of the Arab world or involved in P. affairs.)

A royal Commission under Lord Peel▷, sent out by the British, declared the Mandate to be unworkable and proposed the partition of Palestine into an Arab State (to be united with Transjordan) and a Jewish State, with a British mandated zone to include Jerusalem and Bethlehem and a corridor linking them to the Mediterranean near Jaffa, as well as an enclave near 'Aqaba. Jewish immigration and settlement should be limited to a "political high" of 12,000 *p.a.* in the five years following. The British government accepted these recommendations in July 1937, but the Arabs rejected them and resumed their insurrection. The Jews agreed to consider partition, while protesting against the further limitation put on immigration. The idea of partition was dropped by Britain, following the Woodhead Commission's report (1938) that no partition plan equitable and workable in its details could be elaborated.

Arab violence turned into a full-fledged rebellion in 1937; after Nashashibi and other opposition leaders seceded from the Higher Committee in July, the committee became a tool of the Husseini faction, and terror was increasingly directed against the Arab opposition. The Higher Committee was outlawed on 1 Oct. 1937 and Hajj Amin Husseini dismissed as President of the Muslim Council; he evaded arrest and escaped to Lebanon and Syria, as did Jamal Husseini (some other Arab leaders were arrested and deported).

Some unofficial Arab-Jewish contacts continued, but they failed, as the greatest concession that any Arab leader was willing to make was that the Jews should form 40% of Palestine's population. Once plans for partition were abandoned, the Arab position hardened even further. Late in 1938 the British decided to call a Round Table Conference of Britain, the Jews and the Arabs, to discuss a solution to the Palestine dispute. They invited the Arab states (including, for the first time, Egypt) to participate in the conference, which met in London in Feb. 1939. The Arabs refused to sit down with the Jews at the same table, and the British had to meet separately with them and the Jewish representatives. No agreement was reached, and Britain reverted to rule by decree.

A new White Paper was issued in May, limiting Jewish immigration to 15,000 *p.a.* during the next five years, further immigration to depend on Arab consent, and prohibiting or restricting land purchase by Jews in large parts of P. (implemented by Land Transfer Regulations of 1940). An independent Palestinian State, based on the existing population ratio (a 2:1 Arab majority) and making no provisions for Jewish autonomy or further growth, was to be established within ten years. The League of Nations Mandates Commission denounced the White Paper as "not in accord with" the spirit and purpose of the Mandate. The Jews regarded it as a betrayal of Britain's obligations under the Mandate and the Balfour Declaration and resolved to fight it. They combated the curtailment of immigration by organizing mass illegal immigration.

No World War II battles took place in P. It was feared the Germans might reach P. through either Lebanon and Syria (under Vichy-France until June 1941), or Egypt (until the German defeat at al-'Alamein), and plans were made for guerilla resistance. About 26,000 P. Jews volunteered for the British and Allied forces, but only in 1944 were the Jewish volunteers allowed to form their own Jewish Brigade▷ within the British Army (the *Hagana* was illegal). The violent, armed Jewish resistance that had followed the White Paper of 1939 was suspended for the duration of the war by both the *Hagana* and the dissident *Irgun (T)zeva'i Le'umi*▷ (IZL), with only the extremist Stern Group▷ continuing violent resistance.

Arab participation in the anti-German war effort was less enthusiastic than that of the Jews. The disturbances came to an end in 1939, and some 9,000 P. Arabs volunteered for the British Army. But their leader, Hajj Amin al-Husseini, and many of his associates defected—after anti-British activities in Syria and Iraq in 1940–1—to the Axis. Husseini broadcast pro-German propaganda from Radio Berlin to an eager audience and helped organize Muslims in Yugoslavia for service .with the German Army. He was also reported to have collaborated in planning and organizing the extermination of Jews. Many Arabs openly expressed their hope for an Axis victory.

After the war the future of P. once again became a pressing issue. The White Paper policy was still in force, despite the victory in the 1945 elections of the British Labour Party which had promised understanding towards Jewish aspirations. The problem of the Jewish survivors of the Nazi holocaust was immediate: US President Harry S. Truman▷ was particularly aware of this. British Foreign Secretary Ernest Bevin▷ proposed that the Mandate be transformed into a UN Trusteeship, with Great Britain continuing as trustee; but both the Arabs and the

Jews were now pushing for independence and an end to British rule. The Jews of P. resumed their active struggle against the British White Paper policy—a struggle based, since the Biltmore▷ Programme of 1942, on the explicit demand for a Jewish State, and turning, late in 1945, into violent rebellion sustained by *Hagana* and the national leadership. Dissident Jewish organizations (IZL, Stern Group) advocated and practised more militant methods, including individual acts of terrorism that were rejected categorically by the national leadership.

On 13 Nov. 1945, the USA and Britain announced that a joint Anglo-American Committee would be sent to investigate the problems of the Jewish refugees in Europe and the possibilities for a settlement in P. In 1946 it proposed the admission into P. of 100,000 Jewish refugees but as to P.'s future its recommendations were vague—a continuation of the Mandate or a Trusteeship, with neither Arabs nor Jews allowed independence. Truman accepted—and began pressing for—the admission of the 100,000; but the British hesitated. Further proposals, such as the Morrison-Grady plan (named after Herbert Morrison, Lord President of the Council, and Henry F. Grady, an American special envoy) and later ideas propounded by Bevin, were based on the division of P. into semi-autonomous Jewish and Arab provinces or cantons, with a central government that would remain British and retain wide powers. (These plans proposed the absorption of Jewish refugees in Europe or other countries willing to accept them.) They failed to gain American, Jewish or Arab approval.

As the clash between the Jews and the government became increasingly serious (firm steps against the Jewish national leadership and the *Hagana*, were taken in June 1946), Arab leaders also prepared for the inevitable final struggle. Arab activity, almost at a standstill during the war, was resumed towards its end. In the absence of a large part of the leadership, detained or in the Axis countries, Arab activity was not initially concerned with the major political problems. A "National Fund" (*Sanduq al-Umma*) was organized to prevent the sale of Arab lands to Jews; Mussa al-'Alami▷ set up a rival "Constructive Scheme" to achieve the same aim by the comprehensive development of Arab villages; 'Alami also organized and headed a network of propaganda and information offices abroad. No representative leadership body was established in the absence of the most prominent Husseini leaders. The founders of the Arab League▷ appointed 'Alami to represent the P. Arabs both at its foundation, 1945, and in the League Council. Later in 1945 an "Arab Higher Executive" was established through the mediation of envoys from the Arab states—and after the British

had promised the early release of the detained leaders. Jamal al-Husseini returned to P. in Feb. 1946 and assumed the *de facto* chairmanship of the Executive—officially vacant (for the ex-Mufti, as was well known). As Husseini arbitrarily changed the composition of the Executive, bitter disputes soon arose, and the opposition set up a rival Committee. In June 1946, the League intervened and, simply dissolving the existing bodies, appointed a new Higher Committee, which was extremist and followed the policy of Husseini. Hajj Amin al-Husseini, the ex-Mufti, had escaped in May 1945 from French detention and returned to the ME. He established his headquarters in Cairo and was again considered the top leader.

The P. Arab cause had, in fact, been taken up by the Arab states—called in, since 1939, by Great Britain. Some of the Arab statesmen, taking account of Jewish aspirations for independence, were considering the possibility of an autonomous Jewish canton within a federal framework (that would perhaps include neighbouring countries—Transjordan, Syria—as well). Iraq's Nuri al-Sa'id▷ in a federal plan presented in 1942–3, and Jordan's King 'Abdullah, favoured such ideas. The latter was reported to have conceded a much greater degree of independence to the Jews, and to have had contacts, or even to have reached agreement, with them. However, such cantonal schemes were unacceptable to the other Arab governments, and their authors did not insist on them. The official all-Arab aim in P., as expressed in a "Special Resolution Concerning P." in the Protocol of Alexandria, 1944 (which prepared the groundwork for the establishment of the Arab League) and as repeated throughout 1946–8, remained independence for a *unitary* P., with the Jews as a permanent minority and no more immigration, land purchases or settlement—in fact, an accelerated version of the British White Paper of 1939. The Arab leaders in P. regarded even that as too moderate; they were not prepared to accept the existence of the Jewish population and to guarantee its rights and security in the future Arab P.

Armed conflict was considered inevitable, and Arabs as well as Jews were preparing for it. In P., largely urban, Arab paramilitary groups were formed; these were two rival groups: *al-Futuwwa* (pro-Husseini) and *al-Najjada*▷ (opposition). The Arab states promised aid in the form of money, arms, training, logistics, volunteers, and political pressure. But, at all-Arab conferences in Inshas and Bludan▷ (1946), 'Aley and Cairo (1947), they decided against mounting a fully fledged invasion of P. by the regular Arab armies. In fact, practical preparations, such as the recruitment of volunteers, and the supply of arms and funds were not carried out very enthusiastically in 1946–7.

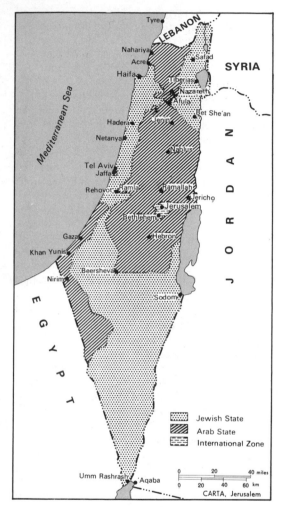

Palestine: the Jewish and Arab states according to the 1947 UN resolution

The British government turned the whole P. problem over to the UN in Apr. 1947. The UN General Assembly sent out its own Committee of Inquiry to P. (UNSCOP). The majority report of the committee proposed the partition of P. into a Jewish State and an Arab State, economically united, and an internationalized Jerusalem. The Jewish State proposed was much larger than that proposed by the Peel Commission, including most of the Negev, the coastal plain and north-eastern Galilee. UNSCOP'S minority plan proposed a federal state with wide autonomy for the Jews who would remain a permanent minority. UNSCOP's majority plan was adopted by the UN General Assembly on 29 Nov. 1947, by 33 votes to 13 with 10 abstentions. The USA, the USSR and France voted in favour of the partition plan, but Britain abstained.

The Arab states and the P. Arab leadership categorically rejected the UN's partition resolution and announced that they would resist its implementation by force. Arab guerilla operations inside P. actually started the day after the UN decision. In Jan. 1948 the guerillas were replenished by a volunteer force—the "Army of Deliverance" (*Jeish al-Inqadh*), largely officers and men seconded from the Syrian and Iraqi armies—again, as in 1936, under Fawzi al-Qawuqji▷; other volunteers were sent to southern P. by the Egyptian "Muslim Brotherhood"▷. Qawuqji's control only extended over the Arab parts of northern and central P., and was resisted by the "Brotherhood" and the Husseini-controlled Palestinian groups, as well as local bands, particularly in the south.

The British were still officially responsible for the maintenance of law and order; but, having declared that they would neither co-operate in the implementation of partition nor allow a UN Commission to supervise it, they did little to prevent the fighting. They hardly interfered with the establishment of Arab control in Arab areas and Jewish control in Jewish areas; they made half-hearted attempts to prevent the establishment of one side's full control over mixed areas and inter-area communications. The Jews felt that, on the whole, British intervention was directed against them; they resented, in particular, the entry of the Transjordanian Army, the "Arab Legion", commanded by British officers, into the fighting in and around Jerusalem. From about March 1948, the British appeared to be interested mainly in the security of their own staff and forces, and in their orderly withdrawal.

The P. Arab military effort crumbled in Apr. 1948, as Jewish forces firmly held the areas allotted to the Jewish State, including most of the Arab towns and villages within them; Jerusalem remained divided, and the control of the road leading to it from the coast was disputed. The failure of the P. Arab guerilla war was the main reason for the new decision taken by the Arab states, at the beginning of May 1948, despite the strong opposition of their military staffs, to invade P. with regular Arab forces.

During the local, guerilla phase of the war, in Feb.-Mar. 1948, thousands of Arab refugees had begun leaving the area of the fighting, and most of the leaders had been among the first to flee, thus contributing to the complete breakdown of the P. Arab body politic; in Apr.-May the thousands of refugees turned into a torrent of hundreds of thousands. The cause of this Arab exodus remains a matter of bitter controversy. Arab spokesmen claim that the refugees were forcibly expelled by the Jews, and adduce cases of expulsion or atrocities, particularly that of Deir

Yassin—a village near Jerusalem, many of whose inhabitants were killed when the village was taken by Jewish forces (dissident, not *Hagana*). Israel spokesmen maintain, on the other hand, that the Jews called on the Arab population to remain and live in peace, that Deir Yassin was an isolated case and publicly denounced, and that the refugees left of their own accord, spurred on by their leaders' example and advice (see, e.g., Haifa▷). What is beyond doubt is that the refugees fled in an atmosphere of fear and hatred. Their number was 550–650,000 in 1948, and most of them stayed within the original boundaries of P.—nearly 200,000 in the Egyptian-occupied Gaza▷ Strip, more than 200,000 in Jordanian-occupied P. (the West Bank▷), and close to 100,000 in Transjordan.

The British Administration was terminated, and British forces evacuated, on 14 May 1948, and the State of Israel proclaimed the same day. The invasion of P. by the regular forces of the Arab states began the same night (see Arab-Israel War▷). The UN Security Council appointed a mediator, the Swedish Count Folke Bernadotte▷ (who put forward a number of ideas, but had made no headway by September, when he was assassinated by Jewish extremists), and ordered a truce that came in force on 11 June but was interrupted by renewed hostilities 8–18 July, 15–31 Oct., and 22 Dec.–7 Jan. 1949. Armistices were negotiated under the auspices of the UN, with Dr. Ralphe Bunche▷ mediating (with Egypt and Jordan at Rhodes; with Lebanon and Syria at border points), and concluded early in 1949.

POPULATION, ECONOMY, SOCIAL STRUCTURE. The country had witnessed rapid development—mostly initiated by Jewish settlement and investment, but of benefit to the whole of the country.

At the beginning of the century P. was poor and backward, suffering from centuries of neglect. Agriculture was primitive and industry practically non-existent. Of the Jewish population (80–100,000 out of 400–500,000), the majority belonged to urban communities of traditional-orthodox Jews engaged mainly in pious study and dependent on charity; about 35,000 were new settlers, 12,000 of whom lived in 44 agricultural settlements. Jewish agricultural settlement, that had begun in the late 19th century, subsequently with the support of Baron Rothschild, was intensified. There was a strong sector of co-operative villages (small-holder co-operatives, *moshavim*, and collectives, *kibbutzim*▷ or *kvutzot*). Land for this settlement was purchased from Arab owners, mostly by the Jewish National Fund▷ (*Keren Kayemet Leyisrael*), for perpetual national ownership (leased to the settlers). By 1945 the Jews owned about 380,000 acres of land and held an additional 65,000 acres

in concession. About 204,000 acres of Jewish land were owned nationally (*i.e.* by the Jewish National Fund).

Claims that large numbers of Arab tenants were displaced, were investigated by the Mandatory Government and proved unfounded: of 3,270 complainants only 664 had been displaced from land sold to Jews (while thousands of Arabs had found employment, markets and economic advancement through Jewish settlement and development. The Hope Simpson Report estimated that less than 25% of P.'s area was cultivable, thus supporting the British Mandatory restrictions on Jewish immigration and settlement. Subsequent developments proved the report wrong.

Jewish settlement and development resulted in such projects as the draining of swamps—e.g. the Hula▷ Valley and the Valley of Jezreel (Ezdraelon); afforestation (also undertaken by the government); the modernization of cultivation methods; urban and industrial development; and an optimal usage of water resources.

During Mandatory times two economies existed side by side. The Arab economy was primitive, rural, partly based on large-scale land ownership, with no attempt at land reform, and with a nomadic or semi-nomadic sector; there was little Arab industry. The Jewish economy was modern, up-to-date methods of agriculture were used and sophisticated industries were developed. Zionist doctrine called for the employment of Jewish labour by Jewish enterprise, to enable a Jewish working class to grow, to develop a nation with a normal and healthy structure and to avoid the creation of a colonial-type society; this policy tended to accentuate the separation between the two economies. The Mandatory Government participated in the economy in the field of public works and communications such as the Haifa▷ port, developed in 1933, but otherwise played little part in economic development. The oil refineries in Haifa were constructed by the Iraq Petroleum Company (largely under British control).

P.'s population almost trebled during the Mandate. The Jewish population increased almost eight-fold, mainly through immigration. The Arab population doubled, mainly through natural increase, but also through the immigration of Arab labour from neighbouring countries (see Table, p. 300).

The Jews had their own health and education systems (their medical services assisting Arabs as well). Nearly 100% of Jewish children, aged 5–14, attended school, and there was little illiteracy. The Jews had fully revived Hebrew as a spoken language; it was used at all educational levels and in public life. Hebrew literature and poetry were flourishing—with

POPULATION OF PALESTINE

Year	Total	Muslims	Jews	Christians
1922 (census)	752,048	589,177	83,790	71,464
1931 (census)	1,033,314	759,700	174,606	88,907
1935 (est.)	1,308,112	836,688	355,157	105,236
1940 (est.)	1,544,530	947,846	463,535	120,587
1946 (est.)	1,912,110	1,143,330	608,230	145,060

a young generation of local-born (*Sabra*) writers growing up next to the older masters mostly of European origin. There were a number of Hebrew daily papers, the most important of which: *Haaretz* (founded 1919) and *Davar* (1925), are still in existence, and a large number of political and literary periodicals. A national theatre, *Habimah*, founded in Moscow 1918, has flourished in Tel Aviv since 1925, and other theatres followed; a Symphony Orchestra was established in 1936. The Hebrew University in Jerusalem was opened in 1925, and an Institute of Technology in Haifa in 1912. A "P. Broadcasting Service" was established by the Mandatory Government in 1936, broadcasting in English, Arabic and Hebrew. From 1945–6, the *Hagana*▷ maintained an underground broadcasting service, in Hebrew and (from 1947) in Arabic, guided by the Jewish national leadership.

The Arab population depended for its health and education services on the Mandatory Government and private institutions (particularly institutions maintained by Christian missionaries). School attendance (5–14) was estimated at 32.5%, the number of children who received some schooling at 48%. No significant specifically Palestinian-Arab literature or culture developed. Many Arab writers were active in P., but none of them achieved great prominence. There was a lively Arab press, both daily and periodical; of those papers regularly appearing for longer periods, the most important were *Filastin* (founded 1911) and *Al-Difa* (1934).

At the end of the War of 1948, Israel occupied 7,993 sq. mi., 77% of pre-1948 P.—about 2,500 sq. mi. more than allotted her in the UN blueprint of 1947. Israel held that the details of that blueprint, which took no account of her security requirements, could only have been implemented in peace and were invalidated by the Arab invasion; Israel contended further that the rounding-out of her area, which had resulted from the war, was vitally necessary for her defence and that she considered the extra areas an integral part of Israel. The Armistice Agreements laid down that the existing lines, while not constituting final borders, could only be changed by mutual consent.

The part of P. not within Israel's boundaries was occupied by Jordan (part of Jerusalem, including the Old City, and the districts of Hebron, Bethlehem, Ramallah, Nablus, Jenin and Tulkarm) and Egypt (the Gaza Strip▷). P. thus ceased to be a political-administrative entity.

All of P.'s pre-1948 Jewish population (600–650,000) was now in Israel (a few villages in Arab-occupied areas and the Old City of Jerusalem having been abandoned). Of pre-1948 P.'s Arab population (c. 1.3m.), about 700,000 had remained in their previous homes—about 150,000 in Israel, and 550,000 in the Arab-occupied parts of P. (400,000 in the Jordanian-occupied part: the West Bank, 100–150,000 in Egyptian-occupied Gaza); 550–650,000 had become refugees—100–150,000 had left P. (mostly for Lebanon and Syria), while the rest had remained within the original borders of their homeland (200,000 in the Gaza Strip, 200,000 in the West Bank, 100,000 in Transjordan).

For post-1948 P. see Israel▷, Jordan▷, West Bank▷, Gaza Strip▷, Arab-Israel Conflict▷, Palestine Arabs▷. (Sh.H.-E.L.-Y.S.)

*PALESTINE ARABS. The demographic development, history, national organizations and movements of the A. of P. (*Falastin* or *Filastin* in Arabic), were, till 1948, an inseparable part of the history of P. and are described in the entry Palestine▷. Until 1920–2, P. was not a clearly defined political and administrative unit, and it is doubtful whether her Arabs identified themselves specifically as A. of P.—opinions differ on this. In any case, under Turkish rule no nationalist Arab movement called explicitly for the independence of P. as a unit, and those few PA active in the Arab nationalist movement had wider aims in the context of a "Greater Syria"▷ or the Fertile Crescent▷.

In 1918–20, during the period when Amir Feisal▷ ruled in Damascus, the PA leaders called their country "Southern Syria" and opposed its separation from Syria; but when Feisal's dream of a greater Syrian kingdom was shattered and the partition of the area into separate states became fact, the PA accepted that fact and began conducting their communal and political activities within the framework of P. The struggle with the British Mandate▷, but first and foremost with the Jews over the future of the country and its government (See Arab-Israel Conflict▷), was a main factor in the emergence of the A. of P. as a body politic.

The number of PA increased under the British Mandate, and parallel with the development of the Jewish National Home, at an unprecedented rate: in less than 30 years, they doubled in number. In 1900, their numbers were estimated at 500–550,000, and by the end of World War I, at 600–650,000 (c. 70,000 were Christians, the rest Muslims); in 1948 they were 1.2–1.3m. (140,000 Christians). This was mostly natural increase made possible by the rapid development of the country's economy, security, public health and medical services. But P. also attracted a good number of Arab migrants—partly seasonal workers, mostly from Transjordan and Syria ("Houranis") of whom only a fraction stayed permanently, and partly immigrants who came to settle; there are no reliable figures, but Arab immigration during the Mandate has been estimated at 100,000 or more.

The PA did not establish binding, all-embracing national institutions, like the Jews' *Knesset Yisrael* with its elected General Assembly and National Council (*Va'ad Le'umi*▷). The Mandatory Government suggested the establishment of an "Arab Agency" (parallel to the "Jewish Agency"▷ provided for in the Mandate), but the proposal was rejected. The PA had communal-religious representation— the Supreme Muslim Council▷ on the one hand and various representative and administrative bodies of the Christian community on the other, and they had economic, professional and cultural institutions, as well as nationalist political organization. The latter never established elected representation organs which were accepted by everyone. It grew out of local and regional self-appointed committees of notables (such as the "Muslim-Christian Committees", in 1919–20), conferences and congresses. In 1920 the Arab Executive▷ led by Mussa Kazem al-Husseini▷ was established as an all-embracing and permanent roof organization; it existed till al-Husseini's death in 1934. Behind this united front, a fierce struggle between rival camps was taking place. The chief bone of contention was the Supreme Muslim Council; its supporters were called *al-Majlisiyin*, "Council Men", but the "Opposition"—*al-Mu'aridin*—opposed the Arab Executive together with the Muslim Council. The supporters of the Council and the Executive were often called the Husseinis▷, after the family of their chief leaders, while the opposition were called the

Nashashibis▷. In the mid-1930s, after the disbanding of the Arab Executive, Arab political parties were formed (see Palestine▷). However, they did not play an important role.

An inclusive roof organization was re-established in Apr. 1936 as the Arab Higher Committee▷. In this committee were represented the two opposing camps; it was composed of the leaders of the six existing parties, and three others (two Christians); the chairman was Hajj Amin al-Husseini▷, the Mufti of Jerusalem. This committee was born out of the nationalist agitation of 1936 which began with a general strike and soon turned into violent "disturbances". The committee directed this struggle, and, when it failed, called in autumn 1936 for mediation and, following the recommendation of the Arab kings, the cessation of the strike and riots. When the disturbances were renewed in 1937, the unity of the PA was destroyed: the opposition, the Nashashibis, opposed their renewal, and seceded from the Higher Committee, which represented from then on the extremists only. The guerilla bands fought their Arab opponents as much as the British and Jews, and the number of Arab victims of this Arab terror was much greater than the number of British or Jewish. The Arab Higher Committee was disbanded and outlawed by the government in Oct. 1937; the Supreme Muslim Council was also dispersed.

The A. of P. emerged from these years of revolt, 1936–9, split into factions and torn by bitter bloodfeuds, deprived of a united organization and of leadership, their leaders in prison or in exile, some of them in Nazi Germany. The war years passed with no political or organizational activity. In 1943–4, when there was talk of renewed activity, the Husseini faction opposed any attempt at political activity or representation during the absence of its leaders. The other factions accepted this ruling, and until the release of Jamal al-Husseini▷, late in 1945, PA organizational and political activity was concentrated in chambers of commerce, propaganda offices and attempts to prevent the sale of Arab land to Jews by developing the Arab village and establishing an Arab national land fund and did not deal with the basic questions concerning the country's future. When the PA were asked to send a representative to the founding meetings of the Arab League▷, 1945, they were unable to agree on a delegate and the league itself had to appoint one (Mussa al-'Alami▷). A new Arab Higher Committee was established by the end of 1945 with the mediation of the Arab League. When Jamal Husseini returned at the beginning of 1946, he assumed (in the name of the ex-Mufti, who was not permitted to return to P.) the leadership of the committee, and soon appointed several of his followers to it. His opponents, angered by his factionalism and dictatorial methods, seceded and formed a rival "High Arab Front". The Arab League had to cut the Gordian knot and, in June 1946, appointed a new Arab Higher Committee—dominated by the Husseinis. The PA no longer retained the command in the struggle for an Arab P.; it had been taken over by the Arab states, who supported the extremist faction among the PA.

The PA adopted an extreme and uncompromising position at the time of the decisive struggle for the country, but they were unprepared in organization and for action. In 1947, they rejected the partition of P., just as they had turned down earlier proposals (including compromise proposals such as a binational▷ state, permanent parity, etc.), and called for war to prevent partition and the establishment of a Jewish State. But the military instrument in their hands was dull; two paramilitary organizations (rival and squabbling) of urban youth—al-Futuwwa under Husseini leadership, and al-Najjada▷, belonging to the opposition; and guerilla-terrorist on the pattern (and partially under the leadership) of 1936–9. The Arab states helped with money, arms, training, operational bases and shelter; provided political and moral support, and even volunteers, (Fawzi al-Qawuqji's▷, "Army of Deliverance"). All this assistance was disproportionate to what was needed to oppose the strength and stubbornness of the Jews.

When the PA's military effort had failed, (see Arab-Israel War of 1948▷), the flight of refugees▷ began, in Feb. 1948; by Apr.–May they had become tens of thousands. The top leaders had been living outside P. since the beginning of the violence; the others, including most of the military leaders, now joined those in flight. By the end of Apr. the PA were a flock without a shepherd, disorganized and leaderless. When the Arab armies invaded P. in mid-May, they no longer found an organized Arab community.

When the battle was over and P. partitioned—disappearing as a political and administrative entity after less than 30 years—the A. of P. found themselves without their own independent State (which they had rejected when it was offered them) and divided into three groups: those in the State of Israel; those who had stayed in the rest of P. under Arab occupation; and refugees. Of the 1.2–1.3m. PA, 700,000 had remained in their previous residences: c. 150,000 in Israel, 400,000 in Judea and Samaria (which had now become the West Bank▷ of the Kingdom of Jordan), and 100–150,000 in the Gaza Strip▷; 500–600,000 had become refugees—of whom all had been uprooted from their places of residence though the great majority had remained in their country: c. 200,000 in the Jordan-occupied West

Bank and 200,000 in the Egypt-occupied Gaza Strip; c. 100,000 moved to Transjordan (originally also part of Mandatory P.), and 50–100,000 to Syria, Lebanon and other Arab countries. The refugees were kept, for political reasons, separate and distinct from the rest of the community in their countries of residence; this applied particularly to those in camps. Those in P. were, despite their separate status of "refugees", an integral part of the general PA community. For only in the Kingdom of Jordan did the refugees receive full civil rights, including the right to vote (although their numbers were not accounted for in the division of the country into constituencies, and the allocation of seats in parliament). For the A. who became citizens of the State of Israel—see Israel▷.

The PA had not opposed the occupation of their country by the armies of the neighbouring countries. Most of them regarded the entry of these armies as brotherly help and deliverance from Jewish domination. Part at least of the PA welcomed their prolonged stay, and its transformation into a permanent occupation and, finally, annexation (formal in the case of the West Bank, de facto in the case of the Gaza Strip). The PA in Gaza—i.e. those under Egyptian control—tried to establish in Gaza a PA political entity: in July 1948, an "Administrative Council for P." was established in Gaza with the approval and under the auspices of the Arab League; in Sept. the Arab Higher Committee established, instead of that council, a "government" calling itself "Government of All P."—i.e. claiming authority also over Israel and the Jordan-administered West Bank. The Gaza government was headed by Ahmad Hilmi, a Septuagenarian and included Jamal Husseini as Foreign Minister, and also the non-Husseinis 'Awni Abd-ul-Hadi▷, and Dr. Hussein al-Khalidi▷. An 86-member "Constituent Assembly" was presided over by Hajj Amin al-Husseini.

However, this experiment of a P. government in Gaza failed. Actually, all the Arab states except Jordan recognized it. But Jordan opposed its existence with all her strength. She was about officially to annex the West Bank and intended to become the only representative and legal successor of the PA entity; consequently, she could not allow a second representative of that same entity, especially a body which would claim the very territories annexed to Jordan. In the Gaza Strip a real government of "All P." could not exist, the more so as even in Gaza the Egyptians did not allow it real authority. The "government" became a group of frustrated politicians; some of its prominent members had already left it in 1948–9; the "Constituent Assembly" was not convened, after Oct. 1948, for a second sitting; and in Sept. 1952 the Arab League Council announced officially that the government had "ceased to operate" and that from now on the heads of the Arab states would represent P. in the League. Egypt continued to avoid the annexation of Gaza to her territory. Some rudiments of local self-government were allowed only after 1958.

In Judea and Samaria (the West Bank) no efforts were made in 1948 to establish a separate P. entity. King 'Abdullah's supporters, led by Ragheb Nashashibi▷ and Muhammad 'Ali al-Ja'bari, the Mayor of Hebron, smoothed the way for annexation while his opponents lay low. The first steps towards formal annexation were taken after the establishment of the Gaza government, and in response to this challenge. Conferences of notables in Oct. and Dec. 1948 offered 'Abdullah the crown of Jerusalem and asked him to take the remnant of Arab P. under his protection. 'Abdullah did not formally accept at once, but he began appointing Palestinians to governmental and administrative positions—first on the West Bank (Ragheb Nashashibi—Governor, Hussam-ul-Din Jarallah—Mufti), and since 1949 also as Jordanian government ministers, diplomatic representatives, etc. In Mar. 1949 the use of the term "Palestine" in official documents was forbidden and the term "West Bank" substituted for it. The formal annexation was completed in Apr. 1950: the Palestinians were made full citizens of Jordan and permitted to vote in parliamentary elections (under an election law, passed in Dec. 1949, that gave equal representation to the two parts of the state); and the new parliament solemnly proclaimed the annexation.

The annexation caused a serious crisis in the Arab League. It was resolved by a face-saving formula: 'Abdullah agreed not to enter into a separate non-aggression pact with Israel which had been negotiated, and the Arab states acquiesced in the annexation, which was described as "temporary", to last until the whole of P. was liberated.

From 1948 to 1967, during 19 years, the PA acquiesced in their political status under Jordan and Egypt. Certainly there was dissatisfaction, perhaps even bitterness, due to autocratic government and restrictions on political activity. The Palestinians formed an element of agitation, opposition and ferment in the Kingdom of Jordan, and they demanded more positions in the government. But in the course of 19 years there was no demand for a PA State, for secession from, or even autonomy within, Jordan; no specifically Palestinian organization was set up with specifically Palestinian aims. On the other hand, PA enjoyed positions at all levels in the Jordanian government.

The situation was different in the Gaza Strip. It had never been annexed to Egypt; the PA did not become part of the Egyptian nation and filled no position in the society, government or administration of Egypt. Egypt kept the Gaza Strip clearly separate and, unlike Jordan, regarded the part of P. in her hands as the nucleus of a separate, independent Palestinian entity. When a "National Union" was established as the only legal political organization in the UAR (Egypt-Syria), in 1958, a similar body was established in Gaza, as a Palestinian National Union; furthermore, it was decided to establish it also in Syria, and to oblige the PA living there to join it. But the "National Union" did not take root in Gaza any more than it had in Egypt and Syria. There were also attempts to establish in Gaza a rudimentary self-government on the Egyptian model: elected local committees which would nominate delegates to a Council of Representatives. True self-government did not grow out of that pyramid of local, district, central committees in Egypt, nor did it in occupied Gaza. Yet in the course of 19 years there was no movement of resistance or opposition to Egyptian rule.

The question of a "P. Entity" was reopened in the late 1950s. It was a basically anti-Jordanian idea, since any separate, distinct Palestinian "entity" would necessarily invalidate Jordan's rule over, and sole representation of, Arab P. Egypt, too, did not cherish the idea of a PA state, since the establishment of such a state in a part of P. could be interpreted as acquiescence in the existence of Israel. During the years of Jordan-Egyptian tension and incessant Egyptian propaganda assault on Jordan, Jordan completely rejected a P. entity and crushed any attempt to organize one. But in the 1960s, young PA became more active both in the armed, terrorist struggle against Israel, and in a renewed demand that the PA be recognized as a distinct nation with its own national "entity".

These were the years of the all-Arab "summit meetings"▷, of inter-Arab reconciliation and co-operation, and of intensification and escalation of the struggle against Israel. The first meeting, Jan. 1964, decided to recognize a Palestinian "entity" that would not be a state or a territorial unit (and therefore would not represent a danger for Jordan, or an invalidation of her rule in P., or an acquiescence in Israel's existence and possession of part of P.) but an extra-territorial national and organizational entity. Thus was established, with the blessing and co-operation of the Arab League and the Arab states, the "Palestine Liberation Organization"▷ (PLO), with Ahmad Shuqeiri▷ as its head. Parallel to or actually within the PLO, a "Palestine Liberation Army." was established. This was more in the nature of a label pinned to Palestinian units already existing within the armies of Egypt, Syria and Iraq than the creation of new forces: the Palestinian units remained under the control of the armies to which they belonged, and the PLA command had no real authority. The establishment of the PLO and the PLA was confirmed again at the second meeting, Sept. 1964, and they were promised finance, support and equipment; afterwards, the PLO often claimed that the funds promised and allocated were not paid out.

In the 1960s, new guerilla and sabotage organizations ("feda'iyin" ▷, see PA guerilla organizations▷) were founded and grew. Their methods, until after 1967, resembled those of the terrorist bands in their early development; but they were supported by the Arab states with finance, equipment, training, recruitment, shelter and, most important of all—bases. Once given the opportunity to operate in and from the Arab countries, they became a complex, wealthy establishment with all the trappings of a regular army (uniforms, administration, military police, pay, medical service, rest camps, etc.). In Jordan and Lebanon they grew increasingly independent until they became a state within a state. The self-assertion of a new feda'iyin establishment, which also introduced new tactics (artillery shelling of settlements in Israel from across the border, terrorist activities and sabotage in countries outside the ME, the hijacking of airplanes), became fully apparent after the Six Day War▷. This self-assertion brought about a confrontation between the feda'iyin establishment and the "host" states—primarily Jordan and Lebanon—even though they had supported and raised it.

As the guerilla organizations expanded, the PLO was drained of content; the extremist and utterly unrealistic speeches of Ahmad Shuqeiri angered the leaders of the Arab states, and, at the end of 1967 he was dismissed and replaced by Yahya Hamudeh, like him a politician and lawyer rather than a charismatic leader. In 1969 the al-Fatah▷ guerilla organization took control of the PLO; Fatah leader Yasser 'Arafat▷ became the chairman of its executive committee, guerilla representatives made up the majority of the Executive and the newly established Central Committee, and the PLO actually became a kind of co-ordinating roof organization of the various rival guerilla formations. In this task it failed, as it was unable to overcome their factionalism and mutual jealousies.

The PA played a passive role in the Six Day War. After the war, most of them found themselves under Israeli administration. Due to a new movement of refugees, there were changes in the geographical distribution of the PA. About 250,000 (some estimates are higher) moved from the West Bank and the Gaza Strip, as new refugees, to the East Bank; among them were about 110,000 old 1948 refugees (including their descendants). The West Bank population, c. 900,000 on the eve of the war, was now c. 600,000 (about 650,000 if East Jerusalem is included), of whom 200–230,000 were 1948 refugees with their families and descendants; 350,000 resided in the Gaza Strip (of whom 250–300,000 were 1948 refugees). The Arabs of Israel now amounted to c. 320,000 without the East Jerusalem Arabs, c. 380,000 if they were included. There were about 800,000 refugees outside Israel-controlled P. (500,000 in Jordan, i.e. the East Bank, c. 150,000 in Syria, 150,000 in Lebanon).

The PA in the West Bank and the Gaza Strip were now administered by an Israeli military government. This administration, though certainly not loved, was liberal and refrained as far as possible from intervening in civil affairs. The municipalities continued to function, and became the nuclei of a civil (though not a political) leadership. Courts and government departments now operated in the framework and under the supervision of the military government. Some officials, judges and lawyers refused to "collaborate", but most of them continued work; apparently the Government of Jordan, with whom they retained contact, advised West Bank leaders to maintain a normal daily civilian life and administration, and continued even to pay its former officials their salaries (so as to demonstrate that it still regarded itself as the legal government). In the area of economic development, especially in agricultural modernization, the military government offered help and training, and this the residents willingly accepted. Many thousands of West Bank and Gaza residents— 30–40,000 by 1970–1—worked in Israel despite attempts of the guerilla organizations to prevent this "collaboration" by acts of terrorism against the Arab workers. The bridges over the Jordan River were open to commercial traffic (especially the export of West Bank and Gaza agricultural products) and the passage of people in both directions—merchants, family visitors, tourists. There was a special programme of summer visits to the West Bank, mostly for students from the Arab countries; the number of PA visits to Jordan (and perhaps to other Arab countries from there), was estimated at c. 100,000 each year, while over 200,000 from Jordan and other Arab states (mostly PA) had visited the West Bank (and many had toured Israel, too).

This surprising co-existence has its limits of course. In the first place, there is the natural opposition of a people to an occupying military government. Israel had effectively to maintain security. Attempts at extensive infiltration by the guerilla organizations were prevented; most acts of sabotage or shelling were carried out from points beyond the border; and although there was doubtless much sympathy for the *feda'iyin*, they were unsuccessful in establishing any real network of underground cells or a resistance movement in the administered territories. Most of the population did not co-operate with these efforts. Most actual sabotage attempts were prevented by Israeli security forces—often by stringent means, such as administrative detention, residence in a place chosen by the military government, destruction of houses in which terrorists or arms had been found. Yet at times of crisis in Jordan, such as the anti-*feda'iyin* operations of Sept. 1970 or summer 1971, PA from Jordan sought refuge in the Israel-occupied West Bank. These included, in 1971, *feda'iyin* who surrendered on reaching Israel.

No new political leadership has emerged among the PA. No overall body was established to represent all the Arabs of the occupied territories (beyond local municipal representation). Israel neither requested nor encouraged the organization of such a political representation (although many Israelis regretted this). Among residents of the administered territories were leaders, dignitaries and former Jordanian politicians—Members of Parliament, ministers, diplomats and mayors. But they did not engage in political activity, they worked out no plan of action, proposed no solutions. Many of them probably favoured peace and some sort of co-existence; but few dared to take the decisive political step and publicly accept the existence of Israel and propose ways of peaceful co-existence with her (be it as supporters of a separate PA State, or as advocates of re-union with Jordan, with the PA as bridge-builders between Israel, Jordan and the other Arab states). And those few who did dare to speak out did not stimulate a movement or create a group of representative leaders. Israel did not encourage political negotiations with the leaders of the occupied territories, or seek out their proposals. They were not authorized to represent Jordan and the Arab states or propose anything on their behalf. On the other hand, if they were proponents of a separate Palestinian State, Israel could not encourage them without sealing off possible openings for future contacts with King Hussein and the Kingdom of Jordan—options which Israel had to retain. In any case, Israel could not create partners for negotiation; they had to emerge through their own strength.

In the 1960s the ideological content of the Palestinian movement was much debated among the leaders of the *feda'iyin* and the PA establishment outside Israel (see Arab-Israel Conflict▷). All were united, as always, in the basic demand that the P. entity must include all of P. and that the destruction of Israel must therefore precede any settlement. However, since 1967, most PA leaders have avoided, at least in their public utterances, reiterating the usual slogans about the (physical) destruction of the Jews of Israel or their expulsion. Beginning with the "P. Charter"▷, of July 1964, they emphasize that it is only the State of Israel, and Zionism, that must be eliminated; those Jews who renounced Zionism or were "liberated" from it, would be allowed to remain in the country and become citizens of the P. State to be created. The wording of the charter implies, on the other hand, that this would apply only to those Jews who were in P. before 1948, or (as in resolutions adopted in 1968) "before the beginning of Zionist penetration"—a date defined in another paragraph as the year 1917; yet, some spokesmen claim that the "offer" applies to all Israel Jews without distinction. This whole debate is, of course, utterly unrealistic, in its disregard of the firm resolve of Israeli Jews to preserve their national independence (over and above their physical survival). Yet even in its internal debates the PA leadership has arrived at no authoritative interpretation concerning this crucial point. Similarly, the revived PA movement has still to issue a clear and binding statement as to whether the future P. State would secede from, be united with, or take over, Jordan. The character and regime of the hoped-for P. State was also much debated. Left-wing organizations advocated a "democratic and secular state with no distinction of nationality, religion or race"; others, though using a similar formulation, shrank from the deletion of the clear definition of future P. as "Arab". *Al-Fatah* and the mainstream of the movement tried to avoid definitions and to postpone the decision until after the "liberation". The left-wing organizations—the "Popular Front for the Liberation of Palestine"▷ and the "Popular Democratic Front for the Liberation of Palestine"▷—emphasized the revolutionary Marxist-Maoist character of the planned state and stressed that the liberation of P. was linked with the destruction of all reactionary Arab regimes and with revolution in all the Arab countries.

King Hussein, who continues to regard Arab P. as part of his domain, has in recent years pledged that after Israel's evacuation of the occupied territories and the return of the West Bank to his Kingdom, the PA will be asked for their views; if they decide for an autonomous West Bank, he will accede to their views, and the kingdom will be reconstituted as a federation. The events of 1969–71 on the East Bank, and the struggle of the Jordanian king, army and government with the PA *feda'iyin* establishment, have made the future of the PA even more uncertain and controversial. The opinion is growing that there can be no settlement of the Arab-Israel conflict without the participation of the PA, without a solution that will satisfy them and allow them an honourable national existence. The PA themselves have not yet revealed the strength and courage for constructive solutions. Even their future relationship with the Kingdom of Jordan has not yet been clarified. More pressing is the problem of their relationship to Israel. As Israel cannot be destroyed, the future of the PA depends on peaceful co-existence with her. Israel will not evacuate the territories she now administers unless she can ensure that co-existence. Yet, the only PA voices that are clearly heard call for the elimination of Israel and the construction of the PA future on her ruins. Wiser voices, counselling peace and co-existence, are, if not silent as in the 1930s and '40s, still few and feeble.   (Y.S.)

*PALESTINE-ARAB GUERILLA ORGANIZATIONS. (*Feda'iyin*). The new PAG movement includes about 40 groups and organizations, some of them with little political or military significance. Apart from *al-Fatah*, *al-Sa'iqa* and the "Palestine Liberation Organization", (see below), each of these organizations numbers only a few dozen to a few hundred members. The movement is a direct descendant of the "Husseini"▷ G. gangs operating in Palestine during the British Mandate, especially in 1936–9, and the unorganized *feda'iyin* gangs active along the Israel-Arab armistice lines in the 1950s. The nucleus out of which the movement grew into its present form was founded in the late 1950s and early 1960s among the P.s in the Persian Gulf, Egypt and Lebanon and among P. students in Europe. All these organizations want to liquidate the State of Israel and establish in its stead a state realizing the national aspirations of the P. people. They have in common the conviction that this objective can be attained only by military means; the desire to revive the nationalist pride of the P.s and to reassert it against Pan-Arabism▷; the conception that the PAG should be a vanguard sweeping the Arab states along with them; and the belief that emphasis should be shifted to a non-conventional "People's Liberation War". Several groups were attracted by the neo-Marxist thesis that the defeat of the existing bourgeois regimes in the Arab countries is an essential pre-condition of victory. The *Feda'i* movement as a whole was established around one organization and in its footsteps. This organization, *al-Fatah*, derives its name from the reversed acronym of *Harakat Tahrir Filastin* (Palestine Liberation Movement): the root *fth* also carries the meaning: conquest.

Fatah coined the slogan of the "P. Revolution" in 1958, and its leaders (most of them graduates of

Egyptian universities compelled to migrate to the Persian Gulf principalities) were establishing underground cells until *c.* 1965, at which time they started to send groups of infiltrators into Israel. Since 1958, *Fatah* has published in Beirut a bulletin called *Filastinuna* ("Our Palestine"). From *c.* 1963 its centre moved to Algeria, and one year later its representatives took over the leadership of the West German and Austrian branches of the General Federation of P. Students. *Fatah* leader Yasser 'Arafat▷, formerly an active member of the "Muslim Brotherhood"▷, collaborated late in 1964 with the *Ba'th*▷ government of Syria, and with their help organized 113 sabotage operations in Israel between Jan. 1965 and June 1967. During that period *Fatah* failed in its efforts to turn itself into a mass movement, but succeeded indirectly in breaking Nasser's▷ doctrine (prevalent since 1957) that military operations against Israel should be undertaken only after long-range preparations, and in undermining the P. organization established on Egyptian initiative—the Palestine Liberation Organization (PLO) headed by Ahmad Shuqeiri▷.

The propaganda disseminated by both *Fatah* and Shuqeiri in favour of a "P. entity" bore fruit after the Six Day War. Within two years, *Fatah* and numerous G. fringe groups recruited thousands of arms-carrying volunteers. With political, financial and military aid from most Arab countries, *Fatah* and its rival-imitators became a fully fledged establishment in Jordan and Lebanon; a state within a state that presented a serious menace to King Hussein's▷ rule in Jordan. They also took command of the refugee camps in Jordan and Lebanon, and of various sectors along the cease-fire lines. The most important G. organizations are:

AL-FATAH. Its origins are described above. *Al-Fatah* apparently equals in military strength all the other organizations together, apart from the "Palestine Liberation Army" (see below). It is headed by a Central Committee, whose prominent members are Yasser 'Arafat (Abu 'Ammar), Khalil al-Wazir (Abu Jihad), Salah Khalaf (Abu Iyad), Faruq al-Qadumi (Abu Lutf), Mamduh Sabri (in charge of military activity), and the brothers Khaled and Hani Hassan. Its military arm, *al-'Assifa* (Thunderstorm), is responsible for about 70% of all P. sabotage activity against Israel. The political organization has overt and secret branches among Palestinians in the Arab world and overseas. The number of active members is approximately 20,000 (but other estimates put its effective membership at much less). Ideologically, *Fatah* is a moderately rightist movement; it has not adopted the doctrine of "scientific socialism" prevailing in other organizations. Officially, it stands for the establishment of a P. democratic, secular, multireligious state after the destruction of the "Zionist Entity" (Israel); the secular-democratic character of that state, and the dropping of its description as explicitly *Arab*, are still heatedly debated. *Fatah* wishes to avoid all discussion of ideology and social doctrine until victory is won.

PALESTINE LIBERATION ORGANIZATION (PLO). Established in 1964 on Egyptian initiative and under the aegis of the Arab League. It was conceived as the all-embracing roof organization, constituting "a P. A. entity" of sorts. However, some of the more extremist groups have boycotted it. Its chairman was Ahmad Shuqeiri and, after his dismissal late in 1967, Yahya Hamuden. The latter remained chairman of the National Council, while control of the Executive Council was taken over, in 1969, by *Fatah*, and 'Arafat became chairman of the Executive. PLO has a regular military arm—"The Palestine Liberation Army"—whose regiments (variously estimated at 10–12,000 strong) are, in fact, under the command of the Egyptian, Syrian and Iraqi general staff respectively and accordingly under the control of the relevant governments. The PLA also maintains Gs. of its own—the "Arab Liberation Forces". Since 1969 the independent character of the PLO has been obliterated in accordance with the systematic policy of the *Fatah*. Yet, *al-Fatah*'s own domination of the PLO seemed to be declining in 1970–71.

THE POPULAR FRONT FOR THE LIBERATION OF PALESTINE (PFLP). This organization evolved in December 1967 from the Arab Nationalist Movement▷ (*Harakat al-Qawmiyyin*) headed by Dr. George Habash▷. His adherents were active before that in sabotage under the names "Heroes of the Return" and "The Young Avengers", and the date of their merger into the PFLP varies in different versions. The organization is active mainly in the Gaza Strip and in sabotage outside the Palestine-Israel area (e.g. in Europe, the hijacking of airliners, etc.). The PFLP has adopted neo-Marxist doctrines, although Dr. Habash and other PFLP leaders started their careers far to the right. Numerically the PFLP is much smaller than *Fatah,* but it controls the network of the "Arab Nationalist Movement". "The Popular Front", considered more extremist than *Fatah,* is *Fatah*'s main competitor for the hegemony of the P. movement. At first it had close ties with Egypt, but since 1968 its chief support has come from Baghdad. It has been split several times, and several splinter groups use its name or parts of its name (e.g. "PFLP—General Command Group", headed by Ahmad Jibril).

THE POPULAR DEMOCRATIC FRONT FOR THE LIBERATION OF PALESTINE (PDFLP). A small organization headed by Nayef Hawatmeh, a Christian of Jordanian Bedouin origin, who seceded from the PFLP in 1968

as a result of a dispute with Dr. Habash about problems of doctrine and leadership. The PDFLP, extremist leftist and inspired by Maoist doctrines, demands an active struggle against the non-leftist Arab governments, especially Jordan.

THE ARAB PALESTINE ORGANIZATION. Headed by Ahmad Za'rur, formerly an officer in the armies of Jordan and Syria, this is another splinter group that formerly co-operated with Dr. Habash and Ahmed Jibril. Its political leanings are unclear.

POPULAR FRONT FOR THE LIBERATION OF PALESTINE—GENERAL COMMAND. Headed by Ahmad Jibril, formerly an officer in the Syrian Army, this group which seceded from the PFLP, previously operated under the name of "Palestine Liberation Front". It is a small organization with obscure political leanings, strong in small but well-trained units.

AL-SA'IQA—The Vanguard of the People's War of Liberation. Palestinian leftist military organization established in 1968 by the *Ba'th* party ruling in Syria. It is, in fact, under the direct command of the Syrian Army and *Ba'th* headquarters in Damascus. Since 1969 its membership has grown considerably and it has turned into the second largest organization, after *Fatah*. It is headed by Muhammad al-Mu'aita and Dafi Jumai'ani. Purges and factional rivalries reflect the factional struggles within the Syrian *Ba'th* party.

THE ARAB LIBERATION FRONT. Palestinian leftist military organization established by the Iraqi *Ba'th* party in 1969. It is headed by Dr. Zeid Haidar.

THE ACTION ORGANIZATION FOR THE LIBERATION OF PALESTINE. Established in 1969 by an extremist leftist group of dissenters from *Fatah* under the leadership of Dr. 'Issam Sartawi.

THE POPULAR STRUGGLE FRONT. A small organization, leftist-*Ba'th* in character, headed by the brothers Subhi and Samir Ghosheh and Bahjat Abu-Gharbiyya.

THE POPULAR LIBERATION FORCES. G. groups established in 1968 by the PLO and its Palestine Liberation

"Al-Fatah" guerilla, in training

A Palestinian guerilla in camouflage uniform

Army. Commanded by Col. Bahjat 'Abd-ul-Amir.

AL-ANSAR. The military arm of the Jordanian Communist Party. Established in Jan. 1970. Headed by Dr Ya'qub Zayyadin.

The main stages in the military activity of these organizations after the Six Day War were: a. "Popular Armed Revolution" (July-Dec. 1967), an attempt to establish G. bases inside the Israel-occupied West Bank▷, and incite mass insurgency. The attempt failed because of lack of co-operation by the local Arab inhabitants and the steps taken by the Israeli Security Forces. Most of the sabotage units were exterminated; survivors withdrew across the Jordan River.

b. Consolidation in the Jordan Valley (Jan.-Apr. 1968) and the establishment of bases in the valley next to the cease-fire line. This bid was foiled by Israeli strikes, culminating in the Karame raid of 21 Mar. 1968.

c. The large bases stage (May-Oct. 1968); large bases were established on the crest of the hills in Jordan (the East Bank) and units were despatched to fire at Israeli troops and settlements across the border, instead of attempting to infiltrate into Israel or the West Bank as before. This bid failed as a result of Israeli air-raids on these bases, beginning with the attack on al-Salt on 4 Aug. 1968.

d. Dispersal: the large bases were dispersed and G. forces were split up into many small units, constantly on the move within Jordanian territory. Some of these units infiltrated into the large refugee camps and in due time took them over.

e. Heavy shelling: in view of their inability to break through the defensive barricades along the Jordan River, the *feda'iyin* began using heavier weapons such as Russian *Katyusha* rockets, 120 mm. mortars and light artillery for long-range shelling across the cease-fire line.

In Oct. 1968 G. groups entered south-eastern Lebanon between the Hermon slopes and the Hasbani River. During 1969 they expanded and moved their bases westwards, reaching the large refugee camps along the coastline. As they began establishing their "state within a state", numerous clashes occurred between them and the Lebanese Army and a grave political crisis shook Lebanon. Finally, the so-called Cairo Agreement was signed on 3 Nov. 1969, laying down general principles for PG's presence and operations in Lebanon. However, this agreement, several times repeated and expanded since, was often broken by the Gs. and created repeated crises (see Lebanon▷).

The constant tension between the *feda'iyin* and the Jordanian government and army erupted, in 1970, several times in serious clashes, culminating in a bloody war in Sept. 1970 and the gradual re-imposition of Jordanian army control (see Jordan▷).

In 1970, the terrorist organizations were active largely in Jordan, which remained their main base, and in Lebanon. In 1971, their constant clashes with Jordanian forces, and Jordanian operations against their "state within a state", prevented active G. operations against Israel from Jordan, and Lebanon became the most active G. base. In other Arab countries PAG activities were restricted to such operations as were permitted by the governments concerned. Committees for co-ordination between the numerous organizations were established, but no efficient method of military or political co-operation was reached. 'Arafat—as *Fatah* leader and chairman of the PLO— attempted to concentrate the main co-ordinating power in his and *Fatah*'s hands and gradually to establish a monopoly of G. activity in PLO-*Fatah*, eliminating other organizations. It is too early to judge to what extent he will succeed.

The G. groups have built hospitals, rest camps and youth centres, established health and social services and published scores of periodicals and bulletins. (E.Y.)

✱PALESTINE CHARTER. A charter of basic principles and an action programme adopted by the Arab Palestine Liberation Organization▷, at its first conference in 1964. Its main and basic principle is the elimination of Israel and the establishment of an Palestinian-Arab State. The clauses dealing with the character and regime of that state and in particular those dealing with the fate and status of the Jews (as well as the question which Jews would be allowed to stay and become citizens), were high-sounding but vague. They were much debated and aroused bitter controversies, but the problem is still unresolved. See

Arab-Israel conflict▷; Palestine Arabs▷; Palestine-Arab Guerilla Organizations▷.   (Y.S.)

PALESTINE, COMMITTEES AND COMMISSIONS. As Palestine became entangled in conflict, various C.s were sent out to investigate the situation: 1. The KING-CRANE C. was sent in 1919, on behalf of the Allies, but including only American members (Henry C. King and Charles R. Crane), to ascertain the wishes of the population as to their future. It reported an overwhelming opposition of the Palestinian (and Syrian) Arabs to Zionism, and their desire for a US Mandate. It submitted recommendations to that effect (not implemented). 2. In 1921, following the disturbances of that year a local C. under SIR THOMAS W. HAYCRAFT reported (Cmd. 1540) that the disturbances were initiated by the Arabs, but implied that the socialist ideas of the Zionists and Zionist policy were mainly responsible. 3. In 1929. a C. under SIR WALTER SHAW investigated the disturbances of 1929. It blamed (Cmd. 2530) the Arabs, but stated that the riots' cause was "the Arab feeling of animosity and hostility towards the Jews consequent upon the disappointment of their political and national aspirations and fear for their economic future". It recommended tighter control over Jewish immigration, an investigation of the agricultural potentialities of Palestine, and a clear statement of British government policy in Palestine. 4. In 1930, an international C. on behalf of the League of Nations investigated the rival claims of Jews and Arabs concerning the WAILING WALL▷. It confirmed the Jewish right to access to the Wall, but accepted British provisional regulations of Oct. 1929 which limited the effectuation of this right. 5. In 1930, SIR JOHN HOPE SIMPSON examined the questions of immigration, land settlement and development. Based on erroneous estimates of the absorptive capacity of the country, he reported (Cmd. 3686) that there was barely any space left for further Jewish immigration. He proposed to modernize local agriculture but was pessimistic about industrial development. 6. In 1931, MR. LEWIS FRENCH concluded that any further immigration would cause serious displacement of the indigenous population. 7. In 1936, after the outbreak of disturbances, or the "Arab Revolt", a Royal C. under LORD PEEL▷ concluded (Cmd. 5479, 1937) that the Mandate could not be fulfilled and therefore proposed to divide Palestine into an Arab State (united with Transjordan) and a Jewish State, while leaving certain districts under British administration. If partition could not be implemented, Jewish immigration should be limited to the political "high" of 12,000 per annum—the first open departure from the principle that the im-

migration quota be determined by Palestine's economic absorptive capacity. Partition was rejected out of hand by the Arabs, and accepted by the Zionists as a basis for further discussions. 8. In 1938, the WOODHEAD C.▷ investigated the details of the Peel partition plan, and reported (Cmd. 5854) that partition was not practical, as any plan would either put many Arabs under Jewish rule or create an unviable Jewish State. 9. In 1946, an ANGLO-AMERICAN C. was sent "to examine political, economic, and social conditions in Palestine as they bear upon the problem of Jewish immigration" and "to examine the position of the Jews in the countries in Europe where they have been the victims of Nazi and Fascist persecution". It proposed (Cmd. 6808) that 100,000 Jewish refugees be admitted to Palestine. It opposed partition and expressed the hope that the two communities would eventually learn to live together. Until then Palestine should be placed under British trusteeship. 10. In 1947, after Britain had submitted the Palestine problem to the UN, the UN SPECIAL COMMITTEE ON PALESTINE (UNSCOP) was formed —composed of representatives of Australia, Canada, Czechoslovakia, Guatemala, India, Iran, Netherlands, Peru, Sweden, Uruguay and Yugoslavia. The majority report (adopted by the General Assembly on 29 Nov. 1947) proposed the partition of Palestine into a Jewish State and an Arab State, and the internationalization of Jerusalem. The minority proposed a federal solution with restricted Jewish immigration (for further details see Palestine▷). 11. The UN General Assembly on 29 Nov. 1947 also established a UN PALESTINE COMMISSION to administer Palestine during the transition period on behalf of the General Assembly and under the guidance of the Security Council, to set up, in consultation with the Jewish and Arab leadership, provisional government councils for the two states, and to assist them in the establishment of democratic representative and legislative bodies. The C. was authorized even to recruit armed militias. It consisted of representatives of Bolivia, Czechoslovakia, Denmark, Panama and the Philippines. Its first meeting was held in Jan. 1948, at which time armed clashes had already broken out in Palestine. The British Mandatory Government refused to co-operate with the C., declaring that until the end of the Mandate, in mid-May 1948, it alone would be responsible for administration and security. The C. never went to Palestine nor fulfilled any function. It was disbanded by the UN General Assembly on 17 May 1948, after the establishment of the State of Israel and the occupation of parts of the country by Egypt and Jordan. 12. In Dec. 1948, the UN General Assembly set up a Palestine Conciliation Commission (PCC) to help the parties to the Arab-Israel conflict arrive at a settlement by peaceful means. The five permanent members of the Security Council (the USA, USSR, Britain, France and Nationalist China) elected as members of the PCC representatives of the USA, France and Turkey. The PCC convened in 1949 a conference of sorts in Lausanne, but, since the Arab representatives refused to meet directly with those of Israel, it confined itself to separate consultations with Arabs and Israelis. From this meeting emerged a statement of principles, the so-called "Protocol of Lausanne"▷, but neither the protocol nor the conference were of value or consequence. The PCC formally exists to this day, but has in fact not been active for many years; the three member states no longer appoint prominent representatives to the commission.   (Sh.H.-Y.S.)

PALESTINE CONCILIATION COMMISSION (PCC). UN commission entrusted with the task of assisting the parties in the Arab-Israel conflict to find a solution. It was set up by the UN General Assembly in Dec. 1948, composed of representatives of US, France and Turkey; it still exists though it has not been active for some years. See Palestine Commissions and Committees▷.   (Y.S.)

PALESTINE CONFLICT, DISPUTE—see Arab-Israel Conflict▷.

***PALESTINE ENTITY.** The notion that the P. Arabs form an ethnic, national group, of their own, was generally accepted from the 1920s to 1948 and recognized by the UN Resolution of 29 Nov. 1947, providing for an Palestinian-Arab State. The notion lay dormant after the 1948 Arab-Israel War, as P. had disappeared as a political-administrative unit and its Arab part had been occupied by Jordan (the West Bank▷) and Egypt (the Gaza Strip▷). Jordan regarded itself as the sole representative of the P. Arabs and any attempt to re-establish a PE was considered an anti-Jordanian move, casting doubt on the annexation of Arab P. to Jordan. The subject was frozen until 1959, when it was brought up again at meetings of the Arab League▷, and led to the establishment of the Palestine Liberation Organization▷. The PLO left the nature of a PE deliberately vague, and made no demand for the establishment of a Palestinian State.

After the Six Day War▷, the rejection of a Palestinian State in only part of P. by the PLO and other Palestinian-Arab organizations became even more outspoken, as its acceptance would imply recognition of Israel's existence. They continued to claim the whole of P. (e.g. 1968 and 1971 resolutions of the Palestine National Council, the supreme organ of the PLO). Nevertheless, the failure of the Arab states to attain a solution of the P. problem that could satisfy the Arabs convinced many Palestinians that they should themselves assume responsibility for their fate, and the notion of a PE gained wider acceptance.

In 1947-8 the Jews had accepted the existence of a P.-Arab nation and its right to an independent state of its own. In its new form, Israel did not support the idea of a PE. However, many Israelis do (despite the fact that the Palestine National Charter rejects the Jews' right to their own state). They maintain that Zionism, itself based on the notion of a "Jewish E." even when the Jews had no territory of their own, should not deny the PE.   (E.L.)

***PALESTINE LIBERATION ORGANIZATION, PLO.** (*Munazzamat Tahrir Filastin*). Organization established in 1964, on the initiative, and with the aid, of the Arab League▷, to represent the Palestine Arabs and to constitute a form of Palestinian "Entity"—short of a separate Palestinian-Arab State (support of which the Kingdom of Jordan would have bitterly resented). The PLO claimed the status of a roof organization for all Palestinian bodies, including the guerilla organizations (*feda'iyin*▷). See Palestine-Arab Guerilla Organizations▷ and Palestine Arabs▷.   (Y.S.)

PALESTINE PROBLEM—see Palestine Arabs▷, Arab-Israel Conflict▷, United Nations Organization▷.

PALESTINE WAR, 1948—see Arab-Israel War of 1948▷.

PALMAH. "Striking force" of the *Hagana*▷ (the Jewish underground self-defence organization in Mandatory Palestine). Established in 1941, as a full-time military force of volunteers, to meet the danger of a German and Italian invasion. In the spring of 1942, a joint Jewish-British programme was adopted to form sabotage and guerilla units partly with the help of British instructors. Nevertheless, for want of funds, only six companies were formed in the first year; volunteers stayed in their homes and only trained a few days a month.

With the passing of the danger, P. became the principal force of the *Hagana* in the struggle against the Mandatory Government. The financial problem was solved by an arrangement, under which the enlisted lived in *kibbutz*▷ settlements where they financed a fortnight of training by a fortnight of work. This combination became the P. symbol—two sheaves and a sword.

Prior to the Arab-Israel War of 1948▷, the P.

numbered 3,000 men in 15 companies forming four battalions. One of the battalions comprised special units: naval, air, and reconnaissance. P. was the élite unit of the *Hagana*, with a high level of training and operational capability. In the first, local guerilla stage of the war, P. was the force that provided protection for the Jewish community while it was gearing itself for full-scale war. But afterwards also, when organized into three brigades, it played a decisive role in the Israeli victory.

The P. was disbanded in Oct. 1948, following a decision of David Ben-Gurion▷ that no unit in the new state's army would retain its separate command. Opponents of the disbandment claimed that this was done in order to wipe off the influence of the *Mapam*▷ party and its leftist *kibbutz* movement. The values of the P. and the principles on which it was based served as an example to *Nahal* (Pioneering and Fighting Youth), which still forms a part of the Israel Defence Forces.   (E. A.-E. L.)

PAN-ARABISM. The aspiration towards Arab unity is one of the main components of Arab nationalism. The Arabic term for unity: *wahda*, has a range of meanings, including solidarity, co-operation and political unity. From several aspects the Arab world forms a single unit with several common denominators; other factors operate for division and the crystallization of separate national units (see Arabs▷; Arab national movement▷; Arab Federation▷).

Before World War I the Pan-Arabists envisaged at most an independent union of the Arab territories then within the Ottoman Empire, *i.e.* the Fertile Crescent▷ (excluding Egypt and the *Maghreb*▷). During World War I Hussein▷, Sharif of Mecca, claimed the whole of the Arabian peninsula and the Fertile Crescent. When these plans for unity failed and separate semi-independent states were set up, PA remained a general political trend with no organizational framework and no immediate practical aims (see Hashemites▷). During the 1920s and 1930s the main proponents of the idea were Feisal▷ I, the Amir 'Abdullah▷ and nationalist politicians such as Shakib Arslan▷ and 'Abd-ul-Rahman Shahbandar▷.

During and after World War II, Hashemite unity projects were revived—Nuri Sa'id's▷ "Blue Book" (1942–3) and King 'Abdullah's "Greater Syria"▷ plan, both limited to the Fertile Crescent. They were sharply opposed by the other Arab states, in particular Egypt. When Egypt became active in the PA movement (1943), she worked for co-operation between independent Arab states (see Arab League▷) and not for their political integration. On the other hand, Egypt called for the full union of the Nile Valley, *i.e.* Egypt and Sudan.

This situation changed in the 1950s when, under Nasser▷, Egypt turned to a PA policy. Her aim was Egyptian hegemony rather than full union, but circumstances pushed her towards the latter. Such a political union occurred between Egypt and Syria in Feb. 1958 (the United Arab Republic▷), through Syrian initiative, but in conformity with Nasser's conditions. The UAR was dissolved by the Syrians on 28 Sept. 1961. As a reaction to the establishment of the UAR an "Arab Federation" was established in Feb. 1958 between Iraq and Jordan, but it fell apart following the July 1958 coup in Iraq. A confederation between the UAR and the Kingdom of Yemen was nominally set up in Mar. 1958, but was never implemented; it was dissolved at the end of 1961. On 17 Apr. 1963 Egypt, Iraq and Syria, the latter two under *Ba'th*▷ regimes, signed an agreement to set up a federation; it was not put into effect and was annulled in July 1963. Agreements which were to lead to union were signed between Egypt and Iraq in May 1964, and between Egypt and Yemen in July 1964, but they, too, were not put into effect. On 8 Nov. 1970 Egypt, Sudan and Libya agreed to establish a federation; Syria joined two weeks later. A final accord was signed on 17 Apr. 1971 between Egypt, Libya and Syria (Sudan was, for internal reasons, not yet ready to join). Plebiscites on 1 Sept. 1971 were to endorse the "Federation of Arab Republics". Each member state was to preserve its identity and sovereignty and maintain its international and diplomatic relations; representation in all federal bodies was to be equal. How far the new federation was to be more than an arrangement for close co-operation between three—later possibly four— separate states, could not yet be anticipated.

All these federal agreements were partial in both character and scope, and not a realization of PA. Military and economic agreements between the Arab states have failed the test of performance. The only inter-Arab framework which has survived is the Arab League▷, which is based on the existence of separate states. The unstable blocs and camps which have coalesced (Hashemite Iraq and Jordan vs. Egypt-Sa'udi Arabia-Syria in the 1950s; *Ba'thist* Iraq and Syria in 1963; the Egypt-Libya-Sudan triangle of 1969–70; the *Maghreb* states) point at divisive rather than integrationist tendencies in the Arab world.

The Pan-Arabists agree on the whole that their final aim is complete and all-embracing unity. But they differ as to the means of its implementation and its stages, as well as to the regime of the proposed union. Some Pan-Arabists advocate revolution, while others prefer mutual agreement and evolution. Some see in a partial union (such as the Fertile Crescent, or the *Maghreb*▷) a first step towards complete union. Some prefer a federation or a confederation; others want a unitary regime and complete integration. Some want union based on the equality of all members; others demand a position of leadership (e.g. Egypt). Some are satisfied, as a first step, with united military and economic frameworks.

Until the 1940s, the particular nationalism of each state was stronger than the all-Arab one, especially in Egypt (the first leader of the *Wafd*▷, Sa'd Zaghlul▷, defined Arab unity as "zero plus zero plus zero"). There were even anti-Arab manifestations (in Arabic—*Shu'ubiyya*), such as Pharaonism▷ in Egypt, Phoenicianism▷ in the Lebanon, and Pan-Syrianism in the Levant, though these were never a serious threat to Arabism. Even today identification with a particular Arab country takes precedence. There are no unhyphenated "Arabs" who do not belong to one of the various Arab nations. In Egypt a separate national movement developed before World War I (Mustafa Kamel) and even today it is still the determining factor. Nasser's continuous failures in the inter-Arab arena occasionally raised in Egypt currents of disappointment with PA and isolationist trends. Pan-Syrian nationalism crystallized in the Syrian Nationalist Party▷ of Anton Sa'adeh▷ which favoured the aim of a Greater Syria (the Fertile Crescent, including the Sinai Peninsula, the Gulf of 'Aqaba and even Cyprus) and considered the "Syrians" a race superior to the Arabs; it claimed that there is no Arab nation, but only various Arabic-speaking nations. Phoenicianism had political meaning only during the French Mandate, but Lebanese separatism is still strong, though it conceives Lebanon within a general Arab framework. In the *Maghreb*, separate national feeling and Pan-*Maghrebism* are stronger than PA feelings.

The fate of PA depends on the interaction between the factors operating for and against union. The following operate for union: the existence of Arab political forces interested in the PA ideology; the common resistance to outside factors (the Western Powers, Israel); a common fate and history, a common language and culture, and Islam. Factors operating against union are: different geographical, economic, social backgrounds; the existence and interests of minorities; psychological factors and local rivalries; the vested interests and traditions of rulers, regimes and existing separate political establishments; particularism that grows stronger the longer an Arab state maintains its separate independence; differences between revolutionary and conservative regimes, and differences of opinion within the revolutionary camp, as well as disputes between neighbours; the historical rivalry between

Pres. Nasser, King Hussein, and Y. 'Arafat meeting, 1970

the Nile Valley and the Valley of the Euphrates. Strong regimes generally oppose union, weak ones are exposed to unionist initiatives from without and within (Syria 1958).

Britain encouraged PA during both world wars, hoping to use it for her own ends, and from 1936–9 onwards also in connection with the Palestine problem. France opposed PA until de Gaulle's pro-Arab *volte face*. The Soviet Union supports a united Arab front against the West and Israel, but it is doubtful whether she would support the abolition of the present structure of states in favour of unions. The rivalry between the Great Powers has restricted their influence on inter-Arab developments. Western support for the conservative Arab governments has acted as a brake against PA pressures.

Israel constitutes a physical barrier between the Arabs of Africa and those of Asia. The hatred for Israel is one of the chief driving forces behind the desire for Arab unity. The Palestinians stand at the centre of PA activity. Nevertheless, there is no unity of interests among the Arab states concerning Palestine; internal Arab conflicts are reflected in the tactics of the struggle against Israel, and the Palestine issue is used in inter-Arab rivalries.

So far, efforts to implement Arab unity have been among the main causes for Arab disunity, instability and upheavals. Hashemite pressure in the direction of PA shook inter-Arab co-operation during the 1940s; in the 1950s and 1960s, Egypt, Syria and Iraq used PA to undermine the regimes and independence of other Arab states, with Egypt interfering even by military force in other Arab countries. The repeated failure of PA raises doubts as to the chances of its fulfilment. The maximum attainable would seem to be co-operation on issues of common interest. No Arab force appears to exist which could impose and maintain a real union for any length of time. (A.G.)

PAN-ISLAM. The idea and doctrine of, and the movement to establish the unity of the Islamic world.

The modern PI movement originated at the end of the nineteenth century. The Turkish Ottoman Sultan Abdülhamid II▷ encouraged it, to help him ward off European influences infiltrating his Empire. He also hoped that the PI movement would prevent the disintegration of his realm from within. The PI idea was propagated by such reformers and thinkers as Jamal-ul-Din al-Afghani.

However, PI was not strong enough to fight off European influences, or to suppress the increased national particularism of the Muslim nations. Western materialism and secularism further weakened the hold of religion, and impaired religious solidarity. Most Muslim people ignored the declaration of Jihad▷ (holy war) by the Ottoman Sultan and Caliph▷ of all the Muslims, on the infidel European powers in 1914. Some Muslims even joined forces with the infidels against him.

Following revolutionary Turkey's dissolution of the caliphate in 1924, PI was reinforced by the desire to restore the caliphate. Various Muslim rulers aspired to the crown of the caliph, but their efforts all failed. PI was rooted in the hearts of many Muslims, but it was not embodied in a political organization. Attempts to direct the PI feeling along political channels such as a PI movement directed against the Zionists in Palestine (e.g. Hajj Amin al-Husseini▷ in the late 1920s and early '30s). perhaps resulted in short-term successes (committees, congresses, resolutions), but did not produce an effective power or movement.

PI activities were renewed after World War II. Conditions appeared more propitious for realizing the movement's aims. Most Muslim countries had become independent, in many countries the Muslim religious establishment acquired a stronger influence and status, and regional and supranational organizational frameworks became acceptable and even fashionable. Pakistan▷ embarked on PI activities, both officially and, even more so, through non-governmental channels. She expected to rally the Islamic countries in her conflict with India. However, she soon abandoned official, governmental attempts to establish a political PI framework, even a limited and loosely knit one. Unofficial PI activities, mainly in the fields of religion and culture, continued but their scope and importance were limited.

The Nasserist▷ regime in Egypt also was active in Muslim countries and fostered close relations with them, as a means in its struggle for leadership of the Muslim, Arab and African worlds (and also to gain support for its domestic fight against the "Muslim Brotherhood"▷, an organization with PI tendencies). For this purpose Egypt makes full use of her religious institutions (such as the al-Azhar▷ University). She

convenes Islamic conferences, provides an education for Muslim clergymen, sends clergymen and teachers abroad and supplies Korans and religious articles to Islamic countries. Egypt also exploits PI in the struggle against Israel (particularly since 1967, with Muslim shrines in Jerusalem under Israeli rule). All these activities have not, however, induced Egypt to support the PI movement ideologically or politically. Egypt is still more opposed to PI political activities when these are instigated by her adversaries. The Ba'th▷ regimes in Syria and Iraq reject all PI initiatives.

The kings of Sa'udi Arabia use their control of Muslim shrines to present themselves as leaders of the Islamic world. In the pilgrimage season (Hajj) at Mecca and Medina, where leaders and notables from the entire Muslim world assemble, they sometimes organize all-Islamic meetings. An attempt by King Feisal▷, in 1965, to broach the idea of an Alliance of Islamic States (in effect, of conservative ones), failed at the start.

Non-Arab Muslim leaders occasionally engage in PI activities to advance their own national or personal aims. The example of Pakistan has been mentioned. The Malaysian leader Tunku 'Abd-ul-Rahman suggested in 1961 the establishment of a "League of Muslim Nations". The idea found little support and died quickly. In 1969, he organized a PI conference in Malaysia, but there was no follow-up. In recent years, a non-governmental group, the "Afro-Asian Islamic Conference", has been active in Indonesia and sponsored two international conferences, but its impact on the Muslim world has been very limited. Turkey, as a secular state, generally adopts a negative attitude to governmental and political PI activities, but sometimes her representatives take part in meetings that do not commit the government.

One common denominator of many Muslim states is their hostility to Israel. Much PI activity has been directed against Israel, and numerous PI conferences have adopted anti-Israel resolutions. The trend to inter-Muslim hostility to Israel was noticeably strengthened by the impact of the Six Day War that left the Muslim holy places in Jerusalem under Israel rule, and particularly after the fire at the al-Aqsa Mosque in 1969. A meeting of heads of states for an official PI conference, that would have been quite impossible before that conflagration, took place in Sept. 1969. Twenty-five heads of Muslim states assembled in Rabat to discuss the consequences and significance of the fire (on the erroneous, or propagandistic, assumption that it was Israel that had set fire to the mosque). Following that first conference, twenty-two Muslim foreign ministers attended a second one at Jidda, Mar. 1970, and decided to establish a permanent secretariat. This was set up at a third conference (Karachi, Dec. 1970), headed by Tunku 'Abd-ul-Rahman, the former Prime Minister of Malaysia, and with its seat in Jidda.

At these conferences Israel was vilified and calls for a *Jihad* were heard. However, differences of opinion and conflicts of interests were also obvious. Syria and Iraq boycotted the conferences; South Yemen—the last two; Egypt attended but grudgingly; and several countries, such as Turkey and the African states, dissociated themselves from the extreme anti-Israel stand, and the permanent secretariat. Calls for a *Jihad* and for the severing of all relations with Israel were rejected. In any case, several Muslim states maintain normal relations with Israel; and even in the case of the others, their anti-Israel attitude is often lip service and propagandist in character.

Various attempts to establish PI economic or professional organizations were made in the 1950s. Now that governments were taking new interest in PI, such efforts were resumed. A conference attended by representatives of 15 Muslim countries (Teheran, Apr. 1971), proposed, for instance, the creation of an Islamic news agency; the Muslim Foreign Ministers' conference will be asked to endorse it.

In recent years the USSR has increased her efforts to make use of the Muslim factor in support of her penetration of Arab and Muslim countries. She has attempted to overcome the opposition of orthodox Muslim circles to Russia and Communism by emphasizing her support for the Arabs and by glowing descriptions of the state of the Muslim religion in Russia. These efforts have led to PI congresses within Russia (the Tashkent Conference, 1970), exchange of visits of religious leaders with the Arab countries, etc.

It appears that, except for emotions of religious solidarity which boil over and then subside once the event that aroused them recedes, the Islamic countries do not have sufficient in common to enable the creation of a PI framework. At times, they are split by even stronger conflicts of interest and views. The countries which hoisted the flag of PI did so for their own purposes and interests, seeking support in their disputes, or to strengthen their national prestige. PI activity in one country may frequently encounter the opposition of a competing Muslim country. The chances of establishing a stable PI political framework exerting real power and influence seem very small.

(Z. R.)

PAN-TURKISM. A movement aiming at the linguistic, cultural, and sometimes political, unity of all Turkish-speaking peoples. The movement (also labelled P.-Turanism—after Turan, the Turks' name for their ancient homeland in Central Asia) sprang up among Turkish intellectuals in the Russian and Ottoman empires towards the end of the 19th century. It was influenced by nationalist ideas, the development of Turcology in Europe, and the increasing contacts between Turks within the Ottoman Empire▷ and those outside it. In Turkey the movement, which numbered many Turkish emigrés from Russia among its adherents, as well as the national philosopher Ziya Gökalp▷, was particularly active during the period of the Young Turks▷. It exercised a strong influence upon some of their leaders, and gained momentum as the theories of Ottomanism and Pan-Islamism▷, aimed at guarding the integrity of the Empire, were seen to be ineffectual. Enver's▷ decision to enter World War I▷ against Russia was partially motivated by his desire to free her Turkish peoples, as were his activities on the Russian front. Atatürk▷ who wanted to maintain good relations with the USSR, discarded PT, preferring to foster loyalty to the Turks' Anatolian homeland. However, during World War II▷, and especially after the German victories in Russia, PT circles resumed their activities; they were suppressed when the tide of war turned. Yet, PT ideas are still alive in Turkey today and at the very least take the form of a strong interest in the fate of Turks outside Turkey (e.g. in Cyprus▷).

(D.K.)

PARIS PEACE CONFERENCE. Post-World War I Conference of the Allied and Associated Powers, who met in Paris from 18 Jan. 1919 to 20 Jan. 1920. The Peace Settlements were embodied in separate treaties with the Central Powers. The one with Turkey—the Treaty of Sèvres▷—was signed only in August 1920 and remained abortive as it was renounced by Turkey's new, nationalist regime. However, Turkey's renunciation of any claims to Syria, Palestine, Mesopotamia and Arabia— which was the abortive treaty's main impact on the ME outside Turkey herself—was incorporated in the Treaty of Lausanne▷, 1923, which replaced it.

An Arab delegation to the PPC was headed by Amir Feisal▷, representing his father, Sharif Hussein▷ of Mecca, King of Hijaz▷, and speaking for Arab nationalism. He was accompanied by T.E. Lawrence▷ as an advisor, and his delegation included Nuri Sa'id▷, Rustum Haidar and 'Awni 'Abd-ul-Hadi▷. Feisal called for Arab independence in the newly freed ex-Ottoman territories. He appeared before the Supreme Council of the C. on 6 Feb. 1919 and also submitted his views in writing. His opinions on Zionist aspirations in Palestine, were those of a moderate prepared to reach a compromise (see Feisal-Weizmann Agreement▷). Other Arab delegations included one from Syria and one from Lebanon; both pleaded for independence under French guidance. The Armenians▷ and Kurds▷ also pleaded their cases.

Jewish representatives appeared before the Council on 27 Feb. 1919. The delegation was headed by Dr. Chaim Weizmann▷, and included Nahum Sokolow, Menahem Ussishkin, André Spire, and the French anti-Zionist Sylvain Lévi, all of whom—except for Lévi—pleaded the Zionist case.

The PPC had to find a compromise between the generally accepted idea of self-determination for all, war-time promises, and war-time imperial plans for a division of the spoils. The compromise resulted in the mandate▷ system. Its details, and the fate of the territories freed from Turkish rule, were decided at the San Remo Conference▷, Apr. 1920. The PPC laid the groundwork for the establishment of the League of Nations▷.   (Sh. H.)

PASSFIELD WHITE PAPER. The British White Paper of 1930 on Palestine is sometimes called PWP—after Lord Passfield (Sidney Webb), the then British Colonial Secretary. See Palestine▷, White Papers▷.
                                                     (Y. S.)

PCC—Palestine Conciliation Commission. See Palestine, Commissions and Committees▷.

PDFLP—see Popular Democratic Front for the Liberation of Palestine▷, see Palestine-Arab Guerilla Organizations▷.

PEACE AND SECURITY, MOVEMENT FOR. An Israeli movement established in 1968 as a counter-weight to the Land of Israel▷ Movement. It advocates that Israel give up territories occupied in the Six Day War▷ in 1967, in return for a genuine peace, and is opposed to any annexation (see Israel▷).   (E. L.)

PEEL, PEEL REPORT. Lord P., a British politician and administrator, headed a Royal Commission sent to Palestine in 1936 to investigate the causes of the 1936 disturbances and to propose a solution to the Palestine problem. In its report, considered to be one of the most penetrating and lucid studies of the problem, the P. Commission recommended the partition of Palestine into a Jewish State, an Arab State to be united with Transjordan, and an area to remain under the British Mandate▷. See Palestine▷, Palestine, Commissions and Committees▷.   (Y. S.)

PEKER, RECEP (1888–1950). Turkish statesman, Prime Minister 1946–47. Born in Istanbul. P. received a military education and took part in the War of Independence, 1920–22, as a staff major. Elected to the National Assembly in 1923, he held several ministerial

posts and was Secretary-General of the Republican People's Party. From 1935 to 1942 he gave lectures on the Turkish revolution at Ankara and Istanbul universities, in which he showed his strong reformist and élitist bias. After World War II, P. headed the faction of his party which opposed a swift transition to multi-party rule. He became Premier in Aug. 1946, maintained an authoritarian rule and clashed with opposing groups in his party and with President Inönü▷. He resigned in Sept. 1947.   (D. K.)

PERIM (Arabic: *Mayum*). Island located in and controlling the Red Sea straits of Bab al-Mandeb▷, between the south-western tip of Arabia and Africa. Area: about 5 sq mi.; no water or vegetation; pop.: 300. Briefly occupied by the British in 1799, as a strategic outpost against Napoleon's plan to advance from Egypt to India, the island was in Britain's permanent possession from 1851 and was administered from Aden▷. P. was used as a coal depot for ships until 1936, and later as a military airfield. In 1967, Britain reportedly intended to retain possession of P., denying her to nascent South Yemen▷. However, Britain gave in to South Yemen's vociferous claim and the latter immediately occupied the island.
                                                     (Y. A. O.)

PERSIA. Alternative name for Iran▷. Derived from Parsa, the capital of the Achaemenid dynasty in the sixth century BC, situated in the area now known as Fars. In 1925 Reza Shah▷ decreed that Iran (Land of the Aryans) alone should be used as the official name of the country (and the Iranian Post Office began returning envelopes addressed to "P."). In 1949 Muhammad Reza Shah▷ ruled that both names might be used, but Iran remained in official use. The language was always, and still is, referred to as Persian.   (B. G.)

PERSIAN GULF. Gulf of the Indian Ocean, separating the Arabian peninsula and the coast of Iran. The shallow strait of Hormuz connects it with the Gulf of 'Oman. It contains a number of islands (of which the largest is Qishm, and the most important, from a historical point of view, Hormuz, near the Iranian port of Bandar 'Abbas). The PG is about 497 mi. long and 124 mi. wide. Its waters are shallow and the maximum depth does not exceed 328 ft. The north-eastern coast, forming part of Iran, is mountainous, almost without streams, but it has a few inlets suitable for harbours. The south-western, Arab, coast is flat and sandy. At its centre, the peninsula of Qatar▷ juts into the sea for 100 mi. The shallowness of the Gulf makes the southern coast unsuitable for harbours, except for a few bays, the

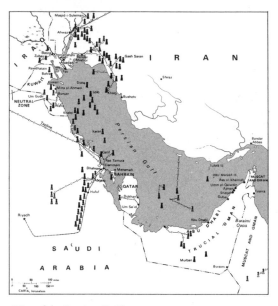

Map of the Persian Gulf

Basra▷ flourished; but all the towns on the coast benefited from this commerce and specialized in the construction of boats of the "Dhow" type.

When the Portugese captured the Bahrain▷ Islands (1507) and Hormuz (1514), European trade moved to the route around the Cape of Good Hope, and the countries on the Gulf returned to local trade in their own products only. The Portugese rule was ended in 1622 by the Persian conquest of Bahrain and Hormuz; the fortress guarding the straits was transferred by the Persians from Hormuz to the port of Bandar 'Abbas. They controlled Bahrain until 1783, when the islands fell under the rule of the Arab al-Khalifa family. Bandar 'Abbas remained the major port of the PG, but Europe's trade with India through the Gulf never recovered its former glory. When, in the seventeenth century, it began once again to develop, the inhabitants of the Gulf shores began to engage in piracy and slave-trading.

The suppression of piracy served in the 19th century as a major pretext for the British penetration of the PG region. Since 1820, numerous agreements for the cessation of piracy were signed between Britain and the various amirs and sheikhs of the Gulf coasts and islands. Later these agreements came to establish British protection over the various rulers, and the entire Gulf area became an area of British influence.

The achievement of status and influence in the PG was a strategic target of both Germany and Russia. The Germans hoped to create an overland route from Berlin, *via* Istanbul and Baghdad, to the PG and planned the extension of the "Baghdad Railway"▷ as far as Kuwait; in order to block this design, Britain, besides other measures, imposed its protection on Kuwait, in a treaty of 1899, which barred Kuwait from granting concessions to other powers without Britain's consent.

After World War I, Britain's position in the PG seemed very strong. Besides protectorate agreements with all the Arab principalities on its southern coast, she enjoyed a decisive influence in Iraq, at first as the Mandatory▷ Power, then as the senior ally. Sa'udi▷ Arabia was also closely linked to Britain—first through a protection pact with Ibn Sa'ud▷ (1915), and later by virtue of the Treaty of Jidda, 1927. Britain also had considerable influence on the tribes of southern Iran (Bakhtiaris▷, Qashqais▷, etc.).

After World War II, the situation changed. Britain was weakened and began to reduce the area of her influence. Independence was granted to all ME countries except the protected principalities of the PG. In the Gulf area, only Kuwait became independent, and British protection was removed, in 1961. The principalities were expected to gain full independence

most important of which is the Bay of Kuwait▷, which served in the past as the chief port of the region. Another bay is at Dubai▷. In the modern oil ports on the PG's Arabian shore ships anchor at a considerable distance from the shore and the oil is conveyed to them by pipes.

At the northernmost extremity of the Gulf, the geological structure of the area continues as a trough, constituting the central basin of Iraq. This is the silt plain of Iraq and Iran, built up by the Shatt al-'Arab▷ (the common estuary of the Euphrates and Tigris) and the Karkheh and Karun rivers in Iran. These rivers carry so much silt that the land encroaches on the sea in the form of marshy tongues at the rate of 164 ft. each year.

The climate of the shores of the Persian Gulf is very hot and completely arid. Only a very small population managed in the past to eke out an existence in the oases and by fishing, boat building and pearl diving. Only on the Shatt al-'Arab shore and in the deltas of the Iranian rivers is a more numerous and dense population possible due to agriculture irrigated by the river waters; these areas, though, are swampy and malaria-ridden.

From antiquity till the Middle Ages, the PG served as an important route for marine trade, through which goods passed from India and China to Kuwait or to the Shatt al-'Arab, and continued from there overland to Arabia, Iraq and Syria, or to the shores of the Mediterranean and thence to Europe. The main gateway for trade with Europe was the Shatt al-'Arab where, in the Middle Ages, the port of at the end of 1971, when the British military presence was to be liquidated and British protection removed (a British decision under review by the Conservative Government since 1970—but unlikely to be basically reversed.)

Far-reaching geopolitical changes were introduced by the discovery of oil in the PG area. In Iran, oil has been produced since the turn of the century, and in Bahrain since 1934. In Kuwait, Sa'udi Arabia and Qatar, oil was discovered before World War II, but its exploitation was deferred until after the war. Since then, the oil industry of the area has developed tremendously—in Iran and in South Iraq, Kuwait and Sa'udi Arabia, Qatar, Abu Dhabi▷, in the Neutral Zone▷ between Kuwait and Sa'udi Arabia and in 'Oman▷, as well as offshore, on the Gulf bed. The PG area possesses the world's potentially greatest oil reserve; in 1968, it produced some 500m. tons of oil, about a quarter of the entire oil production of the world (see oil▷). The development of oil was initially in the hands of British and American companies, with a French company as a minor partner; of late Japanese, German, Italian and other companies have appeared.

The countries on the shores of the PG are: along the entire north-eastern coast—Iran▷; at the north-western extremity—Iraq▷; along the length of the south-western coast, the following countries, from the north-west: Kuwait; Sa'udi Arabia's al-Hasa▷ district (and between the two—the "Neutral Zone"); Qatar; the seven Trucial Coast▷ principalities: Abu Dhabi (Sa'udi Arabia claims a considerable part of Abu Dhabi's coastline), Dubai, Sharja▷, 'Ajman▷, Umm al-Qaiwain▷, Ras al-Khaima▷ and al-Fujaira▷—all seven on the 'Oman peninsula, the tip of which belongs to the Sultanate of Muscat-and-'Oman▷. Al-Fujaira lies on the eastern shore of the peninsula, towards the Gulf of 'Oman and no longer on the PG coast. So does the Sultanate of Muscat-and-'Oman (since 1970—'Oman). Bahrain consists of a group of islands in the PG.

In anticipation of the British withdrawal from the Gulf area and the removal of their protectorates, several plans were advanced. In 1968 it was decided to set up a federation of the seven principalities of the Trucial Coast together with Bahrain and Qatar (UAE—"Union of the Arab Emirates", *Ittihad al-Imarat al-'Arabiyya*). First steps were taken towards implementation, the formulation of a constitution and the establishment of administrative patterns for the federation, but many difficulties and disputes arose, particularly regarding details of the constitution (Where would the federal capital be? Would representation be equal or in accordance with the size of each member state's population? Should a member

state's voice and authority be proportionate to its contribution to the federal treasury?) There are also several vestigial border disputes between the members. Bahrain and Qatar have apparently decided not to join the federation, and in July 1971 six Trucial sheikhdoms decided to go ahead without them (and without the seventh, Ras al-Khaima).

A potential conflict is rooted in Iraq's claim to Kuwait. This demand was raised in 1961, then rescinded in 1963, but it may be raised once again. An Iranian claim to sovereignty over Bahrain was withdrawn in 1970, when Iran accepted the verdict of public opinion in favour of independence as attested to by a UN emissary. The delimitation of offshore, sea-bed borders—especially important with regard to oil rights—has not yet been settled. The island of Abu Mussa▷ is claimed by Sharjah and Iran, the Tumb Islands by Iran and Ras al-Khaima (both disputes involving contradictory oil concessions); Iran has declared that she will take these islands by force, if they are not peacefully handed over. A further conflict which may erupt once again involves the oasis of Buraimi▷, situated partly in Abu Dhabi and partly in Muscat-and-'Oman, which Sa'udi Arabia claims in its entirety.

Behind these disputes over small details lie rivalries that go much deeper. The Arabs regard the PG as the "Arab Gulf" and call it so in Arabic; Iran insists on the Persian character of the Gulf and her own status as the major power in the region. In the face of the threat of a disturbance of the area's stability by leftist-revolutionary forces, Iran and the chief Arab power in the area, Sa'udi Arabia, seem to begin looking for ways to co-operate. Revolutionary groups may be preparing, quite apart from the Persian-Arab dispute, an attack on the oil sheikhs and the two conservative monarchies. Russian interests appear in the area in the wake of the Soviet entrenchment in Iraq and also in the form of visits to the PG by Soviet war ships. Iraq herself, under her leftist Ba'th▷ leadership, supports the underground organizations and "Liberation Fronts" established in the Gulf area (there are no confirmed reports of any rebel operations or activities except for the Dhofar▷ region in 'Oman, in southern Arabia, and the "Imam" of 'Oman—see Muscat-and-'Oman▷, 'Oman▷). Many observers see in these guerilla fronts also the hand of China▷.

(Y.K.–Y.S.)

PFLP—see Popular Front for the Liberation of Palestine▷, see Palestine-Arab Guerilla Organizations▷.

PHALANGES (Arabic: *al-Kata'eb*). A paramilitary youth movement in Lebanon, established in 1936 by Pierre Gemayel▷, George Naccache, Charles

Helou▷, Shafiq Wasif and others, to work for Lebanese independence and to foster a Lebanese national spirit. Although not stated explicitly, it was a Christian Maronite▷ organization, primarily devoted to defending the Maronite community and preserving the Christian character of Lebanon, against the Muslims, who were still questioning the separate independence of Lebanon and the inclusion of predominantly Muslim areas within her borders, and demanding the integration of Lebanon in Pan-Arab▷ schemes. The Ph. adopted a pro-French attitude; but they clashed with the French administration, when France refused to ratify the Franco-Lebanese Treaty of 1936 and to grant independence to Lebanon.

In time the Ph. became a kind of political party, though they still kept their paramilitary structure. In the 1940s, the organization opposed President Bishara al-Khouri▷ and his Pan-Arab policies. The organization was declared illegal in 1949 and until 1952 it operated under another name ("Lebanese Unity Party"). In the 1958 civil war, the Ph. were the principal supporters of President Camille Chamoun▷ against the Muslim Nasserist▷ rebels. After that crisis had ended, the Ph., by the threat of a new civil war, prevented the formation of a government controlled by the former rebels. Since then, they have functioned mainly as a political party led by Gemayel. They have participated in elections since 1951. In that year they won three seats, but only one in 1957. In 1960, when they had emerged as the best organized Maronite group, the Ph. won six seats. In the 1964 elections, their strength dropped to four, but in 1968 it rose to nine. Together with the "National Bloc" (of Raymond Edde▷) and the "National Liberals" (of Camille Chamoun), they formed the "Tripartite Bloc" in the 1966 parliament with over 25 representatives (out of 55). This group seeks to preserve the liberal, democratic and Christian character of Lebanon.

The ideology of the Ph. rests on the premise that Lebanon constitutes a separate historic entity, with an identity of her own and a continuity dating back to the Phoenicians (see Phoenicianism▷). They admit that the Arabic language links Lebanon culturally with the Arabic-speaking countries, but do not attach political significance to this link. Consequently, the Ph. oppose Pan-Arabism and the inclusion of Lebanon in any plans for Arab unity. They believe that Lebanese interests have precedence of general Arab interests, even in regard to Israel—e.g. in the case of the Arab boycott▷ and also in connection with Palestinian-Arab guerilla operations from Lebanese territory. The Ph. support these activities, at least in public, but they oppose their being carried out from Lebanese soil. They fear the *feda'iyin*▷ may involve

Lebanon in a war with Israel which would be contrary to her interests. They oppose also the further acquisition of power by the guerilla establishment, creating in effect a state within a state.

The political organization of the Ph. is effective. Most of its members are Maronites and Greek Catholics recruited from the middle classes and landowning farmers.   (Y. P.)

PHARAONISM. Egyptian doctrine or theory, developed in the 1920s and defining the Egyptian nation as a distinct, independent entity separate from the Arab-Muslim world both politically and culturally. Ph. looked for the sources of Egyptian civilization in its Pharaonic, Mediterranean past. It regarded the Arabs as foreign conquerors and Islam as merely a stage in Egypt's historic experience. It interpreted for instance Ibn Tulun's 9th-century secession from the Baghdad-centred 'Abassid Empire, and the foundation of his independent dynasty in Egypt, as exemplifying Egypt's aspiration to independence. Ph. held that, despite Islamic influences, Egypt retained a distinct, and almost unchanged, Pharaonic genius. This belief was embodied, e.g., in the stories of Tawfiq al-Hakim. The chief representatives of Ph. were Lutfi al-Sayyid, Ahmad Amin, Taha Hussein▷ and Tawfiq al-Hakim. The Ph. movement, which had considerable intellectual influence in the 1920s, did not survive the diffusion of Arab and Islamic doctrines in Egypt during the 1930s.   (S.L.)

PHILBY, H. ST. J. B. (1885–1960). British traveller and orientalist. P. entered Indian government service in 1907. During World War I he served with the British Army in Iraq as head of its political administration unit, 1915–17. In 1917, he was sent on a mission to establish contact with Ibn Sa'ud▷ to ensure his neutrality, restrain him from attacking Britain's ally, the Sharif Hussein▷, and encourage him instead to attack the House of Rashid▷, which supported the Turks. P. continued his journey westward, crossed the Arabian peninsula and reached Jidda. This journey marked the beginning of his research and travels, his exploration of the peninsula, and his long connection with Ibn Sa'ud. In 1920–1, he was Adviser to the Iraqi Ministry of the Interior and, 1921–4, British Resident in Transjordan. He resigned in 1925 and in 1926 settled in Jidda as a businessman. In 1930, he converted to Islam and took the name al-Hajj 'Abdullah. He maintained his ties with Ibn Sa'ud and, according to some sources, was his adviser and a member of his council. P. did much research and wrote many books. In 1932, he became the second European (Bertram Thomas was the first) to cross and map the Rub' al-Khali, the great desert in south-east Sa'udia. In 1954, a year after Ibn Sa'ud's death, he was expelled from Sa'udi Arabia. P. was a controversial personality and frequently clashed with Britain's official representatives. He suggested various solutions to the Palestine problem—e.g. in 1920 to Dr. J. L. Magnes, and during World War II in contacts with Dr. Ch. Weizmann▷; but none of his suggestions bore fruit. (His son was involved in a well-known case of post-World War II espionage for Soviet Russia.)   (Y. S.)

PHOENICIANISM (Sidonism). An ideology which views the Lebanese people as the descendants of the ancient Phoenicians. It asserts their historical connection with the glorious past of the Phoenician merchants and sailors who achieved so high a level of civilization. The main political manifestation of Ph. was in the Phalanges▷; but Ph. also found important linguistic and literary expression. In the 1930s, the Maronite▷ priest Maroun Ghusn, proposed that the Lebanese dialect of Arabic become the written and literary language of Lebanon; he argued that the Lebanese should write in their own language and not in classical Arabic, a foreign language. The great Lebanese poet Sa'id 'Aql went further. He published poems in dialect, and even, in 1961, in Latin characters; those, he maintained, made pronunciation easier and constituted the true national alphabet of Lebanon, since the Latin alphabet developed from the early Canaanite, i.e. Phoenician, script. The school of poets associated with the monthly Shi'r ("Poetry") also believe that poets should write in the true popular language, the spoken dialect.   (Y. P.)

PLO Palestine Liberation Organization▷—see Palestine Arabs▷ and Palestine-Arab Guerilla Organizations▷.

POLITICAL PARTIES IN ME COUNTRIES. If no entry is found under the proper name of the party, see under the country concerned, as well as Socialism▷, Communism▷, Zionism▷, Arab National Movement▷.

*POPULAR DEMOCRATIC FRONT FOR THE LIBERATION OF PALESTINE, PDFLP. Palestinian-Arab guerilla (feda'iyin▷) organization led by Nayef Hawatma. Created in 1968 out of an extreme leftist faction that split away from the Popular Front for the Liberation of Palestine▷. It is considered the most extreme Leftist faction among the terrorist organizations, with a Marxist-Maoist orientation. The PDFLP reportedly receives Chinese aid. See Palestine-Arab Guerilla Organizations▷.
                                                   (Y. S.)

POPULAR FRONT FOR THE LIBERATION OF PALESTINE, PFLP. A Palestinian Arab guerilla (feda'iyin▷) organization, led by Dr. George Habash▷. Founded in 1967 through a merger of several groups. Leftist-Marxist, and extremist both in terrorist activities (including the hijacking of foreign airplanes) and in its revolutionary schemes against the regimes of the Arab states. See Palestine-Arab Guerilla Organizations▷.   (Y. S.)

*POPULATION. In 1970 the population of the ME numbered c. 150m., as compared with 40m. at the beginning of the century. Then, natural increase was estimated at 1.5–2% p.a.; this figure rose to 2–2.5% p.a. between the two World Wars, and to 2.5–3.0% following World War II.

POPULATION OF ME COUNTRIES
(in thousands)

Country	1900	1970
Iran (Persia)	8,000	28,700
Iraq	2,000	9,580
Lebanon	750	2,730
Syria	1,500	6,295
Turkey	10,000	35,200
Egypt	9,700	33,350
Israel	*	2,957
Jordan	**	2,260***
Sa'udi Arabia	n.d.	7,300
Kuwait	n.d.	720
Southern Yemen	n.d.	1,250
Yemen	n.d.	5,000
Libya	n.d.	1,940
Sudan	n.d.	15,600

   * The population of Palestine numbered in 1900 c. 600,000.

 ** The population of Transjordan was estimated at 400,000 in the 1930s and '40s.

*** Including the West Bank▷ (c. 700,000).
                                                   (M. E.)

POPULATION EXCHANGE. The only organized and mutually agreed PE in the ME took place between Turkey and Greece in 1923. Even that agreement was preceded by war and a spontaneous exodus of refugees; it was to some extent but a confirmation of the violent and uncontrollable process that had preceded it. The PE comprised about 1.3 m. Greeks and 400,000 Turks. See Greek-Turkish Relations▷.

A PE took place in effect in 1948, without agreement but as a result of war and the flight of refugees▷, between the nascent State of Israel and the

Arab states. Some 550–650,000 Palestinian Arab refugees left Israel during the 1948 War, while about 500,000 Jews left Arab countries and came to Israel. See Refugees▷; Jews in the ME▷.   (Y.S.)

*PORT SA'ID. Egypt's third largest city and an important port. In 1967, its population was 260,000. The city, located at the northern end of the Suez Canal▷, was built in 1860, while work on the Canal was proceeding, and named after Sa'id, the then ruler of Egypt (d. 1863). Built to provide sleeping quarters for the workers and employees of the Canal Company, PS developed into an industrial city with docks and wharves, oil storage, shipping agencies, etc.

Port Sa'id

It served principally as a harbour for entering, and transit through, the Canal. During the Suez War▷ (1956), PS was heavily bombed, and occupied for a short while by British and French expeditionary forces. After they had evacuated it, the city was rehabilitated and modern quarters were built. The Six Day War▷ gravely affected the city. Once the canal closed, it was deprived of its major function as a port and tourist centre. Many of its inhabitants were evacuated during the fighting in 1968–9.   (O.G.)

PORTSMOUTH, TREATY OF. Draft treaty between Britain and Iraq, signed in Portsmouth on 15 Jan. 1948, to replace the Anglo-Iraqi Treaty of 1930, which was considered by Iraqi nationalists as restricting their independence. In its preamble, the PT emphasized the "complete freedom, equality and independence of Iraq." The British air bases in Habbaniya and Shu'eiba were to be handed over to Iraq. Instead of British bases a Joint Defence Board, with equal representation, was to secure British strategic interests. Despite this advance over the treaty of 1930, the Draft PT was strongly opposed by the political parties in Iraq, who alleged that it granted excessive privileges to Britain. Violent demonstrations erupted in Baghdad and other Iraqi towns. Premier Saleh Jabr▷, who had negotiated the treaty, was compelled to resign, and his successor, Muhammad al-Sadr, repudiated it. (The old treaty of 1930 remained in force until 1955.)   (B.G.)

PPS. Parti Populaire Syrien; *al-Hizb al-Suri al-Qawmi*—see Syrian Nationalist Party▷.

PROTECTORATE. Whether or not the protection and aid accorded a small state by an empire or Great Power amounts to a P. is often a matter of deanition and terminology. The mandate▷ system can be termed a tutorial P. on the part of a Great Power. The treaties Britain signed with various Arab rulers at the beginning of the century, e.g., with Ibn Sa'ud▷ in 1915, and the incomplete agreement contained in the exchange of letters between Hussein b. 'Ali▷, Sharif of Mecca, and Sir Henry MacMahon▷ (1916) provided for a partial, or veiled, P. Genuine British P.s were imposed in the 19th century, through numerous treaties, on the Persian Gulf▷ principalities of Kuwait▷, Bahrain▷, Qatar▷, Trucial 'Oman▷, Muscat-and-'Oman▷.

Full use of the term P. to describe the judicial and political status of a country occurred in the ME only on two occasions. a. Britain named the administration imposed on Egypt in 1914 a P. (she had ruled Egypt actually since 1882, but had previously refrained from describing her occupation as a P.). She took this step when Turkey joined the enemy camp in World War I, to emphasize the end of any formal ties between Egypt and Turkey. The British P. lasted until 1922, when Britain unilaterally declared Egypt independent. b. Britain established a P. over the interior of Aden▷ where she entered into numerous treaties with local sheikhs and sultans. The principalities in the "Eastern P." and the "Western P." were joined together in 1959 into the Federation of South Arabia▷ which in 1967 became the People's Republic of South Yemen▷.

The French occupations of Tunisia (1881–1956) and Morocco (1912–56)—outside the scope of this Encyclopaedia—were also officially termed P.s.   (Y.S.)

PROTESTANTS. Since the 19th century several P. denominations have commenced strong proselytizing activities in the ME—mostly from among the members of other Christian communities. However, the number of converts has remained small. In Ottoman Turkey the persecution of the Armenian▷, Christian minorities also affected the P., most of whom were Armenian converts. Today only about 2,000 P. remain in Istanbul. The strongest P. groups in the ME are in Egypt and Sudan. In Egypt, an Evangelical Church, established mainly by American Presbyterian missionaries, has about 100,000 members, most of whom were formerly Copts▷. The 9,000 members of the Evangelical Church of Syria and Lebanon are also mostly Presbyterians. Several thousand Lutherans, Methodists, Pentecostals, Baptists, Adventists, members of the Church of the Nazarene, and of some minor sects, reside in the ME. The main concentration of Anglicans is in southern Sudan, with about 140,000 adherents. Many of them left as refugees due to the rebellion and its suppression (see Sudan▷). There are a further 10,000 Anglicans in the ME, 5,000 of whom belong to the Arab Episcopal Church of Jordan, Syria and Lebanon.   (Sh. C.)

PROTOCOLS OF THE (LEARNED) ELDERS OF ZION. Forged "P." of an alleged

Jewish world conspiracy. The original version purported to be a report of meetings held at Basle, Switzerland, in 1897 while the first Zionist World Congress was in session. Previous meetings were alleged to have been held in the Prague Jewish cemetery once every 100 years. The P. were inspired *i.a.* by a satire by Maurice Joly on Napoleon III, which was published in 1864. Investigation revealed that the P. were concocted by officials of the Russian secret police. During the 1930s the fact that the P. are a crude forgery was reconfirmed at a long trial in Berne; but their circulation continued and they were widely used by anti-Jewish propagandists, such as Hitler and his disciples, and Palestinian-Arab leaders. In recent years new editions have been produced in Arabic, and other languages, in Egypt (in state-controlled publishing houses) and Lebanon. They are widely circulated, and many Arab leaders in their struggle with Israel seem to be unaware that the P. are a crude invention. (For example, President Nasser has quoted from the P. in interviews and in Aug. 1971 they were "quoted" by the Jordanian government radio).

(Sh. H.-E. L.)

Q

✱QADDHAFI, AL-, MUA'MMAR (b. 1941). Libyan officer and politician, Chairman of the Revolutionary Council, Prime Minister and Minister of Defence since 1969–70. Graduated from Benghazi University (history), 1963, and the Military Academy, 1965. After further military studies in Britain, 1966, Q. joined the signal corps. He participated in the coup of Sept. 1969, which overthrew the Monarchy. He was promoted to the rank of Colonel, appointed Commander-in-Chief of the Armed Forces, and finally Chairman of the Revolutionary Council. Since 16 Jan. 1970 he has also been Prime Minister and Minister of Defence. Under his leadership, Libya has become active in inter-Arab politics, and Q. himself has become well-known to the Arab public. Within the Libyan junta, Q. seems to hold the balance between a pro-Egyptian group and a "nationalist" faction opposing too dominant an Egyptian influence. He stresses his loyalty to Islam and opposition to Communism. In inter-Arab affairs, he follows a most extremist line—e.g. in favour of the Palestinian-Arab *feda'iyin*▷ in their fight against Jordan, advocating (and aiding?) revolution in Morocco, or interfering in Sudan.   (B.G.)

QASHQAIS. Group of semi-nomadic tribes in south Iran, living mainly in the province of Fars▷. Their number is estimated at 150,000. They speak a Turkish dialect. The Q. were semi-independent until Reza Shah's▷ reign: they recognized the suzerainty of the Shah and his prerogative to name the tribal leaders, but actual interference by Teheran in tribal affairs was rare. However, in the mid-1920s Reza Shah, endeavouring to establish a centralized regime, abolished the Q.'s autonomy and forced them—and other tribes—to become sedentary, pay taxes and serve in the army. The Q. revolted unsuccessfully in 1929 and again in 1932. After Reza Shah's abdication, 1941, they reverted to their old nomadic way of life. In 1946 they revolted again, demanding 1. greater representation for Fars in the *Majlis* (Parliament), 2. a provincial council, 3. a railway and 4. the ouster of the three communist *Tudeh*▷ ministers from the cabinet. Only their last request was granted. They supported Mossaddeq▷ in the crisis of 1951–3. They opposed Muhammed Reza Shah's▷ agrarian reforms in 1962–3, but their opposition was crushed by the army.   (B.G.)

QASSEM, 'ABD-UL-KARIM (1914–63). Iraqi officer and politician. Born in Baghdad of a Sunni-Muslim lower middle class family. An army officer, commissioned in 1938, Q. served as a battalion commander with the Iraqi expeditionary forces in the Palestine War of 1948. In about 1956, by then a brigade commander, he was elected Chairman of the Committee of the "Free Officers" who were plotting the overthrow of the Monarchy and an end

General 'Abd-ul-Karim Qassem

to Iraq's Western connections. On 13/14 July 1958, the group under Q. and his confederate Col. 'Abd-ul-Salam 'Aref▷, carried out their revolution. Contrary to the expectations of his fellow-conspirators, Q. declined to form a "Revolutionary Command Council"; he appointed himself Commander-in-Chief, Prime Minister and Acting Minister of Defence. He became in effect dictator and "Sole Leader" (soon to be his semi-official title) of the Republic.

The most important part of his policy was to keep Iraq independent of 'Abd-ul-Nasser's UAR, then at the height of her prestige. He quarrelled with 'Aref over this matter, as well as over the latter's ill-disguised ambition to displace his chief, and in Sept. 1958, 'Aref was removed from office and later tried and sentenced. Nationalist-Nasserist disaffection, soon followed by conspiracy, threw Q. into a working alliance with the communists which reached its peak in the suppression of the Nasserist mutiny of Col. Shawwaf in Mosul, Mar. 1959. However the communists, who had been penetrating the administration, overreached themselves when they began clamouring for participation in Q.'s cabinet and for legalization of their party. Q. began suppressing them, and in the summer of 1959 their fortunes waned.

An attempt, early in 1960, to restore constitutionalism through the revival of political parties, failed; it is doubtful to what extent Q. had taken it seriously in the first place. By then Q. had no supporters left among the political groupings of Iraq. The Kurds▷, under the leadership of Mulla Mustafa Barzani▷, rebelled in the autumn of 1961. They soon controlled the countryside of north-east Iraq in spite of the army's efforts to subdue them. Q.'s unsuccessful claim to Kuwait▷ in 1961, never withdrawn, though not actively carried through, alienated hitherto friendly Arab states and made him look ridiculous at home. His breach with the Iraq Petroleum Co. in Dec. 1961, and the unilateral take-over of about 90% of the latter's concessionary area (though not including any oil fields actually in operation), added to his powerful adversaries. But his most rabid enemies remained the Nasserist-*Ba'thist* nationalists, who had much blood to avenge. A combination of civilian *Ba'thists* and anti-communist officers finally brought about Q.'s downfall on 8/9 Feb. 1963. Q. and three of his closest collaborators were shot.

Q. was genuinely interested in social affairs, and the agrarian reform law of 30 Sept. 1958 will probably be considered a landmark in Iraqi history. He was high strung and became increasingly erratic; his exalted sense of his own mission prevented him from creating a political base to his rule, and earned him the nickname of the "Mad Dictator".　　(U.D.)

✻**QATAR.** Sheikhdom, Amirate (principality) on the Qatar Peninsula of the Persian Gulf's▷ Arabian Coast. Its length from north to south is 105 mi. and its width 25–49 mi. Q. neighbours in the south on Sa'udi-Arabia▷; their common frontier is disputed. Q. is *c.* 7,720 sq. mi. in area. Her population was estimated in 1969 at 70,000; 50,000 in the capital Doha, on the eastern coast. The population subsisted, up to the present century, on grazing, fishing, pearl-diving and some agriculture.

Q.'s sheikhs belong to the house of al-Thani; they are Sunni▷ Muslims of the *Wahhabi*▷ school. They were under a British protectorate established in treaties of 1868 and 1916. In 1968, Q. joined the sheikhdoms attempting to form a Federation of the Trucial Coast▷ and the Persian Gulf, but by 1971 she had abandoned her plan to join the federation. In Apr. 1970, Q. provisionally declared her independence. At the same time, a provisional constitution was proclaimed, providing for government on a modern pattern and an elected advisory council. Q. proclaimed her full independence, and the British protectorate was terminated, on 1 Sept. 1971. Her admission to the UN was expected.

In 1935, an oil concession was granted to a subsidiary of the Iraqi oil company IPC. Oil was discovered in 1939, but, due to the advent of World War II, production did not begin until 1950. Output reached 8.2m. tons in 1960. In the 1960s further concessions were granted, mainly for offshore drilling. "Shell" began production in 1964. In 1969, offshore concessions were granted also to Japanese companies. By 1970, production had reached 17m. tons. Continental oilfields are situated on the west coast of the peninsula and the crude oil is pumped through a pipeline to the port of Umm Sa'id, specially built for the exploration of oil. A small refinery, with a capacity of 30,000 tons for local needs is also located there. The oil royalties, over $100m. are used for services such as education and health, desalination of sea water, and also for economic development: petro-chemical plants, fertilizer production, a cement factory (opened in 1969) and factories for the processing of agricultural products. (Y.K.)

QAVAM AL-SALTANEH, AHMAD (1874–1960). Iranian politician. Prime Minister 1922–3, 1923–4, 1942–3, 1946–7 and July 1952. Q. was Iran's chief negotiator with the USSR during the Azerbaijan crisis of 1945–6 (see Iran▷, political history). In order to appease the Russians he included three Tudeh▷ (communist) ministers in his cabinet and signed an oil agreement with the USSR; however, this was never ratified by the *Majlis* (Parliament). In July 1952 Prime Minister Mossadeq▷ resigned over the Shah's refusal to appoint him also as Minister of War, and Q. was appointed in his stead; but when he had to yield, four days later, to violent pro-Mossadeq demonstrations in Teheran, he tendered his resignation and retired from political life. (B.G.)

QAWUQJI, FAWZI. Syro-Lebanese politician and soldier. Born in Tripoli, Lebanon, Q. served in the Ottoman Army and took part in the Druze Revolt in Syria (1925–7). He was sentenced to death by the French, but fled to Baghdad, where he taught at the Military Academy. In 1936, he came from Syria at the head of volunteers to assist the Arab guerillas in Palestine. His attempts to organize a revolutionary army under his command failed. When the rebellion was ended in the autumn of 1936, through the mediation of the Arab kings, the Palestine government permitted Q. to escape across the border with his troops. In 1941, he took part in the Rashid 'Ali al-Kilani▷ rebellion in Iraq. After it was quelled, he fled to Germany, where he headed one of the Arab offices in Berlin. After World War II, he returned to Syria.

In Jan. 1948 he was appointed by the Arab League▷ as commander of the "Army of Deliverance"— a volunteer force from Arab countries organized in Syria to assist the Palestinian-Arab guerillas. Q.'s force operated in the north and centre of Palestine and tried, without success, to storm Jewish settlements in the Jezreel Valley and Lower Galilee (Tirat Zvi, Mishmar Ha'emek, Ramat Yohanan). His attempts to impose a unified command on all the Arab guerilla forces failed. He had scarcely any influence in the south of the country, although he was called upon to shell Jewish Jerusalem in Apr. 1948. In Oct. 1948, Operation "Hiram" of the Israel Defence Forces forced Q. and his troops to flee to Lebanon. Some of his officers later became prominent in Syria's numerous coups from 1949 onward. (A.L.-O.T.)

QUDSI, AL-, DR. NAZEM. Syrian jurist and politician. Prime Minister, 1949–50; President 1961–3. Born 1906 in Aleppo, Q. studied at the universities of Beirut, Damascus and Geneva, and received his doctorate in international law. He was Syrian envoy to the USA, 1944–6. Q. was one of the leaders of the Aleppo-based "People's Party" in the 1950s, and was several times elected to parliament. He was President of Parliament 1951–3 and 1954–7. Q. held ministerial offices in a number of governments and was three times Prime Minister in 1949–50. When Syria united with Egypt in the UAR▷, 1958, he withdrew from political life. After the dissolution of the UAR in 1961, he was elected President. He was deposed in a military coup in Mar. 1962, but returned to office when it became apparent that the officers who had organized the coup had no programme, suffered from internal dissension and could not form a government. Q. was again deposed in the Ba'th▷ coup of 8 Mar. 1963, and again withdrew from political life. (A.L.-O.T.)

QUWWATLI, AL-, SHUKRI (1892–1967). Syrian politician. President of Syria 1943–9 and 1955–8. Born in Damascus, Q. was active in the Arab nationalist movement from his youth and was

Shukri al-Quwwatli

one of the leaders of the nationalist *al-Fatat* society (1911). During World War I, he was arrested by the Turks because of his activities, and according to some reports sentenced to death. Q. was Governor of Damascus under Amir Feisal▷. The French also condemned him to death, *in absentia*. In the years 1920–31, Q. was in exile in Egypt and Europe and active there on behalf of the nationalists. He returned to Syria in 1931, and became one of the leaders of the "National Bloc", the main faction of the nationalist movement in its struggle for independence. He was among the negotiators of the Franco-Syrian Treaty of 1936, signed but never implemented, and, when the first nationalist government of Syria was established in 1936, he was Minister of Defence and Finance (until 1939).

As leader of the "National Bloc", Q. was elected President of Syria in 1943 and re-elected in 1948. He was deposed by Gen. Husni Za'im▷ in a military coup in March 1949 and spent five years in exile in Egypt, returning to Syria after the fall of Adib Shishakli▷ in 1954. In Aug. 1955, Q. was elected President for the third time. He followed a pronounced pro-Egyptian policy and advocated the forging of closer links with the Soviet Union; the first agreements on Soviet aid to Syria enjoyed his active support. In 1957–8, he was among the advocates of union with Egypt, though he was no longer in the confidence of the young officers who worked for this aim. Once the union had been effected, Q. resigned from office and proposed Nasser▷ as President of the United Arab Republic▷. He then retired from politics and was awarded the honorary title of "First Arab Citizen".   (A.L.-O.T.)

R

*RAS AL-KHAIMA. The northernmost of the seven sheikhdoms on the Trucial Coast▷, 524 sq. mi. in area, with a population of 25,000, mostly living in the port of R. They engage in fishing, boat-building and pearl-diving. The Sheikh of R. has been subject to British protection since the 19th century. A concession to prospect for oil on land and at sea was granted in 1964 to an American company. Part of it was transferred in 1969 to "Shell". R. is involved in a dispute with Iran over the possession of the (two) Tumb Islands in the Persian Gulf. R. decided in 1971 not to join the Trucial Coast Federation (UAE▷).
(Y.K.)

RASHID, HOUSE OF. A family of Sheikhs of the Shammar▷ tribe in north Najd▷, centering on al-Ha'il. The R. family were rivals of the House of Sa'ud▷. During the 1880s, the R.s gained the upper hand, capturing Riyadh▷, the Sa'udi capital. In 1890 and 1891, the heads of the House of Sa'ud were forced to flee to Kuwait, but at the turn of the 20th century, under the leadership of young Ibn Sa'ud▷, they recaptured Riyadh, thereby renewing the struggle for hegemony in the region. The feud was deepened by religious differences, in that the Sa'udis belonged to the Wahhabi▷ sect and the Rashids did not, and also by political factors, as the Rs. remained loyal to the Ottoman Empire, while Ibn Sa'ud made a treaty with the British. After World War I, Ibn Sa'ud was victorious, and, in the autumn of 1921, the Rs. surrendered and renounced all claim to power or influence.   (Y.S.)

RASHID 'ALI—See Kilani, al-, Rashid 'Ali▷

RAZMARA, 'ALI (1901–51). Iranian officer and politician. Prime Minister 1950–51. A graduate of the French Military Academy at Saint Cyr, R. held several military commands in Iran. As Chief of General Staff, 1946–50, he was responsible for the successful entry of Iranian troops into secessionist Azerbaijan▷, Dec. 1946. R. was Prime Minister from June 1950 to Mar. 1951. He received strong support from the Shah and tried to initiate land-reform measures, but was opposed by the powerful group of landowners in the *Majlis* (Parliament). He was assassinated in Mar. 1951 by a member of the fanatical "*Fedayan Islam*"▷ because he had stated in Parliament that Iran was not yet ready for oil nationalization.   (B.G.)

RED LINE AGREEMENT—See Oil in the ME▷ (Iraq, IPC).

RED SEA. Six ME countries border on the shores of the RS: Egypt, Israel, Jordan, Sa'udi Arabia, Yemen, and Sudan (as well as Eritrea, in Ethiopia, which is outside the scope of this Encyclopaedia). A seventh country, Southern Yemen, touches the end of the Bab al-Mandab▷ Straits, connecting the RS with the Indian Ocean, between Africa and the Arabian peninsula. In the north, the RS ends in two inlets, the Gulf of 'Aqaba▷ (Eilat) to the east, and the Gulf of Suez, to the west. The importance of the RS as an international sea route greatly increased with the opening of the Suez Canal▷ in 1869. With the continuing closure of the Canal since 1967, traffic in the RS has greatly decreased.

Several powers regarded control of the RS as most important, particularly Great Britain in her concern for the imperial route to India (as well as the African colonies), and Italy in her ambition to establish an African empire. Italy governed Eritrea from 1889 to 1941 and her efforts to extend her influence across the RS to the Yemen and Sa'udi Arabia gave rise to British concern for many years. The establishment of official relations between the USSR and Yemen and Sa'udia, in the 1920s, caused concern in the West. However, a more real Soviet presence began only in the 1960s, when ports in Sudan and Egypt, as well as in South Yemen, became available to the USSR. The closure of the Suez Canal is a serious obstacle to any Russian efforts to establish bases and a permanent naval and military presence in the RS (and the Indian Ocean).   (Y.S.)

*REFUGEES. Many crises and wars in the ME have forced groups of inhabitants to flee their homes or emigrate and to become R. The Armenians▷ of Eastern Anatolia and the Caucasus foothills were persecuted by the Ottoman Empire and many of them fled, particularly after the pogroms of 1895–6 and the persecutions of 1915–18; they reached most countries of the area, Syria and Lebanon in particular. They settled in their new countries and ceased being R., but they were not entirely assimilated by Arab society and preserved their separate identity.

Turkish R. left the Balkans following the Balkan Wars (1912–13) and World War I. On the other hand, Bulgarian and Greek R. fled from Turkey. The exchange of R. between Turkey and Greece was sanctioned in an agreement on population exchange, 1923 (see Greek-Turkish Relations▷); this agreement remains the only one of its kind in the region. The emigration of Turks from Rumania (in the 1930s) and from Bulgaria (in the 1930s and '50s) was only partially based on agreements. In all these cases, the emigrants were absorbed by their own people.

Many Assyrians▷ became R.—fleeing first from Turkey to Iraq, during World War I, and then from Iraq, after massacres in 1933. Many of them settled in north-east Syria, the Jazira▷, and ceased being R.,

Refugee camp north of 'Amman

though they were not absorbed by the local population.

European Jewish R. were denied entry to Palestine under the British Mandate▷ until 1948, except for a quota determined by the British, which was supposed to be based on the economic absorptive capacity of the country, but was decisively influenced by political considerations. The pressure of the survivors of the Nazi Holocaust, still in European concentration camps, was an important political and moral factor, in the deliberations on the future of Palestine, 1945–7, and in world support for the setting up of a Jewish State. After the establishment of Israel, 1948, there was free and unlimited Jewish immigration; nearly 1.3m. Jewish immigrants included the remnants of European Jewry and also R. from the Arab countries (c. 500,000). Once they reached Israel they were no longer "R.": they immediately became citizens and were accepted as equal partners in building and defending Israel.

The most persistent R. problem in the area, so far unsolved, is that of the Arab R. from those areas of Palestine which in 1948 became Israel, and it is an integral part of the Arab-Israel conflict▷; its origin, the number of R., the right solution are all disputed. It is undisputed that it was the 1948 War that caused the departure of many Arab residents of the areas of Palestine allotted to the State of Israel. Had the Arabs accepted the creation of the State (along with the establishment of their own State in the other half of the country), no R. problem would have arisen. Once the Arab leaders decided to oppose the creation of the State and embarked on hostilities, R. began fleeing from those areas where it was expected the Jews would establish control. There have been persistent Arab claims, that the Jews "expelled" these R. Israeli spokesmen deny such claims and maintain that the R. fled on their own initiative, following the instructions, and even more so the example, of their leaders and in disregard of the pleas and counsel of the Jews. The leaders and the upper and educated class were indeed the first to flee, leaving the masses like a flock without a shepherd.

Figures have been inflated by political propaganda, but it is possible to determine the real numbers of the R. of 1948. In 1948, the Palestine Arabs numbered 1.3m; 400,000 remained in the West Bank▷ occupied by Jordan, 100–150,000 in the Gaza Strip▷, under Egyptian occupation, and 150,000 in Israel. The number, then, of the 1948 refugees cannot have been more than 550–650,000. The usual estimate of the UN agencies is 715–730,000. Most of them left their towns or villages, but remained within their homeland, Palestine: 200,000 in the West Bank, 200,000 in the Gaza-Strip, and 100,000 in Transjordan (which was part of Palestine until separated by the British in 1922). Only 100–150,000 crossed the borders of Palestine, mostly to Syria and Lebanon.

The UN began immediately, in 1948, to aid the R. At the end of 1949, a special agency, the UN Relief and Works Agency (UNRWA)▷ was set up, to administer that aid. The UN still aids the R. through UNRWA. Annual expenditure, at first *c*. $20m, had increased by the 1960s to $40m., the US contributing most of it. Plans were contemplated at first to settle refugees and work out development projects for their rehabilitation and absorption. Several schemes along these lines were prepared in the early 1950s, but the Arab states opposed in principle the rehabilitation and absorption of the R. in their new areas of residence or in Arab lands in general and insisted that they be repatriated to the homes they had abandoned in 1948, or at least be given a free choice — demands Israel found unacceptable. The UN General Assembly resolved that the freedom of choice to return to what was now the State of Israel should be given to those refugees "willing to live at peace with their neighbours." Israel could not rely upon such a distinction, since all requests for repatriation were always accompanied by demonstrations of extreme hostility towards Israel and calls for her destruction. The UN General Assembly consistently referred to either the repatriation of the R. or their resettlement with compensation for their abandoned property. Israel has, from the first, offered such compensation, but the Arab states and the R. have refused to accept it, lest acceptance of compensation be interpreted as renunciation of the demand for repatriation.

Thus the UN—in resolutions repeated in similar versions year after year—regarded repatriation as one of the approaches to a solution and demanded a free choice for each individual R. The Arab states demanded repatriation as the main or only way. Israel, however, could offer only the acceptance of a limited and agreed-upon number of R. (in 1949, she offered to take back 100,000 refugees, but the Arabs rejected the offer); she could not agree to the repatriation of large numbers or to a free choice to be exercised by the refugees (in the existing climate of hatred and indoctrination there was no prospect that individual refugees would be able to choose freely (see Arab-Israel Conflict▷). Meantime, the political implications of the problem and the total opposition of the Arab states to any rehabilitation or resettlement schemes prevented any progress towards rehabilitation and condemned the R. to a life of frustration on the margins of society. (For unregistered *de facto* rehabilitation see below). UNRWA could offer only non-constructive aid:

food and temporary housing in R. camps, and also medical and education facilities (through UNESCO).

The number of R. has grown since 1948 and continues growing. According to the rate of natural increase for the area (2.5–3%), the number of refugees and their descendants should have reached 1m. in 1970 (with no allowance for those who may have found employment and ceased to be refugees). UNRWA lists 1.4m., admitting in its publications that its statistics "do not necessarily reflect the actual R. population owing to factors such as unreported deaths and undetected false registration". Of the 1.4m. on the UNRWA lists, 580,000 are in Palestine, *i.e.* in areas administered by Israel since 1967 — over 300,000 in the Gaza Strip and over 250,000 in the West Bank (according to Israeli statistics, only about 200,000 of these are genuine R. or members of R. families); more than 500,000 in Jordan (including 200,000 refugees who crossed the Jordan from the West Bank in 1967 — half of them R. from 1948, half new R.); 170,000 in Lebanon and 160,000 in Syria. About 800,000 of all the R., or 65%, received full rations from UNRWA. About 950,000 were at one time housed in camps, but now the majority live outside camps. A considerable percentage of breadwinners have found employment. Jordan, already in 1950, granted all refugees in her territory full citizenship, including the unlimited right to work. The other Arab states did not grant such full rights, but did not in fact prevent R. from working. The Persian Gulf principalities, with their expanding oil economies and consequent development of industry and transport, have absorbed tens of thousands of Palestinian R. and provided them with profitable employment. Many of the intelligentsia have found work as teachers, clerks and technicians in the oil sheikhdoms and those other Arab states (Sa'udi Arabia, Libya, etc.) short of educated manpower. Most of them have not given up their status as R. or their UNRWA rations.

UNRWA has been very active in the fields of health and education and particularly in vocational training. Public health among the R. is superior to that among the surrounding ordinary Arab population, and their rate of natural increase is among the highest in the world. The level of school education are higher than those of the non-R. in the host countries. This adds perhaps to the social and host countries. This adds perhaps to the social and political frustration of the R., for despite their superior education and wide possibilities of profitable employment the ruling trend is still to deny them complete absorption or permanent settlement. There are no reliable estimates as to how many refugees have been effectively integrated into the economy and labour force of their host countries, for the Arab states and the R. themselves are anxious to conceal or obscure this process of integration and at any rate, to diminish its political import. However, a sizeable number of R. has probably been integrated at least in employment—in housing conditions little different from those of the surrounding population, and with better health and educational facilities. In contrast to notions prevalent in the early 1950s, it is now evident that the rehabilitation of the R. is primarily a matter of work and housing, and that employment must be mainly urban-industrial, since most R. have lost their rural and agricultural character, and that there is no need for large-scale agricultural settlement or development projects. An overall solution to the Arab R. problem, though economically feasible, remains, of course, primarily a political issue and can be arrived at only with the resolution of the tragic Arab-Israel conflict as a whole.   (Y.S.)

RESTITUTION AGREEMENT. An agreement signed on 10 Sept. 1952 between the Federal Republic of Germany and the State of Israel, under which West Germany undertook to pay DM 3,000m. in goods and services, to help the resettling of "destitute Jewish refugees uprooted from Germany and from territories formerly under German rule" in recognition of the fact that "unspeakable criminal acts were perpetrated against the Jewish people during the National-Socialist regime of terror".

West Germany undertook to pay also a sum of DM 450m. for the benefit of the "Conference on Jewish Material Claims Against Germany", as compensation for the persecution of Jews, deprivation of liberty, compulsory labour, damage to health and to economic prospects. In addition, R. has been paid by 1971, to individual Jews: $8,000m. in total, $1,500m. to Israelis.

Germany made all the agreed eleven annual installments and implemented the agreement in 1965 through an Israeli company specially established for the purpose (the "Israel Mission", also called "R. Company"). Goods to the net value of $741m. were imported into Israel (approximately 9% of total imports in that period), mainly: ships and equipment for electricity supply and transmission, railway, telephone and mining equipment, and oil.

During the period of the agreement, there were no diplomatic relations between the two countries, but the "Mission"—while being officially a German juristic person—enjoyed a *de facto* diplomatic status.'

The RA was the outcome of negotiations which commenced with contacts made by Dr. Nahum Goldmann▷ and the World Jewish Congress. Later,

they were taken up by official Israeli representatives headed by the then Foreign Minister Moshe Sharett▷.

The signing of the agreement was preceded by opposition of unprecedented intensity in Israel, sometimes in the form of violent demonstration inspired by the nationalist *Herut* party, headed by Menahem Begin▷. He claimed—and had much support in Israel and from world Jewry—that because of the Jewish people's sombre historical account with Germany, there should be no contact whatsoever with the Germans, and that it was necessary to refrain from any act (such as the signing of a RA) which could be interpreted as rehabilitating the German people. Even after the signature of the agreement, the boycott—sometimes official—on contacts with Germany continued, apart from those required for the implementation of the agreement. Yet, the agreement was a definite step towards normalisation of relations between the two countries and the subsequent establishment of diplomatic relations between them in 1965.   (E.L.)

✽**REZA SHAH** (1878–1944). King or Emperor (Shah) of Iran 1925–41; founder of the Pahlavi▷ dynasty. Born at Alasht (Mazanderan Province), R. joined the Persian Cossack Brigade and became its Commander with the rank of Colonel. In Feb. 1921 R. (then known as R. Khan) and Ziyya-ul-Din Tabatabai▷ engineered a coup. The latter became Prime Minister and R. served as Minister of War and Commander-in-Chief of the army. In June 1921, R. forced Tabatabai to resign and leave Iran. R. became Prime Minister in 1923; Shah Ahmad, the last monarch of the Qajar dynasty, left for Europe. In 1925, R. had the Shah deposed by the *Majlis* (Parliament). Some wanted to turn Iran into a republic, and R. was for a time reported to favour such a move; but the religious leaders dissuaded him.

In Dec. 1925 R. was proclaimed Shah by the *Majlis*, he chose the name Pahlavi▷ for the new dynasty. RS, inspired partly by Ataturk's▷ reforms in neighbouring Turkey, initiated a series of bold reforms aimed at westernizing the country and making it economically independent. These reforms brought him into conflict with the clergy. Internationally, RS initiated a policy of *rapprochement* with Iran's Muslim neighbours; this culminated in 1937 in the Saadabad▷ Pact (with Iraq, Afghanistan and Turkey). He was suspicious of Britain and the USSR and therefore followed a pro-German policy. In 1941, he turned down a joint Anglo-Soviet demand to let supplies destined for the USSR pass through Iran. The Allies then invaded and occupied Iran, and R. abdicated, Sept. 1941. He was deported to South Africa where he died in 1944.   (B.G.)

*RIAD, MAHMUD (b. 1917). Egyptian officer and politician. Foreign Minister since 1964. A 1939 graduate of the Egyptian military academy and an army career officer. Egyptian representative on the Egypt-Israel Mixed Armistice Commission (1949–52), Director of the Department of Arab Affairs in the Foreign Ministry (1954–5), Ambassador to Syria (1955–8), Presidential Adviser on foreign affairs (1958–61), Deputy Chief of the permanent mission to the UN (1961–2), Ambassador to the UN (1962–4). Foreign Minister since 1964, concurrently Deputy Prime Minister since 1970. R. favours active diplomacy and often travels abroad. He is considered an expert on the Arab-Israel dispute. Despite all changes in high government echelons, R. has maintained his position and seems to be accepted by the various factions. Although R. values Egypt's relations with the West he gives priority to the Soviet-Egyptian alliance and is one of its architects. In the Arab-Israel conflict he is a hard-liner. (A.S.)

Abd-ul-Mun'im Rifa'i (at left) (with Michael Steward, British Foreign Secretary)

1966. R. was Foreign Minister 1968–9, Prime Minister Mar. to Aug. 1969, Deputy Prime Minister and Minister for Foreign Affairs Aug. 1969 to June 1970, Prime Minister June to Sept. 1970. Considered loyal to the king, but respected by the Palestinian guerillas, he was expected to achieve a compromise after the serious clashes in June 1970 between the Jordanian Army and Palestinian guerillas; but as new clashes erupted, in Sept. 1970, he was replaced by a military government. R. is also a Poet and has composed several patriotic verses and songs, especially since the Six Day War. (B.G.)

RIFA'I, SAMIR (1899–1967). Jordanian politician. Born in Safad, Palestine, R. served in the civil service of Mandatory Palestine 1922–5, and of Transjordan 1925–44. He joined the Transjordan government as Minister of the Interior 1943 and Minister of the Royal Court 1950. R. was Prime Minister 1944–5, 1947, 1950–1 and 1956; Deputy Prime Minister and Minister for Foreign Affairs 1957–8; President of the Senate 1959–61; President of the University of Jordan 1962–7. R. was a staunch supporter of the Hashemite dynasty, a conservative and a moderate (including a moderate attitude towards Israel). (B.G.)

RIVER DEVELOPMENT—see Water in the ME▷.

RIYADH, AL-. Capital of Sa'udi-Arabia▷. A desert oasis in Najd▷. Pop.: 169,000 (1967; there are estimates of 300,000 or more). R. was a stronghold of the Wahhabi▷ sect and in 1924 became the capital of the Kingdom of Najd and Hijaz, later Sa'udi Arabia. Its development into a modern city began with the exploitation of the oil resources in the east of the country. Roads were paved, wide avenues laid, and modern commercial premises built, together with palaces and parks. R. is linked by a railway opened in 1951, and by roads to the port of Dammam on the Persian Gulf. A link with the port of Jidda▷ on the Red Sea is being planned. R. has an international airport. (Y.K.)

Mahmud Riad

*RIFA'I, 'ABD-UL-MUN'IM (b. 1917). Jordanian diplomat and politician. Prime Minister, 1969–70. Born in Safad, Palestine and educated at Beirut University, R. held various posts in the Jordanian civil and diplomatic services from 1938 onwards. He was Minister to Teheran 1951–3; Washington 1953–7; Ambassador to Beirut 1957–8; London 1958; to the UN 1962–5; and to the Arab League

*ROGERS, WILLIAM. US Secretary of State in the Nixon administration since 1969. In ME affairs, he is known principally for the "R. Plan", a proposed solution of the Arab-Israel conflict, which he submitted in Oct. 1969 to Egypt, Jordan and Israel (and the Soviet Union). The plan was published in outline in Dec. 1969. Its main points are: Israel to withdraw to the international boundary with Egypt (that of the Mandate period); the Gaza Strip▷ and Sharm al-Sheikh▷ to remain subjects for negotiation, on the assumption that they will not remain under Israeli control; Israel to withdraw to the 1949 armistice lines with Jordan, with slight revisions; the Arab refugees▷ to be accorded the choice between returning to Israel and accepting compensation; in Jerusalem, Jordan to be accorded a status equal to that of Israel in the religious, economic and civil spheres (the R. Plan leaving open the question of Jerusalem's political future). R. does not deal with the questions of the Israel-Syrian frontier and of the Golan Heights▷.

The R. Plan was rejected by the USSR and Egypt as excessively pro-Israel. The plan was also rejected by Israel, as not ensuring her security and unlikely to bring peace nearer.

In June 1970, R. proposed to Egypt, Jordan and Israel that negotiations under the auspices of Ambassador Jarring▷ be resumed—aiming to reach agreement on a just and lasting peace, to be based on mutual recognition of each country's sovereignty, territorial integrity and political independence, and on an Israeli withdrawal from territories occupied in 1967 (in accordance with the Security Council Resolution of 22 Nov. 1967). As a first step, R. proposed that the cease-fire between Israel and Egypt be renewed for a period of at least three months. This proposal came in view of the political impasse, Jarring's failure to promote a settlement, the failure of the Four-Power talks▷, and the rejection of the R. Plan. Military escalation also caused much concern, as it was liable to lead to a Great-Power confrontation, i.e. from early 1970, Soviet involvement in Egypt had increased, Soviet pilots had begun to take part in Egyptian Air Force operations, and sophisticated missiles (SAM 2 and 3) were deployed and manned by Soviet crews.

The R. proposals were accepted by Egypt and Jordan. On 24 July 1970, President Nixon sent "clarifications" to the Prime Minister of Israel: Israel's withdrawal would be to secure and agreed borders, not the pre-June 1967 borders. No withdrawal would be demanded until a contractual, binding peace had been signed; the Arab refugee problem would be solved in a way that would not impair the Jewish character of the State of Israel; the US would ensure that the integrity, sovereignty and security of Israel be safeguarded and the balance of arms preserved.

In the wake of this message, the Israeli government decided to reply affirmatively to the R. initiative concerning peace talks and the cease-fire. At the same time the Israeli government clarified its position on a peace agreement as such and reiterated its rejection of the R. Plan. The acceptance of the R. proposals caused a cabinet crisis and the withdrawal of the Gahal▷ ministers from the coalition.

The cease-fire agreement, which included a military "standstill" for a 30. mi. strip on both sides of the Suez Canal▷, came into force at midnight 7 Aug. 1970. On the morrow it transpired that the same night the Egyptians had moved missiles towards the Canal. Later, fortification works and the movement forward of missiles continued. Israel protested and suspended the Jarring talks but resumed her participation in Jan. 1971 when the USA promised to counter-balance the Egyptian advantage. The talks again came to a deadlock in Feb. 1971. R. now offered the good offices of the USA to achieve an interim arrangement: the reopening of the Suez Canal against a partial Israeli withdrawal. Talks on this continued.   (E.A.-E.L.)

ROOSEVELT, FRANKLIN DELANO (1882–1945). President of the USA, 1933–45. Familiar with the plight of refugees and minority groups in the USA, and of the Jews in Nazi Germany, R. convened, in 1938, the 32-nation Evian Conference on the refugee problem which led to the establishment of the Inter-Governmental Committee for Refugees (succeeded, after World War II, by the War Refugees Board set up to succour victims of Nazism—both Jews and others). R. was generally sympathetic to Zionist aspirations, but in view of Arab opposition to them, he refrained from supporting them fully. During World War II▷ he showed special interest in the ME and an awareness of America's growing oil interests there. He sent personal envoys to report and made contacts. King Ibn Sa'ud▷, neutral during the war, received R.'s emissary, Gen. Patrick Hurley, on several occasions, and accepted a token shipment of lend-lease munitions in 1944. R. met Ibn Sa'ud on board an American cruiser after the Yalta Conference, 1945. The King's hostility to Zionism impressed him and was partly responsible for keeping his Palestine policy vague and uncommitted. (R.'s meeting with the Sultan of Morocco, in Jan. 1943, led Moroccan nationalists to believe that the USA would support them in their struggle against France.)

R.'s wife, Eleanor (Ann) R. (1884–1962) was a

fervent supporter of Zionism, a Patron of Youth Aliyah (the Institute responsible for bringing Jewish refugee children to Israel) and a frequent visitor to Israel. (A.W.-Sh.H.)

ROTHSCHILD, BARON EDMOND DE

(1845–1934). Known as the "Father of the new Jewish settlement in Palestine", after his response, in 1883, to a desperate appeal for help from the Jewish settlements there. He purchased large tracts of land, sent experts and reorganized the settlements' administration on an economic basis.

At the turn of the century R. aided, and took responsibility for 6,000 settlers in 30 villages. His new administration, however, was foreign to the settlers and their vision, who misinterpreted R.'s motives. Its paternalistic methods led to revolts, which ended in independence for the settlements. The lands and assets passed into the ownership of the PICA (Palestine Jewish Colonization Association), which was set up at the Baron's initiative. (E.A.)

*RUMANIA.

R.'s independent position in the Soviet bloc and her direct interest in ME oil brought her into the ME in the mid-1960s, as a factor in her own right. R. was the first Eastern European country to purchase ME oil directly, when she signed an exchange agreement with Iran in 1965. It is not clear to what extent this was a demonstration of R.'s independence from the Soviet Union; since then, other "Comecon" countries have also bought oil directly in the ME. Trade and co-operation agreements between R. and Israel, since Apr. 1967, and also after the Six Day War▷, indicate a policy running counter to the position of the Soviet Union. In some cases, R. took exception to Soviet initiatives on the ME and refused to join them. She alone among the countries of the Soviet bloc maintains diplomatic relations with Israel since June 1967; she even raised these to the ambassadorial level in 1968. R.'s position on a ME settlement is also different from that of the Soviet bloc and the Arab countries: she too, demands total Israeli withdrawal to the borders preceding the Six Day War, but holds that a peace settlement should be reached by direct talks between the two parties. (Y.R.)

*RUSSIA, RUSSIAN (AND SOVIET) INTERESTS AND POLICIES IN THE ME.

Tsarist R. made her first contacts with the ME in the 16th century, when her southward expansion reached the neighbouring Muslim empires of the Ottoman Turks and the Persians; her main drive for expansion began in the 17th century, and has, since 1677, resulted in thirteen wars between R. and her southern neigh-

Nasser meeting with Russian leaders (from left to right), Marshal Grechko, Kosygin and Podgorny, Moscow 1970

bours. R.'s quest for warm-water ports further accentuated the traditional enmity; the Black Sea▷-Bosphorus▷-Dardanelles▷ outlet to the Mediterranean and the Caspian Sea▷-Persian Gulf▷ corridor leading to India attracted Muscovite statesmen, merchants and strategists alike. They sought to exploit European continental rivalries and the internal decay weakening the Turkish and the Persian empires, generally by force but sometimes by diplomacy.

Yet even when militarily successful, R. was prevented from consolidating her territorial gains and political influence either by the unilateral intervention of Great Britain or by a combination of the major European powers. Therefore, in spite of three centuries of aspirations and marginal penetration, it is only since 1955 that Moscow has established a strong presence in the ME, mainly in its Arab countries.

The Treaty of Kutchuk Kainardja (Küçük Kainarca), 1774, ending a Russo-Turkish war, established R. as a recognized Black Sea power. Her constant ambition now became the control of the Turkish Straits—an ambition opposed by Great Britain, which defended Ottoman territorial integrity throughout the 19th century. In some instances R. supported the Turkish Sultan, e.g. in 1798 against the French and in 1833 against the rebellious Egyptian Viceroy Muhammad 'Ali, hoping to gain influence and concessions from Iskelesi, 1833, virtually made Turkey a R. protectorate but Anglo-French opposition prevented its consummation. In general, however, R. advocated the dismemberment of the Ottoman Empire; Tsar Nicholas I urged its partition as early as 1853, only to be rebuffed by London. The Crimean War of

1854–6 grew out of a quarrel between R. and France over the holy places in Palestine and R.'s claim to protect all Orthodox Christians in the Ottoman Empire. The Treaty of Paris, 1856, neutralized the Black Sea, but the Treaty of London, 1871, restored to R. warships their former right to use the Straits in time of peace. In the Treaty of Berlin, 1878, ending another Russo-Turkish war, the powers again prevented R. from gaining all she wanted. R. obtained, though, important border areas in the east: Batum, Kars▷, Ardahan▷.

Imperial R. also assaulted Persia—in 1804–13 and 1826–8—but with scant success. She acquired small pieces of territory, navigation rights on the Caspian Sea, and later growing influence, but was still barred from the Persian Gulf. In 1907 R. and Great Britain agreed to make up their differences in Asia and to divide Persia into three zones; the whole of northern Persia, including Teheran and down to Isfahan and Yazd, came under direct R. influence.

As R. was allied with Britain and France against the Turks and Germany in World War I, she claimed the right to annex—after victory—Constantinople and the Straits, i.e. both shores of the Bosphorus, the Sea of Marmara and the Dardanelles. These claims were accepted by Paris and London (secret agreement of Mar. 1915) in a radical transformation of Western policy; the Western powers also granted R. complete freedom of action in her zone of influence in Persia. In the secret Sykes-Picot▷ Agreement, 1916, R. obtained Western approval for the annexation of most of Eastern Anatolia, as well. In return R. consented to the partitioning of the Arab parts of the Ottoman Empire between her two European allies. However, by the time the Ottoman Empire was defeated, the Revolutionary Bolshevik government in Moscow had renounced all Tsarist territorial claims and gains.

During the interwar period the ME did not figure prominently in Soviet foreign policy. That policy was now conducted on two separate levels. 1. The USSR sought to maintain normal foreign relations. She concluded treaties of friendship with the fully independent ME countries of Turkey, Persia and Afghanistan in 1921; the one with Turkey contained undertones of Soviet support for a fellow-revolutionary; all three treaties had anti-British implications. The USSR, having signed her own treaty with Turkey, was not a party to the Peace Treaty of Lausanne▷, 1923; she signed—but failed to ratify—the Straits Convention appended to the Treaty, which demilitarized the Bosphorus and the Dardanelles and opened them to foreign warships (with certain limitations). The USSR was a signatory to the Montreux▷ Convention on the Straits, 1936, which permitted

their re-fortification and further restricted the right of warships to pass the Straits and enter the Black Sea. The USSR also established consular and diplomatic relations with Sa'udi Arabia and Yemen, in 1926 and 1928 respectively, despite the reactionary nature of these traditionalist monarchies; both missions were withdrawn in 1938. 2. On a different level, the USSR supported revolution everywhere, and particularly in colonial countries, through the Communist International. A Congress of the Peoples of the East, held in Baku in 1920 under the auspices of the "Comintern", called on the inhabitants of the area to rise up against their colonial masters. Communism, however, had little appeal for the peoples of the ME. Its secularist, atheistic elements were anathema to the religious values and beliefs of Muslim society; a proletarian industrial working class did not yet exist; communist cells were suppressed by the existing semi-independent nationalist regimes—with the full support of their Western supporters—Communist doctrine and practice in the colonial and semi-colonial countries were also severely hampered by frequent changes of dogma concerning the relations with the nationalist movement as a whole and its bourgeois or semi-feudal leadership—from "United Front" tactics and co-operation to bitter enmity.

As the USSR resumed the position of a Great Power, further penetration of the ME continued to be a major Soviet interest. In secret negotiations with Nazi Germany during 1940, the USSR made this explicit, declaring that her territorial aspirations centred "south of the national territory of the Soviet Union in the direction of the Indian Ocean" and the Persian Gulf. She also registered her demand for "land and naval bases within range of the Bosphorus and the Dardanelles".

In Aug. 1941, the USSR and Great Britain occupied Persia, for the duration of the war, to prevent her conquest by the Germans, and again divided her into zones (with the Soviet zone much smaller than in 1907). However, in 1945–6 the USSR was reluctant to evacuate; under the protection of her troops separatist regimes were set up in Azerbaijan▷ and Kurdistan▷, and leftists were encouraged throughout Persia. The matter was raised in the UN Security Council, as one of the first post-war East-West crises. When Soviet troops were finally evacuated, in 1946, the separatist regimes collapsed. An oil concession granted by Persia under strong Soviet pressure was rejected by the Persian Parliament in 1947. In 1945 the USSR also demanded bases and special rights in the Turkish Straits, through a revision of the Montreux Convention of 1936, and territorial concessions in the East (Kars, Ardahan)—denouncing the Soviet-Turkish

Treaty of Friendship of 1925 and making the conclusion of a new one conditional upon the acceptance of these demands. They were rejected (the USSR finally withdrew them in 1953). From 1945 onwards the USSR also claimed a share in UN trusteeships to be imposed on the former Italian colonies, particularly Libya—a claim that contributed to the West's preference for independence rather than trusteeship for the territories concerned.

The Cold War was thus introduced into the ME immediately after World War II. The USA reinforced Great Britain in the region by stationing the Sixth Fleet in the Mediterranean and taking on some of the defence and aid commitments Britain was no longer able to discharge. The "Truman▷ Doctrine" of Mar. 1947 committed the USA to aid Greece and Turkey against Communist agression or subversion. The USSR reacted to this Western opposition by falling back upon less direct means to subvert the West's position. She endorsed the partition of Palestine, 1947—as the speediest means to get Great Britain out—recognized Israel and let Czechoslovakia assist her with arms in her crucial struggle for survival, 1948; she encouraged ME nations in conflict with the West—such as Syria and Lebanon, 1945–6, Iran, in her defiance of Western oil interests 1951–3, and Egyptian and Iraqi nationalist governments struggling with Britain. Also, she soon gave increasing support to the Arab states against Israel, whom she came to regard as a protégé of the West. (The USSR's anti-Israel attitude thus reverted, after the brief interlude of 1947–9, to the violent anti-Zionism that had been traditional with the Communist establishment; one factor was the inability of the Soviet regime, after more than 50 years, to resolve its domestic Jewish problem either by assimilation or by territorial autonomy, and a revival of the Jewish national consciousness among the Jews of R. In her growing support for the Arab nationalist governments, the USSR greatly diminished—or at least played down—her support for local Communist parties and for national minorities in conflict with ME governments (such as the Kurds)▷; as such support could not be completely abandoned, Soviet policy continued displaying shifts and contradictions. It was obviously determined by the strategic and political interests of an expanding Great Power rather than by considerations of Communist ideology or solidarity.

As the countries of the ME gained complete independence, the USSR established, during and after World War II, full diplomatic relations with them (before the war she had maintained relations only with Turkey and Iran—and for a number of years with Yemen and Sa'udi Arabia). In the mid-1950s the opportunity came for the USSR to make a major

breakthrough. A revolutionary nationalist Egypt was locked in a bitter struggle with Britain. She was increasingly alienated from the USA—firstly by US pressure for a sponsorship of a ME Defence Treaty▷, and later the Baghdad Pact▷ which Egypt opposed and regarded as a hostile encirclement, then by US reluctance to grant arms on easy terms, and finally by the cancellation of the promised financial assistance for the Aswan Dam▷ project. Intensification of the Arab-Israel conflict also engendered anti-Western feelings to Moscow's profit. The break-through was a large-scale Egyptian-Czechoslovakian arms deal early in 1955. Full Soviet support for Egypt's stand in the Suez crisis of 1956 and similarly for Syria in 1957, accompanied in both cases by threats of military intervention, enhanced the USSR's position as the Arabs' chief supporter against Western imperialism and Israel. The USSR's stand in 1956 was a factor inducing the USA to press Israel to withdraw from Sinai. From 1957–8 the USSR gave ever-increasing military and economic aid to Syria and Egypt and, as a result, expanded her influence in the ME. The subsequent revolutions in the Arab world enlarged the camp of the USSR's clients: Iraq 1958, Algeria 1962, Yemen 1962, South Yemen 1967, Sudan 1969 and Libya 1969—though Egypt remained the USSR's single most important client and ally. Soviet aid was often geared to great show-piece schemes of national prestige, such as the High Dam of Aswan in Egypt and steel plants. The USSR also trained the officers of her Arab allies' armed forces and provided most of their military equipment, thus making them more and more dependent on her.

In the 1960s, the USSR abandoned hostile confrontation with her neighbours, Turkey and Iran, in favour of large-scale economic co-operation, credits and aid. Government leaders of the three states made several visits to each others' countries in the 1960s.

One significant consequence of the *rapprochement* with Turkey and the friendly ties with several Arab countries has been the growing presence of the Soviet fleet in the eastern Mediterranean. By the end of the 1960s it enjoyed free entry and exit through the Turkish Straits and the use of strategic ports in Egypt, Syria and Algeria; other Soviet fleets were welcome guests in Sudan, Yemen, South Yemen and Iraq (but the closure of the Suez Canal since June 1967 has severed the sea link between the former three countries and the latter three).

The Six Day War▷ of June 1967 constitutes another watershed in Soviet relations with the ME. The USSR's policies, and her advice to the Arab states, including allegations of Israeli troop concentrations (certified as false by UN observers), were among the chief factors determining the course of events before and during the crisis, and increasingly so since Moscow has supported the Arab cause against Israel in the UN and in Great-Power talks on the ME. In June 1967 she severed diplomatic relations with Israel. Moreover, the Soviets have, within two years, much more than replaced all military equipment lost in the conflict by the Arab states, both quantitatively and qualitatively. By 1970, the USSR had gone even further by dispatching Soviet officers to train and advise the Egyptian Army, by manning missile sites at several strategic points within Egypt, and by providing Soviet pilots to fly operational missions over Egypt. While the USSR officially accepted the existence of an independent Israel (in her pre-1967 borders, possibly in the even more restricted area proposed by the UN partition plan of 1947, and under certain conditions), she could not support the Palestinian-Arab guerilla organizations striving for the complete elimination of the State of Israel. Lately, however, she has even begun aiding and encouraging the guerillas—possibly, to counteract potential or actual Chinese influence—without explicitly identifying with all their aims.

The USSR fully supports insurgent movements in the Persian Gulf area. However, aiding the revolutionary regimes has not prevented the Kremlin from increasing its contacts with such more or less pro-Western countries as Lebanon, Jordan, Morocco and Tunisia, and aiding such arch-conservative regimes as pre-1962 Yemen.

In 1969–70, as the Arab-Israel crisis was escalating to such a level that a US-Soviet confrontation could no longer be confidently excluded, both powers had a clearly perceived interest in reaching some accommodation. The USSR was apparently prepared to impose, together with the USA, a settlement based on her policy proposals, namely: a complete withdrawal of Israel from all the territories occupied in 1967, a non-belligerency declaration of sorts (not full, contractual peace, containing a complete solution to the Palestine conflict, as demanded by Israel), and UN and Great-Power guarantees and supervision; in summer 1970, the USSR appeared to be pressing such plans—leading also to the re-opening of the Suez Canal, in which she was keenly interested—on her Arab allies, advising them to accept US initiatives that seemed to point in the same direction (e.g. the Rogers▷ Plan).

At the beginning of the 1970s Soviet policy in the ME appeared to have both negative and positive motivations. Negatively, the USSR aimed to weaken if not totally exclude the Western Powers, particularly the USA, from the ME. Positively, it appeared now realistic to envisage a Soviet pre-eminence in

the region—so close to the Soviet homeland and of so great importance for the USSR's global position. Soviet interest in a sphere of secure political influence, in free naval and air passage and bases, in a firm military alliance with countries of the area (and the prevention of any rival military pact directed against the USSR), in favourable trade terms, and in access to ME oil—would seem to indicate undiminished Soviet involvement in the future.   (A. K.)

S

SAADABAD PACT. Treaty of non-aggression between Turkey, Iran, Iraq and Afghanistan, signed at the S. Palace in Teheran on 8 July 1937. Relations between these countries were not very cordial; occasionally they were disturbed by tension and border disputes. In view of the increasing international tension, however, the insecurity felt by small countries after Italy's attack on Ethiopia in 1935 and the West's inaction, the four were anxious to improve their relations and strengthen their mutual security. They were encouraged in their endeavour by the West. The SP did not play an important role; its council never even met after the outbreak of World War II. Signed for five years, to be automatically renewed every five years unless annulled by one of the parties, it was never rescinded, but is not considered valid.   (Y.S.)

SA'ADEH, ANTON (1912–1949). Lebanese politician. Son of a Greek-Orthodox doctor. In 1921, S. went to Brazil and returned to Lebanon only in 1930, as a teacher of German at the American University of Beirut. S. propagated a "Syrian nationalism" in the framework of a greater Syria and was strongly influenced by Fascism. In 1932, he established a "Syrian Nationalist Party"▷, which expounded his doctrines, demanding independence and the eviction of the French. The party was banned and S. was harassed by the authorities until, in the late 1930s, he returned to South America. In 1947, he returned to Lebanon, now independent, but suspected by the authorities, he was kept under surveillance and arrested on several occasions. After Husni Za'im▷ came to power in Syria, S. hoped for his help, but was disappointed. In June 1949, S. escaped to Syria after a clash between members of his party and the "Phalanges"▷ that was described as an attempted coup. Syria extradited him to Lebanon, where he was sentenced to death by a military court and executed.   (Y. P.)

SA'ADIST PARTY. Egyptian party founded in 1937 by a faction of younger leaders seceding from

SABAEANS, SABIANS

the *Wafd*▷. They were led by Mahmud Fahmi al-Nuqrashi▷ and Dr. Ahmad Maher▷ and presented themselves as the true heirs of the *Wafd* leader, Sa'd Zaghlul▷, from whom they took their party's name. The SP became one of the anti-*Wafd* groups relied upon by the king and his court. They formed coalition governments with the Liberal Constitutional Party. The two parties won the 1938 and 1945 elections. They participated in most of the non-*Wafdist* governments, and their leaders headed the government in 1944–6 and 1946–9. Two of them were assassinated (Maher in Feb. 1945, Nuqrashi in December 1948). See Egypt, Parties▷.   (Y.S.)

SABAEANS, SABIANS—see Mandaeans.

SABAH, AL-. The ruling dynasty in Kuwait▷. Its head uses the title of Sheikh or, recently, Amir. (For the branches of the families and its prominent members, see Kuwait▷.)   (Y.S.)

***SABRI, 'ALI** (b. 1920). Egyptian army officer and politician. Graduated from the military academy in 1939. S. was not among the ten founders of the "Free Officers" Group that staged the *coup d'état* in 1952, but was close to them and their liaison officer with the US Embassy before and during the coup. He commenced his climb to power as Director of the President's Office. In 1960, he was appointed Minister for Presidential Affairs. He was Prime Minister 1962–5, Vice-President 1965–7, and Chairman of the "Arab Socialist Union"▷ from 1965. S. converted the ASU into a base for his climb to power. He is credited with the organization of the demonstrations of 9 and 10 June 1967, which "compelled" Nasser▷ to withdraw his resignation. He was dismissed in 1969 from his position of Chairman of the ASU—obviously because of his ambitions and growing power. In 1970, he was made responsible for the air force and its procurement needs.

In contrast to the close relations with the USA that he fostered in the early days of the revolution, S. in the 1960s supported closer relations with the USSR, and a socialist policy more extreme than that laid down by the regime in the National Charter (1962). During his chairmanship of the ASU, he reorganized it into cadres, with Soviet backing. As he came to be considered "Moscow's man", his position in the national leadership was seen as an index of relations between the regime and the USSR. After Nasser's death, in Sept. 1970, he was considered by many as a Soviet-supported candidate for the succession. Though not elected President, S. was included in the new government as one of the two Vice-Presidents. However, in May 1971 he was accused—

'Ali Sabri

together with a large group of other leaders and administrators—of plotting against President Sadat▷, high treason, and various abuses of power; he was dismissed from all government and party posts, and imprisoned. His trial opened in August.   (S. L.)

SACME—see Middle East Defence Organization▷.

***SADAT, AL-, ANWAR** (b. 1918). Egyptian army officer and politician. President of Egypt since 1970. Graduated from the military academy in 1938. During World War II, in 1941–4, he was active in the pro-German underground and was detained. S. was one of the ten leaders of the "Free Officers" Group formed in 1949 and headed by Gamal 'Abd-ul-Nasser▷, who later carried out the July 1952 coup. S. was liaison officer between the "Free Officers" and the "Muslim Brotherhood"▷ and the right-wing "Young Egypt" party, to both of which he had belonged for a while. At the end of 1954, after Nasser had consolidated his rule, S. was banished from the inner circle for about two years—apparently because of his "Muslim Brotherhood" sympathies. S. returned to the leadership group in 1957, as chairman of the "National Union", then Egypt's single party; but in 1958, with the union of Egypt and Syria (as the UAR▷), he in effect lost all authority in the "National Union". S. was Chairman of the National Assembly, Egypt's quasi-parliamentary body, 1959–69. He alone among the "Free Officers" never held a ministerial post. S. was considered closest to Islam among the "Free Officers", and was sent on several missions to Muslim countries and attended Muslim conferences. He also maintained liaison between Egypt and the Yemen. Though he accepted Nasser's principles of Positive Neutralism and Arab Socialism, he has remained a Right-wing nationalist.

In 1969, S. was appointed Vice-President of Egypt, as Nasser's only deputy. On the death of Nasser, in September 1970, when observers anticipated a struggle for power between the right-wing (Zakaria Mohieddin▷) and the left ('Ali Sabri▷), S. was elected President of Egypt and also President of the "Arab Socialist Union"▷, Egypt's only political party. At first considered a rather colourless heir of Nasser, a weak *primus inter pares*, he soon endeavoured to form his own policies—presented as more liberal internally and moderate externally—and establish a firm personal leadership. In May 1971, he announced the discovery of a plot and gross political malpractices, and dismissed and arrested a large number of his colleagues (and rivals), including both a leftist faction ('Ali Sabri), military leaders (Gen. Muhammad Fawzi) and a group of Nasser's close collaborators (Sha'rawi Gum'a, Sami Sharaf). In summer 1971, S. seemed to be firmly in the saddle.   (S.L.)

Anwar Sadat

SA'ID, AL-, NURI (1888–1958). Iraqi politician. Many times Prime Minister. Born in Baghdad to a Sunni-Muslim family of mixed Arab-Kurdish descent. Graduate of Istanbul Military Academy. During World War I, NS, an officer in the Ottoman Army, joined Sharif Hussein's▷ Arab revolt, in

1916, and became Chief-of-Staff in Amir Feisal's▷ regular army commanded by Ja'far al-'Askari▷, his brother-in-law. He remained attached to Feisal after the war, and became the first Chief-of-Staff of the Iraqi Army in 1921. He was Minister of Defence 1922–4 and 1926–8. In 1930 he became Prime Minister for the first time (founding a party—al-'Ahd, "The Covenant"—to support him in Parliament); he negotiated the treaty with Britain which terminated the Mandate and gave Iraq her independence. In all, NS served 14 times as Prime Minister 1930–2, 1939–40, 1941–4, 1946–7, 1949, 1950–2, 1954–7 and 1958, and often held other or additional ministerial offices, particularly as Foreign or Defence Minister. In Feb. 1958 he became Prime Minister of the short-lived Arab Federation▷ of Iraq and Jordan. After the defeat of the Rashid 'Ali▷ movement in 1941, NS was Iraq's leading statesman, whether in or out of office, and the chief representative of the Hashemite▷ establishment. He was murdered in Baghdad during the coup of July 1958.

NS believed, above all, in the need for a loyal alliance with Britain (though he apparently tried to reinsure with Germany for a brief while in the summer of 1940). He feared and hated communism and the USSR. In Arab affairs he was keenly conscious of the age-old rivalry with Egypt. He favoured a Federation of the Fertile Crescent▷ under Iraqi leadership (with a measure of cultural and administrative autonomy for the Jews of Palestine); late in 1942–3 he submitted this scheme to Britain and the Arabs states—but it met with strong Arab (particularly Egyptian) opposition, and he did not pursue the idea. In domestic affairs NS promoted administrative efficiency and long-term economic planning, he did not believe parliamentary democracy to be a suitable form of government for Iraq. He was an autocrat; in his heyday Iraq was a police state, though his regime seems mild and rational in the light of more recent developments. NS had no real understanding of the social and political forces sweeping the Arab world during his last years.   (U.D.)

*SA'IQA, AL- (Arabic: "Lightning"). A Palestinian-Arab guerilla (*feda'iyin*▷) organization established in 1968 in Syria by the ruling *Ba'th*▷ party and the Syrian Army. It is under the direct command of the Syrian Army and its intelligence service, and guided by the *Ba'th* party. It includes Syrian soldiers and volunteers. See Palestine-Arab Guerilla Organizations.   (Y.S.)

SAKA, HASAN (1885–1960). Turkish statesman, Prime Minister 1947–9. Born in Trabzon, S. graduated from the School of Public Service (Mulkiye)

and studied economics and finance in Paris. He was a deputy in the last Ottoman parliament and was elected in 1920 to the first Grand National Assembly. He served in several ministerial posts and was Foreign Member of an influential Sunni-Muslim▷ family in tarian Recep Peker▷ as Premier and held office until Jan. 1949.   (D.K.)

SALAM, SA'EB (b. 1905). Lebanese politician. Member of an influential Sunni Muslim▷ family in Beirut. Graduate of London University. In 1943 and 1947, S. was elected to Parliament. He was Minister of Interior in 1946, and Prime Minister in 1952 and 1953. S. was active also as a businessman and industrialist serving *i.a.* as chairman of Middle Eastern Airlines. In 1956, he was Minister of State in 'Abdullah al-Yafi's▷ government, but resigned together with Yafi in November in protest against the pro-Western policy of President Camille Chamoun▷. From that date he became one of the leaders of the pro-Nasserist▷ opposition. He was defeated in the 1957 elections by Chamoun's supporters who enjoyed government support. In the 1960 election he defeated in Beirut his former ally 'Abdullah al-Yafi with whom he contended for pre-eminence among Beirut's Muslim leaders, and established the first government after the elections. He repeated this victory in 1964. In 1968, he was again elected to parliament, but this time not at al-Yafi's expense. During the 1960s, he led the Beirut bloc of Muslim representatives which opposed Premier Rashid Karameh▷, leader of the Muslim representatives from Tripoli. In Oct. 1970, when Suleiman Franjiyeh▷, supported by S. and his bloc, became President, S. was appointed Prime Minister.   (Y.P.)

✳**SALLAL, AL-, 'ABDULLAH** (b. 1917). Yemeni soldier and politician, of a Zeidi▷ lower-class family. In the 1930s, when a non-tribal army was first organized, S. was sent to the Baghdad Military Academy from which he graduated in 1938. Upon his return to San'a, he was arrested for advocating a change in the Yemeni regime. He was soon released and served in the army. He took part in the abortive coup of 1948, led by al-Wazir, and was sentenced to seven years' imprisonment, but released after a short time and appointed Governor of Hudeida. S. maintained close relations with Prince al-Badr▷ who in the mid-1950s made him commander of his personal guard. When in 1959 Badr temporarily replaced the Imam Ahmad▷ (absent through illness), he made S. commander of the newly established military academy. In Sept. 1962 al-Badr became Imam and appointed S. Commander-in-Chief of the army. S. was the main leader of the revolution of 26 Sept.

1962 and became President of the Republic, a post which he held until 5 Nov. 1967 (though after 1965 his powers were restricted by the nomination of a Republican, i.e. Presidential, Council). S. also held the offices of Prime Minister, 1962–4 and 1966–7, and Foreign Minister, 1963–4 and 1967. During his presidency, S. followed a strongly pro-Egyptian policy and depended upon Egyptian support. He advocated a Union of Yemen with Egypt and concluded several agreements towards that end. He had little influence on the Republican army officers and even less on the Zeidi tribes. When the Egyptians were forced to adopt a policy of appeasement in Yemen, S. was sent to Cairo, Apr. 1965–Sept. 1966. Following the Egyptian withdrawal from Yemen, after the Six Day War▷, S. was overthrown in a bloodless coup, 5 Nov. 1967, and went into exile in Baghdad.
                                            (H.E.)

SAMARIA. The northern part of central Palestine. Principal town: Nablus▷. See West Bank▷.

SAMARITANS. Descendants of the colonists brought to Samaria▷ by the King of Assyria to replace the Hebrews, who had been exiled after the defeat of the Kingdom of Israel, 722 BC. The colonists eventually intermarried with those Jews who had remained in the country and gradually adopted Jewish religious practices. The Samaritans' Holy Book is a slightly altered version of the Pentateuch. They consider Mt. Gerizim, South of Nablus▷ (Shekhem), and not Jerusalem, as sacred. The Samaritans still celebrate Passover by sacrificing sheep on Mt. Gerizim. There are today only about 400 Samaritans, 250 of whom live in Nablus, on the slopes of Mt. Gerizim. Following the establishment of the State of Israel, the remainder settled in Holon, near Tel Aviv.   (Sh.C.)

Samaritans at prayer

SAMUEL, SIR (later **VISCOUNT) HERBERT** (1870–1963). British Liberal statesman. S. recommended to the British government, in 1914, to work towards the creation of a Jewish Palestine, and thus helped in preparing the ground for the Balfour Declaration▷. As first High Commissioner of Palestine 1920–5, he tried to act impartially towards the Jews and Arabs in Palestine; Zionist leaders often accused him of leaning over backwards, as a Jew, to favour the Arabs. The White Paper▷ of 1922 was based on his draft. When his term of office ended, S. wanted to remain in Palestine as a private citizen, but this idea was viewed unfavourably in London. In 1936–8 S. advocated a plan which would have allowed the Jews to reach 40% of the Palestine population within ten years. After the end of World War II he opposed both the division of Palestine into cantons and its partition into two separate states.
(Sh. H.)

SAN REMO CONFERENCE. Convened after World War I, in Apr. 1920, by the principal Allied Powers (Great Britain, France, Italy, Japan, Greece and Belgium) to decide on the Turkish peace treaty and other matters. According to article 22 of the Covenant of the League of Nations▷, founded earlier the same year, the former colonial possessions of Germany and Turkey were to be administered under mandates▷ on behalf of the League. The SRC assigned to France the Mandate for Syria and Lebanon, and to Britain those for Mesopotamia (Iraq) and Palestine, the latter to be administered in accordance with the Balfour Declaration. These mandates were formally confirmed by the League of Nations in 1922. The decision of the SRC was hailed by the Zionists as a further recognition of their claims, while the Arabs denounced it as contrary to the independence promised to them by the Allies. In SR an Anglo-French accord was reached, incidental to the conference, concerning the participation of French interests in the future exploitation of oil in Iraq.
(Sh.H.)

SAN'A. Capital of Yemen. Pop.: *c.* 100,000 mostly Zeidis▷. Situated on the al-Jahal plateau, 7,872 ft. high and surrounded by mountains, which is populated by Zeidi tribesmen. Before the Revolution of 1962 S. was a small walled city serving as market place for the neighbouring tribes, with no paved roads or running water. Since then the city has undergone partial modernization and been connected with the port of Hudeida▷ and the cities of Ta'izz▷ (in the south) and Sa'da (in the north) by modern roads built with Chinese, American and Soviet aid respectively. Following the Egyptian evacuation late in

1967, S. came under Royalist siege but was saved in Feb. 1968 mainly as a result of the renewal of Zeidi tribal support for the Republican regime after the fall of Sallal▷.
(H.E.)

SANUSSI ORDER, SANUSSIS, SANUS-SIYYA. Islamic religious order founded in Mecca in 1837 by Muhammed b. 'Ali al-S., of Algerian origin. A Sunni order (of the Maliki school dominant throughout North Africa), it aims at purging Islam of unorthodox accretions, and returning to the original teachings of the Prophet and the Qur'an. Though orthodox-fundamentalist in their doctrine, the founder and the O. were influenced by various Islamic orders of mysticism—as were the *Mahdiyya*▷ and the *Idrissiyya*▷—(see also Dervish Orders▷). In 1841 al-S. went to Egypt and from there to Tripoli and Benghazi, teaching the new faith and gathering adepts among tribesmen and oasis dwellers. In 1843 he founded the Mother Lodge of the O., *al-Zawiya al-Baida*, on the central Cyrenaican plateau. In 1856 he settled in the oasis of Jaghbub▷, which was to become the centre of the O.

The SO spread its faith through a network of *zawiyas* (monasteries or lodges) set up along caravan highways. It was more successful with the Bedouin, especially those of Cyrenaica▷, than in urban areas and among peasants. Beside rituals and prayers known only to the Learned Brothers, the *Ikhwan*, who live in the *zawiyas*, the SO lays down rules of behaviour in daily life which are austere without being ascetic. S. rituals are simple and discourage religious ecstasy as practised by mystic brotherhoods. They ban the use of musical instruments during religious ceremonies, as well as dancing and singing. The organization of the O. is based on the *zawiyas*, which derive their livelihood from taxation, gifts, endowments, and also agricultural work, and transmit surpluses to Jaghbub and Kufra, for the maintenance of the S. family and the centre of the O.

The founder died in 1859 and was succeeded by his son, al-Sayyid al-Mahdi al-S. Under his leadership the O. spread in the Sahara and Sudan. Its centre was transferred in 1895 from Jaghbub to Kufra▷, then the crossroads of important desert routes. After the death of al-Mahdi, in 1902, leadership of the O. passed to Sayyid Ahmad al-Sharif al-S.▷, the nephew of the founder. During his time, the SO developed into a political force, which mounted relentless resistance against the Italian invaders from 1911 onwards.

As this resistance, aided by the Turks, merged into World War I▷, a rival S. leader, al-Sayyid Muhammad Idris al-S.▷ (the founder's grandson and the second leader's son), decided to support Great Britain

SANUSSI, AL-, AL-SAYYID AHMAD

and the Allies. In 1916, in Egypt, he was recognized by Britain as the "Grand S.", the leader of the SO. When he overcame the rival faction with Allied help, al-Sharif escaped to Turkey, never to return. The O., now under Idris, endeavoured to reach a *modus vivendi* with Italy—S. autonomy in the interior of Cyrenaica, under the overall Italian rule of Libya. But by 1922 these efforts had failed, Idris again became an exile in Egypt and the SO rebelled. This rebellion was crushed by the Italians, gradually and painfully—Jaghbub fell in 1926, most of the other cases in 1928 and Kufra in 1931; the main leader of S. resistance, Idris's brother al-Sayyid Rida, surrendered in 1928; the O. was outlawed and declared dissolved in 1930 (see Libya▷, History).

Resistance, never completely stamped out, was resumed during World War II, with British aid, and the SO as its backbone. The SO was also the main force behind its leader, Idris, in the latter's successful efforts to gain control of Cyrenaica and later, 1951, of the whole of Libya. With Idris as King of Libya, the SO was the mainstay of the regime—though its real strength and influence appeared to decline, inevitably, with the increasing modernization and industrialization of Libya. This decline seems to have been accelerated and intensified under the revolutionary officers' regime after the coup of 1969.

(B.G.-Y.S.)

SANUSSI, AL-, AL-SAYYID AHMAD AL-SHARIF (1873–1933). Grandson of the founder of the S. Order▷. Succeeded Sayyid al-Mahdi al-S. as Head of the Order in 1902. From 1911–12 onwards he was the leader of S. resistance in Cyrenaica▷ against the Italian conquerors. He left Cyrenaica in 1916, after a S. force, under Turkish command, was defeated by the British at Sollum (and after internal disputes over the leadership of the Order). He was taken to Turkey in a German submarine and never returned to Libya. His name was sometimes mentioned as a possible King of Iraq or Syria, but these ideas were abortive. He died in Medina. (B.G.)

SANUSSI, AL-, AL-SAYYID MUHAMMAD IDRIS (b. 1890). Libyan-Sanussi leader, King of Libya 1951–69. Born at Jaghbub, Cyrenaica, Grandson of Muhammad b. 'Ali al-Sanussi, the founder of the S. Order▷. S. established contacts with the British in Egypt in 1914, and stayed in Egypt during World War I, while the S.s' guerilla war against Italy became part of Ottoman Turkey's war against the Allies. In 1916 Britain recognized him as the "Grand S.", the leader of the Order—in place of his uncle, Sayyid Ahmad Sharif al-S.▷, who fought on the other side. After victory, Italy recognized him,

King Idris (with King Paul of Greece)

in the Rajma Agreement of 1920, as Amir of Cyrenaica▷ heading a self-governing regime in the S. oases of Jaghbub▷, Awjila, Jalu and Kufra▷ in the interior of that region. S. accepted the additional title of Amir of Tripolitania▷ offered to him by the Tripolitanian nationalists in 1922. His agreement with the Italians was half-hearted and short-lived. Unable to come to terms with them, he left in 1922 for exile in Cairo, where he remained for 20 years, rallying around him Libyan emigrés and resistance fighters.

When Italy entered World War II, S. called upon all Libyans to co-operate with the Allied forces in a joint effort to drive out the Italians, and initiated the recruitment of a S. force which took part in the North African campaign. In return, and while the war still proceeded, the British recognized his claim to head an independent or autonomous Cyrenaica. In 1949, with British support and under British provisional military government, he proclaimed himself Amir of Cyrenaica. In 1951 the crown of a united Libya was offered to him, and on 7 Oct. 1951 the National Assembly proclaimed him King of Libya. He ascended his throne on 24 Dec. 1951 when Libya became independent. His rule was ultra-conservative; the regime's stability seemed dependent on his person, since he had no children. King Idris was deposed by a military coup on 1 Sep. 1969, while in Turkey for medical treatment, and did not fight for his throne. Late in 1969 he settled in exile in Cairo. (B.G.)

SARAÇOĞLU, ŞÜKRÜ (SHUKRI) (1887–1953). Turkish politician, Prime Minister 1942–6. Born in Ödemis, S. was trained for the civil service and studied economics and political science in Geneva. A deputy for the Republican People's Party in the National Assembly from 1923, he held several ministerial posts. He was Foreign Minister 1938–42, under Celâl Bayar▷ and Refik Saydam, and upon the latter's death in 1942 he became Premier, remaining in this office until replaced by Recep Peker▷ in 1946.

(D.K.)

SARRAJ, 'ABD-UL-HAMID. Syrian officer and politician. Born in Hama, S. studied at the military academy and had advanced training in France. He served in Qawuqji's▷ "Army of Deliverance" in Palestine in 1948. S. was associated with the Ba'th▷ party but did not officially join it. From 1955, he was head of Army Intelligence and the Military Police and was considered the "strongman" of Syria. He played a major part in the union between Syria and Egypt, and, after the establishment of the UAR▷ (1958), he was appointed Minister of the Interior in the "Syrian Region" of the UAR. He enjoyed ever-increasing powers and became, for all practical purposes, the deputy of the UAR President in Syria. Between Sept. 1960 and Aug. 1961, S. headed the Syrian Region's "Executive Council" (*i.e.* Government) and was Minister of the Interior and also Secreatury of the "National Union" (the only political organization) and in charge of the security services. In Aug. 1961, when the separate governments of the "regions" were abolished, he was appointed Vice-President of the UAR, in charge of internal affairs, but, following differences with President Nasser▷, he resigned a month later and returned to Syria. At the time of the officers' coup that resulted in Syria's withdrawal from the UAR, in Sept. 1961, he was arrested. He escaped to Egypt in 1962 and directed attempts from there to bring Syria back to the orbit of Egyptian influence. In 1967, he was appointed head of the National Insurance Institute in Egypt.
(A. L.-O. T.)

*SA'UD, HOUSE OF, DYNASTY. Ruling house in the Arabian peninsula, lending its name to the largest country in the Peninsula, Sa'udi Arabia▷. The family, from the 'Anaza tribe, first ruled the Dar'iya area of Najd▷. Muhammad Ibn Sa'ud ruled Dar'iya 1747–65. He adopted the Wahhabi▷ doctrine and gained control over large sections of the peninsula, introducing the new faith everywhere. His son, 'Abd-ul-'Aziz (ruled 1766–1803), and his grandson, Sa'ud (1803–14) extended their power as far as Iraq and Syria and raided Mecca▷ and Medina▷. During the reign of 'Abdullah Ibn Sa'ud (1814–18) the army of the H. of S. was defeated by Muhammad 'Ali of Egypt, and 'Abdullah was executed in Istanbul. During the years 1818–42, Egyptian-Turkish army units intermittently camped in Najd. During the second half of the 19th century, the H. of S. at times had limited control over the Dar'iya-Riyadh▷ area; the Ottomans and the rival House of Rashid▷ of the Shammar tribe usually prevented a further extension of its power.

In the 1880s, the Rashid family gained the upper hand and in 1890–91 defeated 'Abd-ul-Rahman (1888?–91) and conquered the Dar'iya-Riyadh area. Survivors of the S. family fled from Najd and found refuge in Kuwait. Amongst those who escaped was 'Abd-ul-'Aziz b. 'Abd-ul-Rahman Ibn Sa'ud▷ (1880–1953, ruled 1902–53). In 1902, he returned and gained control of Riyadh. He made a pact with Britain in 1915, and beat the Rashids who in 1921 surrendered to him. In the course of his expansion, he clashed with Hussein▷, the Hashemite▷ Sharif of Mecca and king of Hijaz▷. In 1924, he conquered Hijaz and deposed the Hashemites, and henceforth the H. of S. ruled most of the Arabian peninsula.

From 1922 onward, Ibn Sa'ud was titled Sultan of Najd and her dependencies; in 1926, he proclaimed himself King of Hijaz and Najd, and in 1932 he renamed the area under his control the Sa'udi Arabian Kingdom. He was succeeded at his death in 1953 by his eldest son, Sa'ud b. 'Abd ul 'Aziz▷ (1953 64). Sa'ud tried to appoint his son, Fahad, heir to the throne, but the pressure of his brothers, the remaining sons of 'Abd-ul-'Aziz Ibn Sa'ud, forced him to appoint his brother Feisal▷ instead. Sa'ud's reign was unsuccessful, and, in 1958, he was forced to transfer wide authority to Feisal. In 1964, he was deposed (he died in 1969) and Feisal b. 'Abd-ul-'Aziz ascended the throne. The Crown Prince is, since 1964, their brother, Khaled b. 'Abd-ul-'Aziz.   (Y. A. O.)

*SA'UD b. 'ABD-UL-'AZIZ (1902–69). King of Sa'udi Arabia▷ 1953–64. Eldest son of 'Abd-ul-'Aziz b. 'Abd-ul-Rahman "Ibn Sa'ud"▷. With the con-

King Sa'ud

solidation of the Sa'udi Kingdom, S. became crown prince. He had suffered since childhood from an eye disease and therefore read little and occupied himself mainly with executive affairs and liaison with the tribes. After the death of Ibn Sa'ud in 1953, there were reports of rivalry between S. and his brother Feisal▷, but matters did not come to a head, and S. mounted the throne. During his reign the country underwent, despite its enormous oil revenues, a severe financial crisis, as a result of extravagance and unbridled spending. At the same time, relations with Egypt became strained, and in Mar. 1958 Nasser publicly accused S. of an attempt to organize his assassination. S. was publicly asked to resign in favour of his brother Feisal, and he had to give Feisal extensive authority in internal, foreign and economic affairs. S. was now ruling in name only, Feisal actually holding the reins. S.'s poor health also compelled him to make numerous trips abroad. But he continued struggling. In March 1964, S. demanded that Feisal give up his powers, and a fresh crisis ensued, which left S. his crown but no authority. Soon he was deprived also of his crown. On 2 Nov. 1964, the Council of 'Ulama' deposed S. and appointed Feisal in his place. S. went into exile, living in a number of European countries. In Dec. 1966, he settled in Egypt and became an instrument in Nasser's conflict with Feisal. After the Six Day War, when Nasser was in need of Sa'udi aid that only Feisal could provide, S., no longer of use, was pushed into the background. He died in exile in 1969.

(Y.A.O.)

*SA'UDI ARABIA (also SA'UDIA) (al-Mamlaka al-'Arabiyya al-Sa'udiyya). Kingdom in the Arabian peninsula. Area: 2,100,000 sq. km. (810,600 sq. mi.). Capital: Riyadh▷. The religious capital is Mecca▷. SA borders on Jordan, Iraq, Kuwait, the Persian Gulf principalities, Yemen and South Yemen. On the border with Iraq and with Kuwait there are two "Neutral Zones"▷ in places where no agreement could be reached on boundaries. The country has two coasts: in the east the Persian Gulf, in the west the Gulf of 'Aqaba and the Red Sea. The northern land borders, with Iraq and Jordan, were determined in 1925 in the Hadda and Bahra agreements. Britain played an important role in these agreements and a number of provisional accords. The border with Yemen was finally settled in 1934, after a war. The borders with the Persian Gulf principalities and the Neutral Zone on the Kuwait border are still in dispute. The maritime border with Bahrain was determined in a treaty in 1958. S. is divided into the provinces of Najd▷, Hijaz▷, al-Hasa▷, the northern border, and 'Asir▷.

The population is estimated at 6m., all Arabic speaking. The overwhelming majority are Sunni▷ Muslims belonging to the Wahhabi▷ trend of the Hanbali school. A small Shi'ite▷ community is found in the al-Hasa region and a Yemenite Zeidi▷ minority in the 'Asir region. The majority of the population is tribal, nomadic or semi-nomadic. Population of the major cities (1964 census): Riyadh: 300,000; Mecca: 200,000; Jidda▷: 150,000; Medina▷: 40,000.

The economy was one of desert nomads engaged in camel raising (and raiding), with a few agricultural settlements in oases, and a few towns with some commerce on the coasts and in the nearby hinterland; fishing and shipping developed more on the Persian Gulf than on the Red Sea shore. For many years, a major source of income was the annual Muslim pilgrimage (Hajj) to the holy cities of Mecca and Medina (estimates as to the number of pilgrims from abroad in the 1920s and '30s varied from 50,000 to over 200,000; in the 1960s from 200,000 to 375,000). Beginning with the 1940s, oil production has become the major source of national and individual income and of development resources (see Oil in the ME▷ and below).

POLITICAL HISTORY. SA, in its present form, came into being in 1925–6 and 1932 out of the fusion of various parts of Arabia conquered by 'Abd-ul-'Aziz b. 'Abd-ul-Rahman Ibn Sa'ud▷. On 1 Aug. 1926, Ibn Sa'ud declared himself king of Hijaz after having conquered it in 1924–5 from the Hashemite▷ Sharif Hussein▷ b. 'Ali. This title was added to that of Sultan of Najd and her Dependencies which he had taken in 1922. He appointed his son Sa'ud▷ (the Crown Prince) Governor of Najd and his son Feisal▷ Governor of Hijaz.

Between 1926 and 1932, Ibn Sa'ud introduced a certain stability, both internal and external, throughout most of the Arabian peninsula and integrated Hijaz, which was more developed than Najd and did not willingly accept Wahhabi customs, in his realm. He set up a consultative council (Majlis al-Shura) of sheikhs and notables in Hijaz. Britain recognized his independence in the Treaty of Jidda▷ of 1927. In 1929–30, he put down a rebellion of tribal chieftains and the Ikhwan ("Brethren"—the semi-settled military nuclei of the Wahhabis), who demanded the continuation of conquests beyond the northern borders.

Once stability had been achieved, Ibn Sa'ud decreed the union of the two parts of his kingdom, on 18 Sep. 1932, as the "Kingdom of SA". In his continuing efforts to stabilize the country, Ibn Sa'ud endeavoured to settle the tribes, mainly around the oases, though the setting up of Ikhwan settlements

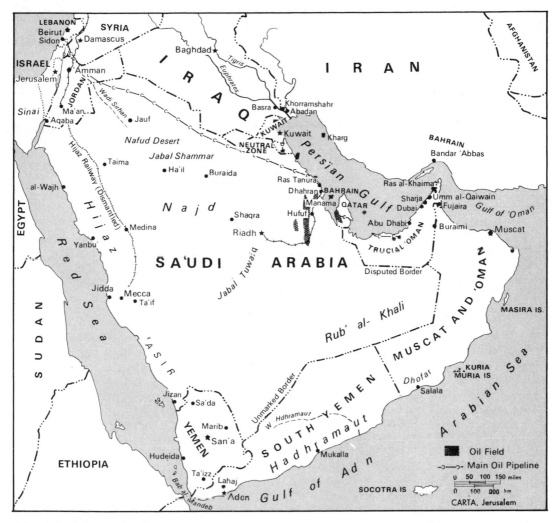

Map of the Arabian peninsula

ceased after the suppression of their revolt. He allotted lands to sheikhs and wealthy merchants to encourage settlement, and in 1947 exempted them from paying rent on these lands. His attitude to the tribes was alternately soft and hard. He granted the sheikhs large sums of money, took their women for his and his sons' wives; on the other hand, he would heavily punish tribes which did not keep order or carried out traditional raids for plunder *(ghazzu)*.

The conquest of Hijaz and the holy cities made SA a focus for all Islam. In 1926, Ibn Sa'ud convened an all-Islamic congress in Mecca. He rejected a proposal by Indian Muslims to turn Hijaz into an all-Islamic protectorate and made for strained relations with Egypt by barring the traditional Egyptian army escort for the Egyptian *Hajj* caravan, as there was no longer any need for such protection. Ibn Sa'ud signed

a series of friendship and non-aggression treaties with Arab countries: Transjordan 1933, Bahrain 1936, Iraq 1936, Egypt 1936 (the last one settled the 1926 dispute over the *Hajj* caravans). On the other hand, there was increasing tension between SA and Yemen. In the 1920s, SA extended her protection over the 'Asir region, taking advantage of internal disputes in the ruling Idrissi⊳ dynasty. In 1933, a revolt of Hassan al-Idrissi was put down and Ibn Sa'ud formally annexed 'Asir to his kingdom. Idrissi fled to Yemen where he received asylum as well as aid in organizing raids across the border. In Mar. 1934, Ibn Sa'ud declared war on Yemen and within a few weeks conquered large portions of the country, including the principal port of Hudeida⊳. On 23 June 1934, he signed a peace treaty agreeing to give up the occupied areas, evacuate Yemen and revert to the *status quo*.

In 1937 he signed a friendship and non-aggression pact with Yemen.

In 1933, Ibn Sa'ud granted the first oil exploration rights to the Standard Oil Company of California, which was joined by the Texas Oil Company in 1934. The two companies jointly formed the "Arabian American Oil Company" (Aramco). Oil was found in the Dhahran, Dammam, and Abqaia areas. Commercial production began in 1937. Production increased after World War II, and became the mainstay of the economy. Production reached 175m. ton in 1970, and royalties—$1,100m.

In World War II Ibn Sa'ud was neutral, though leaning towards the Allies. Even when the Axis powers appeared victorious, he refused to support the anti-British revolt of Rashid 'Ali al-Kilani▷ in Iraq; he pointedly sent his son Mansour to Cairo on the eve of the battle of al-'Alamein▷, and rejected German and Japanese requests for oil concessions. On account of the sharp decline in the number of pilgrims since the late 1930s, he requested—and received—financial aid from the Allies, mostly the USA (by Sept. 1946—$17.5m. in grants and loans). On 1 Mar. 1945, SA "joined" the Allies, without declaring war formally on Germany and while maintaining the neutrality of the holy places; this enabled her to join the UN as a charter member.

During this period, relations between SA and the USA grew increasingly intimate. A US diplomatic representation in SA was established in 1940. Under a 1943 agreement the Americans in 1944–6 built a large air base in Dhahran (with rights to use it for three years); at the same time, a US military mission began training the Sa'udi Army. The US government also decided to lay an oil pipeline from Dhahran to the Mediterranean (the "Tapline"—in fact later built by the oil company). In Feb. 1945, Ibn Sa'ud met President Roosevelt▷ on board an American warship. At the meeting, he stressed his anti-Zionist stand and this appeared to be the only matter at issue between SA and the USA. Ibn Sa'ud remained firm: he opposed President Truman's▷ proposal to permit the immigration to Palestine of 100,000 Jewish survivors of the Holocaust (1946) and resented US support for the partition of Palestine (1947), and US aid to Israel. Yet, in spite of threats of retaliation against American interests, such as stopping the flow of oil, the dispute never really hurt Sa'udi-American relations. In 1949, the US representation in Jidda was raised to ambassadorial level. Under a defence treaty of 1951, US rights at the Dhahran base were extended for five more years; the supply of American arms, and training and military aid continued.

Ibn Sa'ud was absolute ruler of SA, restricted only by Islamic law and custom. Muslim law (Shari'a)▷

was state law, administered by religious courts. The Consultative Council of Hijaz became progressively weaker and eventually was replaced by the king's council, which had no real powers. There was no distinction between the national treasury and the private coffers of the king. This was changed only towards the end of Ibn Sa'ud's life; in 1951–2 the first national budget was published, and the first bank in SA opened shortly after. In Oct. 1953, Ibn Sa'ud set up a modern-style council of ministers, though he kept his right of veto. Despite opposition of the clergy to westernizing innovations, Ibn Sa'ud began a series of development programmes. A railroad was laid between Dammam on the Persian Gulf and Riyadh (completed 1951); a network of roads and internal air communications was developed, the numbers of cars increased, and radio stations were established, first by Aramco and then by the state. Ibn Sa'ud also curbed somewhat Wahhabi fanaticism. The ban on smoking, for example, was never put into effect in Hijaz and was soon abolished throughout the country, and that on music ended with the introduction of radio broadcasts.

'Abd-ul-'Aziz b. 'Abd-ul-Rahman Ibn Sa'ud died on 11 Nov. 1953. Though many expected an immediate struggle among his sons for the succession, his son Sa'ud▷ b. 'Abd-ul-'Aziz had a smooth succession to the throne. Sa'ud attempted to make his eldest son Fahad crown prince, but, in the face of his brothers' opposition, he had to appoint his brother Feisal▷ instead. Under Sa'ud's rule the tempo of change increased. Income from oil passed the $300m.-mark in the mid-1950s. New social strata—workers, clerks, college graduates, army officers—demanded their share of the socio-political cake. Technicians and experts began migrating to S.A. The introduction of modern teachers, mostly foreigners—Palestinians, Egyptians, Lebanese and Syrians—caused much ferment, and in 1955, Sa'ud expelled many of them. The royal family itself was the source of much waste and corruption. Sa'ud built for himself a marble palace in Riyadh which cost $4m. merely to plan, and $140m. to complete. A special plane brought flowers every day to the palace from Asmara in Eritrea. About 350 princes and their relatives lived at royal expense, and they, too, built themselves magnificent palaces and lived a life of extravagance. The royal household alone swallowed 17% of the state revenues. In spite of the large oil earnings, the national deficit in 1957 was $500m., state debts—$400m. and the value of the rial plummeted. The power of Wahhabism declined and a way of life diametrically opposed to its doctrine spread widely.

Sa'ud was also experiencing difficulties in foreign affairs. Immediately after his ascent to the throne, a serious dispute developed with Britain (as the power protecting 'Oman▷) over Buraimi▷. Anglo-Sa'udi relations deteriorated until they were cut off completely in 1956 because of Britain's Suez War▷. SA's rulers had always taken an anti-Hashemite▷ stand in the Arab League▷ and opposed, together with Egypt and Syria, all plans to extend the influence of the rulers of Iraq and Jordan. SA was one of the principal opponents of the Baghdad Pact▷, worked against Iraqi influence in Syria and, together with Egypt, attempted to alienate Jordan from the West. An alliance with a radical-revolutionary Nasserist▷ Egypt, however, with her aspirations to hegemony in the Arab world, could not last long. In 1957–8, relations worsened to an extent that Nasser accused Sa'ud, in Mar. 1958, of organizing an attempt on his life.

This charge added to the unrest in SA resulting from internal crises and the quarrel between Sa'ud and his brother Feisal. On 3 Mar. 1958, Sa'ud was forced to transfer all authority in external and internal matters to Feisal, hitherto Crown Prince and Deputy Prime Minister. Feisal placated Nasser and introduced a number of reforms. He changed the composition of the government and brought four ministries, including the Treasury, under his direct supervision. Royal household expenses were reduced from 17% to 5% of the state budget, the financial situation recovered, and in 1960 there was a surplus balance of $185m. The reforms aroused opposition, mainly among the princes, some of whom objected to the curtailment of their purses, while others, led by Prince Talal, turned radical and demanded more drastic reforms and savings. Aided by these princes, Sa'ud succeeded in bringing about Feisal's resignation in Dec. 1960, and regaining full authority. He promised Talal's group reforms and changes and even appointed him Minister of Finance; but he did not keep his promises and in 1961 dismissed Talal who later fled to Beirut. Because of failing health, however, Sa'ud had to go for medical treatment to America in Nov. 1961, and authority was in effect once more in the hands of Feisal. In Mar. 1962, Sa'ud gained the upper hand again, but in the summer he was compelled to go abroad again for medical treatment. The struggle between the two brothers continued until 1964. In the meantime, Feisal succeeded in removing Sa'ud's supporters from key positions, and in Mar. 1964 Feisal refused to hand over his power to Sa'ud. With the approval of the Council of 'Ulama', all authority was finally taken from Sa'ud and invested in Feisal. On 2 Nov. 1964, Sa'ud was deposed and Feisal was crowned King of SA. His brother, Amir Khaled, was made Crown Prince.

Feisal made use of the machinery of absolute power to weaken power foci that had raised their head under Sa'ud—princes, the clergy, foreigners. He encouraged energetic though gradual development and progress. The network of roads was widened, ports were built and deepened and airports established. Feisal attempted to reduce SA's dependence on Aramco and the oil industry in general. In 1963, Aramco gave up 75% of its concession area, and a national SA oil company, "Petromin", was set up. Other branches of the economy not directly linked to oil were also developed—agriculture, the construction of dams, and mining (e.g. gold mines in Hijaz). The school network was expanded and the education budget grew from $7m. in 1957 to $40m. in 1967. A second university, named after 'Abd-ul-'Aziz Ibn Sa'ud, was opened in Riyadh in 1964 (the first had been inaugurated in 1957 and built in the following years). Feisal also continued efforts to settle the Bedouin. Telecommunications were developed and a third radio station was inaugurated in 1968 in Dammam. The army was also strengthened, mainly the "White Guard"—tribal units, mostly of Najdi tribes, particularly loyal to the king, in charge primarily of internal security. Though this progress is almost wholly opposed to the inclinations of the religious establishment, Feisal took care not to affect their status more than necessary. The *Shari'a* remained the law of the land. Hands of thieves are still cut off, and public executions take place in town centres. A special "Religious Police" enforces the performance of the obligatory prayer and other religious duties.

In his inter-Arab policies, Feisal has attempted to thwart Egyptian attempts to penetrate the Arabian peninsula. When civil war broke out in Yemen in Sept. 1962 and Egypt sent an expeditionary force to help the Republicans, Feisal gave moral and propaganda support and military, financial and political assistance to the Royalists, headed by the Imam al-Badr▷. This support continued until the Egyptians evacuated their troops from Yemen at the end of 1967. In Aden▷ and South Arabia▷, S. supported the underground "South Arabian League" (SAL) which opposed the main-line pro-Nasserist nationalist movement and Egyptian attempts to penetrate and control Aden. As opposed to Nasser's idea of an Arab Union (dominated by Egypt), Feisal advocated an Islamic union embracing more than the Arab world. Thus, SA drew closer to the conservative monarchies of Jordan and Iran, while her relations with Egypt deteriorated in 1966–7. When a number of sabotage attacks occurred in Sa'udi cities and along the pipeline, Egypt was even accused of activating a subversive underground, the "Arabian Peninsula People's Union", APPU (*Ittihad al-Sha'b fi'l-Jazira* al-'*Arabiyya*). Several of the underground activists were executed in early 1967, most of them from the Yemenite minority in 'Asir. The accused confessed, and said they were trained and sent by the Egyptian army in Yemen. On the eve of the Six Day War, SA's declarations against Israel were very extremist, but her participation in the war was minimal. SA sent a brigade to Jordan, but it did not arrive in time and took up positions in southern Jordan when the war was over; it has remained there since. At the Khartoum▷ Conference, following the defeat, SA consented to grant an annual assistance of £50m. to Egypt and Jordan. Open enmity between S. and Egypt ceased after the war. Underground groups ceased their activities (which were anyway very limited in scope) and the war of broadcasts against SA emanating from Radio Cairo died down.

At the Arab summit conference in Rabat, at the end of 1969, Egypt asked S. to double her aid, but S. refused. Since 1969–70 SA actively supports efforts to establish permanent institutions of Pan-Islamic political co-operation, but as these efforts are limited in scope and have lost the anti-Egyptian implications they had in 1965–6, they have not disturbed the Sa'udi-Egyptian *rapprochement*.   (Y.A.O.)

SECURITY COUNCIL—see United Nations▷.

SÈVRES, TREATY OF. Peace T. signed on 10 Aug. 1920 between the Ottoman Empire and her World War I enemies. It obliged the Ottoman government to surrender all non-Turkish provinces in Asia and Africa, renounce all claims to them and to recognize the Allied arrangements for their disposal. The Ottoman government retained Istanbul and most of Anatolia (although parts of Anatolia were divided by the Allies into spheres of influence, in a separate secret agreement at S.); but some of Eastern Anatolia's provinces were to be ceded to an independent Armenia▷. Moreover, the Kurdish areas of south-eastern Anatolia were to be granted autonomy, and later (if recommended by the League of Nations), full independence. Izmir▷ and its surroundings remained under Ottoman sovereignty but they were to be administered by Greece for five years, after which a local parliament or a plebiscite would be entitled to request their incorporation in Greece. The Islands of the Dodecanese were left in Italy's possession, while Imbros and Tenedos were given to Greece.

Under the terms of the T. commercial vessels and warships were to be given complete freedom of navigation in the Straits of the Bosphorus▷ and the Dardanelles▷ in times of peace and war, and an international Straits Commission was to control them. Representatives of Britain, France and Italy would supervise the financial, economic and administrative policy of Turkey. The T., which dismembered not only the Ottoman Empire but also Anatolia, the centre of Turkey proper, and considerably restricted her sovereignty, was never ratified. The nationalist leaders in Anatolia, who replaced the Sultan and his regime, totally rejected the T. Following Turkey's victory in her War of Independence it was superseded by the T. of Lausanne▷, 1923.   (D.K.)

SHABAK. A small minority group in northern Iraq, north of Mosul. They number *c.* 10–15,000. The Sh. are thought to be of Kurdish▷origin, and are close to the Yazidis▷. Their religion is based on Shi'ite Islamic and Yazidi elements.   (Y.S.)

*SHA'BI, AL-, QAHTAN MUHAMMAD (b. 1920). South Yemeni politician. Born in Lahej Sultanate to a lower middle class family, Sh. worked for several years in the Lahej Land Department and became its director in 1955. He left his job in 1958 to work for the nationalist insurgents. He joined the "South Arabian League" (SAL), but left it in 1960 and fled to Yemen. In June 1963 he founded the "National Liberation Front for Occupied South Yemen" (NLF▷), became its leader and in Oct. 1963 proclaimed an armed rebellion. Until Nov. 1967 he fought a guerilla war against the British and the federal authorities, as well as against rival nationalist groups, e.g. FLOSY▷. In 1967 he succeeded in establishing the NLF as the only organization with which the transfer of power was to be negotiated. In Nov. 1967, Sh. headed the NLF delegation to the Geneva independence talks; after independence (granted that same month), he became South Yemen's first President, Prime Minister and Commander-in-Chief of the Armed Forces. As a result of the factional struggles within the government and the NLF, Sh. was deposed in June 1969 and succeeded by more extreme leftists led by Muhammad 'Ali Haitham. He was later expelled from the party, placed under house arrest and finally, in Apr. 1970, imprisoned.   (Y.A.O.)

SHAFE'I, AL-, HUSSEIN (b. 1919). Egyptian officer and politician. Sh. belonged to the "Free Officers" who planned the 1952 coup, and was one of the twelve member of its "Council of the Revolution". For a few months in 1954, he served as Minister of War; from the end of 1954 he was Minister of Social Affairs. After the union with Syria, 1958, he held the same portfolio, together with that of Planning, in the government of the "Egyptian Region" of the United Arab Republic▷. When the separate governments of the two "regions" were abolished in Aug. 1961, he was appointed Vice-President of the UAR. After the dissolution of the union, in 1961, Sh. served as Deputy Prime Minister and Minister of *Waqf*▷ (Endowments) and Social Affairs. In the years 1962–7 he was one of the vice-presidents of Egypt. In 1967, he was Deputy Prime Minister and Minister of Social Affairs and *Waqf*. In 1967–8, he was president of the revolutionary court which tried 55 officers accused of plotting against the President and the State. In 1968–70, Sh. was again Deputy Prime Minister. In Oct. 1970, after the death of President Nasser▷, the new President, Anwar Sadat▷, appointed Sh. one of the two vice-presidents. With the ouster of 'Ali Sabri▷, May 1971, he remained the only Vice-President. Sh. is regarded as a loyal follower of Nasser (now—of Sadat) and conforms to the political and ideological line—pro-Soviet since the late 1950s. He is regarded as colourless and lacking independent political or ideological views.   (Y. S.)

*SHAFE'IS. One of the four main schools of orthodox Sunni▷ Islam▷. Of particular significance in Yemen, because of the confrontation there between the Sunni Sh. and Shi'i Zeidis▷. The Sh. make up about 45% of the population of Yemen (though estimates vary). They live mainly in the coastal strip (the Tihama) and in the southern regions, mostly in towns and villages; very few Sh. belong to the belligerent tribes of Yemen, like the al-Zaranig (near Hudeida) whose power was destroyed in the 1930s by the then Crown Prince (later Imam) Ahmad▷. Throughout history Yemen's Sh. had no military power and were subjected to Zeidi hegemony. They therefore co-operated with the Turkish authorities during the period of Ottoman rule. Some of their intelligentsia played leading roles in the 1962 revolution—e.g. Ahmad Muhammad Nu'man▷ and 'Abd-ul-Rahman al-Beidani. At first, the Republic of 1962 seemed to fulfil Sh. expectations. Legally the *Shafe'iyya* and the *Zeidiyya* were "abolished" and the Egyptian expeditionary force (mostly Sh.) helped to foster and promote young Sh. Gradually, however, the Zeidi element became dominant in the Republic—a process which culminated after the Egyptian withdrawal, late in 1967. Many Sh. army officers, who were extremely dissatisfied if not in open rebellion, were forced to leave Yemen. The establishment of the Republic of South Yemen▷, which is populated largely by Sh. gave great hope to Yemen's Sh., but plans for a union of the two countries have so far failed to materialize; Yemen appears opposed to such a union, and relations between the two countries are tense.   (H.E.)

SHAHBANDAR, Dr. 'ABDUL-RAHMAN.
Syrian politician. Sh. was active in the Arab national-

ist movement from Ottoman times. He was sentenced to death, but escaped. He was one of the founders of the "Syrian Unity Party" in Cairo, 1918, which sought British support for a united Arab kingdom. Sh. was Foreign Minister in the government of Amir Feisal▷ in Damascus, 1920. He played a prominent part in the Druze–Syrian rebellion in 1925–7. When the rebellion was suppressed, he escaped to Egypt, where he remained until granted an amnesty in 1937. He was a staunch opponent of the "National Bloc" and markedly pro-Hashemite▷ and pro-British. During the 1930s, he headed the opposition to the "National Bloc" government. He was murdered in July 1940. Some of the leaders of the "National Bloc" suspected of having organized the murder were charged, and escaped to Iraq; but they were later exonerated and acquitted.   (A.L.-O.T.)

SHARETT (formerly SHERTOK), MOSHE
(1894–1965). Zionist Labour leader, Israeli statesman and writer. Born in Russia, S. immigrated to Palestine with his parents in 1906. He was an officer in the Turkish Army during World War I. He was active in the Labour parties *Ahduth Ha'avodah*▷ and, after 1930, *Mapai*▷. Member of the editorial board of *Davar*, the daily newspaper of the *Histadrut*▷ (Federation of Labour). After the assassination of Dr. Chaim Arlosoroff▷ in 1933, S. was appointed head of the Political Department of the Jewish Agency, becoming chief Zionist spokesman to the British and the Arabs, with whom he frequently met in an attempt to find an agreed solution to the Palestine problem. His stubborn struggle with the British led to the formation of the Jewish Brigade Group▷ in 1944, which participated under his guidance in saving the survivors of the Holocaust and bringing them to Palestine. His arrest, in 1946, by the British (with other members of the Jewish Agency▷ Executive) marked the increasingly violent nature of the Jewish resistance. S. was Foreign Minister from the establishment of the State of Israel, 1948, until 1956 and also Prime Minister 1954–5. His resignation in 1956 was connected with the incompatibility of his moderate policies and the activism of Prime Minister Ben-Gurion▷ (e.g. concerning the events leading to the Sinai War▷, 1956) and presumably the Lavon Affair▷. From 1960 until his death he was Chairman of the Zionist and Jewish Agency Executive, and Chairman of the *Histadrut* publishing house, Israel's largest publisher.   (Sh.H.-E.L.)

SHARI'A (Islamic Law).
Ideally Islamic law is intended to regulate all spheres of life and society without differentiating between personal, civil, criminal law, etc., and theoretically it is eternal and cannot

be changed. In practice, the areas covered by the Sh. have been shrinking at an ever increasing rate in the past 100 years; Islamic law is being superseded by secular legislation.

From the mid-19th century onwards secular laws were enacted in various fields (commercial, criminal, etc.), but not in matters of personal status. In those fields, complete Western codes were adopted, new Western-inspired laws were enacted, or Islamic laws were codified by Western methods (e.g. the Ottoman Civil Code *(Mejelle)*, and the family and succession laws of Qadri Pasha in Egypt). Secular legislation, intended for the civil courts, was ostensibly designed to supplement, not abrogate, the Sh.; from a Muslim point of view this method was less dangerous than reform of the Sh. itself. In the long run, however, secular legislation paved the way for the displacement and restriction of the Sh.

From the second decade of the 20th century the secular legislator began interfering also with the laws of personal status, the core of the Sh. Far-reaching reforms were made, such as compensation for the divorced woman, and the prohibition of polygamy except with the permission of the *qadi* (e.g. by the Syrian Law of Personal Status of 1953). Such reforms were effected, formally, in three principal ways. 1. The adoption of suitable elements from the teachings of Sh. jurists of various schools, lately even from the *Shi'a*, instead of such precepts of the dominant school as did not suit the purposes of the reformers (e.g. the Iraqi Law of Succession of 1963, is based on the Shi'ite system). This method, known as *talfiq* or *takhayyur*, was also used in modern codifications of Islamic law, for the convenience of lawyers who had received a modern secular education. 2. Procedural devices designed to deny legal recognition, and hence legal relief, to certain acts, though they are valid under the Sh. (e.g. Egyptian legislation prohibits the registration of marriages of persons below a minimum age). 3. Penal legislation designed to prevent an act permitted under the Sh. (e.g. the prohibition of polygamy by the Syrian Family Law of 1953).

The reformers could thus claim that basically they were doing no more than refurbishing the Sh. internally. Nationalist factors played a part. The reformers wished to avoid ideological indebtedness and subjugation to the West; consequently they tended to give Western-inspired reforms a local colouring by finding support for them in the vast Islamic legal heritage. The Ottoman Family Law of 1917 is the first modern law of personal status based on this technique. Modern laws followed in Egypt, Jordan, Syria and Iraq.

On the other hand, even in fields outside the Sh.'s jurisdiction and the area of personal status, secular legislation is inspired by the Sh. Civil laws promulgated in recent years in Egypt, Syria and Iraq, state that, in the absence of an express provision of law in a given matter, the principles of Islamic law, custom and natural justice shall be followed. The delimitation of sovereign spheres of religious and secular law, characteristic of the 19th century, has become blurred in the 20th; on the one hand, secular elements have penetrated into family law, and on the other, religious elements have entered into secular law. Yet the importance of the Sh. as a source of legislative inspiration must not be overrated: it is not the only or main source of secular legislation, declarations to the contrary (e.g. the dictum of the Syrian constitutions of 1950 and '53 that Islamic law shall be the main source of legislative inspiration) notwithstanding.

It is doubtful whether the indirect technique so far applied by reformers is sufficient to adapt family law to the changing requirements of modern society. Express substantive legislation from outside the Islamic legal heritage seems unavoidable. It is also doubtful whether the present encounter of Muslim and Western civilization will lead to an Islamization of elements adopted from foreign cultures, as occurred in the formative period of Islamic law. Although the ideological foundations of legal modernism were laid by clerics and religious scholars such as Muhammad 'Abduh, reforms are actually carried out by sovereign parliaments and secular jurists and imposed from above on Sh. functionaries. Government and Parliament now determine the limits of the Sh.'s powers, although orthodox Islam lays down that the Sh. should set the limits of the ruler's powers. The reforms must thus be seen as an extra-Sh. development. The original aim of the modernists was to adapt the Sh. to the needs of present-day society by renewing its traditional mechanism; yet, as soon as they resorted to secular legislation, they left the Islamic legal system. They sought authority for their reforms in the Islamic legal heritage; but the dominant element in those reforms is the influence of Western law.

The area of Sh. jurisdiction was gradually diminished and eventually abolished in some countries. In the 19th century, civil courts were set up that dealt with various areas of law in accordance with secular legislation; mixed courts dealt with foreign nationals, and contributed greatly to the establishment of Western-type legal systems; the jurisdiction of the Sh. Courts became limited to personal status and *waqf* matters; the Sh. Court system was reorganized on the Western pattern; a hierarchy of judicial authorities and appellate courts not previously recognized in Islam were introduced. However, reforms in family law considerably widened the *qadi*'s discretionary power—e.g. in the dissolution of marriages in which there is a great age difference, under the Jordanian law of 1951 and the Syrian law of 1953, and permission for polygamy under the Syrian law of 1953 and the Iraqi law of 1959. The *qadis* thus became the guardians of religious and social ethics, but they are apparently reluctant to use their wide powers.

The secularization of Sh. justice reached its climax with the abolition of the Sh. Courts in Egypt in 1956 and the transfer of their powers to the civil courts. There, Sh. law still governs family matters, but it is applied by civil judges bound by secular rules of evidence and procedure. Sh. *qadis* have been incorporated into the secular judicial system as advisers on matters of personal status. Tunisia, too, has abolished Sh. jurisdiction. Other countries may follow suit. This development will probably entail the codification of family law based on the Western model, and its gradual integration within the civil law.

The Sh.'s power has been further curtailed by government control, secularization or even the complete abolition of various institutions sanctioned by the Sh. Far-reaching reforms have been introduced in the *waqf*, to the extent of its complete abolition in Egypt; the *mufti*, perhaps the most important agency for the development of the Sh. and the preservation of its vitality, is no longer fully independent but implements the government's secular policies; the mosque functionaries—the *Imam*, the *Khatib* and the *Wa'iz*—have been placed under government control. The traditional religious educational institutions are being superseded by secular state institutions; al-Azhar's▷, curriculum and teaching methods, are being secularized; it is gradually becoming a modern university in the European sense, while being harnessed to the internal and external needs of the regime. The state controls the religious establishment and supervises its activities by means of government departments or statutory bodies created specially for the purpose, and it incorporates the religious functionaries into the civil service.

Naturally, the degree of reform of the Sh. and the religious institutions varies from one ME country to another. Turkey went farthest by separating religion from the state and placing it under state jurisdiction. In the first few years after the establishment of the Republic Sh. laws, including the Ottoman Family Law of 1917, were replaced by European codes; the religious courts were abolished; the '*ulama*' were deprived of their power; the administration of the *awqaf* was nationalized; various restrictions were imposed on ritual practices; and finally, in 1928, all references to Islam were removed from the constitution. Although the struggle over the place of religion in Turkish society and the Turkish state has not ended, a restoration of the Sh. and the religious establishment is highly unlikely. The pace of change is generally quicker in Egypt than in the countries of the Fertile Crescent. In these countries, a struggle over the supremacy of the Sh. in matters of personal status is now at its height—with the outcome a foregone conclusion. The position of the Sh. is still unshaken in the Arabian peninsula, although there are signs of an incipient transformation in this area, too.

The powers of the Sh. have also been transformed and diminished in Israel. The *Knesset* (Parliament) passes legislation on family law with a view to achieving equality for women—though without affecting the religious laws of marriage and divorce; in this sensitive area it has preferred procedural regulations and penal sanctions to substantive provisions. This was done in the matters of a minimum marriage age, the prohibition of divorce against the wife's will, and the prohibition of polygamy. Wherever legislation supersedes religious law, the parties are left free—with certain reservations—to litigate under the latter. Thus, in matters of personal status, Israel has a religious and a secular system, based on different norms. In the absence of *muftis* the care for the maintenance of the Sh. and its adaptation to the needs of society has in Israel devolved on the *qadis* of the Sh. Courts. The Sh. Courts have wider powers in matters of personal status and *waqf* than the courts of the other religious communities. Most of the *qadis* recognize the need to introduce reforms in the law of personal status, so long as these do not contradict the express provisions of the Sh. Some *qadis* are inclined to accept birth control and family planning, autopsies for medical purposes, and organ transplants, seeking support for their reforms in other orthodox schools, but some adhere strictly to the Hanafi school traditional among the Muslims of Israel.

Most *qadis* do not oppose reforms of a procedural or penal character by secular legislation so long as no violation of substantive provisions of Islamic law is involved; but they make no effort to initiate such legislation.

In Israel, too, *qadis* tend not to exercise the wide discretion given them by the secular legislator (e.g., the dissolution of the marriage of a girl under 17 or permission for a divorce against the wife's will) wherever such discretion is not supported by Sh. law. But they are inclined to confirm social custom ('*ada*, '*urf*), e.g., in compensation for the divorced woman. The balance between legal theory, once paramount in the development of Islamic law, and the practice of the courts (*'amal*) shows signs of being upset in Israel. The importance of the *qadi* in shaping material law is growing. As the number of *qadis* with a modern, secular education increases, we may expect a reorientation of the status of the Sh. in Israeli Muslim society.							(Ah. Ly.)

SHARIF (Arabic: noble). A man distinguished by his descent from illustrious ancestors. The title refers especially to the descendants of Hassan, the eldest son of the Caliph 'Ali, and Fatima, daughter of the Prophet Muhammad. An especially honoured position in the larger towns of the Arab-Muslim world was that of *Naqib al-Ashraf*, the Head of the Sharifs (in the respective area); the position usually passed from father to son. A branch of Hassan and 'Ali's descendants, bearing the title "Sh.", established itself in Mecca▷ in the 10th century and ruled it independently or semi-independently until 1924, when Hijaz▷ was conquered by Ibn Sa'ud▷. The Hashemites▷ of Jordan (and until 1958 also of Iraq) are descendants of the Shs. of Mecca.
(B. G.)

***SHARJA.** (correct transliteration: al-Shariqa). One of the seven principalities of the Trucial Coast▷, north of Dubai▷. Pop.: 15–20,000, mostly in the port of Sharja. They engage in fishing, boat building and pearl-diving. The sheikhs of Sh. of the house of al-Qassemi, signed several treaties with the British and have been under their protection since the 19th century. Sh. is a British military base and the centre of the military force of the Trucial Coast (the "Trucial Scouts") set up and commanded by the British. Sh. has frontier disputes with Dubai▷ and Muscat-and-'Oman▷. She also disputes with Umm al-Qaiwain▷ and Iran the ownership of the island of Abu Mussa▷, important for strategic reasons and on account of offshore oil concessions. Sh. reached a federal arrangement with Fujaira▷. She is one of the prospective members of a planned federation of Persian Gulf principalities (the "Union of Arab Emirates", UAE). In 1968, Sh. granted oil concessions on land and offshore to 'Shell" and a group of German· companies.							(Y.K.)

SHARM AL-SHEIKH. Small cove on the eastern shore of the Sinai▷ Peninsula, controlling the Straits of Tiran▷. In 1954, the uninhabited place was fortified by Egypt in order to blockade shipping to the Israeli port of Eilat▷. It was taken by Israeli forces in the Sinai campaign▷ of 1956, but was evacuated, under the pressure of the UN and the Great Powers, in 1957. A United Nations Emergency Force▷ was stationed at Sh. to ensure free passage of ships, and did so from 1957 to '67. It withdrew upon Egypt's demand in May 1967. The re-imposition of the Egyptian blockade of the Straits, after the withdrawal of the UNEF, was one of the main causes of the Six Day War▷ of 1967, during which Sh. was again taken by Israel. It has been under Israel occupation since 1967. In view of past experience, and to avoid future clashes over the freedom of shipping in this area, Israel claims the right to keep a force in Sh. and in a strip of territory that would connect it with Israel.							(Y.K.-E.L.)

SHATT AL-'ARAB. River formed by the confluence of the Euphrates▷ and Tigris▷ near Qurna in southern Iraq, and entering the Persian Gulf after a course of 115 mi. About 50 mi. from its mouth the Sh. receives on its left (eastern) bank the Karun River, entirely on Iranian territory. The Sh. carries much of the foreign trade of Iraq (via Basra▷) and Iran (via Khorramshahr▷), and provides the outlet for the southern Iraqi oilfields and the Abadan▷ refineries.

The Sh. has for long been an object of strife between Iraq (previously, the Ottoman Empire) and Iran. According to an agreement concluded in 1937—based on previous Ottoman-Iranian accords—the Sh. is wholly Iraqi territory except for a length of 3 mi. opposite Abadan, where the frontier is considered to run along the thalweg (the line of greatest depth) of the river. This arrangement remained unsatisfactory to both sides, particularly to Iran, and questions of piloting, dues and general procedures continued causing outbursts of the conflict. Grave crises over the Sh. occurred in 1961, 1965 and 1969; during the crisis of Apr. 1969, Iran formally abrogated the agreement of 1937 and served notice that any future accord should grant Iran equal rights and fix the boundary along the thalweg or the medium line of the river.							(U.D.-Y.S.)

SHAW, SIR WALTER. British jurist and administrator, sent to Palestine in 1929 at the head of a Royal Commission to investigate the disturbances of 1929. His report, submitted in 1930, aroused the opposition of the Jewish community and the Zionist leadership. It served as a basis for the White Book of 1930, which was regarded as distinctly anti-Zionist. See Palestine, Committees and Commissions.▷
(Y.S.)

***SHAZAR** (formerly **RUBASHOV**), **SHNEOR ZALMAN.** Born in Russia 1889. Israel's third President. Author, journalist, historian. Received a traditional Jewish education at home, and a secular education from private teachers and at the St. Peters-

Zalman Shazar

burg "Academy for Hebraic Studies". Active from youth in the *Po'alei Zion* ("Workers of Zion") party, Sh. went to Palestine in 1911, but returned to Russia to do his army service. After his discharge he studied history and philosophy at the universities of Freiburg, Strasbourg and Berlin. In Germany Sh. founded the German branch of the *Po'alei Zion* party and worked for the German-Jewish press. He was a member of a *Po'alei Zion* delegation to Palestine in 1919, and drafted its plan, based on the principle of co-operative physical work, for the settlement of a million Jews. Upon his return to Europe, he became one of the leaders of the world bureau of *Po'alei Zion* in Vienna. Sh. returned to Israel in 1924, was elected a member of the Secretariat of the Executive Committee of the *Histadrut*▷, the Federation of Labour, and on the foundation of its daily, *Davar*, joined the editorial board. In 1944, he became its editor-in-chief. He was also active at the central Zionist and labour institutions. Sh. was Minister of Education and Culture, 1949–50, and later a member of the Jewish Agency▷ Executive and Head of its Department for Education and Culture in the Diaspora. In 1963, he succeeded Y. Ben-Zvi▷ as President of Israel. In 1968, he was elected President for a second five year-term.   (E.A.)

SHI'A, SHI'I(TE)S. (Arabic: faction, party). During the early Islamic period the term referred to those Muslims who claimed that 'Ali b. Abi Talib, a cousin of the Prophet Muhammad and the husband of his daughter Fatima, was his legitimate successor (*Khalifa*) as ruler and religious leader. Subsequently it referred to those Muslims who held, in contrast to the mainstream of Islam, the Sunni(te)s▷, that leadership of the Muslim community was divinely vested in the family of the Prophet, *i.e.* 'Ali's descendants *(Ahl al-Beit)*. Those claimed as successors of the Prophet were called Imams▷. The identity of the Imams, their number and the extent of their influence on the community have been the subject of controversy. The term Sh. thus applied to various groups, believing in the Imamate of different Imams, descendants of different lineages within the *Ahl al-Beit*.

In modern Islam, however, the term Sh. refers to the major non-Sunni group which follows the juridical-theological school of the *Ithna'ashariyya*, "the Twelvers", named also *al-Ja'fariyya* after the sixth Imam, Ja'far al-Sadiq (died 765). This school has been the state religion of Persia since the early 16th century. Its adherents include most of the Persians and more than half the Arab population of Iraq, as well as considerable communities in India, Pakistan, Afghanistan, Lebanon, Bahrein and Kuwait. Iraq, India, Pakistan and Lebanon officially recognize *al-Madhhab al-Ja'fari* (the Ja'fari school), and its followers come under the jurisdiction of their own religious institutions, which are fully independent of those of the Sunnis. The Sh. of Lebanon are also called Mutawalis▷ (*Matawila*).

The Sh. maintain that the office of the Imamate has succeeded prophecy and that the Imams are designated and guided of God. The first Imam after the death of Muhammad was 'Ali who was succeeded consecutively by his sons al-Hasan and al-Hussein, the only grandchildren of the Prophet. Al-Hussein was succeeded by nine male lineal descendants, the last of whom is the twelfth Imam, Muhammad Abu'l-Qassem, who did not die but became invisible in early childhood, 873, and will reappear at the end of time as al-Mahdi▷ "to fill the earth with justice".

Since the elevation to the occult of the Imam, the religious and political institutions of the community are considered fallible, as, therefore, are their decrees. The believer is called upon to act as a *mujtahid* in the matter of religious ordinances, namely, to interpret the law by his own personal endeavours, on the basis of the literal text of the Qur'an, the Traditions of the Prophet and the Imams, as codified in the Sh. collections, and in the light of reason. Those who lack the necessary learning (the *muqal-lidun*, "imitators") are required to follow the opinion of a living *mujtahid*. Particularly erudite sages, such as the late Hussein Tabatabai Burujirdi of Qum in Persia and the late Muhsin al-Hakim of Karbala in Iraq, are considered to be "Grand *Mujtahids*". Out of piety many Sh. pay the *Mujtahids* a religious tax, *al-khums*, though by tradition they are exempt from this duty as long as the Imam is hidden.

As for the political ruler, Sh. law considers his power as originating in his own person and/or in other fellow men and forbids his endowment with divine authority.

Apart from the legal and constitutional theories peculiar to the Sh., it differs from Sunnism mainly in the following: the formula of the Witness, *al-Shahada* ("There is no God but Allah, and Muhammad is Allah's apostle"), adds in its Shi'i version "... and 'Ali is the *wali* (helper) of God"; Shi'i daily and ceremonial prayers contain reference to the Imams, and the Sh. permits *mut'a*. a temporary marriage contract. The Sh. differs from Sunni Islam also in certain other legal provisions concerning family law and personal status.

The Sh. beliefs contain elements of tragedy centred on the martyrdom of the third Imam, al-Hussein. The Sh. doctrine of the Imamate has exerted a great influence on Islamic philosophy in general and on Sufism (mystic schools, see Dervish Orders▷) in particular.

The Zeidi(te)s▷ are a non-*Ithna-'ashariyya* Sh. sect. This sect grew out of a schism over the identity of the fifth Imam; it recognizes a living Imam. The *Zeidiyya* rule Yemen. The Sect of Isma'ilis▷ resulted from a schism over the identity of the seventh Imam; one Isma'ili branch also recognizes a living Imam, the Aga Khan. Several sects on the fringe of Islam, e.g. the Druzes▷ and the 'Alawis▷, seceded from the *Isma'iliyya*.

In the late 1950s Sheikh Mahmud Shaltout, the Rector of al-Azhar in Cairo and some of his colleagues, encouraged by President Nasser, advocated a *rapprochement* with the Sh. As a result, Shi'i Law Doctrine (*fiqh*) was introduced into the curriculum of al-Azhar. Shi'i institutions of traditional learning, however, are located mainly in the Shi'i holy cities containing the shrines of the Imams, such as Najaf, Karbala and Kadhimain in Iraq and Qum and Mashhad in Persia. In India Lucknow has for many generations been a centre of Shi'i scholarship and a theological seminar has recently been established in Sidon in southern Lebanon. (Y. E.)

*SHIHAB, FU'AD, GENERAL (b. 1902). Lebanese officer and politician, President of Lebanon 1958–64. Maronite▷ Christian of a renowned family of Amirs. During the Mandate▷, Sh. served in the "Special Troops" recruited by the French, reaching the rank of Lieutenant-Colonel. In 1946, when Lebanon became independent, he was appointed Commander of the Army and did much to build it up into a modern, professional force. In Sept. 1952, when a "National Front" staged demonstrations against the corrupt administration of President Bishara al-Khouri▷, Sh. refused to order the army to suppress the demonstrators, and Khouri was in consequence forced to resign. For an interim period of a few weeks, Sh. served as Prime Minister and Minister of the Interior and Defence. He adopted a similar attitude in the civil war in 1958, when fighting broke out between supporters of President Camille Chamoun▷, who stood for an independent Christian Lebanon, and a Nasserist▷ "National Front". Sh. once again refused to order out the army against the insurgents, holding that it ought to be above the rival camps, and constitute a force for national unity. Sh. thus acquired a reputation for impartiality, and on 31 July 1958 he was elected President for the constitutional term of six years. His election was a compromise, the first step towards a reconciliation of the parties in the civil war. Sh. continued that reconciliation, though somewhat favouring the Nasserist Muslims. In response to their demands, and to appease them, he moved closer to Egypt and her camp. He initiated a series of reforms in the administration, aimed at strengthening the Muslim population, and initiated public works in the backward north and south mainly populated by Muslims. His opponents claimed that he was employing bureaucratic and dictatorial methods, using the Secret Service for his own purpose and emptying the parliamentary system of its content. Even after he retired from the presidency in 1964 (declining urgent offers to arrange for an amendment of the constitution and his election for a second term), Sh. retained much influence through his supporters in Parliament, who formed a Shihabist bloc, through numerous army officers who remained loyal to him, and through the Secret Services. In 1970, he was urged to stand again for the presidency (as permitted by the constitution after an interval of one term), but refused. (Y.P.)

SHISHAKLI, ADIB (1909–64). Syrian officer and politician. President of Syria, 1953–4. Born in Hama. Served in the French "Special Troops" in Syria. In 1948 Sh. was a senior officer in Qawuqji's▷ "Army of Deliverance" which fought the Jews in Palestine. Afterwards, he went back to the Syrian Army. He is said to have been a member of the "Syrian Nationalist Party"▷ of Anton Sa'adeh▷. He played a major part in Husni Za'im's▷ coup in 1949, but was suspected by Za'im of disloyalty and dismissed from the army. He was reinstated by Sami Hinnawi▷, in Aug. 1949. On 19 Dec. 1949 he led a military coup which overthrew Hinnawi. The continued formal existence of parliamentary rule established by

Hinnawi was at first permitted and Sh. assumed only the title of Deputy Chief-of-Staff, though in fact he ruled behind the scenes. Sh. opposed the pro-Iraqi leanings of the "People's Party" then in power, and on 29 Nov. 1951 carried out a second coup. His rule now became more openly dictatorial, although he appointed as a figurehead President and Prime Minister Marshal Fawzi Selo, one of his supporters. He assumed formal power only in June 1953, when he became Premier and had himself elected President in a referendum. The same referendum approved a new constitution, which gave the President wide powers.

Sh. attempted to introduce several economic and social reforms, but did not persist in them. In 1952 he banned all political parties and established an "Arab Liberation Movement" as the single political organization. The ALM did not take root, and the parliament elected under its aegis in 1953 remained a non-representative shadow-body. Since Sh. created order and stability in Syria, the West supported him, and he was considered pro-Western.

In Jan. 1954 resistance to his oppressive regime and his pro-Western policies broke out (at first among the Druzes). On 25 Feb. 1954 a coup forced Sh. to resign. He left Syria and lived in Lebanon, Sa'udia and France. In 1957 he was charged with plotting a coup with the support of Iraq and the West, and was tried *in absentia* several times. In 1960 he emigrated to Brazil. There he was assassinated in 1964 by a Druze in revenge for the bombing of the Druze Mountain during his rule.   (A.L.-O.T.)

*SHUQEIRI, AHMAD. Palestinian-Arab politician. Born 1907 in Acre, son of Sheikh As'ad Sh., a prominent political and Muslim religious figure in mandatory Palestine. A lawyer by profession, Sh. in 1945 headed a Palestinian-Arab propaganda office in the USA, and later in Jerusalem. Briefly a member of the Arab Higher Committee▷ (Mar. to June 1946); Member of the Syrian delegation to the United Nations 1949–50; Under Secretary for political affairs of the Arab League▷ 1951–7; Sa'udi Arabian Minister of State for UN affairs and Ambassador to the UN 1957–62. During his tenure as Ambassador to the UN (Syrian or Sa'udi), he was the most active and vituperative spokesman for the Arab cause against Israel. In 1963 he was the representative of the Palestinian Arabs at the Arab League. When, in 1964, a "Palestine Liberation Organization▷" was established under the auspices of the Arab League, Sh. became its chairman. His leadership of the PLO was considered a failure—he was later particularly blamed for his violent and irresponsibly extremist speeches advocating the physical extermination of the

Jews of Israel—and he was relieved of his post in Feb. 1969. He has since retired from the political scene.   (E.Y.-Y.S.)

SIDQI, BAKR (1890–1937). Iraqi officer and politician. In 1933, as commanding officer of the army in northern Iraq, B.S. crushed the Assyrian▷ rebellion, and was promoted general in consequence. In 1935 he put down several tribal rebellions in southern Iraq. He headed a group of army officers who looked with distaste at the disputes of civilian politicians and wished to emulate their colleagues in Iran and Turkey who had played so prominent a part in modernizing their country. S. collaborated clandestinely with the civilian politician Hikmat Suleiman▷ and the leftist-reformist *Ahali* Group. In Oct. 1936, when he was Acting Chief of General Staff, S. moved military units to Baghdad and forced Prime Minister Yassin al-Hashemi▷ to resign. He became Chief of General Staff, and Hikmat Suleiman, Prime Minister. His was the first straightforward military *coup d'état* in the newly independent Arab countries. S. was the strong man and real ruler of the country, but his reformist plans remained largely unimplemented. S. was assassinated, in Aug. 1937, by a group of dissident officers.   (B.G.)

SIDQI, ISMA'IL (1875–1950). Egyptian politician. S. began his political career as a supporter of Sa'd Zaghlul▷ and accompanied him to exile in the Seychelles in 1919. He subsequently left the *Wafd*▷ and participated in setting up the Liberal Constitutional Party after 1922. He was Minister of the Interior in 1925 on behalf of that party. He was Prime Minister in 1930–3 after the People's Party (*Hizb al-Sha'b*), which he had founded just before the 1931 elections, won. His rule was autocratic; he substituted for the 1923 constitution a more conservative one, and altered the election law. His aim was to strengthen the monarchy and to weaken the *Wafd* party. As a former Prime Minister, he was a member of the delegation which negotiated and signed the Anglo-Egyptian Treaty of 1936. In 1946, he again became Prime Minister. He reached an agreement with the British Foreign Secretary, Ernest Bevin▷, on the evacuation of British forces from Egypt within three years and the establishment of a joint defence council. The agreement was not ratified, as both sides published conflicting interpretations of the clause dealing with the future self-determination of Sudan, and S. was compelled to resign. He never again held government office. S. was also President of the Association of Industrialists and was regarded as a representative of conservative capitalism. He did not believe in Arab unity and, in 1948, had the courage to warn, alone in the Senate against the Egyptian invasion of Palestine. He later published a series of articles in which he advocated an understanding with Israel.   (S.L.)

SINAI PENINSULA. Triangle-shaped desert area, which forms the land bridge between Asia and Africa, bordered in the west by the Suez Canal▷ and the Gulf of Suez, in the east by the Gulf of 'Aqaba▷ (Eilat▷). The rugged mountains in the southern part of S. are, according to some traditions, the site of the Giving of the Law. Area: 23,200 sq. mi. Its population was *c.* 38,000, mostly Bedouin▷, in 1948. After 1948 the Egyptian Army mounted a major military build-up in S. and its population grew to 126,000 (1967). S. was the battle-ground for the wars of 1956 and 1967 (see Sinai War▷, Six Day War▷).

Along the western shore minerals were discovered and exploited: manganese at Um Bugma and oil at Ras Sudar and Abu Rudeis.

S. was part of the Ottoman Empire since 1517. The agreements of 1840–1 (regulating the relations between the Sultan and his autonomous Viceroy of Egypt) left the administration of S. unclear and controversial. While Ottoman sovereignty was uncontested, sporadic Egyptian administration was maintained—at least since the late 1870s—and continued under the British occupation of Egypt (1882). The Sultan claimed that Egyptian temporary rights of administration referred only to the northwestern parts of the Peninsula and to a number of posts in the southern parts, on the pilgrims' route to Mecca, while the central triangle: Suez-'Arish-'Aqaba was under direct Turkish rule.

After 1882 the British on their own initiative claimed for Egypt—and tried to establish *de facto*—fuller rights of possession. British notes of 1892 and 1902 laid down the eastern boundary as a line drawn from al-'Arish or Rafah to 'Aqaba. (A tentative plan to develop the al-'Arish area for Jewish settlement was briefly discussed in 1902–3, but was never put into practice.) When the Turks set up a garrison in Taba, south of 'Aqaba, in 1906, a sharp diplomatic clash with Britain ensued (the "'Aqaba Incident"), and the Sultan, while not renouncing his claim, had to accept the Rafah-'Aqaba line as a border. This line became the boundary of British-Mandated Palestine (1922–48) and—except for its western extremity, where Egypt crossed it to occupy the Gaza Strip▷—the armistice line between Egypt and Israel (1949–67).

In the Six Day War▷, Israel took S. which then contained the major part of the Egyptian Forces. S. has been under Israeli occupation since, with an estimated population of 60,900 (1969–70). Israel has

initiated several projects for the improvement of the conditions of the Bedouin (economic, health, education) and the development of tourism.

Egypt demands a total Israeli withdrawal. Israel insists on the demilitarization of S. in the framework of a peace settlement and her occupation of Sharm al-Sheikh▷ with a territorial link to Israel, to secure free shipping in the Gulf of 'Aqaba.

(Y.K.-E.L.-Y.S.)

SINAI CAMPAIGN (Oct. 1956). The Czech arms deal concluded by Egypt in 1955, and the Suez crisis of summer 1956, created growing tension in the ME. Israel felt herself especially threatened by the Egyptian blockade of Eilat▷ and the Gulf of 'Aqaba, imposed since 1954, the continuous sabotage raids across the Egyptian Armistice lines, and the speeches and statements threatening another round of war and Israel's destruction—all amounting, in Israel's view, to the abrogation of the Armistice Agreement▷ of 1949. Israel's sense of encirclement and immediate mortal danger was deepened by Jordan's adherence to the Egyptian-Syrian military pact and the establishment, in Oct. 1956, of a Unified Military Command of these three countries' forces.

On 29–30 Oct.—in co-ordination with Britain and France in the context of their conflict with Egypt over the Suez Canal▷—Israeli parachute battalions seized the Mitla Pass. Subsequently, three columns set out across the desert, tactically supported by the air force. One, striking south from Eilat along a road hitherto considered impassable, took Sharm al-Sheikh▷, commanding the Straits of Tiran▷. Another column followed the central Sinai road in the direction of Isma'iliya. The northernmost column outflanked the Gaza Strip▷, then turned north, to mop up enemy forces in the Strip, and south-west, along the coastal road in the direction of Qantara. Within 100 hours the massive Egyptian forces in the Sinai Peninsula had been completely routed. Heeding a pre-determined Anglo-French ultimatum, Israel's forces halted 10 mi. east of the Suez Canal. (Meanwhile the Israelis had captured an Egyptian destroyer off Haifa.) Other Arab countries—mutual defence treaties notwithstanding—did not take part in the conflict.

The Security Council was paralysed because of the involvement of two of its permanent members, who had the right to veto any decision. On 2 Nov., and again on 7 Nov., the UN General Assembly called—with rare unanimity of the USA and the USSR—for the immediate withdrawal of Israel's forces to the Armistice Lines; the USSR threatened to use force if the resolution were not heeded. The withdrawal of Anglo-French forces, which had in the meantime in-

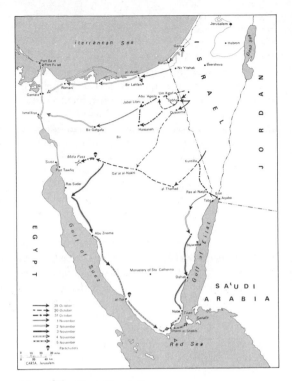

Map of the Sinai Campaign

vaded the Suez Canal Zone, was also demanded On 4 Nov., the Assembly decided to create a UN Emergency Force▷ (UNEF) to replace the withdrawing troops. On 8 Nov. Israel agreed to withdraw upon the conclusion of arrangements with the UN concerning UNEF. By 22 Jan. 1957, she had evacuated all the occupied territory except for the Gaza Strip (occupied by Egypt since 1948, but not considered Egyptian territory) and the Sinai coast facing the Straits of Tiran. Concerning these areas, Israel insisted on safeguards for free navigation and freedom from attack across her borders. In Mar. 1957 the UNEF was stationed along the borders, including the Gaza Strip, and in Sharm al-Sheikh, to provide such "safeguards", and Israel withdrew accordingly. Israel also received certain diplomatic assurances; but the precise extent of the UN and (US) commitment in that respect has remained controversial. The Gaza Strip was, contrary to Israel's expectations, immediately handed over to Egypt, and hostile incursions from the area were soon resumed. Freedom of navigation through the Straits of Tiran was maintained until May 1967 (see UNEF▷, Six Day War▷).   (N. L.)

SIX DAY WAR (5–11 June 1967). Arab-Israel tension rose steadily during the mid-1960s, owing to the constant increase in Jewish casualties resulting

from Arab sabotage and infiltration, pursued with the active encouragement of the Arab states. Sabotage and the shelling of border villages were particularly intensive in early 1967, from Syrian territory, with the active participation of the Syrian Army. On 7 Apr. 1967, Israeli planes struck at Syrian artillery positions and brought down six Syrian MIGs. Syria complained bitterly to Egypt that the latter had not rushed to help her ally, particularly in view of their defence pact of Nov. 1966.

Egypt now announced that she would not tolerate any further Israeli action against Syria, and concentrated large numbers of tanks and infantry units in the Sinai Peninsula close to the Israeli border. Egypt's Soviet ally encouraged her in these war preparations; the USSR warned her of alleged Israeli troop concentrations against Syria (denied by the UN Truce observers). Mid-May statements by Israeli leaders were interpreted by the Russians and Arabs as threats against Syria. On 16 May, Egypt requested the immediate withdrawal of the UN Emergency Force (UNEF) from its position along the Egypt-Israel border and the Straits of Tiran▷, and, on 18 May, from the whole of Sinai. The UN Secretary-General complied with this request (see UNEF▷ for details). While he was on his way to Cairo, for further talks, President Nasser, on 21–22 May, reimposed a blockade in the Gulf of 'Aqaba— kept open since 1957 under the supervision of UNEF —by closing the Straits of Tiran to all shipping to and from Eilat. Israel had repeatedly stated that she would regard such a blockade as a *casus belli*.

The USA and a number of other maritime nations —though not prepared to take practical steps to make President Nasser change his decision—proclaimed that the Straits of Tiran were an international waterway open to free passage by ships of all nations. Egypt proclaimed that she would consider any attempt to break the blockade an act of war. President Nasser tauntingly challenged Israel to war, announcing that Egypt was now strong enough to win it and threatening Israel's destruction. Leaders of the other Arab states made equally bellicose speeches. The Nov. 1966 defence pact with Syria was followed on 30 May and 4 June 1967 by similar pacts with Jordan and Iraq, resulting in Israel's complete encirclement. The Arab states were supported by huge supplies of Soviet military equipment.

In the early hours of 5 June, Israel announced that her radar screens had shown approaching flights of Egyptian planes, and Egyptian armour had moved towards the border. Israel armour struck across the Sinai border, while her Air Force was destroying the Egyptian Air Force. That same morning the Jordanian forces started shelling and carrying out

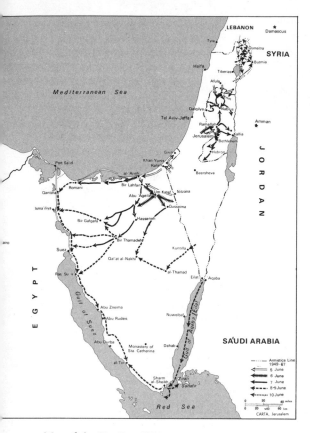

Map of the Six Day War

Tiran had been enforced, was captured on 6 June from the sea; parachutists landed without opposition.

Israel reacted swiftly to Jordan's entry into the war. Reinforcements, rushed to Jerusalem, were able to retake, on 5 June, the UN Headquarters and to link up with the isolated outpost on Mount Scopus▷ in the north, which had since 1949 constituted an Israel enclave behind Jordanian lines. Out of respect for the Holy Places, strict orders were given to minimize damage to the Old City. On 7 June, Israel forces took the Old City of Jerusalem.

By the end of the third day of fighting, Israeli forces had taken all of the Sinai Peninsula, up to the Suez Canal, the Gaza Strip▷ and most of the "West Bank▷" of Jordan. When the UN Security Council, after days of wrangling, called for a cease fire, Israel was the first to accept it. Jordan followed soon after. Egypt, initially rejecting the cease fire, acceded after 24 hours, on Thursday, 8 June. Lebanon had played no significant part in the fighting. Syria, the most militant of the Arab states, was still intensively shelling border villages. An attempt to capture one of them had failed. Now Syria refused to accept the cease fire, relying on the tremendous tactical advantage which the fortifications on the crest and slopes of the

air-raids across the 1949 Armistice Line with Israel; a warning was consequently sent to King Hussein of Jordan to stay out of the war. The warning went unheeded, and subsequently the Jordanian Army attacked and captured the UN Headquarters south of Jerusalem. The Israeli Air Force now took action against Jordan's Air Force. As Syria continued to shell Israeli villages, Syrian airfields were attacked, the same day, and Syria's Air Force largely destroyed. During the first 16 hours of the war the Arab states lost well over 400 planes, as against 19 Israeli planes lost in the air. On that first day of fighting Israel won complete aerial superiority while an almost total news blackout was maintained.

Simultaneously Israeli columns advanced into the Sinai Peninsula, in the direction of Rafah and al-'Arish in the north, Abu 'Ageila, Bir Gafgafa in the centre, and al-Qusseima in the south. A major battle took place on and around the elaborate fortifications of Abu 'Ageila. Bitter fighting took place on the outskirts of Gaza. By the end of 6 June, the Egyptian retreat had become a rout. Sharm al-Sheikh▷, the Egyptian position from which the blockade of the Straits of

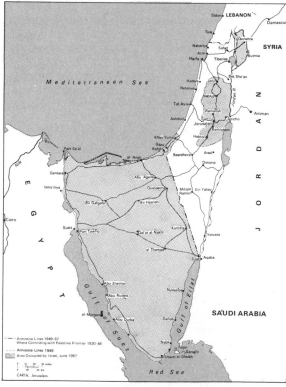

Cease-Fire Lines, June 1967

Golan Heights▷ gave her. However, 20 hours of intensive uphill fighting ended in the capture by Israel forces of the Golan Heights up to and including Quneitra, whereupon the cease fire came into effect also on the Syrian border (on 10 June).

In the course of less than six days, Israel had routed three of its neighbours supported by a number of other Arab countries. Well over 400 Arab planes had been destroyed, over 500 tanks destroyed or captured. Arab military equipment lost included 70% of the heavy equipment of three Arab armies, valued at well over $1,000m. Over 11,500 Egyptians were killed and 5,600 were taken prisoner; Jordan lost about 6,000 (so King Hussein claimed); Syria suffered about 1,000 casualties; over 700 Israelis were killed and 2,500 wounded.

The war left Israel in control of areas over three times her pre-1967 size, and with an Arab population of about one million (in addition to her own Arab 400,000 citizens). In the political struggle which followed, the Arab states demanded the complete evacuation of all territory occupied as a pre-condition for any settlement; Israel, determined not to return to the strategic and tactical situation of a constant threat of war, decided to withdraw only to secure and recognized borders, to be established through a mutually agreed peace settlement.   (N. L.)

SLAVERY. Open chattel-S., full ownership of humans with unlimited rights to bequeath, sell, and trade them, was already forbidden in most ME countries at the start of the twentieth century (Sudan: 1898, Morocco: 1911), except for the Arabian peninsula. However, even in those countries where S. was thus outlawed, many vestiges remained of hidden S. or of semi-S., such as "inherited" domestic servants, indebted tenant-farmers forbidden in effect to leave their master's land, and young girls sold into marriage by their fathers. Cases were also known of slaves who were formally freed, but who preferred the security of remaining attached to the household of their masters.

Open S. survived in the Arabian peninsula at least up to the 1960s. West African countries and Sudan supplied young men and women to the slave markets which were openly held in Arabia. The victims were either sold by their families, abducted by force, or inveigled into slavery. The Pilgrimage to Mecca, *(Hajj)* often served as cover and pretext for slave trading, both as an inducement to the victims to join pilgrims' caravans and as a meeting and market place, where such transactions were carried out. The sale of those accompanying the caravans in this manner, was often calculated as a means of financing the pilgrimage of powerful individuals. S. in Sa'udi

Arabia, Muscat-and-'Oman, and in various principalities along the Persian Gulf coast, the transfer of slaves from Africa to the Arabian peninsula and slave trading were documented as late as the 1950s and '60s. Estimates as to the number of slaves in the Arabian peninsula varied from 700,000 to as many as two or even three million in the 1950s, and from 100,000 to 300,000 and more in the 1960s.

In some Arabian principalities no legal steps have yet been taken to abolish S. In Sa'udi Arabia a 1936 decree imposed certain limitations on slave trade and importation, and forbade the imposition of S. on free men; but it did not forbid S. as such. The complete prohibition of S. was decreed only in Nov. 1962; to facilitate the implementation of its decree, the government allocated funds to compensate owners who freed their slaves. Since then, officially S. no longer exists in Sa'udia, but evidence and reports continue being published that the ban has not yet been put fully into effect. UN agencies also reported several times that Sa'udi Arabia had not replied to questionnaires on S. and that, though she was a party to the 1956 convention banning S., she had yet to ratify it.   (Y. S.)

*SNEH (formerly KLEINBAUM), Dr. MOSHE. Born 1909, in Radzyn, Poland. Graduated from Warsaw University as a physician and was active in the Zionist movement, becoming chairman of the Polish Zionist Organization. Was a member of the left wing of the "General-Zionists" and delegate to several Zionist Congresses. S. immigrated to Israel in 1940 and became a member of the *Hagana*▷ High Command, 1940–6, and its chief, 1941–6. When, in July 1946, the *Hagana* stopped armed resistance against the British and the Zionist Congress failed in December to order its resumption, S. resigned his post as Chief of the High Command, becoming (1947–8) head of the European branch of the Political Department and head of the "illegal" Immigration Department of the Jewish Agency▷. Convinced that the future Jewish State should win Soviet friendship, S. resigned in 1948 from the Jewish Agency Executive to join the leftist *Mapam*▷ (United Workers' Party). He led its left wing which broke away from *Mapam* in 1954 and merged with the Israel Communist Party. When in 1965 the Communist Party split, S. stayed with *Maki*, the predominantly Jewish more moderate faction. Since the Six Day War▷, S. has severely criticized Soviet bloc policies. He regarded the Six Day War as a justified campaign of Israeli self-defence. He was a member of the *Knesset* 1949–65, and again since 1969. He was editor of *Kol Ha'am* (Voice of the People), the daily newspaper of the Israel Communist Party, 1965–9.   (A. W.-E. L.)

SOCIALISM, "ARAB SOCIALISM". As a current of thought S. can trace its history in the Arab ME to the early 20th century. In 1913 the Egyptian writer Salama Mussa published a pamphlet "S.", advocating ideas which were strongly influenced by those of the English Fabian Society. In 1920 Salama Mussa helped found an "Egyptian Socialist Party". But these activities were without influence and the group was short lived and restricted to very small circles. Part of the *al-Ahali* group in Iraq, which took part in the formation of Hikmat Suleiman's▷ government (resulting from a military coup) in summer 1936, drew their inspiration from S. But the group was soon relieved of its position. The term S. also appeared in the names and programmes of several marginal, ephemeral groups and "parties". This tendency became more widespread after World War II (when the name S. was even used by fascist groups; for example, Ahmad Hussein's "Young Egypt" *(Misr al-Fatat)*, with its "Green Shirts", in 1949 changed its name to "Democratic Socialist Party").

After World War II, S. assumed a new importance as a slogan in the programmes of political parties and governments. The increasing popularity of socialist concepts—such as redistribution of wealth, planned development, progressive taxation, expansion of social services and freedom of trade union activities— reflected a growing awareness of the region's economic and social backwardness, of the vast gap between the small, unproductive exploiting classes of the rich, generally (but not quite correctly) called "feudals", and the poverty-stricken masses. However, until the consolidation of the Syrian Ba'th▷ party around 1950, S. represented no more than an amorphous trend. In the ME, unlike Europe, Communism▷ had preceded non-communist S.; the adherents of AS have always been preoccupied with its demarcation from Communism. Generally, regimes professing S. were no less fierce than nationalist-conservative ones in outlawing and jailing communists—even while maintaining intimate relations with the USSR in the spheres of international politics, and economic and military affairs.

From 1961 onwards, "AS", later defined in the "National Charter" of 1962, became the official doctrine of Nasser's▷ Egypt, and the regime's single-party mass-organization was renamed, May 1962, the "Arab Socialist Union"▷.

Generally speaking, Nasser's S. is close to that of the *Ba'th* party of the 1960s although none of the rival trends would admit this. Its principal features are: a high, progressive scale of income tax; a highly developed social legislation in matters of health, education and protection of workers' rights; and mainly—nationalization of basic industries, central banking and foreign trade, a planned economy, and a state monopoly of major economic enterprises.

Unlike Communism, AS does not wholly forbid private ownership of the means of production. It only abolishes private ownership in cases of "exploiting capitalism" (which, in Egypt, meant primarily the nationalization of enterprises owned by foreigners and by non-Muslim Egyptians; far fewer enterprises owned by Egyptian Muslims were expropriated). AS tolerates and sometimes encourages "national capitalism" in certain economic activities; the public sector is dominant but not completely monopolistic. In agriculture—still the main form of property and the largest source of income in most Arab countries—there has been no nationalization at all; all schemes of agrarian reform have meant the redistribution of land among small holders (who are in some cases required to join co-operatives), but never collectivization. AS advocates harmony between the classes, without exploitation, "equality of opportunities" for all, in contrast to Communism's class struggle and the dictatorship of the proletariat. Furthermore, AS encourages religion and repudiates atheism; it is often presented not merely as compatible with religion, particularly Islam, but as the real fulfillment of Islamic doctrine and ethics (and Islam is frequently cited as the most solid base of S.).

While AS, as preached and practised since the 1950s, thus contains conservative elements, particularly in its attitude towards Islam, it definitely has more affinity with the single-party, populist dictatorship of an East-European "Peoples Democracy" than with West-European Social Democracy. Moreover, some of the groups professing AS lean heavily towards Maoism or Castroism—and even some of the regimes in power, such as that ruling South Yemen, are attracted by such trends.

Most of the revolutionary, socialist Arab states have no official constitutions; in the provisional, partial constitutions adopted or in various stages of drafting, S. appears as one of the basic principles (sometimes together with the term "People's Democracy") in Egypt, Syria, Iraq, South Yemen, Sudan, Libya and— outside the scope of this Encyclopaedia—Algeria and Tunisia (where the term does not appear in the constitution, but in the name and principles of the ruling party).

The main Arab political groups and parties, who have professed S. in recent years, are the Arab Socialist Union in Egypt and the rival *Ba'th* parties in Syria and Iraq, the National Liberation Front▷ in South Yemen (and—outside the scope of this Encyclopaedia —the Socialist Dustur Party of Tunisia, and the FLN in Algeria and the rival factions that seceded from it). Attempts by the 'Aref▷ regime in Iraq, 1963–8, to create an Egyptian-type Arab Socialist Union failed. Lebanon's Progressive Socialist Party, led by Kamal Jumblat▷, also professes S. None of these parties is affiliated to an international socialist body, such as the Socialist International—though the International maintains some contact with the Tunisian and Lebanese groups mentioned. S. is also professed by some of the small circles of Maoist-Castroist intellectuals that have evolved around, or out of, the "Arab Nationalist Movement"▷— (Harakat al-Qawmiyin); they maintain close contact with, or control, some of the Palestinian-Arab guerilla groups (such is the Popular Front for the Liberation of Palestine▷ led by Dr. George Habash▷, and the Popular as the Popular Front for the Liberation of Palestine▷ led by Nayef Hawatmeh); South Yemen's National Liberation Front and the liberation fronts it has established in the Persian Gulf area also seem to follow these trends. So does the "Organization of Lebanese Socialists" that seceded in the 1960s from both the Communist Party and the Arab Nationalist Movement.

Thus, the terms and slogans of S. have, since the 1950s, been widely used in the Arab countries—both, for a version of populist military state S., as in Egypt, and in a variety of more extreme Maoist versions. However, in the context both of the nationalist struggle for liberation and of the governance of independent countries by military juntas, often brought to power by coups (Syria, Iraq, Sudan, Libya), factional politics and military might may be more decisive than the fine points of doctrinal and ideological debate in which they are superficially garbed.

In Turkey, S., together with Communism, is illegal and considered subversive, so no group can openly propagate it. Attempts to found socialist parties were suppressed several times. The Turkish Labour Party (Türk Is Partisi), established 1961, is regarded as socialist-leftist. In the elections of 1965, it gained 3–4% of the vote and 15 seats in the 450-member Parliament; in the elections of 1970 it received only 2% of the vote and two seats. In July 1971 it was outlawed. Kemal Ataturk's▷ People's Republican Party (Cumhuriyet Halk Partisi), under Ismet Inönü▷, has since 1964 described itself as left-of-center (with its left wing gaining the upper hand and rightist factions seceding or in opposition to the party leadership) and has absorbed some moderate socialist ideas.

In Persia, public figures interested in S. have been drawn mostly toward the communist Tudeh▷ party, banned since 1949. There have been several attempts to form non-communist socialist groups, such as a "Socialist Tudeh League", led by Khalil Maledi,

in the 1940s, or the "Toilers' Party" of Dr. Muzaffar Baqai and Khalil Maleki, in the 1950s; but democratic, non-communist S. has not become a strong political force. Dr. Mosaddeq's▷ "National Front" of the early 1950s was primarily motivated by nationalism, but its thinking contained some elements of S.; since its suppression by the Shah, in 1953, it has not regained its power.   (E.B.-Y.S.)

S. in Israel, and in the Zionist▷ movement which preceded it, is of the democratic type and European in origin. It is rooted in the tradition of Jewish suffering and rebellion against injustice, and inspired by the biblical prophets' vision of social justice. It grew out of Russian Socialist Zionism, based on the conviction that the Jewish problem could be solved only in a Jewish national territory, i.e. Palestine, and that national and social revival were interdependent.

Nahman Syrkin (1867–1924) was the first, in 1898, to use the term "Jewish Socialist State", and conceived it as being built on co-operative lines, with the help of national capital. He rejected—as did his followers Aharon David Gordon▷ (1856–1922) and Berl Katznelson▷ (1887–1944)—a communist dictatorship of the proletariat and Internationalism (inasmuch as it opposed a national revival). Ber Borochov (1881–1919) based his Socialist Zionism on the doctrines of Marxism and historical materialism. He and his followers, who founded the Po'alei Zion (Workers of Zion) party in 1906, held, without renouncing parliamentary and co-operative institutions, that national liberation could be achieved only through a revolutionary class struggle (part of that of the world's proletariat) to be conducted in Palestine by a newly created Jewish proletariat; that solidarity with the Arab workers should be achieved, and that the improvement of working conditions was the immediate task of the Jewish Labour Movement in Palestine. The party's main leaders were D. Ben-Gurion▷, B. Katznelson, Yitzhak Ben-Zvi▷. (A group of dissidents, establishing a left Po'alei Zion in 1920, sought membership in the Communist International as an autonomous unit, but this demand was rejected by the strictly anti-Zionist communists. The left Po'alei Zion remained a small, marginal faction.)

The mainstream of Zionist-Socialists, Po'alei Zion —merged in 1919–20 with smaller factions into Ahduth Ha'avodah▷ (Unity of Labour)—struggled for "Jewish Labour", i.e. the principle that Jewish enterprises, and particularly plantations and farms, should employ Jewish workers, so as to create a viable economy and a normally structured society and to prevent a colonial-type economy based on Jewish ownership and "native" labour. It also stressed labour settlement in pioneering co-operative villages based on socialist ideals. These endeavours were also stressed by another faction, *Hapo'el Hatza'ir* (The Young Worker), established 1905, which opposed *Po'alei Zion's* Marxist ideology and class struggle. Its members were among the founders of the first collective (*Kibbutz*▷): Degania, 1909 and the first smallholder co-operative (*Moshav*): Nahalal, 1921. Its mentor was A. D. Gordon, who stressed the creative revolutionary value of manual labour, work on the land and the return to nature—both as a moral justification for the Jewish claim to Palestine and as the road to the moral and spiritual revival of the Jewish people. Chaim Arlosoroff▷ (1899–1933), another leader of *Hapo'el Hatza'ir*, advocated Reformist S.

Ahduth Ha'avodah and *Hapo'el Hatza'ir* jointly founded, in 1920, the General Federation of Jewish Labour (*Histadrut*▷), which became the main organization of the Jewish Labour Movement, its trade unions—active also in social security and welfare, co-operatives, settlement and economic enterprise. In 1930 the two parties merged to form *Mapai*▷ (*Mifleget Po'alei Eretz-Israel*, Palestine Workers' Party). Affiliated to the Socialist International, *Mapai* became the leading force both in the *Histadrut* and in the national parliamentary and executive organs of the Jews of Palestine and later of Israel. (For splits of *Mapai*, factions seceding, and their reunion, in 1968, as the Israel Labour Party, see Zionism▷, and Israel▷.)

Hashomer Hatza'ir (The Young Watchman) was a left-wing Socialist party with a Marxist and pro-Soviet orientation. It grew out of a youth movement of the same name, formed a *kibbutz* movement, 1927, and established itself as a political party in 1946. It also advocated a compromise with the Arabs of Palestine on the basis of a bi-national▷ state. It merged with other leftist factions, in 1948, to form *Mapam*▷ (*Mifleget Po'alim Me'uhedet*, United Workers' Party)—see Israel▷, Parties. For the Communist Party in Palestine, and later Israel, see Communism▷.

Within Israel's society and economy—which combines free enterprise in a private sector with a state sector and a co-operative labour sector—socialist ideas and the labour movement have remained strong and influential. (For labour's direct role in the economy, see *Histadrut*▷.) The *kibbutz* and the *moshav* have developed into highly successful nuclei and examples of a new pattern of Socialist co-operative living, arousing much interest outside Israel. *Mapai* (since 1968 the Israel Labour Party) has always been Israel largest single party. Owing to Israel's electoral system of proportional representation, it has never had an absolute majority in Parliament, but in all the coalition governments formed

since the establishment of the State, 1948, it, *i.e.* the Socialist labour movement, has always been the dominant partner; the Premier and the Foreign, Defence and Finance ministers have always been leaders of the Labour Party. The State has, therefore, been fashioned in the image of its social-democratic and welfare-state principles. (E.L.)

*SOCOTRA. Island in the Indian Ocean, *c.* 140 mi. from the Horn of Africa, 250 mi. from the coast of southern Arabia. Area: 1,382 sq. mi. pop.: *c.* 15,000 (Arabs, Africans, some people of Portuguese ancestry). S. came under British protection in the late 19th century when the Mahri Sultanate of Qishn, to which it belonged, became part of the Eastern Aden▷ Protectorate (see South Arabia▷); since Nov. 1967 it has been part of the independent Republic of South Yemen▷. According to 1970 reports, unconfirmed so far, S. has been placed at the disposal of the USSR as a naval base. (Y.S.)

SOUTH ARABIA, FEDERATION OF (*Ittihad al-Janub al-'Arabi*). Formed under British guidance, between 1959 and 1965, out of the majority of the sultanates, amirates and tribal sheikhdoms of the Aden▷ protectorates. By 1965, it comprised an area of *c.* 61,000 sq. mi. and a population of around 700,000, consisting mainly of nomadic tribes. In Feb. 1959, six units of the Western Aden Protectorate formed the "Federation of Arab Amirates of the South". The six were the amirates of Beihan and Dali', the sultanates of Audhali, Fadli and Lower Yafi' and the Sheikhdom of Upper 'Aulaqi. In Apr. 1962 the Federation changed its name to "F. of SA". During the 1960s nine more units of the Western Protectorate joined the F.: the sultanates of Lahaj 1959, Lower 'Aulaqi 1960, Hawshabi 1963 and Upper 'Aulaqi 1965; the sheikhdoms of 'Aqrabi 1960, Sha'ib 1963, 'Alawi and Mufalahi 1965, and the states of Dathina 1960. Fifteen units of the Western Protectorate had now joined; only the Sultanate of Upper Yafi' stayed outside the F. However, of the four principalities of the Eastern Protectorate, only the Sultanate of Wahidi joined, 1962. Aden town, a Crown Colony, decided to join in Sept. 1962 and did so formally in Jan. 1963 (acquiring the status of a Federal State). By 1965 the F. comprised 17 members.

Aden's decision to join was controversial. The nationalists bitterly opposed it, considering it a British plot to submerge the politically advanced and sophisticated town of Aden in the backward, autocratic Federation subservient to the British (see South Yemen▷, Political History). A majority in favour of the F. had been obtained in the Aden Legislative Council only by including a provision enabling Aden to secede within seven years if the Council felt she were being unfairly treated and her interests were being harmed. The Federal political structure indeed reflected Britain's intention of assimilating the potentially revolutionary Aden in the conservative hinterland. The Federal Legislature—named the Federal Council (*Majlis al-Ittihad*)—consisted of 103 members, only 24 of whom were from Aden; and the Executive—the Supreme Federal Council (*Majlis al-Ittihad al-'Ali*)—had 15 members, only four of whom were Adenis. On 29 Nov. 1961 a Federal Army was created out of the former Aden Protectorate Levies, formed in 1928; it was under the nominal control of the federal authorities, but was in fact under British command. On 1 June 1967 the five battalions of the Federal Army joined four battalions of "Federal Guards" (raised by the various petty rulers) to create a 9,000-man strong South Arabian Army.

The Federal structure remained weak: the diverging interests of the various sheikhdoms were dominant and no strong federal establishment was created. The chairmanship of the Executive (*i.e.* Premiership) was held in monthly rotation by the members of the Supreme Council, and no one was prepared to serve as President. The insurgent nationalists regarded the F. as a creation of British colonialism and wanted to destroy it. Their guerilla war, 1963–7, was directed against the F. no less than the British. After 1964, when Britain announced her intention of leaving SA by 1968, the degree of British help to be expected after the envisaged transfer of power to the Federal Government became doubtful and controversial. A treaty between Britain and the F. proposed and tentatively agreed to in 1964, was never ratified. A UN mission which visited Aden in Apr. 1967 did not recognize the Federal Government. Between Aug. and Sept. 1967, the nationalist NLF▷ overran one South Arabian sultanate after another and the Federal authorities collapsed. Britain had to admit that collapse in Sept. 1967 and to negotiate a transfer of power to the NLF. When, on 29 Nov. 1967, independence was attained, the Federal structure was abolished and SA was renamed the "People's Republic of South Yemen". (Y.A.O.)

*SOUTH YEMEN, PEOPLE'S REPUBLIC OF
(since Nov. 1970: People's Democratic Republic of Yemen). Country in the Southern part of the Arabian peninsula, between the Red Sea and the Sultanate of Muscat (Masqat)-and-'Oman. SY is made up of the former Colony of Aden▷ and the Western and Eastern Aden protectorates (including those that had not joined the Federation of South Arabia▷), and the offshore islands of Perim▷. Qamran and Soco-

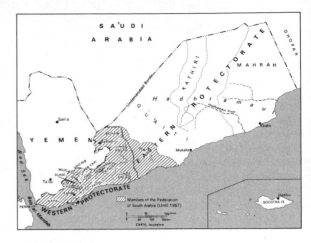

Map of South Yemen

tra▷. She became independent in Nov. 1967. Area: 116,000 sq. mi. SY is bordered by Yemen, Sa'udi Arabia and the Sultanate of Muscat-and-'Oman. The only demarcated border is part of the Yemen border. Pop.: 1.25m. (1967). Main town: Aden—pop.: 250,000 (1965). Capital: *Madinat al-Sha'b* (Arabic: People's Town; former name: *al-Ittihad*), adjacent to Aden. Outside Aden the population is almost 100% Arab, and consists mainly of Shafe'i▷ Sunni Muslims; the population of Aden also includes Yemenis, tribesmen from the hinterland, and non-Arab Indians, Pakistanis and Somalis; nearly all the Europeans and Jews left Aden after independence in 1967. There is a sharp contrast between rich, modern Aden town and the underdeveloped, poor and traditionally tribal hinterland. SY derives its main revenues from Aden harbour and the oil refineries.

POLITICAL HISTORY. Britain briefly took control of Perim Island in 1799 with the intention of preventing Napoleon from passing through the Straits of Bab al-Mandeb▷. In 1839, the Government of Bombay Province, in British India, acquired Aden town from the Sultan of Lahaj, mainly for use as a coal depot. Aden remained under the jurisdiction of the Bombay government till 1932. As its importance grew, particularly after the opening of the Suez Canal, 1869, Britain signed almost 30 separate treaties by which the sultans, sheikhs, sharifs and amirs of the town's hinterland accepted varying degrees of British protection. Most of these were Shafe'i Muslims who resisted the intrusions of both the Zeidi▷ Imams of Yemen and the Ottoman Empire. Backed by Britain, these tribal leaders successfully foiled Ottoman penetration of South Arabia in the 1870s and an attempt to conquer Aden in 1915 (although Ottoman troops succeeded in capturing Lahaj). The Yemeni Imam Yahya▷ claimed that South Arabia was an integral part of Yemen, but his demands were rejected by South Arabia's petty rulers.

In 1932 the administration of Aden was transferred from Bombay Province to the Governor General of India. Five years later, in 1937, Aden became a Crown Colony, and the hinterland was termed the Western and Eastern Aden Protectorates.

Britain maintained stronger contacts with the chiefs of the Western Aden Protectorate, the immediate hinterland of Aden town. In the early 1950s the Colonial Office proposed to create in the Western Protectorate a federation which would later become a member of the British Commonwealth; but this proposition was opposed by the tribal leaders who disliked the increasing British interference. After the Suez crisis of 1956–7, Britain suggested the creation of a federation which would later become an independent Arab state linked with Britain only by treaty. The Sultans, who were under growing leftist and Nasserist pressure, now accepted Britain's offer. In 1959 six sultanates formed the "Federation of Arab Amirates of the South". Other sultanates joined the Federation—which changed its name in Apr. 1962, to the "Federation of South Arabia"▷—and by 1965 there were 17 members; 15 from the Western Protectorate (listed in the entry on South Arabia), one from the Eastern Protectorate and Aden town. This last was transformed from a Crown Colony into a Federal State in January 1963. One sultanate of the Western Protectorate and three of the Eastern Protectorate refused to join the Federation. The Federation had a Legislative Council and an Executive Council; but all attempts to form a strong government failed. The presidency remained vacant and the premiership was held in rotation. A political party, the United National Party (UNP, *al-Hizb al-Ittihadi al-Watani*), had been formed mainly by middle-class pro-British and Federalist Adenis, but it had little influence.

The Eastern Aden Protectorate consists mostly of deserts and barren hills, with some fertile valleys of which the most important is the Hadhramaut. It is made up of the four sultanates of Wahidi, Qu'aiti, Kathiri and Mahra (including the island of Socotra▷). The main town and harbour is Mukalla, in the Qu'aiti State. Sa'udi Arabia claimed the Hadhramaut▷ as part of her territory. Britain was interested in pacifying the area and strengthening it against the Sa'udi claims. Between 1936 and 1939 Harold Ingrans, the British Political Officer in Mukalla, signed about 1,400 treaties with local tribal leaders obliging them to stop fighting among themselves. The chief sultans accepted British protection and the tutelage of the British Governor of Aden. In 1940, Britain raised a military force of *c.* 1,500 men, the Hadhrami Legion. Wahidi was the only one of the four Eastern Protectorate sultanates willing to join the Federation.

In Aden town, administered as a colony, the constitutional progress was that of paternalistic, British-guided gradualism: a Legislative Council, initially composed of "official" (*i.e.* colonial government officers) and non-official members, was established in 1946–7. Reforms of 1955 and 1957 reduced the number of official members and increased, among the non-official ones, the number of elected members, until they formed a majority; the electorate, however, remained restricted. At the same time the Governor's Council, originally consisting of colonial officials only, was gradually enlarged to include representatives of local notables, and finally—members of the Legislative Council; it became a "Council of Ministers" in 1961, and its chairmanship passed from the Governor to a "Chief Minister" in 1963. The British wanted Aden to join the Federation—a highly controversial proposal, as the character and interests of the colony and the tribal sultanates were quite different: the latter were economically and socially backward, under the mediaeval autocracy of their desert chieftains, but enjoyed a larger degree of independence from Britain; while the former was economically more developed, socially sophisticated, politically active, but under a colonial form of government. Yet, in 1962–3 Britain succeeded in persuading the Aden government and Legislative Council to approve Aden's entry into the Federation —with its weight in the Federation's councils much less than that merited by its population, strength and economic contribution. The Crown Colony now became a Federal State and the British Governor's title was chanted to that of High Commissioner.

Nationalists, both in the sultanates of the protectorates and, particularly, among the urban population of Aden, were dissatisfied and clamoured for faster progress towards complete independence and the liquidation of British tutelage and privileges. Most of them believed that violence and insurgency were the only ways to achieve their aims.

The first insurgent organization, formed in 1951 in the Lahaj Sultanate, was the "South Arabian League" (SAL), led by Muhammad 'Ali al-Jifri and Sheikhan al-Habshi and backed by Egypt. Following the Yemen revolution of 1962, Egyptian support was transferred to a new and more militant organization—the NLF▷ (the National Liberation Front for Occupied SY, founded in 1963 and led by Qahtan al-Sha'bi▷. On 14 Oct. 1963 in the Radfan mountains north of Aden, Sha'bi proclaimed an "armed struggle" against the Federation and against any British presence; later the main focus of insurgent activities shifted to Aden town.

In Feb. 1965, the British High Commissioner attempted to appease the insurgents and invited 'Abd-ul-Qawwi Makkawi▷, leader of the opposition in the Legislative Council, to form the Aden government. But insurgent activities increased, Makkawi gave them his open support, and in Sept. 1965 the High Commissioner dismissed Makkawi, the government and the Legislative Council, suspended the constitution and ruled by decree. Makkawi became a voluntary exile.

The Yemeni minority constituting almost half of Aden's population, and deprived of electoral rights provided many insurgents. About 25,000 of them were members of the "Aden Trades Union Congress" (ATUC), led by 'Abdullah al-Asnaj. The first of these trade unions had been organized in 1953 with British support, but gradually ATUC had adopted a leftist and pro-Nasserist line. It also founded, in 1962, a political wing, the "People's Socialist Party" (PSP). In May 1965, the PSP united with the SAL to form the "Organization for the Liberation of the Occupied South" (OLOS). A few months later the SAL, which now supported the sultans and was considered conservative, seceded. Egypt sponsored a successful effort to unite all the insurgent organizations (except for the SAL), and in Jan. 1966, the OLOS—now made up mainly of PSP followers—and the NLF merged to form FLOSY▷ (Front for the Liberation of Occupied SY, *Jabhat Tahrir Janub al-Yaman al-Muhtall*). The deposed Prime Minister, 'Abd-ul-Qawwi Makkawi, headed the Political Bureau, and 'Abdullah Asnaj became Secretary-General. FLOSY continued the "armed struggle" against Britain and the Federation; but it favoured the union of South Arabia with Yemen and it accepted Egyptian guidance. These two issues, and factional struggles, destroyed the recently achieved unity: late in 1966 the NLF split from FLOSY and the two organizations engaged each other in a struggle for supremacy. FLOSY and Egypt did not recognize the separate existence of the NLF (Radio Cairo, for instance, ignored its activities or credited them to FLOSY).

Between 1964 and 1967 insurgent activities had greatly increased. Since the early 1960s, the South Arabian problem had also been raised at the UN—mainly by the Arab states, none of which recognized the Federation. (The Arab League▷ had denounced the Federation as "a creation of British imperialism and colonialism".)

The UN Special Committee on Colonialism (the "Committee of 24"), and subsequently the General Assembly, endorsed in 1963 a report claiming that large parts of the South Arabian population disliked the existing regime and that the Federation was designed to prolong British rule in the area. British-Federal consultations in 1964 resulted in a British promise to grant independence, evacuate South Arabia and hand over power to the Federation by 1968. But in 1965 the UN General Assembly adopted a resolution urging elections and affirming the "inalienable right of the (South Arabian) people to self-determination and freedom from colonial rule" and demanding the "immediate and complete removal of the British bases". A similar resolution was adopted in 1966. Britain accepted the UN resolutions—in Feb. 1966, again stating that she would withdraw by 1968—and agreed to some UN supervision of the election and self-determination process. In Apr. 1967, a UN mission came to Aden for a three weeks stay for consultations concerning the organization of elections; but because of insurgent activities and a dispute with the British and Federal authorities, the mission left after a few days. Both FLOSY and the NLF refused to meet the mission, because it would not forego all contacts with the sultans. The UN mission thus played no part in the shaping of events. In Feb. 1967 the British Foreign Secretary reiterated that Britain would leave South Arabia by 1968, transferring power to the Federal Government, to whom financial and military support was also promised. During summer 1967, most Federal Ministers were out of the country—for discussions with the UN mission (in Europe) and Britain, and to make a (vain) attempt (supported by Britain) to contact the nationalists and arrange for a broad-based coalition of all groups.

Egyptian support for FLOSY was withdrawn after the evacuation of the Egyptian expeditionary force from Yemen, 1967. Seizing this opportunity the NLF took over most of the South Arabian sultanates. When the NLF emerged as the stronger force, the Federal Army and the ATUC gave it their support and the sultans and Federal ministers who were not captured by the NLF fled the country. Egypt, who had previously ignored the NLF, now lent it her support. Britain had, on 5 Sept. 1967, to acknowledge the complete collapse of the Federal regime and to recognize the nationalists as the group with whom Britain would negotiate the transfer of power; in November, she had to state that negotiations would be conducted with the NLF alone. Negotiations were held in Geneva that same month and it was decided that independence would be granted to South Arabia at midnight on 29 Nov. 1967. The new State was named the PR of SY, and Qahtan al-Sha'bi became its first President, Prime Minister and Commander of the Armed Forces. The Republic was immediately admitted to membership of the UN and the Arab League.

The situation in SY deteriorated during her first year of independence. She had few, if any, economic resources of her own; British aid was meagre, and was soon stopped because of incessant disputes; her only economic asset—Aden's position as a transit and refuelling port—was placed in jeopardy by the closure of the Suez Canal. Government attempts to remedy the situation by tax increases and a reduction of salaries were unsuccessful. At the same time, moderate and extreme-leftist factions within the NFL were fighting for power; this caused instability and two unsuccessful rebellions during 1968. In June 1969, a coup replaced President Qahtan al-Sha'bi and his government with a more extremist leftist presidential Council and government under Muhammad 'Ali Haitham and Salem Rabi'.

During these first years an attempt was made to abolish the traditional tribal system by the liquidation of the former sultanates and the re-division of the country into six new governorates. The former sultans, Federal ministers, SAL and FLOSY leaders were purged, jailed or sentenced to death and their property was confiscated. In addition to their past sins they were accused of plotting and attempting rebellion against the new State—in collusion with Sa'udi Arabia and "the imperialists". Though the new country had adopted the name "SY" to show that it wished to be united with Yemen, no practical steps were taken towards this end, and relations with Yemen remained cool and tense. In Nov. 1970 SY renamed herself "People's Democratic Republic of Yemen"—a step resented by Yemen. Relations with Sa'udi Arabia, SY's other neighbour, were hostile; Sa'udi Arabia did not even recognize SY and a border dispute soon arose. Relations with Egypt were correct but reserved; though SY applied for assistance, Egypt gave her little help. Some assistance, economic and particularly military, was given by the USSR; and a close relationship developed between SY and China, who also granted aid. According to unconfirmed reports, the USSR is building a naval base on SY's Socotra Island. Relations with the USA were severed by SY in Oct. 1969. SY also recognized East Germany to symbolize her leftist sympathies. Late in 1969, SY enacted far-reaching measures of nationalization.

SY adopted an extreme anti-Israel line and even threatened to bar Israeli vessels from the Straits of Bab al-Mandeb. A bazooka attack by a Palestinian-Arab guerilla group (the PFLP▷) on a Liberian oil tanker on its way to Israel, June 1971, in this area, seems to have been supported, at least tacitly, by SY. SY is also reported to support actively the revolutionary guerrilla groups operating in the Persian Gulf▷ and particularly in the Dhofar▷ region of Muscat-and-'Oman▷.   (Y.A.O.)

*SOVIET INTERESTS AND POLICIES IN THE ME.—see Russia▷.

SPAIN, SPANISH INTERESTS AND POLICIES IN THE ME. S.'s involvement in ME affairs is mainly due to her part in Moroccan affairs (outside the scope of this Encyclopaedia. S. handed over to Morocco her Protectorate in the north in 1956, and the one in south Morocco in the years following. The Spanish enclave in Sidi Ifni was transferred to Morocco in 1969. The future of Spanish Sahara, south of Morocco, is still in dispute. A number of towns ("presidios") held by S. on Morocco's northern Mediterranean coast (Ceuta, Melilla, and others) are also liable to pose a serious problem; S. views them as S. soil, but it is not likely that Morocco will accept this for long. Despite her colonial past in Morocco and outstanding problems that may become serious conflicts, S. has succeeded in maintaining the status of a friend of Morocco; she even kept fairly good relations with the nationalist movement while still ruling her protectorates.

S.'s Moroccan interests induced her to adopt a position of friendship and support in regard to the other Arab states as well, both in the *Maghreb*▷ and the ME. Even the leftist-revolutionary regimes maintain friendly relations with ultra-rightist S. S. economic interests have penetrated the ME to a limited extent; a S. oil company operated in Kuwait, in co-operation with the national company there. In contrast to the friendly relations with the Arab states, and apparently chiefly because of them, S. has refused to establish official relations with Israel. Israel also hesitated during the first years of her existence, to establish relations because of S.'s fascist past, but in recent years Israel has evidently become interested in normal relations with S.   (Y.S.)

STACK, SIR LEE (1868–1924). British soldier and administrator. Transferred to the Egyptian Army in 1902, and to the Sudan government service in 1904. Served as agent of the Sudanese Government in Cairo and director of military intelligence 1908–14; civil secretary of the Sudanese government 1914–17; Governor-General of Sudan and Commander-in-Chief (*Sirdar*) of the Egyptian Army (1917–24. His assassination in Cairo by an Egyptian nationalist, in Nov. 1924, created a grave crisis in Anglo-Egyptian relations (see Egypt▷, History).   (B.G.)

STERN GROUP (Hebrew: *Lohamei Herut Yisrael*, LHY, "Fighters for the Freedom of Israel"). Zionist militant underground organization founded in Palestine by Avraham S., one of the first commanders of *Irgun (T)zeva'i Le'umi*▷, (IZL, *Etzel*), who broke away in 1939 because IZL had called off its campaign against the British Mandatory authorities for the duration of World War II. S. was killed in 1942 by the British while a prisoner.) S. maintained that Britain's enemies should become allies of the Jews and consequently LHY tried (unsuccessfully) to reach an agreement on co-operation with Italy. Although never numbering more than 300 members, LHY created much trouble for the British authorities.

Except for a short period after World War II (November 1945 to July 1946), when LHY co-operated with the *Hagana*▷ and IZL in militant underground activities against the British, it was banned and denounced by the Jewish national leadership in Palestine. Two of LHY's most dramatic actions were the assassination of Lord Moyne, the British Minister for the ME, in Cairo, on 1 Nov. 1944 (the assailants were tried and executed), and the assassination in Jerusalem in 1948 of the UN Mediator, Count Folke Bernadotte▷ (the assailants remained unknown). The latter operation caused the Israel government to disband LHY and arrest its leaders (they were released soon afterwards). Shortly after this, LHY virtually ceased to exist.   (A. W.-E. L.)

STRAITS. There are a number of politically significant S. in the ME: the S. of Tiran▷, Bab al-Mandab▷, the S. of Hormuz (linking the Persian Gulf with the Gulf of 'Oman). "The S." without specification usually refer to the Bosphorus▷ and the Dardanelles▷.   (Y. S.)

*SUDAN. Republic (since 1969—"Democratic Republic") in north-east Africa. Pop.: 14.3m. (1967 estimate), about two-thirds of whom are Arabic-speaking Muslims and almost one-third Nilotic, Nilo-Hamitic and Sudanic groups, non-Muslim and non-Arab, speaking a variety of Central African languages. The majority of the latter live in the South and are —apart from nearly ½ m. Christians—pagans.

Religion (1967 estimate): Muslims—10,250,000; Animists—3,640,000 ; Catholics—250,000 ; Protestants—150,000 ; Greek Orthodox—18,000 ; Jews—300. Area : 967,500 sq. mi. S. is bordered in the east by Ethiopia and the Red Sea, in the south by Kenya, Uganda and Congo (Kinshasa), in the west by Chad, the Central African Republic and Libya, and in the north by Egypt.

S. has existed as a political entity in its present borders since 1899 (when she was re-conquered by Anglo-Egyptian forces, after the *Mahdi*'s▷ rule). She attained independence in Jan. 1956, and became a member of the UN on 12 Nov. 1956.

S.'s economy is almost entirely agricultural, and to a large extent pastoral. The most important cash crop is cotton which accounts for about half of the country's exports. In the south coffee, tea and tobacco are grown. Between 80% and 90% of the world's supply of gum arabic comes from S. There is, however, little industry.

POLITICAL HISTORY. S.—*Bilad al-S.* (Arabic: "Land of the Blacks")—is the name given by mediaeval Muslim geographers to the region lying south of the Sahara Desert and Egypt. The western part, extending to the Senegal and Niger rivers, was under French domination until the 1960s when this area became the independent states of Chad, Niger and Mali. Eastern S. or S. in the more restricted sense used from the end of the 19th century, comprises the territories south of Egypt, under joint Anglo-Egyptian rule ("Condominium") from 1899 till 1955.

Muhammad 'Ali, the Ottoman Sultan's Viceroy in Egypt, who became an autonomous ruler, coveted S. because of her wealth, especially precious metals and slaves, as well as for reasons of prestige and strategy. Between 1820 and 1822 his expeditionary forces conquered the north-central areas of the country, *i.e.* Nubia, Sennar and Kordofan. A second phase of Egyptian penetration into S. took place during the reign of the Khedive Isma'il (1863–79), when the provinces of Darfur, Bahr al-Ghazal and Equatoria and the Red Sea port of Suakin were added to the Khedivial possessions.

Egyptian rule impoverished S., especially through the slave trade. The bitterness which the population felt towards the occupants was one of the reasons for the rebellion of the *Mahdi*, who took advantage of the power vacuum created by the deposition of the Khedive Isma'il (1879) and the resignation of the dynamic Governor-General of S., Gen. Charles Gordon, an Englishman, who was then in the service of Isma'il.

The rebellion grew out of a fanatical Islamic-revivalist movement. Its leader, Muhammad Ahmad Ibn-'Abdullah, claimed to be the *Mahdi*▷ (Arabic: The Guided One), the divine leader chosen by God at the end of time to fill the earth with justice. In Aug. 1881 the *Mahdi*'s followers (*al-Ansar*▷—Arabic: Helpers, after the first supporters of the Prophet Muhammad) defeated the troops sent against them, later took the initiative and in 1882–83 conquered most of Kordofan, Darfur and the Bahr al-Ghazal. The British, who had occupied Egypt in 1882 (although nominally it remained part of the Ottoman Empire), recommended the evacuation of the rest of S. and re-appointed Gen. Gordon to organize this. Gordon negotiated with the *Mahdi* but failed to reach a compromise. In Jan. 1885, the *Mahdi*'s troops conquered Khartoum and massacred its garrison including Gordon. The *Mahdi* died in the same year and his successor, the *Khalifa* 'Abdullahi, ruled till the liquidation of the *Mahdist* state in 1898.

Map of Sudan

In 1896 the British government decided to re-conquer S., mainly to prevent other powers (Germany, Italy, Belgium and especially France) from taking over the vital area of the sources of the Nile. To avoid conflict with other European powers, the conquest was carried out in Egypt's name, to re-impose Egyptian control over what was described as Egyptian territory temporarily occupied by *Mahdist* rebels. The expeditionary force, composed of British and Egyptian troops under the command of Sir Herbert Kitchener, took Khartoum in Sept. 1898 and by the end of that year the remaining *Mahdist* forces were defeated and the *Khalifa* 'Abdullahi was killed. The *Mahdiyya* later became a peaceful sect, although still very influential; it was opposed by the *Mirghaniyya*▷ or *Khatmiyya*▷ sect.

The foundations of the new regime in S. were laid by an agreement signed by Britain and Egypt in Jan. 1899, establishing their joint rule over S. This form of government was favoured by Britain because the mere restoration of the former Ottoman-Egyptian regime overthrown by the *Mahdist* forces would have left Britain's presence in S. without legal basis; the imposition of British sovereignty, on the other hand, would have aroused the hostility of the Egyptians, the Sudanese, the Ottomans, the French and other European powers. However, the agreement stressed the position acquired by Britain through its participation in the reconquest of S., and gave

Britain *de facto* control. S. was to be governed by a Governor-General, appointed by the Egyptian Khedive on the recommendation of the British Government. The Governor-General, who held both executive and legislative powers, was always British, and until 1926 the post was entrusted to the British C-in-C of the Egyptian Army (the *Sirdar*). In Mar. 1899 Britain also concluded an agreement with France providing for the evacuation of the French forces which had conquered the Sudanese town of Fashoda, an event which brought Britain and France to the brink of war. In 1901 and 1902 agreements were concluded with Italy and Ethiopia respectively, fixing the Sudanese borders with Eritrea and Ethiopia.

Great Britain set up a colonial-type regime in S., the Anglo-Egyptian partnership being virtually fictitious. The administration of the country was carried out along military lines, because there were frequent uprisings and pacification was completed only at the end of World War I.

At a rather late stage a nationalist movement came into being, stimulated by the presence of Egyptian Army officers and civil servants (confined generally to lower and middle ranks). In 1921, 'Ali 'Abd-ul-Latif, a former army officer, created a "Sudanese United Tribes Society", which demanded independence for the Sudanese nation. He was imprisoned and after his release he created, 1924, a "White Flag League" aiming to establish S. not as an independent state but as part of a Nile Valley freed from British occupation and united under the Egyptian Crown. Supported by Egyptian circles both within and outside the country, it organized anti-British demonstrations in which military school cadets were active. The British imprisoned 'Abd-ul-Latif again and suppressed the beginnings of the national movement.

On 19 Nov. 1924 Sir Lee Stack, the Governor-General of S. and *Sirdar* of the Egyptian Army, was assassinated in Cairo by Egyptian nationalists. In retaliation the British compelled all Egyptian troops and civil servants to evacuate S. (amidst renewed anti-British demonstrations). As anti-British agitation was mainly conducted by educated Sudanese in the cities, the British encouraged tribalism and tribal institutions and started ruling through local chiefs and sheikhs, thus creating an alternative to bureaucratic government which would have necessitated the cultivation of a class of urban educated Sudanese. Courses for training Sudanese administrators were discontinued, the Khartoum military college was closed down and harsh discipline was introduced at the Gordon Memorial College of Khartoum, an institution opened in 1902 for the training of artisans and junior officials, which had become a breeding-ground of Sudanese nationalism.

After 1924 Sudanese nationalism stagnated. From the mid-'30s on, its main organization was the "Graduates' Congress' once more based at Gordon College. Nationalist activity was revived after World War II when a decision concerning S.'s future seemed imminent. Nationalism was now faced with the alternatives of an independent state, or "Union of the Nile Valley", i.e. union with Egypt. Those favouring the latter seem to have conceived it as a weapon against Britain rather than as a serious political commitment to Egypt. Most of the supporters of an independent S. joined the Umma (Nation) Party, under 'Abdullah al-Khalil▷, while the pro-Egyptian group, under Isma'il al-Azhari▷, formed the Al-Ashiqqa' (the Brethren), which had grown out of the "Graduates' Congress". (Both camps, though, were continuously splitting into many rival factions.) Of the religious orders, the Mahdist al-Ansar supported independence, while the rival al-Mirghaniyya supported the pro-Egyptian camp.

The British started a gradual transition to partial autonomy by establishing in 1943 an Advisory Council for northern S. In 1948 a Legislative Assembly was established for the whole of S. The transfer of power was slow, however, and caused perilous friction with Egypt which regarded S. as part of a United Nile Valley, whose political future was linked to Egypt, and objected to any form of self-rule under British tutelage. The pro-Egyptian factions in S. also boycotted the legislative elections of 1948 and the assembly deriving from them. (The Sudanese members of the government—the Governor-General's Executive Council—were not, as a rule, political personalities.)

A turning point was the July 1952 coup in Egypt. The new rulers agreed to grant the Sudanese the right of self-determination, as they were eager to get the British out of S. as soon as possible. Late in 1952 they concluded an accord with the Sudanese parties, and on 12 Feb. 1953 Egypt and Britain signed an agreement about the future of S. A transition period of three years was set to prepare the ground for the act of self-determination that would decide the future of S. (independence or union with Egypt). During the transition period the administration would be transferred to the Sudanese, and elections held under international supervision. British and Egyptian troops would be evacuated as soon as the Sudanese Parliament should decide that "Sudanization" was completed and the time for self-determination had come. Two international commissions were to assist that transition. Elections took place in Nov. 1953, and al-Azhari's pro-Egyptian party—by now called "National Unionists"—won an absolute majority. In Jan. 1954 Azhari became the first Prime Minister of S.

The process of Sudanization of the administration was considered completed in Aug. 1955; Parliament demanded the evacuation of British and Egyptian troops and this was effected by Nov. 1955. Parliament and the government also demanded a simplification of the complicated constitutional procedure originally set for self-determination, and in the end it was agreed that S.'s future would be decided by a vote in Parliament. It was now quite clear that al-Azhari and his supporters had changed their minds about a union with Egypt and preferred complete independence. A resolution to that effect was unanimously adopted by Parliament on 19 Dec. 1955 and on 1 Jan. 1956 S. became formally independent.

Soon after achieving independence, Premier al-Azhari lost his parliamentary majority as his "National Unionist Party" split and lost the support of the Khatmiyya order, generally considered pro-Egyptian. He had to form a coalition government that included 'Abdullah Khalil's Umma party. In July 1956 a new coalition was formed by the Umma and the "People's Democratic Party" founded by seceding members of the NUP and supported by the Khatmiyya; 'Abdullah Khalil became Prime Minister. The same coalition returned to power following the elections of Feb. 1958, but its stability was threatened by disagreements between its partners over both domestic and foreign affairs. Thus the suggested appointment of the Mahdist leader 'Abd-ul-Rahman al-Mahdi▷ as President of the Republic was strongly opposed by the PDP and had to be shelved. The Umma party—pro-British and keen to strengthen ties with the West—also clashed with the PDP's pro-Egyptian and neutralist-leftist orientation. The threat of an economic crisis, caused mainly by a poor cotton crop, induced Premier Khalil to appeal for US economic aid; he was opposed by his coalition partners, and to maintain his parliamentary majority, had to win the support of the representatives of the south—in exchange for a pledge to discuss the introduction of a federal constitution. The coalition, and the Premier's position, were again soon threatened by feelers put out by some leaders of his own party for a new coalition with the NUP. In October talks were held in Cairo between President Nasser▷, al-Azhari and PDP leaders, causing further concern to the Prime Minister and to a number of senior army officers who feared the increase of Egypt's political influence in S. On 16 Nov. the two main parties—the Umma and the NUP—agreed to form a coalition. But their agreement was thwarted by a military coup on 17 Nov. 1958. It has been suggested—but never proved—that 'Abdullah Khalil had a hand in the coup.

The leader of the coup, Gen. Ibrahim 'Abbud▷, proclaimed his intention of saving the country from the "degeneration, chaos and instability" into which the rivalries of the parties and the self-seeking intrigues of the politicians had led it. All political parties were abolished and all political activity was banned. Parliament was dissolved and the constitution suspended. A "Supreme Council of the Armed Forces", composed of twelve officers under the leadership of Gen. 'Abbud as President, ruled the country. The council formally delegated to him all legislative, judicial and executive powers, as well as the command of the armed forces. A cabinet of twelve ministers—seven officers and five civilians—was formed, with 'Abbud as Premier.

'Abbud's military dictatorship, which was rather mild and conservative, lasted for nearly six years. Several abortive military coups were crushed by 'Abbud in 1959. Fifteen prominent former politicians were arrested in 1961 for causing agitation and unrest, but they were released a year later. There was no progress towards constitutional rule or the resumption of political life, little economic advance—and the problem of southern S., to be discussed below, appeared to be deteriorating. The southern tribes were in open rebellion since Sept. 1963.

A coup broke out in Oct. 1964 sparked off by the troubles in the southern provinces and by the general discontent with the economic situation, inefficiency and corruption. Politicians, university students and workers started campaigning for an end to military government and the restoration of democracy. On 21 Oct. police fired on demonstrators, killing one student. A general strike was called immediately and Gen. 'Abbud was forced to negotiate with a common front comprising all the old parties and supported by the heads of the two religious orders. It was agreed that 'Abbud would stay on as President but hand over executive power to a transitional government composed of all parties and including, for the first time, the Communist Party and the "Muslim Brotherhood"▷. Within four weeks, however, 'Abbud had to dismiss all his officers. The presidency reverted to a five-member Council.

The transitional government put much emphasis on the problem of southern S. and tried—unsuccessfully—to solve it with the help of southern leaders. The freedom of the press was restored and the ban on political parties was abolished. In June 1965 elections were held, in which all parties, except the PDP, participated. As no party won an absolute majority, a coalition was formed between the Umma party, with 76 seats and the NUP, 53 seats. Muhammad Ahmad Mahjoub (Umma) became Prime Minister and al-Azhari (NUP) permanent chairman of the Presidential Council. The new regime was torn between rightist and leftist factions. In Nov. 1965, the

Communist Party was declared illegal. The decision was contested in court, which declared it null and void. However, after a protracted dispute with the judiciary, the court's judgement was overruled by the Assembly, which reimposed the ban on the Communist Party.

In the meantime, the Umma party was again split. A right wing under the leader of the Mahdiyya Order, the Imam al-Hadi al-Mahdi▷ supported the Premier, Mahjoub, while younger elements followed the Imam's nephew, the progressive Sadeq al-Mahdi▷ who wished to modernize S. He became Prime Minister after a vote of no confidence forced Mahjoub to resign, July 1966. The new government, also a coalition of the Umma and the NUP, was able to improve the economic situation owing to strict controls and loans from the World Bank. It also promised to solve the question of southern S., by a degree of regional autonomy. The drafting of a permanent constitution was speeded up. However, as the Imam withdrew his support from his nephew, one faction of the Umma party voted against the government and it was defeated in the Assembly in May 1967. M. A. Mahjoub again became Premier, supported by a coalition of the NUP and the Imam al-Hadi faction of the Umma; the PDP now also joined (it merged, late in 1967, with the NUP, to form the "Democratic Unionist Party"). This government concluded an arms deal with the USSR and lifted the ban on the Communist Party. It severed diplomatic relations with the UK and the US following the Israel-Arab Six Day War. The coalition was unstable; the presidency was claimed by both Azhari and al-Hadi al-Mahdi; the southern problem was unsolved; and the drafting of the constitution caused considerable controversy. The draft prepared was based on Islam, regionalist decentralization and a strong presidential executive at the centre; it was strongly opposed by the Communists and the PDP. In Jan. 1968, the government decided to dissolve the Assembly.

In Apr. 1968, elections took place. The newly merged "Democratic Unionist Party" won 101 seats, al-Hadi al-Mahdi's faction of the Umma 30 seats and Sadeq al Mahdi's Umma 36. The two former groups formed a government under Mahjoub. This government did not succeed in tackling the three major problems (the economic situation, the permanent constitution and southern S.). Its position was undermined by disputes between the coalition partners and by reports that the two wings of the Umma had reunited and were about to reestablish their conservative rule.

On 25 May 1969 a group of army officers under Col. Ja'far al-Numeiri▷ staged a bloodless coup.

The name of the state was changed to "Democratic Republic of the S.". The Constituent Assembly, the Presidential Council and the transitional constitution were abolished. Absolute powers were vested in a National Revolutionary Council. A former Chief Justice, Abu Bakr 'Awadullah▷, was appointed Prime Minister. His Cabinet contained several Communists. All political parties were abolished and several former ministers were brought to trial on charges of corruption. The new regime proclaimed a policy of "Sudanese Socialism". The state would participate to a greater extent in the economy, while maintaining full freedom for foreign aid and local capital. The struggle against Israel would play an important part in foreign policy.

In Oct. 1969, friction concerning the Communist Party came to a head. During a visit to East Germany, 'Awadullah had declared that the Sudanese revolution could not function without the Communist Party (which had disregarded the ban imposed on political parties and conducted public meetings and propaganda activities—encouraged by its representation in the Cabinet and the Revolutionary Council). Numeiri disavowed his Premier. While prepared to co-operate with the Communists to achieve broader support for his regime, Numeiri feared the internal and external implications of their influence and strove to curtail their power. Numeiri took over as Premier, and 'Awadullah became Foreign Minister and Minister of Justice.

Relations with the Communists—both the official, orthodox Communist Party and vaguely pro-Communist leftist groups—continued plaguing the regime and were at the roots of several coup attempts, changes of government and purges. In Nov. 1970, leading leftists were purged from the government and army—while other leftists continued serving. The Communist Party itself was split on the question of collaboration with the regime (with the main faction, under Secretary-General 'Abd-ul-Khaleq Mahjoub, opposing such collaboration). In July 1971, a group of leftist officers—of those purged in Nov.— actually ousted Numeiri and his regime; they were, however, defeated, after three days, by loyal army units, and Numeiri was reinstated amidst bloody purges of leftists, summary trials and executions (including the top Communist leaders). The crisis also caused some upheaval in S.'s foreign relations—a bitter conflict was developing between S. and the USSR, ambassadors were recalled, and a breach of relations seemed near; Iraq, too was accused of having supported the abortive coup, and relations with her were severed; Libya and Egypt appeared to have helped Numeiri.

No major schemes for economic development or socio-economic reform were undertaken by the post-1969 revolutionary regime, though the general policy is one of nationalization, a socialized, state-supervised economy and a "Nasserist" ideology. The new regime has made no significant progress towards a solution of S.'s most pressing problem—that of the south.

THE PROBLEM OF SOUTHERN SUDAN. The most acute domestic problem is the question of S.'s southern provinces—Equatoria, Bahr al-Ghazal and the Upper Nile, populated by some 4m. non-Arab and non-Muslim Negro tribes, mostly pagan and partly (about 10–15%) Christian. During the Condominium, the (British) government endeavoured to preserve southern S.'s special character and to close it to northern Muslim penetration and domination. On the eve of independence, in 1955, southerners, afraid of northern domination, rebelled, starting with a mutiny of southern troops. The rebellion was suppressed, but a further revolt took place in 1963. In Feb. 1964 the Sudanese government decided to expel all foreign Christian missionaries operating in the south, accusing them of fostering the rebellion. Harsh military action against the rebels and villagers and tribes assisting them caused a great number of southern Sudanese to take refuge in neighbouring countries (the UN High Commissioner for Refugees estimated their number, in July 1969, at over 150,000—40,000 of whom were in the Congo (Kinshasa) and 50,000 in Uganda; other estimates speak of up to 400,000 refugees). The rebellion and its suppression is estimated to have caused the death of hundreds of thousands of people.

The southerners were divided over their plans for the future. some wanted a separate southern state, independent of S. and some a federation with the north, while others were prepared to co-operate with the existing unitary state, perhaps with increased local autonomy and decentralization, and collaborated with the government (in which some southerners usually held ministerial posts).

The new civilian government of Oct. 1964 declared an amnesty in the south. A Round Table Conference was held in Khartoum in Mar. 1965, attended by the government, representatives of southern and northern political parties and observers from seven African states. However no agreement was reached, and the problem of the constitutional future of the south was referred to a committee. The latter recommended a measure of decentralization and regional autonomy—a recommendation endorsed by another conference of political parties. There was now peace in the country so that elections that had had to be postponed in the south in 1965, could be held in 1967. But, in spite of this progress the government was unable to agree to a basic solution to the problem and the rebellion continued.

In 1967–8 the rebels established a Uganda-based "Provisional Government" headed by Aggrey Jaden, and early in 1969 they proclaimed an independent "Nile Republic", headed now, after factional struggles and the ouster of Jaden, by Gordon Mayen. However, some of the rebels inside S. refused to recognize the Uganda-based refugee government; their military arm, the *Anyanya*, proclaimed in mid-1969, their own independent government, the *Anyidi* State, and Gen. Emidio Tafeng Lodongi formed a Revolutionary Council and Government. In 1970–1, Col. Joseph Lagu emerged as the main leader.

The unrest in the south was one of the main reasons for the military coup of May 1969. The new rulers proclaimed their intention of solving the problem of the south by a formula, unspecified so far, of some self-rule within the framework of a united S. They also proclaimed an amnesty and called on the rebels to lay down their arms, and on the refugees to return. None of the rebel organizations has accepted the new regime's vague offers, and no agreement has been reached. The regime claims considerable success in a gradual pacification of the south and maintains that the rebellion is slowly dying down and refugees are returning in increasing numbers; rebel sources deny these claims, and foreign observers and journalists do not substantiate them.

INTERNATIONAL ORIENTATION AND FOREIGN POLICY. During its first years, S.'s government followed a neutralist line, generally with pro-Western sympathies. After the 1958 coup, Gen. 'Abbud carried on the same policy, although he was somewhat less friendly towards the West. The civilian government which succeeded 'Abbud in 1964 started actively supporting revolutionary movements in southern Arabia, Congo and Eritrea. Relations with the German Federal Republic were severed in 1965, after Bonn's decision to establish diplomatic relations with Israel. In June 1967 relations with the West deteriorated further as a result of the Six Day War, and Sudan broke off relations with the USA and UK. Those with Britain had been severed in 1965 over Rhodesia, and re-established in 1966; they were resumed again in Jan. 1968. Relations with the USA, however, remained severed. From 1967–68, the Sudanese government strengthened and intensified relations with the USSR and the Soviet Bloc, including the acceptance of military and economic aid. After the May 1969 coup the new regime also recognized the German Democratic Republic. Relations with the Soviet Bloc·suffered a heavy blow in the crisis of July 1971 (see above).

S. joined the Arab League in 1956. She followed a neutralist policy between the rival Arab blocs. In 1958 a sharp conflict with Egypt arose when the latter tried to take over disputed border areas by force. Egypt was compelled to retreat following Khartoum's firm stand, including a complaint to the UN Security Council. Another, more permanent cause of friction with Egypt was the problem of the distribution of the Nile▷ waters. In 1959 a new agreement was concluded, superseding an Anglo-Egyptian accord of 1929, which had looked after Egyptian interests at the expense of the Sudanese by prohibiting any water and irrigation works in S. without prior Egyptian consent. The new agreement provided for Sudan to receive 18,500m. cubic metres (mcm) compared with 4,500 mcm under the 1929 agreement. (Egypt was to increase her share of the Nile waters from 48,000 to 55,500 mcm.)

After the Arab-Israel Six Day War S. became more active in inter-Arab affairs. The first Arab "summit conference" after the war was held in Khartoum in Sept. 1967. A Sudanese contingent was left with the Egyptian Army at the Suez front. The Sudanese Premier also tried—unsuccessfully—to mediate in the Yemen war.

Following the May 1969 coup, the new ruler, Gen. Numeiri, initiated a policy of close co-operation with Egypt and Libya. Leaders of the three countries met several times to discuss co-operation in the military, economic and cultural spheres. In Nov. 1970 they announced their decision to establish a federation of Egypt, Sudan and Libya. When, in Apr. 1971, the Federation was re-endorsed (with Syria as an additional member), S. was not among its founder-members—apparently because the leftists in the government (and outside it) opposed it. S. is, however, expected to join the Federation soon.

CONSTITUTION. Constitutional developments have been described above (see Political History). First moves towards the development of self-governing institutions, made by the (British) administration beginning in the mid-1940s, led to the elaboration of a "Self-Government Statute"; its major parts were taken over in 1956 as the constitution of an independent S. This provided for an elected Parliament (elections being partially indirect, through tribal and village councils), and an Upper House three-fifths elected and two fifths appointed. As Head of State, a Presidential Council, elected by Parliament, took over from the British Governor-General. This constitution was suspended, 1958–64, and reinstated, 1964–9. During the latter years, a new draft constitution was being prepared and discussed—reportedly providing for a "Democratic Socialist Republic, based on Islam" and for a degree of decentralizing regionalism; it did not, however, come to fruition, before the constitution was re-suspended by the coup of May 1969. The revolutionary regime has not issued constitutional decrees so far.

PRESS, RADIO, TV. The first Sudanese newspaper, *Al-Nil* (The Nile), was founded in 1918 by an immigrant from Lebanon. Before the coup of May 1969, S. had about ten dailies, all published in Khartoum, and some periodicals. After the coup of May 1969 all newspapers were closed down. The government publishes one daily, *Al-Ayyam* (The Days). The government-controlled S. Broadcasting Service broadcasts in Arabic and English. The Television Service broadcasts an Arabic programme of 30 hours per week.

STATISTICS. Area: 967,500, sq. mi. Cultivable: 120m. acres (estimate); cultivated: *c.* 22m. acres (1966). Pop.: 14,355,000 (1967 estimate). Birth-rate: 5.1% (1956 estimate). Natural increase: 2.6%. Life expectancy: 40 years. GNP: S£475m. ($1,363) (1966). National income *p.c.*: S£36 ($103) (1966). Exports: S£81.2m. ($233m.) (1968). Imports: S£91.3m. ($262m.) (1968). Budget: revenue: S£113.5m. ($325.7m.), expenditure: S£100m. ($287m.) (1968/9). Literacy: 18% (1966). % children (6–14) at school: 13% (1965). Doctors: 1 doctor per 24,590 persons (0.04 p/1,000) (1966). Hospital beds: 1 bed per 1,010 persons (0.99 p/1,000) (1965). S£1 US$2.87.   (B.G.-Y.S.)

*SUEZ CANAL. An artificial canal connecting the Mediterranean and the Red Sea. Its length is 101 mi. and it is 43 ft. deep and 796 ft. wide at its narrowest point. Its northern outlet is at the city of Port Sa'id▷ and its southern outlet is at Suez. It passes through lakes the largest of which is the Great Bitter Lake. The SC shortens the distance between Europe and the Far East and Australia by thousands of miles, as compared with the route around the Cape of Good Hope.

The man who conceived the idea of the canal and was its driving force was the French engineer Ferdinand de Lesseps. France gave him support, while Britain, regarding the scheme as a French attempt to challenge her influence in the East, opposed it fiercely (and tried, as an alternative, to develop a land route from the Mediterranean to the Red Sea and, also, a railway from the Syrian coast to Mesopotamia, to link up with Euphrates and Tigris steamers). In Nov. 1854, de Lesseps obtained a concession for the "Universal SC Shipping Company" to dig the canal and operate it for 99 years. Due to British pressure, the Ottoman Sultan, who was nominally the Suzerain of Egypt, refused to approve the concession. A new concession, in Jan. 1856, included an Egyptian undertaking to supply free of charge the labour required

for digging. In 1858, despite British opposition, de Lesseps announced the formation of the SC Company. In Nov. 1858, the Company floated about 400,000 shares at the price of 500 francs each. Half of them were bought by France, and Egypt bought nearly all the other half.

Work began in 1859 under the guidance of French experts; tens of thousands of Egyptian *fallahin* laboured—and many of them perished. In 1866, the Company dispensed, in an agreement with Isma'il, the new Viceroy, with most of the forced labour (*corvée*), against a substantial compensation. The agreement also stressed Egyptian sovereignty over the C. area and, in its wake, the Ottoman "Sublime Porte" confirmed the concession. On 17 Nov. 1869, the SC was inaugurated with great pomp.

The Egyptians held 44% of the ordinary shares, in addition to preference shares which entitled them to 15% of the profits. The Khedive Isma'il got, however, heavily into debt until he had to put up for sale all his shares. The British government bought them in 1875, at the initiative of Disraeli, for *c.* £4m. In 1882, the British occupied Egypt and thereby gained control over the canal zone.

In 1888, the Maritime Powers signed a convention in Constantinople, in which they undertook to keep the SC "always free and open in time of war as in time of peace, to every vessel of commerce or of war, without distinction of flag". With regard to some clauses of the convention, priority was given to Egyptian security needs, but this did not apply to the freedom of passage which was established as an essential principle not limited by any conditions.

The SC became profitable several years after its opening and, by 1920, its profits had paid eight times the original investment. On the eve of World War II, more than 20m. tons of shipping passed through the C. In the 1960s, the total tonnage reached 275m. and the annual income $150–200m. Until 1938, Egypt did not receive any part of the Company's income or profits, because in 1880 she had mortgaged her share of the profits (15%) to French banks. Under agreements in 1937 and 1949 this was corrected to some extent and Egypt began receiving 7% of the profits. Similarly, in 1937 Egypt was given representation on the Board of the Company; this was enlarged in 1949.

The SC is of great military and strategic importance. British reinforcements and equipment (mainly from India and Australia) passed through it during World War I. A Turkish-German attempt to capture the C. in 1915 was driven off. When Britain granted nominal independence to Egypt in 1922, she kept the right to station troops and bases in the C. Zone and to defend it. In the Anglo-Egyptian Treaty of

1936, Egypt recognized Britain's special interests with regard to the SC and agreed to the stationing of British forces of specified type and strength in the C. area; the treaty stressed that this would not be interpreted as occupation or an infringement of Egyptian sovereignty. During World War II, reinforcements for the Allied troops fighting the Germans and Italians in the ME and North Africa, passed through the SC. The Germans tried without success to bomb it.

After World War II, Egypt demanded the evacuation of all British forces and bases from her soil, including the C. Zone. Negotiations met with many difficulties, and a severe crisis resulted in 1951–2 (See Egypt▷, History). Under an Oct. 1954 agreement Britain undertook to evacuate the C. Zone within 20 months; the bases would be maintained with the help of British technicians, and British forces would be permitted to return to them in the event of an attack on a member state of the Arab League▷ or on Turkey (in other words, on any ME country with the exception of Israel). The agreement re-emphasized the freedom of passage, although Egypt had prevented for years the passage of ships to and from Israel. The last British forces evacuated the C. Zone in July 1956.

In the meantime a crisis had arisen in the relations between Egypt and the West and, on 26 July 1956, Egypt nationalized the SC, in retaliation for the discontinuation of promised Western aid. The West European countries, with Britain and France at their head, feared for the freedom of passage through the C., and especially for their vital oil supply route. They were also concerned that Egypt might not be able to maintain the C. or organize navigation through it. Egypt argued that she had only nationalized the Company, as the C. itself was in any case Egyptian property, and no changes would occur in C. passage and arrangements. Negotiations on those arrangements and the safeguarding of international interests, on compensation to the Company and representation on the board of management, ended in failure in late summer 1956, and discussions at the Security Council were of no avail.

At the beginning of Nov. 1956, British and French troops moved into the C. Zone on the pretext of separating Egypt and Israel, then engaged in the Sinai War▷. In the course of the fighting, the Egyptians blocked the C. by sinking 47 ships. Intervention of the UN, and particularly the US and USSR, forced Britain and France completely to withdraw their forces from Egypt (see Suez War▷). In Jan. 1957, Egypt abrogated the Anglo-Egyptian Agreement of 1954 and denied Britain the right to return and operate her bases in the C. Zone. That same

month the Egyptian "SC Authority" began to clear the C. and in Apr. it was re-opened to navigation. In 1957, Egypt also reiterated her undertaking to respect the freedom of navigation and announced details of arrangements for passage through the C. After lengthy negotiations with the Company and shareholders, an agreement on compensation and the mutual settlement of accounts was reached in Apr. 1958. Contrary to fears expressed in 1956, the Egyptians succeeded in running the C. including navigation, without mishap. For a number of years after 1957, Egypt received loans and grants, mainly from the World Bank and Kuwait, for the widening and deepening of the C.

Ever since 1948, Egypt has prevented the passage of ships flying the Israeli flag, and of ships of whatever flag on their way to or from Israel. This blockade, which led to many incidents, was not only contrary to the Constantinople Convention of 1888 and other international agreements (such as the Anglo-Egyptian Treaty and the Egypt-Israel Armistice), but was also on 1 Sept. 1951 explicitly condemned by the UN Security Council, which called on Egypt to "terminate the restrictions on passage", found to be "unjustified interference with the rights of nations to navigate the seas". Egypt ignored the decision, and attempts to get the Security Council to act again were frustrated by a Soviet veto. The blockade of the SC was one of the causes of the Sinai War and the Six Day War▷.

The SC was closed a second time during the June 1967 Six Day War. Israel, whose forces have since 1967 occupied the east bank of the C., has agreed to its immediate reopening—on the assumption that freedom of navigation for the ships of all nations would be secured. Egypt has so far refused this; she also opposes the reopening of the C. as long as Israeli forces are stationed on its east bank. Attempts, 1971, to arrive—through the good offices of the USA —at a separate interim agreement on a partial Israel withdrawal and the reopening of the SC, have not so far succeeded.

The blocking of the SC during the 1956 crisis caused a shortage of oil and oil products, mainly in Europe. The proportion of oil tankers among ships passing through the C. increased between 1957 and 1967—up to 70% of the tonnage of the 21,000 ships which passed in 1966. Since 1967 giant oil tankers, on the route around Africa, serve as the main alternative. As some of these are too big to pass through the SC, it is doubtful if the C. will recover its central position in oil transportation even when it reopens. In any case, despite forebodings, international transport and oil supplies are managing without the SC. The USSR on the other hand, is, for strategic reasons, most interested in the reopening of the C.; it would give her easier access to the Red Sea and the Indian Ocean, and enable her to increase the Soviet presence in these regions, and acquire more strong points and bases.   (O.G.)

SUEZ WAR. (Oct.–Nov. 1956), Military operation ("Operation Musketeer") undertaken by Great Britain and France against Egypt. The operation was originally planned in response to Egypt's nationalization of the Suez Canal Company, on 26 July 1956, in case negotiations should fail to secure the desired safeguards. But in the event it was presented as an operation designed to "separate the belligerents" in the Sinai Campaign▷ (Egypt and Israel) "and to guarantee freedom of transit through the Canal by the ships of all nations".

On 30 Oct., 24 hours after Israeli parachutists had been dropped at the Mitla Pass in Sinai, an Anglo-French ultimatum ordered Israel and Egypt to withdraw ten miles from the east and west banks, respectively, of the Suez Canal and to allow British and French troops to establish themselves along its length. As expected, the ultimatum was accepted by Israel—whose forces had not reached the Canal and apparently had no intention of so doing—and rejected by Egypt. About twelve hours after the expiry of the ultimatum, British and French aircraft operating from Malta, Cyprus and aircraft carriers started bombing Egyptian airfields in the Delta and Canal areas, and an Egyptian frigate was sunk in the Gulf of Suez. President Nasser ordered the blocking of the Canal; this was achieved by sinking 47 ships filled with concrete. However it was only at dawn on 5 Nov., a few hours before the surrender of Sharm al-Sheikh▷ to Israeli troops, when Israel had achieved her objectives and fighting in Sinai had practically stopped, that French and British parachutists were dropped outside Port Sa'id▷; the French and British Armada, which had been based on Malta, arrived off Port Sa'id at dawn on 6 Nov. After very little fighting, lasting only a few hours, the town surrendered; light patrols started south towards Suez.

The UN General Assembly had been pressing for a cease fire since 2 Nov. By now, the outraged reaction of the US government (which had not been consulted prior to the operation), outright threats of intervention from the USSR, mounting internal opposition and financial difficulties, and the fact that the Sinai Campaign, which had served as a pretext, was over—compelled the British government to agree to a cease fire, effective from midnight. The French government, unable to continue alone, reluctantly followed Britain's lead. The UN continued to press for the immediate withdrawal of the invading troops. A UN Emergency Force (UNEF▷) was created temporarily to take over control of the evacuated areas. Port Sa'id was evacuated in December and full possession of the Canal was restored to Egypt.

During the operation Egypt had nationalized British and French (as well as some other foreign and mostly Jewish) properties. Negotiations over claims and counter-claims for compensation—war damage, sequestrated and confiscated properties—dragged on for years (particularly as Egypt had severed diplomatic relations with Britain and France); agreements were reached in Aug. 1958 (with France) and Feb. 1959 (with Britain), and relations were restored in Dec. 1959 (with Britain) and Apr. 1963 (with France—delayed because of Franco-Algerian conflict). Several other Arab countries also severed relations with Britain and France—though none aided Egypt militarily—and only restored them after some time.

The outcome of the Suez War is generally taken as evidence that direct imperial military intervention overseas, of the 19th-century gunboat diplomacy type, is no longer feasible. In particular, Britain and France could no longer apply force without US support. The episode thus marked the end of Britain's position as a Great Power. (France had ceased to be a Great Power in 1940.)   (N.L.-Y.S.)

SULEIMAN, HIKMAT (b. 1889). Turkish-Iraqi politician. Educated at Istanbul University, S. was active in the Ottoman "Union and Progress" Party (the "Young Turks"▷) in the 1900s; his brother was the "Young Turk" leader Mahmud Shevket Pasha, Grand Vezir in 1913, and assassinated the same year. After World War I, S. served as Director-General of Iraqi Posts and Telegraph 1922–5; Minister of Education (later of Interior) in 1925; Speaker of Parliament 1926; Minister of Justice 1928. He was Minister of the Interior in 1933, during the suppression of the Assyrian▷ rebellion. Though of conservative inclination, he joined in 1935 the moderate left-wing and reformist "Ahali" group and became a member of its executive committee. During a visit to Turkey, he also was much impressed by the Kemalist reforms there. He became the "Ahali" group's chief liaison with army officers' circles, under General Bakr Sidqi▷, who envied and wanted to emulate the role played by the army in the reforms carried out by strong rulers in Turkey and Iran. In October 1936, Sidqi engineered a military coup, and H.S. became Prime Minister. The alliance between the Ahali and the army did not last and they left the government, while H.S. carried on as Premier. However, in August 1937, Sidqi was assassinated, and

H. S. had to resign. In February 1939 he was accused by the rightist officers ruling Iraq of plotting to seize power, and sentenced to death, but his sentence was commuted to 5 years' imprisonment, following an intervention from the British Embassy. He played no further part in Iraqi politics. (B.G.)

SULH, AL-, RIYAD (1894–1951). Arab nationalist and Lebanese politician. Prime Minister, 1943–5 and 1951–6. Member of a well-known Sunni▷–Muslim family originating in Beirut and Sidon. He studied law in Beirut and Istanbul. S. was active from his youth in the Arab nationalist movement. He was sentenced to death by a Turkish military court during World War I, but was pardoned. In 1918, he joined the administration set up by Amir Feisal▷ in Damascus and was one of the co-founders of the *Istiqlal*▷ party. When Feisal's rule collapsed, S. escaped from Syria. He worked in Egypt and Geneva for Syrian independence, in the framework of the Syrian-Palestinian Congress. Despite his Pan-Arab▷ views, he was in the 1920s friendly towards Zionism▷ and in 1921 tried to persuade the Palestinian-Arab leaders to accept Britain's Zionist policy. He returned to Lebanon only in 1936, when relations between the nationalist movement and France improved, and rapidly became one of Lebanon's most prominent Sunni-Muslim leaders.

In 1943, S. helped lay the foundations for independent Lebanon by agreeing with the Maronite▷ Christian leader Bishara al-Khouri▷ on a "National Pact" which determined the regime and character of the State—based on an inter-communal equilibrium, the Muslims accepting Lebanon's independence within her existing borders, the Christians the multi-communal character of the State and a degree of integration or alliance with the Arab countries. S. became the first Prime Minister of Independent Lebanon. He held this office for more than five years, 1943–5 and 1946–51. He was highly regarded also in the other Arab countries.

In 1949, while S. was Prime Minister, the right-wing Pan-Syrian leader Anton Sa'adeh▷ was sentenced to death by a military court, in a summary trial, and executed. Sa'adeh's supporters held S. responsible and in revenge assassinated him in July 1951, on a visit to Jordan. (Y.P.)

SULH. AL-, SAMI (1890–1968). Lebanese politician, Prime Minister several times. Born in Acre of a well-known Lebanese Sunni▷–Muslim family, S. studied law in Istanbul and Paris. He first became Prime Minister in 1942–3, under French rule. He was first elected to Parliament in 1943, and was re-elected in 1949, 1951, 1953 and 1957. During the

presidency of Bishara al-Khouri▷ 1943–52, S. generally supported the President. S. was Prime Minister in 1945–6, and again in summer 1952, when President Khouri was deposed; he resigned during that crisis. From 1954, he became the main ally of President Camille Chamoun▷ among the Sunni-Muslim leaders, and the least Pan-Arab▷ of them. He was again Minister in 1954–5 and 1956–8. He joined Chamoun in a journey to Turkey, at the time that the Baghdad Pact▷ was being negotiated, and was suspected of intentions to attach Lebanon to the Pact (a scheme bitterly opposed by many Muslims). The anger of the Muslim leaders increased in 1958 and most of them became opponents of Chamoun; they were Nasserists▷ and supported the integration of Lebanon in an Arab front under Egyptian leadership. S. remained loyal to President Chamoun who appointed him Prime Minister during the 1958 crisis and civil war. S. was violently attacked for his policies during the crisis by the other Muslim politicians and excommunicated by the religious leaders in June 1958. He resigned in Sept. 1958 together with Chamoun, when the President's term of office expired. His influence declined and in 1960 he failed in the elections; he was re-elected in 1964, defeating 'Adnan al-Hakim, the leader of the nationalist-Muslim *Najjada*▷; but in 1968, al-Hakim defeated S. He died the same year. (Y.P.)

SUMMIT CONFERENCES. High-level meetings and conferences between heads of state, or government, have been held in the past also, but in the 1950s and '60s they began to be called SC, and their frequency increased. There have been five full- or nearly full-dress SC of Arab heads of state: 1. Cairo Jan. 1964; 2. Alexandria, Sept. 1964; 3. Casablanca, Sept. 1965; 4. Khartoum, Aug.-Sept. 1967; 5. Rabat, Dec. 1969. "Mini-SC" were held between several heads of Arab states at Tripoli in June 1970, Cairo in Sept. 1970 and Tripoli in July 1971 (mostly about the critical struggle between the King and government of Jordan and the Palestinian guerillas). The Rabat conference of Muslim world leaders, Sept. 1969 (about the fire at the al-Aqsa Mosque in Jerusalem), was also called a SC, because several kings and heads of states and governments participated. The Bandung Conference▷, Apr. 1955, can also be termed a SC. The conferences of non-aligned nations (Belgrade, Sept. 1961; Cairo, Oct. 1964; Lusaka, Sept. 1970; see Neutralism▷) also were SC. (Y.S.)

SUNAY, CEVDET (b. 1900). Turkish officer, and fifth President of the Turkish Republic. Born in Trabzon. S. received a military education, and during World War I served on the Palestinian front. Rising

in the military hierarchy, he was appointed Chief of General Sraff in 1960. S. was elected President in March 1966, after Cemal Gürsel▷ had resigned for reasons of health. Like his predecessor, S. has kept the army formally out of politics but he has, from time to time, transmitted to the civilian politicians the army's views on current affairs, urging action towards internal, social and economic reforms and warning against a departure from the principles of the constitution and a return to the excessive political strife of the Democratic Party's regime. S. seems to have backed the ultimatum, or semi-coup, by which the army chiefs forced, in March 1971, the resignation of the Justice Party's Demirel▷ government and the installation of a new, national coalition regime.
(D.K.)

SUNNI(TE)S. The chief and major stream in Islam, adhering to the accepted *Sunna* ("Tradition"), in contrast to the *Shi'a*▷ (the "Faction", which reserved the leadership of the Muslim community to the descendants of 'Ali and developed traditions of its own). Several schools (*madhhab*, plural *madhahib*) developed within the framework of Sunni Islam; for these and Sunni Islam's marginal schools or sects as well as Sunni-Muslim mysticism and fundamentalist revivalist orders—see Islam▷, *Wahhabiyya*▷, Dervish Orders▷, *Mahdiyya*▷, *Sanussiyya*▷. See also *Shi'a*▷.
(Y.S.)

SUPREME MUSLIM COUNCIL—see Muslim Council, Supreme▷.

SUWEIDI, AL-, TAWFIQ (b. 1890). Iraqi politician and jurist. S. served as Legal Adviser to the Iraqi government 1921–7, Minister of Education 1927–8, Prime Minister and Foreign Minister 1929, Speaker of Parliament 1929–30, Minister to Teheran 1931–3. He was again Foreign Minister 1937–8, 1941 (in the restored pro-British government, after the ouster of Rashid 'Ali al-Kilani), 1950 and 1953, Prime Minister 1946 and 1950, and Deputy Prime Minister 1958. S. also served as Foreign Minister of the short-lived Iraqi-Jordanian "Arab Federation"▷, May–July 1958. After the July 1958 coup he was sentenced to life imprisonment; his sentence was reduced to 10 years, but he was released in July 1961 and left for Lebanon. He belonged to the conservative and pro-British faction loyal to the Hashemite▷ dynasty.
(B.G.)

SYKES-PICOT AGREEMENT. A secret exchange of notes, 1916, among the chief Allies of World War I (Britain, France and Russia), relating to the partition of the Ottoman Empire after its de-

feat. Named after the chief British and French negotiators, Sir Mark Sykes and Charles François George-Picot. Diplomatic exchanges among Britain, France, Russia and Italy, in spring 1915, had preceded the SPA.

According to the A., the non-Turkish provinces of the Ottoman Empire were to be divided as follows: The Arabian peninsula was to become independent. Palestine, west of the Jordan River (excluding the Negev) was to be placed under an international regime; Britain was to control Haifa and Acre and the region between them.

The French sphere was to include two zones. An "A" zone—the interior of Syria, from and including Damascus, Homs, Hama and Aleppo in the west, up to and including the Mosul District in the east— was designated as a French zone of influence; a "Blue" zone—Cilicia in Asia Minor and all of coastal Syria, west of the "A" zone—was to be placed under direct French control.

The British sphere included the "B" zone—the Negev desert in Palestine, the area east of the Jordan River, and central Mesopotamia with a northern arm reaching into Persia and a southern arm descending towards the Persian Gulf—designated as a British zone in influence; a "Red" zone—the provinces of Basra and Baghdad—was to be placed under direct British control (as were Haifa and Acre).

Zones "A" and "B" were envisaged as areas in which semi-independent Arab states or a confederation of Arab states might be established, while France and Britain were to supply advisers and to be accorded economic privileges.

The SPA was approved by Russia in return for Britain and France's recognition of Russia's right to annex Trabzon (Trebizond), Erzerum, Lake Van and Bitlis in Anatolia. The SPA was published—and repudiated—in Nov. 1917 by the Bolsheviks who found it in the Russian Foreign Office Archives. Both Arabs and Zionists strongly criticized the A. as being inconsistent with promises Britain had made to them (the McMahon-Hussein Correspondence▷ and the Balfour Declaration▷, respectively).

The final distribution of the Ottoman territories partially reflected the SPA, but was greatly modified by the Mandate▷ System which abolished any formal, direct possession by the Powers—though it left them full *de facto* control. The SPA's territorial provisions were also changed: Palestine became a British Mandate; Cilicia remained part of Turkey; and France ceded her rights in the Mosul region to Britain (see map, page 291).
(Sh.H.)

*****SYRIA.** Republic in western Asia, bordering on Turkey to the north, Iraq to the east, Jordan to the south, and Israel, Lebanon and the Mediterranean to the west. Official name: The Syrian Arab Republic (*al-Jumhuriyya al-'Arabiyya al-Suriyya*). Pop.: 5.8m. (1968 estimate). Arabic is the official language and common throughout the country, but there are also concentrations of Kurdish, Armenian, Turkish and Aramaic speakers.

Geographic and historic circumstances encouraged the existence of ethnic and ethno-religious groups. Close on 70% of the inhabitants of S. are Sunni(te)▷ Muslims. This number, however, includes more than 400,000 Kurds▷, *c.* 7% of the population, mostly in the north-eastern border region, who are a linguistic-national minority. The largest ethno-religious minority is the 'Alawi(te)▷ community with 500–600,000 members, 10–12% of the population, concentrated in the region of the Mountain of the 'Alawites, in the north-west of the country. The Druzes▷, about 3%, 120–150,000, dwell primarily in the region of Jabal Druze (the Druze Mountain) in southern S. Christians comprise 10% of S.'s population, but they are split into various sects (1968 estimate): Greek Orthodox▷: over 200,000; Armenian▷ Orthodox: over 150,000; Syrian Orthodox (Jacobites▷): 70,000; Greek Catholic: 65,000; Armenian Catholic: 25,000; Syrian Catholic: about 25,000; Maronites▷: 20,000; Protestants: 15,000; Nestorians▷: 15,000; Latins: 5,000; Chaldeans: 5,000. Other religious minorities are the Isma'ilis▷ (50,000); Shi'it(es)▷ (called Mutawalis▷ in Syria—15,000); Yazidis▷ (3,000); and Jews (3,000 —their number decreased as a result of the Arab-Israel conflict; in 1938 there were still 26,350). The number of nomadic Bedouin has dropped to 2–3% of the population. The area of S. is 72,000 sq. mi., including 386 sq. mi. under Israeli administration since June 1967. About one-third of S.'s area is desert or unarable mountainous terrain; one third is pasturable, and one third—about 24,000 sq. mi.—is arable. However, of this area only 10,000 sq. mi. are at present cultivated (some 2.6m. hectares [6.4m. acres]).

The Syrian economy is largely dependent upon agriculture, which accounts for close on 30% of the total national income. The possibilities of agricultural development are still great. At present, grain is mostly grown by extensive cultivation methods, and only a small portion of the cultivated area is irrigated. The major crops are wheat (1.2m. hectares, 3m. acres, 1967), barley (645,000 hectares, 1.5m. acres), cotton (239,000 hectares, 590,260 acres) and olive trees (142,000 hectares, 350,740 acres), as well as sorghum, corn, sugar-beet and tobacco. Fruits are plentiful in the areas of Damascus and Lataqia. Sheep, goats and cattle are also raised. During the past decade, industry in S. has developed at an in-

creased pace and its relative proportion of the national income has risen constantly (13% in 1966), but it still produces mainly consumption goods and is linked to the agricultural produce of the country. The major industrial branches are textiles, hide processing, tobacco, edible oils and cement. The important industrial areas are Damascus, Aleppo, Homs and Lataqia.

At the end of the 1950s, oil was discovered in north-eastern S., and until the beginning of 1969 oil reserves estimated at 1,200m. tons were found. Oil is produced by the government-owned "Syrian General Petroleum Corporation". In 1968, 950,000 tons were produced, in 1970 4.5m. In 1968, a 400 mi., 5m. ton *p.a.* pipeline was completed from the oil-

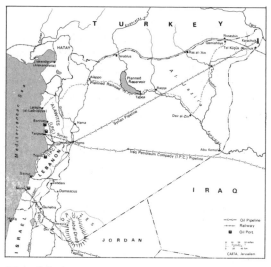

Map of Syria

fields in the east to the refinery in Homs (established in 1959 and producing 1m. tons of oil products in 1966), and thence to the oil port at Tartous▷. Other pipelines traversing Syrian territory are those of the Iraq Petroleum Company from Kirkuk, which branches out at Homs to Tripoli in Lebanon and Baniyas in Syria, and the "Tapline" from Aramco's fields in Sa'udi Arabia to Sidon in Lebanon. In 1968, 73m. tons of oil went through these pipelines. The Syrian government receives transit royalties. Efforts are being made to develop the oilfields and the petro-chemical and fertilizer industries connected with them. S.'s largest development project is the planned $628m. Euphrates▷ Dam. On completion, this dam will permit the irrigation of 1–1.6m. acres to be further expanded at a later stage and produce 200,000 kilowatts of electricity (with extensive expansion at future stages). In 1968, work began to implement the first $260m. stage. The USSR has promised credits totalling some $157m., and Soviet experts supervise construction.

POLITICAL HISTORY. The area known today as S. was part of the Ottoman Empire▷ from 1517 until the end of World War I▷. Most of S. was part of the three provinces (*Vilayet*) of Aleppo, Damascus and Beirut. In fact, effective Ottoman administration did not extend beyond the main cities while the outlying towns and rural areas were ruled by local leaders, to whose control the Ottomans did not object as long as they paid their taxes on time and did not disturb order and security.

With the continuing decline of the Ottoman Empire during the 19th century, Western influence grew—first through economic and cultural penetration, later through political and military intervention France was the power with the most ramified interests in S., a result of steady commercial activity as well as ties with the Catholic, and especially the Maronite, community. Beginning in the 1830s, the Jesuits intensified their educational activity in S., opening many schools and, in 1875, a university in Beirut. American Protestants in 1834 established a modern printing press and in 1866 founded the Syrian Protestant College, later to be named the American University of Beirut. The Ottoman government in the late 19th century also opened a number of modern schools in S.

A cultural revival resulted, which paved the way for the appearance of an Arab nationalist movement on the eve of World War I. The Arab nationalists in S., who organized themselves in semi-secret associations, at first demanded only cultural autonomy, decentralization and an increased participation of the Arab population in Ottoman governmental institutions; but, when they encountered the opposition of the "Young Turks"▷ in power, their aspiration to independence grew. Active nationalists were very few—perhaps hundreds at the most. They were split into factions and their political influence was slight. The fact that the Ottoman Empire joined Germany and Austro-Hungary in the war opened up new possibilities. The British contacted the Arab leader, Sharif Hussein▷ of Mecca, with whom the Syrian nationalists also had been in touch and promised him their support for the establishment of an Arab state which would also include S.; however, S.'s borders remained undetermined, and the British reserved the Western coast lands for a future French administration.

The Syrian nationalists did not take part in the Arab Revolt▷ that erupted in Hijaz in 1916. There was also no uprising in S. itself, but the Turks suspected the nationalists and condemned several of them to death. With the Ottoman collapse in 1918, S. was conquered by Allied forces, including Arab troops commanded by Amir Feisal▷, son of Sharif Hussein. Feisal entered Damascus in Oct. 1918, and, with the encouragement of the British, established an Arab government which gradually took over the administration in the interior of the country. However, S.'s political status remained unclear. In accordance with the McMahon-Hussein▷ correspondence, Britain supported the establishment of an Arab State in her interior. However, the secret Sykes-Picot▷ Agreement of 1916 between Britain, France and Russia earmarked the interior of S. as a French "area of influence", while the coastal areas were to be directly administered by France.

With some flexibility and good will the two agreements might have been reconciled and an Arab State set up in the Syrian interior with semi-independent status and under French influence. But as the French became entrenched on the coast, antagonism between them and the nationalists grew more intense. In July 1919, the "General Syrian Congress" declared S.'s independence, and clashes soon erupted between Arab and French forces. In Mar. 1920, the Congress proclaimed Feisal King of S. (intending, though no borders were precisely defined, a greater S. that would include Lebanon and Palestine). Britain and France did not recognize this declaration of independence and decided, at the San Remo Conference▷ in Apr. 1920, to confer upon France a Mandate▷ over S. French forces began moving toward Damascus and after breaking the Arab resistance at Meisalun (Methalun), entered Damascus on 25 July 1920, putting an end to Feisal's brief rule. The League of Nations endorsed the French Mandate over S. in July 1922.

From the start, the Syrians and particularly the Sunnite▷-Muslim Arab majority, the mainstay of the nationalist movement, hated the French rule imposed on them. As a result, the French tried to weaken this majority and base their government upon the support of the ethnic and religious minorities, especially the Christians of Mount Lebanon. They set up a state of "Greater Lebanon" and added to the Christian majority area—semi-autonomous since 1861—Muslim majority districts in the north, south, Coele S.▷ (*al-Biqa*'—the Valley) and Beirut (see Lebanon▷). Thus S. lost areas of vital importance for her economic viability. The French also divided up the rest of S. into separate administrative units, emphasizing separatist minority interests. The Lataqia▷ region, inhabited chiefly by 'Alawites▷, became a separate administrative unit, as did Jabal Druze▷ and the district of Alexandretta▷ (with a sizeable Turkish minority.) In the rest of S. two different states, that of Aleppo and that of Damascus, were established, linked in a federation. In 1924–5, the states of Damascus and Aleppo were united in the "State of S.", but the separate existence of the three special regions continued.

The various Syrian states were given constitutions and councils, but real authority remained with the French High Commissioner in Beirut and his officials. The French Mandatory government improved public security and administration; but the people of S. rejected it as a foreign rule. Their nationalist opposition erupted into violence several times during the 1920s. In 1925, a local uprising spread from Jabal Druze to other areas of S. and became a national uprising. A national Syrian government was set up in Jabal Druze by the national leader, Dr. 'Abd-ul-Rahman Shahbandar▷. The rebels broke through to Damascus and the city was subsequently shelled by French guns and aircraft. The revolt was finally quelled only in 1927.

The French government now agreed to grant S. independence after the manner of the Anglo-Iraqi agreement of 1922 — i.e. nominal independence based on a treaty granting the Mandatory Power special privileges and particularly the right to maintain troops and bases. Accordingly, France began to encourage increased self-government. In May 1926, Lebanon was declared a republic and granted a constitution and parliamentary institutions. In regard to S., however, similar progress was held up, mainly because nationalist demands far exceeded the concessions that France was willing to make. Only in 1928 did the French High Commissioner do away with military government and allow the holding of elections for a constituent assembly. The elections of Apr. 1928 were won by the "National Bloc" (al-Kutla al-Wataniyya) — a coalition of several nationalist parties, united only by their opposition to the French Mandate. Hashem al-Atassi▷, Prime Minister during Feisal's reign and now leader of the Bloc, was elected President of the Assembly.

The nationalists prepared a draft constitution, which demanded, inter alia, the re-unification of all S. The French High Commissioner refused to endorse this draft, attempts to reach understanding failed, and the Assembly was dissolved in May 1930. The High Commissioner now unilaterally proclaimed a constitution; this established a republican regime in S. and provided for a Chamber of Deputies elected by males aged 20 and older for a four-year term; the Chamber was to elect the President of the Republic, with limited powers; the government was to be responsible to the Chamber. "The obligations contracted by France in respect of S." were to take precedence of the constitution and, in all matters touching

upon these obligations, the constitution was to be applied only with French approval.

The nationalists protested the imposition of this constitution, but public life began to follow its provisions. In Jan. 1932 elections were held and the "National Bloc" lost much of its strength. The French tried once again to replace the Mandate with a Franco-Syrian treaty which would extend nominal independence to S., while safeguarding French interests. However, the nationalist members of the Chamber torpedoed all compromise proposals and the Chamber dissolved in 1934. Again tension increased in French-Syrian relations, until rioting broke out early in 1936.

New efforts to find a political solution brought a Syrian delegation to Paris. The "Popular Front" government of Socialist Leon Blum was more inclined to compromise than its predecessors, and, in Sept. 1936 a Franco-Syrian treaty was signed. After an interim period of three years, S. was to become independent. The territories of Jabal Druze and Lataqia would be incorporated, but maintain a certain degree of autonomy. France's economic status and educational institutions were guaranteed. France alone was to equip and train the Syrian Army to be established and to maintain troops and military bases in S. After the treaty was iniated, elections were held, won again by the "National Bloc". Its leaders now took over the government: Hashem al-Atassi became President, Jamil Mardam▷ Prime Minister, Shukri Quwwatli▷, Sa'dullah Jaberi▷, Fares Khouri▷ ministers. The Lataqia and Jabal Druze districts were incorporated into S. Numerous government posts were gradually transferred to Syrians. The Syrian Chamber ratified the treaty with alacrity; but France tarried, postponed, and finally refused to ratify it.

Close on twenty years of French rule had contributed much to the development of the country. Modern quarters were built in Damascus and Aleppo, a network of roads was laid, the educational and health systems were improved and numerous Syrians received training in the administration of a modern state. The influence of French culture was evident in many spheres, in social customs, in dress. Gradually, economic conditions improved and the standard of living rose. Under the French Mandate S. became a place of refuge for persecuted minorities. Most of S.'s Kurds▷ and Armenians▷ were immigrants of the 1920s and '30s, refugees from Kemalist Turkey; Assyrians▷ settled in S. in the wake of persecution and massacres in Iraq, 1933.

The quest for a political settlement with France continued to cloud economic progress. The nationalists insisted on full independence, but were not united as to how to achieve this aim. The "National

Bloc", their main political faction, suffered from splits and instability. Dr. 'Abd-ul-Rahman Shah-bandar, never a trusted member of the Bloc's dominant faction (he was pro-Hashemite▷ and pro-British), withdrew in 1939 and established a "Popular Organization" *(al-Hai'a al-Sha'biya)*. He was assassinated in 1940; it was apparently a political murder, and it shocked the country and dealt a heavy blow to the beginnings of a parliamentary tradition.

Separatist movements grew with French support, in the Jazira▷ and Jabal Druze. French-Syrian relations suffered as a result of the Alexandretta affair: the district was ceded by the French in the face of the demands and powerful pressure of Turkey; after a brief League of Nations-sponsored autonomy it was finally annexed by Turkey in July 1939. Furious riots followed in S. and President al-Atassi and the government resigned. The French dissolved the Chamber of Deputies, appointed a government of officials, and announced that the Franco-Syrian draft treaty would not be submitted to Parliament for ratification. The administration of the Jabal Druze and Lataqia districts were again separated from S.

After the defeat of France, June 1940, French officials in S. remained loyal to the pro-German Vichy government. The Italians and the Germans penetrated Syria, *i.a.* in the form of a cease-fire supervision-commission, and began preparing airfields and bases and cells of agents and supporters. Their growing domination brought the British to invade S. and Lebanon together with Free French forces in June 1941. General Georges Catroux▷, Free France's new Governor ("Delegate"), proclaimed the termination of the Mandate and the independence of S., but in actuality the French were tardy in transferring the government to the Syrians and in re-establishing parliamentary institutions. Under British and American pressure, they agreed in 1943 to hold elections. The "National Bloc" once again triumphed, and its leader, Shukri Quwwatli, was elected President.

Power was now gradually transferred to the Syrian government and administration. The article of the constitution restricting S.'s sovereignty and granting special privileges to France (Art. 116), was annulled in Jan. 1944 without a struggle (after a fierce struggle over the same issue in Lebanon in Nov. 1943). The separatist autonomy of the Druze and 'Alawite districts was ended. But Franco-Syrian differences erupted around the fate of the "Troupes Speciales", Syrian and Lebanese units within the framework of the French Army in the ME. The French refused to transfer these units to the jurisdiction of the Syrian government and withdrew their own troops unless a treaty were signed guaranteeing

France a preferential status and special privileges (on the lines of the Anglo-Iraqi Treaty of 1930, the Anglo-Egyptian one of 1936—and the Franco-Syrian Treaty of 1936 which had not been ratified). S., however, was no longer prepared to sign any preferential agreement of this type and began to win international support for her attitude.

In 1944, the USSR and the USA recognized S., and Britain did in 1945. The newly-founded Arab League▷, too, unequivocally supported S. S., therefore, began to act like any sovereign state. In Jan. 1945, the establishment of a national army was announced; in Feb. S. declared war on the "Axis" powers and thus became, in Apr., one of the founding members of the United Nations. In May, anti-French riots broke out because France still refused to withdraw her troops, and the French again shelled Damascus. However, a British ultimatum forced the cease fire, and by the end of the year the British and French had agreed on the withdrawal of their troops. This agreement did not satisfy S., as its wording implied a special, privileged status for France in S. and Lebanon, and (together with Lebanon) she lodged in Feb. 1946 a complaint with the UN Security Council. The USSR vetoed a resolution calling for negotiations and a speedy withdrawal; but the parties settled the matter between themselves, and by mid-Apr. 1946 France had withdrawn all her garrisons from S. 17 Apr.—"Withdrawal Day"—still remains S.'s national holiday.

LIST OF FRENCH HIGH COMMISSIONERS AND—SINCE 1941—DELEGATES GENERAL FOR SYRIA AND LEBANON

Gen. Henri E. Gouraud	1919–23
Gen. Maxime Weygand	1923–4
Gen. Maurice Sarrail	1924–5
Henri de Jouvenel	1925–6
Henri Ponsot	1926–33
Damien de Martel	1933–9
Gabriel Puaux	1939–40
Jean Chiappe★	1940
Gen. Henri Dentz★★	1940–1
Gen. Georges Catroux★★★	1941–3
Jean Helleu★★★	1943
Yves Chataigneau★★★	1943–4
Paul Beynet★★★	1944

★ His plane was shot down and he was killed before he took up his post.
★★ Representing the Vichy government.
★★★ Representing Free France—no longer with the title "High Commissioner" (Haut Commissaire) but as "Delegate General" (Délégué Général).

It soon emerged that S. had no strong leadership to guide her first steps in independence. The "National Bloc", the major political force on the road to independence, disintegrated soon after that aim had been realized. Aleppo leaders, centred around the "People's Party", competed with the Damascus leadership and its "National Party". The minorities were loyal first and foremost to their communities, and the tribes to their own leaders. The 1947 elections resulted in a parliament without any strong party or leadership. Many "independent" deputies stood for local and clan interests and were always prepared to support anyone who might give them a temporary advantage. Fundamental problems surfaced due to the lack of internal stability: would S. continue to exist as a separate independent state, or should she unite with the other neighbouring Arab states, particularly Hashemite Jordan and Iraq? In general the Aleppo leadership supported union schemes while the Damascus leaders and most Syrian governments generally opposed them together with Egypt and Sa'udi Arabia. S. became an arena and object of inter-Arab and inter-power conflicts, all of them aggravating the political instability.

A serious crisis occurred as a result of the army's defeat in the Palestine War (1948). Political and military leaders accused each other of responsibility for the débâcle. On 30 Mar. 1949 the commander-in-chief of the armed forces, General Husni al-Za'im▷, carried out a *coup d'état* and deposed the President, Parliament and Government. Za'im declared that he would eliminate wide-spread corruption, institute reforms, and encourage development schemes. In June 1949 he was elected President in a referendum. If he had considered a union with Iraq, Egyptian-Sa'udi pressure soon caused him to abandon this idea. In Aug., Za'im was deposed in another coup by Sami al-Hinnawi▷ (Za'im and his Prime Minister were executed). Hinnawi tended toward union with Iraq; he restored parliament, which was dominated, under his protection, by the Aleppo leadership and adherents of union. Hashem al-Atassi▷ was elected to the presidency. Opponents of union with Iraq incited army units to rebel, and in Dec. 1949 Hinnawi was deposed by Colonel Adib Shishakli▷.

At first, Shishakli preferred to leave the President, Parliament and Government intact and to rule from behind the scenes as Deputy Chief-of-Staff of the army. But the clash between the army's growing intervention in state affairs and the traditional civilian leadership's desire to return the officers to their barracks, created constant tension. In Dec. 1951, Shishakli staged a second coup and established a dictatorial regime. He dissolved Parliament and abolished all parties, establishing a single political

organization of his own, "The Arab Liberation Movement". In July 1953, a referendum approved a new constitution, which granted the President extensive powers, and Shishakli himself was elected to the post. The leaders of all factions were now united in their opposition to Shishakli. In Feb. 1954, a new coup was carried out with the help of a military junta, Shishakli's government collapsed and he fled S. The 1949 Parliament and President Hashem al-Atassi, dismissed by Shishakli in Dec. 1951, were restored. Most of the members again were independents; political stability was still lacking, and one government followed another. In 1955 Shukri al-Quwwatli replaced Atassi as President.

From the mid-1950s leftist elements began to achieve positions of strength, especially the "Arab Socialist Renaissance Party" *(al-Ba'th)* and the Communists. In inter-Arab relations, S. began to adopt an increasingly pro-Egyptian line; in Oct. 1955, a Syro-Egyptian defence pact was signed and a joint command established. A far-reaching Soviet-Syrian *rapprochement* led to economic aid agreements and arms purchases (since Feb. 1956). The Sinai Campaign▷ and the Suez War▷ brought S. even closer to Egypt and the Soviet Union. During the Nov. 1956 hostilities in Egypt, the Syrians blew up the oil pipelines from Iraq and Sa'udi Arabia passing through S. This resulted in tension between S. and these two countries. The pipelines were repaired in Mar. 1957, but S.'s relations with her pro-Western neighbours remained strained. S.'s leftist leadership feared outside intervention. Inside the country, power was increasingly concentrated in the hands of officers with *Ba'th* or communist leanings. These two parties sometimes collaborated, but late in 1957 relations between them deteriorated to the point that a dangerous confrontation seemed imminent. The *Ba'th* leadership found itself in a double danger: it feared a communist take-over from within and the intervention of pro-Western forces (Iraq, Jordan, Turkey, Israel) from without. So the *Ba'th* leadership turned to Egypt and prodded its president, Gamal 'Abd-ul-Nasser▷, into establishing a union of the two countries and thereby saving S.

The union took place in Feb. 1958. The Egyptian President became the President of the United Arab Republic▷ (UAR; *al-Jumhuriyya al-'Arabiyya al-Muttahida*), and S. became the "Syrian Region" of the UAR. At first S. was to a certain extent treated as a distinct entity. Although foreign affairs, security, education and industry were handled by the central government, separate governments of the "regions" dealt with financial and economic matters and more. The provisional constitution (on the Egyptian pattern) granted extensive powers to the President of the

Republic. Political parties in S. were disbanded. Gradually the merger became more complete. Early in 1960, there were elections for local "National Union" committees, and in the summer a single National Assembly was set up—appointed from past members of the Syrian Parliament (one third) and the Egyptian National Assembly (two thirds). In Oct., the authority of the central government was considerably expanded.

The union with Egypt soon became unpopular in S., as Egypt, the bigger, more modern and developed country, increasingly took over control of the Union government. The *Ba'th* party, the major force that had brought about the union, was disappointed at the meagre representation it had in the regime. The upper classes were apprehensive of the socialist policies the UAR government had already introduced in Egypt and was preparing in S. too. On the other hand, left-wing circles were disappointed at the slow pace of the socialist reforms. Above all, Syrian army officers felt that Egyptian officers were taking over key positions, and relegating them to less important posts. A further step toward full integration was made in Aug. 1961, when the separate governments of the two regions were abolished. Similarly, far-reaching steps were taken toward nationalization and reform.

In Sept. 1961, a Syrian officers' junta carried out a coup which resulted in S.'s withdrawal from the UAR and the restoration of her full independence. In Nov., a new temporary constitution was proclaimed in Damascus and general elections were held in Dec.: The Constituent Assembly chosen resembled those that had preceded the Union and lacked political stability; it contained independent members and representatives of the traditional parties. They elected Nazem al-Qudsi▷, a leader of the "People's Party", as President of the Republic. The new regime turned to the right and abolished many of the reforms of the UAR government. This policy caused renewed ferment among the army officers and, in Mar. 1962, a group of officers carried out a further coup, in order to establish a more progressive regime. President al-Qudsi and his civilian administration were at first dismissed; but, due to disunity among the various officer factions and unrest in the cities, they were restored to power. The government was now more leftist—and still less stable. Ministers changed very frequently and the government was more than ever under pressure by the army commanders, who were themselves divided into rival factions (pro-Egyptian against anti-Egyptian; *Ba'th* against right-wing, etc.).

Egypt could not forgive S. for her secession from the Union and refused to recognize it (continuing to call herself the "United Arab Republic"). Mutual complaints shook the Arab League; and when the League refused to accept the Egyptian position, Egypt boycotted it, in 1962–3, for half a year. The *Ba'th* coup that took place in Iraq in Feb. 1963 encouraged the Syrian *Ba'th* and its supporters among the officers to attempt seizing power. On 8 Mar. 1963, they staged another coup. Many of these officers were members of minority groups, 'Alawites and Druzes, but as strong man there emerged after several months of factional struggle the Sunnite general Amin al-Hafez▷, who maintained his leading position by playing off the rival factions against one another. With his rise to power, the *Ba'th* began to purge the army and government of pro-Nasserist elements. This resulted in a Nasserist attempt to overthrow the regime in July 1963; the coup was suppressed.

The *Ba'th* regime in S. endeavoured to establish a united front with the *Ba'th* circles in Iraq, but they had little success; in any case the *Ba'th* regime in Iraq was overthrown in Nov. These upheavals put an end, for the time being, also to the Syrian *Ba'th* efforts to renew the Syrian-Egyptian union—this time in the form of a federation, in which Iraq, too, would have participated; discussions on the plan had been held in spring 1963, immediately after the *Ba'th* had come to power, and resulted in an agreement, but this had not been implemented (see Pan Arabism▷, Arab Federation▷, *Ba'th*▷). Relations with Egypt, which had improved slightly with these discussions, deteriorated again because of the purges of Nasserists in S. and remained cool. The Egyptian-Syrian military pact was renewed only in 1966; the resumption of formal diplomatic relations was decided upon with the signing of this pact and put into effect in spring 1967).

Inside S., the *Ba'th* government began implementing a socialist policy of nationalizing banks and factories and distributing land to the peasants. Merchants' and landowners' riots and protest demonstrations, Feb.–Apr. 1964, were brutally suppressed. In Apr. 1964, a new temporary constitution was proclaimed, defining S. as a "democratic socialist republic, constituting an integral part of the Arab nation".

The *Ba'th* leadership had by now split into two rival factions: one based itself upon the veteral party leadership, which was more moderate in the implementation of the socialist programme and remained loyal to the ideal of Arab unity, hoping, in consequence, for an alignment with Egypt. The rival faction comprised younger party leaders, many of them 'Alawites and Druzes; they pressed for a speedy implementation of socialist principles and regarded Nasser as an enemy. This extremist faction won greater support among the officer's corps (in which minority groups are more numerous than in the general population and were called the "military wing"). Late in 1965, the "moderate", "civilian" faction ousted the extremists from their positions and began to carry out purges. On 23 Feb. 1966, however, the extremists staged a military coup against the old leadership and imprisoned them. Amongst those arrested were Michel 'Aflaq▷, the founder and ideologist of the party, Salah-ul-Din al-Bitar▷, co-founder of the party and head of the deposed government, and General Amin al-Hafez, Chairman of the Presidential Council.

The real power behind the coup was the 'Alawite General, Salah Jadid▷, who was supported by the "regional" (Syrian) leadership of the Ba'th party, Dr. Yussuf Zu'ayyin▷, and Dr. Nur-ul-Din al-Atassi▷. General Hafez Asad▷, Commander of the Air Force and Minister of Defence, was, like Jadid, a powerful figure, and the two men soon became rivals. The elimination of the moderate faction still further restricted the public base of the regime, and this drove it to collaborate with the Communists, and to grant them, for the first time in S.'s history, representation in the government. In the course of 1966, it conducted wide-scale political purges and continued fortifying its positions by entrusting to its loyal supporters all key positions in the army, the central government and the local administration; it also gained control over "popular organizations" such as trade unions, and students', farmers' and women's associations. Nationalization was stepped up; in 1967, the party claimed that one third of the cultivated land in S. had already been redistributed.

In its external policy, the regime strengthened its ties with the Soviet Union. It tried to improve its relations with Egypt. It adopted an extreme line against Israel, and the Israel-S. border became an arena of violent clashes and constant tension—and one of the decisive causes of the Six Day War▷ of June 1967. The war resulted in the occupation of the Golan Heights▷ by Israel forces and their advance to within 38 mi. of Damascus. S. agreed to a cease-fire supervised by the United Nations, but continued to oppose any political settlement of the Arab-Israel conflict. She refused to participate in the Arab summit conference at Khartoum▷ in Aug. 1967. She rejected the Security Council resolution of Nov. 1967, which called for Israel's withdrawal from occupied territories in the framework of a just and lasting peace and refused to co-operate with the UN envoy, Gunnar Jarring▷. S. gave unreserved support—at least in declarations—to the Palestinian guerilla (feda'iyin▷) organizations, and especially the Al-Sa'iqa formation established by her own

Ba'th party and security services; but the guerillas were not allowed to set up an independent establishment in S. and were kept under strict Syrian supervision.

After the Six Day War, splits in the Ba'th leadership continued. Until Oct. 1968, the dominant group was the leftist faction led by Jadid, Prime Minister Yussuf Zu'ayyin, and Foreign Minister Dr. Ibrahim Makhus, who advocated the rapid imposition of Marxist-Socialist principles on society and the economy. This faction was isolated in both S. and the Arab world. In Oct. 1968, a "nationalist" group gained the upper hand; it aimed at reducing S.'s dependence upon the USSR, improving relations with the other Arab states and renewing the battle against Israel. The central figure in this group was Jadid's rival, the 'Alawite General Hafez al-Asad, Minister of Defence.

Asad and his "nationalists" strengthened their position in 1969 as is evident in the arrest of communists in Apr. 1969 and changes in the government in May. Asad had actually taken over control in Feb. 1969, in a kind of semi-coup, but S.'s continued dependence on Soviet military and economic aid, as well as Egyptian pressure, had compelled him to accept a compromise and the continued participation in the government of the leftist faction, in an uncomfortable co-existence between the rival factions. In the growing conflict between the feda'iyin organizations and the governments of Lebanon and Jordan, 1969–70, S. consistently supported the feda'iyin, and relations with these countries deteriorated. S. threatened intervention on several occasions; in Sept. 1970, Syrian forces indeed moved into Jordan to aid the feda'iyin but were repulsed.

In Nov. 1970, General Asad completed the takeover he had to forgo in spring 1969. He was spurred on by the fact that the Ba'th party conference had adopted a resolution in favour of his rival, Jadid, and against himself. President Nur-ul-Din al-Atassi was dismissed and provisionally replaced by Ahmed al-Khatib (who had not been in the top leadership), while Asad himself became Prime Minister. His opponents of the Jadid-Zu'ayyin faction were removed from their government and party posts, and most of them were arrested. In Feb. 1971, a 173-member "People's Council" was convened, which nominated Asad, in Mar., as President of the Republic. He was endorsed, the same month, in a plebiscite (as the only candidate, 96% voting, 99.2% of the votes in favour). In April, Asad divested himself of the Premiership, appointing a loyal follower to the post.

The new regime hastened to mend S.'s relations with the inter-Arab alignments from which its

predecessors had dissociated her. Asad was apparently prepared to abandon S.'s ultra-extremism and align himself with Egypt. In Dec. 1970 he announced that S. would join the proposed Egyptian-Libyan-Sudanese Federation, and in Apr. 1971 S. became a partner to the formal proclamation of the Federation plans, S. mitigated even her position in the Jordan-guerilla dispute—to such an extent that in summer 1971 she sent emissaries to mediate between King Hussein and the *feda'iyin;* these were quickly withdrawn when the King remained stubborn and mediation failed, and S. reverted to an anti-Jordanian attitude—but it was moderate compared with her interventionism before the Asad coup. S. also indicated that she would agree to the revival of the joint "Eastern Command" against Israel.

GOVERNMENT AND POLITICS, CONSTITUTION. For S.'s parliamentary constitution and political parties in the past—see above, History. Since the *Ba'th* coups in 1963 and 1966, the constitution has remained vague. On 1 May 1969, the "regional" (Syrian) leadership of the *Ba'th* party proclaimed a new provisional constitution. This defined S. as "the Arab-Syrian region", a "democratic, popular, socialist and sovereign state and part of the Arab homeland". The regime is "republican". Government institutions are: the People's Council, the President and the Council of Minister, district People's councils, and the Judiciary and Prosecution. "The ruling party in state and society is the Arab Socialist Renaissance *(Ba'th)* Party" and until constitutional government institutions are established, its "regional" (Syrian) leadership is to exercise all the powers of government. A "People's Council" was established, after a short-lived attempt in 1965 to found a representative body, and much talk since 1968, only in 1971 by the Asad regime; but apart from the election of the President it does not seem to fulfill any active function as legislature.

Since the 1966 coup, the body ruling the state has been the 16-member (Syrian) "Regional" leadership of the *Ba'th* party. It determines policy and instructs the government and other public bodies as to its implementation. The party leadership makes appointments to key government and administration posts. The Secretary-General of the party—up to Nov. 1970, Dr. Nur-ul-Din al-Atassi, since 1971, Hafez al-Asad—is also President of the State; 1968–70 he was Prime Minister, too. Other members of the party leadership serve as ministers and army commanders. During Jadid's years of power, his official post was Deputy Secretary-General of the party.

The *Ba'th* party, advocating militant Pan-Arab▷ policies and a rapid socialization of the economy, is,

since 1963, the only party in S. The Communist Party is officially banned, but its activity is more or less tolerated by the authorities, to an extent determined at any given time by the relations between the Communists and the ruling party. It is represented in the Government since 1966. Its leader, Khaled Bakdash▷, is one of the most respected Communist leaders in the Arab World. There is also a pro-Chinese Communist faction, the "Socialist Workers' Party". Pro-Nasserist elements are organized in the "Socialist Unionist" party *(al-Ittihadiyyun al-Ishtirakiyyun).* The "Arab Socialist Democratic Party" of Akram Hourani▷, a former *Ba'th* leader who seceded in 1962 and maintains an anti-Egyptian line, advocates a moderate socialism and the restoration of parliamentary life. The Arab Nationalist Movement"▷ *(al-Qawmiyyun al-'Arab)* is a militant Pan-Arab movement with a leftist Marxist ideology and strongly opposes the *Ba'th* party, despite the ideological proximity of the two. In the past, the "Muslim Brotherhood"▷ movement, advocating the establishment of an Islamic theocracy, was active in S. (it operated at times under different, but similar names, such as the "Islamic Front", etc.), and it still commands a certain popularity. All these factions operate in exile, particularly in Lebanon—and perhaps underground in S. While they are not permitted openly to organize in S., the leftist factions are represented in most Syrian governments.

In the past, S. had a fairly rich and varied press. During the UAR period, 1958–61, it was "guided" and regimented and many papers closed down. Since the *Ba'th coup d'état*, 1963, the press and all other communication media are under strict governmental supervision and most of them are owned by the government or the *Ba'th* party. There is now no major privately owned newspaper. Most publications are mouthpieces of branches of the government or of the party, or religious or trade organizations. The important daily papers are *al-Ba'th*, the official organ of the ruling party (circulation: 16,000), and and *al-Thawra* ("The Revolution"), a government paper (circulation: 20,000). The Syrian broadcasting service broadcasts mainly in Arabic, but also in French, English, Russian, German, Spanish, Portuguese, Turkish and Hebrew.

Damascus Univeristy had, in 1968, 655 teachers and 27,932 students, Aleppo University—197 staff and 4,418 students.

STATISTICS: Area: 72,000 sq. mi. Cultivated area: 10,000 sq. mi., constituting some 14% of the area of S., 42% of the arable area. Pop.: 5.8m. (est. 1968), (6.3m.—later unconfirmed estimates). Birth rate 4.7%; natural increase: 3.2%. Gross national product: *c.* $1,000m. National income *per capita:* $175–200.

Imports: c. $330m., exports: $168m. (1968). Budget: about $200m. Literacy: 35% of the population (est.). Doctors: .1 per 5,080 inhabitants. Hospital beds: 1 per 800 or 1.23 per 1,000 pop. £S2.19 = US $ 1.
(A. L.)

SYRIAC, SYRIAN CHRISTIANS. The S. language is a branch of Aramaic which was spoken in the ME shortly before and at the beginning of the Christian era. The main centre of S.-Aramaic civilization was the town of Edessa. The Syriac tongue has a western and an eastern branch, which differ from one another mainly in the form of the script, the system of vocalization and in pronunciation. Western Syriac is the liturgical tongue of the S. Orthodox (Jacobites▷), the Maronites▷ and the S. Catholics. Eastern S. is used by the Nestorians▷ and the Chaldeans▷. A S. dialect is still spoken in a few villages in Syria and in one village in eastern Turkey.
(Sh.C.)

SYRIAN NATIONALIST PARTY (al-hizb al-suri al-qawmi, Parti Populaire Syrien, PPS). A right-wing pro-Fascist party established in Lebanon by Anton Sa'adeh▷ in 1932. It agitated for the termination of the French Mandate▷ and was proscribed. After independence, the PPS was suspected and harassed both in Lebanon and Syria, since it agitated against Lebanon's existence as a separate state and against Syrian Arab nationalism. It claimed that "Natural Syria"—Syria, Lebanon, Palestine and Transjordan (subsequently also Iraq and Cyprus!)—is a geographic unit with a distinct identity, where a "Syrian nation" has developed through the ages; language is not a determining factor in the creation of nations and therefore the Arabic language used by Syrians does not determine their national identity. The party stood for a totalitarian regime, and for the separation of church and state.

In the 1940s and '50s the PPS had a considerable influence among Western-educated intellectuals, particularly among the Greek Orthodox▷. In 1949 it was accused of a plot and Sa'adeh was summarily tried and executed. The execution of its leader, its persecution by the authorities, the rising wave of Arab nationalism, and internal splits, greatly weakened the party. Members of the party in 1951 assassinated Riyad al-Sulh▷, holding him responsible for the execution of their leader. In the 1950s, the PPS was regarded as right-wing, pro-Western, and even connected with the Hashemite▷ dynasty. Its members were tried in the purges conducted in leftist Syria. In 1958, the party supported Camille Chamoun▷ against Nasserist▷ rebels, as it preferred

an independent Lebanon to her integration in or annexation by a Pan-Arab▷ state, and provided some of the fighters against the rebels. Late in 1961, the PPS was accused of a plot to seize power in Lebanon through a military coup, many of its members were arrested as plotters, and the party—now in decline, with almost no members—went underground. In 1970, there was talk of again permitting the party in Lebanon, and its leader 'Abdullah Sa'adeh made numerous statements; but it is doubtful whether it could attain a position of much influence. (Y.P.)

T

TABATABAI, ZIYA-UL-DIN (1890–1968). Iranian journalist and politician. Born in Yazd, son of an Islamic religious leader. In Feb. 1921, T. engineered, together with Col. Reza Khan (later Reza Shah▷ Pahlavi), a coup which led, four years later, to the ousting of the last Qajar Shah. Although he was considered to be pro-British, T. rejected the British-Iranian draft treaty of 1919 which he considered humiliating to Iran. He concluded a treaty of friendship with the USSR in which the Soviets renounced the capitulations▷ and turned over to Iran all Soviet assets except the Caspian fishing industry. T. planned a series of social reforms which antagonized the big landowners, but had no time to implement them, as disagreement with Reza Khan caused him to resign and leave Iran, 1921. The British granted him asylum in Palestine, where he lived until 1943. After his return to Iran he established a political party, the "National Will" (Irade-i-Melli), which was considered pro-British; though conservative and right-wing, he proposed economic and social reforms. In 1944 he was elected to Parliament (the Majlis). In 1946, he exerted pressure on Premier Qavam al-Saltaneh▷ for the removal of the communist Tudeh▷ ministers from the Iranian Cabinet; that same year he was arrested by Qavam, in an effort to appease the Soviets, and retired from politics. (B.G.)

TA'IZZ. The second, southern capital of Yemen, situated on a high plateau (c. 1,500 mi.). Pop.: c. 90,000, most of whom are Shafe'is▷. Because of its Shafe'i population and its remoteness from the centre of the Zeidi▷ tribes, T. was chosen by Iman Ahmad▷ in 1955 as a second capital and a retreat in case of tribal rebellion. There were no battles around T. in the civil war of 1962–70. However it served as a main base for the FLOSY▷ underground group fighting in Aden▷ (see South Yemen▷). T. was connected to the capital San'a and the port of Hudeida by roads built, with American, West German, and Soviet aid, respectively. (H. E.)

TALAL b. 'ABDULLAH (b. 1909). Former King of Jordan. Born in Mecca. Ascended the throne in 1951, after the assassination of his father, King 'Abdullah▷. T. approved, in Jan. 1952, a change in the constitution, making the cabinet responsible to Parliament. His foreign policy was reported to be aimed at bringing Jordan into line with Egypt, Syria and Sa'udia, and was thus directed against Britain and Iraq. T. was dethroned in Aug. 1952 because of mental illness, and his son Hussein▷ was proclaimed King. T. has since been under care in a mental institution in Istanbul.   (B. G.)

TALÂT PASHA (1874–1921). Turkish political leader. One of the "Young Turks"▷. Ottoman Grand Vizir (Prime Minister), 1917–18. T. was born in Edirne (Adrianople), worked in the telegraph office there, and subsequently became Secretary of Posts and Telegraphs in Salonika. He was one of the first to join the Young Turks' "Committee of Union and Progress" and played an active role in the revolution of 1908; after the revolution he became a deputy in the Ottoman Parliament. He filled various government posts, serving twice as Minister of the Interior. Together with Enver Pasha▷ and Cemal Pasha▷, he formed a "triumvirate" that ruled Turkey from 1913 to 1918, and in 1917 became Grand Vizir, succeeding Sa'id Halim Pasha. He fled the country after the Armistice and was assassinated in 1921 in Berlin by an Armenian.   (D. K.)

Bahjat Talhouni

✳ **TALHOUNI, BAHJAT** (b. 1913). Jordanian jurist and politician. Graduate of Damascus University (Law), T. served as Attorney-General, Magistrate, member and later President of a District Court. He was Minister of the Interior 1953–4, Chief of the Royal Court 1954–60 and 1963–4, Minister for Foreign Affairs 1961–2. T. was Prime Minister 1960–1, 1964–5, Oct. 1967 to Mar. 1969, Aug. 1969 to June 1970. He is considered a moderate Nasserist, though loyal to King Hussein▷, and was thus appointed by the king whenever he needed a Prime Minister who was *persona grata* with Egypt. T. has taken up an equally ambiguous stand towards the Palestinian-Arab guerillas—Jordan's major policy problem in recent years: while loyal to the Jordanian establishment, he is acceptable to the guerillas and seeks an accommodation with them.   (B. G.)

TALL, AL-, 'ABDULLAH (b. 1919). Jordanian officer, from Irbid. In the Palestine War of 1948 he served in the Jerusalem area and became commander of the city with the rank of Lieutenant-Colonel. Strongly anti-Israel and anti-British, he collaborated with Palestinian nationalists and endeavoured to obstruct King 'Abdullah's▷ efforts to reach a peace agreement with Israel. He was suspected of plotting, with Egyptian and Syrian support, to overthrow the regime. In June 1949 T. resigned from the army and in October went to Egypt, where he lived as a political refugee. He was accused of playing a part in the assassination of King 'Abdullah. His memoires contained a bitter attack on the Hashemite dynasty and the Jordanian regime. T. was allowed to return to Jordan in 1965. He settled down in Irbid and abandoned political activity.   (B. G.)

✳ **TALL, AL-, WASFI** (1920–71). Jordanian politician. Educated at the American University of Beirut, T. worked as a teacher, 1941–2. He served in the British Army, 1942–5, reaching the rank of captain. T. joined Mussa 'Alami's▷ Arab propaganda offices in London and Jerusalem, 1945–7. During the Palestine War, 1948, he joined Qawuqji's▷ "Army of Deliverance" and, for a few months, the Syrian Army. He served in the Jordanian Civil and Diplomatic Service from 1949. T. was Ambassador in Iraq, 1961–2. He was Prime Minister and Minister of Defence, Jan. 1962 to Mar. 1963, and Prime Minister Feb. 1965 to Mar. 1967 and Oct. 1970 to Nov. 1971. T. was considered anti-Nasserist and loyal to the king. The royal regime's decisive operations against the guerilla establishment were conducted during his Premiership, in 1971. He was unpopular with the Egyptians. T. was assassinated in Nov. 1971 in Cairo by Palestinian terrorists.   (B. G.)

TAPLINE—see Oil▷ in the ME, appendix: major oil companies.

TARTOUS. Port town in north-west Syria. A new harbour was opened there at the beginning of 1968, bigger than Lataqia▷, Syria's main port. T. is mainly an oil port, the terminus of a 403 mi. oil pipeline from the Jazira▷ oilfields, opened in 1968. The pipeline— 22″ up to the Homs refinery, 18″ from Homs to T.— has a capacity of 4m. tons *p.a.* and can be expanded to 7.5m. tons. Oil tankers of up to 80,000 tons can berth at the harbour. In 1969, T. was linked to the Syrian railroad network.   (A. L.-O. T.)

TASHNAQ (also **DASHNAQ**). A political party that developed among the Armenians▷ dispersed in the ME, particularly in Lebanon and Syria, between the two world wars. Its politics and ideology change according to tactical considerations, but it is usually considered as more moderate and pro-Western than the rival Hantchak▷ party. It is mainly concerned with the interests of the Armenian community.
(Y. S.)

＊**TEHERAN** (or**TEHRAN**). Capital of Iran since 1785. Pop.: *c.* 3m. The city has expanded considerably since the beginning of the 20th century, when its population was about 200,000. Its growth is due mainly to migration from the interior of the country. There are a number of light industries in the T. area such as textiles, cigarettes, leather goods, cement works, sugar, etc. There are two universities: T. University, and the National University.

In Dec. 1943 the first meeting of the Allied "Big Three" (Churchill, Roosevelt and Stalin) took place in T. (the "T. Conference"). An important accord, the "T. Agreement", between the major international oil companies and six oil-producing countries of the Persian Gulf was signed in T. in Feb. 1971, ending an international crisis.   (B. G.)

Tel Aviv

TEL AVIV. The largest town in Israel (pop.: 383,000). Founded in 1909, it grew rapidly after 1921, being the only all-Jewish town in the world. When in 1936 Haifa and Jaffa ports were obstructed by the Arab rebellion, a small port was built in TA (later also used to smuggle Jewish refugees from Europe through the British blockade). In May 1948 David Ben-Gurion▷ declared the establishment of the State of Israel in TA, which served, from 1948 to 1950, as the seat of the Government and Parliament until they moved to the capital, Jerusalem.

TA is the industrial (52% of all enterprises), banking, commercial, press and cultural centre. Its university has 11,500 students (1971) with a second university (4,000 students) in its conurbation.

In 1950 it was municipally united with Jaffa▷ under the name of Tel Aviv-Yafo. With the surrounding suburbs TA forms a rapidly expanding conurbation of 800,000 inhabitants.   (Y. K.)

TIGRIS, RIVER (Turkish: Dicle, Arabic: Dijla). Issues from Lake Hazar in the east of central Anatolia (Turkey) and joins the Euphrates▷ to form the Shatt al-'Arab▷ near Qurna, in southern Iraq, after a course of 1,150 mi. For about 25 mi. the T. forms the frontier between Turkey and Iraq on the left (eastern) bank, and Syria in the west. In northern and central Iraq the T. receives important tributaries, all from the east; chief among them are the Greater Zab, the Lesser Zab and the Diyala. In central and southern Iraq the T. connects up with the Euphrates through a number of channels and natural water courses, generally seasonally. The lower reaches of the T. are largely surrounded by swamps. Important development works based on the T. and its tributaries are the Kut Barrage, completed 1939, and the Samarra Barrage, diverting flood waters into the Wadi Tharthar depression, 1956, the Dokan Dam on the Lesser Zab, 1959, and the Derbendi Khan Dam on the Sirwan (upper Diyala; completed 1963–4). River navigation is important between Mosul and Basra, on the Shatt al-'Arab.   (U. D.)

TIKRITI, AL-, HARDAN 'ABD-UL-GHAF-FAR (1925–71). Iraqi officer and politician. Entered the regular army and joined the air force. During the Qassem▷ regime, 1958–63, T. took up contacts with the clandestine *Ba'th* group and was among the leaders of the coup which overthrew Qassem in February 1963. He became the commander of the air force under the *Ba'th* regime of 1963. After its fall (Nov. 1963) he was appointed Minister of Defence by President 'Abd-ul-Salam 'Aref▷, but soon quarrelled with him; he was exiled as Ambassador to Sweden, but left that post in unclear circumstances.

After the first Bakr▷ coup (17 July 1968), T. became Chief of General Staff and commander of the air force; after Bakr's second coup (30 July 1968) – Deputy Prime Minister and Minister of Defence. In April. 1970 he was appointed Vice-President and gave up the Defence Ministry. He was also a member of the Revolutionary Command Council. T.'s name was often mentioned in connection with factional rivalries and rumoured coup preparations. In Oct. 1970, he was deprived of all his offices and went into exile. His fall was due to his bad relations with President Bakr and *Ba'th* Secretary Sadam Hussein (al-Tikriti). His alleged responsibility for the failure of the Iraqi forces in Jordan to interfere in support of the Palestinian guerillas during the September 1970 fighting between them and Jordanian government forces, served as pretext for his dismissal. T. was assassinated in Kuwait in Mar. 1971.   (U. D.)

TIRAN, STRAITS OF. A narrow passage, connecting the Gulf of 'Aqaba▷ (Eilat▷) with the Red Sea▷. A string of islands here approaches the Sinai▷ coast to a distance of 4.5 mi. The westernmost of these islands is the Island of T. As both the island and the Sinai coast are accompanied by coral reefs, the actual width of the S. is 2.5 mi. Another group of reefs within the S. confines navigability to two narrow passages: Passage Enterprise—near Sinai—3,900 ft. wide and 820 ft. deep; and Grafton Passage—near the island—2,300 ft. wide and up to 230 ft. deep. Other passages, east of the island, are even narrower and shallower. Shipping uses only Passage Enterprise.

The uninhabited and barren Island of T. was occupied by Egypt in 1949 with the approval of its owner, Sa'udi Arabia, in order to close the S. for shipping to the Israeli port of Eilat. Egypt claimed that the S. were within her territorial waters and were not to be considered an international waterway. The legal situation remains controversial. While most countries would concede that the S. are within Egypt's territorial waters, they would insist that straits connecting the high seas with another country's territorial waters are international waterways, through which the right of innocent passage overrides the territorial rights of the riparian country. An International Conference on the Law of the Sea, in 1958, adopted a Convention, articles 4 and 16 of which confirm that principle.

Egyptian gun positions at Sharm al-Sheikh▷ and Ras Nasrani, on the Sinai coast of the S., since the early 1950s blocked the approach to Eilat and controlled all shipping to 'Aqaba. After some attempts at running the blockade, traffic to Eilat virtually ceased until 1956. This blockade was one of the main causes of the Sinai Campaign▷ of 1956, in the course of which Sharm al-Sheikh and Ras Nazrani were occupied. In 1957, upon their evacuation by Israel, units of the United Nations Emergency Force▷ were stationed there, with Egypt's consent, to ensure and observe free passage through the S. of T. Egypt's demand for their withdrawal in May 1967 and the reimposition of the Egyptian blockade were one of the chief causes of the Six Day War▷. Since that war the S. are once more under Israeli control, open to the free passage of all vessels.   (Y. K.-Y. S.-E. L.)

TOBRUK. Mediterranean port in eastern Cyrenaica, Libya. T. became famous during World War II. It was occupied by British troops on 22 Jan. 1941. When they retreated before the Germans under Rommel, in spring 1941, T. was cut off and its garrison (mostly Australians) was besieged for eight months until relieved by the British in Dec. 1941. On 26 May 1942, T. fell in Rommel's second offensive. It was recaptured by Montgomery at the end of 1942. After the war, T. served as a British military and naval base under the Anglo-Libyan treaty of 1953. The revolutionary regime that took power in Libya in Sept. 1969 demanded the evacuation of the base, and Britain agreed. The T. base was evacuated on 28 Mar. 1970.

T. serves as terminus for a 320 mi., 30m. ton British Petroleum Company oil pipeline from the Company's wells inland (opened 1966) and as its oil port (opened 1967).   (O. G.)

TOUQAN. A prominent Palestinian-Arab family of Jordanian origin, centred in Nablus, where the family is known since the 12th century. For generations, it has been competing for supremacy in the town and area with the al-Nimr and 'Abd-ul-Hadi families.

Members of the family served in governmental positions during the Ottoman period. During the Mandate▷, it leaned towards the Nashashibi▷ camp and had close contacts with Amir 'Abdullah▷. Some of its members, though, did not conform to that rule. Hafez Agha T. in the 1920s headed the "Muslim-Christian Society" of Nablus and supported the Husseinis▷. His son, Qadri H. T. (died 1971), a mathematician and author of textbooks, was principal of the "al-Najah" College, a well-known Nablus Arab high school. He also wrote books about national and political problems, and was active in politics. He was Jordanian Foreign Minister 1964–5.

Other members of the T. family served in governmental positions during the Mandatory period and afterwards in the Kingdom of Jordan. Baha'-ul-Din T. was Jordanian Minister in Cairo, 1948–51, and Ankara 1951–4, and Ambassador in London 1956–8, and at the UN in 1958 and since 1971. Jamal T.—a senior administrative official and District Governor— was Foreign Minister in 1954 and Minister of Education in 1957; Taysir T.—Jordanian Ambassador in Libya. The outstanding members of the family in the last generation were Suleiman▷ T. and Ahmad▷ T. who gained prominence in the service of the Kingdom of Jordan.   (Y.P.)

TOUQAN, AHMAD (b. 1903). Palestinian-Jordanian civil servant and politician. Born in Nablus. Educated at Oxford University.

In the 1930s and '40s T. served in various posts in the Department of Education of the Mandatory Government of Palestine. In the early 1950s he held several ministerial posts in the Jordanian Cabinet (Public Works, Education, and briefly—1951—Foreign Affairs). T. served on the staff of UNESCO 1954–63. After returning to Jordanian politics he became Foreign Minister, 1967 and 1969, and served as Deputy Prime Minister 1967–70 and Defence Minister 1969 and 1970. T. was briefly Prime Minister in Sept.-Oct. 1970, taking over from a short-lived military government that had led Jordan into a bloody confrontation with the Palestinian-Arab guerillas. Since Oct. 1970, T. is Chief of the Royal Cabinet. He is considered King Hussein's man, and his premiership was a compromise between pro-guerilla pressure, supported by Pan-Arab mediators, and the army (loyal to the king) which wanted to maintain a firm attitude towards the guerilas' attempts to take over Jordan.   (B.G.)

TOUQAN, SULEIMAN 'ABD-UL-RAZZAQ (1888 or 1890–1958). Palestinian-Arab and Jordanian politician. Educated in Istanbul (law school and military academy), he returned to Nablus to run the family's commercial enterprises (olive oil and soap factories). Mayor of Nablus 1925–48. T. was among the founders of the "National Defence Party", 1934, the political arm of the "Nashashibi"▷ faction, and collaborated with Amir 'Abdullah▷. T. was pro-Jordanian, pro-Iraqi and pro-British; he was considered a moderate in his attitude to the Jews of Palestine. When in 1937–9 Arab nationalist guerilas turned their arms mainly against Arab opposition circles, T. organized counter-guerillas. After 1948, he helped consolidate 'Abdullah's rule in the West Bank▷. From 1950 he was a member, and later Deputy President, of the Jordanian Senate. T. served as Minister of Defence 1951 and 1957, and Minister of the Royal Court 1953–5. From Apr. to July 1957—a period of crisis, after an attempted coup and the restoration of the King's power—he served as Military Governor. He was again Minister of the

Royal Court in 1957–8. In 1958 he served as Minister of Defence in the Federal Government of the (Jordanian-Iraqi) "Arab Federation"▷. He was assassinated in Baghdad during the coup of 14 July 1958 that put an end to Hashemite rule in Iraq.   (B.G.)

TRANSJORDAN (Arabic: *Sharq al-Urdunn*). The area on the east bank of the Jordan, most of which was part of the province (*Vilayet*) of Damascus during the Ottoman period. After World War I T. was included within the boundaries of the British Mandate▷ over Palestine. In 1921 the British decided to establish a Transjordanian entity as an Amirate under 'Abdullah b. Hussein▷ (see also Jordan▷, Political History). At British request, T. was in 1922 excluded from those clauses of the Palestine Mandate which prescribed the foundation of a Jewish National Home, but remained within the Mandate and subordinate to the High Commissioner in Jerusalem, who was represented in 'Amman, the capital of T., by a British Resident. In 1946 Britain granted T. formal independence and 'Abdullah became king. After the occupation of the Arab part of Palestine in 1948, the name of the kingdom was changed to Jordan▷ (The Hashemite Kingdom of Jordan) and the term T. went out of use. What used to be T., 1921–48, is since 1948 often referred to as the East Bank (of the Jordan, within a kingdom situated on both banks).   (B.G.)

TRANSPORT IN THE MIDDLE EAST. The prosperity of the ME in the past was based largely on its location at the crossroads of the world's main routes. Until the discovery of America, the ME was the heart of the known world, the bridge between the three continents. The wares of the Far East in India were traded in the commercial centres of the ME against goods from the Baltic, West Europe, the Mediterranean basin and the ME itself. This commerce used both land and sea routes, but all the routes converged on a few centres such as Constantinople (Istanbul), Cairo, Damascus, Baghdad. The location of these hubs was determined by the topography of south-west Asia, where high mountain ranges make communications difficult and limit free movement to a corridor running north-west to south-west from the eastern Mediterranean coast to the head of the Persian Gulf of the Red Sea. Within the corridor, a number of routes operated throughout history, and also influenced modern transportation routes.

The principal route ran from Constantinople or the ports on the Aegean coast of Anatolia, *via* Adana (or Aleppo), Mosul (formerly Nineveh), Baghdad (formerly Babylon or Ctesiphon), to the head of the Persian Gulf (Susa, Basra). It was along this route that the world's first international road was laid—the "King's Way" of the Persian monarchs, linking Susa with Sardes (near Izmir). The Baghdad Railway▷ in the present century follows a similar route. Another road branched off near Baghdad and led up to the Iranian plateau, through Teheran, and Meshed to Turkestan, the central Asian steppe and China. This route was known as the "Silk Route". Another road started at Aleppo and led southwards to Damascus (with a few narrow secondary roads leading to the Mediterranean ports) and on to Medina, Mecca, and thence to Yemen and the southern coast of Arabia. The southern part of this route was known as the "Incense Route". In the Middle Ages, its northern stretch was known as "Darb al-Hajj", the route of the pilgrims to Mecca, and, in modern times, the Hijaz Railway▷ from Damascus to Medina followed it. Main junctions led from Aleppo to Antiochia (today Antakia) and from Damascus to Tyre or Sidon, Acre, Jaffa, and Egypt. Another lateral road lay along the axis Tripoli-Homs-Palmyra-Baghdad. Parallel to these land roads was the sea route through the Red Sea, from Suez (or, in some periods, Eilat), to Jidda, Aden and Mukalla. In Africa, the Nile served as the sole communications route from the Mediterranean coast to Aswan, with lateral roads to the Red Sea ports of Safaga and Berenice (there is now an Egyptian harbour under construction nearby).

Until the 16th century, Europe's commerce with India and the Far East was carried by sea as far as the Levant ports, from there overland to the Persian Gulf or Red Sea coast, and once again by sea. With the discovery of America and the sea route to India around the Cape of Good Hope, the ME no longer provided a main link for world trade, and henceforth the caravans served only local needs. Modern transport returned to the ME with the cutting of the Suez Canal▷, 1969, which reopened the historic route to the Red Sea and became a "vital artery of the British Empire".

At the end of the 19th century, the construction of railways began—intended mainly to serve local needs. Egypt became the only ME country with a dense rail network. The only railway scheme intended to serve more than local needs was the Baghdad Railway▷. Planning for this railway began in 1873 and a concession was granted in 1899, yet the railway itself reached Baghdad only in 1940. Due to the fragmentation of the ME into many states, and to political and economic friction amongst them, the Baghdad Railway never fulfilled its international role and its main importance lies in its providing the back-bone of Turkey's sparse railway network. (There had been an earlier British plan for a railway linking Syria—Lebanon's ports with the Persian

Gulf, but it was never implemented). Another international rail route, the Hijaz Railway▷, ceased to operate during World War I. Today, only national railway systems exist in the region and there is virtually no international rail traffic. The line between Egypt, Palestine, Syria, Lebanon and Turkey was cut when the Arab States went to war against Israel in 1948. A rail-link between Turkey and Iran is in the planning and construction stage (scheduled for completion 1970–1). Internal railway systems in ME countries consist, in most cases, of a few lines. Equipment is, for the most part, obsolete, and trains are infrequent.

ME road systems are not well developed either. In remote or mountainous regions, access to the villages is usually over unpaved roads or even mule-tracks. A road across the Arabian peninsula (from Dammam on the Persian Gulf, via Riyadh, to Mecca and Jidda) was not completed until 1967. In other ME countries, asphalted roads link only the major cities. In Turkey, a road system linking the major cities was built only recently to meet the strategic requirements of NATO▷. In the Nile Delta, to this day most roads are dirt roads, and the recently built highway along the Nile was a by-product of the Aswan High Dam▷. Inter-country road links are almost non-existent. The only road linking Iraq with the Mediterranean coast runs alongside the oil pipeline, and joins the 'Amman-Damascus road at Mafraq. The first road connecting Turkey and Iran was laid in the 1960s. By contrast, the maritime links of the ME are highly developed and modern ports exist in most countries. Some of them, especially those on the Persian Gulf, serve only for oil transport, but on the Mediterranean cost each country has at least two modern harbours.

The limitations of the transport system described above have prevented the ME from regaining its role of a major transit area, on which its former greatness was based. Yet it has regained such a role to a certain degree with regard to the most modern means of transportation—oil pipelines and air communications. Pipelines follow the ancient routes from the Persian Gulf to the Mediterranean. The "Tapline" links the oilfields of Sa'udi-Arabia with the port of Sidon. The IPC pipeline system brings oil from Iraq to the ports of Tripoli▷ in Lebanon and Baniyas▷ in Syria. More pipelines from the Iran-Iraq region to the Mediterranean are planned. A pipeline brings gas from Iran to the USSR. The Eilat-Ashkelon pipeline transports oil from the Red Sea to the Mediterranean; a Suez-Alexandria pipeline, in the planning stage, will do the same.

In aviation, the ME has also resumed its historic part in T. Most air routes from the USA and Europe to India and the Far East cross the ME. The airports in

Istanbul, Teheran, Cairo and Beirut have become first-class international airports, and Damascus is not far behind; Kuwait, Bahrain, Baghdad have busy international airports. The airport of Tel-Aviv serves Israel's heavy international traffic; its position as a transit point for flights farther east is affected by the Arab countries' barring any aircraft which has touched down at Tel-Aviv from entering their air space—a ban compelling those flights to the Far East that land in Tel-Aviv to bypass Arab air space by flying over Turkey to Teheran. Cairo is also a major junction for flights to East-Africa and its airfield has helped create a new transport route, Moscow-Africa. (Y.K.)

TREATIES, AGREEMENTS—see under the place where they were signed (e.g. Saadabad, Lausanne) or the men who signed them (e.g. Bevin, Sidqi).

TRIPARTITE DECLARATION. A statement issued by the Foreign Ministers of the USA, France and Great Britain on 25 May 1950, recognizing the "need of the Arab states and Israel to maintain a certain level of armed forces for ... their internal security and legitimate self-defence and to permit them to play their part in the defence of the area as a whole". Arms were to be supplied in accordance with these principles, and only to countries pledging themselves not to commit aggression against any other state. The three governments declared that such "assurances have been received from all the states in question" and pledged immediate "action both within and outside the UN", to prevent any violation of frontiers or armistice lines.

While primarily concerned with the Soviet threat to the region, the TD came close to being a guarantee of the territorial *status quo*. Although issued without previous consultation with Israel or the Arab states, it was cautiously welcomed by the government of Israel as a commitment to some Israel-Arab arms balance, a sign that discrimination in the supply of arms would henceforward be corrected, and a guarantee of sorts for the inviolability of her borders. The Arab states, in a joint statement, while 'reaffirming their pacific intentions'', expressed doubts concerning the powers' intentions to intervene and stressed the sovereign right of each state to judge the level of arms it needed.

The TD, originally interpreted as a co-ordinated Western guarantee of ME borders and ME defence, did not live up to such far-reaching expectations. Whatever influence it may have had ceased on the eve of the Six Day War▷ in May 1967, when Britain and France announced that they considered the TD was no longer binding upon them. (N.L.-Y.S.-E.L.)

TRIPOLI. Main city of Northern Lebanon, on the Mediterranean coast. Pop.: *c*. 150,000, or 240,000 if the al-Mina Quarter and the Palestinian refugee camps are included. The IPC oil pipeline, from the Kirkuk region in northern Iraq, has its terminus in T. A refinery has been built alongside the harbour. About 80% of the population are Sunni▷ Muslims, 10% are Greek-Orthodox▷. T. and its environs were annexed to Lebanon on 1 Sept. 1920, with the creation of "Greater Lebanon" by the French (see Lebanon▷, History). The Muslim Arabs opposed the annexation and came only gradually later to accept it—and perhaps not wholeheartedly. T. has remained the centre of opposition to the Christian character and image of Lebanon. Nationalist Arab parties, such as the *Ba'th* party and the Arab Nationalist Movement▷, are concentrated there. (Y.P.)

TRIPOLI (Arabic: *Tarablus al-Gharb*, T. of the West, to distinguish it from *Tarablus al-Sham*, T. of the North, in Lebanon). Capital of Libya▷, and her main port. Pop.: 250,000? 430,000? (conflicting 1970 estimates). During Ottoman and, later, Italian rule T. was the capital of the province of Tripolitania▷. When the Italians merged Cyrenaica▷ and Tripolitania into the colony of Libya, 1934, T. became Libya's capital. During World War II, it was conquered by the Allied forces (Jan. 1943). When Libya became independent, in Dec. 1951, T. became one of her two capitals (with Benghazi). It also maintained its status as provincial capital of Tripolitania until 1963, when the federal provinces were abolished. The military coup of Sept. 1969 started in T., which was declared sole capital of Libya by the new regime. (B.G.)

TRIPOLITANIA. North-western region of Libya▷, with an area of 110,000 sq. mi. and a population of 1.03m. (1964 census). Major city—Tripoli▷. T. consists of a narrow strip of inhabited land along the coast and an extended desert hinterland. In the past, the name T. was sometimes used for the whole of Libya. For T.'s history, government and politics—see Libya▷. (Y.S.)

TRUCIAL COAST (or **TRUCIAL 'OMAN**). A group of seven sheikhdoms or principalities along a peninsula on the southern (Arabian) coast of the Persian Gulf. TC has a length of about 372 mi., but its internal borders facing Sa'udi Arabia and Muscat-and-'Oman▷ are not defined. Its area is estimated at 32,000 sq. mi., the population at 150,000. (The tip of the peninsula belongs to Muscat-and-'Oman, separated by the TC principalities). The region is desert, lacking water resources and farming land. Most of the population is nomadic or engaged in fishing, pearl-diving, boat-building and marine commerce (until the development of the oil economy in the 1960s). The population in the coastal towns includes Iranians, Indians, Pakistanis and Negroes.

In the 18th century, the sheikhs engaged in piracy, and the area became known as the "Pirate Coast". At the beginning of the 19th century, Great Britain began to take military measures, through the government in India, to protect its commerce, and in 1820 imposed on the coastal chiefs an agreement to end piracy. This agreement was expanded in 1853 into a perpetual maritime truce, and the area became known as the "TC". Britain undertook, in these and other treaties with various sheikhs, to provide protection and financial support to the sheikhdoms and their rulers. Subsequently, British political officers were stationed in Dubai▷ and Abu Dhabi▷ (under the chief British Political Resident for the Persian Gulf▷ —at first at Bushire, and since 1946 at Bahrain▷).

The seven principalities of the TC are: Abu Dhabi, Umm al-Qaiwain, Dubai, 'Ajman, Fujaira, Ras al-Khaima and Sharja (see entry for each of them). In 1952, Britain began to organize co-operation between the seven through a quasi-federal permanent council headed by the British Resident. In the 1950s, she established a small British-commanded military police force jointly for the seven with headquarters at Sharja (the "T. Scouts").

With the discovery of oil in the 1960s, the area's economic importance grew. Abu Dhabi especially soon became rich through the discovery of huge quantities of oil. Part of the oil income goes to a joint development fund for the TC principalities, later joined also by Qatar▷ and Bahrain.

In 1966, Britain established a naval base in Sharja to replace the British base in Aden, then due to be evacuated. But in 1968, Britain decided to liquidate her commitments and evacuate her forces "East of Suez", and plans for the Sharja base were curtailed. Britain also decided to remove in 1971 her protection from the TC and the rest of the Persian Gulf principalities.

Preliminary to full independence expected in 1971, it was decided in spring 1968 to form a federation— "Union of Arab Emirates", UAE—to include the seven TC principalities, Qatar and Bahrain. Since 1968, discussions have been in progress on the Federation, its constitution and future form of government. There were many difficult questions—would all partners be of equal weight and importance or would their size and contribution be taken into account? Who would preside over the Federation and where would its capital be located? What would be the authority and power of the Federation in relation to

its component units? Mutual jealousies and old disputes between several of the TC rulers were another obstacle. Both land and offshore border disputes between several of the principalities have assumed a new importance with the discovery of oil in the area. An additional difficulty was Iran's attitude: Iran objected to any political arrangement for the region as long as her claim to three islands also claimed by T. sheikhs (Abu Mussa▷, claimed by both Sharja and Umm al-Qaiwain, and the two Tumb islands claimed by Ras al-Khaima) was not accepted and satisfied.

In 1970, provisional arrangements were made for federation. The Sheikh of Abu Dhabi became President for two years, with Abu Dhabi as a temporary capital until a new one was built on the border between Abu Dhabi and Dubai. A provisional Federal Council was also established. There was, however, no progress towards the implementation of federal plans. Moreover, it transpired that Bahrain was not really prepared to join (certainly not as an equal partner, being more populous than the other sheikhdoms together), and that Qatar, too, would probably not join the UAE. In July 1971 it was therefore announced that preparations would go ahead for the creation of a six-member UAE—without Bahrain and Qatar, and also without Ras al-Khaima.   (Y. K.-Y. S.)

*TRUMAN, HARRY S. (b. 1884). 32nd President of the USA, Apr. 1945–Jan. 1953, Democrat. T. was faced with the Palestine dispute shortly after he became President. He favoured, and pressed for, the admission of 100,000 displaced Jews to Palestine. While he was unwilling to allow the USA to become actively involved in the Palestine problem, he agreed to send the Anglo-American Committee▷, 1945–6, to investigate the problem. When the issue came before the UN in 1947, the USA supported UNSCOP's▷ partition plan, but later attempted to replace it by a trusteeship; however on 14 May 1948, the USA became, on T.'s decision, the first state to recognize Israel.

T.'s main impact on the ME was caused by the T. Doctrine▷—a policy statement of 12 Mar. 1947 pledging US support for "free peoples who are resisting attempted subjugation by armed minorities or outside pressure". The T. Doctrine was meant to apply particularly to Greece and Turkey, for whom T. was asking for an emergency aid appropriation of $400m., and also Iran. (Three months later, American aid—the "Marshall Plan"—went into full operation.)
                                    (Sh. H.-Y. S.)

TRUMPELDOR, JOSEPH (1880–1920). Zionist pioneer and military hero, of Russian-Jewish origin.

T. had lost one of his arms as a Russian officer in the Russo-Japanese war of 1905. He called for collective agricultural settlement in Palestine and for armed Jewish self-defence. He settled in Palestine in 1912, worked in Kibbutz Deganiya, and took part in the defence of Jewish settlements in the Lower Galilee. During World War I, T. helped to organize Jewish volunteers to the Jewish Legion▷ within the British Army. He founded the *Hehalutz*▷ (Hebrew: The Pioneer) movement, 1917, and was active in the foundation of the *Histadrut*▷ (General Federation of Labour). His heroic death in the defence of Tel-Hai (1920) against Arab rioters ("It is good to die for our country") became a symbol of defence for Jewish youth, of both left- and right-wing parties. The Zionist-Revisionist Youth and its sports organization was named after him.   (M. S.-E. L.)

*TUDEH (Persian: "The masses"—nearest Persian equivalent to "Proletariat"). The clandestine Communist Party of Iran. The first Communist Party in Iran was founded in 1920, but it was crushed by Reza Shah▷ in 1930. The T. was established in Oct. 1941 in Northern Iran, then under Soviet occupation. Its founders were mostly liberals, but included a few communists who had been released from prison. T. did not officially define itself as communist, its declared aims being extensive social and economic reforms. In 1944, T. participated in the elections and won eight seats, and in 1946 three T. ministers were included in the cabinet. In 1945 the T., in collaboration with the USSR, tried to take over Azerbaijan▷, then separated from Iran. In order not to endanger T. branches in Iran, the Azerbaijan branch dissolved itself, and two new parties were set up instead: the "Democratic Party of Azerbaijan" and the "Democratic Party of Kurdistan", which proclaimed independent Azerbaijani and Kurdish republics with capitals in Tabriz and Mahabad▷ respectively, Dec. 1945. After the evacuation of Soviet troops from Iran and the entry of Iranian armed forces into the two republics, Dec. 1946, the Iranian authorities began to suppress the T.

In Feb. 1949, after an unsuccessful attempt on the Shah's life by a member, the party was banned. Some of its leaders were arrested, while others fled to Eastern Europe. The party continued its activities in Iran through cover organizations, such as the "Peace Partisans". During the Premiership of Dr. Mossaddeq▷, 1951–3, it operated openly, although it did not obtain a legal status. T. supported Mossaddeq in his oil nationalization policy and shared his hostility towards the Shah. After the fall of Mossaddeq, T. was again banned and driven underground. The social and economic reforms initiated by the Shah and

improved Persian-Soviet relations removed the impetus of T., and the party now operates mainly in exile in Eastern Europe, where it runs a clandestine broadcasting station. Its present programme calls for the overthrow of the "anti-democratic" Government of Iran and for its withdrawal from CENTO▷.
                                                                                    (B. G.)

*TUNISIA. Tunisia—herself outside the scope of this Encyclopaedia—has played a significant part in ME affairs, more than once taking a position opposed to that of most Arab countries. During T.'s struggle for independence, many of her leaders found asylum and a base of operations in Egypt, including Habib Bourguiba▷, leader and President of independent T., and Saleh Ben Yussuf, his principal rival. It was the Arab countries which raised the issue of T. at the UN General Assembly from 1951–2 onwards, in the teeth of vigorous opposition from France; and although the UN debates and resolutions were of no practical and immediate influence, they created a climate of world opinion which helped prepare the way for France's surrender to the demand for independence, in 1956. There was renewed Arab pressure in 1961, at the time of the acute French-Tunisian crisis over Bizerta, and this pressure helped to impose on France a withdrawal and, ultimately, the abandonment of the base.

Yet relations between independent T. and the other Arab states have not always been good; at times they were extremely strained. As early as Oct. 1958, when T. joined the Arab League▷, the T. delegate attacked the expansionist, domineering aspirations of Egypt and accused her leaders of plotting against the T. regime and its President (meaning the political asylum and the base of operations Egypt had accorded to Saleh ben Yussuf, Bourguiba's rival, who had been accused of plotting a *coup d'état*). The T. delegate walked out of the League session, and T. did not return to League meetings until 1961. In 1958, T. also severed diplomatic relations with Egypt and did not re-establish them until 1961, following Egypt's support over the Bizerta crisis. Throughout this period of estrangement, T. continued to accuse Egypt of aspirations to dominate the other Arab states.

T.'s relations with the other *Maghreb*▷ countries have also been tense on more than one occasion. In 1960, Morroco severed diplomatic relations with T. because T. recognized the independence of Mauritania▷, and in 1963 T. severed relations with Algeria, accusing the latter of conspiracy against her regime.

On the Arab-Israel conflict, President Bourguiba adopted a position different from that of most Arab leaders (see Bourguiba). This caused permanent tension, and an acute crisis in 1965 when Bourguiba, on a tour of the ME, vigorously expressed his views both in conversations with leaders and in public, before student audiences and journalists. Several Arab countries recalled their ambassadors and some of them even broke off relations (Syria and Iraq in 1965, Egypt in 1966). Once again, T. suspended her participation in the activities of the Arab League—to a point that Bourguiba was neither present nor represented at the Arab summit conference of Casablanca▷. It was reported at the time that the leaders of the Arab League had indicated to T.'s delegates that their presence was not desired.

T. also differed from the other Arab States on the issue of relations with West Germany. Most of them severed relations with the Federal Republic when the latter established relations with Israel, but T. refused to do so. In this case, Morocco and Libya followed T.'s example. Once again, a campaign of mutual accusations and coarse vituperation ensued.

The crisis of 1967 and the Six Day War brought T. back to the fold. In the frenzied Arab enthusiasm which preceded the outbreak of the war, Bourguiba also gave his blessing to the victorious war. After the defeat, Bourguiba did not attend the Khartoum▷ summit conference, but T. was represented and did not voice reservations regarding the extremist position adopted at the conference (no recognition, no negotiations, no peace with Israel). T.'s relations with the extremist revolutionary camp among the Arab states remained cool and even strained, and diplomatic relations with Syria were severed once again in 1968. T. did, however, maintain normal relations, though somewhat reserved on both sides, with the Arab camp in general and especially with the "moderate" countries (Egypt and Jordan). In autumn 1970, T. even indulged in a measure of all-Arab activity when she sent her Prime Minister, Bahi Ladgham (al-Adgham), to head the inter-Arab commission mediating between Jordan and the Palestinian guerillas. Foreign Minister Masmoudi toured the ME in summer 1971 to a similar purpose.   (Y. S.)

*TURKEY (*Türkiye Cumhuriyeti*), Republic on the eastern Mediterranean. 296,185 sq. mi. Pop.: 35.6m. (1970 estimate). The population is relatively homogeneous, in terms both of religion and ethnic origin, being 99% Muslims and 90% Turks. The Kurds▷, estimated at 7% (1965), constitute the largest ethnic minority, and share their Sunni-Muslim religion with the Turks. About 1% are Arabs, while Greeks▷ (mostly Christian Orthodox) and Armenians▷ (mostly Gregorian) constitute about 0.1–0.2% each. Jews form about 0.1% of the population. There are also other linguistic and ethnic groups in T., com-

posed largely of Muslim immigrants from the Balkans or the Caucasus, but these have become largely assimilated. Figures are cited from the official census, which recognizes the division of the population by language or by religion but, in the interests of national unity, not by ethnic groups. For the same reason, the Kurds are usually referred to officially as "Mountain Turks". Similarly, official Turkish statistics do not make the division of Muslims into Sunni▷ and Shi'i▷ denominations. The number of Shi'i Muslims (or *Alevis*, as they are called in T.) is apparently considerable. Minorities in T., though relatively small in numbers, are concentrated geographically. The Kurds inhabit the south-eastern region, forming a majority in some provinces. The Arabs are found in the provinces bordering on Syria. Greeks, Armenians and Jews are mainly concentrated in Istanbul.

T. is situated on the eastern Mediterranean, astride two continents, Europe and Asia, and controls the only waterways connecting the Black Sea and the Mediterranean: the Straits of the Bosphorus▷ and the Dardanelles▷, and the Sea of Marmara between them. She is thus strategically situated at a most important land and water junction. Most of the country is in Asia and consists of the Anatolian peninsula (Asia Minor), whereas European T. forms a small region (Thrace) at the south-eastern tip of the Balkans. T.'s boundaries are mostly natural sea borders: the Black Sea in the north, the Aegean in the west and the Mediterranean in the south. On land, T. is bordered in the west by Bulgaria and Greece, in the east by the USSR and Iran, and in the south by Iraq and Syria.

T. has a large variety of topographic features— coastal strips encircling high inland plateaux, and a mountainous region in eastern T.—and of climatic conditions, and extreme variations in temperature and rainfall. The interior plateaux and the eastern region are less suitable for human habitation and cultivation and hence are relatively underdeveloped.

Over 70% of T.'s labour force is engaged in agriculture, which accounts for over 35% of the national income. T. raises a wide range of crops and livestock, which virtually supply her home needs. Agricultural products are also her chief export, the most important being cotton, tobacco, dried fruits and nuts. Agriculture, however, has the disadvantage of being dependent on the weather conditions, old-fashioned techniques, poor communications, and the generally small size of farms which are often worked by sharecroppers. These factors, which are more marked in inner and Eastern Anatolia, account for widespread poverty and under-employment, resulting in a movement of population away from the villages to seek work in urban centres, at home and

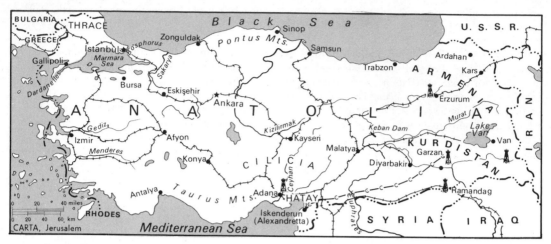

Map of Turkey

abroad. (There are over 200,000 Turkish workers in Europe.) Republican T. has devoted considerable efforts and financial resources to agricultural development by irrigation works, subsidies to farmers, mechanization, farmers' education, and land distribution schemes.

Mining and industry, undeveloped in Ottoman times, now occupy an important and growing role in the Turkish economy, engaging about 8% of the labour force and providing about 18% of the national income. T., alone in the ME, possesses rich and varied mineral deposits, the most important being coal, lignite, iron and chrome. Oil is found in quantities which promise self-sufficiency in the future. Minerals also feature as a large percentage of exports. Industrial production is predominantly in light industry, such as textiles, chemicals, "agricultural industries" and cement, but the existence of minerals has led to the development of heavy industry as well, e.g. iron and steel plants. The development of mining and industry has been regarded as a primary objective in republican T., in her drive for modernization, self-sufficiency and alleviation of rural under-employment. When the Republican People's Party was in power, T. followed a policy of state enterprise and control *(étatism)*. Since the 1950s, however, this has given way to a relaxation of state supervision, the denationalization of some enterprises, and the encouragement of private, including foreign, investment.

The T. Republic inherited from the Ottoman period a very poor network of railways and roads. Of the former, all built and owned by foreign concessionaires, the most important was the Anatolian Railway from Haydarpaşa (opposite Istanbul) to Konya (with a branch line to Ankara) and the Baghdad Railway from Konya to Nusaibin on the Syrian

frontier. Road and rail communications in T. still lag far behind her needs; but there has been much development of communications, which are considered important for reasons of security and economic development. Many roads have been built and improved. All railways were nationalized and new lines laid; one of them, almost completed, links the Turkish and Iranian networks *via* Mus and Tarvan. T. also maintains good maritime coastal communications. The major ports are Istanbul▷, Izmir▷, Mersin, Iskenderun and Izmit. Iskenderun is also the terminal for an oil pipeline from the Batman oilfields. The "Turkish Airlines" link the most important cities of Anatolia and serve some European and ME cities.

Since World War II T. has suffered from a deficit in her foreign trade and balance of payments, as imports, mostly of capital goods for development and industrialization, increased more than exports. Public finances have also suffered, owing to large outlays on defence and development, and low tax revenue (annual income *per capita* is low; approximately $300). Government expenditure has also led to growing inflation. T. was thus forced to seek foreign aid and to devote great energy to development. In 1960 a State Planning Organization was set up, and in 1962 a Five-Year Plan (1963–7) for development was adopted, resulting in a 6.6% increase *p.a.* in the gross national product. A second plan (1968–72) was announced in 1967. Foreign aid came mainly from a consortium of Western countries set up in 1962 by the OECD. In 1963 T. concluded an agreement with the European Economic Community for a preparatory association with its six member countries; this was raised in 1969–70 to associate membership (in a transitional stage). In 1964 T., with Iran and Pakistan, set up an organization for Regional Co-operation and Development (RCD) (see CENTO▷).

The present borders (with the exception of Hatay▷, i.e. the Alexandretta▷ province, and the border with Iraq in the Mosul▷ area) were determined by the Peace Treaty of Lausanne▷ signed in 1923 by T. and the victorious Allies of World War I. The Mosul border was established by League of Nations arbitration late in 1925. In 1939 the province of Alexandretta, previously part of Syria under the French Mandate, was annexed to T. and renamed, in Turkish, Hatay. T. became a member of the League of Nations in 1932, and is a founder member of the UN. She is also a member of the Council of Europe, NATO and CENTO.

POLITICAL HISTORY (FOREIGN RELATIONS). The area which today comprises the Turkish Republic (with the exception of the Kars▷ and Ardahan▷ regions ceded to Russia in 1878) was until the end of World War I part of the Ottoman Empire▷. Owing to nationalist uprisings and the encroachment of the Great Powers the empire had, by the end of the 19th century, lost most of its previous possessions in the Balkans and North Africa. Though the period of Sultan Abdülhamid▷ (1876–1909) was mostly peaceful, European imperialist penetration continued, particularly through the acquisition of economic concessions in mining, communications and public services. A newcomer to the inter-power rivalries in the empire was Germany—favoured by the Sultan as a counterbalance to the other Powers—traditionally Britain, France and Russia. The hunt for concessions led to a continuing diplomatic crisis around the Baghdad Railway▷ concession in 1899 and the years following.

In order to foster loyalty among his Muslim subjects, Sultan Abdülhamid promoted the idea of Pan-Islamism▷; at the same time he upheld the "Ottomanist" principle of equality for the Christians as initiated by the 19th-century reformers. Nevertheless, nationalist ferment among the various ethnic groups within the empire continued to develop and erupted from time to time into armed revolt.

In 1908, a military coup brought the "Young Turks" to power. One of their chief aims was the preservation of the empire's integrity, and later they gradually adopted a rigid policy of Ottomanization. Yet within a few years they were forced to fight several wars and suffer considerable territorial losses. In 1908, Bosnia and Herzegovina were formally annexed by Austria, Bulgaria declared its independence, and Crete was incorporated into Greece. The Italian-Ottoman War of 1911–12 resulted in the loss of Tripolitania▷ and the Dodecanese▷ Islands, and in the Balkan Wars▷ of 1912–13 T. lost Macedonia and Western Thrace. Albania declared its independence in 1912. The direct rule of the empire now extended only to Anatolia, Eastern Thrace and the Arab provinces of Asia.

The decision that the Ottoman Empire should enter World War I▷ on the side of the Central Powers was the work of a small party headed by Enver▷ Pasha. The decision proved fatal, though Ottoman arms were not entirely unsuccessful. The Empire suffered severe losses on the Caucasian front and failed in an attempted invasion of Egypt (1915), but put up a strong defence at Gallipoli▷, forcing the Allied Expeditionary Force to evacuate the peninsula (1915–16). It stopped the British advance in Mesopotamia at Kut al-Amara▷ (1916) and won several battles against Russia in Armenia and Persia (1916). However, new British offensives from Egypt and Mesopotamia (the former helped by the troops of Sharif Hussein▷ who had proclaimed the Arab Revolt▷), resulted in the loss of almost the whole of the Fertile Crescent by the end of 1918. In October 1918, T. was compelled to sign the Armistice of Mudros▷.

The Russian Revolution of 1917 had opened the way for another Ottoman advance towards the Caucasus, and the peace with the Soviets, concluded at Brest Litovsk in March 1918, secured the return of Kars▷, Ardahan▷ and Batum to the Ottoman domain; Batum was returned to the Georgian Republic in a treaty of June 1919 with the Trans-Caucasian Republics; Kars and Ardahan remained Turkish.

Anatolia and the region of Istanbul were still under the control of the Ottoman government. But shortly after, the Armistice Allied forces occupied the Straits and the Istanbul region and, within the next year, British and French forces occupied parts of southeastern Anatolia, the Italians landed at Antalia, and the Greeks at Izmir. At the same time Armenian forces controlled sections of Eastern Anatolia. The occupation of the Istanbul area and various parts of Anatolia conformed ostensibly to the provisions of the armistice, yet these steps were meant to produce *faits accomplis* in line with the secret agreements concluded earlier between the Allies for the partition of Anatolia. The Ottoman government of Sultan Mehmed VI Vahideddin was powerless to prevent this. In Aug. 1920 it was forced to sign the Treaty of Sèvres▷, reducing the territory of T. to some middle and northern parts of Anatolia and Istanbul, and exercising considerable limitations on its sovereignty, including the continued enforcement of the capitulations▷, by which foreign residents had extraterritorial rights, and the opening of the Straits to "every vessel of commerce or war" under the supervision of an International Commission.

However resistance to Allied schemes and the dictated treaty had sprung up in the Turkish provinces, with mass meetings, the organization of societies "for the Defence of Rights", and sporadic guerilla warfare. Turkish national consciousness had already been developed by writers and intellectuals, notably Ziya Gökalp▷, during the last years of the Empire; but it was the experience of foreign, Christian, and particularly Greek, invasion, which gave the resistance its driving force. Organization and leadership were provided by the wartime hero, Mustafa Kemal (Atatürk▷). Two congresses, one in Erzurum in July 1919, and the other in Sivas in September, were convened under his leadership and called for the preservation of the integrity of Turkish territory and full independence. Elections to the Ottoman Parliament in October were won by the Nationalists, and in Jan. 1920 Parliament adopted the "National Pact", based on the resolutions of the two congresses. The growing power of the Nationalists precipitated a confrontation with the Allies and the Ottoman government. In Mar. of that year some of the Nationalist leaders in Istanbul were arrested and exiled by the Allies, who now occupied the city of Istanbul itself, while the Sultan dissolved parliament and had the Nationalists declared rebels. The Nationalists now proceeded to convene, in Ankara (the centre of their activities), the Grand National Assembly with Mustafa Kemal as its president and formed a temporary government.

After this open Nationalist secession from the Ottoman government and defiance of the Allies, the Greeks, encouraged by Britain, began, in June 1920, a successful offensive into Anatolia, captured Bursa and Usak and also occupied Adrianople in Thrace. But the Nationalists were successful against their other adversaries. They defeated an army of the caliphate sent against them by the Sultan, and in May they concluded an armistice with the French. They also drove the Armenians eastward, and Turko-Armenian hostilities ended, in Dec. 1920, in a peace favourable to the Turks. The eastern frontier, leaving the regions of Kars and Ardahan in Turkish hands, was finally fixed in Mar. 1921 in a Treaty of Friendship with the USSR and, in October, Nationalist T. signed the Treaty of Kars with the Soviet republics of Armenia, Georgia and Azerbaijan. The Soviets, in fact, were the first to recognize the Nationalist government and provided very valuable military and financial aid. Dissension among the Allied Powers also helped the Nationalists. Italy, realizing the futility of the struggle, agreed, in Mar. 1921, to withdraw in return for economic concessions. The French followed in October with the Franklin-Bouillon▷ agreement, which fixed the border between T. and Syria.

The main struggle now took place between T. and Greece. The Greeks had resumed their offensive early in 1921, but their advance was twice halted by Ismet Pasha (Inönü▷). After another Greek advance, Mustafa Kemal, the supreme commander, defeated the Greeks on the Sakarya River in September. In August 1922 a Turkish counter-offensive began, and within two weeks the Greeks were swept out of Anatolia. The Turkish forces now turned towards Thrace, still in Greek hands. War between the British and the Nationalist Turks appeared imminent when the latter approached the Straits, still under Allied occupation. Yet both sides agreed to negotiate, and at the Armistice of Mudanya, signed in Oct. 1922, the Allied Powers agreed to a restoration of Turkish sovereignty in Thrace, Istanbul and the Straits, while T. accepted the principle of international control of the Straits.

A new peace conference opened in Lausanne in November. As the sultanate had been abolished in November 1922 (see below), the Nationalists alone represented T. Bargaining was difficult and protracted, but in the end the Nationalists, led at the conference by Ismet Pasha (Inönü), obtained most of their demands. By the Treaty of Lausanne▷, signed in July 1923, T. succeeded in keeping practically all the Turkish provinces, and abolishing virtually all restrictions on her independence, including the capitulations▷. The Straits were to remain open to all vessels of commerce and war, but with certain limitations on the latter; an international commission was to supervise the Straits. In Oct. the last foreign troops evacuated Istanbul and the Republic of T. was proclaimed, with Mustafa Kemal as its first elected president.

T.'s foreign policy during and after the Kemalist period was based on her desire to preserve the hard-won independence and integrity of the state. Kemal's motto, "Peace at home, peace abroad", was regarded as the guarantee of Turkish security, and T. made a great effort to promote good relations with neighbours and world powers alike. Mustafa Kemal gave up all ideas of retaking the Empire's non-Turkish provinces or of pursuing Pan-Islamic▷ or Pan-Turkish▷ policies.

However, T.'s claim to the province of Mosul, demanded by Britain for mandatory Iraq, continued for a time to upset Turko-British relations. But in 1926, following arbitration and a decision by the Council of the League of Nations, T. agreed to renounce her claim in return for a share in Iraq's oil revenues. Relations with the USSR were further strengthened when the two countries signed a Treaty of Friendship and Neutrality in Dec. 1925. Relations with Greece showed a steady improvement. By a special agreement annexed to the Treaty of Lausanne, Turkey and Greece effected an exchange of population (see Greek-Turkish Relations▷). After its completion, they concluded, win 1930, a Treaty of Friendship and Arbitration.

T. reacted to the growing menace from Germany and Italy in the 1930s by contracting various alliances. In August 1932 she joined the League of Nations; two years later, she concluded with Greece, Yugoslavia and Rumania the Balkan Pact▷; and in 1937 she signed at Saadabad▷, a non-aggression pact with Iraq, Iran and Afganistan. The rising Fascist menace also brought about a *rapprochement* with the Western Powers, resulting in their consent, in the Montreux▷ Convention of 1936, to the fortification of the Straits by T., banned under the Treaty of Lausanne. France also consented, in 1939, to the annexation by T. of the Syrian district of Alexandretta▷, partly populated by Turks. To consolidate the ties between T. and the Western Powers, an Anglo-Turkish Declaration of Mutual Assistance was issued in May 1939, and followed shortly afterwards by a non-Aggression Pact with France. In Oct. a tripartite pact was signed between Britain, France and T. Turkish efforts to enter into an alliance with the USSR failed, owing to the German-Soviet pact.

During World War II T. maintained her neutrality. Fearing German superiority she remained inactive even after Italy's entry into the war—although her treaty with the Western Powers specified Turkish intervention if the war reached the Mediterranean. Furthermore German victories induced T. to conclude a Non-Aggression Pact with Germany in June 1941 and later to consent to the sale of chrome ore to Germany. Nevertheless T. did not renounce her Western alliance, continued to sell chrome to Britain, too, and resisted Nazi pressure for closer collaboration. The change in the course of the war did not bring an immediate formal shift in Turkish policy, although economic relations with the West increased. Meetings between President Inönü and Churchill and Roosevelt in the course of 1943 failed to persuade T. to cooperate fully with the West. She insisted that she was not prepared for war. Her fears of Nazi invasion were compounded by the fear of subsequent Soviet liberation. Only in 1944, after the tide of war had definitely turned in favour of the Allies, did T. break off relations with Germany. In Feb. 1945 she declared war on Germany, thus qualifying to participate in the United Nations Conference in San Francisco.

Immediately after the war, Soviet-Turkish relations, already cool following the German-Soviet Pact of 1939, further deteriorated. Angered by Turkish neutrality during the war (and by the wartime activities of Pan-Turkish circles), the USSR,

early in 1945, repudiated her treaty of 1925 with T. She demanded a share in the defence of the Straits and the return of the Kars▷ and Ardahan▷ regions as the price of its renewal. These demands, rejected by T. (and renounced by the USSR only in 1953), placed her firmly in the Western bloc. Since Britain was unable to afford the necessary aid, the USA undertook this responsibility, and thereafter became T.'s principal ally. Beginning in 1947 the USA (within the framework of the Truman▷ Doctrine, the Marshall Plan, and later NATO) gave T. increasing military, economic and technical aid. In 1949 T. became a member of the Council of Europe. A year later to prove her loyalty to Western interests, she despatched a brigade to join the UN forces in the Korean war. In 1952 T. was admitted to NATO as a full member, Izmir becoming the headquarters of the European South-Eastern Command. Subsequently T. and the USA signed several bilateral agreements which provided for American aid and granted the USA bases and installations in the country. In 1959 the two countries signed a formal defence agreement. T. also took part in regional alliances, with the encouragement of the Western Powers. A project to set up a ME Defence Organization▷ in 1951 failed because of Egyptian objections. But in 1955 T. signed a defence alliance with Iraq, known as the Baghdad Pact▷, which soon also included Pakistan, Iran and Britain. Upon Iraq's withdrawal from the treaty following the Qassem revolution of 1958, the headquarters of the Pact moved to Ankara; in 1960 its name was changed to Central Treaty Organization (CENTO▷). In 1954 following an earlier Treaty of Friendship and Co-operation, T. signed a Treaty of Alliance, Political Co-operation and Mutual Assistance with Greece and Yugoslavia.

In the late 1950s the Cyprus▷ question became increasingly important in Turkish foreign policy. In the face of growing Greek terrorism and British plans to leave the island, T. adamantly opposed exclusive Greek rule of the island or union (*Enosis*▷) with Greece. Her motivation was both national-sentimental (the existence of a Turkish minority in the island) and strategic (the danger of a communist take-over). Prolonged discussions resulted in the agreement of Zurich and London, in 1959, by which Cyprus acquired independence and a constitution containing strict safeguards for the Turks' minority rights, August 1960. Order was restored in the island, and Greek-Turkish relations improved. Tension arose again at the end of 1963, when President Makarios of Cyprus revealed plans for constitutional changes and riots between Turkish and Greek Cypriots broke out. Direct Turkish intervention, with the possibility of war between Greece and T., was averted in the summer of 1964 only by American pressure. A measure of order was restored in Mar. 1965, when the UN sent a peace-keeping force to the island; but no final settlement has been reached and relations between Greece and T. have remained cool.

A side-effect of the Cyprus crisis was a serious deterioration in T.'s relations with the USA and a parallel improvement in those with the Soviet bloc. A desire to make T. more flexible in the inter-bloc rivalry—felt already at the end of the 1950s—coincided with the wish to acquire supporters for the Turkish cause in Cyprus as well as to seek new offers of foreign aid. The American and British position during the Cyprus crisis, and especially US President Johnson's note to Premier Inönü warning him against military intervention in Cyprus, June 1964, were bitterly denounced as contrary to the terms of the Turkish-American alliance. Official visits were exchanged with the USSR and other Soviet bloc and neutralist states, and economic and technical agreements were concluded with the USSR.

Hostility toward the USA became a marked feature of a segment of Turkish public opinion (particularly leftist intellectuals and students), and assumed a violent form in militant organizations which attacked American installations and property and even kidnapped American servicemen. This pressure from public opinion compelled the government to adopt a more balanced policy between East and West. With the aim of establishing a relationship of equals with the USA, the government concluded a new defence agreement with her in 1969 which superseded earlier pacts. Despite criticism from the left, the government remained faithful to its NATO and CENTO commitments, which were reconfirmed by the new government of Nihat Erim, 1971 (see below).

In pursuance of a good neighbours' policy, and motivated also by security, economic and global considerations, T. has sought out the friendship of ME countries. Relations with her neighbours to the East—Iran, Pakistan and (until 1958) Iraq—developed after the conclusion of the Baghdad Pact (later CENTO). Yet T.'s role in Western alliances, her recognition of Israel (after a negative vote on the UN Partition Resolution of 1947), Syria's claim to the Hatay Province, differences of regime and of historical background, inhibited close relations with the Arabs, and particularly the leftist, anti-Western ones. There have even been periodical crises. Relations have improved in recent years. In the present Arab-Israel crisis, T. supports the 1967 Security Council Resolution, and identifies herself with its Arab interpretation. T. also took part in the Islamic Solidarity Conferences held in Rabat in 1969 and Jidda in 1970 (a departure from her earlier policy of disengagement from an Islamic foreign orientation).

POLITICAL HISTORY (GOVERNMENT AND POLITICS). In the first quarter of the 20th century, Turkey twice witnessed radical changes in its political regime. Sultan Abdülhamid▷ (1876–1909), had in 1878 suspended the first Ottoman Constitution and dissolved parliament, and his rule, up to the Young Turks'▷ revolution in 1908, was a heavy-handed personal autocracy. It also put renewed emphasis on the Muslim character of the state, although the 19th-century reforms towards secularization and modernization were not discarded. The Young Turks' revolution, in 1908, forced the Sultan to reactivate the Constitution and convene a new parliament; suspecting him of an attempted counter-coup, they deposed him in 1909 and placed Mehmet V Reshad on the throne.

The Young Turks, western and secular in education and outlook, introduced political, economic and social reforms. However, wars and insurrections prevented them from extending these reforms or effectively carrying them out. Though the semblance of democratic procedure remained, the regime soon drifted into a new authoritarianism, led by a triumvirate of Cemal▷ (Jamal), Enver▷ and Talât▷. They limited the power and hold of the traditional Muslim institutions but because of the force of tradition or the dictates of their Islamic policy (trying to keep the Arabs within the framework of the empire) they did not entirely abolish them.

The defeat of the Ottoman Empire did away with the Young Turk regime and the traditional foundations on which the state had rested, and paved the way for the establishment of the modern Turkish national state. The achievement of full independence and territorial integrity made it possible for Nationalist T., under the leadership of Mustafa Kemal, to embark from the start on a far-reaching programme of political, economic and social reform. With the old regime crumbling, and the country destitute, Mustafa Kemal resolved to create a new T. on the Western secular pattern.

The first steps towards reform had been taken during the war of independence when, in Apr. 1920, the Grand National Assembly convened to replace the dissolved Ottoman Parliament. Under a Law of Fundamental Organization, adopted in Jan. 1921, the Assembly was to exercise executive and legislative powers in the name of the sovereign nation. Loyalty was still professed to the Ottoman Sultan, but in Nov. 1921, in the face of the Sultan's fight against the Nationalists, the sultanate was abolished altogether, although a "spiritual" caliphate was to remain in the Ottoman dynasty; as Sultan Mehmed VI Vahideddin fled the country, his cousin Abdülmecid was elected to this office. In Oct. 1923 the Turkish Republic was proclaimed and Mustafa Kemal (Atatürk) elected as its first President, with Ismet Pasha (Inönü) as Premier. Ankara was made the capital. In Mar. 1924 Mustafa Kemal, in line with his already growing programme of secularization, had the Assembly abolish the Caliphate as well and the Ottoman dynasty was exiled from the country. In Apr. 1924 the first Turkish Constitution was promulgated, incorporating and extending the constitutional steps taken so far. Kemal's chief political instrument in Parliament was the People's Party, later renamed Republican People's Party (RPP, *Cümhuriyet Halk Partisi*), formed in Aug. 1923 out of the League for the Defence of the Right of Anatolia and Rumelia.

Following these political reforms, Mustafa Kemal initiated measures of westernization and secularist reform. Along with the caliphate, the office of the *Seyh (Sheikh)-ül-Islam*, i.e. the head of the religious hierarchy, and the Ministry of Religious Affairs and *Evkaf* (Pious Foundations, see *Waqf*▷) were abolished in 1924. All schools were placed under the supervision of the Ministry of Public Instruction, which soon closed all the religious seminaries *(Medrese)*. Religious courts were also closed (see *Shari'a*▷) as, later, were religious orders *(Tarikat*, see Dervish Orders▷), monasteries *(Tekke)* and holy tombs *(Türbe)*. In 1925 the traditional headgear (tarbush, fez) was prohibited and the international calendar and time systems were adopted. New civil, criminal and commercial codes, based on European models, were introduced in 1926. Two of the most radical and far-reaching reforms were made in 1928. One abolished the clause in the Constitution declaring Islam to be the state religion; the other discarded the old Arabic script used in T. in favour of a new one based on the Latin alphabet. Language reform▷ was to proceed further in the 1930s, when the Turkish Language Society simplified the written language and eliminated many of its Arabic and Persian elements. The emancipation of women, already advanced by the introduction of the new civil code, was completed in 1935, when they were accorded full political rights. Other reforms included the requirement that citizens adopt family names, 1934, and the proclamation of Sunday as the weekly day of rest in place of Friday, 1935.

In the field of economics, Atatürk concentrated on developing T.'s rich mineral resources, industry and communications. With the memory of the capitulations still alive, and being unwilling to risk T.'s political independence by the importation of foreign capital, he initiated the policy of *étatism*, by which the state was to be the chief investor and owner of large enterprises and to exercise close control over planning and development. Industrialization was at its height in the 1930s and especially during the first Five-Year Plan in 1934.

Despite Kemal Atatürk's charismatic leadership, he encountered from the start serious opposition to his rule and reforms. At the end of 1924, some of his previous collaborators, such as Rauf (Orbay▷) and Ali Fuad (Cebesoy) organized the conservative "Progressive People's Party". Early in 1925 a Kurdish insurrection broke out in the eastern provinces, motivated by displeasure with Kemal's secularism and by Kurdish nationalism; it was put down by the middle of the year, and its leaders sentenced to death by special "Independence Tribunals", although further disturbances occurred. Accused of complicity in the revolt, the Progressive Party was disbanded. In 1930 another attempt was made (with the consent of Kemal) to organize an opposition, and former Premier Fethi (Okyar▷) was permitted to found a "Liberal Republican Party". This experiment, too, was short-lived. After failing in municipal elections, and accused variously of reactionary leanings and communism, the party was soon dissolved. The RPP continued to rule for the next 15 years unopposed, though a measure of criticism was allowed in the press and in parliament. In 1937 the six major principles of the RPP—republicanism nationalism, populism, *étatism*, secularism, and reformism—were incorporated into the State Constitution. The party made great efforts to inculcate the people with its ideas; one of its methods was the establishment of "People's Houses" in urban areas, or "People's Rooms" in villages, to serve as centres of cultural activity and indoctrination.

Despite all these efforts, large segments of the population were not won over to Kemal Atatürk's policies and reforms. The conservative elements, particularly the peasants, rejected secularism; the commercial classes resented the heavy hand of the government on the economy; others were against the authoritarianism of the RPP and the personal rule of its chief. These signs of opposition increased after Atatürk's death in 1938, under the rule of his successor, President Ismet Inönü. Conditions in T. during World War II accentuated existing grievances. Shortages and rising prices, the levying of a capital tax with punitive measures (directed mainly against the minorities), and repressive measures against the press, all contributed to growing dissatisfaction and a demand for liberalization. This coincided with increasing support for democracy following the victory of the West in the war.

At the end of 1945, Inönü announced his support for a multi-party system and several new parties were established. The most important, as it turned out, was the "Democratic Party" founded in Jan. 1946 by previous members of the RPP, such as Celâl Bayar▷, Adnan Menderes▷, and Refik Koraltan. The party advocated free enterprise and political freedom, and its popular support was soon demonstrated in its handsome showing in the 1946 elections. The desire to steal the thunder from the DP brought about a rift in the RPP and the replacement of authoritarian Premier Recep Peker▷ by Hasan Saka▷ in 1947. It also brought about some liberalization of the political machinery, the economy and religion. However, in the elections of May 1950, the DP—despite a split in its own ranks, in 1948, and the formation of a rival "Nation Party"—gained a large majority. The transfer of power took place peacefully; Celâl Bayer was elected President and Adnan Menderes formed a government.

The victory of the DP was due, to a great extent, to the support it found among the peasant population in T., which remained its chief bulwark throughout its rule. Although outwardly committed to secularism and curbing reactionary manifestations, the DP relaxed the secularist anti-religious attitude of the previous regime. It also assisted the peasants economically with loans, public works, etc. Its supporters among the business classes profited from a relaxation in government controls and the encouragement of local and foreign investment. Helped by increasing foreign aid, and, in agriculture, by favourable weather conditions, the economy was booming in the early 1950s.

The government failed, however, to implement its liberal principles in the political field. In 1953 it confiscated the property of the RPP and closed the People's Houses. Rigid new Press Laws were adopted in 1954 and 1956; critical journalists were prosecuted and newspapers suspended. Politically motivated interference in the judiciary, civil service and academic appointments became commonplace. A turn for the worse in the economic situation, inflation and the growing public debt made the government increasingly unpopular, as did anti-Greek and anti-minority riots in Istanbul in September 1955. In 1955 the DP itself split, and the seceding faction founded the Freedom Party. The decline in the popularity of the DP and its government was shown by the 1957 elections: the DP was returned to power, but with a smaller margin of votes and the RPP made considerable gains. However, the government did not change its policies and growing criticism by the opposition was met with further repression.

Unrest had, meanwhile, spread to the army. Kept out of politics by Atatürk, but loyally Kemalist as a body, army officers became restive in the face of the deterioration of the economy, the growing internal tensions, and the failure of the government to preserve Kemalist principles. In 1959 and early 1960, the confrontation between the RPP and the DP and its government became critical, leading to violence. The most serious incident occurred in April 1960, when troops were ordered to prevent Ismet Inönü, the leader of the opposition, from conducting a political tour. Following the arrest of several officers, Gen. Cemal Gürsel▷, Commander of the Land Forces, who had been in contact with army conspirators, resigned. The government set up a commission of inquiry into the activities of the opposition, and subsequently banned all political activity. By the end of the month, students were holding demonstrations, resulting in clashes, casualties and the imposition of martial law. The use of the army in repressing the opposition hastened the crisis. On 27 May 1960 the army staged a bloodless coup that brought the ten-year rule of the DP to an end.

From May 1960 until Oct. 1961 T. was ruled by a "National Unity Committee" composed of the leading rebel officers, with Cemal Gürsel as President of the Republic, Premier and Minister of Defence. The DP was banned and its leaders put on trial, charged with breaches of the constitution, responsibility for the 1955 riots and corruption. In the trial, held from Oct. 1960 to May 1961 on the island of Yassiada near Istanbul, 15 leaders were sentenced to death and about 430 to prison terms (including 31 to life terms). Menderes and two of his ministers were executed, while 12 death sentences were commuted to prison for life (including Bayar); 138 were acquitted. The NUC also purged the armed forces and the academic staff of the universities and established a State Planning Organization.

The NUC ruled through a largely civilian cabinet and declared its aim to be the return of the country to democratic rule. Fourteen radical members of the NUC who favoured long-term military rule and wide reform were purged in Nov. 1960. In January political parties were permitted to resume their activities and several new parties came into being. The same month, a Constituent Assembly was convened (with the NUC as the Upper House), to draft a new constitution that would prevent future governments from such abuses of power as those perpetrated by the old regime. The new Constitution—drafted with help of a special commission of experts and professors —was approved by a national referendum in July 1961. Elections were held in Oct. 1961 and gave the RPP 173 seats in the 450-member Assembly and 36 in the 150-member Senate. Second in the elections came the newly formed "Justice Party" (Adalet Partisi), founded by Gen. Ragip Gümüşpala and considered the successor of the outlawed DP—with 158 seats in the Assembly, and 70 in the Senate.

Cemal Gürsel was elected President, and Ismet Inonu formed a RPP-JP coalition government.

The first years of the Second Republic brought no full return to civilian rule and political stability. The army still kept an eye on political developments. The NUC members became partners in the regime by being nominated life members of the Senate, and when, in May 1966, Gürsel's health deteriorated, the Chief-of-Staff, Gen. Cevdet Sunay▷, was elected President. Two abortive coups, in Feb. 1962 and May 1963, both led by Col. Tâlat Aydemir, showed that some officer's groups still wanted to take the reins of power into their own hands. As no single party had a majority in the Assembly, coalition governments were necessary, and frequent crises ensued.

The RPP-JP coalition, supported by the army, fell in May 1962, over a heated debate on a proposed amnesty for the political prisoners of the Yassiada trials. The issue was later settled by a second Inönü cabinet, formed in coalition with the minor parties and without the JP, by the deduction of four years from the jail sentences, leading to the release of many convicts. (Subsequently all the prisoners, including Celâl Bayar, were released on various grounds.) The government also adopted the first Five-Year Plan, providing for a wide-scale development programme. Disenchantment with the RPP and their own failure in local elections, in Nov. 1963, induced the minor parties to leave the government. A third Inönü government had to rely on the support of independents; it fell in February 1965. This time an independent senator, Suat Ürgüplü▷, formed an interim government, until the elections, composed of all parties except the RPP, with the leading role assumed by the JP, whose leader, Süleyman Demirel▷, became Deputy Premier.

Elections in Oct. 1965 were won by the JP, which gained, with 240 seats, an absolute majority, and Demirel formed a JP government. The RPP, with only 134 seats, was once again reduced to a minor role. A Socialist party, the "Turkish Workers' Party", participated for the first time in general Turkish elections and won 15 seats. The JP's growth and final election to office showed that it had gained the votes of the previous supporters of the DP—first and foremost the conservative, religiously-minded masses of the peasantry—who had been indifferent or hostile to the 1960 revolution. These elements have given the JP successive victories in various elections in recent years. In the general election of Oct. 1969, the party increased its number of seats in the Assembly from 240 to 256, compared with the 143 held by the RPP; the remaining seats were held by minor parties and independents.

Demirel, aware of the suspicions which he and his party aroused in the army, tried to steer a careful course and avoid the excesses and mistakes of the DP. He committed himself to furthering economic development and social reform and also maintained political liberalism and freedom of expression. In foreign relations he conducted a balanced policy vis-à-vis the East and the West, asserting T.'s freedom of action. He also paid careful attention to the army's views, for instance in postponing the restoration of political rights to DP leaders (they were finally restored in Nov. 1969).

Nevertheless, criticism of Demirel and his government became increasingly severe. Frequent splits in his Justice party, both for political and personal reasons, gradually reduced his majority in parliament. The most serious split occurred with the defection of the right-wing deputies under the leadership of Saadettin Bilgic in Feb. 1970 (forcing Demirel to resign and form a new government). The most vehement critics of the government came from among the intellectual classes who clung to Kemalist and Socialist principles and accused the government of ruinous economic policies (entailing inflation and a worsening balance of payments), a failure to introduce social (particularly land) reform and yielding to foreign capitalism and American domination. These critics belonged to the RPP, the Workers' Party, Student and youth organizations, and Leftist labour unions. Militant youth organizations, in particular, became a continuous embarrassment to the government, striking or taking to the streets on issues of university reform as well as internal and foreign policy. By 1970, student riots and clashes between rightist and leftist groups had become the order of the day, resulting in bloodshed, the closure of the universities and the imposition of martial law. Matters came to a head in the early months of 1971 when militant leftist youth organizations ("The Revolutionary Youth" and the "Turkish People's Liberation Army")—some of their members trained by Palestinian-Arab guerilla organizations—were responsible for a series of explosions, bank robberies and kidnappings of US servicemen (subsequently released). The government seemed to be unable to curb the violence.

Signs were once more evident of the army's displeasure with the current scene and the government's conduct, and of its increasing determination to intervene in a decisive manner. Impelled partly by these motives, and partly from fear of a more radical army coup, the Commander-in-Chief, Gen. Memduh Tağmaç, and three other prominent military leaders, handed to the President and leaders of parliament on 12 Mar. 1971 an ultimatum threatening a military take-over unless a strong national government was formed which would end the anarchy and initiate economic and social reforms. Demirel resigned at once, and, although political parties did not hesitate to voice criticism of the army's action, they complied with its wishes. Nihat Erim▷, a moderate RPP member, resigned from his party and became Prime Minister. By early Apr. he had received a vote of confidence for his cabinet composed of some JP, RPP, and Reliance Party deputies, but based largely on independent experts and technocrats. (The left wing of the RPP and the right wing of the JP opposed the new coalition).

The government promised to crack down on the anarchist movements, to initiate reforms and prepare for general elections. Erim had to deal with continuing cases of violence, culminating in the kidnapping and murder of the Israeli Consul-General in Istanbul in May. True to its pledges, the government adopted a harsh line toward the trouble-makers. Martial Law was decreed late in April, and in May there began a crackdown not only on the extreme student left and their guerilla groups, but on the whole left—including the arrest of many liberal, left-of-centre intellectuals and purges of army and government services. The Turkish Labour Party was outlawed (as was an extremist right-wing group). Trial were begun. The Constitution was being amended to make the Executive stronger and restrict some freedoms. In summer 1971 it appeared that violence had been halted and the government was in control.

CONSTITUTION, GOVERNMENT AND POLITICS. T.'s Constitution of 1961 endeavours to prevent a return to authoritarian government by detailing the liberties and rights of the citizen (including social and economic rights) and introducing a strong system of checks and balances. In this it shows a marked change from the previous constitutions of 1876 and 1924. It proclaims T. to be a "nationalist, democratic, secular and social state", and unalterably a Republic. Legislative Power is vested in the Grand National Assembly, which is composed of the National Assembly and the Senate. The National Assembly, which is supreme, has 450 members, elected for a four-year-term. The Senate has "natural", established members—15 appointed by the President, the members of the NUC of 1960, and ex-presidents—as well as 150 members elected for six years (one-third of the elected and appointed Senators retire every two years). The Executive function is carried out by the President of the Republic, elected by the Grand National Assembly for seven years, and a Council of Ministers. The Constitution stresses the independence of the Courts and sets up a High Council of Judges, to prevent external pressures on the judiciary, and a Constitutional Court to decide on the constitutionality of laws. The electoral system, as introduced in 1961 and later amended, provided for proportional representation in the National Assembly (later extended to the Senate). The Political Parties Law of 1965 obliged the parties to maintain a democratic internal organization and adequate finances, and to uphold the basic principles of the Republic. Amendments restricting some of the freedoms held to be excessive and to have been abused, were being prepared in summer 1971.

Political parties in T. are relatively well organized. Despite the creation of several new parties, and frequent splits, there has been in recent years a tendency towards bipolarity in Turkish politics. The chief contenders have been the "Justice Party", under the leadership of Süleyman Demirel, which is liberal-conservative, advocates private enterprise, and is supported by the peasantry and the commercial and industrialist classes; and the "Republican People's Party", under the leadership of Ismet Inönü, which advocates state enterprise, describes itself as left-of-centre and is supported by the urban intelligentsia. Other parties include the "Reliance Party" (centre; leader—Turhan Feyzioğlu); the "Nation Party" (conservative; leader—Osman Bölükbaşi); the "National Action Party" (rightist; leader—Alpaslan Türkeş); the "United Party" (rightist; leader—Mustafa Timisi); the "New Turkey Party" (rightist; leader—Yusuf Azizoğlu); the "Turkish Workers Party" (Marxist; leader—Behice Boran, outlawed July 1971); the "National Order Party" (conservative-rightist; leader—Necmettin Erbakan; outlawed May 1971); the "Democratic Party" (re-established late in 1970 by right-wingers seceding from the Justice Party; leader—Ferruh Bozbeyli). The Communist Party is banned.

PRESS, RADIO, TV. T. has a variegated and lively press, devoting much space to political criticism and public affairs. The freedom of the press, which in the past was often infringed, is secured by the constitution. While most newspapers are independent, some are associated with political parties—especially *Ulus* which supports the RPP, and *Adalet* and *Son Havadis* which support the JP. Of the independent dailies, *Milliyet*, *Cümhuriyet* and *Akşam* lean to the left and are most influential, *Hürriyet* (the most popular) is moderate, and *Tercüman*, conservative. *Hayat* is a popular illustrated weekly magazine. Like the press, lively publishing houses—issuing both original and translated books—are in general concentrated in Istanbul. Radio and the newly established part-time TV are controlled by the public "Association of Radio and Television". Three major broadcasting stations operate, in Istanbul, Ankara and Izmir.

Istanbul is no longer the only centre for higher education, although it still retains the richest libraries and the Ottoman archives. There are seven universities in T., all administered by the state, and autonomous by law. These are the Ankara U., the ME Technical University, (Ankara), Hacettepe U. (Ankara), Istanbul U., Istanbul Technical U., Aegean U. (Izmir), Atatürk U. (Erzurum) and Black Sea U. (Trabzon). There are other, private higher institutions of learning.

STATISTICS. Area: 296,185 sq. mi. Pop.: 35.6m. (1970 estimate). Natural increase: 2.6% (1960, '65 censuses). Gross National Product: T£113,870m. ($12,430) at current prices, T£84,085m. ($9550) at constant 1961 prices (both 1968 estimates); $14,400m. (1969 estimate). National Income p.c.: T£2,665 (c. $300) (1968 estimate), $347 (1969 estimate). Imports: $801.2m.; exports: $536.8m. (1969). Budget: T£ 26,670m. ($2963) (1968). Literacy—adult population (aged 6 +): c. 40%. Doctors: 1 per 2,820 population. Hospital beds: 1 per 571 pop., or 1.735 per 1,000 pop. (1967). T £15 = $1 (since summer 1970; previously T £9 = $1).   (D.K.)

TURKISH LANGUAGE REFORM. The R. of the TL was one of Kemal Atatürk's▷ greatest achievements. After their Islamization, the Turks had begun writing T.—which belongs to the Altaic group of Ls.—in the Arabic script and adopted a large number of words and grammatical and syntactical forms from both Arabic and Persian, the Ls. of the contemporary Muslim civilization. These borrowings, ill-suited to the phonological, grammatical and syntactical structure of T., particularly affected the Ottoman literary and official L., which was enriched but became cumbersome, unintelligible to the common people and required years of study, including the study of Arabic and Persian. Under the impact of Europe, and with the movement towards modernization, 19th century Ottoman writers began advocating the simplification of T. in order to spread literacy and education. The emergence of a T. national consciousness in the late 19th and early 20th centuries further intensified the campaign for LR The increase in the number of T. publications, the development of the press and some individual efforts led to a considerable simplification of the literary L.; but hardly any official action was taken until the advent of the Republic, after World War I.

Atatürk's L. revolution began in Nov. 1928 when Parliament adopted a new T. alphabet based on Latin characters. The change, in line with Atatürk's Rs. towards secularization and westernization, was enforced within a few months. In July 1932 a T. Linguistic Society was founded which initiated an ambitious programme of purifying the L. of all its foreign forms, and of most of the Arabic and Persian words. The foreign vocabulary was replaced by pure T. words taken from dialects and other Turkic Ls. or else invented. The Society's puristic approach to LR encountered serious opposition; it was claimed, e.g., that the newly created vocabulary was not assisting the simplification of the language and remained unintelligible to the people. Since 1949 the Society has followed a more moderate course, and the TL of today, both spoken and written, still contains a significant number of words of Arabic and Persian origin.   (D.K.)

U

UAE—see Union of Arab Emirates▷.

UAR—see United Arab Republic▷.

UGANDA PLAN. In 1903 Joseph Chamberlain, British Colonial Secretary, suggested to the Zionist leader, Theodor Herzl▷ that a large Jewish settlement enjoying full autonomy might be established in U. in East Africa. (During the previous year Chamberlain had raised the possibility of settlement in al-'Arish.) Herzl submitted the proposal to the Sixth Zionist Congress, 1903, which decided to send a commission to investigate Uganda, despite the strong objections of many Zionists, particularly from Eastern Europe, and their charge that the mere consideration of any settlement outside Palestine would be a betrayal of the Zionist cause. In 1905 the Commission reported that U. was unsuitable and the Seventh Zionist Congress overwhelmingly rejected the offer. The major reason for its rejection was that most Zionists believed the Jewish national revival could materialize only in Palestine. (Some of those who disagreed seceded and founded a "Territorialist" movement.)   (Sh.H.)

*UMM AL-QAIWAIN. The smallest of the seven sheikhdoms of the Trucial Coast▷. Area: c. 289 sq. mi; pop.: c. 3,000, mostly nomads. Situated between Ras al-Khaima▷ and Sharja▷ along a narrow coastal strip, it lacks modern harbour facilities. The Sheikh of U. al-Q.—a British Protectorate since the 19th century—granted oil-prospecting rights in 1969 to the Shell Company and the American "Occidental" Co. (with some offshore delimitation disputes with Sharja). U. al-Q. plans to join the UAE▷ Federation.   (Y.K.)

UN—see United Nations Organization▷.

*UNEF—see United Nations Emergency Forces▷.

UNIATE. The U. communities of the ME comprise the Greek▷ Catholic ("Melkite"), Maronite▷, Syrian▷ Catholic, Armenian▷ Catholic, Coptic▷ Catholic and Ethiopian▷ Catholic churches. These churches resulted from the union of parts of the Eastern Orthodox and Monophysite▷ churches with the Roman Catholic Church. The U. churches recognize the supreme authority of the Pope and believe in the dogmas of the Roman Catholic Church, but maintain their own liturgies and customs. The U. churches are headed by patriarchs, who enjoy a large measure of autonomy within the Catholic Church. They depend on the Vatican Congregation for the Oriental Churches. See also Catholics▷.   (Sh. C.)

UNION OF ARAB EMIRATES. Planned Federation of Persian Gulf▷ sheikhdoms, principalities. Conceived in 1968 as a federation of nine (Bahrain, Qatar and the seven Trucial Coast▷ sheikhdoms of Adu Dhabi, Dubai, Sharja, Umm al-Qaiwain, 'Ajman, Fujaira, Ras al-Khaima). Bahrain and Qatar decided not to join, and 1971 plans envisage a federation of six Trucial sheikhdoms (without Ras al-Khaima). See Trucial Coast▷, Persian Gulf▷, Arab Federation▷.   (Y. S.)

UNITED ARAB REPUBLIC (UAR). Syria and Egypt merged in Feb. 1958 to form the UAR. It broke up in Sept. 1961, when Syria seceded following a military coup. Egypt continued officially calling herself the UAR until Sept. 1971.

The initiative for the union came from Syria, while Egypt sought political co-ordination and a dominating influence, but not a full union. President Nasser▷ agreed to the union on condition it would be based on his terms, and the Syrians accepted this condition without fully clarifying its meaning. Syria was pushed into a hasty union by fear lest the Syrian body politic disintegrate due to the increasing conflict of social groups, intensified by growing army interference and inter-Arab and international pressure. Syria feared a Communist take-over on the one hand, and rightist pro-Western domination, on the other, compounded by intervention on the part of pro-Western neighbouring countries (Turkey, Iraq, Israel) supported by the USA. The idea of union was not new for Syria; ever since her creation as a separate state, union with one or another Arab country had been discussed—though it was generally Iraq rather than Egypt. Now, a growing faction in the leadership and officers' corps saw union with Egypt as the only way out.

The UAR was built according to the constitutional patterns of the Egyptian regime—a presidential regime, whose representative institutions are not elected along democratic multi-party lines and enjoy very limited power. The UAR National Assembly was to be appointed by the President and at least one half of its members were to be former members of the assemblies in Syria and Egypt. The executive was virtually left to the discretion of the President, Gamal 'Abd-ul-Nasser, who was elected President by an overwhelming majority—in a referendum and as a single candidate—and who set up a small central government appointed to deal only with defence, foreign affairs, education and "national guidance", and industrialization, and two "regional" governments for the Egyptian "region" and the Syrian "region". There were initially only eight ministers in the central government—seven Egyptians and one Syrian. Four vice-presidents were appointed—two Egyptians and two Syrians. At the end of 1958, the central government was expanded to 21 members (14 Egyptians, 7 Syrians), and its powers were increased by abolishing the distinction between matters handled by the central government and matters under the jurisdiction of the "regions". The UAR government was not a success and in the three years of its existence changes were, on several occasions, made both in the division of authority and in the composition of the Cabinet.

A single political organization, the "National Union", was to replace the parties still active in Syria at the time of the union—this was one of Nasser's conditions for Egypt's merger with Syria. The parties were ordered to disband—including those which had pressed for the union and brought it about, led by the Ba'th▷. The Ba'th leaders had anticipated that they would become the ideological mentors of the UAR regime. Nasser, however, was unwilling to share power and tried to shape his rule in Syria on the Egyptian pattern—a group of loyal aides in the army and administration, and a single popular organization to provide mass support (but unable to become a political power group). The "National Union", however, failed to take roots.

Egyptian rule in Syria aroused bitterness and opposition. The placing of Egyptian officers in key positions in the Syrian Army without a similar posting of Syrian officers in the Egyptian Army, the trend towards centralization which put ever more power in the hands of the central government and Egypt, the application of Egyptian economic policy in Syria—beginning with land reform and some nationalization and culminating in July 1961 in far-reaching nationalization measures and a turn to full socialism—hurt the Syrian political élite, both civilian and military, the bourgeoisie and the middle class. The political élite, which had supported the union in 1958, changed its views after three years of Egyptian rule and realized that Syria had lost her independence and political identity.

The counter-coup of Sept. 1961 was led by a group of Syrian officers in key positions. The group exploited the ferment caused by the nationalization laws of July 1961, the increasing bitterness in the army as a result of Egyptian dominance and the power struggle between Marshal 'Amer▷ and the Syrian, 'Abd-ul-Hamid Sarraj▷. Initially, the coup leaders did not demand the break-up of the Union, but were willing to discuss changes in the structure of government and a proper division of powers. But Nasser was not prepared to compromise with them, and Syria seceded.

Egypt regarded the secession as an illegal act of rebellion and refused to recognize Syria's renewed independence. The conflict led to a serious crisis in the Arab League▷ in summer 1962, and Egypt boycotted League meetings for six months. There was a partial normalization in spring 1963, when the Syrian *Ba'th* government began discussions with Egypt on a renewed union (with the addition of Iraq, and on a federal pattern; this union scheme failed—see Arab Federation▷). Official diplomatic relations between Egypt and Syria were resumed only at the end of 1966, when a new defence treaty was also signed.

A federation of Egypt, Syria, Libya and possibly also Sudan, planned in 1971, may also be called UAR—"Union (or rather Federation—both termed *Ittihad* in Arabic) of Arab Republics".   (S.L.-Y.S.)

*UNITED NATIONS ORGANIZATION (UN).

Seven countries of the ME were founder-members of the UN, 1945 (five of them Arab): Egypt, Iran, Iraq, Lebanon, Sa'udi Arabia, Syria and Turkey. The following eight countries of the area have since been admitted: Yemen 1947; Israel 1949; Libya 1955; Jordan 1955; Sudan 1956; Cyprus 1960; Kuwait 1963; South Yemen 1967. Of the Arab countries of the Maghreb not covered by this Encyclopaedia, Morocco and Tunisia were admitted in 1956, Algeria in 1962. Thus, Arab countries have 14 votes at the UN. The admission of Bahrain, Qatar and 'Oman was expected in 1971.

PALESTINE PROBLEM. The UN has, since its establishment in 1945, dealt continuously with many ME problems. The one most persistently on its agenda has been the Palestine▷ question. Great Britain referred it to the UN in April 1947, after having failed to reconcile Jewish and Arab interests. In May 1947, the General Assembly (GA) set up a "Special Committee on Palestine" (UNSCOP) to study the problem and make recommendations.

UNSCOP was given full powers to investigate all relevant questions, in Palestine and wherever else it deemed useful (despite Arab objections to UNSCOP's implied authority to visit the displaced persons' camps in Europe, thus linking the Palestine with the Jewish refugee problem).

UNSCOP submitted its report on 31 Aug. 1947 to the GA, which adopted on 29. Nov. 1947 the plan recommended by UNSCOP's majority, viz. the partition of Palestine into independent Jewish and Arab states, linked in an economic union; Jerusalem was to become an international enclave under UN trusteeship (a minority report had favoured a united federal Palestine). The recommendations were adopted by a vote of 33 in favour (including the USA, the USSR and France), to 13 against and 10 abstentions (including Britain). A UN Palestine Commission of five nations was set up, to aid the establishment of transitional regimes in the two states gaining independence; but the British Palestine administration refused to co-operate and the Commission never came to Palestine (and was disbanded by the GA in May 1948).

Since the proposed partition was opposed by force by the Arabs, and hostilities broke out immediately, a special session of the GA was convened in April-May 1948. The Security Council (SC) was seized with the Palestine problem at the same time. Both considered an American proposal to shelve or postpone partition in favour of a new trusteeship, as well as other proposals for a temporary administration under UN auspices; they came, however, to nought.

Late in April, the SC established a Jerusalem Truce Commission composed of the US, French and Belgian Consuls-General in Jerusalem, to supervise the truce. In mid-May, the GA decided to appoint a Mediator, and the permanent members of the SC (*i.e.* the Big Five Powers) nominated the Swedish Count Folke Bernadotte.

As the British Mandate expired on 14 May 1948, and the State of Israel was proclaimed, the Arab states invaded Palestine and a full-fledged war broke out (see Arab-Israel War, 1948▷). At the end of May the SC called for a four-week truce which went into effect on 11 June. The SC also established a UN Truce Observers' Corps. The Arab states refused to prolong the truce and fighting was resumed; the SC again called for a cease-fire which went into effect on 18 July. In the meantime Count Bernadotte made proposals for a settlement (see Bernadotte▷); these were rejected by both sides (and, later in the year, by the GA Political Committee as well). Count Bernadotte was assassinated by Jewish terrorists on 17 Sept. 1948. The UN

Under-Secretary-General, Dr. Ralph Bunche▷, an American, succeeded him as acting mediator. Large-scale fighting broke out again in the Negev in October, lasting until December. The SC again called, in several resolutions, for a cease-fire and an Armistice. Negotiations were held under the chairmanship of the acting Mediator in spring 1949 and resulted in separate Armistice Agreements (Egypt-Israel 24 Feb.; Lebanon-Israel 23 Mar.; Jordan-Israel 3 Apr.; Syria-Israel 20 July). The General Armistice Agreements (GAA) banned all hostilities, defined demarcation lines and set up Mixed Armistice Commissions (MAC) to consider complaints of breaches of the GAAs. The four MACs were each composed of representatives of the parties and the Chief-of-Staff of the UN Truce Observers, or his representative, as chairman responsible to the SC.

On 11 Dec. 1948, the GA adopted resolution 194 (III), which *i.a.* provided for: a. the establishment of a Conciliation Commission (PCC) of three members (France, Turkey and the USA were selected by the five permanent members of the SC), to assume the functions of the Mediator and the Truce Commission and to assist the parties to achieve a final settlement; b. the protection of the Holy Places; c. the SC to ensure Jerusalem's demilitarizaton and the PCC to make proposals for an international regime in Jerusalem; d. the resolution also called on the parties to seek agreement by negotiations either with the PCC or directly; e. the PCC was to facilitate the repatriation or resettlement of the Palestine refugees▷, or payment of compensation to them. (This provision, implying that the choice between the two would be with the individual refugees was to become a focus of debate on the refugee question in later GAs; it was repeated, in one form or another, by most annual sessions of the GA.)

In the summer of 1949, the PCC arranged for negotiations with Israeli and Arab delegations at Lausanne▷. However, the conference (which never led to Arab-Israel negotiations or meetings) ended in deadlock, as Israeli and Arab attitudes remained irreconcilable.

Israel was admitted to the UN on 11 May 1949. JERUSALEM: In Dec. 1949 the GA reaffirmed the establishment of an international regime in Jerusalem as a *corpus separatum*, to be administered by the Trusteeship Council. However, the two governments directly concerned, Israel and Jordan, refused to accept such internationalization; the Trusteeship Council made no progress in its deliberations and reported to the GA in 1950 the failure of its mission. Swedish proposals for a "functional" international-

ization rather than a territorial administrative one were accepted by Israel, but rejected by the Arab states, and were not voted by the GA. Technically, the original GA resolution on the internationalization of Jerusalem remained in force, though no further efforts were made to implement it. During the Six Day War▷ of 1967, the city was reunited under Israeli administration. During the Special Emergency Session of the GA convened after the war, two resolutions were passed calling upon Israel to rescind the measures it had taken and to refrain from changing the status of the city. These resolutions were later affirmed by SC resolutions.

THE ARMISTICE REGIME: The transition to permanent peace as foreseen in the Armistice Agreements of 1949 did not materialize, and in the following years border clashes, Arab infiltration, sabotage, and Israeli retaliation resulted in a long list of complaints to the MACs and the SC. In its consideration of these complaints, the SC was assisted by the UN Truce Supervision Organization (UNTSO), composed of military observers seconded from different armies and headed by a Chief-of-Staff who also chaired the four MACs. While the MACs often condemned the acts of Arab infiltration and and sabotage, the SC—before which only major complaints were usually raised—mostly condemned Istaeli retaliatory action without giving equal weight to the sabotage action that caused it and its cumulative magnitude (see Arab-Israel Conflict▷). This was largely due to the Soviet veto, generally applied with an anti-Israeli bias.

Another aspect of the Arab-Israel conflict which caused UN bodies to intervene was the closing of the Suez Canal▷ to Israeli shipping, and to foreign ships *en route* to and from Israel. This blockade was termed unlawful, and Egypt was called upon to terminate the restrictions, in a SC resolution in Sept. 1951. The call was not heeded.

Sabotage incursions, the Suez blockade, coupled with a blockade of the Gulf of Aqaba (Eilat▷) (see Tiran▷), and the encirclement of Israel by huge troop concentrations caused a flare-up at the end of Oct. 1956, when Israeli forces struck at bases of the infiltrators in the Gaza Strip and the Sinai Peninsula (see Sinai Campaign▷). Some days later, British and French forces intervened in Egypt (see Suez War▷). As the SC, alerted by the USA and USSR, was paralyzed by the British and French veto, an emergency session of the GA was convened. This session, and the regular session shortly afterwards, accompanied by heavy American and Soviet pressure, brought about the withdrawal of all foreign troops from Egyptian territory and established a UN Emergency Force (UNEF)▷, initially to replace the foreign troops and, later, to patrol the lines between Egypt and Israel. Comparative quiet prevailed along the Egyptian-Israel lines until spring 1967.

Jordan-Israel Armistice lines also caused frequent UN debate. Here there were, in addition to border clashes, sabotage and retaliation, special problems arising out of the division of Jerusalem▷ and the existence of special arrangements for particular areas—such as Mt. Scopus▷ and the area around UNTSO's headquarters. The holding of Israel Independence Day parades in Jerusalem also caused Jordanian complaints. The UN was unable to arrange for the implementation of the special agreements on Jerusalem incorporated in the Armistice Agreements (see Jerusalem▷; Arab-Israel War▷).

The Syria-Israel lines also had their special problem—the existence of three demilitarized zones. Israel maintained that these were under full Israel sovereignty, with their demilitarization as the only limitation, while Syria claimed rights and a standing in the zones and the status of a protector of local Arab farmers. Frequent clashes were brought to the attention of the MAC and sometimes the SC. Syria often fired upon Israeli fishermen on the Sea of Galilee▷ (Lake Tiberias), wholly within Israel borders, another matter for UN debate.

A major question at issue was the utilization of the waters of the Jordan River▷. Disputes over the diversion of these waters, as well as the drainage of the Hula▷ swamps, caused Syria to complain to the MAC and the SC. The drainage was completed by Israel with SC endorsement; however, the SC questioned Israel's plan to divert the waters of the Jordan at a point within the Demilitarized Zone, and Israel, to avoid trouble and interference, shifted the point of diversion to the western shore of the Sea of Galilee, outside the Demilitarized Zone.

The crises of May 1967, Egypt's reimposition of a blockade on the Straits of Tiran and request for the removal of UNEF (see Six Day War▷, UNEF▷), caused another flurry of UN activity. The SC convened to discuss the situation, but did not take any action. After the Six Day War broke out, the SC called for a cease-fire along all frontiers; this was accepted by all the belligerents (except Algeria, Kuwait and Iraq) and went into effect on 10 June 1967. A special emergency session of the GA was called to discuss the situation but no resolution on ways to solve the crisis received the required majority; the GA could only request Israel to facilitate the return of the persons displaced by the recent fighting, to refrain from changing the status of Jerusalem (which had been unified under Israeli administration) and to cancel measures taken towards a formal

unification or annexation. In Nov. 1967, the SC discussed the situation and on 22 Nov. unanimously adopted resolution No. 242 which called for "the establishment of a just and lasting peace," a "withdrawal of Israeli armed forces from territories occupied," the "termination of all claims or states of belligerency and respect for and acknowledgment of the sovereignty, territorial integrity and political independence of every State in the area and their right to live in peace within secure and recognized boundaries free from threats or acts of force." The resolution also affirmed the necessity for the freedom of navigation through "international waterways in the area," and a "just settlement of the refugee problem." It asked the UN Secretary-General to designate a "Special Representative" to "promote agreement and assist efforts to achieve a peaceful and accepted settlement." Ambassador Gunnar Jarring▷ of Sweden was asked to undertake this mission and has been engaged on it ever since. The GA and the SC too have continued to deal with the Arab-Israel conflict—the "Palestine question."   (I.M.)

The problem of Palestine and the Arab-Israel conflict has occupied the UN and its various organs more than any other issue. There have, however, been other ME questions and disputes which were raised at the UN by the countries involved. These problems and disputes are discussed in the entries on each of the countries concerned. They are listed here only briefly to summarize UN involvement in ME affairs.

SYRIA AND LEBANON: The first to turn to the SC, complaining, in Feb. 1946, of the failure of Britain and France to withdraw their military forces. No binding decision was reached, because of a Soviet veto, but the debate helped resolve the dispute. Syria's problems were raised again in autumn 1957, this time in the GA, when she complained of a threat to her independence by Turkey, Iraq, Israel and the Western Powers. Lebanon complained to the SC in May 1958, that Egypt was endangering ME peace by interfering in her internal affairs, i.a. through the "infiltration of armed bands" and the "participation of UAR nationals in acts of terrorism and rebellion". The UN deliberations on this complaint resulted in the setting-up of an international observers' force which remained in Lebanon for several months, but achieved little.

IRAN: A complaint was lodged by Iran against the USSR in Mar. 1946 because the latter refused to withdraw her military forces at the agreed time. (They were withdrawn later.) Iran's dispute with the British Petroleum Company in 1952-4 was not discussed at the UN, but was brought before the International Court of Justice in The Hague, which ruled that it had no jurisdiction in the case.

EGYPT: Brought her dispute with Britain to the SC in summer 1947. It concerned the evacuation of British forces and the future of Sudan; no decisions were taken and the problems were not resolved. The Suez Canal crisis of 1956 was dealt with both in the SC and the GA. The Suez War▷ and the Sinai Campaign▷ were raised primarily in the Assembly (because of the British and French veto in the SC); its debates resulted in the setting up of an Emergency Force (UNEF▷).

Egypt appeared before the SC as the defendant (apart from the Arab-Israel conflict) in four complaints raised by Arab states: in Feb. 1958 by Sudan; in May 1958 by Lebanon; shortly thereafter by Jordan; and in summer 1963 by Sa'udi Arabia. All these problems were resolved—or left unresolved—by the Arab states themselves without a UN decision on the merits of the issues.

KUWAIT: Complained in June 1961 to the SC about an Iraqi threat to her independence as soon as it had been granted; the dispute was also finally resolved outside the UN.

LIBYA: Came up for discussion in the UN in 1948-9. It was in fact the GA which determined her future, deciding to grant her independence, rather than submit her to foreign rule or trusteeship, and to establish one united State of Libya with a federal structure.

YEMEN: The problem of Yemen was raised at the UN in 1962, following the outbreak of revolution and civil war and Egypt's armed intervention. The UN set up an international military observers' group to supervise the withdrawal of both Sa'udi Arabian and Egyptian forces intervening in Yemen; these observers served from summer 1963 to Sept. 1964. The SC also inconclusively debated incidents and border skirmishes between Yemen and the British Protectorate of Aden.

SOUTH ARABIA: The Special UN Committee for Non-Self-Governing Territories dealt with the questions of Aden and South Arabia from 1963 onwards. They were also brought up the same year at the GA. The Assembly recommended the evacuation of South Arabia by British forces, refused to consider the South Arabian Federation as an independent state whose establishment would have solved the problem of the area, and recommended UN supervision of elections and the transition to independence. A UN committee tried to implement such supervision in 1967, but the events which led to the independence of South Yemen moved so rapidly that the Committee could exert no influence.

'OMAN: The anti-colonial majority in the UN succeeded in getting the UN to intervene in the problems of Muscat-and-'Oman in 1960-1 (a previous attempt, in 1957, had failed). From 1961 onwards, the General Assembly recommended the evacuation of British forces from the principality. Britain, and the Sultan who had asked Britain to send troops to his aid, took no account of this recommendation, which they regarded as unwarranted interference in the affairs of an independent country. The UN also tried to investigate, through sub-committees and a special envoy of the Secretary-General, the dispute between the Sultan of Muscat-and-'Oman and the Imam of 'Oman, but reached no conclusions on this problem.

BAHRAIN: An envoy sent by the UN Secretary-General in 1970 prepared a public opinion poll on the future of Bahrain, following a proposal by the Shah of Iran and with the agreement of Britain and the Sheikh of Bahrain. He concluded that the majority wanted independence (and not annexation to Iran).

CYPRUS: The fundamental issue of Cyprus was solved through direct negotiations between the countries and national forces involved. But the renewed dispute between the government and the Greek Cypriots on the one hand and the Turkish Cypriots on the other, was brought in 1964 before the UN. A UN mediator failed to find a tangible solution. An international emergency peace-keeping force was sent to Cyprus in 1964, and its continued existence is confirmed every six months.

SUDAN: Sudanese issues were raised at the UN only in connection with Sudan's above-mentioned complaint against Egypt in 1958. The suppression and subsequent rebellion of the Negro tribes in south Sudan have not been raised at the UN by any one of the bodies struggling for the liberation of peoples; the south Sudan rebels themselves turned to the UN only in 1970 and the Committee for Non-Self-Governing Territories has promised to give them a hearing.

MAGHREB: Outside the scope of this Encyclopaedia, the UN dealt with the struggle of Morocco and Tunisia for independence from 1951-2 and with the Algerian problem from 1955. UN intervention did not produce tangible immediate results, but contributed to the creation of an atmosphere in which the French had to grant full independence to the *Maghreb* countries.

Besides UN discussions of ME political problems, and of complaints by or against ME countries, various UN institutions and, in particular, its special agencies were engaged in the area in many fields of activity: health, education, labour relations, development, transportation, etc. The UN and its special agencies made various attempts to set up regional centres to stimulate regional co-operation by all the ME countries (as through similar centres in the Far East, Africa, Latin America); these efforts all failed due to the refusal of the Arab states to co-operate in any way with Israel, and their opposition to any regional co-operation which would include Israel.   (Y. S.)

*UNITED NATIONS EMERGENCY FORCE (Palestine) (UNEF). Established 1956–7, following a decision of the UN General Assembly of 5 Nov. 1956, "to secure and supervise the cessation of hostilities" which had resulted from the Anglo-French Suez War▷ and the Israeli Sinai Campaign▷. Egypt agreed to the stationing of the UNEF in Egypt and the Egyptian-occupied Gaza Strip▷; Israel declined to have it on her territory. UN Secretary-General Dag Hammerskjold was instructed to establish and supervise the F. Brazil, Canada, Colombia, Denmark, Finland, India, Indonesia, Norway, Sweden and Yugoslavia supplied troops to UNEF (Indonesia withdrew in 1957). Its strength, at first over 6,000 men, was later reduced to c. 3,400. The financing of the F., from a special UN budget raised by member states, ran into difficulties. An advisory opinion of the International Court, in 1962, declared the contribution of UN members to the financing of the F. to be obligatory, but the Soviet Bloc refused to pay its share.

Initially, UNEF replaced the withdrawing troops of the three occupying states and briefly administered the Gaza Strip. Its permanent task was to patrol the Egyptian side of the 1949 Egypt-Israel armistice demarcation line and to prevent—by its presence rather than by direct action—clashes, particularly those caused by the penetration of Arab *feda'iyin*▷ (commandos) into Israel. A UNEF detachment was stationed at Sharm al-Sheikh▷ on the Straits of Tiran▷, to ensure the free passage of shipping in the Straits.

During the crisis of May 1967, Egypt requested the withdrawal of UNEF. Initially, 16 May, she only asked for its withdrawal from the border (interpreted to include Sharm al-Sheikh). UNEF's commander replied that he could accept orders concerning the deployment of the F. only from the UN Secretary-General. The Secretary-General, U Thant, endorsed that position and asked for clarification: if Egypt wanted a temporary withdrawal from the line or parts of it, her request would be unacceptable and considered as "tantamount to a request for the complete withdrawal of UNEF"; if she "intended to mean a general withdrawal of UNEF", her request would be complied with but

should have been addressed to the Secretary-General. On 17 May Egyptian local commanders ordered the immediate evacuation of UNEF posts, including that at Sharm al-Sheikh, and Egyptian forces took up positions on the border (UNEF now found itself behind them); U Thant warned that if these orders were maintained, he would "have no choice but to order the withdrawal of UNEF". On 18 May Egypt informed the Secretary-General that she had decided to "terminate the presence of UNEF" on her territory and requested its withdrawal; the same day, she asked the countries that had supplied contingents to UNEF to withdraw their troops.

U Thant consulted the UNEF Advisory Committee and again came to the conclusion that the Egyptian request was legitimate and that, in the absence of any proposal to convene the UN General Assembly or the Security Council, it had to be complied with. This decision has aroused considerable controversy; Israel in particular thought the removal of UNEF at Egypt's unilateral request—without even the Security Council's approval—was unjustified and incompatible with the assurances she had received in 1957.   (Sh.H.-Y.S.)

UNITED NATIONS OBSERVERS. On several occasions of armed conflict ended or suspended by a truce or an armistice, or in cases of complaints of outside military intervention denied by the party accused, the UN Security Council decided to send military observers (as distinct from an emergency force) to the conflict area, to check the actual situation and report on it. Such observers—military officers from various countries—have been sent to the Israel-Arab borders since 1948 (see Arab-Israel Conflict▷; United Nations Organization▷)—first as a Truce Supervision Organization (UNTSO); then 1949–67 as Armistice Observers (still titled UNTSO); and since 1967 as cease-fire observers—under a Chief-of-Staff responsible to the UN Secretary-General and the Security Council. Observers were briefly posted also to Lebanon in 1958, and to Yemen in 1963–4. On the other hand, the UN forces sent to the Israel-Egyptian borders, 1957–67, and to Cyprus, since 1964, were emergency forces, not observers.   (Y.S.)

UNITED NATIONS RELIEF AND WORKS AGENCY FOR PALESTINE REFUGEES IN THE NEAR EAST, UNRWA. An Agency established by the UN General Assembly in Dec. 1949 to aid and rehabilitate the Arab refugees from Palestine. The Agency, with an average annual budget of $34-40m. (more in recent years), from the beginning was torn between two approaches:

aid and rehabilitation. Some of its directors, and even more the states that contributed the funds for its budget (always headed by the USA), wished to channel assistance towards rehabilitation, constructive employment and resettlement. But all such rehabilitation plans had political import in that the Arab states, who pressed for the return of all the refugees to what had in the meanwhile become the State of Israel, opposed any resettlement and, therefore, any project of rehabilitation or employment which might be construed as a permanent arrangement. UNRWA (and the contributing states and the UN) yielded to this fundamental position of the Arab states and concentrated most of UNRWA's activity in assistance and services: rations and housing in camps to the needy, education (in co-operation with UNESCO, the United Nations Educational, Scientific and Cultural Organization), health. Attempts in UN assemblies and institutions to decide that such perpetually unproductive aid should be terminated and the pace of the refugees' rehabilitation accelerated, always failed for political reasons. UNRWA presents an annual report to the UN. See Refugees▷.   (Y.S.)

*UNITED STATES OF AMERICA, US INTERESTS AND POLICIES IN THE ME.
The USA first showed direct political interest in the ME following World War I, earlier links having been restricted chiefly to religious missions and educational institutions connected with them (notably the American University of Beirut). Of President Wilson's▷ Fourteen Points intended to establish US war aims and guide the Peace Settlement in 1918–19, one dealt specifically with the disposition of the Ottoman Empire. Two study groups were sent by President Wilson to the ME—the King-Crane Mission▷ to Syria and Palestine, and the Harbord Mission to Armenia. However, as the USA shunned direct involvement or a Great-Power role in the ME (and was anyhow retreating into isolationism), their recommendations were not acted upon, and they remained until *c.* 1941 almost isolated manifestations of a direct American political interest in the ME. A possible exception was the American-British Convention of 1924, in which the USA associated herself with the Palestine Mandate, *i.e.* the Jewish National Home. At the same time, the USA took strong action to enable US companies to participate in the development of ME oil resources; her struggle led to an agreement with Britain by which the Standard Oil Company of New Jersey and other companies obtained a share in Iraq's oil resources. The same companies later joined another group that had obtained a concession in the 1930s

(wholly American) in Sa'udi Arabia. Bahrain oil, too, was developed by a wholly American company, Kuwait oil—by an Anglo-American partnership.

In World War II, the USA had for the first time a military commitment in the area, including an expeditionary force in Iran (for purposes of implementing Lend-Lease to the USSR) and an air base at Dhahran in Sa'udi Arabia (completed after the war). This, US oil interests, and her increasing role as a Great Power in international affairs, led to further political involvement. Plans were made to finance and operate an oil pipeline from Sa'udi Arabia to the Mediterranean (eventually implemented by private interests, the oil companies, rather than the government); a US economic minister for the ME was nominated in 1944, and a regional petroleum attaché appointed to the US Embassy in Cairo. Among a series of important wartime contacts with ME rulers and governments were President Roosevelt's▷ talks with Arab leaders, including King Ibn Sa'ud▷, in Feb. 1945, immediately after the Yalta Conference.

Upon the conclusion of the war, the USA—eager to disengage from global commitments except for Western Europe and the Far East—was content that Britain remain the principal foreign power in the ME. It was only when Britain found herself unable to retain her position that the USA moved in, and even then she preferred limited steps affecting only the country or issue in question. In the late 1960s, the USA was still supporting Britain wherever the latter could make a show of withstanding anti-Western pressure.

In 1946, the USA endeavoured to solve the Iranian crisis within the framework of the UN; yet, in the event, only an unambiguous statement on the part of the USA that she was prepared to resort to force if necessary, secured the withdrawal of Soviet forces from Iran. The first direct American commitment in the area was the Truman▷ Doctrine of March 1947, which extended aid (military and economic) to Greece and Turkey, and in effect to Iran also; these three countries have received since 1947 by far the greatest share of US aid to the ME; aid to Iran continued until 1967, that to Greece and Turkey is still being maintained.

While American relations with Turkey and Iran were clear-cut and considered mutually beneficial, US relations with the other states of the region were vague and more flexible, in the absence of a constant and basic mutual interest. These states, not directly contiguous with Soviet territory and not, until the mid-1950s, the object of Soviet expansionism, were neither considered by the USA as legitimate recipients of large-scale aid nor, for their part, willing to become involved in the Powers' inter-bloc rivalry. However, Egypt, Sa'udi Arabia, Lebanon, Jordan, Iraq, Libya and Israel did enter into aid agreements with the USA under "Point Four" (technical aid) or subsequent acts which, in fact, continued combining economic aid with a policy designed to lead to the containment of the USSR.

American-Arab relations were made additionally intricate by the establishment of the State of Israel in 1948 and the concomitant Arab-Israel conflict. The USA had been less consistent than the USSR in her advocacy of a Jewish State and had even—after the acceptance, in Nov. 1947, of partition and Jewish Statehood—proposed in Mar. 1948 a trusteeship for an undivided Palestine as an alternative. However, once Israel was established, the USA found herself inextricably committed to the state's well-being and security: nor was the Administration able to turn its back on this commitment in view of domestic opinion (both Jewish and non-Jewish).

At the same time, the USA considered her relations with the Arab world a national interest more fundamental than her support of Israel. In order to mitigate the latter and to stress the predominance of her Western allies, and notably Britain, in the region, the USA joined Britain and France in the Tripartite Declaration▷ of May 1950, which supported and half-guaranteed the sovereignty and territorial integrity of all ME states and sought to co-ordinate the supply of arms to the Arab states and Israel.

In Oct. 1951, the USA, together with Britain, France and Turkey (which had just joined NATO), officially proposed to Egypt that she join them in forming a Middle East Defence Organization▷ or Command. (The other Arab states and Israel were informed, with the possibility of their later admission implied.) The proposal, implicitly but clearly directed against the USSR, was rejected, as were other, similar ideas. A new impetus was given to these plans in 1953 by the new Secretary of State, John Foster Dulles▷, who toured the ME in an attempt to persuade the states of the region to form a Western-oriented treaty organization on the lines of NATO▷ and what was to become SEATO. Dulles found, however, that the Arab states, Iraq excepted, were under no fear of the Soviet Union, and turned his attention to the countries of the "Northern Tier"▷ where a Soviet threat was a very relevant consideration. In Apr. 1954, the USA agreed to give military assistance to Iraq, and in May to Pakistan (the latter preceded by a Turco-Pakistani agreement), and in 1955 the Baghdad Pact▷ was set up comprising Britain, Turkey, Iraq, Pakistan and Iran. The USA at no stage became a full member of the pact (called

CENTO▷ after 1959, when Iraq withdrew), but participated in its major committees.

This apparent achievement of Western diplomacy alienated Egypt and her allies, who regarded the Pact as a move to split the Arab world, bring it into the cold war and force a Western imperial hegemony on it. The conditions imposed by the USA on arms supplies also offended the sensivities of the states of the area and particularly of Nasser's Egypt. The latter also resented the participation of Iraq and Pakistan in the Pact. This alienation provided the chief opening for Soviet penetration of the area and concomitant anti-American feeling.

The dilemmas of the USA *vis-à-vis* the ME were evident in the inconsistencies of her policy in late 1956. On the one hand, she wished to appear mainly as a supporter of Britain, as her role in the Baghdad Pact made clear; on the other, she was not prepared to collaborate with Britain and France in the extreme measures these two powers considered inevitable. It was Dulles who announced in July that the USA, and thus in effect also the International Bank, was retracting her offer to aid Egypt in constructing the Aswan▷ High Dam; but it was also Dulles who stated that the USA was free from the stigma of colonialism and would not go with Britain to the extent of resorting to force against Egypt. After the Suez War▷, the USA, whose stand had saved Egypt and forced Britain and France (and Israel, too) to withdraw, received no thanks and virtually no political gain.

Fallacious analysis and a doubtful assessment of regional trends are again evident in the Eisenhower Doctrine▷, followed by the American stance in the Syrian-Turkish crisis of 1957. US aid to Jordan, in the crisis of Apr. 1957, halted further radicalization and a Nasserist take-over; the USA took upon herself the major part of subsidizing the Kingdom State of Jordan. US aid to Lebanon, in July 1958, had the requisite immediate effect of preventing the radicalization of the regime; but the actual landing of US troops obfuscated the achievement. An American gain during this period was the severance of the Sa'udi-Egyptian alliance since 1957.

The USA, however, recovered some of her prestige in the Arab world after the crisis of 1957–8. The year 1959–63 saw both a crisis in Soviet-Arab relations and a renewed American effort to come to an understanding with the Arab world, and first and foremost with President Nasser. Under Kennedy there seemed to be a chance that the USA might succeed both in detaching herself from local conflicts and mitigating them, and in convincing the local governments of the need for peaceful development and eventually a measure of regional co-operation.

However, with the improvement of Soviet-Arab relations as from 1964, American ME policies became once more a reaction to Soviet initiatives, rather than the pursuit of any US-stimulated constructive line. As first the "progressive" Arab states and later, after June 1967, almost the entire politically-expressive Arab world opted for a pro-Soviet orientation, concurrently with the Soviet exacerbation of the Arab-Israeli conflict and the Soviet polarization of the role of the two Super Powers in that conflict, the USA found herself in an increasingly complex and difficult position in the Arab world. She became not only associated with attempts at undermining the national sovereignty of the ME states but identified with the one adversary of the entire Arab world, Israel. The USA has not always agreed with Israel either on some of the basic issues at stake or on several Israeli military and political initiatives; moreover, influential circles in the USA have always called for an Arab-oriented ME policy; yet the USA cannot accept a considerable part of the Arab stand on the Arab-Israel conflict. Moreover, since 1967 the USA has come increasingly to regard Israel, with Turkey and Iran, as the sole significant and reliable ally in the region.

The ever-increasing Soviet ME presence has made the USA aware of the need to be in a position to fulfil her commitments in the area. In the late 1960s, in view of the Vietnam war, the USA was wary of involvement in other parts of the world, especially in an area not considered as directly affecting her own national security. Yet the USA had certain obligations vis-à-vis a number of ME states, namely Turkey, Iran, Jordan, Lebanon, Sa'udi Arabia and Israel. Moreover, the USA cannot allow her own considerable investments and direct interests in the area to be threatened, especially insofar as the issues are no longer in essence between an external power and the local states, but rather between the two Super Powers. The stress laid by President Nixon on the strength of the Sixth Fleet, in 1970 still the strongest military factor in the area, must be seen as part of the global strategy of one Super Power in the face of constant encroachment by the other into spheres that have hitherto been considered neutral in the cold war.

Present US policy in the ME remains primarily concerned with the area's strategic importance and its oil resources. As to oil, American or partially American oil companies have been heavily involved in ME oil production and marketing, and American investment is extensive; also, while the USA does not need ME oil for her own consumption, she is intent on preserving its steady flow to her West-European allies. Strategic considerations were mainly two: a. the need for uninterrupted communications through the area, a vital nexus of the world's water- and airways; b. the possibility of a strike against the Soviet Union—exposed to such a strike on her Turkish and Iranian frontiers and accessible in her southern parts from the Mediterranean itself.

(Y. R.)

UNSCOP (United Nations Special Committee on Palestine, 1947)—see Palestine, Committees and Commissions▷, United Nations▷.

UNTSO—see United Nations Observers▷.

ÜRGÜPLÜ, ALI SUAT HAYRI (b. 1903). Turkish politician, Prime Minister, 1965. Ü. studied Law at the University of Istanbul and filled various judical positions. In 1939 he was elected to the National Assembly on the RPP list, and was Minister of Customs and Monopolies (1943–6). He later joined the Democratic Party and held various diplomatic posts. In 1961, as an Independent, he was elected Speaker of the Senate. Ü. became Prime Minister in Feb. 1965, after Inönü's resignation. He formed a coalition cabinet with the Justice Party and smaller groups, but excluding the Republican People's Party. After the Justice Party won the general election in 1965, he was replaced by Süleyman Demirel▷. (D.K.)

USA—see United States of America▷.

USSR—see Russia▷.

V

VA'AD LEUMI. National Council of the Palestine Jewish Community (*Knesset Yisrael*) elected by its Assembly of Deputies (*Assefat Hanivharim*). It was set up in 1920 (and recognized by the British in 1926) with rights of administration and taxation over the Jewish Community, whose members were, however, entitled to opt out of community affiliation. The VL dealt with local government of Jewish settlements, education, health, welfare and religion. It represented (generally following policies set by the Jewish Agency▷) the Jewish Community before the Mandatory Government and the Commissions of Inquiry on Palestine. Upon the establishment of Israel, the Provisional Government took over the rights and obligations of the VL. (Sh.H.)

VATICAN. As centre of the Roman Catholic Church, the V. takes a deep interest in the affairs of the ME, because of the presence there of Holy Places▷ and sites connected with the activities of the Apostles.

It is concerned for the welfare of a million and a half Catholics in the area. The Holy See also maintains hundreds of educational and charitable institutions in the ME, intended not only for Catholics, but also for missionary purposes among other creeds. In addition the V. maintains special relief agencies in the ME for assistance to refugees and displaced persons.

The V. has diplomatic representatives in most countries of the ME: a Nuncio in Lebanon, and pro-Nuncios in Egypt, Syria, Iraq, Iran and Turkey. An Apostolic Delegate has his seat in Jerusalem and is in charge of Catholic interests in Israel, Jordan and Cyprus. The V.'s relations with Israel have not been formalized up to now—mainly because of the Jerusalem▷ problem.   (Sh.C.)

W

WAFD (Arabic: "Delegation"). Egyptian nationalist political party, which evolved from the nationalist delegation sent by the leaders to the British in 1919 to negotiate Egyptian independence and Anglo-Egyptian relations. The W., led by Ahmad Sa'd Zaghlul▷ until his death in 1927 and thereafter by Mustafa Nahhas▷, was considered the principal nationalist party. It was modernistic in internal and social matters, bourgeois-democratic in ideology and for many years fought the King and Court circles, because of their attempt to reduce parliamentary power. The W. was in power for only short periods— in 1924, 1928, 1930 (each time for several months only), 1936–7, 1942–4, and 1950 to Jan. 1952. The W. won the elections of 1924, 1926, 1929, 1936, 1942 and 1950. While initially considered anti-British, the British eventually regarded it as the group most representative of Egyptian nationalism and tried to reach an agreement specifically with the W. Such an agreement was concluded in 1936. In 1942, the British compelled King Farouq▷ to dismiss his government and appoint Nahhas, the W. leader, Prime Minister, in the hope that the W. government would co-operate with the British war more willingly and efficiently. It was the W. which, in 1951, precipitated a severe crisis in Anglo-Egyptian relations. In 1953, in common with all other political parties, the W. was banned by the new regime of army officers. See Egypt▷, Political History.   (Y.S.)

WAHHABIS, WAHHABIYYA. Ultra-conservative puritan Sunni▷-Muslim movement which arose in the Arabian peninsula in the second half of the 18th century. Its founder was Muhammad Ibn 'Abd-ul-Wahhab (1691 or 1703–1791) from 'Uweina in Najd▷, of the Banu Sanan tribe (Banu Tamim

tribal federation). His teaching was rejected by his township, but adopted and propagated by Muhammad Ibn Sa'ud of the 'Anaza tribe who ruled (1747–65) in the neighbouring Dar'iya region. The W. call themselves *Muwahhidun*, believers in the one-ness of God. They are Sunni Muslims of the Hanbali school, greatly influenced by the teachings of Ibn Taimiyya (d. 1328). They claimed the Muslims had abandoned their faith in one God and distorted their religion through innovations which run counter to pure Islamic faith. The W. accepted only what is written of the *Qur'an* and the early *Sunna* and rejected all later developments and interpretations in Islamic theology and mysticism. Since there can be no mediation between man and God, they violently rejected veneration of saints and tombs. They forbade the decoration of mosques and banned luxuries and ostentation, and even tobacco and coffee. They considered all Muslims who did not accept their interdicts as heretics.

Ibn Sa'ud accepted their beliefs and spread them by conquest and expansion in Najd. During the reigns of his son and grandson, the W. began to raid other regions: 'Asir, parts of Yemen and Hijaz. In 1802–3, they conquered Karbala in Southern Iraq, the holy city of the Shi'ite▷ Muslims, and destroyed the mosque of the tomb of Hussein b. 'Ali venerated by the *Shi'a*. In 1803–4, the W. seized Mecca and Medina and destroyed the Ka'ba and the Mosque of the Tomb of the Prophet sacred to all Muslims. They also harassed the *Hajj* caravans of the pilgrims and at times prevented their entry to Mecca.

The Ottoman Sultan then ordered Muhammad 'Ali, Governor of Egypt, to take action against the W. In 1811 and 1812, Muhammad 'Ali sent military expeditions to the Arabian peninsula, conquered Mecca and Medina and, later on, all Hijaz. In 1818, Dar'iya in Najd, the last W. centre, was captured and their leader 'Abdullah b. Sa'ud was imprisoned and later executed in Istanbul.

As a religious movement, the W. influenced other similar sects of orthodox, fundamentalist Islam (*Idrissiyya▷*, *Mahdiyya▷*, *Sanussiyya▷*) and their influence reached as far as India and even China. But they never recovered from the defeat of 1912–18. A branch of the House of Sa'ud▷ maintained a limited rule in the Riyadh region but was blocked by the House of Rashid▷ of the Shammar tribe, and at the end of the century Riyadh was conquered by the Rashidis and the remnants of the House of Sa'ud fled to Kuwait. At the beginning of the 20th century, 'Abd-ul-'Aziz Ibn Sa'ud▷ succeeded in recapturing Najd and conquering, thereafter, most of the Arabian peninsula, and he did so, nominally, in the cause of the W. He even tried to settle an order of the W., the

"Brethren" (*Ikhwan*), in fortified villages. However, the W. beliefs were only one aspect of his conquests and Wahhabism became more moderate, with many interdicts abolished and forgotten. Officially, Wahhabism still rules in Sa'udi Arabia but, in practice, the religious leaders are slowly losing their power and influence. (Y.A.O.)

WAILING WALL. Built by King Herod about 20 BCE as an outer, western wall, the WW is the only remnant of the Jerusalem Temple area buildings destroyed by the Romans in 70 CE. It is the most hallowed site in Judaism, to which, throughout its history, Jewish pilgrims have come to lament the loss of their homeland and pray for redemption. In 1928 Muslim leaders challenged the right of Jews to bring prayer appurtenances to the WW; the Jews disputed the right of the Muslim *Waqf*▷ to build on that part of the Temple Mount (*Haram al-Sharif* with the Mosques of *al-Aqsa* and the Dome of the Rock, sacred to Islam) immediately overlooking the WW. A British White Paper in Nov. 1928, followed by detailed regulations in Oct. 1929, confirmed the Jews' right to pray, but forbade any change in the *status quo*, thus accepting the Muslim claim that no benches, screens etc. could be brought.

In Aug. 1929 incidents occurred at the WW. Rumours inflated by tales of alleged Jewish plans to appropriate the *Haram al-Sharif*, led to severe Arab

At the Wailing Wall

attacks on Jews all over Palestine. These disturbances resulted in a League of Nations Commission, 1930, which endorsed the Government regulations of Oct. 1929; a British Commission of Inquiry (under Sir Walter Shaw); and the White Paper▷ of 1930, which limited Jewish immigration. Restrictions of Jewish prayer rights were maintained.

Under Jordanian rule, 1948–67, Israelis were denied access to the Wall, contrary to the express terms of the Jordan-Israel Armistice Agreement. Since the Six Day War of June 1967, free access to their holy places in Jerusalem has been given by Israel to members of all religions. The WW is again a place of Jewish pilgrimage, though Jews are not allowed to pray on the Temple Mount to avoid inflammation of Muslim feelings. (Y.K.-E.L.-Y.S.)

WAQF (Plural: *awqaf*). Muslim religious foundation or endowment. Property dedicated as W. is given for all time and may not be subjected to any transaction, sale, inheritance, gift, etc. Its formal ownership is controversial in Islamic law, but this is of no practical significance; its income is used for the purpose indicated in the W. deed (*waqfiyya*), which may be the welfare of the dedicator's family (*W. dhurri* or *ahli*) or support for public worship, education, social relief, etc., (*W. kheiri*). The W. is administered by a custodian (*mutawalli*, *nazir*), as laid down by the dedicator.

The W. has, with the blessing of Islam, established itself as a form of religious charity, although its basis in the sources of Islamic law, the *Qur'an* and the *Sunna*, is somewhat flimsy. Its main aim has been to prevent the fragmentation of family property through inheritance (especially to daughters married into other families), government expropriation, and loss through indebtedness.

The tying-up of property by dedication withdraws it from the private and national markets (although there are legal devices for circumventing this restriction), and in countries where the W. represents a considerable portion of the agricultural landed property (such as Egypt before the military coup), it is a serious drawback of the agrarian system, with manifold economic, social and political implications. The W. has also been a source of corruption, chiefly among the administrators and in the *Shari'a*▷ courts, which have exclusive jurisdiction in W. matters. In the course of time the original purpose of a W. may cease to apply, but, because of its eternal sanction, it cannot be changed.

In the 20th century, public criticism of the W.'s ill-effects on the economy and society increased, but prior to the military coups the Arab governments opposed far-reaching reforms, as did the religious

establishment. Reforms were confined to the introduction of supervision of the W. administration by
special ministries, and amendments to the W. relating
only to future endowments: limitation of its validity
in time; permission for the dedicator to revoke the
establishment of the W.; prohibition of exclusion of
legal heirs from rights of enjoyment, and abrogation
of restrictions on the dedicator designed to circum-
vent the laws of succession; administration of the
W. by the beneficiaries; investment of the proceeds
of sale or exchange *(Amwal al-Badal)* for constructive purposes and winding-up of *awqaf* irretrievably
ruined by neglect. These reforms were based on a
combination of elements from various *Shari'a*▷
schools. Egypt was the first to introduce such reforms
(1946). Lebanon followed suit in 1947. As these reforms were not applied to existing *awqaf*, they had
little effect.

The military regimes in Syria and Egypt introduced more radical reforms of the W., eventually
resulting in its abolition. Besides economic and social
motivations, both regimes wanted to overthrow the
traditional leadership, which was closely bound up
with the agrarian system. In 1949, Syria abolished
the family W. and the combined W. (part
dhurri and part *kheiri*) and prohibited the founding of
new *awqaf*. Family *awqaf* were to be distributed mainly to the beneficiaries; the administration of those
parts of combined *awqaf* intended for charitable purposes was nationalized. In the wake of Syria, Egypt
abolished the family W. in 1952, and nationalized the
administration of all *awqaf kheiriyya* (except those
administered by their founders) in 1953; the Ministry
of W. was authorized to use the income of W.
property for purposes other than those indicated in
the W. deed. Finally, in 1957, properties were wholly
nationalized, to be distributed within the framework
of the agrarian reform, and proceeds of sale or exchange were ear-marked for development projects.
In Iraq, a special Ministry of W. Affairs was set up
in 1924, but material changes in the W. have so far
not taken place.

In 1924, Republican Turkey abolished the W.
Ministry and transferred W. affairs to a special department under the direct control of the Prime Minister. The aim was to nationalize the W. and use its
income for religious and other public purposes, but
although the *Shari'a* had been completely abrogated,
the W., which derives its sanctions from the *Shari'a*,
still exists.

In Mandatory Palestine, W. income, except where
a private *mutawalli* was appointed, was under the
jurisdiction of the Supreme Muslim Council▷. It was
used by its leaders, under Hajj Amin al-Husseini▷,
to gain political influence and finance nationalist ac-

tivities. In 1937, the Council's authority was transferred to a government-appointed committee. In
Israel, far-reaching changes were introduced in *awqaf*
in cases where their administrators or beneficiaries
had become absentees in 1948. A law of 1965 provided for the transfer of family *awqaf* to the beneficiaries' full ownership; W. *kheiri* property was
transferred to the ownership of Muslim boards of
trustees but these were not authorized to carry out
transactions affecting mosques.   (Ah.Ly.)

WATER IN THE ME. W. is scarce and therefore
greatly valued in the ME. Its importance increases
with the degree of aridity of the country concerned:
Few countries in the ME are without desert, and in
most of them more than two-thirds of the area are
arid (See Table 1).

Aridity is not the sole obstacle to agriculture
(others are mountainous topography, swamps, ster-
ile soils); but throughout history it has provided the
main challenge to human endeavour. The empires of
antiquity (Egypt, Babylon, Assyria) were based mainly on the harnessing of rivers and elaborate irrigation
systems. In modern times the importance of irrigation is greater still, as the products of traditional
agriculture, based upon winter rains, cannot compete
in world markets with the products of temperate
regions, whereas crops grown under irrigation are
able to utilize the high solar radiation of the ME
region. The main modern export crops of the ME—
cotton, citrus, sub-tropical fruit, vegetables, tobacco—are all grown under irrigation, while the
traditional products—wheat, barley, olive oil, figs—
all grown in areas of winter rains, have lost much of
their economic significance. In most countries of the
ME more than half the population still engages in
agriculture, and the improvement of farming by the
development of irrigation is therefore the main instrument for the raising of the low living standard.

As Table 1 shows, only the countries of the great
rivers, Egypt and Iraq, irrigate more than half of their
cultivated lands. In the Arabian peninsula almost all
cultivation is done in oases, except for the south-
western tip, where summer rainfall over the Yemen
and the 'Assir region of Sa'udi Arabia makes the
growing of unirrigated crops possible. In all other
countries of the ME only up to one quarter of the
cultivated area is irrigated and much can be done
through the development of new sources of W.

The main sources of W. for irrigation are springs
and rivers originating within the ME itself, except
for the Nile▷ whose sources lie in equatorial and
monsoonal Africa. The main source area is in the
mountains of Armenia▷, situated for the greater part
in Turkey. Because of their great elevation—with

Table 1. ARIDITY AND IRRIGATED AREAS IN THE ME (1966)

Country	Area (1,000 sq. mi.)	% of arid land	Cultivated lands— % of tot. area	Irrigated lands— % of cultivated lands
Arab. penins. (excl. Yemen)	1,042	98	1	70
Egypt	372	100	3	100
Iran	625	65	11	12
Iraq	171	70	13	50
Israel	8	60	23	27
Jordan	37	85	6	10
Lebanon	4	—	27	26
Sudan	967	55	7	4
Syria	71	65	28	14
Turkey	301	5	24	6
Yemen	76	70	?	?

Table 2. THE LARGE RIVERS IN THE ME

River	Length mi.	Catchment area (1,000 sq. mi.)	Volume p.a. mcm	Countries
Nile	4,142		83,100	East Africa, Sudan, Egypt
Euphrates	1,676	138	25,000	Turkey, Syria, Iraq
Tigris	1,148	139	38,000	Turkey, Syria, Iraq
Kizil Irmak	714	58	n.a.	Turkey
Karun	528	22	20,000	Iran
Sakariya	491	n.a.	n.a.	Turkey
Safid Rud	487	21	19,000	Iran
Orontes	355	n.a.	540	Syria, Turkey
Seyhan	348	n.a.	n.a.	Lebanon, Turkey
Ceyhan	292	n.a.	n.a.	Turkey
Yesil Irmak	258	n.a.	n.a.	Turkey
Litani	106	0.85	700	Lebanon
Jordan	160	6.3*	1,125*	Lebanon, Syria
		3.4**	560**	Israel, Jordan
Yarmuk	50	2.8	475	Syria, Jordan, Israel

n.a.   not available
*   including the Yarmuk
**   excluding the Yarmuk

many peaks above 9,843 ft. above sea level and a maximum height of 16,917 ft. in Mount Ararat, they induce large amounts of rainfall, which is preserved in the form of snow throughout the winter. Many parts of the highlands receive a precipitation of up to 78″ annually, and the slopes towards the Black Sea even up to 156″. The Armenian rains feed a large number of rivers, among them the Kizil Irmak and Yesil Irmak within Turkey, the Euphrates▷ and Tigris▷ and their tributaries and the Aras▷ (Araxes) which forms the boundary of Turkey and Iran with the Soviet Union. The combined quantity of W. carried by these rivers exceeds that of the Nile. The mountain ranges of Iran also produce a large number of streams and rivers; those, however, flow mainly into the inland deserts, where they evaporate in salt marshes. Only the Karun River reaches the coast of the Persian Gulf, where it joins the swampy delta of

Table 3. MAJOR WATER PROJECTS IN THE ME

Project.	River	Storage capacity mcm	Area irrigated (1,000 acres)	Electricity generated (megawatt)	Year of completion
Egypt					
Aswan	Nile	5,300	All Egypt	340	1939
Aswan High Dam	Nile	150,000	All Egypt	2100	1970
Isna	Nile		321		1947
Nag' Hammadi	Nile	★	86		1930
Asyut	Nile	★	766		1902
Muhammad 'Ali	Nile	★	All delta		1939
Sudan					
Sennar	Blue Nile	1,000	988		1925
Jabal Awliya	White Nile	3,500	n.a.		1935
Russeires	Blue Nile	2,500	n.a.	n.a.	1966
Khasm al-Ghirba	Atbara	n.a.	519	n.a.	(u.c.)
Turkey					
Seyhan Dam	Seyhan	n.a.	356	248	1956
Sariyar	Sakarya	★★		80	1956
Demir Köprü	Gediz	n.a.	190	69	1958
Hirfanli	Kizil Irmak	n.a.	83	128	1958
Sile	Sile	n.a.	74	—	1957
Keban	Euphrates	26,000	n.a.	620–1240	u.c.
Iran					
Muhammad Reza Shah Dam	Karun	n.a.	586	n.a.	u.c.
Dezful	Dez	3,300	556	130–520	1964
Manjil	Safid Rud	1,690	296	80	1960
Teheran Water Supply	Karaj	200	22	110	1962
Dorudzan	Kur	875	109	109	u.c.
Syria					
Homs Lake	Orontes	n.a.	54		1952
Ghab Marshes	Orontes	★★★	161		1963
Euphrates Dam (Al-Tabqa)	Euphrates	8,000	988–1,482		u.c.
Iraq					
Hindiya	Euphrates	★			1913
Kut al-Amara	Tigris	★			1939
Habbaniya Lake	Euphrates	★★			1956
Wadi Tharthar	Tigris	★★			1956
Dokan Dam	Little Zab	6,300	790		1959
Darban-i-Khan	Diyala	3,250	804	112	1964
Bekhme Dam	Great Zab	3,825	597		u.c.

u.c.   under construction
n.a.   data not available
★   no storage; purpose: distribution of river waters
★★   no storage; purpose: flood control, diversion
★★★   no storage; purpose: drainage

Israel, the National Water Carrier, Pumping Station (under construction)

the Shatt al-ʿArab▷. From the mountain ranges which fringe the Anatolian plateau, a large number of rivers radiate towards the surrounding seas. The Lebanon and Anti-Lebanon ranges on the Levant coast constitute a minor source region, providing the headwaters of the Orontes▷ and Litani▷ as well as the sources of the Jordan▷ and the rivers of Damascus▷. A list of the main rivers of the ME and their annual average discharge is given in Table 2.

In addition to the utilization of rivers for irrigation, modern technology has facilitated the pumping of W. from deep seated horizions of groundwater. Methods of transporting W. to the fields vary from the primitive to the most elaborate. In Upper Egypt and in the Sudan the type of contraption still most often seen, the *shaduf*, has been in use in the region for millennia. It consists of a bucket made of goatskin attached to a wooden beam; its lifting capacity is 2.5 cu.m of W. to a height of 6 ft. in one work-hour. A much more advanced installation is the *saqiyya*, a W.-wheel driven by animals with an output of about 20–40 cu.m per hour; but its disadvantage is that it requires capital investment, in the form of a working animal, and the growing of fodder on land which would otherwise yield food crops. In Iran, irrigation has been based since antiquity on *qanats*, which reach a groundwater horizion by access tunnels, sometimes several miles long.

a groundwater horizion by access tunnels, sometimes on minimum capital and maximum labour invest-

ment, because manpower for agriculture is abundant. In areas of labour scarcity, as in Iraq since the development of the oil industry, mechanical pumping has been installed. In Iran also many *qanats* are being replaced by pumping, as the traditional form of W.-supply was wasteful of W. and necessitated frequent repairs. In countries of developed commercial agriculture, such as Israel, Lebanon and parts of Syria, groundwater sources are utilized by modern pumping methods, using pressure pipes and sprinklers.

Modern irrigation systems are often based on the construction of dams, which usually serve a number of purposes in addition to irrigation—mainly flood control and the generation of power. As small rivers run dry in summer, and only the largest provide a sufficient perennial flow, dams must be large. A large reservoir is usually also necessary, to provide sufficient volume of water to balance the variations in flow between dry and rainy seasons. A list of the main irrigation projects in the ME is given in Table 3.

The modernization of W.-supply with the aid of dams and pipes raises new economic problems. Irrigation has been based in the past on the free flow of W. into channels by gravity and its raising and transfer to the fields by primitive methods. Where W. is pumped into channels, as in Iraq, the peasant pays the owner of the pump (a landlord or the state) a share of the crop; but his cash income will not enable him to pay even a minimal price for W. in money. It is only in areas of commercialized modern farming that the farmer can afford to pay cash for his W. consumption. Most of the capital investment in modern dams or pumping installations cannot therefore be recovered through payment by the peasants, and it is mainly the power generated which provides for the payment of interest and eventual recovery of the capital invested.

Large projects of river development may produce political conflict between riverine neighbours and necessitate agreement on the combined use of W. Thus the Nile dams in Sudan—particularly those on the Blue Nile intended for Sudan's benefit (those on the White Nile benefit Egypt)—were built by Britain against Egypt's opposition. The Sennar Dam on the Blue Nile was completed in 1925, but an agreement on the use of its W. was signed only in 1929. A new agreement, which put its W. completely under the control of Sudan, was signed in 1959 (see Nile▷). The dam on the White Nile at Jabal Awliya was completed in 1935 and its W. placed completely at the disposal of Egypt. The new Egypt-Sudan agreement of 1959, necessitated by the construction of the High Dam at Aswan▷ and Sudan's insistent demands, puts at the disposal of the Sudan 18,500m. cu.m *p.a.*, leaving c. 55,500m. cu.m to Egypt downstream. Sudan now controls both dams, Sennar and Jabal Awliya, and is constructing two additional dams at Russeires on the Blue Nile (inaugurated 1966) and Khasm al-Ghirba on the Atbara. Egypt's own dams, being downstream, have raised no international problems. Likewise, Syria is downstream from Lebanon on the Orontes River; her development plans on the river are being pursued with no prior agreement with Lebanon. However, Syria is also going ahead, with Soviet aid, with plans to construct a large dam on the Euphrates River, though no agreement with Iraq, downstream, has been signed. Plans for a large dam on the upper Euphrates at Keban in Turkey may create future friction between Turkey and Syria and/or Iraq. Iraq being downstream, no international problems were raised by her own dams (see Euphrates▷, Tigris▷).

Severe conflict broke out between Israel and her Arab neighbours over the W. of the Jordan River. Although tentative agreements on the equitable distribution of its W., and other points at issue, had been reached in 1955 through the mediation of an American business leader, Eric Johnston▷ (see Jordan River▷), the Arab states refused to finalize the agreement. When Israel went ahead with her Jordan diversion plans (proclaiming she would not take more than her share under the Johnston Plan), the Arab states threatened to divert the sources of the river. The Six Day War▷ put a stop to this element of the conflict.

Iran is in perpetual conflict with Iraq over navigation and boundary problems on the Shatt al-'Arab▷. She has agreed with the Soviet Union on common projects along the Aras▷ river which forms their joint boundary.   (Y.K.)

WEIZMANN, CHAIM (1874–1952). Professor of chemistry and Zionist leader. First President of Israel (1948–52). Born in Russia, W. was active in the Zionist Movement from its inception. In 1903 he was one of the founders of the Democratic Faction which advocated "Practical Zionism" (see Zionism▷). In 1904 W. migrated to Britain where he played an influential role in the discussions towards the issuance of the Balfour Declaration▷ in 1917.

From 1920 to 1948, with only a short break (1931–5), W. was President of the Zionist Organization. His moderate policy of full co-operation with the British government was the main cause for his defeat at the 1931 Congress. W. also advocated moderation with regard to the Arabs; until 1937, he propagated a political parity between the two peoples in Palestine irrespective of their relative numerical strength. From 1937, he supported partition and separate states—preferably within the framework of a ME federation.

W. supported, together with David Ben-Gurion▷, the Biltmore Programme▷ calling for a Jewish Commonwealth in Palestine; but Ben-Gurion accused W. of often acting independently. W.'s moderate policies were not in accord with the violent

Chaim Weizmann

struggle which was developing; his absence from Palestine aggravated his lack of contact with colleagues there. However, he retained considerable prestige and was in the forefront of the final struggle (1946–8) for the creation of the State of Israel. In May 1948 W. became Israel's first President (sworn in on 16 Feb. 1949), but due to the merely representative nature of the office and his poor health he did not play an active part in policy making.

W.'s favourite projects were the Hebrew University of Jerusalem, opened in 1925, and the W. Institute of Science in Rehovot, opened in 1934. His autobiography, "Trial and Error" (1949), is an important human and Zionist document. (Sh.H.)

WEST BANK. Name given by the Jordanian government to the Palestinian territory (2,270 sq.mi.), west of the River Jordan, which Jordan seized during the Arab-Israel War▷ of 1948. According to a UN Assembly Resolution of 1947, the territory was to have become an independent Arab State by the side of the Jewish State. The Israel-Jordan Armistice Agreement of 1949 left it under Jordanian rule, without fixing rights or permanent frontiers (which were to be determined in a peace settlement). At the time of its formal annexation by Jordan (Apr. 1950, see Jordan▷; Palestine Arabs▷), the WB had c. 400,000 residents and some 200,000 refugees who had fled from Israeli territory during the war.

The annexation was formally recognized only by Britain and Pakistan, although other nations maintained official relations with Jordan in its enlarged borders. It was strongly opposed by the Arab League▷, which, in a compromise solution, treated the WB as "a trust in Jordan's hands until the Palestine case is fully solved in the interests of its inhabitants". Israel, for her part, considers the annexation invalid and contrary to international law, as it was the consequence of an aggression undertaken to annul the 1947 UN Resolution.

Because of their higher economic and cultural level and more developed political awareness, the WB inhabitants felt superior to those of the East Bank. They opposed Jordanian restrictions on the freedom of political organization, and advocated greater parliamentary control of the executive. At the same time they held important posts in the Jordanian administration and never attempted to establish an autonomous state of their own. The WB became an integral part of the Jordanian economy, responsible, in the mid-1960s, for 60–85% of Jordan's agricultural products and 48% of the industrial, thereby providing about 35% of the kingdom's GNP, over 40% of the government's revenue and one-third of its foreign currency income.

Between 1948 and 1967 the WB served as a base and refuge for Arab saboteurs and guerillas, both local and from other countries. They would cross the border to attack Israeli settlements, often under covering fire of the Jordanian Army.

In the Six Day War▷ the WB, including East Jerusalem, was occupied by Israeli forces (7 June 1967). On 28 June 1967 Israeli administration, law and jurisdiction were extended to include East Jerusalem and the surrounding area, comprising some 68,000 residents. The rest of the WB was placed under military government.

In 1966 the WB population, including East Jerusalem, had been 860,000. During the Six Day War 200,000 refugees crossed to the East Bank, leaving in September 1967 a population of 595,900. On 31 Dec. 1970 it was 609,700 (32,000 of them Christians). As against a natural increase of 24,000 a year, other residents left for the East Bank with the permission of the Israeli authorities. Mobility in seeking employment opportunities abroad was common also under Jordanian rule (e.g. 63,000 in 1961), but during 1969–70 more returned to the WB than left it. The population includes a controversial number of refugees who had abandoned their Israeli dwellings in 1948. According to figures of the United Nations Relief and Works Agency (UNRWA) the figure for 1967 was c. 270,000. Israeli figures—defining as refugees members of a family whose head was born in Israel—put the number at 106,000 or, according to a wider definition, some 180,000.

There has been surprisingly little subversive activity on the WB, or collaboration with terrorists infiltrating from Jordan and Syria. Israel minimizes her presence, limits her intervention in internal affairs, and maintains a policy of "open bridges" between the WB and the Arab states. This policy—after the initial period of adjustment marked by a few shopkeepers' and school strikes—brought about an atmosphere of order and tranquility. 280,416 West Bankers visited the East Bank (until 31 Mar. 1971) and 130,359 Arabs from Arab countries came to the WB (including summer visits of 94,830 Arab students). These mutual visits were occasionally stopped by the Jordanian government, but renewed under WB pressure.

Local government is fully in the hands of local authorities which co-operate with the Military Government. The WB inhabitants, however, are still in a dilemma concerning their political future. Some local leaders favour an autonomous WB—separated from Jordan or associated with her—within the framework of a settlement with Israel. Many others hold that any settlement with Israel will be practicable only if accepted by the Arab states, at the least by Jordan, and in particular by Egypt. Jordan's sanguinary campaign since Sept. 1970 against Palestinian terrorists within her borders was vehemently resented in the WB and lessened the chances of a solution based on political union between the two Bs.; King Hussein has implied he might establish an autonomous WB within the framework of a federal association with Jordan. Israel, for her part, has shown no enthusiasm for setting up an autonomous Palestinian State on the WB. She would prefer to deal with a single unit east of her frontier; she has stressed that Jerusalem must remain united and Israel-administered, and indicated that the River Jordan should be her security (though not necessarily her political) frontier. Meanwhile Israel has established security settlements along the River Jordan and has begun to build a Jewish suburb next to the town of Hebron.

Israel's principal economic aim has been to provide employment for the population and to ensure the free flow of goods. In 1970, out of a labour force of 140,000 (average), only 2.6% were unemployed (in 1961, under Jordanian rule, unemployment was 7%). The average daily wage rose to I£6.70 (1969) (I£ 4.90 for a farm labourer under Jordanian rule). Some 23,000 a day find employment in Israel (Jan. 1971), through newly opened labour exchanges (there were none under Jordanian rule). In 1969 and 1970, over 5,000 persons were taught metal-work, sewing, and building trades at professional training centres.

The WB exports and imports goods to and from both Israel and the Arab countries (across the Jordan bridges). In 1970 total WB exports amounted to I£146m. (41% to Israel, 41% to Jordan and 18% to other Arab states and other countries). Imports to the WB (half of them by UNRWA and public institutions) amounted to approximately I£293m. in 1970—I£252m. from Israel, I£13m. i.e. 4.4% from the East Bank. The WB GNP was I£472m. in 1969 (IL656m. in 1966). However, the population in 1969 was only 70% of the population in 1966. *Per capita* production increased therefore despite the Six Day War. The sense of economic and political security in the WB is indicated by the small difference between the official exchange rate of the Jordanian dinar (I£11.75) and the free market rate I£11.50).

The Israeli administration has not altered school curricula, except for the deletion from text-books of incitement against Israel. In 1971–2 there were c. 190,000 pupils (167,000 before the Six Day War)— a significant increase despite the drop in population. The number of teachers rose by 80% and the number of classes by 72%.

Two daily newspapers are published in the WB (one of them openly advocating an Israeli withdrawal from the occupied territories, including Jerusalem), and also one political weekly, three monthlies and two "internal publications". Two additional weeklies and a medical publication are being planned.

The budget of the military administration in 1971–2 was approximately I£96m. (I£16m. for development). About I£48m. were not covered by revenues. In accordance with the Israeli policy of non-intervention, only 391 (4.7%) out of 9,236 military administration personnel are Israelis. (E.L.)

WHEELUS FIELD. American Air Force base near Tripoli (Libya). Built originally by the Italians and known as Mellaha Field, it was enlarged after World War II by the Americans and renamed WF (after an American Air Force officer). It was the largest American air base in the eastern hemisphere; at its peak period it was manned by c. 6,000 personnel with 4,500 dependents. US rights to the base, in return for US aid, was confirmed in a 1954 agreement with Libya. Libyan nationalists soon began clamouring for its evacuation. In Dec. 1969 the new Republican Government of Libya and the USA reached agreement regarding its evacuation. WF was evacuated in June 1970 and its installations handed over to Libya. (B.G.)

WHITE PAPERS. Statements of British policy. Among those concerning the ME: 1. The WP of 1922 (Cmd. 1700) denied that the Balfour Declaration▷ meant to turn Palestine into a Jewish State, promised to foster self-government in Palestine and limited Jewish immigration to the economic absorptive capacity of the country. The Zionists accepted the WP; the Arab leaders rejected it.

2. In 1928, a Memorandum published (Cmd. 3229) by the Colonial Secretary (sometimes referred to as a WP) stated that the *status quo* which had prevailed under the Ottomans should be maintained at the Wailing Wall▷.

3. The WP of 1930 (Cmd. 3692) re-emphasized the "dual obligation" of the Mandate, and re-interpreted more rigidly the economic absorptive capacity regarding immigration. The Arabs were moderately pleased with the WP. As the Jews protested against it as being contrary to the Mandate and Britain's commitment, British policy was reinterpreted in a letter from Prime Minister MacDonald to Weizmann (1931): Jewish immigration would not be stopped, and there would be no change in the interpretation of economic absorptive capacity.

4. A WP of July 1937 (Cmd. 5513), following the Peel Report, tentatively adopted partition as official policy, but this plan was dropped in 1938 (Cmd. 5893).

5. The WP of 1939 (Cmd. 6019) allowed only 75,000 Jewish immigrants to enter Palestine during the following five years, with further immigration to depend on Arab consent, restricted Jewish land purchases, and declared the government's intention of granting Palestine, in which the Arabs would remain the majority, independence after ten years. The Mandates Commission of the League of Nations denounced the WP as "not in accord with" the spirit of the Mandate and its purpose; the Zionists fought it tooth and nail. The Arabs were reserved as they had wanted immediate independence and a complete halt to immigration, but they accepted it. The 1939 WP remained official British policy until the end of the Mandate.   (Sh.H.)

WILSON, SIR ARNOLD TALBOT (1884–1940). British colonial administrator, politician and writer. As an army officer W. carried out survey and intelligence work in south-west Persia, 1907–14. He was Political Officer with the British Expeditionary Forces in Mesopotamia, 1914–18, and Acting Civil Commissioner for Mesopotamia during the absence of Sir Percy Z. Cox▷ in Teheran, 1918–20. W. was an able and energetic administrator but he fell foul of the Iraqi nationalists, and London considered the insurrection of 1920 to be largely due to his misinterpretation of the spirit of the times. After his recall he entered the service of the Anglo-Persian Oil Company and later was a Conservative member of the British Parliament. He published a number of books on the ME; the most interesting is "Loyalties", 1930, an account of, and apologia for, his work in Mesopotamia. In World War II, W. volunteered for the RAF and was shot down over France.
(U.D.)

WILSON, WOODROW (1856–1924). Democratic President of the USA, 1912–19. Under his leadership the USA entered World War I▷ (6 Apr. 1917), following unrestricted German U-boat attacks. Under the influence of Louis D. Brandeis, W. approved the Balfour Declaration▷. His famous "14 Points" of 8 Jan. 1918 emphasized the right of national self-determination for all peoples and called for the establishment of a League of Nations▷. W. tried to bring his idealism to bear at the Paris Peace Conference▷, and was instrumental in the replacement of old-fashioned imperialist domination or influence by the mandate▷ system. He also sent the King-Crane Commission▷ to investigate the wishes of the inhabitants of Palestine and Syria. But his efforts to associate the USA actively with international politics were frustrated by the refusal of the US Senate to ratify the Versailles Treaty and the Covenant of the League.   (Sh.H.)

WINGATE, ORDE CHARLES (1903–44). British captain who adopted the cause of Jewish self-defence as his own and organized, during the Arab revolt of 1936–9, units of young Jewish volunteers known as the Special Night Squads. They successfully used unorthodox counter-guerilla tactics, which still influence Israel military training. Removed from Palestine for his pro-Jewish activities, W. used the methods he had developed, during World War II as a brigadier in Ethiopia and Burma. He was killed in an aircrash in Burma.   (A.W.)

WOMEN. W. in the ME have had, since antiquity, an inferior legal status and social standing, and have not enjoyed equality of rights with men. Some have attributed this primarily to the influence and laws of Islam. Historically, such an attribution is unjust, since Islam improved the status of women, in comparison with their situation prior to its emergence, and increased and defined their rights. However, in comparison with the rights women now enjoy in contemporary Western civilization, Islam has turned into a restrictive factor (see *Shari'a*▷). The same applies, *mutatis mutandis*, to other religions. Historically, Christianity and in particular Judaism alleviated the situation of women and gave them increased rights in antiquity; but both have become restrictive in contemporary society. Yet, women's inferior social standing and legal inequality were not the products of religion but of specific social circumstances. The fact that these restrictions have survived longer in the ME than in Europe is another instance of a general historical phenomenon: social and economic development, since the end of the Middle Ages, has been slower in the ME than in Europe.

The absence of equal rights for women expressed itself, till a generation or two back, in many forms: polygamy (in Islam and certain branches of Oriental Jewry) and the case with which husbands could divorce their wives, limitations on woman's rights to own property and, in case of divorce, on her right to her own children; the denial of all political and civil rights to women; the payment of bridal money to the bride's father (not to the bride)—*i.e.* the virtual purchase of brides; the denial of education to girls; women's socially inferior position, her confinement to the inner chambers of the house and the veiling of her face; a severe, punitive attitude to women accused of sexual relations before or outside marriage, as compared with permissiveness where men were concerned. It goes without saying that, in spite of these and many other restrictions, women have had great social influence in the ME, through their domestic management, their bringing up of the children, and their actual influence on the men.

At the end of the 19th century, a movement for improving the condition of women slowly emerged in Turkey, Iran and the Arab countries. At first it was concerned principally with education—and those who wanted to send their daughters to school could be quite conservative in other spheres and oppose any change in women's civic or social status. As to its educational aims, the reform movements succeeded. Certainly, even today there are parents, mainly in the villages, who do not send their daughters to school, either because they are needed for work, or because of excessive conservatism. Yet wherever compulsory education is the law—and that means most ME countries—it applies to both sexes. The actual percentage of girls attending school still does not fully correspond to their percentage in the age-group population; but in several countries (Israel, Turkey and Egypt) it approaches half the school population, and at any rate exceeds 40 percent, while in other countries (Jordan, Iraq) it exceeds 30 percent. Since the 1920s, institutions of higher learning and universities, including even the Islamic al-Azhar▷ University, have opened their doors to women.

Gradually, the movement began to concern itself also with the social situation of women. The first and main targets of the reform were polygamy and the easiness of divorce for men. Even the more conservative revivalists of Islam, such as Muhammad 'Abdu▷, fought polygamy, deriving authority for their struggle from the Koran itself. The best known among the fighters for women's rights was the Egyptian Qassem Amin (1865–1908); he also was the author of several books on the subject. In the 1920s women themselves began gradually to take the initiative in the fight for equal rights and to found their own women's organizations.

ME states began slowly to respond by changing their laws. Kemal Atatürk's▷ Turkey went to the revolutionary extreme: in 1924 she abolished the Shari'a▷ and introduced a civil code (adapted from the Swiss) which covered matters of personal status, family, etc. Under this law polygamy was abolished and outlawed. A campaign was also started against the veil. Polygamy is banned, outside Turkey, only in Tunisia and Israel. Other countries of the area adopted more cautious, conservative attitudes— whether, like Sa'udi Arabia, they did not introduce any significant reforms concerning women's status, or attempted to relate such reforms as were instituted to Muslim law and to apply them but slowly and conservatively. In some Muslim countries, for example, wide authority was given to Muslim judges (Qadis) to make divorce more difficult and conditional on the safeguarding of the wife's rights, and the husband's right to divorce his wife without legal act or sanction was abolished or limited. In Syria, the Qadis were authorized to restrict a man's right to take an additional wife and to refuse sanction to such a marriage. In most Muslim countries, laws were passed fixing a minimum age for marriage. In some countries, rights of women to inherit and own property were extended (on these improvements see Shari'a▷).

There have been rapid changes in the civic and political rights of women, especially since the 1950s. At present women formally enjoy equal, or almost equal, civic rights in all ME countries, except Sa'udi Arabia, Jordan, Kuwait and the Persian Gulf, and Yemen. Kemalist Turkey was the first, in 1934, to extend to women the franchise. Israel did so at her foundation in 1948 (women had enjoyed equal rights in the pre-State Jewish national institutions), and so did Cyprus, 1960. Among the Arab states, Syria was the first to confer the franchise on women; in the 1949 Election Law and the 1950 Constitution this right was limited to women who had finished a primary school (an educational qualification not required of men); women also could not be elected. This last discrimination was removed in 1953, and women have been able to stand for Parliament since 1954 (but there have been no elections in Syria since 1961). Lebanon granted the vote to women in 1953 (until 1957 only men were *obliged* to vote); Egypt, in 1956 (but there have been no real, multi-party and multi-candidate elections since then); Iraq, in 1964 (there have been no elections in Iraq since 1958); Libya, in 1963; Sudan in 1965. Iran also conferred the franchise on women in 1963. Appropriate legislation has long been promised in Jordan, but has not yet been enacted.

There are still very few women MPs in the ME. In Israel, ten women were elected to the Sixth *Knesset*, 1965, eight to the Seventh, 1969 (out of 120 members). In Egypt, five women were, in 1957, among the 1,318 permitted to present their candidacy for the National Assembly and two out of 350 elected were women; in 1964, eight were elected. In Lebanon, the first woman was elected to Parliament in a by-election in 1963.

Women have been members of the government in Israel, Iran, Iraq, Egypt, Turkey and Cyprus. In Israel a woman has been Prime Minister since 1969. In no country of the ME is the part women play so far in public and political life proportionate to their numbers.   (Y.S.)

WOODHEAD, SIR JOHN. British administrator, sent to Palestine in 1938 at the head of a commission, to work out details of the Partition Plan proposed by the Peel▷ Commission. In his report, W. concluded that partition could not be carried out without doing injustice to either Jews or Arabs. See Palestine▷, Committees and Commissions▷.   (Y.S.)

WORLD WAR I. The ME entered the W. as a result of Turkish involvement with Germany. Germany had given the Ottoman Empire▷ military and economic aid before the W. and secured an alliance with her on 2 Aug. 1914. The Turks closed the Straits of the Bosphorus▷ and the Dardanelles▷ on 26 September. Late in October they bombarded Odessa and Sebastopol—without any declaration of war. The *Entente* Powers—Britain, France and Russia —now severed relations with Turkey and declared war on her.

By the end of 1914 Britain had annexed Cyprus and proclaimed Egypt a British Protectorate (both had been occupied by Britain since the late 19th century). The Turks proclaimed a *Jihad*▷, a holy war, against the infidels. In Dec. they occupied parts of north-west Persia and the Sinai Peninsula; early in 1915 they attacked the Suez Canal. British forces invaded Mesopotamia in 1914 (from the Persian Gulf) and occupied its southern parts.

The Allies mounted an unsuccessful campaign in the Dardanelles and Gallipoli▷, 1915, while the British lost several battles to the Turks in Mesopotamia, 1915–16. Meanwhile the *Entente* Powers had begun discussing the disposition of the Ottoman Empire. It was agreed that Russia would occupy the Straits with Constantinople and north-eastern Anatolia; Italy was to obtain south-west Anatolia; and the subjection of major parts of the Empire to British or French domination or indirect control was blue-printed in the Sykes-Picot Agreement▷, 1916.

David Lloyd George, who became Prime Minister of Britain late in 1916, favoured the expulsion of the Turks from Palestine in order to force them out of the W. The ME, until then considered a marginal front, became a major theatre of war. In June 1916 an Arab Revolt▷ against the Turks—pre-arranged in the McMahon-Hussein Correspondence▷—broke out in Hijaz▷, pinning down Turkish forces and causing Turkey to loose both territory and Arab support (though most Arabs in the Fertile Crescent▷ remained loyal to the Turks).

The British began advancing through Sinai into Palestine late in 1916 but were halted in the Gaza area. In 1917 the Turks retreated. On 11 Mar. the British captured Baghdad and the Turks retreated from the parts of Persia they had occupied. The advance into Palestine was now resumed under the command of Gen. Allenby▷. The Arab troops from Hijaz captured ʿAqaba▷ in July 1917 and became Allenby's right wing, advancing northwards in the

area east of the Jordan River. Jerusalem surrendered to Allenby on 9 Dec. A last British offensive, in Sept. 1918 (the Battle of Megiddo), broke Turkish resistance. On 1 Oct. Damascus was conquered, on 7 Oct. Beirut, on 26 Oct. Aleppo, and on 30 Oct. 1918 the war was ended by the Armistice of Mudros▷.

WWI brought the Ottoman Empire to an end. The Arabs immediately gained complete independence in most of the Arabian peninsula: Hijaz, the Sultanate of Najd▷ (ruled by Ibn Saʿud▷ and later to be united with Hijaz as Saʿudi Arabia) and Yemen. Egypt, released from Ottoman sovereignty became nominally independent in 1922 and started the final phase of her struggle for full independence. The Arabs of the Fertile Crescent were placed under mandates▷ and were, for the time being, under the effective rule of Britain or France. However, they were to achieve full independence within two to three decades. In Palestine the Zionists were given a chance to develop a Jewish National Home and the Jewish-Arab struggle for the future of the country began in earnest. Turkey turned her back on her imperial past and inaugurated a rapid programme of modernization.   (Sh.H.)

WORLD WAR II. Most of the ME was not directly involved in the fighting in WWII. There was, however, until 1942, a constant danger of German and Italian penetration into the area. The Third Reich had wooed the Arabs during the years preceding the W. and many of them shared its enmity towards Britain and the Jews. Italy had also broadcast anti-British propaganda in Arabic over Radio Bari for several years and did not disguise her ambitions in the Mediterranean area and the ME.

Italy had 215,000 troops in Libya and another 200,000 in Italian East Africa. These troops posed, at least in theory, a threat to the Allies' Egyptian flank. German forces joined the Italian armies in Libya in Feb. 1941, under Gen. Rommel, after a first Italian offensive, late in 1940, had been repelled and a British counter-offensive (under Gen. Wavell) had resulted in the conquest of Cyrenaica. A German-Italian counter-offensive, in spring 1941, expelled the British from Cyrenaica and halted at the borders of Egypt (cutting off Tobruk▷). A second British offensive (under Gen. Cunningham and Gen. Ritchie), late in 1941, again took all of Cyrenaica, halting in the al-ʿAgheila area. A third German-Italian offensive began in Jan. 1942 and led to the reoccupation of Cyrenaica; the offensive was resumed in May, penetrated Egypt and was halted in July at al-ʿAlamein▷, Egypt's last line of defence. The third, and final, British counter-offensive (under Gen. Montgomery) began in Oct.;

it was one of the decisive turning points of the W. Cyrenaica was captured by November and—with an Allied invasion of north-west Africa (Morocco and Algeria)—the German-Italian forces were compelled to face giant pincers, closing in on them on two fronts simultaneously. All of Libya up to the Tunisian border was captured by Jan. 1943. The threat of a massive German-Italian invasion through North Africa was removed.

While large segments of Arab public opinion were openly sympathetic to the Axis and eagerly awaiting their victory, the Arab governments remained officially neutral. Egypt was committed by the Anglo-Egyptian Treaty of 1936 to aiding Britain in the event of war, mainly by putting her territory and communications at Britain's disposal. Egypt broke off diplomatic relations with Germany in Sept. 1939 and those with Italy in June 1940, but did not declare war, even when Egyptian territory was invaded. (In Apr. 1940 the opposition *Wafd* party attempted—unsuccessfully—to obtain a British commitment to a post-W. political solution agreeing with Egyptian demands, as the price for her entry into the W.) The Egyptian government of 1939–40 was openly pro-Axis; so was the Chief-of-Staff (who tried in 1940 to defect to Italy and was captured). British pressure forced the government's replacement, but collaboration with Axis agents was rife. In Feb. 1942, British intervention forced King Farouq to appoint a *Wadf* government. Yet, only when an Allied victory had become certain did Egypt commit herself to the Allies—by signing the Atlantic Charter, on 14 Nov. 1943; in Feb. 1945, she declared war on Germany (the Premier responsible was assassinated).

After France's defeat, 1940, Mandatory Syria and Lebanon were governed by the Vichy government and increasingly at the disposal of German and Italian preparations for a Me invasion. They were conquered by the British and Free French in June 1941.

Iraq caused more trouble. German influence in Iraq had been mounting in the years preceding the W. and reached its peak in Apr. 1941 when Rashid 'Ali al-Kilani▷, a right-wing pro-German politician supported by the colonels who were the *de facto* rulers of Iraq, staged a coup. As Iraq refused to grant Britain full use of her facilities (as agreed in the Treaty of 1930), fighting broke out between British and Iraqi troops, culminating in British victory and Rashid 'Ali's flight (to Italy and Germany, where he became—with the ex-Mufti of Jerusalem—the Nazis' chief Arab propagandist). Though the pro-British regime was restored in June 1941, Iraq declared war against the Axis only in Jan. 1943.

Ibn Sa'ud remained neutral and did not even formally sever relations with Germany and Italy (though he closed the Italian Legation in 1942). Only in Mar. 1945 did he proclaim Sa'udi Arabia's "adhesion" to the Allies—making it clear that because of the sanctity of the holy places under her guardianship this should not be regarded as a declaration of war. Yemen, too, remained neutral.

Palestinian Arabs, influenced by Hajj Amin al-Husseini▷ (in exile since 1937, but never replaced as their main leader) were largely pro-German; Husseini was the Germans' chief Arab propagandist in Berlin. Only 9,000 Palestinian-Arab volunteers joined the British forces and there was a high incidence of desertion. The Jews naturally held that, whatever their differences with Britain, the defeat of the Third Reich was the most urgent consideration. About 26,000 Palestinian Jews volunteered for the Allied forces and in 1944 were permitted to create their own Jewish Brigade▷.

Turkey remained neutral despite Allied efforts to bring her into the W. She broke off relations with Germany in Aug. 1944 and declared war on Germany and Japan only late in Feb. 1945.

Iran had fallen under German influence during the 1930s and the early W. years. She was occupied in Aug. 1941 by Soviet and British forces to prevent her oil resources falling into German hands and to enable the transport of supplies to the USSR through her territory. In Sept. 1943 Iran declared war against Germany. Teheran was the meeting place, from 28 Nov. to 1 Dec. 1943, of Stalin, Roosevelt and Churchill.

WWII accelerated the acquisition of independence by all ME countries; made the Jewish problem even more urgent, thus bringing the Palestine conflict to a climax; caused the eclipse of French and the decline of British domination; and generated a growing interest by the USA and the USSR in the ME, preparatory to their entry into the area as the new major powers.   (Sh.H.-Y.S.)

Y

YAFI, AL-, 'ABDULLAH (b. 1901). Lebanese politician. A leader of the Sunni▷-Muslim community in Beirut. Y. studied law in Paris. He was elected to Parliament in 1932 to represent Beirut, and first served as Prime Minister in 1938–9. Since 1943, he has been elected to various parliaments; he was Minister of Justice 1946–7 and Prime Minister, 1951–2. In 1952, Y. allied himself with Camille Chamoun▷ in the opposition front that brought down the President, Bishara al-Khouri▷. After Chamoun was elected President, he appointed Y. Prime Minister in 1953. He was again Prime Minister in 1956 but, during the 1956 Suez crisis, when President

Chamoun refused to sever diplomatic relations with Great Britain and France Y. resigned and became one of the strongest opponents of the pro-Western Chamoun. In 1958, he was defeated in parliamentary elections, together with other Opposition leaders. His hostility to Chamoun increased and he adopted a pro-Egyptian and Nasserist▷ line, advocating the integration of Lebanon in an Arab alignment under Egyptian leadership; he enthusiastically welcomed the merger of Egypt and Syria as the UAR▷, which he saw as "the best guarantee of Lebanon's existence". When civil war broke out in Spring 1958, he was one of the leaders of the rebellion. After the civil war died down, a bitter rivalry ensued for the premiership between Y. and Sa'eb Salam▷, his colleague in the revolutionary leadership. This rivalry led to Y.'s defeat in the 1960 and 1964 elections. He was again Prime Minister in 1966 and 1968. In 1968 he was re-elected to Parliament.   (Y. P.)

YAHYA HAMID-UL-DIN (1869–1948). Imam of Yemen. Scion of a noble family of the Zeidi▷ sect of Shi'ite▷ Islam. Elected Imam▷—head of the sect, and ruler—in 1904. He continued a rebellion against the Ottoman Empire▷ that had been simmering for years and by an agreement of 1911 obtained wide autonomy in the interior under nominal Turkish sovereignty. The Imam remained loyal to the Empire during World War I, but gained complete independence for Yemen without a struggle in 1918. A dispute over the principality of 'Asir▷ in 1934 led to war between Yemen and Sa'udi Arabia, resulting in the Imam's defeat and final loss of the disputed regions. Y.'s rule was authoritarian and ultra-conservative. He prevented economic or social modernization and opposed any attempt to create a modern administration or a representative system other than the traditional council of notables. He even hesitated to maintain regular economic or diplomatic ties with other nations and tried to keep Yemen closed to foreign influence. His harsh administration drove many antagonists of the regime into exile and caused periodic rebellions and plots inside the country. Y. was assassinated during a revolt—otherwise unsuccessful —in 1948.   (Y. S.)

YAHYA (AL-TIKRITI), TAHER. Iraqi officer and politician. Born 1913 at Tikrit (northern Iraq). An officer in the regular army, Y. was accused of subversion and dismissed. He was a member of the Free Officers committee that prepared the coup of July 1958; after the coup he was Director-General of Police in Gen. Qassem's▷ new regime. He took part in the Nasserist-nationalist mutiny of Mar. 1959, headed by Col. Shawwaf, and was dismissed. Y. was

amongst the leaders of the coup which overthrew Qassem in Feb. 1963. He became Chief of General Staff under the Ba'th▷ regime of 1963. After the Ba'th was removed by President 'Abd-ul-Salam 'Aref▷, Y. was appointed Prime Minister, in which office he served 1963–5 and 1967–8, until the coup of 17 July 1968. Detained by the new Ba'th regime, he was not brought to trial, despite incessant rumours of an impending trial, and was reportedly released in Nov. 1970.   (U.D.)

YARMUK RIVER. A tributary of the Jordan▷ River, joining it south of Lake Kinneret (the Sea of Galilee▷). For most of its length (of c. 49 mi.) the Y.R. forms the boundary between Syria and the Hashemite Kingdom of Jordan. It carries an average annual water volume of c. 475 m. cubic metres (mcm). A development project initiated by the government of Jordan in the early 1950s, the Y. Scheme, aims to divert the waters of the Y. to the *Ghor* (Jordan Valley). The USA, willing to aid and finance this scheme, initiated several plans for a joint, or co-ordinated, use of the waters of the Jordan and its tributaries (including the Y.). Attempts by Eric Johnston▷, representative of US President Eisenhower, in 1953–5, to obtain the agreement of Israel, Syria, Lebanon and Jordan to such a scheme were successful on the technical level, but ultimately failed as the Arab states were not prepared, for political reasons, to agree to any scheme co-ordinated with, and beneficial to, Israel (see Jordan▷ River).

Jordan and Israel therefore proceeded with their own irrigation development schemes. According to the Jordanian plan the Y. was to be dammed at al-Mukheiba and its waters were to be stored, diverted into a main open canal running down the eastern side of the Jordan Valley, and supplied to a network of smaller channels. In a later stage, water was also to be piped over a bridge to a parallel canal running down the western side of the valley. The East Bank canal was completed, in 1964, at a cost of c. $16m. It is about 50 mi. long and could irrigate an estimated 28,000 acres. (Some estimates were much higher.) Water from several smaller eastern tributaries of the Jordan—some of it stored in small dammed reservoirs built in the later 1960s—is added to the East *Ghor* Canal at various points.

Work on the large Mukheiba storage dam and lake, which had begun in 1966, was interrupted by the Six Day War and the Israeli occupation of the northern bank of the Y. up to a point close to the Mukheiba. The main *Ghor* Canal was damaged several times in 1969–70 as the Palestinian guerillas, sometimes supported by Jordanian artillery, brought the war to the Jordan Valley by shelling Israel's villages and attracting return fire. Israel did not object to the repair of the canal following Jordanian pledges—which were not always honoured—that guerilla action in this sector would be prevented.

(B.G.-Y.S.)

YAZIDIS. A small minority—an estimated 20–40,000—in northern Iraq, in the Jabal Sinjar and Sheikhan region, north of Mosul. They are probably of Kurdish extraction, though opinions differ. They speak a Kurdish dialect, but use Arabic in their religious rites. Their religion includes Muslim, Christian and magical elements; it sees Satan—symbolized by the peacock—as a strong force contending with God, to be appeased by man. The Y. are sometimes called "devil-worshippers".

(Y.S.)

＊YEMEN. Country, since 1962: Republic, in south-west Arabia. The area of Y. as she emerged during the reign of Imam Yahya▷ Hamid-ul-Din is about 73,000 sq. mi. She is bordered by Sa'udi Arabia▷ in the north and north-east, the People's Republic of South Yemen▷ (formerly the Federation of South Arabia▷) in the south-east and south, and the Red Sea▷ in the west. Y. consists largely of high plateaux broken in the north by deep, fertile valleys. The narrow, coastal strip, called the *Tihama*, is hot and dry. Intensive mountain terracing has enabled Y. to produce coffee, millet, maize, oats, sorghum, rice, etc.; in the mountains fruit is also grown, while cotton is cultivated in the *Tihama*. Livestock (sheep, cattle, goats, mules, donkeys and camels) is also bred. Nearly 90% of the population earn their living from agriculture; industry and business are still in their infancy.

The population of Y. is estimated to be about 5m., all of whom—apart from a few descendants of Hamitic and Negroid peoples from eastern Africa in the *Tihama*—are Arabs. About 55% of the population belong to the Zeidi▷ sect of Shi'i▷ Islam while the rest are Sunni▷ Muslims of the Shafe'i▷ school, and a few Shi'i Isma'ilis▷. (There are no reliable statistics and estimates differ.) 5–10% of the population live in towns. Most of the rural population belongs to about 75 tribes nominally affiliated to tribal confederations of which the most important are those of Hashid and Bakil.

Most of the tribes claim descent from Qahtan, the legendary father of the ancient tribes of South Arabia; the rest are related to the north Arabian 'Adnani tribes which migrated to Y. following the rise of Islam. The Yemeni tribe under its sheikh is an almost independent political unit with its own volunteer army and judicial system. As approximately 80%

of the tribes, including the strongest ones, are Zeidis, the Zeidi Imam—who is nominally elected by the Zeidi *Sada* (plural of *Sayyid:* descendants of the *Khalifa* 'Ali and his son Hussein)—was able to establish a Zeidi hegemony over the non-militant urban Shafe'is.

POLITICAL HISTORY. The Ottoman Empire claim sovereignty over Y. and officially considered her an Ottoman province. In fact the Empire controlled and garrisoned only the coast. In the interior, there was, since the 1890s, a continuous rebellion, intensified after 1904 under a new Imam, Yahya Hamid-ul-Din. In 1911 the Turks had to conclude with the Imam an agreement restoring to the interior *de facto* autonomy under nominal Ottoman sovereignty. During World War I, Y. remained loyal to the Ottoman *Khalifa* (Caliph) and the Imam refrained from hindering Turkish operations from Y. against the British in Aden. The dismemberment of the Ottoman Empire after the war automatically gave Y. complete independence.

The Imams Yahya Hamid-ul-Din (1904–48) and Ahmad b. Yahyia▷ (1948–62) endeavoured to keep Y. isolated from the modern world. Foreigners were forbidden to enter the country and no modernization or economic development was allowed. Relations with neighbouring Sa'udi Arabia were hostile and resulted in war, 1934, over 'Asir▷; the Imam's tribal army was defeated. In the south, border disputes led to a permanent conflict with the British in Aden, which continued, despite the 1934 San'a Treaty, up to the British evacuation of South Arabia in 1968. (The first British diplomatic representative was sent to San'a in 1951.) The Anglo-Y. conflict enabled Fascist Italy to become the main foreign power to have real contact with Y. (Treaties were signed in 1926 and 1927.) Britain was disturbed both by Italian penetration—especially after Italy's conquest of Ethiopia, 1936—and by the official relations Y. established with the USSR, 1928. However the Soviet mission was withdrawn in 1938, and Italy lost her special interest in the Red Sea following the loss of Ethiopia, 1941, in World War II▷ (in which Y. remained neutral). In the 1950s Y. attempted to introduce some degree of modernization by improving relations with the USSR and the People's Republic of China and accepting their aid. In 1958 Y., under Imam Ahmad, formally joined the UAR▷, the union of Egypt and Syria (in a federation that was never implemented).

The Imams established a centralist regime in San'a—encouraging popular beliefs in their spiritual power, paying subsidies to strong tribes and subduing rebellious ones through military expeditions in the 1920s and '30s. Taking the tribal sheikhs' oldest sons as hostages to guarantee their fathers' good behaviour, they built a central tribal army mobilized in rotation for short periods. This army was encamped near San'a and used mainly to pacify Zeidi tribes and enforce taxation in Shafe'i areas. They used the de-tribalized Zeidi élite of nobles and religious dignitaries —the *Sada*—as the administrative and religious backbone of their regime. At the same time, they barred any foreign capital or enterprise and tried to prevent any modernization.

This political structure, built almost exclusively on the Zeidi tribes yet simultaneously strictly controlling them, began to fall apart in the 1940s and '50s. Tribal unrest increased; there were several tribal rebellions, and finally two attempted coups in 1948 and 1955. During the former Imam Yahya was assassinated, but his son Ahmad subdued the rebels and assumed the imamate. In the second coup Imam Ahmad was forced to leave San'a, but he was saved by his eldest son Muhammad al-Badr▷, who mobilized the northern tribes of Bakil. Two of the Royal princes, 'Abdullah and 'Abbas, were involved in the 1955 coup and executed. These attempted coups, launched mainly by disappointed royal princes, would-be reformers among the *Sada* and young officers, hastened the establishment of a new central, non-tribal army. Young officers were sent abroad for their military education, mainly to Baghdad (among them 'Abdullah al-Sallal▷, Hamud al-Ja'ifi, Hassan al-'Amri▷). The urban élite, en-couraged by Shafe'i unrest, began to demonstrate its interest in modernization; some of its members went into exile and began a propaganda campaign against the Imam's regime; prominent among them were the Zeidi notables Mahmud al-Zubeiri and Quadi 'Abd-ul-Rahman al-Iryani▷ and the Shafe'i Ahmad Muhammad Nu'man▷. The last three years of Imam Ahmad's reign were marked by intensive unrest. Seven days after Ahmad's death, on 26 Sept. 1962, the new Imam Muhammad al-Badr was over-thrown by a military coup but managed to escape to the northern mountains.

The young officers who overthrew al-Badr pro-claimed a "People's Republic of Y." (*al-Jumhuriyya al-Yamaniyya al-Sha'biyya*). Motivated by Nasserist aspirations, they called for a total change in Y.'s economic, social and religious structure; knowing Y.'s tribal character they thought it necessary to seek outside help. Thus, a few days after the coup, an Egyptian expeditionary force landed in Hudeida and the so-called "civil" war in Y. began (see below). The Revolutionaries, under Sallal, sought to model their institutions on those of Egypt by setting up a President ('Abdullah Sallel), a Revolutionary Council and an Executive Council. Unsuccessful attempts were made to establish a "People's Organization";

early in 1967 a "People's Revolutionary Union" was founded in San'a, but it failed to take root and was abolished ten months later, following the Egyptian evacuation. A temporary constitution was published in Apr. 1963.

The non-militant Shafe'i population was en-couraged by the anti-tribalism of the San'a government as well as by the presence of the Egyptian Army (mostly Sunni-Shafe'i like themselves). A young member of their intelligentsia, 'Abd-ul-Rahman al-Beidani achieved high office in the government and, as Foreign Minister and a generally accepted economic expert, he began to rival Sallal. Beidani claimed to represent the Shafe'i population and enjoyed close contacts with Egypt (as a relative of the Egyptian leader Anwar al-Sadat▷). In Cairo he asked for a more strongly anti-Zeidi policy. In Sept. 1963 the Egyptians, having fought for a year with militant Zeidi tribes and realizing that the Zeidis were the real power in Y., detained Beidani in Cairo; he has not returned to Y. since. Shafe'i hopes to abolish Zeidi hegemony were rekindled only in 1967–8 following the Egyptian evacuation and the establishment of the Republic of South Yemen (which is Shafe'i-populated).

The Republican regime underwent frequent personal and factional changes—resulting largely from shifting Egyptian support. When on the offensive, the Egyptians supported the leftist officers, e.g. 'Abdullah al-Sallal, Hassan al-'Amri, 'Abdullah Juzeilan, Hamud al-Ja'ifi; when on the defensive and seeking to appease the Zeidi tribes they invited Sallal for protracted "medical treatment" in Cairo and appointed non-revolutionary and moderate liberals like Nu'man, Iryani and Zubeiri to lead the Republic. Thus, Sallal held office until Aug. 1963 when he was flown to Cairo, while Zubeiri, Iryani (now Vice-President) and Nu'man organized a pro-Republican tribal conference ('Amran, Sept. 1963). In Jan. 1964 Sallal returned and 'Amri was appointed Prime Minister. In Apr. 1965, again, following Egyptian defeats, Nu'man was made Prime Minister and organized, together with Iryani (Zubeiri had been murdered in April), a pro-Republican conference of Zeidi tribes at Khamir; there it was resolved to establish a truly independent Republic, free from foreign interference and led by elected elders under a rotating presidency. In June 1965 Iryani and Nu'man were forced to resign and the leadership of the government was again taken over by Sallal. A month later he had to transfer the office to Hassan al-'Amri, and following the Jidda Agreement in August (see below) he was again flown to Cairo. 'Amri, Iryani and Nu'man again headed the San'a regime, thus appeasing the Zeidi tribes. In Sept. 1966 Sallal was returned to San'a and the above three leaders were flown to Cairo where they were detained until Oct. 1967.

When Egypt planned her evacuation of Y. following the Six Day War, she released 'Amri, Nu'man and Iryani. Sallal left Y. for exile on 4 Nov. 1967. Following Sallal's fall and the Egyptian evacuation, a new regime was established in San'a. Iryani became Head of a new Republican Council. The regime derived its main support from the military power of the tribes, particularly the Hashid. The paramount chief of this tribal confederation, Sheikh Hussein al-Ahmar, had been executed by Imam Ahmad in 1960, and his son and successor, 'Abdullah al-Ahmar, had refused to join either the Royalists or Sallal's Egyptian-backed regime. Al-Ahmar's newly won support was one of the main reasons that San'a did not fall to the Royalist assault in late 1967 and early 1968 (see below). Together with Iryani, al-Ahmar became the real leader in San'a and many Zeidi tribes, under their hitherto pro-Royalist sheikhs, followed him and joined the new Republic. Hassan al-'Amri, who organized the defence of the besieged capital, thereby acquiring a considerable reputation, co-operated with Iryani and Ahmar in their new politics of compromise with Zeidi tribalism.

For the Shafe'is, who had for five years fought with the Republican Army and provided some of its best commanders, the Egyptian evacuation and the establishment of the new regime came as a hard blow, and they were extremely bitter. This situation resulted in two inter-army clashes in March and Aug. 1968 in which Ahmar's tribal warriors joined Zeidi soldiers against leftist Shafe'i officers. The latter were subdued and some 40 under 'Abd-ul-Raqib 'Abd-ul-Wahhab were expelled from Y. Since the end of the war, Zeidi-Shafe'i relations—which also reflected the struggle between revolutionary centralism and moderate tribalism—seem to have been the Republic's main problem.

From 1962 to 1969–70, the Royalists maintained their own regime in parts of the country. After the Sept. 1962 coup Imam al-Badr was at first believed to be dead and his uncle Prince Hassan b. Yahya, formerly a rival of his father and opposed to al-Badr's succession, proclaimed himself Imam. However, when Badr emerged alive, Prince Hassan recognized him as Imam and was appointed Prime Minister and Commander-in-Chief. The government formed in Oct. 1962, included some of the *Sada*, e.g. *Qadi* Ahmad al-Siyyaghi and Ahmad al-Shami. Princes Muhammad and 'Abdullah b. Hussein, and Hassan and 'Abdullah b. Hassan, were sent to the northern mountains to lead the tribes in the campaign. Since the Republic was identified with the Egyptian presence, the Zeidi tribes, though they had hitherto fought the imamate soon began to join the Royalist camp. This led to an increase in the power of the young princes in command of the tribes; the ablest among them, Prince Muhammad b. Hussein, began in 1964 to train a semi-regular tribal army. Moreover, Iman Badr often left Y. for medical treatment, and Prince Hassan b. Yahya was old. These factors led to a certain division of power, and even pressure for some democratization within the Royalist camp. In Jan. 1965 the Imam published a "Royalist National Charter" designed to come into force after the Royalist victory. It promised to establish a legislative assembly to limit the power of the imamate.

In Aug. 1966 Imam al-Badr was virtually deposed when a new "imamate council" was formed at a tribal conference organized by Prince Muhammad b. Hussein. Prince Muhammad was appointed Vice-President of this Council, and since Imam al-Badr was in Sa'udi Arabia from Apr. 1965 to Oct. 1968, he was now the real leader of the Royalists. Prince Muhammad commanded the Royalist offensive against San'a in late 1967 and early 1968. In June 1968 he appointed the members of a new "imamate council" and a new government under his premiership, but after failing to achieve further military successes he was overthrown in early 1969 by the Imam who had returned to Y. in Oct. 1968.

The war between the Royalist and Republican camps was not really a civil war. The Egyptian Army was the war's main protagonist. The Egyptian expeditionary forces in Y. were estimated at about 15,000 in late Oct. 1962, 25,000 in Jan. 1963, 50,000 in Nov. 1963 and 70,000 in Aug. 1965. Following the Jidda Agreement of Aug. 1965 this number was reduced to about 30,000. The force was evacuated in 1967, after the Six Day War, the last soldier officially leaving Hudeida on 15 Dec. 1967. The involvement of a foreign army was the main reason the Royalists were able to attract and retain support. Almost all the belligerent Zeidi tribes fought the Egyptians and joined the royal princes, not because they wanted to revive the Imam's rule but, because the Royal family was a unifying element in the war against the Egyptians. The Sa'udi government supplied the Royalists with war materials and gold. The main purpose of the Egyptian military campaigns was to cut off the two sources of Royalist strength: the tribes and the Sa'udi supplies, *i.e.* to close Y.'s northern and eastern borders. In winter and spring 1962–3, Egyptian forces tried to subdue the tribal guerillas in the eastern regions of Harib, Marib and al-Jauf and in the north around the ancient capital of Sa'da.

In response to a UN initiative, Sa'udi Arabia and

Egypt signed, on 29 Apr. 1963, the "Bunker Agreement" to end foreign intervention. UN observers were posted along the Y.-Sa'udi border; but foreign intervention did not cease, and the war continued. The agreement was renounced by the Sa'udi government in Nov. 1963. Fighting continued during 1964 with partial Egyptian successes. A Y. reconciliation congress in the Sudanese town of Erkwith, Oct. 1964, proved abortive because both sides insisted on their original demands—the Royalists on the revival of the imamate and the evacuation of Egyptian troops, and the Republicans on the "continuation of the revolutionary way" and the exclusion of the Imamic Hamid-ul-Din family. In spring and summer 1965 the Royalists gained the upper hand. They captured Harib and Marib in February and defeated large Egyptian forces in Jabal al-Akhdar, isolating the Egyptian garrison in the al-Jauf area.

In Aug. 1965 President Nasser and King Feisal signed the "Jidda Agreement" to end the war. Sa'udi supplies were to be stopped and Egyptian forces to be evacuated within a year; the future regime of Y. was to be determined by a plebiscite in Nov. 1966; Royalist and Republican delegates were to meet and discuss the type of regime to be set up during the transition period. In Nov. 1965 delegates met in the north-western town of Harad but achieved no results. This was mainly due to a change in Egyptian policy. Egypt had stopped appeasing Sa'udi Arabia, and, following reports of British plans to withdraw from Aden (officially announced in Feb. 1966), decided to remain in Y. in order to achieve her long-term plans—and publicly announced this decision.

In Mar.-Apr. 1966 Egypt evacuated her forces—except for a number of strongholds—to the San'a-Hudeida-Ta'izz triangle, leaving the main tribal areas to their own rule—and to the new moderate regime simultaneously established in San'a. When the Egyptian Army was evacuated from his southern border, King Feisal stopped giving subsidies and supplies to the young Y. princes who wanted to continue fighting. Seeing no more Egyptian soldiers and receiving no more money and arms from the Royalists, many Zeidi tribes switched their allegiance to the San'a government. The Royalists managed to organize only small-scale and ineffective operations, while the Egyptians concentrated on bombing the Royalist tribes. The bombing was intensified following Sallal's return to power in Sept. 1966 (there were several reports, confirmed by the International Red Cross on 2 June 1967, that poison gas had been used), and many of the tribes returned to the Royalist camp.

Egypt's defeat in the Six Day War changed the course of the Y. War. In Aug. 1967 King Feisal and President Nasser agreed at the Khartoum Summit Conference to end the war. Soon afterwards the Egyptian Army was removed from San'a and Ta'izz and concentrated in Hudeida, from which its evacuation began in October 1967. The Royalists, under the command of Prince Muhammad b. Hussein, marched on San'a and laid siege to it in early Dec. 1967.

Following the Egyptian evacuation and the change of regime in San'a many Yemeni tribes, mainly of the Hashid Confederation, were mobilized to save the capital. The Republican Army, which had previously left the main conduct of the war to the Egyptians, demonstrated its fighting ability around San'a, supported also by civilian volunteers. The siege was lifted. In February 1968 the road from San'a to Hudeida was opened, and in early 1969 the road to Ta'izz. After the Egyptian evacuation the Y. war really became a local, civil war—in many cases a diplomatic one, in which the various tribes continued to change sides, and to obtain rewards and subsidies from both sides without much fighting. In fact the war began to peter out in 1969.

Inter-Arab efforts to end the war were resumed, mainly by a Tripartite Committee established by the Khartoum agreement; but they were again abortive and ceased early in 1968. In 1969, however, the policy of appeasing Sa'udi Arabia followed by Iryani and 'Amri was successful and Sa'udi support for the Royalists was reduced. Drought and starvation, intense in 1970, also greatly weakened the Royalist tribes. In Mar. 1970 the Republican Prime Minister visited Jidda for the Islamic Foreign Ministers' Conference, and a general reconciliation agreement was prepared. In May, the former Royalist Foreign Minister Ahmad al-Shami—who had previously advocated reconciliation with San'a and agreed to exclude the Hamid-ul-Din family (thus following Sa'udi policy)—came to San'a with 30 Royalist leaders, none of whom were members of the Royal family. Although the Royal princes and some of their tribal supporters continued to resist, the war was ended and former Royalists were admitted to the Republican regime—Shami and the moderate Republican Ahmad Muhammad Nu'man joined the three-member Republican Council, four Royalists joined the government, and twelve were co-opted to the National Council. (Shami and Nu'man were not included when the Republican Council was re-formed in Apr. 1971, with three members only, under Iryani; Nu'man became Prime Minister, but resigned in July.)

The Republican victory also ended a diplomatic struggle between the two camps over world recognition and international relations. After the coup of 26 Sept. 1962 the Republic was immediately recognized by almost all the Arab countries—except Sa'udi Arabia and Jordan (the latter recognized the Republic in 1964)—and the Soviet Bloc, which also gave the Republic military aid, mainly through Egypt. In Dec. 1962 the USA also recognized the Republic, and, the same month, the UN accepted the credentials of the Republican delegation as the true representatives of Y. Britain and France refrained from recognizing the Republic. Despite US recognition US-Y. relations were not warm and the Republic severed relations in spring 1967. Sa'udi Arabia continued to recognize the Royalists and her aid enabled them to continue their struggle. After the Royalist military defeat, the establishment of the new post-1967 Republican regime and the settlement of 1970, most of the countries still recognizing the Royalists withdrew that recognition in favour of the Republic. Britain, France and Sa'udi Arabia extended their recognition in July 1970.   (H.E.)

YEMEN, PEOPLE'S DEMOCRATIC RE-PUBLIC OF —see South Yemen▷.

YOUNG TURKS.
Group of Ottoman officers, officials and intellectuals who, in 1908, revolted against the regime of Sultan Abdülhamid II▷ and, except for six months, ruled the Empire from then until the end of World War I. The opposition movement dates back to 1889, when a secret society was formed by students of the military medical school to fight against the Sultan's absolutist and tyrannical regime. Students from other institutes joined the society but the police began to crack down on the revolutionaries and many of them had to escape abroad. In European capitals and in Cairo, the exiles (the most prominent of whom were Ahmed Riza and Murad Bey) formed a number of societies and published periodicals which were smuggled into the Ottoman Empire. In 1899 they were joined by the Sultan's own brother and two of his sons (one of whom, Sabahettin, later rose to a position of leadership). In the early 20th century, particularly after 1906, many new secret societies were organized by officers and officials within the Empire itself. In 1907 a loose umbrella organization of these groups was established, called the "Committee of Union and Progress" (CUP).

The revolution itself was carried out by the strongest society, located in Salonika. Military unrest reached its peak in summer 1908, when several high-ranking officers in Macedonia defected. The Sultan failed to prevent the mutiny from spreading and on 24 July he yielded to the officers' demands by reactivating the Constitution of 1876 and Parliamentary institutions. From then until the end of World War I, the CUP, now a political party, was the dominant force in the government. Its hold was strengthened when a conservative counter revolution failed in Apr. 1909 and led to the deposition of the Sultan and his replacement by his compliant brother Mehmed Reşad.

The YT' revolution gave rise to great hopes for brotherhood and equality among all the nations of the Empire; but the CUP. gradually became centralistic and authoritarian. It was committed to the preservation of the Empire and tried to achieve this by a harsh policy of Ottomanism, the prohibition of nation-oriented organizations and the compulsory dissemination of the Turkish language. It was therefore opposed by more liberal groups and non-Muslim non-Turkish elements supporting decentralization. In 1911 liberal opposition in parliament came together in the Liberal Union. Parliament was dissolved and new elections were won by the CUP.; but an officers' coup in July 1912 ousted the party. In a counter coup, in Jan. 1913, led by Enver▷, the CUP regained power, and from then until 1918 the state was in fact ruled by a military dictatorship headed by a triumvirate of Enver, Cemal▷ and Talât▷.

The YT, despite their efforts, did not succeed in preserving the integrity of the Empire. In 1908, soon after the Revolution, Austria-Hungary annexed Bosnia and Hertzogovina, Bulgaria declared her independence, and Greece incorporated Crete. The Ottoman-Italian War of 1911–12 led to the loss of Tripolitania and the Dodecanese Islands, Albania rebelled, 1910, and gained her independence, 1912, and in the Balkan Wars▷ of 1912–13 Turkey lost almost all her European territories. The YT decision to join World War I on the losing side hastened the final dissolution of the Empire. Though promoting Pan-Islamist ideas, the government was unable to prevent the Arab revolt of Sharif Hussein▷ of Mecca in 1916, and by the end of the war the Arab provinces occupied by Allied and Arab troops, had been irrevocably detached from the Empire. The YT leaders fled the country, and though they later tried to re-establish their rule, the new nationalist forces remained in power.

The YT introduced important measures of modernization. They organized provincial administration, 1913, passed new land laws and encouraged local industry and economic development. They were educated in military and secular schools and therefore attempted to reduce the influence of religion on state affairs, adopting, for example, a new liberal family law, 1917. By maintaining at least the outward forms of parliamentarianism, elections and party life, they permeated the country with the principles of democratic procedure. Finally, the relative freedom of expression allowed by them led to the crystallization of various ideologies, among which were those of secularism and Turkish nationalism (the latter founded by Ziya Gokalp▷). In fact the YT did the groundwork for the radical reforms of Atatürk.

(D.K.)

*YUGOSLAVIA. National security requirements on the one hand, and an important role in "Third World" politics on the other, have given Y. a direct interest in the ME. Because of her long and vulnerable coastline, Y. objects to the two Super Powers' naval presence in the Mediterranean, especially in times of crisis between Moscow and Belgrade. Y.'s stand on the Palestine question in 1947–8 combined support —*i.a.* as a member of the UN Special Committee on Palestine—for a federated bi-national state (*i.e.* a pro-Arab solution of Palestine's political future) with important practical help for the Jews of Palestine and the State of Israel. Since then maintaining correct bilateral relations with Israel until 1967, her political attitude to the Arab-Israel conflict has been consistently pro-Arab. President Tito's personal relationship with President 'Abd-ul-Nasser was a main axis of the "non-aligned" world, notably from 1956 to 1968; in that year the condonement by Egypt and other Arab countries of the Warsaw Pact invasion of Czechoslovakia caused an Arab-Yugoslav estrangement. In 1967 Y. associated herself with the USSR in her support for the Arab countries and headed a non-aligned effort at the Special Emergency Session of the UN General Assembly to put through a resolution that would be acceptable to the Arabs. She proposed a ME settlement on strongly pro-Arab lines, in connection with which Tito visited Egypt, Syria and Iraq; he also laid his proposals before each of the Four Powers. Y. severed, in 1967, official relations with Israel.   (Y.R.)

Z

ZAGHLUL, (AHMAD) SA'D (1860–1927). Egyptian politician and main leader of Egyptian nationalism. Born in a *fellahin* family in the Delta region. Studied law. At the beginning of the century Z. was one of the young modernists who opposed the conservative-Islamic current. Z. was in 1906 appointed Minister of Education and then Minister of Justice. He headed the nationalist movement at the end of World War I and led the delegation (Arabic: *Wafd*) in Nov. 1918, which demanded full independence; The *Wafd*▷, the main proponent of national struggle, evolved from this delegation in 1919. In

attempts to suppress national ferment, the British exiled Z. twice, once in Mar. 1919 to Malta (released in Apr.) and again in 1922 to Aden and Gibraltar. In Sept. 1923, Z. took part in the first election campaign in nominally independent Egypt. His *Wafd* gained a large majority and in Jan. 1924, Z. was appointed Prime Minister. In Nov. 1924, a fanatic member of the *Wafd* assassinated Sir Lee Stack▷, Governor-General of Sudan and Commander (*Sirdar*) of the Egyptian Army. The British High Commissioner, Lord Allenby▷, issued an ultimatum to the government embodying humiliating conditions and extreme demands. Z. refused to submit to the ultimatum and resigned. In 1925, Z. was elected President of the new Parliament, and, Parliament was thereupon dissolved by the anti-Wajd government. In 1926, the *Wafd* again won the election; the British prevented Z.'s appointment as Prime Minister, but he was elected President of Parliament. His death in Sept. 1927 was a great blow to the nationalist movement.   (O.G.)

ZAHEDI, FAZLOLLAH, MAJ.-GEN. (1890– 1963). Iranian officer and politician; Prime Minister 1953–5. Born in Hamadan into a great land-owning family. Educated at the Military Academy of Teheran. Z. held various army posts from 1916. He was arrested in 1942 by the British (then occupying most of Iran) for alleged pro-German activities and exiled to Palestine and later to India, 1943–5. Z. became Chief of Police in 1949 and Minister of the Interior 1950–51. In Aug. 1953 he headed a coup which ousted Prime Minister Mossaddeq▷ and restored the Shah to power. Following the coup he became Prime Minister and held office until 1955. He lived in Switzerland in 1955–7 and served as Iran's Permanent Representative to the Geneva Offices of the UN 1960–63.   (B.G.)

ZA'IM, HUSNI (1889 or 1896–1949). Syrian army officer and politician. President of Syria in 1949. Born in Aleppo, of Kurdish origin. Z. served in the Ottoman Army and then in the "Special Forces" formed by the French authorities in Syria; as he remained, during World War II, loyal to the Vichy government, he was detained by the British after the occupation of Syria in 1941. After his release he returned to the Army. After the Palestine War, 1948, Z. was appointed Chief-of-Staff of the Syrian Army, with the rank of Brigadier. On 30 Mar. 1949, Z. carried out the first military coup in Syria, deposed President Quwwatli▷ and dissolved parliament. In June, Z. held a referendum, in which he was elected President with wide powers. He dissolved all political parties and set up a dictatorship. He had ambitious plans for reforms similar to those of Atatürk▷ in Turkey, but no time to work out a programme. He was the first Arab leader to give women the franchise. He tried to separate state and religion. In foreign affairs, he was pro-French and strengthened relations with Egypt, Sa'udi Arabia and Turkey. On 14 Aug. 1949, his regime was toppled by a coup staged by Col. Sami Hinnawi▷. A military court sentenced Z. to death together with his Prime Minister, Muhsin al-Barazi▷, and the sentence was immediately carried out.   (A. L.-O. T.)

*ZEIDIS, ZEIDIYYA. A branch of Shi'ite▷ Islam, dominating Yemen▷. The Z. are distinguished from other Shi'ites by their recognition of Zeid b. 'Ali, the grandson of al-Hussein b. 'Ali (killed in 740, while fighting the Umayyad *Khalifa*), as the fifth *Khalifa* (Caliph) and Imam▷. Unlike other groups of the *Shi'a* the Z. recognize a continuing line of living, apparent imams. Their Imam must be a member of *Ahl al-Beit*, i.e., a descendant of 'Ali, both learned and able to fight. He is elected by the Z. *Sada* (plural of *Sayyid*, descendants of the *Khalifa* 'Ali and his son Hussein)—a custom that caused many crises and schisms in the two Zeidi states: one on the Caspian Sea up to about 1126, and Yemen from the early days of Islam until the present. The election rule has twice been broken in modern Yemen by the imams Yahya▷ and Ahmad▷, who appointed their elder sons to succeed them.

In modern times the Z. of Yemen fought many wars with the Ottoman Turks, during which the town of San'a often changed hands; while the Ottomans controlled the coastal areas, the Z. usually managed to maintain some degree of autonomy in the interior or else rebelled. Internal rifts often resulted in several rival *Imams* contending for power. The founder of the modern State of Yemen, Yahya Hamid-ul-Din, elected Imam in 1904, continued a rebellion against the Turks and secured his autonomy in the interior. He took San'a and obtained full independence only in 1918, upon the dissolution of the Ottoman Empire. Under his rule (1918–48) the hegemony of the Z. was re-established.

The Z. form about 55% of the population of Yemen (though there are conflicting estimates), and about 80% of the belligerent tribes, of whom the strongest are the confederations of Hashid and Bakil. Z. doctrine also reinforced both the tribal sheikh's power within his tribe, and his submission to the Imam. Thus the Z. were the military and social, though not the economic, élite of the new Kingdom. There are estimated to be 300,000 non-tribal Z. *Sada*. They provide the administrative, judicial and religious backbone of the Kingdom. Some of their

families, mainly the al-Wazir clan, claimed the imamate from the Hamid-ul-Din Dynasty and were responsible for some political crises, (e.g. the abortive coup of 1948 in which the Imam Yahya was killed).

The Republican regime established in 1962 abolished the imamate and the *Sada* hegemony. However as the Z. tribes continued to be the strongest element and the main military force in the civil war, the Republican regime also had to rely on them and gradually revive and recognize their hegemony. The position of the imamate after the Republican-Royalist reconciliation of 1970 is unclear; but it is conceivable that even in a Republican Yemen the Zeidi imamate may survive as a spiritual institution.   (H.E.)

ZIONISM. Movement of Jewish national revival calling for the return of the Jewish people to Palestine. The name (coined by the Viennese Jewish writer Nathan Birnbaum in 1885) is derived from "Zion", one of the biblical names for Jerusalem.

The yearning to return to Zion existed throughout the two millennia of the Jewish Diaspora, and is an integral part of the Jewish religion and the Messianic belief. In fact, there have always been Jews in Palestine, and a trickle of Jewish immigration has never ceased to flow.

Modern Z. grew out of 1. 19th century nationalist thought, 2. the westernization of the Jews resulting from their emancipation, 3. disappointment with attempts to become assimilated, and 4. the persistence and intensification of anti-Semitism. The "fathers" of Z. were Moses Hess (1812–75), Rabbi Hirsch Kalischer (1795–1874), Yehuda Leib Pinsker (1821–91), and Dr. Theodor Herzl▷ (1860–1904). Hess, a German socialist and one-time associate of Marx, advocated the establishment of a just society and the normalization of Jewish economic and social life in its own state. Rabbi Kalischer believed that the Messiah would come only after a large part of the Jewish people was reassembled in Palestine. Many other Jewish writers of the 19th century expressed the idea of a national revival in Palestine. Pinsker, in his book "Auto-Emancipation" (1882), held that not an emancipation granted by others, but only the territorial concentration of the Jewish nation, could solve the abnormal Jewish position. In the late 19th century, the *Hovevei Zion* (Hebrew: Lovers of Zion) movement, based mainly in Russia, and given further impetus by the pogroms and persecution taking place there, encouraged Jews to go and settle in Palestine; young pioneers began immigrating to Palestine in the 1880s (the *Bilu* group).

Shocked by the Dreyfus case and the growth of anti-Semitism, Herzl▷ published his "Judenstaat" ("The Jewish State") in 1896 and founded the World

Zionist Organization at the first Zionist Congress in Basle in 1897. The "Basle Programme" stated: "The aim of Z. is to create for the Jewish people a home in Palestine secured by public law . . .".

Z. was bitterly opposed by many. The proponents of assimilation denied the existence of a Jewish nation and insisted that the Jews were simply a religious group belonging ethnically to the nations of their respective countries. Many Jewish socialists endorsed such assimilationist ideas. Other socialists—particularly in Eastern Europe, where the Jewish masses obviously could not be assimilated—accepted the existence of a Jewish national minority (with Yiddish—not Hebrew—as its national language), but held that its problem would be solved in the Diaspora with the advent of socialism; socialists organized the "Bund"—Z.'s main adversary in the public life of East European and American Jewry. Later, Jewish communists adopted a similar, violently anti-Z. stand. While many of the Social-Democratic parties gradually became more sympathetic, the Communist parties have remained bitterly hostile to Z. Z. was also opposed by ultra-orthodox groups who denounced it as blasphemous interference in the will of God.

Until his death in 1904 Herzl attempted to obtain from the Ottoman Sultan a charter for the Jews to settle, and set up a state, in Palestine—although he was ready to consider settlement in other places, too, e.g., Uganda▷ (the Uganda plan was rejected by the Zionist Congress; its supporters seceded and founded a "Territorialist" movement). As Herzl's diplomatic efforts failed to obtain immediate success, many Zionists (headed by Weizmann▷) advocated immigration, settlement and practical work in Palestine as a step toward statehood ("Practical Z." as against "Political Z."). An office was set up in Jaffa, Palestine, in 1908, to foster settlement, and the first settlements under Zionist auspices were founded from 1910 onwards. The issuance of the Balfour Declaration▷ by the British government, on 2 Nov. 1917, and the establishment of the British Mandate over Palestine (1922) resolved the dispute between "Practical" and "Political" Z.: both activities should take place simultaneously ("Z. of Synthesis").

World War I created much controversy within the Zionist Movement as to whether to support the *Entente*, the Central Powers, or to remain neutral. The Balfour Declaration—supported by Britain's principal allies—decided the issue.

Priorities in Z. also caused much debate. Did the term "National Home" imply that Z.'s main aims were the establishment of a state, and the immigration to Palestine of all Jews or most of them? Or was the aim creation of only a national "cultural centre" (as

envisaged by Ahad Ha'am▷), not necessarily with a Jewish majority? The European Holocaust of World War II, the failure of attempts to reach an agreement with Arab leaders, and the assumption that statehood was now attainable, induced the Zionist leaders (especially Ben-Gurion▷) in 1942 to call for the first time for the creation of a "Jewish Commonwealth" in Palestine (the Biltmore Programme▷). It was obvious that the establishment of a Jewish State would entail the partition of the country. Partition had already been accepted after a bitter dispute among Zionists in 1937 (see Palestine▷). The right-wing Zionist Revisionists▷ under Jabotinsky▷, who had always advocated statehood in the whole of Palestine (and Transjordan) seceded in 1935. An independent Jewish State had become politically realistic in the 1930s, as the Jewish community in Palestine was growing through immigration, while the imminence of Nazi barbarities greatly increased its urgency. The Arab revolt of 1936–9 strengthened the Jews' resolve and compelled them to devote more efforts to self-defence; their underground military organization, *Hagana*▷, in existence since 1920, grew into a country-wide, united, formation under national discipline.

Until 1939 the Zionists co-operated with the British despite "the whittling down of Britain's original commitment". The White Paper of 1939 (see White Papers▷; Palestine▷) forced the Jews of Palestine, under their Zionist leadership, to adopt a policy of non-co-operation, while giving Britain every assistance in her war against Germany. After World War II they intensified the struggle culminating in the final clash of 1945–7.

Efforts were made by the Zionists to foster co-operation and understanding with the Arabs, and the Zionists deeply regretted the bitter hostility that came to determine Arab attitudes—after tentative agreement was briefly and hopefully reached in 1918–20 (see Feisal-Weizmann Agreement▷). The Zionists held that neither nation should dominate the other, searched for agreed solutions within a united Palestine (including the idea of a bi-national▷ perpetual party), and held numerous meetings with Arab leaders. The demand for a Jewish State in a partitioned Palestine was adopted only when all efforts towards an agreement failed.

The Zionists' main financial organization is *Keren Hayesod*▷ (Foundation Fund), established in 1920 to finance settlement and immigration. The Jewish National Fund▷, founded 1901, is concerned mainly with the acquisition and improvement of land, and afforestation. In 1929, the Zionist Organization succeeded in harnessing the support of non-Zionist groups, particularly in America, for its work in Palestine through the establishment of the Jewish Agency▷, provided for in the Mandate. The ultra-religious *Agudath Israel*▷ and the communists, as well as assimilationist anti-Zionist groups, remained outside the Zionist Organization.

Labour (see Socialism▷) and non-Labour ("General") groups, as well as religious-orthodox ones, were formed within the Zionist Organization. *Po'alei Zion* ("The Workers of Zion") was a socialist faction, based on the tenets of Marxism; it was founded in 1905–6 by Russian Jews. Its Palestinian branch merged with smaller groups in 1919 to form *Ahduth Ha'avodah*▷ ("Labour Unity")—with a leftist faction seceding as Po'alei Zion Smol ("Leftist Workers of Zion"). *Hapo'el Hatza'ir* ("The Young Worker"), founded in 1905 in Palestine, was socialist but non-Marxist and avoided "class warfare" and doctrinal disputes, as it believed these to be premature prior to the re-establishment of the Jewish people in its land. The group encouraged settlement and glorified physical labour. It considered A. D. Gordon▷ as its mentor. In 1920 *Hapo'el Hatza'ir* and *Ahduth Ha'avodah* founded the General Federation of Jewish Labour (*Histadrut*▷). Both groups actively fostered co-operative settlement (collective: *kibbutz*▷, *kvutza*, and small-holders: *moshav*) and Jewish labour in all fields of the economy. In 1930 the two factions merged to form the Palestine Workers' Party, *Mapai*▷—with David Ben-Gurion▷, Berl Katznelson▷, Chaim Arlosoroff▷ and Moshe Sharett▷ (Shertok) as its chief leaders.

Hashomer Hatza'ir ("The Young Watchman"), another socialist group, was founded in 1913 in Galicia as a youth organization. It developed a more pronounced Marxist-leftist line in the 1920s in Palestine. It founded *kibbutzim* (collective farms), organized since 1927 under the umbrella organization *Hakibbutz Ha'artzi*. It advocated a bi-national socialist state in Palestine as the only solution to the Jewish-Arab conflict. Appearing since 1946 also as a political party, it united in 1948 with other Marxist groups to form *Mapam*▷ ("United Workers' Party"). *Mapam* included a group that had seceded in 1944 from *Mapai*, taking the old name *Ahduth Ha'avodah*, and merged in 1946 with left *Po'alei Zion;* it seceded from *Mapam* in 1959 (see Israel▷).

The "General Zionists" advocated Zionism without class or social ideology. They were a middle-class party of the centre and right, closely associated with capitalistic industry and farming. In 1935, the group split into two factions: left-of-centre, which gave Weizmann its full support, and right-of-centre.

Mizrahi▷ was founded in 1902 by religious Zionists. *Hapo'el Hamizrahi*▷ was established in 1922 as a religious workers' organization.

The Zionist-Revisionists▷, led by V. Z. Jabotinsky▷, were extreme right-wing nationalists, who wanted to establish a Jewish state in Palestine (on both sides of the Jordan), by force—if need be. They seceded in 1935 to form a "New Zionist Organization", with its own military organization, the *Irgun (T)zeva'i Le'umi*▷ (IZL, *Etzel*). A small "Jewish State Party" left the Revisionists in order to remain within the Zionist Organization, which the Revisionists rejoined in 1946.

All the parties mentioned maintain youth movements of their own. After 1948, most of these groups became political parties in the State of Israel—besides continuing as factions within the Zionist Organization. Since Israel's establishment, the Jewish Agency▷ continues, under a special status, to function as a means to implement Zionist aspirations in the fields of immigration, land improvement and settlement but does not participate in the government of Israel.
(Sh.H.-E.L.-Y.S.)

PRESIDENTS OF THE WORLD ZIONIST ORGANIZATION

Dr. Theodor Herzl	1897–1904
David Wolffsohn	1905–11
Prof. Otto Warburg	1911–20
Prof. Chaim Weizmann	1920–31
Nahum Sokolow	1931–35
Prof. Chaim Weizmann	1935–46
No president	1946–56
Dr. Nahum Goldmann	1956–68
No president	1968–

ZIONIST REVISIONISTS. Party established in 1925 by Ze'ev Jabotinsky▷, who opposed the moderate political line taken by the Zionist Organization under Chaim Weizmann▷. Its main aims were: the immediate establishment of a Jewish State in Palestine on both sides of the Jordan; the revival of the Jewish Legion▷; nationalist and military youth education (hence the establishment of the ZR youth movement—*Betar*); political instead of practical activity. In the economic sphere, the ZR were conservatives; they favoured compulsory arbitration in labour disputes.

The ZR were the strongest group opposing the Zionist Organization and the Jewish community institutions in Palestine. Relations between the *Histadrut*▷ (General Federation of Labour) and the ZR worsened particularly in the 1930s. Hostility reached its peak after the assassination of Chaim Arlosoroff▷ in 1933 and the arrest of two *Betar* members as suspects (who were later acquitted).

In 1933, the ZR party established an independent

trade union, the National Labour Federation. Numerically small, it rejects class symbols, aims at normalizing labour relations and has the same political aim as the ZR party, It maintains a health insurance fund, and is active in similar fields to the *Histadrut*▷. (A Revisionist list had first taken part in elections to the *Histadrut* Convention, in 1927.)

As a result of the worsening dissension, the ZR broke away from the Zionist Organization and, in 1935, founded the New Zionist Organization; but its political activities (including a ten-year programme for the evacuation of 1.5m. Jews from Europe to Palestine) were not of great consequence.

Two militant underground organizations were established from the ranks of the ZR—*Irgun (T)zeva'i Le'umi* (IZL) and the Stern Group▷ (LHY).

In 1946 the Revisionists returned to the Zionist Organization. In the elections to the First *Knesset* (Parliament), they failed to return a single member. Within a short time, they merged with the *Herut*▷ party under Menahem Begin▷.   (E.A.)

ZOROASTRIANS, ZOROASTRIANISM.

Z. was the official religion of Iran from the time of the Achaemenides (sixth century BC) until the Muslim conquest (seventh century CE). Its legendary founder was Zoroaster or Zarathustra (who probably lived in the late seventh and early sixth centuries BC). He reformed ancient Indo-Iranian polytheism and introduced a highly elaborate code of ethics which has influenced Greek thought, late Judaism, Christianity and Islam. Z. propounds a cosmic battle between the spirits of good (Ahura-Mazda) and evil (Ahriman). At times outlawed and persecuted, the Zs. in Iran number today *c*. 30,000; most of them are merchants and live in Yazd, Kerman and Tehran. About another 130,000 Z. live in Bombay, India, where they are called Parsees.   (B.G.)

*ZU'AYYIN, YUSSUF. Syrian politician. Born in Abu Kamal in the Euphrates region. Studied medicine at Damascus University and practised as a physician. Member of both the "national"(*i.e.* all-Arab), and "regional" (Syrian) leadership of the *Ba'th*▷ party. Z. was Minister of Agrarian Reform in the government of Amin Hafez▷ in 1963; member of the Presidential Council, 1964–5; Prime Minister in 1965. He was deposed at the end of 1965, when Bitar▷ and his "moderate" faction connected with the all-Arab *Ba'th* leadership tried to return to power. Z. supported the countercoup of the "military wing", the extremist faction headed by Gen. Salah Jadid▷, who deposed the Hafez-Bitar group in Feb. 1966. Following the coup and until Oct. 1968, Z. was Prime Minister under the auspices of the ruling military junta of generals Jadid and Asad▷. He introduced communists into his government and encouraged closer relations with the USSR. Loyal to Jadid and his faction, Z. has been out of power since late 1968, when Asad gained the upper hand. During that time, he was active in the political leadership of the Syrian-sponsored al-Sa'iqa▷ Palestinian guerilla formation. Since Gen. Asad's take-over, Nov. 1970, Z. has been under arrest.   (A.L.-O.T.)

SUPPLEMENT 1971–1974

A

'ABD-UL-FATAH ISMA'IL AL-JAWFI. Secretary-General of the NFL▷ of South Yemen▷, member of the Central Committee and ideological leader of the party. Began career as teacher; took part in struggle against the British in Aden▷ in 1967. Minister of Culture, National Guidance and Unity in al-Sha'bi▷ Government. Author of NFL political programme submitted by leftist-radicals to the Mar. 1968 party congress. Expelled from the Government in April 1968 following a dispute with the army.

A returned to the party leadership in Aug. 1968, his position growing stronger following the expulsion of al-Sha'bi in June 1969. In Dec. 1969, A was nominated a member of the Residential Council. In Jan. 1970, he was nominated a member of the Executive Committee, and in May 1971, in addition to being Secretary-General of the party, became President of the Supreme National Council. A visited East European countries on several occasions.
(T.Y.)

'ABD-UL-QUDDUS, IHSAN. Born 1913. Egyptian journalist and prominent writer; Chairman of the Executive Board of the *Akhbar al-Yawm* newspaper foundation since 1966, and editor of the weekly of the same name.

His artist mother, Fatma al-Yussuf, founded the *Rose al-Yussuf* weekly, which he later headed. In 1958 A was appointed chief editor of the weekly, keeping this position even after it was nationalized. His standing and influence increased under Sadat▷ and since 1973 A has acted as spokesman of the Egyptian President.
(Al.S.)

★ABU DHABI. A senior member-state of the Union of Arab Emirates▷ which was formed in Dec. 1971. The main initiator of the forming of the Union, the management and finance of which are mainly AD's responsibility. During 1969 and 1970, the border disputes with Dubai▷, Qatar▷ and Ras al-Khaima▷ were settled. Negotiations on a sea-border agreement with Iran▷ began in Sept. 1971. In June 1970 Sa'udi Arabia▷ renewed demands for ownership of the oasis of Buraimi▷, but there were no further developments on this subject. In 1971 the ruler commenced steps to enlarge participation in the Government beyond the ruling family: In July 1971 the first cabinet of 16 ministers (of whom three were of the ruling family) was established. In Oct. 1971 the first session of the Advisory National Council, appointed by the ruler, took place. Among its 50 members, not one is of the ruling al-Nahian▷ family.

AD continues to develop its army, the largest and most experienced of the Emirate armies.

In Mar. 1972, AD signed an agreement for participation in 25% of the shares of the oil▷ companies operating there. However, following the example of Kuwait▷, AD demanded a revision of the agreement and ownership of 51% of the oil companies' shares. In July 1973 AD began the construction of its own oil refinery, which will alleviate dependence on neighbouring refineries.
(V.E.)

'ADAL, PROF. YAHYA. Iranian physician and politician. Born 1908; studied medicine at University of Paris; professor at Teheran University Faculty of Medicine, and personal physician to the Shah. A founder of the Mardom▷ party, A became its Secretary-General in 1960, and its President in 1971. Elected to the Senate in 1963.
(D.M.)

★'AFLAQ, MICHEL. Again in exile, A maintains ties with the Ba'th▷ regime in Iraq▷. In 1971 A was sentenced to death *in absentia* by the Syrian Supreme Court of State Security, for plotting against the regime, but was pardoned later. (O.T.)

★AFRICA. In 1971 the A states attempted to play a more active role in the ME dispute. In June 1971 the Organization of African Unity▷ came out in support of the Jarring▷ mediation effort and adopted an unequivocal resolution calling upon Israel to implement UN Resolution 242▷ and to withdraw from all territories occupied in 1967. A delegation of A heads of state unsuccessfully tried to mediate between Israel and Egypt in Nov. 1971. During 1972 there was an increased Arab, especially Libyan▷, pressure on the A states to sever diplomatic relations with Israel▷. Uganda was the first to do so, followed mainly by countries with Muslim populations and countries open to Arab pressure or dependent upon Arab aid. During the Yom Kippur War▷ nearly all the other A states, including many quite friendly, broke off diplomatic relations with Israel.
(O.Y.)

AHMAR, AL-, 'ABDULLAH BIN HUSSEIN.
Chairman of Advisory Council of the Legislature of
Yemen▷. Chief of Hashid tribal confederation;
son of previous Chief of the confederation,
Sheikh Hussein Ibn Nasser al-Ahmar, who was
executed (together with his eldest son) by the Imam
Ahmad at the end of 1969. After the 1962 *coup*
and the establishment of the Republic, A gave it his
support. During the first years A took part in the
Egyptian military campaign at the head of some
2,000 warriors. On behalf of the Republic, A served
as Governor of the Hajja district (controlled in any
case by his tribes). From 1963 on A was the ally of
the moderates in the Republican camp, such as al-
Iryani▷, al-Zubeiri and al-Nu'man▷. A recruited
support for the moderate wing in the Republic by
means of tribal conferences which he summoned,
including those of Sept. 1963, Mar. 1965, May 1965
(the Hamar conference, at the capital of the Hashid
district) and Jan. 1967. At these conferences A called
for Egyptian removal from Yemen and the establishment of an Advisory Council to manage the affairs
of the Republic, formed mainly of tribal representatives, religious elders and other conservative
elements. In Oct. 1966, when Sallal▷ returned to
Yemen as a result of the Egyptian toughening of
their anti-Royalist and anti-tribal line, Sallal attempted to arrest A, who was then in San'a▷. A
escaped to his tribal district, which became the
centre for the Republican forces opposing Sallal.
After the Egyptian evacuation, following the Six
Day War▷, A returned to San'a with his warriors,
and was one of the chief factors in the removal of
Sallal in Nov. 1967.

Together with al-Iryani, A became the mainstay
of the new moderate-conservative regime in San'a.
In late 1967 and early 1968, his tribes played an
important role in lifting the Royalist siege of San'a.
A, as Commander of the Yemeni Forces, organized
support for the Republic among the important
tribes in Hamar. During 1968, with the decline of
Royalist prestige due to the removal of the Imam,
A succeeded in bringing most of the north-western
tribes of Yemen over to the Republican camp.
Since then A has been the representative of tribal
support of the Republic and, as such, is apparently
the most influential person in San'a.

The 1970 Constitution, granting supreme powers
to the Advisory Council (in which the influence of
tribal sheikhs is paramount), was in fact the implementation of some of the demands made by A since
1963. Since Mar. 1971, A has been Chairman of the
Advisory Council, elected for a four year period.
The ill-fated attempt of al-'Amri▷ to depose or
limit the Council (Aug. 1971), which cost him his
political career, served as a test of A's standing
within the Republican leadership, from which A
emerged with the upper hand. (H.E.)

*AHRAM, AL-. During recent years, due to the
political stand of its chief editor, Heykal▷, A was
more representative of the right-wing political line
than of the general stand of the Egyptian regime.
Since 1967 Heykal attempted to advance his personal-
political influence by means of research institutes,
established within the framework of the newspaper,
such as the Institute for Palestinian Studies, the
Institute for Strategic Problems and, after the death
of Nasser▷, the Institute for the Legacy of Nasser,
headed by Nasser's daughter, Huda 'Abd-ul-Nasser.

In 1974 Heykal was dismissed from his position
as chief editor and chairman of the board of directors
of A. In his place, 'Abd-ul-Qadir Hatim▷ was
appointed as chairman of the board and 'Ali Amin▷
as chief editor. Heykal's dismissal was the result of
his opposition to the political stand of Sadat▷. (S.L.)

*'AJMAN. A sheikhdom, member state of the
Union of Arab Emirates▷. (Y.K.)

*ALGERIA. During 1971 the process of State
control over most French economic interests in the
country, especially oil▷ companies, was completed.
An agreement signed with France▷ settled this
matter following a lengthy dispute. British▷ and
US▷ interests were also nationalized. All meaningful agitation against Boumedienne's▷ regime
during this period was confined to the universities
and the State enjoyed relative quiet. Boumedienne
continued to play an active role, though less active
than that of his predecessor, in ME affairs and in
the Arab-Israel conflict▷. A's proximity to both
Egypt▷ and other radical countries and elements in
the Arab World accords her a special position
within the present constellation of inter-Arab
relations and, indeed, the Arab Summit conference▷
following the Yom Kippur War▷ was held there.
(O.Y.)

'ALI, AHMAD ISMA'IL. Egyptian Minister of
Defence since Oct. 1972. On 19 Feb., 1974, following
the Yom Kippur War▷, A was promoted to the
rank of *Mushir* (Marshal). Born 1913; attended
military college with Nasser▷; graduated
Command-and-Staff School 1950; received advanced
training in Russia▷ 1957 and the Nasser Academy
1965. Following the Six Day War▷, A commanded the Infantry Corps; appointed Chief of
Operations 1968, and Chief of Staff Mar. 1969.
Dismissed following an Israeli raid on the Red Sea

area (Sept. 1969). Sadat's▷ dismissal of the Sabri▷-Gum'a group led to A's appointment as Chief of Intelligence and then Minister of Defence. A is considered Sadat's confidant.   (Al.S.)

'ALI NASSER MUHAMMAD HUSNI. Prime Minister of South Yemen▷. Born 1939; began career as a school-teacher; appointed Governor of Kuria-Muria▷, Perim▷ and Qamaran islands in the southern Red Sea▷ and Indian Ocean. Governor of the Second District of South Yemen in 1968, and was later appointed Minister for Local Civil Administration Affairs; Minister of Defence from 1969 to Aug. 1971, when appointed Prime Minister and member of Residential Council, replacing Muhammad 'Ali Haitham▷. Member of the Executive Board and the Control Committee of the NFL▷.
                                                  (T.Y.)

★ALLON, YIGAL. A contender for the position of Prime Minister following Golda Meir▷. It was suggested in both the Israeli press and abroad that A was involved in negotiations with Jordan▷, including clandestine meetings with Hussein▷. A was reappointed Deputy Prime Minister and Minister of Education and Culture in Meir's Government of Mar. 1974. In May 1974 A was appointed Deputy Prime Minister and Foreign Minister in Rabin's Government.   (A.W.)

★'AMMAN. A became a battle-ground during the civil war in Jordan▷ in Sept. 1970. The eradication of the Palestinian-Arab guerillas▷ from refugee▷ camps was carried out slowly and systematically. Several districts, especially the refugee camps around it, were destroyed, and thousands of civilians were killed or wounded. The rebuilding of the camps was begun only in 1971, and in that year life in A returned to normal.   (O.Y.)

★'AMMASH, SALAH MAHDI. Removed from office as Iraqi▷ Vice-President, following the dispute with Sadam Hussein al-Takriti▷ and was appointed Ambassador to Russia▷.   (U.D.)

★'AMRI, AL-HASSAN. As Yemeni▷ Chief of Staff of the Armed Forces and Member of the Residential Council, A found himself in a strong position to defend the interests of the non-tribal faction. A was appointed Prime Minister in 1971, and formed a Cabinet considered to be of central-leftist character, but was dimissed after five days, being accused of intending to dissolve the Advisory Council. Charged with murder, A faced execution but instead was expelled from Yemen.   (H.E.)

★'AQABA. A enjoyed relative peace during the civil war of 1970; the strife brought it prosperity, following the closure of the Syria▷-Jordan▷ border and making A the main port of entry to the country. The new port, constructed with British▷ financial assistance, was opened on 13 May, 1972; a new international airport was built north of the town in 1973.   (O.Y.)

★ARAB-ISRAEL CONFLICT. The Yom Kippur War▷ was the most important single development in the A-IC since 1970. Between 1970 and late 1972, the Arab partners to the conflict sensed their impotence; Egypt▷ under Sadat▷ was weak internally and externally, and was unable to renew its "war of attrition". Egyptian foreign policy had reached a dead-end when Sadat expelled the majority of Soviet advisers from his country in July 1972. With the conclusion of the civil war in Jordan▷, pressure on Israel eased also from that quarter. Attacks by Palestinian-Arab guerillas▷ against Israeli targets outside the ME were the only continued pressure against Israel during this period.

This situation began changing toward late 1972, and especially during 1973, with the strengthening of international standing of the Arab States, and the utilization of this factor for the benefit of those Arab countries in direct conflict with Israel. Most important were the world's increasing dependence on Arab oil▷, the growing foreign currency reserves in several of the Arab oil producing states, the support of the Eastern Bloc, and Israel's declining position with Western European States and in the Third World.

Under these circumstances, two major approaches to the continued struggle against Israel developed. The first, upheld mainly by Libya▷, proposed to concentrate greater might in Arab hands and then launch a full-scale war against Israel. The second, sponsored primarily by Sadat, aimed at establishing an Arab allied front to enable Egypt to go to war (even if it yielded no more than partial military successes, it would enable Egypt to utilize all the above factors to impose a settlement upon Israel acceptable to the Arabs). The latter approach somewhat postponed Arab long-range objectives. Meanwhile, Egyptian activity centred on intermediate goals, the most important of which were the return of territories occupied by Israel during the Six Day War▷.

It is still too early to evaluate the full impact of the Yom Kippur War on the long-range course of the A-IC. The initial success attained by the Arab armies in that war may reduce Israel's deterrent capacity and encourage the Arabs in their hope for a military victory in a further round. But the significance of the war's closing stages may well indicate Arab failure to maintain initial advantages even under favourable circumstances and should lead them to understand the futility of additional armed encounters.

The various efforts to reach a settlement since that war (the Six Point Agreement▷, the Kilometre 101 talks▷, the Separation of Forces Agreements▷ and the Geneva Peace Conference▷) have only sharpened the differences between the above two approaches in the Arab world. Libya and Iraq▷ oppose all negotion or political agreement with Israel, and they boycotted the Algiers Arab Summit▷, convened after the war to legitimize Egyptian policy vis-à-vis Israel. Syrian policy in negotiations with Israel has generally been coordinated with that of Egypt. Some of the Palestinian organizations have accepted the Egyptian approach and expressed their willingness to attend the Geneva Peace Conference. Others, however, favour the Libya-Iraq approach.

Public debate has also been raging in Israel since the Yom Kippur War. There are various Israeli approaches to the significance of the war and its results, concerning future prospects. The central problem is evaluation of Egypt's true intentions: Does Sadat really want a settlement, or is his present positive approach only a tactical device to obtain Israeli withdrawal, to be followed by continued Arab efforts under conditions more favourable to them? (It.R.)

*ARAB LEAGUE. By 1973, the AL had twenty member states; upon achieving independence, Bahrain▷, Qatar▷, the Federation of Arab Emirates▷ and Oman▷ had joined, as had Mauritania▷ and Somalia▷. (O.T.)

*ARAB NATIONAL MOVEMENT. After the death of Nasser▷, chief leader of messianic Arab nationalism, the dynamic element of Pan-Arabism▷ lessened, while in Egypt▷ itself patriotism grew stronger. The Libyan▷ ruler Mu'ammar Qaddhafi▷ has sought to take Nasser's place as leader of revolutionary Pan-Arabism. The substantial importance of the Palestinians▷ in ANM rose after the Six Day War▷. (A.G.)

*ARAB SOCIALIST UNION. With the rise of Sadat▷ to the Egyptian Presidency, fertile ground was created for friction and conflict between him and the "centre of power" formed by the ASU Executive Committee. His chief opponent was 'Ali Sabri▷. This turned into open conflict in the spring 1971 due to the opposition of Sadat's enemies to his planned federation with Libya▷ and Syria▷, and to his policy towards the superpowers and the conflict with Israel. In May 1971 this led to the removal of his opponents from the Executive Committee and the Central Committee. New elections were held in July-Aug. 1971 for the ASU institutions, "from top to bottom", resulting in the election of a new Central Committee, but not a Supreme Executive Committee. Since then mediocre personalities have been appointed to the position of First Secretary of the Central Committee: Dr. 'Abd-ul-Salam al-Zayyat (May-Aug. 1971), Dr. 'Aziz Sidqi▷ (Aug. 1971-Jan. 1972), Sayyid Mar'i▷ (Jan. 1972-Mar. 1973) and Dr. Hafez Ghanem (since Mar. 1973). (Al.S.)

ARAB SUMMIT CONFERENCES. Meetings of the rulers of Arab States have been convened since the 1940s, due to the Arab League's▷ weakness and inability to make binding decisions. The immediate reason for such gatherings usually lay in the "Palestine problem" or the Arab-Israel Conflict▷. Three periods may be differentiated: The first, before the formation of the State of Israel▷, covers two meetings. In May 1946 five states (Egypt, Syria, Iraq, Sa'udi Arabia and Jordan) met at Inshas, Egypt; and in June of that year Prime Ministers and Foreign Ministers gathered at Baludan▷, Syria.

The second period was during the 1960s. The immediate reason was the demand to oppose construction of the National Water Carrier in Israel, but the background was furnished by sharp conflicts then raging within the Arab world. Three summit meetings took place, setting up military and technical action groups (an organization to divert Jordan waters, a joint Arab military command, the Palestine Liberation Organization▷ and the Palestine Liberation Army). (a) The Cairo summit of Jan. 1964, called by Nasser▷, was attended by 13 Arab States; (b) the Alexandria summit took place in Sept. 1964; and (c) the Casablanca summit, in Sept. 1964, was the last to be held before the Six Day War. The failure of the last again fanned the flames of conflict in Yemen▷.

The third period came after the Arab defeat in the Six Day War▷. Summit meetings were called in order to support the "confrontation states" in their efforts to regain territory lost by them. So far, three such meetings have taken place: (a) The Khartoum summit (Aug.-Sept. 1967), one of the most important meetings, allocated financial aid to Egypt, Jordan and the PLO and decided on the famous "three noes" (no recognition of Israel, no negotiations and no peace). This summit also settled the Yemen conflict reaffirmed concern for the Palestinians. (b) Rabat summit (Dec. 1969) was considered a complete failure, because of disagreement on the means and methods to be used against Israel. (c) The Algiers summit (Nov. 1973) was the first to meet after the Yom Kippur War▷. Two radical states, Iraq and Libya, refused to participate. The purpose of the meeting was to ratify Egyptian and Syrian participation in the Geneva Peace Conference▷, under the terms of UN Resolution 338▷. The most important result was the *de facto* repeal of the Khartoum "noes", by approving the achievement of a "just" peace, predicated upon the return of all occupied territories and the recognition of Palestinian rights.   (Al.S.)

*ARAB UNITY. During recent years several attempts were made to establish unions and federations in the Arab world. On 1 Sept., 1971, a loose federation was established between Egypt▷, Syria▷ and Libya▷. This Federation of Arab Republics▷ had judicial institutions, a Presidential Council, Parliament, Government, etc. From its inception, relations between the member countries were not close and it did not withstand the crucial test of the Yom Kippur War▷, which Egypt and Syria initiated without consulting Libya. During Aug. 1972–Aug. 1973, al-Qaddhafi▷, the Libyan ruler, forced upon Egypt an agreement towards merger between the two countries. However, relations between the two remained strained and Egypt evaded implementation of the agreement. Qaddhafi on his part attempted, and again failed, to form a union with Tunisia▷. On 28 Nov., 1972, Yemen▷ and South Yemen▷ signed an agreement towards union, following an armed dispute between the two countries; so far, however, no progress has been made towards its implementation. The only successful undertaking in this sphere is the federation established by seven sheikhdoms on the Persian Gulf, in Dec. 1971, under the name of the Union of Arab Emirates▷.

During recent years, the dynamic drive of Pan-Arabism▷ has come to a halt and al-Qaddhafi has been the only leader to continue attempting its implementation. This abatement of tension has facilitated inter-Arab cooperation which found prominent expression during the Yom Kippur War.

It is albeit clear that the use of oil▷ as a political weapon, the most important manifestation of this cooperation, was also in line with the particular interests of some of the Arab oil producing states.   (A.G.)

*'ARAFAT, YASSER. A is continuing his protracted struggle with the leftist terrorist organizations, especially in the matter of contacts with the governments of Egypt▷ and Syria▷. A openly claims that all ideological controversies should be postponed until the destruction of the State of Israel is achieved. His opponents accuse him of conservatism in tactics and reactionary views in ideology, a result of his closeness to the Muslim Brotherhood▷.   (E.Y.)

*ARMED FORCES IN THE ME. EGYPT: In April 1971, Russia▷ was noted to have supplied Egypt with MIG-23 and *c.* 150 other MIG aircraft. After the signing of a Soviet-Egyptian Friendship Pact on 27 May, 1971, Russia▷ supplied Egypt with further arms, including *c.* 100 MIG 21 aircraft. The Minister of War, Muhammad, Sadeq, was appointed Supreme Commander of the armies of Egypt and Syria on 17 Oct., 1971. Soviet arms shipments to Egypt lessened at the end of 1971, at the time of the counterrevolution in Sudan. On 4 Nov., 1971, Sadat▷ appointed himself Supreme Commander of Egypt's armed forces, and it was disclosed that Russia had supplied Egypt with medium bombers carrying air-to-ground missiles. The subsequent rift in Soviet-Egyptian relations led to the expulsion of Russian advisers from Egypt, in May 1972. In Aug. 1972. Egypt sought to buy arms from Britain▷. During the period following the cease-fire of Aug. 1970, Egypt absorbed large quantities of war equipment and began training troops on divisional and army levels. The quality of officers in the Egyptian army improved with the mobilization of university students, while detailed plans for war were drawn up with the aid of Russian advisers. When the Yom Kippur War▷ broke out, on 6 Oct., 1973, the army was fully prepared; it numbered *c.* 300,000 men, supported by a large number of reservists. Its striking force consisted of two armoured divisions and several independent armoured brigades, amounting to 2,000 tanks and eight infantry divisions (of which three were mechanized). In addition, 1,000 artillery pieces were deployed in six brigades, and there were 26 commando companies and two paratroop brigades. The infantry was well supplied with anti-tank weapons, primarily of the "Sagger" and "Snapper" types. Other weapons included anti-aircraft shoulder missiles ("Strella", SAM-7). There were also dozens of "Frog" and "Scud" ground-to-ground missiles.

The air force totalled 23,000 men, 420 combat aircraft, of which 210 were MIG-21, 180 Sukhoi-7 and 25 Tupolev-16 and -18 bombers (the latter types armed with air-to-ground missiles of the "Kelt" type); 200 helicopters, 70 aircraft and 200 trainers.

Deployment of ground-to-air missiles included 130 batteries, mostly SAM-2 and SAM-3, as well as the mobile SAM-6 batteries; in addition, there was a dense deployment of 37 mm and 57 mm anti-aircraft guns.

The 15,000 man Egyptian navy had five destroyers, 12 submarines, 19 missile boats ("Osa" and "Komar" types) and other vessels.

In the Yom Kippur War, Egyptian losses were about a third of the abovementioned equipment. However, these were replaced within two months after the cease-fire; thus, by early 1974 the army had about 25% more arms and equipment than it had before the war. The loss of many trained soldiers is the main problem facing the army. The Separation of Forces Agreement▷ facilitated reconstruction and reorganization of the army, and it freed the encircled Third Army for effective service.

SYRIA: During 1971 Russia▷ supplied Syria with MIG-21 aircraft; in addition, 50 combat aircraft were received from Egypt, in accord with an agreement signed on 1 June, 1971. On 17 Oct., 1971, Egyptian War Minister Sadeq was appointed Supreme Commander of the Egyptian and Syrian armies; in 1972, Ahmad Isma'il 'Ali▷ replaced him.

From late 1970 on, the army underwent intensive reorganization, and within the following three years its overall strength was doubled, especially in tanks. The army was reorganized into divisional units, and was trained under the supervision of Soviet experts. In the Damascus▷ region and on the Golan front, a network of anti-aircraft missiles and artillery was formed, and the air force made more effective. When the Yom Kippur War▷ broke out, the army numbered 200,000 men (including many reservists); it had two armoured divisions and two independent armoured brigades, accounting for more than 1,200 tanks; three infantry divisions reinforced with tank units and armoured cars, trained commando units, and paratroop battalions. Its seven artillery brigades had hundreds of cannon, and its anti-aircraft weapons included 12–20 SAM-2 and SAM-3 missile batteries; infantry forces had SAM-7 shoulder missiles and anti-tank missiles of the "Sagger" and "Snapper" types.

The air force, numbering 10,000 men, had over 400 combat aircraft, including 210 MIG-21, 180 Sukhoi-7 and 25 Ilyushin bombers; 50 helicopters and c. 10 transport aircraft.

The navy remained small; its 2,000 men served and manned 12 missile boats ("Osa" and "Komar" types), and several other small vessels.

After the Yom Kippur War, in which about 50% of the army's equipment was lost, Russia replaced and supplemented the losses, but the army still suffers from the loss of trained troops. By early 1974, however, the armed forces were as strong in equipment as they had been at the outbreak of the war.

IRAQ: No great increases took place in Iraq's army. Two divisions, one armoured and one mechanized, took part in the Yom Kippur War▷, the former losing most of its tanks in the fighting. The Iraqi force left Syrian territory with the cease-fire, but in Jan. 1974 Iraq was reported to have agreed to stationing troops on Syrian soil should this again become necessary.

JORDAN: The army emerged victorious in the civil war of Sept. 1970, and had held the incursions of Syrian troops though it suffered losses in men and equipment. From 1971 on, Jordan began expanding its armed forces, receiving additional arms from the US▷. In 1972, Jordan received dozens of Patton M-48 tanks, and about 20 F-5 combat aircraft. A new armoured division was built up, so that it had two such divisions by Oct. 1973, at which time there were three infantry divisions as well as commando units and the Royal Guard. During the Yom Kippur War▷ only the 40th Armoured Brigade took part in the fighting, on the Syrian front, losing 27 tanks in one battle. After the war, Jordan requested military equipment from the US, and was assured of aircraft and various categories of new equipment.

LEBANON: The army's chief task was to police Palestine-Arab guerilla▷ activities in the country. There was essentially no new development of the army in this period. When the IDF raided Beirut in April 1973, the army was strongly criticized for inadequately defending the city. The army took no part in the Yom Kippur War▷, though a major radar station at Jebel Baruk, which had been put at the disposal of the Syrians, was destroyed by Israel aircraft.

LIBYA: By May 1971, Libya had received 20 Mirage fighter aircraft from France▷, and Libyan pilots were trained in France. Libyan troops took part in the Yom Kippur War▷, on the Egyptian front, being withdrawn only after the Separation of Forces Agreement▷, in Jan. 1974.

MOROCCO: Morocco sent a brigade to the Syrian front during the Yom Kippur War▷; it suffered heavy losses in the fighting.

ISRAEL: Following the cease-fire of Aug. 1970, the IDF was considerably strengthened with new US▷ equipment. Armoured brigades and the air force were the principal beneficiaries, while the navy was transformed into an effective missile-boat force (largely of Israeli manufacture). The IDF was partly reorganized, as well.

Up to Oct. 1973, much of the army's operations were against Palestine-Arab▷ terrorist bases in Lebanon▷. During this period there was relative quiet along the cease-fire lines and, except for several incidents along the Suez Canal▷ and on the Golan Heights▷, the military situation remained unchanged till the Yom Kippur War▷.

In Oct. 1973, the IDF numbered 100,000 men and reserve forces estimated at c. 400,000 men. The London Institute of Strategic Studies has estimated Israeli ground forces to include 10–12 armoured brigades (1,500 tanks), as follows: 400 Patton M-48, 200 M-60, 600 Centurion, 200 Sherman (improved and "super-Shermans"), 100 Soviet tanks (T-54 and T-55, captured in the Six Day War▷). The IDF also had 18 infantry brigades, 10 of which were mechanized, 4,000 armoured cars and half-tracks, and three paratroop brigades. Artillery included four to five brigades, 400 mobile artillery pieces, and hundreds of cannon and field pieces. A considerable number of ground-to-ground missiles of the "Jericho" type, with a range of 600 km, were also reported.

The air force was composed of 16,000 men, and 4,000 reservists. Its c. 420 combat aircraft included 120 "Phantoms" (F-4), 180 "Skyhawks" (A-4), 24 Israeli manufactured fighter aircraft ("Barak"), 18 "Super-Mysteres" and 72 "Mirage" aircraft (C-3); 74 helicopters (Sikorski CH-53, Super-Frelon and Bell 203); 60 transport aircraft (Dakota, Nord, Stratocruiser, Hercules) and 80 trainers (Super-Fouga "Magister") and other patrol aircraft. Israeli combat aircraft were equipped with both US and Israeli missiles. Air force anti-aircraft units had various weapons, including 10 batteries of "Hawk" missiles.

The 4,500 man navy had one destroyer, three submarines, 13 missile boats ("Saar" type, manufactured in Israel and equipped with "Gabriel" missiles), 10 torpedo and landing boats, and other vessels.

The IDF lost 2,600 men during the Yom Kippur War, as well as c. 400 tanks, 100 aircraft, and other equipment. Most of these losses were replaced within two months, beginning with the US airlift during the war. Following the signing of the Separation of Forces Agreement▷, in Jan. 1974, about half of the reservists were released from active service along the cease-fire lines.   (O.Y.)

★ARMY OFFICERS IN POLITICS. Several changes within the framework of military and semi-military regimes in Arab countries have taken place. In Egypt▷, Sadat▷ imposed his authority on the army; in Syria▷ the military character of the Ba'th▷ regime became more pronounced and in Iraq▷ the Ba'th regime of Tikriti▷ succeeded in bringing the military under party rule.

In Sudan▷ a Communist▷ inspired *coup d'état* failed in July 1972. In Iraq the Chief of Military Intelligence headed an unsuccessful *coup d'état* in 1973. Several units of the Jordan▷ army were unruly in Feb. 1974, due to pay conditions; their feelings, however, were also directed against some of the army chiefs.   (O.Y.)

★ASAD, HAFEZ. Upon gaining control of the Government in Syria▷ in Nov. 1970, following a bloodless military *coup*, A established a Government headed by himself; he commenced the implementation of an "open" policy, which he had long been advocating. This stood for more moderation and liberalization in internal politics and in the economy, as well as more active Syrian participation in Arab affairs, after a period of several years of extreme isolation.

In Mar. 1971, A as sole candidate was elected President of Syria in a referendum in which he gained 99.2% of the vote. According to an amendment of the Syrian Constitution, presidential powers were augmented and his term of office extended to a seven-year period. This was the first time in Syrian history that the presidency was held by a member of the Alawite▷ minority, rather than by a member of the Sunnite▷ majority.

In contrast to the collective leadership of the Ba'th▷ party which ruled Syria until Nov. 1970, A became prominent as an individual leader concentrating power in his own hands. He enlarged the basis of his public support by being elected by referendum (hitherto the President had been appointed by the Ba'th leadership), the establishment of a People's Council (a legislative body in which other parties apart from the Ba'th were represented) and the forming of a National-Progressive Front (a political entity comprising a number of left-wing parties, headed by the Ba'th, and the only legal political body in Syria), in Mar. 1972. A is the Secretary-General of this Front, as well as the Secretary-General of the Ba'th Party.

A also began promoting the personality cult which arose around him: He is called "The great leader" by communications media, and the lake formed by the Euphrates▷ Dam is called "Lake Asad" (similar to "Lake Nasser" formed by the Aswan Dam▷ in Egypt). Despite several plots against his regime (including an attempt on his life), which were foiled, it appears that A holds complete control of Government in Syria, with the assistance of the Minister of Defence (and ex-Chief of Staff) Mustafa Tallas▷ and a group of army officers who owe him personal loyalty and are headed by his brother, Rif'at Asad. A's decision to initiate, together with Egypt, the Yom Kippur War▷ against Israel, strengthened his position and prestige in Syria and in the Arab world. However, the results of that war, together with the political pressures being applied on Syria, have resulted in a certain degree of opposition within the Ba'th Party and even within the army, which serves as the mainstay of support for A's rule. (O.T.)

★'ASIR. The end of the Yemen▷ war in 1967, recognition of the Yemeni Republic by Sa'udi Arabia▷, and collaboration between the two countries, brought a solution of the A problem. During the visit of Yemeni President Iryani▷ to Sa'udi Arabia in Mar. 1973, the possibility of a Yemeni declaration recognizing A as a part of Sa'udi Arabia was discussed. (H.E.)

★ASNAJ, AL-, 'ABDULLAH. A carried out activities against the regime in South Yemen▷ mainly from Sa'udi Arabia▷ and Yemen. For a time he was considered a political officer of FLOSY▷, but he was removed from the leadership in Jan. 1970 due to his opposition to attempts on behalf of some of the FLOSY leaders to achieve a reconciliation with the NLF▷. In Aug. 1971 A was appointed Minister for Foreign Affairs in the Government of Hassan al-'Amri▷ in Yemen, an appointment which aroused great resentment in South Yemen in view of the tense relations between the two countries. In Sept. 1971 A was appointed Minister of Economy in the Government of Muhsin al-'Ayni, a position he holds still today. (T.Y.)

ATASSI, AL-, JAMAL. A physician and ex-member of the Ba'th▷ party. A holds the position of Secretary-General of the Arab Socialist Union Party in Syria▷ (a Nasserist party participating in the Government in Syria since the rise of Asad▷ in Nov. 1970). (O.T.)

★ATASSI, AL-, NUR-UL-DIN. After the Nov. 1970 coup in Syria▷, A was detained without trial for two and a half years. In mid-1973 A was released and departed for exile in Libya. (O.T.)

★'AWADULLA, ABU-BAKR. Following the reorganization of the Sudan▷ regime in Oct. 1971, A was appointed Vice-President. He resigned in May 1973, while on a private visit to Cairo, giving ill health as the reason; however, it is thought that A's

dispute with Numeiri▷ over the Egypt-Libya-Syria federation, which A supported, was the true reason behind his resignation. A subsequently has not returned to Sudan. (E.S.)

AYYUBI, AL-, MAHMOUD. Syrian politician, one of the leaders of the Ba'th. Born 1932; Minister of Education 1969–71; Deputy Prime Minister 1970–1. In April 1971, A was appointed Deputy to the President of Syria▷ and took part in contacts with Egypt▷ and Libya▷ toward the forming of a federation. A was one of the formulators of the Constitution of the federation in June 1971. Participated in attempts to settle the crisis between Sudan▷ and Russia in Aug. 1971, after the ill-fated Communist▷ coup there. In Dec. 1972 A formed a new Government at the request of Asad. (O.Y.)

B

★BAB AL-MANDEB. Since the closure of the Suez Canal▷, in 1967, the strategic and economic importance of the BM straits declined. South Yemen▷ repeatedly declared its determination to prevent passage of Israel▷ vessels. In June 1971, members of the Popular Front for the Liberation of Palestine▷ attacked the tanker Coral Sea, apparently with the encouragement of South Yemen, who had maintained contacts with member states of the Arab League▷ concerning the possible closure of the straits in time of war. In Mar. 1973 rumours appeared that an Israel force had taken up positions on one of the islands in the straits; this was denied by both Yemen▷ and South Yemen, as well as by Israel. At the outbreak of the Yom Kippur War▷, the straits were closed to Israel shipping by an Egyptian flotilla, although Egypt had not declared a formal blockade. This step increased the importance of the straits in the Arab-Israel Conflict▷. The straits were opened to shipping to and from Israel after the Six Points Agreement▷ was signed. (T.Y.)

★BAHRAIN. According to the 1971 census, the population was 216,800, of which 88,800 are in the capital city. Petroleum production reached 3.8m tons in 1971, to which may be added 1.5m tons from an offshore field held jointly with Sa'udi Arabia▷. The oil▷ refinery produced 12.8m tons in 1971. An aluminium refinery, based on the use of natural gas, has been under construction since 1969; partial production began in 1970, and final annual output is planned at 120,000 tons.

Agreements on maritime borders were signed, in

1970 with Qatar▷ and in 1971 with Iran▷.

B became independent in Aug. 1971 and subsequently left the Union of Arab Emirates▷. A small US▷ naval force, formerly stationed at the British▷ naval base, remained in B after the British departure. B also signed a new treaty of friendship with Britain.

After independence, democratization of Government institutions began: A Cabinet took the place of the Administrative Council; elections to a 45-member Constitutional Assembly were held in Dec. 1972, and the Constitution formulated by this body was made public in June 1973. It gave women the right to vote — a sphere in which B is ahead of all other Persian Gulf▷ states, except Iran. General elections to the 30-member National Assembly first took place in Dec. 1973; these were held on a personal basis, since political parties are illegal. Ministers appointed by the ruling Sheikh also are members of the Assembly. Key ministries remained in the hands of members of the ruling al-Khalifa family.

In 1973, construction of a drydock for giant tankers at B was approved by the Organization of Arab Petroleum Exporting Countries▷.

(Y.K. & V.E.)

BAJBUJ MUHAMMED JABER. Deputy Director-General of the National Executive of the Ba'th▷ party in Syria▷. The Director-General is Asad▷, and thus routine management of party affairs is actually B's responsibility.   (O.Y.)

*BAKDASH, KHALED. His stand favouring cooperation with the Ba'th▷ regime under Asad▷ almost split the Syrian▷ Communist party▷; some of the party's younger members vigorously opposed this line, as well as B's traditional leadership. Ultimately this was settled with the aid of the Soviet Communist party, and the Syrian Communist party continues to participate in the Government. B is a member of the Executive of the National Progressive Front (of leftist parties, led by the Ba'th, which alone is allowed to operate legally in Syria), established in 1972; B was elected as a representative of the Front on the Syrian Popular Council   (O.T.)

*BARAZANI, MULLA MUSTAFA. The group of Kurds▷ headed by Talabani joined B early in 1972, accepting his leadership; however, unity was not maintained for long, since another group split from B's camp at the end of 1972. He himself escaped two attempts on his life, in 1971 and in 1972; apparently, both were instigated by the Iraqi▷ authorities. The Mar. 1970 agreement

concluded between B and the Government is not being implemented. A number of serious collisions have taken place since then with the Iraqi army, and recently these have developed into fulfledged fighting.   (O.Y.)

BAR-LEV, HAIM. Former Chief of Staff, IDF, and now Minister of Commerce, Industry and Development. Born in Yugoslavia 1924; came to Palestine 1939; since 1942 involved in defence activities, originally in the Palmah▷, where B-L participated in the Arab-Israel War of 1948▷ as battalion commander. B-L remained in the IDF where he held several important positions. During the Sinai Campaign▷, B-L commanded an armoured brigade in the northern part of Sinai. Shortly before the Six Day War▷, B-L was recalled from abroad to be appointed deputy to the Chief of Staff. In 1968 B-L became Chief of Staff; under his command, the IDF conducted its struggle against terrorists, as well as the "war of attrition" against Egypt▷. The line of defensive positions along the eastern bank of the Suez Canal▷, the so-called Bar-Lev Line▷, is named after him. In 1972 B-L concluded his army service and was coopted into the Cabinet as Minister of Commerce and Industry. During the Yom Kippur War▷, B-L was recalled and appointed GOC Southern Front. At the end of that war B-L returned to his Government post. When the new cabinet was formed in Mar. 1974, B-L entered his present post.   (O.Y.)

*BAR-LEV LINE. During the Yom Kippur War▷, the Bar-Lev▷ Line was penetrated by the Egyptian army, which crossed the Suez Canal▷ and captured essentially all the strongholds along its eastern bank. They continue to hold the line, in accordance with the Separation of Forces Agreement▷.   (E.A.)

*BASES, FOREIGN MILITARY. US: After the closure of its bases in Libya▷, the only US bases left in the area are in Turkey▷ and Sa'udi Arabia▷. The US Navy has users' rights at the port of Bahrain▷. During 1973-4 there was talk of establishing a new US base at the Diego Garcia Islands in the Indian Ocean.

RUSSIA: Reports of a new Soviet base at Socotra▷ were proven unfounded during this period. The most important recent event in this context was the summer 1971 expulsion of Soviet military advisers from Egypt▷, after disagreements with Sadat▷. Subsequently, the special rights enjoyed by Russia concerning the use of Egyptian naval and air bases (mainly Marsa Matruh and Cairo-West) were restricted, but not cancelled. During this same period relations between Russia and Syria▷ became closer, resulting in additional rights on Syrian bases. During the Yom Kippur War▷ the Soviets again used many Egyptian and Syrian bases for the resupply of these two countries' armies; however, the Egyptian bases remained under Egyptian control. (O.Y.)

*BA'TH, AL-. Frequent splits in the B ranks, overall changes in the Arab world, lack of ideological innovation within the party and the concentration of its regimes on their individual problems, greatly reduced B influence as representative of a Pan-Arab▷ ideological movement. Despite this, the name Ba'th still carries considerable political weight and its organization is still of importance. Several factions compete for the position as its "true" representative:

(a) The present Syrian▷ regime, headed by Asad▷. Immediately after its *coup* in Nov. 1970, this regime established a national command, as well as a Pan-Arab command for the B, claiming to be legitimate heir of the B which had ruled Syria since 1963. This has led to Asad's general recognition as the legitimate spokesman of the B.

(b) The regime in power in Iraq▷ since 1968, related to a faction of the short-lived B regime of 1963. To strengthen its own position, the Iraqi leadership leans on the support of several of the historic B leadership, which had been deposed during the revolution in Syria in Feb. 1966. Despite this, and in spite of the Pan-Arab party command which it maintains, this regime is generally considered Iraqi.

(c) The followers of Jadid▷ who fled Syria and now publish their own organ in Lebanon▷. Lacking official backing, their influence is limited.

The formal framework for the maintenance of B unity and continuity is its Pan-Arab organization. The last Pan-Arab conference took place in Dec. 1970. Asad is the present Secretary-General of the B connected with his regime, and 'Abdullah al-Ahmar▷ is his deputy. (I.R.)

*BAZZAZ, AL-, DR. 'ABD-UL-RAHMAN. Died in Baghdad in July 1973. (R.G.)

*BEGIN, MENAHEM. After *Gahal*▷ left the National Unity Cabinet in Aug. 1970, B and his party rejoined the opposition. When Maj.-Gen. Ariel Sharon retired from active service, in the summer of 1973, negotiations began between *Gahal,* the Free Centre, the State List and the Land of Israel Movement▷ for the creation of a parlia-

mentary bloc in opposition to the Alignment▷. B opposed this step, but finally accepted it, and the *Likud*▷ was formed. After the Yom Kippur War▷, B strongly attacked Prime Minister Golda Meir▷ for not having mobilized the reserves in time; during the election campaign of Dec. 1973, argument between the parties was violent, and the *Likud* proposed the establishment of a National Unity Government; efforts to this end continued even after the elections and B's attitude became more extreme once it was clear that the Alignment might set up a minority cabinet. B protested against the manner in which the Cabinet was formed, mirroring its previous composition. (O.Y.)

*BEN-GURION, DAVID. Refrained from active participation in political affairs, appearing only rarely in public. B-G continued to concentrate on writing his memoirs until Nov. 1973, when he fell ill. B-G died on 1 Dec., 1973, and was buried at Sde Boqer. (O.Y.)

*BITAR, SALAH-UL-DIN. Remained in exile and engaged mainly in writing. In Jan. 1969, the Supreme State Security Court in Syria▷ tried B *in absentia* for his part in an alleged conspiracy against the Ba'th▷ regime and sentenced him to life imprisonment with hard labour. (O.T.)

BLACK PANTHERS. An Israel▷ organization formed early in 1971 by youth in Jerusalem, with the aim of protesting against social and community discrimination. The BP organized street demonstrations, several of which ended in violence. *Knesset* member Shalom Cohen joined the BP and ran in the 1973 elections at the head of the BP list, the "Israel Democratic BP".

One BP leader, Eddie Malka, organized a splinter movement which ran in the 1973 elections under the name of the "Blue-and-White Panthers". Neither list gained representation in the *Knesset*. Before the split, 24 BP representatives were elected at the *Histadrut*▷ conference in Sept. 1973. (O.Y.)

BOUMEDIENNE, HOUARI (BEN HARU-WA, MUHAMMAD). President of Algeria▷. Born 1923; educated at Institute of Muslim Studies in Constantine, at Zeitouna University in Tunisia, and at al-Azhar▷ in Cairo. His military education was at the École de Guerre in Paris.

Col. B was at first in charge of a school. Later he moved to Cairo where he underwent military training, as a member of the FLN. In 1955 B assumed a leading position in the Algerian Liberation Movement, and was appointed commander of the FLN's

Fifth District in Oran. In 1960 B became Supreme Commander of the FLN but was removed from this post shortly before the 1962 referendum on the future of Algeria. After independence, B became Defence Minister, in the first Government established in Sept. 1962. During 1963–5 B also served as Deputy President of the Council of Ministers. B maintained himself in these two positions, in spite of frequent changes in Government.

In 1965 B assumed full power and arrested his predecessor, Ben Bella. Since then B has been President of Algeria and Chairman of its Revolutionary Council. After the death of Nasser▷, B became one of the outstanding Arab leaders. In the Arab-Israel conflict▷, he follows an extreme line and supports the terrorist organizations, as well as the PLO▷ and its leader 'Arafat▷. On the issue of Maghreb▷ unity, B holds that the region is not yet ready for federation since Algeria is the only revolutionary state there.

B has become very active in inter-Arab affairs, where he plays a central role. In the Yom Kippur War▷ B actively supported many of the steps taken by Sadat▷ and Asad▷, and units of his army participated in the conflict. After that war, B hosted the Arab Summit Conference▷ which decided on future strategy; a summit attended by Egypt, Syria, Sa'udi Arabia and Algeria later discussed the same issues.   (O.Y.)

★BOURGUIBA, HABIB. The question of B's political succession is the focal point of Tunisian▷ internal politics in recent years. B removed two of his close associates from positions of power — Ahmad ben Saleh and Bahi Ladgham — possibly because he feared their growing influence. B, seventy in July 1973, is not in good health and spends considerable time abroad for medical treatment.   (O.Y.)

BOUTEFLIKA, 'ABD-UL-'AZIZ. Algerian statesman, Foreign Minister since 1963. Born 1935 in Algeria▷; educated at Algerian and Moroccan schools; participated in the Algerian revolt and rose to Captain in the Liberation Army, where he became acquainted with Boumedienne▷. After independence (July 1962), B was appointed Minister for Youth and Sports, and several months later became Foreign Minister. B is active in the Government party and was elected to the Political Bureau of the Liberation Front (1964).

In the conflict between Ben Bella and Boumedienne, B sided with the latter because of his opposition to the Marxist tendencies favoured by Ben Bella and his supporters in the party. When Ben Bella was removed from office, B was appointed

to the Revolutionary Council, of which Boumedienne was head, and B has been Foreign Minister since then. He follows pragmatic anti-Communist lines, but favours cooperation with the Eastern Bloc and with China▷. B is opposed to domination of the Mediterranean area by the superpowers.   (Al.S.)

★BRITAIN. On 31 Oct., 1970, the Foreign Secretary, Sir Alec Douglas Home, restated the principles of B's ME policy. Despite B claims that these were in keeping with UN Resolution 242▷, Israel felt that B was moving once again toward the Arab point of view, particularly since Home argued that at least some of the refugees▷ should be allowed to return to Israeli territory. Relations with Egypt▷ took a turn for the better in 1971 when an agreement was reached on compensation for B property nationalized in 1960–4, and the Egyptian Foreign Minister emphasized that B had an important role to play in the ME.

With the outbreak of the Yom Kippur War▷, B took a more moderate stand than France▷, refusing publicly to accuse either side for opening hostilities, but declaring an absolute arms embargo on the belligerents. B tried to influence the course of the crisis but was side-tracked by the two superpowers. B also refused the US landing-rights on B soil for the airlift of arms to Israel. B efforts to participate in the new UNEF▷ and in the Geneva Peace Conference▷ were thwarted by the superpowers and Israel. Together with France, B was responsible for the publication of the EEC▷ declaration of 6 Nov., 1973, but subsequently lost interest in a common policy when it became evident that many of the Common Market member-states (headed by West Germany) were in favour of a common front against the Arab oil▷ embargo and a common energy policy; B feared that her relatively good relations with the Arab oil producers would be harmed. Unlike France, however, B has agreed to participate in a US initiative for a common Western front to face the Arab oil producers.

(Sh.H.)

C

★CHAMOUN, CAMILLE. The Tripartite Alliance fell apart after the 1970 presidential elections in Lebanon▷. C continued his activity, in cooperation with the Phalanges▷, at times in opposition to the Government and sometimes in its support. In the 1972 parliamentary elections C's National Liberal Party lost most of its seats (11 in 1968; 2 in 1972). C adopts a rightish stand on the Palestine-Arab guerilla organizations▷. Sometimes he expresses support for them, provided it does not prejudice the sovereignty, integrity and unity of Lebanon. (H.Z.)

★CHINA. C's ME policy continued along previous lines. Diplomatic relations were established with several Arab States, and C continued to nurture connections with the Palestine-Arab guerilla organizations▷ and South Yemen▷. C attempted to exploit tensions existing between Russia▷ and Sudan▷ (1971), and between Russia and Egypt▷ (1972). (O.Y.)

★CLERIDES GLAFKOS — See Cyprus.

★COMMUNISM, COMMUNIST PARTIES IN THE ME. No essential change in the status of the CPs in the Arab world has taken place. In July 1971 the Sudan▷ CP persuaded leftist army officers▷ to carry out a *coup d'état* against the Numeiri▷ regime; after initial success, the *coup* failed and the large Sudan CP was dealt a severe blow.

In Iraq▷ a front consisting of the CP and the Ba'th▷ was formed in 1973. As in Syria▷, the CP gained a minor say in Government in return for the use of their name. In Syria, the Ba'th-CP partnership continues, on a broader basis, and the CP is presently part of the National Progressive Front. Cooperation with the Ba'th resulted in severe criticism of Bakdash▷ by radical elements within the CP, and brought it to the verge of a split. In Jordan▷, CP opponents of the traditional leader Fuad Nasser also caused a split. In Lebanon▷ the CP enjoys relative freedom since Kamal Jumblat▷ became Minister of Interior, enabling it to hold public gatherings and conventions. (O.Y.)

★CYPRUS. During 1970–3, various attempts to reconcile the Turkish and Greek communities, and within the Greek community, failed. Proposals submitted by Glafkos Clerides in Dec. 1970 and Jan. 1971 were rejected by the Turkish Cypriots. Relations between the Government and Parliament deteriorated and a crisis was prevented only by a compromise worked out by Makarios▷. UN mediation between the communities continued until it, too, reached an impasse, in Sept. 1971; both sides, however, showed an interest in the continuation of talks. Gen. Grivas▷, one-time EOKA▷ leader, secretly returned to Cyprus in late 1971, and there were rumours of a new, intense struggle between him and Makarios. Greece was opposed to the C Government's anti-Grivas measures, and arms ordered from Czechoslovakia were handed over to the UN. Makarios also agreed to some changes in

his Government, after receiving assurances that he would not be deposed by force.

In Mar. 1972 the three members of the Holy Synod of the Orthodox Church, with Greek Government backing, declared that Makarios must resign since, as an Archbishop, he could not serve as President. Makarios, supported by a majority of the Greek community, strongly resisted this move. Spiro Kyprianou, Minister for Foreign Affairs and a strong supporter of Makarios, resigned under pressure, and the new Cabinet formed in June included only three ministers carried over from the previous Government. A fourth round of intercommunal talks commenced in June 1972, mediated by UN Secretary-General Waldheim. The mandate for UNEF▷ presence in C was renewed at this time, up to Dec. 1972.

Terrorist activities initiated by Grivas occurred in 1972–3, culminating in Feb. 1973 with attacks on 18 police stations. The Minister of Justice was kidnapped in July and later released, and the threat to the Makarios regime was at its height. Makarios was re-elected as President in Feb. 1973, and the death of Grivas in early 1974 facilitated a period of relative quiet on the island. (O.Y.)

D

★DAYAN, MOSHE. D suffered a serious blow to his personal popularity and prestige as a result of the Yom Kippur War▷, and Israel▷ was seriously divided on the issue of his parliamentary responsibility for the circumstances attending the outbreak of war and his resignation as Minister of Defence. D was publicly attacked by fellow-members of the Alignment▷, and initially he declined to join the new Government formed by Golda Meir▷ in the wake of the 1973 elections. After pressure from other members of the party, including the Prime Minister, D agreed to be reappointed Minister of Defence. In Mar. 1974, the release of a partial report by a Government Commission of Enquiry into the Yom Kippur War created strong public criticism of both D and the Prime Minister, leading to the Government's resignation. (A.W.)

★DEMIREL, SÜLEYMAN. In his years as Prime Minister of Turkey▷, D did not manage to institute major changes in social legislation. His weakness allowed anarchistic groups to resume terrorist activity throughout the country. In Mar. 1971 the army leaders forced him to resign, demanding the establishment of a strong reform Government, and D was replaced by Erim▷. (D.K.)

DÉTENTE. A policy directed toward the reduction of tension between the superpowers and their allies, expressing a willingness to cooperate on matters of common interest even though the basic causes for the East-West split have not and are not likely to be eliminated. (The term détente was first applied, in both West and East, from the mid-1960s on. Previously, terms such as "peaceful coexistence" in the East, and "disengagement" in the West, were used to describe similar policies.) One of the subjects on which some measure of cooperation has been deemed necessary is the prevention of local conflicts, such as that of the ME, from developing into a confrontation between the two superpowers. Concerning the ME, D implies efforts by both the US▷ and Russia▷ to force moderation on their respective clients. Contrary to the spirit of détente, Russia took no measures to prevent the outbreak of the Yom Kippur War▷ and, on the contrary, after the commencement of hostilities continued vast shipments of arms to both Syria and Egypt. The US reaction of a massive arms airlift to Israel and the success of Israel's counter-offensive, both in the Golan▷ and on the West Bank of the Suez Canal▷, restored Soviet interest in common action with the US to stop the fighting and to bring about negotiations between the two sides. The Grade Three Alert declared for US armed forces on 25 Oct., 1973, was meant, among other purposes, to dissuade Russia from sending forces to the ME. Though the two superpowers have acted according to the rules of brinkmanship rather than the spirit of D, they have at least managed to keep each other's involvement under control.   (Sh.H.)

*DUBAI. A leading member-state of the Union of Arab Emirates▷, established in Dec. 1971. In 1970, D's population was estimated at 70,000. Its harbour, Port Rashid, has been developed into one of the ME's largest and most modern facilities. Oil▷ production stands at about 5m tons *p.a.*

In May 1971, D opened the largest and most modern air terminal in the Persian Gulf▷ area. In Dec. 1972, D left the Organization of Arab Petroleum Exporting Countries▷, in protest against its decision to build its large drydock at Bahrain▷. At the same time, D began building a drydock of its own.   (Y.K. & V.E.)

E

EASTERN FRONT. This military framework — intended to unite Arab military forces on the eastern front against Israel — never advanced beyond

planning to an operational stage. A joint command for the EF, established in southern Syria, was to control the armies of Syria▷, Iraq▷ and Jordan▷, in coordination with Egypt▷. However, this organization was eliminated in Sept. 1970 by the civil war in Jordan, even before it really came into existence; at that time, Syria and Jordan actively fought each other and the Iraqi army departed from Jordan. Since then no active steps have been taken to re-establish the EF.

On 28 Dec., 1971, Jordan's Prime Minister, Ahmad al-Lawzi▷, made establishment of the EF conditional upon placing all Arab armed forces stationed in his country under Jordanian control. Iraq did not indicate any willingness to return her troops to Jordan, and relations between Syria and Jordan were tense until mid-1973. Tensions also existed between the Ba'th▷ regimes in Syria and Iraq. All these factors rendered cooperation in an EF under a single joint command difficult.

During the Yom Kippur War▷, both Jordan and Iraq sent forces to the Syrian front in the second week of fighting. Iraq's troops left Syria upon Syria's unilateral decision to accept the cease-fire.
                                        (O.Y.)

*EBAN, ABBA. E's stand as Foreign Minister suffered a serious setback after the Yom Kippur War▷, when all but three African▷ and many Asian states severed diplomatic relations with Israel▷ despite enjoying considerable Israeli aid and technical assistance. E was reappointed Foreign Minister in Meir's▷ Government of Mar. 1974, which has since resigned.   (A.W.)

ECEVIT, BULENT. Turkish politician, Prime Minister of Turkey▷ 1974. Born in Istanbul 1925; studied at Robert College. Journalist and writer, and in 1957 became representative to the National Assembly on behalf of the Peoples Republican Party. Served in governments of Inönü▷ in 1961–5 as Minister of Labour. As leader of the left-wing of his party, E persuaded it to adopt the "left-of-centre" doctrine and became Secretary-General of the party in 1966. In 1972 E forced veteran party leader Inönü to resign and took his place. In the 1973 elections the Republic Party gained victory and, after lengthy negotiations, E formed a coalition Government with the National Security Party, in Jan. 1974.   (D.K.)

*EGYPT. Sadat's▷ policy has been marked by a pragmatism contrasting clearly with the ideological, messianic character of Nasserist▷ policy. From his rise to office, Sadat has understood E's political and economic problems, but his solutions lacked the sophistication characteristic of Nasser and his system. In public, Sadat has defined two major problems: the need to free occupied territories and the rebuilding of E. His efforts toward a political solution which would quickly return lands lost in the Six Day War▷ failed. In internal matters, he considered it his regime's central objective to reconstitute the social and economic structure of the country. Moving away from Nasserist policies, Sadat stressed E's own national and social characteristics, while abandoning the revolutionary pioneering role in the Arab world.

In July 1971 Sadat submitted a ten-year development programme to the National Congress of the Arab Socialist Union▷, designed to double the GNP. This plan emphasized the creation of more jobs for the country's increasing population, in both agriculture and industry, as well as the improvement of services. The adoption of a permanent Constitution, in Sept. 1971, was another step forward. This Constitution increases the power of the National Assembly, provides guarantees of personal freedom and establishes the independence of the judiciary.

A third stage in the liberalization process instituted by Sadat was in the sphere of banking and the finance system. This came in addition to various guarantees extended to domestic and foreign capital, and was intended to attract both foreign and Arab investors, encouraging greater activity on the part of the private sector.

The continued conflict with Israel▷ prevented the execution of many of these changes in practice, especially in connection with proposed development. Neither foreign nor Arab capital has come into Egypt in any significant quantity. Sadat became convinced that the conflict with Israel must be given top priority, and that the only solution lay in military action. This line of reasoning led him directly to the Yom Kippur War▷.   (S.L.)

*EILAT. Export and import data for 1972: 406,000 tons export; 300,000 tons import (excluding oil). The Eilat-Ashkelon oil▷ pipeline, 42 inches in diameter, has a planned capacity of 60m tons *p.a.*
(Y.K.)

EGYPTIAN ARAB REPUBLIC — See United Arab Republic.

ELIAV, ARYEH (LYOVA). Born in Moscow 1921; came to Palestine 1924; during Second World War served in the British Army. After demobilization, E was active in bringing Jewish immigrants to Palestine and commanded illegal immigrant ships. During the Arab-Israel War of 1948▷, E served in the Navy with the rank of Lieut-Col. During the 1950s, E headed the team which developed the Lakhish and Arad districts. During the Sinai Campaign▷, E commanded an operation to rescue the Jewish population of Port Sa'id▷. First Secretary of the Israel Embassy in Russia 1958–60; member of *Knesset* since 1965; Deputy Minister of Commerce and Industry, and later of Absorption. In 1966–71, E was Secretary-General of the Alignment▷.

After the Six Day War▷, E formed a plan for the solution of the Arab-Israel Conflict▷ in a spirit of compromise and recognition of the existence of a Palestine Entity▷. A prominent leader of the "dove" element in Israel, E published his views in a book in 1972, leading to much public debate.
(E.A.)

*ENOSIS. This slogan of Cypriot union with Greece reappeared with the return of Gen. Grivas▷ to Cyprus▷ in late 1971. Since his death early in 1974, pressure for E has weakened, at least for the present.   (O.Y.)

*EOKA. This Cypriot underground organization resumed its activities after the return of Gen. Grivas▷ to the island in late 1971. His supporters reorganized and commenced large-scale terrorist activities against the authorities, reaching a peak during Feb. 1973 when 18 police stations over the island were blown up. This posed a serious threat to Government authority. Among other activities, Grivas' men kidnapped the Minister of Justice, in July 1973. After Grivas' death, early in 1974, relative quiet returned to the island, due to confusion among the terrorist ranks.   (O.Y.)

ERIM, NIHAT. Turkish politician and jurisprudent; Prime Minister 1971–2. Born 1912 in north-western Anatolia; studied law in Istanbul and Paris, and held the position of Professor of Law at Ankara▷ University. Elected in 1945 to the National Assembly as representative of the Republican Party, and appointed to several ministerial posts. After the Democrats came to power in 1950, E returned to teaching, though he continued party activity and represented Turkey▷ at international organizations and conferences. Appointed Prime Minister in Mar. 1971, following an ultimatum by the army chiefs, which resulted in the fall of the Demirel▷ Government. E resigned from his party and formed a coalition Government with a wide basis, composed partly of independent experts. The Government succeeded, to a certain extent, in reducing the anarchy which prevailed as a result of terrorist activities, but failed to realize its social-economic reform plans. E resigned in April 1972.

(D.K.)

ERITREA. The rise of the Numeiri▷ regime in Sudan▷ appears to be connected with the intensification of the activities of the E Liberation Front. Serious fighting was reported during the rainy seasons (May–Sept.) of 1969 and 1970. According to Radio Damascus in mid-May 1970, the Ethiopian▷ Government was forced to send the Imperial Guard to E, where it lost 200 soldiers in one battle with the Front. Drastic retaliatory action resulted in a flow of Eritrean refugees to Sudan. During this period offices of the Front were opened in Aden, Baghdad, Beirut, Khartoum and Mogadisho, in addition to the original office in Damascus. Since 1970, Libya▷ has taken first place in supporting the efforts of the Front, at the same time undermining the senior status of Ethiopia within the Organization of African Unity▷. However, it appears that the decisive role was played by neighbouring Sudan, though since settlement of the southern Sudan problem, in Mar. 1972, the Front has apparently received little active support from Khartoum.

A spokesman for the Front claimed that between April and Sept. 1973, his forces had carried out regular actions against the "occupying forces" and had succeeded in killing an Ethiopian colonel. The Secretary-General, Osman Saleh, continued his activities under the Libyan aegis, mainly from the stage of the Fourth Conference of Muslim Foreign Ministers, held in Tripoli▷ in May 1973.   (H.E.)

ETHIOPIA. Following the Yom Kippur War▷, E broke off diplomatic relations with Israel▷ in an attempt to preserve her status in Africa▷. E tried to preserve her relations with her Muslim neighbours, despite Libyan▷ attempts to undermine her position. It is as yet not possible to determine whether this has influenced the aid given by the Muslim states to subversive activities in Eritrea▷. The fact that Somalia▷ has joined the Arab League▷, in early 1974, has not improved chances for neighbourly relations in the Horn of Africa.

The undermining of the stability of the Emperor's rule, in Feb. 1974, raises the question of the future of Eritrea in consequence of a possible change of regime in E. Whatever the developments, it must be borne in mind that much of the struggle against the central Government is based on tribal–ethnic, rather than religious or national, motives; and that over half of the population in Eritrea is Christian Tigrine.   (H.E.)

EUROPEAN ECONOMIC COMMUNITY. The ME was a prime political problem for which the EEC attempted to formulate a common foreign policy. Following the Yom Kippur War▷ the EEC sought to convince the Arab oil▷ producing countries to lift their partial embargo on oil shipments to Western Europe. This resulted in a joint declaration published on 6 Nov., 1973, generally considered to be pro-Arab since it implied total Israeli withdrawal from the occupied territories, and mentioned the "legitimate rights of the Palestinians". The declaration was welcomed by the Arabs, but Israel argued that it made no attempt to encourage negotiations between the two sides. The declaration was not followed by any concrete common policy, due mainly to differences of opinion and the tendency of France▷ and Britain▷ to be uncooperative on questions connected with oil supply.

During 1969–72, economic ties between the EEC and the countries of the ME constituted some 7% of the EEC's world total (5% in 1969). The rise in ME imports from the EEC is especially conspicuous, in 1972, more than $8,135m, and ME exports to the EEC stood at $4,646m ($2,620m imports and $5,154 m exports in 1969). EEC exports to the ME constituted some 4.9% of the EEC's total in 1972. EEC exports to the Arab countries rose to 3% of the annual exports; Israel▷ absorbed over 0.65% of the EEC exports and Iran▷ and Turkey▷ absorbed over 1.2%. An increase in the importance of Israel and the Arab countries to the EEC lie in the absorption of its commodities, as opposed to no change in the relative importance of Iran and Turkey. From the point of view of the ME countries, the EEC supplied some 34% of their annual imports in 1972 (as against 39% in 1969).

In 1972 the EEC supplied some 32% of the total annual imports of the Arab countries (as against 30% in 1969), compared with Israel, Iran and Turkey who imported more than 35% of their total annual imports from the EEC (as against 31% in 1969).

EEC imports from the ME rose to 8.5% of overall EEC imports in 1972, largely due to a steady rise in the purchase of oil▷. The Arab countries supplied approximately 6.8% of the overall EEC imports in 1972, as against 0.3% supplied by Israel and approximately 1.4% supplied by Iran and Turkey. In 1972 the Arab countries exported some 44% of their total annual export to the EEC (as against 41% in 1969), compared with Israel, Iran and Turkey which exported over 32% of their annual exports to the EEC (as against more than 33⅓% in 1969).

The EEC continued its contacts with the ME countries, signing agreements and/or trade arrangements:

(a) Five-year preference agreements were signed with Israel, Egypt and Lebanon, by which mutual customs rebates were granted. The EEC granted customs rebates of 40–50% on various industrial commodities and 25–40% on agricultural produce, compared with customs rebates of 40–50% granted by the three countries to the EEC.

(b) Arrangements were made with Iran according to which exports to the EEC would not suffer. This was a change on the part of the EEC for, up to Nov. 1973, there had been opposition to granting of appreciable customs rebates on various Iranian goods. In early Feb. 1974, negotiations were still underway between the EEC and Iran on a new trade agreement.   (Sh.H. & M.E.)

F

FAHMY, ISMA'IL. Egyptian Foreign Minister since Nov. 1973. Born in Cairo 1922; graduated from Cairo University 1945; joined staff of Foreign Office; served at UN as head of Department on International Institutions 1964, and as Chairman of Political Committee of General Assembly 1967. Ambassador to Austria 1968; Deputy Foreign Minister 1968. In May 1969 F was suspended from office following a wave of criticism directed at him after *al-Ahram*▷ had conducted a symposium strongly criticizing Russia's▷ policy in the ME. After Russian technical and military advisers were expelled from Egypt▷ in July 1972, F was reinstated and became Minister of Tourism (Mar. 1973). During the Yom Kippur War▷, F was acting Foreign Minister, al-Zayyat▷ being then abroad.

In Feb. 1974, F took on the job of President's Secretary of Information. Today F is considered to be one of the rising stars in Sadat's▷ Government, representing liberal, pro-Western orientation in Egypt.   (Al.S.)

★FATAH. Among the F leaders who died or were killed in recent years are Memduh Sadam ("Abu Sabri"), the military boss; Najjar Yussuf ("Abu Yussuf"), head of intelligence and responsible for cells in Lebanon▷; Kamal 'Adwan, in charge of activities within the Israel-occupied territories; and 'Abd-ul-Fatah 'Isa Hamoud.

Since 1971 there has been a behind-the-scenes struggle in the F leadership. Despite minor insurrections and revolts, a true rift was avoided thanks to the leaders' flexibility and the intentional obscurity

surrounding all questions of a problematic or political nature.   (E.Y.)

★FAWZI, MAHMOUD. Served as Prime Minister of Egypt▷ till Jan. 1972, at which time he was appointed Vice-President.   (S.L.)

★FEDERATION OF ARAB REPUBLICS. One of several attempts to achieve Arab unity▷, and appears to be in force till now. The FAR agreement was signed in Benghazi on 17 April, 1971, the signatories being the Presidents of Egypt▷, Syria▷ and Libya▷. The Sudan▷ President took part in the initial deliberations, but withdrew on 14 April. The political background for the alliance was the Tripoli▷ Agreement of Dec. 1969, wherein Egypt, Libya and Sudan declared their intention of deepening the collaboration between them with the purpose of future unification.

While Nasser▷ ruled Egypt, little was done to change Egypt's relations with Sudan and Libya. When Sadat▷ came to power, however, the situation changed; and on 8 Nov., 1970, Egypt, Sudan and Libya signed a declaration "toward the establishment of a tripartite federation". After Asad▷ took over in Syria he, too, signed this declaration.

Egypt's entry into the FAR led to a Government crisis, solved only upon the expulsion of the Sabri▷-Gum'a-Sharaf▷ faction from the Government.

In Aug. 1971, Syrian, Egyptian and Libyan representatives met in Damascus to forge the FAR Constitution. It was approved in the three countries in plebiscites held on 1 Sept., 1971. So far, this Constitution has provided for a common Presidential Council, whose members are the Presidents of the three countries, with Egypt's ruler as Council President. There is a federated government, sitting in Cairo, and whose Prime Minister is a Syrian statesman, al-Khatib▷. This government has as yet no real authority, being more of a representational body than anything else. There is also a People's Federal Council, a body of 60 members with 20 representatives from each member-state; this Council, also sitting in Cairo, is chaired by a somewhat obscure Libyan.

Despite the various economic and technical agreements, the FAR is not yet viable, due to substantial political differences separating its leaders. Thus, the Presidential Council does not convene regularly; no Federal Court has been established; and the three member-states have yet to decide on a common foreign and domestic policy.   (Al.S.)

★FEISAL b. 'ABD-UL-'AZIZ. F's prestige in

the Arab world increased after he began collaborating with Sadat▷ and Asad▷, particularly in 1973, during which he sharply denounced Israel▷ and Zionism▷. Putting an oil embargo into effect against the US increased F's importance — quite out of proportion to his role in Arab international relations or in the Arab-Israel Conflict▷.   (O.Y.)

*FOREIGN ECONOMIC AID. During 1970–3 the nations of the ME received more than $4,100m in economic aid from other nations, in the form of grants and credit. Of this total, more than $2,000m came from Western countries (OECD in the table below); more than $1,900m came from countries of the Soviet bloc, and more than $130m came from China▷. These figures are based on a study of the various agreements and assurances made regarding economic aid; fulfilment was not always identical with the promises — especially where the Communist states are concerned; various estimates rate Communist aid at about a third of the pledges in 1970–3.   (M.E.)

*FOUR-POWER TALKS. The activity of this forum has ceased and the initiative towards a solution in the ME has passed almost entirely into the hands of the US, especially after the appointment of Kissinger▷ as Secretary of State.

*FRAMJIYEH, SULEIMAN. During his term as Lebanese▷ President, F leaned heavily on the support of the Central (Parliamentary) Bloc, manoeuvring between the Right faction and the (former) Shihabists▷. The basis of his political power is broader than that of his predecessor, Helou▷, and the Presidency has been strengthened under his rule.   (O.Y.)

*FRANCE. F efforts to get the EEC▷ to formulate a joint ME policy in 1971 failed because of internal disagreement and US hostility. When the Yom Kippur War▷ broke out, F did not hide her pro-Arab position. However, all of F's efforts to influence the development of the crisis came to nothing. The fighting did not prevent F from sending arms to

GOVERNMENTAL ECONOMIC AID* TO ME COUNTRIES 1970–3 (IN $ MILLIONS)

	Countries extending aid					
	OECD States		Soviet bloc			
Countries receiving aid	Total	US share	Total	USSR share	Red China	General total
Non-Arab states						
Iran	393	202	369	—	—	762
Israel	727	668	—	—	—	726
Turkey	326	27	—	—	—	326
TOTALS	1,445	897	369	—	—	1,814
Arab states						
Egypt	111	—	533	313	—	644
Iraq	145	—	731	385	40	916
Jordan	165	45	—	—	—	165
Lebanon	14	3	—	—	—	14
South Yemen	—	—	77	36	43	120
Sudan	86	14	108	40	35	229
Syria	54	—	105	—	14	173
Yemen	28	—	15	15	—	43
TOTALS	640**	62	1,569	789	132	2,341**
ME TOTALS	2,085**	959	1,938	789	132	4,155**

*   Including loans and grants from governments, banks and other governmental instutions.
**   Including $37m granted to the Persian Gulf principalities by OECD nations.

Arab states who were officially non-belligerents (even after Israel claimed to have shot down several Libyan▷ Mirage aircraft over Sinai). When the Arab oil▷ embargo was declared, F was singled out for preferential treatment for her "friendly" policy. However, F did not succeed in breaking the monopoly of the superpowers in managing the crisis. Israeli, as well as US and Soviet, opposition ensured that F troops would not participate in the new UNEF▷. F was also not invited to participate at the Geneva Peace Conference▷. Her efforts, together with Britain▷, to get the EEC to follow her own pro-Arab policy merely resulted in the declaration of 6 Nov., 1973, which — though regarded as anti-Israel by the Israelis and by the Arabs as a step in the right direction — was not followed up.

F has argued that the Geneva Peace Conference and the Separation of Forces Agreement▷ will not lead to a satisfactory solution. Since Sec. 1973, F has reached special agreements with both Sa'udi Arabia▷ and Libya, by which F will receive fixed quantities of oil in exchange for military equipment and sophisticated technological aid.   (Sh.H.)

*FUJAIRA. A member of the Union' of Arab Emirates. Population: *c.* 10,000.   (Y.K.)

G

*GAHAL. After leaving the National Unity Government, G returned to the opposition. G lost some ground to Shmuel Tamir, whose Free Centre attacked it for being passive *vis-à-vis* Government policy. When Maj. Gen. (Res.) Ariel Sharon initiated contacts that were to lead to the establishment of the *Likud▷*, tensions developed between Herut▷ and the Liberal faction within G, Begin▷ and his associates opposing the creation of the broader framework. These disagreements finally were settled and in the summer of 1973 the *Likud* came into existence, incorporating G, the Free Centre, the State List and the Land of Israel Movement▷. G remained the dominant element within the *Likud*, providing the majority of its representatives in the *Knesset* elected on 31 Dec., 1973. (O.Y.)

GALILI, ISRAEL. Born in Russia 1911; came to Palestine 1914. A founder of the *No'ar 'Oved* youth movement and of Kibbutz Na'an, to which he still belongs. One of the heads of the Haganah▷ prior to the State of Israel. After the split of Mapai▷ in 1944, G was among the leaders of *Ahduth Ha'avodah▷*, and when that party joined *Hashomer*

Hatzair in 1948 to form the United Workers' Party *(Mapam▷)*. G was one of its outstanding personalities. When *Mapam* split, in 1954, G became Secretary-General of *Ahduth Ha'avodah*. G has been *Knesset* member since 1949, and joined the Cabinet as Minister without Portfolio in 1965. G has generally been considered to be one of those determining Israel's▷ foreign and defence policies and a close confidant of Prime Minister Golda Meir▷.

When conflict within the Alignment▷ intensified during the summer of 1973, in connection with the formulation of the party's platform for the upcoming elections, G formulated a document later adopted by the party Secretariat. This "G document" states principles of action in the occupied territories. When the Alignment came to decide on its election platform after the Yom Kippur War▷, it decided on Fourteen Points.   (E.A.)

GAMASY, AL-, 'ABD-UL-GHANI. Since Dec. 1973, Chief of Staff of the Egyptian Army, promoted to Lieut.-Gen. on 19 Feb., 1974. Born 1921; graduated from Military Academy 1939; completed Staff and Command School 1950; studied in US, Russia and at the Nasser Academy 1966. Maj.-Gen. 1965. Military posts included command of an armoured brigade, staff officer at General Staff and with field formations. Appointed Head of Operations Section 1972, in which position G prepared plans for the Yom Kippur War▷.

G came to be known abroad when he represented Egypt▷ at the discussions with Gen. Yariv▷ at Kilometre 101▷.

In his present post, G replaced the Egyptian Yom Kippur War Chief of Staff, Sa'd al-Din al-Shadhili.   (Al.S.)

*GAZA STRIP. Terrorist activity reached its peak in late 1970 and early 1971 in the GS; in 1971 the IDF launched a systematic effort to stamp this activity out, including the stationing of additional troops in the area, the opening of new access roads in the refugee▷ camps and the relocation of thousands of refugees. On 23 Sept., 1971, Rashad al-Shawa was appointed Mayor of Gaza town, and in Mar. 1972 civil administration of the GS was separated from the military. Several paramilitary *Nahal* settlements have been established in the GS, and relative calm has come to the area for the first time since 1967. Al-Shawa was forced to resign on 22 Oct., 1972, because of his opposition to the military administration. New plans for the large-scale transfer of refugees from the GS camps to other areas were initiated late in 1972. During the

Yom Kippur War▷, a state of relative calm prevailed in the GS and the population remained passive.   (O.Y.)

✱GEMAYEL (JUMAYYIL), PIERRE. Re-elected President of the Phalange▷, in Nov. 1971, G has maintained his support of the traditional institutions and policies in Lebanon▷. This was manifested primarily in G's insistence on a strong Lebanese position *vis-à-vis* the Palestinian Arab guerilla organizations▷ active on and operating from Lebanese territory.   (O.Y.)

GENEVA CONVENTIONS. A series of four multilateral treaties for the protection of war victims, signed in Geneva on 12 Aug., 1949, the first three of which had previous versions.

Both Israel and her Arab neighbours have often accused each other of contravening the letter of the GC. Following the Six Day War▷, Israel was accused of breaking several articles in the Fourth Convention (dealing with the protection of civilian persons in time of war) and in particular articles 49 (deportations from occupied territories) and 53 (destruction of property belonging to inhabitants of occupied territories).

Following the Yom Kippur War▷, Israel accused Syria and Egypt of actions contrary to the Third Convention (treatment of prisoners of war), citing the following articles in particular: 13 (humane treatment of prisoners). 110 (immediate repatriation of seriously wounded or ill prisoners of war), 118 (speedy release and repatriation of prisoners of war after cessation of active hostilities), 122 (prompt publication of lists of prisoners), 126 (visits to prisoners and their places of internment by represent-atives of the International Committee of the Red Cross▷). Syria, in turn, accused Israel of breaking article 17 of the First Convention (relief of wounded and sick in armies in the field), in connection with the burial of soldiers killed in action.   (Sh.H.)

GENEVA PEACE CONFERENCE (officially, "Peace Conference on the Middle East"). Ever since the end of the Arab-Israel War of 1948▷, Israel has called for direct negotiations with the Arab States, prerequisite to a peace treaty. The Arab States persistantly refused such negotiations with Israel, to end the state of belligerency or to recognize the State of Israel.

UN Security Council Resolution 338▷, calling for a cease-fire to end the Yom Kippur War▷, also called for negotiations "between the parties con-cerned under appropriate auspices aimed at establish-ing a just and durable peace in the ME". Egypt and Jordan finally agreed to participate in an official peace conference with Israel on condition that other states would be present and discussions would not be direct. They explained the purpose of the con-ference as a means to obtain Israeli withdrawal from occupied Arab territories. Syria refused to participate, while Israel stated that it should not sit with Syria unless the latter published the lists of Israeli POWs taken during the Yom Kippur War and allowed rep-resentatives of the Red Cross to visit them. The Arab States wanted Britain▷ and France▷ to be invited but neither Israel nor the superpowers agreed. Nor were representatives of the Palestine Arabs▷ invited. The opening session of the GPC took place at the Council Chamber of the Palais des Nations in Geneva on 21 Dec., 1973. The Secretary-General of the UN, Kurt Waldheim, took the chair with the Foreign Ministers of the two superpowers acting as co-chairmen. Due to Arab opposition to sit with Israel at a round-table the participating delegations sat at separate tables arranged in hexagonal pattern, with one table left empty for the Syrian delegation. Under the full blaze of television cameras and the press, the six participants made opening speeches. Following the ceremonial opening the conference was adjourned "until after the *Knesset* elections in Israel". An Egyptian-Israel Military Committee began meeting in Geneva on 26 Dec., 1973, under the chairmanship of Gen. Siilasvuo▷, to discuss separation of forces, but the final agreement on this subject was reached elsewhere, through the diplo-matic efforts of Kissinger▷. The GPC is a definite departure from the course of the ME conflict in the past.   (Sh.H.)

✱GERMANY. Since 1969, the West German Government headed by Willi Brandt, with Free Democrat Walter Scheel as Foreign Minister, has tried to carry out an even-handed policy in the ME. By mid-1972 the Federal Republic had re-established diplomatic relations with most of the Arab States. During visits to Israel▷, by Scheel in 1971 and by Brandt in June 1973, the two statesmen tried to emphasize the normalcy of G-Israel relations. However, Israel has refused to recognize the term "normal" as applicable or acceptable in describing relations between the two nations.

Since 1970 G has been the scene of two murderous attacks by Palestine-Arab guerillas▷, one at Munich airport in Feb. 1970, and the other during the Munich Olympic Games in Sept. 1972, when 11 Israeli sportsmen were murdered. West German aircraft and passengers have been involved in several hijackings by Palestinian terrorists and the G Government has tended to accede to demands of hijackers on each occasion.

During the Yom Kippur War▷, G declared neutrality but refrained from public objection to the US arms-lift, part of which took off from US bases in G, until after the cease-fire. The Federal Republic signed the EEC▷ declaration of 6 Nov., 1973, but unlike Britain▷ and France▷ has strongly supported a common European energy policy and has been much more wary of submitting to the Arab oil▷ embargo.   (Sh.H.)

★GEZIRA. Syria's▷ oil▷ fields are located in the north-eastern part of the G. In 1972 these produced 5.72m tons of crude oil. Development of the G will greatly be furthered by the completion of a railroad from the port of Lataqia▷, through Aleppo to Deir al-Zor and Qamishliye.   (O.T.)

★GOLAN, GOLAN HEIGHTS. Since the area came under Israeli control, in consequence of the Six Day War▷, 14 agricultural settlements have been established there, partly of a paramilitary nature. During the Yom Kippur War▷ the Syrian▷ army initially overran part of the GH, but was repulsed during the second stage of fighting. Israel forces also expanded the area under their control in the north by some 20 km, to the peak of Mount Hermon and to near the Sa‘sa crossroads.   (Y.K.)

★GRIVAS, GEN. GEORGE. Returned secretly to Cyprus▷ at the end of 1971. His supporters then renewed terrorist activity, posing a very real threat to the regime of Makarios▷. G's death, early in 1974, was followed by the first period of relative quiet on the island in over two years.   (O.Y.)

GROMYKO, ANDREI ANDREYEVICH. Born 1909. Foreign Minister of Russia▷ since 1957 and one of the architects of Soviet ME policy, G has held ranking posts in the Soviet Foreign Ministry since 1930. On the international scene, G's first ranking post was as head of the delegation to the Dumbarton Oaks Conference in 1944, when the decision to establish the UN was taken. In 1945 G participated in the Yalta and Potsdam Conferences, where Europe's post-Second World War map was drawn, and in the UN Founding Conference at San Francisco. In 1946–8, G was permanent Soviet delegate on the Security Council and in this capacity he delivered the address expressing Soviet support for the establishment of a Jewish State in Israel. Under Khrushchev, G represented the USSR at many international gatherings and accompanied his leaders on important trips abroad, such as the visit to Britain with

Bulganin in 1956, and the meeting with Kennedy in 1961.

G frequently met with Nasser▷ in the early 1960s and visited the ME shortly before the Six Day War▷. He played an active role in negotiations with the US on the cease-fire in the Yom Kippur War▷. G has visited the ME several times since then, apparently in an effort to crystallize Soviet policy in this area.   (Am.S.)

H

★HABASH, DR. GEORGE. After the Yom Kippur War▷, H followed an extremist line in opposition to any agreement with Israel. He opposed the cease-fire, the Geneva Peace Converence▷ and the Separation of Forces Agreements▷, calling for continued armed conflict, with or without the support of the Arab governments.   (E.Y.)

HADDAM, ‘ABD-UL-HALIM. Deputy Prime Minister and Foreign Minister of Syria▷. One of the leaders of the Ba‘th▷ party's civilian section. Previously, H held various lower party posts, also serving as the Damascus District Commissioner.
                                         (O.Y.)

★HADHRAMAUT. Ever since the independence of the Republic of South Yemen▷, H has been a hotbed of revolt against the new regime. Leftist extremists with pro-China▷ tendencies managed to strike root in the area, especially in the port of Mukalla, to conduct propaganda and engage in confiscation and nationalization activities. All this was supported by Chinese influence, reaching H mainly by way of Zanzibar, where a large H community lives.

Such Leftist activity led to conflicts with the central Government in Aden▷, in Mar.-June 1968 and the first half of 1969, resulting even in armed uprisings. These were supported partly by the Popular Front for the Liberation of Oman▷, active in the Dhofar▷ region; factions of the rebellion also joined with tribal uprisings elsewhere in the country. The unrest resulted in changes of governors and the despatch of army units loyal to the Government, in turn leading to friction with local tribal armed forces.   (T.Y.)

★HAFEZ, AMIN. Exiled from Syria▷; connected with the Iraqi▷ Ba‘th▷ party. Sentenced to death *in absentia* in Aug. 1971, by the Syrian Supreme Court of State Security, for having conspired with Iraqi help against the Syrian regime. Later

this sentence was reduced to life imprisonment.
(O.T.)

HA'OLAM HAZEH — KOAH HADASH (MERI). This party split in 1972, when Shalom Cohen left it and joined up with the Black Panthers▷ Uri Avneri, head of the list, was not re-elected in the Dec. 1973 *Knesset* election; for the first time since 1965 the party remained without *Knesset* representation.   (O.Y.)

*HASHEMITES. In the course of his armed conflict with the Palestinian-Arab guerilla organizations▷, Hussein▷ enjoyed the confidence of the entire H family. During his absence in Jan. 1971, his brother Hasan (Crown Prince) carried on the struggle with full H support. However, this unanimity did not last, since some family members failed to agree with Hussein's attempts to make peace with the Palestinians. According to some reports, some members of the royal family criticized the Mar. 1972 plan for federation, as well as Hussein's marriage to a daughter of the Touqan▷ family, resulting in some tension. Hussein's father Talal▷, hospitalized in a mental institution in Turkey, died in July 1972.   (O.Y.)

HATIM, DR. 'ABD-UL-QADIR. Deputy Prime Minister of Egypt▷ and Minister of Information. Also appointed Chairman of the Board of Directors of the *al-Ahram*▷ Publishing House when Heykal▷ was removed from that position, on 1 Feb., 1974. Born in 1917, H was one of the Free Officers who deposed King Farouq▷. Graduated from Military College 1939; completed Staff Officers' Training 1952. In 1947 H obtained a degree in Political Economy (B.A.) from the University of London, and in 1953 in Political Science (M.A.) and in Information Science (Ph.D.) from Cairo University.

When the Free Officers first assumed power, H became Nasser's▷ Assistant for Press Affairs. Leaving the army in 1957 with the rank of Colonel, H became member of the National Assembly. In 1959 H was appointed State Minister for Information and Broadcasting; in 1962 H was appointed Deputy Prime Minister for Culture, National Guidance and Tourism. A year later H became member of the Secretariat of the Arab Socialist Union▷.

H returned to high Government office in May 1971, when the 'Ali Sabri▷ group was deposed; he was given the position of Deputy Prime Minister and Minister of Information. H is considered a moderate nationalist who favours Pan-Arab▷ policies.   (Al.S.)

HAWATMA, NAIF. Leader of the Popular Democratic Front for the Liberation of Palestine (PDFLP)▷, an extremist terrorist organization established after H and his Leftist adherents were expelled from the Popular Front for the Liberation of Palestine (PFLP)▷ in Feb. 1969. A Christian born in Jordan, H is a Marxist and was an active member of the *Kawmiyun al-Arab* movement, in which he led the Left wing since the early 1960s. The disagreements between Left and Right were taken into the PFLP, with its establishment in 1967 under the leadership of Dr. George Habash▷. The open break came about a year later and H set up his own organization, holding Marxist opinions and extremist in relation to the Arab-Israel Conflict▷. In recent years the PDFLP has not carried out much terrorist activity, its main distinction being ideological innovation. Conflict between H and Habash has been bitter, H threatening the latter's standing as main rival to 'Arafat▷. H has criticized 'Arafat frequently for his dependence on the Arab governments, and was trying to develop an independent ideological line concerning Israel▷ in the wake of the Yom Kippur War▷.   (O.Y.)

HAYTHAM, MUHAMMAD 'ALI. Politician in South Yemen▷, member of the Central Committee of the NLP▷. About 40, formerly a school teacher. Appointed Minister of Interior in Qahtan al-Sha'bi's▷ Government in 1967, remaining in this post until dismissed by al-Sha'bi in 1969 for his links with the extreme Leftist wing of the party. When al-Sha'bi was overthrown, in June 1969, H became Prime Minister; in Dec. 1969 he became one of the three members of the Presidential Council, and since Sept. 1970 is Deputy Chairman of this body. In Jan. 1970 H became a member of the party's Executive Committee; a year later he also took over the Foreign Ministry. In Aug. 1971 H was deprived of his Government positions, in consequence of differences of opinion among the ruling group.   (T.Y.)

*HEYKAL, MUHAMMAD HASSANEIN. Under Sadat▷, H lost much of the influence and standing he had possessed under Nasser▷. H never concealed his opinion that Sadat was not a suitable heir to Nasser's mantle, though he supported Sadat against 'Ali Sabri▷ in 1971. H did not hesitate to express his disagreements with Sadat publicly and several times published articles giving his independent opinions on international policies, Israel▷, the superpowers and inter-Arab relations. This led Sadat to make it clear that H did not necessarily represent the regime; at the same time he encouraged

H's veteran rival, Ihsan 'Abd-ul-Qudus▷, editor of *Akhbar al-Yawm*.

On 1 Feb., 1974, Sadat fired H from the post of Editor of *al-Ahram*▷, after that paper had carried signed editorials critical of Sadat's policy on Israel (Separation of Forces Agreement▷) and on rapprochement with the US. He appointed H as his Assistant for Press Affairs, a post devoid of all authority. H also stopped publishing his weekly column "Frankly Speaking", which had appeared for years. In spite of all, many believe that H's departure from *al-Ahram* does not yet mark the end of his journalistic career.   (O.G.)

*HIJAZ RAILWAY. In April 1970, the Supreme Committee for the Rehabilitation of the HR convened in 'Amman. with the participation of transportation ministers from Syria, Jordan and Sa'udi Arabia. Apparently this gathering had no practical results, and except for such occasional talks, nothing has been done to rebuild the destroyed sections of the railway.   (T.Y.)

*HOURANI, AL-, AKRAM. H's faction has participated in the Syrian▷ regime and was represented in the Government since Asad▷ came to power in Nov. 1970. However, H himself did not return to Syria and was not given any official position.   (O.T.)

*HOVEYDA, AMIR 'ABBAS. Prime Minister of Iran▷ since 26 Jan, 1965 — a period longer than that of any of his 38 predecessors since the beginning of Constitutional Government in the country, around the turn of the century. H's success results from the Shah's full confidence in him and the close cooperation between them. His ability to put into practice the principles of the Shah's "White Revolution" has also earned him the support of his party.   (D.M.)

*HUDEIDA. Its importance as a port city has led H to be developed intensively. The town's significance, for both Yemen's▷ economy and global strategy, is likely to increase once the Suez Canal▷ is reopened.   (H.E.)

*HUSSEIN b. TALAL. H emerged from the 1970 civil war as sole ruler of Jordan▷, but remained isolated in the Arab world. His most important problems were the restoration of public security, pacification of the Palestinians on both sides of the River Jordan and breaking out of his isolation in the Arab world. His measures included the Mar. 1972 proposal for a federation between the West and East Banks of the Jordan, and his marriage to a daughter of the Touqan▷ family of Nablus▷. The Yom Kippur War▷ and attempts to find a political solution to the Arab-Israel Conflict▷ again posed difficult problems for H. Arab recognition of the PLO▷ as the only legitimate representative of the Palestinians constituted a blow to H's standing and to the stability of his regime.   (O.Y.)

HUSSEIN, SADAM. — See Tikriti, Al-, Sadam Hussein.

*HUSSEINI, AL-, HAJJ (MUHAMMAD) AMIN. In recent years a resident of Beirut and completely inactive in Palestinian politics. The Hashemite regime in Jordan▷ made several unsuccessful attempts to use him as counterweight to Shuqeiri▷and, later, to 'Arafat▷.   (O.Y.)

I

*INDIA. After the decline of the Neutralist bloc's international standing, I's ME policy was motivated primarily by the desire to win Arab support for its struggle against Pakistan▷. India was disappointed in this respect during its war with Pakistan in Dec. 1971: Jordan and Libya extended aid to Pakistan, although Soviet aircraft were ferried to I by way of Egypt. The Indian disappointment did not result in any change of its ME policy.   (O.Y.)

*INDUSTRIALIZATION. During 1968–73, the process of industrialization in the ME continued at an increased pace. During the same period there was a slow development, or perhaps even a complete standstill, in agriculture, and accelerated development within the services sectors. This was reflected both in the growth of the industrial labour force (a fact which itself required larger scale investments than in the past), and in the percentage of the GNP accounted for by industry, not only in the oil▷ producing countries, but also in other ME nations.

In 1973 the industrial labour force totalled more than 3.25m (as against 2.5m in 1968). Industry (excluding oil) accounted for less than 12% of the GNP of Libya▷, Jordan▷, Iraq▷, Sa'udi Arabia▷ and Sudan▷ in 1973, as against 16–23% in Turkey▷, Lebanon▷, Syria▷, Israel▷ and Egypt.   (M.E.)

*İNÖNÜ, ISMET. The increasing influence of the left-wing leader of the Republican People's Party, Ecevit Bulent▷, resulted in I's resignation from the party presidency and his complete resignation of the party in 1972. Inönü died in 1973.   (D.K.)

INTERNATIONALIZATION. In terms of international law, an internationalized territory is either one which has a special status and regime created for it by multilateral treaty while an international organization becomes responsible for its protection, or is given to the administration of an international organization or an organ thereof.

According to the Sykes-Picot Agreement▷ of 1916, Palestine▷ was to have come under an arrangement of the former variety. The latter status was proposed for Jerusalem▷ by the UN Partition Plan of 1947, and again in 1950 by the Trusteeship Council of the UN. Neither plan was implemented though the I of Jerusalem is still officially supported by many states, and most vigorously by various Christian Churches who would rather have the Holy Places▷ of Christianity outside the territory of the Arab-Israel Conflict▷.

After the Yom Kippur War▷, a suggestion was raised to internationalize the Sinai Peninsula▷, but this is unlikely to be accepted as a solution by Egypt▷, who claims full sovereignty over the area.
(Sh.H.)

IQBAL, DR. MANOUCHEHR. Still serving in early 1974 as Chairman of the Board of Directors of the National Iranian Oil Company. His position within the company and the importance of oil▷ in politics make his function one of the most important in present-day Iran▷.   (D.M.)

IRAN. POLITICAL HISTORY: The centrepiece of the Shah's policy in I is implementation of the overall economic and social revolution known as the "White Revolution" or "Revolution of the Shah and the People". The revolution, the six original stages of which were implemented in Jan. 1963, strives for the realization from above of far-reaching reforms which will result in bridging the gap between I and the developed countries. In recent years the Shah has been successful in restraining the opposition of the landowners by a policy of creating conditions for their participation in the revolution and of Government incentive for investment of their money in new industrial projects. The Shah adopted a policy of co-existence with religious circles by leaving them complete freedom in religious affairs. The Shah also emphasizes that the White Revolution derives its inspiration from the sources of Islam▷. The ability to control this opposition and the primary achievements of the White Revolution resulted in further consolidation of the Shah's position. In Oct. 1967 this was expressed by his formal coronation, after 26 years of *de facto* rule. In Oct. 1971 splendid ceremonies were held

in celebration of 2,500 years of the Iranian dynasty, with a two-fold objective: demonstration of I's power to the outside world with emphasis on achievements during the rule of the Shah, and a display before the people of the history of their country to encourage cooperation in the progress of I toward reoccupying "the place she deserves among the world's family of nations". From the Shah's point of view this was an opportunity to display the achievements of his country before the world and the people, and to portray himself as the successor of Xerxes the Great. World press reaction to the celebrations, however, was not favourable.

Along with consolidation of his personal position there has been in recent years increased opposition from the Left aimed at the White Revolution and at the Shah. The tough stand adopted against them by the Institute for National Security has forced them to transfer their bases of activity outside I. Their main activity is within the framework of the Confederation of Iranian Students Abroad.

POLICY AND GOVERNMENT: Simultaneously with the consolidation of his personal position, the Shah was also active in consolidating the foundations of his Government, while encouraging the activities of the political parties. The Shah is striving to give his country the image of a constitutional monarchy with elements of a parliamentary democracy. The activities of political parties are legal and even receive encouragement, provided they accept the principles of the White Revolution.

In the 1971 elections the ruling party, *Iran Novin*▷ ("New Iran") won 229 seats in the *Majlis* (Lower Assembly) out of a total of 268 seats, and 27 out of the 30 elected seats in the Senate (Upper House). The main opposition party, *Mardom* (People's) party▷ suffered a setback with 37 seats in the *Majlis* and two in the Senate. The Iranians Party▷ gained one seat in the *Majlis*; this party split off from the Pan-Iran Party▷ on grounds of the Iranian renunciation of its claim to Bahrain▷ and on the issue of the Persian Gulf▷. One Independent representative was elected to the *Majlis* and another to the Senate. With the aim of transferring partial authority into the hands of the people, local elections were held in 1968–70 for town and district councils, in which the ruling party gained decisive victory. Up to 1973, village councils were established in 37,202 villages (out of a total of 50,000).

Despite the setback of the opposition party, it enjoys the support of the Shah, who encourages its activities and striving toward the forming of a Government. In contrast to the support of the Shah for the political parties, there is a decided lack of political awareness in Iranian society; this lack of political tradition hinders the masses from joining political parties.

IMPLEMENTATION OF THE WHITE REVOLUTION: The most important part of the White Revolution is implementation of agrarian reform. This was carried out according to the principles of the Law of 1962 (laid down by Dr. Arsanjani▷), and brought about the end of the previous system of land-ownership. In Sept. 1971 the Government announced the end of the stage of sale of lands, upon which implementation of the next stage was commenced, the objective of which is to introduce mechanization and the establishment of economic cultivation units in order to make cultivation more efficient, regulate agricultural output and prevent division of lands (as in the case of inheritance) into uneconomical units. Together with agrarian reform, the reform in education plays a central part in the White Revolution. The objective of this plan is two-fold: To raise the standard of general education and to steer the educational system toward providing trained manpower according to social-economic needs.

An important part in the spread of education was played by units of the Literacy Corps which functioned within the framework of the Revolutionary Units. These groups of soldier-teachers spread literacy among the children and adults of the villages. The White Revolution also resulted in improvement of the status of women. The main achievements in this sphere were granting women the right of vote (1963), determination of the Empress as regent (1967), inclusion of a woman in the Government (1968), and the recruitment of women into military service within the framework of the Revolutionary Units (1968).

ECONOMIC DEVELOPMENT: Implementation of the White Revolution was accompanied by accelerated economic progress, resulting mainly from political stability, income from natural resources (especially oil▷), and increased economic planning.

After implementation of two economic plans, each lasting seven years, economic planning proceeded within the framework of five-year plans (the third plan, 1963–8, the fourth 1968–73, and the fifth commenced in Mar. 1973 and is to end in Mar. 1978). During the last ten years, in which the third and fourth plans were carried out, the per-capita income increased by 530% (from $97 to $513), and is planned to reach $650 by Mar. 1975. During the fourth plan the GNP increased at a rate of 11% *p.a.* at steady prices. During this period, there was a steady increase in the share of industry in the GNP, as opposed to agriculture, and there was also a pronounced rise in investments made by private

and Government sectors in industrial projects. The most important phase of industrial activity was inauguration of the steel complex at Isfahan, in Mar. 1973, established with Russian▷ cooperation. Efforts within the agricultural sector are aimed at reduction of manpower, while increasing production. In 1973, 57.5% of the population lived in rural areas; this included some 40% of the manpower employed in agriculture, while the share of agriculture in the GNP was only 16%.

The most important factor in economic activity is the oil▷ industry. I has stated clearly that it will not use oil as a political weapon and, indeed, has refrained from doing so. On the other hand, she sees in her oil an important economic weapon and plays a decisive role in the determination of its price. The significance of the oil price rise may be illustrated in the following example: With the presentation of the proposed budget for 1974/5 (in late 1973), income from oil for that year was estimated at $6,300m; however, when the process of approval was finished (in early 1974), this income was estimated at some $14,000m, and in Feb. 1974 at $16,000m.

FOREIGN POLICY AND DEFENCE: Simultaneous with the crystallization of internal policy principles, the White Revolution also formed principles for foreign policy. Toward the superpowers it advocates "straddling the fence" while improving relations with them and making the most of the advantages to be had from relations with each, without becoming dependent on any of them.

During the period under discussion there was further improvement of relations with Russia, with continued mutual visits: In Oct. 1971 President Podgorny participated in the celebrations in honour of 2,500 years of the Iranian dynasty; in Oct. 1972 the Shah and the Empress visited Russia and signed a 15-year agreement for economic-technical cooperation and a 5-year agreement for cultural cooperation. In Mar. 1973 Kosygin visited I for the inauguration of the steel complex in Isfahan; in 1973 Prime Minister Hoveyda▷ twice visited Moscow and in Oct. 1973 an agreement was signed for laying a new natural gas pipeline from I to the Soviet Union, in addition to one operating since 1971. Despite these visits, and despite the fact that the Shah has twice defined the border with Russia as one of "peace and friendship", the attitude of I toward the Soviet Union remains ambivalent. Soviet relations with Iraq▷ (especially after the Feb. 1972 agreement) and with India▷ continue to increase Iranian misgivings. During the period under discussion relations were also improved with other Communist countries; Ties were formed with

North Korea and North Vietnam. Relations with European socialist countries continued to improve. In Dec. 1972 agreement was reached for establishment of relations between I and East Germany. In 1971 I also formed ties with Communist China▷, commencing with the visit of Princesses Ashraf Pahlevi and Fatma Pahlevi to China (April–May 1971). In Aug. 1971 both countries declared mutual recognition and in Oct. 1971 embassies were established. In Sept. 1972 the Empress, the Prime Minister and a number of Iranian Ministers visited China. In June 1973 the Chinese Foreign Minister visited Teheran. Despite improvement of relations with Russia and the Communist Bloc, I viewed herself as closer to the West politically, culturally and socially. During Nixon's▷ Presidency, there has been a further improvement of relations between I and the US, based on common interests and mutual understanding. Indeed, I serves as an ideal example of implementation of the Nixon Doctrine▷. I, as a stable country with the interest and capability for self-defence, represents an entity defending US interests in an extremely sensitive strategic area. It therefore deserves aid, even more so when it is not given *gratis*.

In recent years I has made considerable efforts to strengthen her military power. This expansion has been implemented in two parallel spheres — acquisition of the most modern arms available (other than nuclear) and an attempt to raise the professional standard of military personnel to a capability of operating modern and sophisticated equipment. In fiscal 1973/4, I allocated 28% of her budget for defence, and in fiscal 1974/5, 28.8%. Special emphasis in the arms procurement plan was given to equipment for the air force and navy, arms being sought from several sources. Strengthening the army has special significance in the Persian Gulf▷. With all of I's oil export passing through the Gulf, I views it as a lifeline and seeks to uphold absolute freedom of navigation in the Gulf, to prevent any interference with the Iranian economy. Toward the British evacuation (in late 1971), I declared that the countries bordering on the Persian Gulf should be responsible for the freedom and security of the Gulf.

An important stumbling block was removed when I gave up her claim to Bahrain and recognized its independence (29 Aug., 1971). In Nov. 1971, diplomatic relations were established between I and Bahrain, followed by development of close economic ties. In contrast, I insisted on realizing ownership of three islands in the Straits of Hormuz (Little and Great Tumb, and Bu Musa). This demand was based on historical claim but was chiefly influenced by strategic-economic interests vital to I. During

the night of 29 Nov., 1971, I landed military forces on the islands and raised her flag over them. This was preceded by diplomatic softening-up and propaganda, and did not meet any actual opposition, or even significant verbal opposition, constituting a victory for Iranian diplomacy. After the problem of the islands was solved, it was possible to establish the Union of Arab Emirates▷, and I was one of the first countries to grant it recognition.

During the Yom Kippur War▷, I acceded to Iraq's▷ request for renewal of diplomatic relations, which had officially been severed after occupation of the Gulf islands on 1 Dec., 1971, though in fact suspended already in Jan. 1970, following disputes over the Shatt al-'Arab▷. Renewal of relations was not accompanied by a solution of the controversial problems and therefore, even simultaneously with the exchange of ambassadors (in Feb. 1974), there were armed border disputes. Apart from a possible solution to the Shatt al-'Arab issue, I sees in the renewed relations with Iraq a chance for the return to Iraq of Iranian citizens expelled after the occupation of the Gulf islands.

During the period under review ties were formed with countries and sheikhdoms in the area with whom I had previously had no relations: Lebanon▷ (July 1971) and Qatar▷ (Oct. 1971). Relations with Kuwait▷, suspended following occupation of the Gulf islands, normalized in Dec. 1972. Relations with Syria▷, at the level of chargés-des-affaires since 1965 (following a statement by the Syrian Prime Minister to the effect that Khuzistan▷ was Arab territory), returned to ambassadorial level in Oct. 1973. Relations with Egypt▷ also improved, as did those with Afghanistan (upon solution in Mar. 1973 of the dispute over the Helmand river). Relations with other countries in the area continued to improve; among Islamic countries, relations only with Libya▷ and South Yemen▷ remained strained.

In the sphere of the Arab-Israel Conflict▷, Iran has continued her policy adopted since June 1967: Emphasis on need for return of all territories occupied by Israel while indicating the existence of Israel as a fact to be recognized. Despite pressure on the Shah to sever relations with Israel, increased during and after the Yom Kippur War, the Shah did not give in. He has stated that I's relations with Israel are of economic nature and therefore have nothing to do with politics. He has also stated that these relations concern only I.

Despite the Shah's support for the idea of Islamic Unity (as opposed to Arab Unity▷), he avoided participation in the Conference of Islamic Heads of State in Lahore (Feb. 1974).

STATISTICS: Pop.: 32,650,000 (Nov. 1973 est.) of which 32m Muslims; 260,000 Armenians; 30,000 Assyrians; 40,000 other Christians; 85,000 Jews; 35,000 Zoroastrians and 200,000 others. Natural increase: 3%. Urban population 42.5% (as opposed to 35% at the beginning of the White Revolution)

Literacy: Age group 10–44, 50% (as opposed to 24% in 1963); number of primary school-children in 1972/3: 646,000 (as opposed to 338,600 in 1962/3); number of university students in 1972/3: 108,000 (as opposed to 24,000 in 1962/3).

Manpower employment according to sectors in Jan. 1973: Agriculture 40%; industry 30%; commerce and services 30% (as opposed, respectively, to 55%, 21.2% and 23.8% in Jan. 1963). Exports in 1972/3: $2,962m; imports $2,864m. Est. price index in 1972/3: 138.6% (on basis of 100% in 1959/60).

Transport and vehicles: In Jan. 1973 there were 24 airports, three of which international. Total of vehicles in Jan. 1973: Private automobiles, 450,000; taxis and hire-cars, 13,500; buses, 3,000.

Tourism: Number of tourists in 1972/3, 425,000 (as opposed to 74,228 in 1962/3 and 298,411 in 1968/9)

Hospital beds: In 1973, 13.6 beds per 1000 inhabitants (as opposed to 9.7 in 1963).

Currency: US $ is equal to 68.60–68.85 Rials (purchasing and selling price, respectively). (D.M.)

IRANIANS PARTY. Following his resignation from the Pan-Iran party⊳ in 1970, Dr. Fazlollah Sadr, together with Dr. Nazem Vadi'i, established the Iranians Party. In the 1971 elections this party gained one seat in the *Majlis*. It aims to bring intellectuals and members of the younger generation into its ranks. At the present stage, its activities are concentrated in Teheran⊳ alone. The party organ, "The Newspaper of the Iranians", was founded in 1972 (D.M.)

IRAN NOVIN ("NEW IRAN") PARTY. The present ruling party in Iran⊳. Founded in 1963 by members of the Progressive Centre. The fact that members of other parties, as well as independents, joined the INP granted it an absolute majority in the 21st *Majlis* (1963–7). In Mar. 1964 the Secretary-General of the INP, Hasan 'Ali Mansur, formed a Government based on INP members. After his murder in Jan. 1965 his place was taken by Hoveyda⊳ as Prime Minister and Ataollah Khosravani (Minister of Labour) as Secretary-General of the INP (until 1969). The INP maintained its absolute majority in elections held in 1967 and 1971. In the elections for Municipal and Provincial Councils (1968–72), the INP also obtained an absolute majority.

The INP sees the realization of the White Revolution as its primary objective and it aspires to draw into its ranks a majority of citizens of all age groups and from all sectors and districts, under the slogan "National unity under the principles of the White Revolution". However, lack of a well-developed political awareness, as well as other factors, prevents a mass response.

Organizational changes within the INP took place in 1971, among them the appointment of the Prime Minister as Chairman of the Political Bureau and the doubling of members of the Executive Committee and the Political Bureau. (D.M.)

*IRAQ. Since 1971, power in I has been increasingly concentrated in the hands of Sadam Hussein al-Tikriti⊳, Assistant Secretary-General of the I Ba'th⊳, actual ruler of the country instead of President Bakr⊳, whose health has declined. Hussein's two serious rivals — Hardan 'Abd-ul-Ghaffar el-Tikriti⊳ and Salah 'Ammash⊳ — have been dismissed and the former assassinated. A series of plots was suppressed in a rather bloody manner in subsequent years.

In April 1972, a treaty of friendship was signed with Russia⊳, which made I the Arab state closest to the Soviet bloc. In that same year, far-reaching measures were taken against Western oil⊳ companies, with no clear-cut situation developing.

The I expeditionary force in northern Jordan⊳, stationed there since the Six Day War⊳, was recalled in late 1970, following the suppression of the Palestinian-Arab guerillas⊳ there. During the Yom Kippur War⊳, I sent two divisions to the Syrian front, which took an active part in the fighting, being recalled after the Separation of Forces Agreements⊳.

I's relations with Iran⊳ have remained tense, with occasional crises and outbreaks. The problem of the Kurds⊳ came to a new climax in early 1974, with intense fighting on a broad front.

STATISTICS: Pop.: *c.* 10m (est. 1973). GNP: ID 1,000m ($2,800m) (1969). National Income *p.c.*: *c.* ID 100 ($280) (est. 1969). Exports: ID 24.7m ($71.2m) (including re-exports, excluding crude oil) (1970). Imports: ID 181.6m ($508.5m) (1970). Revenue: ID 373m ($1,044.4m); expenditure: ID 373m ($1,044.4m) (1971/2). (U.D.)

*IRYANI, AL-, SAYYID 'ABD-UL-RAHMAN. Serving as Yemeni⊳ President since 1967. I's position appears to be quite secure. As of late 1971 there have been several reports that he is not in good health. (H.E.)

ISMA'IL, MUHAMMAD HAFEZ. Until Feb. 1974, adviser to Sadat▷ on matters of national security and Chief of the Presidential Cabinet with rank of Deputy Prime Minister. Removed to deplomatic post following undermining of his status.

Born in 1918; son of family of army officers; his father served as a General in the Royalist Egyptian army. I graduated from the Military Academy 1937 and advanced to the rank of Maj.-Gen. (Liwa) 1958. In Sept. 1960 I was transferred to the Ministry of Foreign Affairs, serving as Under-Secretary for Foreign Affairs 1960; Ambassador to Britain until the severance of political relations 1964–5; Ambassador to Italy 1967; and Ambassador to France 1968. Recalled to Cairo from his post in France in April 1970, I was appointed Chief of General Intelligence. After the death of Nasser▷ I was appointed Minister of State for Inter-Ministerial Cooperation (Nov. 1970) and Minister for Foreign Affairs (May 1971) in the Government of Mahmoud Fawzi▷. In Sept. 1971 I was reappointed Adviser to the President on affairs of national security and, as such, was considered the architect of Egypt's security and superpower policy up to the Yom Kippur War▷.

(Al.S.)

*ISRAEL. The principal event during recent years was the Yom Kippur War▷, the conduct and results of which already have exerted considerable influence on I's internal and external policies. Until Oct. 1973, social problems dominated the election campaign; after the war, interest focussed on foreign and defence policy, as well as on the conduct of the war.

POLITICS. The most important developments since the elections of 1969 were the establishment of the Likud▷ bloc of Rightist parties, the increasing tensions between the groups that constitute the Alignment▷ party and the absolute decline of extremist Leftist groups, such as Siah▷ and Matzpen▷.

The Likud was formed on the initiative of Maj.-Gen. (Res.) Ariel Sharon, who retired from active service in the summer of 1973, to join the Liberal Party▷, opening discussions with the Free Centre and the State List. After the Likud was formally set up, it was joined by the Land of Israel Movement▷.

Within the Alignment, conflict increased between "doves" and "hawks", in each of the three component factions. Several compromises after crises broke out did not enhance the party's unity, and differences only intensified after the Dec. 1973 elections, in anticipation of the new Cabinet's formation.

Knesset elections were postponed from 29 Oct. to 31 Dec., 1973, because of the Yom Kippur War. They were held in the shadow of the mehdal ("omission, oversight") — the alleged failures to prepare against the Arab attack in spite of ample warnings. The damage I suffered from the Arab gain of surprise thus was blamed on the political leadership. The actual election campaign was short; 22 lists participated, of which only ten won Knesset seats: Alignment 51; Likud 39; National Religious Party▷ (NRP) 10; Torah Front (Agudath Israel and Poalei Agudath Israel) 5; Independent Liberals 4; New Communist List (Rakah) 4; Shulamit Aloni's Civil Rights List 3; Arab lists linked with Alignment 2; Bedouin 1; Moked 1. The Alignment lost six seats, while the Likud gained eight. The NRP lost two seats and Rakah gained one. The greatest surprise was the large number of votes gained by the Civil Rights List, a new contender without links to any of the existing parties; this was generally considered a vote of protest against the Establishment.

These developments caused considerable difficulties in the formation of a new Cabinet, negotiations taking nearly two months. One of the possibilities was a National Unity Government, as proposed by the Likud and supported by the NRP, but opposed by the Alignment (with the exception of the Rafi▷ faction); another envisaged a minority Cabinet, backed by 58 representatives of the Alignment, the Minority lists and the Independent Liberals. The entire process was accompanied by crises within the individual parties: Dayan▷ and Peres at one time refused to join the new Government; in the NRP the Young Guard opposed veteran leadership, and matters were complicated even more by the Chief Rabbinate Council, which opposed NRP participation in the Cabinet unless the "Who is a Jew" issue were settled in the spirit of Jewish Orthodoxy. Early in Mar. 1974 a Cabinet was formed, with the participation of the Alignment, the Independent Liberals and NRP. In April, the release of a partial report by the Commission of Enquiry set up the Government in the wake of the Yom Kippur War, created a Government crisis, leading to the resignation of Prime Minister Golda Meir▷.

I's international position became more difficult in the 1970s, and ground was lost in both Africa▷ and Western Europe. This was emphasized during the Yom Kippur War, when the Arab states used oil▷ as a political weapon. Arab pressure resulted in the almost complete diplomatic break between the African states and I, while many European and "unaligned" states proclaimed support of the Arab aims.

IMMIGRATION AND SOCIAL PROBLEMS: From 1948 till the end of 1973, 1,750,000 Jews had immigrated to I from all parts of the world. Until 1967 the majority had come from Eastern Europe (excepting the Soviet Union), North Africa, Iraq▷ and Yemen▷. In the latter 1960s the Soviet authorities eased their immigration restrictions under the impact of world opinion and of Soviet Jewry's constant demand for emigration rights. Until 1971 few persons were permitted to leave, though since then more permits are granted; in 1973 some 40,000 Soviet Jews came to I. The Six Day War▷ enhanced feelings of solidarity in the US and other Western countries as well, bringing some 50,000 Western immigrants to I by the end of 1973.

Government investment in immigrant absorption amounted to c. IL3,500m in 1972. Benefits given to new arrivals, mainly housing and employment, aroused jealousy among certain elements in I, especially among the Oriental communities. Thus, the Black Panther▷ movement demanded greater attention to the needs of the underprivileged already in I, including rights equal to those of new immigrants. The 1974/5 budget allocates IL3,000m to housing — 35%, for new immigrants, 35% for newly-weds and 30% for slum clearance.

Defence requirements increased substantially after the Yom Kippur War▷. The cost of the war itself has been estimated at IL30,000m, resulting in a considerable increase of I's national debts. The 1974/5 defence budget amounts to IL14,000m (in addition to indirect defence expenditures) — about 50% of the total budget. This has raised taxation considerably, with Government revenue amounting to 54% of the national income.

STATISTICS (1973): Area: 20.770 sq. km (8,017 sq. mi); cultivated area: 20.34%–4,225 sq.km (1,630 sq.mi). Population: 3,300,000. Birth rate: 3.41%; natural increase: 2.79%. Life expectancy: Jews — males 69.8, females 73.4; non-Jews: males 68.4, females 70.9. Infant mortality: 24.2 per 1000 births. GNP (1972): IL 28,958m. National income p.c. (1972): IL 7,494. Foreign trade (1972): Imports (goods and services): IL 12,699m; exports (goods and services): IL 2,911m. Budget (1974/5): IL 35,000m. Population over 14 never schooled (1972): Jews 8.8%; non-Jews 33.6%. Children (6–14) at school (1972): Jews 94.5%; non-Jews 84.6%. Doctors: 2.3 per 1000; hospital beds: 8 per 1000. Rate of exchange: IL 4.20 = $1.

POPULATION: In 1973, of the 3,300,000 inhabitants in Israel, 2,760,000 were Jews and 480,000 non-Jews (and 75,000 in East Jerusalem). Non-Jews constituted 14,5% of the total population, according to the following breakdown:

		% of total population	% of non-Jewish population
Muslims	360,000	10.8	75
Christians	80,000	2.5	16.5
Druze and others	40,000	1.25	8.25

Additional data: Population of major cities (1973): Jerusalem 305,000; Tel Aviv 363,000. Urban Population as % of total: Jews 90%; non-Jews 50%.

JEWISH POPULATION BY ORIGIN:	Nov. 1948	%	Dec. 1972	%
Israel	253,700	35.4	1,305,400	48
ME and Asia	57,800	8.1	318,000	11.7
Egypt and Africa	12,200	1.7	358,300	13.2
Europe-America	393,000	54.8	743,000	27.5

(E.A.)

MINORITIES (1970–4): Natural increase stood at about 4% p.a., due to a high birthrate (45 per 1000) and a low death rate (6 per 1000). The birthrate has been showing a slight decline since 1970 though not yet indicating family planning. In future a decline may be expected in both birthrate and natural increase, due to rising educational levels and penetration of Western values into Arab villages. There has been significant expansion of education among Arab girls, which undoubtedly will also exert its influence.

The high birthrate affects the age structure of the Arab population, resulting in a high proportion of young persons. Some 70% of all the Arabs in Israel were born after 1948.

The focus of the economic activity of the Arab population is shifting from village to city, with an increasing number travelling to urban jobs. Sedentarization has increased during this period among the Bedouin▷ of both the Negev▷ and Galilee.

NON-JEWISH POPULATION OF ISRAEL (1969–73) (IN 1000s):

	Total	Muslims	Christians	Druze, etc.
1969	422.7	314.5	73.5	34.6
1970	440.0	328.6	75.5	35.9
1972	476.9	358.6	79.6	38.7
1973 (est. 31 Dec.)	514.1	388.8	83.7	41.6

The integration of I Arabs in I life continued during the three years prior to the Yom Kippur War, without any solutions being found to the problems of a minority, the nation of which they are part being hostile to the state in which they live. However, even among extremist circles the belief that I could be wiped out steadily lost ground. This was accompanied by increasing pressure for the practice of equal rights. Demands for the development of educational facilities in the Arab sector increased, as did those for suitable employment opportunities for Arab graduates. Greater efforts were made to eliminate limitations on membership in political organizations formerly closed to Arabs, such as the Hebrew Writers' Union and the Labour Party (which until now operated in the Arab sector by way of affiliated lists). After much debate, the party opened its ranks to Arabs on the basis of full equality. Even before this two Arab *Knesset* members

had been appointed Deputy Ministers: 'Abd-ul-'Aziz Zou'bi, of Health (deceased early 1974) and Sheikh Jaber Mou'adi, of Communications. Kamal Mansour, a Druze leader, became special Adviser to the President, and 32-year old Zaydan Atasha, became the first Druze to hold a post in the I diplomatic service (Consul for Information in New York).

During the summer of 1972 the demand again arose to allow Arabs evacuated from Birim and Iqrit in 1948 to return to their villages near the Lebanese border. This was supported by a broad Jewish-Arab movement in which Yussuf Raya, Bishop of the Greek-Catholic community, was most active (attempting to consolidate his position of leadership among all I Arabs). Demonstrations of solidarity focussed on the fundamental problem of I.s Arabs, concentrating on the assurance of fundamental rights for the minorities, to enable them to participate in the life of the country.

NON-JEWISH POPULATION BY TYPE OF SETTLEMENT (1970–2):

	1970			1972		
	No. of settlements	Population ('000)	%	No. of settlements	Population ('000)	%
Total urban						
population	11	188.4	42.8	16	237.1	49.7
Cities	8	161.2	36.6	8	170.6	35.8
Others	3	27.2	6.2	8	66.4	13.9
Total rural						
population	99	251.6	57.2	96	239.8	50.2
Large villages	42	165.0	37.6	38	145.9	30.6
Small villages	56	45.8	10.4	57	47.1	9.9
Moshavim and kibbutzim	—	0.6	0.1	—	0.6	0.1
Bedouin tribes	—	38.4	8.7	—	44.0	9.2
Institutions, etc.	1	0.1	—	1	0.1	—
Outside settlements	—	1.7	0.4	—	2.0	0.4
Total	110	440.0	100.0	112	476.8	100.0

The Government was in agreement with these objectives, and during this period greater efforts were exerted toward integration. Large amounts were allocated for fundamental services in all Arab villages; at the same time, recognition is ripening that more must be done to dull the sense of bitterness among educated Arabs, mainly by providing satisfactory spheres of activity.

In Aug. 1972 the Cabinet held its first thorough discussion of the problems of I Arabs, much of which focussed on the employment of educated Arabs and on the settlement of land ownership in the Negev▷. On the one hand, the country's Arabs look at their future in the Jewish state with a greater degree of realism; on the other hand, Arab society itself is undergoing change. Urban jobs have already reduced the pre-eminence of agriculture; and the centre of economic gravity has shifted from the villages to the cities, with no current process of urbanization. Arab workers continue to live in the villages, returning at the end of each day of work. This has opened an important channel for the penetration of new values that stand in conflict with established traditions. The same may be said for the organs of the State of I which have become active in the villages. All this contributes to the weakening of social traditions; the extended family, for instance, is on the decline, while the individual gains ground. The younger generation seeks a place among the leadership — a conflict of generations that has yet to reach its decision. Indeed, Arab society in I is still in transition.

During this period recognition of membership in a Palestine Entity▷ increased, without infringing upon the desire to become integrated in I life. The internal conflicts did not cause many young Arabs to join in terrorist activity, but it often imposed a difficult choice upon them. Those who did join or support the terrorist organizations often had personal motives. An exceptional phenomenon was the joint Jewish-Arab terrorist group uncovered in the northern part of I in 1972, before it had engaged in any overt activity. In East Jerusalem▷, tensions between Jews and Arabs were on the decrease.

A special law for the compensation of East Jerusalem Arabs, in consideration of property owned by them before 1948 and abandoned in I, was prepared by the Cabinet. This proposal has not yet been made law, but preliminary estimates place the amount of compensation at many hundreds of millions of I pounds. The potential beneficiaries to this compensation received the proposal coolly, considering the basic assessment too low and the period of payment too long.

Arab journalism developed in Jerusalem: Al-Quds ("Jerusalem") continued to be published by Mahmoud Abu Zuluf; and al-Sha'b ("The People") first appeared on 23 July, 1972, published by Hamoud Ya'ish, one of the owners of the defunct al-Jihad ("The Holy War"), published under Jordanian rule. The latter is extremely hostile to I, and has serialized an aggressive book aimed at the Zionist state; nor does it hesitate to call for a war of destruction against I.

A new weekly, al-Fajr ("The Dawn"), made its first appearance on 7 April, 1972, edited by Yussuf ("Joe") Nasser, who considered himself the representative of young intellectuals, anxious to establish a Palestine Entity in opposition to both Jordan▷ and I. To this end, a new leadership was to be evolved from among the Palestine Arabs▷. Because of its aggressive editorial policies, the weekly was in danger of being closed by the authorities, and also aroused much opposition among supporters of Hashemite▷ rule. Yussuf Nasser was kidnapped by persons unknown in Feb. 1974. At the time of writing, his disappearance had not been solved.

During the last four years education in the Arab sector developed rapidly. The number of educational institutions increased from 257 (1969/70) to 338 (1972/3). An additional Teacher Training College was opened in the "Triangle", where 750 teachers will be trained over the next seven years. The Arab college in Haifa was expanded. Total attendance at Arab schools increased from 110,500 in 1969/70 to 133,300 in 1972/3. More than a thousand I Arabs attend the several universities in the country, including an increasing number of women.

The Yom Kippur War▷ interrupted a steadily growing acceptance of the political reality, which was regarded as likely to endure. I Arabs once again felt themselves caught between hammer and anvil; as soon as war broke out, there were expressions of solidarity with I, but not on a broad front. Most of the Arab population remained silent, and the younger Arabs were once again deeply troubled. Extreme nationalist circles hoped for the destruction of I, and even moderates felt sympathy for the Arab armies attacking I on two fronts. No truly hostile acts occurred, but after the war doubts were raised whether I would be able to hold out in the long run. Renewed Soviet penetration of the ME led to a certain resurgence on the part of Rakah▷, as could be seen from the results of the Dec. 1973 elections.

The Yom Kippur War interrupted the elections campaign, in progress among I's Arabs since early fall, and resulted in fairly sharp changes in voting trends. The general elections to the Histadrut▷, on

11 Sept., 1973, brought a 4% drop in the Arab votes for *Rakah*, despite some 20,000 new voters to the rolls. By Dec., when *Knesset* elections took place, this trend was reversed completely: *Rakah* won 7% more Arab votes, while Zionist parties lost some 10% in this sector. Interestingly, this success on the part of *Rakah* was not duplicated in the concurrent voting for local authorities. The Arab voter preferred to split his vote, on the local level awarding it on the basis of family or personal ties. This reflects the present state of transition of Arab society in I: On the local level ties of blood still dominate, but in the broader framework, nationalist and class feelings have replaced traditional loyalties.

RESULTS OF KNESSET ELECTIONS IN THE ARAB SECTOR (1969 and 1973):

	1969	1973
Registered voters	141,000	174,000
Participation	82%	77%
Valid votes	119,000	134,000
Vote for Zionist parties	84,000	86,000
Vote for *Rakah*	36,000	49,000

(O.S.)

ITALY. Italian oil▷ companies, even though late in entering the ME oil race, have gained a foothold through joint venture agreements (which were not previously customary). Such an agreement was signed between a subsidiary of ENI (Ente Nazionale Idrocarburi) and Egypt▷ in Feb. 1957, between AGIP (Azienda Generale Italiana Petroli) and Iran▷ in July 1957, and between another ENI subsidiary and Sa'udi Arabia▷ in Dec. 1967.

Since the Six Day War▷, I has succeeded in carrying on a neutral and even-handed policy toward the ME conflict, which has been dictated by conflicting opinions within her coalition governments. Attempts to act as mediator between Israel and the Arab states, often with the aid of Tunisia, have not met with success. Like the other West European states, I has suffered from the oil embargo and joined in the EEC▷ statement on the ME in Nov. 1973. She has also been subject to pressure by Libya▷ and the Arab League▷ boycott committee. Since 1970 I has become a centre for Palestine-Arab guerillas▷ acting both within her territory and in other parts of Europe.   (Sh.H.)

J

JA'BARI, AL-, SHEIKH MUHAMMAD 'ALI.

Mayor of Hebron under Jordan▷ and under Israel▷ since the Six Day War▷, one of the more important leaders of the Palestine Arabs▷ in Judaea and Samaria and the outstanding personality in the Hebron area. Participated in the 1929 pogrom in Hebron, was the moving spirit behind the 1948 Hebron Conference which incorporated the West Bank of the Jordan into the Hashemite▷ Kingdom and supported the rulers of Jordan until 1967; was several times Minister in the Jordan Cabinet. In the Six Day War, J surrendered Hebron to the IDF, and since then has conducted a cautius policy of cooperation with Israel, as well as with Hussein▷.

J has frequently met with Minister of Defence Dayan▷. J was the first mayor of any of the occupied towns to visit Tel Aviv▷, on 23 Aug., 1971. In Aug. 1971 J also participated in the first gathering of mayors from Judaea and Samaria to be held after 1967.

J's political line has not been consistent since 1967; at times he favoured the establishment of a Palestine Entity▷, to exist side-by-side with Israel, but he has also stressed loyalty to Hussein. J opposed the establishment of Kiryat Arba', a Jewish settlement on the outskirts of Hebron, and has spoken at length on preserving the Arab character of Judaea and Samaria under Israel control.   (O.Y.)

*JADID, SALLAH. Has been imprisoned since his overthrow by Asad▷, in Nov. 1970, but has not yet been brought to trial.   (O.T.)

JALOUD 'ABD-UL-SALAM. Libyan politician and army officer (Major), member of the Revolutionary Council since its establishment in Sept. 1969 and Prime Minister of Libya▷ since July 1972. Born in 1941; participated actively in the military *coup* against Idris▷ and is considered second only to Qaddafi▷. Appointed Deputy Prime Minister, Minister of Interior and Minister for Local Authorities, Jan. 1970; Minister for Economic Affairs Oct. 1970; and acting Minister of Industry and Finance Aug. 1971. J is one of the better-known members of the revolutionary Government and acts as its roving representative. J has visited the Soviet Union, East Bloc countries and Western Europe, usually in connection with aid and arms procurement treaties.   (Al.S.)

JAMIL, GEN. NAJJI. Commander in Chief, Syrian air force, since the end of 1970; a leader of the Ba'th▷ party in Syria▷. J is a confidant and leading supporter of Asad▷, his predecessor as commander of the air force.   (O.Y.)

*JAPAN. J's dependence on ME oil▷ supplies continued to shape its ME policy. This became increasingly clear after the Yom Kippur War▷, when J had to resist strong Arab pressure to break off diplomatic relations with Israel▷. J issued several declarations in support of Arab policy and offered economic and technical aid to Arab countries, in partial appeasement.   (O.Y.)

*JARRING, DR. GUNNAR. Retired from diplomatic service in Nov. 1973.   (Sh.H.)

*JERUSALEM. Pop. in 1973: 325,000. When Pan-Arab▷ and Pan-Islamic▷ feelings reached new heights after the Yom Kippur War▷, Arab states re-emphasized demands for Muslim control over the eastern part of the city. Feisal▷ of Sa'udi Arabia was among the most uncompromising spokesmen of J's Muslim character; an official resolution to this effect was adopted at the Conference of Muslim States, held at Lahore, Pakistan, in Feb. 1974.   (E.A.)

*JORDAN, KINGDOM OF. Arab governments reacted strongly to the expulsion of the Palestine-Arab guerilla organizations▷, intensifying Hussein's▷isolation. Armed encounters occurred between J and Syria▷ in Aug. 1971, followed by a break in diplomatic relations. The consequent closure of the Syrian border posed severe economic problems for J, most of its overseas imports coming from Beirut *via* Syria territory. However, relations with Iraq▷ improved, easing J's position somewhat. Sa'udi Arabia▷ attempted to mediate between J and the Palestinians, and the latter began operations against the J Government, primarily in unsuccessful hijack attempts against the J national airline. Prime Minister Wasfi Tall▷ was assassinated on 28 Nov. 1971, when in Cairo for a meeting of the Arab League▷. (The assassins, of the Black September organization, were soon freed by the Egyptians.) The new Prime Minister was Ahmad al-Lawzi▷.

Hussein made several efforts to break out of his isolation, the most important of which was his federation plan announced in Mar. 1972, designed to attract Palestinian support. This envisaged the creation of two autonomous regions — Transjordan, with its capital at 'Amman▷ ; and the West Bank, with its capital in Jerusalem▷ — with a federal Government seated in 'Amman. The proposal was received with considerable criticism abroad, especially in Egypt▷, where it was interpreted as preparatory to a separate J settlement with Israel.

On 26 May, 1973, Zayd al-Rifa'i▷ became Prime Minister. That summer a rapprochement was achieved with both Syria and Egypt, easing Hussein's external isolation. The Palestine organizations, however, remained hostile and continued to call for the king's overthrow; an attempt to take over Government installations in 'Amman failed in Feb. 1973.

In the Yom Kippur War▷, a J expeditionary force saw action on the Syrian front. Hussein appears not to have been privy to the Egyptian-Syrian plan and consequently maintained quiet on his country's long border with Israel. His isolation in the Arab world again intensified after the Arab Summit Conference▷ in Algiers, in Dec. 1973, which recognized the Palestine Liberation Organization▷ as the only representative of the Palestine Arabs▷. This resolution posed a direct threat to Hussein and his regime. J participated in the opening sessions of the Geneva Peace Conference▷ in Dec. 1973, but the question of Palestinian representation there continued to complicate Hussein's relations with the Arab world.

Official data place J's population at 2.4m (28 Mar., 1972), with about 700,000 on the West Bank▷. The economy suffered seriously from the Sept. 1970 civil war, trade practically ground to a standstill in the major towns, and imports through Beirut ceased. In Nov. 1970 the Minister of Finance estimated the cost of the civil war at £29m. Several Western states, mainly the US, promised aid for the rehabilitation of the economy, and Sa'udi Arabia provided financing.

Repairs on the Ghor canal were begun in May 1971, and villagers began to return to the Jordan river valley. Settlement of refugees was undertaken at Karameh and other places in the area. The Syrian blocade of J was removed, in effect, in April 1972. Inauguration of the new port of 'Aqaba▷, in 1972, also enhanced economic development potential.   (O.Y.)

JORDAN NATIONAL UNION. A political quasi-party organization, established in Jordan▷ in late 1971. Similar in structure to the Arab Socialist Union▷ in Egypt and is the only legal political body in Jordan. Its establishment, after the removal of the Palestine-Arab guerillas▷ from the country, was meant to create a popular basis for the support of Hussein▷ and the Hashemite▷ establishment, as well as to serve as a "pressure valve" for groups interested in taking active political action but unable to do so within a party framework.

The President of the JNU is Hussein. The Executive Committee has 36 members, 18 from either bank of the Jordan river. Under it is the Union Council, with 360 members (one-third from the East Bank, one third from the West Bank and one third appointed). The JNO has branches and offices in all districts and subdistricts in Jordan. Elections were held in Aug.-Sept. 1972 for the Union Council, on an area basis with each subdistrict being allocated a number of seats. The Union Council elected the Executive Committee from among its members, in Oct. 1972. In 1973 the prestige of the JNU declined, and a change of name, to the Arab National Union, did not succeed in extricating it from its lack of vitality.   (Y.N.)

*JUMBLAT, KAMAL. While holding the sensitive post of Minister of Interior, in 1970, J initiated policies that left him open to strong criticism; J had permitted the Palestine-Arab guerilla organizations▷ to carry on their activities, as well as other organizations and parties declared illegal in Lebanon▷. After leaving the Cabinet, J generally took a strongly oppositionist line.

J continued to be active also outside Lebanese politics. For instance, he attempted to mediate between the Soviet Union and Syria and Egypt, when tensions existed between them, and participated in several leftist international congresses. In 1972 J was re-elected to the Lebanese Parliament, and in the same year was also awarded the Lenin Peace Prize.   (O.Y.)

K

KALALI, DR. MANOUCHEHR. Iranian politician. Studied law and economics at University of Teheran; completed PhD at University of Paris. Since 1967 *Iran Novin*▷ member of *Majlis. Iran Novin* Secretary-General in Sept. 1969; joined Cabinet as Minister without Portfolio in Nov. 1971.   (D.M.)

*KARAMEH, RASHID. Since Franjiyeh's▷ election to the Presidency, K's political influence has waned. A sharp critic of the present administration, K has lost ground even in his own constituency of Tripoli▷, due to increasing influence of the radical elements.   (O.Y.)

KATZIR (KATCHALSKI), PROF. EPHRAIM. President of the State of Israel▷. Born in Russia 1916; immigrated to Palestine 1925; graduate of the Hebrew University in Jerusalem; research work in Bio-Physics, alongside activity in the Haganah▷ and in the Mapai▷ party. During

the Arab-Israel War of 1948▷, K was in the IDF Scientific Corps. During the 1960s, K served as Chief Scientist of the Ministry of Defence. From 1951 was head of the Bio-Physics Institute at the Weizmann Institute, Rehovot; Member of the Academy of Sciences, and of the National Council for Research and Development. Elected President in 1973, succeeding Zalman Shazar▷.   (E.A.)

KAZZAR, AL-, NAZEM. Chief of Security Services in Iraq▷. Led unsuccessful *coup d'état* in 1973, in which the Minister of Defence, Hamed Shihab▷, was killed. K was executed for his role in the attempt.   (O.Y.)

KHALATABRI, DR. 'ABBAS. Iranian statesman; born in 1912; since 1966, member of the Foreign Office staff; represented Iran▷ at various European capitals, the UN and CENTO▷. Appointed Deputy Foreign Minister Jan. 1970, and Foreign Minister 1971. Continued policy of "national independence", which resulted in improved relations with the superpowers, as well as with neighbouring countries.   (D.M.)

KHATIB, AL-, AHMAD. In Syrian Ba'th▷ party leadership. Born in 1931; teacher in southern Syria▷, later heading the Syrian Teachers' Union. President of Syria Feb. 1970, after rise of Asad▷; resigned in Mar. 1971. Chosen Prime Minister of Federation of Arab Republics▷ Dec. 1971.   (O.Y.)

KHOULI, AL-, HASAN SABRI. Adviser to Sadat▷ on Arab affairs, with the rank of Minister. Filled almost the same position under Nasser▷. Born in 1921; member of the Free Officers. In the Arab-Israel War of 1948▷, K was wounded while serving under Nasser. Served as Chairman of the Egyptian-Israeli Mixed Armistice Commission. Retired from active military service 1958, with rank of Col., and became Nasser's Secretary for Information. In the early 1960s, K became head of the presidential Palestine Office, and later the President's Public Relations Officer. Since 1964, K was Nasser's, and later Sadat's, personal representative for special assignments, including the follow-up committee of the 1964 Arab Summit Conference▷, the problems of the Palestine-Arab guerilla organizations▷ (1970) and relations with Jordan▷ and Syria▷ (1972, 1973).   (Al.S.)

KILOMETRE 101 TALKS. The direct discussions between senior Israeli and Egyptian army officers, resulting in stabilization of the cease-fire following the Yom Kippur War▷ and leading to the Separation of Forces Agreement▷ with Egypt▷. Two days after the acceptance of the cease-fire, Israel▷ suggested the talks. It was therefore agreed that meetings be held under UN auspices at a point along the cease-fire line west of the Suez Canal, to discuss procedures for the passage of non-military supplies to the besieged Egyptian Third Army and the town of Suez. On 28 Oct., 1973, Israeli and Egyptian officers met at K 101 of the Cairo-Suez road.

Under US pressure, Israel permitted the passage of regular food convoys to the Third Army, the truck drivers being UNEF▷ soldiers. The Israeli representative to the talks, Gen. Yariv▷, and the Egyptian representative, Gen. Gamasy▷, discussed mainly the matter of supplies to the Third Army, as well as the exchange of POWs. Until 11 Nov., there were differences of opinion on the latter, with Egypt refusing to present a list of POWs prior to Israeli withdrawal to the 22 Oct. lines. The Six-Point Agreement▷ was signed on 11 Nov. at K 101 by Yariv and Gamasy, in the presence of Gen. Siilasvuo▷, settling the issue. The Agreement stabilized the cease-fire, arranged for an exchange of POWs and ensured supplies to the Third Army. Two other subjects (ending of the Bab al-Mandeb▷ blockade and further peace talks) were verbally agreed upon. Three control points along the Cairo-Suez road were handed over to the UNEF.

Contacts for the stabilization of the cease-fire continued during Nov. 1973, but talks were suspended on 29 Nov., after continued Egyptian demands for Israeli withdrawal to the 22 Oct. lines. An Israeli suggestion that both sides withdraw to their respective banks of the Suez Canal▷ met a priori Egyptian rejection. Contacts for the renewal of talks were held between Siilasvuo, Dayan▷ and Gen. Ahmad Isma'il 'Ali▷ in early Dec., though no results were achieved. UN Secretary-General Waldheim was also unsuccessful in his efforts toward renewed talks. Gen. Yariv stated on 1 Dec. that there remained differences of opinion on reduction of Egyptian forces on the East Bank of the Canal, Israeli withdrawal from the West Bank, the disengagement line between the forces and a timetable for the disengagement. Violations of the cease-fire continued throughout Nov. and Dec. and in early Dec. there were even fears of impeding full-scale warfare. The talks were reported to have been terminated by Kissinger▷ who wanted the issue of disengagement to be the first stage of the Geneva Peace Conference▷, after Israel had agreed to a disengagement of forces in Nov. Sadat▷ agreed to Kissinger's suggestion on 13 Dec. The Geneva conference began on 21 Dec. and on 26 Dec. dis-

cussion commenced between officers of both sides on the issue of disengagement; these ended without results in early Jan. In mid-Jan., Kissinger arrived in the ME for discussions with both sides on disengagement, resulting on 18 Jan. in the signing of an agreement at K 101 by the Chiefs of Staff of both armies, Gen. El'azar and Gen. Gamasy. Detailed talks on related matters were held between senior officers up to 28 Jan. Withdrawal of Israeli forces from the southern sector of the territory west of the Suez Canal commenced on 25 Jan. On 28 Jan. the tent at K 101, which had served for the talks, together with the entire Cairo-Suez road, was handed over to the UN and subsequently to the Egyptians. (O.Y.)

KISSINGER, PROF. HENRY A. U.S. Secretary of State since 3 Sept., 1973 (first Secretary of State of Jewish origin). Born in 1923; immigrated from Germany to US in 1938. After receiving PhD from Harvard University, K embarked on an academic career and wrote extensively on US foreign policy, NATO, and Metternich's diplomacy. Became Nixon's▷ Assistant for National Security 1970. Conducted talks in Paris with North Vietnamese representative Le Duc Tho, concluding in an agreement in Jan. 1973 to end the war in Vietnam (for which both negotiators were awarded the Nobel Peace Prize). K visited both Moscow and Peking to prepare the way for Nixon's historic visits there in 1972.

During the Yom Kippur War▷, when the extent of Soviet arms shipments to Syria and Egypt became known, the US administration decided on massive arms air-lifts to Israel. K then helped bring about the cease-fire of 22 Oct., the Egyptian-Israeli discussions at Kilometre 101▷, and the Geneva Peace Conference▷. K subsequently served as a catalyst in negotiations toward the Separation of Forces Agreements▷ between Israel and Egypt, and Israel and Syria — bringing open hostilities to a close. Since the Yom Kippur War, K has visited the ME several times and has received both Israel and Arab leaders in Washington. K has set as his goals the achievement of a lasting peace between Israel and the Arabs and the improvement of the US position with the Arab states, symbolized by the restoration of diplomatic relations with Egypt.

Concerning the oil▷ embargo declared by the Arab oil▷ producing states after the Yom Kippur War, K has taken a non-compromising attitude, refusing to change US policy toward Israel and the ME. (Sh.H.)

KOLLEK, THEODORE (TEDDY). Born in

Vienna in 1911; active in the Zionist movement; member of kibbutz 'Ein-Gev; active in rescue of European Jews during Second World War. Minister at Israel Embassy in Washington 1951; Director-General of Prime Minister's Office 1952–64. Mayor of Jerusalem▷ since 1966.

K fostered the unification of Jerusalem after the Six Day War▷ and was responsible for the policy of tolerance among all sectors of the population, as well as accelerated development in the city, devoting special attention to preservation of cultural values of the various communities.   (I.G.)

KORUTÜRK, FAHRI. Sixth President of Turkey▷. Commander of the Navy; Ambassador to Moscow and Madrid. Elected President in April 1973 as joint candidate of the "Justice", "Republican" and "Republican Trust" parties, after Sundy's▷ term of office had expired and the army's candidate had failed in repeated balloting in the National Assembly.   (D.K.)

KÜÇÜK, DR. FAZIL. In the Feb. 1973 Cyprus elections, K was not re-elected.   (O.Y.)

*KUWAIT. In Jan. 1971, 41,000 voters elected the third National Council, which had gained stature and adopted independent political stands (more extreme than those of the Government) on inter-Arab and domestic issues. (For example, the Council demanded nationalization of the oil▷ industry.) Compulsory military service was enacted in 1973, for all males aged 18 to 30.

The number of aliens, mostly Palestine Arabs▷, has increased considerably since the Six Day War▷, constituting a major internal problem. Their inferior status is carefully maintained by the Government; K citizenship is difficult to obtain, and non-citizens cannot vote, are not accepted in any army framework, cannot be employed by any Government agency (except by special contract specifying early replacement by qualified K citizens). Foreign corporations must be 51% K owned. Further, aliens are often subjected to arrest, investigation and explusion whenever a crisis occurs.

Official statistics (somewhat tendentious) placed the population at the end of 1972 at 860,000 (83% K citizens and 17% aliens).

Government policy on oil is affected by several domestic and external factors. New estimates of K's oil reserves, prepared early in 1972, found that these were being used up rapidly, leading to Government instructions not to increase output. Furthermore, the Government announced that it would not renew agreements with foreign oil companies

and would attempt to reduce existing concessions, transferring them mainly to the K National Oil Co. In late 1972 an agreement was reached whereby K would obtain 25% of the foreign companies' shares; where the National Council refused to ratify this, it was abrogated by the Government. In renewed negotiations in July 1973, 60% of the shares were demanded and, unofficially, it was reported that this was accepted. After the Yom Kippur War▷, K played an active role in reducing oil output by the OAPEC▷.

Discussion on the maritime border with Iran▷, on the continental shelf in the Persian Gulf▷, reached agreement in 1970; no final conclusion was reached, however, due to pressure from Iraq▷, who argued that the proposed treaty would infringe on her territorial waters, and thus she threatened not to recognize it. In Mar. 1973 active conflict broke out on the K-Iraq border, the Iraqi forces invading K territory near Umm-Qasr; Iraq also demanded that K relinquish two islands controlling the entrance to that port. Besides mutual withdrawal of forces, no progress was made toward a settlement by the end of 1973.

Two major factors have led to K's recent additional importance in the Arab world: The radical Arab regimes are becoming increasingly dependent upon K's financial support, which has been expanding since 1967, and all the more so since the Yom Kippur War; further, the K regime has followed a cautious, neutral but nevertheless active inter-Arab policy, frequently offering to mediate in local and inter-Arab disputes.   (V.E.)

L

LAGU, MAJ.-GEN. JOSEPH. Of the Madi tribe in southern Sudan▷. Fled the country in 1963; returning in 1968, L joined the *Anyanya* rebels in eastern Equatoria, and by 1970 was one of their outstanding leaders. In Jan. 1971 L organized and headed the South Sudan Liberation Movement, which sought to become the roof-organization, both political and military, of all the rebel forces in the south. L played a central role in the conclusion of the 1972 Addis Ababa agreement bringing fighting in the south to an end. Following this, he was placed in command of all the southern units incorporated in the Sudanese armed forces.   (E.S.)

*LAND OF ISRAEL MOVEMENT. Before the 1973 *Knesset* elections, the LIM joined the *Likud*▷ and one of its leaders, Maj.-Gen. (Res.) Avraham Yoffe, was elected to the *Knesset*.   (E.A.)

★LATAQIA. Pop.: 126,000 (Sept. 1970). In 1971, the port handled some 1.63m tons. (O.T.)

LAWZI, AL-, AHMAD. Jordanian politician. Born in 'Amman in 1925; teacher, early 1950s; joined civil services 1953; during next decade worked at the Royal Court, and the Ministry of Foreign Affairs; member of Parliament 1961. L joined Bahjat Talhouni's▷ Cabinet as Minister without Portfolio in 1964. In the two Cabinets headed by Sa'd Jum'a, L was Minister for Municipal Affairs; Minister of Finance under Wasfi Tall▷ in 1971. In the interim periods, L was a member of the Senate. After Tall's assassination in 1971, L became Prime Minister, until May 1973. (Y.N.)

★LEBANON. After Franjiyeh's▷ rise to the presidency, and the appointment of his associate, Saeb Salam▷, as Prime Minister, the Cabinet was composed of non-parliamentary experts, most of them young men — in contrast to Lebanese tradition — rather than experienced political leaders. The newly-elected Speaker of the Parliament, Kamal al-As'ad, also supported Franjiyeh's policies and worked for their implementation.

The 1972 elections enhanced the Centre's power; the Left also made progress, even "ideological" parties not purely Lebanese. Between the elections and June 1973, three Cabinets were formed under different Prime Ministers. The President's son, Tony Franjiyeh, is a member of the present Cabinet, headed by Taqi al-Din al-Sulh▷.

The most immediate problem facing Franjiyeh when he came into office was his relations with the Palestine-Arab guerilla organizations▷. His approach has been more definite than that of his predecessor, but he also stresses his support, in principle, of their activities. As a rule, all the Cabinets between 1970 and 1973 informed the terrorists of their adherence to the Cairo Agreement, and of their desire to make additional compacts for the implementation of that document. Nevertheless, the Cairo Agreement was not observed: Terrorist attacks and the consequent reprisals by Israel resulted in the flight of villagers from southern Lebanon, mainly in 1970. Relatively violent encounters between the guerilla organizations and the Lebanese army occurred in the Spring of 1973. (H.Z.)

★LIBYA. Several political trials were held in L in 1970 and 1971. A conspiracy was uncovered in July 1970 (the "Abha" conspiracy) in which Monarchists and other elements sought to overthrow the Qaddhafi▷ regime; the conspirators were brought to trial in 1971. Corruption trials were held in 1970–2,

including that of ex-King Idris▷, who was sentenced to death in *absentia*.

Since 1971 Qaddhafi has appeared to be undisputed ruler of L, though there are rumours of disagreement within the Revolutionary Council. Union with Egypt▷ is probably a major point of dispute, as are the means of executing the Revolution and possibly also L's international orientation. These disagreements were probably behind Qaddhafi's resignations and the frequent changes in top offices. Between Sept. 1970 and Aug. 1971, the Revolutionary Council has clearly strengthened its hold on various important offices; this process was later reversed, however, culminating in the Jaloud▷ Cabinet of July 1972. Qaddhafi's resignations in Jan. and Oct. 1971 were mere manoeuvres to stabilize his own position and force his views on his associates.

In 1971, the Arab Socialist Union▷ was organized in L, as the country's only legal political party. The "cultural revolution" was proclaimed in April 1973, to realize the regime's revolutionary objectives, revolving around five principles: religious law to replace secular law; elimination of Communism▷ and Conservatism; arming the people, including organized Popular Resistance Forces; administrative reform; and advancement of Islamic thought. Application of these principles was entrusted to Popular Committees subsequently established; these soon took over enterprises and certain institutions, burning some foreign libraries, and taking control of communications media, schools and banks.

On the inter-Arab plane, L continued a dynamic foreign policy. A quadrilateral federation — Federation of Arab Republics▷ — Egypt, Syria, Sudan and L — was proposed in Nov. 1970; though Sudan soon left the negotiations, the three other countries held a plebiscite on 1 Nov. 1971, and ratified the Federation's Constitution; steps were also taken to advance economic, technological and cultural co-operation. However, this rather loose arrangement did not satisfy Qaddhafi, who favoured full, immediate union with Egypt. Agreement in principle was reached in Sept. 1972, but neither that nor the popular procession from Tripoli to Cairo, in July 1973, led to the realization of his programme.

Qaddhafi voiced violent criticism of the Arab conduct of the Yom Kippur War▷, possibly because he had not been consulted in its prosecution. In consequence, he turned to the Maghreb▷ in his search for worthy allies. In Jan. 1974, a declaration proclaiming the immediate union of L and Tunisia▷, but a day later it became clear that this would end like all previous attempts at union.

Changes in policy led to tension with Algeria▷

and a deterioration of relations with Morocco▷; the latter resulted from Qaddhafi's involvement in the July 1971 conspiracy against King Hasan.

In the Arab-Israel Conflict▷, Qaddhafi (alongside Iraqi▷ and several Palestine-Arab guerilla organizations) represents the most radical approach, criticizing the limited objectives set by Egypt in the Yom Kippur War effort, as well as any attempts to reach agreement with Israel, no matter how favourable for the Arabs or how temporary.

L's foreign policy in general remains anti-Western. Qaddhafi has been quite active on the African▷ scene and in the Mediterranean (Malta▷, Cyprus▷), as well as in Muslim countries (for example, supporting the Muslim opposition in the Philippines).
(E.S.)

LIKUD. Parliamentary bloc uniting most of the Rightist parties in Israel▷; its component bodies are *Gahal*▷, the State List, the Free Centre and the Land of Israel Movement▷. Established in late summer of 1973 at the initiative of Maj.-Gen. (Res.) Ariel Sharon, only prolonged and difficult negotiations settled differences between the constituent groups. In the Dec. 1973 elections, L posed a real threat to the Alignment▷, proposing the establishment of a National Unity Government. L won 39 of the 120 *Knesset* seats (32 total in the previous session). After the elections, L continued its demand for a broad coalition, strongly criticizing all efforts to set up a minority Cabinet.
(O.Y.)

M

*MAGHREB, AL-. In recent years, Libya▷ was the most active factor in inter-M relations. In July 1971, Libya backed opponents of the regime in Morocco▷, leading to a deterioration in relations. After failure to effect a union with Egypt▷, Qaddhafi▷ sought union with Tunisia, in Jan. 1974; this also ended in failure and aroused the opposition of both Algeria▷ and Morocco.
(O.Y.)

*MAHDI, MAHDIYYA. Sadeq al-Mahdi returned to Sudan▷ at the end of 1972, and was immediately put under house arrest. In Jan. 1973 he was suspected of participating in a conspiracy to overthrow the Numeiri▷ regime, leading to his imprisonment. In May 1973 he was released, after ratification of the new Constitution, which prohibits incarceration without trial.
(E.S.)

*MAHJOUB, MUHAMMAD AHMAD. Died in 1969.

MAJALI, AL-, HABIS. Appointed Supreme Commander (Field Marshal) of Jordan's▷ armed forces shortly before the civil war in Sept. 1970; Military Governor, in charge of rooting out the Palestine-Arab guerillas. Hence, one of the most hated opponents of the Palestine Arabs▷.
(O.Y.)

*MAKARIOS, ARCHBISHOP. M found manoeuvring between the Turkish minority in Cyprus▷, the Greek Government and the supporters of extremist Gen. Grivas▷ a most difficult matter. His position became even more difficult when Grivas returned to the island in late 1971. In Mar. 1972 three members of the Greek Orthodox Synod declared that M could not continue to serve as both President and Archbishop. M rejected this, though he yielded on certain points. In February 1973 M was re-elected for another term as President.
(O.Y.)

MAKKAWWI, 'ABD-UL-QAWWI. Head of FLOSY▷ faction favouring compromise with the NLF▷. In Jan. 1970 M successfully overthrew 'Abdullah al-Asnaj▷, who had opposed any agreement. In Jan. 1971, South Yemen▷ Minister of Defence, 'Ali Nasser Muhammad Husni▷, offered M a post in that country's government service, possibly in the diplomatic corps. M refused, since a personal appointment would solve nothing; rather, M demanded the incorporation of his party's leadership in the regime. M apparently remains outside South Yemen and continues in opposition.
(T.Y.)

MAJTOUM, AL-, RASHID b. SA'ID. Ruler of Dubai▷. Born in 1914; ascended to rule upon his father's death in 1958. Since Dec. 1971, Vice-President of the Union of Arab Emirates▷.   (V.E.)

MARDOM PARTY. Founded in Iran▷ in 1957, by Dr. Asdallah 'Alam, with the Shah's support, in an attempt to rehabilitate the country's political system. In the 1960 general elctions, the MP won 40 seats in the *Majlis*; in the return elections it achieved 50 seats. Dr. 'Alam resigned in 1961, and was replaced by Dr. Yahya 'Adel▷.

Ideologically the MP differs from the Government party, *Iran Novin*▷. Both parties favour the White Revolution, but differ on its implementation.

In spite of its having lost ground in parliamentary elections, the MP has gained encouragement from the Shah's favouring a two- or multi-party regime. The Prime Minister also favours party activity, believing in the necessity of a moderate opposition for the orderly operation of a political system.

In 1971 'Ali Kani became the party's secretary, and under him the MP strongly attacked *Iran Novin* and the Hoveyda▷ Government. 'Ali Kani has been succeeded by Nasser Amri. The MP publishes two periodicals.   (D.M.)

MAR'I, SAYYIN. Born in 1913; agricultural engineer since 1937; engaged in agricultural planning, reform and the Aswan High Dam in Egypt▷. Minister for Land Reform 1956–61; Deputy Prime Minister for Agricultural Affairs 1968–71; Secretary-General of Arab Socialist Union▷ in summer 1971-Mar. 1973. M's appointment to the latter was one reason behind unrest among Leftist students, who regarded him a "feudalist" landowner. M was subsequently given the symbolic appointment of Presidential Adviser. However, events have shown that M has remained close to Sadat▷ (his son married Sadat's daughter). In 1974 M was proposed for the position of Secretary of the Food and Agriculture Organization.   (Al.S.)

★MAURITANIA. M policies have steadily approached those of the Arab world and have led the country to join the Arab League▷, at the end of 1973.   (O.Y.)

★MEIR, GOLDA. M suffered a major blow to her popularity and support following the Yom Kippur War▷, and in the general elections of Dec. 1973 the Alignment▷ under her leadership lost seven seats. After strenuous negotiations and having surmounted crisis after crisis, in Mar. 1974 M managed to form a new three-party coalition Government which commanded a slim majority in the *Knesset*.

In Mar. 1974, the release of a partial report by a Government Commission of Enquiry set up to investigate the Yom Kippur War▷ created strong public criticism in the wake of which M resigned as Prime Minister. Yitzhaq Rabin▷ was selected by the Alignment as candidate for setting up a new Government.   (A.W.)

MELEN, FARIT. Prime Minister of Turkey▷ 1972-3. Born in Van in 1906; studied Political Science at University of Ankara; served in the Ministry of Finance; elected as Republican People's Party representative to National Assembly 1950; Minister of Finance under Inönü▷ 1962–5. Left his party in 1966 to found, with others, the Republican Reliance Party. Minister of Defence under Erim▷ 1971. M became Prime Minister upon Erim's resignation in 1972, continuing his policies of social and economic reform as well as the re-establishment

of public order. After Korutürk▷ was elected to the Presidency, in April 1973, M resigned and was replaced by Naim Talu▷.   (D.K.)

★MIDDLE EAST. GEOGRAPHY AND GEOPOLITICS: Like Europe, the ME is characterized by interrelationships of land and sea. There is a high ration of coastline per unit of land area; indeed, the ME is sometimes regarded as an isthmus, connecting larger land masses. No spot in the ME is more than 700 km from the sea. These characteristics, as well as the ME's relative location, have in all periods encouraged commercial ties and cultural exchange between the three adjacent continents — Europe, Asia and Africa, creating a desirability for controlling the ME among the major powers outside this area.

ME physical geography is largely dominated by two phenomena: Almost all coasts have mountain ranges near by, which separate the sea from the interior; and most interior regions are deserts. Throughout history this has led to different, mutually opposed foci of civilization: (a) populations located along the narrow coastal strips depended on relations with other countries, but lacked the manpower, or the extensive land areas necessary to become major powers; (b) nomadic societies in the desert areas, with low population densities, supporting themselves by trade; these occasionally became military concentrations capable of making a decisive impact on the entire area; (c) mountain dwellers with independent civilizations and a strong national consciousness, of limited organizational potential because of low population densities and difficult lines of communication; such areas became refuges (Lebanon▷, Armenia▷, Kurdistan▷, Yemen▷); (d) river valley civilizations, along the Nile▷, Tigris▷, and Euphrates▷, where populations were dense, technological organization very necessary, and both military and economic power could be accumulated; at various times, these became the dominant political powers; (e) the extensive highlands of Iran▷ and Anatolia allowed for high population densities and facile transport, both supporting the concentration of forces sufficient for the establishment of sizable empires.

The power foci mentioned in (d) and (e) above, are hundreds of km apart, forming a semicircle around the desert heartland. Each of them, at different times, constituted the central political power controlling much of the ME. The area's geographical centre, however, is located in the desert and is almost entirely unpopulated. This can explain why processes common elsewhere — the rise of political and economic forces at the centre, capable of uniting outlying areas — did not occur in the ME. During most historical periods the ME was divided into hostile political entities, or else hegemony came from without: Greece, Rome, Byzantium, the Crusaders and the Western powers.

In terms of world history, the ME was almost always of central importance. Prior to the Roman Empire, it was almost the only locale where political organization and cultural development made progress. Later, with the rise of the West and the East (especially India), the ME became a meeting point, and all contacts between the large centres of organized civilization passed through it. The discovery of America and the shift of trade with India to the Cape route, made the ME a backwater, as far as the world powers' interest was concerned. This began to change during the late 18th and early 19th centuries, and subsequently the Suez Canal▷ restored the area to the world transportation map. In the two World Wars, the major powers expressed renewed interest in the ME.

The ME is again a focal point of world interest, due to its geographical position, its religious significance (see Holy Places), and its wealth in oil▷, containing the world's largest known reserves.
(Y.K.)

MOKED. Political movement in Israel▷, established in the summer of 1973. Its component elements are *Maki* (Israel Communist Party) and several Leftist groups organized as the Blue-Red Movement. M participated in the Dec. 1973 elections, sending the head of its list, Meir Pa'il, to the *Knesset*. (O.Y.)

★MOROCCO. King Hasan's regime managed to overcome two attempts at revolution, in July 1971 and in Aug. 1972. The former resulted in deteriorating relations with Libya▷, ending in a break of diplomatic relations. The second attempt was followed by the suicide of Gen. Ofkir, till then considered the King's right-hand man.

Internal problems apparently motivated M's more active role in the Arab-Israel Conflict▷. M sent a brigade to Syria▷ in 1973, which fought in the Yom Kippur War▷. (O.Y.)

MUHAMMAD REZA SHAH (PAHLAVI). In Oct. 1971, amid great splendour, the Shah celebrated the 2,500th anniversary of the Iranian dynasty. The festivities were a clear expression of the Shah's desire to demonstrate his country's achievements, at both home and abroad. His greatest achievement is the White Revolution, carried out as it is under his personal initiative. This may be regarded as an attempt to neutralize opposition to the Shah's rule

by carrying out urgently needed social and economic reforms "from the top".

The wide popular support which the Shah enjoys, due both to his achievements and to traditional sentiments of homage and respect, has largely discouraged opposition movements. The Shah also takes active steps to block opposition groups in Iran▷ and their freedom of organization.

The Shah has also had successes in his foreign policy; pursuing a policy of national independence, he has improved Iran's relations with both the great powers and with countries with whom Iran had previously had poor rapport. (D.M.)

★MUSLIM BROTHERHOOD. Since the death of Nasser▷, relations between the regime and individual members of the MB have improved. Egyptians in exile who had belonged in the past to the organization were permitted to return to the country. Nevertheless, activities within the framework of the MB are still illegal and it carries on its activities from countries outside Egypt▷, such as Sa'udi Arabia, Lebanon and Sudan. (Al.S.)

N

★NABULSI, AL-, SULEIMAN. Not among the thirty new members of the Jordanian▷ Senate, appointed by Hussein▷ in Sept. 1971. From 1972 on N dropped out of public life, both within his country and abroad. (O.Y.)

★NAGIB, GEN. MUHAMMAD. N was under house arrest from 1954 till 1973, when he was released by Sadat▷. N subsequently denied having authored the book published under his name in 1955, *Egypt's Destiny*; he explained that it was based on various interviews, but that he himself had not read it before publication. Since then N has written his own memoirs. (S.L.)

NAHIAN, AL-, SHEIKH ZEID IBN SULTAN. Ruler of Abu Dhabi▷. Born in 1918. Since Dec. 1971 functioned as President of the Union of Arab Emirates▷. During 1946–66, N was Governor of the Eastern District, al-'Ain. (V.E.)

★NATIONAL LIBERATION FRONT FOR OCCUPIED SOUTH YEMEN — See National Front for the Liberation of South Yemen.

NATIONAL FRONT FOR THE LIBERATION OF SOUTH YEMEN. In Nov. 1967, the NLF▷ changed its name. Upon assuming political power in June 1969, the extremist faction of the NF gained the party and its ideology complete authority over all public institutions, including the army and all citizens of South Yemen▷. This was formulated at the party's congresses held in Mar. 1968, and in Mar. 1972. The NF is the only political body legally permitted to exist in South Yemen, and its leaders are responsible for forming their country's policy. The NF includes the Central Committee (formerly the general leadership), today numbering 310 members and mostly representative of the various regions and districts, is selected by the party. An Executive Committee, chosen by the Central Committee, is composed of ten members and reflects the various power grouping within the party. The Constitution of Nov. 1970 defines the jurisdiction of the state and party organs; in practice, however, the Supreme People's Council, which is to become the Legislative Branch of the Government, as well as the members of the Presidential Council and the Cabinet itself, are all appointed by the party leadership.   (T.Y.)

*NATO. Since the Six Day War▷, NATO members have become increasingly concerned by considerable growth of the Russian Mediterranean Fleet. During the Yom Kippur War▷, the US asked several NATO members for landing facilities for US aircraft taking part in the massive arms air-lift to Israel▷, but only Portugal acquiesced— leading to increased tension within NATO. (Sh.H.)

NEW ISRAEL LEFT. This movement has been conspicuous in its actions of protest against the policies of the Israel▷ Government in the occupied territories and toward the Arab sector in the country. In the summer of 1973 the movement split, some of its members joining *Moked*▷ and others the *Ha'olam Hazeh-Koah Hadash*▷ movement.   (O.Y.)

NIXON, RICHARD M. President of the US. Born in 1913; admitted to the bar 1937; Vice-President 1952–60; Republican candidate for Presidency 1960, and again in 1968, when he was elected; re-elected for second term 1972.

During N's term of office, the US▷ has increased its involvement in ME affairs more than ever before, as reflected in massive sales of arms and equipment to Israel▷, and in US efforts at mediation in the Arab-Israel Conflict▷.

In June, 1974 N visited Egypt▷, Sa'udi Arabia▷, Syria▷, Israel▷ and Jordan.   (Sh.H.)

NIXON DOCTRINE, THE. Never formulated as such, the ND consists of three guiding principles,

emphasized during Nixon's▷ first term as US President in connection with the war in Vietnam: (a) The US will fulfill all its treaty commitments; (b) the US will protect allies and other states whose survival is considered vital to her security from the threat of a nuclear power (i.e. Russia and China); (c) the US will provide military and economic assistance to states to whom she has committed herself by treaty, in the event of their facing aggression by a non-nuclear state. In the latter event the state being attacked must, however, supply the manpower for the conduct of the war. Though relations between the US▷ and Israel▷ have never been formalized by treaties of a political or military 'character, the conduct of the US Government during the Yom Kippur War▷ implied that Israel is considered to be covered by the ND.   (Sh.H.)

*NORTHERN TIER. CENTO▷ continued to comprise Iran▷, Pakistan▷, Turkey▷ and Britain▷, with the US▷ as an Associate Member. The alliance continued its normal activities in the military and strategic spheres, with large-scale economic development plans being implemented in all NT countries and in Pakistan. The 1970 budget of the organization was approximately $1m. The 18th meeting of Ministers from member countries took place in Ankara▷, in May 1971.   (O.Y.)

*NU'MAN, AHMAD MUHAMMAD. Following the first Yemeni▷ elections in Mar. 1971, N formed a Cabinet in May, but resigned two months later. Appointed adviser to the Republican Council in Jan. 1972, and in Feb. 1973 was chosen to be representative for San'a to the planned Yemeni Union with South Yemen▷.

N's son, Muhammad Ahmad Nu'man, has recently become a leading figure in Yemeni politics, rising from the position of Ambassador to Paris to the office of Deputy Prime Minister and Foreign Minister in the Government of Qadi 'Abdullah al-Hajari, set up late in 1972.   (H.E.)

*NUMEIRI, MUHAMMAD JA'FAR. After the abortive revolt in July 1971, N disbanded the National Revolutionary Council and instituted Presidential rule, N being elected President in Oct. 1971. N also became head of the political bureau of the Sudanese Socialist Union, set up in Feb. 1972. When his Minister of Defence resigned in Feb. 1972, N assumed this portfolio but two months later transferred it, as well as command of the army, to Maj.-Gen. 'Awad Halfallah. In Aug. 1973, N was promoted to the rank of General of the Armies. Despite national crises and various conspiracies against, N instituted reforms and took steps to weaken Rightist elements (particularly supporters of the Mahdi▷), as well as extreme Left groups (especially the Communists▷). In Mar. 1972, N reached an accord stopping fighting in the south of Sudan, a central problem for the successive regimes from the first moment of Sudan's▷ independence.

(E.S.)

O

OIL IN THE ME. Generally speaking, the major development concerning ME oil in recent years has been the rise of its international importance. As a result, the economic and political bargaining power of the region's oil producers has increased, accompanied by a steep rise in oil prices and, hence, income to these producers. The oil-producing nations have, in addition, achieved much greater control over the exploitation of their oil fields.

Following Libya's▷ decision in 1970 to cut down its oil production, to obtain higher prices per barrel of exported oil, the Teheran agreements signed at the beginning of 1971 continued this policy for the ME in general. The oil price rise encouraged the giant oil companies to raise their fuel prices, thereby increasing their margins of profit for 1972–3. During this period, the US also began importing petroleum from the ME and North Africa, resulting in still more bargaining power for the producers. Some of these countries, such as Algeria▷, Libya and Iraq▷, either completely or partially nationalized the foreign oil companies' property, while in other ME countries the oil companies "voluntarily" relinquished some control over their fields. Iran▷ assumed complete control over its oil production, and other Persian Gulf▷ nations won a 25% control over profits and oil production of the foreign companies early in 1972. The energy crisis and the oil sanctions applied by the Arab nations during the Yom Kippur War▷, led to world-wide oil shortages, enabling the oil-producing nations to raise their prices unilaterally by as much as 450%. Cutbacks in oil production by the Arab states made it virtually impossible for the large oil companies to supply demands, and the oil-importing countries entered direct negotiations with the oil-producing nations of the ME and North Africa. This opened up still larger markets to the oil-producing countries, who thus demanded further ownership and control of production. At the beginning of 1974 both Kuwait▷ and Qatar▷ gained control of 60% of their oil production, and the other nations in this region will soon probably own at least as much of their oil fields, and eventually attain complete

ownership. The large oil companies will probably continue buying most of the ME oil. The above raised the oil revenues of the ME and North African states from $5,000m in 1968 to $9,200m in 1971, and $17,000m in 1973. Expected income for 1974 has been estimated at $66,000m — more than a third of the world's currency reserves at the end of 1973!

The economic and political power welded by the ME nations, manifest in acts such as the oil embargo and the unilateral oil price rise, rests on the fact that they possess about 55% of the world's known oil reserves, and that the ME is considered to be the only region capable of increasing its oil production sufficiently to supply future needs of the Western nations. Western Europe imported from the ME and North Africa, in the first half of 1973, c. 90% of its oil imports (of which 15% came from Iran). The four largest ME oil-producers (Sa'udi Arabia▷, Iran, Kuwait and Iraq) together control almost half of the world's known oil reserves, while Sa'udi Arabia alone has one fifth of those reserves. Of the world's oil exports in 1972, the ME nations accounted for 987.5m tons, or 80% of the world total. This percentage is increasing.

OIL-PRODUCING COUNTRIES. IRAN: In 1973, oil output increased to 300m tons. In mid-1973, Iran assumed control over the oil consortium which had enjoyed full oil rights since 1954, promising to sell her petroleum to the various member companies of the consortium, except for an agreed percentage for local consumption and self-marketing. The latter percentage is to increase as follows: from 10m tons in 1973 to 75m tons by 1981. On its part, the oil consortium undertook to lend Iran the funds for increasing its oil output to 400m tons by 1976.

Iran's oil revenues came to $1,934m in 1971, and to $3,883m in 1973. Iran today has facilities to refine 33m tons of petroleum *p.a.* By early 1974, negotiations were in progress for construction of two giant oil refineries, each capable of handling 25m tons *p.a.*, one to be constructed by a German firm and the other by a Japanese firm.

IRAQ: Oil output has increased to 76m tons in 1971 and 94.4m tons in 1973. Much of Iraq's oil is exported through pipelines, the capacity of which has also been increased. By late 1973 the pipelines were transporting 60m tons, and it has been decided to increase this to 70m tons.

Iraq has decided to build a 160 km pipeline from the Rumaila oil field to Fao port on the Persian Gulf, as well as a 655 km pipeline to connect its northern wells with the port in the south. The latter pipeline will handle 50m tons of oil *p.a.* An oil pipeline of 30m tons annual capacity is planned to the Turkish port of Dörtyol. Iraq also intends to deepen its port as Fao, to facilitate oil tankers of 350,000 tons when loaded; this alone will increase its oil export capacity by 80m tons *p.a.*

The Government company now controlling the oil fields (formerly owned by the IPC) has expanded drilling at North Rumaila, with the aid of Soviet bloc nations. Since April 1972, this field has produced some 18m tons *p.a.*

In mid-1972, Iraq nationalized IPC wells in the Kirkuk⊳ region, which account for some two-thirds of the oil from this part of the country. Iraq is now marketing this oil herself. Following Iraq's nationalization of the oil wells, Syria⊳ and Lebanon⊳ have nationalized their portions of the IPC pipelines passing through their territories; Lebanon has also nationalized the company's refinery at Tripoli⊳. The oil fields south of Rumaila and at Zubair were not nationalized, but the IPC undertook to increase oil output there from 33m tons (1972) to 80m tons by 1976.

SA'UDI ARABIA: In 1971, oil output reached 238m tons, and in 1973, 370.8m tons. The foremost oil-producing nation in the ME, Sa'udi Arabia's known oil reserves are 132m barrels (but unofficial estimates are even higher). Thus, Sa'udi Arabia plays a leading role among the Arab oil-producing countries and, indeed, initiated the embargo on oil exports which the Arab nations put into effect during the Yom Kippur War⊳. Oil revenues have increased from $966m in 1968 to $2,100m in 1971 and $4,915m in 1973! Estimated revenues for 1974 reached $20,000m!

In addition to the oil export refinery at Ras Tanura, there is a small refinery at Jidda⊳ (c. 600,000 tons *p.a.*) serving local consumption. Sa'udi Arabia is now establishing, with foreign aid, a large petro-chemical enterprise, with an output geared to markets abroad.

KUWAIT: In 1971, oil ouput reached 145m tons. Kuwait decided to freeze production at that level, to prevent rapid depletion of its oil reserves. The annual capacity of the refinery near Mina al-Ahmadi was 15m tons in 1973, while that of the refinery at Shuaiba was increased to 6–7m tons *p.a.*

Early in 1974, Kuwait assumed 60% ownership of the foreign oil companies in its territory, intending to attain full ownership in the next few years. Oil revenues reached $1.439m in 1971, and $2,131m in 1973.

THE NEUTRAL ZONE: Oil output has attained 27m tons *p.a.*, but in 1973 dropped to 25.3m tons.

QATAR: In 1971 oil output rose to 21.5m tons, while in 1973 it came to 27.7m tons. Oil revenues increased from $184m in 1971, to $358m in 1973.

ABU DHABI: In 1971 oil output reached 46.7 m tons,

and in 1973 it rose to 64.3m tons. Oil revenues rose from $418m in 1971 to $1,038 m in 1973.

DUBAI: Oil output rose from 6.2m tons in 1971 to 11m tons in 1973.

'OMAN: In 1973, oil exports reached 13.5m tons.

EGYPT: Technical difficulties in the Morgan oil fields led to a decrease in oil output, from 14m tons in 1971 to 9m tons in 1973.

Oil prospecting licenses were granted to two US companies (Mobil Oil and Exxon) and to several smaller companies from Japan and West Germany. With an eye to the reopening of the Suez Canal⊳, Egypt decided to build several pipelines, including two parallel 42-inch pipes, each capable of supplying 40m tons of oil *p.a.*. The first is to be laid within two years and the second to be ready two-and-a-half years later. They are to connect the Gulf of Suez and Alexandria⊳, a distance of 330 km. The US Bechtel company will install the pipeline for $345m. Financing of the undertaking is underwritten by an Arab company set up for the purpose ($400m capital). Egypt is to put half of the capital; Sa'udi Arabia, Kuwait and Abu Dhabi will put up $60m each, and Qatar has promised $20m. Egypt anticipates that these pipelines will add some $150m *p.a.* to its treasury.

LIBYA: Qaddafi's⊳ new Government has compelled the foreign oil companies to increase Libya's percentage by cutting down on their production. The smaller, independent companies, which had no alternative sources outside Libya, soon acceded to these demands, and the larger companies followed not long after. Libya's success made other ME oil-producing nations realize their negotiating power, and they, too, quickly demanded and received large increases in their oil revenues. Being closer to European markets than the other oil producers, Libya obtained still more favourable terms as seen in the Tripoli Agreement. However, far from being satisfied, Libya began nationalizing foreign oil companies, one-by-one, whether by seizing a 51% interest or by outright confiscation. Inasmuch as Libya was not able to put its huge oil revenues to productive use, Qaddafi continued to curtail Libyan oil output, which dropped from 160m tons in 1970 to 105m tons in 1973. Income from oil, however, rose from $1,295m in 1970 to $1,766m in 1971, and $2,210m in 1973.

ISRAEL: In 1973, oil output at the Heletz field dropped to a mere 37,000 tons, while the output of national gas in the Arad region dropped to 49,115 tons. MARKETING: The oil fields found in the Sinai Peninsula⊳ produced about 4.5m tons in 1967, and about 5m tons in 1973. The Eilat⊳– Ashkelon pipeline began operating in 1970, when

11m tons of oil flowed through it. In 1971, it handled 19m tons; in 1972, 25.5m tons. By mid-1973, this pipeline was transporting 45m tons *p.a.*, and the construction of additional installations could increase this to 60m tons *p.a.* Until the Suez Canal is enlarged sufficiently for super-tankers, the Eilat-Ashkelon pipeline will remain of importance.

In addition to the Haifa refineries, a refinery at Ashdod began operating in mid-1973, with a capacity of 4.25m tons *p.a.*, fed by the Eilat-Ashkelon pipeline. These two refineries are connected to a pipe network which transports petroleum products to the main consumption centres of the country. This network was particularly efficient during the Yom Kippur War▷, when most of the petrol trucks were mobilized by the IDF.

SYRIA: In 1971 oil output had risen to 6m tons, but two years later it was down to 5.2m tons. The carrying capacity of the pipeline to Tartus▷, constructed in 1968, is now 7m tons *p.a.* The refinery at Homs, with a 27m tons *p.a.* capacity, was destroyed in the Yom Kippur War▷.

TURKEY: Oil output in 1973 was at the 1969 level, while the capacity of the Mersin refinery rose to 4.5m tons *p.a.* Recently a refinery was built at Izmit, with a 6.5m ton capacity *p.a.* This brings Turkey's refining capacity to about 16m tons *p.a.* Turkey and Iraq have agreed to commence construction, in July 1974, of a Kirkuk-Dörtyol pipeline, to transport 30m tons *p.a.* ultimately; it will cost about $30m.

OIL TRANSPORT IN THE ME: The closing of the Suez Canal▷ encouraged the building of super-tankers capable of transporting 250,000–500,000 tons of oil. These vessels will not be able to pass through the canal until it is sufficiently widened.

The pipelines connecting Iraq and Sa'udi Arabia to Mediterranean ports convey about 85m tons *p.a.* The Eilat-Ashkelon pipeline can presently handle 45m tons *p.a.*, with an ultimate capacity estimated at 60m tons. Egypt is to construct a pipeline to transport 80m tons *p.a.*, while Iraq and Turkey are to construct a pipeline with a capacity of 30m tons *p.a.*

OIL IN THE ME'S ECONOMY: The huge oil revenues which the oil-producing nations expect in coming years are estimated in the hundreds of billions of dollars, which should hasten development of their national economies and raise standards of living there. Meanwhile the treasuries of Sa'udi Arabia, Kuwait and Libya will be overflowing with surplus capital. The oil-producing nations must invest this capital in a secure and profitable manner in the industrialized nations of the world, unless they decide to decrease their oil production, thereby

causing permanent shortages of oil the world over. A policy of this latter nature (even more than the present inflationary spiral of oil prices) would have the effect of speeding up development of alternative sources of energy in the West, with a resulting lessening in dependence upon ME oil.

OIL PRODUCTION (millions of tons *p.a.*)

	1970	1971	1972	1973
Abu Dhabi	33.28	44.79	50.0	64.27
Algeria	47.25	36.34	52.0	51.77
Bahrain	3.83	3.73	3.5	3.18
Egypt	16.40	14.70	11.0	9.0
Iran	191.66	227.34	254.0	300.0
Iraq	76.55	84.0	67.0	94.41
Israel	0.077	0.062	0.050	0.037
Kuwait	137.39	146.78	152.0	144.51
Neutral Zone	26.72	29.11	30.3	25.37
Libya	159.20	132.25	105.00	105.83
Morocco	0.046	0.022	0.030	0.045
Oman	17.16	14.10	13.60	13.59
Qatar	17.25	20.20	23.30	27.77
Sa'udi Arabia	176.85	223.51	285.50	370.89
Syria	4.35	5.25	5.3	5.28
Tunisia	4.15	4.09	4.10	4.35
Turkey	3.46	3.25	3.50	3.25

(M.C.)

*‘**OMAN.** British▷ withdrawal from the Persian Gulf▷, completed by the end of 1971, led to increased British forces in bases in O. To secure rule over the entire country, the O Government called back political exiles and granted amnesty to rebels willing to surrender. Reconciliation talks with Imam Ghaleb and the Popular Front for the Liberation of ‘Oman and the Occupied Arab Gulf▷, mediated by Kuwait▷, were initiated in 1972 and 1973. In organization and armaments, the army was adapted for operations in the mountainous terrain where the main centres of resistance were located. In addition to British support, military and financial assistance was enlisted from Iran▷, Sa'udi Arabia▷ and Libya▷.

Late in 1971, Government forces gained a foothold in parts of Dhofar▷. The Popular Front attempted to fan open revolt in the northern parts of the country, relying on the followers of the exiled Imam; this was frustrated early in 1973. Armed clashes occurred between South Yemen▷ and O in an attempt to block supply lines to the Popular Front. The dispute between the two states was brought before the UN on the initiative of

South Yemen. In 1972 an agreement on the control of the Hormuz Straits, at the entrance to the Persian Gulf▷, was reached between O and Iran▷; this ceded the island of Ghanam to Iran. Iranian forces are rumoured to be present in Ras Masandam. (The agreement was probaly reached in exchange for armed Iranian assistance to the Sultan of O.)

Despite Imam Ghaleb's endeavours to prevent it, O was admitted to the Arab League▷ in Sept. 1971. (Until then the Imam had been recognized by the League as the official representative of O.) O became a member of the UN in 1971. (V.E.)

ORGANIZATION OF AFRICAN UNITY, RELATIONS WITH THE ME.

The OAU was formed at a summit meeting of African▷ heads of state in Addis Ababa in May 1963. The main emphasis in the charter of the OAU was put on African unity; the sovereignty, territorial integrity and independence of the various states; the need to uproot colonialism in all its forms and to free those areas in Africa which had not yet attained independence; cooperation in economic development and the settlement of disputes by peaceful means. At the time of its establishment, the OAU numbered 32 member states. At present, after additional states have joined upon their attainment of independence, there are 41 members: all the Black African states, as well as six Arab states in Africa — Algeria▷, Egypt▷, Libya▷, Morocco▷, Sudan▷ and Tunisia▷. The joining of countries governed by whites, such as Angola, Mozambique, Rhodesia and South Africa, is prohibited on ideological grounds.

Despite Arab pressure for the condemnation of Israel▷, especially after the Six Day War▷, the OAU did not adopt an active stand on the Arab-Israel Conflict▷ throughout the sixties (only Guinea broke off relations with Israel in 1967). The OAU remained content with passing resolutions affording support of UN Security Council Resolution 242▷ and called for "the withdrawal of foreign military forces and the demilitarization of occupied Arab territories".

At the summit meeting in Addis Ababa in June 1971, the OAU took a more active stand in connection with the Arab-Israel Conflict. In addition to the sharply worded resolutions, a committee of ten was appointed to assist in the implementation of the Security Council's resolution and the renewal of the Jarring▷ mission. Members of this committee were countries known for their friendship toward the Arabs, toward Israel or toward both parties: Cameroon, Ethiopia, Ivory Coast, Kenya, Liberia, Mauritania. Nigeria, Senegal, Tanzania and Zaire.

Four heads of state were chosen from among this group (Senegal, Cameroon, Zaire and Nigeria) to represent the OAU as a fact-finding delegation to Israel and Egypt.

From the early seventies, the influence of the Arab countries within the OAU has steadily increased, as reflected in the election of Muhammad Ould Dadda of Mauritania as President of the Council of African Heads of State in 1971, and the election of King Hasan II of Morocco in 1972. Qaddhafi▷ of Libya headed an unsuccessful campaign at the OAU summit conference of 1973 for the transfer of the OAU centre from Addis Ababa to Cairo or to another location, since he considered Ethiopia was too friendly with Israel. The cumulative influence of Arab political and economic pressure at the OAU summit (May 1973), the Conference of Non-Aligned States, in Algeria (Sept. 1973) and in the UN Security Council (Sept. 1973), as well as the Yom Kippur War▷, resulted in a majority of African states breaking off diplomatic relations with Israel, in Oct.–Nov. 1973. Representatives of the African states expressed "solidarity" with Egypt, whose "territorial integrity had been violated" by the IDF. The African states thought their support would result in a renewed Arab effort in the struggle against "colonial racist" regimes in southern Africa. (S.G.)

ORGANIZATION OF ARAB PETROLEUM EXPORTING COUNTRIES.

Established in 1968 by the largest Arab oil▷ producers, Sa'udi Arabia▷, Kuwait▷ and Libya▷, with the declared objective of preventing Nasser▷ from again using their oil for the attainment of Egyptian political aims, as he tried to do during the Six Day War▷. In order to prevent Egypt▷ from joining the organization, it was laid down in its articles that only Arab countries which derive their main income from oil could join. Due to the "boycotting" of Egypt by the three Royalist countries, Iraq▷ refused to join the organization. However, at the time of the officer's *coup* in Libya there was a far-reaching change in the orientation of the OAPEC and, one after the other, militant Arab countries such as Iraq and Algeria▷ (and ultimately also Egypt) joined the organization. With the outbreak of the Yom Kippur War▷, OAPEC became the main initiator of the Arab oil sanctions and the use of oil as a political weapon.

In 1972 the organization controlled 50.5% of the oil reserves, 27% of oil production and 60% of oil commerce in the world. Its main strength derives from the fact that the large Arab oil producers were the only ones capable of increasing their production at the rate required to fulfil Western oil requirements as predicted before the Yom Kippur War. It is the aim of the Arab oil producing countries to turn the OAPEC into an economic organization, which would operate a jointly-owned fleet of oil tankers and undertake other economic projects. The first example of such a project is a shipyard for super-tankers, now under construction in Bahrain▷.

(M.Ch.)

ORGANIZATION OF PETROLEUM EXPORTING COUNTRIES. Established in 1960 in reaction of the decision of the large Western oil▷ companies to reduce the declared price of crude oil in the Persian Gulf▷ area, as a result of the reduction in the prices of oil products on the international market. The founding members were Iran▷, Iraq▷, Sa'udi Arabia▷, Kuwait▷ and Venezuela. The stated objective of the organization was to bring about a return of the declared prices, which served as a basis for the calculation of their income from each barrel of oil exported, to its previous level. During the first year of its existence, OPEC in fact was content to prevent further deterioration of the declared prices and to obtain relatively small advantages for its members. Other oil exporters later joined OPEC: Qatar▷ in 1961; Indonesia in 1962; Libya▷ in 1962; Abu Dhabi▷ in 1967; Algeria▷ in 1969; Nigeria in 1972; Equador in 1973 and Gabon in 1973 (as an associate member).

As a result of the rapid increase in world oil consumption, it became apparent that the major source for the oil requirements of the Western world were the OPEC member countries. This resulted in an increase in the bargaining power of OPEC, and it obtained large rises in the price of oil and in the overall income of its members. The Teheran and Tripoli agreements signed in the beginning of 1971 assured OPEC members of additional agreed prices up to 1975.

The organization of OPEC as a cartel reached its climax during the Yom Kippur War▷, when it exploited the world oil shortage, created by the sanctions imposed by the Arab countries, to increase the price of oil by 450% in complete disregard of the 1971 agreements.

Mutual support promised by members of the organization to one another allowed several (Algeria, Libya, Iraq) to nationalize Western oil companies' property without risking retaliatory action. Other members, without resorting to formal nationaliza-tion, received increasing portions (25–51%) of the assets of foreign oil companies and of their oil produced by means of a "partnership agreement"

which came into effect early in 1972. Kuwait, which refused to ratify this agreement, gained 60% ownership of the foreign oil companies operating in the sheikhdom in early 1974. It is to be assumed that the other oil producers in the ME will soon make similar gains. In 1972 OPEC controlled 66% of the world oil reserves, 41.5% of world oil production and 90% of the oil in world commerce.   (M.Ch.)

P

PAHLAVI, FARAH (DIBA) Queen of Iran▷. Born in Teheran 1938; daughter of an army officer. Studied architecture in Paris 1957; married Muhammad Reza Shah▷ 1959. In the Regency Law of 1967, the Queen was designated as the regent to rule Iran (as head of a Regency Council) in the event of the Shah's death before the Crown Prince had reached maturity. (Should she remarry in the meantime, this act would be seen as her resignation from the regency.) The Queen plays an important role in the advancement of women in Iran.   (D.M.)

*PAKISTAN. Most Arab nations supported P in its Bangladesh conflict. Toward the end of 1971, both Libya▷ and Jordan▷ sent US built aircraft to P. Egypt▷ remained neutral, but Russia▷ sent aircraft to India through Egypt. Algeria▷ supported P both before and after the war, while Jordan's relations with P were strengthened during 1972. Egyptian-P relations remained friendly throughout.

During Feb. and May 1972, P's President, 'Ali Bhutto, visited several Arab capitals to foster Arab support.   (O.Y.)

*PALESTINE-ARAB GUERILLA ORGAN-IZATIONS. With the additional failure of the PAGO in Jordan▷ in their fight for their strong-holds, they were completely expelled from that country in Jult 1971, after having been forced out of the Jarash-Ajloun hills in the north.

Lebanon▷ has since become the main base for all the PAGO, while their rear and training bases have been transferred to Syria▷ and, to a lesser extent, to other Arab countries, mainly Libya▷. The latter commenced, in mid-1973, to form her own guerilla groups, outside the framework of the PLO▷ In this situation, the PAGO were, in fact, forced to stop intensive activities along the borders of Israel▷, and toward the end of 1972 there was relative quiet—the result of pressure by Arab governments and the method of massive retaliation developed by the IDF. This led to an increase in terrorist activities abroad, carried out mainly by the Popular Front▷ and the Fatah▷, for which a special arm, the Black September, was formed. The most conspicuous events in this context were the murder of Israeli sportsmen during the Olympic Games in Munich (Sept. 1972) and a series of aircraft hijackings and acts of sabotage all over the world, some of them carried out with the assistance of non-Arab terrorist organizations such as the Japanese "Red Army", the Eritrea▷ rebels and the German Bader-Meinhoff group.

During the Yom Kippur War▷, the PAGO fulfilled a marginal function only, chiefly in harrassment shellings and infiltration through the Lebanese border. Immediately after the war there was again relative quiet, with a return to the method of terrorist activities abroad and an unsuccessful attempt to revive their networks in the West Bank▷ and the Gaza Strip▷. On the other hand a new stage in the political activities of the PAGO was initiated — an effort to deprive Jordan of the authority to represent the population of the territories held by Israel at the Geneva Peace Conference▷. The Arab Summit Conference▷ in Algeria in Dec. 1973 adopted a resolution recognizing the PLO as the "only authorized representative" of the Palestine Arabs▷, and hence the PAGO leaders are striving for widespread international recognition and the assurance of their status, or at least the non-harming of their status, in any eventual agreement between Israel and her Arab neighbours.

(E.Y.)

*PALESTINE ARABS. During 1970–3, the position of Hussein▷ in Jordan▷ was strengthened and at the same time the Palestine-Arab guerilla organizations▷, whose centres were removed to other Arab countries, were weakened. Guerilla activities within Israel▷ came to a virtual halt due to insufficient strength to break through the security measures adopted against infiltration and due to the refusal of the population of the Israel-occupied territories to be carried away by extremist circles, together with an increasing feeling as to their futility.

The process of coming to terms with the reality of Israel rule continued steadily, and there was a gradual weakening of the expectation for a meaningful change. Nevertheless, the guerilla organizations did not cease activities, especially in the Gaza Strip▷, during 1970–1. From 1971 on, such activities were weakened as a result of special measures adopted by the Israel authorities, including the thinning out of the refugee▷ camps and the concentration of economic resources to hasten relief of the poverty in the area.

From then on the interest of the population of the occupied territories was centred on the activities of the guerilla organizations abroad, where their successes in hitting Israeli targets increased their prestige without its resulting in expressions of active identification. The movement which boycotted Israeli rule subsided completely. In early 1973 it was apparent that even the lawyers in the West Bank, the "last bastion", were inclined to stop their protracted strike, after actual breaches had appeared previously. Life in the occupied territories continued as usual. The rate of development of infrastructural services increased and the standard of agriculture was raised by introduction of modern methods and new strains of crops. During the period under review there was an increase in the population, with a rise in the rate of natural increase. The trend toward emigration, characteristic of the West Bank▷ during Jordanian rule and during the first years of Israeli control, came to a stop. Even in the Gaza Strip there was a conspicuous demographic change.

During these years there was an increase in commerce across the Jordan river, in both directions. Overall exports at the end of 1972 totalled IL 121.1m as against only IL 60.2m in 1970. Imports from Jordan showed no appreciable increase and were confined to merchandise to the value of IL 19.1m, chiefly industrial products. From time to time there were provisional attempts by the Jordanian Government to limit the movement of goods across the bridges by prohibition or by taxation, as occurred in late 1972. However, summer visits became an extensive tourist movement: As opposed to 6,000 visitors in 1967, 106,000 persons crossed the bridges in 1971. Their permits allowed them to stay in the occupied territories from June to Oct., and they made many trips across the "Green Line" into Israel proper. In 1972, nearly all requests for summer visits were approved and even "friends" invited by inhabitants of the territories were permitted entry. Some 15% of the tourists came from countries which have no borders with Israel, including Libya, Algeria, Morocco, Iraq and the oil sheikhdoms. During 1972–3, some 150,000 Arab "tourists" arrived yearly. They travelled throughout Israel, with a tendency toward visiting towns which in the past had been centres of the Palestinian population.

In 1973 the military governorate commenced the introduction of new arrangements to enable visits to the territories and to Israel during the whole of the year. This led to increased contact between the population of the occupied territories and Israeli Arabs. As of July 1971 there was full freedom of movement on either side of the "Green Line" and nearly all barriers were removed. Two economies developed side-by-side, with mutual supplementation. Apart from dates grown in the Gaza Strip, there seem to have been no crops in the occupied territories threatening competition with those grown in Israel. Exports to Israel in 1972 came to IL 157.2m, as opposed to IL 73.2m in 1970. The volume of imports was greater, reaching IL 544.2m in 1972, as against IL 290.9m in 1970. Imports from Israel were mainly industrial commodities (IL 456.9m). Surplus of imports over exports in trade with Israel reached IL 387m in 1972.

During recent years there has been an increased demand in the Israeli economy for hired labour from the occupied territories. Many labourers from Judaea and Samaria, the Gaza Strip and North Sinai came to work on farming settlements, in construction and in industrial plants. By stages, many of them tended toward finding temporary lodgings in the vicinity of their places of work. At times new "suburbs" of Arab labourers were set up. On this background there were serious disputes between Israeli Arab villages and the labourers from the territories. In Jewish settlements social tensions also arose in this respect, against which the Government took large-scale measures in 1972–3. However, it would appear that these measures could not contain this process or its many consequences. The Yom Kippur War▷ "drove out" the Arab labourers from the territories back to their homes, though after the cease-fire they began returning by stages and the process of settlement, together with its side-effects, started again, albeit on a smaller scale. The average daily wage of the Arab labourer from the territories reached IL 17.2 in 1972, as against IL 11.8 in 1970.

In the three years prior to the outbreak of the Yom Kippur War, security restrictions were reduced by stages, both in the West Bank and in the Gaza Strip. Several of the members of the guerilla organizations were released from prison, or their sentences reduced. The number of people under administrative arrest, which in the period immediately after the occupation stood at several hundreds, was also reduced. (At present this number stands between 20 and 30.) The practise of exiling people to Jordan has ceased and some 50 "veteran" exiles were allowed to return to their homes. The governorate resorted to this method again only after the Yom Kippur War, to stop hostile organization.

The atmosphere of tranquility which prevailed up to Oct. 1973 encouraged the establishment of new projects and the expansion of economic activity. As from 1970 there was increased activity among

politicians for the establishment of a university on the West Bank. A preparatory committee, headed by al-Ja'bari▷, prepared the ground though following a lengthy campaign the Mayor of Hebron announced his withdrawal from the plan, after the revealing of internal differences of opinion among key personalities, and organizational difficulties in the implementation of the plan. The crowning point in the process of the return to normalcy were the municipal elections held in Judaea and Samaria. in 1972 (the first time under Israeli rule), following a lengthy hesitation due to misgivings that the population would react by a complete boycott. Up to the last moment there was the threat of abstention, chiefly due to internal disputes among the leaders of Nablus. However, the lively participation in the elections was a sign of the desire for normal conditions. The election campaigns and voting were orderly. The results of the elections proved that the mayors of the towns had gained the trust of the population, and there were no drastic changes.

During the first days of the Yom Kippur War there was an atmosphere of excitement manifested by hoarding of food, dissemination of rumours, hesitancy to use Israeli currency and individual cases of violence against Israelis. However, the administration reacted swiftly and within two to three days the initial excitement subsided. Shops were assured of plentiful food supplies and a "demonstrative quality" of staples, which had run out during the first few hours of the war. The continued supply dispelled fears and also greatly reduced crowds of potential customers in shops. The military governors were diligent in preserving the continuation of day-to-day activities and at the height of the initial battles they met with local leaders to discuss long-range development plans. Loans were approved, budgets granted for various projects and the population was gradually convinced that the Israeli administration was "here to stay". Jordan's abstention from attacking Israel certainly assisted in tempering the population, and the open bridges across the Jordan river were additional proof of the lack of immediate danger.

During the month of the war there were high powered "private" consultations among leading figures in Judaea and Samaria, apparently mere "situation evaluations". There was a tendency in widespread circles to refrain from cooperation with Israel, leading to difficulties with Arab truck owners on the West Bank, who demanded prohibitive prices for placing their vehicles at the service of the Israeli economy. Tension in the occupied territories increased in the period following the war, with the strengthening of the overall opinion that Israel was about to make a complete withdrawal. Following this mood there was a noticeable general move toward "filling the vacuum". There was appreciable activity among the mayors and, in opposition, increased activity on behalf of the Communist Party. In mid-Nov. 1973, the Communists disseminated proclamations in which the PLO▷ was presented as representing the PA. Together with this there was a demand from the National Council of the PLO to enlarge its circle of representation in order to broaden the basis of popular support and to strengthen its position. There is no doubt that the Communist Party seeks to penetrate this organization and to thus gain political strongholds. Hussein's▷ position has fluctuated from the defence of his right to rule in the West Bank to being prepared for far-reaching concessions.   (O.S.)

*PALESTINE CHARTER. The PC was reformulated and ratified by the Palestine National Council at its conference in Cairo in July 1968. The new draft was more detailed and explained points which had remained obscure in the previous version. Concerning the right of Jews to live in Palestine, para. 6 of the new draft determines that only Jews who lived in Palestine before the "Zionist intrusion" (1917) would be considered as Palestinians.   (J.N.)

*PALESTINE ENTITY. The Yom Kippur War▷ and the initial steps taken in its wake toward a settlement (Geneva Peace Conference▷) increased the importance of the problem of the PE. Hussein's▷ standing as representative of the Palestinian Arabs▷ on the West Bank▷ weakened. The Algiers Arab Summit Conference▷ of Nov. 1973 recognized the PLO▷ as the only legitimate representative of the Palestinian people. A similar resolution was adopted by the World Moslem Conference at Lahore in Feb. 1974. Contacts and discussions in anticipation of the reconvening of the Geneva Conference raised the possibility of representations of the West Bank and the Gaza Strip▷. Such proposals are supported by some leaders of the Palestine-Arab guerilla organizations▷, in the beliefs that they will be able to control the representations.

On the West Bank and in the Gaza Strip, support for the PLO has increased somewhat since the last war, but many local leaders remain attached to the Hashemite▷ regime. These propose that any Palestinian entity to be established maintain close ties with Jordan▷.   (E.A.)

*PALESTINE LIBERATION ORGANIZA-TION. Following the Yom Kippur War▷ there

was an increased demand for the establishment of a Palestine Government-in-exile, whether as a replacement for the PLO or as one of its organs. Sadat▷ made a public statement calling for such a move and several of the Palestine-Arab guerilla▷ leaders voiced support.   (E.Y.)

PAN-IRAN PARTY. Extreme Right party in Iran▷, established during the Second World War; it disappeared temporarily from public view after the Mossaddeq▷ era, reactivating once again after 1960. The mould of the PIP is somewhat militaristic, its members wearing a distinctive uniform; the role of the leader and his importance is constantly stressed. Racial or Pan-Iranian motives play an important part in the PIP ideological platform, which favours uniting all elements (including Kurds▷ and Iranians in the Persian Gulf▷) under a single political entity. The PIP supports the White Revolution, but holds that the Government and the ruling party have failed in their application of the Shah's concepts.

In 1970, the PIP attacked the Government, voting against relinquishing Bahrain▷, "the 14th province of Iran". Dr. Fazlollah Sadr, who abstained from the voting, was expelled from the PIP, and the same year set up the Iranians Party▷. The political power of the PIP declined in the 1967 elections, and it was not represented in the 1971 elections.   (D.M.)

PARTIAL AGREEMENT. Joint Israel-US-Egypt attempt to break the deadlock in the ME conflict between 1970 and 1972. These efforts have been variously named — "interim solution", "Sadat's February 1972 initiative", "proximity talks" and "partial settlement". Such efforts to reach a settlement with US aid failed because of the varying objectives and motives of the · parties. However, after the Yom Kippur War▷, the Separation of Forces Agreements▷ were concluded and carried out on the Egyptian and Syrian fronts, in effect based on similar assumptions raised in earlier initiatives.

In Oct.-Dec. 1970, Israel adopted decisions aimed at strengthening and prolonging the cease-fire agreement achieved with the aid of US Secretary of State William Rogers▷ in Aug. 1970, intending this to be a step toward the cessation of hostilities. In this context, Israel Defence Minister Dayan▷ on 3 Oct., 1970, proposed a settlement in Sinai which would be acceptable to Israel and Egypt. Dayan intended a gradual Israel withdrawal from the Suez Canal▷, demilitarization of a zone 10–20 mi. wide and opening the Canal to traffic. Though *al-*

Ahram▷ described this proposal as unrealistic, Sadat▷ countered with a proposal of his own on 4 Feb., 1971, calling for Israeli withdrawal from the east bank of the Canal as the first step in the execution of all the provisions of UN Resolution 242▷, according to a timetable to be established. On his part, Sadat promised to begin clearing the Suez Canal immediately, and to open it to international traffic. In an interview (15 Feb., 1971), Sadat explained that he meant an Israeli withdrawal to "behind el-Arish".

Israel raised its own proposal and then welcomed the principles behind the Egyptian offer, for various reasons: (a) After the cease-fire of Aug. 1970, the Egyptians immediately violated that agreement's provisions and advanced their missile installations to the shores of the Suez Canal. This led Israel to refuse renewed discussions with Dr. Jarring▷, who acted under the provisions of UN Resolution 242. When the cease-fire period neared its end (Dec. 1970), Israel's proposal aimed at preventing the renewal of the War of Attrition.

(b) Sadat's rise to power, in Oct. 1970, encouraged Israel to try and win his confidence by proposing a move that would yield him a significant political achievement and also result in reduced tension between the two countries. By withdrawing from the bank of the Canal, Israel also wanted to separate the two armies and remove the constant affront to Egyptian morale, posed by Israel flags flying in the face of Egyptian forces.

(c) Israel hoped that a partial agreement would move Egypt toward development and rehabilitation of the Suez Canal — trends that would relieve pressures for renewed warfare without giving Egypt a military advantage.

Egypt, for its part, hoped to achieve the following from Sadat's initiative: (a) The first stage in an Israel withdrawal from all occupied territories. (Later Egypt attempted to tie her agreement to a partial settlement with an Israel undertaking to withdraw to the international boundary, or an affirmative Israel reply to Dr. Jarring's memorandum of 8 Feb., 1971.) (b) A clear military advantage, by moving Egyptian forces to the east bank of the Canal at no cost whatsoever. This would give her a powerful position in attempting to force further withdrawal, or in the reopening of hostilities. (c) Israel-US relations would be undermined through the utilization of US aid in achieving a partial settlement. Several times in 1971 the Egyptian President declared that he hoped the US would stop supplying arms to Israel and that he assigned much greater importance to the attitude of the US than to that of Israel.

The US attempted to utilize the motives of both parties in order to break the deadlock in the ME conflict, to reduce tension in the area and the danger of superpower confrontation, as well as trying to gain a foothold in Egypt after Nasser's death.

Jordan, Syria and the Palestine Arabs, all of whom consider themselves to be sides to the conflict, opposed these moves and criticized them as "partial" solutions.

After Sadat had made his proposal, intensive bilateral talks were held between the US and Israel, and between the US and Egypt. Rogers visited Egypt on 4 May, and Israel on 6 May, 1971. Sisco▷ came to Egypt on 9 May, 1971, and spent five days in Israel, from 1 Aug., 1971. Sterner was in Egypt from 4–16 July, 1971. In addition, both Egyptian and Israeli leaders travelled to the US for talks with the State Department. The major points of disagreement concerned the move of Egyptian forces to the east bank of the Suez Canal, and the way in which any partial settlement would relate to a final agreement.

The conclusion of a Cooperation and Friendship Treaty between Egypt and Russia▷, on 27 May, 1971, slowed US activity somewhat. Several times in the course of 1971 and 1972, Sadat said that the US initiative was renewed only after he had agreed to renew diplomatic relations with the US and to eject Soviet personnel from Egypt at the conclusion of the first stage of any partial settlement; Sadat also explained that Egypt's attitude had not changed in consequence of the treaty signed with Russia.

After Sisco returned from Israel, anti-US propaganda intensified in Egypt. Sadat termed US activity a trick and an attempt at leading him astray (Sept. 1971). In Oct. 1971, Rogers made a new six-point proposal in a speech at the UN General Assembly, aimed at overcoming the differences between Israel and Egypt. The US also proposed "proximity talks" between the two parties, to be held in New York in order to accelerate the pace of negotiations. Initially Israel disagreed with Rogers' six points and conducted negotiations on them with the US. Only after explanations were received did Israel agree to them.

Egypt was about to agree to proximity talks and even appointed Mourad Ghaleb to head its delegation; however, after Sadat's visit to Moscow in Oct. 1971, *al-Ahram*▷ wrote on 5 Nov., 1971, that proximity talks were worse than the 1949 Rhodes Armistice▷ talks had been. Sadat rejected the US proposal by using the US explanation that they would act as catalyst, rather than in a more active role. In a Jan. 1972 speech he again attacked the US for having "misrepresented" his initiative, turning it into a partial settlement, and finally to a "partial agreement about a partial settlement". On that occasion Sadat announced breaking contact with the US on this subject, bringing all significant efforts to a close, until the Separation of Forces Agreement▷ of Feb. 1974.   (Al.S.)

PERES, SHIM'ON — See RAFI.

*POPULAR DEMOCRATIC FRONT FOR THE LIBERATION OF PALESTINE. In spite of its generally extremist attitudes, the PDFLP follows a moderate policy on military tactics. Thus, it objects to terrorist attacks outside the ME. It also favours the establishment of a Palestinian state on the West Bank▷ and in the Gaza Strip▷, and proposes to create contacts with anti-Zionist circles in Israel▷.   (E.Y.)

POPULAR FRONT FOR THE LIBERATION OF 'OMAN AND THE OCCUPIED ARAB GULF. Underground organization with leftist revolutionary tendencies, active mainly in the Sultanate of 'Oman▷. The PFLOOAG's origins are in Dhofar▷, where a revolt took place in 1966, demanding autonomy and even complete separation from the Sultanate. The character of the organization changed over the years, and it came to assume a Communist and Maoist line, with support obtained from South Yemen▷, as well as from China▷. The PFLOOAG's long-range objectives now go far beyond the confines of Dhofar and include seizure of power in all 'Oman, as well as the overthrow of the pro-Western royal regimes in the Persian Gulf▷ area. Conflict between the PFLOOAG and the Government has intensified since Sultan Qabus'▷ accession to power in 1970; the latter was successful in obtaining military assistance from Iran▷ and economic aid from Sa'udi Arabia▷. In 1973, the PELOOAG established contacts with the supporters of the exiled Imam in Yemen▷.   (U.E.)

*POPULATION. In 1973 the population of the ME numbered c. 167m. In several countries the rate of natural increase rose due to improved medical services.

POPULATION OF ME COUNTRIES —

1973 ('000)

Iran	32,600	Sa'udi Arabia	7,900
Iraq	9,300	Jordan*	1,680
Lebanon	3,100	Kuwait	970
Syria	6,900	South Yemen	1,550
Turkey	37,900	Yemen	6,200
Egypt	35,600	Libya	2,150
Israel*	3,150	Sudan	16,900

* Excluding the West Bank, with a population of c. 720,000, and the Gaza Strip, with a population of c. 350,000.

(M.E.)

*PORT SA'ID. After the Yom Kippur War▷, PS was included in the plan for reconstruction of towns along the Suez Canal▷, calling for the erection of new commercial plants; widening the harbour; and the construction of a tunnel to connect this region to the Sinai Peninsula▷.   (O.G.)

Q

QABUS b. SA'ID. Governor of 'Oman▷ sultanate in the Persian Gulf▷. Born 1942; an Ibadi Sunnite▷. Received military training in Britain; served in British army till 1966; returned to 'Oman 1966, and held under house arrest by his father, Sa'id▷. In July 1970 Q assumed power by deposing his father, and changed the state's name to the "'Oman Sultanate". Carried out reforms in Government institutions, in education, in the army and in economic development.   (N.E.)

*QADDHAFI, AL-, MU'AMMAR. Q ceased to be Prime Minister in July 1972, continuing, however, to rule Libya▷ as Chairman of the Revolutionary Council. In the years under review, Q continued his active foreign policy, his attempts to attain a position of leadership within the Arab world and to play an international role in areas beyond the ME (Africa▷, the Maghreb▷, non-ME Islamic states).

(E.S.)

QASIMI, AL-, SAQR b. MUHAMMAD. Since 1972 ruler of Sharja▷. Elected by the Supreme Council of the Union of Arab Emirates▷ after an attempted *coup d'état* during which the previous ruler, his brother, was killed.   (A.W.)

*QATAR. In Feb. 1972 the ruler was deposed by his cousin, the Crown Prince, seeking to implement the reforms declared in 1970. In April 1972 a 20-member Advisory Council was appointed, eventually to be replaced by an elected council. In 1971 oil▷ production reached 17.2m tons, with revenues at over $200m p.a. In Jan. 1973 an agreement was signed with the oil companies operating in Q territory, by which 20% of the companies' shares reverted to Q.   (V.E. & Y.K.)

R

RABI', 'ALI SALEM. Chairman of the Presidential Council in the Republic of South Yemen▷. Born 1934; began career as school teacher; studied law; active in FLOSY▷ against the British▷ 1963–7; exiled under Qahtan al-Sha'bi▷ for having participated in revolt. Chairman of the Presidential Council and Supreme Commander of the Armed Forces since June 1969. Member of the Executive Committee 1970, and of the Central Committee of the National Front for the Liberation of South Yemen▷. R is identified as the leader of the pro-Chinese▷ faction in the regime; his power is based mainly on supporters from workers and farmers, in rural party branches outside Aden▷.   (T.Y.)

RABIN, YITZHAQ. Born in Jerusalem 1922. Israeli military and political figure. Educated at an agricultural school and joined the *Palmach*▷ 1940, participating in several clandestine operations including commando raids on Atlith prison-camp and Jenin police-station, and eventually became Deputy Commander of the *Palmach*. In the Arab-Israel War of 1948▷, R served as Commander of the Harel Brigade which fought in and around Jerusalem▷. After the war R became Chief of Operations and in 1956 Commander of the Northern Sector. R was appointed Chief of Staff 1964 and led the IDF in the Six Day War▷. After resigning from the army in 1968, R was appointed Ambassador to the US, serving with considerable personal success until 1973. R then joined the Alignment▷ party, was elected to the *Knesset* in Dec. 1973, and was appointed Minister of Labour in Golda Meir's▷ Government of Mar. 1974. After Meir's resignation, in April 1974, R was elected the Alignment candidate to form a new Government.   (A.W.)

RAFI. This faction within the Alignment▷ remained in support of Moshe Dayan▷. However, in 1973, those R members who did not join the Alignment formed the State List and as such joined the *Likud*▷. After the Yom Kippur War▷, Dayan and Shimon Peres threatened not to join the Government to be formed and many R members supported the establishment of a National Unity Government.   (O.Y.)

RAKAH. This Israeli▷ party has become stronger in the Arab sector, especially since the Yom Kippur War▷. In the Dec. 1973 elections, R representation in the *Knesset* was increased to four seats.   (O.Y.)

*RAS AL-KHAIMA. At first refused to join the Union of Arab Emirates▷ when it was formed in Dec. 1971, in protest against Iranian▷ occupation of the two Tumb islands, which RK claimed. Key positions in the administration of the Union were also demanded. In Feb. 1972 RK gave up her claim on the islands and joined the Union.   (V.E.)

*REFUGEES. The condition of the Palestinian refugees in the Arab countries has not changed materially, with the exception of those in the Gaza Strip▷, who have been thinned out and partly sent to other areas by the Israeli▷ authorities. Following the Yom Kippur War▷, two new refugee problems arose, one in Syria▷ and the other in Egypt▷ : (a) Tens of thousands of peasants living in the agricultural buffer area conquered by the IDF west of the Suez Canal fled their homes after the Egyptian army had cut their main water canal, thus in effect putting an end to agriculture in the region; these refugees left for the Nile Delta and Cairo. With the signing of the Separation of Forces Agreement▷ and the departure of Israeli forces from the west bank of the canal, these people began returning to their homes. Egyptian plans call for the resettling of the Suez Canal▷ towns by hundreds of thousands of refugees who had left the region in June 1967, and during the War of Attrition. These refugees have been living in overcrowded conditions in Cairo's▷ slums, and constituted a serious social problem.

(b) In Syria, some 15,000 Syrian subjects abandoned the area of the enclave conquered by the IDF during the Yom Kippur War, moving toward Damascus. One of Syria's conditions for agreeing to a Separation of Forces Agreement▷ with Israel was that a part of these refugees would be allowed to return to their homes.   (O.Y.)

RIYAD, MAHMOUD. Secretary of the Arab League▷ since the end of the tenure of office of 'Abd-ul-Khaleq Hassuna▷, in May 1972. Born 1917; graduated Military Academy 1939; in Arab-Israel War of 1948▷, and at Rhodes Armistice▷ talks between Egypt▷ and Israel▷; later a member of the Israel Egyptian Mixed Armistice Commission. An architect of the United Arab Republic▷; Egyptian Ambassador to Syria; later Adviser on Foreign Affairs to Nasser▷; Egyptian representative to the UN and Egyptian Minister for Foreign Affairs 1964–Jan. 1972; subsequently appointed Adviser on Foreign Affairs to Sadat▷.

R is considered loyal to the regime in his outlook. Nevertheless, he is considered a supporter of Egypt's Pan-Arab▷ orientation.   (Al.S.)

RIFA'I, AL-, 'ABD-UL-MUN'IM. R resigned from politics after Sept. 1970; since then he has served as personal representative of Hussein▷ to Egypt and Syria in attempts to improve relations with Jordan▷. Sent to Russia▷ in Nov. 1971; and visited Egypt in July 1972 and May 1973, after having been appointed Jordan representative to the Arab League▷.   (O.Y.)

RIFA'I, AL- ZAYD. Jordanian▷ diplomat and politician. Born in 'Amman 1936; graduate of Victoria College, Alexandria (where he first became friendly with Hussein▷); Foreign Service 1957–65; transferred to the Royal Court where he served variously, including as Minister of the Royal Court 1970. Ambassador to Britain 1971, where he was slightly infured by Palestine-Arab guerillas▷.

Prime Minister of Jordan since May 1973. R is considered a close adviser to Hussein and enjoys his confidence.   (O.Y.)

*ROGERS, WILLIAM. In the summer of 1973, some months after Nixon▷ was elected to his second term of office, R resigned from his post as US Secretary of State, and was succeeded by Dr. Kissinger▷.   (E.A.)

*RUMANIA. There was no change in R's basic stand on the ME conflict, though a slight move was made toward the Arab point of view. During a tour of Arab countries, in Feb. 1974, R leader Ceausescu called for the establishment of a Palestine state. On the whole, R developed political and economic ties with the Arab countries. Relations between R and Israel were marked by visits of Golda Meir▷ in 1972 and of Abba Eban▷ following the Yom Kippur War▷.   (O.Y.)

*RUSSIA, INTERESTS AND POLICIES IN THE ME. From 1970 to July 1972, there was an increased R involvement in Egypt▷ in strategic, operational and tactical spheres. On the tactical level the R advisers increased their efforts in training the armies of Egypt and Syria▷. On the operational level they established an anti-aircraft missile system, the control system of which was operated by R advisers. On the strategic level, R naval forces in the Mediterranean reached 40–60 vessels. The extent of R operational involvement may be gauged by an aerial dog-fight in which IDF aircraft shot down four or five Egyptian aircraft flown by R pilots.

Sadat▷ visited R on 1–2 Mar., 1971. Relations between R and Egypt later deteriorated due to Sadat's policy and R foreign policy. This occurred in two main spheres: On the one hand there was increased tension between R advisers and their Egyptian trainees and on the other hand there were increased differences of opinion between the role R agreed to play (as an arms supplier, and in her military presence in Egypt) and the role which Sadat wished her to play. The R instructors seem not to have been satisfied with living conditions in Egypt or with the achievements of the forces being trained. There were hints that Sadat wanted R to supply offensive weapons, namely surface-to-surface missiles and advanced types of aircraft, and to give a clear definition of the practical military support she would be prepared to render if and when Egypt crossed the Suez Canal▷. While the tension between Egypt and R increased, conditions were created for further rapprochement between R and the US. The preference given by R to the détente▷ made her suspect, from the Egyptian point of view. All these elements led to an open rift in R-Egyptian relations; an indication of this rift could be observed during the crisis in Sudan▷, when R supported the Communist Party▷ and Sadat supported Numeiri▷.

The India▷-Pakistan▷ war in Dec. 1971 added to the tension between Egypt and R. Though a "treaty of friendship and cooperation" was signed on 28 May, 1971, and Sadat continued to visit R (Oct. 1971, Feb. 1972, April 1972), on 18 July, 1972, the expulsion of R advisers from Egypt was announced.

With the deterioration of relations with Egypt, R moved its centre of activity from the southern ME to the north. In 1972 a "friendship and cooperation" treaty was signed with Iraq▷, and serious attention was devoted to Syria▷. This largely accelerated the intensified struggle for power in the Persian Gulf▷ and over the oil▷ pipelines. After the Nixon▷-Brezhniev meeting in May 1972, and the expulsion of R advisers from Egypt, there were several attempts to widen the R basis for cooperation by means of economic aid and aid in the development of local economic resources (such as the Euphrates▷ dam, aid in oil prospecting and drilling in Iraq, and the training of technicians in Iran▷). With the aggravation of the energy crisis there was an increased interest in the re-opening of the Suez Canal▷ and in the gateway to the Persian Gulf▷. Before and during the Yom Kippur War▷, R found herself involved in Arab policy in a different manner than prior to July 1972. Greater importance was attached to the supply of arms — the need for quick delivery according to precise timetables and from the point of view of profitability (for the arms received by Syria and Egypt during the 1973 war were actually paid for).

The question as to whether R was an active or passive partner to the planning which preceded the Yom Kippur War is at present unresolved. On the one hand, R instructors were involved in preparing the Egyptian and Syrian armies and it is difficult to assume that they were not aware of the preparations. On the other hand, due to the détente, the exact date of the attack may have been kept secret even from R. In addition, R also employed methods of her own to keep track of events in the ME, unconnected with the intelligence supplied by the Arabs. However, no actual deployment of R forces was noticeable up to the beginning of the war.

Since Oct. 1973, R has been striving to have a larger say in the fate of the ME. To all appearances, the US and R are cooperating in attempts to find a durable solution to the ME problem. In fact, however, each of the superpowers is seeking to gain political and economic advantages to serve its own interests. So far R has taken no action which could endanger the cease-fire or the agreements already obtained between the Arabs and Israel.   (Am.S.)

S

SAB, DR. MUHAMMAD. Iranian statesman. Born in Kerman 1924; studied education, University of Teheran; doctorate in Business Administration at University of Southern California. A founder of the Iran Novim▷ party, S served in the *Majlis* since 1963. Governor of Isfahan and Gilan provinces 1965–71. In May 1971 S was made Minister of Information and in Sept. 1971 became Minister of Interior, one of the most important posts in the Government.   (D.M.)

SABAH, AL-, JABER AHMAD. Born 1928. Kuwaiti▷ Prime Minister 1965; Heir Apparent since June 1966. Also head of the Supreme Defence Council.   (V.E.)

SABAH, AL-, SABAH AL-SALEM. Ruler of Kuwait▷. Born 1915; Heir Apparent 1961–5; Prime Minister 1963–5. Came to power following the death of his brother, in Nov. 1965, as twelfth ruler of the al-Sabah▷ dynasty.   (V.E.)

★SABRI, 'ALI. Sentenced to death for his part in the anti-Sadat▷ plot; this sentence was commuted to life imprisonment with hard labour.

★SADAT, AL-, ANWAR. S has emerged as a right-wing Liberal, an enthusiastic nationalist with deep religious leanings. As Chairman of Egypt's▷ National Assembly, S had permitted members considerable freedom to express their ideas, in spite of the fact that Nasser's▷ Presidential regime allowed for little influence or activity on the part of the Assembly. As President of Egypt, S extended the authority of the National Assembly, under the Constitution of 1971. During his first three years as President, S instituted many other liberal changes. After the arrest of the leftist faction (May 1971), S introduced various changes in Egypt's political, economic and social life, generally tending to greater liberalization, with more authority given to the various political bodies, as well as to economic groups.

Six years of "cold war" with Israel▷ ended with the Yom Kippur War▷; though ending with no clear victory for either side, it left Egypt with certain political gains. In foreign policy, S has achieved a new political balance in Egypt's relations with the two super-powers. S was successful in limiting Russian▷ military and political influence within his country, though such influence had naturally accelerated following the Six Day War▷. S expelled the Russian experts and military advisers from Egypt in 1972, and subsequently allowed the US a more direct role in influencing Egypt's foreign policy and national economy.   (S.L.)

SA'ID b. TAIMUR. Born 1910; Governor of Muscat-and-'Oman▷ in the Persian Gulf▷ 1938–70. Received education in India and Iraq. During his rule, the Sultanate underwent little progress or economic development, and outside influence was discouraged. S was deposed by his son, Qabus▷, in July 1970, was exiled and died abroad in 1972. (V.E.)

★SA'IQA, AL-. After the change of Government in Syria▷, in Nov. 1970, the two men placed in charge of S were Suhair Muhsin and Sami al-'Attari.   (E.Y.)

SALIM, MEMDUH. Egyptian Deputy Prime Minister and Minister of Interior since May 1971. Born 1920; served in the Egyptian Police. In 1967, S began activities in regional government; in Dec. 1970 S was appointed district governor of Alexandria▷.

In May 1971, S was asked by Sadat▷ to prepare the legal foundations for ousting the Sabri▷ group; his success rewarded him with his post in the Cabinet and later he was made Deputy Prime Minister. S is also a member of the Arab Socialist Union▷, and the Council for Civil Defence. A technocrat, S is among Sadat's most loyal supporters.   (Al.S.)

*SALLAL, AL-, 'ABDULLAH. In Nov. 1972, it was announced in Cairo that S and his former deputy, 'Abdullah Juzilan, were members of a political body in exile calling itself the National Democratic Front of Yemen.   (H.E.)

SAMMARAI, 'ABD-UL-HALEQ. Member of Iraqi▷ Revolutionary Council. In 1972–3, S was Gen. Bakr's▷ sometime emissary to various Arab countries. S was arrested on charges that he knew of the Nazem Qazzar▷ plot against the Government; sentenced to death, he was later released.
(O.Y.)

*SAPIR (KOZLOVSKY), PINHAS. Born in Poland 1909; active in leadership of *Hechalutz* movement prior to immigrating to Palestine in 1929. Later chosen manager of *Mekorot* Water Company. During the Arab-Israel War of 1948▷, S was Director-General of the Defence Ministry, and for several years after Israel's▷ independence was Director-General of the Ministry of Finance. Minister of Commerce and Industry 1955; Minister of Finance in Levi Eshkol's▷ Cabinet; Secretary of the Alignment▷ 1968. S was reappointed Minister of Finance after the 1969 elections, and continued as such in Golda Meir's▷ Cabinet after the Dec. 1973 elections as well. Sapir is considered the "strong-man" of the Alignment, and had often been considered a candidate for Prime Minister.   (E.A.)

SAQQAF, AL-, 'OMAR. Sa'udi Arabian▷ statesman. Born 1923; in diplomatic service; served as Permanent Secretary for Foreign Affairs. S was Feisal's▷ personal emissary abroad and, in April 1968, was appointed Foreign Secretary.   (T.Y.)

*SA'UD, HOUSE OF. Sources opposed to the present rule in Sa'udi Arabia▷ report that a struggle is already under way among Feisal's▷ brothers over the succession. According to these sources, one group vying for power is led by Feisal's chief deputy, Crown Prince Khaled b. 'Abd-ul-'Aziz. The latter commands the security services and has been called Sa'udi Arabia's "strong-man". In Mar. 1970, after several unsuccessful attempts to replace Feisal and change the form of government, there was talk of dividing the present powers of the king so that Khaled would be President, while Fahed would serve as Prime Minister and Foreign Minister. No concrete steps, however, were taken in this direction.

Two other princes involved in Sa'udi Arabia's political life are Sultan b. 'Abd-ul-'Aziz, Minister of Defence and aviation, and the Inspector-General of the army, and Sultan's deputy since July 1969, Tariki b. 'Abd-ul-'Aziz.   (T.Y.)

*SA'UD b. 'ABD-UL-'AZIZ. Following S's death in 1969, a struggle took place within the royal family over his wealth, a considerable part of which was located abroad. Feisal▷ gave instructions to freeze this capital for the benefit of Sa'udi Arabia's treasury.   (T.Y.)

*SA'UDI ARABIA. In 1969–70 several unsuccessful attempts to overthrow Feisal▷ were made by underground opposition, mainly petty air-force officers and oil▷ company employees in Dhahran▷, supported by the opposition outside SA, mainly in South Yemen▷ and Syria▷. Feisal continued his policy of slow modernization. Efforts have been made to develop educational, health, welfare and communications services, and to settle the Bedouin▷. In foreign affairs, SA continues to play a dominant role in the Arabian Peninsula. SA recognition of the Republican regime in Yemen▷, in July 1970, following the treaty between the Monarchists and, the Republicans, was achieved under SA auspices. SA's influence in the Arab world grew considerably. In her relations with Egypt▷, especially after Sadat's▷ rise, there was a marked improvement and SA has extended to Egypt considerable economic aid. Collaboration with Egypt is clearly evident in the use of oil as a political and economic weapon as a supplement to the Egyptian military effort against Israel.

SA's standpoint in the Arab-Israel Conflict▷ is based on three demands: (a) Israeli return to the June 1967 borders; (b) realization of the rights of the Palestinians; and (c) the return of the Holy Places▷ of Islam to Arab control. Feisal visited several African▷ countries in Nov. 1972, in an effort to build a broad Islamic front against Israel. Relations with the Palestine-Arab guerilla organizations▷ are quite selective, supporting 'Arafat's▷ PLO▷, but strongly opposing Habash's▷ Popular Front for the Liberation of Palestine▷ and Hawatma's▷ Popular Democratic Front for the Liberation of Palestine▷ — regarding them as too extreme and too leftish.

SA's relations with Syria▷ have deteriorated sharply, aggravated in May 1970 by the blowing up of the Tapline. Trade between the two countries dropped, flights were cancelled and SA threatened to stop aid to Jordan▷, Egypt and the Palestine terrorist organizations. Relations with Syria improved by early 1971, and SA tried to mediate between Jordan and the terrorist organizations, missions from the Jordan Government and the

Palestinian organizations visiting Jidda in Sept. 1971. Following the Yom Kippur War▷, relations with Jordan deteriorated when SA, with other Arab states, recognized the PLO as the only legitimate representative of the Palestine Arabs. (T.Y.)

SEPARATION OF FORCES AGREEMENTS.

ISRAEL-EGYPT: Following the Six-Point Agreement▷ reached at the Kilometre 101 talks▷, and after the opening moves in the Geneva Peace Conference▷, the Chiefs of Staff of Israel and Egypt met on 18 Jan. 1974, at Kilometre 101 on the Suez-Cairo road and signed an agreement for the separation of the armed forces of the two countries along the Suez Canal▷. This agreement resulted from mutual concessions, as well as the active mediatory efforts of US Secretary of State Kissinger▷; it provided for Israeli withdrawal from the area occupied west of the Canal in the last days of the Yom Kippur War▷, the establishment of a 10 km buffer-zone between the two armies, under UNEF▷ supervision, and the thinning out forces in defined areas east and west of the buffer-zone. West of the Canal, Egypt could maintain unlimited forces, though anti-aircraft missiles were not to be placed in positions effective beyond the Egyptian "thinned-out" zone, where Egypt was allowed eight infantry battalions (70,000 men), 30 tanks and 36 short-range cannon. Israel forces in the Israeli thinned-out zone were to be of similar size, but east of it no limits were placed on Israel.

The agreement provided 28 days for the execution of its thinning-out and separation provisions, which would start after five days of technical and clarification talks between representatives of the two armies. Execution of all parts of the agreement were to take no longer than seven weeks. UNEF troops stationed in the buffer zone and charged with the inspection of the thinned-out zones on either side were to lend the agreement credibility. In addition the two parties were permitted to conduct aerial surveillance flights over their own lines.

The importance of this agreement lay in its preventing accidental or intentional local encounters which could deteriorate into fullfledged war. Furthermore, it removed the Israeli encirclement of the Egyptian Third Army, as well as enabled demobilization of some Israel reserves.

Egypt stressed that this agreement constituted a technical military step not to be interpreted as an expression of Egypt's attitude to the conflict in general, and warned against any attempt to freeze the situation along the lines newly-occupied by the two sides. On the other hand, Israel emphasized that painstaking implementation of all provisions in the agreement, as well as the normalization of civilian life along the Suez Canal, would constitute the test of Egypt's true intentions. (H.S.)

ISRAEL-SYRIA: On 30 May, 1974, a SFA was initialed; the agreement, reached through the mediation of Dr. Kissinger▷, included an undertaking to cease all "hostile acts". Israel was to withdraw from the territory captured during the Yom Kippur War▷ and from the town of Kuneitra and an adjacent area. A UN buffer-zone would separate the two armies, and would be manned by 1,250 men of a UN Disengagement Observer Forces (UNDOF). In the first 10 km zone, each side would be allowed to hold 6,000 troops, 75 tanks and 36 light cannon. In the next 10 km zone, neither side would be allowed to keep long-range artillery, ground-to-ground missiles or Katyusha rockets, and no more than 450 tanks were permitted. For 25 km from the disengagement line, no anti-aircraft missiles could be kept. Civilians were to return to the areas returned to Syria outright and to parts of the buffer-zone (Kuneitra and its environs) though in the buffer-zone only a Syrian civilian administration would be allowed. Syria refused to undertake to prevent Palestine-Arab guerillas▷ from operating from its territory, but Asad▷ is believed to have given a verbal undertaking to Kissinger on the subject.

Following the signing of the agreement in Geneva, on 31 May, 1974, exchange of POWs began. (Sh.H.)

SHA'BI, AL-, QHATAN MUHAMMAD. In Oct. 1970, former senior members of the South Yemen▷ Government under S, who had been arrested with him and accused of plotting against the regime, were tried. S was not among those accused, perhaps out of fear that it would lead to a popular uprising. As far as is known, S has not appeared in public since his arrest. (T.Y.)

SHARAF, SAMI 'ABD-UL-RAUF. Egyptian intelligence officer and politician. Born 1929; after the 1952 revolution served in President Nasser's▷ Office, holding several staff positions. Left army with rank of Major in 1954 to manage the President's Information Office. Operated behind scenes till April 1970, when S was appointed Minister of State for the Presidency of the Republic; continued as such even after Nasser's death, until dismissed in May 1971 for his part in an attempt to overthrow Sadat▷. Sentenced to prison and confiscation of property. (Al.S.)

SHA'RAWI, GUM'A. Deputy Prime Minister

SEPARATION OF FORCES

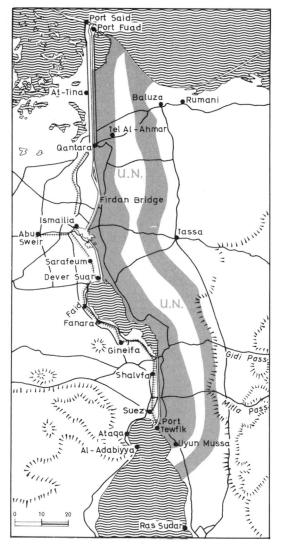

on Southern Front   on Northern Front

and Minister of Interior of Egypt▷ until May 1971, when dimissed, arrested and sentenced to life imprisonment and confiscation of property, for plotting the overthrow of Sadat▷, in collaboration with 'Ali Sabri▷. Born 1920; instructor at Military Academy; graduate of Staff and Command School 1951; staff and intelligence positions until 1961, when appointed Governor of the Suez District; appointed Minister in the joint Iraqi-Egyptian council 1964; Minister of State in Prime Minister's Office, for coordinating between Government and Arab Socialist Union▷ 1965; appointed Secretary of ASU 1965; a founder of the party's "secret service", active within the ASU and subordinate to the President; appointed Minister of Interior Sept. 1966, a position he held until his dismissal in May 1971. Following Nasser's▷ death, S became Deputy Prime Minister for Services Sector, in addition to his function as Minister of Interior. Considered one of the most influential persons in Egypt▷ during the final period of Nasser's rule. S was known for his pro-Russian inclinations.

(Al.S.)

SHARJA. Member of the Union of Arab Emirates▷. Pop.: 31,500 (1968). In Nov. 1972, Iranian troops landed on Abu Musa island which, according to an agreement with Iran▷, belongs to Sharja. In Jan. 1972 this agreement served as a pretext for an attempted *coup* by the deposed ruler, which failed due to intervention of the Union army. The ruler of Sharja was killed in the fighting and a new ruler was elected by the Supreme Council of the Union.

Commercial quantities of oil▷ were discovered along the shores of Abu Musa in Aug. 1972. Income from this oil was to have been divided equally between Sharja and Iran. (Y.K. & V.E.)

*SHAZAR, SHNEOR ZALMAN. S's second term of office as President of the State of Israel▷ expired in 1973. A two-term restriction prevented him from re-election, and Ephraim Katzir▷ subsequently was elected in his stead. Since his retirement, S has concentrated on writing and on maintaining links with Jewish communities outside Israel. (E.A.)

SHEIKH, AL-, AHMAD AL-SHAFI'. A leader of the Railway Workers' Union established in Sudan▷ in 1948. Elected Secretary of the Sudan Trade Union Federation 1959. Arrested and sentenced to five years imprisonment in Dec. 1958 for activities in the Sudan Communist Party▷. While in prison, elected Deputy Chairman of World Trade Union Federation, when the 'Abbud▷ regime was toppled in Oct. 1964, S was elected representative of the Sudanese workers in the interim Government which served until April 1965. Following the ban on the Communist Party, in late 1965, the party split; S was a leader of the faction advocating circumvention of the ban by creating a wider basis for the party within the framework of a Socialist party. S thereby became a founder of the Socialist party in Sudan, in Jan. 1967.

S supported the Numeiri▷ *coup d'état* in 1969 and despite fluctuating relations with Numeiri's regime, continued to serve as President of the Sudanese Trade Union Federation until July 1971. Received the Lenin Peace Prize in May 1970. Executed in July 1971, after having been found guilty of participation in the *coup d'état* which threatened to depose Numeiri. S's wife, Fatima Ahmad Ibrahim, also an active Communist, headed the Sudanese Women's Federation. (E.S.)

*SHIHAB, FUAD. Died on 25 April, 1973. (H.Z.)

*SHUQEIRI, AHMAD. Since the Yom Kippur War▷, S has continued to publish his political opinions from time to time. His main thesis is the rejection of any agreement with Israel▷ and a demand to refrain from forming a Palestine Government-in-exile. (E.Y.)

SIDQI, DR. 'AZIZ. Egyptian politician, Assistant to President Sadat▷ since Mar. 1973. Born 1920; graduated from engineering college 1944; completed education in US; began political career under revolutionary regime; appointed Minister of Industry 1956, 1961; member of Aswan Dam▷ Committee 1958; head of National Oil▷ Institute 1961; member of Supreme Executive Committee, Arab Socialist Union▷ 1962; Deputy Prime Minister for Oil▷ Development, Light Industry and Natural Resources 1964; and member of the Ministerial Committee for Science. In 1965 friction between S and 'Ali Sabri▷ led to his dropping out of public life for a year. In 1966 S was appointed Presidential Adviser for Production and Industrial Development, and again became Minister of Industry in 1967.

After the expulsion of the Sabri faction in May 1971, S served for two months as Secretary of the Arab Socialist Union; he was Deputy Prime Minister and Minister of Economy in the Government of Mahmoud Fawzi▷. From Jan. 1972 till Mar. 1973 S was Prime Minister. S is known as the "father of modern industry in Egypt", a reputation which he encourages. (Al.S.)

SIILASVUO, LT.-GEN. P.H. ENSIO. Born in Helsinki 1922. Commander of UNEF▷ since 25 Oct., 1973. Completed Officers' Training College 1945. Commander of Finnish UN contingent in Sinai 1957. Staff Officer, UN Observer Mission in Lebanon▷ 1958; Commander of Finnish UN contingent in Cyprus 1964–5; Chief of Foreign Operations, General Staff Headquarters 1967; Assistant Commander and later Commander of UNTSO 1970–24 Oct., 1973.

When the UNEF▷ was re-established on 25 Oct. 1973, in accordance with UN Security Council Resolution 340▷, S was appointed its Commander. As such, S chaired discussions at Kilometre 101▷, leading to the Six-Point Agreement▷, during discussions of the Israeli-Egyptian Military Committee which began in Geneva on 26 Dec., 1973, and during the final stages of discussions on the Separation of Forces Agreement▷ between Israel and Egypt.   (Sh.H.)

SISCO, JOSEPH J. US Under-Secretary of State for Political Affairs since Jan. 1974. Born 1919; joined Department of State in 1951; Assistant Secretary of State for International Organization Affairs 1965–9, in which capacity S participated in the US delegation to the UN General Assembly during discussions on the ME in 1967; Assistant Secretary of State for Near-Eastern and South-Asian Affairs 1969–74, in which capacity S has a hand in the formulation of the US ME policy under both Rogers▷ and Kissinger▷. During Kissinger's mediation efforts, since the Yom Kippur War▷, S has been close at hand though never in the limelight.   (Sh.H.)

SIX-POINT AGREEMENT. Following UN Security Council Resolution 338▷, which called for a cease-fire to end the Yom Kippur War▷, discussions began between Israeli and Egyptian officers at Kilometre 101▷. On 11 Nov., 1973, an official Six-Point Cease-fire Agreement was signed by Gen. Aharon Yariv▷ and Gen. Muhammad 'Abd-ul-Ghani al-Gamasy▷. The six points were as follows:

"(1) Egypt and Israel agree to observe scrupulously the cease-fire called for by the UN Security Council." In fact until the Separation of Forces Agreement▷ was signed on 18 Jan., 1974, the Egyptians constantly broke the cease-fire and officially announced a war of attrition until Israel would agree to withdraw from the territories occupied during the Six Day War▷.

"(2) Both sides agree that discussions between them will begin immediately to settle the question of the return to the Oct. 22 positions in the framework of agreement on the disengagement and separation of forces under the auspices of the UN." Officially, the cease-fire called for by Resolution 338 was to have come into effect on the morning of 22 Oct., 1973; however, fighting continued during that day and Israeli forces completely surrounded the Egyptian Third Army. Israel claimed that Egypt was to blame for the non-observance of the cease-fire and that it was impossible to determine where the forces of either side had in fact stood when the cease-fire was to have come into effect. Egypt argued that Israel had purposely continued fighting on 22 Oct. Discussions on the disengagement and separation of forces carried on at Kilometre 101 were subsequently moved to Geneva and finally brought to a successful conclusion through the mediation of Dr. Kissinger▷.

"(3) The town of Suez will receive daily supplies of food, water and medicine. All wounded civilians in the town of Suez will be evacuated." Since the Cairo-Suez road had fallen into Israeli hands, Suez town was in fact cut off from supplies. In accord with this third point, Israel allowed UN-driven vehicles to bring supplies to the inhabitants remaining in Suez. Wounded civilians were evacuated.

"(4) There shall be no impediment to the movement of non-military supplies to the East Bank." A large part of the Egyptian Third Army, which had crossed the Suez Canal during the Yom Kippur War, had found itself besieged when the cease-fire came into effect. In accordance with Point 4, Israel allowed UN-driven Egyptian vehicles to bring non-military supplies to the besieged Egyptian forces.

"(5) The Israeli checkpoints on the Cairo-Suez Road will be replaced by UN checkpoints. At the Suez end of the road, Israeli officers can participate with the UN to supervise the non-military nature of the cargo at the bank of the Canal." An incident developed between Israeli and Finnish UNEF troops when the latter tried to construct a barrier at Kilometre 119, on the outskirts of Suez, where Israel claimed she had a right to remain to supervise the nature of the supplies entering the town. Otherwise, Point 5 was implemented without difficulties.

"(6) As soon as the UN checkpoints are established on the Cairo-Suez Road there will be an exchange of all POWs including wounded." The exchange of prisoners between Israel and Egypt begun on 5 Nov., 1973, and ended on 22 Nov., 1973, and was carried out by the International Red Cross▷.   (Sh.H.)

*SNEH, DR. MOSHE. Died in 1972.   (E.A.)

★SOCOTRA. Rumours began to spread in 1970 that South Yemen▷ was about to grant Russia▷ the right to erect military bases on S, but when a delegation of foreign diplomats and newspapermen visited the island the following year, at the invitation of the Government, this was found to be baseless. One reporter wrote that the island lacked minimum requirements for a military base, such as a harbour, airfields, etc.   (O.Y.)

★SOUTH YEMEN, PEOPLE'S REPUBLIC OF. After the overthrow of President Qahtan al-Sh'abi▷, in June 1969, power remained in the hands of the radical wing of the NLF▷. This radicalization led to significant changes in the character of the country, intensifying processes begun in the first year of independence. This group, headed by the NLF Secretary-General 'Abd-ul-Fattah Isma'il al-Jawfi▷, Muhammad 'Ali Haytham▷ and Salem Rabi'▷, bases its policies on the assumption that SY society is just beginning to free itself from the bonds of a backward colonial past. To shake this off and to achieve true liberation, several radical steps are to be taken. Internally, this included the establishment of new Government institutions, such as the Supreme People's Council (formed in May 1971 on the basis of the 1970 Constitution), the Cabinet and the Presidential Council; all these were made subject to the party. Reorganizations took place in the army and police (two power foci formerly based on traditional tribal elements), political commissars were appointed and a Popular Militia was formed in mid-1970. The latter has the double role of providing an auxiliary armed force loyal to the regime, while employing its members mostly in industry and agriculture. In the economic sphere, the new policy included the confiscation of land owned by tribal chiefs, the prohibition of hired labour, lower wages, large-scale confiscations of foreign firms and private businesses. The trade unions, formerly foci of ferment, were brought under Government control when several of their leaders were replaced by men loyal to the regime (early 1971).

All these steps were accompanied by violent controversies within the ruling group, where personal and tribal conflicts assumed the form of ideological struggle. There were pro-Russian and pro-Chinese wings, the latter led by Salem Rabi' and based on the party cells in the more backward tribal areas, as opposed to the urban centre of Aden▷. Prime Minister Muhammad 'Ali Haytham was overthrown in Aug. 1971, and his place was taken by 'Ali Nasser Muhammad Husni▷. This change was made partly to dampen tense relations between the

two factions in preparation for the Fifth Party Congress in Mar. 1972, where resolutions expressed the establishment of the Leftist ideology.

Since independence there has been constant struggle against oppositionists and underground organizations; some of these are active within the country, especially in the third and fifth districts, and include local military units and tribal elements with long warlike traditions. To some extent such elements also exist abroad: Members of FLOSY▷, former sultans and cashiered army officers have managed, with some success, to set up a National Front organization; they enjoy financial and other support from Sa'udi Arabia and Yemen▷, and also receive help from some tribes in SY. In spite of this, the underground groups are heavily divided. In addition, the tribal elements on which they are based have lost ground, as the central Government destroys their organizational framework, confiscates lands, removes their representative elements from positions of influence and incorporates them in military organizations subject to the party.

The label of "extreme revolutionary" assumed by SY also finds expression in its foreign policy. Relations with other Arab countries are very complicated, since even the so-called progressive Arab countries are insufficiently revolutionary. There is also the sharp conflict with Sa'udi Arabia, which considers the SY regime a danger to Islam. Several pitched battles were fought along the border between the two countries in late 1969 and early 1970, and relations continue to be tense. With Republican Yemen, relations also are generally tense in spite of former "revolutionary" mutual aid and agreement in principle on the establishment of a "united Yemen". At times, this tension results even in hostile acts. SY has adopted the position that its regime represents the "true" Yemen, and consequently has changed its official name from "People's Republic of SY" to "Popular Democratic Republic of Y" (Nov. 1970).

In Oct. 1972 the two Yemens declared union, but this was not carried out. Most of the foreign aid SY receives is from Russia and other East European countries. From China▷, assistance is received for agriculture, industry and medicine.

(T.Y.)

★SUDAN. Since Numeiri▷ assumed control in May 1969, there were several unsuccessful attempts to oust him. During his first year of rule, the opposition sprang mainly from traditional political forces, especially the Muslim Brotherhood▷ and the *Ansar*▷. The struggle came to a head in Mar. 1970, when Numeiri's visit to a region widely settled by the Ansar sparked off a revolt at Juba. Numeiri exploited such local incidents to ruthlessly suppress opposition, hitting savagely at the Ansar. In the revolt, the Imam al-Hadi al-Mahdi was killed, and Sadiq al-Mahdi was banished to Egypt. Private property was confiscated and many members of the Muslim Brotherhood and the Ansar were arrested. Numeiri was then free to tackle his leftist opponents. In April 1970 the Secretary-General of the Communist Party▷ was banished to Egypt, and then a gradual dismissal began of Communists and all individuals of leftist views from key offices. In Nov. 1970 three Communists, all members of the Revolutionary Council, were removed from office; army officers suspected of leftist tendencies were dismissed, and members of the Executive Committee of the Communist Party were arrested. In July 1971, an abortive *coup* took place, when Numeiri's opponents (among them many Communists) seized control for three days (July 19–22), national unrest reaching a new height. Tension between Numeiri and the Communists mounted steadily, for Numeiri sought to make the Sudanese Socialist Union sole political party in S. A second point of conflict was Numeiri's desire to bring S into the Egypt-Libya-Syria Federation of Arab Republics▷.

With the suppression of the July revolt, Numeiri began reorganization of his regime. In Oct. 1971 the Revolutionary Council was disbanded; a referendum was conducted, resulting in Numeiri's election as President of the Republic. In Jan. 1972 the first conference of the Sudanese Socialist Union was held, approving a temporary constitution. In Oct. 1972 elections were held for the S's People's Assembly, intended to prepare and ratify the permanent Constitution. These elections led to changes in the executive branch of Government — in the Cabinet and the political bureau of the Sudanese Socialist Union. In May 1973 the permanent Constitution was ratified and further changes in Government structure. The Constitution recognizes Islam as the principal religion of S; Christianity is mentioned as the faith of many Sudanese. The one-party system is upheld as the only accepted method toward political change. These steps did not, however, succeed in completely destroying pockets of opposition, nor did they completely stabilize it. Further attempts were made on Numeiri's life against his regime, his strongest opponents being army officers and various political elements which had constantly opposed him. In Aug. 1973, when Numeiri was absent from the country, S went through another upheaval, because of rising inflation and economic difficulties. In spite of various attempts to introduce economic and social reforms, including such measures as nationalization of industries (as early as 1970), economic problems persist. Today, indeed, there is a tendency toward private enterprise.

SOUTHERN SUDAN: In Jan. 1971, Joseph Lagu▷, rebel leader in the south, announced the formation of the Movement for Liberation of Southern S, yet another step in the uniting of opposition to the regime, but also a part of the militarization dominating S political life. Soon after Numeiri seized power, he devised a plan for setting the problem of the south, principally the granting of regional autonomy within a unified S. He made several attempts to negotiate with the southern rebels, and brought southerners into his Government. However, clashes continued between the S army and the rebel forces, and only after Numeiri felt he was rid of most of his political enemies did he seek seriously to solve his differences with the rebels—early in 1972. In Mar. 1972 agreement was reached with the rebel leaders (the "Addis Ababa agreement"), which provided for the granting of self-rule to the three southern provinces, while the central Government was to continue to direct S's army, foreign affairs, and national security. Cessation of hostilities was declared, refugees began to be resettled in their former homes, and the *Anyanya* armed forces were absorbed into the regular army. A transitory government in the south, the Supreme Executive Council, was set up, its chosen President, Abel Alir, being a southerner who had once been Vice-President to Numeiri. The Constitution ratified in May 1973 confirmed independent rule in the south. In Nov. 1973, elections were held in southern S to choose representatives to a People's Assembly for the three southern provinces, following which a permanent Government was established, calling itself the Supreme Executive Council of the Southern Region.

FOREIGN POLICY: After the May 1969 revolution, the new regime recognized the East German Republic and relations with Russia▷ were strengthened; sympathy for Russia dropped, however, after the July 1971 revolt, which many Sudanese felt was Russian inspired. Though diplomatic relations with Russia were resumed in 1973, ties were not as strong as formerly. At the same time S drew closer to the West, establishing diplomatic relations with West Germany in Dec. 1971 and with the US in mid-1972.

In her inter-Arab relations, S did not join the federation established between Egypt, Libya and Syria in Sept. 1971, though the most vociferous opponents of this federation (the Communists) had been silenced in July 1971. The southern

Government was against S joining this federation, and Numeiri himself felt that his policy of balance between his Islamic and his African identity might be threatened by joining it. Indeed, some time later relations between S and Egypt and Libya worsened, until Numeiri initiated efforts to restabilize them. Following the Yom Kippur War▷, and the growing rift between Egypt and Libya, there were rumours that Egypt and S would draw closer to one another, and would perhaps even unite in a loose federation.

PRESS, RADIO, TV: Following the May 1969 revolt, all newspapers were closed; several were permitted to reopen a few days later, but only under strong Government censorship. In Aug. 1970, all newspapers and news agencies were nationalized by special Government decree.   (E.S.)

★SUEZ CANAL. On 16 Oct., 1973, while the Yom Kippur War▷ was still in progress, Sadat▷ announced that Egypt▷ was prepared to begin work immediately on the opening of the canal to international traffic from all nations, on condition that Israel▷ vacate the Sinai Peninsula▷. His promise was somewhat theoretical at the time, since Israeli troops still occupied the canal's west bank. Actual clearance work became feasible only in Mar. 1974, after the Separation of Forces Agreement▷.

Upon the disengagement of forces, Israel was convinced that Egyptian willingness to invest heavily in the clearance of the canal, and her readiness to normalize civilian life in the towns along the canal, would be a test of Egyptian sincerity in working toward a state of peace.

Egypt decided on the following course of action: In the first of two stages, to last 4–6 months, the canal would be cleared of mines and shells, the bridges built during the Yom Kippur War would be dismantled, wreckage of some 80 sunken vessels would be cleared and the canal would be dredged of sand that had accumulated; further, the 15 ships trapped in the Great Bitter Lake since the Six Day War would be removed. For the implementation of stage one, Egypt received a loan of $140m from Japan at the end of 1973, and entered into negotiations with foreign companies to dredge and refurbish the canal. US and British naval forces are assisting in the initial clearance work, as well.

In stage two, to take 6–8 years, the canal will be enlarged to enable passage of 28,500 vessels p.a. (as compared with 25,000 vessels till now). A deeper and wider canal will also permit passage of ships of up to 290,000 tons (as compared with the maximum of 60,000 tons in 1967). This will permit passage of the oil▷ super-tankers, which presently circumnavigate Africa in their passage from the Persian Gulf to Europe.

It is estimated that the task will cost about £500m. While the work of enlarging the canal is proceeding, smaller vessels and tankers will be able to use it. Even during this development work, royalties received by the Canal Authority should rise by at least 10% p.a., as they did previous to 1967, and it is believed that by 1980, Egypt's revenue from the canal will amount to more than £230m p.a.

Egypt also plans the rebuilding of the towns partly destroyed during the "War of Attrition". Five tunnels under the canal, part of a master plan for development of the Sinai Peninsula, are also planned.

The Separation of Forces Agreement makes no provision for assurance that ships carrying the Israel flag would be permitted to use the reopened canal; such passage, however, would most likely be a condition in any peace settlement with Egypt.
                                                              (O.G.)

SULH, AL-, TAQI AL-DIN. Prime Minister of Lebanon▷. Born 1909 to an influential Sunnite▷ family; studied at American University and St. Joseph's University, Beirut. Minister of Interior 1964–5; elected to Parliament 1957 and again in 1964. Headed Council for Foreign Relations in Lebanon from 1964; President of the Nidal al-Qawmi party.

S was asked by President Franjiyeh▷ to form a new Government on 21 June 1973.   (O.Y.)

★SUNDY, CEVDET. Completed term as President of Turkey▷ in Mar. 1973, being succeeded by Fahri Korutürk▷.   (D.K.)

★SYRIA. After the Nov. 1970 *coup*, Asad▷, supported by Gen. Tallas▷, announced Syria's new policy of "openness". Within the country the new policy meant that leftist groups would be accepted in the Government within the framework of a Progressive National Front under Ba'th▷ direction; political prisoners would be released; harsh laws would be repealed; a more liberal economic policy would be instituted; and the general standard of living would be raised. Ahmad al-Khatib▷, who was then Chairman of the Syrian Assembly, was appointed Prime Minister of the Federation of Arab Republics▷, which had been declared in April 1971, uniting Egypt▷, Libya▷ and Syria.

The new regime also repaired the Tapline▷ (not in use since May 1970), renewed diplomatic relations with Tunisia▷ (Feb. 1971) and Morocco▷ (Mar. 1971); improved relations with Lebanon▷, and broadened economic ties with Sa'udi Arabia⊳ and the Persian Gulf⊳ states. Relations with Iraq⊳, however, remained tense, because of opposite tendencies of the Ba'th party in either country, as well as Iraq's friendship for the deposed Ba'th leaders in S (such as 'Aflaq⊳ and Hafez⊳).

Russia⊳ was forced to accept Asad's *fait accompli*, though she had supported his political enemies. Already in Feb. 1971 Asad visited Russia, at which time the Russian leaders assured him of continued military and economic assistance; Asad, however, was adamant in refusing to sign a friendship pact, as Egypt and Iraq had already done. In mid-1972, when Russian experts and advisers were expelled from Egypt, Asad resisted Egyptian and Libyan pressure for a like move, even mediating in the Egyptian-Russian disagreement.

The S policy of "openness" led to restored diplomatic relations with Rumania⊳ (Oct. 1972) and Britain⊳ (May 1973). Economic and other agreements were made with the states of the European Economic Community⊳, particularly France⊳ and Italy⊳. Connections with African⊳, Asian and American countries were also broadened, and economic agreements and political rapprochement with the nations of Eastern Europe were encouraged. Improvement of relations with the US came only later, and proceeded slowly.

INTERNAL DEVELOPMENTS: The Ba'th party continued to be the ruling political party, but the newly-established Government bodies changed the character of former institutions. This reduced the political power of the Ba'th. Asad also encouraged the formation of a "personality cult" around himself. As a consequence he is accepted by most Syrians and by various other Arab nations as his country's sole leader. All the while, the army remained Asad's most loyal supporter.

On 21 Nov., 1970, Asad formed a new Government. Ahmad al-Khatib⊳, a man of little political importance, was appointed President. In Feb. 1971 the People's Assembly was appointed as S's legislative body according to the temporary constitution of May 1969; the Assembly numbered 173 members, 87 of them Ba'th followers and the rest chosen from various leftist and independent groups. Al-Khatib resigned from the Presidency and was chosen Chairman of the Assembly.

On 12 Mar., 1971, a referendum was held to select a President, Asad being the sole candidate. Gaining 99.2% of the votes cast, he was elected for a seven-year term. The President's powers had previously been strengthened by the temporary constitution: The Cabinet would be responsible to the President, who would have the right to dissolve the Assembly and rule by decree under certain conditions or eventualities.

In early April 1971, Mahmoud al-Ayyubi⊳ was appointed Vice-President and a new Cabinet was formed, headed by Gen. 'Abd-ul-Rahman Khleifawi, formerly of the General Staff and Minister of Interior in the preceding Government. The new Cabinet continued the policies laid down by Asad.

In May 1971, a national conference of the Ba'th party reaffirmed Asad's policies. Asad was chosen to be the Secretary-General of the party, with 'Abdullah al-Ahmar⊳ as his deputy. In Aug. 1971, another national conference of the Ba'th (Pan-Arab) took place, also confirming Asad's policies and further chosing him as Secretary-General of the Ba'th leadership in S.

From mid-1971 negotiations began for setting up a Progressive National Front which in effect would rule the country; these bore fruit in Mar. 1972. The Front's members came from the following groups: The Ba'th party; the Communist Party, the Arab Socialist Union⊳, the movement of socialist associations (former pro-Nasserite parties), and the Arab Socialist Party (of Akram al-Horani⊳). The Front's leadership was a group of 17 men — nine from the Ba'th and two men from each of the other parties. Asad himself was appointed Secretary-General. Ba'th control of the Front was thus assured, and the other parties were prevented from activity among the students and soldiers, or putting out their own newspapers. The Front's constitution grants the Secretary-General (necessarily also Secretary of the Ba'th) wide powers. The establishment of the Progressive Front was presented as an important step toward Pan-Arab unity⊳, and as a means of strengthening S against Israel.

On 3–4 Mar., 1972, another Cabinet was appointed, again under Khleifawi. Mustafa Tallas⊳ was appointed Minister of Defence, and a new Chief of Staff, Yusuf Sahur, was appointed. In Dec. 1972, Khleifawi resigned on grounds of ill health, and a new Cabinet was formed by the Vice-President, Ayyubi; it was very similar to its predecessor, the demoninant personalities being the Minister of Defence and the two Deputy Prime Ministers (Foreign Minister 'Abd-ul-Halim Haddam⊳, and Minister of Agriculture Muhammad Hidr.

In Mar. 1973, a permanent Constitution was presented for the approval of the people in a referendum. This caused a furour among conservative Sunnites⊳ in the country because, instead of declaring Islam to be the state religion, the constitutional wording was that "Islamic law is a vital source for legislation." Actually, Sunnite unrest rose long before the referendum was declared, for Asad was of 'Alawi▷ origin, as was Salah Jadid before him. In Sunnite eyes, the Ba'th party was a secular party at best (if not anti-religious), besides being opposed to the bourgeoisie. Sunnite opposition soon led to violent street demonstrations in Hama, which the army soon suppressed. Demonstrations and strikes quickly spread to other cities, with a call for the removal of the "'Alawi regime". Some Sunnites urged the people to boycott the referendum. In the end, however, as a result of a judicious blend of suppression and appeasement, opposition subsided and the referendum was held on 12 Mar., 1972, under such close supervision that the Constitution was confirmed by an overwhelming majority.

As stated in the Constitution, S is a "sovereign, democratic, popular, socialist state, and a member of the Federation of Arab Republics▷; she is part of the Arab family of peoples, within which she is determined to work for the realization of the complete unity of the Arab people everywhere; Islamic Law is a vital source for legislation, and the official language is Arabic." It goes on to declare the Ba'th party as "the party which guides the state and society, and which stands at the head of the National Progressive Front". The economic system is described as a "planned socialist economy". The National Assembly is the country's legislative body, its members being elected for a term of four years by direct, national, secret ballot. At least half the members of the legislature must be of the working class. The executive branch of Government comprises the President and the Cabinet. The President must be a Syrian Arab, and must be supported by the national leadership of the Ba'th party. He is elected in a national referendum, for a term of seven years. The President, as in the US, has wide administrative powers but, further, he can dissolve the Legislature and rule by decree under certain conditions. The Cabinet is responsible to him, and he is the Supreme Commander of the country's armed forces.

On 25 May, 1973, elections were held to choose representatives to the Legislature according to the new Constitution. These were the first elections since 1971, and the turnout of voters was fairly low. Only those candidates who were members of the National Progressive Front had the right to advertise their candidacy, and thus of the 186 representatives elected (among them 5 women), 122 were members of the Ba'th party.

In the past few years, S's economic base has developed appreciably, largely through assistance received from Russia and other East European states. In July 1973, the first stage of construction of the Euphrates▷ Dam was completed. Several smaller dams were built in rural areas; the oil▷ refinery at Homs was enlarged; and cement and phosphate factories were built. Transportation services were also expanded: An international airport was built in Damascus▷; the port at Tartous▷ was expanded, and a new terminal for S's oil pipeline established there; a railroad was built from Lataqia▷ through Aleppo▷ to the Euphrates river; and the network of roads was expanded. Oil production east of the Gezira▷ region rose to reach c. 6m tons p.a., of which 4m tons were exported.

The economy suffered considerably during the Yom Kippur War▷: Oil terminals at Tartous and Baniyas▷ were heavily damaged, while the oil refinery and main powerhouse near Homs were destroyed. The Government estimated the damage to its economy in hundreds of millions of dollars. S has requested the aid of wealthy Arab states in rebuilding its economy, and has received assurances of considerable financial assistance.

STATISTICS: Pop.: 6.3m (Sept. 1970); 6.7m (est. 1972); Damascus — 835,000; Aleppo — 636,000. GNP 1972: S£ 6,843m (c. $1,600m). Income p.c.: c. $300. Imports (1972): S£ 2,061m (c. $480m). Exports (1972): S£ 1,098m (c. $255m). National budget (1973): S£ 3,413m (c. $850m). (O.T.)

T

★TALHOUNI, BAHJAT. T was appointed a member of the Jordan▷ Senate by Hussein▷ in May 1973. His political standing improved after Oct. 1973, with Hussein's search for rapprochement with Egypt▷. (O.Y.)

TALLAS, MUSTAFA. Syrian Minister of Defence and member of Ba'th▷ party Command. Graduated from War College; studied Law; author of books on guerilla warfare; President of Military Tribunals in Damascus▷ and Hama 1964; Chief of Staff and Deputy to the then Minister of Defence, Asad▷, in 1968. Subsequently Minister of Defence. T is one of Asad's closest associates. (O.Y.)

TALU, NAIM. Turkish stateman. Prime Minister 1973, 1974. Former Governor of National Bank, and Minister of Commerce in the Melen▷ Government. T established a coalition Cabinet in April 1973 with the Justice Party and the Republican Reliance Party. In spite of its moderately Rightist character, this Government enacted extensive reform legislation. In Jan. 1974 T was replaced by Bülent Ecevit▷ as Prime Minister of Turkey▷.

★TEHERAN. Pop.: 3.8m (est. 1973). The city's rapid development, and the lack of careful advanced planning, resulted in serious urban problems, in transport, housing and other areas, In Dec. 1969, the Government approved a 25-year masterplan, to be carried out in a series of 5-year plans.   (D.K.)

THANI, AL-, AHMAD b. 'ALI. Ruler of Qatar▷ in the Persian Gulf▷ 1960–72. A Sunnite▷ Wahhabi▷. Deposed by his cousin, the Crown Prince, in a coup d'état.   (V.E.)

THANI, AL-, KHALIFA b. HAMAD. Ruler of Qatar▷ in the Persian Gulf▷. Born 1935; a Sunnite▷ Wahhabi▷. Came to power in Feb. 1972 in a coup d'état. Previously the Crown Prince, Minister of Finance and Oil▷, and Prime Minister.   (V.E.)

TIKRITI, AL-, SADAM HUSSEIN. Deputy Chairman of the Revolutionary Command Council in Iraq▷ and, for all practical purposes, the most influential person within the Ba'th▷ regime there. T led the civilian sector of the Ba'th in Iraq and succeeded in establishing the party system within the army. T visited Russia▷ in Feb. 1972. He applies methods of personal terrorism against opponents in Iraq and in exile. His cousin, Hardan al-Takriti▷, was assassinated by T's agents in Kuwait▷, in Mar. 1971.   (O.Y.)

★TRUCIAL COAST — See Union of Arab Emirates.

★TRUMAN, HARRY S. Died 12 Dec., 1972.

★TUDEH. In the mid-1960s, the T split into two factions, one pro-Russian and the other pro-Chinese. The pro-Russian faction is the more moderate toward the Government, mainly because of improved Iran▷-Russia▷ relations. Although it accuses the Shah of an "anti-democratic approach, it opposes extremist movements and all terrorist and guerilla activities. Cooperation between this group and Iraqi▷ Communists▷ has increased recently. In Nov. 1973 the two parties issued a joint proclamation in Baghdad, opposing China▷ and Iran, and praising Russia. The joint group operates two secret radion stations and several newspapers.

The pro-Chinese faction further splintered into: the Tudah Party Revolutionary Organization and the Marxist-Leninist Storm Organization.

The Iranian Government has taken a hard line, especially against the pro-Chinese faction, whose members are not infrequently sentenced to death or prolonged imprisonment. Strong Government action against them has caused a shift of much of their activity abroad, especially among the many Iranian students attending foreign universities. Leadership of the Confederation of Iranian Students Living Abroad is in the hands of the pro-Chinese faction. Their activities reached a peak during the festivities held in Iran in Oct. 1971. Actual membership is quite small.   (D.M.)

★TUNISIA. In 1971–4, the main issue in T internal politics concerned Bourguiba's succession. Till late 1970, Bahi al-Adgham was considered the designated successor; he has lost favour, however, and was replaced by Hedi Nouira, who became the Prime Minister in Nov. 1970.

T, like Morocco▷, felt the pressures applied by Libyan leader Qaddhafi▷, which apparently caused Bourguiba to adopt a more radical stand in his inter-Arab politics, as expressed in his attacks on Hussein▷ and the regime in Jordan▷ in 1973.

Relations with Libya▷ reached a surprising turning point in Feb. 1974, when an agreement for federation was signed between the two countries. Within a few days, however, it was apparent that Foreign Minister Masmoudi had gone beyond his authority and T backed out of the agreement.   (O.Y.)

TURKEY. GOVERNMENT AND POLITICS. Demirel's▷ inability to implement economic and social reforms, and mainly the anarchy perpetrated by leftist and rightist terrorist groups (the most conspicuous of which was the leftist Turkish People's Liberation Army), resulted ultimately in army intervention. In Mar. 1971 the Chiefs of Staff issued an ultimatum threatening that the army would take the Government over if a strong national and reformist Government were not formed immediately. Demirel was forced to resign and a new supra-party Government, comprising also a large number of technocrats, was formed by Nihat Erim▷, who resigned from the Republican People's Party. This Government adopted a tough stand against the terrorist groups, while strengthening and extending the martial laws. However, the Government's reformist plans were unacceptable to wide political circles and Erim resigned in Dec. 1971 and again, after another term as Prime Minister, in April 1972. A new Government was formed by Farit Melen▷, of the Reliance Party. The Melen Government continued Erim's reformist line and succeeded in putting a near complete stop to terrorism. The army continued to keep close watch on the Government and toward the end of

President Sunay's▷ term of office, was active in campaigning for the election of the ex-Chief of Staff, Fahri Gürler, as President. However, his candidacy was rejected by the members of the National Council in repeated ballots, until a compromise candidate, Fahri Korutürk▷, was elected. The new Government formed by Naim Talu▷ was a coalition of the Justice Party and the Republican Reliance Party and, despite its moderate composition, succeeded in bringing about large-scale reform legislation. The Oct. 1973 elections resulted, against all expectations, in the victory of the Republican People's Party, though not gaining it an absolute majority. Continued efforts to form a Government were successful only in Jan. 1974, following a warning from the army. The new Government was a coalition of the Republican People's Party and the National Order Party, and was headed by Bülent Ecevit▷.

STATISTICS: Pop.: 36m (1970). Natural increase: 2.7% (1965 and 1970). GNP: T£ 223,355m (at current prices; T£ 143,784 at constant 1968 prices, 1972 est.). National product p.c.: T£ 6,035 (at current prices); T£ 3,885 (at constant 1968 prices, 1972 est.). Exports: $855m (1972); imports: $1,562.6m (1972). Budget: T£ 50,000m (1972/3). Literacy: 49% (1970). Doctors: 10,895 or 1 per 2,881 (1965). Hospital beds: 173.5 per 100,000 (1967). T£ 14 = $1.

(D.K.)

U

UMMA. Political party in Sudan▷, established in 1945. In actual fact, the political arm of the al-Ansar▷ movement, the successors of the Mahdi▷. This party was the focus of supporters of the idea of an independent Sudan, as opposed to the idea of union with Egypt. At the time of its establishment the party was headed by 'Abdullah Khalili▷. After the death of Siddiq al-Mahdi in 1961, and upon the renewal of legal political activity in Sudan after the civil revolution of 1964, Sadeq al-Mahdi became the political leader of al-Ansar while his uncle, the Imam al-Hadi, served as its spiritual leader. In the summer of 1966 the party was split due to a struggle for prominence between the two personalities, finding expression in a series of changes of Government since July 1966, when Sadeq deposed Prime Minister Muhammad Ahmad Mahjoub▷ and the latter caused the resignation of Sadeq in May 1967.

The faction of the Imam al-Hadi, under Mahjoub's political leadership, formed part of the Government coalition up to and after the elections of April

1968. These elections reduced the number of seats of the party in the Assembly and indicated a lessening of its influence due to the split. As a result, a rapprochement between the two factions commenced in late 1968, leading to their re-unification in April 1969. In May 1969, with the coming into power of Numeiri's▷ regime, the party, together with all other political parties, was dissolved. (E.K.)

*UMM AL-QAIWAIN. Pop.: c. 4,000 (est. 1972), mostly nomads. No oil has so far been discovered in this sheikhdom, and there are differences of opinion with the neighbouring states as to offshore prospecting rights. (Y.K.)

*UNION OF ARAB EMIRATES. In December 1971, the establishment of a federation of six Arab principalities in the Persian Gulf▷ was proclaimed, including Abu Dhabi▷, Dubai▷, Sharja▷, Umm al-Qaiwain▷, 'Ajman▷ and Fujaira▷. In Feb. 1972, Ras al-Khaima▷ also joined the Union, which thus came to cover some 83,000 sq.km, with an estimated population of 210,000 in 1970.

In final form the union comprises seven principalities, though as set up in the Dubai Agreement of 1968, it also included Qatar▷ and Bahrain▷. The two latter in effect left the union in Aug. and Sept. 1971, when they formally declared their independence. Their withdrawal enabled the smooth establishment of the union, for most of the difficulties hindering federation were due to their demands for prominence within the union.

Active mediation on the part of Sa'udi Arabia▷ and Kuwait▷, as well as British assistance, facilitated federation. The two former states regarded the union as a security measure in the area, in view of Britain's withdrawal at the end of 1971. A second consideration, however, was the threat of leftist, revolutionary forces from the north (i.e. Iraq▷), and from the south (South Yemen▷), and the National Front for the Liberation of 'Oman and the Occupied Arab Gulf▷.

Britain's interest in a federation was related to its global policy of maintaining a pro-Western orientation in the politics of the region as a means of preventing Communist▷ penetration of both the Persian Gulf▷ and the Indian Ocean. (The US had no interest in replacing the British military presence in the region.) There were strong economic motives as well, for Britain imported most of its oil from this part of the world.

Iran▷, on her part, activated her claim to ownership of three islands at the entrance to the Persian Gulf, in the summer of 1970; her demands were based on a "historical right" and on her view of her duty to help defend the security of the Gulf, as the strongest state in the region. In this connection, Iran noted its readiness to relinquish claim to Bahrain.

As the date of British evacuation drew near, Iran further pressed its demands until they were more ultimatum than claim. In Nov. 1971, just before the union came into being, an Iranian military force landed on the island of Abu Musa, in accordance with an agreement previously signed between Iran and Sharja, allowing Iranian occupation but retaining sovereignty for Sharja. A yearly compensation was also to be paid by Iran for the use of the island and, should oil be discovered there, the two states agreed to share in its profits equally. Shortly after, a second Iranian force occupied the two Tumb islands without previously receiving the permission of Ras al-Khaima. These occupations, it appears with the permission of the British, coincided with the penultimate day of Britain's defence treaties in the Gulf. This timing of the occupation of the islands thus prevented the act from being considered a weakness of an impotent union. Actually, the only practical effect was that Ras al-Khaima refused to join the union that year, together with its demand that the principalities break off diplomatic relations with Iran until the islands were returned.

The temporary constitution of the union, confirmed on the day the union was proclaimed, sets down that the principalities each retain a large measure of independence. All international agreements previously signed between one of the principalities and foreign power remained valid, and the members reserved the right to conclude similar agreements in future, on the sole condition that agreements with foreign organizations or countries do no harm to the union or its character. Islam▷ is declared the official religion, and the Shari'a▷ its main source of law; Arabic is the official language. All inhabitants of the union enjoy a common citizenship. The union's capital, Al-Karameh, is to be built between Abu Dhabi and Dubai. Taxes and customs duty are to be unified, while customs barriers still existing between the principalities are declared void.

The union has an army under a united command, as well as additional security forces. The individual principalities have the right to form separate armies of their own, trained to cooperate with the union army.

Abu Dhabi and Dubai have taken over most of the key offices, being the largest as well as the most developed of the principalities. The traditional enmity between them has been neutralized by a division of most of the offices equally between them.

Abu Dhabi's ruler has been chosen President, while the Vice-President is from Dubai. In addition, these two principalities reserve a power of veto in the Supreme Council. Representatives from Dubai have been chosen as Prime Minister, Deputy Prime Minister, Minister of Finance, Commerce and Industry and Minister of Defence. The Minister of Interior, Foreign Minister and Commander of the Army are from Abu Dhabi. Moreover, Abu Dhabi is represented in the National Federal Council by more seats than the other principalities.

In Jan. 1972, the union army employed for the first time, to protect the internal security of one of the principalities, and a potential revolution in Sharja was foiled. The Supreme Council elected a temporary ruler for Sharja, to replace the slain ruler; and the rebels were brought to the union capital. The crushing of this revolt (sparked by opposition to the relinquishing of Abu Musa to Iran), Shaja was kept in the union, while the possibility of war with Iran was avoided.

In June 1972 and Aug. 1973, armed tribal disputes broke out in three of the emirates. In both instances the President intervened and Enquiry Commissions were set up to settle the disputes.

In more peripheral matters, efforts to bring Bahrain and Qatar into the union continue, and there is increased cooperation, economically, culturally and in transportation, with the other countries of the Persian Gulf. Thus, in 1973 the union proposed a regional defence treaty; this was made and immediately after the UAE became a member of the Arab League▷, establishing diplomatic relations with the various Arab nations. When the Yom Kippur War▷ erupted, the union assisted the combatant Arab states financially, and was included in the oil▷ embargo against the Western countries.

The international orientation of the union continues to be toward the West. Britain enjoys the status of a "privileged nation" cemented by a new treaty of friendship and by Britain's hand in building up the union army. As a result of pressure from the neighbouring Arab states, mainly Sa'udi Arabia, the union has relinquished the idea of establishing diplomatic relations with Russia▷; and its contacts with countries in the Eastern Bloc are limited to a few commercial ventures.   (V.E.)

*UNITED ARAB REPUBLIC. The name UAR was officially abolished in the 1971 Constitution. Egypt▷ then adopted the name Egyptian Arab Republic.   (Al.S.)

UNITED NATIONS DISENGAGEMENT OBSERVER FORCES. The UNDOF was established to implement and oversee the Separation of Forces Agreement▷ between Israel and Syria.

(R.G.)

★UNITED NATIONS EMERGENCY FORCE (PALESTINE). Following the cease-fire agreement of 22 Oct., 1973, which terminated the Yom Kippur War▷, the UN Security Council voted in favour of the dispatch of a new UNEF to the ME under Maj-Gen. Siilasvuo▷ of Finland. It was agreed that the new force would not include troops of the five permanent members of the Security Council. Austria, Canada, Finland, Ghana, Indonesia, Ireland, Nepal, Panama, Peru, Poland and Sweden agreed to participate in the new force.

The UNEF set up observation posts on both sides of the Suez Canal▷, along the Cairo-Suez road and along the Israel-Syrian cease-fire line. Discussions opened between Israeli and Egyptian officers, at Kilometre 101▷, on 28 Oct., 1973, under UNEF auspices, and supply convoys for the Egyptian Third Army and the town of Suez were driven by UNEF troops. The UNEF also assisted in the Israel-Egypt Separation of Forces Agreement▷ — the field implementation of which involved withdrawal of Israeli forces and reoccupation by Egyptian forces in territories on the west bank and along the east bank of the Suez Canal, and regular patrols in the buffer-zones between the two disengaged armies. It was proposed that the UNEF serve a similar role for the Israel-Syria disengagement, and part of the UNEF, renamed UN disengagement Observer Forces (UNDOF), has set about implementing that Separation of Forces Agreement▷.

(Sh.H.)

★UNITED NATIONS ORGANIZATION. The main UN activities in the ME continued to be associated with the Arab-Israel Conflict▷, concentrating on the renewal of the Jarring▷ mission. The UN Secretary-General served as chairman of the opening session of the Geneva Peace Conference▷ in Dec. 1973.

(O.Y.)

UN RESOLUTION 242. From 7–20 Nov. 1967, four draft resolutions on the ME were presented to the UN Security Council, the first by the US, the second by India▷, Mali and Nigeria jointly, the third by Russia and the fourth by Britain▷. The British draft, adopted on 22 Nov., was worded as follows: "The Security Council.

(1) Affirms that the fulfilment of Charter principles required the establishment of a just and lasting peace in the ME which should include the application of both the following principles: (a) Withdrawal of Israeli armed forces from territories occupied in the recent conflict; (b) Termination of all claims or states of belligerency and respect for and acknowledgement of the sovereignty, territorial integrity and political independence of every State in the area and their right to live in peace within secure and recognized boundaries free from threats or acts of force;

(2) Affirms further the necessity (a) For guaranteeing freedom of navigation through international waterways in the area; (b) For achieving a just settlement of the refugee problem; (c) For guaranteeing the territorial inviolability and political independence of every State in the area, through measures including the establishment of demilitarized zones.

(3) Requests the Secretary General to designate a Special Representative to proceed to the ME to establish and maintain contacts with the States concerned in order to promote agreement and assist efforts to achieve a peaceful and accepted settlement in accordance with the provisions and principles in this resolution.

(4) Requests the Secretary General to report to the Security Council on the progress of the efforts of the special Representative as soon as possible."

Resolution 242 is continuously referred to as the basis for a "just peace" in the ME though there is disagreement as to whether article 1(a) implies that Israel need not withdraw from all the territories it occupied. In accordance with article 3, the Jarring▷ mission was initiated.

(Sh.H.)

UN RESOLUTIONS 338, 339, 340. Three resolutions of the UN Security Council on the ME, adopted on 22, 23 and 25 Oct., 1973, respectively. R 338 calls for a cease-fire to end the Yom Kippur War▷, followed by the implementation of UN Resolution 242▷ and negotiations "between the parties concerned under appropriate auspices aimed at establishing a just and durable peace in the ME."

R 339 calls for the return of all forces to the positions held when the cease-fire was to come into force and called for the dispatch of UN observers to the area.

R 340 calls, *inter alia*, for the establishment of a new UNEF▷ for the ME.

(Sh.H.)

★US, INTERESTS AND POLITICS IN THE ME. The concept of the Nixon▷ administration regarding the ME found expression in 1970 when the US initiated a cease-fire in the Egyptian-Israeli sector. This "Rogers▷ Plan" served as an instrument putting an end to the War of Attrition in Aug. 1970 (it was accepted by Russia despite its US origin, since Russia was seeking a way out of her over-involvement in Egypt, during the last half year of the war. However, within a few weeks the US found that Russia and Egypt had together violated the article in the agreement which determined a status quo in the Suez Canal zone. These developments served as the background for the tough stand adopted by the US during the civil war which broke out in Jordan▷ in Sept. 1970 and the Syrian military intervention, as a result of which the US threatened direct involvement.   (O.Y.)

In the spring of 1971 the US sought to intermediate between the parties of the Arab-Israel Conflict▷ by suggesting an interim agreement based on Israeli withdrawal from the banks of the Suez Canal and its opening by Egypt. However, despite indications from both Egypt and Israel that they would sustain an agreement of this kind, Sadat▷, Egypt's new President, in the end rejected the US suggestion.

Despite improved US relations with several lesser Arab states (such as Sudan▷ and Yemen▷), the US found herself unable to quieten the main focal points of tension in the ME. Even after the expulsion of Russian military advisers from Egypt, in July 1972, the US did not agree to various Arab requests for arms and/or effective US pressure on Israel for withdrawal from the territories occupied in 1967. Even the summit talks held by Nixon and Brezhniev in May 1972 and June 1973, within the frame work of the détente▷, did nothing to change the position of the US in the ME, and the area did not play a central part in the talks.

Upon the outbreak of the Yom Kippur War▷, the superpowers remained in constant contact, with both of them simultaneously operating intensive arms airlifts to their respective clients. The cease-fire was also obtained through the combined efforts of the two superpowers. However, despite the Russian-US coordination, it appears that the status of the US within the Arab world, and perhaps also within NATO▷, was the main victim of the war, since the US bore the brunt of the Arab oil▷ embargo, which succeeded in widening breaches within NATO to the point of confrontation between the US and her Western European allies.

On the other hand, in the months following the war the US position in the Arab world improved. The initiatives of the new Secretary of State, Dr. Henry Kissinger▷, made her the senior partner in the Russian-US preparations for the Geneva Peace Conference▷ and in paving the way for the Separation of Forces Agreements▷. Diplomatic relations with Egypt were renewed and it appears that both countries are entering into an era of intensive co-operation in the political and economic spheres, an achievement which has taken most of the political sting out of the Arab oil embargo.

Present US policy toward the ME remains guided, first and foremost, by the strategic importance of the area and its oil resources. The issue of strategic importance comprises three consideration: (a) The need for unobstructed transport through the area, which constitutes a vital crossroads for the world sea and air lanes. (b) The possibility of an attack against the southern part of the Soviet Union through the Mediterranean and through Turkey▷ and Iran▷. (c) The need for a certain exent of control over ME oil▷, in which the US has large-scale investments. The oil companies with US ownership or partnership play an important part in the production and marketing of ME oil. Despite the fact that the US does not need ME oil for her own consumption, she desires to maintain a constant flow of oil to her West European allies.   (Y.R.)

V

VINOGRADOV, VLADIMIR MIKHAILO-VICH. Born 1921; Russian Ambassador to Japan 1962–4; Deputy Foreign Minister since 1967. V came to Egypt▷ as Soviet Ambassador in Oct. 1970, about one month after his predecessor, Sergei Alexandrovich Vinogradov, passed away. Just as the latter's name is linked with the Six Day War▷, so that of the former is connected with increased Russian▷ military presence in Egypt during the "War of Attrition" and the Yom Kippur War▷. V also represented Russia at the Geneva Peace Conference▷.   (Am.S.)

W

WHITE REVOLUTION — See Iran.

Y

YAMANI, AL-, AHMAD ZAKI. Sa'udi Arabian▷ diplomat. Born 1930; studied at Cairo, New York and Harvard University. Government Legal Adviser 1958–60; appointed Minister for Petroleum and Natural Resources 1962; Director of Aramco 1962; Chairman of General Petroleum and Mineral Organization 1963; Chairman of Sa'udi Arabian Fertilizer Company 1966; Secretary-General of Organization of Petroleum Exporting Countries▷ 1968–9.

When Sa'udi Arabia placed an embargo on oil▷

shipments to the US, in Oct. 1973, Y travelled widely to explain the Arab utilization of oil as a political weapon.   (T.Y.)

YARIV, AHARON. Born in Riga 1920; came to Palestine 1935; joined *Haganah*▷ 1938 and the British Army 1941. Served in the Jewish Brigade▷, reaching the rank of Captain; took part in organizing "illegal" immigration to Palestine, as well as *Haganah* arms procurement activities. After his discharge from the British army, Y studied at the Training Institute of the Jewish Agency's Political Department, in preparation for diplomatic service.

In the Arab-Israel War of 1948, Y commanded a battalion in the North; his later military posts include Military Attache in Washington 1957; and head of Military Intelligence 1964-72. After retiring from active service, in Sept. 1972, Y became the Prime Minister's Special Assistant for Combatting Arab Terror. After the Yom Kippur War▷, Y headed the Israel delegation to the Kilometre 101 talks▷. Elected to the *Knesset* on behalf of the Alignment▷, in Dec. 1973; served as Minister of Transport in the Mar. 1974 Cabinet. From June 1974, he served as Information Minister in Rabin's Government.   (E.A.)

*YEMEN. During 1970 all the Royalist princes and Imam al-Badr▷ left Y and since then have had no direct influence on affairs there. In Oct. 1971 some tribes in the San'a area are reported to have declared a new Imam from the al-Marwani family. In early 1973 the sons of Imam Ahmad were taking legal action in Paris to obtain their share of more than £1m deposited there by their father in 1957. The Y Government claimed this sum as well.

Ambassadors were exchanged with Sa'udi Arabia in Oct. 1970 (for the first time since the 1962 *coup*) and immediately afterwards there were repeated reports of agreements for economic aid, cultural exchanges, aviation agreements, etc. This understanding culminated with the visit of President Iryani▷ and his Prime Minister the Qadi 'Abdullah al-Hajari, to Riyadh in Mar. 1973, which led to an agreement on the Yemeni-Sa'udi border as determined in 1934 (relinquishing the Y claim to 'Asir▷). This Sa'udi orientation enabled Iryani's regime to restore the Imamate, partly overcome severe financial difficulties (an accumulated debt of $185m in July 1971) and find indirect support against the "revolutionary" factions and their potential allies in Aden▷.

The reliance of the Y regime on traditional — Zeidi▷ and tribal — decentralist circles led somewhat to decentralization of authority. On 28 Dec., 1970,

President Iryani declared a new Y Constitution before the National Assembly (provisional laws had been laid down by Sallal▷ on 13 April, 1963, 7 Jan., 1964, and on other occasions). Y was declared an Islamic Arab republic based on parliamentary democracy, with Islam as the state religion and the Shari'a▷ as the basis for its laws, and formed part of the Arab nation. The Constitution mentions equal rights for all (including women), freedom of expression and that the right to rule derives from the people. It also determines the institutions of the Republic: The National Assembly was replaced by an Advisory Council comprising 179 members, 20 of whom are chosen by the President and the rest elected in their districts every four years. The Constitution gives the Advisory Council legislative powers and control over the executive authorities (the Republican Council, headed by the President, and the Council of Ministers). It also forbids political parties. Elections to the Advisory Council, held in Mar. 1971, strengthened the tribal-conservative element. 'Abdullah al-Ahmar▷, chief of the Hashid tribal confederation, was elected Chairman of the Advisory Council. During its first meetings at the end of the same month, this body reduced the number of Republican Council members to three and elected Iryani as Chairman, Sheikh Muhammad 'Ali 'Osman and Gen. Hassan al-'Amri▷ as its members. The moderate Shafe'i, Ahmad Muhammad Nu'man▷, formed a new Government in May 1971 (replacing Muhsin al-'Ayni), gaining the confidence of the Advisory Council and declaring a decidedly pro-Sa'udi stand.

The combination of the Zeidi officers' cadre, tribal members and moderate circles, upon which the Iryani-'Amri-Nu'man partnership relied, was apparently not homogeneous. In late July 1971 there were reports of agitation in military circles against corruption and inefficiency in the administration, and Nu'man tendered his resignation. In Aug. 1971, Gen. Hassan al-'Amri (also a member of the Republican Council and Supreme Commander of the Armed Forces) formed a new Government. Senior members of this Government were 'Abdullah al-Asnaj▷, a South Yemeni▷ Shafe'i and the leader-in-exile of FLOSY▷, and Muhammad Sa'id al-'Attar, a Marxist. Al-'Amri declared the need for an "administrative revolution" (an anti-tribal stand) and the necessity for solving economic problems by means of international (i.e. not only Sa'udi) aid. This centralistic-leftist Government was apparently formed without the authorization of the Advisory Council, and lasted a mere four days. Al-'Amri was deposed and accused of aiming to dissolve the Advisory Council. He was exiled the same week, after having also been suspected of the murder of an innocent citizen. Republican army circles received an additional blow when President Iryani abolished the function of Supreme Commander, in Sept. 1971. He appointed Brig. Muhammad al-Iryani as Deputy Supreme Commander. The re-appointment of Muhsin al-'Ayni as Prime Minister and Minister for Foreign Affairs, on 18 Sept., 1971, appeared to be a compromise choice of a moderate acceptable to all elements within the regime. He remained Prime Minister until late Dec. 1972, during which time he was the main executor of Iryani's policies: Recruitment of economic aid from all over the world; implementation of a declared neutralist policy while improving relations with the West and with China▷, at the same time a cooling-off of relations with Russia▷; good neighbourly relations, including the acceptance of aid, with both conservative Sa'udi Arabia and revolutionary South Yemen. In explanation of his resignation, Muhsin al-'Ayni accused the Advisory Council of "deliberately causing the failure of attempts toward union with South Yemen".

Relations with South Yemen are closely connected with the internal power struggle in the Republic. Attempts at negotiation between San'a and Aden have only emphasised the differences between the centralistic "revolutionary" regime in the South (with a Shafe'i majority) and that in Y proper. The change of name of the People's Republic of South Yemen to the People's Democratic Republic of Yemen on 30 Nov., 1970, was symptomatic of the worsening of relations between the two countries. Oppositionary elements of either regime found refuge in the territory of the other. Border incidents commenced in Mar. 1972, culminating in Sept. in large-scale fighting, employing armour and air power. With the mediation of inter-Arab elements (mainly Kuwait▷ and the Arab League▷), the two Prime Ministers, Muhsin al-'Ayni and 'Ali Nasser▷, agreed to a union on 28 Oct., 1972, in Cairo. This agreement was later signed at Tripoli▷ by Presidents Iryani and Salem 'Ali Rabi'▷. Since then there have been joint committees (economic, military, legal, etc.) which were to have presented a detailed plan for union toward the end of 1973. On 26 Feb., 1973, eleven leading politicians in San'a were elected to a political body named the Union of Yemen, to have served apparently as the executive authority of the unified country, upon its establishment. However, in mid-1973 there were reports of difficulties in the implementation of the union and in the working of the committees, and it was stated that they would not

finish their work by the end of the year. In late May 1973 there were again reports of serious border incidents. On 30 May. 1973, a Shafe'i member of the Republican Council, Sheikh Muhammad 'Ali 'Osman, was murdered in Ta'izz▷, and Radio San'a accused "elements from across the border" of the deed. The Aden Government was ordered to refrain from sending representatives to 'Osman's funeral, due to the prevailing tension. On 1 July, 1973, the Deputy Supreme Commander of the Y army stated that, since the signing of the Union agreement, there had been some 1,000 Y casualties in 360 acts of sabotage.

The basic disparity between the attitudes of conservative San'a and revolutionary Aden — as to the nature of their future combined Government — serves to express the internal balance of political forces in Y. It is clearly apparent that the influential Zeidi tribal circles see no advantage in an actual merger with the Shafe'i south.

The new Prime Minister, 'Abdullah al-Hajari, was sworn into office on 1 Jan., 1973. When he presented the principles of his Government, at the end of the same month, the new Prime Minister made no mention of the Union. In early Feb. 1973 he gained the approval of the Advisory Council (with a majority of 110 votes against 14 abstentions). Al-Hajari (who is also a member of the Republican Council since al-'Amri was removed in 1971) appears to have adopted a rather independent stand and, according to reports during the second half of 1973, has shown interest in a new (anti-tribal?) administrative drive.   (H.E.)

YOM KIPPUR WAR (RAMADHAN WAR).

In Sept. 1973, indications were noted by Israeli intelligence of a build-up on both the Egyptian and Syrian fronts. These were passed off as routine major exercises which had been taking place at frequent intervals along the borders, and particularly along the Suez Canal▷ front. This assessment reconciled with an Israeli intelligence estimate that the Arab armies were not yet ready for a major all-out war, and that their leadership was not capable of launching it. This estimate was aided by a highly effective deception plan mounted by the Egyptians and the Syrians parallel to their actual military preparations.

Early on Saturday, 6 Oct., 1973, news was received confirming finally that war was about to break out on the same day. At 14:00 the Syrian▷ and Egyptian▷ armies attacked simultaneously with their total forces, thus beginning the Yom Kippur War. Throughout the Jewish holy day of Yom Kippur, Israel▷ mobilized her forces. One of the miscalculations made by the Arabs was to launch the war on this day, when the entire manpower of the country was available either at home or in synagogue, and thus saving many valuable hours of mobilization, which were to prove vital at a later stage.

On the northern front the battle began with Syrian air attacks and a heavy artillery bombardment of the Israeli front line and headquarters. Three Syrian infantry divisions moved across the cease-fire line and hundreds of Syrian tanks deployed in an attack on Israeli positions in the Golan▷. Behind these three divisions, two Syrian armoured divisions were ready to follow up. The Israeli line, a series of fortifications acting as outposts and observation points and supported in each case by a small force of tanks, was held and, apart from a position on Mount Hermon, not one fortification surrendered, though three were evacuated under orders.

The battle opened with an Israeli force of approximately 180 tanks holding the line against a major Syrian armoured assault which developed into an attack of some 1,400 tanks. With the opening of the attack, Syrian helicopters landed in the area of Mount Hermon, bringing infantry forces to attack the Israeli positions there. Within a matter of hours, the position was overrun and taken.

The major battle was fought in the area of Nafekh, where the Syrians developed a major thrust, reaching to within 10 km of the confluence of the Jordan into the Sea of Galilee. On the central axis, the Syrian forces reached the area of the Nafekh camp. On Sunday, 7 Oct., heavy fighting continued all along the line with heavy losses sustained by both sides. At this stage, the Israeli Northern Command received another division under its command, enabling it to counterattack on Monday, 8 Oct. A heavy battle raged along the route between El Al and Rafid on Monday and Tuesday, 8–9 Oct. By Wednesday, 10 Oct., at 10:00, Israeli forces had driven the Syrians back to the 1967 cease-fire lines, after inflicting very heavy casualties.

In the northern sector, both sides were wavering when one of the Israeli positions behind the Syrian lines, reported that Syrian supply convoys were withdrawing. The Syrian attack had been broken, and in the area facing the Israeli Seventh Brigade, known as the Valley of Tears north of Kuneitra, some 300 Syrian tanks and armoured personnel carriers were either abandoned or burnt out.

In the central sector, another Israeli division maintained the pressure around the area of Nafekh and along the Tapline route, along which the major Syrian effort had advanced. Pushing in a south-easterly direction, this division gradually drove the Syrians back toward Hushniya. At this point, on Tuesday and Wednesday, 9–10 Oct., a two-division effort from the north and south boxed the Syrian forces in the general area of Hushniya, destroying a considerable number of tanks in very heavy fighting. By Wednesday, 10 Oct., Israeli forces here, too, had regained the 1967 cease-fire line on the Golan Heights, and the attacking Syrian forces had been either destroyed or driven out of the area.

By Wednesday, 10 Oct., the Syrians had been pushed out entirely from the Golan Heights and the Israelis had closed in on the cease-fire line along its entire length.

On Thursday, 11 Oct., an Israeli counter-attack was launched into Syria. One Israeli division broke into Syrian positions in the area of Jubata, while another attacked along the heavily fortified main Damascus route. On Friday, 12 Oct., Israeli forces operating in the northern sector reached Mazraat Beit Jann and established defence positions. To the south, the other Israeli division widened its area of penetration, advancing towards Knaker; it was at this time that the Iraqi▷ forces which had just entered Syria reached the area of battle. The first two Iraqi armoured divisions advanced towards the flank of the advancing Israeli division, and battle commenced at 3:00 hours, resulting in Iraqi withdrawal, leaving some 80 tanks destroyed on the field. The Israeli forces exploited their success and reached the area near Kafr Shams.

On Saturday, 13 Oct., Israeli paratroopers captured the vital hill of Tel Shams. In the meantime, Jordanian▷ forces had entered Syria to support the Iraqis on their left flank in the counter-attack against the Israelis. These counter-attacks by the combined Arab forces (Syrian, Iraqi and Jordanian) were of little avail, for the Israelis now held a very strong line.

On 21–22 Oct., Israeli forces mounted an operation to recapture the Mount Hermon position, and on 22 Oct., both the Israeli and the Syrian positions on the mount were occupied by them.

In the battle for the Golan Heights and the attack into Syria, the Syrian army lost approximately 1,100 tanks; some 867 of these were in the Golan area, inside the 1967 cease-fire line, including a large number of the latest model T-62 Russian▷ tanks. About 370 Syrian soldiers and 65 Israeli soldiers were taken prisoner by the opposing sides.

At all stages of the fighting, the Israel air force supported the ground forces, and at a later stage engaged strategic targets within Syria. By the end of the first week the Syrian air force, much of which had been destroyed, ceased to be an element

YOM KIPPUR WAR — SOUTHERN FRONT

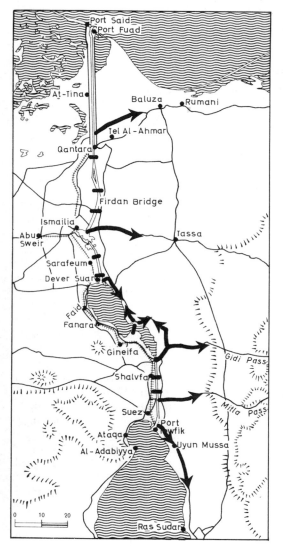

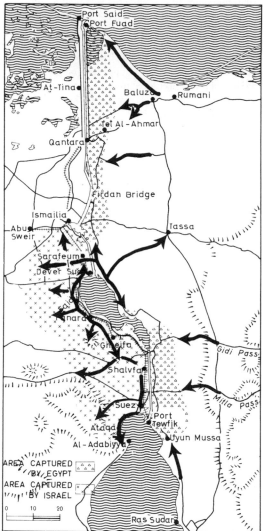

Phase 1 — Egyptian Attack   *Phase 2 — Repulse of Egyptian Army*

on the battlefield. Furthermore, the Syrian missile system, too, was largely destroyed, freeing the Israeli air force to deal with strategic targets deep in Syria, particularly in the Mediterranean ports and in Damascus▷ and other cities.

The Israeli forces concluded the battle holding the strategic heights of Mount Hermon, dominating the entire area between the battlefield and the capital, Damascus, as well as positions as far eastward as Tel Shams, placing the outskirts of Damascus within Israeli artillery range. This was the situation

when the Syrian command agreed to a cease-fire, as requested by the UN Security Council on 22 Oct., 1973.

Simultaneous with the Syrian attack, at 14:00 on Yom Kippur day, 6 Oct., 1973, five Egyptian infantry divisions crossed the Suez Canal▷ — some 70,000 troops against the less than 500 Israeli troops holding the Bar-Lev line▷. A clever plan of deception led the Israeli command to believe that all the preparations, which were clearly visible, were in fact part of a major Egyptian military exercise.

YOM KIPPUR WAR — NORTHERN FRONT

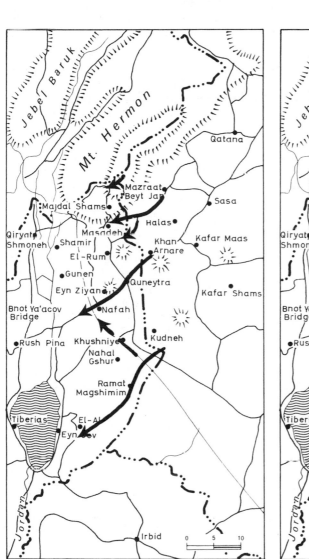

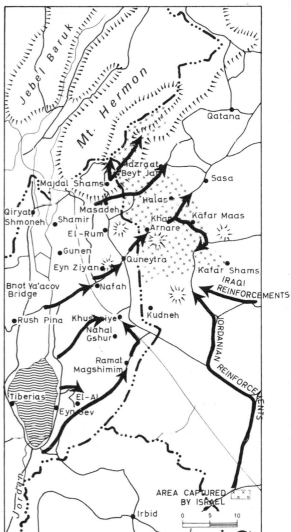

Phase 1 — Syrian Attack   *Phase 2 — Repulse of Syrian Army*

The Israeli line was under intense shelling and air attack. Israeli armoured forces rushed to occupy positions by 16:00, but by this time the Egyptian infantry had already crossed the Canal, by-passing the widely dispersed Israeli fortifications of the Bar-Lev line. As Israeli armoured forces approached their previously prepared positions, now occupied by Egyptian troops, they were met by hails of anti-tank Sagger-type missiles, causing heavy casualties to the tanks of the initial Israeli counter-assault.

The Egyptians set up three major bridgeheads across the Canal: One in the north, basing on Kantara; one in the centre, basing on Ismailia; and one in the south, in the area of the Great Bitter Lake and the town of Suez. The northern and central efforts were made by the Second Egyptian Army, while the southern one was by the Third Egyptian Army. The entire Egyptian operation was carried out under cover of a dense anti-aircraft missile system which caused heavy casualties to the Israel air force, particularly because it forced the

Israel aircraft to fly low and thus expose themselves to the more effective conventional anti-aircraft guns. Efforts were made by Israeli forces to reach units besieged in fortifications of the Bar-Lev line, leading to very heavy casualties. Most of the Bar-Lev line had been either captured or abandoned by the third day of battle. The most northerly positions, in the area of Baluza, succeeded in holding out during the entire war. The most southerly position, at Port Tewfiq, held out for most of the week, surrendering only after it had run out of ammunition and supplies.

On Monday, 8 Oct., the Israeli front was divided into three divisional areas: the northern sector (under Maj.-Gen. Adan); the central sector (under Maj.-Gen. Sharon); and the southern sector (under Maj.-Gen. Mandler). On this day, the northern force attacked toward the area of the Firdan bridge, opposite Ismailia, but was held by the Egyptians. Pitched battled continued, with the Egyptians throwing heavy infantry concentrations with anti-tank missiles against the Israeli armour, inflicting casualties. The Israeli forces quickly adapted themselves to this new type of warfare, soon reducing their losses.

On Sunday, 14 Oct., the Egyptian army mounted a major tank offensive and all day long a heavy tank battle raged. with the Egyptians endeavouring to break out at four different points. The major battle was waged on the central sector, where some 110 Egyptian tanks were destroyed that day. In the northern sector, as well as in the south, the Egyptian Third Army made a determined attempt to break out southwards along the Gulf of Suez, towards the oil fields at Abu Rudais. The Israeli air force knocked out the greater part of an Egyptian brigade here, stopping the Egyptian thrust; they lost over 200 tanks in this day's assault, which failed to achieve any advance.

On the night of 15/16 Oct., Israeli paratroopers led Sharon's division across the Suez Canal, establishing themselves in Egypt proper on the west bank of the Canal. On the morrow they were joined by elements of an armoured brigade, which began to widen the perimeter. Egyptian forces on the west bank of the Canal were taken by surprise, offering little opposition. In preparation for the crossing, Sharon's forces had launched an attack which brought them to the water's edge; however, the area had not been cleared of Egyptian forces, which were in a position to prevent any advance toward the Canal. The northern Israeli division, which had been designated to follow through after bridges had been laid across the Canal, was therefore obliged to postpone its operation and engage the Egyptians on the east bank, in the area of the Israeli breakthrough, to secure a corridor to the Canal, widen it and mop up any Egyptian units there. At the same time an Egyptian armoured brigade moved up from the Third Army area along the Great Bitter Lake, though it was soon destroyed. By this time Sharon's force was reinforced on the west bank of the Canal, and it began pushing northwards. One of the fiercest battles of the war, at the "Chinese Farm", was fought at the northern part of the corridor across to the Canal. In the meantime, despite intense Egyptian bombardment, and artillery and air attacks, the Israelis brought up bridging equipment and two bridges were thrown across the Canal.

On 16–17 Oct., the northern Israeli division cleared the main routes to the bridging areas, as well as the corridor leading to them. This force then built bridges and crossed the Canal on the night of 17/18 Oct. Its first mission was to destroy as many anti-aircraft missile sites as possible and to advance in the general direction of the Genifa Hills, southward. On the same night Egyptian commando battalions unsuccessfully counter-attacked from Ismailia southwards against the paratrooper brigade which had crossed the Canal initially. Large-scale air battles developed in the meantime, the Israeli air force achieving the upper hand.

During the fighting at the end of the first week, Maj.-Gen. Mandler was killed, his command being taken over by Maj.-Gen. Magen. In the evening of 19 Oct., this southern division crossed the bridges, bringing the total Israeli forces on the west bank of the Suez Canal to three divisions. Sharon's force drove through the cultivated area surrounding the Sweet Water Canal towards Ismailia, at the same time endeavouring to remain parallel to the Israeli forces on the east bank of the Canal, which had encountered very heavy opposition from the Egyptian Second Army. The northern Israeli force was directed toward Genifa-Suez, clearing the area of the west bank of the Bitter Lakes and the west bank of the Canal itself. The southern Israeli force, in a broad sweep to the west of the Genifa Hills, approached the port of Adabia on the Gulf of Suez. Sharon's force, which at this stage had advanced some 6 km northward of the bridges, began to widen the Israeli bridgehead and push toward Ismailia. By 22 Oct., they had pushed northward to the water purification plant of Ismailia. They also attacked northward on the east bank of the Suez Canal, in an endeavour to clear the area between the Great Bitter Lake and Lake Timsah, though they were not entirely successful.

The northern Israeli division continued southwards along the Suez Canal between the Bitter Lakes and the town of Suez, in constant touch with Egyptian forces on both banks of the Canal. The southern Israeli division reached the Cairo-Suez road, cutting it early on 22 Oct.

On 21 Oct., the UN Security Council, hastily convened by Russia, called for an immediate cease-fire, to come into effect at 17:58 on 22 Oct. By the time the cease-fire as accepted by both Egypt and Israel came into effect, the Egyptian Third Army found itself cut off and surrounded. Fighting continued after the cease-fire, with units of the entrapped Egyptian Third Army trying to break out of the Israeli ring. The southern Israeli force consolidated its gains, closing the ring by taking Adabia on the Gulf of Suez. The northern Israeli force cleared the entire water edge and reached the outskirts of the town of Suez. Israeli forces moved into the town of Suez assuming that fighting was over, but came against Egyptian strongpoints and suffered heavy casualties.

Fighting finally ceased on 24 Oct., with Egyptian forces holding two major bridgeheads along the east bank of the Suez Canal, for a depth of some 10 km, and with the Israeli forces occupying some 1,600 sq.km inside Egypt proper, from the outskirts of Ismailia in the north to the Mount Ataka and Adabia in the south, reaching a most westerly point some 70 km east of Cairo. The surrounded Egyptian Third Army had some 20,000 troops and approximately 300 tanks on the east bank of the Canal, opposite the town of Suez and, indeed, but for the Security Council cease-fire resolution, it would have been doomed, for the Israeli forces could have wiped it out within a matter of days.

Thus the war concluded on the Egyptian front, with the Egyptians celebrating their initial success in crossing the Canal and their subsequent maintaining of the east bank of the Canal. On the other hand, Israeli forces had effected a counter-attack which gave them a good bargaining position with a view to future negotiations. In the battle with Egypt, over 1,000 Egyptian tanks were destroyed and vast quantities of equipment were captured by the Israelis, in addition to 8,000 prisoners taken. Some 240 Israeli prisoners were taken by the Egyptians. A POW exchange was effected following the Six Point Agreement▷.

In several naval battles during the war, including the first missile battles in naval history, Israeli naval forces destroyed most of the Syrian Navy and part of the Egyptian Navy, gaining complete control of the seas, in both the Mediterranean and the Red Sea.

On 22 Oct., 1973, the UN Security Council

passed UN Resolution 338▷ and on 11 Nov., 1973, a Six Point (cease-fire) Agreement▷ was signed between Egypt and Israel at Kilometre 101▷ on the Suez-Cairo road. The Geneva Peace Conference▷ opened on 18 Dec., 1973, with Egypt, Jordan and Israel participating, under the auspices of the US▷ and Russia. During Jan. 1974, negotiations over an Egypt-Israel disengagement took place, with US Secretary of State Kissinger▷ playing the main part in mediating between the two points of view. On 18 Jan. a Disengagement of Forces Agreement▷ was signed between Egypt and Israel, which by 5 Mar. had been fully implemented. Subsequently, negotiations were set afoot toward a similar arrangement between Syria and Israel. The Israelis announced negotiations could be held only after lists of Israeli POWs in Syria were handed over to Israel. Following the complying of this condition, as well as Red Cross▷ visits to the prisoners, initial disengagement talks were opened, mediated by Dr. Kissinger. Agreement was reached on 30 May, and disengagement was implemented during June 1974.

The Yom Kippur War has changed many concepts on modern warfare. Sophisticated anti-aircraft missiles, such as the SAM-6 Russian missile employed by the Egyptians and Syrians, proved to be very effective and had an important bearing on the air war.

From a purely military point of view, the war began under the worst possible circumstances for Israel, and under the best possible circumstances that the Arab forces could have envisaged, but the final result was a military victory for Israel. Loss of life on both sides was heavy, with an estimated 3,500 Syrians, 15,000 Egyptians and 2,700 Israelis killed. (For the political background of the Yom Kippur War, see Arab-Israel Conflict.)   (H.H.)

*YUGOSLAVIA. Close relations between Y and several Arab regimes continued during 1971-4, though not as close as the personal contact between Nasser▷ and Tito had been. In 1971 Y criticized the friendship treaty between Egypt▷ and Russia▷. During the Yom Kippur War▷ the Russian airlift to Egypt and Syria flew through Y airspace. (O.Y.)

YUNIS, ABU BAKR. Libyan▷ army officer and politician; member of the Revolutionary Command Council since its establishment in 1969. Considered among those closest to Qaddhafi▷; appointed Deputy Commander in Chief of the army Dec. 1969; Chief of Staff since Jan. 1970.

Y supports closer relations with Egypt, including military co-operation. He was awarded Egypt's

"Star of Sinai" decoration in Feb. 1974, in recognition for his role in extending Libyan aid during the Yom Kippur War▷. (Al.S.)

Z

ZAYYAT, AL-, MUHAMMAD HASAN. Egyptian writer, diplomat and politician. Born in Damietta 1915; completed secondary school in Egypt; studied history in France; PhD from Oxford 1947. Upon returning to Egypt▷, Z became head of the Faculty of Oriental Studies at the University of Alexandria▷. Married daughter of Taha Hussein, the famous writer. In 1950 Z joined the staff of the Foreign Office and since then has held several important posts: Deputy Head of the Egyptian UN Delegation 1962; Ambassador to India 1964; and Deputy Foreign Minister 1964.

In 1967 Z became Presidential spokesman and also began to be active in the Arab Union▷, where he participated in the committee planning its reorganization. Z returned to the Foreign Office in 1969 and served three years as Egypt's Ambassador to the UN. During this period Z was in charge of relations with Dr. Jarring▷. In Jan. 1972 Z became Minister of State for Information and, in Sept. 1972, Foreign Minister. Z was away from Egypt during the Yom Kippur War, when he was replaced by Isma'il Fahmy▷. Later, Z became Sadat's▷ Adviser on Foreign Affairs. (Al.S.)

ZAZA, 'ALI. Syrian Minister of Interior, Brig.-Gen. and a Ba'th▷ leader. The position held by Z is of extreme importance for it also holds responsibility for internal security in Syria▷. (O.Y.)

★ZEIDIS, ZEIDIYYA. Even since Egyptian forces left Yemen▷ and Sallal▷ fell in 1967, hegemony has been in the hands of the Z tribes, mainly by virtue of the position held by Iryani▷ and the head of the Hashid tribe, 'Abdullah al-Ahmar▷. However, this leadership tends not to stress the Z in political contexts, since that would have made it necessary to restore the Imamate. The Dec. 1970 Constitution defines Yemen as an Islamic state, without mentioning specific Islamic sects.

Apparently the Z concept, in its political sense, still exists among certain tribes in the northern part of the country. At the end of 1971, several Z tribes reportedly declared a new Imam in the Sa'da region, chosen from the al-Marwani family. (H.E.)

★ZU'AYYIN, YUSSUF. Since the *coup* of 23 Feb. 1966, Z headed the "civilian section" of the Ba'th▷ in Syria▷, and was one of Asad's▷ major rivals in the power struggle within the party. In Sept. 1970 he was Secretary-General of al-Sa'iqa▷, and thus was largely responsible for Syrian intervention in the civil war in Jordan▷. When Asad came to power, in Nov. 1970, Z was removed from all his posts, arrested and consequently freed. Z was re-arrested in June 1971 and accused of subversive activity against the Asad regime. Z has been imprisoned since then, without being brought to trial. (O.T.)